Leith's Cookery Bible

BY PRUE LEITH
& CAROLINE WALDEGRAVE

First published in Great Britain in 1991
Bloomsbury Publishing Limited, 2 Soho Square,
London W1V 5DE

A CIP catalogue record for this book
is available from the British Library

ISBN 0 7475 1044 X

10 9 8 7 6

Edited and designed by
Toucan Books Limited, London

Photographer: Andrea Heselton
Assisted by: Sarah Mac, Nesa Mladjenovic
Stylist: Roisin Nield
Home Economists: Polly Tyrer,
Fiona Trail Stevenson, Jackie Brewer
Assisted by: Louise Bacon

Printed in Great Britain by The Bath Press, Avon

Contents

Acknowledgements

This book is officially by Prue Leith and me. In fact this is not really true. The book is the result of 16 years in the life of Leith's School of Food and Wine. Teachers, students and friends alike have all contributed. Recipes have been unashamedly adapted from magazines, newspaper articles and other cookery books.

We see or hear of a recipe that we like the idea of and then test it and adapt it as we see fit. It then undergoes a more rigorous testing as it is cooked by 96 students, all of whom follow it to the letter, and we certainly know if we've got it wrong! It then gets re-written and becomes part of the bible.

We have acknowledged other people's recipes when we can - but sometimes, I'm afraid, we no longer know where they first came from, and hope their creators will forgive us. Prue and I are not trying to take the credit for these recipes. We have simply tried to build up the collection which we now rather grandly call our bible.

Past and present staff have contributed enormously to this end and I would particularly like to acknowledge the work of the following people: Sally Proctor, Fiona Burrell, Caroline Yates, Barbara Stevenson, Charlotte Lyon, Sarah Staughton, Alison Cavaliero, Lesley Waters, Richard Harvey.

We would also like to thank Judy van der Sande and Maureen Flynn for all their very hard work typing the often illegible manuscript. This book could not have been produced without the editorial expertise of Linda Sontag and Heather Thomas.

Finally, we would like to thank all those people who helped so much with the production of this book. Polly Tyrer, Fiona Trail Stevenson and Jackie Brewer all cooked the food for the photographs that were taken by Andrea Heselton and styled by Roisin Nield. They were a joy to work with, as was Kate Simunek, who drew the pictures. The mushrooms in the colour photograph of wild mushrooms were identified by Antonio Carlucci of the Neal Street Restaurant. The 'bible' was produced by Toucan Books, and I feel indebted to the work of Rosanna Greenstreet who calmly filtered all the inevitable changes that we made, and to Robert Sackville West who worked so hard, so efficiently and so charmingly to produce this book.

CAROLINE WALDEGRAVE

Foreword

THERE are not many cookbooks whose recipes are tested over and over again by 100 students and 15 teachers. However, this book has been 5 years in the making and can probably claim to include the most tried, tested and true set of instructions ever offered to the keen cook, greedy gourmet or addicted recipe reader.

What we have tried to do in this book is to reproduce the style of cooking taught at Leith's School. Frankly, we threw out recipes, however classic and time-honoured, if the teachers and students did not like the results. This has meant the demise of rock buns, nut cutlets and many an uninspiring stew. It has also meant the inclusion of dozens of 'new classics' – the fresh imaginative cooking that has been such an inspiration and fillip to modern chefs. It has meant that Oriental, Indian, Mexican and vegetarian dishes have come into their own. It has meant due regard for healthy eating, alongside the *haute cuisine* of rich butter sauces and cream-laden puddings.

What we have guarded determinedly against is gimmickiness or pretentiousness. Thus, we have included a fruit coulis only when it improves the flavour as well as the appearance of a dessert. We have kept garnishes, decorations and trimmings to the edible and relevant minimum. For example, a twist of lemon on a fillet of fish does nothing for the diner, who cannot squeeze it, nor for the fish, which it clutters up or obscures.

The whole point of cooking, it seems to us, is to lift food from the merely nutritive to the positively pleasurable. There was never a good cook with a Calvinist heart. By which I don't mean that good cooks are profligate, extravagant or wasteful. Waste is as painful to a true cook as second-rate ingredients are.

Another thread running through the recipes, however simple or grand, is the love of doing things well. For there really is great satisfaction for the cook (more, perhaps, even than for the diner) in a perfectly balanced and executed meal. There is no buzz quite like that of surveying a buffet, every dish of which you have got exactly right, before the marauding guests descend. That feeling of pride and pleasure is worth all the hard work.

But of course this book is more a practical manual than a paean to the joy of creativity. It is essentially the tool by which such pleasures (and profit) are reached. It will be, we hope, the mentor and guide of newly fledged cooks, and will become the trusted old friend and helpmeet of experienced chefs. The editor, Caroline Waldegrave, and her team of teachers have put into it everything we think a professional might need to for reference, and enough to turn the amateur into a pro!

Above all, I hope that this book will spread the gospel: good cooking is enjoyable and rewarding for everyone – not least the cook.

PRUE LEITH

All about Cooking

CONVERSION TABLES

The tables below are approximate, and do not conform in all respects to the official conversions, but we have found them convenient for cooking.

Weight

Imperial	Metric	Imperial	Metric
1/4oz	7-8g	1/2oz	15g
3/4oz	20g	1oz	30g
2oz	55g	3oz	85g
4oz (1/4lb)	110g	5oz	140g
6oz	170g	7oz	200g
8oz (1/2lb)	225g	9oz	255g
10oz	285g	11oz	310g
12oz (3/4lb)	340g	13oz	370g
14oz	400g	15oz	425g
16oz (1lb)	450g	1 1/4lb	560g
1 1/2lb	675g	2lb	900g
3lb	1.35 kg	4lb	1.8 kg
5lb	2.3 kg	6lb	2.7 kg
7lb	3.2 kg	8lb	3.6 kg
9lb	4.0 kg	10lb	4.5 kg

Liquid measures

Imperial	ml	fl oz
1 3/4 pints	1000 (1 litre)	35
1 pint	570	20
3/4 pint	425	15
1/2 pint	290	10
1/3 pint	190	6.6
1/4 pint (1 gill)	150	5
	56	2
2 scant tablespoons	28	1
1 teaspoon	5	

Lengths

Imperial	Metric
1/2in	1cm
1in	2.5cm
2in	5cm
6in	15cm
12in	30cm

Oven temperatures

°C	°F	Gas mark
70	150	1/4
80	175	1/4
100	200	1/2
110	225	1/2
130	250	1
140	275	1
150	300	2
170	325	3
180	350	4
190	375	5
200	400	6
220	425	7
230	450	8
240	475	8
250	500	9
270	525	9
290	550	9

Approximate American/European conversions

Commodity	USA	Metric	Imperial
Flour	1 cup	140g	5oz
Caster and granulated sugar	1 cup	225g	8oz
Caster and granulated sugar	2 level tablespoons	30g	1oz
Brown sugar	1 cup	170g	6oz
Butter/margarine/lard	1 cup	225g	8oz
Sultanas/raisins	1 cup	200g	7oz
Currants	1 cup	140g	5oz
Ground almonds	1 cup	110g	4oz
Golden syrup	1 cup	340g	12oz
Uncooked rice	1 cup	200g	7oz

NOTE: In American recipes, when quantities are stated as spoons, 'level' spoons are meant. English recipes (and those in this book) call for rounded spoons except where stated otherwise. This means that 2 American tablespoons equal 1 English tablespoon.

Useful measurements

Measurement	Metric	Imperial
1 American cup	225ml	8 fl oz
1 egg	56ml	2 fl oz
1 egg white	28ml	1 fl oz
1 rounded tablespoon flour	30g	1oz
1 rounded tablespoon cornflour	30g	1oz
1 rounded tablespoon sugar	30g	1oz
2 rounded tablespoons breadcrumbs	30g	1oz
2 level teaspoons gelatine	8g	1/4oz

30g/1oz granular (packet) aspic sets 570ml (1 pint) liquid.

15g/1/2oz powdered gelatine, or 4 leaves, will set 570ml (1 pint) liquid.

(However, in hot weather, or if the liquid is very acid, like lemon juice, or if the jelly contains solid pieces of fruit or meat and is to be turned out of the dish or mould, 20g/3/4oz should be used.)

Wine quantities

Imperial	ml	fl oz
Average wine bottle	730	25
1 glass wine	100	3
1 glass port or sherry	70	2
1 glass liqueur	45	1

Catering Quantities

FEW PEOPLE accurately weigh or measure quantities as a control-conscious chef must do, but when catering for large numbers it is useful to know how much food to allow per person. As a general rule, the more people you are catering for the less food per head you need to provide, e.g. 255g/8oz stewing beef per head is essential for 4 people, but 170g/6oz per head would feed 60 people.

SOUP

Allow 290ml/1/2 pint soup a head, depending on the size of the bowl.

POULTRY

Chicken and turkey Allow 450g/1lb per person, weighed when plucked and drawn. An average chicken serves 4 people on the bone and 6 people off the bone.
Duck A 3kg/6lb bird will feed 3-4 people; a 2kg/4lb bird will feed 2 people. 1 duck makes enough pâté for 6 people.
Goose Allow 3.4kg/8lb for 4 people; 6.9kg/15lb for 7 people.

GAME

Pheasant Allow 1 bird for 2 people (roast); 1 bird for 3 people (casseroled).
Pigeon Allow 1 bird per person.
Grouse Allow 1 young grouse per person (roast); 2 birds for 3 people (casseroled).
Quail Allow 2 small birds per person or 1 large boned stuffed bird served on a croûton.
Partridge Allow 1 bird per person.
Venison Allow 170g/6oz lean meat per person; 2kg/4lb cut of haunch weighed on the bone for 8-9 people.
Steaks Allow 170g/6oz per person.

MEAT

LAMB OR MUTTON

Casseroled 285g/10oz per person (boneless, with fat trimmed away).
Roast leg 1.35kg/3lb for 3-4 people; 2kg/4lb for 4-5 people; 3kg/6lb for 7-8 people.
Roast shoulder 2kg/4lb shoulder for 5-6 people; 3kg/6lb shoulder for 7-9 people.
Roast breast 450g/1lb for 2 people.
Grilled best end cutlets 3-4 person.
Grilled loin chops 2 per person.

BEEF

Stewed 225g/8oz boneless trimmed meat per person.
Roast (off the bone) If serving men only, 225g/8oz per person; if serving men and women, 200g/7oz per person.
Roast (on the bone) 340g/12oz per person
Roast whole fillet 2kg/4lb piece for 10 people.
Grilled steaks 200-225g/7-8oz per person depending on appetite.

PORK

Casseroled 170g/6oz per person.
Roast leg or loin (off the bone) 200g/7oz per person.
Roast leg or loin (on the bone): 340g/12oz per person.
2 average fillets will feed 3-4 people.
Grilled 1 x 170g/6oz chop or cutlet per person.

VEAL

Stews or pies 225g/8oz pie veal per person.
Fried 1 x 170g/6oz escalope per person.

MINCED MEAT

170g/6oz per person for shepherd's pie, hamburgers, etc.

110g/4oz per person for steak tartare.
85g/3oz per person for lasagne, cannelloni etc.
110g/4oz per person for moussaka.
55g/2oz per person for spaghetti.

FISH

Whole large fish (e.g. sea bass, salmon, whole haddock), weighed uncleaned, with head on: 340-450g/12oz-1lb per person.
Cutlets and steaks 170g/6oz per person.
Fillets (e.g. sole, lemon sole, plaice): 3 small fillets per person (total weight about 170g/6oz).
Whole small fish (e.g. trout, slip soles, small plaice, small mackerel, herring) 225-340g/8-12oz weighed with heads for main course; 170g/6oz for first course.
Fish off the bone (in fish pie, with sauce, etc) 170g/6oz per person.

SHELLFISH

Prawns 55-85g/2-3oz per person as a first course; 140g/5oz per person as a main course.
Mixed shellfish 55-85g/2-3oz per person as a first course; 140g/5oz per person as a main course.

VEGETABLES

Weighed before preparation and cooking, and assuming 3 vegetables, including potatoes, served with a main course: 110g/4oz per person, except (per person):
French beans 85g/3oz.
Peas 85g/3oz.
Spinach 340g/12oz.
Potatoes 3 small (roast); 170g/6oz (mashed); 10-15 (Parisienne); 5 (château); 1 large or 2 small (baked); 110g/4oz (new).

RICE

Plain, boiled or fried 55g/2oz (weighed before cooking) or 1 breakfast cup (measured after cooking).
In risotto or pilaf 30g/1oz per person (weighed before cooking) for first course; 55g/2oz per person for main course.

NOTE: As a general rule men eat more potatoes and less 'greens' than women!

SALADS

Obviously, the more salads served, the less guests will eat of any one salad. Allow 1 large portion of salad, in total, per head – e.g. if only one salad is served make sure there is enough for 1 helping each. Conversely if 100 guests are to choose from 5 different salads, allow a total of 150 portions – i.e. 30 portions of each salad.

Tomato salad 450g/1lb tomatoes (average 6 tomatoes), sliced, serves 4 people.
Coleslaw. 1 small cabbage, finely shredded, serves 10-12 people.
Grated carrot salad 450g/1lb carrots, grated, serves 6 people.
Potato salad 450g/1lb potatoes (weighed before cooking) serves 5 people.
Green salad Allow a loose handful of leaves for each person (i.e. a large Cos lettuce will serve 8, a large Webb's will serve 10, a Dutch hothouse 'butterhead' will serve 4).

SANDWICHES

2 slices of bread make 1 round of sandwiches.
Cucumber 1 cucumber makes 15 rounds.
Egg 1 hardboiled egg makes 1 round.
Ham Allow $^{3}/_{4}$oz/20g for each round.
Mustard and cress For egg and cress sandwiches, 1 punnet makes 20 rounds.
Tomatoes 450g/1lb makes 9 rounds.
Smoked salmon Allow $^{3}/_{4}$oz/20g for each round.

COCKTAIL PARTIES

Allow 10 cocktail canapés per head.
Allow 14 cocktail canapés per head if served at lunchtime when guests are unlikely to go on to a meal.
Allow 4-5 canapés with pre-lunch or pre-dinner drinks.
Allow 8 cocktail canapés, plus 4 miniature sweet cakes or pastries per head for a wedding reception.

PUDDINGS

Cooking apples Allow 225g/8oz a head for puddings.
Fruit salad Allow 8 oranges, 2 apples, 2 bananas and 450g/1lb grapes for 8 people.
Mousses Allow 290ml/$^{1}/_{2}$pint double cream inside and 290ml/$^{1}/_{2}$pint to decorate a mousse for 8 people.
Strawberries Allow 110g/4oz a head.

MISCELLANEOUS

Brown bread and butter $1\frac{1}{2}$ slices (3 triangular pieces) per person.

French bread 1 large loaf for 10 people; 1 small loaf for 6 people.

Cheese After a meal, if serving one blue-veined, one hard and one cream cheese: 85g/3oz per person for up to 8 people; 55g/2oz per person for up to 20 people; 30g/1oz per person for over 20 people.

At a wine and cheese party : 110g/4oz per person for up to 8 people; 85g/3oz per person for up to 20 people; 55g/2oz per person for over 20 people. Inevitably, if catering for small numbers, there will be cheese left over but this is unavoidable if the host is not to look mean.

Biscuits 3 each for up to 10 people; 2 each for up to 30 people; 1 each for over 30 people.

Butter 30g/1oz per person if bread is served with the meal; 45g/1oz per person if cheese is served as well.

Cream 15ml/1 tablespoon per person for coffee; 45ml/3 tablespoons per person for pudding or dessert.

Milk 570ml/1 pint for 18-20 cups of tea.

Sliced bread A large loaf, thinly sliced, generally makes 18-20 slices.

Butter 30g/1oz soft butter will cover 8 large bread slices.

Sausages 450g/1lb is the equivalent of 32 cocktail sausages; 16 chipolata sausages; 8 pork sausages.

Bouchées 675g/$1\frac{1}{2}$lb packet puff pastry makes 60 bouchées.

Chicken livers 450g/1lb chicken livers will be enough for 60 bacon and chicken liver rolls.

Dates 50 fresh dates weigh about 450g/1lb.

Prunes A prune (with stone) weighs about 10g/$\frac{1}{3}$oz.

Mushrooms A button mushroom weighs about 7g/$\frac{1}{4}$oz

Bacon A good sized rasher weighs about 30g/1oz.

Button onions A button onion weighs about 15g/$\frac{1}{2}$oz.

Choux pastry 6 egg choux paste makes 150 baby éclairs. They will need 570ml/1 pint cream and 225g/8oz chocolate.

Short pastry 1.25kg/2lb pastry will line 150 tartlets.

Planning a Party

COOKING for a party can be daunting, but if you are well prepared it can also be terrific fun and it is deeply satisfying to look at perfectly presented food and realize that the occasion is going to be a success.

Forward planning

1. Decide where you are going to have the party, decide on a convenient date and book the venue.
2. Decide on the type of party - cocktail party, buffet, sit-down dinner, dancing or disco.
3. Work out how many people can come to the party. Allow 3 square metres/10 square feet per person for a sit-down party and 2 square metres/6 square feet for a drinks party.
4. If chairs have to be removed to allow space for dancing, make sure that you hire stackable chairs.
5. Is the kitchen area big enough? Are there good reheating facilities or should you hire extra ovens?
6. Are there adequate toilet facilities or will you need to hire a portacabin?
7. Think about the colour scheme, particularly if you are having a marquee that has to be ordered well in advance.
8. Get invitations printed - and expect one-third refusals.
9. If the party is a commercial event, organize a licence and extend your employer's liability insurance.
10. If the party is for a charity, set up a committee to organize the tombola, programme advertising, and most importantly the sale of tickets.

Medium-term planning

1. Plan the menu.
2. Work out the hire list. Once you know the menu it is simple to work out how many knives, forks, plates, coffee cups and glasses you will need and how many chairs and tables to hire, but don't forget any of the following:

4 or 5 extra place settings
serving dishes and cloths
butter dishes
serving trays for food and glasses
serving spoons and forks
$1^{1/2}$ glasses a head for a cocktail party
menu holders (if required)
cake stand (for a wedding)
coffee urns for a big party
table mats
knife and board for lemons
ice buckets
water jugs
corkscrews
coffee pots, milk jugs, sugar bowls, teaspoons
punch bowl and ladle
tablecloth and napkins
cocktail shakers
ashtrays, plenty, all the same size
dustbins in which to chill wine
salt and pepper pots (check that they are full)
bread baskets
plate stackers (for piling up plates of ready plated food)
fruit baskets
coat rail and hangers
candlesticks
drugget (cloth for the floor behind the bar)
stand for the seating plan
extra ovens or hot cupboards

Establish that the hired linen is returned dirty and agree a delivery time.
3. Hire a van to deliver food if necessary - start saving boxes to deliver food in.
4. Plan the wine to go with the menu (see pages 79-80). Allow a bottle a head and hope to have

some left over. Order it on sale or return and only chill wine as you need it so that the labels don't drop off. Many wine firms will supply ready-chilled wine and glasses.
5. Book a master of ceremonies if necessary.
6. Book staff if necessary. The general rule is that for silver service, one waitress can cope with 6 people, and for butler service one waitress can look after 10 people. At a buffet, one waitress can look after 25 people. One barman can cope with 30 people if it is a full bar and with 50 people for a single bar. Decide whether you need to hire kitchen staff, kitchen porters, cloakroom ladies, security staff or any other help. Decide on the kind of staff you want.
7. Think about parking arrangements. Do you need to give car registration numbers to security? Find out from what time you can have access and from what time you can lay the tables. Check what time you need to leave the building and the latest time you can have the hired equipment collected in the morning. Check how the equipment can be delivered to the right place - is there a goods lift etc?
8. Hire and order flower arrangements and table decorations as necessary.
9. Order the band, discotheque, casino, etc. Discuss electrical requirements.
10. Go to the party venue and make a plan of action so that you can establish if there are any gaps in your forward planning scheme.

A week before the party

1. Order the food (see catering quantities pages 10-12) to arrive 2 days before the party. Don't forget to order sandwiches for the staff.
2. Order the ice. Champagne is generally served colder than wine. Make sure that the containers for ice are delivered before the ice arrives.
3. Order other drinks, such as orange juice, mineral water and whisky.
4. Talk over the plan of the party with a friend to make sure there are no gaps.

A day before the party

1. Prepare as much of the food as you can. Separate into small batches to cool as quickly as possible and chill well. The easiest way to cook in large quantities is to do one process at a time. If making sandwiches make all the fillings, soften all the butter, butter all the bread and then put all the sandwiches together.
2. Get all the equipment you need to take with you. This may include:

matches
loo paper, cloakroom soap and towels, flowers for loos
cling film
kitchen paper
tin foil
dustbin liners (lots)
knives, whisks, fish slices, etc.
carving knife and fork
electric carving knife
oven gloves
tea towels
washing-up liquid
mop and bucket
broom and dustpan and brush
J-cloths
plenty of boxes for taking home dirty equipment
first-aid box
pins
screwdriver
needles and cotton
rubber gloves
chopping boards
scissors
lemons
petty cash (for tipping people)
tea bags, milk, sugar for staff
cold drinks for staff

On the day of the party

1. Get someone to the venue reasonably early to check off the deliveries, sign slips, persuade people to take equipment to the right place and generally organize the setting up and laying of tables, the seating plan, the flowers, the microphone, the lighting, the table decorations, tidying the cloakroom and warding off potential problems.
2. Meanwhile, finish off all the cooking, pack up the food, undecorated, and deliver it with all the equipment and garnishes.
3. Set up an efficient working kitchen, work tidily and stick to a time plan.
4. Serve the food by the agreed method and enjoy the party.

Dictionary of Cooking Terms and Kitchen French

Abats French for offal (hearts, livers, brains, tripe, etc.). Americans call them 'variety meats'.
Bake blind To bake a flan case while empty. In order to prevent the sides falling in or the base bubbling up, the pastry is usually lined with paper and filled with 'blind beans'. See below.
Bain-marie A baking tin half-filled with hot water in which terrines, custards, etc. stand while cooking. The food is protected from direct fierce heat and cooks in a gentle, steamy atmosphere. Also a large container that will hold a number of pans standing in hot water, used to keep soups, sauces, etc. hot without further cooking.
Bard To tie bacon or pork fat over a joint of meat, game bird or poultry, to be roasted. This helps to prevent the flesh from drying out.
Baste To spoon over liquid (sometimes stock, sometimes fat) during cooking to prevent drying out and to promote flavour.
Bavarois Creamy pudding made with eggs and cream and set with gelatine.
Beignets Fritters.
Beurre manié Butter and flour in equal quantities worked together to a soft paste, and used as a liaison or thickening for liquids. Small pieces are whisked into boiling liquid. As the butter melts it disperses the flour evenly through the liquid, thereby thickening it without causing lumps.
Beurre noisette Browned butter; *see* Noisette.
Bisque Shellfish soup, smooth and thickened.
Blanch Originally, to whiten by boiling, e.g. briefly to boil sweetbreads or brains to remove traces of blood, or to boil almonds to make the brown skin easy to remove, leaving the nuts white. Now commonly used to mean parboiling, as in blanching vegetables when they are parboiled prior to freezing, or precooked so that they have only to be reheated before serving.
Blanquette A stew made without prior frying of the meat. Usually used for lamb, chicken or veal. The sauce is often thickened with an egg and cream liaison.
Blind beans Dried beans, peas, rice or pasta used to temporarily fill pastry cases during baking.
Bouchées Small puff pastry cases like miniature vol-au-vents.
Bouillon Broth or uncleared stock.
Bouquet garni Parsley stalks, small bay leaf, fresh thyme, celery stalk, sometimes with a blade of mace, tied together with string and used to flavour stews etc. Removed before serving.
Braise To bake or stew slowly on a bed of vegetables in a covered pan.
Brunoise Vegetables cut into very small dice.
Canapé A small bread or biscuit base, sometimes fried, spread or covered with savoury paste, egg, etc., used for cocktail titbits or as an accompaniment to meat dishes. Sometimes used to denote the base only, as in champignons sur canapé.
Caramel Sugar cooked to a toffee.
Chapelux Browned breadcrumbs.
Châteaubriand Roast fillet steak from the thick

end for 2 people or more.
Chine To remove the backbone from a rack of ribs. Carving is almost impossible if the butcher has not 'chined' the meat.
Clarified butter Butter that has been separated from milk particles and other impurities which cause it to look cloudy when melted, and to burn easily when heated.
Collops Small slices of meat, taken from a tender cut such as neck of lamb.
Concasser To chop roughly.
Consommé Clear soup.
Coulis Essentially a thick sauce, e.g. coulis de tomatoes, thick tomato sauce; raspberry coulis, raspberry sauce.
Court bouillon Liquid used for cooking fish.
Cream To beat ingredients together, such as butter and fat when making a sponge cake.
Crêpes Thin French pancakes.
Crepin Pigs caul.
Croquettes Pâté of mashed potato and possibly poultry, fish or meat, formed into small balls or patties, coated in egg and breadcrumbs and deep-fried.
Croustade Bread case dipped in butter and baked until crisp. Used to contain hot savoury mixtures for a canapé, savoury or as a garnish.
Croûte Literally crust. Sometimes a pastry case, as in fillet of beef en croûte, sometimes toasted or fried bread, as in Scotch woodcock or scrambled eggs on toast.
Croûtons Small evenly sized cubes of fried bread used as a soup garnish and occasionally in other dishes.
Dariole Small castle-shaped mould used for moulding rice salads and sometimes for cooking cake mixtures.
Déglacer To loosen and liquefy the fat, sediment and browned juices stuck at the bottom of a frying pan or saucepan by adding liquid (usually stock, water or wine) and stirring while boiling.
Deglaze See Déglacer.
Dégorger To extract the juices from meat, fish or vegetables, generally by salting then soaking or washing. Usually done to remove indigestible or strong-tasting juices.
Dépouiller To skim off the scum from a sauce or stock: a splash of cold stock is added to the boiling liquid. This helps to bring scum and fat to the surface, which can then be skimmed more easily.
Dropping consistency The consistency where a mixture will drop reluctantly from a spoon, neither pouring off nor obstinately adhering.
Duxelles Finely chopped raw mushrooms, sometimes with chopped shallots or chopped ham, often used as a stuffing.
Egg wash Beaten raw egg, sometimes with salt, used for glazing pastry to give it a shine when baked.
Emulsion A stable suspension of fat and other liquid, e.g. mayonnaise, hollandaise.
Entrecôte Sirloin steak.
Entrée Traditionally a dish served before the main course, but usually served as a main course today.
Entremet Dessert or sweet course, excluding pastry sweets.
Escalop A thin slice of meat, sometimes beaten out flat to make it thinner and larger.
Farce Stuffing.
Fecule Farinaceous thickening, usually arrowroot or cornflour.
Flamber To set alcohol alight. Usually to burn off the alcohol, but frequently simply for dramatic effect. (Past tense flambé or flambée; English: to flame.)
Flame See Flamber.
Fleurons Crescents of puff pastry, generally used to garnish fish or poultry.
Fold To mix with a gentle lifting motion, rather than to stir vigorously. The aim is to avoid beating out air while mixing.
Frappé Iced, or set in a bed of crushed ice.
Fricassé White stew made with cooked or raw poultry, meat or rabbit and a velouté sauce, sometimes thickened with cream and egg yolks.
Fumet Strong-flavoured liquor used for flavouring sauces. Usually the liquid in which fish has been poached, or the liquid that has run from fish during baking. Sometimes used of meat or truffle-flavoured liquors.
Glace de viande Reduced brown stock, very strong in flavour, used for adding body and colour to sauces.
Glaze To cover with a thin layer of shiny jellied meat juices (for roast turkey), melted jam (for fruit flans) or syrup (for rum baba).
Gratiner To brown under a grill after the surface of the dish has been sprinkled with breadcrumbs and butter and, sometimes, cheese. Dishes finished like this are sometimes

called gratinée or au gratin.
Hors d'oeuvre Usually simply means the first course. Sometimes used to denote a variety or selection of many savoury titbits served with drinks, or a mixed first course (hors d'oeuvres variés).
Infuse To steep or heat gently to extract flavour, as when infusing milk with onion slices.
Julienne Vegetables or citrus rind cut in thin matchstick shapes or very fine shreds.
Jus or jus de viande God's gravy, i.e. juices that occur naturally in cooking, not a made-up sauce. Also juice.
Jus lié Thickened gravy.
Knock down or knock back To punch or knead out the air in risen dough so that it resumes its pre-risen bulk.
Knock up To separate slightly the layers of raw puff pastry with the blade of a knife to facilitate rising during cooking.
Lard To thread strips of bacon fat (or sometimes anchovy) through meat to give it flavour, and, in the case of fat, to make up any deficiency in very lean meat.
Lardons Small strips or cubes of pork fat or bacon generally used as a garnish.
Liaison Ingredients for binding together and thickening sauce, soup or other liquid, e.g. roux, beurre manié, egg yolk and cream, blood.
Macédoine Small diced mixed vegetables, usually containing some root vegetables. Sometimes used of fruit meaning a fruit salad.
Macerate To soak food in a syrup or liquid to allow flavours to mix.
Mandolin Frame of metal or wood with adjustable blades set in it for finely slicing cucumbers, potatoes, etc.
Marinade The liquid described below. Usually contains oil, onion, bay leaf and vinegar or wine.
Marinate To soak meat, fish or vegetables before cooking in acidulated liquid containing flavourings and herbs. This gives flavour and tenderizes the meat.
Marmite French word for a covered earthenware soup container in which the soup is both cooked and served.
Medallions Small rounds of meat, evenly cut. Also small round biscuits. Occasionally used of vegetables if cut in flat round discs.
Mirepoix The bed of braising vegetables described under Braise.
Mortifier To hang meat, poultry or game.
Moule-à-manqué French cake tin with sloping sides. The resulting cake has a wider base than top, and is about 2.5cm/1 inch high.
Napper To coat, mask or cover, e.g. éclairs nappées with hot chocolate sauce.
Needleshreds Fine, evenly cut shreds of citrus rind (French julienne) generally used as a garnish.
Noisette Literally 'nut'. Usually means nut-brown, as in beurre noisette, i.e. butter browned over heat to a nut colour. Also hazelnut.
Also boneless rack of lamb rolled and tied, cut into neat rounds.
Nouvelle cuisine Style of cooking that promotes light and delicate dishes often using unusual combinations of very fresh ingredients, attractively arranged.
Oyster Small piece of meat found on either side of the backbone of a chicken. Said to be the best flavoured flesh. (Also a bivalve mollusc!)
Panade or panada Very thick mixture used as a base for soufflés or fish cakes, etc., usually made from milk, butter and flour.
Paner To egg and crumb any ingredients before frying.
Papillote A wrapping of paper in which fish or meat is cooked to contain the aroma and flavour. The dish is brought to the table still wrapped up. Foil is sometimes used, but as it does not puff up dramatically, it is less satisfactory.
Parboil To half-boil or partially soften by boiling.
Parisienne Potato (sometimes with other ingredients) scooped into small balls with a melon baller and, usually, fried.
Pass To strain or push through a sieve.
Pâte The basic mixture or paste, often used of uncooked pastry, dough, uncooked meringue, etc.
Pâté A savoury paste of liver, pork, game, etc.
Pâtisserie Sweet cakes and pastries. Also, cake shop.
Paupiette Beef (or pork or veal) olive, i.e. a thin layer of meat, spread with a soft farce, rolled up, tied with string and cooked slowly.
Piquer To insert in meats or poultry a large julienne of fat, bacon, ham, truffle, etc.
Poussin Baby chicken.
Praline Almonds cooked in sugar until the

mixture caramelizes, cooled and crushed to a powder. Used for flavouring desserts and ice cream.
Prove To put dough or yeasted mixture to rise before baking.
Purée Liquidized, sieved or finely mashed fruit or vegetables.
Quenelles A fine minced fish or meat mixture formed into small portions and poached. Served in a sauce, or as a garnish to other dishes.
Ragout A stew.
Réchauffée A reheated dish made with previously cooked food.
Reduce To reduce the amount of liquid by rapid boiling, causing evaporation and a consequent strengthening of flavour in the remaining liquid.
Refresh To hold boiled green vegetables under a cold tap, or to dunk them immediately in cold water to prevent their cooking further in their own steam, and to set the colour.
Relax or rest Of pastry: to set aside in a cool place to allow the gluten (which will have expanded during rolling) to contract. This lessens the danger of shrinking in the oven. Of batters: to set aside to allow the starch cells to swell, giving a lighter result when cooked.
Render To melt solid fat (e.g. beef, pork) slowly in the oven.
Repere Flour mixed with water or white of egg used to seal pans when cooking something slowly, such as lamb ragout.
Revenir To fry meat or vegetables quickly in hot fat in order to warm them through.
Roux A basic liaison or thickening for a sauce or soup. Melted butter to which flour has been added.
Rouille Garlic and oil emulsion used as flavouring.
Salamander A hot oven or grill used for browning or glazing the tops of cooked dishes, or a hot iron or poker for branding the top with lines or a criss-cross pattern.
Salmis A game stew sometimes made with cooked game, or partially roasted game.
Sauter Method of frying in a deep-frying pan or sautoir. The food is continually tossed or shaken so that it browns quickly and evenly.
Sautoir Deep-frying pan with a lid used for recipes that require fast frying and then slower cooking (with the lid on).
Scald Of milk: to heat until on the point of boiling, when some movement can be seen at the edges of the pan but there is no overall bubbling. Of muslin, cloths, etc.: to dunk in clean boiling water, generally to sterilize.
Seal or seize To brown meat rapidly usually in fat, for flavour and colour.
Season Of food: to flavour, generally with salt and pepper. Of iron frying pans, griddles, etc.: to prepare new equipment for use by placing over high heat, generally coated with oil and sprinkled with salt. This prevents subsequent rusting and sticking.
Slake To mix flour, arrowroot, cornflour or custard powder to a thin paste with a small quantity of cold water.
Soft ball The term used to describe sugar syrup reduced by boiling to sufficient thickness to form soft balls when dropped into cold water and rubbed between finger and thumb.
Supreme Choice piece of poultry (usually from the breast).
Sweat To cook gently, usually in butter or oil, but sometimes in the food's own juices, without frying or browning.
Tammy A fine muslin cloth through which sauces are sometimes forced. After this treatment they look beautifully smooth and shiny. Tammy cloths have recently been replaced by blenders or liquidizers, which give much the same effect.
Tammy strainer A fine mesh strainer, conical in shape, used to produce the effect described under Tammy.
Terrine Pâté or minced mixture baked or steamed in a loaf tin or earthenware container.
To the thread Of sugar boiling. Term used to denote degree of thickness achieved when reducing syrup, i.e. the syrup will form threads if tested between finger and thumb. Short thread: about 1cm/$^1/_2$inch; long thread: 5cm/2 inches or more.
Timbale A dish that has been cooked in a castle-shaped mould, or a dish served piled up high.
Tomalley Greenish lobster liver. Creamy and delicious.
Tournedos Fillet steak. Usually refers to a one-portion piece of grilled fillet.
To turn vegetables To shape carrots or turnips to a small barrel shape. To cut mushrooms into a decorative spiral pattern.

To turn olives To remove the olive stone with a spiral cutting movement.
Velouté See under Sauces, page 222.
Vol-au-vent A large pastry case made from puff pastry with high raised sides and a deep hollow centre into which is put chicken, fish, etc.
Well A hollow or dip made in a pile or bowlful of flour, exposing the tabletop or the bottom of the bowl, into which other ingredients are placed prior to mixing.
Zest The thin-coloured skin of an orange or lemon, used to give flavour. It is very thinly pared without any of the bitter white pith.

Classic garnishes

Americaine For fish. Slices of lobster tail and slices of truffles.
Anglaise Braised vegetables such as carrots, turnips and quartered celery hearts (used to garnish boiled salted beef).
Aurore A flame-coloured sauce obtained by adding fresh tomato purée to a béchamel sauce: used for eggs, vegetables and fish.
Bolognaise A rich sauce made from chicken livers or minced beef flavoured with mushrooms and tomatoes. Usually served with pasta.
Bonne femme To cook in a simple way. Usually, of chicken, sautéed and served with white wine gravy, bacon cubes, button onions and garnished with croquette potatoes. Of soup, a simple purée of vegetables with stock. Of fish, white wine sauce, usually with mushrooms; and served with buttered mashed potatoes.
Boulangère Potatoes and onions sliced and cooked in the oven in stock. Often served with mutton.
Bouquetière Groups of very small carrots, turnips, French beans, cauliflower florets, button onions, asparagus tips, etc. Sometimes served with a thin demi-glace or gravy. Usually accompanies beef or lamb entrées.
Bourgeoise Fried diced bacon, glazed carrots and button onions. Sometimes red wine is used in the sauce. Used for beef and liver dishes.
Bourguignonne Button mushrooms and small onions in a sauce made with red wine (Burgundy). Used for beef and egg dishes.
Bretonne Haricot beans whole or in a purée. Sometimes a purée of root vegetables. Usually served with a gigot (leg) of lamb.
Chasseur Sautéed mushrooms added to a sauté of chicken or veal.
Chiffonnade Chopped lettuce or sorrel cooked in butter to garnish soup.
Choron Artichoke bottoms filled with peas.
Clamart Garnish of artichoke hearts filled with buttered petits pois. Sometimes a purée of peas, or simply buttered peas.
Doria A garnish of cucumber, usually fried in butter.
DuBarry Denotes the use of cauliflower; potage DuBarry is cauliflower soup. Also, cooked cauliflower florets masked with mornay sauce and browned under grill, used for meat entrées.
Flamande Red cabbage and glazed small onions used with pork and beef.
Florentine Spinach purée, or leaf spinach. Also a 16th-century name for a pie.
Hongroise Normally implies the addition of paprika.
Indienne Flavoured with curry powder.
Jardinière Garnished with fresh vegetables.
Joinville Slices of truffle, crayfish tails and mushrooms with a lobster sauce, used for fish dishes.
Lyonnaise Denotes the use of onions as garnish – the onions are frequently sliced and fried.
Meunière Of fish, lightly dusted with flour, then fried and served with beurre noisette and lemon juice; also frequently (but not classically) chopped parsley.
Milanese With a tomato sauce, sometimes including shredded ham, tongue and mushrooms. Frequently served with pasta.
Minute Food quickly cooked, either fried or grilled. Usually applied to a thin entrecôte steak.
Mornay With a cheese sauce.
Nantua With a lobster sauce.
Napolitana Tomato sauce and Parmesan cheese (for pasta). May also mean a three-coloured ice cream.
Niçoise Name given to many dishes consisting of ingredients common in the South of France, e.g. tomatoes, olives, garlic, fish, olive oil.
Normande Garnish of mussels, shrimps, oysters and mushrooms. Or creamy sauce containing cider or Calvados, and sometimes apples.
Parmentier Denotes the use of potato as a base or garnish.
Paysanne Literally, peasant. Usually denotes the

use of carrots and turnips sliced across in rounds.
Portuguaise Denotes the use of tomatoes or tomato purée.
Princesse Denotes the use of asparagus (usually on breast of chicken).
Printanière Early spring vegetables cooked and used as a garnish, usually in separate groups.
Provençal Denotes the use of garlic, and sometimes tomatoes and/or olives.
Rossini With collops of foie gras and truffles tossed in butter, served with a rich meat glaze.
St Germain Denotes the use of peas, sometimes with pommes Parisienne.
Soubise Onion purée, frequently mixed with a béchamel sauce.
Vichy Garnish of small glazed carrots.

Methods of cooking

WAYS OF COOKING MEAT

THE TOUGHER the meat, or the larger its volume, the more slowly it must be cooked. The quick methods of cooking – frying, deep-fat frying and grilling – are suitable for small pieces of tender meat, whereas the slower methods – braising, stewing, etc. – are best for the tougher cuts.

Three factors determine the toughness of a particular cut of meat: the age of the animal (the older it is the tougher it will be); the activity of the particular joint (the neck, shoulders, chest and legs are used far more than the back of a quadruped and are therefore tougher); and finally the texture of the fibres.

Muscle tissue is made up of long thin cells or muscle fibres bound together by sheets of connective tissue. Individual fibres can be as long as the whole muscle. Bundles of fibres are organized in groups to form an individual muscle. The lengthways structure of muscles is what we call the grain of the meat. It is easier to carve and chew in the direction of the grain. That is why we cut across the grain to make for easier chewing. The connective tissue is the harness of the muscle and is seen as gristle, tendons, etc. Connective tissue is made up of three main proteins: collagen, which can be converted by long, slow cooking into gelatine; elastin, which is elastic and not changed by heat; and reticulen, which is fibrous and not changed by heat.

Tender cuts of meat such as sirloin steak have relatively few connective tissues and as they cook the meat fibres shrink and lose moisture. When overcooked, the juices finally dry up and a once tender piece of meat becomes well done, tough and dry. However, a tough joint of meat such as oxtail, which has a lot of connective tissue, can become very moist during cooking. The collagen is converted into gelatine and the meat becomes almost sticky in its succulence.

As we like our meat to be tender and juicy rather than dry and tough, it is important to cook it in such a way as to minimize fluid loss and to maximize the conversion of the tough collagen in the connective tissue into water-soluble gelatine.

It is possible to tenderize meat before cooking it. This can be done by damaging the meat physically: cutting, pounding and grinding to break down the structure of muscle bundles. It can also be done by marinating. The acid in citrus fruit or wine produces protein-digesting enzymes that can break down muscle and connective tissue.

POT-ROASTING

Pot-roasting is not really roasting at all but baking food enclosed in a pot, either in the oven or over a low heat. It is an old, economical method of cooking that was much used in the days before there were many domestic ovens. Roasting proper is a much faster, 'dry' method, used for cooking choicer, more tender cuts of meat and poultry by exposing them to direct heat. Pot-roasting involves cooking meat in its own juices and might better be called a simpler, quicker version of braising. It is ideal for cooking joints with plenty of connective tissue. A tender joint will toughen when pot-roasted or braised.

Traditionally there is very little liquid in a pot-roast, other than the fat needed for browning, as moisture from the meat provides most of the liquid during cooking.

A casserole with a tightly fitting lid creates a small oven. Steam is formed inside the pot from the moisture given off by the added liquid or by the food itself, and this tenderizes and cooks the meat. If the lid does not fit tightly, the steam can escape. Similarly, if the casserole or pan is too large, the liquid spreads over too large an area and is more likely to boil away. To make sure a lid fits tightly, cover the top of the pan with a piece of greaseproof paper and place the lid on top, jamming it down firmly.

If you have a flameproof casserole, you can brown meat on the hob and pot-roast in the oven in one vessel. Otherwise, brown the meat in a frying pan and transfer it with all the pan juices to a casserole for pot-roasting.

A traditional pot-roasting 'trick' is to cook the browned meat on a piece of pork rind. This adds flavour, and prevents the meat scorching. Coarsely cut root vegetables are sometimes placed under the meat for the same reason. They can either be raw or browned in the same fat as the meat, though the meat should be removed from the pan while browning the vegetables. Once cooked, they can be served with the meat.

One way to ensure tender meat is to marinate it before cooking. A mixture of oil, wine and other flavourings penetrates the outer layer of the meat when it is left to marinate overnight in the refrigerator. The acid in the marinade also helps to break down tough fibres, and the oil prevents moisture evaporation and adds richness. Save some of the marinade to use as the cooking liquid.

Another way to make sure that a large piece of pot-roasted meat is succulent is to lard it. This is especially important with some lean joints such as the beef 'leg of mutton' cut. Cut thin strips of pork back fat longer than the joint and thread them all the way through the meat about 1cm/½inch apart. This is easily done with a larding needle which, when removed, leaves the strips of fat in place. As the meat cooks, the fat partially melts, making the meat juicy and adding flavour and richness to the sauce. As long as the meat cooks slowly, the liquid in the pan is not likely to boil or, more importantly, to evaporate. This liquid becomes a richly flavoured sauce for the meat after cooking. Any vegetables cooked with the meat will help to thicken it.

Transfer the pot-roasted joint to a warmed serving dish or board to carve and remove any strings or skewers. If there is too much liquid left in the pan, simply reduce it by boiling or thicken it with beurre manié (see page 217). Serve it separately.

GRILLING

Intense heat is the secret of successful grilling. Although this method requires active attention from the cook, its advantages are that the food cooks quickly and the charred surface gives great flavour.

To produce succulent, perfectly grilled meat with a crisp brown outside and pink juicy inside, it is absolutely essential to preheat the grill to its highest setting. This may take 10 or even 20 minutes for a grill on a good domestic cooker. Under a cooler grill, the meat's surface will not brown quickly, leaving the meat tasteless and unattractive by the time it is cooked through. If the grill cannot be adequately preheated to quickly brown meat and fish, save it for toast and fry the steaks instead.

Over an open charcoal fire, it may take 2 hours before the embers are flameless yet burn with the necessary intensity. But their fierce heat will cook a small lamb cutlet perfectly in 2 minutes and the charcoal will give it a wonderfully smoky flavour. Charcoal, when ready, glows bright red in the dark and has an ashy grey look in daylight.

Unlike braising, grilling will not tenderize meat, so only tender, choice cuts should be grilled. They should not be much thicker than 5cm/2 inches because of the high temperatures involved. Any thicker and the meat will remain cold and raw when the outside is black. Even so, unless the cut of meat is fairly thin, once it browns it must be moved further away from the heat source so that the interior can cook before the surface burns. Basting with the delicious pan juices or with olive oil or butter adds flavour and shine. Turning is necessary for even cooking, and should be done halfway through the estimated cooking time, when the first surface is attractively brown.

When grilling over, rather than under, heat, use a fine grill rack or wire mesh grill to support delicate cuts of fish and grease the grill rack or mesh well. Fish cuts can be wrapped in greased foil and cooked over heat, but they then cook in their own steam rather than grill in the true sense.

The following points should be remembered when grilling:

1. Take food out of the refrigerator or freezer in plenty of time to have it at room temperature before grilling. An almost frozen steak will still be cold inside when the outside is brown and sizzling. This is particularly important if the steak is to be served very rare (blue).
2. Do not salt food much in advance. The salt draws moisture from the food. Salt after, during or immediately before grilling.
3. Brush the food with butter, oil or a mixture of the two to keep it moist and to speed the browning process. This is also essential to keep delicate foods such as fish from sticking.
4. The more well done meat or fish is, the tougher it will be to the touch and the palate.
5. To avoid piercing the meat and allowing the juices to escape, turn the grilling food with tongs or spoons, not a sharp instrument.
6. Serve immediately. Grilled food, even if well sealed, inevitably loses moisture, dries up and toughens if kept hot for any length of time.

GRILLING STEAKS

All grilled meats should be well browned on the surface, but the varying degrees of 'doneness' are defined as follows:

BLUE The inside is almost raw (but hot).
RARE Red inside with plenty of red juices running freely.
MEDIUM RARE As rare, but with fewer free-flowing juices and a paler centre.
MEDIUM Pink in the centre with juices set.
WELL DONE The centre is beige but the flesh is still juicy.

The best way to tell if meat is done is by its texture. Feel the meat by pressing firmly with a finger. Rare steak feels soft, almost raw; medium steak is firmer with some resilience to it; well done steak feels very firm. With practice there will soon be no need to cut-and-peep.

COOKING TIME FOR STEAKS varies with the heat of the grill, the distance of the food from the heat, the thickness of the cut and its fat content. The density of the meat also affects the cooking time. Open-textured steak such as sirloin will cook faster than the same thickness and weight of the closer textured rump.

GRILLING FISH

Lay the fish steaks and fillets on greased foil on the grill rack, and set close under the preheated grill. This prevents the delicate flesh from sticking to the rack and breaking up when turned.

FRYING AND SAUTEING

Frying, sometimes referred to as 'shallow frying', and sautéing are both quick cooking methods which are suitable for small, not-too-thick, tender pieces of meat and other foods. The difference between the two methods is the amount of fat used in cooking. For sautéing, an almost dry pan with no more than 15ml/1 tablespoon of fat is used; for frying, food is cooked in up to 5mm/¼ inch of fat.

The processes are similar to grilling but when grilling small pieces of meat some fat is lost into the pan juices which may or may not be eaten with the meat. In frying, the meat cooks in fat, at least some of which is eaten with the meat. For this reason the fat used for frying is an important consideration as its distinctive flavour – or the lack of it – will affect the taste of the dish. Olive oil, butter, bacon dripping, lard and beef dripping will each flavour fried foods, while corn, safflower, peanut and most other vegetable oils have little or no flavour. Potatoes fried in goose fat may taste delicious, but not when they are served with fish.

When choosing a fat, remember that some can be heated to much higher temperatures than others before they break down and start to burn. For example, clarified butter – butter with all its milk solids removed (see page 631) – can be heated to a higher temperature than untreated butter; pure bacon dripping, lard, beef dripping and solid frying fat can generally withstand more heat than margarine, butter or vegetable oil. Fats tend to lose their molecular structure ('break down') if heated for too long, and this causes them to smoke (and smell) unpleasantly at a lower temperature than when fresh. Eventually they will give an unpleasant flavour to any food fried in them. However, even solid fresh fats (if they contain an emulsifier) will smoke and burn at cooler temperatures than pure fats without additives.

FRYING

Techniques vary depending on the texture and size of the food and the effect the cook wishes to achieve. For instance, when frying steaks or chops remember to:

1. Fry in an uncovered wide pan. A lid traps the steam and the food stews or steams rather than frying crisply.
2. Preheat the fat. If the fat is cool when the food is put into it, the food will not brown. It will then lack flavour, look unattractive and might even absorb some of the cool fat and become too greasy.
3. Fry a little at a time. Adding too much food at one time to hot fat lowers the temperature and, again, hinders the browning.
4. Fry fast until the meat is completely browned on all sides. Then turn down to moderate heat to cook the inside through.

Fried food should be served as soon as possible after cooking. Juices gradually seep out and meat toughens on standing; potatoes lose their crispness, becoming leathery and tough skinned; fritters deflate, and everything loses its newly fried shine.

Fish is cooked à la meunière by dusting it with flour and shallow-frying in butter until it is brown on both sides. The slight coating of flour helps to prevent sticking and adds crispness to the skin. The fish is then put on a warm platter. Chopped parsley, lemon juice, salt and pepper are added to the butter in the pan and, once sizzling, this is poured over the fish.

STIFFENING Some recipes require gentle frying without a coating of flour. When this method is used, the fat, though hot, is not fearsomely so and the food can be gently fried to a very pale brown, or cooked without browning. This is particularly useful with kidneys and liver, which tend to burst and become grainy if fried too fast; with shellfish, which toughens if subjected to fierce heat, and with thin slices of fish (e.g. salmon to be served in a sorrel sauce), where the the taste of butter-frying is required without a browned surface.

ENGLISH BREAKFAST FRYING Eggs should be fried in clean fat. Frying them in a pan in which bacon or sausages have been cooking leads to sticking and possible breaking of the yolks. If eggs are to be fried in the same pan as other items, fry the bacon, ham, sausages, potatoes, mushrooms and bread first as these will all keep in a warm oven for a few minutes. Tip the fat into a cup. Rinse the pan, removing any stuck sediment, dry it, then pour the fat back into the pan. Using enough sizzling fat to spoon over the eggs speeds up the process and prevents the edges of the whites overcooking before the thicker parts are set.

Sausages generally have skins which, as the stuffing expands in the hot pan, can burst or split open. Avoid this by pricking them carefully all over with a thin needle (large holes like those made by the prongs of a fork provide weak points where the skin will split), and/or by cooking slowly. Shake the pan with rapid but careful side-to-side or forward-and-backward movements; this will dislodge any pieces that are stuck with less damage than a prodding utensil. Fry the sausages slowly until evenly browned all over and firm to the touch.

Bacon rashers can be fried in an almost dry pan as they readily produce their own fat. However, they cook faster and more evenly in shallow fat.

GLAZING VEGETABLES Vegetables are sometimes given a final shiny, slightly sweet glaze by frying them in a mixture of butter and sugar. The sugar melts and caramelizes to a pale toffee and the vegetables brown in the butter and caramel mixture. Constant shaking of the pan is necessary to prevent burning and sticking. This method is particularly successful with shallots, baby onions, mushrooms and root vegetables.

SAUTEING is used on its own to cook foods such as chicken pieces, mushrooms or apple rings, but is most frequently used in conjunction with other forms of cooking. For example, whole small onions may be sautéed to brown them before they are added to liquid in a stew or a sauce. Sautéing is also employed after boiling to give cooked or partially cooked foods, such as potatoes, a lightly browned and buttered exterior.

Browning gives a sautéed dish its essential character. After browning, some meats, such as liver or veal slices, are often removed and then served with a relatively small amount of well-flavoured sauce which has been made in the same pan. Meats such as pork chops or chicken pieces may be given an initial browning and then be cooked with added ingredients that will eventually form the sauce. The range of such sauces is almost endless – as various as the liquids and other flavourings that can be used in making them. Stages in sautéing are as follows:

1. Fry the main ingredient together with any others, browning them in minimal fat. Remove them from the pan and keep them hot.
2. Deglaze (see page 16) the pan with a liquid such as stock, cream or wine.
3. Add the flavourings for the sauce.
4. If the initial browning has cooked the main ingredients sufficiently, reduce the sauce by rapid boiling and pour it over the dish. Garnish and serve immediately.
5. If the main ingredients need further cooking, simmer them in the sauce until they are tender, then proceed as above.

DEEP-FRYING

Deep-frying is one of the fastest possible methods of cooking small, tender cuts of meat and fish. It is also suitable for many vegetables, and for dough mixtures such as fritters and doughnuts.

Because of the very high temperatures the fat reaches, most foods are given a protective coating before frying. This seals in their juices and prevents overcooking, as well as too much spluttering of the hot fat, caused by moisture rapidly vaporizing on the surface of uncoated wet food.

Some foods, such as potato crisps, are in and out of the hot fat so quickly that they do not need any coating. Chips are given a first frying at a low temperature to cook them through, then a second frying at a higher temperature to brown them.

Most other foods need a coating, either of flour or crumbs or a flour-and-liquid batter. While the coating fries to a crisp brown, the food inside stays moist and tender. One of the pleasures of deep-fried food is the contrast between interior and exterior. For the driest and crispest coating, drain off all excess fat on absorbent paper after cooking and serve as soon as possible.

If the coating covers the food completely, as it should, the flavour of the fried food will not contaminate the fat, which may then be used again. Filter the fat clean of any food particles after frying. As soon as it shows signs of breaking down, by becoming dark, odorous or cloudy, it should be replaced. Such fat smokes and burns at a lower temperature than fresh fat, smells stale and gives an unpleasant flavour to anything cooked in it.

BATTER Batter is a farinaceous mixture of a thick liquid consistency. It is used to give a crisp protective coating to food that might otherwise burn or splatter when deep- or shallow-fried.

USING A DEEP-FRYER

1. If the deep-fryer is not thermostatically controlled, use a thermometer or test the temperature of the fat by dropping a cube of bread into it. If the bread browns in 60 seconds, the fat is about 182°C/360°F and suitable for gentle frying; if it browns in 40 seconds, the oil is moderately hot, about 190°C/375°F; if it browns in 20 seconds, the fat is very hot, about 195°C/385°F. If the bread cube browns in 10 seconds, the fat is dangerously hot and should be cooled down. Turn off the heat and fry several slices of bread in it to speed up the cooling.
2. Cook food in small amounts. Adding too many pieces at one time lowers the temperature of the fat so that the coating will not form a crisp crust. The food then absorbs fat and loses its juices into the cooking fat. This is particularly important if you are frying food that is still frozen, such as fish fingers, commercially prepared chips or Chinese spring rolls, which will of course greatly cool the fat. However, do not attempt to remedy this problem by frying in very hot fat. Comparatively cool fat is needed (about 180°C/350°F) to allow the inside to thaw and cook before the coating browns.
3. Drain the cooked food well on absorbent paper.
4. If the food is not served right away, spread it out in a single layer on a hot baking sheet or

tray and keep it uncovered in a warm oven with the door ajar to allow the free circulation of air. Covering or enclosing the food will make the crust soggy. Try not to fry far ahead of serving.
5. Add salt, or a sprinkling of caster sugar if the food is sweet, after frying. This accentuates the flavour and the dry, crisp texture.
6. After use, cool the fat and strain it through muslin or a coffee filter paper. This removes food particles which, if left in the fat, will become black and burned with repeated fryings. As soon as the fat becomes at all dark, it should be changed, as it is beginning to break down, will smoke readily and give a rancid flavour to fried food.

BRAISING

Braising, in the true sense of the word, is a method of slowly cooking meat on a mirepoix, a thick bed of finely diced mixed vegetables with the addition of strong stock. In practice, the term braising is often confused with pot-roasting, as in both methods food is cooked slowly in a pan with a tightly fitting lid to give deliciously tender results. The main difference is that pot-roasted food is cooked with little, if any, liquid other than the fat used for browning the ingredients, and braising involves some liquid and at least some cut-up vegetables to add moisture to the pan, even if a true mirepoix is not used. A pot-roast should taste 'roasted' and be decidedly fattier than a braise, which is closer to a stew and depends more on juices and stocks than on fat for flavour.

Braising can also mean 'sweating'. This is a method of gently cooking vegetables, frequently onions and shallots, in butter or oil in a covered pan, which is shaken frequently to prevent burning and sticking. Once cooked through, softened and exuding their juices but not coloured, the vegetables are usually added to stews, sauces or soups, to which they give a subtle flavouring but no colouring. For example, to 'braise' red cabbage, a finely chopped onion is sweated in butter until tender, then shredded cabbage, a little vinegar, sugar, apple and seasonings are added. These are left over a low heat, covered tightly, to sweat for 2-3 hours. The red cabbage is then 'braised', even though neither meat nor mirepoix have been included.

Occasionally the term braising is used to mean baking in a covered pan with only a little liquid. Braised celery heart, for example, consists of quarters of celery head cooked in a little stock in a covered pan in the oven. Braised fennel is cooked with lemon juice, butter and stock.

Beef fillet and sirloin or lamb best end should be roasted or grilled, but otherwise whole joints or smaller pieces of meat can with advantage be braised. The meat should be fairly lean and any fat that melts into the stock should be skimmed off before serving. Poultry may be braised unless it is old and tough, when stewing or poaching are more suitable cooking methods, as all the flesh, which will tend to be stringy and dry, is submerged in liquid.

The vegetables for the mirepoix should be browned quickly in hot fat and stirred constantly to ensure even colouring, then transferred to a heavy-based casserole or pan. The meat can be browned in the same fat before it is placed on top of the vegetables and stock is added. As the vegetables cook they will disintegrate, helping to thicken the stock.

Making a strong, reduced, well-flavoured stock is time-consuming, but it is one of the key factors in good braising. The best stock is one made from chopped-up beef shin bones that have been browned all over and then simmered and skimmed frequently for hours (see page 218).

As with pot-roasting, meat may be marinated overnight in the refrigerator and large pieces of exceptionally lean meat may be larded to ensure that they remain moist. Dry the meat well before browning it.

The exacting and by no means easy steps for braising red meat to the ideal tenderness and almost sticky juiciness are as follows:

1. Fry the mirepoix of vegetables and a few tablespoons of diced salt pork or bacon slowly in oil and butter, shaking the pan and stirring until they are evenly browned all over.
2. Brown the meat on all sides and place it on top of the vegetable bed in a heavy casserole.
3. Add stock, made from gelatinous meats such as knuckle of veal or beef shin bones, to cover the meat. If the stock is not rich and solidly set when cold, the braise will not have the correct 'melting' stickiness. Then stew, without basting, until half-cooked.
4. Lift out the meat, strain the stock, and discard

the mirepoix, which will by now have imparted all of its flavour.
5. Return the meat to the casserole and reduce the stock by rapid boiling until it is thick and syrupy, then pour it over the meat.
6. There will no longer be enough stock to cover the meat and there is a danger, even in a covered pan, of the exposed top drying out, so turn the meat every 15 minutes and baste it with the stock.

By the end of the cooking time, when the meat is tender, the stock should be so reduced as to provide a shiny coating that will not run off the meat. It will penetrate the flesh, moistening it and giving it the slightly glutinous texture of perfectly braised meat.

STEWING

The term 'stew' is so widely used that it can mean almost anything. A 'stew' is essentially food that has been slowly and gently cooked in plenty of liquid. Most cooks envisage meat cut into smallish pieces before cooking, as in our beef stew with suet crust, but the term is sometimes used for sliced, sautéed meat or poultry served in a sauce, or for a whole joint or bird poached in liquid. Many stews require preliminary frying of the meat, and sometimes of onions, shallots, carrots or mushrooms too. This gives a richer flavour to the ingredients and adds colour and flavour to the sauce, which will be made on top of the browned sediment and dried-on juices sticking to the pan after frying. These are called 'brown' stews. 'White' stews are made without preliminary browning and are less rich, less fatty, altogether gentler, and more easily digestible, than brown ones.

Both brown and white stews are served in their cooking liquid, which is usually thickened to a syrupy sauce.

The principles of shallow-frying (see page 23) apply to the preliminary frying for a brown stew. If the sauce is not to taste insipid, or be pale in colour, you must start with a good even colour on both sides of each slice or all sides of each cube of meat. Good stews are made or lost in the early stages - so take care to fry only a few pieces as a time, to keep the temperature hot enough to sizzle and to take the time to get an even colour. Deglaze the pan as often as necessary. Deglazing serves three essential purposes: it prevents the stuck sediment in the pan from burning; it allows the capture of the flavour of that sediment and its incorporation into the sauce; and it cleans the pan ready for the next batch of meat.

Beef stew with suet crust is a traditional stew, classically made. But the same principles can be used to make a lamb navarin, for example. Follow the same procedure, using lean cubes of lamb instead of the beef and omitting the suet crust. Young spring vegetables such as broad beans, French beans, tiny whole carrots, peas or sprigs of cauliflower, can be added to the stew for the last 10 minutes of stewing time to give a navarin d'agneau printanier.

BOILING AND POACHING

BOILING is a blanket term for cooking food submerged in liquid by one of several techniques: from fast, agitated bubbling - a rolling boil - to a gentle simmer, when bubbles will appear in one part of the pan only, or to the barest tremble of the liquid, which is poaching. The techniques suit different foods and achieve different effects.

Cooking green vegetables quickly in rapidly boiling water in an open pan tenderizes them, yet makes sure they retain their crispness and bright colour. The water should be well salted (15ml/1 level tablespoon for every 1.75 litres/3 pints), as it then boils at a higher temperature, cooking the vegetables even more quickly.

Rapid boiling in an open pan protects the vivid colours of some vegetables, such as artichokes, while enhancing the colours of others, such as peas and spinach. When covered, discoloration can be caused by enzymes from the vegetables, which collect in the condensation on the lid and fall back into the water. The best method is to bring the water to the boil without the vegetables, add the vegetables and cover with a lid to bring them back to the boil as fast as possible, then remove the lid to allow the escape of steam.

Vegetables that would be damaged by vigorous boiling are cooked by the more gentle simmering methods. Vegetables unlikely to discolour, like potatoes, carrots, parsnips, beetroot and other root vegetables, are traditionally cooked in a covered pan to preserve heat and contain fuel costs. Hence the adage: 'If it grows in the light, cook it in the open; if it grows in the dark, keep it covered.'

REFRESHING Once cooked, 'refresh' the vegetables by rinsing them briefly under cold water, then put them in a warm serving dish. 'Refreshing' prevents further cooking by the heat retained in the vegetables, and thus sets the colour. Vegetables that hold their colour well, such as carrots, or small quantities of vegetables, such as French beans for 4 people, do not need refreshing, but for large quantities it is vital, especially if there is to be any delay before serving. They can be reheated briefly before serving by any of the following methods: by being dipped in boiling water; by rapid steaming; by being given 30 to 60 seconds in a microwave oven; by being tossed quickly in butter over high heat. Slow reheating in the oven will discolour most green vegetables, frozen peas being the exception, although even these will eventually lose their brilliant hue.

BLANCHING Some foods, especially vegetables and fruit, are immersed in boiling water without being fully cooked. This is called 'blanching' and has various uses:

1. To remove strong flavours, e.g. from liver or kidneys before frying.
2. To facilitate the removal of skin, e.g. from tomatoes or peaches.
3. To lessen the salt content, e.g. from ham before cooking.
4. To destroy enzymes in vegetables destined for the freezer and to prevent discoloration.
5. To shorten the roasting time of vegetables such as potatoes, onions and parsnips by parboiling first.
6. Simply to semi-cook or soften food, e.g. fennel in salad.

FAST BOILING Rice and pasta cook well at a good rolling boil. The boiling water expands the starch granules and makes them tender, while the rapid agitation keeps the pieces of pasta or rice grains from sticking together or to the pan. Adding 15ml/1 tablespoon of oil to the water also helps to prevent sticking. Long-grain rice boiled in a large pan of heavily salted water takes 10 to 11 minutes to cook. The grains should then mash to a paste when pressed between the thumb and index finger, though a little 'bite' is preferable to an all-over soft texture.

Similarly, pasta should always be cooked 'al dente', i.e. firm to the bite. Remember that fresh or homemade pasta, which already contains moisture, cooks 4 times faster than the dried commercial equivalents. The cooking time also depends on the thickness. Dried vermicelli cooks in 2-3 minutes, while dried lasagne takes 15-16.

Sometimes rapid boiling is used to drive off moisture and reduce liquids to a thicker consistency. With sugar mixtures, the essential high temperatures are most rapidly achieved by a galloping boil.

EGGS are often boiled, yet there is considerable confusion about the correct method of doing this. The easiest and most foolproof is as follows:

1. Prick the rounded end of the egg with an egg-pricker or a needle to allow air to escape.
2. Bring a pan of water to the boil. Have the eggs at room temperature. (If chilled, add 30 seconds to cooking time.)
3. Carefully lower the eggs into the water on a perforated spoon.
4. Time the cooking from the moment of immersion, keeping the water simmering or gently boiling, and not boiling too vigorously, which tends to crack the shells and toughen the whites.

Three minutes will cook a medium-sized egg until the white is barely set; indeed, the white closest to the yolk will still be slightly jelly-like. Four minutes gives a runny yolk and a just-set white. Six minutes gives a well-set white and moist but runny yolk (set on the rim and thick but wet inside). Eight minutes gives a nicely hardboiled egg. Ten minutes will give a yolk sufficiently cooked to be dry and crumbly when mashed. Fifteen minutes will give a yellow-green rim to the dry yolk and make the white tough and unpalatable.

SIMMERING Dried pulses are also cooked by boiling. As there is no colour loss to worry about, and the process is a long one, they may be simmered rather than fast-boiled. Rapidly boiling water evaporates very fast, risking boiling dry and burning. They may even, with advantage, be slowly stewed – cooked in a covered pan in liquid that only partially covers them – either on top of the stove or in the oven. If the proportion of liquid to pulses is right, they absorb all the liquid during cooking. There is nothing to throw away and little loss of taste and nutrients. The amount of water needed obviously depends on the age, and therefore dryness, of the pulses and the speed of boiling, but twice the volume of water to pulses is a good guide.

It is often recommended that pulses be soaked in water before cooking, but this is not always necessary, especially if the pulses are last season's crop. Dried beans that are known to be 2-3 years old can be cooked without any prior soaking, but they will absorb more water, take longer to become tender, and will not taste as good as fresher pulses. As a general rule, soaking is a good idea, especially for the larger beans.

Pressure-cooking works well for pulses and eliminates the need for soaking. Pressure cookers vary and it is obviously sensible to consult the manufacturer's instructions. As a general rule, 450g/1lb of dried peas or beans, unsoaked, will need 1 litre/2 pints water and will cook in 30 minutes at 7kg/15lb pressure.

Like pulses, some vegetables can be slowly stewed until all the liquid is either absorbed or has evaporated. For example, even-sized pieces of carrot can be put in very lightly salted water with a lump of butter. The carrots are cooked slowly so that when all the water has evaporated they are just tender, and coated in the butter. They are then called Vichy carrots.

POACHING is also long, slow, gentle cooking, but the food is generally completely submerged in liquid that is barely trembling, either on top of the stove or in the oven. It is an excellent method for delicate items, such as fish or soft fruit, which would break up if subjected to vigorous agitation.

Tough meat becomes more tender and succulent the more slowly it is cooked. A cut such as oxtail takes at least 3 hours of simmering on top of the stove until it is acceptably tender. Poached in the oven at 150°C/300°F/gas mark 2 for 5 hours, it would be even more tender, falling from the bone and gelatinous.

A ham or large piece of bacon is cooked when the meat has shrunk back from the bone or, if boneless, when the whole thing has visibly shrunk in size by about one-fifth. The rind or skin will then peel off easily and a skewer will penetrate the meat unimpeded. But until you are experienced and confident, it is wise to stick to the cooking times given in recipes.

STEAMING

Steaming is the cooking of food in hot vapours over boiling liquid (usually water) rather than in liquid. It occurs to some extent in braising and pot-roasting, because of the closed pans and the relatively small amounts of liquid used. In true steaming, however, the food never touches the liquid, so the loss of many vitamins is significantly reduced. Furthermore, steamed food is not browned first, so it can be cooked without fat. This makes the food more easily digestible and particularly suitable for invalids and those on low-fat diets. The method has regained great favour with the new-wave nouvelle cuisine chefs because of its simplicity and purity. But excellent ingredients are essential for steaming – there is no help to be had from browning, so the food must taste good without such assistance.

A variety of equipment for steaming food is available. Most common are oval or round steamers, which are like double saucepans, except that the top has holes in its base. Steam from boiling water in the lower pan rises through the holes to cook the food, while the lid on the upper pan keeps in the steam.

Another popular steaming device is a stainless steel or aluminium basket that opens and folds shut and is used with an ordinary lidded saucepan. The basket stands on its own short legs to keep it clear of the boiling water. It fits inside most saucepans and is particularly suitable for foods that do not need much cooking time as the water underneath the short legs would otherwise have to be replaced too frequently. The saucepan must have a tightly fitting lid.

VEGETABLES are the food most commonly steamed as they cook quickly and retain more of their colour and texture this way. Careful timing is essential as steamed food can be tasteless if even slightly overcooked. Today steaming times for vegetables are short, giving bright-coloured, 'al dente', palpably fresh results. Some vegetables can be steamed in their own juices. Spinach, for example, may be trimmed and put wet from washing into a covered saucepan over medium heat, and shaken occasionally until limp and cooked, but still very green. This takes about 5 minutes.

Potatoes that tend to break up when boiled before they are cooked are best steamed; choose potatoes that are about the same size, as they cook at the same time. If they are very large or of different sizes, cut them into bite-sized pieces before steaming. For most other root vegetables, such as turnips, parsnips and swedes, cut them into 1cm/½inch dice and steam them until tender before seasoning and adding butter to serve.

FISH AND POULTRY Steaming fish is simple and quick and always produces a delicate result if the fish is not allowed to overcook. Put the food on a piece of muslin or cheesecloth to prevent it sticking to the steamer bottom. Oval steamers and folding baskets are suitable for small quantities of fish, but for larger fish or cooking many small fish, shellfish, fish steaks or fillets, a fish kettle (usually used for poaching fish) may be used. Made of metal, these come in sizes to take whole fish on a perforated rack inside the kettle. Ramekins can be placed under the rack to keep it well above the boiling liquid. Whole fish can be stuffed and cooked over liquid in a covered kettle on top of the stove. Allow about 8 minutes per 450g/1lb of fish.

Delicate poultry such as chicken breasts or whole small quail may be steamed similarly.

Plate steaming is an excellent method of cooking small quantities of fish in their own juices. Put the fish fillets or steaks on a lightly buttered plate, season well and cover with another upturned buttered plate or buttered aluminium foil. Set the covered plate on top of a pan of gently boiling water or on a trivet inside a large frying pan of bubbling water and cook for 8-10 minutes, depending on the thickenss of the fish.

STEAMED PUDDINGS Traditional English sweet and savoury puddings (particularly suet crust puddings) are also cooked by steaming, but here the food is cooked in a container heated by steam. This gives the suet mixture its distinctive soft, open texture. The easiest way to cook the pudding is to put its container in a saucepan with hot water that comes halfway up the sides of the container. The pan is covered and cooked over low heat to steam gently for a long time, and water is added to the pan as necessary. Take care to put a band of folded foil under the basin with ends projecting up the sides to act as handles.

CHINESE COOKING traditionally involves a good deal of steaming. Fish, shellfish and tender cuts of meat, often wrapped in pastry or vegetable leaves, are quickly steamed. Food in one or more stacked rattan or metal baskets with a lid is placed over steaming liquid in a pan or wok for quick cooking.

Food presentation

If food looks delicious, people are predisposed to think that it tastes delicious. If you have spent a long time cooking, it is a shame just to dump the food on a plate. At Leith's School we have gradually developed a set of rules which can be used as guidelines when presenting food. Fashion may dictate the method - be it stylish nouvelle cuisine or chunky real food - but the guidelines are the same.

1. Keep it simple
Over-decorated food often looks messed about - no longer appetizing, but like an uncertain work of art. The more cluttered the plate, the less attractive it inevitably becomes.

2. Keep it fresh
Nothing looks more off-putting than tired food. Salad wilts when dressed in advance; sautéed potatoes become dull and dry when kept warm for hours, and whipped cream goes buttery in a warm room, so don't risk it.

3. Keep it relevant
A sprig of fresh watercress complements lamb cutlets nicely. The texture, taste and colour all do something for the lamb. But scratchy sprigs of parsley, though they might provide the colour, are unpleasant to eat. Gherkins cut into

fans do nothing for salads, tomato slices do not improve the look of a platter of sandwiches – they rather serve to confuse and distract the eye. It is better by far to dish up a plate of chicken mayonnaise with a couple of suitable salads to provide the colour and contrast needed, than to decorate it with undressed tomato waterlilies or inedible baskets made out of lemon skins and filled with frozen sweetcorn.

4. Centre height

Dishes served on platters, such as chicken sauté, meringues, profiteroles or even a bean salad, are best given 'centre height' – arranged so the mound of food is higher in the middle with sides sloping down. Coat carefully and evenly with the sauce, if any. Do not overload serving platters with food, which makes dishing up difficult. Once breached, an over-large pile of food looks unattractive.

5. Contrasting rows

Biscuits, petits fours, little cakes and cocktail canapés all look good if arranged in rows, each row consisting of one variety, rather than dotted about. Pay attention to contrasting colour, taking care, say, not to put 2 rows of chocolate biscuits side by side, or 2 rows of white sandwiches.

6. Diagonal lines

Diamond shapes and diagonal lines are easier to achieve than straight ones. The eye is more conscious of unevenness in verticals, horizontals and rectangles.

7. Not too many colours

As with any design, it is easier to get a pleasing effect if the colours are controlled – say, just green and white, or just pink and green, or chocolate and coffee colours or even 2 shades of one colour. Coffee icing and hazelnuts give a cake an elegant look. Adding multi-coloured icings to a cake, or every available garnish to a salad, tends to look garish. There are exceptions of course: a colourful salad Niçoise can be as pleasing to the eye as a dish of candy-coated chocolate drops.

8. Contrasting the simple and the elaborate

If the dish or bowl is elaborately decorated, contrastingly simple food tends to show it off better. A Victorian fruit epergne with ornate stem and silver carving will look stunning filled with fresh strawberries. Conversely, a plain white plate sets off pretty food design to perfection.

9. Uneven numbers

As a rule, uneven numbers of, say, rosettes of cream on a cake, baked apples in a long dish, or portions of meat on a platter look better than even numbers. This is especially true of small numbers. Five and three invariably look better than four, but there is little difference in effect between 11 and 12.

10. A generous look

Tiny piped cream stars, or sparsely dotted nuts, or mean-looking chocolate curls on a cake look amateurish and stingy.

11. Avoid clumsiness

On the other hand, the temptation to cram the last spoonful of rice into the bowl, or squeeze the last slice of pâté on to the dish leads to a clumsy look, and can be daunting to the diner.

12. Overlapping

Chops, steaks, sliced meats, even rashers of bacon, look best evenly overlapping. This way, more of them can be fitted comfortably on the serving dish than if placed side by side.

13. Best side uppermost

Usually the side of a steak or a cutlet that is grilled or fried first looks the best, and should be placed uppermost. Bones are generally unsightly and, if they cannot be clipped off or removed, should be tucked out of the way.

Healthy Eating

BY CAROLINE WALDEGRAVE

'HEALTHY' recipes form an integral part of this book, in that you will find some that are low in saturated fat, sugar and salt. It is not a health book as it is designed to cover all aspects of cooking that most of us need to know about. However, I am very keen on bringing up my children as healthily as possible and many of our ex-students are asked to cook carefully for overweight, over-stressed businessmen.

Nutritionists seem to have changed their advice dramatically over the past few years and this can be very confusing. But in fact they are responding to the considerable advance in knowledge made recently as well as to changing social conditioning. Earlier this century, the national diet was high in inexpensive carbohydrate foods like bread and potatoes and often dangerously low in the more costly protein foods like meat. The more affluent post-war years have seen a great change in the way the nation eats, however, and now the danger is seen to be not exactly too much protein, but too much saturated fat in the diet. Saturated fat comes from high-protein foods like meat and cheese as well as from more obvious sources like butter and cream. Moreover, we no longer eat enough carbohydrate to provide adequate dietary fibre.

We are told now to reduce our intake of saturated fat, but we are also sometimes told that a small increase in polyunsaturated fat may be a good thing. What is the difference between these 2 types of fat? It is a matter of the chemical structure of the fatty acids that make them up. Fatty acids are long chains of carbon atoms joined by a chemical bond, which may be either double or single. A fatty acid with no double bonds is called saturated; where there is only one double bond it is known as mono-unsaturated, and where there are two or more, polyunsaturated. Most fats are made up of a mixture of many fatty acids. For example, the fat in butter is 63 per cent saturated, 3 per cent polyunsaturated and 34 per cent mono-unsaturated fatty acids. So when you hear that butter is a 'saturated fat', what it really means is that it is higher in saturated fat than in any other kind. Unsaturated bonds can be converted back into single (saturated) bonds by a process called hydrogenation; a food that undergoes this process, therefore, will become higher in saturated fats. Hydrogenation is used in some food-refining processes to make liquid fats solidify.

Why are saturated fats now considered to be bad for us? Medical research suggests that a high level of saturated fat in the blood blocks and damages the arteries and impedes blood circulation. This increases the risk of cardio-vascular disease, which is one of the major killers in this country. Polyunsaturated fat makes the blood less 'sticky' and so prevents it from attaching itself to arterial walls and causing blockages. Thus it has a beneficial effect on health, unless you eat so much of it that your weight starts to become a health problem. Mono-unsaturated fat has no effect on the blood.

Saturated fat is also thought to be a factor in the level of cholesterol in the blood. Cholesterol is a common source of confusion. It is a substance associated with fat and can originate in two ways.

Blood (serum) cholesterol is manufactured by the human liver and is an essential part of all healthy cells. The liver makes enough cholesterol for our needs, and in some people a high level of saturated fat in the diet makes the liver produce more cholesterol than is needed by the body.

Dietary cholesterol is cholesterol found in foods. Animal foods that are high in saturated fat are also high in cholesterol; some low-fat foods contain high levels as well. You should be concerned about eating too much fat overall, but not about eating prawns, brains, liver and kidney which, although high in cholesterol, are low in other fats. The important point is still to reduce the proportion of saturated fats in your diet.

All fat is fattening, that is, high in calories: 1 gram of fat releases about 9 calories, while 1 gram of carbohydrate releases only about 4. Calories are a unit of heat energy, but if the food you eat releases more calories than you need, your body will store the extra energy as body fat. If you are trying to lose weight, cutting fats out of your diet is therefore the best way. You would find it hard, and it would be foolish, to cut them out entirely, as some intake of fat is essential to several metabolic processes.

It is now recommended that no more than 30-35 per cent of daily calories should come from fats of any sort, even if you are not trying to lose weight. Fat in the diet comes from many sources, from the obvious fatty foods such as butter, cream and cheese to hidden sources such as many ready-prepared and processed foods. Meat products, such as sausages, pork pies and so on, are generally high in fat, and especially high in saturates. Some cuts of meat are very fatty and, again, the fat is mostly saturated. The leanest meats are chicken - especially when skinned - turkey, rabbit, game, liver and kidney. Many fish, such as tuna, salmon, herrings and mackerel, are oily, but the fat is mainly mono-unsaturated and polyunsaturated. If you buy fish canned in oil, however, drain away the oil as it may be high in saturated fat unless, for example, soya oil is used. White fish and shellfish are low in fat.

Nutritionists also advise us to reduce the amount of sugar we eat. Too much sugar has no direct link with heart disease, but sugar is quite fattening and obesity is a major cause of heart disease. Sugar is also bad for your teeth. The calories released by sugar are 'empty', that is, they provide no nutritional advantages.

I am always amazed when I go into health food shops. They are often stuffed full of jars of honey (another form of sugar), 'healthy bars' (often full of more sugar) and mueslis (often far from free of sugar). Also in health food shops you sometimes see cheesey pies (full of saturated fat) and carob cakes (full of another form of sugar). Sometimes they also have spring rolls and samosas (often deep-fried and actually tasting greasy).

The basic message is to cut down on fat, saturated fat in particular, sugar, salt and processed foods. And to increase your intake of fresh fruit, vegetables and cereals. Obviously one must not go 'over the top' by sprinkling bran on everything. Apart from making food fairly unpalatable, this can cause diarrhoea and bowel obstructions. Eating no salt at all would be harmful and everything would taste deadly dull.

At home, I avoid saturated fats in my cooking. This means I do not use butter, lard, cream, dripping, coconut oil, blended cooking fat, mixed blended vegetable oil, solid vegetable fat, or margarines unless they are labelled 'high in polyunsaturated fat'. For general cooking purposes I use sunflower or grapeseed oil as they are both high in polyunsaturated fat. Corn oil is also a good choice but it has a strong flavour, and safflower is high in polyunsaturated fat but very expensive. For special occasions, I buy walnut oil, as it is fairly high in polyunsaturated fat and tastes delicious, as does hazelnut oil, which is high in mono-unsaturated fatty acids. I also like to use extra virgin olive oil, which is high in mono-unsaturated fatty acids. Use a polyunsaturated margarine instead of butter, but don't try using a low-fat spread in cooking, because these tend to separate on contact with heat.

When cooking conventionally, cream is often an important part of a recipe. Cream is high in saturated fat, so I use low-fat natural yoghurt, buttermilk, low fat soft cheese (quark), tofu, fromage frais and cottage cheese in place of cream.

Greek yoghurt is higher in fat than ordinary natural yoghurt but makes a very good cream substitute for special occasions when you would normally serve cream as an accompaniment.

Unfortunately none of these substitutes is capable of remaining stable if boiled, so they must be added at the last minute. Cottage cheese must be whizzed or sieved before use and the others should be slaked. Greek yoghurt can be momentarily boiled.

Skimmed milk can easily be substituted for full-fat milk and after a couple of weeks you will not notice the difference. Nuts are a high-fat food although their fat is mainly mono-unsaturated and polyunsaturated. There are two exceptions: coconut is saturated fat and chestnuts are very low in fat.

Of all the foods high in saturated fats, cheese is the one I find hardest to give up. On the whole I try to eat low-fat cheese such as quark or cottage cheese, but for a treat I have Brie and, for a real treat, farmhouse Cheddar. Looking at labels on cheese can be confusing, as in other parts of Europe the fat content is measured at a different stage in the manufacturing process. They measure the amount of fat in the 'dry matter', that is, the fat content of the cheese minus water. Many French cheeses, like Brie, have a high water content. Here in Britain the amount of fat given per 100g is the amount of fat you actually eat. When you see a Brie labelled in the French way as containing 45 per cent fat, it is only about 23 per cent fat by British standards: that is, the same as the rather bland Edam that dieters have always been told to eat.

A change to healthy eating can involve imitating conventional recipes in a healthier way, making shepherd's pie with more vegetables and less mince, for example. But there are some dishes that you cannot imitate. What is the point of a yoghurt-based crème brûlée? Or a carob, polyunsaturated oil, wholemeal flour and raw sugar chocolate cake? Either you allow yourself the occasional treat, or you try to find equally sophisticated puddings that are low in fat. You want, after all, to keep to your new way of eating. Although after 10 years of healthy eating my taste buds have learned to appreciate slightly different tastes, it has taken time and patience: much better to go slowly and stick to it than be too dramatic and too restrictive and then give it up. Begin by allowing yourself occasional treats: after six months you will not want them any more! The gentle and almost subversive route to health is a smooth path.

Fat contents of various foods

Bacon	Fat (g/100g)
Collar joint, boiled, lean and fat	27.0
Collar joint, boiled, lean only	9.7
Gammon, boiled or grilled, lean and fat	18.9
Gammon, boiled or grilled, lean only	5.5
Rashers, grilled, lean only	18.9
Rashers, back, lean and fat	33.8
Rashers, streaky, lean and fat	36.0
Rashers, middle, lean and fat	35.1

Beef	
Brisket, boiled, lean and fat	23.9
Forerib, roast, lean and fat	28.8
Forerib, roast, lean only	12.6
Rump steak, grilled, lean and fat	12.1
Rump steak, grilled, lean only	6.0
Stewing steak, lean and fat	11.0
Topside, roast, lean and fat	12.0
Topside, roast, lean only	4.4

Lamb		
Breast, roast, lean and fat		37.1
Breast, roast, lean only		16.6
Chops, grilled, lean and fat	without bone	29.0
Chops, grilled, lean only	without bone	12.3
Leg, roast, lean and fat		17.9
Leg, roast, lean only		8.1
Scrag and neck, stewed, lean and fat		21.1
Scrag and neck, stewed, lean only		15.7

Pork		
Chops, grilled, lean and fat	without bone	24.2
Chops, grilled, lean only	without bone	10.7
Leg, roast, lean and fat		19.8
Leg, roast, lean only		6.9

Veal	Fat (g/100g)
Cutlets, grilled	5.0
Fillet, roast	11.5

Chicken	
Roast, meat and skin	14.0
Roast, meat only	5.5

Grouse	
Roast	3 - 5

Partridge	
Roast	4 - 7

Pheasant	
Roast	5 - 10

Pigeon	
Roast	5 - 13

Turkey	
Roast, meat and skin	6.5
Roast, meat only	2.7

Rabbit	
Stewed	3 - 7

Hare	
Stewed	3 - 7

Offal	
Hearts, stewed	3 - 6
Kidneys	5 - 7
Liver, grilled etc.	5

Cooking Fat	Total fat content (g/100g)
Butter	82.0
Margarine	82.0
Gold	40.7
Outline	40.7
Low-fat spreads	40.7
Cream, single	21.2
Cream, soured	21.2
Cream, whipping	35.0
Cream, double	48.2

Cheese	
Camembert, Brie, etc.	23.2
Cheddar, Cheshire, Gruyère, Emmental, etc.	33.5
Danish Blue, Roquefort, etc.	29.2
Edam, Gouda, St.Paulin, etc.	22.9
Parmesan	29.7
Stilton	40.0
Cream cheese	47.4
Low-fat Cottage Cheese (see carton)	0-4
Medium-fat Curd Cheese	25
Medium-fat Mozzarella, etc.	25

Fish	
Eel, stewed	13.2
Herring, grilled	13.0
Bloater, grilled	12.9
Kipper, baked	6.2
Mackerel, grilled	6.2
Salmon, steamed	13.0
Sardines, canned (drained)	13.0
Sprats, grilled (estimated value)	13.0
Trout, steamed	3.0
Tuna, canned (includes oil)	22.0
Tuna, canned (drained, estimated value)	13.0

Nutrition BY ALISON CAVALIERO

A REGULAR intake of food enables the body to work, grow and repair itself, and therefore the kind of food consumed can affect the efficiency of the body processes: from the vital mending of bones, healing of wounds and making of red blood cells, to the more noticeable general physical appearance and energy levels.

The types of food we consume each day are linked in the most complicated and intricate way. Each food source is reliant on another and, whatever the food, it can be broken down into these basic constituents: carbohydrates; fat; proteins; vitamins and minerals. These elements must be included in the diet in the right proportions, according to individual needs. If, for example, supplies of carbohydrate are low, the body will quickly metabolize fat and, in extreme cases, this could cause a disturbance in the body's acid balance, a condition known as acidosis. If, at the same time, reserves of fat and dietary protein are low, there will not be enough protein to replace body tissue and wasting will result, a phenomenon known as protein calorie malnutrition - the most prevalent kind of malnutrition in the world.

Carbohydrates

Carbohydrates are the principal sources of energy for all mammals, accounting for 80 per cent of calorie intake in many countries. They contribute a great deal to the taste and texture of food and also provide vital supplies of fibre. The modern diet is often seriously lacking in fibre. Carbohydrates are to be found in the familiar daily foods: bread, breakfast cereals, potatoes, rice, pasta, fruit and vegetables. Starch is the main form of carbohydrate present in all these foodstuffs. It is insoluble in water and indigestible unless cooked by itself or with liquid, when the starch cells burst out and gelatinize, improving digestibility, taste and texture. As fruit ripens, starch is converted to sugar which gives fruit its natural sweetness.

High consumption of processed or refined carbohydrates in white bread, cake and biscuits may result, over a period of time, in the system being prone to constipation or more seriously, in extreme cases, colitis, diverticulitis, hiatus hernia and even cancer of the bowel. Refined carbohydrates give the body short bursts of energy that are used up quickly; thus, to satisfy the body's need for sustenance, their intake will be increased. This situation has led to an unusual way of consuming food, perhaps anything from 5-10 small intakes per day from fizzy drinks, crisps and chocolate bars to hamburgers and other take-away 'fast' foods. The healthier and more satisfying alternative would be to have regular meals with plenty of fresh fruit and vegetables which would eliminate the need to consume these 'empty calories' which are lacking in nutritional goodness and contribute little to a balanced, healthy diet.

Most of us do not get sufficient fibre in our diet. Fibre is the indigestible material that makes up the cell walls in plants, and adds roughage and bulk to our diet. It helps keep our bowels healthy and regular, absorbs toxic waste products in the gut and helps eliminate them from the body, thereby protecting us against colitis, appendicitis, diverticular disease, ulcers and bowel cancer. And by adding bulk to your diet, you feel full up more quickly and don't want to eat high-calorie refined foods. Good sources of fibre are: wholemeal bread and wholegrain cereals, brown rice, jacket potatoes, beans, pulses, seeds, many fresh fruits and vegetables.

Carbohydrates, like fat, produce heat. Small amounts will play an important part in the structure of connective and nerve tissues, in the activity of hormones, in the immune system and in the general process by which one cell recognizes another. Once eaten, carbohydrates are converted into glucose, which is the body's preferred fuel. This circulates through the blood to all cells in the body. Whereas most tissue can burn fat for energy, the brain and other nervous tissue can use only glucose. Blood glucose levels are critical to the healthy and efficient functioning of the body, and disorders of the complex hormone system that regulate this, could give rise to diseases such as diabetes.

Natural sugars

The main sugar in food is sucrose, which is divided into glucose, fructose, maltose and lactose. These in turn are divided into two groups:

MONOSACCHARIDES (simple sugars) e.g. fructose, glucose, galactose
These are the sorts of sugars found naturally in foods, for example, fruit, vegetables and honey. Because they are natural sources containing sweetness as well as amounts of starch, vitamins, minerals, protein and fibre, they give the body more to work on and, as a result, are broken down and used more gradually.

DISACCHARIDES (refined sugar)
This is the sort that comes from sugar cane. As it is processed, it will give a more immediate burst of energy. The processing chain is a very long one so it is best to use raw cane sugar. As this is near the beginning of the process, it will contain more goodness. To ensure that you buy the true product, look for the country of origin marked on the packet, thus avoiding dyed white sugar.

Sugar, whatever the source, will provide the same amount of calories regardless of the degree of sweetness. The extra 'empty' calories are due to the fact that more refined sugar is required to satisfy desire because it is used up by the body more quickly.

There is an increased awareness about the health risks associated with eating too much sugar, and many people try to eat less by cutting down its use in hot drinks, buying reduced sugar jams and tinned fruit in natural juice. However, without it, many processed foods would not exist. Sugar has extraordinary properties, keeping gluten soft in cakes and biscuits, strengthening the structure of egg whites for meringues and acting as a food for yeast, to name a few. This is where the danger could lie. If the diet depends heavily on processed and refined sweet and savoury foods, the personal intake of sugar could be alarmingly high. Much of the sugar we eat is 'hidden' in processed foods and we may not even be aware of its presence if we do not read the labels carefully. In 1910, approximately 25 per cent of sugar consumption was hidden in commercial foods. Today that figure has risen to 70 per cent, which in extreme cases could mean an annual consumption of 50kg per person.

Food sources: These can be divided into refined and unrefined carbohydrates.
Unrefined carbohydrates include: Baked jacket potatoes, wholemeal bread, root vegetables, dried beans and peas, brown rice, wholewheat pasta, porridge oats, buckwheat, bulghur wheat, sprouted grains and seeds.
Refined carbohydrates include: Sugar, cakes, biscuits, white rice, white bread, etc.

Fats

Like carbohydrates, fats are used as an energy source, and form an important layer of fatty deposits, known as the adipose layer. This protects nerve tissue and delicate organs, acts as insulation helping to maintain the correct body temperature, and enables fat-soluble vitamins to circulate through the body. Fats store twice as much energy in a given volume as carbohydrates. For example, 450g/1lb of fat will provide enough calories for 1-2 days of activity. Therefore when physically active, fat can be useful, but if little or no exercise is taken, the excess will be stored in the body.

Fat is a popular element of food providing flavour, a smooth texture and a sensation of fullness – the very desirable properties that encourage over-eating. In the developed world, fat accounts for 40 per cent of the total calorie intake, whereas the figure is as low as 10 per cent in the developing countries. It is possible to have very little fat in the diet and remain perfectly healthy. The average woman is approximately 25 per cent fat; the average man 15 per cent fat. This difference accounts for varying nutritional needs. The adipose layer is continually changing, as there is a constant breakdown of fat. When synthesis exceeds breakdown, weight will be put on. Fats are not soluble in water (the body's chemical medium) and thus they have to be processed specially during digestion, being broken down into small droplets. The complexity of fat assimilation has one major effect: because it is a slow digestive process, it delays the reoccurrence of hunger. This is one reason why fatty foods seem especially filling and satisfying.

Fats do more than just store energy. Certain fatty acids are converted by the body into phospholipids (in which the brain, liver and nervous system are very rich) and these provide the base material for cell membranes, enabling the transportation of other molecules in and out of the cells to take place, plus providing essential fatty acids – those that cannot be made by the body.

Fats themselves are often 'hidden' in the diet in the form of 'invisible' fats. As well as butter, oil and margarine, there are invisible fats found in nuts, seeds and lean meat, for example. These can be divided into 2 groups: saturated (those that are usually hard at room temperature, generally of animal origin); and polyunsaturated fats found in most vegetable margarines using oils like soya and peanut. These may be of benefit to the heart and skin as they help to reduce the stickiness of the blood and can lower the levels of blood fats. Mono-unsaturated fats are not as well known as polyunsaturated; the best-known example is olive oil. Traditional peasant cultures use a great deal of this type of oil in the diet. The Mediterranean diet is a fine example, the result being a very low incidence of coronary heart disease.

Food sources: Vegetable and seed oils, nuts, oily fish (e.g. mackerel and herring), cheese, milk, cream, butter, lard, margarine, fat on meat, yoghurt.

Hidden fats are found in: Sauces, cakes, biscuits, mayonnaise, chocolate, pastry, processed meat products etc.

Cholesterol

Cholesterol came to the public's attention when studies were published linking saturated fats with the development of heart disease. Cholesterol is similar to but not actually a fat, coming from a different chemical family – the lipids.

It is found in high quantities in animal-based products, for example, liver, kidneys, heart, egg yolks and shellfish. It is a well-known fact that excessive quantities in the diet lead to deposits building up on the walls of the blood vessels, which may eventually cause circulatory problems. However, cholesterol is not always harmful. It is, in fact, an important molecule as the body makes quantities of it to produce the nucleus of vitamin D and other regulatory hormones. Indeed, if there is not sufficient cholesterol in the diet, the body compensates by producing more. Together with bile salts, it also contributes to the fluidity of cell membranes.

Most cholesterol production takes place in the liver and intestine, and because the body processes it independently of dietary intake (it appears to be raised by ingestion of saturated fat), it usually results in excessive quantities being present. The body finds it difficult to get rid of cholesterol once it is in the system – it cannot be broken down and very little is excreted. This situation is made worse by evidence that physical inactivity and emotional stress increase cholesterol levels. The modern Western diet provides on average an intake of 6-8 times the actual nutritional requirements of fat for all bodily processes. One tablespoon of vegetable oil is sufficient to carry the fat-soluble vitamins and linoleic acid needed for daily life. Reducing fat in the diet is made more difficult by the fact that two-thirds of it will be of the invisible kind. Therefore the foods to be aware of are meat, cheese, deep-fried foods, sauces, mayonnaise, avocado pears, nuts, seeds, snacks and convenience foods.

Protein

The World Health Organisation suggests that the average person requires 40g of protein per day, yet the average person in the West consumes 90g. The body needs protein because these foods are the only ones that contain nitrogen, sulphur and phosphorous, which are vital for life. They are needed for the body's construction, growth and repair of skin, nails, hair, cartilage, tendons, bones and muscles. Protein helps maintain the metabolic balance by regulating insulin, hormones, antibodies and haemoglobin. As these are continually worn away, so regular protein in the diet is in demand by the body. Protein therefore provides the correct environment for bodily processes to continue.

Protein foods are made up of amino acids, which are small organic chemicals. When food containing protein is digested, it is broken down into its constituent amino acids, which are subsequently absorbed and new proteins are made. The human body can make some amino acids, but others have to be obtained from the diet – these are known as essential amino acids. Adults need 8 of these and growing children 9-10; the body will be able to make the rest (non-essential amino acids). The quality of the protein will depend on its ability to supply all the essential amino acids in the required amounts. For a long time, animal protein was regarded as a first-class protein, while vegetable sources – nuts, seeds, pulses and grains – were thought of as inferior as they lacked an essential amino acid (second-class proteins). However, it is now recognized that provided that the vegetable sources are used in combination with each other, i.e. grain and pulse, nut and grain for example, they do provide a complete protein.

The amount of protein recommended by the experts has varied over the years. Recent research shows that a much lower daily intake is sufficient for all bodily requirements. The average man needs only to consume 55-85g/2-3oz, the average woman 55-70g/2-2½oz per day, depending on their type of work. This quantity can be obtained from as little as 570ml/1 pint of milk with 55g/2oz of cheese, for example, which suggests that many people eat excessive amounts. Too much will be neither harmful nor beneficial. It is thought that calcium may be required to counterbalance lack of protein; an excess is thought to put a strain on the kidneys as they have to cope with the higher load of residue from protein breakdown.

Food sources: Meat, fish, poultry, offal, eggs, cheese, milk, yoghurt, wholegrain bread and cereals, brown rice, beans, lentils, split peas, nuts and seeds.

Vitamins and minerals

The nickname 'limey' originated in the 1800s when the British Navy decreed that limes should be part of ships' rations to prevent scurvy on board after it was discovered that the disease could be cured by vitamin C. Many other diseases and medical conditions are caused by vitamin deficiencies, and so it is essential to get the recommended daily amounts from your diet in order to maintain good health. Vitamins are required only in small quantities, their function being to perform specific roles in the metabolic process: for example, regulation of growth, tissue replacement and general cellular activity. A well-balanced diet which includes plenty of fresh fruit and vegetables correctly prepared and cooked should provide all the basic requirements without the necessity for vitamin and mineral supplements.

Vitamins are divided into 2 groups:

FAT-SOLUBLE VITAMINS

For these to be absorbed efficiently by the body, small amounts of fat need to be present in the diet.

VITAMIN A: This is needed for growth and resistance to disease. Deficiency leads to dryness around the eyes.
Food sources of vitamin A: Milk, cheese, butter, margarine, eggs, liver, kidney, fish liver oils, dark green leafy vegetables, carrots, dried apricots, yellow vegetables and fruit.

VITAMIN D: This controls the absorption of the calcium and phosphorous needed for healthy bones and teeth. Vitamin D is also absorbed by the action of sunlight on the skin.

Food sources of vitamin D: Fish liver oils (e.g. sardine, herring, salmon, tuna), milk, yoghurt, egg yolks, fortified margarine, cheese and butter.

VITAMINS E & K: Vitamin E is needed for fertility and helps to prevent premature ageing, while Vitaimin K is needed for clotting of blood.
Food sources of vitamins E and K: Wheatgerm, avocado pears, vegetable oils, wholegrain cereals, eggs, soya beans, leafy green vegetables, yoghurt, molasses, alfalfa seeds.

WATER-SOLUBLE VITAMINS

These are more unstable than the fat-soluble kind, as they can be lost in food processing and cookery, e.g. through milling of flour, cooking or soaking water, destruction by heat and sensitivity to oxygen. Great care is therefore needed when preparing fruit and vegetables.

VITAMIN B COMPLEX: This is composed of 13 different constituents needed in varying proportions including thiamine (B1), riboflavin (B2) and niacin (B3). They are vital for the utilization of carbohydrates and the functioning of the nervous system. Vitamin B6 is important for the metabolism and formation of red blood cells. Deficiency leads to weakness.
Food sources of vitamin B1 (thiamine): Meat, liver, kidney, wholegrain cereals and bread, milk, brewer's yeast, beans, brown rice, wheatgerm, lentils and eggs.
Food sources of vitamin B2 (riboflavin): Milk, cheese, eggs, liver, nuts, dark green leafy vegetables, beans, mushrooms, wholemeal bread, avocado pears and yoghurt.
Food sources of vitamin B3 (niacin): Liver, kidney, sardines, nuts, meat, fish, poultry, eggs, milk, wholegrain cereals and bread, dried apricots, dates and prunes, avocado pear, potatoes, swede and parsnip.
Food sources of vitamin B6 (pyridoxine): Wholegrain cereals and bread, liver, kidney, meat, mackerel, fish, nuts, eggs, milk, bananas.

VITAMIN C This is very sensitive to heat, air and alkalis. The older the food, the lower the vitamin C levels. Vitamin C is necessary for healthy skin and muscles, efficient brain and nerve function and helps prevent infection.
Food sources of vitamin C: Citrus fruits, blackcurrants, strawberries, dark green leafy vegetables, potatoes, tomatoes, peppers and cauliflower.

ESSENTIAL MINERALS

These are found in even smaller amounts than vitamins, but even so they are vital for good health.

IRON: This forms part of the haemoglobin – needed for carrying oxygen around the body. Our bodies are unable to use all sources of iron with equal efficiency: animal sources are utilized more easily than vegetable sources. A lot of the iron we eat is not absorbed fully by the body, but eating iron-rich foods together with a source of vitamin C can increase absorption. For example, you can do this by eating a fresh orange and watercress salad with liver.
Food sources of iron: liver, kidney, meat, dark green leafy vegetables, egg yolk, dried apricots, peas and beans.

CALCIUM: In combination with phosphorous, this gives strength to bones and teeth. When the intake of calcium is greater than the body's requirements, excess is stored in the bones, and therefore, when there is a shortfall, this stored supply meets the demand. It is essential for the clotting of blood and transmission of nerve impulses to the muscle.
Food sources of calcium: milk, cheese, yoghurt, sardines, eggs, leafy green vegetables and beans.

MAGNESIUM: This is found in your bones and is needed to synthesize the protein in your body. It also helps build healthy teeth and makes nerves and muscles work properly, and helps combat stress.
Food sources of magnesium: Brown rice, oatmeal, dark green leafy vegetables, nuts, peas, beans, lemons, grapefruit and seafood.

ZINC: You need this mineral for growth, strong bones and a good appetite. People on a diet of highly processed foods often get too little zinc.
Food sources of zinc: Liver, seafood, seeds, meat, eggs, mushrooms, wholegrain cereals and beans.

Other important minerals that should be included in the diet are iodine and potassium. However, not all minerals are good for us and you should learn to distinguish between the beneficial and the harmful ones. Some metals are toxic and can build up in your body. These include aluminium, lead, copper, cadmium and mercury.

WATER

This is an essential constituent of every body tissue and cell. The body's tissue is 60 per cent water, and since all its processes take place in a fluid medium it follows that plain water should be a vital part of the daily diet. Water forms the basis of the body fluid, i.e. blood plasma, lymph and tissue fluid. It also acts as a solvent for the important salts of sodium and potassium and other vitamins and minerals necessary for metabolism. Water is required for the elimination of excess salts and the waste products that dissolve in it.

SPECIAL DIETS

There are many people who require special diets for cultural, ethical, religious or medical reasons, so it is important when cooking for other people to find out whether they have any dietary restrictions. Whether cooking professionally or for friends, it is essential to stick to the rules. In extreme cases 'cheating' could be harmful: for instance, someone on a gluten-free diet who is given wheat flour could become seriously ill.

HINDUS

Most Hindus are vegetarian and many do not eat eggs. The cow is sacred to Hindus and thus no Hindu will ever eat beef. Most cheese is to be avoided because it is often made with animal rennet. Butter, vegetable oil and ghee are used for frying. Lard and dripping are not allowed.

JUDAISM

The degree to which Jews stick to the dietary rules varies considerably and strictly Orthodox kosher Jews cannot eat in a catering establishment unless it has been passed by a rabbi. Even cooking utensils have to be kosher. When Moses came down from Mount Sinai he gave the waiting Jewish women the code of culinary practice that has existed ever since. Originally it was a code of hygiene. It forbade shellfish (including squid and octopus), pork, rabbit, carrion (i.e. an animal that has died of its own accord), birds of prey, and creatures that crawl on their bellies. The code permitted beasts that chew the cud and have cloven hooves, as long as the animal was killed by Jewish slaughter methods (i.e. stunned and purged of its blood), fish with scales and fins, and herbivorous birds. Thus beef, lamb, goat, turkey, chicken, duck (not wild), goose, pheasant and partridge are permitted.

Foods of animal and dairy origin cannot be combined during cooking and may not be served together. Dairy foods can only be served after meat if a specific number of hours has elapsed between the two foods. This can be difficult and explains why in many Jewish cookery books synthetic cream is used for puddings, and why chicken fat is often used in place of butter when cooking meat. Savoury white sauces are sometimes made from stock, egg yolk and cornflour instead of the traditional roux-based white sauce.

MUSLIMS All meat can be eaten except pork and any carnivorous animal. Meat has to be slaughtered according to Muslim law and must come from a Halal butcher. Muslims avoid many prepared cakes, biscuits, ice creams and pastries which may contain either lard or fats from animals not slaughtered in the correct way. However, fish, eggs and dairy foods are permitted. No alcohol is allowed even as an ingredient in a recipe.

Medical modification

The following information is meant only as a basic guideline, and you should always seek professional help and advice when preparing special diets for medical conditions.

GLUTEN FREE

Specifically for coeliacs. Gluten is a protein found in wheat, rye, oats and barley so all these cereals and any food that contains them (such as cakes, bread, pasta) must not be eaten. A gluten-free diet must be followed for life, even when the symptoms disappear. The diet must be adhered to or the symptoms will reappear.

The important thing is to eliminate flour from the diet. A special gluten-free flour is available from chemists, and a range of gluten-free products can be obtained on prescription. Rice flour, wheat starch, soya flour, potato flour, maize flour and gluten-free baking powder can be used for making cakes and breads. Do not use any meat products as they may well have gluten in them; use only fresh or frozen plain meats and fish. Check the labels on cereals and all manufactured products including instant coffee, sweets and packet soups. It is a difficult diet and needs adventurous recipes!

ULCERS

If you have an ulcer you should eat nothing too hot nor too cold, nothing too spicy nor too sweet. In other words, treat yourself gently. Eat little and often, chew slowly and drink some milk. Eat wholefoods and avoid fried foods, strong tea and coffee. Drink plenty of liquid in between meals.

HIATUS HERNIA

Sufferers should eat small light meals - little and often - containing high-fibre foods, and drink plenty of liquids.

DIABETES

This affects one in 75 people, to a lesser or greater degree, so professional advice must be followed rigidly. The basic rules are to reduce your intake of foods high in calories, all sugar (including products containing sugar or glucose), saturated fats and low-fibre food. Diabetics should increase their intake of wholefoods, fresh fruits and vegetables. All diabetic products are forbidden with the exception of diabetic fruit products. Diabetics are advised to eat little and often. All labels of manufactured foods and medicines (such as cough linctus) have to be read carefully to avoid mistakes.

GOUT

This is a painful disease, and very often the medical advice to those who have had gout is to stick to a low-purine (i.e. low in nucleic acid) diet for the rest of their lives. Again, professional advice must be sought, but the basic recommendations are to eat only a small amount of meat or fish a day and to avoid the following: offal, gravies and meat extracts, sardines, meat or broth soups, wholemeal bread, crispbreads or biscuits, wholemeal cereals (including porridge), spinach, peas, mushrooms, strawberries, asparagus, cauliflower, dried fruit and vegetables, nuts, Ovaltine and all chocolate. Alcohol should also be restricted.

HEART DISEASE

Follow the diet as described in Healthy Eating (see page 32) but be careful to avoid foods that are low in saturated fat but high in cholesterol such as most offals and all shellfish. Also do not eat many egg yolks in any form - mayonnaise, for example.

CONVALESCENCE

Drink plenty of liquids; iron replacement may be necessary; and the general advice is to eat red meats, offal, fish (especially oily fish), pulses and bread.

Food safety

Food safety and hygiene are essential in the kitchen as many foods may contain harmful organisms. The cook must be aware of these bacteria and of how to prevent them multiplying to dangerous levels in food which would cause food poisoning.

Salmonella is one of the commonest causes of food poisoning and is most often brought into the kitchen on poultry and meat. Campylobacter (the symptoms of which may not appear for 10 days) usually enters on raw poultry. Clostridium perfringens is often present on raw meats, or unwashed vegetables. The origin of Staphylococcus aureus is usually the food handler with inadequately covered skin infections. The latter two organisms can produce illness within a few hours of eating. Listeria is commonly found in many foods but listeriosis is very rare as most people's immunity copes well. Special dietary advice regarding listeriosis applies only to vulnerable groups who are particularly at risk. These are pregnant women and those with underlying illness which results in impaired resistance to infection. These special groups are advised to avoid soft ripened cheeses of the Brie, Camembert and blue vein types and pâtés and to reheat cooked chilled meals and ready-to-eat poultry until piping hot rather than eat them cold.

PREVENTING THE GROWTH OF BACTERIA

Bacteria will grow to toxic levels if given the chance. What they need to do their evil work is warmth, time and moisture, and the ideal conditions, from the bugs' point of view, would be lukewarm food left out in a hot kitchen for several hours. A tiny (and therefore harmless) colony of bacteria could multiply rapidly to such an extent that anyone eating that food could become very ill or hospitalized. If the victim was a baby (with an immune system not fully developed) or an elderly person or invalid (whose immunity might be impaired), death could result.

Fortunately there are some easy steps to take to prevent food poisoning. You can wash off bacteria (such as listeria from salad vegetables etc.); you can kill the organisms with heat; you can arrest their growth by refrigeration; and you can prevent cross-contamination by practising good hygiene in the kitchen.

THE GOLDEN RULES ARE:

BUYING Buy only very fresh food from suppliers you can trust.

WASHING Wash all food if it is to be eaten raw. It is good practice to wash all fruits and vegetables, even if they are to be peeled, as they could contaminate other foods. If you buy free-range eggs wash them just before cooking – salmonella is more likely to be present on the egg shell than in the egg.

REFRIGERATION Refrigerate all meat, fish and chicken, all dairy products and eggs. Until the discovery of salmonella in eggs, refrigeration of eggs was not thought to be necessary. The danger is still small, but why take any unnecessary risks? Besides, eggs lose their freshness and become stale much more quickly when they are not stored in a fridge.

Keep food refrigerated as much as you can. Never leave it on the side in the kitchen waiting to be used, and never leave cold, cooked food at room temperature for more than an hour or so.

Although the original cooking will have destroyed any bacteria, the food can be re-infected and, if left in a warm atmosphere, can become harmful.

Do not put hot food in the refrigerator. It will warm up the atmosphere inside the fridge and encourage the growth of any bacteria present in other foods in the cabinet.

As far as possible, always keep raw and cooked food separated until serving. Bacteria can enter the kitchen on raw food, and then can be transferred to cooked food where they might easily be left to multiply in peace if the food is not to be re-cooked.

COOKING Cook food sufficiently to kill any bacteria that may be present. In particular chicken, chopped meats, rolled joints, burgers and reformed steaks must be cooked thoroughly as food-poisoning bacteria may be present in the centres of these. If cooking for the very young, the very old or the infirm, egg yolks should be cooked hard. (Soft-cooked eggs may not have reached a sufficiently high temperature to kill salmonella.)

RAW MEAT AND FISH Consumption of raw meat and fish carries a risk of food poisoning. Meat and fish that are traditionally served raw, such as sushi and steak tartare, must be of the freshest, best quality, and should be prepared and eaten on the day they are purchased. Some traditional dishes, such as gravad lax, smoked salmon, or Parma ham, although they are raw, can be kept safely under refrigeration because they have been cured either with salt or smoke, or both.

REHEATING If reheating food, make sure that you serve it really hot, i.e. near boiling point, even right in the middle.

Do not pour hot sauces on to cold food unless you are going to reheat it right through at once. Don't add warm food to cold food. Don't mix yesterday's soup with today's without reboiling. Always reheat any mixture immediately if adding two things of different temperatures together. Remember that the cool one might contain a few bacteria, and the hot one will provide enough heat to start them multiplying, but not enough to kill them.

Reboil stocks, soups and sauces frequently in hot weather. Even in winter, reboil them every three days. In theory, you can keep the same stockpot on the go for ever if you reboil it every time you add anything to it. And remember that the stronger the stock, the firmer it will set to a jelly, and the better it will keep in the fridge. If reheating aspic, bring it to the boil, then let it cool enough to use.

KEEPING FOOD WARM If food must be kept warm, first make sure that it is heated through sufficiently to kill all bacteria; then keep it really hot, not lukewarm. Do not pour a warm sauce over, say, cold poached eggs and keep them warm in a hot cupboard.

FREEZING Do not refreeze completely thawed food without cooking it first. Although the freezing and thawing does no harm, it is easy to forget just how many periods at room temperature the food has had, and therefore it is impossible to guess how large the concentration of bacteria may be. Never refreeze chicken that has been frozen and thawed.

COOKING FROM FROZEN Do not cook large items (e.g. whole chickens) when frozen. When the bird looks cooked, the inside (where salmonella is most likely to be present on the surface of the cavity) may still be lukewarm and raw. For the same reason, it is unwise to stuff large birds. The stuffing may prevent the heat from penetrating the cavity and killing any bacteria present.

THAWING Thaw food slowly in the fridge, or in a leakproof plastic bag under cold water. Do not try to thaw things fast by putting them in a warming drawer or under hot water. The outer layer will stay at incubating temperature too long. However, microwaving to thaw is safe because it is so fast that the bacteria do not have time to breed. But cook the food as soon as it is thawed, just in case your microwave has warmed it up too much.

COOLING Cool large quantities of food fast. If a stew is left to cool in a heavy pan, the centre of it will provide perfect bacteria breeding conditions: warmth, moisture and time. And a stir with a non-sterile wooden spoon could easily provide the parent bacteria to start the colony. Commercial caterers cool food in a blast chiller, but small kitchens do not have this luxury. So either tip the stew into shallow flat containers to cool, or cool the pot fast by standing it in a bowl in the sink, and continuously running the cold tap into the bowl, to keep the waterjacket round the pan cool. Give it an occasional stir to speed things up.

Neither should you leave food covered with a heavy lid. Open food cools quicker. If you want to avoid the food drying out or forming a skin, place some wet greaseproof paper (which is thin enough not to hinder cooling) flat on the surface of the food.

WRAPPING Take care when wrapping hot food in polythene – if there are any air spaces between the food and the film, greenhouse-like incubating conditions will be produced. Instead, wrap the food loosely in foil, and refrigerate as soon as it is cold.

UTENSILS Don't use the same knife or board for raw and cooked food without washing it between jobs. If you have just jointed a raw chicken and then you slice cooked beef with the same knife, you could transfer bacteria from the chicken to the beef. The micro-organisms in the chicken will get cooked to death, but they could grow with impunity in the beef. Caterers have separate fridges and boards, and large-production kitchens very often have separate kitchens and separate cooks. The home cook, however, who is dealing with small quantities of food that are cooked, eaten or refrigerated fast, need not go to such lengths but should practise good food hygiene and take sensible precautions, always washing utensils thoroughly after use.

Keep the kitchen clean. This means washing tools in near-boiling water often, scrubbing boards and surfaces with detergent, washing out the fridge weekly with weak bleach, and making sure that tea towels and cloths are changed as soon as they are dirty or damp. A damp cloth left over a warm cooker, or a crack in the wooden handle of a much-used knife provides the perfect incubating conditions for germs.

'OFF FOODS' Don't ever serve food that smells or looks at all peculiar. Although salmonella is completely tasteless and has no discernible odour, unpleasant odours or appearance are an indication of age and poor condition, and food-poisoning organisms are likely to be present along with the ones causing the obvious deterioration. Always err on the safe side and throw out any food that looks or smells dubious - don't take risks.

SALMONELLA IN EGGS Consumption of raw eggs or uncooked dishes made from them, such as home-made mayonnaise, mousse and ice cream, carries the risk of food poisoning. However, if you do use raw eggs to make these dishes make sure you use only the freshest eggs, that the dishes are eaten as soon as possible after making and that they are never left for more than one hour at room temperature.

For healthy people there is little risk from eating eggs which are cooked however prepared - boiled, fried, scrambled or poached. Vulnerable people such as the elderly, the sick, babies, toddlers and pregnant women should only eat eggs that have been thoroughly cooked until the white and yolk are solid. These vulnerable people should avoid egg recipes which require light cooking such as meringues and hollandaise sauce.

Lightly cooked egg dishes should be eaten as soon as possible after cooking and if the dishes are not for immediate use they should be stored in the refrigerator after cooling. Pasteurised egg, which is free from harmful bacteria, is often used by caterers in making these dishes and is available as a useful alternative in the home.

POISONOUS FOODS Some foods are naturally poisonous and must be treated with care. For example, red kidney beans mut be boiled for 10 minutes to destroy an enzyme which is potentially fatal. Cooking the beans until soft at a very low temperature is not sufficient to do this, so, if using a 'slow cooker', give the beans a good boil before putting them into the pot.

Green potato skins, rhubarb leaves and many wild mushrooms are mildly poisonous and can cause gastric upsets to some people. Indeed, a few wild mushrooms are lethal. Do not cook any mushrooms that are not purchased from a reputable supplier, unless you are certain they are safe. Do not gather and cook wild mushrooms unless you have the knowledge to distinguish between the safe and poisonous varieties.

Choosing and storing produce

THIS CHAPTER is not meant to be a guide to household management – I am not going to suggest that I tell people how to organize their shopping. However, I thought it might be helpful to offer you a few guidelines on how to recognize good-quality food and how best to store it. For freezability, please see the chapter on freezing (see page 571).

Meat

When choosing meat, the general principle is to look for signs that it has come from a young animal. It should not be too fatty, the joints should be reasonably small, it should be of a firm texture and not have too much gristle, although obviously there are different expectations about the quantity of acceptable fat and gristle depending on the particular cut of meat. Meat should never be slimy; it should be moist but not gelatinous and it should not smell. Any exposed bones should be pinky blue in colour and the paler the fat the better.

STORAGE

Always allow meat to breathe, so if it comes tightly wrapped up, pierce the cling film and refrigerate for not more than 2 or 3 days. Raw meat should always be stored at the bottom of the refrigerator so that no raw blood can drop on to cooked food – this can be a cause of food poisoning.

BEEF

Generally you should look for a deep, dull red piece of meat rather than a bright, orange-red joint. This is difficult in a supermarket because managers assume that their customers want 'bright' meat so there is much use of clever lighting as well as the widespread use of adding anti-oxidants. The fat on beef should be a creamy yellow colour. Scotch beef is reputed to be better than other varieties and it comes with a price to match.

VEAL

The flesh should be pale pink, soft, but not flabby, and finely grained. There should be a very little creamy white fat. Do not worry if there is a lot of gelatinous tissue around the meat as this is a natural characteristic of a very immature animal. Dutch veal is generally considered to be the best.

LAMB

The colour of the meat varies with the breed of lamb. The fat should be creamy white, it should not be oily, and if it is yellow it indicates old age. All joints should be plump rather than long and thin. The skin should be pliable; not hard and wrinkled. Welsh or English lamb is considered to be superior to New Zealand lamb.

PORK

The meat should be pale pink, close grained and firm to the touch. It should not have enlarged glands or abscesses (pigs kept too close together, reasonably enough, bite each other).The fat should be firm and white, not oily, and without a greyish tinge. There should be an even covering of fat. Try to find free-range pork; it has an excellent flavour.

OFFAL
Offal has often been called 'awful offal' in the past, but at last it is gaining the recognition it deserves as a delicacy. It tends to be low in fat and high in iron and is very healthy. All offal must be eaten very fresh.

LIVER
It should not have a strong smell; it should be shiny and a little bloody.

CALVES' LIVER It should be a pale milky brown colour with a fine even texture. Dutch liver is considered better than English.

LAMBS' LIVER This is darker in colour than calves' liver.

PIGS' LIVER This is dark and close textured. It is used in pâtés and terrines.

OX LIVER This is dark bluish-brown with a very strong flavour. Used occasionally in stews and pies but it is very inferior to other sorts of liver and is best avoided.

KIDNEY
Kidneys are sold loose or still in their suet. To store kidneys, remove them from the suet and refrigerate for a maximum of 24 hours. Make sure that they are not tightly wrapped in cling film - they must be allowed to breathe.

VEAL KIDNEYS These are delicious. They should be a pale milky brown with a creamy white suet. They look rather like a bunch of grapes.

LAMBS' KIDNEYS These are medium brown, faintly bluish, firm textured and egg shaped.

PIGS' KIDNEYS These are pale brown with a rather strong flavour, similar in shape to lambs' kidneys.

OX KIDNEYS These look like huge veal kidneys but are much darker in colour. They are only suitable for pies and puddings.

SWEETBREADS As with all offal, the calves' sweetbreads are the best, then the lambs' and then the ox breads. Pigs' sweetbreads are not sold.

HEADS AND BRAINS
CALVES' HEADS These are sometimes available if ordered specially. They are used mainly for boiling and serving hot. Salted, they are used for brawn.

CALVES' BRAINS The most delicate and expensive: they are soaked and blanched to remove all traces of blood before cooking, and skinned of membrane and sinew after blanching. They are excellent fried plain or in a crumb coating and have an almost creamy texture when cooked.

PIGS' HEADS These are used for brawn, fresh or salted, and can be used for sausages. The cheeks of certain long-faced breeds of pig are lightly salted and sold as Bath Chaps. They are rather fatty, but have a good flavour, and are usually eaten crumbed and fried, or cold like ham. A pig's head is sometimes used on banqueting tables as a stand-in for the now unavailable boar's head. Pigs' brains are sold in the heads.

SHEEP'S HEADS These can be boiled or stewed for use in broths and pie fillings, but are seldom available, and involve a lot of labour for very little meat.

SHEEP'S BRAINS These are less fine and delicate than calves', but more readily available. They are treated in exactly the same way.

OX CHEEK: This is sold for brawns and stews.

HEART
Heart is highly nutritious, but needs slow cooking to tenderize it. It is also very lean, and requires a sauce or plenty of basting to keep it moist. Hearts must be cleaned of all sinew and the tubes removed before cooking.

OX HEART This is large, very tough, strongly flavoured, coarse and muscular and bluish-red. It is generally used chopped or minced with other ingredients - perhaps for a filling or pie.

LAMBS' HEARTS: The smallest and most tender of the hearts, but stuffing to add flavour, slow cooking and careful basting are still necessary to moisten and tenderize the naturally lean and tough flesh.

PLUCK

The pluck is the name given to the lights (lungs), liver, pancreas and spleen. Today, lights are sold generally for pet food. The liver is sold separately. Sheep's pluck is sometimes minced for haggis.

FEET AND TROTTERS

CALVES' FEET These are seldom sold to the public. They are good for stock and calf's foot jelly due to the high concentration of gelatine present in it. Pigs' trotters are high in gelatine, and good for setting stocks, and for brawn. They can be boned, stuffed, braised, served hot with mustard sauce, or hot or cold with vinaigrette. Sheep's trotters and ox feet are not sold. Cow heel is treated before sale, and looks and tastes similar to tripe. It consists of the whole foot and heel of the animal.

TRIPE

Tripe can come from all cud-chewing animals, being the first and second stomachs, but in practice only ox tripe is sold. The first stomach (blanket tripe) is smooth, the second honeycombed.

Tripe is sold parboiled, but needs further long boiling to tenderize it. It is wise to ask the butcher how much more boiling it will need. Grey, slimy, flabby, strong-smelling tripe should be avoided. It should be thick, firm and very white. Tripe can be stewed, boiled or deep-fried. A specialist taste, it's either loved or loathed.

OXTAIL

Oxtail is sold skinned and usually jointed. Choose fat large tails with plenty of meat on them. Cow tails, which are skinny and rather tasteless, are sometimes passed off as oxtail. The meat should be dark and lean, and the fat creamy white and firm. Oxtail is high in gelatine content, so it cooks to a tender, almost sticky, stew. It is good for soups and very rich in flavour.

MARROW BONES

Marrow bones are from the thigh and shoulder bones of beef. They are sawn across in short cylinders by the butcher. They are boiled whole and served in a napkin, the diner extracting the soft rich marrow and eating it on toast. Marrow is also used as a flavouring in other dishes, such as entrecôte à la Bordelaise, where it moistens and flavours the steak.

BLOOD

Pigs' blood is used in the making of black pudding. It is mixed with fat, and stuffed into intestines like a sausage.

TONGUE

To get a pig's tongue you must buy the whole head, while calves' tongues are very rarely available. Ox and lambs' tongues can be bought, however.

OX TONGUE: It should feel soft to the touch, even though it might have a rough and pigmented skin.

LAMBS' TONGUES They are very small and are generally sold by the pound or kilo. They should be pale pink, but the roughish skin may be pigmented light or dark grey.

Game

If you want to roast your game, try and buy young tender birds or animals. You can recognize a young bird by its smooth legs, pliable feet and beaks. If it has already been plucked, feel it for pliability in the backbone. See the end of this section for a seasonal table for the various kinds of game.

STORAGE

If it has not been hung already, you should hang game, undrawn (except for rabbits, which are paunched as soon as they are killed), in a cool, dry place. Birds are hung by the neck and animals by the feet. The hanging time varies according to the animal and the weather, but a rough guide is given below with a brief description of each bird or animal. The less well hung it is, the easier it is to pluck and draw. If the game is already prepared, store it loosely wrapped in the bottom of the refrigerator.

GROUSE:

Hanging time: anything from 2-10 days.

After 2 days it does not have a strong flavour

but after 10 it will be very 'gamey'. Red or Scottish grouse is considered the best. Allow one grouse per head.

PHEASANT:
Hanging time: 3-8 days.
As with most game birds the hen pheasant is juicier than the cock. Pheasant is fairly mild in terms of 'gameyness'. Allow one pheasant to 2-3 people .

PARTRIDGE:
Hanging time: 3-4 days.
I think that a partridge, particularly the grey British as opposed to the French red leg, is the nicest of all game birds. Plucked birds should have a pale skin and plump breast. Allow one partridge per head (some people can eat 2).

WILD DUCK, TEAL AND WIDGEON:
Wild duck varies in size from the large mallard to the tiny teal. All wild duck should be eaten fresh. It tends to be rather dry and can have a fishy flavour. This can be overcome by stuffing the cavity with an orange, by marinating or by parboiling the plucked bird.

PIGEON AND SQUAB:
These are in season all the year round. Squab are fledgling pigeons. The pigeon breast should be moist, glistening dark red meat. It is difficult to judge the age of a pigeon by its appearance so you have to trust the game dealer. Allow one pigeon per head or 3 breasts each.

SNIPE:
Hanging time: 4 days.
This is a small bird with a long bill which is sometimes served pushed into the body of the bird, like a skewer, draining the head through the legs before roasting. It is traditionally roasted ungutted and served on a croûte. Snipe are very hard to find unless you shoot them yourself.

WOODCOCK:
Like the snipe, it is also roasted undrawn. It is very rarely available to buy: you have to be given woodcock as a present by a rather good shot.

QUAIL:
Eat quail fresh – preferably 24 hours after being killed. Most of today's quails are farmed and should look plump for their size. They have a slightly gamey flavour. Allow 2 quails per person.

VENISON:
Hanging time: 3-10 days.
Venison should be a good deep red colour with a firm texture and should not be slimy. It should be moist but not gelatinous with very little fat, and it therefore needs to be cooked carefully. Venison that has been hung for 3 days tastes like rather delicious beef. However, once it has been hung for 10 days it has a very gamey flavour.

Seasonal Table for Game

Grouse	12 August-10 December
Pheasant	1 October-1 February
Partridge	1 September-1 February
Wild duck, teal and widgeon	Various, starting in August and finishing in March
Pigeon and squab	In season all-year round
Snipe	August-January
Woodcock	October-January
Quail	Available all-year round
Rabbit	Wild or farmed available all year
Hare	September-March
Venison	Seasons are complicated; however, frozen venison is often available all-year round

Statutory Close Seasons for Deer

Species	Sex	England and Wales	Scotland
Red	Stags	1 May-31 July	21 October-30 June
	Hinds	1 March-31 October	16 February-20 October
Fallow	Bucks	1 May-31 July	1 May-31 July
	Does	1 March-31 October	16 February-20 October
Roe	Bucks	1 November-31 March	21 October-31 March
	Does	1 March-31 October	1 April-20 October
Sika	Stags	1 May-31 July	21 October-30 June
	Hinds	1 March-31 October	16 February-20 October
Red/Sika	Stags		21 October-30 June
Hybrids	Hinds		16 February-20 October
In addition The British Deer Society recommends the following Close Seasons for which there is no statutory provision at present			
Muntjac	Bucks Does	1 March-31 October	
Chinese Water Deer	Bucks Does	1 March-31 October 1 March-31 October	

RABBIT:

Hanging time: 24 hours.
Wild or farmed rabbit is available all the year round. Rabbits are paunched (gutted) as soon as they are killed. Wild rabbit is gamier and less tender than a farmed rabbit, whose flesh is pale white, rather like that of a chicken. If the rabbit has not been skinned, look for smooth, sharp claws and delicate soft ears.

HARE:

Hanging time: 5-6 days, unpaunched.
September-March. If the hare has not been skinned, look for smooth sharp claws and delicate soft ears. A leveret (young hare) has a hardly noticeable hare lip – this becomes deeper and more pronounced in an older animal. If the hare has been skinned, look for deep claret flesh. Only young tender joints of hare are suitable for roasting, and even they need much basting. Older hares and the tougher joints, on the other hand, are traditionally made into jugged hare.

Poultry

STORAGE OF ALL POULTRY

If the bird has been sold with giblets remove them as soon as you get home, and unwrap the bird so that it can breathe. Store at the bottom of the refrigerator for not more than 2-3 days.

CHICKENS

The more you spend on a chicken, the better it will probably taste. A frozen supermarket bird, battery raised and fed on fishmeal until the moment of slaughter, has little chance of tasting good, however well cooked. Try to buy free-range birds. They may look scrawnier than the plump-breasted oven-ready bird but the flavour is far superior.

POUSSINS These are 4-6 weeks old. They serve one person and look appetizing but have very little flavour.

DOUBLE POUSSINS These are 6-10 weeks old. They serve 2 people and have quite a good flavour.

SPRING CHICKENS These are 10-12 weeks old. They serve 3 people and have a similar flavour to that of double poussins.

ROASTERS These are usually over 3 months old and can have an excellent flavour as long as they have been reasonably raised. They normally serve 4 people.

CORN-FED CHICKENS These are normally free-range chickens fed on corn. They are yellow in colour and have a very good flavour. The French corn-fed chickens generally seem to have a better flavour than the English ones.

POULET NOIR This is a French black-legged chicken. It is more like a guinea fowl than a chicken in both shape and texture. The poulet noir is more expensive than a conventional chicken but is really worth the occasional burst of extravagance.

CAPONS These were castrated cockerels who, having lost their interest in sex, ate voraciously and became very plump and tender. They have been banned by the EEC.

BOILING FOWLS These are very rare today. They require long, slow cooking and have an excellent flavour.

DUCK

Most ducks sold today are ducklings of 7-9 weeks. A 1.8kg/4lb duck feeds only 2-3 people. Young duck is delicious, but do not buy frozen duck as you will not be able to judge the pliability of the backbone, which is the tell-tale sign of age. The skin of a fresh duck should be dry, soft and smooth. It should not be slimy and should not smell strongly. The Aylesbury duck is a very superior bird.

GOOSE

This is at its best when it weighs 4.6kg/10lb, i.e. when it is 6-9 months old. A goose can be utterly delicious but make sure that you choose a young bird as old geese can be very tough. Fresh goose has a clean white skin, which is soft and dry to the touch.

TURKEY

Try to buy fresh rather than frozen turkeys as they tend to have a better flavour. The flesh should be snow white and firm, and the skin dry and soft. A turkey can often smell a little high. Remove all the giblets as soon as possible because they deteriorate quickly, and wipe the bird inside and out before storing.

GUINEA FOWL

This is normally a little smaller than the average-sized chicken and looks rather scrawny. The taste is that of a very delicious, slightly gamey chicken. Be warned: it needs careful cooking as it should have very little fat.

Dairy products

EGGS

CHICKEN EGGS There is no nutritional difference between a battery and a free-range egg, but somehow the idea of a battery egg is depressing. If the box says 'farm eggs' it simply means battery-farmed eggs. You cannot judge the freshness of an egg from its outward appearance so buy eggs from somewhere with a rapid turnover. You can test for freshness by breaking an egg into a saucer: the yolk should be well domed and there should be 2 distinct layers of egg white, the inner circle being rather gelatinous and the outer circle a little thinner. When an egg is stale, the yolk is flatter and the 2 layers of white intermingle. Store eggs pointed-end downwards so that the air pocket in the rounded end is uppermost. They should keep for a minimum of 2 weeks in the refrigerator. If the eggs have been separated, the whites can be frozen and the yolks kept refrigerated for 2-3 days. Cover them with a little cold water to prevent a hard crust from forming, then cover with cling film.

Eggs can be tainted easily so keep them well separated from other foods. The easiest thing is to keep them in the egg box in which they have been bought.

GOOSE, DUCK, PLOVER, GULLS, TURKEY AND QUAIL EGGS All eggs should be stored in the same way as chicken eggs. The following eggs are now available fresh from farms, from specialist shops and from the occasional supermarket.

TURKEY, GOOSE AND DUCK EGGS These have too strong a flavour to be eaten in the normal way as eggs but are useful for cooking. Goose eggs make particularly good sponge cakes.

QUAIL, GUINEA FOWL AND GULLS EGG These make very good first courses served with celery salt, paprika, brown bread and butter. Quail eggs take 3 minutes to boil, guinea fowl eggs take 5, and gulls eggs are always sold ready cooked and are only in season in May and June.

MILK, CREAM AND YOGHURT

Always refrigerate milk as quickly as possible and keep it covered as it can easily be tainted by other foods in the refrigerator. An open bottle or carton of milk will go off more quickly than an unopened one. Milk keeps for about 3 days. Milk is standardized by its fat content. Most milk has been pasteurized to kill off harmful bacteria.

SKIMMED MILK A thin, slightly grey-coloured milk from which virtually all the fat has been removed. It goes off a little more quickly than 'fattier' milks.

SEMI-SKIMMED MILK As skimmed milk but with a little more fat.

'REGULAR' MILK This is the standard milk with about 3.8 per cent fat.

'RAW' MILK This unpasteurized milk is very rarely available.

HOMOGENIZED MILK This has been pasteurized and then homogenized to distribute the cream evenly throughout the milk. It has a particularly unpleasant flavour.

LONG-LIFE MILK This is milk that has been sterilized or heat treated to give it a long shelf life. It is a useful emergency stopgap but has a rather nasty flavour. Once opened, treat as fresh.

BUTTER

This is either salted or unsalted, and either pasteurized or ripened. Most English and New Zealand butter is pasteurized. Whether you buy salted or unsalted depends on your personal taste, but unsalted butter is better (although more expensive) for cooking as it contains less sediment and is consequently less likely to burn. It should be used for all butter sauces.

Unsalted butter will keep for only 2 weeks whereas salted butter can be kept for up to 4 weeks. It must always be refrigerated and should be kept tightly wrapped to prevent it drying out or becoming tainted by other foods in the refrigerator.

CHEESE

CHOOSING CHEESE Many shops proudly sell unpasteurized cheese. However, I have married into a farmhouse cheesemaking family where this foodie fad is met with scorn and derision. If the milk is not pasteurized it is probably not filtered either as the filter is an integral part of the pasteurizing machine. It might have been filtered into the milk lorry but there will be lots of twigs, hairs and worse still left in the milk. Pasteurization does not change the consistency or the taste of the milk; it only heats it up to 74°C/160°F (boiling is 100°C/212°F) and it simply kills any bugs. No responsible parent would give their children unpasteurized milk, nor should they give them unpasteurized cheese. A certain cynicism exists in my in-laws' minds – they suggest that not all cheese labelled 'unpasteurized' is in fact so. There is a logical problem in keeping the milk fresh long enough to make the cheese.

It is difficult to choose cheese in a supermarket if it has been tightly wrapped in cling film and is deceptively coloured by supermarket lighting.

HARD CHEESE (E.G. CHEDDAR, DOUBLE GLOUCESTER) Try to find a mature cheese that has a rind. It should have a good strong smell but should not smell of whey (i.e. sour milk) and nor should it smell of ammonia. If there is no odour at all, it is probably too bland. It should feel hard rather than soft and should not be sweaty, or have any mould or be cracked.

SOFT FRESH CHEESES (E.G. COTTAGE CHEESE, CURD CHEESE) They should look and smell fresh and the packaging should be undamaged.

SOFT MATURED CHEESES (E.G. BRIE, CAMEMBERT) There are a huge number of soft matured cheeses available but many of them are rather dull. I think that the best are Brie and Camembert, but I fear that the imitation Somerset Brie bears little resemblance to the real thing. Buy a soft runny cheese that does not have a chalky white rind. If it has a strong smell of ammonia do not buy it as it will have an unpleasant flavour.

FIRM MATURED CHEESES (E.G. PONT L'EVEQUE, REBLOCHON) These cheeses can vary from the rather tasteless (Port Salut) to the utterly delicious and very strong Pont l'Eveque. Firm matured cheeses should be pale, creamy and fairly firm in texture.

BLUE CHEESES (E.G. STILTON, ROQUEFORT) These cheeses can be soft or firm, and should have strong blue veins with no brown blotches.

STORING CHEESE

Ideally cheese should be kept in a larder, but as few houses have one, the next best thing is to wrap it tightly in cling film and keep it in the refrigerator. If left in the warmth of a centrally heated house it will sweat.

YOGHURT

CHOOSING YOGHURT There are many different types of yoghurt now widely available. Take no notice of the labels that proudly say 'live' – all yoghurt is live unless specified as having been pasteurized, in which case it cannot be used as a starter for making your own yoghurt. Most yoghurt is labelled 'low fat' as it is made from skimmed milk. Greek yoghurt, which is now widely available in supermarkets as well as delicatessens, is a little higher in fat than most yoghurts but the taste is utterly delicious.

STORAGE

Store in the refrigerator for 3-4 days. Note that Greek yoghurts tends to go off more quickly than other yoghurts.

Fish

For fish classifications and methods of preparation see the chapter on fish (page 237).

Fish must be purchased and eaten when it is still very fresh. Some fish is frozen on board trawlers, so do not be put off buying a frozen fish as it may well be significantly fresher than a 'fresh' fish. It is easy to tell if fish is fresh, firstly by its smell – if it has a strong fishy smell it is probably quite stale. Scaly fish should have plenty of scales and all fish should have bright eyes, red gills and firm flesh. If you press your finger into a fish and the flesh does not spring back immediately into place it is probably not fresh.

Shellfish are often sold alive in order to guarantee freshness – if buying raw shellfish, I would opt for frozen rather than for dead raw shellfish. Chinese supermarkets are often the best place to buy good-quality raw frozen shellfish. If you want to buy cooked shellfish it must be very fresh. Some fishmongers will buy and cook lobsters and crayfish to order. Cooked 'shell-on' prawns are delicious but they must be bought from a reputable source and eaten on the day of purchase. If you just need a few cooked prawns for a recipe, I would recomend that you buy frozen ones and defrost them slowly sprinkled with a little lemon juice and freshly ground black pepper.

STORING FISH

Store fish, gutted, for as short a time as possible. Refrigerate it, lightly covered with cling film, and eat on the day of purchase. Smoked fish will keep for a couple of days and vacuum-packed smoked fish will stay fresh for much longer (see the sell-by date), but as with all 'long-life' products it must be treated as fresh once opened. To store live shellfish, such as crabs, lobsters and oysters (curved side down to prevent them losing their juices), put them on a tray in the bottom of the refrigerator and cover with a damp cloth. They can be kept overnight. Mussels can be kept in a large bucket of cold water. Give them some oatmeal to eat as this will help to 'clean' them.

Vegetables and herbs

See the vegetable chapter (page 191) for detailed descriptions and uses for vegetables and herbs.

CHOOSING

The most important thing about choosing vegetables is that they should be young and fresh. Old-fashioned gardeners and many producers take pride in their enormous turnips and giant parsnips but, in fact, nothing can be nicer than a tiny, roasted parsnip or a minute braised turnip. The only vegetables that I like reasonably old (but not stale) are carrots. Young carrots can be rather flavourless compared to large, deep orange ones. Very old carrots, however, are horrid as they have woody cores.

TO CHOOSE GOOD-QUALITY VEGETABLES It is obvious by a carrot's wrinkled skin that it is old, or by a lettuce's limp leaves that it has wilted. As a general rule of thumb, the vegetables you choose should be small (of their type), brightly coloured, unwrinkled, unblemished and should look 'alert' - for example, pea pods should snap open. Fruit vegetables, such as tomatoes, avocado pears and aubergines, can be large but they should still look and feel ripe. They should also feel heavy for their size.

STORING

Unwrap any vegetables that have been sold tightly wrapped in cling film. Store them in the warmest part of the refrigerator (i.e. the salad compartment) or in a larder. The air in a refrigerator is very dry and, to prevent de-hydration, you should store root vegetables (which like to be in the dark) in brown paper bags, and above-ground vegetables in polythene bags. Make sure that the vegetables are not squeezed into too small a space. If there is no room in the refrigerator and the vegetables have to be kept in a warm room do not put them in polythene bags as they will sweat and rot. Small packets of fresh herbs will keep in their cartons for a day or 2. Large bunches can be kept in polythene bags or, like flowers, in jugs of water. Watercress is best kept leaves downwards in a jug of water.

Choosing fruit

It is fairly easy to choose good-quality fresh fruit - it should look alive, be bright skinned and, usually, be heavy for its size. It should also have a fairly strong scent without being overpowering. Some fruits, such as pears, are very rarely perfect in the shops as they are only ripe for one day and should therefore be purchased in advance and ripened at home.

STORING FRUIT

SOFT FRUIT Do not store for more than 2 days in the refrigerator. Do not prepare until ready for use - an unhulled strawberry will keep longer than a hulled one. If the fruit cannot be used in time, freeze and use for dishes such as ice creams, purées and pies.

CITRUS FRUITS AND HARD FRUITS Ideally these should be kept refrigerated in polythene bags. If there is no room in the refrigerator, do not leave them in polythene bags as they will rot.
To store these fruits for more than a week: wrap each piece of fruit individually in newspaper and place in a box in a cool place. Some fruits, (especially if under-ripe), such as quinces, apples and pears, will keep well like this for 2-3 months. Citrus fruits can be kept for 2-3 weeks. Seville oranges will only keep for 1 week but may be frozen. (Freezing will not spoil the marmalade.)

BANANAS AND AVOCADO PEARS Do not refrigerate but leave in a cool place.

STONE FRUITS (EG. APRICOTS, PLUMS, GRAPES, ETC.) Store in a cool place, preferably the refrigerator.

NOTE: Strong-smelling fruit, such as cut pineapple or melon, must be well wrapped if kept in the refrigerator as their fragrance will taint cheese, butter and milk.

Larder ingredients BY C. WALDEGRAVE

I HAVE called this section larder ingredients, not that many people, especially 'townees' like me, have larders any more, but the word conjures up a pleasing image of a cool room filled with stone storage jars. This section describes our store room at Leith's School - i.e. the basic dry ingredients that are useful to have to hand, and where necessary I have made a few notes.

MUSTARD

Buy in small pots - once opened, mustard deteriorates quite rapidly. We have smooth Dijon mustard. Dry English mustard is also useful for cheese sauces, mayonnaise and some spicy recipes.

VINEGAR

We keep Dufrais white wine vinegar as a basic ingredient although other flavoured ones, e.g. herb vinegars are a welcome additional ingredient. Malt vinegar is very useful for cleaning and the occasional recipe.

FLOURS

We have 100 per cent wholemeal (once opened it goes off quite quickly so keep in a sealed container), 85 per cent wholemeal, strong flour, plain flour, granary flour, self-raising flour, cornflour, arrowroot and rice flour.

OILS

Sunflower is good for general cooking use; extra virgin olive oil for special salads; and sesame oil for Chinese dishes. We usually have some hazelnut, walnut and sometimes pinenut oil in the refrigerator. The expensive oils tend to deteriorate quite quickly and so should be bought in small jars.

PASTA

Dried pasta keeps well in sealed containers and we always have a selection of different shapes. The versatility and reliability of dried pasta makes it a useful standby ingredient.

DRIED HERBS AND SPICES

Ideally, all herbs and spices should be fresh, but in practice this is not possible. Store them out of the sunlight and buy in small jars from a supermarket with a quick turnover as they go stale quite quickly. At Leith's we have the following herbs and spices:

Herbs	**Spices**
Bay leaves	Whole and ground nutmeg
Herbes de Provence	Whole and ground cinnamon
Rosemary	Whole and ground mace
Tarragon	Whole and ground cardamom
Oregano	Vanilla pods
	Juniper berries
	Cloves
	Coriander
	Cumin
	Turmeric
	Saffron
	Chilli
	Paprika
	Cayenne

BOTTLES

Soy sauce, Worcestershire sauce, Heinz tomato ketchup, vanilla essence, rose water, orange blossom water.

TINS

Plum tomatoes, flageolet beans, kidney beans, chick peas, tuna fish, sardines, anchovies, smoked oysters, red peppers, green peppercorns, petits pois, water chestnuts, palm hearts and sweetcorn kernels.

GRAINS
Basmati rice (brown and white), Uncle Ben's long grain rice, risotto rice, pudding rice, brown rice, couscous, cracked wheat (burghul), semolina and polenta.

NUTS
Almonds, ground, nibbed, flaked and whole; walnuts, halved; hazelnuts, whole; pinenuts, whole.

SEEDS
Sesame, poppy, mustard, pumpkin.

JAMS
Apricot, redcurrant jelly – for glazing. Honey.

SUGAR
Granulated, caster, icing, preserving, demerara, lump and muscovado.

CHOCOLATE
Chocolate Menier.

GELATINE
Leaf and powder.

DRIED FRUIT
Raisins, currants, sultanas, apples, apricots and prunes. Try to find those that have not been treated with sulphur dioxide.

COFFEE AND TEA
Earl Grey, camomile and PG Tips, Melitta filter coffee, Gold Blend instant and Café Hag decaffeinated.

Freezing

FREEZING is a method of preserving food – not indefinitely, but for some weeks or months. Bacterial action, which causes spoilage, is prevented by keeping the food at extremely low temperatures. Note that some deterioration in the taste, texture and colour of the food will take place if food is kept frozen for longer than the recommended times. Providing that the simple instructions for freezing are followed religiously, many foods can be stored successfully without any loss of nutritional value or quality.

Rapid freezing

The quicker the freezing process, the smaller will be the ice crystals formed in the food. Large ice crystals, resulting from slow freezing, damage the cell walls of the food itself, and consequently,when it is thawed, liquid will be lost, including some soluble nutrients. Meat, in particular, will lose moisture on thawing if frozen too slowly, and will be dry when cooked.

PACKING THE FREEZER

In order to facilitate rapid freezing, only small amounts of unfrozen food should be put into the freezer at one time. Large quantities of food at room temperature would raise the temperature in the freezer and, inevitably, the freezing process would be slower. For the same reason, food should not be packed in large parcels, and the items should be separated in the freezing compartment, allowing the air to circulate around them. Once they are frozen, however, they can be – and indeed should be for economy's sake – packed tightly together with as little space between them as possible. A full freezer costs less to run than a half-empty one. Many freezers contain a fast-freeze compartment for the actual freezing process, and larger compartments for storage.

WRAPPING THE FOOD

Because the cold atmosphere of a freezer is very drying, and direct contact with the icy air causes 'freezer burn' (dry discoloured patches) on some foods, most foods need careful wrapping before freezing. Heavyweight polythene bags are the cheapest and best wrappers, because it is possible to see through them, and they take various shapes of food without creating too many air spaces. However, any airtight container will suffice. Foil is sometimes used, as are rigid plastic containers, old yoghurt cartons, bowls with lids, etc.

Whatever container you use, it must be robust enough to withstand some rough handling in the freezer, and it must be possible to label it clearly. Freezer labels, or polythene bags with white labels on which it is possible to write with a freezer pen, are best. Once the food is packed into the container, as closely wrapped as possible, it should be labelled with the contents and the date, and frozen immediately. Liquids can be poured into a polythene bag set in square containers and frozen. Once solid, the bag is lifted out of the outer container and thus stored. This means fewer kitchen containers are out of use because they are in the freezer, and liquids can be stored in space-saving rectangular shapes. Liquids in plastic tubs or containers should be frozen with a 2.5cm/ 1 inch gap between bowl and lid to allow for expansion. Food should be used up in the right order – for example, peas frozen last week should not be eaten before the batch that was frozen 2 months ago. To facilitate this, a record or inventory of what is in the freezer can be kept on it, in it or near it, with additions and subtractions made each time food is put in or taken out.

Open Freezing

If frozen in a mass, fruit and vegetables will emerge from the freezer in a solid block. This can be inconvenient for thawing in a hurry, or if only a small quantity of the food is needed. For this reason, many foods are frozen on open trays so that each raspberry, pea, broad bean or sprig of cauliflower is individually frozen before packing into bags. The frozen produce will then be free flowing and separate. Use this method for sausages, beefburgers, breadcrumbs, bread rolls, etc. as well as for fruit and vegetables. Decorated cakes and puddings can be open frozen, then packed when the decoration is hard enough to withstand the tight wrapping around it.

Mass Freezing

If the food to be frozen is not suitable for open freezing, make sure that the block is not too thick. This will make cooking and thawing easier and quicker. For example, meatballs in tomato sauce should be laid one deep in a plastic box, not piled one on top of each other; spinach should be in a flattish pack so that it can be cooked from frozen (a thick block would mean overcooked outside leaves while the middle was still frozen). Air should be excluded as far as possible. This is especially important with casseroles, where the chicken or meat should be coated or covered completely by the sauce. Otherwise, the meat may become dry and fall apart on reheating.

Thawing

Thawing should be as slow as possible. Rapid thawing leads to loss of moisture and subsequent dryness or tastelessness of the food. However, it it sometimes imperative to thaw food in a hurry. To do this, put it into an air-tight polythene bag and dunk it in cold, not hot, water. Hot water tends to cook the outside of the food and encourages bacterial activity which would cause the food to go bad if not completely cooked immediately. Meat should be thawed completely, and should be at room temperature before it is cooked.

Re-freezing Frozen Food

Freezing does not kill bacteria present in food; it simply inhibits growth. So when food is removed from the freezer the bacteria in it will multiply normally. When put back, the now considerably increased population of bacteria will cease breeding, to start afresh when the food is brought back into the warmth. For this reason, frozen food manufacturers caution purchasers not to re-freeze the product once it has been thawed. They are justly nervous that if the food is taken in and out of the freezer, it could contain germs in dangerous concentrations. However, the cook may still regard the product as being perfectly fresh because it has just emerged from the freezer. The foods most likely to cause illness are commercial ice cream and seafood, as both deteriorate rapidly. But this is not to say that no food should ever be re-frozen. It is merely a matter of common sense.

Foods That Cannot Be Frozen Successfully

Although most food will be prevented from going bad if kept at freezing point, some foods cannot be frozen successfully as the texture is ruined by freezing. This is particularly true of foods with a high water content. However, some of these may be frozen if wanted for soups or purées, in which case they should normally be frozen in purée form. Examples are bananas, cucumbers, lettuce and watercress.

Emulsions such as mayonnaise or hollandaise sauce do not freeze successfully as they separate when thawed.

Yoghurt, milk and cream can be frozen but will not be totally smooth when thawed. Double cream freezes better if whipped first. Storage time: 4 months.

Eggs cannot be frozen in the shell, but both whites and yolks freeze well, either lightly beaten together or separated. Storage time: 9 months.

Jelly, both savoury and sweet, loses its texture if frozen, and would have to be reboiled and allowed to set again after thawing if required jellied.

Strawberries keep their colour and flavour well, but become soft on thawing.

Vegetables

Where a choice of times is given, the shorter time is for smaller vegetables, the longer for larger ones

Vegetable		Blanching time in minutes	Storage time in months
Asparagus	Do not tie in bunches	3-4	12
Artichoke (globe)	Remove stalks and outer tough leaves	7	6
Artichoke (Jerusalem)	Freeze once cooked into a purée	-	6
Beans, broad	Sort by size	3	12
Beans, French	Trim ends	2-3	12
Beans, runner	Slice thickly	1½-2	6
Beetroot	Freeze completely cooked and skinned. Slice if large	-	6
Broccoli	Trim stalks	2½-4	12
Brussels sprouts	Choose small, firm sprouts. Remove outer leaves	4-6	12
Carrots	Choose small young ones with good colour. Scrape. Freeze whole	5-6	12
Cauliflower	Break heads into sprigs	3-4	6
Celery	Will be soft when thawed, but good for soups and stews	3	12
Corn on the cob	Remove husks and silks	6-10	9
Courgettes	Use only very small ones. Do not peel	1	12
Kale	Remove stalks	1	6
Leeks	Finely slice; chop in chunks or leave whole	1-3	12
Mushrooms	Do not peel. Freeze unblanched for up to 1 month. For longer storage, cook in butter	-	4
Onions	Store unblanched onions, sliced or chopped, for up to 3 months. Sliced or chopped onions can be blanched in water or oil. Button onions can be blanched whole	1-3	5
Peas	Choose young, very fresh peas	1-2	12
Potatoes	Chips: blanch in oil. Boiled or mashed: freeze cooked and cold	4	6
Root vegetables	Cut into chunks; blanch, or cook completely	3	12
Spinach	Move about in water to separate leaves	1	12
Tomatoes	Do not blanch. Freeze whole, in slices or as juice or purée, cooked or raw		

Melon is too watery to remain crisp when thawed. It is best frozen in balls in syrup, but even this is not totally satisfactory.
Tomatoes emerge mushy when thawed, but are good for soups and sauces. One bonus of freezing tomatoes whole is that they skin well if placed, still frozen, under a running hot tap. They can, of course, be frozen as purée or juice.
Fats, or foods with a high fat content, freeze less successfully as a rule than less fatty foods. They have a tendency to develop a slightly rancid flavour if stored for more than 3 months.

Foods That Freeze Successfully

Most foods freeze well if some care is taken with wrapping etc. But some foods freeze so well that no one would ever know that they had been frozen. Baked or raw pastries, breads, bread or biscuit doughs, cakes and sandwiches containing not-too-wet fillings, are good examples. As a general rule, raw food keeps better and longer than cooked food. But cooked food, especially if well covered in a sauce, or under a potato or pastry crust, keeps well.
Vegetables freeze well if they are to be eaten cooked. They cannot be frozen if intended to be eaten raw. In order to prevent enzyme activity, green vegetables are boiled briefly, then cooled rapidly, before freezing. They may be frozen without this 'blanching' but their storage time would be reduced, and it is foolish to lose food through lazy freezing. Only the best vegetables, very fresh, should be used. They should be washed, or picked over, or otherwise prepared as if for immediate cooking. A large saucepan of water is brought to a rapid boil, and the vegetables (not more than 450g/1lb or so at a time) lowered into it. Accurate timing of the blanching process is important: the minutes are counted from the time the water reboils. As soon as the time is up, the vegetables are lifted out, and immediately cooled in a sink full of cold water, if possible. Once stone cold, the vegetables are lifted out, drained well, patted dry if necessary, and frozen. The same blanching water can be used for several batches of vegetables. Some vegetables (onions, mushrooms, potatoes) may be cooked completely in butter or blanched in oil instead of water. They are allowed to cool normally before freezing.
Fruits (storage time: 9 months) Only freeze fruit that is in prime condition. Unripe, over-ripe or blemished fruit gives poor results. There are 3 methods generally used to freeze raw fruit. (Cooked fruit may also be frozen whole or puréed.)

OPEN FREEZING

Suitable for most soft fruit such as raspberries and currants. Spread the fruit out on a baking sheet or tray and place in the freezer uncovered. When hard, pack into polythene bags or a rigid container, with or without adding sugar.

PUREE

Suitable for any fruits. Stew the fruit and mash, liquidize or sieve. Allow the purée to cool. Pack into containers, leaving head space, cover, label and freeze. Raw purées freeze well, too.

DRY SUGAR PACK

Suitable for most fruit to be used in cooked puddings. Prepare the fruit, toss it in sugar and freeze, with any juices that may have run from it during preparation. Care should be taken to exclude air, which may cause discoloration of the fruit.

HERBS

(Storage time: 3 months) Herbs should be frozen dry in small polythene bags or packets, or chopped finely, put into ice trays and just covered with water. The frozen cubes can be transferred to labelled bags.

MEAT AND FISH

(Storage time: raw meat, 9 months; cooked meat, 4 months; raw fish, 5 months; cooked fish, 3 months) Special care should be taken in wrapping to prevent freezer burn.

CAKES AND BREAD

(Storage time: 12 months) Both raw and cooked doughs and pastries freeze well.

STOCKS

Reduce stocks by boiling rapidly until very concentrated. Freeze in ice trays and when defrosted use as stock cubes.

Equipment and utensils

WHEN BUYING kitchen equipment, the basic rule for standard items is to buy the best that you can possibly afford. Good kitchen equipment will probably last for 15 years and is worth the investment. When buying small or specialist equipment that may be used once only, be as economical or extravagant as your purse dictates.

The following is not intended to be a complete list of the kitchen equipment available, but includes all the utensils that the home cook could possibly want, while excluding certain specialist items like preserving and cake-decorating equipment, barbecues, smokers and storage equipment.

UTENSILS

The following items of equipment are essential for any cook:

1 cook's knife with 18cm/7 inch blade
1 cook's knife with 7.5cm/3 inch blade
1 filleting knife with 14cm/5 inch blade
1 fruit knife
1 carbon-steel knife
1 palette knife
1 large saucepan 21cm/8 inch diameter with lid
1 medium saucepan 19cm/7 inch diameter with lid
1 small saucepan 12cm/5 inch diameter
1 frying pan with 20cm/8 inch diameter base
1 colander
2 wooden spoons
1 fish slice
1 rubber spatula
1 sieve (bowl strainer)
1 potato peeler
1 set of scales
1 measuring jug
1 pair poultry shears
3 gradated pudding basins
1 cheese grater
1 wooden board
1 roasting pan
1 salad bowl

OTHER KITCHEN EQUIPMENT

The home cook will also find the following items useful, and often time- or labour-saving:

Bottle opener
Bottle stopper
Breadboard and knife
Can opener Wall-mounted ones are easiest to use and cannot be mislaid.
Casserole dishes Buy several sizes as food must be cooked in the right-sized pot or it will dry out during the long slow cooking. Make sure that the lids fit tightly. We recommend dishes made of enamelled cast iron (or other heavy duty metal) as they can be used on the hob and in the oven. Earthenware and heat-resistant glass must not be put on to the hob.
Chicken brick This is a clay container for cooking chicken in its own juices and makes for very succulent birds. Never wash it with detergent, which will be absorbed into the brick and taint the food.
Clock This is essential for accurate timing and to avoid guesswork.
Coffee maker There are a huge variety of coffee machines available on the market, but almost the nicest and simplest way to make coffee is to pour boiling water into a large earthenware jug. Add 4 heaped tablespoons of medium ground coffee per 570ml/1 pint water, stir once or twice with a large spoon and leave to stand and infuse in a warm place for 5 minutes. The coffee will sink to the bottom of the jug. Pour, through a small strainer, into prewarmed cups.
Cafétière This is a glass jug with a central plunger. The coffee is made by infusion (as in

the jug method) but the plunger isolates the ground coffee and acts as a filter.
Filter Filter systems range from the simple drip filter with jug to sophisticated electric machines. Use fine ground coffee. Experts recommend that you choose a machine that doesn't use filter paper, which gives the coffee a poor flavour. The ultimate in coffee-filter machines is the one that grinds and filters in one process – and does not use filter paper.
Percolator This does not make very good coffee. If you have one, use medium ground beans.
Corkscrew Choose one with a very thin sharp coil that disturbs the wine as little as possible.
Electric kettle
Freezer Chest freezers are cheaper than upright freezers, but are less convenient to use and lose more energy when they are opened. Upright freezers take up less floor space than chest freezers.
Microwave oven This can be very useful for defrosting food (like loaves of bread and packets of butter), reheating precooked vegetables and melting butter, chocolate and jam. But we would not recommend them for cooking unless you are in a rush.
Oven Choose the largest (think of the Christmas turkey!) and best oven that you can afford. You are not likely to replace it often. If you can, buy a double oven so that food can be cooked at different temperatures. Gadgets can often be a snare – as they often go wrong. So choose an oven with only the gadgets that you are sure you will find useful. Make sure that it is easy to clean with no dirt traps. Ideally, buy one with a self-cleaning oven. Check that it has a good grill.
Fan-circulated ovens The less efficient fan-assisted ovens and convection ovens (rather than radiant ovens) heat up very quickly. Fan ovens can be run at up to 20 per cent lower temperatures than conventional ovens.
Oven cloth/gloves
Refrigerator Choose the largest refrigerator that

Types of Fuel: Advantages and Disadvantages

	Gas	Electricity	Solid Fuel
Expense	Cheaper than electricity		Cheaper than gas or electricity
Hobs	Quick to heat	Needs preheating	Provides a constant source of heat.
	Any pans can be used	Some ceramic hobs need flat-based saucepans	Needs very flat, very heavy saucepans
Ovens	Drier heat than electricity therefore better for roasts, cakes and meringues.		Excellent for long, slow cooking
	Uneven heat; top of oven hotter than bottom, though this can be very useful	Even heat throughout oven	Temperature of oven can be guaranteed, but normally there are only three settings from which to choose
	The flame can go out at low-temperature settings	Good for low simmering	Good for low simmering, but the hotplate is not always hot enough for fast frying. **Room heating**: can make the kitchen too hot in the summer, but is an excellent radiator in the winter

will fit into your kitchen; you can never have enough fridge space. Make sure that it is easy to clean and sturdy. The ice tray should be made of strong, flexible rubber.
Salad spinner Almost a 'spin-dryer' for salad leaves, this is operated by a handle. It is a cheap and very useful piece of kitchen equipment.
Salt and pepper mills Choose wooden ones with matt screw-tops rather than handles.
Tea towels You can never have enough.
Timer Buy the type that you hang around your neck – that way it goes with you when you leave the kitchen.
Toaster This uses less energy than a grill.
Vegetable brush

MEASURING AND WEIGHING

It is essential to have accurate weighing and measuring equipment for successful cooking. Useful charts can be found on page 8. The following measuring equipment is necessary for accuracy and good results.

American cup measures American recipes call for cups or parts of a cup. A cup is 8 fl oz. A set of cup measures is available from specialist kitchen shops in multiples of one cup.
Measuring jug Buy a large jug, so that you can measure both large and small quantities, with both imperial and metric gradations.
Scales Balance scales last a lifetime and are more accurate than other types. They are used with expensive, but very accurate, metal weights, which can be imperial or metric.
Thermometers The thermometers on the market fall into the following broad categories:
Freezer thermometer To check that the freezer is running at the required temperature.
Meat thermometer This is particularly useful when roasting a large joint. It helps to indicate the degree of 'closeness'.
Oven thermometer For the accurate measurement of oven temperature.
Sugar or deep-fat thermometer This gauges when fat is ready for deep-frying and indicates the degree of 'crack' of boiling sugar. It is normally made of glass, so it should be warmed before use.

POTS, PANS AND OTHER VESSELS

Always buy as heavy a pan as you can afford. The very best ones are made of copper with tin lining, or heavy aluminium or steel. Heavy pans conduct heat better and more evenly than light ones. A cheap pan might last two years, but it will dent and burn. A good, heavy pan could last 50 years and will not burn easily. Buy pans that are stable when empty, the right size for your burners or hot plates and have lids that fit well. If you have an Aga or range, you will need heavy pans with flat bases that conduct the heat evenly across the surface. You can buy these from specialist dealers and cookware shops.

Colander Choose a large standing colander; the legs keep the contents clear of draining liquid and it frees hands to empty heavy pans.
Double saucepan This is for making delicate sauces and melting chocolate. The bottom saucepan is very useful for boiling eggs if your other saucepans are made of heavy aluminium, in which eggs tend to discolour. The handles of both pans are angled towards each other to facilitate picking them up as one unit.
Fish kettle Buy a fish kettle with a steaming platform. The kettle is made to accommodate the shape of a large fish, and should be big enough to hold one at least 50cm/20 inches long. The matching platform should fit well and have handles that stand proud of the liquid.
Frying pan For general use, choose a heavy-duty pan with a 20cm/8 inch diameter base.
Crêpe pan This is a small, round-edged frying pan used only for making French pancakes. The ideal size has a 15cm/6 inch diameter base.
Deep-fat frying pan This is thicker and deeper than a roasting pan. Make sure that it is big enough for all your needs (including frying pieces of fish, etc.), has good handles and a fine mesh to keep the fat free of food particles.
Omelette pan A small carbon-steel frying pan with edges curving into the base, making the folding and serving of omelettes easier. Keep it just for omelettes.
Girdle This is a heavy aluminium, iron or steel plate for girdle (pronounced 'griddle') scones and crumpets. Make sure that the base is thick and quite flat. The handle should drop down for easy storage.
Heat diffuser This is made of a circular piece of metal with a wooden handle to reduce heat under glass and earthenware vessels on top of the stove, and for controlled simmering.

Paella pan This broad, shallow, flat-bottomed, two-handled pan gets its name from the traditional Spanish rice dish. (The paella is cooked and served in the pan.) Pans are usually made of cast iron.
Pan rest A wooden triangle that prevents hot pans from marking work surfaces.
Pizza plate A round, metal baking sheet with a slightly raised lip to support the edges of the pizza crust. Buy two. The most common size is 25cm/10 inch diameter.
Pressure cooker This is extremely useful for speeding up cooking processes and wonderful for making preserves.
Roasting pans and racks Get several sizes, but make sure that the large one fits into your oven; a small roast in a large pan allows the juices to spread too thinly and burn. Choose pans made of heavy tin steel with rolled edges and high sides. Many new ovens are supplied with roasting pans. Buy roasting racks to fit.
Saucepans Buy 3 or 4 saucepans ranging in capacity from 1½ pints to 10-12 pints. They should be deep and straight-sided to hold the heat well and minimize evaporation. A sloping-sided saucepan (without a lid) is invaluable for making sauces.
Sauté pan This is like a frying pan with deeper, straighter sides which allow for vigorous shaking of food. It is used for sauté dishes such as chicken casseroles. Buy one with a 30cm/12 inch diameter base, and one with a 20cm/8 inch diameter base.
Splash guard A fine wire mesh with a long handle which covers pans but allows steam to escape. It is very useful when frying.
Steamers You can buy steamers in the form of a saucepan with a second, perforated pan that fits on top. This is rather more expensive than the readily available perforated steamer top, with lid, with gradated bottom that fits onto any saucepan.
Chinese rice steamer A perforated aluminium, hinged, spherical container that is attached to the side of a saucepan for steaming rice.
Folding steaming platform This perforated platform stands on legs with adjustable, folding side panels and is particularly useful for steaming small quantities of vegetables. It fits into any size of saucepan.
Steaming basket for wok A small bamboo cage that fits neatly into the wok, leaving about a 5cm/2inch gap between it and the wok's base.
Stock pot A deep and straight-sided pot for long slow cooking with minimal evaporation. It can be made of light aluminium as it will be used essentially for boiling. Choose one that holds at least 8.5 litres/15 pints. Some pots have small taps near the bottom to draw off fat-free stock.
Wok Buy a wok set complete with a lid, stand and scoop. Choose one made of carbon iron, with a round bottom, wooden handles and domed lid. The best size is 35cm/14 inches.

KNIVES AND CUTTING IMPLEMENTS

The basic principle when buying a knife is to choose one that feels comfortable in your hand: heavy and well balanced. Pivot the handle/blade junction on the edge of the open hand – the handle should fall back gently into the palm.

The part of the blade that extends into the handle of the knife is called the tang. Those knives that have a full tang running the whole length of the handle give the best overall balance; blades that are not riveted in place in this way inevitably come loose. The heads of the rivets should be flush with the surface of the handle as this makes for easy cleaning.

Carbon-steel knives are easy to sharpen and stay sharp for a long time. However, they rust easily and must be wiped clean and dried immediately after use. They also discolour, especially from onions and highly acidic food. Stainless steel knives are strong, do not rust and can be used on onions and highly acidic food. Unfortunately, they are difficult to sharpen and blunt readily. High-carbon stainless steel knives have all the advantages of carbon-steel and stainless steel knives, and none of the disadvantages, but they are very expensive.

Knives must be looked after carefully. Always wipe clean and dry them immediately after use. Sharpen them regularly with a steel suitable for the type of knife. Do not store them in a drawer – they will damage each other's blades and may cut your hands. Use a wooden knife block. When carbon-steel knives get very stained, clean them with half a lemon sprinkled with salt. If that does not work, use a scouring pad, but only occasionally. To remove rust, rub the blade with a burnt cork.

Apple corer Choose one with a sharp, strong and rigid stainless steel blade to withstand the force and torsion when coring.
Boning knife The thin, very rigid blade must be at least 10cm/4 inches long, and particularly sharp, especially at the tip, which does most of the work.
Canelle knife A stainless steel blade with a sharpened notch for cutting decorative grooves.
Carbon steel The bigger the better. Choose one that has a good guard at the hilt and a handle with a good grip. Steels do wear out eventually, after several years.
Carving knife and fork The knife should have a broad and rigid blade at least 20cm/8 inches long. The fork should be about 25cm/10 inches long. If the prongs are curved, they can be useful for roasts - for larger roasts, longer, straighter prongs are necessary. The guard, which is essential, protects you against the knife slipping.
Cheese wire The simplest is a stainless steel wire with 2 wooden handles. Cheese wires are useful only for slicing large pieces of cheese.
Cherry stoner Choose a sturdy stainless steel stoner - very useful for stoning both cherries and olives.
Chinese cleaver This is similar to a meat cleaver but with a finer, sharper edge for precise slicing and chopping.
Chip cutter This is only for people who eat a lot of chips. After the potatoes are peeled, the chip cutter is pushed down on top of each potato. Perfect chips emerge.
Citrus zester A wooden-handled implement with stainless steel blade which has a row of holes with sharpened edges to remove the zest-filled top layer of citrus fruits, leaving the bitter pith behind. Various sizes are available.
Clam knife This is similar to an oyster knife, but with a longer, more blunted blade and rounded tip.
Cook's knife A cook's knife has a gentle curve from the blade to the tip giving a neatly pointed end for fine work. Using the tip as a pivot, the blade gives an efficient chopping action. On a large cook's knife, the broad, heavy flat of the blade makes a useful mallet. Cooks' knives come in a wide variety of sizes from a 25cm/ 10 inch blade to a 7.5cm/3 inch blade. The small one is particularly useful for boning small birds and fine work like dicing shallots.
Double-handled herb chopper or 'mezzaluna' A double-handled knife with a wide curved stainless steel blade. Use for chopping herbs. It can come with up to 4 blades in parallel for chopping herbs in bulk.
Egg pricker This has a steel pin for pricking eggs to prevent cracking during boiling. It is invaluable.
Egg slicer A stainless steel wire cutter that will slice an egg without crumbling the yolk.
Filleting knife Choose a pointed straight-edged filleting knife with a fine, flexible blade that is about 14cm/5 inches long.
Food mill A hand-operated mill for puréeing. Choose one with several discs of different gauges.
Freezer knife This has a rigid blade at least 30cm/12 inches long, serrated deeply on both sides and used like a saw. It has a hooked tip for prising and lifting.
Fruit knife This has a stainless steel blade with a serrated edge to cut through skins and 'saw' slices without squashing delicate fruit and a sharp tip for piercing skins prior to peeling.
Grapefruit knife This has a stainless steel, slightly flexible blade, serrated and curved to fit the shape of the fruit.
Graters Hand-held graters come in a variety of shapes and sizes. We recommend a stainless box-shaped grater for general purposes, a tiny conical grater for nutmeg and a hand-operated rotary grater for cheese. Use a pastry brush rather than a knife to clean the faces of the graters.
Lobster crackers These are for cracking lobsters' legs. They look rather like pliers and can also be used to remove small bones from smoked salmon.
Lobster pick A steel prong for getting meat out of lobsters' legs and claws.
Mandoline A mandoline grater is useful both for slicing and grating. It has adjustable steel blades - 1 rippled and 1 straight - and is mounted on a wooden or plastic base. Food processors have, to a certain degree, replaced mandolines but they are still useful for small quantities.
Meat cleaver Buy one that is as heavy as you can handle with ease. For storage, hang by the hole in the blade.
Melon baller A small stainless steel metal scoop

with a wooden handle used for making balls from potatoes and melons.
Mincers Choose one with a clamp rather than a suction base. Sharpen or replace the blades regularly. Ensure that they come apart easily for cleaning.
Oyster knife For opening oysters. Short, rigid, pointed blade with a good grip and a guard to save hands if the knife slips.
Palette knife The blade should be sturdy and evenly flexible along its full length and have a blunt edge for easing under cakes and breads. It is also useful for smoothing iced surfaces. Buy a large one.
Paring knife A small stainless steel blade (7.5cm/ 3 inch) for peeling soft fruit or vegetables.
Potato peeler There are 2 types of potato peeler: the swivel type has a blade that pivots freely to adapt to the shape of the item being peeled. One with a double cutting edge means that you can peel in both directions. The fixed-blade type is used like a knife. Left-handed people must choose a left-handed peeler. This type can also be used for extracting bones from salmon. Both have pointed ends for clipping out eyes, but neither type can be sharpened well.
Poultry shears These can be used both as scissors and shears. They should be made of stainless steel because they are often immersed in water and you don't want them to rust. They should be at least 25cm/10 inches long to cope with all varieties and sizes of birds. The notch cracks bones; the spring keeps the blade open between cuts, and one blade is usually serrated for cutting cartilage.
Saw A lightweight saw can be very useful for sawing large thigh bones or frozen meat. Get the kind with a replaceable blade.
Scissors Choose kitchen scissors that can be unscrewed for easy cleaning and sharpening. Make sure that the blades meet smoothly along their full length.
Smoked salmon/ham knife The blade should be at least 25cm/10 inches long, and only slightly flexible. The blade often has indentations to reduce friction and keep thin slices intact.

BAKEWARE AND MOULDS

There is a large variety of moulds available on the market, many of which have been designed with a specific use in mind, but inevitably, they are not always used for that purpose. For instance, how many people own both a ring mould and a savarin mould? Moulds that are intended for baking, like terrines and cake tins, are made of a fairly heavy-duty material, whereas moulds that are intended for chilling are usually made of thinner more malleable metal.

The following list does not cover all the moulds available, but only those that it would be fun or useful to own. It also includes many of the different cake tins, baking sheets and flan rings that you can purchase.

Angel cake tin The central funnel allows for better conduction of heat. Choose a non-stick tin as angel cakes tend to stick.
Baking sheets You will need several. Make sure that they fit into your oven. Heavy steel sheets with one lip are suitable for most uses: you can slide reluctant flans off them and the lip makes for easier handling. A lipped baking sheet is useful when there is the likelihood of an overflow.
Blind beans Ceramic baking beans are for baking blind and can be re-used continually. Uncooked rice is a perfectly good substitute.
Bombe mould For moulding ice cream and making ice-cream bombes. The best ones have a vacuum-release top; otherwise they are very difficult to dislodge.
Brioche tins Fluted, tinned metal moulds for making brioches. They come in a variety of sizes and some have funnelled centres to aid the conduction of heat.
Cake moulds These are made of steel and come in a variety of shapes and sizes - chickens, rabbits, etc. They are held together by clips.
Cake racks They are either rectangular (for all types of baked food) or circular (specifically for cakes). They are used for cooling cakes and biscuits without sweating. Buy one that is large and stands fairly high off the work surface.
Charlotte mould A classic shaped mould for charlotte pudding. It can be used hot for apple charlotte, say, or cold for charlotte russe.
Confectionery mould A rubber mould with 50 or more holes in several different shapes for sweet mixtures. Its flexibility makes for easy unmoulding.

Copper bowl An expensive and non-essential piece of kitchenware equipment. It is unlined and used solely for holding egg whites while they are being whisked. Some people say that there is a chemical reaction between the egg whites and copper that aids beating.
Coeur à la crème mould A porcelain heart-shaped mould with a perforated base to drain the whey produced when making coeurs à la crème.
Dariole moulds These small, deep sloping-sided tins are used for individual hot mousses and timbales. Many people use ramekins instead, but these metal dariole moulds are better because the heat is conducted quickly throughout.
Deep cake tin Buy 2 of these - 1 square, 1 round - for fruit cakes. Make sure that they are heavy-duty for long, slow baking. Select ones with loose bottoms.
Easter egg moulds Stainless steel, glass or plastic moulds, either plain or patterned.
Fish mousse mould A metal or porcelain fish-shaped mould for fish mousses set with gelatine.
Flan rings Buy several metal flan rings, plain and fluted, of different sizes. They are preferable to porcelain flan dishes for pastry as they conduct heat well, thereby preventing soggy pastry.
Flour dredger or sifter Buy one with a handle. Better still, buy 2 - a big one and a small-holed one - for heavy and light dredging.
Folding pâté tin Metal with folding sides for pies and pâté en croûte.
Jelly moulds There is a large variety of metal decorative jelly moulds, often made of copper with a tin lining. However, they are very rarely ovenproof.
Loaf tin This can also be used for terrines.
Madeleine sheet This is similar to a patty tin, but shaped for making madeleines.
Marble slab An ideal surface on which to make pastry, as it stays cool.
Mixing bowls Get several different sizes of white china pudding basins and one larger ceramic mixing bowl.
Moule-à-manqué For French génoise cake. The sloping sides ease unmoulding and decoration.
Pastry brush Buy a good quality small paint brush with thick, tightly packed bristles that will not shed. A shaving brush also makes a good pastry brush as it is very soft and will stand upright when you are not using it.
Pastry cutters Buy an assortment of metal cutters, round, fluted, plain, animal shapes, ornamental shapes, etc. The top edge is rolled to safeguard fingers and to keep the shape rigid. The cutting edge must be sharp.
Pastry moulds Buy a variety of different shaped metal moulds for tarts, tartlets, boat-shaped moulds, petit fours moulds etc.
Patty tin The larger the better - all the moulds need not be filled.
Pie dishes Get a large and a small pie dish - usually deep, glazed ceramic dishes. They must be deep so that the filling can cook before the crust burns.
Piping bag and nozzle Nylon bags with sewn seams last longer than plastic bags. Buy both a small and a large bag and a selection of metal nozzles.
Raised pie mould A wooden block to shape hot watercrust pastry and make a traditional raised pie.
Raised pie tin This is not for traditionally raised pies, but for pies that are to be decorated and made to look like a raised pie. The sides unclip and detach from the base. The advantage of these tins is that you can use a pâte à pâté pastry for making a raised pie; this rich pastry would not hold its shape if baked as a self-supporting raised pie.
Ramekin dishes These small soufflé dishes are for individual servings.
Ring mould These jelly moulds have a hole in the centre which can be filled with a suitable accompaniment.
Rolling pin Buy a wooden pin without handles that gives even pressure, covers the maximum surface area and is easy to wipe clean. Buy a fairly long one.
Sandwich tins Buy 2 20cm/8 inch diameter tins for Victoria sandwich cake. Tins with levers ease unmoulding.
Savarin mould or ring mould for jellies The ring mould shape gives maximum surface for good heat conduction.
Soufflé dishes Get 2 or 3 soufflé dishes ranging from 0.5 litre/$^3/_4$ pint to 1 litre/1$^3/_4$ pints. They must have straight sides, be good and deep for high rising and made of very fine porcelain to

aid conduction of heat.

Sponge finger sheet This is similar to a madeleine sheet, but shaped for making sponge fingers.

Spring form tin Use when unmoulding is difficult. The sides unclip.

Spring form tube tin For kugelhopf; the funnel helps to get heat to the centre of the tin and the clips ease unmoulding.

Swiss roll tin Make sure that the sides are at least 2.5cm/1 inch high. The tin should be 35 x 25cm/14 x 10 inches.

Terrine Make sure that the lid has a steam hole. A terrine can also be used as a pie dish.

Wooden board Choose a large, thick one made of maple or another hard wood. Make sure that it is reinforced. Ideally, the grain of the main part should run in the opposite direction to that on the reinforced ends.

FOOD PROCESSING MACHINES

The following machines should be considered.

Deep-fryer Buy an electric thermostatically controlled deep-fryer with a charcoal filter lid, which prevents smells in the kitchen. Make sure that it is easy to clean.

Food mixer Although food mixers have been superseded by food processors, they are remarkably versatile and have a huge variety of attachments, the most useful of which are: mincer, liquidizer, coffee grinder, electric sieve (which gives perfect mashed potatoes), can opener, sausage maker, dough hook and juice extractor. Buy a heavy-duty model with rotating whisks that reach to the bottom of the bowl and are capable of whisking very small quantities.

Hand-held whisk An electric hand-held whisk is a very useful piece of kitchen equipment. Buy one with a heavy-duty motor. It is ideal for making whisked sponge cakes and mayonnaise.

Ice-cream machines Electric ice-cream machines make wonderful ice creams and sorbets and are very easy to use. However, they are expensive and take up a lot of space.

Liquidizer This often comes as an attachment to a food mixer but can be bought as a separate machine. Liquidizers are better for blending soups than food processors, but other than that they have become outdated. Choose a large liquidizer made of clear roughened glass or heavyweight plastic.

Pasta machine Buy a hand-operated machine for kneading, rolling and cutting pasta dough. It should be made of rust-resistant metal and be able to be clamped securely to a work surface. Choose one with rollers that adjust to several positions to alter the thickness of the dough and with rotary cutters that give a range of different widths of cut strips. Electric machines are available but are very expensive.

Processor and julienne attachment This is not an essential piece of equipment, but once you have used one you cannot live without it! It chops, slices, grates, minces, shreds and beats. It does not whip egg whites successfully, though. Choose the most compact model that you can find with as quiet a motor as possible. It should have a circuit breaker to prevent over-heating or burning out. Choose one that will not operate unless the cover is in position.

HAND TOOLS AND SIEVES

Basting spoon Choose a large one with a pierced or hooked handle if you want to hang it up. It should be heavy-duty, deep and long-handled.

Bowl strainer (sieve) Choose a stainless steel sieve as carbon steel discolours some purées, and nylon sieves break easily, sometimes melt and look old relatively quickly. Double-mesh strainers are used for very fine puréeing. Make sure that the sieve will sit securely.

Bulb baster A syringe-type baster in plastic with a rubber bulb. It is also useful for skimming off fat or for extracting fat-free stock from under a layer of fat. Wash and dry carefully.

Conical strainer (Chinois or tammy strainer) There are 2 types of conical strainer: a firm metal one for heavy purées and a wire mesh one for straining large quantities of liquid into a single stream.

Drum sieve This is good for sifting but not easy to clean, so it is not suitable for making purées.

Fish slice Make sure that it has a pierced or hooked handle if you want to hang it up. Choose one that is broad enough to lift and turn large objects.

Fruit juice press Very useful for squeezing quantities of citrus fruits.

Funnel Get one that is heat-resistant, with a wide flared top and a tube that fits narrow bottles.

Garlic press This is best with thick handles and a pivoted pressing foot. Some have cherry or olive stoners integrated in the handle. Garlic presses are invaluable in the kitchen as the smell of garlic is difficult to remove from wooden boards or a pestle and mortar.
Ice-cream scoop Spring action, moulds ice cream or firm vegetable purées into a ball shape.
Ladle Make sure that it has a pierced or hooked handle if you want to hang it up. Choose one with a large bowl and long handle.
Larding needle Lengths of lard are gripped by the teeth at the end of the needle. The lard is then threaded through the meat.
Lemon squeezer There are 2 types of lemon squeezer. One is made of glass or toughened plastic for squeezing citrus fruits, but the plastic ones with a container underneath are the most useful. The other is a wooden gadget used to push into fruit halves for extracting a few drops.
Meat-tenderizing mallet A spiked wooden mallet for flattening and tenderizing meat by breaking down the meat fibres.
Metal tongs For lifting and turning food. These are particularly useful when grilling. Make sure that the ends meet.
Pasta wheel Useful for cutting pasta.
Pastry blender A wooden handle with circular-shaped wires for easy blending.
Perforated jam skimmer A flat perforated spoon for removing fat from liquids and scum from jams and stock.
Perforated spoon Choose a large one with a pierced or hooked handle if you want to hang it up. It is excellent for lifting poached food out of the poaching liquid.
Pestle and mortar A pestle crushes herbs and spices in a mortar bowl. Stone is more effective than glass or wood, as wooden mortars tend to absorb flavours. Stone has the advantage of being heavy and has an excellent rough texture for fine grinding. The pestle and mortar must be made of the same material, or one will grind away the other.
Potato masher Although we recommend making potato purées by pushing the cooked potato through a bowl strainer, a potato masher can be very useful when you are in a hurry.
Scraper The best are steel with a metal handle for scraping pastry boards clean. Scrapers are also invaluable for scraping up vegetables after chopping.
Skewers Metal butchers' skewers are used to hold meat in place. Metal kebab skewers are used for grilling and should be about 40cm/ 16 inches long.
Spaghetti rake This looks like a giant wooden hairbrush. The spaghetti does not slip off the wooden prongs.
Spatulas These come in rubber or wood. The rubber variety is more effective than the wooden type. Choose one with a long wooden handle, making it ideal for getting the last bits of food out of jars and for scraping bowls. A wooden spatula is particularly useful for use on non-stick saucepans.
Steak batt This is flat and made of metal or wood.
Trussing needle A large metal needle with a large eye for sewing up stuffed meat and poultry.
Waffle iron An aluminium or cast-iron toaster or waffle iron for use on an open-flame burner. Check that the 2 halves fit smoothly and that the handles are long and insulated.
Whisk A device for beating air in and lumps out of a mixture. But you need the right type for the job in hand.
Balloon whisk A simply designed whisk of several loops of wire. The large heavy-duty ones with a wooden handle are the best for whisking in plenty of air.
Flat whisk A neat efficient whisk which is ideal for shallow whisking.
Sauce whisk A tiny flat whisk which is invaluable for whisking out lumps from sauces and mounting sauces with butter.
Wire 'spider' or ladle Used for lifting solids from liquids.
Wooden spoons Get a good assortment of sizes – the ones with long handles are sturdier and better beaters than are short-handled ones.
Wooden spoon with hole This allows liquid to pass through and prevents spillage during stirring.
Wooden spoon with square corner This is particularly useful for getting into the corners of saucepans.

Wine

BY RICHARD HARVEY M.W.

IN BRITAIN we are fortunate in having the widest selection of wines for sale in the most varied outlets in the world. Being only a minor producer of wine, we are less prone to the natural chauvinism that exists in most wine-growing regions and countries. The assiduous research of the buyers for British importers has resulted in an enormous range of wines now being available not only in specialist wine shops but also in most supermarkets and off-licences. So where should you go to buy wine, whether it's for everyday consumption or a special occasion?

Where to buy

SUPERMARKETS

These account for most of the retail wine sales in the UK. They have been responsible for bringing wine to many new consumers, with the result that, today, no matter where you live, there is a wide range of wines available. By virtue of their size, the major supermarket groups have great buying power with the result that they can offer the customer very competitive prices. However, their size is also a disadvantage in that normally they are required to buy from the larger producers, and therefore cannot realistically offer the often more characterful wines made by smaller growers.

The second, and more important, disadvantage to buying in a supermarket is the lack of any personal advice. Many stores have overcome this to a small extent by the use of information slips on the shelves, or on back labels of the bottles, often using the Wine Development Board's Wine Taste Guides, but this is rarely sufficient for the really interested consumer. The supermarkets, therefore, are the place to buy everyday drinking wines at affordable prices at the lower end of the price scale as well as their own label champagnes and fortified wines. (The best supermarket groups for wine at the moment are Sainsbury's, Tesco and Waitrose.)

RETAIL CHAINS

These groups have suffered most from the development and rapid growth of wine sales through the supermarkets over the last 20 years. Although having similar buying power to the supermarkets, they have tended to become simply outlets for the major brands of their parent companies (for example, Allied Lyons owns Victoria Wine and Grand Metropolitan, Peter Dominic). Although these stores can offer personal advice, it is all too rarely knowledgeable. The notable exception is Oddbins, the idiosyncratic chain that was bought by Seagrams, but has so far been allowed to follow its own successful path, offering a wide and interesting range of wines, and with knowledgeable and enthusiastic staff on hand to advise the customer. The other chains seem to have finally woken up and there are now many better stores, such as Thresher's, and their Wine Rack stores.

SPECIALIST

The specialist wine merchants, with perhaps only one or two outlets, or even working from home, have proliferated over the last 20 years, since the major brewery groups bought up most of the existing wine-merchant businesses in the 1960s. Some of these specialists offer the most comprehensive range of wines available, such as Lay and Wheeler of Colchester, or perhaps specialize in the wines of a particular country or region, such as Yapp's of Mere which sells wines mainly from the Rhône and Loire Valleys of France. What these specialists can offer is expert advice, since often, especially in the case of one-man bands, you will be buying from the person who has actually visited the vineyard and selected the wine. Whilst these specialists often cannot compete in price at the lower end of the scale with the supermarkets, what they can offer is wines, often only available in small quantities, that really have an individual character. These are certainly the places to buy once you have exhausted the supermarkets' more basic ranges.

MAIL ORDER

This area was for a long time the domain principally of the Wine Society, founded in 1874. It remains the largest operator in this field, but has been joined by many of the specialist merchants mentioned above. This is a good way to buy wine if you do not live near a good wine shop, and many of the wine lists sent out by firms who offer this service are extremely informative. However, the consumer has to bear the cost of delivery, either directly or indirectly, and this can add to the cost significantly for small orders of the less expensive wines. Also, the minimum quantity that you can order is a dozen bottles, although usually these can be mixed.

AUCTIONS

Wine auctions have also developed very much during the last 20 years, although they have existed since the nineteenth century. The majority of wine sold at auction, mostly through Christie's and Sotheby's, is fine claret and vintage port, but there are other smaller auctions around the country that also offer a range of everyday wine. The problem with many of these sales is that the auctioneers are not as fastidious as they might be in respect of the provenance of the wine. In all too many cases, the wine has been badly stored, or it is simply stock that a wine merchant has been unable to sell himself. The other disadvantage is that normally lot sizes are in the order of 2 to 5 dozen cases. However, for the purchaser, or group of purchasers, who know specifically which fine wine they want to buy, the major London auction houses can be cheaper than a traditional merchant.

What to buy

Having decided where to buy, the next question is what to buy. Normally, the first criterion in the mind of the consumer is price. So it is worth examining how the cost of a bottle of wine is determined. In the United Kingdom, we have high rates of excise duty based on the alcoholic strength of the product (and a higher rate for sparkling wines). Because this tax is not related to the cost of the wine, a significantly high percentage of the selling price of less expensive wines is made up by the fixed costs, as the table below shows.

How the retail price is made up

Retail price	**£3.00**	**£5.00**	**£8.00**
Duty and VAT	45%	33%	25%
Shipping, distribution and retailing	30%	33%	35%
Wine	25%	33%	40%

It is apparent therefore that the least expensive wines offer the least value in terms of wine for money.

READING THE LABEL

In the absence of any personal advice from an expert, the consumer's buying choice must be based on the information given on the label. This can be very informative, although only a minimum of information has to be given by law: the country of origin of the wine, the quantity in the bottle (a standard bottle is now 75 centilitres), the alcoholic strength, the name and address of the responsible bottler, and, for wines produced within the E.E.C., the quality of the wine. This latter designation is important as it distinguishes quality wines produced from a specified region from table wines that have no specific geographical designation.

The name and address of the bottler is also a good guide to the quality of the wine within the bottle, and it is worth looking for wines labelled as being bottled by the grower, or at the domaine, estate or château. Apart from giving greater assurance of authenticity, such wines

Wine Labels

Country	Description of table wine	Description of regional wine	Description of quality wine	Description of top-quality wine
France	Vin de table	Vin du pays	V.D.Q.S. (Vin Délimité de Qualité Supérieur)	A.O.C. (Appellation d'Origine Contrôlée)
Italy	Vino da tavola		D.O.C. (Denominazione di Origine Controllata)	D.O.C.G. (Denominazione di Origine Controllata e Garantita)
Germany	Deutscher Tafelwein	Landwein	Qba (Qualitätswein bestimmter Anbaugebiete)	Qmp (Qualitätswein mit Prädikat)
Spain	Vino de Mesa	Vino de la tierra	D.O. (Denominación de Origen)	D.O.C (Denominación de Origen Calificada)
Portugal			Regio Demarcada	

will normally have more individual character than blends put together by large merchant houses. Most French, Italian, German and Spanish wines are named after the region, or village, in which they are produced. The grape variety is sometimes indicated, especially if it is not the norm for the area or, as in Germany, if the same named wine can be produced from different varieties. The quality-wine laws of France and Italy specify the permissible varieties for any particular quality wine.

By contrast, the wines produced in what is called the New World (United States, Australia, New Zealand, South Africa and South America) are usually named after the grape variety, as a producer may make several wines in the same region from a number of different grape varieties.

What is wine?

Wine is the alcoholic drink resulting from the fermentation of the sugars in the grape by natural yeasts. The alcoholic content of most wines is between 8 per cent and 15 per cent alcohol by volume. The wine may be white, pink (rosé) or red. It may be the produce of only one year (a vintage wine) or a blend of wines produced in different years (a non-vintage wine).

The style of any particular wine is influenced by the following factors: the climatic conditions in which the grapes are grown; the soil in which the vine's roots develop; the particular grape variety grown; the methods used to cultivate the vine; the techniques used to make the wine; and any particular variations that occur from year to year. The climatic conditions mean that grapes which receive higher levels of sunshine will have higher degrees of sugar, and thus the resulting wines will be higher in alcohol (generally described as fuller wines).

Conversely, wines produced from grapes grown in cooler climates will be lower in alcohol, higher in acidity, and normally described as being lighter. Cooler climates are generally better suited to the production of white wines, which require a balance of acidity to give them a fresh, crisp style.

White wine is produced only from the juice of the grape, which is usually colourless, so that either white or black grapes can be used. Red wine achieves its colour from the skins

Some useful terms:

France

Sec - dry
Demi-sec - medium-sweet
Doux - sweet
Moelleux - sweet
Brut - very dry (sparkling wine)
Blanc de Blancs - white wine produced only from white grapes
Supérieur - normally 0.5° or 1.0° higher in alcohol

Italy

Secco - dry
Amarone - dry (literally bitter)
Abboccato - medium-sweet
Amabile - medium-sweet
Dolce - sweet
Recioto - wine made from selected (i.e. riper) bunches of grapes
Riserva - wine that has undergone a longer period of ageing
Classico - wines that come from the best part of the denomination

Germany

Kabinett - grower's selection
Spätlese - late-picked grapes with more sugar
Auslese - selected bunches of very ripe grapes
Beerenauslese - selected berries
Trockenbeerenauslese - selected berries with the greatest concentration of sugar
Trocken - dry
Halbtrocken - medium-dry (most German wines are medium to sweet)

Spain

Crianza - wine that has not been aged in cask
Riserva - wine aged in cask
Gran Riserva - wine aged in cask for a longer period

remaining in contact with the juice for a period of time. In addition to colour, the skins also give tannin to the wine - a natural acid, which diminishes in time but can often make young red wines appear quite rough and dry. Pink or rosé wines are produced from a very brief contact with the red grape skins.

Sweetness in wines is achieved either by not fully fermenting the grape sugars into alcohol, thereby leaving residual sugar in the wine, or by adding a concentration of unfermented grape juice to the wine prior to bottling, which is the usual practice for German and English wines. Almost all red wines are dry, but white and rosé wines can be dry, medium or sweet. Sparkling wines are produced by inducing a second fermentation in the wine and retaining the carbon dioxide gas that is produced naturally. Champagne, the best-known sparkling wine, can only be produced in the delimited Champagne region of north-eastern France by secondary fermentation in the bottle (called the *méthode champenoise*).

Fortified wines are made by the addition of grape spirit either during or after fermentation. This spirit is normally brandy, the distillate of wine. These wines are normally between 15 and 20 per cent alcohol by volume and include: sherry, which can be dry, medium or sweet; port, which is normally sweet (although a little dry white port is made); Madeira; Marsala; and the sweet Muscat wines from the South of France.

Major Wine-Producing Areas

WHITE WINES

FRANCE produces many of the greatest white wines of the world, both dry and sweet. The Loire Valley produces mostly crisp, dry white wines, such as Muscadet and the Sauvignon-based Sancerre and Pouilly-Fumé, with their fresh, almost tart, gooseberry flavour. Burgundy is the home of the classic white wines produced from the Chardonnay grape - from Chablis in the north to Mâcon and Pouilly-Fuissé in the south, with the finest, most concentrated and richest wines coming from Meursault and Puligny-Montrachet in the middle, just south of the town of Beaune. Alsace produces fine, fruity wines, which, because they come mostly from German grape varieties, are often confused with German wines. They are mostly dry with a wonderful, intense, spicy flavour. Bordeaux, although producing some good dry white wine in Entre-Deux-Mers and Graves, is best known for the lusciously sweet dessert wines made in Sauternes and Barsac, from grapes that have achieved a super-rich concentration of sugars.

GERMANY is best known for its slightly sweet, delicate and fruity white wines, the best of which are made from the Riesling grape. They also produce drier styles, called trocken or halbtrocken, but these tend to be rather hard and acidic.

ITALY produces a vast range of white wines, mostly inexpensive and easy to drink like Soave, Frascati and Orvieto. More interesting wines can be found in the north of the country and Tuscany, often from French grape varieties.

SPAIN has turned its production mostly from heavy, oaked, alcoholic white wines to fresher, crisper styles.

PORTUGAL is best known for Vinho Verde, traditionally a light, slightly acidic wine, which is usually white and sweetened for the British market.

AUSTRALIA makes very good, ripe, buttery wines from Chardonnay grapes, and lighter more lemony-tasting wines from Semillon.

NEW ZEALAND produces very fine examples of Chardonnay and particularly good Sauvignon, the equal of Sancerre or Pouilly-Fumé.

CALIFORNIA also makes Chardonnay- and Sauvignon-based wines which are generally fuller and fatter than those of New Zealand, due to the hotter climate.

RED WINES

FRANCE, traditionally recognized as producing the finest red wines in the world, be they Bordeaux or Burgundy, now faces competition from around the world. Claret, the English term for red wines from Bordeaux, is made predominantly from the Cabernet-Sauvignon grape in the Médoc and Graves, and the Merlot grape in St Emilion and Pomerol. The wines are, at their best, deeply coloured, tannic when young, with the characteristic blackcurranty flavour of the Cabernet. Bordeaux is an enormous wine-producing region which also offers a vast variety of good-value red wines, often under a château label. Burgundy, in contrast, produces only a fraction of the quantity of red wines made in Bordeaux, and is generally expensive. The finest wines, from the Pinot Noir grape, produced in well-known villages such as Nuits-St-Georges, Gevrey-Chambertin or Beaune, are softer and generally lighter than those of Bordeaux, with a raspberry fruitiness which matures quicker than the more tannic Cabernet. Beaujolais, France's best-known red wine, has been devalued by the excessive production of wine sold as Nouveau, but true Beaujolais is an excellent, drinkable wine from the Gamay grape. The Rhône Valley makes deeply coloured, rich spicy reds from the Syrah grape, such as Hermitage, and, in the south, wines like Châteaneuf-du-Pape have a full, peppery alcoholic flavour derived from the Grenache grape. The South of France, in the past the source of vast quantities of unexciting table wines, is now producing much better, more interesting wines, such as Corbières and Minervois.

ITALY generally makes better red wines than white, whether traditional ones such as Chianti, Barolo or Barbaresco or new wines made outside the DOC laws and labelled simply as Vino da Tavola. The traditional wines were made exclusively to accompany the local cuisine, and can often appear somewhat tannic and astringent to the unaccustomed palate, without the balance of a cuisine based predominantly on olive oil.

SPAIN is best known for Rioja. This, like most Spanish reds, is a full, soft wine, with the pronounced oaky flavour that comes from being aged in barrels.

AUSTRALIA'S best red wines come from the Cabernet-Sauvignon and Shiraz (Syrah) grapes. They are rich, very concentrated wines with masses of ripe fruit flavours.

CALIFORNIA has also produced some very fine wines from the Cabernet-Sauvignon, which, with the warmer temperatures, tend to be softer and riper than those from Bordeaux, with less tannin.

BULGARIA has become a leader in inexpensive red wines, particularly Cabernet-Sauvignon. The better ones have a geographical designation.

ROSE WINES

Rosé wines often do not receive the appreciation they deserve in Britain - the best known is an indifferent branded wine from Portugal. There are, however, some fine dry rosé wines produced in France - the best, such as Tavel, coming from the southern Rhône. Other very good examples are made in the Languedoc, but the wines of the Côtes de Provence are rather over-priced in relation to their quality.

SPARKLING WINES

Whilst few people would dispute the supremacy of the best producers of Champagne, there are also some very good sparkling wines made by the méthode champenoise, which are available at half the price, or less, of Champagne. Saumur and Vouvray in the Loire make fine examples from the local Chenin and Cabernet grapes, with some Chardonnay. Spain produces good wines in the Penedes region south of Barcelona, which are labelled as Cava if made by the méthode champenoise. There are also some very good sparkling wines made in Italy, Australia and California.

FORTIFIED WINES

SHERRY denotes a wine that can only come from a delimited area around the town of Jerez in Andalucía, in Spain. Although not dissimilar wines are made in Cyprus and South Africa, for example, they do not have the classic flavours associated with true sherry. The drier styles, fino, manzanilla and amontillado, make excellent aperitifs, whereas the full, sweeter oloroso-based wines are better after a meal.

PORT is the traditional after-dinner drink. The most common styles, ruby and tawny (relating to their colour), are being overtaken in favour by higher quality Vintage Character (an older ruby-style), 10-, 20- and 30-year-old tawnies, and vintage and late-bottled vintage ports. This last style is wine from a single, but not necessarily vintage, year which avoids the necessity for decanting, an essential requirement for a vintage or crusted port, which has matured for years in the bottle.

MADEIRA AND MARSALA are fortified wines which today are somewhat out of favour as drinks, although appreciated in the kitchen. The sweet, fortified Muscat wines from the South of France, such as Beaumes-de-Venise, are popular as dessert wines in the United Kingdom, although in France they are drunk as aperitifs (as with many sweet wines, and even port).

Storing wine

It is important that any wine that is going to be kept for longer than a few weeks should be stored correctly. Only a limited number of houses nowadays have underground wine cellars, but reasonably similar conditions can be simulated in many other parts of a house. The following criteria should be observed:

TEMPERATURE The ideal temperature for storing wine is 12°C/55°F. It is important to maintain a constant temperature - for example, it is better for the wine to be stored at 10°C/50°F or 14°C/60°F than to fluctuate between 7-16°C/45-65°F. Wine stored at a higher temperature will mature quicker than if stored at a lower temperature.

HUMIDITY A high degree of humidity is good for the wine, although not for the labels, so an ideal compromise is around 75-80 per cent humidity.

LIGHT Ultra-violet light damages wine so it should be stored in a dark place.

SMELL Wine can become tainted by smell through the cork, so a clean atmosphere is important.

VIBRATION The maturation of a wine can be upset by vibration, so minimal movement of the wine is recommended.

Finally, it is important to remember to store all wine bottles on their sides. The wine keeps the cork moist and thereby prevents contraction, which would allow air to enter as wine leaks out and result in oxidation of the wine.

It is worth bearing in mind that many wine merchants offer a cellerage service, usually for wines purchased from them. Certainly, those people who regularly buy wine en primeur (i.e. the year following the vintage) and are therefore looking for long-term storage should ensure that the wines are stored properly, even if they have to pay for it.

Serving wine

TEMPERATURE

White and rosé wines are normally served chilled (at about 7°C/45°F). The best way to chill a white wine is to put it in the fridge for an hour or two. If time is of the essence, 10 minutes in a freezer or 20 minutes in an ice-bucket with water and ice will normally suffice. Remember that too cold a temperature will mask much of the flavour or scent in a wine. Red wines are normally served at what is called 'room' temperature (about 16°C/65°F). It is important to bring red wines up to room temperature gradually and certainly not to 'cook' them by trying to heat them quickly on a stove or in boiling water. Light red wines, such as Beaujolais or Valpolicella, are, however, best served cool, at around 12°C/55°F, and, as a general rule, the fuller the red wine the warmer it should be - up to the 16°C/65°F mark.

OPENING

Red wines also improve by being opened some time before serving. This is because they have generally been aged longer in the bottle than white or rosé wines and benefit from a period of breathing to lose any 'bottle stink' that might have developed. Usually an hour or two before serving is sufficient, but, again, the fuller or heavier the wine, the more benefit it will gain from being opened longer. For example, wines such as Barolo can be opened 6 hours before serving. With very old wines, it is safest not to open them more than an hour before serving as they can deteriorate very quickly.

DECANTING

Red wines will also start to throw a sediment in the bottle after about 5 years ageing and any red wine 10 or more years old will usually have sufficient deposit to warrant decanting. This is easily done by first allowing the bottle to stand for 24-48 hours, and then, after opening, pouring it steadily in one movement into the decanter, allowing the sediment to catch in the shoulder of the bottle. A candle behind the bottle can help to show up the sediment but is not really necessary. Decanting also helps a wine to breathe by aeration as it is poured, thereby losing any 'bottle stink' that may have developed.

CORKSCREWS

The best corkscrews are those with a broad metal spiral rather than the thick screw type which tend to pull straight through the cork. The 'waiter's friend' complete with a knife for cutting the foil, or the 'screw-pull', and its accompanying foil cutter, which are more expensive, are probably the best available.

SPARKLING WINES

These should be served well-chilled, at 5-7°C/ 40-45°F. The cooler temperature helps to reduce the pressure of carbon dioxide gas in the bottle and thereby makes opening the bottle easier. Similarly, the bottle should not be shaken prior to opening. The secret to opening a bottle of sparkling wine successfully is to hold it an angle of 45 degrees, remove the foil and wire cage from the cork, always keeping your thumb over the cork for safety, and then, holding the cork firmly in one hand, twist the bottle carefully and allow the pressure inside to ease the cork out gently. Always have a glass ready, and keep the bottle at a 45-degree angle if the wine starts to froth out.

FORTIFIED WINES

These are mostly served at room temperature, with the exception of pale dry fino or manzanilla sherries which should always be served chilled.

KEEPING WINE FRESH

Once a bottle of wine is opened, it will not keep at its best for very long - older wines will deteriorate in a matter of hours. There are various products available that claim to maintain the freshness of a wine, but it is always possible to decant a half-finished bottle into a smaller container as it is the amount of oxygen available to it that causes the deterioration.

Fortified wines, with the exception of light, dry sherries, will last a little longer than table wines because of their higher alcohol content. Any half-drunk bottle will keep better at a cool temperature.

OXIDIZED AND CORKY WINE:
It is quite rare to find a bottle of wine that is faulty – but problems do arise sometimes. The most common fault is oxidation of the wine, usually as a result of poor storage. The wine smells tired and stale; white wines are particularly susceptible to this condition. At its extreme, the wine becomes what is called 'maderized' (due to its colour turning almost brown). A wine that is corked, i.e. one that smells very woody and musty, is the result of a diseased cork, and not one that has bits of cork floating in it as a result of opening the bottle! Very small, sugar-like crystals are often found in wine, both red and white. These are tartaric acid crystals, which have precipitated out due to the wine being subjected to a cold temperature. They are completely harmless and can easily be left in the bottom of the bottle or glass. Most everyday wines are refrigerated prior to bottling specifically to avoid this phenomenon. They are, in fact, part of a natural sediment which consumers seem to find acceptable in red wines, but not in white.

GLASSES
Choosing glasses for serving wine is usually the result of aesthetic rather than vinous consideration. However, there are factors that should be borne in mind by those who wish to gain the maximum pleasure from wine. The best glasses are the simplest: they should be made of clear thin glass, narrower at the lip than in the bowl to concentrate the bouquet of the wine, with a sufficiently long stem so that the wine is not affected by the temperature of your hand. Finally, good wine glasses should be generous in size so that they do not need to be more than two-thirds filled, thereby allowing room for the bouquet to develop. Glasses for white wines are normally smaller than those for red wines, which usually have more aromas. Glasses for sparkling wines should be of the tall tulip shape rather than the flatter, saucer style, as with less surface area of wine, the sparkle will not dissipate into the atmosphere so quickly. Finally, always make sure that glasses are clean and do not smell of detergents.

Wines for special occasions

Choosing and ordering wine for a large party or a special occasion such as a wedding can often appear a daunting prospect, especially as it is usually one of a whole myriad of jobs that have to be done. However, a few simple guidelines will help to make the exercise one of the simplest.

The first thing is to decide what you want to serve: sparkling wines, white, red, even ports and liqueurs. Then, when you have an idea of numbers of guests, calculate roughly how many bottles you will need. A 75cl bottle gives between 6-7 glasses of wine, depending on the size; a litre bottle 8-10 glasses. Usually people drink two-thirds white wine to one-third red. Most good wine merchants are happy to supply on a 'sale or return' basis and will be able to provide glasses and also ice to chill the white or sparkling wines. Remember, though, that if you want to return bottles they should not have been left in an ice-bath where the labels become damaged. It is also important to have a good quantity of non-alcoholic drinks, such as mineral water and orange juice, at large events. Always ensure that you have sufficient staff both to open and serve the wines. People are normally reluctant to help themselves but invariably irritated by holding an empty glass. As a guide, for 50-60 people, you need two staff just to serve the drinks.

Tasting wine

It is possible to derive much more pleasure from wine by learning a little more about how to taste properly. Cooks, who are used to tasting food, can quickly become expert at tasting wine. The three senses of sight, smell and taste are used.

SIGHT A wine, first of all, should look bright and clear. White wines can be very pale, usually indicating a cool climate, such as a Moselle or Loire, or greeny-yellow such as Chablis. Deeper coloured, more yellowy wines will usually indicate a hotter climate, such as Australia or California. As white wines age, they take on a more golden colour; browning indicates that the wine has probably oxidized either through age or poor storage. Red wines start with a bright purple colour and, as they age, pass through stages of ruby or cherry red, and finally turn to brick or tawny-red. Wines from hotter climates will usually have a fuller, deeper colour than those from cooler climates as a result of the greater ripening of the grapes.

THE SMELL This is also known as the bouquet of a wine, and is the second indication of its character. First of all, any faults in the wine will be apparent. It is also a good idea to swirl the wine around in the glass, thereby releasing more of the aromas. The smell may give indications of the particular grape variety (some of which have very distinctive characteristics – blackcurrants for Cabernet-Sauvignon, gooseberries for Sauvignon). Also, some indication of the levels of alcohol and acidity, as well as sweetness and fruit flavours, will be noticeable.

THE TASTE This should be a confirmation and development of the sight and smell. The primary elements to look for in a wine are sweetness, fruit flavours, alcohol, acidity and, in the case of red wines, tannin. The more these elements are in balance, the more complete the wine will appear, although you should remember that high levels of tannin in many young red wines will diminish in time. It is important to take a good mouthful, to really swirl it around your tongue and draw in some air through your teeth to maximize the potential of the wine.

Finally, it is important to appreciate the length of time the taste remains after you have swallowed or spat out the wine. This is known as the 'after taste' or 'finish'.

A dictionary of tasting terms

APPEARANCE

Bright All wines in sound condition should be bright.
Colour White wines can be:
Pale Usually indicating they come from a cool climate.
Straw-yellow A deeper colour from a hot climate.
Green Usually indicates a young wine.
Purple The colour of young red wine, turning **ruby or cherry red** before becoming **brick red or tawny.**
Deep-coloured Wines that usually come from hot climates.

SMELL

Bouquet The particular smell of a wine.
Fruity Attractive fruit quality, not necessarily:
Grapey Aroma produced by certain grape varieties.
Stalky Green, woody smell often found in young wine.
Dumb Little smell, usually from a young or undeveloped wine.
Corked Distinct smell of cork – the result of a diseased cork leading to a wine becoming:
Oxidized... or worse.
Maderized White wine turned brown in colour.
Acetic/vinegary Excess volatile acidity.
Sulphury Excess of sulphur used in the wine's production.

TASTE

Acidity Natural component of wine. High acid wines are described as **crisp, green, sharp, tart.** Low acid wines taste **flabby** and lack **freshness.**
Alcohol Indicated by the weight of a wine. Low-alcohol wines tend to be **light**.
Extract The soluble solids in a wine. Wines with plenty of extract and alcohol are described as having plenty of **body,** or as being **big** wines. These tend to come from hot climates and will usually have more alcohol and extract than those from cool climates.
Heavy Wine with too much alcohol and extract.
Thin Wine with little extract or flavour.
Flavour The particular taste of a wine. Useful terms in this area are:
Fruity Not necessarily grape tastes.
Nutty Found in full, dry white wines.
Peppery Raw taste often found in young red wine, but also from certain grape varieties.
Spicy Rich taste found in certain grape varieties.
Ripe Wine made from mature grapes – or a wine ready to drink.
Rich Full fruit flavour with alcohol and extract, not necessarily sweet.
Round No rough edges.
Smooth No rough edges.
Soft No rough edges.
Supple No rough edges.
Neutral Bland flavour.
Oxidized Flat, stale taste – the result of the

wine's exposure to air.
Mouldy Off flavour.
Musty Off flavour.
Woody Off flavour.
Dry Wine with all grape sugars fermented out.
Sweet Wine with high sugar content.
Tannin Tannic acid derived from grape skins during fermentation therefore found only in young red wines. Leaves dry taste in mouth and around teeth. Wine with an excess of tannin is described as **hard or tough**.
Finish The end-taste of a wine. The time it lasts is described as **length**.

Wine and food

The essential criterion in matching wine and food is that the two should complement each other. A light wine will be killed by strong food, just as a full, rich wine will overpower a light dish. A wine high in acid will help to cut through any oiliness in the food, yet a sweet wine will balance a sweet course. So it is important to be able to appreciate the elements in a wine so as to match it to the food as follows:

Dry to sweet
Light to full
Low acid to high acid
Fresh, young and fruity to mature and dry
Hard and tannic to soft and mellow

However, there are many surprising combinations that work well, the most famous being Sauternes with foie gras. So do not be afraid to experiment – you may well discover some wonderful combinations.

The following charts are intended only as a guideline, but will help those who are uncertain to gain confidence.

Wine style	Style of food
Very dry white (Muscadet, Sancerre, Sauvignon-grape wines, Chablis)	Shellfish, salmon, oily fish
Dry white (Soave, Frascati,Burgundy, Chardonnay wines)	White fish
Spicy dry white (Alsace, some dry German and English wines)	Smoked fish
Medium dry white (Moselle, Vouvray, Vinho Verde)	Chicken
Medium sweet white (German Spätlese/Auslese, Italian Moscato)	Soft creamy cheese Fruit and fruit puddings
Sweet white (Sauternes, Barsac, Muscat de Beaumes de Venise)	Foie gras Rich puddings Chocolate puddings
Rosé (Tavel, Provence)	Bouillabaise Cold meats
Light red (Beaujolais, Valpolicella)	Chicken, veal, pork
Soft red (Burgundy)	Pork, duck
Medium red (Claret, Côtes du Rhône, Chianti, Rioja)	Lamb Game birds
Full red (Châteauneuf du Pape, Cabernet-Sauvignon wines)	Beef
Very full red (Crozes-Hermitage, Barolo, Australian Shiraz)	Rich stews Venison

Food	Style of Wine	Suggestion
Fish dishes		
Terrine	Light dry white	Chablis
Soups	Crisp dry white	Sancerre/Pouilly Fumé/
Mayonnaise		Burgundy
Buttery sauce		
Smoked	Spicy white	Alsace Tokay/Riesling
Chinese-style		
Barbecued		
Chicken dishes		
Mayonnaise	Light, dry white	Soave/Moselle
Buttery sauce		
Chinese-style	Full white	Mâcon
Roast	Light, red and fruity	Beaujolais
Casserole		
Barbecued/Indian/	Fuller red	Côtes du Rhône
Tandoori		
Veal		
Buttery sauce	Light, fruity red	Valpolicella
Roast		
Casserole	Fuller red	Chianti Classico
Pork		
Buttery sauce	Light red	Beaujolais Villages
Spicy/Chinese style		
Stewed/cassoulet	Full red	Corbières
Roast	Medium red	Burgundy
Barbecued		
Lamb		
With hollandaise	Light to medium red	Chinon/Bourgueil
Stewed	Fuller red	Claret/Rioja
Roast		
Spiced/curried/barbecued	Spicy red	Crozes-Hermitage
Beef		
With hollandaise	Medium red	Burgundy
Casserole	Fuller red	Rhône/Châteauneuf
Roast		du Pape
Spiced/barbecued	Full, spicy red	Australian Shiraz
		Australian/Californian
		Cabernet Sauvignon

Traditional Dishes

Caviar

30g/1oz per person

Leave the caviar in its pot. Chill, and stand on a napkin. Serve 5ml/1 teaspoon on to each guest's plate, and offer, from another platter, wedges of lemon, chopped hardboiled egg white and sieved yolk (in separate piles), chopped parsley and chopped raw onion. Serve with hot toast.

Brown Shrimps

150ml/$^1/_4$ pint per person

Serve the shrimps in piles, unshelled, on individual plates with hot bread, good butter, lemon wedges and salt and black pepper. The guests shell their own shrimps. Provide finger bowls.

Potted Shrimps

1 small pot per person

Warm the pots gently in the oven, and when the butter is just melted, or at least soft, turn out on to individual plates. Offer toast (no butter) and lemon wedges separately, and a knife and fork to eat them with. This is the traditional way of serving shrimps, but today they are sometimes turned out cold and eaten, like pâté, on rather than with the toast. They are better just warm however. Do not re-chill them once melted.

Gulls Eggs

2 per person

Hardboil the eggs by boiling them for 8 minutes. Plovers eggs (4 per person): boil for 6 minutes. Quails eggs (6 per person): boil for 4 minutes. Serve in a basket lined with lettuce leaves or a napkin, and offer sea or rock salt, celery salt or oriental salt, black pepper and cayenne pepper separately. Serve brown bread and butter. The guests peel the eggs and eat them with their fingers.

Oysters

9 or 12 per person

Serve 6 each if there is a big meal to come, but oyster lovers like a lot! Order the oysters and ask for them to be opened only when you are there to collect them, or as late as possible. Keep refrigerated until serving. If the fishmonger has not loosened the oysters from the bottom shell, do so with a sharp knife. Check that there are no bits of shell or grit on the saucer-shaped bottom shells, but leave any sea water or juices with them. Discard the top shells. Put the oysters on to oyster plates, or failing them, on to dinner plates covered by a napkin to keep them from tipping or rolling. Hand Tabasco sauce, or chilli pepper, black pepper, white pepper, wedges of lemon and vinegar separately, and serve with brown bread and butter. The diner eats the oysters with a fork, and drinks the juice from the shell as from a cup.

Oursins (Sea Urchins)

3 per person

Serve exactly as oysters, with the same accompaniments, but with a teaspoon for the guest to extract the flesh. The fishmonger cuts off the top of the shell, like the top of a boiled egg.

Smoked Salmon

75g/3oz per person

Arrange slices in a single layer on dinner plates. Hand lemon wedges or halves and brown bread and butter separately. To slice smoked salmon: use a salmon or ham knife. Put the fish skin-side down on the board. Slice the top thin layer of smoked skin-like flesh off, then feel for the row of lateral bones whose tips will be sticking like pins straight up in a row between the two fillets of flesh, in a line running the length of the fish. Pull them out, one by one, with tweezers or pliers. Then slice the flesh horizontally in paper-thin pieces. Keep covered or painted with salad oil.

Smoked Trout

1 per person

Use scissors to cut the smoked skin carefully round the neck and tail before loosening it with the fingers and peeling it off, leaving head and tail intact. Serve on individual plates with lemon wedges, handing brown bread and butter and horseradish sauce separately.

Smoked Mackerel

half a fish per person

Peel the fish and carefully lift the fillets off the backbone. There will be 4 of them. Arrange 2 per person on plates with lemon wedges and hand mustard, mayonnaise or horseradish sauce separately.

Asparagus

6 fat or 12 thin spears per person

Cut off the woody ends. Peel the fibrous stalks. Wash well. Tie in bundles. Boil in an asparagus cooker (the stalks stand in the water, the tips cook in the steam), or simmer lying down in salted water in a frying pan, until the stalk is tender halfway down. Drain well. Serve from a platter lined with a napkin to absorb the moisture. Hand melted clarified butter, hollandaise or beurre blanc separately if hot; vinaigrette if cold.

Globe Artichokes

1 per person

Twist and pull the stalk off the artichoke very close to the base so that it will stand without rolling. Trim off straight the tips of the bottom few rows of leaves if they are hard or cracked and anyway if the tip spines are prickly. Leave the smaller higher leaves. Boil for 45 minutes in salted water with a cut-up lemon and 15ml/1 tablespoon oil. When a leaf (not an outside one) will pull out easily, drain the artichokes upside down. When cool enough to handle, prise open the middle leaves and lift out the central cluster of tiny leaves. Using a teaspoon scrape out the fibrous 'choke' and discard it. Serve the artichokes on individual plates on a folded napkin. Give each guest a small pot of clarified melted butter if the artichokes are hot, or vinaigrette dressing if cold. The guest pulls the leaves off the flowerhead, dips the flesh end into the butter or sauce, eats the softer part with his fingers and discards the leaves.

Soups

Gazpacho I

This recipe assumes that the cook has a blender or liquidizer.

SERVES 6
900g/2lb fresh, very ripe tomatoes, peeled
1 large mild Spanish onion
2 red peppers
1 small cucumber
1 thick slice white bread, the crust cut off
1 egg yolk
2 large garlic cloves
90ml/6 tablespoons olive oil
15ml/1 tablespoon tarragon vinegar
450g/1lb tin Italian peeled tomatoes
15ml/1 tablespoon tomato purée
freshly ground black pepper
plenty of salt (preferably sea salt)

To serve:
1 large bowl croûtons

1. Chop or dice finely a small amount of the fresh tomato, onion, red pepper, and cucumber and put in separate small bowls for garnish. Roughly chop the remaining vegetables to prepare them for the liquidizer.
2. Put the bread, egg yolk and garlic into the liquidizer. Turn it on and add the oil in a thin steady stream while the machine is running. You should end up with a thick mayonnaise-like emulsion.
3. Add the vinegar and then gradually add all the soup ingredients in batches and blend until smooth.
4. Sieve the soup to remove the tomato seeds and check for flavouring.

NOTE: Gazpacho should be served icy cold with the small bowls of chopped vegetables and fried croûtons handed separately. Sometimes crushed ice is added to the soup at the last minute.

If you prefer a thinner soup, dilute it with iced water or tomato juice.

CRISP DRY WHITE

Gazpacho II

This recipe is by Christopher Buey from *The Taste of Health* and is lower in fat than the previous recipe.

SERVES 4
ice cubes
285g/10oz tomatoes
1/2 cucumber
1/2 green pepper
1/2 sweet red pepper
1 medium sized onion
570ml/1 pint tomato juice (tinned or fresh)
1 garlic clove
30ml/2 tablespoons tarragon vinegar
salt and freshly ground black pepper
30ml/2 tablespoons olive oil
15ml/1 tablespoon fresh herbs, such as parsley, chervil, tarragon, chives

1. Cut all the vegetables into chunks. Set aside a little of each for the garnish.
2. Place half the tomato juice in a liquidizer or processor with the vegetables and garlic, and liquidize for 2-3 minutes. Gradually add the rest of the juice, the vinegar, salt and pepper and finish with the olive oil.
3. Add the ice cubes to the soup and refrigerate it for 10 minutes.
4. Remove the ice cubes and serve the soup garnished with the reserved chopped raw vegetables and herbs.

CALIFORNIAN CHARDONNAY

Avocado Pear Soup

This soup is an acquired taste: some of us love it, others loathe it.

SERVES 4
4 avocado pears
10ml/2 teaspoons onion juice
salt and freshly ground black pepper
1 litre/1 3/4 pints cold chicken stock
juice of 1 lemon

1. Skin and stone the avocado pears and mash to a purée with a fork. Liquidize with the onion juice, salt and pepper, stock and lemon juice. Chill.

Lebanese Cucumber and Yoghurt Soup

SERVES 4
1 large cucumber, peeled
290ml/½ pint single cream
140g/5 fl oz carton yoghurt
30ml/2 tablespoons tarragon vinegar
15ml/1 tablespoon chopped mint
salt and pepper

1. Grate the cucumber coarsely.
2. Stir in the rest of the ingredients and season to taste.
3. Chill for 2 hours before serving.

NOTE: This soup may be garnished with cold croûtons; chopped chives; a spoonful of soured cream added just before serving; chopped gherkins; a few pink shrimps. It is also good flavoured with garlic.

WHITE BURGUNDY

Chilled Cream Cheese Soup

SERVES 4
340g/12oz can jellied consommé
170g/6oz mild cream cheese
5ml/1 teaspoon curry powder
squeeze of lemon juice

1. Reserve 1 cupful of consommé for the top.
2. Liquidize the remaining consommé with the cheese, curry powder and a squeeze of lemon juice. Pour into cocotte dishes.
3. Chill until set.
4. Spoon over the remaining consommé (which should be cool, on the point of setting) and chill again until ready to serve.

NOTE: Some tinned consommé will not set. Test it by chilling for an hour. If the soup is still liquid, melt 5ml/1 teaspoon powdered gelatine in the consommé and allow to cool. Consommé with 'serve hot' on the label is generally non-setting.

WHITE BURGUNDY

Simple Vegetable Soup

SERVES 8
45g/1½ oz butter
225g/8oz onions, chopped
450g/1 lb carrots, chopped
225g/8oz potatoes, chopped
110g/4 oz celery, chopped
425ml/¾ pint milk
860ml/1½ pints water
salt and freshly ground black pepper

1. Melt the butter in a large heavy pan with 30ml/2 tablespoons water. Add all the chopped vegetables, stir and cover with a lid. Cook slowly until soft but not coloured, stirring occasionally. This will take about 30 minutes.
2. Add the milk and water. Season with salt and pepper and simmer, without a lid, for 15 minutes.
3. Liquidize the soup and pass through a sieve.
4. Pour into the rinsed-out saucepan. Season to taste and add water if the soup is too thick. Reheat carefully.

DRY WHITE/LIGHT RED

Creamy Vegetable Soup

SERVES 4
225g/8oz leeks, finely sliced
30g/1oz butter
225g/8oz onions, very finely sliced
1 small head celery, finely sliced
1 large potato, peeled and finely sliced
570ml/1 pint chicken stock
salt, pepper and nutmeg
290ml/½ pint creamy milk
15ml/1 tablespoon thin cream
15ml/1 tablespoon port (optional, but very good)

1. Melt the butter in a very large pan. Add the onions, leeks, celery, and potatoes and sweat with the lid on, stirring occasionally, until the whole mass is soft and cooked (about 40 minutes).
2. Add the stock, bring to the boil stirring, and boil for 1 minute. Add the salt, pepper and nutmeg to taste and simmer gently for 20 minutes.
3. Liquidize the soup in an electric blender and pass through a sieve.
4. Add the milk, reheat, and add the cream and port. Use white port if you would prefer the soup not to go faintly pink.

NOTE: Do not add all the milk if the soup looks too thin.

NOTE: The soup is good hot, too. Reheat without boiling.

WHITE LOIRE/SAUVIGNON

Iced Vichyssoise Soup

SERVES 4
55g/2oz butter
1 medium onion, finely chopped
the white part of 3 large or 5 small leeks, chopped
110g/4oz potatoes, peeled and sliced
salt and pepper
290ml/½ pint chicken stock
290ml/½ pint creamy milk
30ml/2 tablespoons cream
chopped chives

1. Melt the butter in a heavy-bottomed pan and add the chopped onion and leek.
2. Sweat the vegetables for 15 minutes or so. The vegetables must soften without crisping or browning.
3. Add the potatoes, salt and pepper and the stock. Simmer until the potatoes are soft.
4. Liquidize the soup and push it through a sieve.
5. Add the milk and cream. (Check the consistency before adding all the milk.)
6. Check the seasoning. Chill.
7. Add the chives just before serving, and perhaps a swirl more cream.

WHITE BURGUNDY

Cold Cucumber Soup

SERVES 4
2 cucumbers, peeled and sliced
290ml/½ pint water
salt and freshly ground black pepper
30g/1oz flour
570ml/1 pint chicken stock
1 bay leaf
2 cloves
140g/5 fl oz carton soured cream
15ml/1 tablespoon chopped fresh dill
finely grated rind of 1 lemon

1. Cook the cucumber in the water until tender. Liquidize or push through a sieve and add salt and pepper to taste.
2. Mix the flour with 60ml/4 tablespoons of stock. Heat the remaining stock.
3. Add a little of the hot stock to the flour/stock mixture and return this to the pan. Stir until the liquid boils and thickens.
4. Add the cucumber purée, bay leaf and cloves. Bring slowly to the boil and simmer for 2 minutes. Strain into a bowl.
5. Allow to cool. Stir in the soured cream, dill and grated lemon rind. Chill before serving.

MUSCADET/SAUVIGNON

Artichoke Soup

SERVES 4
55g/2oz butter
1 medium onion, sliced
675g/1½ lb Jerusalem artichokes
570ml/1 pint milk
570ml/1 pint water
salt and freshly ground black pepper

1. Melt the butter in a saucepan and gently cook the onion in it until soft but not coloured.
2. Peel the artichokes and leave in a bowl of cold acidulated water (water with lemon juice or

vinegar added) to prevent discoloration.
3. Slice the artichokes and add to the pan. Continue cooking, covered, for about 10 minutes, giving an occasional stir.
4. Add the milk and water, season well and simmer for a further 20 minutes. Do not allow it to boil, or it will curdle.
5. Liquidize and push through a sieve. Check for seasoning – this soup needs plenty of salt and pepper.

LIGHT WHITE ALSACE

Pea Soup

SERVES 4
15g/½oz butter
1 onion, finely chopped
1 potato, peeled and diced
340g/12oz frozen peas
1 litre/2 pints chicken stock or water
salt and freshly ground black pepper
60ml/4 tablespoons single cream

1. Put the butter into a large saucepan, melt over a gentle heat and add the onion and potato. Cover with a piece of greased greaseproof paper and leave to sweat for 10 minutes.
2. Add the peas, stock, salt and pepper. Bring to the boil and simmer slowly for 15 minutes.
3. Remove the soup from the heat, liquidize it very well and pour it through a sieve into a clean saucepan.
4. Reheat for 1-2 minutes, add the cream and taste for seasoning.

ROSE/LIGHT RED

Lettuce and Dill Soup

SERVES 4-6
3 lettuces, washed
30g/1oz butter
225g/8oz onion, very finely sliced
400g/14oz potatoes, peeled and finely sliced
1 litre/2 pints chicken stock (*see page 219*)
salt, pepper and nutmeg
1 bunch fresh dill, roughly chopped
30ml/2 tablespoons single cream

1. Shred the lettuces finely. Melt the butter in a large saucepan and add the onion and potato. Cover and cook slowly (sweat) for 10 minutes.
2. Add the stock, bring to the boil, season with salt, pepper and nutmeg and simmer gently for 5 minutes.
3. Add the lettuce, and simmer for 10 minutes.
4. Add the dill, and simmer for 1 minute.
5. Liquidize the soup in an electric blender and push through a sieve into a rinsed-out saucepan.
6. Bring back to the boil, add the cream and tip into a warm soup tureen.

LIGHT DRY WHITE

Stilton Soup

SERVES 4
1 medium onion, finely chopped
2 sticks celery, finely choppped
55g/2oz butter
45g/1½oz flour
75ml/5 tablespoons white wine
1 litre/1¾ pints white stock (chicken or veal)
290ml/½ pint milk
225g/8oz Stilton cheese, grated or crumbled
30ml/2 tablespoons cream
salt and pepper

1. Soften the onion and celery in the butter over gentle heat. Add the flour and cook for 1 minute.
2. Take off the heat and stir in the wine and stock. Return to the heat and bring slowly to the boil, stirring continuously until the soup thickens. Simmer for 25 minutes.
3. Add the milk and simmer for 2 minutes. Remove from the heat and whisk in the Stilton. Liquidize and push through a sieve.
4. Add the cream and salt and pepper. Reheat the soup, taking care not to let it boil, or it will curdle.

NOTE I: White port, well chilled, is delicious with this soup.
NOTE II: The soup can be served chilled. In this event streak the cream into the soup just before serving, giving it an attractive marbled appearance.

BEAUJOLAIS

Mushroom Soup

SERVES 4

55g/2oz butter
340g/12oz flat black mushrooms, chopped
45ml/3 tablespoons chopped fresh parsley
1/2 garlic clove, crushed
2 large slices bread, crusts removed, crumbled
860ml/1 1/2 pints good chicken stock
pinch of ground nutmeg or mace
salt and plenty of freshly ground black pepper
150ml/1/4 pint cream

1. Melt the butter in a very large thick saucepan.
2. Add the mushrooms and most of the parsley. Cook gently, stirring, until soft. Add the garlic and the bread. Stir until the bread and mushrooms are well mixed, then add the stock, nutmeg or mace and salt and pepper to taste. Bring to simmering point and cook slowly for 10 minutes.
3. Liquidize the soup or put it through a vegetable mill. If the soup is to be served cold, allow to cool, sprinkle on the parsley and swirl in the cream. Alternatively, add the parsley and cream and reheat.

Chinese Mushroom Broth

SERVES 4

85g/3oz Chinese black mushrooms (dried)
860ml/1 1/2 pints chicken stock
30ml/2 tablespoons soy sauce
1 spring onion, finely sliced
sesame oil

1. Soak the mushrooms, caps up, in a bowl of warm water until they are soft; this takes about 30 minutes. Squeeze to remove excess water. Remove the stems and cut each cap into 5mm/1/4 inch slices.
2. Put the stock, soy sauce and mushrooms into a small saucepan, bring to the boil and simmer for 15 minutes.
3. Sprinkle on the spring onion and about 4 drops of sesame oil. Serve.

DRY SHERRY

Chilled Beetroot Soup with Soured Cream

SERVES 4

1kg/2 1/4lb raw beetroot, washed
salt and freshly ground black pepper
570-860ml/1-1 1/2 pints chicken stock (see page 219)
5-10ml/1-2 teaspoons ground cumin or caraway
caster sugar
salt and pepper
285g/10oz soured cream
fresh herbs, chopped

1. Place the whole raw beetroots in a large pan of cold water, and season with salt and pepper. Bring to the boil and cook until 'al dente'. This will take about 1 hour – depending on the size of the beetroots.
2. Drain and leave to cool.
3. Peel, cut roughly into small pieces and liquidize in a blender or food processor.
4. Push the purée through a fine sieve, and then add the chicken stock to give a thick consistency which will still easily run from a spoon.
5. Season the soup to taste with ground cumin or caraway, caster sugar, salt and freshly ground black pepper.
6. Ladle the beetroot soup into three-quarters of an ice-cold soup plate, holding the plate at an angle. Then ladle the soured cream into the remaining (uppermost) quarter of the plate, gently lowering the plate as you do so.
7. 'Feather' the cream into the beetroot soup at the 'join' using a toothpick or thin skewer. Sprinkle with fresh herbs. Serve cold.

ALSACE TOKAY

Clear Borscht

SERVES 6

900g/2lb raw beetroot
1.7 litres/3 pints chicken stock
6 peppercorns
8 coriander seeds
2.5ml/1/2 teaspoon fennel seeds
1 parsley stalk, bruised
1 onion, chopped

1 carrot, peeled and chopped
1 garlic clove, unpeeled
salt and freshly ground black pepper
20ml/4 teaspoons malt vinegar
15ml/1 tablespoon sugar

1. Wash and peel the beetroot and cut each one into 4.
2. Put the beetroot into a large clean saucepan with the stock.
3. Put the peppercorns, coriander seeds and fennel seeds into a small piece of muslin and tie up. Add to the saucepan with the parsley stalk. Bring to the boil and simmer for 1 hour.
4. Add the onion, carrot, garlic, salt and pepper and cook very slowly for a further 20 minutes. Add the vinegar and sugar. Taste and season as necessary.
5. Strain the soup through a muslin-lined sieve into a clean saucepan. Reheat and pour into individual soup bowls.

LIGHT ALSACE WHITE

Lentil Soup

SERVES 4
340g/12oz orange lentils
1 litre/2 pints water
1 small bacon bone or 1 stock cube
1 bay leaf
55g/2oz onion, sliced
1 parsley stalk
45-60ml/3-4 tablespoons cream
chopped fresh mint

1. Wash the lentils and drain them. Put them in a pan with the water, bacon bone or stock cube, bay leaf, onion and parsley stalk, and boil for about 30 minutes.
2. When the lentils are soft, remove the bone etc. Liquidize and sieve the soup.
3. Return the soup to the pan with the cream and heat up. Serve with a little chopped mint.

LIGHT RED

Corn Chowder

SERVES 4
110g/4oz streaky bacon, rindless, chopped
1 large potato, peeled and diced
30g/1oz butter
3 sticks celery, chopped
1 large onion, chopped
1 large green pepper, deseeded and chopped
1 bay leaf
30g/1oz flour
570ml/1 pint milk
4 ears corn on the cob
salt and pepper
chopped parlsey

1. Fry the bacon in the butter. When brown but not brittle add the vegetables and the bay leaf. Turn down the heat and cook slowly until the onion looks soft and transparent.
2. Draw the pan from the heat; mix in the flour, cook for 1 minute and then add the milk.
3. Return the pan to the heat; stir until boiling.
4. Scrape the kernels from the cobs and add them to the soup. Scrape the cobs with a sharp knife to extract all the juice and add this too. Season with salt and pepper to taste. Simmer for 5 minutes or until the vegetables are soft but not broken.
5. Serve sprinkled with chopped parsley.

DRY WHITE

Provençal Fish Soup

SERVES 6-8
45ml/3 tablespoons olive oil
2 onions, sliced
1 garlic clove, crushed
2 leeks, sliced
1 litre/2 pints water
trimmings from the fish (head, skin, bones)
3 tomatoes, peeled and quartered
bouquet garni (celery, parsley, bay leaf, sprig of thyme)
pinch of saffron
salt and freshly ground black pepper
10-12 live mussels
1kg/2lb white fish fillets (any Mediterranean fish or haddock or brill or plaice or cod)
seasoned flour
15ml/1 tablespoon tomato purée

For the rouille (garlic paste):
1 green pepper
1 dry chilli pepper, or a few drops of Tabasco
150ml/¼ pint water
2 garlic cloves, crushed
1 canned pimento cap
45ml/3 tablespoons olive oil
15ml/1 tablespoon stale breadcrumbs

1. Start with the soup: heat the oil in a large pan. Add the onion, garlic and leeks and cook until soft but not coloured. Add the water, fish trimmings, tomatoes, bouquet garni, saffron, salt and pepper. Cook uncovered over a moderate heat for 30 minutes but no longer.
2. Scrub the mussels well, removing their 'beards' and discarding any that do not shut when tapped on the sink edge.
3. Meanwhile prepare the rouille: simmer the pepper and chilli in a little water for 10 minutes. Drain and dry well. Grind the pepper, chilli, garlic and pimento in a pestle and mortar to a smooth paste or blend finely in a liquidizer. Beat in the olive oil drip by drip. Add enough breadcrumbs to make the sauce hold its shape, and add the Tabasco if the chilli was omitted. Taste and season with salt if necessary.
4. Strain the fish bouillon into a clean saucepan, pressing the fish trimmings and vegetables to extract all their juices.
5. Cut the fish fillets into bite-sized cubes and toss them in seasoned flour. Add to the bouillon with the tomato purée.
6. Simmer for 5 minutes and add the mussels. Simmer until all the shells have opened. Taste and season.
7. Pour the soup into a tureen and hand the rouille separately. (If the rouille is very thick and paste-like, a little of the hot soup can be added to thin it slightly.)

RHONE OR PROVENCAL WHITE

Prawn Bisque

SERVES 4
900g/2lb unshelled cooked prawns
30ml/2 tablespoons oil
110g/4oz butter
2 shallots, chopped
juice of ½ lemon
45ml/3 tablespoons brandy
1 litre/2 pints well-flavoured fish stock (page 219)
1 bay leaf
1 parsley stalk
blade of mace
45g/1½oz flour
salt and pepper
Tabasco sauce
45ml/3 tablespoons cream

1. Shell all but 4 of the prawns, and reserve the shells. Wash the prawns, remove the dark vein and reserve any roe.
2. In a large heavy pan heat the oil, add 30g/1oz of the butter and fry the prawn shells for 2 minutes. Add the shallots, lemon juice and brandy and continue to cook for a further 2 minutes. Add the stock, bay leaf, parsley stalk and blade of mace and cook for 30 minutes (this will help to give the bisque flavour and colour).
3. Meanwhile blend or pound together all the shelled prawns with about 45g/1½oz butter and any reserved roe.
4. Melt the remaining butter. Add the flour and cook for 30 seconds. Strain in the stock and bring slowly to the boil, stirring constantly. Simmer for 2 minutes, strain in the pan juices, and whisk in the prawn butter.
5. Season with salt, pepper and Tabasco. Add the cream and the reserved prawns.

NOTE : If there is no roe to be found, whisk 15ml/1 tablespoon tomato purée into the bisque to give it a better colour.

CHABLIS

Lobster Bisque

SERVES 4
1 live lobster (675g/1½lb)
30ml/2 tablespoons oil
110g/4oz butter
2 shallots, chopped
juice of ½ lemon
45ml/3 tablespoons brandy
1 bay leaf
1 parsley stalk
blade of mace

1 litre/2 pints fish or vegetable stock
45g/1½oz flour
45ml/3 tablespoons cream
salt and pepper
pinch of cayenne pepper

1. Set the oven to 180°C/350°F/gas mark 4.
2. Kill the lobster by pushing a sharp knife through its nerve centre (marked by a well-defined cross on the back of the head).

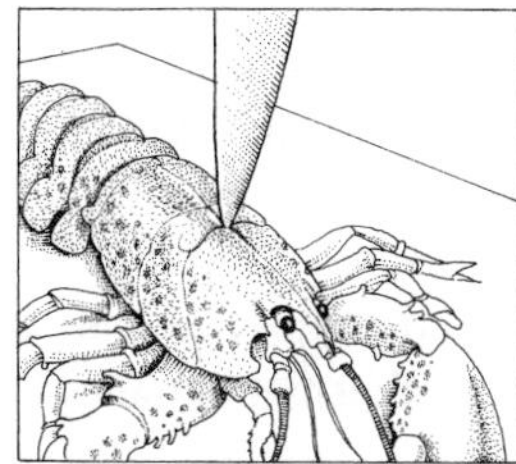

Push a sharp knife through the lobster's nerve centre

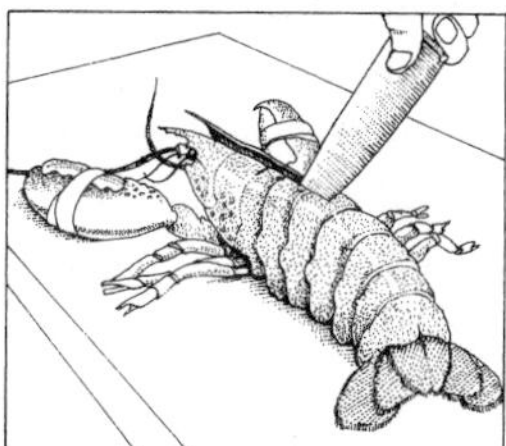
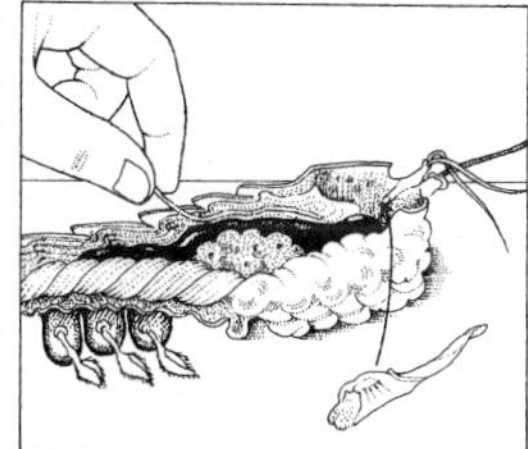

Split the lobster in half and remove the stomach sac

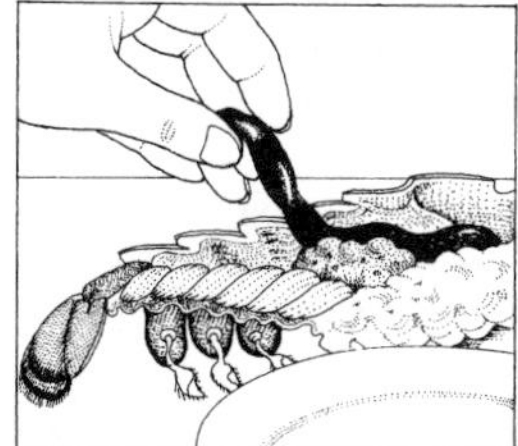

Remove the thread-like intestine and the greeny black roe

3. Lay the lobster flat out and split it in half lengthwise. Remove and discard the little stomach sac from the head and the thread-like intestine. Remove the coral (if any) and reserve.
4. In a large ovenproof pan heat the oil with 30g/1oz of the butter. Sauté the lobster, flesh side down, for 5 minutes. Add the shallot, lemon juice and brandy. Cover and place the pan in the oven for 15 minutes.
5. Remove all the meat from the lobster, adding the greenish creamy paste from the head.
6. Break up the shells in the pan, add the bay leaf, parsley stalk, mace and stock, and simmer for 30 minutes. Set aside. (This will help to give the bisque flavour and colour.)
7. Meanwhile blend or pound together all but a small chunk of the lobster meat with about 45g/1½oz butter and the coral. Cut the reserved meat into neat dice and set aside for garnish.
8. Strain the stock. Melt the remaining butter, add the flour and cook for 30 seconds. Add the stock and bring slowly to the boil, stirring all the time. Simmer for 2 minutes, add the pan juices and whisk in the lobster butter.
9. Add the cream and finally the lobster pieces. Taste and add salt or pepper if necessary. Serve sprinkled with a pinch of cayenne pepper.

CHABLIS

Bouillabaisse

Recipes for this Mediterranean stew are many and varied according to the availability of fish and vegetables. The sad truth is that it is only possible to make a real bouillabaisse on or near the Mediterranean coast. Imitations made at home never have quite the freshness and authenticity of the original.

This recipe is an adaptation of many recipes but we have relied mostly on Jane Grigson's recipe in *Fish Cookery*.

Use a selection of the following kinds of fish: rascasse, bay scallops, mussels, monkfish, conger eel, John Dory, gurnard, crayfish, lobster, Dublin Bay prawns, scampi.

Traditionally the fish are cooked and served unfilleted but they can be skinned and filleted if preferred. The cooking time would need to be reduced accordingly.

SERVES 10
2.7kg/6lb fresh fish, cleaned
150ml/¼ pint good quality olive oil
2 onions, chopped
2 cloves garlic, crushed
the white part of 2 leeks, chopped
1 small bulb fennel, sliced
1 small green chilli, deseeded and chopped
2 very large tomatoes, peeled and chopped
7 filaments of saffron, dissolved in 60ml/4 tablespoons hot water
cayenne pepper

salt
3 litres/5 pints fish stock (see page 219)
small bunch fresh parsley

To garnish:
10 slices French bread, toasted lightly in the oven, fried in olive oil and rubbed with garlic
bowl of rouille (see page 92)
bowl of aïoli (garlic mayonnaise – see page 385)

1. Put the oil into a large saucepan. Add the onions, leeks, garlic, fennel and chilli. Sweat for 5 minutes.
2. Add the tomatoes, saffron tea, cayenne pepper, salt, fish stock and parsley. Bring to the boil and boil well to enable the oil and water to thicken together. Reduce to a simmer.
3. Gradually add the fish. The conger eel will take about 20 minutes to cook; the crayfish about 15 minutes; unfilleted white fish will take about 10 minutes, and most shellfish will take 5 minutes.
4. Remove the fish to a hot serving dish, split the crayfish head in two, slice the tail. Leave the shellfish unshelled. Taste and season the soup.
5. Bring the soup to the boil and boil hard for a few moments to emulsify the liquid, then strain into a warmed soup tureen. Serve immediately with the fish, hot bread, rouille and aïoli.

ROSE DE PROVENCE, WHITE RHONE

Cock-a-Leekie Soup

SERVES 6
This is an unthickened chicken broth, and it should have plenty of chicken and leeks in it. At the end of the cooking process there should be about 1 litre/1¾ pints of soup.

6 prunes
1.5 kg/3lb chicken
10ml/2 teaspoons salt
freshly ground black pepper
1 bay leaf
few parsley stalks
6 leeks, cut into matchsticks
chopped parsley

1. Soak the prunes in cold water for 6 hours. Remove the stones.
2. Joint the chicken and place the pieces in a pan with enough water to cover them generously. Reserve the giblets. Add salt and pepper, bay leaf, giblets (except the liver) and parsley. Bring to the boil and skim. Cover and simmer for about 45 minutes.
3. Skim the fat from the soup, add the leeks and prunes and simmer for a further 45 minutes.
4. Remove the chicken, giblets, bay leaf and parsley stalks. Skin the chicken and cut the flesh into small neat dice. Add the diced chicken to the soup.
5. Check the seasoning and serve hot with a little chopped parsley sprinkled over at the last minute.

NOTE I: It is sometimes desirable to use the chicken breast for a dish on its own, and it seems a pity to put it in a soup. But of course it can be used. Chicken portions (thighs and drumsticks) can be bought more cheaply than whole chickens, but this means no giblets. Best of all, use a boiling fowl, but remember this will need a total of 3 hours simmering, with the water being topped up as necessary.
NOTE II: If there is no time to soak the prunes they may be cooked whole in the soup and the stones removed afterwards.

LIGHT RED

French Onion Soup

SERVES 4-6
55g/2oz butter
450g/1lb onions, sliced
½ garlic clove, crushed
5ml/1 teaspoon flour
2.5 litres/4 ½ pints good stock, preferably beef
salt and freshly ground black pepper
55g/2oz Gruyère cheese, grated
5ml/1 teaspoon dry English mustard
4 slices French bread

1. Melt the butter in a large heavy pan and slowly brown the onions and garlic: this should take at least 1 hour and the onions should

become meltingly soft and greatly reduced in quantity. They must also be evenly golden brown all over and transparent.
2. Stir in the flour and cook for 1 minute.
3. Add the stock and stir until boiling. Season with salt and pepper and simmer for 20-30 minutes.
4. Set the oven to 200°C/400°F/gas mark 6.
5. Mix the Gruyère with the mustard and pepper. Spread this on the bread slices and put them on the bottom of an earthenware tureen. Pour over the soup. The bread will rise to the top. Put the soup (uncovered) in the oven until well browned and bubbling.

BEAUJOLAIS

Beef Consommé

SERVES 6
1.75litres/3 pints very well-flavoured beef bouillon (page 218)
whites of 3 eggs plus shells
salt and pepper
75ml/5 tablespoons sherry or Madeira

1. Place the bouillon and sherry in a large clean metal saucepan. Place over a gentle heat. Season very well.
2. Put the crushed shells and the egg whites into the bouillon. Place over the heat and whisk steadily with a balloon whisk until the mixture boils. Stop whisking immediately and take the pan off the heat. Allow the mixture to subside. Take care not to break the crust formed by the egg white.
3. Bring the consommé just up to the boil again and then again allow to subside. Repeat this once more. (The egg white will trap the sediment in the stock and clear the soup.) Allow to cool for 2 minutes.
4. Fix a double layer of fine muslin over a clean basin and carefully strain the soup through it, taking care to hold the egg white crust back. When all the liquid is through (or almost all of it) allow the egg white to slip into the muslin. Then strain the soup again – this time through both egg-white crust and cloth. Do not try to hurry the process by squeezing the cloth as this will produce murky soup: it must be allowed to drip through at its own pace. The consommé is now ready for serving.

NOTE : To serve the consommé en gelée (jellied), pour the liquid into a shallow pan or tray to cool and refrigerate until set. Chop roughly with a knife and spoon into ice-cold soup cups. Serve with a wedge of lemon and toast.

DRY SHERRY

Garnishes for Consommé

AUX POINTES DES ASPERGES
Place cooked asparagus tips at the bottom of a hot tureen and pour the soup over.

A LA JULIENNE
Add mixed carrot, turnip, leek and celery cut into julienne strips to the consommé and cook until tender. Chopped chervil or parsley is sometimes added at the last minute.

LADY CURZON
Chill the consommé in ovenproof cups. Flavour 30ml/2 tablespoons double cream with curry powder, salt and pepper and pour over each consommé. Place under a hot grill to brown the top. Put into a warm oven to heat the soup.

AUX PROFITEROLES
Season choux pastry with Parmesan, mustard and cayenne, pipe in pea-size pieces and bake until crisp. Place in the bottom of a hot tureen, pour the soup over and serve immediately before the profiteroles can become soggy.

AUX QUENELLES
Poach small chicken quenelles in stock. Float these in the consommé and sprinkle with chopped chervil or parsley.

AUX VERMICELLI
Cook vermicelli in stock until tender. Rinse well, place in a hot tureen and pour the soup over. (Other small-size pastas are also used.)

Consommé Royale

SERVES 6

consommé (page 95)
1 egg white
60ml/4 tablespoons cream
salt and pepper

1. Mix the egg white with a fork and beat in the cream and seasoning.
2. Place in an ovenproof dish and stand in a pan of gently simmering water until set.
3. Cool, cut into neat strips and add to the consommé just before serving.

Spicy Tomato Soup

SERVES 4

15g/1/2oz butter
1/2 onion, finely chopped
15g/1/2oz flour
200g/7oz can tomatoes
425ml/3/4 pint chicken stock
1 bay leaf
pinch of nutmeg
salt and freshly ground black pepper
2.5ml/1/2 teaspoon paprika
1 clove
2.5ml/1/2 teaspoon sugar
squeeze of lemon
15-30ml/1-2 tablespoons port
110g/4oz fresh tomatoes, skinned, deseeded and slivered

1. Melt the butter. Add the onion and cook gently until pale yellow and transparent.
2. Stir in the flour, cook for 1 minute, then add the canned tomatoes and stock. Stir until the mixture boils.
3. Add the bay leaf, nutmeg, a pinch each of salt, and pepper, the paprika, clove, sugar and squeeze of lemon.
4. Simmer, stirring occasionally, for 30 minutes.
5. Push the soup through a sieve and return it to the saucepan.
6. Add the port, and the fresh tomatoes. Reheat and adjust the seasoning.

AUSTRALIAN CHARDONNAY

Leith's Restaurant's Tomato and Basil Soup

SERVES 6

2.3kg/5lb tomatoes
24 large basil leaves
170g/6oz salted butter
salt and freshly ground black pepper
85g/3oz fromage blanc

1. Make a small slit in the skin of each tomato and blanch in boiling water for 5-7 seconds. They are ready to peel when the skin starts to lift away from the knife slits. Skin, then halve the tomatoes scooping the seeds and juice into a sieve set over a bowl. Sieve the juice and reserve, then cut the tomato flesh into small strips.
2. Roughly chop all but 6 of the basil leaves. Put the tomato strips, reserved juice and chopped basil into a large deep frying pan. Add 55g/2oz of the butter and place over a medium heat, shaking the pan and stirring.
3. When the tomato strips start to break up, turn up the heat and briskly stir in the rest of the butter. When all the butter has been added, the tomatoes should be only half cooked. Season with salt and pepper.
4. Fill individual soup bowls with the tomato soup, then spoon fromage blanc into the middle of each bowl. Garnish each soup bowl with a fresh basil leaf and serve at once.

SOAVE

Watercress and Potato Soup

SERVES 4

30g/1oz butter
1 medium onion, chopped
225g/8oz potatoes, diced
570ml/1 pint chicken stock
2 bunches of watercress, trimmed and chopped
290ml/1/2 pint creamy milk
salt and freshly ground black pepper
pinch of nutmeg
fresh chives

1. Melt the butter, add the onion and cook slowly until soft but not coloured. Add the potatoes and chicken stock and simmer for 10 minutes or until the potatoes are tender.
2. Add the watercress to the stock and simmer for 30 seconds.
3. Liquidize the soup and push it through a sieve. Pour into the rinsed-out pan.
4. Add enough of the milk to get the required consistency and season to taste with salt, pepper and nutmeg. Reheat until the soup is just below boiling point.
5. Serve in a warmed soup tureen. Garnish with chopped chives.

WHITE LOIRE

Carrot and Coriander Soup with Puff Pastry Tops

SERVES 4
675g/1½lb carrots, peeled and sliced
1 onion, finely chopped
15g/½oz butter
1 bay leaf
1 litre/2 pints chicken stock or water
salt and freshly ground black pepper
15ml/1 tablespoon chopped fresh parsley
15ml/1 tablespoon chopped fresh coriander
60ml/4 tablespoons double cream
puff pastry made with 225g/8oz flour (see page 528)
beaten egg

1. Put the carrots and onion into a saucepan with the butter. Sweat for 10 minutes or until beginning to soften. Add the bay leaf, stock, salt and pepper. Bring up to the boil and simmer as slowly as possible for 25 minutes.
2. Add the parsley and coriander and simmer for a further 2-3 minutes. Remove the bay leaf.
3. Liquidize the soup and push through a sieve into a clean saucepan. Check the consistency. If a little thin, reduce it by rapid boiling, if a little thick, add extra water.
4. Add the cream and season to taste. Leave to get absolutely cold.
5. Set the oven to 220°C/425°F/gas mark 7.
6. Put 200ml/7 fl oz of the cold soup into 4 large ovenproof soup bowls.
7. Roll out the pastry very thinly and cut out 4 circles a little larger than the rim of the bowl (allowing about 1cm/½ inch extra). Brush a little of the beaten egg around the edge of each circle and use this to attach the pastry to the bowl, pressing firmly to make a good seal. Trim off any uneven edges. Brush the pastry with remaining egg glaze. Chill well.
8. Place the soup bowls on a baking sheet and bake near the top of the oven for 20 minutes until well risen and golden brown.

AUSTRALIAN/NEW ZEALAND SAUVIGNON BLANC

Minestrone

SERVES 6
85g/3oz dried haricot beans
15ml/1 tablespoon oil
3 rashers rindless streaky bacon, diced
2 garlic cloves, crushed
1 large onion, sliced
2 carrots, diced
stick of celery, chopped
2 medium potatoes, peeled and diced
1.4 litres/2 pints beef or chicken stock (see page 219)
bouquet garni (3 leaves fresh basil, 2 parsley stalks, bay leaf, tied together with string)
15ml/1 tablespoon tomato purée
110g/4oz white cabbage
3 large tomatoes, skinned and chopped
55g/2oz broken spaghetti or other small pasta
salt and freshly ground black pepper
freshly grated Parmesan cheese

1. Soak the beans in cold water for 3-4 hours.
2. Heat the oil in a heavy pan, add the bacon and garlic, onion, carrot and celery and cook for 2 minutes, stirring. Add the potato and cook until the oil has been absorbed and the vegetables are soft.
3. Add the stock, bring to the boil, add the bouquet garni, tomato purée and drained beans. Simmer for 45 minutes.
4. Add the cabbage, tomato and spaghetti and continue to simmer for a further 15 minutes, or until the beans are soft and the spaghetti is tender.

5. Just before serving remove the herbs, taste and season as necessary with salt and pepper. Serve sprinkled with grated Parmesan cheese.

LIGHT CHIANTI OR VALPOLICELLA

New England Clam Chowder

SERVES 6

3 rashers rindless streaky bacon, chopped
55g/2oz butter
1 large or 2 medium onions, chopped
stick of celery, chopped
1 leek, chopped
48 clams (soft-or hard-shelled)
425ml/¾ pint water
3 medium potatoes, peeled and finely diced
425ml/¾ pint creamy milk
pinch of thyme
small piece of bay leaf
salt and freshly ground black pepper
30g/1oz flour
60ml/4 tablespoons cream

1. Put the bacon into a heavy saucepan and fry in its own fat until crisp and slightly brown.
2. Add half the butter and the onion, celery and leek. Cook slowly until the vegetables are softened and just beginning to brown.
3. While the vegetables are cooking, scrub the clams well, using a brush to remove any sand. Put the clean clams into a second saucepan and pour on the water. Cook slowly until the shells have opened wide (about 10 minutes).
4. Lift out the clams and reserve their liquid. Remove the clams from their shells and chop the flesh. Strain the cooking liquid through a fine cloth to remove any sand.
5. Add the potato, milk, thyme and bay leaf to the onion mixture and season with salt and pepper. If the potatoes are not covered by the liquid top up with a little water. Cover the pan and simmer gently until the potatoes are almost tender (about 12 minutes).
6. Meanwhile, melt the rest of the butter and stir in the flour. Cook gently for 30 seconds, then draw the pan off the heat and stir in the strained liquid reserved from poaching the clams. Stir steadily until the mixture boils. Simmer for 2 minutes. Add the clams.
7. Stir the thickened clam liquid into the chowder. Taste, adding more seasoning if necessary. Stir in the cream and serve at once.

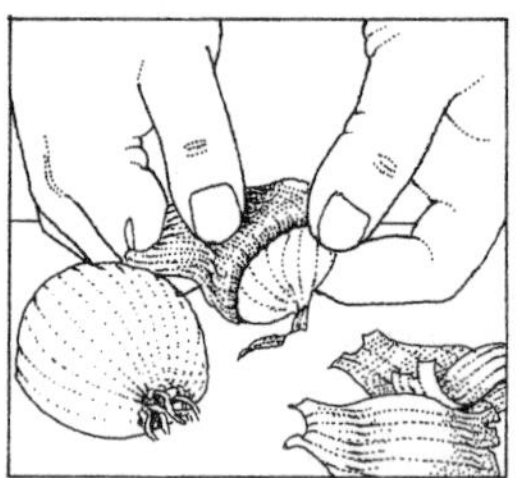
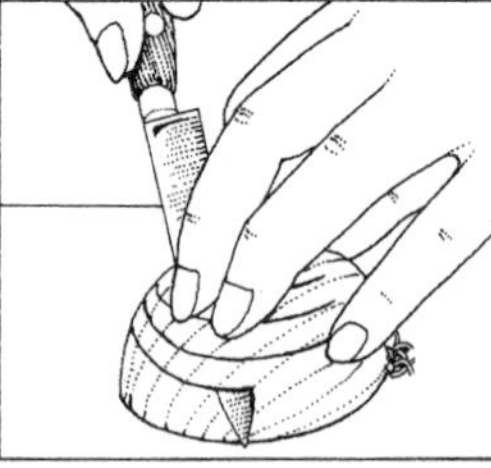

Peel from the pointed end and cut horizontal slices

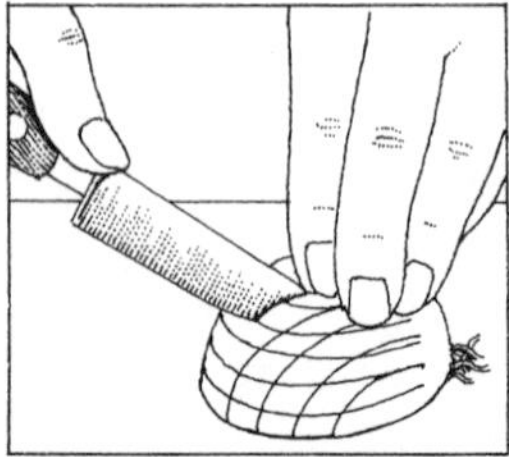
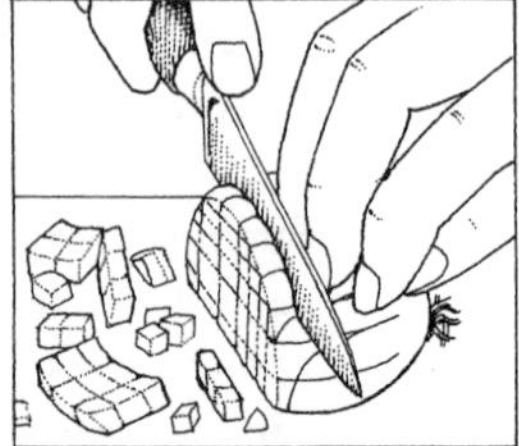

Cut vertical slices, leaving the root intact

NOTE: Canned clams can be used as a substitute for fresh clams. They should be added once the soup has cooked, and simmered for 3-4 minutes before serving. If using canned clams, substitute good fish stock for water.

CALIFORNIAN SAUVIGNON

Soupe au Pistou

This is a Mediterranean peasant soup which calls for fresh basil and very fresh garlic.

SERVES 6

450g/1lb dried haricot beans, soaked overnight
30ml/2 tablespoons oil (preferably olive)
225g/8oz potatoes, peeled and diced
2 leeks, finely sliced
2 carrots, finely sliced
110g/4oz green beans, sliced or chopped
1.7 litres/3 pints chicken stock
5ml/1 teaspoon salt
2.5ml/½ teaspoon coarsely ground black pepper
30ml/2 tablespoons vermicelli or other small pasta
ripe tomatoes, peeled and chopped

For the pistou:
4 garlic cloves, crushed
60ml/4 tablespoons fresh chopped basil
45ml/3 tablespoons olive oil

To serve:
grated Gruyère cheese

1. Cook the beans in boiling water for about 1 hour, until half tender.
2. Heat the oil and add the potatoes, leeks and carrots. Cover and cook gently until the vegetables are soft.
3. Add the half-cooked dried beans, the green beans, chicken stock and pepper. Simmer until the haricot beans are soft (about 1 1/2 hours). Add the pasta and tomatoes and cook for a further 10 minutes, or until the pasta is tender. Allow to cool a little before adding the pistou.
4. Make the pistou: put the garlic and the basil in a mortar or liquidizer and pound to a paste. Add the oil, drop by drop (as when making mayonnaise), mixing all the time, to form an emulsion. Just before serving, stir the pistou into the soup. Hand the cheese separately.

NOTE: Recipes for this soup vary along the Mediterranean according to local tradition and the season. Courgettes, cabbage and onions sometimes make their appearance. The Italian version of pesto (page 228). from which pistou is derived, is sometimes added to the soup, which is itself a version of the Italian minestrone.

RED OR ROSE DE PROVENCE

Egg First Courses

Egg Mayonnaise

SERVES 4

290ml/½ pint mayonnaise (see page 224
water
6 hardboiled eggs (see below)

For the garnish:
strips of cucumber skin or chopped parsley
paprika pepper

1. Thin the mayonnaise slightly by adding a little water – to reluctant dropping consistency.
2. Cut the eggs in half lengthwise and arrange, cut side down, on a plate. Carefully coat each egg with mayonnaise.
3. Decorate every other egg with a small diamond shape cut from cucumber skin or a neat sprinkling of chopped parsley. Decorate the remaining eggs with paprika pepper.

NOTE: Thin strips of anchovy fillet in a criss-cross pattern, stoned black olives, rings of radish or watercress leaves all make suitable garnishes for egg mayonnaise.

GERMAN RIESLING

Hardboiled Eggs

There are two tried and tested methods for boiling an egg:
1. If you are cooking a lot of eggs put them into a saucepan, pour over boiling water and simmer for 12 minutes.
2. If you are just boiling one or two eggs put them into a saucepan of cold water, bring the water up to the boil and then simmer for 10 minutes.

Once the eggs are cooked, drain and put to cool in a bowl of cold water.

NOTE I: If you have an egg prick, prick the rounded end of the raw egg to allow the air under the shell to escape. This will prevent cracking when boiling.
NOTE II: Fresh eggs take longer to cook than stale eggs. Add 30 seconds if the eggs are new and 30 seconds if they are straight from the refrigerator.

Portuguese Eggs

SERVES 4

4 hardboiled eggs (see above)
45g/½oz butter
15ml/1 tablespoon chopped fresh parsley
salt and pepper
4 ripe tomatoes, skinned and sliced
1 garlic clove, crushed
290ml/½ pint coating consistency béchamel sauce (see page 221)
45g/1½ oz strong Cheddar or Gruyère, grated
15ml/1 tablespoon dried crumbs

1. Set the oven to 200°C/400°F/gas mark 6. Light the grill.
2. Cut the eggs in half lengthwise and sieve the yolks.
3. Cream half the butter well and beat in the yolks, parsley and seasoning. Taste.
4. Pile this mixture back into the egg whites and press together until they resemble hardboiled eggs.
5. Fry the tomato slices briefly in a frying pan with the garlic and remaining butter. When barely cooked lay them in a heatproof dish.
6. Place the eggs on top of the tomatoes and coat with the béchamel sauce. Sprinkle with cheese and crumbs.
7. Bake in the oven for 10 minutes and then place under the grill to brown.

RHONE OR PROVENCE RED

Scrambled Eggs on Anchovy Toast

SERVES 1

2 eggs
15ml/1 tablespoon cream or creamy milk
salt and freshly ground black pepper
1 slice of crustless buttered toast, spread with anchovy paste
15ml/1 tablespoon butter

1. In a bowl mix together the eggs, cream or milk, salt and pepper.
2. Get the toast ready. Put on a heated plate and keep warm.

3. Melt the butter in a saucepan. Tip in the egg mixture and using a wooden spoon keep it constantly moving until thickened and creamy.
4. Pile on to the prepared toast and serve immediately.

DRY GERMAN WHITE

Smoked Salmon and Scrambled Eggs

Most recipes for smoked salmon and scrambled eggs suggest chopping up the smoked salmon and adding it to the eggs just before they are ready to serve. We serve the salmon cold as we feel warm smoked salmon can taste a little like smoked ham.

SERVES 4
170g/6oz Scotch smoked salmon
salt and freshly ground black pepper
8 eggs
60ml/4 tablespoons cream
30g/1oz butter

1. Divide the smoked salmon into 4 and arrange on one half of 4 side plates. Grind over a little black pepper.
2. Mix together the eggs, cream, salt and pepper. Beat well.
3. Melt the butter in a small saucepan. Tip in the egg mixture and using a wooden spoon stir constantly until thickened and creamy, but still fairly wet.
4. Pile on to the plates and serve immediately.

ALSACE WHITE

Plain French Omelette

SERVES 1
3 eggs
salt and freshly ground black pepper
pinch of grated Parmesan cheese (optional)
15ml/1 tablespoon cold water
15g/½oz butter

1. Break the eggs into a bowl and with a fork mix in the seasoning, Parmesan and water.
2. Melt the butter in a heavy 15cm/6 inch frying pan and swirl it around so that the bottom and sides are coated. When foaming, pour in the egg mixture.
3. Hold the frying-pan handle in your left hand and move it gently back and forth over the heat. At the same time, with a wooden spoon, move the mixture slowly, scraping up large creamy flakes of egg mixture. As you do this some of the liquid egg from the middle of the omelette will run to the sides of the pan. Tilt the pan to help this process. Leave over the heat until the bottom has set and the top is creamy. Remove from the heat.
4. With a fork or palette knife fold the nearside edge of the omelette over to the centre and then flick the whole omelette over on to a warmed plate with the folded edges on the underside. Alternatively, fold the omelette in two and slide it on to the plate.

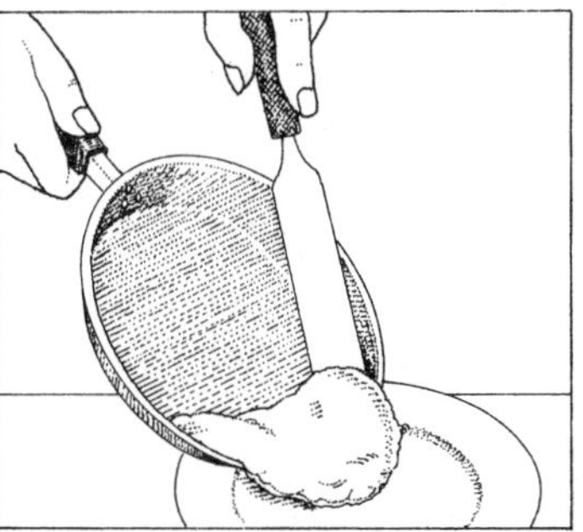

Fold the omelette in two and slide it on to the plate

NOTE: Grated cheese, fresh chopped herbs, fried mushrooms or other flavourings can be added to the basic omelette mixture.

LIGHT RED

Omelette Arnold Bennett

SERVES 4
1 slice onion
1-2 slices carrot
1 bay leaf
4 peppercorns
150ml/$^1/_4$ pint milk
110g/4oz smoked haddock
45g/1$^1/_2$ oz butter
15g/$^1/_2$ oz flour
3 eggs, separated
45ml/3 tablespoons single cream
pepper
15ml/1 tablespoon grated Parmesan cheese

1. Put the onion, carrot, bay leaf, peppercorns and milk in a saucepan and heat slowly.
2. When the milk is well flavoured, add the haddock and poach gently for 10 minutes or until the fish is just cooked.
3. Take out the fish, skin, bone and flake it. Reserve the cooking liquor.
4. Melt 15g/$^1/_2$oz of the butter in a small pan, add the flour and stir over heat for 1 minute.
5. Add 150ml/$^1/_4$ pint of the strained cooking milk. Stir until boiling.
6. Beat the egg yolks with 30ml/2 tablespoons of the cream. Season with pepper only (do not add salt as the haddock is salty). Stir into the sauce. Add the haddock carefully.
7. Whisk the egg whites and fold into the haddock. Add half the cheese.
8. Turn on the grill to a high heat.
9. Melt the remaining butter in an omelette pan over a good heat, tipping the pan so that the bottom and sides are coated. When the foaming begins to subside quickly pour in the egg mixture.
10. When the omelette is fairly firm, sprinkle on the remaining cheese, pour over the remaining tablespoon of cream and brown quickly under the pre-heated grill.
11. Slide on to a hot dish.

ALSACE WHITE

Herb Omelette Salad

SERVES 2-4
For the omelette:
5 eggs
45ml/3 tablespoons olive oil
1 tablespoon chopped parsley
salt and freshly ground black pepper

For the salad:
2 red peppers, quartered and deseeded
2 large tomatoes, peeled and cut into strips
1 cucumber, peeled, deseeded and cut into strips
1 head of lettuce
1 bunch chives, roughly chopped
12 basil leaves, chopped

For the dressing:
1 garlic clove , crushed
2 anchovy fillets, mashed
5ml/1 teaspoon Dijon mustard
30ml/2 tablespoons wine vinegar
120ml/8 tablespoons olive oil
freshly ground black pepper
10 small black olives, stoned

1. To make the omelette: in a bowl mix together the eggs, 30ml/2 tablespoons of the olive oil, the parsley, salt and pepper.
2. Use the remaining oil to fry the omelette. Lightly grease the base of an omelette pan. When hot, add enough of the omelette mixture to cover the base of the pan. The omelette mixture should be the thickness of a pancake. Cook the omelette for about 1 minute. Slide on to a plate to cool. Continue to cook the remaining omelette mixture.
3. When cool, cut the omelettes into thin strips.
4. Meanwhile, prepare the salad. Place the peppers under a hot grill. When charred, hold under cold running water and scrape off the skin, then cut it into 1cm/$^1/_2$inch strips.
5. To prepare the dressing, mix together all the ingredients, and whizz in a liquidizer. Season.
6. Mix together all the salad ingredients, the omelette strips and the herbs. Add the dressing and toss well.
7. Pile on to a serving dish, and scatter over the black olives.

LIGHT TO MEDIUM RED

Tortilla

SERVES 4
450g/1lb floury potatoes, peeled and finely sliced
1 small onion, finely sliced
salt and freshly ground black pepper
4 eggs, beaten
oil for frying

1. Heat about 1cm/½inch of oil in a frying pan, add the potatoes and onions, season with salt and pepper and fry slowly until soft, but not coloured. This may take up to 20 minutes.
2. Tip all the oil, but for a thin film, out of the pan and pour into the egg mixture. Beat, then pour the egg mixture into the pan.
3. Cook the omelette over a moderate heat until it is set and then slip on to a plate. Turn it over and put it back into the frying pan with the uncooked side down.
4. Cook for a further minute and then turn out on to a serving plate. Serve warm or cold, cut into wedges.

NOTE: Frying the potatoes from raw is the usual Spanish method. But if the potatoes are small and waxy it is better to boil them first, then slice and fry. Boiled potatoes give a light, soft omelette.

RED RIOJA

Frittata (Italian Omelette)

SERVES 2
225g/8oz red onions, sliced very finely
45ml/3 tablespoons oil
3 eggs
30g/1oz fresh Parmesan cheese, grated
salt and freshly ground black pepper
20g/¾oz butter

1. Cook the onions slowly in the oil until reduced in quantity, soft, and a rich golden brown colour. Tip the onions into a sieve over a bowl.
2. Beat the eggs until lightly mixed. Mix all but 3 tablespoons of the eggs with the onions, cheese, salt and pepper. Mix well.
3. Melt the butter in an 18cm/6 inch frying pan over a medium heat. When foaming, add the egg and onion mixture. Reduce the heat to very low.
4. Cook very slowly for 15 minutes. The eggs should be set and the surface runny. Pour over the reserved egg. Place under a hot grill until set but not brown. Loosen with a spatula and slide on to a round dish. Serve cut into wedges.

LIGHT CHIANTI

Baked Eggs

SERVES 4
4 medium-sized eggs at room temperature
salt and freshly ground black pepper
20ml/4 teaspoons single cream
15g/½oz butter

1. Set the oven to 180°C/350°F/gas mark 4.
2. Brush 4 cocotte dishes with butter and stand them in a roasting tin or ovenproof dish of hot water (a bain-marie).
3. Break an egg carefully into each dish and season with salt and pepper. Spoon over a little cream and place a knob of butter on top.
4. Place in the centre of the oven, uncovered, for about 12 minutes. The whites should be set and the yolks runny.

NOTE I: The eggs will continue cooking for a short time after removing from the oven, so be very careful not to overcook
NOTE II: Tarragon eggs can be made by adding 2 leaves tarragon to each egg before spooning over the cream.

LIGHT RED

Baked Eggs with Mushrooms

SERVES 4

45g/1 1/2oz butter
1 shallot, finely chopped
110g/4oz mushrooms, finely chopped
10ml/2 teaspoons chopped fresh parsley
salt and freshly ground white pepper
4 eggs
60ml/4 tablespoons cream or creamy milk

1. Set the oven to 180°C/350°F/gas mark 4. Lightly butter 4 ramekin or cocotte dishes.
2. Melt half the remaining butter, add the shallot and cook until very soft but not coloured.
3. Add the rest of the butter with the mushrooms. Cook slowly over a gentle heat until the mushrooms are soft. Add the parsley and season to taste with salt and pepper.
4. Divide this mixture between the 4 cocotte dishes, make a dip in each cocotte and break an egg into each. Spoon 15ml/1 tablespoon cream on to each egg and season with salt and pepper.
5. Stand the dishes in a bain-marie and bake in the oven for 10-12 minutes, until the whites are just set and the yolks still runny.

LIGHT RED

Oeufs Florentine

Eggs for poaching must be very fresh; if not, a little vinegar can be added to the water to help the white coagulate but this will have an adverse effect on the taste.

SERVES 4

450g/1lb leaf spinach, cooked and chopped
salt and freshly ground black pepper
15g/1/2oz melted butter
good pinch of nutmeg
4 eggs, chilled
290ml/1/2pint mornay sauce (see page 221)
little extra grated cheese
browned crumbs

1. Turn the spinach in the melted butter. Season with salt, pepper and nutmeg. Place in the bottom of an ovenproof dish.
2. Set the oven to 150°C/300°F/gas mark 2 and heat the grill.
3. Poach the eggs: three-quarters fill a large shallow pan with water. Bring to the boil, then lower the temperature to a simmer. Break an egg into a cup and slip it into the water. Immediately raise the temperature slightly so that the bubbles help to draw the white round the yolk. Poach for about 3 minutes, and lift out with a perforated spoon.
4. Trim the whites neatly with a pair of scissors or a stainless steel knife and drain thoroughly by shaking the perforated spoon.
5. Arrange the eggs on top of the spinach and coat with the cheese sauce. Sprinkle over the cheese and crumbs.
6. Brown the top under a hot grill.

LIGHT RED

Scotch Eggs

SERVES 4

340g/12oz good quality sausagemeat
salt and pepper
4 hardboiled eggs, shelled (see page 102)
flour
oil for frying
beaten egg
30ml/2 tablespoons dried white breadcrumbs

1. Season the sausagemeat with salt and pepper. Divide it into 4.
2. Roll the eggs in flour. Dip your hands in a little water and mould the sausagemeat around each egg making sure they are completely and evenly covered.
3. Place at least 3.5cm/1 1/2inches of oil in a fryer and begin to heat it up slowly.
4. Dip the eggs in seasoned flour, brush with beaten egg and coat with breadcrumbs.
5. Place the prepared eggs in the wire basket and when the oil is hot enough to fizzle gently when a breadcrumb is added to it put in the eggs and fry for about 10 minutes. Drain well.

MEDIUM RED

Danish Egg Salad

SERVES 2
4 large ripe tomatoes
15ml/1 tablespoon chopped fresh parsley
French dressing (see page 228)
1 French omelette, cooled (see page 103)
12 small black olives, stoned
watercress, trimmed

1. Scald the tomatoes in boiling water for 10 seconds and peel them. Cut the flesh into slices. Arrange them neatly on a plate.
2. Mix the parsley with the dressing.
3. Cut the omelette into neat strips and lay on top of the tomatoes. Scatter over the black olives. Spoon over the French dressing and garnish with watercress.

DRY GERMAN WHITE

Quail Eggs en Croustade

SERVES 4
8 quail eggs
4 thin slices bread
unsalted butter
1 shallot, finely chopped
1 rasher rindless streaky bacon, finely chopped
85g/3oz flat mushrooms, finely chopped
chopped parsley
salt and freshly ground black pepper
beurre blanc (see page 227)

1. Cut the bread in circles with a large fluted pastry cutter and press very firmly into large patty tins. Brush with melted unsalted butter. Bake at 170°C/325°F/gas mark 3 for 15 minutes. Remove from the tins, turn upside down and bake for a further 10 minutes or until crisp and lightly browned.
2. Meanwhile prepare the duxelles: cook the shallot and bacon in butter. Add the mushrooms and cook for a further 2 minutes. Boil away the liquid. Add the parsley and season to taste with salt and pepper. The mixture should be very dry.
3. Poach the quail eggs in water (break 2 eggs at a time on to a saucer and then tip carefully into the saucepan, and poach for approximately 2 minutes).
4. Divide the duxelles mixture between the croustades. Place 2 eggs on top of each and coat with the beurre blanc.

LIGHT RED

Vegetable and salad first courses

Stuffed Cream Cheese Tomatoes

SERVES 2
4 tomatoes, peeled
110g/4oz good cream cheese or sieved cheese
15ml/1 tablespoon chopped fresh mint
squeeze of lemon
1/4 garlic clove, crushed
salt and freshly ground black pepper
15ml/1 tablespoon chopped fresh parsley
French dressing (see page 228)
sprigs of watercress

1. Slice a quarter of each tomato off at the rounded end. Scoop out the flesh and seeds. Discard the seeds and coarsely chop the flesh. Leave the tomatoes to drain while making the filling.
2. Mix a little of the flesh with the cream cheese, mint, lemon, garlic and the salt and pepper.
3. Fill the hollow tomatoes with this mixture and stick the tops back at a jaunty angle. Arrange on a plate.
4. Add the parsley to the dressing and shake or mix well. Spoon this over the tomatoes, and garnish with the watercress.
5. Serve with brown bread and butter.

LIGHT RED

Stuffed Courgettes

SERVES 4
170g/6oz frozen prawns
lemon juice
salt and pepper
4 medium courgettes
2 tomatoes, skinned and chopped
30g/1oz butter
1 small onion, very finely chopped
5ml/1 teaspoon finely chopped fresh parsley
290ml/1/2 pint cheese (mornay) sauce (page 221)
little grated cheese
handful of browned crumbs

1. Defrost the prawns, preferably overnight, and season with lemon juice and pepper.
2. Wash the courgettes and cut off the ends. Place them whole in a pan of boiling salted water and simmer until barely tender. Cool in a colander under cold running water.
3. Split the courgettes lengthways and, using a melon baller or spoon, remove a 'channel' of flesh down the middle of each half courgette. Reserve the scooped-out flesh.
4. Drain the shells very well, otherwise the whole dish will become watery.
5. Heat the oven to 200°C/400°F/gas mark 6.
6. Roughly chop the reserved courgette flesh.
7. Melt the butter in a frying pan and add the onion. Fry gently until very soft. Add the tomatoes and courgette flesh and continue to cook without colouring until the ingredients are soft, then allow to cool completely.
8. Stir in the parsley and prawns and season to taste.
9. Place a spoonful of this mixture in each courgette shell and lay in a buttered ovenproof dish. Coat each courgette with a spoonful of cheese sauce and sprinkle over a little grated cheese and browned crumbs.
10. Heat up the grill.
11. Put the dish in the preheated oven for 15 minutes and then under the grill until delicately browned.

RHONE OR PROVENCE RED

Stuffed Mushrooms

SERVES 4
55g/2oz butter
2 rashers of streaky rindless bacon, finely diced
1 shallot, chopped
85g/3oz chicken livers, trimmed and diced
8 large flat mushrooms, stalks removed and chopped
1 garlic clove, crushed
1 tomato, skinned and finely chopped
2.5ml/1/2 teaspoon chopped fresh parsley
salt and pepper
dried white breadcrumbs
oil for shallow frying
8 slices French bread
chopped fresh parsley to garnish

1. Heat up the grill.
2. In a saucepan, melt half the butter and when foaming add the bacon and shallot. Fry gently

until the shallot is soft.
3. Add the livers, increase the temperature, and fry rapidly until the livers start to brown.
4. Add the mushroom stalks and garlic. Cook for 1-2 minutes.
5. Add the tomato and parsley. Season.
6. Place the mushroom tops, smooth side down, on the grill pan, brush with the rest of the butter, and grill for 1 minute, turn over and grill for a further minute.
7. Fill the mushrooms with the stuffing and sprinkle over the breadcrumbs.
8. Heat the oil in a frying pan and fry the bread slices until a golden brown on each side. Drain well.
9. As the bread fries place the mushrooms back under the grill for a minute to reheat them.
10. Place the mushrooms on the rounds of fried bread and sprinkle with chopped parsley.

RED BORDEAUX

Stuffed Vine Leaves (Dolmades)

SERVES 8
about 30 small young vine leaves
1 onion, finely chopped
30ml/2 tablespoons olive oil
225g/8oz cooked rice
pinch of allspice
2.5ml/½ teaspoon chopped fresh mint
salt and freshly ground black pepper
chicken stock (see page 219)
15ml/1 tablespoon lemon juice
plain yoghurt or tomato sauce (see page 231)

1. Plunge the vine leaves into a pan of boiling salted water for 10 seconds. Rinse under cold water and drain well. Lay the leaves, smooth side up, side by side on a tabletop or board.
2. Fry the onion in the oil until soft but not coloured. Mix together the onion (with its oil), the rice, allspice and mint. Season with salt and pepper.
3. Lay a teaspoon of rice on each leaf and roll up the leaf, tucking in the ends to make a small parcel. Squeeze the rolls in the palm of your hand – this will ensure that the dolmades hold their shape and will not need tying up. Pack all the dolmades into a wide saucepan and add enough stock to half-cover them. Sprinkle over the lemon juice. Cover tightly, preferably with a small plate that fits inside the pan (which will prevent the dolmades moving during cooking) and a lid. Simmer for 1 hour.
4. Lift out the dolmades with a perforated spoon and arrange on a serving dish. Chill. Coat with yoghurt or tomato sauce.

NOTE: Dolmades may be served hot, with the yoghurt or sauce handed separately.

CHIANTI

Avocado Pears Stuffed with Crab

SERVES 4
2 ripe avocado pears
French dressing (see page 228)
170g/6oz white crab meat
1 dessert apple, peeled and chopped
stick of celery, finely chopped
45ml/3 tablespoons mayonnaise (page 224)
15ml/1 tablespoon cream
5ml/1 teaspoon finely grated lemon rind
salt and pepper

1. Split the avocados, remove the stones and immediately brush the cut surface with French dressing to prevent discolouring.
2. Sort through the crab meat to remove any pieces of inedible cartilage.
3. Mix crab, apple and celery with the mayonnaise lightened by the addition of the cream and grated rind of lemon. Season with salt and pepper to taste and pile into the avocado halves.

WHITE LOIRE

Avocado Pear with Strawberry Vinaigrette

SERVES 4

2 avocado pears
90ml/6 tablespoons oil
30ml/2 tablespoons lemon juice
4 strawberries
salt and pepper
pinch of sugar

1. Make the dressing. Liquidize together the oil, lemon juice, strawberries, salt, pepper and sugar. It should become fairly thick. Taste and add more sugar or salt as required.
2. Cut the avocado pears in half. Remove the stones and skin. Lay rounded side up and slice fairly finely or cut into fans.
3. Spoon the dressing on to 4 side plates, making sure that the base of each plate is completely covered. Arrange overlapping slices of avocado pear on top of the strawberry dressing.

Tzatziki

Recipes for this are legion: some have mint; some do not call for garlic.

SERVES 6

1 medium cucumber
570ml/1 pint low-fat plain yoghurt
1 garlic clove, crushed
freshly ground black pepper

1. Cut the cucumber into very fine dice. Place in a sieve, sprinkle liberally with salt and leave to 'degorge' for 30 minutes. Rinse very well, drain and pat dry.
2. Mix the cucumber with the yoghurt, garlic and plenty of black pepper.

NOTE: The yoghurt can be thickened by draining it in a muslin-lined sieve; this will make for a creamier finish.

WHITE ALSACE

Aubergine Loaf

340g/12oz aubergines, peeled and diced
2 garlic cloves, crushed and fried in 15ml/½ tablespoon of olive oil
2 eggs
225ml/8 fl oz Greek yoghurt
pinch of ground cumin
30g/1oz creamed coconut
salt and pepper

1. Set the oven to 150°C/300°F/gas mark 2. Oil a 450g/1lb loaf tin and line with greaseproof paper.
2. Steam the aubergines for about 10 minutes or until softened.
3. Mix together the garlic, eggs, yoghurt, cumin, coconut, salt and pepper. Add the aubergines.
4. Pour into the prepared loaf tin and cover with foil. Place in a bain-marie in the preheated oven for 40 minutes or until firm.
5. Allow to cool and serve cut in slices with a tomato sauce or salad.

MEDIUM RED

Tomato Chartreuse (Jellied Tomato Ring)

SERVES 4

560g/1¼lb canned tomatoes
10ml/2 teaspoons tomato purée
salt and freshly ground white pepper
pinch of sugar
1 garlic clove
1 bay leaf
2 parsley stalks
about 6 leaves fresh basil
6 peppercorns
tomato juice
30ml/2 tablespoons water
15g/½oz gelatine
squeeze of lemon juice

For the garnish:
French dressing (see page 228)
about 30 fresh mint leaves

To serve:
brown bread and butter

1. Put the tomatoes, purée, salt, pepper and sugar into a thick saucepan. Add the garlic, bay leaf, parsley stalks, herbs and peppercorns. Simmer gently for 15 minutes.
2. Strain the mixture into a measuring jug. Make up to 425ml/3/4 pint with tomato juice. Taste and season well. Allow to cool.
3. Put the water into a small heavy saucepan and sprinkle over the gelatine. Leave to sponge.
4. Wet a ring mould, jelly mould or savarin tin.
5. When the gelatine is soft and spongy, dissolve it over a gentle heat until clear and warm. Stir into the tomato mixture, add a squeeze of lemon juice, and pour into the wetted mould. Leave in the refrigerator to set for at least 2 hours.
6. Liquidize the French dressing with all but 10 of the mint leaves.
7. Turn out the jelly on to a round plate: dip the bottom of the mould briefly into hot water, put the plate over the jelly, and turn plate and jelly over together so that the jelly falls out on to the plate.
8. Pour the green French dressing into the centre of the jelly and decorate the jelly with attractively arranged mint leaves. Serve with bread and butter.

CALIFORNIAN SAUVIGNON

Tomato, Avocado and Mozzarella Salad

55g/2oz tomatoes per person, skinned and sliced
55g/2oz mozzarella cheese per person, sliced
1/4 avocado pear per person, sliced
fresh basil, finely chopped
French dressing (see page 228)
black olives
salt and freshly ground black pepper

1. Lay the tomato, avocado pear and cheese in overlapping slices.
2. Add the basil to the dressing. Pour over the salad and sprinkle with a few olives. Season well with salt and plenty of freshly ground black pepper.

SOAVE/FRASCATI

Mushroom and Prawn Salad

SERVES 4
170g/6oz prawns
lemon juice
freshly ground black pepper
170g/6oz button mushrooms, sliced

For the French dressing:
45ml/3 tablespoons olive oil
15ml/1 tablespoon lemon juice
1/2 garlic clove, crushed
salt and freshly ground black pepper
10ml/2 teaspoons chopped fresh mint

For the garnish:
5ml/1 teaspoon chopped fresh parsley

1. Sprinkle the frozen prawns liberally with lemon juice and black pepper and leave to defrost.
2. Mix together the ingredients for the French dressing and add the mushrooms. Leave to marinate for 6 hours.
3. Add the prawns, mix well and put into a clean serving dish. Garnish with the parsley.

CHABLIS

Three-pea Salad

SERVES 8
110g/4oz brown lentils
110g/4oz chickpeas, soaked for 3 hours
110g/4oz split green peas
150ml/1/4 pint French dressing (see page 228)
5ml/1 teaspoon chopped fresh mint
15ml/1 tablespoon chopped fresh parsley
5ml/1 teaspoon French mustard
salt

1. Cook the lentils, chickpeas and split green peas in separate pans of boiling water. The lentils and split peas will take anything from 30 to 75 minutes, and the chickpeas up to 2 hours. Rinse them all under cold water and drain well.
2. Shake the dressing in a jar until well emulsified and divide equally between three

cups. To one cup add the mint; to another, the parsley; and to the third, the mustard. Add a good pinch of salt to each. Toss the chickpeas in the parsley vinaigrette, the split peas in the minty dressing and the lentils in the mustard one.
3. Arrange the piles of dressed peas on a serving dish or hors d'oeuvres tray.

NOTE: Other pulses, such as soya beans, red kidney beans and haricot beans are good treated similarly.

ALSACE WHITE

Shell Salad

This recipe has been adapted from *Cooking with Michael Smith.*

SERVES 4
110g/4oz Mediterranean prawns
1 avocado pear, sliced
2 oranges, cut into segments
110g/4oz cooked mangetout
110g/4oz cooked cauliflower florets
French dressing
chopped chives
chopped parsley
salt and pepper

1. Mix all the ingredients together, season and serve, well chilled, on individual plates.

WHITE LOIRE

Peasant Salad

SERVES 4
1 curly endive lettuce
110g/4oz piece of rindless bacon
2 slices thick white bread, crusts removed
oil
French dressing made with plenty of garlic

1. Wash and trim the lettuce. Spin dry.
2. Cut the bacon and bread into 2 cm/3/4inch cubes.
3. Fry the bacon in oil until it begins to brown, then add the bread and fry until brown and crisp.
4. Toss together and serve immediately.

ALSACE WHITE/LIGHT RED

Melon, Cucumber and Tomato Salad

6 tomatoes, peeled, deseeded and slivered
1 cucumber, cubed
1 medium-sized ripe melon, deseeded and cut into balls
French dressing (see page 228)
15ml/1 tablespoon chopped mint

1. Mix all the ingredients together with the French dressing and chopped mint. Serve well chilled.

Foie Gras and Artichoke Heart Salad

SERVES 6
2 handfuls bitter salad leaves
French dressing (see page 228)
4 artichoke hearts, still warm
110g/4oz pâté de foie gras

1. Wash, pick over and pull to smallish pieces the bitter salad leaves. Dry well. Toss in some of the French dressing and arrange on 6 side plates.
2. Slice the still warm artichoke hearts and toss in the remaining French dressing. Pile them on top of the salad leaves.
3. Slice the foie gras very finely and arrange the slices on top of the artichoke hearts. Serve immediately.

MOSELLE

Bean and Scallop Salad

SERVES 6
225g/8oz small French beans
225g/8oz broad beans
1 shallot, finely chopped
2.5ml/½ teaspoon finely chopped thyme leaves
French dressing (see page 228)
12 scallops
seasoned flour
15g/½oz butter
1 rasher streaky bacon, grilled

1. Blanch the French beans in rapidly boiling salted water for 3-4 minutes. Rinse under cold water and drain very well.
2. Boil the broad beans in the same water for 6 minutes. Rinse under cold water and drain. Carefully remove their skins leaving only the green inner beans.
3. Toss the beans, shallot and thyme in the French dressing. Divide between 6 side plates.
4. Clean the scallops, saving any juices and removing the muscular white frill found opposite the orange roe. Rinse off any black matter. Separate the roes from the body and slice both in half horizontally. Dip the scallops in seasoned flour and fry lightly in butter.
5. Tip the warm scallops over the beans and serve scattered with chopped bacon.

DRY WHITE

Bacon and Quail Egg Salad

SERVES 6
12 quail eggs, raw
3 rashers rindless streaky smoked bacon
2 handfuls very young spinach or beet leaves
1 handful young dandelion leaves, or watercress if not available
30ml/2 tablespoons oil for frying
1 slice bread
French dressing (see page 228)

1. Wash, pick over and pull to small pieces the spinach and dandelion leaves, discarding any stalks or thick ribs. Dry well. Toss in the dressing and arrange on 6 side plates.
2. Break the quail eggs carefully on to a plate. Get a frying pan or shallow sauté pan of water bubbling on the heat. Slide the eggs into it. Reduce the heat and poach for 1 minute. Remove from the pan and slip into a bowl of warm water until ready for use.
3. Cut the bacon across into thin strips. Brown them rapidly in the oil. Remove them. Cut the bread into small dice and fry in the hot fat until evenly browned. Remove with a perforated spoon and drain on absorbent paper.
4. Arrange 2 well-drained eggs per person on the salads. Add a sprinkling of bacon, then the fried croûtons, still warm, and serve at once.

DRY WHITE

Bean and Foie Gras Salad

SERVES 6
225g/8oz small French beans
225g/8oz button mushrooms
French dressing (see page 228)
1 shallot, finely chopped
15ml/1 tablespoon fresh chopped mint
170g/6oz pâté de foie gras

1. Top and tail the beans and blanch them in rapidly boiling salted water for 3-4 minutes. Rinse under cold water and drain very well.
2. Slice the button mushrooms finely and toss in the French dressing with the shallot, mint and beans. Arrange on six side plates.
3. Slice the pâté de foie gras into thin slices. Arrange on top of the salad.

MEDIUM DRY WHITE

Pinenut and Duck Breast Salad

SERVES 4

2 handfuls bitter salad leaves (e.g. mâche, watercress, chicory, radicchio)
30ml/2 tablespoons French dressing, made with walnut oil
15ml/1 tablespoon unsalted butter
1 raw duck breast, skinned and split horizontally into 2
55g/2oz pinenuts

1. Wash, pick over and pull into smallish pieces the bitter salad leaves. Dry well. Toss in the dressing and arrange on 4 side plates.
2. Heat the butter in a frying pan until it has ceased to foam. Add the duck breast pieces and fry fairly fast to brown on both sides – about 3 minutes in all. They are done when they feel firm when pressed and are pink, not blue, when cut. Lift out on to a board.
3. Put the pinenuts into the frying pan and shake over the heat until pale brown and crisp.
4. Cut the duck diagonally into thin slices. Return them, and any juices, to the pan, toss briefly and scatter over the salads.
Serve at once.

LIGHT/SOFT RED

Grilled Pepper Salad

SERVES 4

6 large peppers – 2 red, 2 yellow, 2 green
3 hardboiled eggs
6 anchovy fillets
30ml/2 tablespoons extra virgin olive oil
freshly ground black pepper

1. Cut the peppers into quarters and remove the stalks, inner membranes and seeds. Heat the grill to its highest temperature.
2. Grill the peppers, skin side uppermost, until the skin is black and blistered. With a small knife, scrape off all the skin.
3. Cut the flesh into shapes like petals, and arrange them like a flower on a flat round dish, garnishing with the hardboiled eggs, cut into quarters, and the anchovy fillets. Pour over the olive oil and sprinkle with a little black pepper.

ALSACE WHITE

Duck Liver and Mangetout Salad

SERVES 6

450g/1lb mangetout, topped and tailed
225g/8oz duck livers
salad leaves (radicchio or middle leaves of cos)
3 spring onions, finely chopped
French dressing (see page 228)
15g/½oz butter

1. Blanch the mangetout in rapidly boiling salted water for 3-4 minutes. Rinse under cold water and drain very well.
2. Pick over the duck livers.
3. Toss the salad leaves, spring onions and mangetout in the French dressing. Drain off any excess dressing and arrange on 6 side plates.
4. Just before serving, slice the livers and sauté them in a little butter for 1 minute – they should become just firm but not cooked. Lift them out of the pan with a perforated spoon and arrange on top of the salad.

CLARET

Mango and Lobster Salad

SERVES 4

4 handfuls bitter salad leaves such as endive, lamb's lettuce and radicchio
French dressing (see page 228)
2 ripe mangoes
2 x 450g/1lb cooked lobster

1. Wash the salad leaves and dry. Toss in some of the French dressing and arrange on 4 plates.
2. Cut a thick slice from each side of the mangoes, keeping as close to the stone as possible.
3. Carefully peel off the skin and slice horizontally.

4. Cut the heads and claws off the lobsters and remove the shell rather like peeling a large prawn. Cut the body flesh into neat slices or 'collops'. Crack the claws but leave whole.
5. Arrange alternate slices of lobster and mango on each diner's plate. Pour over the remaining French dressing and garnish with a claw.

WHITE BURGUNDY

Scallop and Rocket Salad

SERVES 4
12 scallops
seasoned flour
hazelnut oil
balsamic vinegar
chives
large handful of rocket leaves, cleaned

1. Clean the scallops. Remove the muscular white frill found opposite the orange roe. Rinse off any black matter. Slice them in half horizontally, trying to keep the roe attached to the scallop.
2. Dip the scallops into seasoned flour. Heat some hazelnut oil in a frying pan and fry the scallops quickly on both sides until lightly browned and just cooked. Sprinkle over some balsamic vinegar.
3. Tip the scallops on to the rocket leaves. Turn lightly and place on to 4 individual plates

DRY WHITE

Salade Tiède

SERVES 4
1 small frisée lettuce
1 small oakleaf lettuce
1 bunch watercress
1 small radicchio
2 heads chicory
French dressing (see page 228)
60ml/4 tablespoons olive oil
110g/4oz piece of rindless bacon, diced
5 spring onions
150ml/1/4 pint olive oil
4 slices white bread, cut into 1 cm/1/2 inch cubes
225g/8oz chicken livers, cleaned
15ml/1 tablespoon tarragon vinegar
1 bunch chervil, roughly chopped

1. Toss the salad in the well-seasoned French dressing and divide it between 4 dinner plates.
2. Heat 1 tablespoon olive oil in a frying pan and cook the bacon until it is evenly browned all over. Lift it out with a perforated spoon and keep it warm in the oven.
3. Cook the spring onions in the frying pan quickly for 1 minute and keep them warm in the oven.
4. Heat the 150ml/1/4 pint oil in another frying pan and cook the bread until golden brown. Drain well and sprinkle with a little salt. Keep the croûtons warm in a low oven.
5. Add the remaining olive oil to the first frying pan and gently cook the livers until slightly stiffened and fairly firm but not hard to the touch. They should be light brown on the outside and pink in the middle.
6. Add the tarragon vinegar to the pan and shake the livers in the vinegar for 10 seconds.
7. Scatter the croûtons, the bacon, the spring onions and finally the livers over the salad. Sprinkle the salad with the chervil and serve immediately.

SPICY DRY WHITE

Italian Bread Salad

SERVES 6
225g/8oz Italian bread (see page 565)
1 large red onion, peeled and roughly chopped
3 sticks celery, roughly chopped
1/2 cucumber, peeled, sliced and deseeded
10 leaves basil, roughly chopped
30ml/2 tablespoons capers, drained
salt and pepper
450g/1lb beef tomatoes, peeled and finely chopped
100ml/4 fl oz good quality olive oil
15-30ml/1-2 tablespoons red wine vinegar

To serve:
5 basil leaves
radicchio

1. Soak the bread in cold water for half an hour. Squeeze out the water and put the bread on a large flat dish.
2. Lay the onion on top of the bread followed by the celery, cucumber, basil leaves, capers and tomato.
3. Cover and refrigerate for at least 2 hours.
4. Transfer to a large bowl. Add salt and pepper to taste, then the olive oil and wine vinegar. Toss very well, sprinkle over the remaining basil leaves, then garnish with a few radicchio leaves.

DRY WHITE

Smoked Chicken Salad

SERVES 4
1 small smoked chicken
85g/3oz butter
5ml/1 teaspoon chopped parsley
salt and pepper
radicchio and lamb's lettuce leaves
5ml/1 teaspoon dry English mustard
French dressing (see page 228)

1. Separate the legs from the body of the chicken.
2. Mince or pound the leg flesh (without the skin) in a food processor with the butter and parsley. Season with salt and pepper.
3. Shape this pâté into a cylinder and roll up in a piece of foil. Chill, then unwrap and cut into slices.
4. Carve the chicken breast in thin slices and divide them between 4 dessert or side plates, overlapping the slices attractively.
5. Add a slice or two of the pâté to each plate and a few crisp salad leaves.
6. Add the mustard to the French dressing and whisk until smooth. Spoon a little dressing over each salad before serving.

SPICY/MEDIUM DRY WHITE

Scallop and Asparagus Salad

SERVES 4
225g/8oz young asparagus, trimmed
salt and freshly ground black pepper
12 scallops
endive
radicchio
lamb's lettuce
French dressing (see page 228)
unsalted butter
lemon juice

1. Cook the asparagus in boiling salted water until just tender. Drain well.
2. Clean the scallops, remove the muscular white frill found opposite the roe. Rinse off any black matter. Separate the roes from the body and slice both in half horizontally.

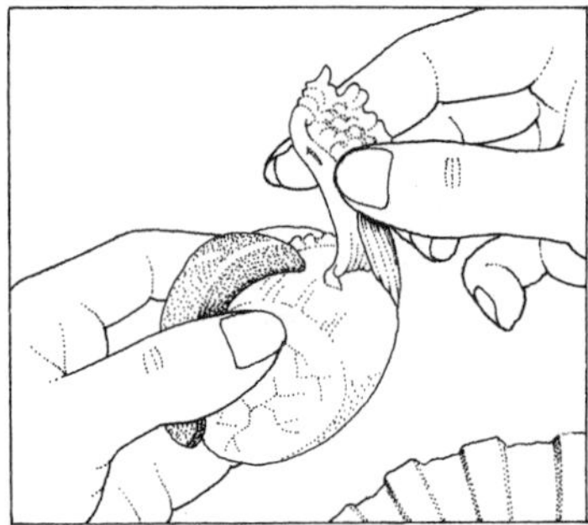

Remove the muscular white frill found opposite the roe

3. Toss the well-washed salad leaves in French dressing and divide between 4 plates.
4. Arrange the still warm asparagus on top of the salad leaves.
5. Fry the scallops quickly in a little butter. Cool slightly, add the lemon juice, salt and pepper.
6. Divide the scallops, with their pan juices, between the 4 salad plates.

WHITE LOIRE

Vegetable Pasta

SERVES 4
4 medium courgettes
4 carrots
French dressing (see page 228)
15ml/1 tablespoon finely chopped chives

1. Peel the carrots, then continue using the potato peeler and shred the carrots into long thin ribbons.
2. Top and tail the courgettes, then proceed as for the carrots, and shred the courgettes into long thin ribbons.
3. Toss the carrots and courgettes in the French dressing at least 2 hours before serving so that the vegetables begin to curl.
4. Arrange on individual plates garnished with the chives.

Tabouleh

Recipes for this are legion. The important thing is that it should be green and have a good lemon flavour.

SERVES 4
110g/4oz cracked wheat
1 tomato, peeled, deseeded and chopped
1/2 cucumber, chopped
10 leaves fresh mint, finely chopped
good handful of fresh parsley, finely chopped
1 shallot, finely chopped
45ml/3 tablespoons olive oil
salt and freshly ground black pepper
lemon juice

1. Soak the wheat in cold water for 15 minutes – it will expand greatly. Drain and wrap in a clean tea towel. Squeeze out the moisture. Spread the wheat on a tray to dry further.
2. Mix all the ingredients together, adding salt, pepper and plenty of lemon juice to taste.

Crudités

A selection of:
celery
green pepper
cauliflower
radishes
button mushrooms
spring onions
carrots
asparagus
cherry tomatoes
tiny mangetout
baby sweetcorns
young turnips
black olives

For the dressing:
1 garlic clove, crushed (optional)
150ml/1/4 pint mayonnaise (see page 224)

1. Prepare the vegetables, making sure they are perfectly clean, and as far as possible evenly sized.
Celery: wash and cut into sticks.
Pepper: wipe and cut into strips, discarding the seeds.
Cauliflower: wash and break into florets. Peel the stalks if tough.
Radishes: wash and trim off the root and long leaves, but leave a little of the green stalk.
Mushrooms: wash. Peel only if the skins are tough. Quarter if large.
Spring onions: wash. Cut off most of the green part, and the beard (roots). Leave whole, or cut in half lengthways if large.
Carrots: peel and cut into sticks the same shape and size as the celery.
Asparagus: peel the tough outer stalk and trim away the hard root ends.
Turnip: peel and cut into strips. (Use young turnips only.)
Black olives: stone with a cherry stoner if desired.
2. Mix the garlic (if using) with the mayonnaise. Spoon it into a small serving bowl.
3. Arrange the raw prepared vegetables and the olives in neat clumps on a tray or flat platter with the bowl of mayonnaise dip in the centre.

Cucumber with Soured Cream

1 medium cucumber

For the dressing:
45ml/3 tablespoons oil
15ml/1 tablespoon wine vinegar
salt and pepper
pinch of sugar
15ml/1 level tablespoon chopped mint

For the topping:
55g/2oz soft cream cheese
30ml/2 tablespoons soured cream
1 small garlic clove, crushed
juice of 1/2 lemon

1. Slice the cucumber finely. Sprinkle the slices lightly with salt and leave for 20 minutes.
2. Put the dressing ingredients in a screw-top jar and shake until well emulsified.
3. Beat the cream cheese until soft, then gradually stir in the soured cream. Add the garlic, and season with salt, pepper and lemon juice to taste.
4. Rinse, drain and dry the cucumber thoroughly. Toss the slices in the French dressing and put them into a serving dish, or on to individual plates. Spoon the cream cheese mixture on top.

NOTE: This makes a good salad, with others, for a party, or can be served with hot bread and butter as a light first course.

MEDIUM DRY WHITE

Marinated Italian Aubergines and Courgettes

This recipe has been adapted from a similar recipe by Sophie Grigson.

SERVES 8
450g/1lb small courgettes (yellow or green)
450g/1lb small aubergines
salt and freshly ground black pepper
olive oil
1 large onion, roughly chopped
1 carrot, diced
5 sage leaves, roughly torn
juice of 1 lemon
60ml/4 tablespoons white wine
240ml/8 fl oz white wine vinegar
3 juniper berries
1 bay leaf
2 sprigs parsley

1. Trim the ends off the courgettes and aubergines and cut into quarters lengthways.
2. Place in a colander, sprinkle with salt and leave to degorge for 30 minutes.
3. Rinse and dry the vegetables and fry in olive oil until lightly browned and just tender. The aubergines will take considerably longer to cook than the courgettes. Transfer, skin side up, to an ovenproof dish.
4. Meanwhile, put the remaining ingredients into a large saucepan. Bring them up to the boil and simmer for 2 minutes.
5. When all the courgettes and aubergines are cooked, reheat the vinegar marinade and pour it over the vegetables. Leave to cool. Cover and refrigerate for 2 days.
6. Remove and discard any bedraggled herbs and vegetables. Bring back to room temperature before serving.

Aubergines Robert

SERVES 4
2 aubergines
150ml/1/4 pint French dressing *(see page 228)*
5ml/1 teaspoon chopped fresh chives

1. Slice the aubergines and soak them in the dressing for 2 hours.
2. Heat the grill.
3. Grill the aubergines on both sides until pale brown. Sprinkle well with chives and more dressing and grill again for 1 minute or until golden brown. Turn the slices over, sprinkle again with dressing and chives, and grill to a good brown.
4. Allow to cool. Chill well before serving.

ROSE

Grilled Aubergines with Pesto

SERVES 4
2 medium aubergines, sliced
salt
150ml/1/4 pint French dressing *(see page 228)*
parsley pesto sauce *(see page 228)*
10ml/2 teaspoons French mustard

1. Sprinkle the aubergine slices liberally with salt and leave for 30 minutes.
2. Make the French dressing and season with the mustard.
3. Rinse the aubergines, drain and dry well. Soak them in the French dressing for 2 hours. Drain well.
4. Heat the grill.
5. Grill the aubergines for about 10 minutes on each side, or until soft and pale brown.
6. Spread one side of the aubergine with the pesto sauce and return to the grill for 1 minute.
7. Arrange on a round plate.

LIGHT RED/ROSE

Vegetable Surprises

SERVES 4
2 large carrots, peeled and sliced thinly lengthways
1 small mouli, peeled and sliced thinly lengthways
2 large courgettes, sliced thinly lengthways
8 leaves spinach, stems removed
225g/8oz silken tofu
15ml/1 tablespoon light soy sauce
2 small beetroot, peeled and cut into julienne strips
8 basil leaves
8 spring onions, cut into 5cm/2 inch julienne strips

For the sauce:
400g/14oz natural yoghurt
1 garlic clove, crushed
15ml/1 tablespoon chopped fresh coriander
30ml/2 tablespoons Indonesian soy sauce (kecap manis) or light soy sauce
ground cumin
salt and freshly ground black pepper

To garnish:
mustard cress

1. Blanch and refresh the carrots, mouli and courgette slices. Drain well and dry on absorbent paper.
2. Cut the spinach leaves into 8 x 5cm/2 inch squares. Refresh, drain and dry on absorbent paper.
3. Mix together the tofu and light soy sauce.
4. Lay the spinach leaves out on the work top. Cover with the julienne of beetroot, the basil leaves, spring onions and a dollop of tofu and soy sauce. Roll up to form a cylinder.
5. Roll each cylinder first in a courgette slice, then in a mouli slice and finally in a carrot slice. The julienne of vegetables should sprout out of the roll of sliced vegetables.
6. Wrap the rolls tightly in cling wrap and leave to stand in the refrigerator for at least 1 hour.
7. Mix together the yoghurt, garlic, coriander and soy sauce. Season to taste with the cumin, salt and pepper. Chill before serving.
8. Unwrap the vegetable surprises and arrange on a plate. Place a dollop of sauce on each plate and garnish with the mustard cress.

DRY WHITE

Niçoise Vegetables

SERVES 4-6
1 bay leaf
sprig of thyme
1/2 cauliflower, broken into florets
110g/4oz French beans, topped, tailed and halved
110g/4oz carrots, cut into julienne
2 large courgettes, cut into julienne
about 8 button mushrooms, trimmed
about 8 button onions, peeled
2 tomatoes, skinned and quartered

For the vinaigrette dressing:
90ml/6 tablespoons olive oil
30ml/2 tablespoons wine vinegar
2.5ml/1/2 teaspoon salt
2.5ml/1/2 teaspoon freshly ground black pepper
15ml/1 tablespoon fresh mixed chopped herbs (parsley, mint, tarragon, chives)
1 garlic clove, crushed

1. Combine the dressing ingredients in a screw-top jar and shake well.
2. Place a pan of salted water on to boil, adding the bay leaf and thyme. In it, one variety at a time, cook all the vegetables except the tomatoes, until just 'al dente'. As soon as they are cooked, lift them out of the water with a perforated spoon and dunk them in a bowl of cold water to stop further cooking and set the colour.

3. Drain the vegetables very well, toss them in the vinaigrette, and put them and the tomatoes on a serving dish. Chill before serving.

NOTE: Peeling onions after boiling is easier than before, but the boiling water should not be used to cook the other vegetables – it will be murky brown.

DRY WHITE

Celeriac Rémoulade

SERVES 4

450g/1lb celeriac
45ml/3 tablespoons mayonnaise (see page 224)
2.5ml/½ teaspoon Dijon mustard
10ml/2 teaspoons finely chopped gherkin
10ml/2 teaspoons finely chopped fresh tarragon or chervil
10ml/2 teaspoons finely chopped capers
1 anchovy fillet, finely chopped

1. Mix together all the ingredients except the celeriac.
2. Peel the celeriac and cut into very fine matchsticks. Blanch briefly in boiling water, refresh and drain well. Mix with the sauce, before it has time to discolour.
3. Turn into a clean dish.

NOTE: Rémoulade sauce is a mayonnaise with a predominantly mustard flavour. The other ingredients, though good, are not always present.

SPICY DRY WHITE

Mushrooms à la Grecque

SERVES 4

425ml/¾ pint water
30ml/2 tablespoons tomato purée
30ml/2 tablespoons olive oil
30ml/2 tablespoons white wine
2 shallots, finely chopped
1 garlic clove, crushed
6 coriander seeds
2.5ml/½ teaspoon dried or 5ml/1 teaspoon chopped fresh fennel
6 peppercorns
small pinch of salt
pinch of sugar
good squeeze of lemon juice
450g/1lb button mushrooms, wiped and trimmed
10ml/2 teaspoons chopped parsley

1. Place all the ingredients except the mushrooms and parsley in a saucepan and simmer gently for 15-20 minutes.
2. Add the mushrooms and simmer for 10 minutes. Remove the mushrooms. Taste.
3. Unless it tastes very strong, reduce the liquid by boiling to about 190ml/⅓ pint. Put the mushrooms back and allow to cool.
4. Check the seasoning and tip into a shallow bowl or dish. Sprinkle with chopped parsley.

BEAUJOLAIS

Mushroom Roulade

SERVES 4-6

450g/1lb mature black cap mushrooms
30g/1oz butter
30g/1oz flour
1 teaspoon tomato purée
1 teaspoon mushroom ketchup (optional)
pinch of freshly grated nutmeg
salt and freshly ground black pepper
4 eggs, separated

For the filling:
225g/8oz cream cheese
60ml/4 tablespoons fromage frais or natural yoghurt
4 medium spring onions, finely sliced
15ml/1 tablespoon chopped herbs (e.g. parsley, thyme, sage, chervil)
salt and freshly ground black pepper

1. Preheat the oven to 200°C/400°F/gas mark 6. Place the mushrooms in a food processor with 15ml/1 tablespoon water. Process until very finely chopped.
2. Melt the butter in a large saucepan, add the flour and cook together for half a minute.
3. Add the chopped mushrooms and stir well. Heat steadily and cook, stirring occasionally,

until the mushrooms are fairly dry. (They will, at first, throw out a lot of liquid which needs to be evaporated.) This may take up to 20 minutes. Meanwhile, line a large roasting tin with a double sheet of greased greaseproof paper or silicone paper, letting the edges stick up over the sides of the tin.
4. Remove from the heat and add the tomato purée, mushroom ketchup, nutmeg, and salt and pepper to taste. Stir in the egg yolks and turn into a large bowl.
5. In another large bowl whip the egg whites with a balloon whisk until they will hold their shape. Take a spoonful of egg white and add to the mushroom mixture, stirring it in to loosen the mixture.
6. Fold the remaining egg whites into the mixture and carefully spread the mixture into the prepared roasting tin, taking care not to lose any air.
7. Place in the preheated oven for approximately 12 minutes, or until the roulade is firm to the touch.
8. Meanwhile, prepare the filling. With a wooden spoon, let down the cream cheese carefully with the fromage frais, stirring well to ensure no lumps are left. Add the spring onions, herbs, salt and pepper.
9. When the roulade is cooked, turn it on to a piece of greaseproof paper, trim the edges, spread over the filling and roll it up carefully, letting it rest on the seam. Wrap tightly with the greaseproof paper and place in the refrigerator for about half an hour or until cold.

LIGHT RED

Spinach Roulade

SERVES 4
450g/1lb fresh spinach, or 170g/6oz frozen leaf spinach, cooked and chopped
4 eggs, separated
15g/½oz butter
salt and freshly ground black pepper
pinch of nutmeg

For the filling:
15g/½ oz butter
170g/6oz mushrooms, chopped
15g/½ oz flour
150ml/¼ pint milk
60ml/4 tablespoons cream
15ml/1 tablespoon chopped fresh parsley
salt and freshly ground black pepper

1. Line a roasting tin with a double layer of lightly greased greaseproof paper. Allow the edges to stick above the sides of the tin.
2. Melt the butter for the filling and gently cook the mushrooms in it. Remove the pan from the heat, add the flour and mix well. Return the pan to the heat and cook for half a minute. Add the milk and bring to the boil, stirring continually until you have a fairly thick creamy sauce. Add the cream and parsley and season to taste. Beat in the butter.
3. Set the oven to 190°C/375°F/gas mark 5.
4. To make the roulade, gradually beat the egg yolks and butter into the spinach and season with salt, pepper and nutmeg. Whisk the egg whites until stiff but not dry and fold them into the spinach. Pour this mixture into the prepared roasting tin, spread it flat. Bake for 10-12 minutes or until it feels dry to the touch.
5. Put a piece of greaseproof paper on top of a tea towel. Turn the roulade out on to the paper and remove the original piece of paper. Spread the filling on to the roulade and roll it up as you would a Swiss roll, removing the paper as you go. Serve whole on a warmed dish.

SOFT RED

Spinach Roulade with Smoked Salmon and Soured Cream

SERVES 4
450g/1lb fresh spinach, or 170g/6oz frozen leaf spinach, cooked and chopped
15g/½oz butter
4 eggs, separated
salt and freshly ground black pepper
pinch of nutmeg
For the filling:
285g/10 oz thick soured cream
110g/4oz smoked salmon, chopped
10ml/2 teaspoons chopped fresh dill

1. Set the oven to 190°C/375°F/gas mark 5. Take a large roasting pan and cut a double layer of greaseproof paper slightly larger than the tin. Lay this in the tin. Don't worry if the ends stick up untidily around the sides. Brush the paper lightly with oil or melted butter.
2. To make the roulade, beat the butter and egg yolks into the spinach and season with salt, pepper and nutmeg. Whisk the egg whites until stiff but not dry and fold them into the spinach. Pour this mixture into the prepared roasting tin, spread it flat. Bake for 10-12 minutes or until it feels dry to the touch.
3. Mix together the filling ingredients.
4. Turn the roulade out on to a piece of greaseproof paper and remove the original piece of paper. Spread the filling on to the roulade and roll it up as you would a Swiss roll, removing the paper as you go. Wet the paper, wrap the roulade up tightly in it and return to the oven for 5 minutes. Serve on a warm dish.

NOTE: Extra soured cream can be served separately with this dish.

DRY WHITE

Spinach and Ricotta Strudels

These strudels can easily be made with bought filo pastry.

SERVES 6
450g/1lb fresh spinach, cooked and chopped
170g/6oz ricotta cheese
1 egg, lightly beaten
salt and black pepper
grated nutmeg
340g/12oz filo or strudel pastry
melted butter

1. Set the oven to 200°C/400°F/gas mark 6.
2. Mix the spinach with the ricotta cheese, egg, salt, pepper, and nutmeg to taste.
3. Cut the strudel leaves to 13cm/5 inch squares. Brush each square immediately with melted butter. Lay 2 or 3 squares on top of each other.
4. Put a spoonful of the spinach mixture on each piece of pastry. Fold the sides of the pastry over slightly to prevent the filling escaping during cooking, then roll the strudels up rather like a Swiss roll.
6. Brush with more melted butter and bake in the prepared oven on a greased baking sheet for 15 minutes.

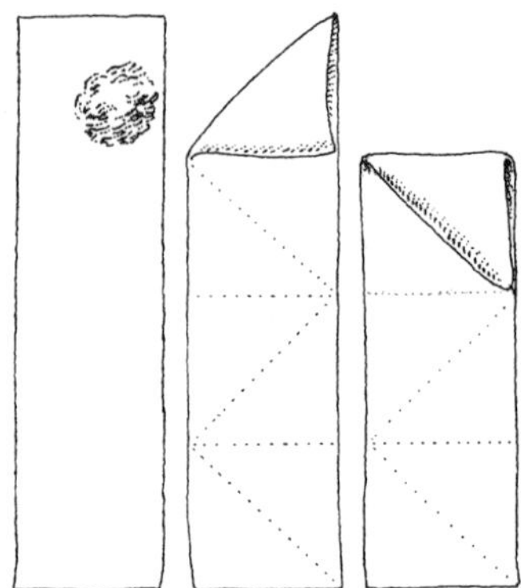

Put a spoonful of filling in the top right-hand corner and fold the pastry into successive triangles

NOTE: Alternatively, the strudel pastry can be cut into long strips, a spoonful of the filling placed in the top right-hand corner and the pastry rolled into successive triangles as illustrated.

SPICY DRY WHITE/LIGHT RED

Spinach Moulds

SERVES 6
30g/1oz butter
675g/1½lb spinach leaves, destalked and washed
225g/8oz ricotta cheese
30g/1oz Gruyère, grated
30g/1oz Parmesan, grated
2 eggs
60ml/4 tablespoons single cream
grated nutmeg
salt and freshly ground black pepper

1. Lightly butter 6 ramekin dishes.
2. Blanch 10 spinach leaves, refresh, drain and dry well.
3. Arrange the leaves inside the ramekin dishes, overlapping the edges.
4. Cook the remaining leaves for 2 minutes, drain very well by squeezing between 2 plates. Chop

finely. Set the oven to 200°C/400°F/gas mark 6.
5. Mix together the cheeses, eggs, cream and seasoning.
6. Fill the ramekin dishes with alternate layers of the cheese mixture and the spinach. Fold over the spinach leaves.
7. Dot butter on each ramekin. Set in a bain-marie and bake for 25-30 minutes. Rest for 2 minutes before unmoulding.

SPICY DRY WHITE/LIGHT RED

Spinach Timbale

SERVES 4-6
675g/1½lb fresh spinach
30g/1oz butter
85g/3oz fresh white breadcrumbs, sieved
2 eggs, beaten
1 egg yolk
pinch of ground nutmeg
salt and freshly ground black pepper
345ml/12 fl oz milk

To serve:
tomato dressing (see page 228)

1. Wash the spinach well and remove the tough stalks. Blanch, refresh and drain 15 of the biggest and best leaves. Put the rest of the still wet spinach into a saucepan with a lid and, holding the pan in one hand and the lid on with the other, shake and toss the spinach over heat until it is soft and reduced in quantity.
2. Squeeze all the water from the spinach, pressing it between 2 plates. Tip on to a board and chop very finely. Butter a 15cm/6 inch cake tin or soufflé dish and line it with the whole spinach leaves.
3. In a saucepan melt the butter, add the spinach and stir until very dry looking. Take off the heat and add the breadcrumbs, eggs, egg yolk, nutmeg and seasoning.
4. Heat the milk and stir it into the mixture.
5. Spoon the spinach mixture into the cake tin and cover with buttered foil or greaseproof paper.
6. Heat the oven to 180°C/350°F/gas mark 4. Stand the cake tin in a roasting pan full of boiling water. Transfer both roasting tin and spinach mould to the oven and bake for 45 minutes or until the mixture is firm.
7. Turn out on a hot serving dish.

NOTE: Individual spinach timbales can be made in ramekin dishes. They will take 20-30 minutes to cook. The finer the china, the more quickly the mixture will cook.

SPICY DRY WHITE

Sweet Potato and Spinach Pots

SERVES 6
900g/2lb sweet potatoes
salt and freshly ground black pepper
45g/1½oz butter, plus a little extra for spreading
2 egg yolks
170g/6oz fresh spinach (choose as large leaves as possible)

To garnish:
225g/8oz cherry tomatoes, halved

1. Wash and peel the potatoes and cook in lightly salted boiling water until tender, about 20-30 minutes. Drain well.
2. Mash the potatoes and add the butter, egg yolks, salt and pepper. Mash until smooth.
3. Preheat the oven to 180°C/350°F/gas mark 4.
4. Lightly butter 6 ramekin dishes.
5. Wash the spinach, remove any tough stalks and blanch in boiling water until just tender. Refresh thoroughly and drain well.
6. Line the ramekin dishes with the spinach leaves. Spoon the sweet potato mixture into the centre and fold the spinach leaves over the mixture to cover.
7. Place the ramekins in a roasting tin and pour boiling water into this to a depth of 1cm/½ inch.
8. Bake for 30-40 minutes or until the potato mixture is heated right through and set.
9. Invert on a warm plate, garnish with the cherry tomatoes and serve.

MEDIUM DRY WHITE

Carrot and Spinach Timbales

SERVES 6

340g/12oz carrots, peeled and sliced
2 eggs, beaten
290ml/½ pint double cream
salt and freshly ground black pepper
pinch of cumin
340g/12oz spinach, tough stalks removed
pinch of nutmeg

1. Cook the carrots in boiling salted water until very tender. Drain well, whizz in a food processor and push through a sieve. Cool.
2. Stir in half the beaten egg, and half the double cream, and season with cumin, salt and pepper.
3. Cook the spinach in a very little boiling water until tender. Drain very well, cool slightly and whizz in a food processor with the remaining beaten egg and cream. Season with grated nutmeg, salt and pepper.
4. Line the bottom of 6 timbale moulds or ramekins with circles of greased greaseproof paper. Spoon in the thicker of the two purées, and carefully pile on the other purée.
5. Preheat the oven to 180°C/350°F/gas mark 4. Cook the timbales in a bain-marie for about 40 minutes or until set. Turn out to serve.

NOTE: If spinach is not available, broccoli can be used in its place.

MEDIUM DRY WHITE

Carrot and Gruyère Timbales

SERVES 4

170g/6oz grated carrot
85g/3oz grated Gruyère cheese
1 egg, beaten
salt and freshly ground black pepper
2.5ml/½ teaspoon dry English mustard
30ml/2 tablespoons double cream
butter

To serve:
tomato sauce (see page 231)

1. Set the oven to 190°C/375°F/gas mark 5.
2. Blanch the carrot in boiling water for 30 seconds. Refresh under cold running water and drain well on absorbent paper. Mix together the carrot, cheese, egg, salt, pepper, mustard and cream. Beat well.
3. Butter 4 dariole moulds and pour in the carrot and cheese mixture. Cover with lids and put the moulds into a roasting tin half filled with very hot water.
4. Bake for 20 minutes. Carefully turn each mould out on a serving dish or plate. Hand the tomato sauce separately.

LIGHT RED

Courgette Timbales

SERVES 6

450g/1lb courgettes
salt and freshly ground black pepper
2 eggs
1 egg yolk
55g/2oz fresh white breadcrumbs, sieved
290ml/½ pint milk
15ml/1 tablespoon fresh thyme, chopped

1. Set the oven to 170°C/325°F/gas mark 3.
2. Oil and line 6 ramekin dishes with a disc of lightly oiled greaseproof paper.
3. Top, tail and grate the courgettes. Sprinkle sparingly with salt. Leave in a sieve for half an hour. Rinse and dry well on kitchen paper.
4. Lightly beat the eggs and egg yolk together. Add the breadcrumbs, milk, thyme and courgettes. Season well with salt and pepper.
5. Pour into the prepared ramekin dishes. Cover with lightly oiled greaseproof paper and place in a hot bain-marie. Put in the centre of the preheated oven for 40 minutes or until the timbales are set.
6. Serve warm.

DRY WHITE

Courgette and Carrot Roulade

SERVES 6
110g/4oz carrots
110g/4oz courgettes
4 eggs, separated

For the filling:
110g/4oz cream cheese
30ml/2 tablespoons yoghurt
4 spring onions, finely sliced
1 tablespoon finely chopped mixed herbs, e.g. parsley, thyme
grated rind of 1/2 lemon
salt and freshly ground black pepper

1. Put a double layer of lightly oiled greaseproof paper into a large roasting tin. Set the oven to 190°C/375°F/gas mark 5.
2. Grate the carrots and courgettes, mix them together with the egg yolks and season well with salt and pepper. Whisk the egg whites to medium peaks and fold them carefully into the carrots and courgettes.
3. Pour this mixture into the lined roasting tin, spread it flat. Bake for 10-12 minutes or until it feels dry to the touch.
4. Meanwhile, mix together the ingredients for the filling. Season to taste.
5. When the roulade is cooked, turn it out on to a clean sheet of greaseproof paper. Trim the edges, spread with the filling and roll up carefully. Serve cold.

DRY WHITE

Vegetable Terrine

SERVES 8
10 large fresh spinach leaves
550g/1lb 2oz large carrots, peeled and sliced
salt and freshly ground pepper
grated rind and juice of 1/2 lemon
4 small turnips, peeled and sliced
60ml/4 tablespoons water
30g/1oz or 2 envelopes of gelatine
1 large ripe avocado pear

1. Wash the spinach very well and remove the tough stalks. Put it into a saucepan, without any extra water; cover and cook the spinach for 3 minutes. Remove the leaves, refresh in cold water and leave to drain on absorbent paper. Use the leaves to line a nonstick 1kg/2lb loaf tin.
2. Cook the carrots in the minimum quantity of water. When they are tender, drain and process them until they are absolutely smooth. Season the carrots and add the lemon rind.
3. Cook the turnips in the minimum quantity of water. When they are completely tender, drain them well and process until they are absolutely smooth. Season.
4. Put 60ml/4 tablespoons of water into a small saucepan, sprinkle on the gelatine and set it aside for 5 minutes to become spongy.
5. Dissolve the gelatine over a gentle heat; when it is clear and warm stir two-thirds of it into the carrot purée and the remaining third into the turnip purée.
6. Spoon half the carrot purée into the loaf tin, smooth it down, cover the tin and leave it to set in the refrigerator.
7. Peel and slice the avocado, sprinkle it with lemon juice and arrange half of it on top of the carrot purée. Cover it carefully with the turnip purée, smooth the purée down and leave the terrine to set in the refrigerator.
8. Arrange the rest of the avocado on top of the turnip. Cover it with the remaining carrot purée, smooth the top down and refrigerate the terrine again.
9. To serve: place a large plate over the loaf tin. Turn the tin and plate over together. Remove the tin and slice the terrine with a serrated knife.

MEDIUM DRY WHITE

Leek Terrine with Stilton Dressing and Griddled Scallops

SERVES 8
9 leeks, cleaned and boiled in salted water until tender
radicchio leaves (or any other chicory salad)
60ml/4 tablespoons olive oil

15ml/1 tablespoon wine vinegar
5ml/1 teaspoon English mustard
55g/2oz crumbled Stilton
salt, pepper

To serve:
4 scallops, cleaned
unsalted butter

1. Cut the leeks in half lengthways. Lay the leeks lengthways in a 450g/1lb loaf tin, making sure they lie head-to-tail, half of them one way, half the other.
2. Put another loaf tin on top to press them down, turn both tins upside-down so the water can drain out, turn over again, and put a 900g/2lb weight on top to press it. Leave for 4 hours.
3. Meanwhile, prepare the dressing. Mix together the oil, vinegar, mustard and Stilton and season with salt and pepper.
4. Cut the scallops in half horizontally. Season with freshly ground black pepper.
5. Unmould the terrine and carefully cut into slices. Lay a slice on 8 individual plates. Quickly fry or griddle the scallops in butter and arrange beside the terrine. Surround with the salad leaves and serve with the dressing.

DRY WHITE

Vegetables in Aspic

SERVES 8
This is a complicated recipe but a very pretty dish that justifies the effort. Other vegetables can obviously be substituted depending on availability of ingredients.

2 small artichokes, washed and with stems removed
225g/8oz carrots, peeled, sliced and boiled
225g/8oz courgettes, peeled, sliced and boiled
225g/8oz turnips, peeled, sliced and boiled
110g/4oz French beans, topped, tailed and boiled
225g/8oz asparagus, scraped and cooked until tender
725ml/1¼ pints well-flavoured aspic (see page 219)

For the sweet pepper sauce:
1 onion, sliced
15ml/1 tablespoon sunflower oil
2 tomatoes, peeled, deseeded and cut into 8
1 sweet red pepper, peeled (by singeing over a flame), deseeded and cut into strips
1 garlic clove, crushed
1 bouquet garni

1. Cook the artichokes in boiling salted water for about 45 minutes. Leave to drain.
2. Meanwhile, make the sauce. Cook the onion in the oil until just beginning to soften. Add the tomatoes, red pepper, garlic and bouquet garni. Add 60ml/4 tablespoons of water and season lightly. Cover and cook slowly for 20 minutes. Liquidize until smooth and push through a sieve. Chill.
3. Remove the leaves from the artichokes and slice the hearts. Drain all the vegetables very well, keeping them separate.
4. Melt the aspic very gently. Pour about 5mm/¼inch into the base of a well-chilled loaf tin. Leave to set.
5. Pour 60ml/4 tablespoons of aspic into a deep dish or soup plate and dip the asparagus spears in it until they are thoroughly soaked. Arrange on top of the aspic in the tin. Pour in a little more aspic and leave to set.
6. Gradually layer up all the vegetables and aspic in the loaf tin, finishing with a smooth layer of aspic. Leave to become completely set.
7. To serve, dip the tin briefly in hot water. Invert a serving dish over the tin and turn both over together. Give a sharp shake and remove the tin. Hand the chilled sauce separately.

NOTE I: An alternative method is to make 4 individual vegetables in aspic in small soup bowls. The pepper sauce can be spread on the base of four side plates and an individual vegetable in aspic unmoulded on top.
NOTE II: Cook the vegetables in minimal amounts of water so that they need little or no draining. This will prevent too much leaching out of vitamins.

DRY WHITE

Above: Provençal Fish Soup.

Above: Herb Omelette Salad. Right: Aubergine Loaf.

Left: Mango and Lobster Salad. Above: Marinated Italian Aubergines and Courgettes.

Above: Aubergine Charlotte. Right: Red Pepper Bavarois with Red Pepper Salad.

Left: Terrine de Ratatouille Niçoise. Above: Leith's Restaurant's Artichoke and Green Olive Pie.

Above: Jamś Californian Vegetables. Right: Potato Cakes with Smoked Salmon.

Left: Ceviche. Above: Squid Salad with Cucumber and Cumin.

Above: Arbroath Smokies Pots. Right: Easy Fish Quenelles

Above: Wild Mushrooms. 1. St George. 2. Velvet shank. 3. Blackening Russula. 4. Cep. 5. Wood blewit. 6. Shiitake. 7. Oyster (pink). 8. Oyster (yellow). 9. Chanterelle. 10. Oyster (wild). 11. Morel. 12. Fairy Ring Champignon.

Mousses and Soufflés

Tuna Fish Mousse

SERVES 4
10ml/2 teaspoons gelatine
285g/10oz tinned tuna fish
150ml/1/4pint mayonnaise (see page 224), or plain yoghurt
salt and freshly ground black pepper
1/2 garlic clove, crushed
lemon juice
15ml/1 tablespoon chopped parsley
150ml/1/4 pint double cream, lightly whipped
oil for greasing

For the garnish:
slices of cucumber
stoned black olives

1. In a small saucepan, soak the gelatine in 30ml/2 tablespoons water.
2. Oil a mould for the mousse and leave it to drain upside down.
3. Pour off the oil from the tuna fish and flake the fish with a fork. Mash to a pulp. Stir in the mayonnaise or yoghurt, seasoning, garlic, lemon juice and parsley.
4. Melt the gelatine over a gentle heat and, when clear and runny, stir into the mixture.
5. Fold in the cream. Pour into the mould. Refrigerate until set.
6. To turn out, invert a serving dish over the mould and then turn both the dish and the mould over together. Give both a sharp shake, and remove the mould.
7. Decorate with slices of cucumber and stoned black olives.

NOTE I: If the mousse is to stand for more than an hour after decorating, the cucumber slices should be degorged, i.e. salted, allowed to stand for 30 minutes, rinsed well and patted dry. If this is not done the cucumber will weep when left on the sides of the mousse.

SPICY DRY WHITE

Egg Mousse

SERVES 4
15ml/1 tablespoon water
10ml/2 teaspoons gelatine
6 hardboiled eggs
90ml/6 tablespoons mayonnaise (see page 224)
10ml/2 teaspoons anchovy essence
45ml/3 tablespoons double cream, lightly whipped
salt and pepper
cayenne

For the garnish:
slices of cucumber

1. Put the water into a small heavy saucepan and sprinkle over the gelatine. Leave for 10 minutes.
2. Oil a soufflé dish or mould and leave it upside down to drain.
3. Chop the eggs and mix them with the mayonnaise, anchovy essence and cream, and season with salt, pepper and cayenne.
4. Dissolve the gelatine over gentle heat and when runny and clear stir it into the mixture.
5. Pour into the mould or dish. Put in the refrigerator until set.
6. Loosen the mousse round the edge, using fingers or thumb, and turn out on to a plate.

NOTE: If the mousse is to stand for more than an hour after decorating, the cucumber slices should be degorged, i.e. salted, allowed to stand for 30 minutes, rinsed well and patted dry. If this is not done the cucumber will weep when left on the sides of the mousse.

PROVENCE ROSE

Haddock Mousse

SERVES 6
225g/8oz haddock
150ml/1/4 pint milk
2 slices onion
1 bay leaf
6 peppercorns
15g/1/2oz butter
15g/1/2oz flour
45ml/3 tablespoons water

8g/¼oz gelatine
2 hardboiled eggs
150ml/¼ pint double cream, lightly whipped
45ml/3 tablespoons mayonnaise (see page 224)
salt and pepper
5ml/1 teaspoon anchovy essence

For the garnish:
thin cucumber slices

1. Set the oven to 180°C/350°F/gas mark 4. Oil a 10cm/4 inch soufflé dish and stand upside down to drain off the excess.
2. Place the haddock in an ovenproof dish. Pour over the milk and put in onion, bay leaf and peppercorns. Cover and poach in the oven for 20-30 minutes, or until the haddock is cooked.
3. Skin the haddock and strain the milk into a bowl.
4. Melt the butter and add the flour. Stir over a gentle heat for 1 minute. Take off the heat and add the milk the fish was cooked in. Return to the heat and stir continuously, gently bringing to the boil. You should now have a very thick white sauce. Set aside to cool.
5. Pour the water into a small thick-bottomed pan and sprinkle over the gelatine. Set aside to 'sponge' for 10 minutes.
6. Meanwhile chop the hardboiled eggs. Flake the fish carefully, removing any bones.
7. Mix the cream and mayonnaise with the cooled sauce, the eggs and the fish. Season to taste with salt, pepper and anchovy essence.
8. Put the gelatine pan over a gentle heat until it is clear and warm. Using a large metal spoon stir the gelatine thoroughly into the fish mixture. Add the cream. Pour into the prepared soufflé dish. Cover and put in the refrigerator to set, preferably overnight.
9. To turn the mousse out, wet a plate and place over the top of the dish. Turn dish and plate over together and give a sharp jerk downwards. The mousse should come out immediately. (Wetting the plate makes it easier to shift the mousse, should it not turn out in the centre). Decorate with the cucumber.

NOTE: If the mousse is to stand for more than an hour after decorating, the cucumber slices should be degorged, i.e. salted, allowed to stand for 30 minutes, rinsed well and patted dry. If this is not done the cucumber will weep when left on the sides of the mousse.

MUSCADET

Cucumber Mousse

SERVES 4
1 large cucumber, peeled if preferred
110g/4oz full fat cream cheese
150ml/¼ pint double cream, whipped or yoghurt or soured cream
salt and freshly ground black pepper
pinch of grated nutmeg
juice of 1 lemon
15g/½oz gelatine
150ml/¼ pint chicken or vegetable stock

1. Grate the cucumber, reserving about 2.5cm/1 inch to slice for decoration. Put the grated cucumber into a sieve. Leave to drain for 15 minutes.
2. Oil a soufflé dish or mould, and stand upside down to drain off excess.
3. Beat together the cream cheese and whipped cream, yoghurt or soured cream. Mix in the grated cucumber and season with salt, pepper and nutmeg. Add the lemon juice.
4. In a small pan, soak the gelatine in the stock. When spongy, warm over a very gentle heat until clear and add to the cucumber mixture, mixing gently but thoroughly.
5. Pour into the prepared mould and chill in the refrigerator until set.
6. To turn out, invert a plate over the mould and turn plate and mould over together. Give a sharp shake to dislodge the mousse. Decorate with slices of cucumber.

NOTE I: If a velvety texture is required, blend the cucumber with the yoghurt or cream in a liquidizer.
NOTE II: This mousse does not keep well. Eat within 24 hours.

DRY WHITE

Red Pepper Bavarois with Red Pepper Salad

SERVES 8

3 red peppers, quartered and deseeded
3 small garlic, cloves, finely chopped
1 onion, finely sliced
15ml/1 tablespoon olive oil
salt and freshly ground black pepper
4 large egg yolks
290ml/1/2 pint milk
20g/3/4oz gelatine
150ml/1/4 pint double cream
150ml/1/4 pint natural low-fat yoghurt
5ml/1 teaspoon chilli sauce

To serve:
red pepper salad (see page 212)

1. Preheat the grill to its highest setting. Grill the peppers, skin side up, until they are blistered and blackened all over. Place under cold running water and remove the skins. Cut the peppers into strips.
2. Cook the peppers, garlic and onion gently in the olive oil until soft but not brown. Allow to cool and then purée in a food processor and push through a sieve. Season with salt and pepper.
3. Beat the egg yolks. Put the milk into a saucepan and heat until scalding. Pour on to the egg yolks stirring all the time. Return the mixture to the saucepan and heat gently until the custard coats the back of a wooden spoon. Do not allow it to boil. Strain into the purée.
4. Put 45ml/3 tablespoons water into a saucepan, sprinkle on the gelatine and leave it to sponge for 5 minutes. Lightly oil a charlotte mould or 20cm/9 inch cake tin. Heat the gelatine gently until clear and warm. Add it to the purée. Allow to cool and thicken.
5. Whip the cream lightly and mix it with the yoghurt and the chilli sauce.
6. Fold the cream mixture into the custard and pour into the prepared mould. Refrigerate until set.
7. Dip the mould quickly into very hot water and turn out on to a plate. Serve with the red pepper salad.

MEDIUM DRY WHITE

Avocado Pear Mousse with Prawns

SERVES 4

15g/1/2oz powdered gelatine
2 ripe avocado pears
150ml/1/4 pint mayonnaise (see page 224)
lemon juice
salt and freshly ground black pepper
5ml/1 teaspoon onion juice (optional)
150ml/1/4 pint double cream, lightly whipped
85g/3oz peeled, cooked prawns
French dressing (see page 228)

1. In a small saucepan soak the gelatine in 45ml/3 tablespoons of cold water.
2. Peel the avocado pears and mash or purée until smooth. Add the mayonnaise, lemon juice, salt and pepper and onion juice.
3. Dissolve the gelatine over a gentle heat. When warm and clear stir into the avocado mixture. Fold in the whipped cream with a large metal spoon.
4. Pour into a lightly oiled ring mould and refrigerate until set.
5. Turn out on to a round serving plate. Mix the prawns with the French dressing and pile into the centre of the mousse. Serve with brown bread and butter.

SPICY DRY WHITE

Smoked Trout Mousse

SERVES 4

2 large smoked trout
150ml/1/4 pint double cream, lightly whipped
squeeze of lemon juice
2.5ml/1/2 teaspoon horseradish cream
freshly ground black pepper
4 slices smoked salmon
buttered brown bread

1. Cut the the heads and tails off the fish. Skin the fish and remove the bones. Mince or pound the flesh and mix with the whipped cream, lemon juice, horseradish and pepper to taste.
2. Shape the mixture into a shallow mound, on a serving plate. Cover neatly with the

slices of smoked salmon.
3. Serve with brown bread and butter.

NOTE: Individual mousses can be made by covering small mounds of mousse with a slice of smoked salmon.

SPICY DRY WHITE

Cheese Soufflé

SERVES 2
40g/1¼oz butter
dry white breadcrumbs
30g/1oz flour
2.5ml/½ teaspoon made English mustard
pinch of cayenne pepper
290ml/½ pint milk
85g/3oz strong Cheddar or Gruyère cheese, grated
4 eggs, separated
salt and pepper

1. Set the oven to 200°C/400°F/gas mark 6. Melt a knob of the butter and brush out a 15cm/6 inch soufflé dish with it. Dust lightly with the breadcrumbs.
2. Melt the rest of the butter in a saucepan and stir in the flour, mustard and cayenne pepper. Cook for 45 seconds. Add the milk and cook, stirring vigorously, for 2 minutes. The mixture will get very thick and leave the sides of the pan. Take it off the heat.
3. Stir in the cheese, egg yolks, salt and pepper. Taste; the mixture should be very well seasoned.
4. Whisk the egg whites until stiff, but not dry, and mix a spoonful into the mixture. Then fold in the rest and pour into the soufflé dish, which should be about two-thirds full. Run your finger around the top of the soufflé mixture. This gives a 'top hat' appearance to the cooked soufflé.
5. Bake for 25-30 minutes and serve straight away. (Do not test to see if the soufflé is done for a least 20 minutes. Then open the oven just wide enough to get your hand in and give the soufflé a slight shove. If it wobbles alarmingly, cook a further 5 minutes.)

SPICY DRY WHITE

Courgette Soufflé

SERVES 4
melted butter
625g/1lb 6oz small dark green courgettes
salt
55g/2oz unsalted butter
45g/1½oz flour
150ml/¼ pint milk infused with a slice of onion
30g/1oz fresh Parmesan cheese, grated
30g/1oz Cheddar cheese, grated
2 egg yolks
4 egg whites

1. Preheat the oven to 180°C/350°F/gas mark 4 and brush 6 ramekin dishes with butter.
2. Trim the courgettes. Slice 450g/1lb of them very finely. Place in a colander or sieve and sprinkle with 25ml/1½ teaspoons of salt. Mix in well and allow to drain for at least an hour.
3. Cut the remaining courgettes into 6mm/¼ inch dice. Salt and drain.
4. Rinse the sliced courgettes and put in a pan with 150ml/¼ pint water. Bring to the boil and cook for 5 minutes. Liquidize until smooth.
5. Melt 45g/1½oz butter in a medium-sized saucepan, add the flour and cook over a gentle heat for about 3 minutes, stirring occasionally. Cool slightly.
6. Gradually add the flavoured milk and courgette purée to the flour and butter. Bring up to the boil and cook gently for about 15 minutes, stirring occasionally. Add more water to the sauce if it gets too thick. Remove from the heat.
7. Add the grated cheeses, stir well, allow to cool slightly and then beat in the egg yolks.
8. Melt the remaining butter in a small pan and cook the rinsed, drained and diced courgettes until slightly brown and crisp.
9. Season the sauce and whisk the egg whites until medium peaks are formed. Fold them carefully into the courgette sauce.
10. Half fill each ramekin with the soufflé mixture. Divide the diced courgettes between the ramekins and cover with the remaining mixture.
11. Place the ramekins in a roasting tin half filled with boiling water and put into the top of the oven.
12. Bake for 25-30 minutes until well risen and brown on the top. Serve immediately.

Twice-baked Cheese Soufflé

These little soufflés are wonderfully rich. They can be cooked a few hours before dinner and then re-baked at the last minute.

SERVES 6
290ml/1/2 pint milk
slice of onion
pinch of nutmeg
45g/1 1/2oz butter
45g/1 1/2oz flour
pinch of dry English mustard
110g/4oz strong Cheddar, grated
3 eggs, separated
salt and pepper
190ml/1/3 pint single cream

1. Preheat the oven to 180°C/350°F/gas mark 4. Heat the milk slowly with the onion and nutmeg. Remove the onion.
2. Melt the butter and stir in the flour. Gradually add the milk, off the heat, whisking until smooth.
3. Return to the heat and stir until the sauce boils and thickens. Stop cooking and add the mustard, three-quarters of the cheese and finally the egg yolks. Add salt and pepper.
4. Generously butter 6 teacups or ramekins.
5. Whisk the egg whites until stiff, and fold into the cheese mixture. Spoon into the cups to fill two-thirds full. Stand the cups in a roasting tin of boiling water and bake at 180°C/350°F/gas mark 4 for 15 minutes or until the mixture is set. Allow to sink and cool.
6. Run a knife round the soufflés to loosen them. Turn them out on to your hand, giving the cups a sharp jerk. Put them, upside down, on a serving dish.
7. Twenty minutes before serving, sprinkle the remaining cheese on top. Season the cream with salt and pepper and pour all over the soufflés, coating them completely. Put the dish into a hot oven, 220°C/425°F/gas mark 7, for 10 minutes or until the soufflé tops are pale gold. Serve fast before they sink.

SPICY DRY WHITE

Cauliflower and Stilton Pudding

SERVES 4
1 medium cauliflower
150ml/1/4 pint milk
30g/1oz butter
30g/1oz flour
salt and pepper
nutmeg
55g/2oz Stilton, crumbled
4 eggs
15ml/1 tablespoon grated Cheddar cheese
15ml/1 tablespoon dried breadcrumbs

1. Cut the cauliflower into florets and cook them in a pan of boiling salted water until tender. Drain well and liquidize or sieve to a pulp with the milk.
2. Melt the butter, stir in the flour and cook, stirring, for 1 minute. Pour in the cauliflower purée. Stir until the sauce is boiling and has thickened. Taste and season very well.
3. Butter a 15cm/6 inch soufflé dish and set the oven to 180°C/350°F/gas mark 4.
4. Stir in the Stilton off the heat, returning the pan to the heat only if it does not melt, but being careful not to boil the mixture. Allow to cool slightly.
5. Separate the eggs and beat the yolks into the cauliflower mixture.
6. Whisk the whites until stiff but not dry and fold into the mixture. Pour into the buttered soufflé dish.
7. Sprinkle with cheese and crumbs. Bake in a bain-marie for 20-25 minutes or until well risen, brown on top and fairly steady when given a slight shake. If it wobbles alarmingly, give it another 5 minutes.

MEDIUM DRY WHITE

Haddock and Spinach Soufflé

This is more of a 'pudding' than a soufflé.

SERVES 4
melted butter, for greasing
30ml/2 tablespoons fresh white breadcrumbs
170g/6oz smoked haddock fillet
290ml/½ pint milk
1 bay leaf
½ small onion
6 peppercorns
450g/1lb fresh spinach
30g/1oz butter
30g/1oz flour
salt and freshly ground black pepper
pinch of mustard powder
4 large eggs, separated

1. Preheat the oven to 200°C/400°F/gas mark 6 and place a baking tray on the middle shelf. Brush a 1.2 litre/2 pint soufflé dish with the melted butter and coat with the breadcrumbs.
2. Lay the smoked haddock in a shallow ovenproof dish and pour on half the milk. Add the bay leaf, onion and peppercorns, cover lightly with a lid or foil and bake in the oven for 20-30 minutes, or until the fish is cooked.
3. Strain the milk through a sieve and reserve. Mash the haddock finely with the back of a fork, then set it aside.
4. Rinse and shake excess water from the spinach and put it into a large non-aluminium pan. Set it over a low heat and cook gently for 3-4 minutes or until soft. Drain very well, cool a little, then chop finely.
5. Melt the butter, stir in the flour and cook for 30 seconds. Take the pan from the heat and gradually add the reserved and the remaining milk. Return the pan to the heat and bring the sauce to the boil. Simmer it for 1 minute and then remove it from the heat, season and add the mustard powder.
6 Allow the sauce to cool slightly and then beat in the egg yolks. Stir in the mashed haddock and spinach.
7. Whisk the egg whites until they are stiff. Fold 2 large spoonfuls into the sauce to slacken it, then gently fold in the remaining egg whites. Spoon the mixture into the prepared soufflé dish, place on the heated baking tray and cook for 25 minutes or until well risen and rich brown in colour. Serve immediately.

VERY DRY WHITE

Gruyère Spoonbread with Vegetables and Butter Sauce

This recipe has been adapted from a recipe cooked at the school by a Mouton Cadet competition entrant.

Spoonbread is a cornmeal-based dish similar to a soufflé but with a denser texture; it is less fragile and temperamental than a soufflé. It is an old American dish based on native American Indian cooking. Other green vegetables can be substituted if broccoli and courgettes are not to hand.

SERVES 6
For the Gruyère spoonbread:
570ml/1 pint milk
150ml/¼ pint double cream
125g/4½oz fine white or yellow cornmeal
70g/2½oz butter
5ml/1 teaspoon salt
2.5ml/½ teaspoon nutmeg
5ml/1 teaspoon paprika
170g/6oz Gruyère cheese, grated
4 eggs, separated

For the vegetables:
110g/4oz dried flageolet beans
450g/1lb broccoli
½ small radicchio lettuce
3 small courgettes, cut into batons
70g/2½oz chopped walnuts
butter for sautéing

For the butter sauce:
70g/2½oz shallots, finely chopped
150ml/¼ pint wine vinegar or white wine
salt and freshly ground black pepper to taste
285g/10oz butter

For the salad:
1 large head of frisée
juice of 1 lemon
150ml/1/4 pint olive oil

NOTE: Other green vegetables can be used – spinach, asparagus, peas, etc. – what's important is that they should be fresh.

1. Boil the dried flageolets for 10 minutes then simmer for one hour or until tender. Drain and set aside. Boil the broccoli until 'al dente'. Cut into bite-sized pieces.
2 For the spoonbread, bring the milk and cream to the boil and reduce the heat. Gradually add cornmeal, stirring constantly until thick, 3-5 minutes.
3. Remove from the heat and stir in the butter, salt, nutmeg, paprika, cheese and egg yolks. The batter can be prepared in advance up to this point, and stored in the refrigerator until 45 minutes before serving.
4. Whisk the egg whites until stiff but not dry, and fold them into the cornmeal mixture. Pour gently into a well-buttered 1.5 litre/3 pint ring mould, and bake at 175°C/350°F/gas mark 4 for 30-40 minutes. The top should be crusty and the centre soft.
5. Sauté the walnuts in butter for 2 minutes over medium heat. Add the courgettes and sauté for a further minute. Pull off approximately half the leaves of the radicchio and tear into smaller bits. Add to the pan, along with the broccoli and flageolet beans, and sauté until the radicchio leaves turn dark and lose their bitternesss – about 5 minutes.
6. For the butter sauce cook the shallots and vinegar over high heat until reduced by about half. Turn down the heat and add the butter slowly, in little pieces, whisking constantly until creamy, about 10 minutes.
7. Unmould the spoonbread as soon as it comes out of the oven on to a platter, and gently heap the vegetables into the centre and around the edges of the platter. Pour the butter sauce over the vegetables. Serve with the remaining frisée dressed with lemon juice and olive oil.

DRY WHITE

Pâtés and Terrines

Sardine and Lemon Pâté

SERVES 6-8
110g/4oz butter
225g/8oz tinned sardines
110g/4oz cream cheese
2.5ml/1/2 teaspoon French mustard
juice of 1/2 lemon
salt and freshly ground black pepper
6 black olives, stoned

1. Beat the butter until soft and creamy.
2. Add the sardines with their oil and beat.
3. Add the cream cheese, mustard, lemon, salt and plenty of pepper and mix well. (Alternatively all the above ingredients can be combined in a blender.)
4. Pile on to a dish and garnish with black olives. Serve with hot toast.

MUSCADET

Smoked Trout Pâté

This recipe is a low-fat version of smoked trout mousse (page 132). It is also delicious made with smoked salmon.

SERVES 4
2 smoked trout
170g/6oz low-fat cottage cheese, well drained
5ml/1 teaspoon grated horseradish
black pepper
lemon juice

1. Skin and bone the trout.
2. If you have a food processor blend all the ingredients together. If not, mince the trout or chop very finely. Sieve the cottage cheese and beat in the trout. Add the horseradish and the black pepper and lemon juice to taste.
3. Pile into a dish and refrigerate for 3 hours.

SPICY DRY WHITE

Kipper Pâté

SERVES 4
340g/12oz kipper fillets
85g/3oz unsalted butter, softened
85g/3oz cream cheese
freshly ground black pepper
lemon juice
4 black olives, or 4 slices lemon

1. Skin and mince the kipper fillets.
2. Beat the butter until very creamy (but do not melt it) and beat in the cream cheese. Add the kippers and beat well.
3. Beat until completely incorporated.
4. Season well with black pepper and lemon juice.
5. Pile into a dish and garnish with slivers of black olive or slices of lemon.

SPICY DRY WHITE

Potted Turkey

SERVES 4
225g/8oz smoked turkey
110g/4oz butter, clarified and cooled (see below)
pepper

1. Mince the turkey and pound it with three-quarters of the butter. Season with pepper.
2. Press the mixture tightly into small pots, making sure that there are no air spaces.
3. Melt the remaining butter, allow to cool until on the point of setting and pour over the pots. Leave to set. Store in a cool place. It will keep for 2 weeks or more in a refrigerator.

NOTE: To clarify butter, heat until foaming, then strain through a piece of muslin.

ROSE/LIGHT RED

Chicken Liver Pâté I

SERVES 6
225g/8oz butter
1 large onion, very finely chopped
1 large garlic clove, crushed
450g/1lb chicken livers or 225g/8oz duck livers and 225g/8oz chicken livers
salt and freshly ground black pepper
85g/3oz clarified butter (if the pâté is to be stored)

1. Melt half the butter in a large thick frying pan and gently fry the onion until soft and transparent.
2. Add the garlic and continue cooking for a further minute.
3. Discard any discoloured pieces of liver as they will be bitter. Rinse under water.
4. Add the livers to the pan and cook, turning to brown them lightly on all sides, for 8 minutes or so, when they should be firm and cooked.
5. Add salt and plenty of pepper.
6. Mince the mixture or liquidize it in an electric blender with the rest of the butter. Put it into an earthenware dish or pot.
7. If the pâté is to be kept for more than 3 days cover the top with a layer of clarified butter.

NOTE: If making large quantities of chicken liver pâté simply bake all the ingredients together under foil or a lid at 190°C/375°F/gas mark 5 for 40 minutes. Cool for 15 minutes and then liquidize or process.

CLARET

Chicken Liver Pâté II

This is a low-fat version of the classic chicken liver pâté.

SERVES 4
170g/6oz cleaned chicken livers
290ml/½ pint chicken stock
1 small onion, finely chopped
1 garlic clove, crushed
1 sprig fresh thyme
225g/8oz cottage cheese
15ml/1 tablespoon brandy
freshly ground black pepper
5ml/1 teaspoon fresh thyme leaves

1. Put the livers, stock, onion, garlic and thyme together in a small pan. Bring gradually up to the boil. Cover and simmer slowly for 20 minutes – the water should barely move. Allow to cool. Tip into a sieve. Remove the thyme.
2. Liquidize the contents of the sieve, with the cottage cheese, brandy, black pepper and fresh thyme leaves. Pour into a small pot, spread flat and leave to chill and harden in the refrigerator.

MEDIUM RED

Smooth Duck Pâté

SERVES 6
1 x 2.3kg/5lb duck
1 bay leaf
1 carrot, sliced
1 onion, peeled and sliced
blade of mace
10 peppercorns
1 stick celery, sliced
15ml/1 tablespoon fresh sage, chopped
salt and freshly ground black pepper
60-85g/2½-3oz butter, softened
grated rind and juice of 1 orange
85g/3oz clarified butter

1. Put the duck into a saucepan with the bay leaf, carrot, onion, mace, peppercorns and celery and cover with water. Bring to the boil and poach for 1½-2 hours until the duck is tender, when the legs will feel loose and wobbly. Allow to cool in the liquid.
2. Remove the duck from the stock. Strain the stock and reserve. Flesh the duck, discarding the skin and bones. Cut up the flesh and place in a food processor with the sage, salt and pepper. Whizz until smooth. Add the butter, rind and juice of the orange and 75ml/5 tablespoons of the reserved stock. Taste and add more seasoning if required.
3. Spread the pâté flat in a serving dish, cover and leave to cool. When completely cold, melt the clarified butter and pour it over the top of the pâté.

RED BURGUNDY

Taramasalata

SERVES 6
1 slice of white bread, crusts removed
110g/4oz bottled smoked cod roe, or 225g/8oz fresh smoked soft roe
1 large garlic clove, crushed
about 150ml/$^1/_4$ pint each salad oil and olive oil
freshly ground black pepper
juice of $^1/_2$ lemon

1. Hold the bread slice under the tap to wet it. Squeeze dry and put it in a bowl with the cod roe and the garlic (if fresh roe is used the skin should be discarded first). With a wooden spoon or electric whisk, beat very well.
2. Now add the oils very slowly, almost drop by drop (as with mayonnaise), beating all the time. The idea is to form a smooth emulsion, and adding the oil too fast will result in a rather oily, curdled mixture.
3. The amount of oil added is a matter of personal taste: the more you add, the paler and creamier the mixture becomes and the more delicate the flavour. Stop when you think the right balance is achieved.
4. Add black pepper and lemon juice to taste. If it seems too thick or bitter add a little hot water.

NOTE: Taramasalata can be served as a spread for cocktail snacks, or with toast or fresh rolls, but it is best served as a first course with hot Greek bread (pitta).
NOTE II: If it begins to separate, add a little boiling water.

RETSINA OR DRY WHITE

Hummus

This is a spicy hummus and has been adapted from a recipe by one of Leith's most popular guest lecturers, Claudia Roden.

SERVES 4
225g/8oz chickpeas
salt and freshly ground black pepper
10ml/2 teaspoons ground cumin
2 cloves garlic, crushed
juice of 1 lemon
60ml/4 tablespoons olive oil
pinch of cayenne pepper
Greek parsley to garnish

1. Soak the chickpeas overnight in cold water.
2. Drain and cook slowly in clean water for 1-1$^1/_2$ hours. Add the salt towards the end of cooking. Drain and reserve the cooking liquor.
3. Cool for a few minutes and tip into a food processor. Whizz and add the remaining ingredients. Add enough of the cooking liquor to produce a soft cream.
4. Serve on a flat plate garnished with the Greek parsley. Hand hot pitta bread separately.

RETSINA OR DRY WHITE

Tuna Fish Pâté

SERVES 8
225g/8oz boned tuna fish
170g/6oz butter, softened
5ml/1 teaspoon anchovy essence
a little lemon juice
salt and freshly ground black pepper
nasturtium leaves or thin slices cucumber

1. Mash the tuna fish. Add the butter, mixing very well. Season with anchovy, lemon juice, salt and pepper.
2. Pile into a soufflé dish, spread it flat and garnish with nasturtium leaves or cucumber.

NOTE: Young nasturtium leaves look very pretty as a garnish and are delicious and peppery to eat. This pâté is good served with hot buttered toast.

MUSCADET

Stilton and Walnut Pâté

I was given this recipe by Mrs Levis at the Sign of the Angel in Lacock.

SERVES 6
340g/12oz Stilton
450g/1lb Philadelphia cheese
110g/4oz unsalted butter, melted
85g/3oz walnuts
1 glass port
15ml/1 tablespoon chopped chives
salt and freshly ground black pepper

1. Grate or crumble the Stilton cheese. Beat it with the cream cheese. Add the melted butter. Reserve 6 walnuts, chop the rest and add to the pâté.
2. Add the port and chives and season to taste. Pile into a nonstick loaf tin. Cover and refrigerate overnight.
3. Turn out and decorate with the reserved walnuts.

GERMAN WHITE

Guacamole

SERVES 4
2 ripe avocado pears
5ml/1 teaspoon onion juice
juice of $^1/_2$ lemon
10ml/2 teaspoons tomato chutney
10ml/2 teaspoons olive oil
2.5ml/$^1/_2$ teaspoon ground coriander
salt and freshly ground black pepper
1 garlic clove, crushed
Tabasco
hot buttered toast

1. Peel the avocado pears and mash them with a fork.
2. Season with the onion juice, lemon juice, tomato chutney, oil, coriander, salt, pepper, garlic and Tabasco.
3. Serve with toast.

Aubergine Caviar

SERVES 8
4 medium aubergines
60ml/4 tablespoons good quality olive oil
4 garlic cloves
30ml/2 tablespoons chopped fresh parsley
salt and freshly ground black pepper
lemon juice to taste

1. Set the oven to 190°C/375°F/gas mark 5.
2. Brush the aubergines with a little oil and bake them until soft (40-60 minutes). After 20 minutes add the whole garlic cloves.
3. Allow the aubergines and garlic to cool.
4. Peel the aubergines, put the flesh into a clean cloth and squeeze dry to extract all the bitter juices.
5. Skin the garlic and put into a food processor with the aubergine flesh, parsley, salt and pepper. Purée until smooth.
6. Gradually beat in the remaining olive oil and when the mixture is stiff stir in the lemon juice and season to taste.
7. Chill in the refrigerator for 2 hours before serving.

Harlequin Omelette

This recipe has been adapted from Roger Vergé's *Cuisine of the Sun.*

SERVES 4-6
75ml/5 tablespoons olive oil
400g/14oz very ripe tomatoes, peeled, deseeded and diced
a pinch of thyme flowers
salt and pepper
500g/1lb 2oz fresh spinach, well washed
2 garlic cloves, peeled
9 eggs
75g/2$^1/_2$oz Gruyère cheese, grated
120ml/8 tablespoons whipping cream
nutmeg

1. Preheat the oven to 180°C/350°F/gas mark 4.
2. Heat 30ml/2 tablespoons olive oil in a medium-sized saucepan. Add the tomato together with the thyme and a pinch of salt and allow to cook until the moisture from the

tomato has evaporated completely.

3. Put 45ml/3 tablespoons olive oil into a larger saucepan and add the spinach, the garlic and a pinch of salt. Stir with a wooden spoon and cook until the moisture has completely evaporated.

4. When the tomatoes and spinach are cooked put them on 2 separate plates, remove the garlic from the spinach, chop finely and allow to cool.

5. Get out 3 bowls and break 3 eggs into each. Add the spinach, 3 tablespoons cream, a grating of nutmeg and salt and pepper to the eggs in the first bowl and whisk everything together. Add the tomatoes, 2 tablespoons cream and salt and pepper to the eggs in the second bowl and whisk. Add the grated Gruyère, 3 tablespoons cream and salt and pepper to the eggs in the third bowl and whisk.

6. Lightly oil the inside of a terrine, and pour in the tomato mixture. Stand the dish in a bain-marie half filled with hot water and cook in the preheated oven for 30 minutes.

7. Very gently, pour in the cheese mixture and return to the oven for a further 10 minutes. Finally pour in the spinach mixture and cook for 20 minutes more.

8. When the omelette is cooked, let it rest for 10-15 minutes in a warm place before turning it out on to a dish. Serve warm, cutting it into slices or wedges according to the shape of the dish it was cooked in.

NOTE I: This omelette can also be served cold, as a first course, with a little extra virgin olive oil sprinkled on each slice.

NOTE II : Cooking times for each 'omelette' can vary so check that the tomato is just set before adding the cheese and that the cheese is just set before adding the spinach.

DRY WHITE

Terrine de Ratatouille Niçoise

SERVES 10-12

20 large spinach leaves, blanched and refreshed
salt and pepper
2 red peppers
2 yellow peppers
2 green peppers
2 aubergines
1 bulb fennel
3 medium courgettes
olive oil

For the mousse:
olive oil
1/2 onion, roughly chopped
2 cloves of new season garlic, crushed
3 red peppers, chopped
2 tomatoes, chopped
2 tablespoons tomato purée
12 basil leaves
a sprig of thyme
15ml/1 tablespoon sugar
150ml/1/4 pint dry white wine
290ml/1/2 pint water
10 leaves gelatine, soaked in cold water

For the basil sauce:
25 fresh basil leaves
150ml/1/4 pint mayonnaise
150ml/1/4 pint single cream
lemon juice to taste
salt and pepper

1. Line a 900g/2lb terrine mould first with cling film, then line it with the spinach leaves, overlapping each other neatly without any gaps. Season lightly.

2. Prepare the vegetables as follows. Peppers: cook in olive oil in the oven at 220°C/425°F/gas mark 7 for 20-25 minutes. Cool, then remove the skins and seeds. Aubergines: cut into 4 lengthways. Cook in olive oil in the oven at 220°C/425°F/gas mark 7 for 20 minutes. Fennel: peel and separate the layers and blanch in boiling water for 5-8 minutes. Refresh in iced water and dry. Courgettes: cut into 4 lengthways and shape neatly into pencil thickness. Blanch and refresh, then dry.

3. Prepare the mousse: heat a little oil in a pan, add the onion, garlic, peppers, tomatoes and tomato purée. Season with herbs and sugar, and cook for 4-5 minutes.

4. Add the white wine and cook until reduced by half. Add the water and cook gently on the edge of the stove until the vegetables are well cooked, about 15-20 minutes.

5. When cooked, add the soaked gelatine,

remove the pan from the heat and allow to cool.
6. Purée the mixture in a liquidizer, then pass the purée through a fine sieve. Allow to cool completely and adjust the seasoning.
7. Prepare the terrine: pour 30ml/2 tablespoons mousse into the bottom of the spinach-lined mould, cut the yellow peppers to size and cover the terrine from end to end. Season as you go.
8. Pour another 2 tablespoons of mousse on top, then add the aubergine, skin side down first to make a good colour contrast, then another 2 tablespoons of mousse followed by the courgettes. Repeat the process, alternating layers of mousse and vegetable in the following sequence: red pepper, fennel, green pepper, aubergine, yellow pepper. Finish with a layer of mousse.
9. Fold over the spinach leaves carefully to seal the terrine, then cover with cling film. Press the terrine with a weight for 8-24 hours in the refrigerator.
10. Prepare the basil sauce: place all the ingredients in a liquidizer and blend well. Adjust seasoning and consistency.
11. Pour a little sauce on to a plate, cut a slice of terrine and place it on the sauce. Serve chilled.

ROSE/DRY WHITE

Plaice and Spinach Terrine

This is a very low-fat terrine

SERVES 4
900g/2lb fresh spinach
1 large or 2 small plaice, skinned and filleted
salt and freshly ground black pepper
a bunch of tarragon, chopped
45ml/3 tablespoons water

To serve::
carrot and cardamom sauce

1. Preheat the oven to 350°F/180°C/gas mark 4.
2. Wash the spinach well and remove the stalks. Put it into a saucepan, cover the pan and cook for 4 minutes, shaking the pan regularly. Remove 6 large leaves. Refresh them under cold running water and leave to drain on absorbent paper. Drain the remaining spinach well, pressing out all the water. Tip it on to a board and chop it roughly.
3. Use the reserved spinach leaves to line a 225g/8oz nonstick loaf tin. Remember that the inside of the leaves should face the inside of the tin.
4. Layer the chopped spinach and plaice fillets in the tin. Season with salt, pepper and tarragon as you go. Finish with a layer of spinach.
5. Fold the whole spinach leaves over the chopped spinach.
6. Pour in the water. Cover the tin with wet greaseproof paper and place it in a bain-marie. Bake for 30 minutes. Leave the terrine to cool in the tin for a further 30 minutes.
7. Drain off the excess liquid. Leave the terrine to become completely cold. Turn it on to a plate.
8. Serve the terrine with carrot and cardamom sauce.

FULL DRY WHITE

Chicken and Spinach Terrine

SERVES 4
2 chicken breasts, skinned and boned
900g/2lb fresh spinach, cooked and chopped
1 bunch tarragon, chopped
white stock

1. Heat the oven to 180°C/350°F/gas mark 4.
2. Slice the chicken breasts horizontally.
3. Layer up the spinach, tarragon and chicken in a small nonstick loaf tin. Pour in a little chicken stock.
3. Place the loaf tin in a roasting tin of hot water, cover with damp greaseproof paper and bake for 1 hour. Allow to cool for 30 minutes. Drain very well.
4. To turn out, invert a serving dish over the loaf tin and then turn both the dish and the tin over together. Give both a sharp shake and remove the tin.

LIGHT RED

Pork and Liver Terrine

Make this terrine the day before serving.

SERVES 6
110g/4oz pigs liver, minced
225g/8oz rindless belly of pork, minced
225g/8oz lean veal, minced
2 shallots, finely chopped
1 garlic clove, crushed
10ml/2 teaspoons brandy
pinch of allspice
salt and freshly ground black pepper
225g/8oz streaky rindless bacon, in thin rashers
110g/4oz chicken livers, cleaned
2 bay leaves

1. Set the oven to 170°C/325°F/gas mark 3.
2. Mix together the pigs liver, belly pork, veal, shallots, garlic, brandy and allspice. Season with salt and pepper.
3. Line a medium-sized terrine or loaf tin with the bacon.
4. Tip in half the prepared mixture and spread it flat.
5. Trim any discoloured parts from the chicken livers, then place in an even layer over the mixture and top up with the other half of the mixture. Lay the bay leaves on the surface.
6. Cover with a piece of greased greaseproof paper. Stand in a roasting tin of hot water (bain-marie) and bake for 1½-2 hours. The mixture should feel fairly firm to the touch.
7. Remove from the roasting pan and place a weight on the terrine (a can of fruit in a second terrine will do) and leave overnight to cool and harden. Then refrigerate until needed, and turn out on to a plate to serve.

NOTE: Foil may be used to cover the baking terrine, but it must be well greased, or lined with a butter wrapper or other paper. If this is not done the foil will corrode into small holes while baking, and the top of the terrine will be covered in metallic spots.

CLARET

Provençal Lamb Terrine

SERVES 8
12 large spinach leaves
400g/14oz lamb fillet
salt and pepper
15ml/1 tablespoon chopped fresh rosemary
15ml/1 tablespoon chopped fresh thyme
15ml/1 tablespoon oil
1 large aubergine
10ml/2 teaspoons salt
90ml/6 tablespoons olive oil
1 large red pepper
1 large yellow pepper
6 medium courgettes
1 large fennel bulb
30g/1oz butter
1 onion, finely chopped
4 garlic cloves, crushed
1 bay leaf
800g/28 oz tin plum tomatoes, liquidized and sieved
1 teaspoon tomato purée
8 basil leaves, torn
30g/1oz gelatine
85ml/3fl oz water
6 tinned artichoke hearts, cut in half
3 ripe tomatoes peeled, seeded and quartered
15ml/1 tablespoon extra chopped herbs

To serve:
450g/1lb cherry tomatoes
45g/1½oz pinenuts, toasted
basil leaves
thyme leaves
French dressing (see page 228)

1. Wash the spinach and blanch in boiling water for a few seconds. Refresh with cold water and pat dry. Remove the tough stalks.
2. Trim any fat off the lamb and cut into 1cm/½inch strips. Season with salt, pepper, rosemary and thyme.
3. Heat 15ml/1 tablespoon oil in a frying pan and quickly fry the lamb so that the strips are brown on the outside but pink in the middle. This will take about 2 minutes.
4. Cut the aubergine in half lengthways and cut each half again lengthways into 4 or 5 equal pieces. Salt lightly and leave to degorge for 30

minutes. Heat the olive oil in a frying pan. Rinse and dry the aubergine and cook each piece until golden brown and soft. Drain on kitchen paper.
5. Cut the peppers in half. Remove the seeds and core and cut into quarters. Place under a hot grill until the skins are blackened and scorched. Remove the skins.
6. Trim the courgettes and cut in half lengthways. Pull the fennel bulb apart. Blanch both in boiling water and then refresh under cold running water.
7. Melt the butter in a saucepan and sweat the onion over a low heat until soft. Add the garlic, bay leaf, tomatoes and tomato purée. Simmer for 10 minutes and add the basil. Remove the bay leaf.
8. Dissolve the gelatine in the water and add to the tomato sauce.
9. Line a 2 litre/3½ pint terrine or loaf tin with the spinach leaves, leaving some overhanging the edge. Spread a layer of tomato sauce over the spinach and layer the vegetables and lamb in the following order, coating each layer with a film of sauce to bind: aubergine, yellow pepper, red pepper, courgettes, fennel, artichokes, lamb fillets and tomatoes. Season carefully between the layers with salt, pepper and fresh herbs.
10. Fold over the spinach, tap firmly to settle the layers. Weight the top and refrigerate overnight to set.
11. Serve at room temperature, garnished with the cherry tomato and pinenut salad.

COTES DU RHONE

Chicken Terrine

SERVES 4
butter for greasing
2 chicken breasts
2 eggs, beaten
salt and ground white pepper
grated zest of 1 orange
60ml/4 tablespoons double cream
30g/1oz fresh white breadcrumbs

For the garnish:
bitter leaves tossed in French dressing

To serve:
tomato vinaigrette (see page 228)

1. Heat the oven to 170°C/325°F/gas mark 3. Butter a 450g/1lb loaf tin. Finely mince the chicken breasts. Place in a large mixing bowl and stir in the eggs, seasoning, orange rind, double cream and breadcrumbs.
2. Place the loaf tin in a roasting tin. Butter 2 strips of greaseproof paper. Use 1 to line the loaf tin. Spoon the mixture into the loaf tin and cover with the other strip of greaseproof paper, buttered side down. Put water in the roasting tin to come halfway up the sides of the loaf tin. Cook for 1 hour until firm.
3. When the terrine is cooked, carefully unmould it and cut it into slices using a sharp knife. Serve it hot, or allow to cool. Garnish with the bitter leaves.
4. Hand the tomato vinaigrette separately.

DRY WHITE/ROSE

Goose Liver Terrine

This traditional terrine has to be made from the liver of a fattened goose. The recipe has been adapted from *Pâtés and Terrines*, published by Hamlyn. More seasoning, such as allspice, can be added if required. Do not use too much alcohol, as it can give the liver an overpowering flavour.

SERVES 12
1 fattened goose liver weighing about 790g/1¾lb
5ml/1 teaspoon salt
freshly ground white pepper
225ml/8fl oz port
dash of brandy or Armagnac

Optional extravagant extra:
110g/4oz cooked black truffles

1. Break up the goose liver into several pieces and where necessary remove any skin or blood vessels.
2. Knead the trimmed liver until soft. Season with salt and white pepper and a little allspice if required.
3. Put the liver into a bowl and add the port and brandy or Armagnac. Work the liver lightly to incorporate the alcohol, cover and leave to marinate in the fridge overnight.

4. Set the oven to 140°C/275°F/gas mark 1.
5. Arrange the pieces of marinated liver in a 1 litre/1¾ pint terrine. Arrange the pieces individually and press them down lightly so that there are no pockets of air. If you are using the truffles, place them in a row in the centre of the terrine so they come out in the centre of each slice.
6. Flatten the top of the terrine, using your hands to press the pieces down quite firmly but gently. Cover with a lid. If you have no lid cover first with a piece of damp greaseproof paper and then tin foil. Tin foil on its own sometimes corrodes.
7. Place in a bain-marie of warm water (80°C/176°F) in the preheated oven and bake for 40 minutes. The temperature of the bain-marie is critical and should be checked once or twice during the cooking of the terrine.
8. Leave to stand for at least a day before turning out.
9. Remove any fat, turn out and serve in slices.

SPICY DRY WHITE

Venison Terrine and Cumberland Sauce

SERVES 8
225g/8oz back pork fat
225g/8oz lean pork
225g/8oz lean venison
1 onion, finely chopped
1 garlic clove, crushed
8 juniper berries, crushed
2.5ml/½ teaspoon ground mace
2.5ml/½ teaspoon ground allspice
60ml/4 tablespoons red wine
30ml/2 tablespoons brandy
salt and freshly ground black pepper
2 eggs
285g/10oz streaky bacon, cut very thin and stretched with a knife

To serve:
Cumberland sauce (see page 232)

1. Cut half the pork fat into small dice. Mince the pork, remaining fat and venison and mix with the onion, garlic, cubed fat, crushed juniper berries, spices, wine, brandy, seasoning and eggs. Beat very well, check for seasoning.
2. Line 1 litre/1¾ pint terrine with streaky bacon and fill with mixture. Cover with the remaining bacon slices.
3. Leave in a cool place for at least 3 hours for the flavour to develop – the longer the better.
4. Set the oven to 170°C/325°F/gas mark 3.
5. Put the covered terrine in a bain-marie (a roasting tin half filled with boiling water). Cook in the preheated oven for 1½-2 hours. It is cooked when the terrine shrinks away from the side of the dish and no pink juices come out when pierced with a skewer.
6. Keep the terrine in the refrigerator for a couple of days to mature the flavour.
7. Serve alone or with Cumberland sauce.

FULL RED

Fruit First Courses

Pears with Stilton and Poppy Seed Dressing

SERVES 4

55g/2oz Stilton cheese
55g/2oz cream cheese
4 ripe dessert pears, washed but not peeled
1 small bunch of watercress, washed

For the dressing:
45ml/3 tablespoons oil
15ml/1 tablespoon lemon juice
10ml/2 teaspoons poppy seeds, toasted
salt and freshly ground black pepper

1. Put all the dressing ingredients together in a screw-top jar and shake until well emulsified. Taste and add more seasoning if necessary.
2. Beat together the Stilton and cream cheese until soft. Spoon into a forcing bag fitted with a plain large nozzle.
3. With an apple corer, remove the centre of the pears. Pipe in the cheese mixture. Place in the refrigerator until ready to serve (at least 2 hours).
4. Slice each pear across into thin round slices. Spoon over the poppy seed dressing and garnish with watercress.

NOTE: To toast the poppy seeds, place in a heavy saucepan over a moderate heat for a couple of minutes.

SPICY DRY WHITE

Pineapple with Tarragon Sabayon

SERVES 4

1 fresh pineapple
caster sugar

For the dressing:
1 egg
45ml/3 tablespoons tarragon vinegar
30ml/2 tablespoons caster sugar
pinch of salt
30ml/2 tablespoons lightly whipped cream

1. Slice the pineapple in half lengthways, cutting through the fruit and the leaves. Using a grapefruit knife, cut out the flesh in one piece from each pineapple half. Remove the woody core and discard it. Slice the flesh and return it upside down to the pineapple shell (i.e. rounded side up). Sprinkle with sugar and leave it to stand while preparing the dressing.
2. Put the egg into a bowl with the vinegar and sugar and a pinch of salt. Stand the bowl over a pan of simmering water and stir slowly until lightly thickened, then whisk continuously until thick and creamy. Allow to cool.
3. Stir in the cream and spoon the dressing over the pineapple.

Grape and Grapefruit Cocktail

SERVES 4

2 grapefruit
110g/4oz white grapes
5ml/1 teaspoon sugar
15ml/1 tablespoon oil
15ml/1 tablespoon chopped fresh mint
salt and freshly ground black pepper
30g/1oz flaked almonds, browned

1. Halve the grapefruit and, using a grapefruit knife, remove all the segments, leaving the membranes attached to the shell. Put the segments, with the juice, in a bowl.
2. Dip the grapes for 4 seconds in boiling water and peel them. Cut them in half lengthways and discard the pips. Add the grapes to the grapefruit with the sugar, oil, mint, salt and pepper. Leave for at least 30 minutes.
3. Pull the membrane from the grapefruit shells and fill the shells with mixture.
4. Scatter the almonds on top. Serve with brown bread and butter.

NOTE : If the grapes are soft-skinned and nice looking do not bother to peel them.

Melon and Prawn Cocktail

SERVES 6

1 small honeydew melon
450g/1lb cooked peeled prawns, plus 6 unpeeled prawns for garnish
150ml/1/4 pint thick mayonnaise
30ml/2 tablespoons double cream
15ml/1 tablespoon tomato ketchup
1 drop Tabasco, or a pinch of cayenne
5ml/1 teaspoon lemon juice
a few tarragon leaves, finely chopped
fresh chervil

1. Cut the melon into 6. Remove the skin and cut the flesh so that it can be attractively arranged on 6 small plates.
2. Mix together the mayonnaise, cream, ketchup, Tabasco, lemon juice and chopped tarragon. Add the peeled prawns.
3. Taste, and add salt and pepper if necessary.
4. Arrange the prawns beside the melon.
5. Remove the legs and roe (if any) from the whole prawns, and arrange on top of the prawn mayonnaise. Sprinkle with the chervil.

MUSCADET

Flans, Tarts and Yeast-Based First Courses

Quiche Lorraine

SERVES 2
rich shortcrust pastry made with 110g/4oz flour (see page 525)

For the filling:
1/2 small onion, finely chopped
55g/2oz bacon, diced
7.5g/1/4oz butter
75ml/5 tablespoons milk
75ml/5 tablespoons single cream
1 egg
1 egg yolk
30g/1oz strong Cheddar or Gruyère, grated
salt and pepper

1. Roll out the pastry and line a flan ring about 15cm/6 inches in diameter. Leave in the fridge for about 45 minutes to relax – this prevents shrinkage during cooking.
2. Set the oven to 190°C/375°F/gas mark 5. Bake the pastry case blind (see below).
3. Fry the onion and bacon gently in the butter. When cooked but not coloured, drain well.
4. Mix together the milk, cream and eggs. Add the onion, bacon and half the cheese. Season with salt and pepper (the bacon and cheese are both salty, so be careful not to overseason).
5. Turn down the oven to 150°C/300°F/gas mark 2.
6. Pour the mixture into the prepared flan ring and sprinkle over the remaining cheese. Place the flan in the middle of the heated oven and bake for about 40 minutes.
7. Remove the flan ring and bake for a further 5 minutes to allow the pastry to brown. The top should be golden and set.
8. Serve hot or cold.

NOTE: To bake blind, line the raw pastry case with a piece of foil or a double sheet of greaseproof paper and fill it with dried lentils, beans, rice or even pebbles or coins. This is to prevent the pastry bubbling up during cooking. When the pastry is half cooked (about 15 minutes) the 'blind beans' can be removed and the empty pastry case further dried out in the oven. The beans can be re-used indefinitely.

WHITE ALSACE

Spinach Flan

SERVES 2
rich shortcrust pastry made with 110g/4oz flour (see page 525)

For the filling:
1/2 onion, finely chopped
15g/1/2oz butter
75ml/5 tablespoons milk
75ml/5 tablespoons single cream
1 egg
1 egg yolk
340g/12oz spinach, cooked and chopped
30g/1oz cheese strong Cheddar or Gruyère, grated
salt and pepper

1. Roll out the pastry and line a flan ring about 15cm/6 inches in diameter. Leave in the refrigerator for about 45 minutes to relax – this prevents shrinkage during cooking.
2. Set the oven to 200°C/400°F/gas mark 6.
3. Bake the pastry case blind for 10-15 minutes and remove from the oven.
4. Reduce the heat to 150°C/300°F/gas mark 2.
5. Fry the onion slowly in the butter. When thoroughly cooked but not coloured, drain well.
6. Mix together the milk, cream and eggs. Add the onion, spinach and three-quarters of the cheese. Season carefully with salt and pepper (the cheese is salty, so be careful not to overseason).
7. Pour the mixture into the prepared flan case and sprinkle over the remaining cheese. Place the flan in the middle of the oven and bake for 30-40 minutes.
8. Remove the flan ring to allow the sides of the pastry to cook evenly and colour. Bake for a further 5 minutes until the filling is brown and set.
9. Serve hot or cold.

LIGHT RED

Onion Tart

SERVES 4

rich shortcrust pastry made with 225g/8oz flour quantity (see page 525)
55g/2oz butter
15ml/1 tablespoon olive oil
675g/1½lb onions, sliced
2 eggs
2 egg yolks
150ml/¼ pint single cream
salt and pepper
grated nutmeg

1. Preheat the oven to 200°C/400°F/gas mark 6.
2. Roll out the pastry and line a 20cm/8 inch flan ring with it. Leave in the refrigerator to relax for 20 minutes.
3. Melt the butter, add the oil and onions and cook very slowly until soft but not coloured. This may take up to 30 minutes. Leave to cool.
4. Bake the pastry case blind, then turn the oven down to 175°C/350°F/gas mark 4.
5. Mix together the eggs, cream and onions. Season to taste with salt and pepper. Pour into the pastry case and sprinkle with nutmeg. Bake until golden and just set, about 20 minutes.

BEAUJOLAIS/ALSACE WHITE

Leek and Bacon Flan with Mustard

SERVES 4

rich shortcrust pastry made with 170g/6oz flour (see page 525)

For the filling:
15g/½oz butter
white of 5 small or 3 large leeks, washed and finely chopped
55g/2oz bacon, derinded and chopped
2 egg yolks
150ml/¼ pint double cream
salt and pepper
good quality coarse-grain mustard
fresh Parmesan cheese, grated

1. Roll out the pastry and line a 20cm/8 inch flan ring. Leave in the refrigerator to relax for 30 minutes.
2. Set the oven to 190°C/375°F/gas mark 5.
3. Bake the pastry case blind. Remove from the oven and turn it down to 170°C/325°F/gas mark 3.
4. Melt the butter and cook the leeks until fairly soft. In a second pan fry the bacon, in its own fat, until it begins to brown. Drain well on absorbent paper.
6. Mix together the egg yolks and cream. Add the leeks and bacon. Season with salt and pepper.
7. Spread a fairly thick layer of mustard on the base of the flan and then pour in the filling. Sprinkle evenly with Parmesan. Bake for 30 minutes or until the filling is set and golden brown.

VERY DRY WHITE

Leek en Croûte with Mushroom Sauce

SERVES 4

900g/2lb leeks, trimmed and finely sliced
30g/1oz butter
45ml/3 tablespoons double cream
salt and freshly ground black pepper
puff pastry made with 450g/1lb flour (see page 528)
4 basil leaves
1 egg yolk

To serve:
mushroom sauce (see page 229)

1. Melt the butter in a sauté pan and add the leeks. Cook gently for 1 minute and then add the cream and salt. Cook, stirring occasionally, for approximately 15 minutes or until the leeks have softened and any juices have evaporated. Season with salt and pepper and allow to cool completely.
2. Flour the work surface lightly. Roll the pastry to the thickness of a coin. Using a 10cm/4 inch and a 13cm/5 inch cutter, cut out 4 rounds of each size. If you need to re-roll the pastry, lay the scraps on top of each other and re-roll.

3. Take the 4 smaller circles and divide the leeks between them, leaving a 1cm/½inch border clear. Top each mound of leeks with a basil leaf. Dampen the edges lightly with water.
4. Take the larger circles of pastry and carefully place over the filling, ensuring no air is trapped inside. Press the edges lightly together, knock up and crimp the edges.
5. Brush with the egg yolk and then using the back of a sharp knife, mark a criss-cross pattern on the top.
6. Put the leeks en croûtes on a baking sheet and chill in the refrigerator for 30 minutes.
7. Meanwhile, preheat the oven to 200°C/400°F/gas mark 6.
8. Bake the leeks en croûtes in the oven for 15-20 minutes or until they are risen and brown.
9. To serve: put a leek en croûte on each diner's plate and spoon a little sauce around the edge.

DRY WHITE

Creamy Fish Flan with Burnt Hollandaise

SERVES 4
shortcrust pastry made with 170g/6oz flour (see page 525)
1 small onion, finely chopped
30g/1oz butter
30g/1oz flour
1 bay leaf
290ml/½ pint milk
salt and freshly ground black pepper
1 egg
225g/8oz white fish, cooked and flaked
15ml/1 tablespoon chopped fresh parsley
squeeze of lemon juice
hollandaise sauce made with 55g/2oz butter (see page 225)

1. Set the oven to 190°C/375°F/gas mark 5. Line a 20cm/8 inch flan ring with pastry and bake blind.
2. Reduce the oven temperature to 180°C/350°F/gas mark 4.
3. Cook the onion in the butter until soft but not coloured. Add the flour and bay leaf. Cook, stirring, for 1 minute. Remove from the heat, stir in the milk, and bring slowly to the boil, stirring continuously. Taste and season as necessary. Simmer for 2 minutes, remove the bay leaf and allow to cool for 5 minutes.
4. Separate the egg and beat the yolk into the sauce. Stir in the fish, parsley and lemon juice to taste. Whisk the egg white until stiff but not dry and fold into the mixture. Pour into the pastry case. Bake until firm and set (about 25 minutes).
5. Heat up the grill 10 minutes before the flan is cooked.
6. Prepare the hollandaise sauce and spoon over the flan. Put the flan under the grill until the top is nicely browned. Serve at once.

CHABLIS

Spinach and Olive Tart

This recipe has been adapted from Roger Vergé's *Entertaining in the French Style.*

SERVES 6
Provençale pastry made with 340g/12oz flour (see page 532)
30ml/2 tablespoons virgin olive oil
2 onions, finely chopped
450g/1lb fresh spinach, cooked and chopped
3 garlic cloves, crushed
3 eggs
45ml/3 tablespoons double cream
salt and pepper
340g/12oz small black Niçoise olives in oil, pitted
5ml/1 teaspoon fresh thyme leaves

1. Set the oven to 200°C/400°F/gas mark 6.
2. Heat the oil, add the onions, and cook over a low heat for about 15 minutes until beginning to soften and brown. Add the spinach and garlic and continue to cook over low heat until all the liquid has evaporated. This will take about 8 minutes. Leave to cool.
3. Beat the eggs with the cream. Add the onion and spinach mixture. Mix well and season lightly to taste.
4. Roll out about half of the pastry and use it to line the base of a 30cm/12 inch loose-bottomed flan ring. Bake for 15 minutes.

5. Roll the remaining pastry into strips about 1cm/½inch wide and twist into 'ropes'. Put the part-baked flan base back into the flan ring and arrange the 'ropes' of pastry around the edge of the base. Bake for a further 15 minutes.
6. Reduce the heat to 180°C/350°F/gas mark 4.
7. Pour the spinach and onion mixture into the flan case and spread it evenly over the base. Bake for 10 minutes. Remove the flan ring to allow the sides of the pastry to cook and sprinkle the olives evenly over the tart. Dust with the fresh thyme leaves and bake for a further 5 minutes.
8. Serve hot or cold.

PROVENCE ROSE

Mushroom and Ricotta Tart

SERVES 6
herby wholemeal pastry made with 225g/8oz flour (see page 527)
225g/8oz medium-sized mushrooms, stalks removed
30g/1oz butter
juice of ½ lemon
900g/2lb ricotta cheese
10ml/2 teaspoons tinned green peppercorns, crushed
1 garlic clove, crushed
3 eggs
60ml/4 tablespoons double cream
60ml/4 tablespoons mixed fresh chopped herbs, such as chives, parsley, dill and sage, salt and freshly ground black pepper

1. Preheat the oven to 400°F/200°C/gas mark 6.
2. Roll out the pastry and use it to line a 28cm/11 inch flan ring. Chill in the refrigerator for 30 minutes.
3. Bake the pastry blind, and turn down the oven to 150°C/300°F/gas mark 3.
4. Cook the mushrooms in half the butter and the lemon juice for about 5 minutes. Allow them to cool.
5. Beat together the ricotta cheese, peppercorns, garlic, eggs, cream and herbs. Season to taste with salt and pepper.
6. Carefully spoon the mixture into the flan ring. Smooth it flat.
7. Place the mushrooms, stalk side down, on top of the filling. Brush with the remaining butter, melted, and cook for 30 minutes. Serve hot.

LIGHT RED

Leith's Restaurant's Artichoke and Green Olive Pie

SERVES 6-8
10 fresh globe artichokes
30g/1oz butter
10 shallots, finely diced
2 small garlic cloves, crushed
fresh thyme, chopped
fresh sage, chopped
60ml/4 tablespoons dry white vermouth, or white wine
150ml/¼ pint double cream
170g/6oz green olives, chopped
salt and freshly ground black pepper
225g/8oz puff pastry (see page 528)
1 egg, beaten

1. Peel the artichokes to the core and put them immediately into acidulated water.
2. Preheat the oven to 190°C/375°F/gas mark 5.
3. Cut the artichokes into 5mm/¼inch cubes and cook in the butter very slowly, with the shallots, garlic, thyme and sage, until soft.
4. Add the vermouth or wine. Add the cream and reduce, by boiling, to a coating consistency. Stir the sauce every so often to prevent it from catching on the bottom of the saucepan.
5. Add the olives and season to taste. Leave to cool.
6. Line a 20cm/8 inch flan ring with pastry. Pile in the artichoke and olive mixture and cover the pie with the remaining pastry.
7. Brush with beaten egg and bake for 15-20 minutes or until golden brown.

DRY WHITE

Provençal Filos

Lyn Hall came to demonstrate at Leith's School and meant to cook these filo 'fingers' for our students. Unfortunately she ran out of time and so didn't do them; we decided to try them anyway and found them delicious.

SERVES 4
3 sheets filo pastry
1 small aubergine, finely sliced into semicircles
2 small courgettes, finely sliced into semicircles
3 small tomatoes, finely sliced, deseeded and cut into semi-circles
60ml/4 tablespoons olive oil
5ml/1 teaspoon fresh thyme leaves
5ml/1 teaspoon fresh oregano, chopped
salt and freshly ground black pepper

1. Preheat the oven to 200°C/400°F/gas mark 6.
2. Cut the filo sheets into rectangles about 7.5cm/3 inches wide.
3. Layer 3 or 4 sheets of lightly oiled filo pastry on top of each other on an oiled baking sheet.
4. Lay the vegetables in overlapping rows on the pastry.
5. Brush lightly with olive oil and sprinkle with the herbs, salt and pepper.
6. Bake for 15-20 minutes.
7. Trim off the sides, cut into fingers and serve warm.

PROVENCE ROSE

Brioche Stuffed with Wild Mushrooms

SERVES 4
brioche dough made with 225g/8oz flour (see page 569), but omit sugar

For the filling:
340g/12oz wild mushrooms, sliced
20g/¾oz butter
15ml/1 tablespoon chopped fresh parsley
squeeze of lemon juice
salt and freshly ground black pepper
60ml/4 tablespoons double cream

To glaze:
a little beaten egg

1. Grease a large brioche mould. Roll three-quarters of the dough into a ball and put it into the tin. Make a dip in the centre. Roll the remaining dough into a ball and press into the prepared dip. Press a wooden spoon handle through the smaller of the 2 balls into the brioche base to anchor the top in place while it bakes.
2. Cover with greased polythene and leave in a warm place until risen to the top of the tin. This will take about 30 minutes.
3. Set the oven to 220°C/425°F/gas mark 7.
4. Meanwhile make the filling. Fry the mushrooms slowly in the butter for 1 minute. Add the parsley, lemon juice, salt and pepper and cream. Taste and set aside.
5. Brush the brioche with beaten egg and bake for 25 minutes. Remove the 'top knot' and some of the inside brioche dough.
6. Heat up the mushroom filling and spoon it into the brioche cavity. It does not matter if it does not all fit in as the final dish looks very attractive if served with some of the filling on the side of the plate. Replace the top and serve immediately.

WHITE ALSACE

Blinis

MAKES 25 BLINIS
225g/8oz wholemeal flour
225g/8oz plain flour
salt
3 eggs
45g/1½oz fresh yeast
10ml/2 teaspoons sugar
720ml/1¼ pints warm milk
15ml/1 tablespoon melted butter
lard for frying

1. Sift the flours into a bowl, add the salt and any bran left in the sieve.
2. Make a hollow in the centre and drop in 2 whole eggs and 1 egg yolk, reserving 1 egg white.
3. Cream the yeast with the sugar and add the milk. Mix well.

4. Pour the yeasty milk gradually into the flours and mix to a smooth batter. Add the melted butter.
5. Cover with a sheet of greased polythene or a cloth and leave in a warm place for 1 hour.
6. Just before cooking, whisk the remaining egg white and fold it into the mixture.
7. Grease a heavy frying pan lightly with oil. Heat it gently over steady heat. When the frying pan is hot, pour enough of the batter on to the surface to make a blini the size of a saucer. When bubbles rise, turn it over and cook the other side to a light brown.
9. Keep the blinis warm in a cool oven between sheets of greaseproof paper.

TO SERVE:
CAVIAR: Butter the hot blini, place a spoonful of caviar (or Danish lumpfish roe) on top and surround with soured cream. Serve at once.
SMOKED SALMON: Butter the hot blini, spread liberally with soured cream and place a roll of smoked salmon on top. Serve at once.
PICKLED HERRING: Mix herring fillets with soured cream. Butter the blini and top with the herring and soured cream mixture. Serve at once.

NOTE I: If using dried yeast use half the amount called for, mix it with 45ml/3 tablespoons of the liquid (warmed to blood temperature) and 5ml/1 teaspoon of sugar. Leave until frothy, about 15 minutes, then proceed. If the yeast does not froth it is dead and unusable.
NOTE II: Blinis are very good made with buckwheat flour in place of some or all of the wholemeal flour. They can also be made with white flour.

VERY DRY OR SPICY WHITE

Fish First Courses

Marinated Kipper Fillets

SERVES 4

8 kipper fillets
1 medium onion, sliced
2 bay leaves
freshly ground black pepper
5ml/1 teaspoon mustard powder
150ml/¼ pint olive oil
5ml/1 teaspoon brown sugar
30ml/2 tablespoons lemon juice

To serve:
lemon wedges
brown bread and butter

1. Skin the kipper fillets and cut into wide strips on the diagonal.
2. In a small dish layer the fillets with the onion and bay leaves, grinding black pepper between the layers.
3. Place the mustard, olive oil, sugar and lemon juice in a jar with a lid and shake vigorously. Pour over the fillets.
5. Cover the dish well with a lid or plastic film and leave refrigerated for at least 2 days, preferably a week.
6. Drain off most of the oil and discard the onion and bay leaves.
7. Serve with lemon wedges. Hand brown bread and butter separately.

VERY DRY WHITE

Gravad Lax

This Scandinavian pickled salmon is best made with a whole fish. The recipe is for a 2.25kg/5lb salmon which would serve 15-20 people, but it can be made with a pound or two of salmon fillet. The fillet should come from a large fish – the larger the fish the oilier and better flavoured. Frozen salmon gives good results.

SERVES 20

1 salmon, filleted and de-boned but not skinned
olive oil
about 45ml/3 tablespoons granulated sugar
22ml/1½ tablespoons coarse sea salt
15ml/1 tablespoon brandy
15ml/1 tablespoon chopped fresh dill
crushed white peppercorns

To serve:
mustard sauce (see page 228)

1. Smear the sides of salmon all over with olive oil. Put one of them skin side down on a board.
2. Mix together 2 parts granulated sugar and 1 part sea salt and pack this mixture in a layer on the flesh side of the fillet. Sprinkle with brandy to moisten and cover the top with chopped dill – there should be enough dill to completely cover the sugar/salt. Sprinkle heavily with the peppercorns.
3. Put the second side on top of the first, skin side up, so that you have a salmon sandwich with a thick sugar and dill filling.
4. Wrap the whole thing up very tightly in 2 or 3 layers of foil and put it in a tray or dish with a good lip. Put another tray on top and weight it down with a couple of large cans of fruit or something heavy. Leave for 4 hours at room temperature.
5. Unwrap the parcel, taking care not to lose any of the juice, turn the whole sandwich over and re-wrap. Weight down again for a further 4 hours and then refrigerate.
6. The gravad lax will be ready when it has been marinating for at least 12 hours. Slice the salmon thinly and serve with the juices that have run from the fish. Hand brown bread and butter and mustard sauce separately.

SANCERRE/SAUVIGNON

Smoked Salmon and Oyster Mushrooms

SERVES 4

340g/12oz oyster mushrooms, sliced
hazelnut oil
15ml/1 tablespoon finely chopped chives
salt and freshly ground black pepper
340g/12oz good quality smoked salmon

1. Fry the mushrooms slowly in hazelnut oil for about 2 minutes. Add the chives and season to taste with salt and pepper.
2. Arrange the mushrooms in the centre of 4 plates and surround, rather like a castle wall, with the salmon. Leave it to 'sit' for 2 minutes so that the smoked salmon becomes warmed by the mushrooms.

SANCERRE/SAUVIGNON

Potato Cakes with Smoked Salmon

MAKES 8
450g/1lb floury potatoes, peeled and cut in half
55g/2oz butter, melted
1 egg yolk
salt and freshly ground black pepper
15ml/1 tablespoon creamed horseradish
30ml/2 tablespoons mayonnaise
30ml/2 tablespoons soured cream
grated rind of 1/2 lemon
225g/8oz smoked salmon, cut into strips
55g/2oz salmon roe
small bunch of chives, snipped
flour

1. Set the oven to 180°C/350°F/gas mark 4.
2. Cook the potatoes until just tender. Drain and cool.
3. Mash the potatoes, add the butter and egg yolk and stir until well mixed. Season.
4. Divide the mixture into 8 and with floured hands shape into flattish circles about 9cm/4 1/2 inches in diameter.
5. Place on a lightly oiled baking sheet, bake for 20 minutes, turn over and bake for a further 20 minutes.
6. Meanwhile prepare the filling. Mix together the horseradish, mayonnaise, soured cream and lemon rind, and season to taste.
7. Sandwich the potato cakes together with the filling and the sliced smoked salmon. Garnish each one with salmon roe and chives.

VERY DRY WHITE

Moules Marinières

SERVES 4
2 kg/4lb mussels (or 2 litres/4 pints)
2 medium onions, chopped
2 shallots, chopped
2 garlic cloves, chopped
15ml/1 tablespoon chopped parsley
150ml/1/4 pint water
150ml/1/4 pint white wine
45g/1 1/2oz butter
salt and freshly ground black pepper
extra parsley to garnish

1. Clean the mussels by scrubbing them well under a running tap. Pull away the 'beard' (seaweed-like threads). Throw away any mussels that are cracked or that remain open when tapped.
2. Simmer the onion, shallot, garlic, parsley, water and wine together for 10-15 minutes. Add the mussels, put on the lid and leave to steam over a gentle heat until the shells open, shaking the pan occasionally. This should take about 5 minutes. Tip the mussels into a colander set over a bowl.
3. Throw away any mussels that have not opened. Pour the mussel liquid from the bowl into a saucepan. Boil and reduce well. Lower the heat and whisk in the butter, then season to taste.
4. Transfer the mussels to a soup tureen or wide bowl, pour over the sauce and sprinkle with extra chopped parsley.

NOTE I: Moules marinières recipes vary from port to port in France. In Normandy cream is sometimes added to the sauce instead of, or as well as, butter. Sometimes the juice is thickened by the addition of beurre manié. Herbs other than parsley are frequently used in sophisticated restaurants. Sometimes one mussel shell from each mussel is removed and discarded after cooking, as is the 'rubber band' found round the mussel. The mussels are served in the remaining shells, neatly piled on a dish.
NOTE II: Extra soup plates or bowls should be provided to take the pile of discarded shells.

MUSCADET

Baked Mussels Provençal

SERVES 4

2 kg/4lb mussels
290ml/½pint water
1 onion, chopped
few sprigs of fresh parsley
1 bay leaf
170g/6oz butter
2 small garlic cloves, crushed
1 shallot, finely chopped
45ml/3 tablespoons finely chopped fresh parsley
30ml/2 tablespoons Gruyère cheese, grated
30ml/2 tablespoons dried browned crumbs

1. Scrub the mussels well, discarding any that are cracked or will not close when tapped.
2. In a large saucepan heat the water, onion, parsley and bay leaf. When simmering add the mussels and cover. Shake the pan occasionally until the mussels have opened. This should take about 2 minutes.
3. Strain through a colander, discarding any mussels which have not opened.
4. Completely open the shells, throwing away the top half. Remove the 'rubber band' around each mussel.
5. Heat the oven to 200°C/400°F/gas mark 6.
6. Cream the butter, stir in the garlic, shallot and parsley. Spread each mussel with the garlic butter and place on a flat ovenproof serving dish. Mix the cheese with the breadcrumbs and sprinkle the mixture over each shell.
7. Bake in the oven until hot and browned. This should take about 10 minutes.

NOTE: The water in which the mussels were stewed will make an excellent base for a fish sauce or soup.

VERY DRY WHITE

Grilled Oysters

SERVES 4

24 oysters
150ml/¼ pint single cream
Parmesan cheese
cayenne pepper
melted butter
dry breadcrumbs

1. Open the oysters: wrap a teatowel around your left hand. Place an oyster on your palm with the flat side upwards. Slip a short, wide-bladed kitchen or oyster knife under the hinge and push it into the oyster. Press the middle fingers of your left hand on to the shell and with your right hand jerk up the knife and prise the two shells apart. Free the oyster from its base.
2. Heat the grill.
3. Rinse and dry the bottom shells, spoon a little cream into each and return the oysters. Sprinkle with Parmesan cheese, a very little cayenne, melted butter and dry breadcrumbs. Grill for 3-4 minutes or until hot and lightly browned.

CHAMPAGNE OR CHABLIS

Steamed Clams

4-6 soft-shelled clams per person, depending on size

1. Clean the clams thoroughly with a brush under running water.
2. Place the clams on a flat heatproof dish.
3. Put the dish in a steamer and allow to steam for 7-8 minutes or until the shells open.

DRY WHITE

Goujons with Tartare Sauce

85g/3oz white fish fillets per person
oil for deep-frying
seasoned flour
beaten egg
dry white crumbs
salt

tartare sauce (see page 224)
lemon wedges

1. Cut the fish, across the grain of the fish or on the slant if possible, into finger-like strips.
2. Heat the oil until a crumb will sizzle in it.
3. Dip the fish into the seasoned flour, then into the beaten egg, and toss in the breadcrumbs.
4. Fry a few goujons at a time until crisp and golden brown. Drain well on absorbent paper and sprinkle with salt. Serve with tartare sauce and lemon wedges.

LOIRE WHITE

Ceviche

SERVES 4
450g/1lb fillet of monkfish, halibut or salmon, skinned and cut into thin slices or small strips
1 onion, sliced
juice of 2 lemons or 4 limes
15ml/1 tablespoon good quality olive oil
pinch of cayenne pepper
1 fresh chilli, deseeded and cut into strips (optional)
15ml/1 tablespoon chopped fresh dill or chives
1 avocado pear, peeled and sliced
1 tomato, peeled and cut into fine strips
1/2 yellow pepper, cut into fine strips
salt and freshly ground black pepper

1. Put the fish, onion, lemon juice, oil, cayenne pepper, chilli and half the dill or chives in a dish and leave in a cool place for 6 hours, giving an occasional stir. (If the fish is really finely sliced, as little as 30 minutes will do; it is ready as soon as it looks 'cooked' – opaque white rather than glassy.)
2. Remove the raw onion from the marinade.
3. Season with salt and freshly ground black pepper. Arrange on a serving dish with the avocado pear, tomato and pepper, and sprinkle liberally with the remaining dill or chives.

CHABLIS

Tuna Fish and Pasta Salad

SERVES 8
85g/3oz pasta shells
salt and freshly ground black pepper
oil and lemon, for cooking
150ml/1/4 pint French dressing (see page 228)
1x200g/7oz tin flageolet beans, rinsed and drained
1x200g/7oz tin borlotti beans, rinsed and drained
1x200g/7oz tin red kidney beans, rinsed and drained
1 bunch spring onions, chopped diagonally
1 box mustard and cress
15ml/1 tablespoon chopped fresh chives
15ml/1 tablespoon finely chopped fresh parsley
squeeze of lemon juice
1x200g/7oz tin tuna fish, drained
15 small black Niçoise olives

1. Cook the pasta in plenty of boiling salted water, with 15ml/1 tablespoon oil and 1 slice of lemon, until just tender. This will take about 10 minutes.
2. Drain and rinse the pasta well under running cold water.
3. Soak the pasta in the French dressing for 30 minutes, seasoning well.
4. Mix the pasta with the beans, spring onions, half the mustard and cress, half the chives and parsley and the lemon juice.
5. Add the tuna fish and gently mix so as not to break up the flesh.
6. Pile into a serving dish and scatter over the remaining herbs, the black olives and the mustard and cress.

VERY DRY WHITE

Fish Niçoise

SERVES 4
4 fillets of pink trout
grapeseed oil
black pepper
110g/4oz French beans, topped, tailed and blanched
1 small cauliflower, broken into florets and blanched
4 tomatoes, skinned, deseeded, and cut into slivers
8 black olives, stoned

To serve:
French dressing, made with hazelnut oil

1. Heat the grill to the highest temperature.
2. Brush the trout fillets with a little oil, season with pepper and grill until tender, 2-3 minutes on each side. Heat a meat skewer until red hot and use it to score a lattice pattern on each fillet. Leave to cool.
3. Arrange the fish, beans, cauliflower, tomatoes and olives on a plate. Pour over the dressing.

DRY WHITE

Smoked Salmon and Pasta Salad

SERVES 4
110g/4oz fresh green and white tagliatelli
sunflower oil, for cooking
110g/4oz good quality smoked salmon, cut into fine strips
4 tomatoes, skinned, deseeded, and cut into slivers
French dressing (see page 228)
fresh dill

1. Cook the pasta in plenty of rapidly boiling water with 30ml/2 tablespoons of oil. When cooked, drain and pour boiling water over it. Leave to cool.
2. Mix together the pasta, smoked salmon, tomatoes and French dressing. Arrange on 4 individual plates and decorate each with a sprig of fresh dill.

WHITE LOIRE

Marinated Salmon and Melon Salad

A simple, light and refreshing first course.

SERVES 6
225g/8oz piece fresh salmon
juice of 1 lime
18 green peppercorns
2 handfuls bitter salad leaves
1 small melon
French dressing (see page 228)
salt and freshly ground pepper

1. Slice the salmon finely and marinate overnight in the lime juice and green peppercorns. Turn occasionally.
2. Wash and spin dry the salad leaves.
3. Cut the melon in half. Scoop out the seeds. Cut into quarters, cut off the skin and slice finely. Toss the salad leaves in the French dressing, arrange on 6 small plates and cover with salmon and melon. Season well with salt and pepper.

Saumon Mariné et Fromage Blanc au Poivre

SERVES 4
1 small bunch of dill
225g/8 oz filleted fresh salmon
10ml/2 teaspoons green peppercorns, well rinsed
1 shallot, very finely chopped
15ml/1 tablespoon coarse sea salt
60ml/4 tablespoons olive oil
60ml/4 tablespoons fromage blanc
15ml/1 tablespoon whipped cream
15ml/1 tablespoon chopped fresh herbs, e.g. chives, chervil, tarragon
salt
juice of 1 lemon

To serve:
hot toast

1. Blanch the dill, reserving 1 sprig for decoration.
2. Slice the salmon finely and marinate with the dill, half the green peppercorns, the shallot, sea salt and olive oil for 30 minutes.
3. Remove the salmon from the marinade and scrape down, making sure there is no salt left.
4. Divide the salmon between 4 plates and leave in the fridge.
5. Drain the fromage blanc, add the whipped cream, fresh herbs, remaining peppercorns and salt to taste. Form this mixture into quenelle shapes using 2 dessertspoons and place 1 quenelle on each plate.

6. Just before serving, brush the salmon with the lemon juice and garnish with the reserved dill. Serve at once with hot toast.

LIGHT WHITE

Italian Seafood Salad

SERVES 6
450g/1lb fresh squid
a few slices onion
a few parsley stalks
1 bay leaf
2 slices lemon
salt
1 medium leek
1 medium carrot
55g/2oz cooked peeled prawns
55g/2oz cooked cockles
55g/2oz white button mushrooms, finely sliced

For the dressing:
15ml/1 tablespoon good quality olive oil
30ml/2 tablespoons mild salad oil
5ml/1 teaspoon wine vinegar
5ml/1 teaspoon fresh lemon juice
salt and freshly ground black pepper
1 small garlic clove, crushed
15ml/1 tablespoon finely chopped parsley

1. Ask the fishmonger to gut and skin the squid. Alternatively tackle it yourself – it is rather messy, but quite easy. Remove the blood (ink) and the entrails under cold running water – they will come out easily. Remove the clear plastic-like piece of cartilage that runs the length of the body on the inside. Cut off and throw away the head (it is the round middle bit with two large eyes). Scrape off the pinkish-purple outside skin – a fine membrane – from the body and the tentacles. Don't worry if you cannot get all the tentacles completely clear of it. Wash the body and tentacles to remove all traces of ink: you should now have a perfectly clean, white, empty squid.
2. Cut it into thin strips. Put them in a saucepan and just cover with water. Add the onion, parsley stalks, bay leaf, lemon slices and a pinch of salt. Simmer gently until the squid is tender. This can take up to 1 hour for strips cut from a large squid. Drain well.

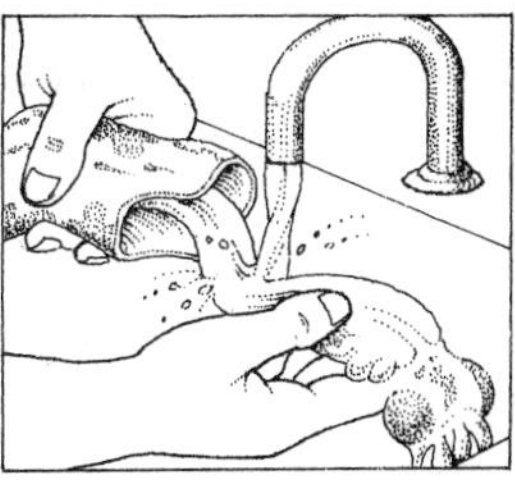
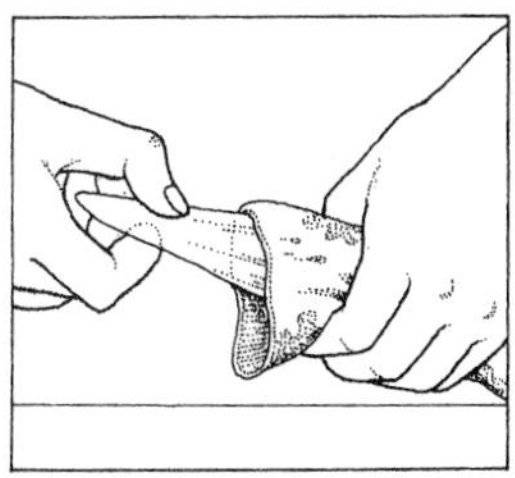

Remove the entrails and cartilage

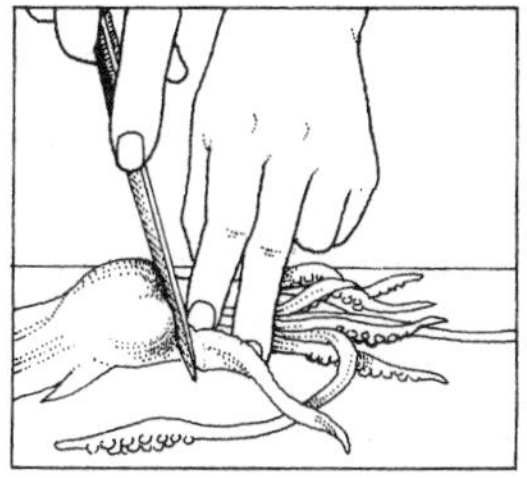
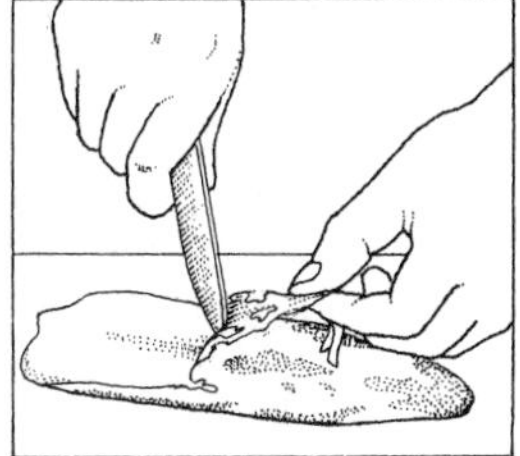

Cut off the head and scrape away the membrane

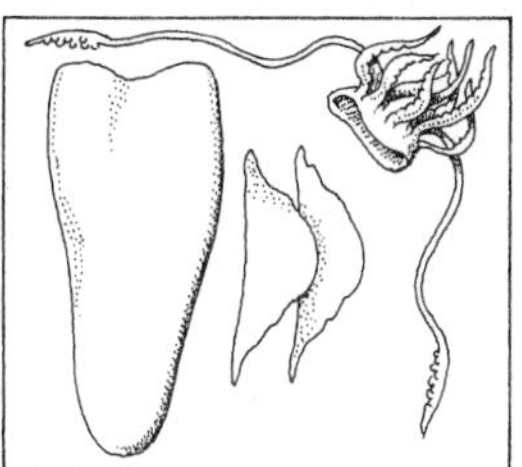

Body, fins and tentacles

3. Wash the leek and discard the tough outside leaves and the dark green part. Shred the rest finely and plunge it into boiling salted water for 1 minute until just tender but still bright green. Rinse under running cold water to set the bright colour. Drain well.
4. Peel the carrot. With a potato peeler shred it into long thin ribbons.
5. Combine the ingredients for the dressing in a screw-top jar and shake well.
6. When the squid is cool drain it (but keep the fish stock for some future soup or sauce – it is delicious), discard the onion, bay leaf, lemon slices and parsley stalks and put the squid into a bowl. Add prawns, cockles, mushrooms, carrot strips, leek and dressing. Chill well before serving.

NOTE: Other seafood can be used too.
FRESH COCKLES: Leave for 1 hour in salty water and turn often to rid them of sand before cooking as for mussels.
MUSSELS: Scrub well under running water. Pull away the 'beard' and discard any that are

broken or which will not close when tapped. Put in a heavy pan with a little white wine, cover, and shake over heat for 5 minutes until the shells have opened. Discard any that remain closed. Remove the mussels from the shells and discard the 'rubber bands'.

FROZEN COOKED PRAWNS: Thaw slowly, season with lemon juice, salt and black pepper.

FROZEN RAW 'SCAMPI': simmer in a court bouillon for 3-4 minutes.

RAW WHOLE PRAWNS: Simmer for 4 minutes in a court bouillon. (The shells will be bright red when they are cooked.) Shell carefully. If using any whole for decoration, remove the legs and any roe after cooking.

SOAVE/FRASCATI

Squid Salad with Cucumber and Cumin

SERVES 4

450g/1 lb squid
150ml/1/4 pint water
150ml/1/4 pint dry white wine
1 onion, chopped
bay leaf

For the salad:
1 cucumber
6 spring onions, finely sliced

For the dressing:
5ml/1 teaspoon Dijon mustard
30ml/2 tablespoons crème fraiche, or Greek yoghurt
30ml/2 tablespoons olive oil
2.5ml/1/2 teaspoon cumin
salt and freshly ground black pepper
juice of 1 lime
15ml/1 tablespoon chopped mint and chives

1. Clean the squid (see page 165). Chop the tentacles into 2.5cm / 1 inch lengths and cut the body into rings.
2. Place the water, wine, onion and bay leaf in a saucepan, bring to the boil and simmer for 10 minutes. Allow to cool, then add the squid and bring to the boil again. Remove from the heat, leave to stand for 5 minutes and then lift out the squid and allow to cool.
3. Peel the cucumber and cut into 4. Using an apple corer, remove the seeds and then slice the cucumber into rings about the same size as the squid rings.
4. Make the dressing by mixing all the ingredients together, and check the seasoning.
5. Toss the squid, cucumber, and spring onion in the dressing.

DRY WHITE

Arbroath Smokies Pots

This recipe has been taken from *La Potinière and Friends* by David and Hilary Brown.

SERVES 6

3 large Arbroath smokies
3 eggs
290ml/1/2 pint fromage frais
juice of 1/2 lemon
salt and freshly ground black pepper
melted butter

To serve:
tomato, basil and olive oil sauce (see page 230)
sprigs of dill

1. Preheat the oven to 160°C / 325°F / gas mark 3.
2. Place the smokies on an ovenproof dish and place in the oven for 10 minutes.
3. Remove from the oven and carefully remove the skin and bones.
4. Place the flesh in the bowl of a food processor and process until smooth. Add the eggs one at a time and continue to blend. Gradually add the fromage frais, lemon juice and seasonings to taste. Be careful with the salt.
5. Brush 6 ramekin dishes with melted butter and line the bases with a circle of greased greaseproof paper.
6. Divide the fish mixture between the dishes and place them in a roasting tin half filled with boiling water. Place the tin in the middle of the oven.

7. Bake for 35-40 minutes or until set.
8. Meanwhile, make the sauce.
9. Remove the mousses from the oven and allow to rest for 2 minutes. Run a knife around the edges of the dishes and turn the mousses out on to warm plates.
10. Spoon a tablespoon of the warm sauce over each mousse and decorate with a sprig of dill.

SPICY DRY WHITE

Easy Fish Quenelles

SERVES 4

675g/1½lb fish fillet (turbot, salmon, haddock or any lean fish)
2 egg whites
4 slices white bread, with the crusts cut off
milk
salt, pepper and cayenne
170ml/6 fl oz double cream
court bouillon or fish stock (see page 219)
fish beurre blanc (see page 227)

To garnish:
slivers of peeled tomatoes
whole chervil leaves

1. Process the fish well in a food processor, adding a little egg white if necessary. Soak the bread in milk, squeeze dryish and beat into the fish. Season with the pepper only.
2. Remove from the processor. Season with salt. Place in a large bowl set in a roasting tin of ice. Beat well and gradually add first the egg white and then the cream, making sure that the mixture remains fairly firm. Taste – it should be well seasoned.
3. Heat the court bouillon or fish stock.
4. Using 2 wet dessertspoons, mould the mixture into 12 egg shapes and drop them into the hot court bouillon or fish stock. Poach for 3-5 minutes or until the quenelles feel firm to the touch.
5. Flood the base of 4 plates with the beurre blanc and arrange 3 quenelles on each plate. Garnish with the tomatoes and whole chervil leaves.

NOTE: In this recipe much of the beating is done over ice. This is to prevent the mixture from splitting, which it may do in a food processor, especially if you are working with large quantities in hot weather.

WHITE LOIRE

Pain de Poisson

SERVES 4

285g/10oz sole or haddock (filleted weight)
1 egg white
230ml/8 fl oz double cream
salt, freshly ground white and black pepper
cayenne
1 egg
55g/2oz fresh white breadcrumbs
30ml/2 tablespoons chopped fresh parsley
15ml/1 tablespoon chopped fresh tarragon and chives, mixed

To serve:
hollandaise sauce (see page 225)

1. Set the oven to 150°C/300°F/gas mark 2.
2. Skin the fish and remove any bones. Cut into pieces and pound in a food processor. Add one egg white and process well. Remove to a bowl and gradually beat in approximately two-thirds of the double cream. Everything should be very cold. If not, place the bowl over iced water as the cream is added. Season well with salt, white pepper and cayenne. Place in the refrigerator.
3. Whisk the egg and add the rest of the cream. Add the breadcrumbs and herbs. Season with salt and freshly ground black pepper.
4. Oil a 450g/1lb loaf tin and line the base with a piece of greaseproof paper cut to size and also lightly oiled.
5. Spread the fish mixture round the base and sides to approximately 1cm/½ inch thickness.
6. Place the herb mixture in the middle and cover with the remaining fish.
7. Cover with a double sheet of wet greaseproof paper. Place in a bain-marie and bake in the preheated oven for 1-1¼ hours

WHITE BURGUNDY

Fish Terrine with Chive and Lemon Dressing

This recipe is very quick to make in a food processor.

SERVES 6

680g/1½lb filleted, skinned sole
10ml/2 teaspoons green peppercorns
1 large carrot, peeled and cut into batons
45g/1½oz French beans, topped and tailed
3 egg whites, lightly beaten
salt and pepper
290ml/½ pint double cream
15g/½oz butter

For the dressing:
1 large bunch chives
1 carton soured cream
290ml/½ pint mayonnaise (see page 224)
salt and freshly ground black pepper
juice of ½ lemon

1. Rinse the green peppercorns under cold running water for 2-3 minutes. Drain well. Steam the carrots and beans over boiling water until very tender. Rinse under cold running water and drain on absorbent paper.
2. Set the oven to 175°C/350°F/gas mark 4. Pound the sole fillets in a food processor with a little egg white. Season with salt. Place in a large bowl set in a roasting tin of ice. Beat well and gradually add first the remaining egg whites and then the cream, making sure that the mixture remains fairly firm. Beat in the pepper. Taste: it should be well seasoned.
3. Lightly butter a medium-sized loaf tin or terrine, line the base with greaseproof paper and spoon in a quarter of the fish mixture. Spread it flat with a spatula. Arrange 4 parallel lines of green beans down the length of the tin. Cover with a second quarter of the fish mixture. Spread flat. Arrange 4 parallel lines of carrot sticks immediately above the beans. Cover with a third quarter of the fish mixture. Spread flat. Arrange 4 parallel lines of green peppercorns immediately above the carrots. Cover with the remaining fish mixture and smooth over with a spatula. Cover with a piece of damp greaseproof paper.
4. Stand the terrine in a roasting tin of nearly boiling water. Bake for 35 minutes. Remove from the oven, leave to cool and refrigerate overnight.
5. To make the sauce, put the chives and soured cream into a liquidizer and whizz until pale green. Remove from the liquidizer and mix with the mayonnaise and season to taste with salt, pepper and lemon juice.
6. To serve, invert a plate or wooden board over the terrine and turn the whole thing over. Give a gentle shake and remove the tin. Cut into even slices. Serve with the chive sauce and garnish with watercress.

NOTE: If you do not have a food processor the fish should be pushed through a sieve before adding the egg whites (quite a task!).

MUSCADET

Pâté of Fish Tricolour

If whiting is not available, any white fish can be used.

SERVES 4

For the fish mousse:
675g/1½ lb fillet of skinned whiting
2 egg whites
5ml/1 teaspoon salt
2.5ml/½ teaspoon freshly ground white pepper
425ml/¾ pint double cream

For the fish:
170g/6oz salmon fillet
4 large fillets of sole (about 140g/5oz each), skinned and lightly pounded

For the herb mousse:
4-5 shallots, peeled and coarsely chopped
225ml/8 fl oz dry white wine
pinch of freshly ground white pepper
2.5ml/½ teaspoon salt
110g/4oz spinach leaves
1 small bunch watercress leaves, chopped
10ml/2 teaspoons fresh chopped tarragon, chives or any other herb
30ml/2 tablespoons fresh chopped parsley

For the sauce:
1 large tomato, peeled, deseeded and roughly chopped
2.5ml/1/2 teaspoon good paprika
dash of cayenne pepper
5ml/1 teaspoon salt
pinch of freshly ground white pepper
15ml/1 tablespoon good red wine vinegar
1 egg yolk
225ml/8 fl oz virgin olive oil,

TO PREPARE THE FISH MOUSSE:
1. Set the oven to 140°C/275°F/gas mark 1.
2. Place the whiting in the bowl of a food processor and process for 1 minute, with the egg whites, salt and pepper, slowly pouring in half the double cream.
3. Fold the remaining cream into the fish mixture.

TO PREPARE THE HERB MOUSSE:
4. Put the shallots, white wine, pepper and salt in a saucepan and bring to the boil, then reduce by boiling rapidly to 45ml/3 tablespoons. Add the spinach and cook until the liquid is reduced to 15ml/1 tablespoon.
5. Put into a clean food processor bowl with the watercress, tarragon and parsley. Process until smooth, then mix with 45ml/3 tablespoons of the whiting mousse.

TO ASSEMBLE THE TERRINE:
6. Grease a 1.7 litre/3 pint mould or 2 x 450 g/1 lb loaf tins with butter and line the bottom with greaseproof paper. Line the bottom and sides of the mould with 1cm/1/2inch of the fish mousse.
7. Cut the salmon fillet into 1cm/1/2inch slices and line the fish mousse with a layer of the salmon slices.
8. Sprinkle with salt and pepper and spread a thin layer of fish mousse on top.
9. Place half the pounded fillets of sole over the fish mousse.
10. Place the herb mousse in the centre.
11. Cover with the remaining fillets of sole, spread with some more fish mousse and slices of salmon.
12. Thinly cover the last layer of salmon with the remaining fish mousse, smooth the top and cover with bakewell paper. Place wet greaseproof paper over the top.
13. Place the mould or loaf tins in a bain-marie, three-quarters filled with hot water. Bake for 1 1/2 hours. Allow to cool.

MEANWHILE, PREPARE THE SAUCE:
14. Combine all the sauce ingredients, except the oil, in a food processor and blend until smooth. Add the oil slowly with the machine running as for mayonnaise. Taste for seasonings. If it is too thick, then thin down to a creamy consistency with a little lukewarm water.

TO SERVE:
15. Unmould the cooled pâté and cut into 5mm/1/4 inch slices. Spread about 30ml/2 tablespoons of the sauce on to the base of each plate. Arrange a slice of the pâté on top of the sauce.

The finished layers of the pâté

NOTE: This pâté is quite difficult to slice – if you have an electric carving knife it makes life much easier.

CHABLIS

Thai Deep-fried Noodle Balls

MAKES 22
200g/7oz egg noodles or fine spaghetti
salt and freshly ground black pepper
400g/14oz crab meat
4 large eggs
60ml/4 tablespoons coriander leaves, chopped
55g/2oz Parmesan, grated
70g/2 1/2oz plain flour
1 onion, sliced into fine rings
3 garlic cloves, crushed
oil for deep-frying

For the sauce:
125ml/4½ fl oz Thai sweet chilli sauce
½ cucumber, peeled, deseeded and finely diced
55ml/2 fl oz rice vinegar

1. Cook the egg noodles in plenty of salted boiling water until just cooked. Drain well then cut into small lengths.
2. Put the remaining ingredients except for the oil into a large bowl and mix to a firm, slightly sticky mixture.
3. Mould the mixture into balls about the size of a golf ball. Chill well.
4. Preheat the oil for deep-frying to 160°C/ 300°F. Fry about 4 balls at a time, being careful not to overload the fryer as this will reduce the temperature of the oil. Fry until golden brown. Drain well on kitchen paper.
5. Meanwhile make the sauce by mixing the ingredients together in a small bowl.
6. To serve: arrange 3 Thai noodle balls on individual plates with a small dish of sauce. Offer the remaining balls separately.

FULL DRY WHITE

Scallop Mousse with Crayfish Sauce

This recipe has been adapted from Michel Guérard's *Cuisine Gourmande.*

SERVES 4
225g/8oz scallops
salt and white pepper
1 egg
340ml/12 fl oz double cream
30g/1oz butter, melted

For the sauce:
30ml/2 tablespoons olive oil
45ml/3 tablespoons groundnut oil
20 deep frozen freshwater crayfish
2 small carrots, peeled and diced
½ onion, peeled and chopped
1 shallot, peeled and chopped
1 unpeeled garlic clove, crushed
bouquet garni
30ml/2 tablespoons Armagnac
30ml/2 tablespoons port
200ml/7 fl oz dry white wine
2 tomatoes, peeled, quartered, deseeded and diced
15ml/1 tablespoon tomato purée
salt and freshly ground black pepper
290ml/½ pint double cream
5ml/1 teaspoon freshly chopped tarragon

To serve:
a few sprigs lamb's lettuce

1. Remove the tough muscle (found opposite the roe) from the scallops. Process the scallops briefly with salt and pepper. When smooth, add the egg and process for 1 minute. Refrigerate until fairly firm, about 30 minutes.
2. Now process in the cream. The mousse should be fairly thick. Check the seasoning.
3. Set the oven to 170°C/325°F/gas mark 3. Brush 4 ramekins with melted butter and fill with the scallop mousse. Place in a roasting tin half filled with hot water and bake for 30 minutes. Once cooked, remove from the oven and keep warm in the bain-marie.
4. To make the sauce: heat the oils in a very large sauté pan, add the crayfish and cook, covered with a lid, for 10-12 minutes or until red and cooked. Remove from the heat and take the crayfish out of the sauté pan. Shell them and remove the intestinal thread but do not throw away the shells.
5. Pound the shells in a mortar (or grind in a processor). Add to the sauté pan with the vegetables, garlic and bouquet garni. Cook slowly without browning. Add the Armagnac and port and simmer until reduced by half.
6. Add the wine, tomato and tomato purée. Season with salt and pepper and reduce by a third by rapid boiling.
7. Add the cream and tarragon and simmer slowly for 10 minutes. Stir every so often to prevent the sauce 'catching'.
8. Push the sauce through a fine sieve, pressing well to extract all the flavour.
9. Arrange 5 shelled crayfish on each diner's plate. Turn out the warm mousses beside them.
10. Just before serving, coat each mousse with the hot sauce and decorate with a sprig of lamb's lettuce.

WHITE BURGUNDY

Meat First Courses

Minted Pigeon Balls

SERVES 6

3 pigeons
85g/3 oz unsalted butter, well chilled
2 small shallots, finely chopped
fresh mint leaves
170g/6oz piece streaky bacon
fresh thyme and a few leaves of rosemary
a little brandy
salt and freshly ground black pepper

1. Skin the pigeons and take the flesh off the bones. Keep the carcases for stock or soup.
2. Cut 75g/2½oz of the butter into cubes the size of a hazelnut and put them in the freezer or a very cold fridge.
3. Cook the shallots in the remaining butter until soft.
4. Blanch the mint leaves in boiling water, refresh and drain well.
5. Put the pigeon flesh, bacon, shallots, thyme, rosemary and brandy together in the food processor and work until smooth.
6. Remove the butter from the freezer. Moisten your fingers with water and shape pigeon mixture around each butter cube. Place a mint leaf firmly on each ball.
7. Put the balls on a steamer rack over boiling water and steam, covered, for 8 minutes. Serve.

Snails with Garlic Butter

SERVES 4

170g/6oz butter
juice of ½ lemon
30ml/2 tablespoons chopped fresh parsley
6 garlic cloves
salt
24 snails and 24 shells

1. Soften the butter and beat in the lemon juice and parsley. Crush the garlic with salt and beat this into the butter. Leave in a cool place.
2. Push a snail, tail first, into each shell with a teaspoon handle. Fill the remaining cavity of the shell with the garlic butter, scraping off the top neatly. Keep in the refrigerator until needed.
3. Set the oven to 200°C/400°F/gas mark 6. Place a snail, butter upwards, in each indentation of 4 snail dishes and cook in the oven for 8 minutes or until the butter has completely melted and starts to sizzle, but no longer. Overcooking snails toughens them.
4. Serve immediately with fresh French bread.

NOTE: Because preparing fresh snails is a specialized and long process, ready-to-use snails are bought in cans, even by the top French restaurants. Shells are bought separately and can be reused.

Chinese Chicken Balls

SERVES 4-6

450g/1lb chicken flesh, finely minced
4 large spring onions, chopped
2.5cm/1inch piece of root ginger, finely chopped
1 garlic clove, crushed
1 small green chilli, deseeded and finely chopped
30ml/2 tablespoons soy sauce
15ml/1 tablespoon wine vinegar
2.5ml/½ teaspoon ground, roasted Szechwan peppercorns
1 egg, lightly beaten
570ml/1 pint chicken stock

To serve:
150ml/¼ pint low-fat plain yoghurt
5ml/1 teaspoon sesame oil
a dash of Tabasco

To garnish:
a small bunch of watercress

1. Mix together the chicken, spring onion, ginger, garlic, chilli, soy sauce, vinegar and peppercorns. Taste and season if required. Add the egg and beat well.
2. With wet hands shape into balls the size of ping pong balls and place in the top half of a steamer – on a plate if the holes are large. Put the stock in the bottom half of the steamer. Bring to the boil and steam the balls for 20 minutes.
3. Meanwhile, make the sauce: mix the yoghurt, oil andTabasco and pour it into a small dish.
4. Serve the balls on a warm plate, garnished with sprigs of watercress.

Wonton and Pancake First Courses

Chicken and Spring Onion Wontons

MAKES 12 WONTONS

For the stuffing:
140g/5oz chicken flesh
5 spring onions, finely sliced
10ml/2 teaspoons soy sauce
a few drops of sesame oil
salt and freshly ground black pepper

110g/4oz packet wonton skins
oil for frying

For the garnish:
30ml/2 tablespoons peanut oil
30ml/2 tablespoons sesame seeds
5ml/1 teaspoon grated ginger
10 spring onions, finely sliced

1. To make the stuffing, finely chop or process the chicken flesh. Place in a bowl and add the spring onions, soy sauce, sesame oil, salt and pepper. Mix well.
2. Place a teaspoon of the stuffing in the centre of a wonton skin. Brush the edges of the skin with water and place a second skin on top, then press the edges together to seal. Repeat until all the filling and wonton skins are used.
3. Cook the stuffed wonton skins in boiling salted water for 2 minutes. Drain, then refresh under cold running water. When cold, drain well and toss in a little peanut oil.
4. When ready to serve, fry the wontons. Heat 45ml/3 tablespoons oil in a frying pan and cook the wontons until golden brown on both sides. You may well need to add extra oil for each batch of wontons.
5. For the garnish, heat the oil in a frying pan, add the sesame seeds and cook, stirring until just turning brown. Add the ginger and spring onions and cook for a further 2 minutes.
6. Arrange the stuffed wonton skins on a serving dish and scatter the garnish over the top.

WHITE ALSACE

Pork and Chinese Leaf Wonton Stuffing

This is an alternative filling for the chicken and spring onion wontons (above).

MAKES 12 WONTONS

25g/8oz Chinese leaves
5ml/1 teaspoon salt
freshly ground black pepper
110g/4oz pork, finely chopped
5ml/1 teaspoon Shaoxing wine, or medium dry sherry
3 spring onions, finely chopped
15ml/1 tablespoon sesame oil
15ml/1 tablespoon corn oil

1. Chop the Chinese leaves very finely, discarding any tough stalks, and put into a bowl. Cover with water and add half the salt. Leave for 30 minutes.
2. Mix together the remaining salt, the pepper, pork, spring onions, sesame and corn oil and wine. Beat well.
3. Drain the cabbage, squeeze dry and add to the pork mixture. Mix thoroughly.
4. Follow the recipe above to stuff and cook the wontons.

WHITE ALSACE

Peking Pancakes with Duck, Pork and Prawn Fillings

SERVES 6

For the Peking pancakes:
450/1lb plain flour
290ml/½ pint very hot water
30ml/2 tablespoons sesame oil

For the prawn filling:
225g/8oz prawns
15ml/1 tablespoon finely chopped spring onions
5 cm/2 inch piece of root ginger, finely chopped
15ml/1 tablespoon dry sherry
5ml/1 teaspoon soy sauce
15ml/1 tablespoon chicken stock

For the Peking duck:
1 young duckling
1 lemon
1 litre/2 pints water
45ml/3 tablespoons honey
45ml/3 tablespoons soy sauce
150ml/$^1/_4$ pint dry sherry

For the pork and cashew filling:
340g/12oz minced pork
15ml/1 tablespoon oil
$^1/_2$ red chilli
55g/2oz cashew nuts
30ml/2 tablespoons soy sauce
15ml/1 tablespoon dry sherry
5ml/1 teaspoon sugar
salt and black pepper

To serve:
hoisin sauce
2 bunches spring onions, cleaned and cut into fine strips
$^1/_2$ cucumber, cut into fine sticks

1. Prepare the duck on the day before cooking. Wash and dry it well with kitchen paper. Slice the lemon thickly and put it in a pan with the remaining ingredients. Bring to the boil and simmer for about 30 minutes.
2. Ladle the honey and lemon syrup over the duck several times, until it is completely coated with the mixture. Hang the duck in a cool, well ventilated place and leave to dry overnight. Place a roasting tin underneath it to catch any drips.
3. The following day, prepare the pancakes: sift the flour into a large bowl. Gradually add enough of the hot water to form a soft but not sticky dough. Knead the dough for 10 minutes until it is soft and smooth, cover it with a damp cloth and leave for 30 minutes.
4. After the dough has rested, knead it again for 5 minutes. Shape it into 2 sausages, each about 30 cm/12 inches long, and cut each roll into 2cm/1 inch pieces. Shape each piece into a ball.
5. Take 2 balls at a time and dip one side of one ball in the sesame oil, put the oiled side on top of the other ball and roll the 2 together into a 15 cm/6 inch circle.
6. Heat a heavy frying pan or griddle and cook the pancake until it has dried on one side, then cook the other side. Remove from the pan and peel the 2 sides apart. Continue to roll and cook the pancakes. Cover tightly in plastic wrap until you are ready to use them.
7. To finish the duck: heat the oven to 250°C/500°F/gas mark 9. Place the duck breast-side up on a wire rack. Stand the rack over a roasting tin filled with 150 ml/$^1/_4$ pint water. Cook the duck for 15 minutes, then turn the oven down to 180°C/350°F/gas mark 4 and continue to cook for 1 hour or until the juices from the cavity are no longer pink. Allow the duck to stand for 10 minutes, then remove the meat from the bone and cut both meat and skin into neat slices. Keep warm.
8. Prepare the prawn filling: put the spring onions, root ginger, sherry, soy sauce and chicken stock together in a frying pan or wok. Bring to the boil and simmer for 2 minutes. Add the prawns and cook for a further 2 minutes. Turn into a heated serving dish and keep warm in a low oven.
9. Prepare the pork and cashew filling: heat the oil in a frying pan or wok, add the chilli and fry until it turns dark, then remove from the pan. Stir-fry the pork in the oil, breaking up any lumps of meat. Remove the pork from the pan and drain off all but 15ml/1 tablespoon of the fat. When the fat is very hot, add the cashew nuts and stir-fry for 1 minute. Return the pork to the pan and add the soy sauce, sherry and sugar, and season with salt and black pepper. Continue to stir-fry for 5 minutes or until the meat is cooked. Turn into a serving dish and keep warm.
10. To serve the pancakes: give each guest a tiny dish of hoisin sauce. Dry the spring onion and cucumber well and put into serving dishes. Steam the pancakes to reheat them and serve at once with the various hot fillings. The guests help themselves to duck, spring onions and cucumber (dipped into hoisin sauce if they like) or to the other fillings, wrap them in the pancakes and eat with chopsticks or fingers.

SPICY DRY WHITE

Special Spring Rolls

MAKES 16 ROLLS
16 spring roll wrappers

For the filling:
55g/2oz beansprouts
55g/2oz French beans
55g/2oz carrots, peeled and cut into julienne
1 stick celery, de-stringed and cut into julienne
1 courgette, cut into julienne
110g/4oz lean veal or pork, cut into fine julienne
15ml/1 tablespoon oil
1 x 1cm/½ inch piece root ginger, peeled and sliced
1 garlic clove, peeled and sliced
15ml/1 tablespoon soy sauce
salt and freshly ground black pepper

To cook:
lightly beaten egg white
oil for deep-frying

1. First prepare the filling. Blanch the beansprouts in boiling water for 15 seconds. Drain and refresh. Top and tail the French beans and cut them in half lengthways. Mix the sprouts and beans with the carrots, celery and courgette.
2. Mix in the veal or pork.
3. Heat the oil in a wok, add the ginger and garlic and cook over a gentle heat for 2 minutes. Remove the ginger and garlic – the oil should by now be well infused with their flavour.
4. Increase the temperature and quickly stir-fry the meat and vegetables. Season with the soy sauce, salt and pepper. Leave to cool.
5. Divide the filling between the spring roll wrappers. Put the filling in the centre of the wrapper and fold 2 opposite corners on top of it. Then roll up from one of the exposed corners to the other to form rolls.

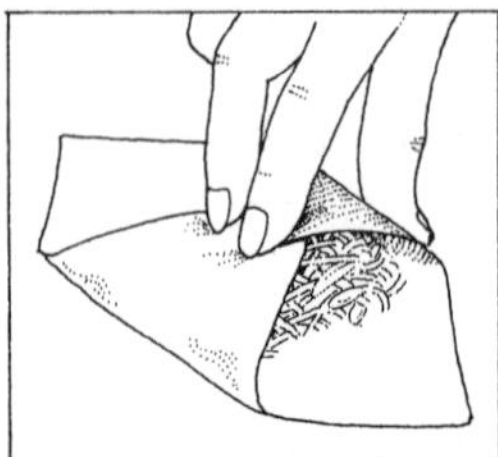
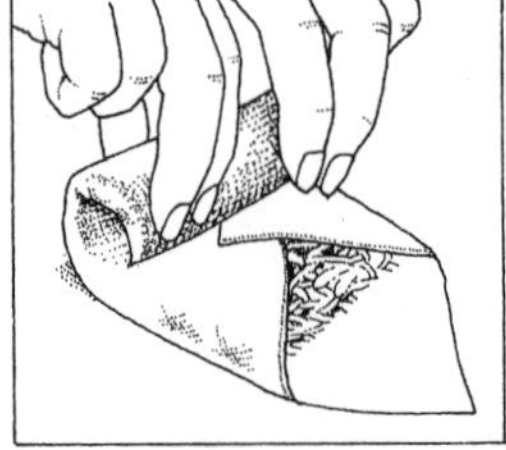

Put the filling in the centre and fold and roll up

6. Brush the rolls with the beaten egg white.
7. Heat the oil until a crumb will sizzle vigorously in it and add the spring rolls. Fry until golden brown and then drain well on absorbent paper. Sprinkle with salt, and serve.

WHITE ALSACE

Spring Pancake Rolls with Chinese Vegetables

This has been adapted from a recipe by Paul Gayler in *Take Six More Cooks.*

MAKES 20
2 medium large celeriacs
a squeeze of lemon juice
30g/1oz mouli (Chinese radish)
¼ red pepper
¼ green pepper
¼ yellow pepper
2 carrots
30g/1oz beansprouts
3 spring onions
30g/1oz mangetout
30g/1oz butter
a little sesame oil
2.5ml/¼ teaspoon crushed garlic
a small piece of root ginger
2 egg yolks
60ml/4 tablespoons arrowroot
60ml/4 tablespoons clarified butter (see page 138, for frying
fresh coriander leaves for garnish

For the tomato coriander sauce:
55g/2oz butter
2 shallots, finely chopped
2 garlic cloves, crushed
4 tomatoes, roughly chopped
15ml/1 tablespoon tomato purée
75ml/5 tablespoons sherry vinegar
150ml/¼ pint white wine
290ml/½ pint water
30ml/2 tablespoons soy sauce
10 fresh coriander leaves, finely shredded

1. Peel the celeriacs and slice them into very thin rounds, preferably on a slicing machine. Blanch the celeriac in boiling water with a squeeze of lemon juice for 10 seconds, then plunge into iced water to refresh. Remove, drain and dry on a clean cloth.
2. For the filling, finely shred all the other vegetables. Heat the butter and the sesame oil in a frying pan. Add the crushed garlic, then the shredded vegetables and the ginger. Cook for 2-3 minutes, keeping the vegetables crisp. Remove the ingredients from the pan and allow to cool.
3. Prepare the celeriac pancake rolls: place 2 circles of celeriac overlapping on a clean surface. If using smaller celeriacs, you may need several circles. Bind the egg yolks and arrowroot together to form a paste and brush this mixture lightly around the edge of the celeriac circles.
4. Place a portion of Chinese vegetables in the centre of the celeriac circles, roll up to form a pancake roll. Leave in the refrigerator for 30 minutes to set.
5. Prepare the sauce: put the butter, shallots, and garlic in a pan and cook together without colouring. Add the tomatoes and the tomato purée, and cook for a further 5 minutes.
6. Add the sherry vinegar and white wine and cook until reduced by half. Pour in the water, cover with a lid and cook gently for 20 minutes.
7. When ready, pass the sauce through a fine sieve. Finish by adding the soy sauce and the coriander leaves.
8. Fry the celeriac pancake rolls in the clarified butter until golden. Arrange 2 on each diner's plate and pour a little of the coriander and tomato sauce alongside.
9. Garnish with fresh coriander leaves and serve immediately.

NOTE I: Smaller versions of these rolls make excellent hot canapés.
NOTE II : If celeriac is not available, filo pastry, spring roll wrappers or wonton skins can be used in its place.

WHITE ALSACE

Savoury Stuffed Pancakes

SERVES 4
12 pancakes (see page 533)
450g/1lb smoked haddock
290ml/½ pint milk
1 bay leaf
1 slice of onion
3-4 peppercorns
1 parsley stalk
salt and pepper
15g/½oz butter
15g/½oz flour
pinch of mustard
pinch of cayenne
55g/2oz Cheddar cheese, grated
5ml/1 teaspoon chopped fresh tarragon
30g/1oz melted butter
dry white breadcrumbs
15ml/1 tablespoon grated fresh Parmesan

1. Heat the oven to 190°C/375°F/gas mark 5.
2. Place the smoked haddock skin side up in an ovenproof dish with the milk, bay leaf, onion, peppercorns, parsley stalk, salt and pepper.
3. Cover the dish and cook for 15 minutes or until the fish will flake easily with a fork.
4. Strain off the liquor and flake the fish, taking care to remove any bones and skin.
5. Melt the butter, add the flour, mustard and cayenne and cook for 1 minute. Draw the pan aside, pour on the liquor and bring to the boil, stirring continuously.
6. Remove the sauce from the heat, stir in half the grated cheese and season with salt, pepper and tarragon. Stir in the fish. Heat the grill.
7. Place a good spoonful of the fish mixture on each pancake and roll up. Lay the pancakes side by side in a buttered ovenproof dish. Brush with melted butter. Sprinkle with the remaining Cheddar cheese, the breadcrumbs and the Parmesan cheese.
8. Place under the hot grill until well browned.

BEAUJOLAIS

Other First Courses

Toasted Goats Cheese with Sesame Seeds

SERVES 6

6 small or 3 medium goats cheeses (crotin)
85g/3oz sesame seeds, lightly toasted
6 slices wholemeal toast, cut into circles just larger than the cheese
2 heads radicchio, washed and dried

For the dressing:
30ml/2 tablespoons olive oil
30ml/2 tablespoons white wine vinegar
1 garlic clove, crushed
30ml/2 tablespoons chopped chives
salt and freshly ground black pepper

1. Preheat the oven to 200°C/400°F/gas mark 6.
2. If you have 3 medium goats cheeses, cut them in half horizontally. Roll the cheeses in the sesame seeds until completely coated.
3. Place the circles of toast on a baking tray and place the cheeses on top. Bake for 5-10 minutes, until the cheese is soft and on the point of melting.
4. Meanwhile, combine all the ingredients for the dressing and mix well. Separate the radicchio into leaves and toss in the dressing. Arrange on 6 plates with the hot toast and cheese on each leaf.

SAUVIGNON BLANC

Goats Cheese with Sesame Seeds in Filo

SERVES 6

6 small or 3 medium goats cheeses (crotin)
85g/3oz sesame seeds, lightly toasted
3 sheets filo pastry
30g/1oz melted butter
2 heads radicchio

For the dressing:
30ml/2 tablespoons olive oil
30ml/2 tablespoons white wine vinegar
1 garlic clove, crushed
30ml/2 tablespoons chopped chives
salt and freshly ground black pepper

1. Preheat the oven to 200°C/400°F/gas mark 6. If you have 3 medium goats cheeses, cut them in half horizontally. Roll the cheese in the sesame seeds until completely coated.
2. Spread out the filo pastry, brush with butter and cut into 12 x 15cm/6 inch squares. Layer one square on top of another. Place a whole or half goats cheese in the centre of each. Draw up the pastry to form 'Dick Whittington' sacks. Lightly dot the outside of the pastry with the melted butter and place on a baking sheet in the hot oven for 5 minutes.
3. Meanwhile, combine all the ingredients for the dressing and mix well. Separate the radicchio into leaves and toss in the dressing. Arrange on 6 plates with the filo parcels.

WHITE LOIRE

Fried Polenta

Polenta is a classical dish of Northern Italy. It can be eaten as soon as it is cooked, served with roasts, grills, casseroles or poultry. Or it can be left to cool, sliced and then grilled or fried. This recipe is for fried polenta. It is particularly good served with fried wild mushrooms.

SERVES 4-6

2 litres/3½ pints water
10ml/2 teaspoons salt
285g/10oz coarse cornmeal/maize flour/polenta
oil

1. Put the water and salt into a large saucepan and bring to the boil.
2. Remove from the heat and sprinkle on the cornmeal, whisking quickly to avoid lumps. Reduce the heat.
3. Return the pan to the heat and cover it as the mixture will bubble and spatter.
4. Continue cooking until the polenta is very thick, approximately 35-40 minutes, stirring often to prevent sticking and burning.
5. The polenta can be served at this stage piled high on a plate, or it can be fried as below.
6. Lightly oil a shallow tin 28cm x 18cm/11 x 7 inches. Spread the mixture out evenly, allow to cool, and refrigerate for about 1 hour.
7. Turn the polenta out of the tin, and cut into

4cm/1½ inch slices.

8. Fill a large deep frying pan with enough oil to come 2cm/¾inch up the sides of the pan. Heat until very hot.

9. Add the polenta slices, being careful not to overcrowd the pan as this will make turning difficult, reduce the heat and fry gently until golden brown on both sides. Remove with a fish slice, taking care to drain off excess oil.

YOUNG RED

Spinach Gnocchi

SERVES 6

170g/6oz fresh spinach, cooked and chopped
225g/8oz ricotta cheese
85g/3oz Parmesan cheese
1 egg
salt and freshly ground black pepper
a good grating of freshly ground nutmeg
flour
45g/1½oz butter, melted

1. Combine the spinach, ricotta and half the Parmesan cheese in a bowl with the egg, salt, pepper and nutmeg. Mix thoroughly.

2. Place a large pan of salted water on the heat and bring up to simmering point.

3. Meanwhile shape the mixture into egg shapes using a tablespoon and the palm of your hand. Roll the gnocchi lightly in flour. Place them in the simmering water a few at a time and poach gently until they come to the surface, approximately 2-3 minutes.

4. Heat the grill. Remove the gnocchi from the pan with a slotted spoon, allowing excess liquid to drain off. Arrange in an ovenproof dish.

5. Pour over the melted butter, and sprinkle with the remaining Parmesan cheese. Place under the grill for a few minutes until the cheese turns golden brown. Serve immediately.

SOAVE

Fried Gnocchi

SERVES 6

570ml/1 pint milk
1 onion, sliced
1 clove
1 bay leaf
6 parsley stalks
110g/4oz semolina
200g/7oz strong Cheddar cheese
30ml/2 tablespoons fresh grated Parmesan cheese
15ml/1 tablespoon chopped fresh parsley
salt and freshly ground black pepper
pinch of dried mustard
pinch of cayenne
oil for deep-frying
beaten egg
dried white breadcrumbs

1. Infuse the milk with the onion, clove, bay leaf and parsley stalks over a very gentle heat for 7 minutes. Bring up to boiling point, then strain.

2. Sprinkle in the semolina, stirring steadily, and cook, still stirring, until the mixture is thick (about 1 minute). Draw the pan off the heat and add the cheeses, parsley, salt, pepper, mustard and cayenne. Taste: it should be well seasoned. Spread this mixture into a neat round on a wet plate and leave to chill for 30 minutes.

3. Cut the gnocchi paste into 8 equal wedges. Chill.

4. Heat the oil until a crumb will sizzle vigorously in it. Dip the gnocchi into beaten egg and coat with breadcrumbs.

5. Deep-fry in hot oil until golden brown (about 2 minutes). Drain well on absorbent paper. Sprinkle with salt and serve.

NOTE I: A thin tomato sauce (see page 231) is good with fried gnocchi.

NOTE II: If you do not like the idea of deep-frying, bake the gnocchi at 190°C/375°F/gas mark 5 for 20 minutes, and then grill until well browned on both sides.

LIGHT RED ITALIAN

Gnocchi alla Romana

SERVES 4-6

1 litre/1¾ pints milk
7.5ml/1½ teaspoons salt
a good grating of fresh nutmeg
225g/8oz coarse-ground semolina
3 egg yolks
85g/3oz Parmesan cheese, freshly grated
85g/3oz butter

1. Lightly oil an oven tray.
2. In a large saucepan, bring the milk, salt and nutmeg to the boil, remove from the heat and sprinkle over the semolina, stirring continually with a wooden spoon.
3. Reduce the heat and return the pan to the heat. Continue to cook, uncovered, for 10-15 minutes, stirring occasionally to prevent burning and sticking. The spoon should be able to stand upright, unsupported in the mixture. Remove from the heat. Cool slightly.
4. Beat in the egg yolks, 30g/1oz of the cheese and 30g/1oz of the butter. Taste and season.
5. Pile into the prepared tin and smooth over with a wet spatula to about 5mm/¼ inch thick. Refrigerate for about 1-1½ hours until the semolina is firm.
6. Set the oven to 230°C/450°F/gas mark 8. Melt the butter and lightly brush a shallow ovenproof dish with a little of it.
7. Cut the semolina into circles using a 4cm/1½ inch plain pastry cutter. Arrange these discs overlapping each other slightly in the prepared dish.
8. Pour over the remaining butter and sprinkle with the remaining Parmesan cheese. Bake for 15-20 minutes or until crisp and golden brown.

LIGHT RED ITALIAN

Tempura

SERVES 4

For the batter:
225g/8oz flour
2 small egg yolks
340ml/12 fl oz water
pinch of salt

1 small aubergine
1 medium courgette cut into batons
110g/4oz baby sweetcorn, halved lengthways
225g/8oz scampi, seasoned with lemon juice and black pepper
oil for deep-frying

For the sauce:
10ml/2 teaspoons sesame oil
30ml/2 tablespoons red wine vinegar
30ml/2 tablespoons soy sauce
45ml/3 tablespoons ginger syrup (from a jar of preserved ginger)
30ml/2 tablespoons runny honey
1 small bunch spring onions, shredded

1. Slice the aubergine thinly, score the flesh lightly and place in a colander, sprinkling each layer with salt. Leave to 'degorge' for half an hour.
2. Mix all the ingredients together for the sauce, except for the spring onions.
3. Heat the oil for deep-frying until a crumb will sizzle vigorously in it.
4. Wash the aubergines well and pat dry on kitchen paper.
5. When the oil is hot mix the batter ingredients together – it should not be smooth.
6. Dip the prepared ingredients into the batter and deep-fry in small batches. Drain well on kitchen paper and sprinkle lightly with salt. Arrange on a large serving dish.
7. Scatter the shredded spring onions on top of the sauce and hand separately.

SPICY DRY WHITE

Farinaceous

Boiled Rice

55g/2oz long-grain white rice per person
slice of lemon
15ml/1 tablespoon oil

1. Take a large saucepan and fill it with salted water (1 cup of rice will need at least 6 cups of water, but the exact quantities do not matter as long as there is plenty of water). Bring to a rolling boil.
2. Tip in the rice and stir until the water re-boils. Add the lemon slice and oil.
3. Boil for exactly 10 minutes and then test: the rice should be neither hard nor mushy, but firm to the bite: 'al dente'.
4. Drain the rice in a colander or sieve, and swish plenty of hot water through it.
5. Stand the colander on the draining board. With the handle of a wooden spoon, make a few draining holes through the pile of rice to help the water and steam escape. Alternatively, turn the mass of rice over every few minutes with a spoon.

NOTE: If the rice is required for a salad, it may be rinsed in cold water after cooking, but it will need longer to drain dry - if the water is hot it steams dry faster.

Boiled Brown Rice

Brown rices vary enormously, and though this method is suitable for the majority of them, some may require longer, slower cooking.

55g/2oz brown rice per person
salt

1. Cook the rice in a large amount of boiling salted water for 20 minutes. Drain well.

Basmati Rice I

Allow 55g/2oz of rice per head. Soak it in cold water for about 1 hour. Drain, rinse under cold running water, drain well. Put it in a saucepan and add enough cold water to cover, a pinch of salt, a cinnamon stick, 5ml/1 teaspoon lightly fried mustard seeds, and the crushed seeds from 2 or 3 cardamom pods. Bring it to the boil, cover and simmer until the rice is cooked and the water absorbed. This will take 6-9 minutes. Remove the cinnamon stick.

Basmati Rice II

Allow 55g/2oz rice per head. Soak it in cold water for about 1 hour. Drain, rinse well and drain again. Put into a saucepan with a pinch of salt. Add enough cold water to just cover the rice. Bring it up to the boil, simmer for 4-5 minutes, cover and remove from the heat. After about 10 minutes the rice should be perfectly cooked and all the water absorbed.

Noodles with Red Peppers

SERVES 4
1 medium red pepper, quartered and deseeded
225g/8oz fettucine noodles
15ml/1 tablespoon olive oil
salt and freshly ground black pepper

1. Grill the pepper until the skin is black and blistered. Cool, remove the skin and slice.
2. Cook the pasta in plenty of rapidly boiling salted water for about 6 minutes, until tender but not too soft. Drain and leave in the colander.
3. Heat the oil, add the peppers and shake over the heat until sizzling. Add the pasta and pile into a warmed serving dish. Season with plenty of pepper.

DRY WHITE

Potatoes in Coconut Milk

This recipe has been adapted from *Curries and Oriental Cookery* by Josceline Dimbleby.

SERVES 4
55g/2oz unsweetened desiccated coconut
290ml/$^1/_2$ pint milk
675g/1$^1/_2$lb potatoes, peeled and cut into chunks
salt
1 small green chilli
2-3 small bay leaves
3 x 2.5cm/1 inch sticks cinnamon

1. Put the coconut in a bowl. Bring the milk to the boil and pour on to the coconut, stir and leave on one side.
2. Boil the potatoes in salted water for 7-10 minutes, until just cooked but not breaking up, and drain.
3. Cut open the chilli under running water, discard the seeds and stem and chop the flesh finely.
4. Return the drained potatoes to a saucepan and strain the coconut milk over them through a fine sieve, pressing to extract all the liquid. Add the bay leaves, the chilli, a little salt and the cinnamon sticks. Bring to the boil and simmer for 8-10 minutes. Transfer to a serving dish.

Fondant Potatoes

SERVES 4
900g/2lb potatoes
110g/4oz butter
2 bay leaves
200ml/$^1/_3$ pint chicken stock (see page 219)
salt and freshly ground black pepper

1. Wash and peel the potatoes and then turn into 8-sided barrel shapes.
2. Melt the butter in a sauté pan, add the potatoes and lightly brown on all sides.
3. Add the bay leaves, chicken stock, salt and pepper and cover with wet greaseproof paper. Cook over a low heat for about 40 minutes, when the stock should have been absorbed and the potatoes are tender.
4. Carefully lift the potatoes out of the pan and place in a warmed serving dish. Pour over any remaining butter and juices from the sauté pan.

Roast Potatoes

SERVES 4
900g/2lb potatoes
salt
60ml/4 tablespoons dripping or oil

1. Wash and peel the potatoes and, if they are large, cut them into 5cm/2 inch pieces.
2. Bring them to the boil in salted water. Simmer for 5 minutes.
3. Drain them and shake them in the sieve to roughen and slightly crumble the surface of each potato. (This produces deliciously crunchy potatoes that can be kept warm for up to 2 hours without coming to any harm. Potatoes roasted without this preliminary boiling and scratching tend to become tough and hard if not eaten straight away.)
4. Melt the fat in a roasting pan and add the potatoes, turning them so that they are coated all over.
5. Roast, basting occasionally, and turning the potatoes over at half-time. See note below.

NOTE: Potatoes can be roasted at almost any temperature, usually taking 1 hour in a hot oven, or 1$^1/_2$ hours in a medium one. They should be basted and turned over once or twice during cooking, and they are done when a skewer glides easily into them. Potatoes roasted in the same pan as the meat have the best flavour, but this is not always possible if the joint or bird is very large, or if liquid has been added to the pan.

Château Potatoes

SERVES 4
675g/1$^1/_2$lb small even-sized potatoes
oil or beef dripping
salt and freshly ground black pepper

1. Wash and peel the potatoes. Trim each one into a barrel.
2. Set the oven to 190°C/375°F/gas mark 5.
3. Heat a few spoons of oil or dripping in a sauté pan. Add the potatoes and brown gently on all sides (shaking the pan constantly) until they are just brown. Season with salt and pepper.
4. Cover the pan and place in the oven for about 30 minutes or until the potatoes are tender. (Alternatively, they can be cooked on the hob, but care must be taken that they do not burn: shake the pan frequently. Do not remove the lid as this allows the steam to escape, and the potatoes will fry rather than cook gently.)

Baked Potatoes with Chives and Soured Cream

SERVES 1
1 large potato, well scrubbed
salt and pepper
30ml/2 tablespoons soured cream
5ml/1 teaspoon chopped chives

1. Prick the potatoes with a fork to prevent them from bursting in the oven.
2. Bake in a fairly hot oven at 200°C/400°F/gas mark 6 for 1 hour or until a skewer glides easily through the largest potato.
3. Mix the remaining ingredients together and season with salt and pepper.
4. Split the potatoes without cutting them quite in half and fill with the soured cream mixture.
5. Serve immediately and hand the extra soured cream separately.

NOTE: There is some controversy about preparing potatoes for baking: oiling and wrapping them in foil gives a soft shiny skin, wetting them with water and sprinkling them with salt gives a dull very crisp skin.

Boulangère Potatoes

SERVES 4
675g/1½lb potatoes, very thinly sliced
45g/1oz butter
1 small onion, very thinly sliced
salt and freshly ground black pepper
290ml/½ pint chicken stock

1. Heat the oven to 170°C/325°F/gas mark 3.
2. Butter a pie dish and arrange the potatoes in layers with the onion, adding a little salt and pepper as you go.
3. Arrange the top layer of potatoes in overlapping slices.
4. Dot with the rest of the butter and pour in the stock. Press the potatoes down firmly – they should be completely submerged in the stock.
5. Bake in the oven for about 1½ hours or until the potatoes are tender and the top browned.

Leith's Good Foods' Dauphinoise Potatoes

900g/2lb old floury potatoes, peeled and finely sliced
1 onion, finely sliced
1 garlic clove, crushed (optional)
15g/½oz butter
425ml/¾ pint mixed single and double cream
150ml/¼ pint soured cream, let down to double cream consistency with milk
salt and freshly ground black pepper

1. Preheat the oven to 170°C/325°F/gas mark 3.
2. Cook the onions and garlic in the butter until soft but not brown.
3. Layer up the potatoes and creams with the onions and seasoning in a lightly buttered dish, and bake in the oven for 1½ hours.

Pommes Anna

SERVES 4
675g/1½lb potatoes, peeled and finely sliced
55g/2oz butter, clarified (see page 138)
salt and pepper
grated nutmeg

1. Heat the oven to 190°C/375°F/gas mark 5. Brush a heavy ovenproof pan with the butter.
2. Arrange a neat layer of overlapping potato slices on the bottom of the pan. Brush the potatoes with the melted butter and season well with salt, pepper and nutmeg.
3. Continue to layer the potatoes, butter and seasoning until all the potatoes have been used. Finish with butter and seasoning.
4. Hold the pan over direct medium heat for 2 minutes to brown the bottom layer of potatoes.
5. Take off and cover with greased paper and a lid or foil. Bake in the oven for about 45 minutes.
6. When the potatoes are tender, invert a serving plate over the pan and turn the potatoes out so that the neat first layer is now on top.

Individual Pommes Anna

450g/1lb potatoes, peeled and finely sliced
45g/1½oz unsalted butter
salt and freshly ground black pepper
grated nutmeg

1. Heat the oven to 220°C/425°F/gas mark 7. Brush 12 individual patty tins with the melted butter.
2. Arrange one slice of potato on the bottom of the patty tin and then neatly overlap the slices with more melted butter and seasoning. You need 8 layers of potatoes.
3. Bake in the top of the oven for 30 minutes or until golden brown.
4. When the potatoes are tender, remove from the patty tin and serve immediately.

Mashed Potatoes

SERVES 4
675g/1½lb potatoes, peeled
about 290ml/½ pint milk
55g/2oz butter
salt and pepper
a little grated nutmeg

1. Boil the potatoes in salted water until tender. Drain thoroughly.
2. Push the potatoes through a sieve or mouli. Return them to the dry saucepan. Heat carefully, stirring to allow the potato to steam dry.
3. Push the mass of potato to one side of the pan. Put the exposed part of the pan over direct heat and pour in the milk. Tilt the pan to allow the milk to boil without burning the potato.
4. When the milk is boiling, or near it, beat it into the potato. Add the butter. Season with salt, pepper and nutmeg.

NOTE I: This recipe is for very soft mashed potatoes. If you want a stiffer consistency add less milk.
NOTE II: For mashed potatoes with olive oil, add half the quantity of milk, as above, then beat in 150ml/¼ pint olive oil instead of the butter and season to taste.

Fried Rice

SERVES 4
120ml/8 tablespoons polished rice
55g/2oz pine kernels (optional)
oil
salt and pepper
2 spring onions, finely chopped

1. Bring a large saucepan full of salted water to the boil and tip in the rice. Stir, bring back to the boil, and cook for 10 minutes or until the rice is just tender.
2. Fry the pine kernels in 15ml/1 tablespoon oil until lightly browned all over.
3. Rinse plenty of hot water through the rice to remove the excess starch and drain well. While it is draining, turn it over occasionally with a spoon to allow trapped steam to escape.
4. Pour 45ml/3 tablespoons oil into the frying pan with the pine kernals. Put in the rice, now quite dry. Fry, turning all the time to brown evenly. Season to taste.
5. Stir in the spring onions.

NOTE: 'Easy cook' or polished rice is much easier to fry evenly.

Sauté Potatoes

SERVES 4
675g/1½lb potatoes
30ml/2 tablespoons oil
45g/1½oz butter
salt and freshly ground black pepper
15ml/1 tablespoon chopped fresh parsley or rosemary

1. Cook the potatoes until tender in boiling salted water. Drain and allow to dry. Cut into 2.5cm/1 inch irregular chunks.
2. Heat the oil in a large sauté or frying pan, add the butter and wait for the bubbles to disappear. Add all the potatoes at once.
3. Add the salt and pepper and shake the potatoes gently over the heat while they slowly fry to a pale brown. Turn them only occasionally or they will break up too much. They should anyway be fairly dry and crumbly.
4. When delicately brown and crisp add the parsley or rosemary and tip into a warmed serving dish.

Pommes Parisienne

SERVES 4
6 large potatoes, peeled
30ml/2 tablespoons oil
knob of butter
salt

1. Scoop the potatoes into small balls with a melon baller. As you prepare the balls drop them into a bowl of cold water to prevent discolouring. Float a plate on top to keep them submerged.
2. Heat the oil in a sauté pan and add the butter. Dry the potato balls well and toss them in the pan until completely coated with fat. Fry very slowly until they are browned and tender, shaking the pan frequently to prevent them sticking.
3. Drain well, sprinkle with salt and serve immediately.

NOTE: Allow 15 Parisienne potatoes per head. The larger the potatoes, the easier it is to scoop them into balls.

Chips

SERVES 4
657g/1½lb potatoes
oil for frying
salt

1. Cut the potatoes into 5 x 1cm/2 x ½ inch sticks. Keep them in a bowl of cold water until ready for cooking. This will prevent any discoloration and remove excess starch, which tends to stick the chips together.
2. Heat the oil to a medium temperature – when a croûton of bread is dropped in it should fizzle gently.
3. Dry the potatoes carefully and place a few at a time in the chip basket – too may will stick together.
4. Fry for 7-8 minutes until soft. Remove from the oil.
5. Heat the oil again until a croûton of bread will fizzle and brown in just 30 seconds.
6. Repeat the frying process in the hotter oil until the chips are well browned and crisp.
7. Drain the chips on absorbent paper. Sprinkle with salt.
8. Serve immediately. Do not cover the chips or they will lose their crispness.

NOTE: Chips are cooked in two stages because if the fat is hot enough to crisp and brown the chips, the process is so quick that the middle of the potato will not be cooked. On the other hand, if the oil is cooler, although the chip will cook through, it will be soggy. The second frying, to create the crisp brown outside, should be done just before serving.

Game Chips

SERVES 4
450g/1lb large potatoes
oil for frying
salt

1. Wash and peel the potatoes. If you want even-sized chips trim each potato into a cylinder shape.
2. Slice them very finely across the cylinder, preferably on a mandolin. Soak in cold water for

30 minutes to remove the excess starch – this will prevent them from discolouring or sticking together.
3. Heat the oil until a crumb will sizzle vigorously in it.
4. Dry the chips very thoroughly on a tea towel.
5. Lower a basket of chips into the hot oil. They are cooked when they rise to the surface and are golden brown.
6. Drain on absorbent paper, sprinkle with salt and serve immediately.

NOTE: Commercial plain potato crisps will do very well as game chips. Simply heat them, uncovered, in a moderate oven.

Matchstick Potatoes (Pommes Allumettes)

SERVES 4
450g/1lb potatoes
oil for deep-frying
salt

1. Wash and peel the potatoes. Cut them into tiny even matchsticks and soak in cold water for 15 minutes. This is to remove the excess starch and will prevent the potatoes from sticking together. Dry them very thoroughly with a tea towel.
2. Heat the oil until a crumb dropped in the fat sizzles vigorously. Fry the chips for 2-3 minutes, until golden brown and crisp. Drain on absorbent paper. Sprinkle with salt and serve at once.

Game Chip Baskets Filled with Chestnuts

SERVES 4
675g/1½lb potatoes
oil for deep-frying
45g/1½oz butter
30g/1oz pinenuts
400g/14oz tin whole unsweetened chestnuts
handful of raisins
small bunch of white grapes, halved and pips removed

1. Peel the potatoes. Slice finely using a mandolin or a patterned cutter so that the finished basket will look like woven straw.
2. Dip a small wire strainer or sieve into the oil to get it well greased. Heat the oil until a crumb will sizzle vigorously in it.
3. Line the strainer with potato slices overlapping each other. Using a small ladle to prevent the chips floating away from the strainer as you cook them, deep-fry the 'basket' until golden and crisp.
4. Drain well on absorbent paper.
5. Melt the butter and add the pinenuts. Brown them lightly, then add the chestnuts, raisins and grapes. Fry until hot.
6. Fill the baskets with this mixture just before serving.

NOTE: A gadget for making the baskets is available in shops selling to the catering trade, but the sieve and ladle method works perfectly well.

Baked Potatoes with Cheese

SERVES 4
450g/1lb potatoes
butter
salt and freshly ground black pepper
85g/3oz Gruyère or strong Cheddar cheese, grated
15ml/1 tablespoon grated Parmesan cheese
150ml/¼pint double cream
1 egg, beaten

1. Peel and cut the potatoes into slices about the thickness of a coin. Soak in a bowl of cold water for 15 minutes. This removes some of the starch and prevents the slices sticking together.
2. Heat the oven to 180°C/350°F/gas mark 4. Butter an ovenproof pie dish.
3. Drain and dry the potatoes and place a layer in the bottom of the pie dish. Sprinkle with salt, pepper and cheese. Continue to layer potatoes, seasoning and cheese, reserving a little cheese for the end, until the dish is nearly full.
4. Mix the cream with the beaten egg, season with salt and pepper and pour over the potatoes.

5. Sprinkle on the remaining grated cheese and place a few knobs of butter on top.
6. Bake in the oven for $1^1/2$ hours until the potatoes are tender and the top is brown and crisp. Test with a skewer.

Rösti Potatoes

SERVES 4
1 Spanish onion, finely chopped
55g/2oz streaky bacon, finely chopped
oil
675g/$1^1/2$lb large potatoes, peeled and parboiled
salt and freshly ground black pepper
butter

1. Take a 23cm/9 inch frying pan and put into it the onion and bacon and 15ml/1 tablespoon oil.
2. Cook slowly over gentle heat until the onion is transparent and soft but not coloured. Remove from the heat.
3. Coarsely grate the potatoes. Season with salt and pepper. Fork in the onion and bacon.
4. Heat 15ml/1 tablespoon mixed butter and oil in the frying pan. Add the potato mixture. Pat it lightly into a flat cake with straight sides.
5. Fry gently until the underside is crusty and golden brown (about 15 minutes). Shake the pan every so often to ensure that the cake does not stick.
6. Place a plate larger than the frying pan over the pan and turn both plate and pan over to tip the rösti out on to the plate. Slip it immediately back into the pan to cook the other side for 5 minutes. Place in a warm oven for 15 minutes, if necessary. Serve on a large flat dish, cut into wedges like a cake.

NOTE I: Finely grated raw carrots are sometimes added to the mixture. The potato cake can be baked in the oven at 190°C/375°F/gas mark 5 for about 30 minutes rather than fried.
NOTE II: Very old large floury potatoes need not be parboiled before grating. The boiling is to remove some of the sticky starch present in small young waxy potatoes.

Individual Rösti Potatoes

SERVES 4-6
1 Spanish onion, finely chopped
30ml/2 tablespoons oil
2 slices smoked ham
675g/$1^1/2$lb large potatoes, peeled and parboiled for 10 minutes
salt and freshly ground black pepper
30g/1oz butter, melted

1. Cook the onion in half of the oil until soft but not coloured.
2. Set the oven to 200°C/400°F/gas mark 6.
3. Cut the ham into short fine strips. Grate the potatoes coarsely and mix with the onion, ham, salt and pepper.
4. Divide the mixture into 12 and place in patty tins. Spoon over the melted butter and bake for about 15 minutes until golden brown.

Brown Rice Pilaf with Sesame Seeds

SERVES 4-6
1 small onion, finely chopped
30g/1oz butter
225g/8oz brown rice
720ml/$1^1/4$ pints chicken or vegetable stock
45ml/3 tablespoons toasted sesame seeds
15ml/1 tablespoon chopped mixed fresh herbs
salt and freshly ground black pepper
paprika

1. Cook the onion in the butter until it is soft but not coloured.
2. Add the rice and fry, stirring, until it is slightly opaque, about 3 minutes.
3. Add the stock, seeds, herbs, salt and pepper. Bring to the boil, cover and cook very slowly for 45 minutes, by which time the liquid should be completely absorbed and the rice tender.
4. Serve sprinkled with a little paprika.

Vegetables

Vegetables

VEGETABLES in Britain are usually served as an accompaniment to a main meat course. It is worth considering them, however, as first courses on their own, or as main courses if served in sufficient variety or with a sauce. For a salad or first course they may be served raw or cooked, warm or cold, and with a dressing.

TO PREPARE VEGETABLES

Always wash vegetables before preparing them. Vegetables are an excellent source of vitamins and minerals but these can easily be leached if the vegetables are cut up too far in advance of cooking, if they are left to soak in cold water (vitamin C particularly is lost in this way), if they are cut up with a blunt knife, which damages the cells, or if they are cooked with bicarbonate of soda in an attempt to preserve colour.

FRESH GREEN VEGETABLES

BLANCHING AND REFRESHING. This method of cooking vegetables is commonly used in restaurants where some advance preparation is vital. It is worth doing when coping with a large selection of vegetables.

Boil the vegetables separately: bring the water to a good boil and drop in the vegetables. Use enough water to barely cover them and add 5ml/1 teaspoon of salt for each 570ml/1 pint of water. Boil as rapidly as you dare (delicate vegetables like broccoli can break up if too rapidly boiled). As soon as they are tender, but not yet totally soft, drain them and rinse in cold water to prevent further cooking and to set the colour. This is called refreshing. Just before serving toss the vegetables separately in melted butter over a good heat.

NOTE: As the cooking liquid contains much of the vitamins and minerals it should, if possible, be preserved and used for soups or sauces.

BOILING. Follow the same procedure as above. Drain the vegetables (without refreshing) and dish up. Brush with melted butter if required.

SWEATING. Put the prepared vegetables in a heavy saucepan with 15ml/1 tablespoon of butter or oil. Cover tightly with a lid. Cook very slowly. Shake the pan frequently until the vegetables are tender. Add salt and dish up.

STEAMING. Steaming in a proper steamer is an excellent method of cooking root vegetables, but is less successful with green ones as their bright colour is sometimes lost. It is nutritionally superior to boiling – although vegetables take longer to cook, there is no leaching of vitamins or minerals into the water.

STIR-FRYING. This cooking method, much beloved of Chinese cooks, is excellent for green vegetables. It preserves vitamins and minerals, and the vegetables remain bright in colour. The disadvantage is that you must stand over the cooking vegetables all the time.

Slice the vegetables as finely as you can, put in a large deep-sided frying pan (the Chinese wok is perfect) with a splash of oil. Toss the vegetables in the hot oil over a fierce heat. Shake the pan, and stir and turn the vegetables continually until they are just tender. Sprinkle with salt and serve.

FRESH NON-GREEN VEGETABLES

BOILING. Put the vegetables into cold salted water and bring slowly to the boil. Cook covered, until completely tender. With the exception of carrots (which are good with a bit of bite to them), root vegetables should be cooked until tender. Drain and brush with melted butter if required. New potatoes are usually put into boiling salted water.

REFRESHING. It is sometimes advisable to rinse carrots briefly in cold water after cooking, as this sets the bright colour, but it is not necessary.

SWEATING OR HALF-STEAMING. Slice the vegetables fairly thickly. Cook them slowly in a covered saucepan with butter or oil. They will absorb more fat than green vegetables. This is a very good method for mushrooms.

STEAMING. This is excellent for all root vegetables, particularly for large potatoes, which might otherwise break up while boiling.

DRIED PULSES

Dried peas and beans (lentils, split peas, chickpeas, green peas, black-eyed peas, haricot beans, lima beans, butter beans, brown beans, red kidney, beans etc.) are generally cheaper than their fresh or tinned equivalents, are easy to cook and very nutritious. They should be bought from grocers with a good turnover, and as a rule small butter beans are better than large ones.

Most pulses need soaking until softened and swollen before cooking. Soaking can take as much as 12 hours (butter beans) or as little as 20 minutes (lentils). Do not soak for more than 12 hours in case the beans start germinating or fermenting. If there is no time for preliminary soaking, unsoaked pulses may be cooked either in a pressure cooker or very slowly; but remember that enough water must be used to allow the beans first to swell and then to cook. Preliminary soaking is less hazardous.

To cook the pulses, cover them with fresh cold water, bring to the boil and simmer for 5 minutes. Change the water and cook until tender. Boiling times vary according to the age and size of the pulses: new season's pulses will cook faster. Small lentils may take as little as 15 minutes and large haricot beans or chickpeas can take as long as 2 hours.

NOTE: Red kidney beans must be fast boiled for at least 15 minutes to destroy dangerous toxins.

Cabbage with Caraway

SERVES 4

450g/1lb white cabbage, finely sliced
30g/1oz butter
2 onions, sliced
15ml/1 teaspoon caraway seeds
5ml/1 teaspoon vinegar or lemon juice
salt and freshly ground black pepper

1. Melt the butter in a frying pan and add the sliced onion. Cook over a gentle heat until soft but not coloured.
2. Put the cabbage into a pan of boiling salted water. Simmer for about 5 minutes until tender and drain well.
3. Add the caraway seeds and vinegar to the onion and cook gently for 1 more minute.
4. Stir this into the drained cabbage and season well with salt and pepper.

Brussels Sprouts and Chestnuts

SERVES 4

450g/1lb very small Brussels sprouts
225g/8oz fresh chestnuts
45g/1½oz butter
salt, freshly ground black pepper and nutmeg

1. Wash and trim the sprouts, paring the stalks and removing the outside leaves if necessary.

2. Make a slit in the skin of each chestnut and put them into a pan of cold water. Bring to the boil, simmer for 10 minutes and then take off the heat. Remove 1 or 2 nuts at a time and peel. The skins come off easily if the chestnuts are hot but not too cooked.
3. Melt the butter in a frying pan, and slowly fry the chestnuts, which will break up a little until brown.
4. Bring a large pan of salted water to the boil, and tip in the sprouts. Boil fairly fast until they are cooked, but not soggy: the flavour changes disastrously if boiled too long. Drain them well.
5. Mix the sprouts and chestnuts together gently, adding the butter from the frying pan. Season with salt, pepper and nutmeg.

Vichy Carrots

SERVES 4
560g/1 1/4lb carrots
150ml/1/4 pint water
10ml/2 teaspoons butter
2.5ml/1/2 teaspoon salt
5ml/1 teaspoon sugar
freshly ground black pepper
10ml/2 teaspoons chopped mint and parsley, mixed

1. Peel the carrots and cut them into slices or even-sized barrel shapes; or if they are very young leave them whole.
2. Put everything except the pepper and herbs into a saucepan and boil until the water has almost evaporated and the carrots are tender. Then turn down the heat and allow the carrots to brown slightly in the remaining butter and sugar, watching to make sure they do not burn.
3. Season with pepper and mix in the herbs.

NOTE : It is important not to oversalt the water. When the water has evaporated the entire quantity of salt will remain with the carrots.

Courgettes with Garlic and Tomato

SERVES 4
4 large courgettes
30g/1oz butter
1 onion, finely chopped
1 garlic clove, crushed
30ml/2 tablespoons tomato purée
15ml/1 tablespoon white wine
15ml/1 teaspoon fresh basil, chopped
salt and freshly ground black pepper

1. Cut the courgettes into 2.5cm/1 inch chunks.
2. Put into a sieve over a pan of boiling water, or into a proper steamer, cover and steam for 5 minutes or until just tender.
3. Melt the butter, add the onion and garlic and cook gently until the onion is soft but not coloured. Add the courgettes, the tomato purée, wine and basil, and season with salt and pepper.
4. Cover and cook, shaking the pan frequently to prevent sticking and burning, over a moderate heat for about 5 minutes.
5. Taste and season again if necessary. Serve hot or cold.

Mushrooms with Lemon and Parsley

SERVES 4
675g/1 1/2lb button mushrooms, halved
juice of 1/2 lemon
150ml/1/4 pint chicken stock
15ml/1 tablespoon chopped parsley

1. Cook the mushrooms in a covered pan with the lemon juice and stock for about 3 minutes until tender.
2. Lift the mushrooms, with a perforated spoon, into a warmed serving dish. Reduce the cooking liquor by boiling rapidly to 45-60ml/3-4 tablespoons. Add the parsley and pour it over the mushrooms.

Broccoli Tower

SERVES 4-6
450g/1lb green broccoli
450g/1lb cauliflower
butter
salt and pepper

1. Butter a 1litre/2 pint pudding basin heavily. Break the broccoli and cauliflower into florets and boil, unsalted, until just cooked. Arrange a few cauliflower florets, stalks up, in the bottom of the pudding basin. Then arrange a ring of green florets of broccoli on top of them, stalks inwards. Continue the white/green layers in this way, filling the middle with uneven-sized pieces and keeping the even ones for the edge.
2. Add salt, pepper and a little melted butter as you go. When full, press down well with a saucer. Reheat for 3 minutes in a microwave, or 20 minutes in a steamer, then carefully turn out.

Glazed Vegetables

SERVES 6-8
450g/1lb large potatoes
450g/1lb carrots
450g/1lb turnips
12 button onions
15ml/1 tablespoon bacon or pork dripping
2.5ml/½ teaspoon sugar
salt and freshly ground black pepper
55g/2oz butter
110g/4oz button mushrooms
juice of ½ lemon
15ml/1 tablespoon chopped fresh parsley

1. Wash and peel the potatoes, carrots and turnips. Using a melon scoop, scoop the flesh of the potato into balls. Dry them in a clean cloth. Trim the carrots and turnips into small barrel shapes.
2. Peel the onions. Dipping them into boiling water for 10 seconds makes this easier.
3. Heat the oven to 200°C/400°F/gas mark 6.
4. Put the prepared vegetables in a roasting pan and baste with the dripping. Roast, shaking the pan occasionally and turning the vegetables over, for 45 minutes.
5. When the vegetables are tender, put the roasting pan over direct heat, add the sugar and shake the pan until browned to a good even colour. Season with salt and pepper. Keep warm.
6. Melt the butter over a good heat and toss the mushrooms in it. Shake the pan to make sure that every mushroom is coated with butter. When they are beginning to brown, add the lemon juice and allow this to sizzle and evaporate a little. Add salt and pepper and the chopped parsley.
7. Serve the vegetables mixed together on a heated dish.

NOTE I: If these vegetables are to accompany a roast meat, the root vegetables can be cooked in the meat roasting tin. Add them about 30 minutes before the meat is due to come out.
NOTE II: The root vegetables can be 'pot roasted' instead of cooked in the oven. This is a good idea if nothing else is being baked or roasted at the time, when it would be wasteful to heat the oven just for this dish. In a heavy casserole or pan toss the vegetables in the fat. Cover with a lid, and turn the heat down low. Cook like this for 20 minutes or until the vegetables are tender, giving the pan a shake every now and then to prevent sticking. When they are cooked, brown them with the sugar, and fry the mushrooms etc. as described above.

Provençal Tomatoes

SERVES 4
4 medium tomatoes
55g/2oz butter
1 onion, finely chopped
½ garlic clove, crushed
60ml/4 tablespoons stale white breadcrumbs
salt and freshly ground black pepper
pinch of nutmeg
10ml/2 teaspoons chopped fresh parsley
5ml/1 teaspoon chopped tarragon
chopped parsley to garnish

1. Heat the oven to 200°C/400°F/gas mark 6.
2. Cut the tomatoes in half horizontally. Spoon out and strain the tomato pulp.
3. Melt half the butter and gently cook the onion in it until soft. Add the garlic and cook for 1 more minute.

4. Mix the breadcrumbs, seasoning, nutmeg, herbs, and onion mixture together with a fork. Add enough strained tomato to make a wet but not soggy stuffing.
5. Pile the breadcrumb mixture into the tomatoes and place a knob of the remaining butter on each.
6. Put the tomatoes in an ovenproof dish and bake in the oven for about 20 minutes or until the breadcrumbs are golden.
7. Sprinkle with chopped parsley.

Bashed Neeps

SERVES 4
675g/1½lb swedes
salt and freshly ground black pepper
30-55g/1-2oz butter
grated nutmeg

1. Peel and cut the swedes into chunks.
2. Boil the swedes in salted water until tender.
3. Drain well.
4. Push through a sieve or mash with a potato masher. Beat in salt, pepper, butter and grated nutmeg.

NOTE: The Scots call a swede a neep (or turnip). Very confusing.

Celeriac Purée

SERVES 4
2 medium potatoes
225g/8oz celeriac
290ml/½ pint milk
55g/2oz butter
salt and white pepper

1. Wash and peel the potatoes and place them in a pan of cold salted water. Bring to the boil, cover and simmer for about 25 minutes until tender.
2. Meanwhile, wash the celeriac, peel it and cut into chunks. Simmer slowly in the milk for about 20-30 minutes until tender.
3. Mash the celeriac with its milk, which should by now be much reduced.
4. Drain the potatoes and mash or sieve them. Place the potatoes and celeriac together in a pan. Beat over a gentle heat, adding the butter as you mix. Add salt and pepper to taste.
5. Pile into a serving dish and serve at once.

Purée Clamart

SERVES 4
1 medium onion
45g/1½oz butter
150ml/¼ pint strong chicken stock
450g/1lb frozen or podded fresh peas
salt and pepper
225g/8oz mashed potato (see page 187)

1. Chop the onion finely and put it with the butter, stock and peas in a saucepan. Add a little salt and pepper. Cover the saucepan and simmer the ingredients until the peas are tender. If the peas are fresh, or frozen in a solid block, it may be necessary to add a splash more stock during cooking as the cooking time will be longer.
2. Liquidize the peas with any remaining juice, or push through a sieve. Turn into a bowl.
3. Gradually beat the potato into the peas. The purée should be soft but able to hold its shape. Taste for seasoning and turn into a warm dish.

Carrot and Chervil Purée

SERVES 4
450g/1lb carrots
570ml/1 pint stock
2 cardamom pods, crushed
1 bay leaf
30ml/2 tablespoons fromage blanc (or substitute)
15ml/1 tablespoon chopped fresh chervil

1. Peel and slice the carrots. Cook in the stock with the cardamom and bay leaf for 20 minutes, or until really soft.
2. Allow to cool slightly, remove the cardamom pod and bay leaf. Drain well but reserve a little of the liquor.
3. Liquidize the carrots with the fromage blanc to make a firm but soft purée. If too firm add a little of the reserved cooking liquor. Add the chervil and season to taste.

Jams Californian Vegetables

This recipe was inspired by Jams Restaurant, New York, where they serve a similar beautifully colourful selection of attractively prepared vegetables.

SERVES 4

12 small new potatoes, washed but not peeled
12 baby carrots, or 3 carrots peeled and cut into diagonal slices
1/4 red pepper, cut into 4 strips
1/4 yellow pepper, cut into 4 strips
4 baby corncobs
4 button turnips
16 French beans, topped and tailed
4 broccoli florets
2 courgettes, cut into 12 diagonal slices
12 strips of cucumber, deseeded
12 radishes
30g/1oz butter
freshly ground black pepper

1. Cook the potatoes and carrots in boiling salted water until just tender. Drain.
2. Blanch the rest of the vegetables except the cucumber in boiling salted water for 2 minutes. Drain.
3. Melt the butter in a sauté pan, add the pepper and toss all the vegetables in it until lightly glazed. Pile on to a warmed serving dish or divide between 4 warmed plates and serve immediately.

Petits Pois à la Française

SERVES 4

225g/8oz peas, shelled (use frozen peas if fresh are not available)
1 large mild onion, very finely sliced
1 small lettuce, shredded
150ml/1/4 pint water
30g/1oz butter
handful each of fresh mint and parsley
1/2 garlic clove, crushed (optional)
salt, freshly ground black pepper
5ml/1 teaspoon sugar

1. Mix the peas, onion and lettuce in a heavy casserole. Add the water, butter, mint, parsley, garlic (if using), salt and pepper and sugar.
2. Cover tightly. Put a double seal of greaseproof paper over the pan before pushing down the lid to make a good seal.
3. Cook for about 30 minutes on a very gentle heat until the peas are almost mushy or, better still, bake in a slow oven at 170°C/325°F/gas mark 3 for 1-2 hours.

NOTE: The liquid may be thickened by the addition of beurre manié (see page 217) if preferred, but care should be taken not to mash the peas while stirring.

Vegetable Stew

SERVES 6

110g/4oz haricot beans
55g/2oz butter
3 small whole onions, peeled
2 leeks, washed and cut up
2 courgettes, cut in chunks
2 medium carrots, peeled and cut into chunks
2 sticks celery, cut in chunks
3 small tomatoes, peeled and quartered
290ml/1/2 pint vegetable stock
3 new potatoes, cut into chunks
salt and freshly ground black pepper
1/4 cauliflower, broken into florets
10ml/2 teaspoons flour
10ml/2 teaspoons chopped fresh parsley
10ml/2 teaspoons chopped fresh mint

To serve:
brown rice (see page 184)

1. Soak the haricot beans for 3 hours. Cook them in fresh boiling water until tender, 1-2 hours. Drain well.
2. Melt half the butter, add the onions and cook them slowly for 1 minute, then add the leeks, courgettes, carrots, celery and tomatoes. Pour on the stock and bring to the boil. Add the potatoes, season with salt and pepper and simmer for about 30 minutes. Add the cauliflower and beans and continue to simmer for about 15 minutes until all the vegetables are tender.

3. Mix the remaining butter and the flour to a paste (beurre manié). Slip a little at a time down the side of the pan and into the mixture, stirring gently. When all the beurre manié has been added you should have a smooth, slightly thickened sauce for the vegetables. Simmer the stew for 3 minutes to cook the flour. Add the parsley and mint. Taste and season as required. Serve with brown rice.

Braised Celery

SERVES 4
1 head celery, cut into batons
15g/1/2oz butter
1 small onion, finely chopped
1 carrot, finely chopped
290ml/1/2 pint chicken stock
1 bay leaf
salt and freshly ground black pepper
15g/1/2oz butter
15g/1/2oz flour

1. Heat the oven to 180°C/350°F/gas mark 4.
2. Melt the butter in a heavy roasting pan and cook the onions and carrots in it until soft but not coloured.
3. Add the celery, stock, bay leaf, salt and pepper and bring to the boil.
4. Cover with a lid or foil and bake in the oven for about 30 minutes until tender.
5. Mix the butter and the flour together to a smooth paste (beurre manié).
6. When the celery is tender place the roasting tin over direct heat. When the liquid boils stir in a little of the beurre manié to thicken the sauce. Do not add too much at a time. Stir until boiling.
7. Simmer for 2 minutes to cook the flour. Taste and adjust the seasoning if necessary.
8. Remove the bay leaf. Transfer celery and liquid to a warmed serving dish.

Ratatouille

SERVES 4
2 small aubergines
2 courgettes
olive oil
1 large onion, sliced
1 garlic clove, crushed
1 medium green pepper, sliced
1 small red pepper, sliced
6 tomatoes, peeled, quartered and deseeded
salt and freshly ground black pepper
pinch of crushed coriander
15ml/1 tablespoon chopped fresh basil (optional)

1. Wipe the aubergines and courgettes and cut into bite-sized chunks. Degorge (sprinkle with salt and leave to drain for about 30 minutes). Rinse away the salt and dry the vegetables well.
2. Melt a little oil in a pan and add the onions and garlic. When soft but not brown, add the aubergine and fry to a pale brown, adding more oil if necessary. Add the peppers and courgettes, cover and cook gently for 25 minutes.
3. Add the tomatoes, salt if necessary, pepper and coriander. Cook, covered, for about 20 minutes.
4. Dish up and sprinkle with basil. Serve hot or well chilled.

NOTE: If you are making large quantities of ratatouille try this catering trick. Deep-fry the aubergines, peppers and courgettes in oil. Drain them and put into the saucepan with the onions, which you have gently fried in olive oil, and the tomatoes. Cook, covered, for 10 minutes with the flavourings. Deep-frying saves a lot of time, but the oil must be clean.

Red Ratatouille

SERVES 4
1 medium aubergine
olive oil
2 red onions, sliced
1 garlic clove, crushed
1 large red pepper, sliced
400g/14oz tin of tomatoes
salt and freshly ground black pepper
crushed coriander
15ml/1 tablespoon chopped purple basil (optional)

1. Wipe the aubergine, cut into bite-sized chunks and degorge (sprinkle with salt and leave to drain for about 30 minutes). Rinse away the salt and dry the aubergine well.
2. Heat a little oil in a pan and add the onions and garlic. When soft but not brown, add the aubergine and fry to a pale brown. Add the red pepper and fry for another couple of minutes over a low heat until the pepper softens a little.
3. Add the tinned tomatoes, salt, pepper and a pinch of crushed coriander. Cover with a lid and simmer gently for about 20 minutes until the vegetables have softened but not broken up. (If the ratatouille is too wet, remove the lid and reduce the juices.)
4. Check seasoning and serve sprinkled with chopped purple basil.

Red Cabbage

SERVES 6
1 small red cabbage
1 onion, sliced
30g/1oz butter
1 small cooking apple, peeled and sliced
1 small dessert apple, peeled and sliced
10ml/2 teaspoons brown sugar
10ml/2 teaspoons vinegar
pinch of ground cloves
salt and freshly ground black pepper

1. Shred the cabbage and discard the hard stalks. Rinse well.
2. In a large saucepan, fry the onion in the butter until it begins to soften.
3. Add the drained but still wet cabbage, the apples, sugar, vinegar and cloves, and season with salt and pepper.
4. Cover tightly and cook very slowly, mixing well and stirring every 15 minutes or so. Cook for 2 hours, or until the whole mass is soft and reduced in bulk. (During the cooking it may be necessary to add a little water.)
5. Taste and add more salt, pepper or sugar if necessary.

Lentils with Cloves

SERVES 4
2 large onions, sliced
3 large carrots, sliced
1 garlic clove, crushed
sunflower oil
225g/8oz brown lentils
750ml/1¼ pints white or vegetable stock
15ml/1 tablespoon tomato purée
15ml/1 tablespoon dried Provençal herbs
6 cloves, tied up in a piece of muslin
black pepper

1. Brown the onions, carrots and garlic in a minimum amount of sunflower oil in a nonstick frying pan.
2. Heat the oven to 170°C/325°F/gas mark 3.
3. Transfer the onion mixture to an ovenproof dish. Add the lentils, stock, tomato purée, herbs and cloves. Bring gradually up to the boil. Stir well and season with pepper.
4. Cook in the preheated oven for 1¼ hours, or until the lentils are just tender and the stock absorbed. Check every so often that all is well – you can never rely completely on a pulse recipe for either cooking times or liquor quantities.

Roast Parsnips

SERVES 4
675g/1½lb parsnips
oil
salt and freshly ground black pepper

1. Heat the oven to 200°C/400°F/gas mark 6.
2. Wash and peel the parsnips. Cut in half lengthways.
3. Boil in salted water for 5 minutes. Drain well.
4. Heat 1cm/½ inch of oil in a roasting tin in the oven. When the oil is hot, add the parsnips. Season with salt and pepper.
5. Roast the parsnips, basting and turning during cooking until they are crisp and golden brown – this will take about 30 minutes.

Cauliflower Cheese

SERVES 4-6
1 large or 2 small cauliflowers
290ml/½ pint mornay sauce (see page 221)
15ml/1 tablespoon grated Cheddar cheese
15ml/1 tablespoon dried white breadcrumbs

1. Break the cauliflower into florets and cook in boiling salted water until just tender. Drain well.
2. Heat up the grill.
3. Reheat the mornay sauce. Put the cauliflower into an ovenproof dish and coat with the cheese sauce.
4. Sprinkle with the cheese and breadcrumbs and place under the grill until brown.

Vegetable Mornay

SERVES 6
1 small cauliflower
salt
225g/8oz shelled peas, or 1 small packet frozen peas
450g/1lb carrots, peeled and cut into batons
3 tomatoes, skinned and halved
570ml/1 pint mornay sauce (see page 221)

To finish:
dry white breadcrumbs
grated cheese

1. Break the cauliflower into sprigs and cook them in boiling salted water until just tender, but not soft.
2. Boil the peas. Boil the carrots in salted water until just tender. Heat the oven to 230°C/450°F/gas mark 8.
3. Put all the vegetables into an ovenproof dish.
4. Heat the mornay sauce and pour it over the vegetables. Sprinkle with the breadcrumbs and cheese.
5. Bake the vegetables until bubbling and brown on top. If necessary, the finished dish can be briefly grilled.

Salsify (or Scorzonera) in Mornay Sauce

Salsify and scorzonera are classified as different vegetables but they taste very alike and are treated similarly, the only practical difference being that salsify is peeled before cooking and scorzonera afterwards. In fact both may be peeled before cooking, but the flavour of scorzonera boiled in its skin is said to be superior.

SERVES 4
12 roots salsify or scorzonera
salt
lemon juice (for salsify only)
290ml/ ½ pint mornay sauce (see page 221)
grated cheese
dried white breadcrumbs

1. For salsify, wash, peel and cut each root into 3-4 pieces.
2. Place in a pan with a cupful of salted water with a little lemon juice and simmer, with a tightly closed lid, for 12-20 minutes, or until tender, topping up with water if necessary.
3. Drain well and arrange in a serving dish.
4. Coat with the hot mornay sauce, sprinkle with grated cheese and breadcrumbs and brown under the grill.

1. For scorzonera, wash and cut each root into 3-4 pieces.
2. Place unpeeled into a pan of boiling salted water and simmer until tender, 15-20 minutes.
3. Drain well and peel off the skin.
4. Proceed as for salsify.

Hot Raw Beetroot

SERVES 4
450g/1lb raw beetroot
55g/2oz butter
salt and coarsely ground black pepper
squeeze of lemon

1. Peel the beetroot and put it through the julienne blade of a processor or grate it on a coarse cheese grater or mandolin.
2. Melt the butter. Toss the beetroot in it for 2 minutes until hot but by no means cooked.
3. Season with salt and pepper and a sprinkle of lemon juice.

NOTE: Raw beetroot in a mustardy vinaigrette is very good too.

Cooked Cucumber with Dill

SERVES 4
2 cucumbers
salt and pepper
30g/1oz butter
10ml/2 teaspoons chopped fresh dill
squeeze of lemon juice

1. Peel the cucumbers and cut into 1cm/½ inch cubes.
2. Drop them into boiling salted water and cook for 3 minutes.
3. Rinse under cold running water and drain well.
4. Melt the butter in a frying pan and when foaming add the cucumber and dill.
5. When the cucumber is beginning to turn a delicate brown, reduce the heat, season with pepper and lemon juice and shake briefly.

NOTE: If cucumbers are cheap and plentiful it is worth shaping them into balls with a melon baller – wasteful but very pretty.

Spinach Bhajee

SERVES 4
900g/2lb fresh spinach, cooked and chopped
45ml/3 tablespoons oil
1 medium onion, finely chopped
1 green chilli, deseeded and chopped
1 garlic clove, crushed
2.5cm/1 inch piece root ginger, grated
10ml/2 teaspoons ground coriander
5ml/1 teaspoon ground cumin
6 cardamom pods
1 tomato, deseeded and sliced
salt and freshly ground black pepper

1. Heat the oil and fry the onion until it is golden. Add the chilli, garlic, ginger and spices and cook together for 1 minute.
2. Add the spinach and tomato and stir over a gentle heat for about 6 minutes. Season with salt and pepper. If necessary, boil away any extra liquid.

Cauliflower Fritters

SERVES 4
1 large cauliflower
lemon juice
freshly ground black pepper
oil for deep-frying
150ml/¼ pint fritter batter (see page 534)

To serve:
290ml/½ pint tomato sauce (see page 231)

1. Cut the cauliflower into florets. Boil them in salted water for 3 minutes.
2. Drain the florets well. When dry, sprinkle liberally with lemon juice and season with black pepper.
3. Heat the oil until a crumb will sizzle in it.
4. Dip each piece of cauliflower in the seasoned fritter batter and drop carefully into the hot oil.
5. The batter will puff up and the cauliflower is ready when golden brown. Drain well and serve immediately with tomato sauce.

NOTE: Although this dish makes a good vegetable accompaniment to plain meat dishes, it is delicious on its own as a lunchtime dish, or as a first course for a more elaborate meal.

French Beans with Almonds

SERVES 4
450g/1lb whole French beans, topped and tailed
salt and freshly ground black pepper
20g/¾oz butter
30g/1oz flaked almonds
squeeze of lemon juice

1. Place the beans in a pan of boiling salted water and cook until just tender.
2. Meanwhile melt the butter and, when foaming, add the almonds. Fry until golden brown, cool for 30 seconds, then add the lemon juice.
3. Drain the beans well and mix with the buttery almonds. Sprinkle with pepper.

Baked Tomatoes

SERVES 4
4 tomatoes
butter
salt and freshly ground black pepper

1. Heat the oven to 190°C/375°F/gas mark 5.
2. Remove the stalk from the tomatoes. With a sharp knife cut a shallow cross in the rounded end of each tomato.
3. Brush with a little melted butter and season with salt and pepper.
4. Put the tomatoes in a roasting dish and bake for about 10 minutes, until soft but not out of shape.

Piedmont Beans

SERVES 4
900g/2lb French beans, topped and tailed
salt and freshly ground black pepper
45g/1oz butter
1 garlic clove
1 egg
55g/2oz Edam or Gruyère cheese, grated
Parmesan cheese
dry white crumbs

1. Heat the oven to 180°C/350°F/gas mark 4. Butter an ovenproof serving dish.
2. Place the beans in a pan of boiling salted water and cook until just tender. Drain well and mince or push through a vegetable mill, or chop finely.
3. Melt the butter and, when frothing, add the beans and garlic. Shake over the heat for 1 minute. Tip into a mixing bowl.
4. Separate the egg and beat the yolk and cheese into the bean mixture. Taste and season with salt and pepper. Be careful not to overseason as cheese is salty.
5. Whisk the egg white until stiff but not dry. Using a large metal spoon fold into the beans.
6. Turn the mixture into the ovenproof dish and sprinkle with Parmesan and breadcrumbs. Bake for 40 minutes.

Mjadara

SERVES 4
225g/8oz brown lentils, soaked for 2 hours
1 litre/2 pints salted water
55g/2oz long-grain rice
30ml/2 tablespoons olive oil or vegetable oil
1 large onion, finely sliced
salt

For the garnish:
raw onion rings, finely sliced
raw tomato, finely sliced

1. Drain the lentils and cook in the salted water for about 1 hour or until just tender but not broken.
2. Add the rice and stir, making sure that there is enough water to cook it. Cook for about 20 minutes until the rice is tender. At the end of the cooking time the water should be absorbed by the rice and lentils. If it is not, boil the mixture rapidly until the liquid is reduced to leave the cereals moist but not swimming.
3. While the rice is cooking, heat the oil in a frying pan and cook the onion very slowly until soft and just brown. Pour this into the rice and lentil dish, stir well and season with salt.
4. Transfer to a warmed flat dish. Garnish with the onion and tomato rings.

NOTE: This is a Middle Eastern peasant dish. It is good served with a finely sliced cabbage salad dressed with yoghurt, lemon and garlic.

Vegetable Couscous

Couscous is made from wheat. It is similar to semolina, but coarser. It is available in specialist shops.

SERVES 4
110g/4oz chickpeas
110g/4oz couscous
425ml/¾ pint vegetable stock
salt and freshly ground black pepper
4 button onions, peeled
2 leeks, coarsely chopped
1 carrot, peeled and coarsely chopped
stick of celery, coarsely chopped
2 courgettes, coarsely chopped
4 tomatoes, peeled and cut into quarters
5ml/1 teaspoon chopped fresh mint
10ml/2 teaspoons chopped fresh parsley
pinch of dried oregano
pinch of saffron or a few shreds soaked in 15ml/1 tablespoon water

For the sauce:
30ml/2 tablespoons hot stock
5ml/1 teaspoon cumin
5ml/1 teaspoon ground coriander
2.5ml/½ teaspoon chilli powder
30ml/2 tablespoons tomato purée

1. Soak the chickpeas for 3 hours. Drain them and simmer for 1-2 hours in fresh salted water until tender. Drain well.
2. Cover the couscous with 230ml/8 fl oz cold water and leave to absorb the liquid for 20 minutes.
3. Put the stock, salt, pepper and onions in a large saucepan. Bring slowly to the boil and add the leeks, carrots and celery.
4. Set the couscous to steam in a muslin-lined sieve or couscoussière above the cooking vegetables. Cover the sieve with foil or a cloth to prevent too much steam escaping and simmer for 30 minutes.
5. Add the courgettes to the vegetables. Fork through the couscous to remove any lumps and return the lid. Cook for 2 minutes.
6. Add the tomatoes, mint, parsley and oregano to the vegetable mixture and again cover and cook for 2 minutes. Pour the couscous into a dish and keep warm.
7. Add the chickpeas and saffron, with its water if soaked, to the vegetables, and heat for 2 minutes. Drain off some of the stock.
8. For the sauce, mix the hot stock with the cumin, coriander, chilli powder and tomato purée.
9. Spread the couscous over a flat serving dish and pile the vegetables, with a cupful or so of stock, on the top. Serve the spiced sauce separately.

Zucchini Fritters

SERVES 4
450g/1lb courgettes (zucchini)
flour
salt and freshly ground black pepper
oil for deep-frying
2 egg whites

1. Cut the courgettes into thin chip-like strips. Sprinkle with salt and leave for 30 minutes. Rinse, drain and dry.
2. Season the flour well with salt and pepper.
3. Heat the oil until a crumb will sizzle vigorously in it.
4. Whisk the egg whites until stiff but not dry.
5. Put the courgettes in a sieve. Add the seasoned flour and toss them in it. Then turn them in the egg white.
6. Fry a few at a time until brown. Drain on absorbent paper. Season with salt and pepper. Serve immediately.

Seaweed

This recipe has been adapted from Yan Kit So's excellent *Classic Chinese* cookbook. She says: 'This Northern dish uses a special kind of seaweed which is not available elsewhere. However, the adapted ingredients used below do produce the desired delicious result.'

SERVES 4
450g/1lb spring greens
oil for deep-frying
2.5ml/¼ teaspoon salt
10ml/2 teaspoons sugar

1. Remove and discard the tough stalks from the spring greens. Wash, then lay them out on a large tray to dry thoroughly.
2. Fold 6-7 leaves, or however many you can handle at a time, into a neat roll and, using a sharp knife, slice very finely into shreds. Lay out on the tray again to dry. The drier the better.
3. Heat a deep-fat fryer until a cube of stale bread will brown in 40 seconds. Add half the spring greens and fry for 30 seconds or until bright green and crisp. Remove with a large strainer and deep-fry the remaining spring greens.
4. Sprinkle with salt and sugar and mix thoroughly.

Broad Beans and Bacon

SERVES 4
3 rashers rindless streaky bacon
450g/1lb shelled broad beans
butter
salt and freshly ground black pepper
15ml/1 tablespoon chopped fresh thyme or savory

1. Dice the bacon and fry the pieces in their own fat until crisp and brown but not brittle.
2. Boil the beans in salted water for 8 minutes. Drain well and toss in melted butter. Season with salt and pepper, and stir in the diced bacon, any bacon fat, and the chopped savory or thyme.

NOTE: Tough large broad beans are delicious if the inner skins are removed after boiling. Boil the beans as usual then run under cold water until cool enough to handle. Slip off the skins and put the bright green beans into a frying pan with the butter, bacon and savory or thyme. Toss carefully to reheat, as they are inclined to break up.

Spring Cabbage with Cream and Nutmeg

SERVES 4-6
675g/1½lb spring cabbage
salt and freshly ground black pepper
pinch of grated nutmeg
15g/¼oz butter
30ml/2 tablespoons soured cream

1. Shred the cabbage finely and rinse it. Place in salted boiling water and return to the boil. Boil rapidly for 3-5 minutes until slightly soft but crunchy.
2. Drain the cabbage well, then return it to the heat to evaporate excess moisture, shaking the pan and tossing the cabbage so it dries but does not burn.
3. Sprinkle with black pepper and nutmeg. Toss in the butter. Take off the heat, and stir in the soured cream.

Salads

Everything Green Salad

1 lettuce (any kind)
French dressing (see page 228)

Choice of the following:
green pepper
cucumber
fennel
celery
chicory
spring onions
watercress
green beans
peas
5ml/1 teaspoon chopped fresh mint, parlsey or chives

1. Prepare the salad ingredients.
Lettuce: Wash, drain and shake to allow to drip dry. Do not twist or wring the leaves together, which bruises them, but break each lettuce leaf individually and place in a salad bowl.
Green pepper: Wash, cut off the top and remove the seeds. Slice finely.
Cucumber: Peel or not, as desired. Slice finely.
Fennel: Wash and shave into thin slices.
Celery: Wash and chop together with a few young leaves.
Chicory: Wipe with a damp cloth. Remove the tough core with a sharp knife and cut each head at an angle into 3 or 4 pieces.
Spring onions: Wash and peel. Chop half the green stalks finely. Keep the white part with the rest of the salad.
Watercress: Wash and pick over, discarding the thick stalks and any yellow leaves.
Beans and peas: Cook in boiling salted water until just tender and cool under cold running water. Drain well and pat dry in a tea towel.
2. Add the chopped herbs and the chopped spring onion tops (if used) to the dressing.
3. Mix the salad ingredients together and just before serving toss them in French dressing.

Frilly Bitter Salad

slightly bitter leaves: watercress; young kale; curly endive; young spinach; chicory; lamb's lettuce; radicchio; rocket; frisée

For the dressing:
45ml/3 tablespoons salad oil
15ml/1 tablespoon olive oil
15ml/1 tablespoon red wine vinegar
5ml/1 teaspoon French mustard
salt and pepper

1. Put the dressing ingredients into a screw-top jar and shake well.
2. Wash and dry the salad leaves, discarding any tough stalks.
3. Toss the salad in the dressing and tip into a clean bowl.

Caesar Salad

SERVES 4
2 large garlic cloves
150ml/$^1/_4$ pint olive oil
2 anchovy fillets, finely chopped
30ml/2 tablespoons lemon juice
dry English mustard
freshly ground black pepper
1 egg
2 slices bread, cubed, crusts removed
1 cos lettuce
2 tablespoons fresh Parmesan cheese, grated

1. Crush the garlic and mix with the olive oil. Leave to stand for 10 minutes. Strain off 45ml/3 tablespoons of the olive oil to make the dressing.
2. Add it to the anchovy fillets, lemon juice, mustard, pepper and raw egg and blend in a liquidizer.
3. Pour the remaining oil and the garlic into a frying pan. Heat slowly. When the garlic shreds begin to sizzle add the diced bread and fry, turning frequently with a fish slice or spoon, until the croûtons are crisp and brown. With a perforated spoon, lift out the croûtons and drain and allow to cool on absorbent paper.
4. Toss the lettuce in the dressing. Sprinkle over the croûtons and cheese.

Tomato and Basil Salad

SERVES 4
6 tomatoes, skinned and sliced
8-10 leaves of fresh basil, coarsely chopped
French dressing (see page 228)

1. Arrange the tomatoes on a plate.
2. Mix the dressing and basil together and spoon over the tomatoes.
3. Chill for 1-2 hours before serving.

Carrot and Mint Salad

SERVES 4
8 large carrots
2.5ml/½ teaspoon caster sugar
large pinch of cumin powder
French dressing (see page 228)
30ml/2 tablespoons chopped fresh mint

1. Mix the sugar and cumin powder with the dressing.
2. Peel the carrots and grate coarsely into the French dressing.
3. Add the mint and toss the salad well. Taste and season with salt and pepper if necessary.

Fennel and Walnut Salad

SERVES 6
2 large or 3 small bulbs of fennel
110g/4oz fresh shelled walnuts, coarsely chopped
15ml/1 tablespoon chopped marjoram
French dressing made with hazelnut oil (see page 228)

1. Remove the feathery green tops of the fennel and put aside. Wash, then finely slice the fennel heads, discarding any tough outer leaves or discoloured bits.
2. Blanch the fennel in boiling water for 3-4 minutes to soften slightly. Refresh by running under cold water until cool. Drain well on absorbent paper, or dry in a tea towel.
3. Mix together the fennel, nuts and marjoram and moisten with a little French dressing. Pile into a salad bowl.
4. Chop the green leaves of the fennel and scatter them over the salad.

Fennel, Red Onion and Red Pepper Salad

SERVES 4-6
1 large or 2 small heads fennel
1 red pepper
½ medium-sized red onion, sliced

For the dressing:
15ml/1 tablespoon wine vinegar
45ml/3 tablespoons salad oil
pinch of mustard
salt and freshly ground black pepper

1. Remove the feathery green tops of the fennel and put aside. Finely slice the fennel heads, discarding any tough outer leaves. Blanch in boiling salted water for 1 minute. Refresh under cold running water. Drain well.
2. Remove and discard the seeds and inner pith from the pepper. Cut the flesh into quarters. Place, skin side up, under a very hot grill. Grill until very black. Cool, skin and cut into strips.
3. Mix all the dressing ingredients in a jar, shaking well to form an emulsion.
4. Toss everything in the dressing and tip into a clean salad bowl. Chop the green leaves and scatter over the salad.

Carrot and Poppy Seed Salad

SERVES 4

4 large carrots
French dressing made with hazelnut oil (see page 228)
2 spring onions, chopped
10ml/2 teaspoons poppy seeds

1. Peel the carrots into ribbons. Toss in the French dressing with the onions.
2. Put the poppy seeds into a heavy saucepan and place over a moderate heat. Cover and dry-roast them for 2 minutes. Leave to cool, then sprinkle over the salad.

Japanese-style Cucumber and Carrot Salad

This recipe is by Madhur Jaffrey from *The Taste of Health.*

SERVES 4-6

1 large cucumber
1 small carrot
15ml/1 tablespoon unhulled sesame seeds
30ml/2 tablespoons soy sauce
20ml/2 dessertspoons distilled white vinegar

1. Peel the cucumber and cut it diagonally into wafer-thin, long, oval shapes. Put them in a bowl.
2. Peel the carrot and cut this similarly. Put in the bowl with the cucumber.
3. Put the sesame seeds in a small cast-iron frying pan and place it over a low heat. Cook, shaking the pan, until the sesame seeds begin to brown evenly; it takes just a few minutes. When they start popping, they are ready.You can also spread the sesame seeds out on a tray and roast them under the grill. They should turn just a shade darker.
4. Pour the soy sauce and vinegar over the salad, and mix thoroughly. Sprinkle on the sesame seeds and mix again. Serve immediately.

Chinese Cabbage and Apple Salad

SERVES 4

450g/1lb Chinese cabbage (Chinese leaves)
2 dessert apples
chopped parsley

For the dressing:
45ml/3 tablespoons oil
15ml/1 tablespoon vinegar
45ml/3 tablespoons chopped fresh mint
30ml/2 tablespoons soured cream
salt and freshly ground black pepper

1. Mix all the ingredients for the dressing together in a screw-top jar and shake until well emulsified. Season well.
2. Shred the cabbage finely and slice the apples but do not peel them.
3. Toss the cabbage and apple in the dressing.
4. Tip into a wooden salad bowl and sprinkle with plenty of chopped parsley.

Mushroom and Coriander Seed Salad

SERVES 4

225g/8oz button mushrooms
French dressing (see page 228)
10ml/2 teaspoons coriander seed
1 onion, sliced
sunflower oil
plenty of freshly ground pepper

1. Wipe the mushrooms, slice fairly finely and leave to marinate in the French dressing.
2. Crush the coriander seeds very well indeed in a pestle and mortar and add the mushrooms. Leave for 2 hours.
3. Cook the onion until soft but not brown in a nonstick frying pan in a minimum amount of oil. Cook and add to the mushrooms and season well.

Spinach Salad with Bacon and Yoghurt

SERVES 4
450g/1lb fresh young spinach
6 rashers rindless streaky bacon

For the dressing:
30-45ml/2-3 tablespoons plain yoghurt
30ml/2 tablespoons oil
10ml/2 teaspoons vinegar
5ml/1 teaspoon French mustard
1/2 garlic clove, crushed
salt, pepper and sugar

1. Heat the grill.
2. Wash the spinach and remove the stalks. Drain well and shred finely.
3. Grill the bacon for about 2 minutes on each side until brown and crispy. Cool, then chop up.
4. Mix all the ingredients for the dressing together.
5. Toss the spinach and bacon in the dressing just before serving.

Salade Niçoise

SERVES 3-6
3 tomatoes, skinned and quartered
225g/8oz cooked French beans
200g/7oz tin tuna fish
1/2 mild onion, thinly sliced
1 green pepper, deseeded and sliced
12 radishes
1 lettuce heart
6 anchovy fillets, split lengthways
2 hardboiled eggs, quartered lengthways
8 black olives

For the dressing:
15ml/1 tablespoon wine vinegar
45ml/3 tablespoons olive oil
salt and freshly ground black pepper
1/2 garlic clove, crushed
15ml/1 tablespoon finely chopped fresh herbs

1. Put all the dressing ingredients into a large bowl and whisk well.
2. Reserving a few colourful ingredients for the top, put all the rest of the salad ingredients into the bowl. Turn them gently in the dressing. Do not over-mix.
3. Tip carefully into a clean salad bowl and put the reserved ingredients on the top.

Bean and Bean Salad

SERVES 4
450g/1lb fresh French beans, topped and tailed
450g/1lb cooked or tinned haricot beans or butter beans
30ml/2 tablespoons chopped fresh basil, or spring onion tops
15ml/1 tablespoon lemon juice
salt and freshly ground pepper
1 small garlic clove, crushed
45ml/3 tablespoons salad oil

1. Boil the French beans in salted water until just tender. Drain and swish under the cold tap to prevent further cooking and preserve their colour. Drain well.
2. Drain the haricot or butter beans if they are tinned and rinse away any starchy water. When they are dry mix them with the cooked French beans and put into a dish.
3. Place the basil or spring onions in a jar, add the lemon juice, seasoning, garlic and oil and shake vigorously. Pour over the salad.

NOTE: All types of beans are good – fresh broad beans (especially if the inner skins are removed after cooking), dried lima, tinned flageolets, etc.

Watercress Salad with Croûtons

SERVES 4-5
oil for deep-frying
4 slices white bread, crusts removed, cubed
2 bunches watercress, trimmed

For the dressing:
45ml/3 tablespoons oil
15ml/1 tablespoon vinegar
salt and pepper
1/2 garlic clove, crushed

5ml/1 teaspoon chopped fresh parsley
pinch of sugar (optional)

1. Combine all the dressing ingredients in a screw-top jar and shake well.
2. Make the croûtons: heat the oil until a crumb will sizzle vigorously in it. Fry the bread until golden brown and crisp. Drain well on absorbent paper. Sprinkle lightly with salt.
3. Just before serving toss the watercress in the French dressing, tip into a clean salad bowl and sprinkle the warm croûtons on top.

Salad of Roast Tomatoes and Spring Onions

SERVES 4
10 medium-sized ripe tomatoes, blanched and peeled
olive oil
salt and freshly ground black pepper
sugar to taste
sprig of thyme
30g/1oz butter
1/2 bunch spring onions, trimmed and cleaned, cut on the cross

For the dressing:
5ml/1 teaspoon Dijon mustard
10ml/2 teaspoons each of tarragon and white wine vinegars
30ml/2 tablespoons olive oil
45ml/3 tablespoons vegetable oil
1/2 bunch flat leaf parsley, chopped, for garnish

1. Preheat the oven to 200°C/400°F/gas mark 6. Cut the tomatoes in half vertically and scoop out the seeds. Drain thoroughly on absorbent paper.
2. Brush a baking sheet with olive oil. Arrange the tomatoes cut side up on the tray. Season with salt and pepper and sugar. Scatter with branches of thyme and drizzle over more olive oil.
3. Roast for 10-15 minutes until the flesh just gives when touched.
4. Arrange 5 tomato halves on each plate, cut side down.
5. Melt the butter in a frying pan and sauté the spring onions for about 2 minutes, scatter around the roasted tomatoes.
6. Whisk the dressing ingredients together, check the seasoning, and drizzle over the tomatoes. Garnish with parsley.

NOTE: This dish is ideally made with plum tomatoes.

Pasta and Red Pepper Salad

SERVES 4
225g/8oz pasta, preferably spirals
2 red peppers
110g/4oz broccoli
French dressing (see page 228)
chopped sage

1. Cook the pasta in plenty of boiling salted water with 15ml/1 tablespoon oil. When tender drain well and leave to cool.
2. Cut the peppers into quarters and remove the stalk, inner membrane and seeds. Heat the grill to its highest temperature.
3. Grill the peppers, skin side uppermost, until the skin is black and blistered. With a small knife, remove all the skin. Cut into strips.
4. Cook the broccoli in boiling salted water. Refresh under cold running water. Drain well and leave to cool.
5. Toss the pasta, pepper, broccoli, French dressing and sage together.

Rice Salad

Almost any vegetables can be added to cold cooked rice to make a salad, but it is important to have approximately equal quantities of rice and vegetables, or the result may be lifeless and stodgy. The dressing should moisten, not soak, the dish.

SERVES 8
225g/8oz long-grain rice
110g/4oz frozen peas
1/2 green pepper, deseeded and chopped
1/2 red pepper, deseeded and chopped

small stick of celery, chopped
1/4 cucumber, peeled and chopped
2 tomatoes, skinned and quartered
a few black olives
finely chopped fresh parsley, mint, chives or dill

For the dressing:
45ml/3 tablespoons salad oil
15ml/1 tablespoon vinegar
1/2 small onion, very finely chopped
salt and pepper

1. Boil the rice in plenty of water until just tender (about 10 minutes). Rinse in boiling water and leave to drain well.
2. Cook the peas.
3. Put the dressing ingredients into a screw-top jar and shake well.
4. Mix everything together and add salt and pepper if necessary.

NOTE: Rice salad looks pretty when turned out of a ring mould, jelly mould, or even a mixing bowl. Push it down firmly in the oiled mould, then invert it on to a dish. If simply served in a bowl or on a dish, keep back a few olives and tomato pieces for the top.

Potato Salad

SERVES 4
675g/1 1/2lb new potatoes
sprig of mint
60ml/4 tablespoons French dressing (see page 228)
140ml/5 fl oz carton soured cream
15ml/1 tablespoon mayonnaise (page 224)
30ml/2 tablespoons fresh chopped chives

1. Boil the potatoes with the mint in a pan of salted water until just tender. Do not peel small new potatoes. Peel larger potatoes after boiling. Drain well. Cut up if large.
2. Toss in the French dressing while still hot. Leave to cool.
3. Mix the soured cream and the mayonnaise together. Add half the chives.
4. Turn the potatoes in this creamy dressing and tip into a salad bowl.
5. Sprinkle liberally with the rest of the chives.

Barley and Beetroot Salad

SERVES 4
30g/1oz barley
1 large beetroot, cooked and chopped
1/2 small onion, very finely chopped
1/2 green apple, chopped
French dressing (see page 228)
110g/4oz lettuce or white cabbage, shredded

1. Boil the barley in plenty of salted water for about 1 hour, until tender. Drain well.
2. Toss the barley with the beetroot, onion and apple in the French dressing. Serve on a bed of shredded lettuce.

New Potatoes Vinaigrette

SERVES 4
675g/1 1/2lb small new potatoes
small bunch of fresh mint
French dressing (see page 228)
15ml/1 tablespoon chopped chives
1 shallot, finely chopped

1. Wash the potatoes and scrape them, but do not peel. Cook in boiling salted water with a sprig of mint until tender. Chop 8-10 mint leaves finely.
2. Mix the French dressing with the mint, chives and shallot.
3. Drain the potatoes well and toss immediately in the French dressing. Leave to cool and toss again just before serving. Decorate with leaves of fresh mint.

NOTE: There is always controversy about peeling new potatoes. The best, very new, pale ones need little more than washing. Most need scraping, and some – usually large, dark and patently not very new – need peeling after cooking.

Coleslaw with Raisins and Walnuts

SERVES 4

225g/8oz hard white cabbage, finely shredded
3 small carrots, coarsely grated
45ml/3 tablespoons mayonnaise (see page 224)
5ml/1 teaspoon French mustard
5ml/1 teaspoon sugar
salt and pepper
15ml/1 tablespoon raisins
15ml/1 tablespoon chopped walnuts

1. Toss the cabbage and carrots together in a bowl.
2. Mix the mayonnaise with all the remaining ingredients and, using your hands, combine it with the cabbage and carrots.

NOTE: Mayonnaise for coleslaw is delicious made with cider vinegar.

Orange and Watercress Salad

SERVES 4

6 oranges
large bunch watercress, trimmed

1. Peel the oranges with a knife as you would an apple, making sure that all the pith is removed. Reserve the juice.
2. Cut the oranges into slices horizontally, removing all the pips, or cut into segments.
3. Arrange the oranges and watercress attractively on a plate and spoon over the reserved orange juice.

Orange and Frisée Salad

SERVES 4

2 oranges, peeled with pith removed
1 small frisée

For the dressing:
45ml/3 tablespoons hazelnut oil
15ml/1 tablespoon raspberry vinegar
salt and freshly ground black pepper

1. Segment the oranges and keep the juice.
2. Select the palest bits of the frisée, rip into manageable pieces.
3. Make the dressing, add the reserved orange juice.
4. Toss the frisée in the dressing and pile into the centre of a serving plate.
5. Arrange the orange segments neatly around the edge.

Avocado, Apple and Lettuce Salad

SERVES 4

1 eating apple
French dressing (see page 228)
1 ripe avocado pear
1 small cos or round lettuce

1. Cut the unpeeled apple into chunks, and put straight into the French dressing.
2. Peel and cut the avocado into cubes and turn carefully with the apple in the French dressing until completely coated.
3. Toss the lettuce with the avocado and apple.

Red Pepper Salad

SERVES 4

4 red peppers
1 clove garlic
1/2 teaspoon salt
45ml/3 tablespoons extra virgin olive oil
4 anchovies
5ml/1 teaspoon chopped fresh oregano
45ml/3 tablespoons stoned black olives

1. Preheat the grill to its highest setting. Cut the peppers into quarters and remove the seeds and any pith. Grill the skin side of the peppers until they are blistered and blackened all over. Place under running cold water and remove the skins. Cut the peppers into strips.

2. Crush the clove of garlic with the salt, add the olive oil and anchovies. Mash well together. Add the oregano and toss in the red pepper strips. Mix with the black olives.

Grilled Radicchio Salad

SERVES 4
2 large radicchio, cut into 8 wedges each

For the dressing:
45ml/3 tablespoons hazelnut or walnut oil
15ml/1 tablespoon balsamic, sherry or raspberry vinegar
chopped chives

1. Preheat the grill.
2. Toss the radicchio in the dressing.
3. Grill half of the wedges until brown around the edges but pink in the middle.
4. Toss the grilled radicchio with the ungrilled radicchio and add the chives. Serve immediately.

Quinoa and Lime Salad

SERVES 8
255g/9oz quinoa
720ml/1 1/4 pints water
salt

For the dressing:
juice of 6 limes
125ml/4 fl oz groundnut oil
Salt and freshly ground black pepper
15ml/1 tablespoon sugar
15ml/1tablespoon dry-roasted Szechuan peppercorns, ground
4 small garlic cloves, crushed
15ml/1 tablespoon each flat parsley, basil and coriander

To serve:
10 Kalamata olives, stoned and slivered
140g/5oz cooked kidney beans
1 radicchio
small bunch basil or coriander

1. Rinse and drain the quinoa well before use to remove bitterness. It can then be lightly toasted in oil to enhance the flavour, if you wish.
2. Put the quinoa in a pan with the water and salt, bring to the boil then reduce the heat, cover and cook for 15-20 minutes or until the liquid has been absorbed and the quinoa looks transparent. If all the liquid has not been absorbed, drain well.
3. Remove from the heat and fluff up with a fork. Allow to cool.
4. Make the dressing: put the ingredients into a liquidizer and blend until smooth, then season well to make a strong dressing.
5. Mix the dressing with the quinoa and mix in most of the olives and the kidney beans, reserving a few for garnish.
6. Line a serving bowl with the radicchio leaves, spoon in the quinoa, scatter over the reserved olives and kidney beans and garnish with either fresh basil or coriander.

NOTE I: Quinoa is a grain similar to tapioca. It is available in large supermarkets and health food shops.
NOTE II: This dressing is also very good with hot or cold pasta. It should be made on the day that it is eaten. It loses some of its brilliant green if kept overnight.

Stocks and Savoury Sauces

Stocks and Savoury Sauces

BEHIND every great soup and behind many a sauce, stands a good strong stock. Stock is flavoured liquid, and the basic flavour can be fish, poultry, meat or vegetable. Stock cubes and bouillon mixes are usually over salty and they lack the intensely 'real' flavour of properly made stock. Also, they generally come in two universal flavours, chicken and beef, making much of the cook's food taste the same. As an emergency measure, or to strengthen a rather weak stock, they are most useful. But a good cook should be able to make a perfect stock.

MAKING A STOCK

The secret of stocks is slow, gentle simmering. If the liquid is the slightest bit greasy, vigorous boiling will produce a murky, fatty stock. Skimming, especially for meat stocks, is vital: as fat and scum rise to the surface they should be lifted off with a perforated spoon, perhaps every 10 or 15 minutes.

Rich, brown, stocks are made by first frying or baking the bones, vegetables and scraps of meat until a good, dark, even brown. Only then does the cook proceed with the gentle simmering. Care must be taken not to burn the bones or vegetables: one burned carrot can ruin a gallon of stock. Brown stocks are usually made from red meats or veal, and sometimes only from vegetables for vegetarian dishes.

White stocks are more delicate and are made by simmering only. They are usually based on white poultry or vegetables. The longer meat stocks are simmered the better flavoured they will be. A stockpot will simmer all day in a restaurant, being skimmed or topped up with water as the chef passes it, and only strained before closing time. However, it is important not to just keep adding bits and pieces to the stockpot and to keep it going on the back burner for days, because the pot will become cluttered with cooked-out bones and vegetables that have long since given up any flavour. At least three, and up to eight hours over the gentlest flame, or in the bottom oven of an Aga, is plenty.

In the Aga, skimming is unnecessary - as the liquid hardly moves there is no danger of fat being bubbled into the stock, and it can be lifted off the top when cold.

Fish stocks should never be simmered for more than 30 minutes. After this the bones begin to impart a bitter flavour to the liquid. For a stronger flavour the stock can be strained, skimmed of any scum or fat, and then boiled down to reduce and concentrate it.

Similarly, vegetable stocks do not need long cooking. As they contain very little fat, even if the vegetables have been browned in butter before simmering, they are easily skimmed, and can then be boiled rapidly to concentrate the flavour. An hour's simmering or half an hour's rapid boiling is generally enough.

THE BONES. Most households rarely have anything other than the cooked bones from a roast available for stocks. These will make good stock, but it will be weaker than that made with raw bones. Raw bones are very often free from the butcher, or can be had very cheaply. Get them chopped into manageable small pieces in the shop. A little raw meat, the bloodier the better, gives a rich, very clear liquid.

WATER. The water must be cold, as if it is hot the fat in the bones will melt immediately and when the stock begins to boil much of the fat will be bubbled into the stock. The stock will then be murky, have an unattractive smell and a nasty flavour. Cold water encourages the fat to rise to the surface; it can then be skimmed.

JELLIED STOCK. Veal bones produce a particularly good stock that will set to a jelly. A pig's trotter added to any stock will have the same jellying effect. Jellied stock will keep longer than liquid stock, but in any event stocks should be re-boiled every two or three days if kept refrigerated, or every day if kept in a larder, to prevent them going bad.

SALT. Do not add salt to stock. It may be used later for something that is already salty, or boiled down to a concentrated glaze (glace de viande), in which case the glaze would be over-salted if the stock contained salt. (Salt does not boil off with the water, but remains in the pan.)

STORAGE. A good way of storing a large batch of stock is to boil it down to double strength, and to add water only when using. Or stock can be boiled down to a thick syrupy glaze, which can be used like stock cubes. Many cooks freeze the glaze in ice cube trays, then turn the frozen cubes into a plastic box in the freezer. They will keep for at least a year if fat-free.

SAUCES

Larousse defines a sauce as a 'liquid seasoning for food', and this covers anything from juices in a frying pan to complicated and sophisticated emulsions.

FLOUR-THICKENED SAUCES. The commonest English sauces are those thickened with flour, and these are undoubtedly the most practical for the home cook. The secret is not to make them too thick (by not adding too much flour), to beat them well and to give them a good boil after they have thickened to make them shine. They will also look professionally shiny if they are finished by whizzing in a liquidizer, or if they are 'mounted' with a little extra butter, gradually incorporated in dice, at the end.

The butter and flour base of a sauce is called a roux. In a white roux, the butter and flour are mixed over a gentle heat without browning; in a blond roux, they are allowed to cook to a biscuit colour; and in a brown roux, they are cooked until distinctly brown.

Another way of thickening a sauce with flour is to make a beurre manié. Equal quantities of butter and flour are kneaded to a smooth paste and whisked into a boiling liquid. As the butter melts the flour is evenly distributed throughout the sauce, thickening the liquid without allowing lumps to form. Cornflour or arrowroot are also useful thickeners. They are 'slaked' (mixed to a paste with cold water, stock or milk), added to a hot liquid and allowed to boil to thicken it for a couple of minutes.

EMULSIONS AND LIAISONS. Emulsions are liquids that contain tiny droplets of oil or fat evenly distributed in suspension. Like liaisons, they may be unstable.

STABLE EMULSIONS. Mayonnaise is the best known of the cold and stable emulsion sauces, in which oil is beaten into egg yolks and held in suspension. If the oil is added too fast the sauce will curdle.

WARM EMULSIONS. The most stable warm emulsions, like cold emulsions, are based on egg yolks and butter. The best known is hollandaise. Great care has to be taken not to allow the sauce to curdle.

EGGLESS EMULSIONS. These have become the more fashionable butter sauces. The classic is beurre blanc. Eggless emulsions curdle very easily, so great care should be taken to follow the recipe precisely.

UNSTABLE EMULSIONS. French dressing will emulsify if whizzed or whisked together, but will separate back to its component parts after about 15 minutes.

SABAYONS. Egg yolks are whisked over heat and the flavouring ingredient is gradually whisked in. The suspension is temporary and most sabayons collapse after 30-40 minutes.

LIAISONS. Egg yolk can be mixed with cream to form a liaison. It is then used to thicken and enrich sauces. The yolks must not boil or the sauce will curdle.

Sauce table

Flour-thickened		Emulsions		Combinations and other
Mother	Daughter	Mother	Daughter	
White sauce	Anchovy	**Mayonnaise**	Aïoli	Apple sauce
	Béchamel		Remoulade	Tomato sauce
	Cardinale		Tartare	Mint sauce
	Crème		Andalouse	
	Egg		Elizabeth	**Savoury butters -**
	Cheese			Almond, Anchovy,
	Onion	**Hollandaise**	Bearnaise	Garlic, Green,
	Parsley		Charon	Maitre d'hotel,
	Green		Moutarde	Mint and mustard
			Mousseline	
Blond (velouté)	Aurore			Cumberland sauce
	Poulette	**Beurre blanc**	Chicken	Yoghurt sauce, Cranberry sauce
	Suprême		Fish	Bread sauce, Horseradish cream
	Mushroom		Orange	Soured cream, Onion and mint
			Saffron	Tomato and cream sauce
Brown	Chasseur			Red pepper, Black bean sauce
	Robert	**French dressing**		Ginger and tomato sauce
	Madeira			Uncooked pasta sauce
	Bordelaise			Exotic sauce
	Poivrade			Tomato and whisky sauce
	Diane			Salsa Pizzaiola, Salsa Romesco
	Reforme			
	Perigueux			**Sabayons –**
				Leek and watercress
				Liaisons –
				As in Blanquette de Veau
				Reduction and Pan sauces –
				Wild mushroom sauce

Brown Stock

900g/2lb beef bones
1 onion, peeled and chopped, skin reserved
2 carrots, roughly chopped
15ml/1 tablespoon oil
parsley stalks
2 bay leaves
6 black peppercorns

1. Preheat the oven to 220°C/425°F/gas mark 7.
2. Put the beef bones in a roasting tin and brown in the oven. This may take up to 1 hour.
3. Brown the onion and carrots in the oil in a large stock pot. It is essential that they do not burn.
4. When the bones are well browned add them to the vegetables with the onion skins, parsley stalks, bay leaves and black peppercorns. Cover with cold water and bring very slowly to the boil, skimming off any scum as it rises to the surface.
5. When clear of scum, simmer gently for 3-4 hours, or even longer, skimming off the fat as necessary and topping up with water if the level gets very low. The longer it simmers, and the more the liquid reduces by evaporation, the stronger the stock will be.
6. Strain, cool and lift off any remaining fat.

Glace de Viande

570ml/1 pint brown stock (see page 218), absolutely free of fat

1. In a heavy-bottomed saucepan reduce the brown stock by boiling over a steady heat until thick, clear and syrupy.
2. Pour into small pots. When cold cover with polythene or jam covers and secure.
3. Keep in the refrigerator until ready for use.

NOTE: Glace de viande keeps for several weeks and is very useful for enriching sauces.

White Stock

onion, sliced
celery, sliced
carrot, sliced
chicken or veal bones, skin or flesh
parsley
thyme
bay leaf
peppercorns

1. Put all the ingredients into a saucepan. Cover generously with water and bring to the boil slowly. Skim off any fat, and/or scum.
2. Simmer for 2-3 hours, skimming frequently and topping up the water level if necessary. The liquid should reduce to half the original quantity.
3. Strain, cool and lift off all the fat.

Aspic

1 litre/2 pints white stock
2 egg shells, crushed
2 egg whites
15-30g/½-1oz gelatine, if necessary

1. Lift or skim any fat from the stock.
2. Put the stock into a large saucepan and sprinkle on the gelatine. If the stock is liquid when chilled, use 30g/1oz gelatine; if the stock is set when chilled, gelatine will not be necessary. Put over a gentle heat to dissolve. Allow to cool.
3. Put the shells and egg whites into the stock. Place over the heat and whisk steadily with a balloon whisk until the mixture begins to boil. Stop whisking immediately and draw the pan off the heat. Allow the mixture to subside. Take care not to break the crust formed by the egg white.
4. Bring the aspic just to the boil again, and again allow to subside. Repeat this once more (the egg white will trap the sediment in the stock and clear the aspic). Allow to cool for 2 minutes.
5. Fix a double layer of fine muslin over a clean basin and carefully strain the aspic through it, taking care to hold the egg-white crust back. When all the liquid is through (or almost all of it) allow the egg white to slip into the muslin. Then strain the aspic again – this time through both egg white crust and cloth. Do not try to hurry the process by squeezing the cloth, or murky aspic will result.

Court Bouillon

1.14 litre/2 pints water
150ml/¼ pint vinegar
1 carrot, sliced
1 onion, sliced
1 stick celery
12 peppercorns
2 bay leaves
30ml/2 tablespoons salad oil
salt

1. Bring all the ingredients to the boil and simmer for 20 minutes.
2. Allow the liquid to cool and place the fish, meat or vegetables in it, then bring slowly to simmering point.

Fish Stock

onion, sliced
carrot, sliced
celery, sliced
fish bones, skins, fins, heads or tails, crustacean shells (e.g. prawn shells, mussel shells, etc.)
parsley stalks
bay leaf
pinch of fresh thyme
pepper

1. Put all the ingredients together in a pan, with water to cover, and bring to the boil. Turn down to simmer and skim off any scum.
2. Simmer for 20 minutes if the fish bones are small, 30 minutes if large. Strain.

NOTE: The flavour of fish stock is impaired if the bones are cooked for too long. Once strained, however, it may be strengthened by further boiling and reducing.

Fish Glaze

Fish glaze (glace de poisson) is simply very well-reduced, very well strained fish stock, which is used to flavour and enhance fish sauces. It can be kept refrigerated for about 3 days or frozen in ice cube trays and used as required.

Horseradish Cream

150ml/1/4 pint double cream
15-30ml/1-2 tablespoons grated fresh horseradish
10ml/2 teaspoons wine vinegar
2.5ml/1/2 teaspoon made English mustard
salt and pepper
sugar to taste

1. Lightly whip the cream and add the remaining ingredients.

Uncooked Pasta Sauce

This sauce should be served on the day after it has been made in order to allow the flavours to develop. It can be served with hot or cold pasta.

6 large tomatoes, finely chopped
1 red onion, finely chopped
2 garlic cloves, finely chopped
60ml/4 tablespoons chopped fresh basil
15ml/1 tablespoon chopped parsley
90ml/6 tablespoons extra virgin olive oil
juice of 1/2 lemon
salt and freshly ground black pepper

1. Put the tomatoes into a sieve and drain them for 30 minutes.
2. Mix the tomatoes with the onion, garlic and herbs. Add the oil and lemon juice. Season to taste with salt and pepper.

Ginger and Tomato Sauce

This is a very simple sauce that can be used to accompany fish, chicken, pasta and vegetable dishes. This quantity fills two sauceboats. Simply process or liquidize together the following ingredients.

400g/14oz canned tomatoes
3 spring onions
10ml/2 teaspoons very finely chopped fresh ginger
1 large garlic clove
30ml/2 tablespoons fresh lime juice
10ml/2 teaspoons caster sugar
1 fresh green chilli, deseeded (under cold running water), and chopped
30ml/2 tablespoons roughly chopped fresh coriander
salt and freshly ground black pepper

Tomato and Cream Sauce

3 large tomatoes, peeled, deseeded and finely diced
45ml/3 tablespoons double cream
5ml/1 teaspoon wine vinegar
5ml/1 teaspoon strong Dijon mustard
10 leaves fresh tarragon, finely chopped
15ml/1 tablespoon finely chopped parsley
5ml/1 teaspoon finely chopped chervil
5ml/1 teaspoon cognac
salt, cayenne, pepper or Tabasco

1. Put the tomatoes into a sieve and leave to drain.
2. Pour the cream into a bowl and add the mustard, wine vinegar, cognac, salt and cayenne pepper or Tabasco. Whisk until the cream just thickens, but do not let it separate.
3. Add the tomatoes, parsley, tarragon and chervil. Add salt if necessary. Keep in a cold place and serve in a sauceboat.

White Sauce

This is a quick and easy basic white sauce.

20g/¾oz butter
20g/¾oz flour
pinch of dry mustard
290ml/½ pint creamy milk
salt and white pepper

1. Melt the butter in a thick saucepan.
2. Add the flour and the mustard and stir over the heat for 1 minute. Draw the pan off the heat, pour in the milk and mix well.
3. Return the sauce to the heat and stir continually until boiling.
4. Simmer for 2-3 minutes and season with salt and pepper.

Béchamel Sauce

290ml/½ pint creamy milk
slice of onion
blade of mace
a few fresh parsley stalks
4 peppercorns
1 bay leaf
30g/1oz butter
20g/¾oz flour
salt and white pepper

1. Place the milk with the onion, mace, parsley, peppercorns and bay leaf in a saucepan and slowly bring to simmering point.
2. Lower the temperature and allow the flavour to infuse for 8-10 minutes.
3. Melt 20g/¾oz butter in a thick saucepan, stir in the flour and stir over heat for 1 minute.
4. Remove from the heat. Strain in the infused milk and mix well.
5. Return the sauce to the heat and stir or whisk continuously until boiling. Add the remaining butter and beat very well (this will help to make the sauce shiny).
6. Simmer, stirring well, for 3 minutes.
7. Taste and season.

NOTE: To make a professionally shiny béchamel sauce, pass through a tammy strainer before use or whizz in a liquidizer.

Mornay Sauce (Cheese Sauce)

20g/¾oz butter
20g/¾oz flour
pinch of dry English mustard
pinch of cayenne pepper
290ml/½ pint milk
55g/2oz Gruyère or strong Cheddar cheese, grated
15g/½oz Parmesan cheese, grated
salt and pepper

1. Melt the butter and stir in the flour, mustard and cayenne pepper. Cook, stirring, for 1 minute. Draw the pan off the heat. Pour in the milk and mix well.
2. Return the pan to the heat and stir until boiling. Simmer, stirring well, for 2 minutes.
3. Add all the cheese, and mix well, but do not re-boil.
4. Season with salt and pepper as necessary.

Parsley Sauce

290ml/½ pint creamy milk
slice of onion
good handful of fresh parsley
4 peppercorns
1 bay leaf
20g/¾oz butter
20g/¾oz flour
salt and pepper

1. Put the milk, onion, parsley stalks (but not leaves), peppercorns and bay leaf in a saucepan and slowly bring to simmering point.
2. Lower the temperature and allow the flavour to infuse for about 10 minutes.
3. Melt the butter in a thick saucepan, stir in the flour and cook, stirring, for 1 minute.
4. Remove from the heat. Strain in the infused milk and mix well.
5. Return the sauce to the heat and stir continuously until boiling, then simmer for 2-3 minutes. Taste and season.
6. Chop the parsley leaves very finely and stir into the hot sauce.

Soubise Sauce

For the soubise:
30g/1oz butter
60ml/4 tablespoons water
225g/8oz onions, very finely chopped
60ml/4 tablespoons cream

For the béchamel sauce:
20g/3/4oz butter
bay leaf
20g/3/4oz flour
290ml/1/2 pint milk

1. To make the soubise, melt the butter in a heavy pan. Add the water and the onions and cook very slowly, preferably covered with a lid to create a steamy atmosphere. The onions should become very soft and transparent, but on no account brown. Add the cream.
2. Now prepare the béchamel: melt the butter, add the bay leaf and flour and cook, stirring, for 1 minute. Draw off the heat, and stir in the milk. Return to the heat and bring slowly to the boil, stirring continuously. Simmer for 2 minutes. Remove the bay leaf and mix with the soubise.

NOTE: This sauce can be liquidized in a blender or pushed through a sieve if a smooth texture is desired.

Green Sauce

Delicious with cauliflower, pasta and fish.

30g/1oz butter
30g/1oz flour
290ml/1/2 pint milk
salt and pepper
bunch of watercress, trimmed and chopped

1. Melt the butter and stir in the flour. Cook, stirring, for 1 minute.
2. Remove from the heat, pour in the milk. Mix well. Return to the heat and stir continuously until boiling. Simmer for 2 minutes.
3. Add the watercress to the sauce. Cook for 1 minute. Taste and season as required.
4. Liquidize the sauce thoroughly. Do not keep it warm for too long - the colour dulls.

English Egg Sauce

3 hardboiled eggs
45g/1 1/2oz butter
45g/1 1/2oz flour
570ml/1 pint fish or chicken stock
45ml/3 tablespoons cream
60ml/4 tablespoons chopped fresh parsley
salt and freshly ground black pepper

1. Using a stainless steel knife, chop the eggs roughly.
2. Melt the butter in a saucepan. Stir in the flour and cook for 1 minute. Remove from the heat, add the stock and mix well.
3. Return the sauce to the heat and stir continuously until boiling, then simmer for 2-3 minutes, stirring occasionally.
4. Just before serving, add the remaining ingredients and season to taste. This sauce does not keep warm well.

NOTE: The liquid in which fish or chicken is cooked is suitable as stock. Chicken stock will do for veal, fish or chicken dishes, but fish stock is only good for fish dishes of course.

Velouté Sauce

20g/3/4oz butter
20g/3/4oz flour
290ml/1/2 pint white stock, strained and well skimmed (see page 219)
salt, pepper
a few drops of lemon juice

1. Melt the butter, add the flour and cook, stirring, over a gentle heat until straw coloured. Remove from the heat. Add the stock and mix well.
2. Return to the heat. Bring to the boil, stirring, and simmer until slightly syrupy and opaque. Taste and add seasoning and lemon juice.

Sauce Espagnole

60ml/4 tablespoons oil
2 small carrots, finely chopped
1 onion, finely chopped
1 stick celery, finely chopped
10ml/1 dessertspoon flour
570ml/1 pint brown stock
2.5ml/½ teaspoon tomato purée
a few mushroom stalks
bouquet garni of 2 parsley stalks, bay leaves, blade of mace

1. Heat the oil in a heavy saucepan, add the vegetables and fry until brown.
2. Stir in the flour and continue to cook slowly, stirring occasionally with a metal spoon, scraping the bottom of the pan to loosen the sediment. Cook to a good russet brown.
3. Draw aside, add three-quarters of the stock, the tomato purée, mushroom stalks and the bouquet garni.
4. Return to the heat, bring to the boil, half-cover and simmer for 30 minutes.
5. Skim twice to remove scum: add a splash of cold stock to the boiling liquid to help bring the scum and fat to the surface. Tilting the pan slightly, skim the surface with a large metal spoon. Strain.

Demi-glace Sauce

Demi-glace sauce is a refined sauce espagnole and is made by simmering together equal quantities of sauce espagnole and brown stock. Reduce by boiling to half its original quantity. Skim off any impurities as they rise to the surface and pass through a fine chinois (conical strainer), re-boil and taste for seasoning.

Sauce Robert

15ml/1 tablespoon chopped onion
a little butter
150ml/¼ pint vinegar
290ml/½ pint demi-glace (above)
3 gherkins, chopped
5ml/1 teaspoon French mustard
5ml/1 teaspoon chopped fresh parsley

1. Soften the onion in the butter in a heavy pan over gentle heat. Add the vinegar and boil until the liquid has reduced to 15ml/1 tablespoon. Pour in the sauce espagnole, stir, and simmer for 15 minutes.
2. Immediately before serving, add the gherkin, mustard and parsley.

Madeira Sauce

45ml/3 tablespoons Madeira
5ml/1 teaspoon glace de viande (see page 219)
290ml/½ pint sauce espagnole (see above)
nut of butter

1. Place the Madeira and glace de viande together in a small heavy pan. Boil until reduced by half.
2. Add the demi-glace and heat up.
3. Beat in the nut of butter.

Sauce Poivrade

15ml/1 tablespoon oil
1 small onion, chopped
1 shallot, chopped
1 small carrot, chopped
45ml/3 tablespoons red wine
75ml/5 tablespoons vinegar
2 parsley stalks
1 bay leaf
15g½oz butter
15g/½oz flour
290ml/½ pint beef stock (cold)
4 juniper berries, crushed
salt and freshly ground black pepper

1. Heat the oil and soften the onion, shallot and carrots in it. Add the wine, vinegar, parsley stalks and bay leaf and boil over a moderate heat to reduce to 30ml/2 tablespoons. Set aside.
2. Melt the butter, stir in the flour and cook until a pale biscuit brown. Pour on the stock. Bring to the boil, stirring well. Add the wine and vegetables and simmer for 30 minutes.
3. Add the juniper berries and seasoning. Simmer for a further 10 minutes. Strain through a very fine sieve, tammy strainer or piece of muslin into a clean pan. Return to the heat and

simmer for 20 minutes. The sauce should be thick and syrupy. Taste for seasoning.

Mayonnaise

2 egg yolks
salt and pepper
5ml/1 teaspoon pale mustard
290ml/½ pint olive oil, or 150ml/¼ pint each olive and salad oil
squeeze of lemon juice
15ml/1 tablespoon wine vinegar

1. Put the yolks into a bowl with a pinch of salt and the mustard and beat well with a wooden spoon.
2. Add the oil, literally drop by drop, beating all the time. The mixture should be very thick by the time half the oil is added.
3. Beat in the lemon juice.
4. Resume pouring in the oil, going rather more confidently now, but alternating the dribbles of oil with small quantities of vinegar.
5. Add salt and pepper to taste.

NOTE: If the mixture curdles, another egg yolk should be beaten in a separate bowl, and the curdled mixture beaten drop by drop into it.

Elizabeth Sauce

This sauce was invented by the staff at the Cordon Bleu School for the Coronation in 1953 and has become a classic.

1 small onion, chopped
10ml/2 teaspoons oil
10ml/2 teaspoons curry powder
2.5ml/½ teaspoon tomato purée
45ml/3 tablespoons water
1 small bay leaf
60ml/4 tablespoons red wine
salt and pepper
10ml/2 teaspoons apricot jam
1 slice lemon
5ml/1 teaspoon lemon juice
290ml/½ pint mayonnaise (see page 224)
30ml/2 tablespoons double cream

1. Cook the onion gently for 10 minutes in the oil.
2. Add the curry powder and fry gently for 1 minute.
3. Add the tomato purée, water, bay leaf, wine, salt, pepper, jam, lemon slice and juice and simmer for 8 minutes.
4. Strain the mixture, pushing as much as possible through the sieve. Leave to cool.
5. When cold, use this sauce to flavour the mayonnaise to the desired strength.
6. Half-whip the cream and stir into the sauce.

NOTE: This sauce is also delicious made with Greek yoghurt instead of mayonnaise.

Green Mayonnaise

bunch of watercress
290ml/½ pint mayonnaise (see page 224)
salt and freshly ground black pepper

1. Pick over the watercress to remove stalks and yellowed leaves. Wash well. Dry thoroughly and chop very finely.
2. Add to the mayonnaise and season to taste.

NOTE: Cooked and very well-drained spinach can be used instead of watercress.

Tartare Sauce

150ml/¼ pint mayonnaise (see page 224)
15ml/1 tablespoon chopped capers
15ml/1 tablespoon chopped gherkins
15ml/1 tablespoon chopped fresh parsley
1 shallot, finely chopped
squeeze of lemon juice
salt and pepper

1. Mix everything together. Taste and add salt or pepper as necessary.

NOTE: Chopped hardboiled eggs make a delicious addition.

Rémoulade Sauce

150ml/¼ pint mayonnaise (see page 224)
5ml/1 teaspoon Dijon mustard
7ml/½ tablespoon finely chopped capers
7ml/½ tablespoon finely chopped gherkin
7ml/½ tablespoon finely chopped fresh tarragon or chervil
1 anchovy fillet, finely chopped

1. Mix all the ingredients together.

NOTE: Rémoulade sauce is a mayonnaise with a predominantly mustard flavour. The other ingredients, though good, are not always present.

Hollandaise Sauce

45ml/3 tablespoons wine vinegar
6 peppercorns
1 bay leaf
blade of mace
2 egg yolks
salt
110g/4oz softened unsalted butter
lemon juice

1. Place the vinegar, peppercorns, bay leaf and mace in a small heavy saucepan and reduce by simmering to 15ml/1 tablespoon.
2. Cream the egg yolks with a pinch of salt and a nut of butter in a small bowl. Set in a bain-marie on a gentle heat. With a wooden spoon beat the mixture until slightly thickened, taking care that the water immediately around the bowl does not boil. Mix well.
3. Strain on the reduced vinegar. Mix well. Stir over the heat until slightly thickened. Beat in the softened butter bit by bit, increasing the temperature as the sauce thickens and you add more butter, but take care that the water does not boil.
4. When the sauce has become light and thick take it off the heat and beat or whisk for 1 minute. Taste for seasoning and add lemon juice, and salt if necessary. Keep warm by standing the bowl in hot water. Serve warm.

NOTE: Hollandaise sauce will set too firmly if allowed to get cold and it will curdle if overheated. It can be made in larger quantities in either a liquidizer or a food processor: simply put the eggs and salt into the blender and blend lightly. Add the hot reduction, allow to thicken slightly. Set aside. When ready to serve, pour in warm melted butter, slowly allowing the sauce to thicken as you pour.

Easy Hollandaise Sauce

This sauce is fairly foolproof. It takes at least 10 minutes to make.

45ml/3 tablespoons wine vinegar
6 peppercorns
1 bay leaf
blade of mace
30ml/2 tablespoons water
1 egg
2 egg yolks
110g/4oz melted unsalted butter
lemon juice
salt

1. Put the vinegar, peppercorns, bay leaf and mace in a small saucepan and reduce by boiling until only 15ml/1 tablespoon remains. Take the pan off the heat, remove the solid ingredients and add the water.
2. Put the eggs and yolks into the pan. Whisk, off the heat, until thick and fluffy.
3. Return to a gentle heat and, whisking continuously, slowly add the melted butter. Keep whisking, removing from the heat if the sauce gets more than warm, until the sauce is a thick emulsion. This may take up to 10 minutes. Remove from the heat and add lemon juice and salt to taste.

Béarnaise Sauce

45ml/3 tablespoons wine vinegar
6 peppercorns
1 bay leaf
1 small shallot, chopped

sprig of fresh tarragon
sprig of fresh chervil
2 egg yolks
salt and pepper
110g/4oz unsalted butter, softened
5ml/1 teaspoon chopped fresh tarragon
5ml/1 teaspoon chopped fresh chervil
nut of glace de viande (see page 219)

1. Place the vinegar, peppercorns, bay leaf, shallot, tarragon and chervil in a heavy saucepan and reduce over medium heat to 15ml/1 tablespoon.
2. In a small bowl cream the egg yolks with a pinch of salt and a nut of butter. Set the bowl in a bain-marie over a gentle heat. With a wooden spoon, beat the mixture until slightly thickened.
3. Strain on the reduced vinegar. Mix well and beat until thickened. Beat in the remaining butter bit by bit, increasing the temperature as the sauce thickens and you add more butter, but take care that the water does not boil immediately round the bowl.
4. When all the butter is added, stir in the chopped tarragon, chervil and glace de viande. Taste for seasoning.

NOTE: See the note at the end of hollandaise sauce for cooking in larger quantities.

Herby Hollandaise Sauce

1 shallot, finely chopped
30ml/2 tablespoons chopped fresh tarragon
30ml/2 tablespoons chopped fresh chervil or parsley
60ml/4 tablespoons wine vinegar
6 peppercorns
1 bay leaf
3 large egg yolks
170g/6oz unsalted butter
pinch of salt
pinch of cayenne
lemon juice

1. Put the shallot, half the tarragon and chervil, the wine vinegar, peppercorns and bay leaf into a small saucepan and simmer until the liquid is reduced to about 15ml/1 tablespoon. Cool slightly and strain into a small pudding basin. Add the egg yolks and mix well.
2. Fit the basin over a saucepan of water, making sure that the water does not touch the bottom of the basin. (Alternatively set the basin in one end of a roasting tin full of water. Place the empty end of the tin over enough heat to make the water bubble only in that area, leaving the water immediately around your basin hot but not bubbling.) Get the water under and around the bowl to simmering point, stirring the egg yolk mixture with a wooden spoon all the time. Allow to thicken slightly and then gradually add the butter, a teaspoon at a time. The trick is to add the next small blob of butter only when the last one is safely absorbed without curdling. The mixture must stay warm enough for the egg yolk to thicken slightly but must never boil if it will curdle. When all the butter is absorbed you should have a sauce the consistency of soft mayonnaise. Add salt, cayenne and lemon juice (very little) to taste. Stir in the remaining herbs. Serve in a warmed sauce boat.

NOTE: See the note at the end of hollandaise sauce for cooking in larger quantities.

Herb and Cream Hollandaise Sauce

The addition of cream to the hollandaise sauce means that it is stabilized and can be gently reheated, though it will curdle if allowed to boil. This recipe has glace de poisson in it, so is only suitable for fish dishes.

hollandaise sauce made with 2 eggs (see page 225)
5ml/1 teaspoon fish glaze (see page 220)
85ml/3 fl oz double cream
15ml/1 tablespoon chopped fresh herbs, such as chives, chervil, tarragon and fennel

1. Make the hollandaise sauce, stir in the fish glaze, double cream and herbs.
2. Reheat over a very gentle heat as and when required.

Beurre Blanc

225g/8oz unsalted butter
15ml/1 tablespoon chopped shallot
45ml/3 tablespoons wine vinegar
45ml/3 tablespoons water
salt, white pepper
squeeze of lemon

1. Chill the butter then cut it in 3 lengthways, then across into thin slices. Keep cold.
2. Put the shallot, vinegar and water into a thick-bottomed sauté pan or small shallow saucepan. Boil until about 30ml/2 tablespoons remain. Strain and return to the saucepan.
3. Lower the heat under the pan. Using a wire whisk and plenty of vigorous continuous whisking, gradually add the butter, piece by piece. The process should take about 5 minutes and the sauce should become thick, creamy and pale – rather like a thin hollandaise. Add salt, pepper and lemon juice.

Saffron Beurre Blanc

3 shallots, finely chopped
240ml/8 fl oz dry white wine
110g/4oz butter, chilled and cubed
15ml/1 tablespoon double cream
salt and white pepper
good pinch of saffron, steeped in 30ml/2 tablespoons hot water for 30 minutes
15ml/1 tablespoon lemon juice

1. Put the shallots and wine into a saucepan and simmer until reduced by one-third.
2. Add the butter, bit by bit, whisking all the time. Add the cream, salt, pepper and saffron. Sharpen the flavour with a very little lemon juice.

Fish Beurre Blanc

225g/8oz unsalted butter
1 shallot, finely chopped
75ml/5 tablespoons very strong fish stock (see page 219)
15ml/1 tablespoon white wine vinegar
salt and ground white pepper
squeeze of lemon

1. Chill the butter then cut it in 3 lengthways, then across into thin slices. Keep cold.
2. Put the shallot, stock and vinegar into a small heavy saucepan and boil until reduced to 30ml/2 tablespoons. Strain and return to the pan.
3. Keep the stock hot, not boiling. Using a wire whisk and plenty of continuous whisking, gradually add the butter, piece by piece. The process should take about 5 minutes and the sauce should become thick, creamy and pale, rather like a thin hollandaise. Add the salt, pepper and lemon juice to taste.

Chicken Beurre Blanc

225g/8oz butter, unsalted
1 shallot, finely chopped
75ml/5 tablespoons very strong chicken stock
15ml/1 tablespoon white wine vinegar
salt and ground white pepper
squeeze of lemon

1. Chill the butter then cut it in 3 lengthways, then across into thin slices. Keep cold.
2. Put the shallot, stock and vinegar into a small heavy saucepan and boil until reduced to 30ml/2 tablespoons. Strain and return to the pan.
3. Keep the stock hot but not boiling. Using a wire whisk and plenty of continuous whisking, gradually add the butter, piece by piece. The process should take about 5 minutes and the sauce should become thick, creamy and pale, rather like a thin hollandaise. Add salt, pepper and lemon juice to taste.

Orange Beurre Blanc

110g/4oz unsalted butter
75ml/3 fl oz white wine
juice of 2 oranges
rind of 1 orange
15ml/1 tablespoon chopped parsley
100ml/4 fl oz double cream
salt and pepper

1. Cut the butter into small even-sized pieces and chill.
2. Put the wine, orange juice and rind into a small saucepan, bring to the boil and reduce to

45ml/3 tablespoons.
3. Lower the heat under the pan. Using a wire whisk and plenty of vigorous continuous whisking, gradually add the butter piece by piece. This process should take about 5 minutes, and the sauce should become thick and creamy.
4. Add the parsley and cream and season to taste.

NOTE: This sauce is fairly sweet. If preferred a little lemon juice can be used in place of some of the orange juice.

French Dressing (Vinaigrette)

45ml/3 tablespoons salad oil
15ml/1 tablespoon wine vinegar
salt and pepper

1. Put all the ingredients into a screw-top jar. Before using, shake until well emulsified.

NOTE I: This dressing can be flavoured with crushed garlic, mustard, a pinch of sugar, chopped fresh herbs, etc., as desired.
NOTE II: If kept refrigerated, the dressing will more easily form an emulsion when whisked or shaken, and has a slightly thicker consistency.

Tomato Dressing

1 tomato
60ml/4 tablespoons oil
15ml/1 tablespoon water
15ml/1 tablespoon tarragon vinegar
small pinch of English mustard
small pinch of sugar

1. Chop the tomato and whizz in a liquidizer with the remaining ingredients.
2. When well emulsified push through a sieve. If the dressing looks as though it might separate add a little very cold water.

Pesto Sauce

2 garlic cloves
2 large cups basil leaves
55g/2oz pinenuts
55g/2oz fresh Parmesan cheese, finely grated
150ml/1/4 pint olive oil
salt

1. In a liquidizer or mortar, grind the garlic and basil together to a paste. Add the nuts, cheese, oil and plenty of salt. Keep in a covered jar in a cool place.

NOTE: Pesto is sometimes made with walnuts instead of pinenuts, and the nuts may be pounded with the other ingredients to give a smooth paste.

Parsley Pesto

2 garlic cloves
1 large handful freshly picked parsley, roughly chopped
30g/1oz blanched almonds
150ml/1/4 pint olive oil
55g/2oz Cheddar cheese, finely grated

1. Process or liquidize the garlic and parsley together to a paste.
2. Whizz in the nuts, then add the olive oil slowly with the motor still running. Whizz in the cheese quickly.
3. Keep in a covered jar in a cool place.

Mustard Sauce

90ml/6 tablespoons oil
30ml/2 tablespoons wine vinegar
15ml/1 tablespoon Dijon mustard
15ml/1 tablespoon chopped dill
salt and pepper

1. Put all the ingredients together in a screw-top jar. Cover and shake until well emulsified.

Red Wine and Mushroom Sauce

1 onion, chopped
15g/½oz butter
55g/2oz flat mushrooms
15ml/1 tablespoon plain flour
90ml/6 tablespoons red wine
290ml/½ pint beef stock

1. In a saucepan gently sweat the onions in the butter. Add the mushrooms and cook for 2 minutes. Stir in the flour and cook for 30 seconds. Add the red wine and stock, slowly stirring all the time. Bring to the boil and simmer for at least 5 minutes.

Wild Mushroom Sauce

30g/1oz butter
2 shallots, chopped
110g/4oz wild mushrooms (e.g. horn of plenty, chanterelles, etc.)
55g/2oz flat mushrooms, sliced
425ml/¾ pint brown stock (see page 218)
1 glass dry white wine
170g/6oz unsalted butter, chilled and cut into small pieces

1. Melt the butter in a sauté pan, add the shallots and cook until soft. Increase the heat and cook until golden brown.
2. Add the mushrooms and cook for 1-2 minutes.
3. Add the stock and wine. Remove the mushrooms with a draining spoon and reserve. Boil the stock and wine to reduce to about 150ml/¼ pint. Reduce the heat under the pan.
4. Using a small wire whisk and plenty of vigorous continuous whisking, gradually add the butter, piece by piece. This process should take about 5 minutes and the sauce should become thick and creamy. Taste and season with salt and pepper if necessary.
5. Return the mushrooms to the sauce and serve.

Mushroom Sauce

2 handfuls of mixed herbs (tarragon, parsley, chervil)
150ml/¼ pint chicken stock (see page 219)
220ml/8 fl oz double cream
30g/1oz butter
110g/4oz button mushrooms
110g/4oz oyster mushrooms
salt and pepper

1. Drop the herbs into a pan of boiling salted water. Bring back to the boil and then strain through a sieve. Pour cold water on to the herbs and squeeze out any excess moisture. Put into a liquidizer.
2. Put the stock and cream into a saucepan, bring up to the boil and simmer until a coating consistency is achieved. Pour into the liquidizer and liquidize with the herbs until smooth and green.
3. Melt the butter in a sauté pan and cook the mushrooms until soft and any liquid has evaporated. Add the herb sauce to the pan and reheat. Season with salt and freshly ground black pepper.

Tomato and Whisky Sauce

900g/2lb tomatoes
90ml/6 tablespoons whisky
3 garlic cloves, crushed
salt and pepper

1. Chop the tomatoes and place in a saucepan with the other ingredients. Simmer for 20 minutes.

Salsa Pizzaiola

This recipe has been taken from *A Taste of Venice* by Jeanette Nance Nordio

1 onion, chopped
30ml/2 tablespoons olive oil
3-4 garlic cloves, chopped
1kg/2¼lb tin plum tomatoes
30ml/2 tablespoons tomato purée

10ml/2 teaspoons dried oregano
5ml/1 teaspoon dried basil
1 bay leaf
10ml/2 teaspoons sugar
salt and pepper

1. Fry the onion in the oil until transparent.
2. Add the garlic and cook for a further minute, then stir in the tomatoes with their liquid, the tomato purée, oregano, basil, bay leaf, and sugar. Season with salt and pepper. Bring to the boil and then cook very gently for about 1 hour.
3. Remove the bay leaf and check the seasoning. This sauce should be quite thick and rough but you could purée it if you wish.

Salsa Romesco

290ml/1/2 pint olive oil
2 green peppers, deseeded and sliced
5 tomatoes, chopped
3 garlic cloves, crushed
1 dried red chilli
20 hazelnuts, roasted and ground
15ml/1 tablespoon white wine vinegar
salt and freshly ground black pepper

1. Heat the oil, cook the peppers, tomatoes, garlic and chilli for 5 minutes.
2. Add the hazelnuts and vinegar, put into a liquidizer and blend until smooth. Season to taste.

Tomato, Basil and Olive Oil Sauce

55ml/2 fl oz olive oil
1 garlic clove, flattened but not crushed
2 medium tomatoes, peeled, seeded and finely chopped
4 large basil leaves
salt and pepper

1. Place the oil and the garlic in a small saucepan and place over a gentle heat to infuse for a few minutes.
2. Remove the garlic and add the tomatoes and basil. Season with salt and pepper.
3. Serve warm.

Tomato and Mint Salsa

1 shallot, finely diced
15ml/1 tablespoon red wine vinegar (white wine vinegar can be used)
45ml/3 tablespoons extra-virgin olive oil
4 tomatoes, peeled, deseeded and finely chopped
1 garlic clove, crushed
15ml/1 tablespoon chopped mint
salt and freshly ground black pepper

1. Mix together the shallot, vinegar and oil and allow to stand for 10 minutes. Add the tomatoes, garlic and mint and season with salt and pepper.

Thick Onion and Mint Sauce

1 large Spanish onion
55g/2oz butter
45ml/3 tablespoons water
30ml/2 tablespoons chopped mint
salt and freshly ground black pepper

1. Chop the onion very finely. Cook slowly in the butter and water until very soft but not coloured. Push through a sieve, or liquidize in a blender.
2. Mix in the mint and season with salt and pepper.

Exotic Sauce

This sauce has been adapted from a recipe by Josceline Dimbleby. It is a very useful accompaniment to fish, chicken or veal.

2 large green chillies, finely chopped
450g/1lb tomatoes, peeled and chopped
2-3 garlic cloves, crushed
5ml/1 teaspoon ground cardamom
10ml/2 teaspoons caster sugar
15ml/1 tablespoon tomato purée
juice of 1/2 lemon
15ml/1 tablespoon chopped coriander
110g/4oz button mushrooms, thinly sliced
salt and pepper

1. Put the chillies, tomatoes, garlic, cardamom, sugar, tomato purée and lemon juice into a saucepan. Bring up to the boil and simmer for 10 minutes.
2. Add the coriander and mushrooms. Season to taste with salt and pepper.

NOTE: If this sauce is too thick it can be thinned to the required consistency with water.

Fresh Tomato Sauce I

1 large onion, finely chopped
45ml/3 tablespoons oil
10 tomatoes, peeled, deseeded and chopped
salt and freshly ground black pepper
pinch of sugar
150g/1/4 pint chicken stock (see page 219)
5ml/1 teaspoon fresh thyme leaves

1. Cook the onion in the oil for 3 minutes. Add the tomatoes, salt, pepper and sugar, and cook for a further 25 minutes. Add the stock and cook for 5 minutes.
2. Liquidize the sauce and push through a sieve. If it is too thin, reduce, by boiling rapidly, to the desired consistency. Take care: it will spit and has a tendency to catch.
3. Add the thyme. Taste and adjust the seasoning if necessary.

Tomato Sauce II

400g/14oz can plum tomatoes
1 small onion, chopped
1 small carrot, chopped
1 stick celery, chopped
1/2 garlic clove, crushed
1 bay leaf
parsley stalks
salt and pepper
juice of 1/2 lemon
dash of Worcestershire sauce
5ml/1 teaspoon sugar
5ml/1 teaspoon chopped basil or thyme

1. Put all the ingredients together in a thick-bottomed pan, cover and simmer over medium heat for 30 minutes.
2. Liquidize and sieve the sauce and return it to the pan.
3. If it is too thin, reduce by boiling rapidly. Check the seasoning, adding more salt or sugar if necessary.

Barbecue Sauce

This sauce is particularly suitable for fried, barbecued, grilled or roasted pork. Brush some of the sauce on the meat and heat the remainder and use as a sauce.

55g/2oz unsalted butter
4 spring onions, white part only, finely sliced
5ml/1 teaspoon finely grated lime rind
5ml/1 teaspoon finely grated, peeled fresh ginger
juice of 2 oranges, strained
75ml/2 1/2 fl oz soy sauce
30g/2oz brown sugar
75ml/2 1/2 fl oz water
10ml/2 teaspoons cornflour

1. Melt the butter in a saucepan and add the spring onions. Sweat for 3 minutes or until soft.
2. Add the lime rind, ginger, orange juice, soy sauce and sugar and simmer for 5 minutes.
3. Mix the water with the cornflour and add to the glaze mixture, mix well. Return to the heat, stir constantly up to the boil and simmer gently for 4 minutes. Use as required.

Red Pepper Sauce

1 onion, finely chopped
15ml/1 tablespoon sunflower oil
2 tomatoes, peeled and deseeded
1 red pepper, peeled (by singeing over a flame), deseeded and cut into strips
1 garlic clove, crushed
1 bouquet garni
90ml/6 tablespoons water
salt and pepper

1. Cook the onion in the oil until just beginning to soften. Add the tomatoes, red pepper, garlic

and bouquet garni. Add the water and season lightly. Cover and cook slowly for 20 minutes.
2. Liquidize until smooth and push through a sieve. Chill.

Black Bean Sauce

45ml/3 tablespoons fermented black beans
2 spring onions, chopped
15ml/1 tablespoon sunflower oil
1 garlic clove, sliced
2.5 cm/1 inch piece root ginger, peeled and sliced
30ml/2 tablespoons soy sauce
30ml/2 tablespoons sherry
5ml/1 teaspoon sugar
290ml/½ pint water
10ml/2 teaspoons sesame oil

1. Wash the beans again and again.
2. Heat the oil in a saucepan, add the spring onions, garlic and ginger and cook for 1 minute.
3. Add the soy sauce, sherry, beans, sugar and water. Bring slowly to the boil, then simmer for 15 minutes to allow the flavour to infuse.
4. Stir in the sesame oil. Use as required.

Apple Sauce

450g/1lb cooking apples
finely grated rind of ¼ lemon
45ml/3 tablespoons water
10ml/2 teaspoons sugar
15g/½oz butter

1. Peel, quarter, core and slice the apples.
2. Place in a heavy saucepan with the lemon rind, water and sugar. Cover with a lid and cook very slowly until the apples are soft.
3. Beat in the butter, cool slightly and add extra sugar if required. Serve hot or cold.

Mint Sauce

large handful of fresh mint
30ml/2 tablespoons caster sugar
30ml/2 tablespoons hot water
30ml/2 tablespoons vinegar

1. Wash the mint and shake it dry. Remove the stalks, and chop the leaves finely. Place in a bowl with the sugar.
2. Pour on the hot water and leave for 5 minutes to dissolve the sugar. Add the vinegar and leave to soak for 1-2 hours.

Bread Sauce

1 large onion, peeled
6 cloves
290ml/½ pint milk
1 bay leaf
10 peppercorns, or 1 pinch of white pepper
pinch of nutmeg
salt
55g/2oz fresh white breadcrumbs
55g/2oz butter
30ml/2 tablespoons cream (optional)

1. Cut the onion in half. Stick the cloves into the onion pieces and put with the milk and bay leaf into a saucepan.
2. Add the peppercorns, nutmeg, and a good pinch of salt. Leave to stand for 30 minutes, then bring it to the boil very slowly.
3. Take the milk from the heat and strain it on to the breadcrumbs. Add the butter and cream. Mix and return to the saucepan.
4. Reheat the sauce carefully without boiling.
5. If it has become too thick, beat in more hot milk. It should be creamy.

Cumberland Sauce

2 oranges
1 lemon
225g/8oz redcurrant jelly
1 shallot, chopped
150ml/¼pint port or red wine
2.5ml/½ teaspoon pale mustard
pinch of cayenne pepper
pinch of ground ginger

1. Peel 1 orange and the lemon, removing only the outer skin. Cut the rind into fine shreds.
2. Squeeze the fruit juice and strain into a pan. Then add the remaining ingredients with the needleshreds. Simmer for 10 minutes and cool.

Dips and Savoury Butters

Dips and Savoury Butters

SOFT pâtés, dips and spreads are useful served with raw vegetables (crudités), biscuits or toast, or on cocktail canapés. Tartare dip is good with fried fish or chicken, and cream cheese dip is delicious on iced consommé. Quantities in these recipes would fill two good-sized cups.

Flavoured butters are good served with grilled or fried fish or shellfish, or with plainly grilled chicken or meat dishes. They are also excellent with hot toast or bread. After preparation the butter should be shaped into a cylinder, rolled up in foil or damp greaseproof paper and chilled in the refrigerator. It can then be sliced and used as required. If it is to be kept for more than 2 days it should be frozen.

Avocado Dip

2 avocados, mashed
1 garlic clove, crushed
15ml/1 tablespoon chopped fresh chives
225g/8oz cream cheese
juice of 1/2 lemon

1. Combine everything together, beat well, and season to taste.

Tartare Dip

30ml/2 tablespoons chopped gherkins
30ml/2 tablespoons chopped capers
15ml/1 tablespoon chopped fresh parsley
1/2 small onion, finely chopped
290ml/1/2 pint mayonnaise *(see page 224)*
salt and freshly ground black pepper
squeeze of lemon

1. Mix the gherkins, parsley, capers and onion with the mayonnaise. Season with salt, pepper and lemon juice.

Cream Cheese Dip

225g/8oz cream cheese
15ml/1 tablespoon soured cream
30ml/2 tablespoons chopped fresh chives
salt and freshly ground black pepper
a little milk

1. Mix the cream cheese with the soured cream and chives, season with salt and pepper and add enough milk to bring the dip to the required consistency.

Blue Cheese Dip

225g/8oz blue cheese
1 shallot, very finely chopped
15ml/1 teaspoon vinegar
salt and freshly ground black pepper
60ml/4 tablespoons soured cream

1. Beat the cheese with a wooden spoon and mix in the shallot and vinegar. Season with salt and pepper and beat in the soured cream.

Mustard Dip

150ml/1/4 pint mayonnaise (see page 224)
150ml/1/4 pint soured cream
30ml/2 tablespoons moutarde de Meaux or other mustard with the seeds

1. Combine all the ingredients.

Almond Butter

55g/2oz butter
30g/1oz ground almonds
squeeze of lemon
salt and white pepper

1. Beat the butter to a light cream. Mix the almonds with the lemon juice and beat this paste into the softened butter. Season to taste. Chill.

Anchovy Butter

2 anchovy fillets
1/2 garlic clove
55g/2oz butter
freshly ground black pepper
anchovy essence

1. Pound the anchovies and garlic and mix well with the butter. Season with pepper and anchovy essence. Chill.

Garlic Butter

55g/2oz butter
1 large garlic clove, crushed with salt
30ml/2 tablespoons lemon juice
salt and pepper

1. Beat all the ingredients together. Chill.

Green Butter

2 sprigs watercress
small bunch of fresh tarragon
sprig of parsley
salt and pepper
55g/2oz butter
1 shallot, minced

1. Blanch the watercress, tarragon and parsley for 30 seconds in boiling salted water. Refresh under cold running water. Drain well and pat dry. Chop very finely.
2. Cream the butter and beat in the shallot, watercress and herbs. Add salt and pepper. Chill.

Maître d'Hôtel Butter

55g/2oz butter
10ml/2 teaspoons lemon juice
5ml/1 teaspoon finely chopped parsley
salt and pepper

1. Cream the butter, stir in the lemon juice and parsley and season to taste. Mix well and chill.

Mint and Mustard Butter

110g/4oz butter
5ml/1 teaspoon Dijon mustard
15ml/1 tablespoon finely chopped fresh mint
salt and freshly ground black pepper

1. Cream the butter until very soft and beat in the mustard and mint.
2. Season with salt and pepper. Chill.

Fish

Fish

FRESHWATER fish are divided into coarse fish, fished mainly for sport and generally thrown back live into the rivers, and game fish, which are caught both for sport and commercially. Much freshwater fish in fact comes from fish farms. Many freshwater fish, such as bass, sturgeon, sea trout and salmon spend most of their adult lives in the sea, swimming back up the rivers to spawn, but they are still classified as freshwater fish despite the fact that most of them are caught by trawl in the sea. Coarse river fish, such as roach, gudgeon and tench are not sold commercially and are seldom eaten except by anglers' families.

Most of our fish comes from the sea. As the fishing industry 'modernizes' it is increasingly difficult to get locally caught fish. Fish is frozen or deep-chilled on trawlers and immediately exported. For the cook this is sad. Fish is a valuable source of protein, vitamin D (in oily fish), calcium and phosphorus (especially found in the edible bones of whitebait, sardines, etc.), iodine, fluorine and some of the B vitamins. Fish contains very little fat, and even oily fish seldom has more than 20 per cent fat content. The fat in fish is polyunsaturated and contains essential fatty acids that cannot be obtained elsewhere.

Like meat, fish is composed of muscle fibres that vary in length and thickness according to type. For example, lobster has long and coarse fibres and herring very fine fibres.

The fibres are generally shorter than in meat and are packed in flakes with very little connective tissue between them. The fat is dispersed among the fibres. The connective tissue is very thin and is quickly converted to gelatine when cooked. Because of its structure, fish is naturally more tender than meat and over-vigorous or overlong cooking will cause dryness and disintegration as the connective tissue dissolves and the flakes fall apart. The protein in the fibres coagulates, the fish begins to shrink and the juices are extracted - in dry heat there is a more rapid loss of juices. In moist heat soluble nutrients and flavouring minerals are lost into the liquid making an overcooked fish dry, tough and tasteless.

Fish should be cooked quickly by grilling or frying, or slowly by poaching. If frying or grilling, the fish should be protected from the fierce heat by seasoned flour, beaten egg, breadcrumbs or a batter. If poaching, use a well-seasoned court bouillon and then use this liquid to make the sauce so that none of the flavour is lost. Do drain fish well after it has been poached, and do not keep warm as it will dry out and become tough and tasteless. Fish does not keep well and should be eaten as fresh as possible. A plausible theory explaining this is that as fish live in cold water, they are cold-blooded and their enzymes work at very low temperatures. Thus they continue, unlike meat, to deteriorate in the refrigerator.

PREPARATION FOR COOKING

REMOVING THE SCALES. Large fish have dry scales which should be removed before cooking. To do this, scrape a large knife the wrong way along the fish (from tail to head). This can be a messy business as the scales tend to fly about; it can be cleanly done in a plastic carrier bag to prvent this. However, unless you are buying fish from a wholesale market, the fishmonger will do it for you.

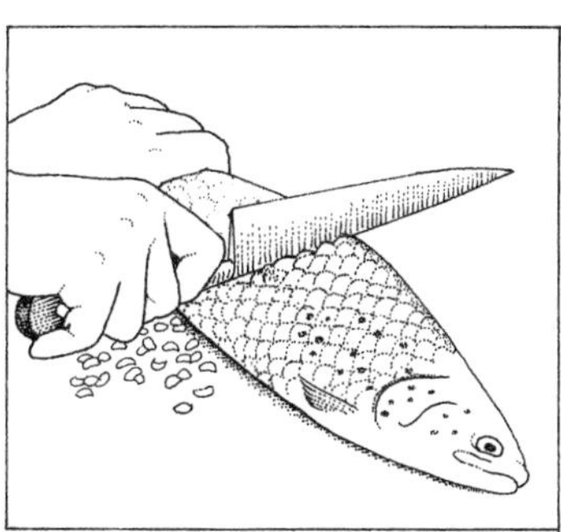

Remove the scales with the back of a knife

GUTTING AND CLEANING. The fishmonger will probably clean the fish, but if you are to do it yourself you will need a very sharp knife. Fish skin blunts knives faster than anything else. If the fish is to be stuffed or filleted it does not matter how big a slit you make to remove the entrails. If it is to be left whole, the shorter the slit the better. Start just below the head and slit through the soft belly skin. After pulling out the innards, wash the fish under cold water. If it is large, and of the round type, make sure all the dark blood along the spinal column is removed. Now carefully cut away the gills. Take care not to cut off the head if you want to serve the fish whole. If you do not, cut off head and tail now. To remove the fins, cut the skin round them, take a good grip (if you salt your fingers well it will stop them slipping) and yank sharply towards the head. This will pull the fin bones out with the fin.

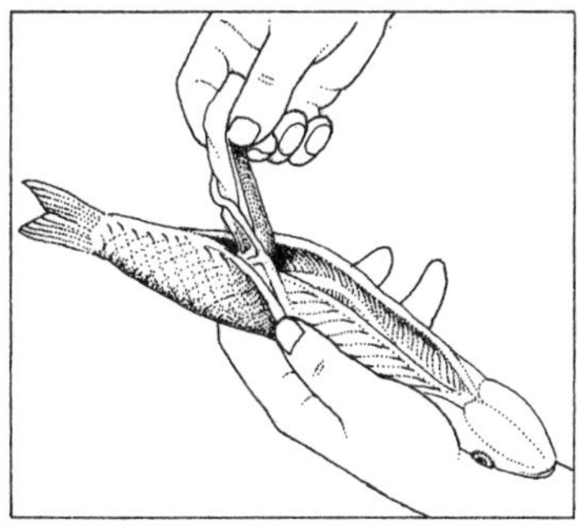

Remove the innards and wash thoroughly

SKINNING AND FILLETING FLAT FISH. Fish skin is easier to remove after cooking. But sometimes the fish must be skinned beforehand. Most whole fish are not skinned or filleted before grilling, but sole (and lemon sole, witch and plaice) are skinned on at least the dark side, and sometimes on both sides. To do this, make a crosswise slit through the skin at the tail, and push a finger in. You will now be able to run the finger round the edge of the fish loosening the skin. When you have done this on both edges, salt your fingers to prevent slipping, take a firm grip of the skin at the tail end with one hand, and with the other hold the fish down. Give a quick strong yank, peeling the skin back towards the head. If necessary, do the same to the other side.

Flat fish are generally filleted into four half-fillets. To do this, lay the fish on a board with the tail towards you. Cut through the flesh to the backbone along the length of the fish. Then, with a sharp pliable knife, cut the left-hand fillet away from the bone, keeping the blade almost flat against the bones of the fish. Then swivel the fish round so the head is towards you and cut away the second fillet in the same way. Turn the fish over and repeat the process on the other side. (If you are left-handed, tackle the right-hand fillet first.)

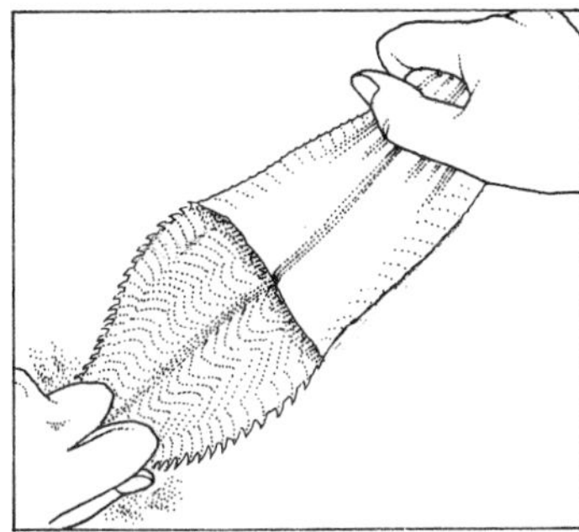

Remove the skin from a flat fish in one piece

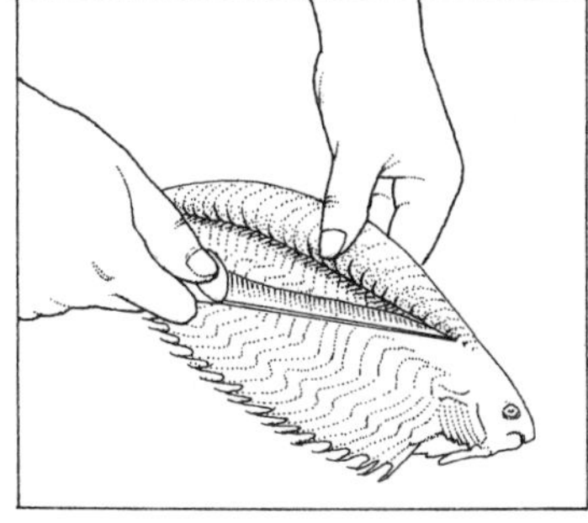

To fillet a flat fish, stroke the flesh away from the bones

FILLETING AND SKINNING ROUND FISH. Round fish are filleted before skinning. If they are to be cooked whole, they are cooked with the skin, but this may be carefully peeled off after cooking, as in the case of a whole poached salmon. To fillet a round fish, lay it on a board and cut through the flesh down to the backbone from the head to the tail. Insert a sharp pliable knife between the flesh and the bones, and slice the fillet away from the bones, working with short strokes from the backbone and from the head end. Remember to keep the knife as flat as possible, and to keep it against the bones. When the fillet is almost off the fish you will need to cut through the belly skin to detach it completely. Very large round fish can be filleted in four, following the flat fish method, or the whole side can be lifted as described here, and then split in two once off the fish.

TO SKIN A FISH FILLET. Put it skin side down on a board. Hold the tip down firmly, using a good pinch of salt to help get a firm grip. With a sharp, heavy, straight knife, cut through the flesh, close to the tip, taking care not to go right through the skin. Hold the knife at rightangles to the fish fillet, with the blade almost upright. With a gently sawing motion, work the flesh from the skin, pushing the fillet off rather than cutting it. The reason for keeping the knife almost upright is to lessen the danger of cutting through the skin, but with practice it is possible to flatten the knife slightly, so that the sharp edge is foremost, and simply slide it forward, without the sawing motion.

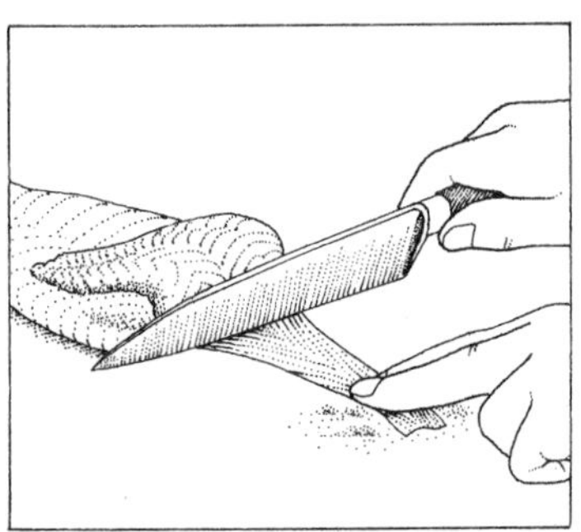

To skin a fillet, grip the tail with one hand and push the flesh off the fillet with a knife

TO BONE SMALL FISH. Split the fish open completely, clean thoroughly and lay, skin side up, on a board. With the heel of your hand, press down firmly on the backbone of the fish. This will loosen it. Turn it over, cut through the backbone near the head, and pull it out with all the side bones, or nearly all the sidebones attached to it.

SKINNING EEL. Cut through the skin round the neck and slit the skin down the length of the body. Hang the eel up by its head - a stout hook through the eyes is best. Using a cloth to get a good grip, pull hard to peel off the skin from neck to tail.

STUFFING FISH. Round fish are more suitable for stuffing whole than flat fish, as there is more space in the body cavity after gutting. Stuffings usually contain breadcrumbs, which swell during cooking, so care should be taken not to overfill the fish. Fish fillets can be sandwiched with stuffing, or rolled up round the mixture. Well-flavoured expensive fish is less often stuffed than the most tasteless varieties, which need the additional flavour of an aromatic filling.

SLICING SMOKED SALMON. Place the side of salmon, skin side down, on a board. Run the tips of the fingers of one hand over the surface of the flesh to locate the ends of the small bones. Pull the bones out with tweezers or pliers. Now slice the flesh in horizontal paper-thin slices, using a long, sharp ham knife. The slices should be long and wide. It is customary to remove the central narrow stripe of brownish flesh, but this is not strictly necessary - it tastes excellent. If the whole side is not to be sliced, place a piece of plastic wrap on the cut surface of the remaining salmon to prevent drying out.

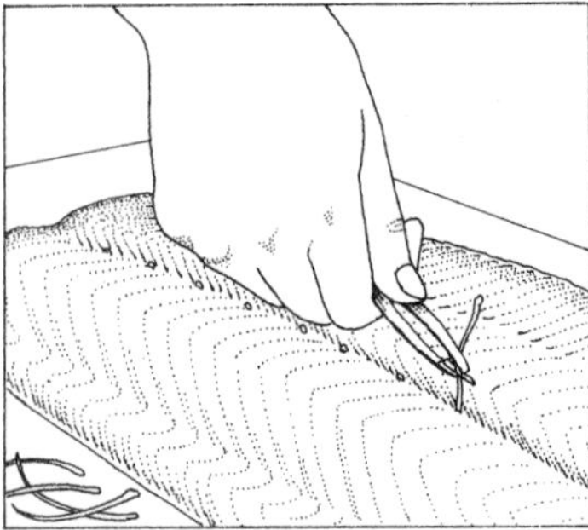

Remove the bones with tweezers or pliers

Grilled Fish Cutlets

This recipe is suitable for brill, cod, halibut, haddock, turbot or salmon cutlets. The pieces of fish should, if possible, be cut to a uniform thickness.

SERVES 4
4 x 170g/6oz fish cutlets
melted butter
freshly ground black pepper
juice of 1/2 lemon

For the garnish:
parsley sprigs or watercress
lemon wedges

1. Heat the grill. Brush the cutlets and the bottom of the grill pan with melted butter. Season the cutlets with pepper and lemon juice. Lay them in the grill tray (not on the wire tray where they might stick).
2. Grill them until pale brown. Turn over and brush with more melted butter. Season again with pepper and lemon juice and grill for a further 3 minutes or until cooked. They will feel firm to the touch, and the flesh will flake easily.
3. Serve on a heated dish with the pan juices poured over, garnished with parsley or watercress and lemon wedges.

CRISP DRY WHITE

Cod with Spring Onions and Ginger Sauce

Any firm white fish such as halibut, haddock, monkfish or turbot can be used for this recipe – the firmer the fish, the easier it is to cook.

SERVES 2-3
450g/1lb cod fillet
2 garlic cloves, slivered
1 cm/1/2 inch root ginger, slivered
8-10 spring onions, shredded
sesame oil for frying

For the marinade:
15ml/1 tablespoon soy sauce mixed with 1 tablespoon sherry

For the sauce:
2.5ml/1/2 teaspoon ground ginger
2.5ml/1/2 teaspoon caster sugar
15ml/1 tablespoon soy sauce
15ml/1 tablespoon sherry

1. Cut the fish fillets into strips the size of your little finger.
2. Add the fish to the marinade and leave it to stand for 30 minutes.
3. Mix all the ingredients for the sauce together and set aside.
4. Heat a sauté pan (preferably nonstick), add a little oil, and when hot add the garlic and ginger. Cook quickly until the garlic is lightly browned. Lower the heat and add the fish, in its marinade, and fry briefly. Pour in the sauce, stir and add the spring onions. Serve immediately.

SPICY DRY WHITE

Dressed Crab

SERVES 3
900g/2lb live crab

To season:
salt and freshly ground black pepper
lemon juice
mustard
breadcrumbs
cooked egg yolks, sieved
parsley

To serve:
mayonnaise (see page 224)
tartare sauce (see page 224)
brown bread and butter

1. Place the crab in a pan of well-salted water (about 170g/6oz salt to 2.5 litres/4 pints water), cover and bring to the boil. Simmer, allowing 15 minutes to each 450g/1lb crab. Remove from the pan and allow to cool.
2. Lay the crab on its back. Twist off the legs and claws. Cracking round the natural line (visible

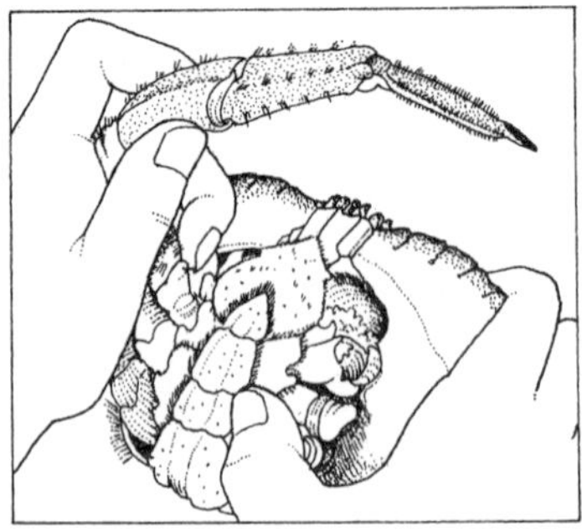
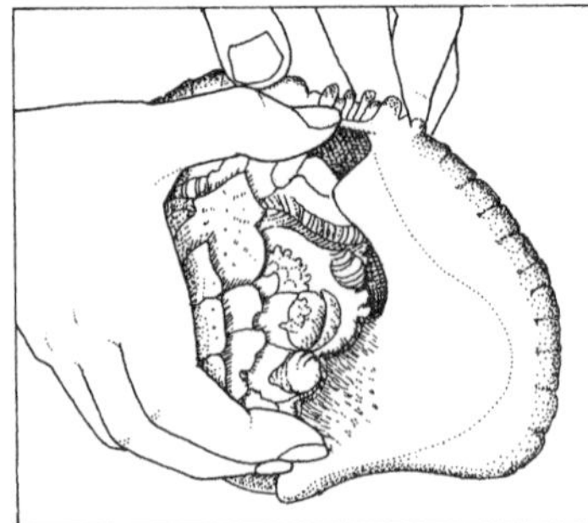
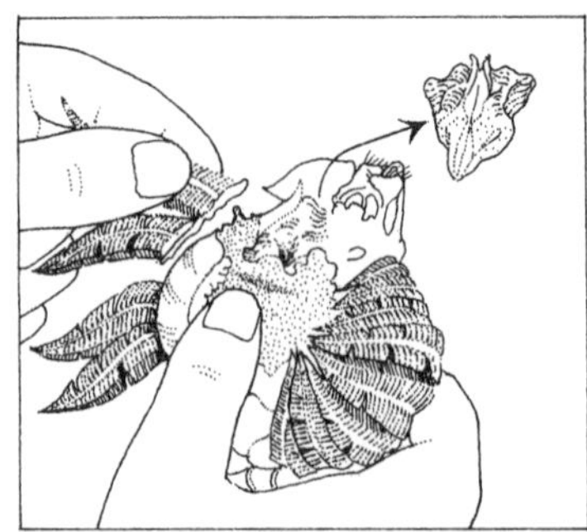

Twist off the legs and claws; remove and throw away the pale belly shell; discard the spongy lungs and small stomach sac

near the edge), remove the pale belly shell and discard it. Remove and throw away the small sac at the top of the crab body and the spongy lungs which line the edge (they look rather like grey fish gills).

3. Have 2 bowls ready, one for white meat, one for brown. Lift out the body of the crab, cut into 2 or 4 pieces and carefully pick out all the meat that you can. This is fiddly and could take up to 15 minutes. If you have a lobster 'pick' it can be very useful. Wash and dry the shell.

4. Crack the large claws, remove the meat and put it into the white meat bowl.

5. With a lobster pick or toothpick poke out the remaining meat from the legs, and add it to the white meat in the bowl.

6. To dress the crab: cream the brown meat, season with lemon juice, salt, pepper and mustard. Add enough breadcrumbs to bind the mixture. Arrange this down the centre of the shell and pile the white meat up at each side. Decorate with neat lines of egg yolk and parsley.

7. Place on a serving plate with the claws. Serve mayonnaise or tartare sauce and brown bread and butter.

LOIRE WHITE

Eel Pie

SERVES 6

puff pastry made with 340g/12oz flour (see page 528)
900g/2lb smoked eel, skinned and boned
900g/2lb fresh spinach, cooked and chopped
grated nutmeg
freshly ground black pepper

For the sauce:
55g/2oz unsalted butter
15g/½oz flour
150ml/¼ pint milk
2 egg yolks
beaten egg

1. Set the oven to 200°C/400°F/gas mark 6.

2. Take one-third of the pastry and roll it out to a rectangle, 15 x 20cm/6 x 8 inches. Place on a wet baking tray and prick with a fork. Bake for about 20 minutes until golden brown. Do not turn the oven off. Leave the pastry on a wire rack to cool.

3. Season the spinach with nutmeg and pepper.

4. To make the sauce: melt 15g/½oz butter, add the flour and cook for 30 seconds. Draw off the heat and stir in the milk. Return to the heat and stir until boiling.

5. Cool slightly, then beat in the rest of the butter and the egg yolks. Season with the pepper.

6. Arrange half the spinach on the cooked pastry base and cover with the eel. Spread the béchamel sauce over the eel and cover with remaining spinach.

7. Roll the remaining pastry on a floured board into a 'blanket' large enough to overlap the edges of the whole pie. Lay it gently over the spinach. With a sharp knife cut off the corners to the size of the pie. Reserve the trimmings.

8. Lift one side of the overlapping pastry and brush the underside with a little beaten egg. Tuck the 'blanket' neatly underneath the cooked base. Repeat with the other three sides.

9. Shape the trimmings into leaves. Brush the whole pie with beaten egg. Lay on the pastry leaves and brush again.

10. Bake for 40-45 minutes. Serve hot or cold.

NOTE: To counteract the saltiness of the smoked eel, salt is not added to the sauce or to the spinach.

Haddock Filling for Gougère

SERVES 4

340g/12oz smoked haddock fillet, cooked and flaked
4 tomatoes, skinned, deseeded and slivered
45g/1oz butter
30g/1oz flour
290ml/½ pint milk
freshly ground black pepper
30ml/2 tablespoons chopped fresh parsley
60ml/4 tablespoons cream
1 gougère case, see page 286

1. Melt the butter. Add the flour, stir well and draw off the heat.
2. Add the milk, pepper, parsley and cream. Return to the heat and stir until boiling. Simmer for 1-2 minutes.
3. Stir in the haddock and tomatoes. Use as required.

Haddock with Tomatoes and Chives

SERVES 4

4 x 170g/6oz fresh haddock fillets
salt and freshly ground black pepper
290ml/½ pint fish stock (see page 219)
150ml/¼ pint white wine
30g/1oz butter
30g/1oz flour
150ml/¼ pint cream
2 large tomatoes, skinned, deseeded and cut into slivers
15ml/1 tablespoon chopped parsley
15ml/1 tablespoon chopped chives

1. Set the oven to 180°C/350°F/gas mark 4. Wash and season the fillets.
2. Lay the fish skin side up in an ovenproof dish. Pour over the strained fish stock and the wine. Cover with buttered greaseproof paper or foil and bake in the oven for 15-20 minutes.
3. Lift out the fish. Strain the cooking liquor into a small heavy saucepan and boil rapidly until reduced to 290ml/½pint.
4. Melt the butter in another saucepan, add the flour and stir for 1 minute. Draw off the heat and strain in the reduced fish liquor. Return to the heat, bring slowly up to the boil, and simmer for 2 minutes. Take off the heat. Add salt and pepper to taste, and the cream, tomatoes, parsley and chives.
5. Skin the fish and lay in a serving dish. Pour over the sauce.

MUSCADET

Haddock with English Egg Sauce

SERVES 4

900g/2lb haddock fillets
570ml/1 pint milk
1 onion, sliced
bouquet garni
salt and pepper

To serve:
570ml/1 pint English egg sauce , made with the reserved cooking liquor (see page 222)

1. Set the oven to 170°C/325°F/gas mark 3.
2. Wash the fish, scrape off any scales and lay skin side up in a roasting tin.
3. Pour in the milk and add the onion, bouquet garni and seasoning.
4. Cover the dish with greased paper or a lid and bake in the oven for 30 minutes, until the fish is tender to the touch of a skewer.
5. Take out the fish, skin, drain and remove any bones. Reserve the fish liquor for the sauce. Arrange the fish on a flat ovenproof dish.
6. Cover again with the paper and keep warm while you make the sauce.
7. Pour the sauce over the fish and serve.

NOTE: Cooking times for baking fillets of fish depend on the size of the fillets, the type of roasting tin and the heat of the milk as well as the oven temperature.

DRY WHITE

Halibut au Gratin

SERVES 4

4 halibut steaks

For the court bouillon:
570ml/1 pint water
30ml/2 tablespoons vinegar
1 carrot, sliced
1 onion, sliced
4 cloves
salt
6 peppercorns
parsley stalk
sprig of thyme
bay leaf

For the sauce:
30g/1oz butter
20g/3/4oz flour
150ml/1/4 pint fish liquor
150ml/1/4 pint milk

For the topping:
dried breadcrumbs
30g/1oz Gruyère or strong Cheddar cheese, grated

1. Make up the court bouillon: combine the ingredients, bring to the boil, simmer for 10 minutes and allow to cool.
2. Set the oven to 180°C/350°F/gas mark 4. Place the halibut steaks in a buttered dish. Strain on the court bouillon and cover with a piece of greased paper, foil or a lid. Poach in the oven or over a gentle heat for 10-15 minutes. Reduce the oven temperature to 70°C/150°F/gas mark 1.
3. Lift out the fish. Strain the fish liquor into a saucepan and reduce it by rapid boiling to 150ml/1/4 pint.
4. Skin the fish and take out the bone. Drain well. Place them on an ovenproof serving dish, cover, and return to the oven.
5. Heat up the grill.
6. Make the sauce: melt the butter in a small pan and stir in the flour. Cook for 1 minute and then remove from the heat. Pour in the fish stock and milk. Return to the heat and bring slowly to the boil, stirring until you have a smooth creamy sauce. Simmer for 2 minutes. Season with salt and pepper as necessary.
7. Spoon the sauce over the fish. Sprinkle with breadcrumbs and grated cheese.
8. Grill until well browned.

WHITE BURGUNDY

Langoustine in Filo with Herb Butter

SERVES 4

8 langoustines
85g/3oz unsalted butter
6 garlic cloves, 4 bruised and 2 finely chopped
15ml/1 tablespoon of finely chopped parsley
4 slices of white bread
4 sheets of filo pastry
salt and pepper
1 egg, beaten
1 lemon, cut into wedges

1. Bring a pan of water up to the boil. Put the langoustines in the water and bring back to simmering point. Remove the langoustines and allow them to cool.
2. Remove the head, shells and legs from the langoustines. Remove the digestive tract (a black vein running down the back of the langoustine).
3. Gently melt the butter and add the 4 bruised cloves of garlic. Allow them to infuse for as long as possible – at least 30 minutes. Remove the garlic cloves, chopped garlic and the parsley.
4. Set the oven to 170°C/325°F/gas mark 3.
5. Cut 4 x 5cm/2 inch rounds from the bread and dry out in the oven until crisp.
6. Cut a sheet of filo in half and trim each half into squares of approximately 17.5cm/7 inches.
7. Brush each square with the herb butter and place one on top of the other at an angle.
8. Put a piece of the crisp bread in the middle. Dip 2 langoustines into the herb butter. Place them on the bread and season with salt and pepper.
9. Gather the corners of the pastry together to form a 'Dick Whittington sack'. Brush with egg

glaze. Repeat for the other 3 parcels. Refrigerate until required.

10. Turn up the oven to 220°C/425°F/gas mark 7 and cook the parcels on a baking sheet for 5 minutes or until they are a rich brown.

11. Remove from the oven and serve immediately with lemon wedges.

WHITE LOIRE

Boiled Lobster

SERVES 4

2 x 900g/2 lb live lobsters

For the court bouillon:
1 litre/2 pints water
225g/8oz carrots, sliced
1 medium onion, sliced
1 bay leaf
sprig of thyme
30g/1oz salt
150ml/1/4 pint wine vinegar
bunch of parsley
10 peppercorns

To serve hot:
hollandaise sauce (see page 225), or melted butter

To serve cold:
mayonnaise (see page 224)

1. Simmer all the court bouillon ingredients together for 30 minutes.

2. Weigh the lobsters, then put them into the court bouillon.

3. Bring to the boil, cover and simmer for 10 minutes per 450g/1lb. Lift out. Allow to cool before splitting if to be served cold.

4. Split the lobsters in half, remove the stomach sac near the head and the dark thread running the length of the body.

5. Serve with hollandaise sauce or melted butter if to be eaten hot, with mayonnaise if cold.

NOTE: A fresh live lobster goes bright red when cooked and the tail lightens considerably.

CHABLIS

Lobster and Chicken Salad

SERVES 4

2 x 340g/12oz cooked lobsters
225/8oz cooked chicken meat
a few drops anchovy essence
juice of 1/2 lemon
a few drops of Tabasco sauce
290ml/1/2 pint mayonnaise (see page 224)
15ml/1 tablespoon cream
2 hardboiled eggs
15ml/1 tablespoon chopped parsley
1 hearty lettuce
French dressing (page 228)

1. Place each cold lobster with the head to your left and the tail spread out flat to your right. Hold firmly by the head and with a very sharp knife push the point of the blade into the cross on the top of the head. Carefully cut all the way down the shell to the end of the tail. Turn the lobster around and split the head in 2. Remove the small bag or stomach sac in the head. Remove the intestine, which is a thin grey or black line running down through the tail meat.

2. Take out the remaining lobster meat and chop roughly. Place in a bowl. Crack the claws and remove the meat.

3. Take the chicken off the bone and cut into dice about the same size as the lobster meat. Add the anchovy essence, lemon juice and Tabasco to the mayonnaise and mix half of it with the lobster meat and chicken. Pile this mixture into the lobster shells.

4. Add the cream to the remaining mayonnaise and coat it neatly over each shell. Place on a serving dish.

5. Halve the hardboiled eggs and sieve the yolks. Mix the yolks with the chopped parsley and sprinkle over the lobsters.

6. Remove the outer leaves of the lettuce, wash, dry and shred coarsely. Shred the egg whites and toss with the lettuce and French dressing. Surround the lobsters with the salad.

WHITE BURGUNDY

Grilled Lobster with Red Butter Sauce

SERVES 4
4 small live lobsters
unsalted butter, melted
cayenne pepper

For the butter sauce:
1 shallot, finely chopped
150ml/$^1/_4$ pint dry white wine
5ml/1 teaspoon fish glaze (see page 220)
110g/4oz unsalted butter, chilled and diced
the coral from the lobster
45ml/3 tablespoons double cream
5ml/1 teaspoon tomato purée

To garnish:
watercress, trimmed

1. Begin to prepare the butter sauce: put the shallot into a small saucepan with the white wine. Cook slowly until the liquid is reduced to half its original quantity. Strain into a clean pan. Add the fish glaze and set aside.
2. Next kill the lobsters. Push a sharp strong knife through the nerve centre of each lobster. This is a well-defined cross on the back of its head. When the middle of the cross is pierced the lobster will die instantly, although it will still move alarmingly.
3. Lay the lobsters out flat and split in half lengthways. Remove the stomach sac from near the head and remove the threadlike intestine. Do not mistake roe (or coral), which may or may not be present, for the intestine, which is tiny. The roe, when cooked, will be bright red and has an excellent flavour. Reserve it for the sauce. Do not throw away the soft grey green flesh near the head either – it is the liver (or tomalley) and quite delicious.
4. Heat up the grill.
5. Brush the lobster with butter and season with cayenne pepper. Place under the grill, cut side uppermost first, for 5-10 minutes a side, depending on size, until the lobster is a good bright red.
6. While the lobster is cooking, continue with the butter sauce. Mix 5ml/1 teaspoon of the butter with the coral. Set aside.
7. When the lobsters are cooked, crack the claws, without removing them from the body if possible, with a claw cracker or by covering with a cloth and hitting gently with a rolling pin. Keep the lobsters warm while finishing the sauce.
8. Warm up the reduced wine and fish glaze. Using a wire whisk and plenty of vigorous continuous whisking, add the butter bit by bit. The process should take about 2 minutes and the sauce should thicken considerably. Do not allow it to get too hot.
9. Whisk in the coral and cream, and any pan juices from the grill. Add a little tomato purée to brighten up the colour. Taste and season as required.
10. Arrange the lobsters on a large oval dish. Garnish with watercress and hand the sauce separately.

CHABLIS

Lobster Fricassée with Tarragon Cream Sauce

2 lobsters (about 450g/1lb each)
45g/1$^1/_2$oz unsalted butter
1 shallot, finely chopped
290ml/$^1/_2$ pint fromage frais
30ml/2 tablespoons double cream
2 sprigs of tarragon
salt and freshly ground black pepper

1. Cut the lobsters in half lengthways. Remove the stomach sac and the entrails that run in a line down the tail. Crack the claws.
2. Melt the butter in a sauté pan and add the shallot. Cook gently until softened and slightly brown.
3. Add the lobster halves, shell side down, and pour the fromage frais and double cream over them. Add the tarragon stems, stripped of their leaves, and simmer over a low heat until the cream comes up to the boil. Cover the pan and turn the heat down very low. Cook for 10 minutes.
4. Remove the lobsters from the cream. Carefully pull the tail meat out of the shells in one piece. Remove the claw meat. Place it all in a medium saucepan and set aside.

5. Crack or cut up all the lobster shells and add to the cream in the sauté pan. Bring to the boil over a moderate heat. Remove from the heat and pass the sauce through a very fine sieve into the saucepan containing the lobster meat. Season with salt and pepper and the reserved tarragon leaves.
6. Heat the fricassée very gently and serve.
7. If making this in advance, allow the fricassée to cool and refrigerate. About 10 minutes before serving, heat very gently in a saucepan.

CRISP DRY WHITE

Mackerel with Gooseberry Sauce

SERVES 4
4 x 225g/8oz mackerel

For the gooseberry sauce:
340g/12oz young gooseberries
30g/1oz sugar
30g/1oz butter
pinch of ground ginger

For the garnish:
lemon wedges

1. Heat up the grill.
2. Clean the fish, cut off the fins and make 2 or 3 diagonal slashes into the flesh through the skin.
3. Meanwhile, prepare the gooseberry sauce. Top and tail the berries and place them in a pan with a little water and the sugar. Simmer until tender.
4. Push the berries through a sieve. Beat in the butter and ginger and taste for sweetness.
5. Grill the mackerel for about 5 minutes a side, depending on size, or until cooked.
6. Arrange the mackerel on a serving dish. Garnish with lemon wedges. Hand the sauce separately.

ALSACE WHITE

Spicy Fish Curry

Any firm white fish will do for this curry. Be very careful not to overcook the fish as it will begin to fall apart and look unattractive. It is a fairly mild curry but it can be made hotter by using an extra green chilli. Remove the seeds of the green chilli under cold running water.

675g/1½lb monkfish, filleted and skinned
1 x 1cm/½ inch piece fresh ginger, slivered
1 garlic clove, crushed
sunflower oil
1 large onion, sliced
1 green pepper, deseeded and sliced
1 green chilli, deseeded and chopped
5ml/1 teaspoon ground cumin
5ml/1 teaspoon ground coriander
5ml/1 teaspoon ground cinnamon
5ml/1 teaspoon turmeric
water
110g/4oz Greek yoghurt
fresh mint

1. Cut the monkfish into 2.5cm/1 inch cubes.
2. Fry the fish in a nonstick pan in a little sunflower oil with the ginger and garlic. Remove from the pan. Add the onion, pepper and green chilli and allow to soften without browning for 2-3 minutes. Add the dry spices and cook for a further 2 minutes. Stir regularly and add a little extra oil if they are getting too dry.
3. Take the pan off the heat. Return the fish, ginger and garlic. Add enough water to half cover the fish and vegetables and bring gradually up to the boil. Season well. Simmer for 10 minutes. Remove the fish with a slotted spoon. Reduce the sauce, by boiling rapidly to a syrupy consistency.
4. Beat the yoghurt with a little water, add some of the hot fish juices, mix well and return to the pan. Bring up to the boil but do not allow it to get too hot. Return the fish to the saucepan.
5. Pile into a warm serving dish and serve decorated with roughly chopped fresh mint.

SPICY DRY WHITE

Lotte à l'Americaine

This is one of the best ways of serving monkfish, which like lobster has a firm enough flesh to marry well with the strong flavours of the sauce.

This recipe has been adapted from *Fish Cookery* by Jane Grigson.

SERVES 6
1.35kg/3lb monkfish, filleted, and cubed
seasoned flour
2 shallots, chopped
3 onions, chopped
1 large garlic clove, chopped
120ml/8 tablespoons olive oil
90ml/6 tablespoons brandy
425ml/3/4 pint dry white wine
340g/12oz large ripe tomatoes, peeled and chopped
15ml/1 tablespoon tomato purée
5ml/1 teaspoon sugar
cayenne pepper
salt, pepper
chopped parsley and tarragon to garnish

1. Toss the monkfish in seasoned flour.
2. Meanwhile fry the shallot, onion and garlic in the oil until they begin to colour. Add the fish; when it is lightly browned, warm half of the brandy, set it alight and pour it into the pan, stirring the contents about in the flames. When these die down, remove the fish to a warm plate.
3. Pour the wine into the pan, add the tomatoes, tomato purée, sugar and seasonings. Boil hard for 20-30 minutes to reduce to a well-flavoured sauce – it must not be watery. Return the fish to the sauce and simmer gently until cooked, about 8 minutes, adding the remaining brandy at the same time. Arrange on a hot serving dish, sprinkle with parsley and tarragon.

WHITE BURGUNDY

Monkfish with Herby Hollandaise

SERVES 4
900g/2lb monkfish, skinned and filleted

For the court bouillon:
570ml/1 pint water
75ml/5 tablespoons wine vinegar
1 carrot, sliced
1 onion, sliced
bunch of parsley
1 bay leaf
stick of celery
6 peppercorns
2.5ml/1/2 teaspoon salt

To finish:
herby hollandaise sauce (see page 226)
sprigs of chervil

1. Put all the court bouillon ingredients into a saucepan and bring to the boil. Simmer for 30 minutes. Strain and cool the liquid.
2. Put the fish into a saucepan, pour over the court bouillon and put on the heat. Cover with a lid and bring slowly to simmering point. Now turn down the heat and let the fish poach. The water should barely move; it must not boil. Poach for 20 minutes.
3. Lift out the fish. Remove any remaining skin or bones.
4. Arrange the fish on a warm serving dish. Coat over the herby hollandaise and decorate with chervil leaves.

MUSCADET

Monkfish Salad with Exotic Sauce

This recipe has been adapted from *The Josceline Dimbleby Collection* published for Sainsburys. It is one of our most popular recipes and is ideal for a cold buffet.

SERVES 10
1.25kg/2^{1}/2lb monkfish, skinned and cubed
60ml/4 tablespoons olive oil
2 large green chillies, deseeded and chopped
450g/1lb tomatoes, skinned and chopped
2-3 garlic cloves, finely chopped
5ml/1 teaspoon ground cardamom
10ml/2 teaspoons caster sugar
15ml/1 tablespoon tomato purée
juice of 1/2 lemon
salt
a good bunch of fresh coriander leaves
110g/4oz button mushrooms, finely sliced

1. Heat the oil in a large frying pan and cook the fish over a medium heat for 5-7 minutes, turning gently. Turn off the heat, remove the fish with a slotted spoon and leave on one side in a mixing bowl. Leave the fish juices in the frying pan.
2. Pour any juices that have drained from the fish into the mixing bowl back into the frying pan. Bring the juices to the boil and add the chillies, garlic, tomatoes, cardamom, sugar, tomato purée and lemon juice. Stir and allow to simmer over a low heat for 7-10 minutes until the tomato is soft. Season to taste with salt and turn off the heat.
3. Chop about three-quarters of the coriander and stir into the hot sauce. Pour the sauce over the fish in the bowl and gently mix in. Stir the sliced mushrooms into the mixture. Leave until cold.
4. When the salad has cooled, pile it into a clean dish. Pull the whole leaves off the remaining sprigs of coriander and scatter them over the fish.

NOTE: The sauce can be made on its own and used with chicken or veal dishes (see page 230).

AUSTRALIAN/CALIFORNIAN CHARDONNAY

Girardet's Red Mullet with Rosemary Sauce

This recipe was published by Robert Carrier in the *Sunday Express.*

SERVES 4
4 red mullets, 140-200g/5-7oz each
290ml/1/2 pint double cream
60ml/4 tablespoons butter
2 medium-sized shallots, finely chopped
1 rosemary sprig, cut into 4
1 glass dry white wine
juice of 1/2 lemon
salt and freshly ground black pepper
30ml/2 tablespoons olive oil

To garnish:
sprigs of fresh rosemary

1. Scale and fillet the mullets, and remove the pin-sized bones along the centre of the fillets. Finely chop the fish livers. Chop the fish heads, bones and trimmings.
2. To make the stock: melt half the butter in a thick-bottomed saucepan, add the fish trimmings, and simmer for 2-3 minutes, pressing them into the butter with the back of a wooden spoon to extract all the juices.
3. Add the shallots and continue to simmer for a further 2 minutes, stirring constantly. Add the rosemary, wine and an equal quantity of water and simmer for a further 7 minutes. Remove the rosemary and discard.
4. Pass the stock through a fine sieve into a clean pan, pressing down with a wooden spoon to extract all the juices. Set the pan over a high heat and reduce the stock by boiling rapidly to half its original quantity.
5. Pour the reduced stock on to the double cream. Return to the pan and continue to reduce until the sauce is thick enough to coat the back of a wooden spoon, stirring frequently to prevent the sauce from catching.
6. Remove the pan from the heat and gradually beat in the remaining butter, a little at a time. Add the chopped fish livers and lemon juice and season with salt and pepper to taste. Keep warm.
7. To cook the fish fillets: heat 2 thick-bottomed frying pans. Pour half the olive oil into each pan and arrange 4 fillets, red skin side down, in each pan. Season generously with salt and pepper. Cook gently for 2 minutes.
8. To serve: cover 4 heated plates with the sauce; place 2 fillets on each plate, with rosy skin uppermost, and garnish with the sprigs of fresh rosemary.

WHITE ALSACE

Red Mullet with Fennel and Chives

This is a very low-fat fish dish.

SERVES 4
4 red mullet, cleaned

For the fish stock:
the fish trimmings
1 litre/2 pints water
1 stick of celery, sliced
1 onion, sliced
1 bay leaf
3 slices of lemon
6 black peppercorns
1 glass of dry white wine
1 small fennel bulb, chopped, tops reserved
1 bunch of chives

1. Prepare the mullet. Remove the scales and cut off the head and tail. Using a sharp filleting knife, cut down either side of the backbone. Lift off the two fillets and remove any remaining small bones.
2. Clean the fish heads, tails and trimmings and put into a large saucepan with the water, celery, onion, bay leaf, lemon slices and peppercorns. Bring gradually up to the boil and simmer very slowly for 20 minutes.
3. Strain, pushing the trimmings well into the bottom of the sieve to extract as much flavour as possible, into a large flat saucepan.
4. Put the fish fillets in the saucepan, skin side uppermost, with the white wine and fennel, and simmer very slowly for 2 minutes.
5. Remove the fish with a fish slice and keep warm. Meanwhile, boil the fish stock rapidly until reduced to 150ml/$^1/_4$ pint. Add the chives and pour over the fish fillets. Decorate with a little of the feathery fennel tops.

WHITE RHONE OR PROVENCE

Dry-fried Prawns with Coriander

This has been adapted from a recipe by Yan Kit So.

SERVES 4
450g/1lb raw, medium-sized prawns in their shells, weighed without heads
5 garlic cloves
2.5cm/1 inch root ginger
45-60ml/ 3-4 tablespoons oil
15ml/1 tablespoon dry sherry
3 spring onions, chopped
15ml/1 tablespoon chopped fresh coriander

For the marinade:
2.5ml/$^1/_2$ teaspoon salt
5ml/1 teaspoon sugar
15-30ml/1-2 tablespoons thin soya sauce
10ml/2 teaspoons Worcestershire sauce
10ml/2 teaspoons oil
pepper

1. With a small sharp knife slit along the backs of the prawns and remove the black vein. Cut off the legs. Wash and pat dry.
2. Mix together the marinade ingredients and add the prawns. Leave to stand for at least 30 minutes.
3. Bruise the garlic with a rolling pin, remove the skin and leave the cloves flattened but whole. Peel the ginger and bruise it with a rolling pin.
4. Heat a wok or heavy sauté pan until it is very hot. Add the oil and swirl it about. Fry the garlic and ginger for about 1 minute, remove and discard.
5. Add the prawns. Spread them out in a single layer and fry for about 1 minute. Reduce the heat if they begin to burn. Turn over to fry the other side for about 1 minute. Turn up the heat if necessary. Splash in the sherry. The prawns are cooked when they have turned red and curled up. Sprinkle with the spring onion and coriander. Stir once or twice and serve immediately.

DRY WHITE

Prawn Pilaf

SERVES 4

790g/$1\frac{3}{4}$lb cooked prawns in their shells
570ml/1 pint water
small glass white wine
salt and freshly ground black pepper
1 slice lemon
3-4 parsley stalks
110g/4oz butter
1 medium onion, finely chopped
225g/8oz long-grain rice, washed
2 hardboiled eggs, chopped
15ml/1 tablespoon chopped fresh parsley

1. Shell all but 3 of the prawns. Reserve the prawns and put the shells into a saucepan with the water, wine, salt and pepper, lemon and parsley stalks. Bring to the boil and simmer for 15 minutes. Strain and keep the liquid to cook the rice in.
2. Melt 85g/3oz of the butter and in it gently cook the onion until soft. Add the rice and fry slowly until the rice looks opaque. Add the liquid. Bring to the boil, stirring with a fork. Cover and simmer gently for 25 minutes, until the rice is tender and the water absorbed.
3. Meanwhile, melt the remaining butter, add the shelled prawns and eggs and heat through. Season with salt, pepper and lemon juice. Fork the shelled prawns and eggs into the pilaf rice. Pile into a serving dish and sprinkle with plenty of chopped parsley. Put the unshelled prawns on top and serve.

NOTE I: Ideally, prawn pilaf should be made with raw prawns with their shells, but they are often difficult to get hold of. If you do get them, simply cook the prawns for 4 minutes in the water and wine. Remove from the liquid and then follow the recipe as before.
NOTE II: If the pilaf is to be kept warm, do not garnish with the parsley and whole prawns until serving. The parsley dries out and the prawns go chalky white.

DRY WHITE

Prawns in Coconut Sauce

SERVES 4

450g/1lb shell-on raw prawns
10ml/2 teaspoons coriander seeds
2.5ml/$\frac{1}{2}$ teaspoon peppercorns
a few fenugreek seeds
30ml/2 tablespoons oil
a few mustard seeds
2 garlic cloves, slivered
3 shallots, chopped
5ml/1 teaspoon grated fresh ginger
150ml/$\frac{1}{4}$ pint water
5ml/1 teaspoon paprika
pinch of cayenne
pinch of turmeric
salt
10ml/2 teaspoons lemon juice
110g/4oz creamed coconut
fresh coriander leaves

1. Peel the prawns and remove the veins. Rinse them out quickly under running water and pat them dry with absorbent paper. Cover and refrigerate.
2. Heat a small, cast-iron frying pan over medium heat. When hot, put in the coriander seeds, peppercorns and fenugreek seeds. Stir for about 1 minute or until lightly roasted. Remove from the heat and grind in a clean grinder. Set aside.
3. Heat the oil in a large frying pan. When hot, put in the mustard seeds. As soon as the seeds begin to pop (this takes just a few seconds), stir once and add the garlic and shallots. Stir and fry until the shallots are lightly browned. Put in the ginger and stir once. Now add the water, the paprika, cayenne, turmeric, salt, the ground spice mixture and the lemon juice. Bring to the boil then simmer for 5 minutes.
4. Fold in the prawns and stir until they just turn opaque. Stir in the creamed coconut. As soon as the liquid begins to bubble, turn off the heat and serve garnished with coriander leaves.

FULL DRY WHITE

Salmon with Fish Mousseline and Tomato Sauce

SERVES 4

4 x 110g/4oz tail end slices of fresh salmon
110g/4oz fresh salmon trimmings
2 egg yolks
150ml/¼ pint double cream
15ml/1 tablespoon Pernod
15ml/1 tablespoon very finely chopped chives
salt and white pepper
ground nutmeg

For the sauce:
1 shallot, chopped
250ml/8 fl oz dry white wine
2 large tomatoes, skinned and deseeded
10ml/2 teaspoons tomato purée
15g/½oz butter

To garnish:
small bunch of chervil

1. Prepare the salmon slices: cut them in half horizontally and remove any grey flesh. Place each one between two pieces of cling film and batter them slightly so that they increase their size by about a quarter.
2. You should now have 8 thin pieces of salmon shaped like flattened triangles.
3. Now prepare the mousse filling. Put the salmon trimmings into a food processor with the egg yolks. Process quickly, then add half the cream and process again. Season with the Pernod, chives, salt, pepper and nutmeg. Chill for 20 minutes.
4. Set the oven to 200°C/400°F/gas mark 6.
5. Divide the filling between the 8 pieces of salmon and roll them up like cones. The thin end will be a tight roll and the thicker end will be a looser roll.
6. Put the salmon cones into a lightly greased baking dish. Sprinkle with the very finely chopped shallots, pour over half the wine, cover and bake for 10 minutes.
7. Meanwhile cut the tomatoes into julienne strips and leave them to drain in a sieve.
8. Remove the salmon fillets to a warm place while you make the sauce.
9. Reduce the cooking liquor, by boiling rapidly, add the tomato purée and the remaining wine and cream. The sauce should be fairly thin.
10. Melt the butter in a frying pan and heat the tomatoes through very quickly.
11. Partially flood the base of 4 dinner plates with the sauce. Slice the cones of salmon and arrange 2 cones on each plate. Garnish with the warm tomatoes and the leaves of chervil.

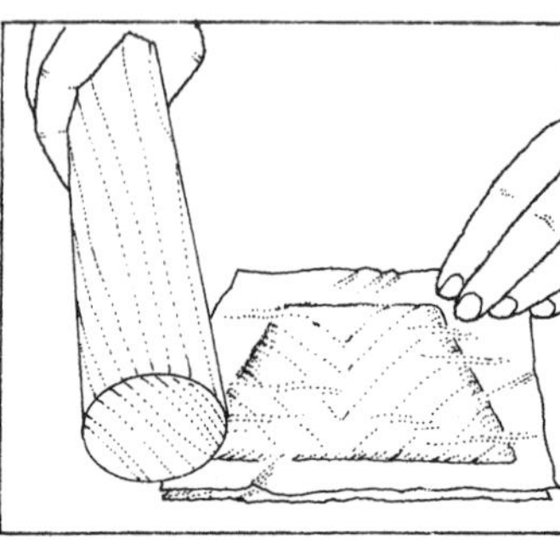

The pieces of salmon should be shaped like flattened triangles

SANCERRE/POUILLY-FUME

Salmon in Filo Pastry with Watercress Mousseline

SERVES 6

900g/2lb fillet of salmon, skinned
110g/4oz watercress, trimmed
8 eggs
55ml/2 fl oz single cream
100ml/3½ fl oz fish stock (see page 219)
salt and freshly ground black pepper
olive oil
1 x 400g/14oz packet filo pastry
15ml/1 tablespoon cumin seeds
15ml/1 tablespoon lemon juice

1. Place the watercress in a sieve and dunk in boiling water to blanch it. Remove after 2 seconds and refresh under cold running water. Drain well.
2. Liquidize together the watercress, eggs, cream, fish stock, salt and pepper until smooth and pale green.
3. Heat the oven to 400°F/200°C/gas mark 6.

4. Brush an ovenproof dish large enough to take the salmon in one layer with olive oil. Line it with a sheet of filo pastry (it will have a lot of overlap). Brush the pastry with oil. Bake for 5 minutes.
5. Cut out 12 sheets of filo the size of the dish. Arrange them on the bottom of the dish, brushing each with oil as you go. Sprinkle with the cumin seeds and spoon over half the watercress mixture.
6. Lay the salmon on top of the watercress in a single layer. Sprinkle with black pepper and lemon juice. Spoon over the remaining watercress cream. Smooth the surface.
7. Arrange 4 sheets of filo pastry on top of the watercress mousseline, brushing with oil as you go. Fold over the overlapping piece of pastry, trim to get a good fit, brush with more oil and cover with the last piece of filo. Brush with oil. Score the surface of the pastry into diamond shapes.
8. Bake for 35-40 minutes until golden brown. Serve hot or cold.

CRISP DRY WHITE

Salmon Steaks with Tomato and Basil

SERVES 4
4 x 170g/6oz salmon steaks
10 tomatoes, roughly chopped
1 onion, chopped
30ml/2 tablespoons water
30ml/2 tablespoons chopped basil
55g/2oz pinenuts
sunflower oil
5 spring onions, chopped

1. Wipe the salmon steaks. Put each one on a fairly large, lightly oiled, round piece of tin foil. Set the oven to 175°C/350°F/gas mark 4.
2. Put the tomatoes in a large saucepan with the onion and water. Cook very slowly until quite a lot of liquid seeps out of the tomatoes. Increase the heat and simmer for 15 minutes. Liquidize and push through a sieve into a clean saucepan. Reduce, by rapid boiling, to a thick consistency, allow to cool slightly and add the basil.
3. Divide the tomato mixture between the salmon steaks, wrap up in the foil and bake in the oven for 15-20 minutes.
4. Meanwhile, cook the pinenuts in a little sunflower oil, being careful not to let them burn.
5. Just before serving, open the parcels slightly and sprinkle each one first with pine kernels and then with the spring onions.

FULL DRY WHITE

Grilled Gravad Lax with Saffron Noodles

SERVES 6
900g/2lb filleted salmon
170g/6oz sea salt
170g/6oz caster sugar
15g/½oz freshly ground white peppercorns
1 bunch fresh dill, chopped

To serve:
saffron noodles (see page 533)
55g/2oz butter, melted
salt and freshly ground black pepper
200ml/7fl oz crème fraîche or fromage frais
1 bunch chives, chopped

1. Make sure all the bones are removed from the salmon.
2. Mix the salt and sugar and pepper together. Lay half the chopped dill in the bottom of a non-metallic dish large enough to hold the salmon fillets. Sprinkle half the salt and sugar mixture evenly over the dill.
3. Place the salmon fillets, flesh side down, on top of the cure. Cover with the remaining dill, salt and sugar. Cover tightly and refrigerate for 24 hours.
4. Remove the salmon from the cure, clean off the dill and cure and pat the fish dry with kitchen paper. Remove the skin and slice the fish on the diagonal into 5mm/¼ inch thick pieces.
5. Heat the grill and place a sheet of well-buttered foil on the top of the grilling tray. Place the salmon slices on the foil and grill very quickly on one side so that the salmon is barely cooked.

6. Meanwhile, boil the pasta in plenty of boiling salted water for about 5-6 minutes until 'al dente'. Drain well, toss with melted butter and season with salt and pepper.
7. Place a pile of noodles on 6 warm plates and arrange 3 slices of grilled salmon on top of each plate. Spoon on the crème fraîche and sprinkle with chopped chives. Serve immediately.

CHARDONNAY

Summer Salmon en Papillote with Lime and Chives

SERVES 4
8 x 85g/3oz thin flat pieces of salmon fillet
8 tomatoes, peeled and thinly sliced
salt and freshly ground black pepper
fish beurre blanc (see page 227)
oil
2 limes
1 small bunch chives, chopped very finely
55g/2oz butter, melted
30ml/2 tablespoons dry white wine

To serve:
4 small sprigs watercress

1. Heat the oven to 220°C/425°F/gas mark 7.
2. Sandwich the fillets of salmon with the tomato slices. Season well with salt and pepper.
3. Place each sandwich on one half of a 20cm/8 inch circle of oiled tin foil.
4. Slice one of the limes in 8 and squeeze the juice from the second lime.
5. Put 2 slices of lime and a sprinkling of chives on each sandwich and sprinkle with the lime juice, melted butter and dry white wine.
6. Fold over the free half of the tin foil to make a parcel rather like an apple turnover. There must be space inside for circulation of air. Twist and press hard to make a good seal.
7. Lightly brush a baking sheet with oil and put it into the oven for 5 minutes to heat. Then carefully put the papillotes on the baking sheet, taking care that they do not touch each other. Bake for 12 minutes.
8. Unwrap the sandwiches and place on individual hot plates. Garnish with small sprigs of watercress. Hand the sauce separately.

CALIFORNIAN SAUVIGNON BLANC

Salmon en Croûte

SERVES 10
1 x 2.3 kg/5lb salmon
puff pastry made with 450g/1lb flour (see page 528)
a few tablespoons fine semolina
butter
lemon juice
tarragon leaves
white pepper and salt
beaten egg

For the stock:
2 slices onion
1 bay leaf
small bunch of parsley
6 peppercorns
salt
bones, skin and head from the salmon
water

For the sauce:
55g/2oz butter
20g/¾oz flour
290ml/½ pint fish stock (see page 219)
50ml/½ glass white wine
5ml/1 teaspoon chopped fresh tarragon or parsley
30ml/2 tablespoons double cream

1. Fillet the fish, keeping the 4 fillets as intact as possible. Skin the fillets.
2. Use the bones and other trimmings for the stock. Put all the ingredients for the stock into a saucepan and simmer for 30 minutes. Strain, measure, and reduce, by boiling to 290ml/½ pint.
3. Heat the oven to 230°C/450°F/gas mark 8.
4. Roll out a third of the pastry into a long thin piece, about the thickness of a coin. Cut it to roughly the size and shape of the original salmon.
5. Place on a wet baking sheet, and prick all over. Leave in a cool place for 15 minutes. Bake it in the hot oven until brown and crisp. If,

when you turn it over, it is soggy underneath, put it back in the oven, soggy side up, for a few minutes. Allow to cool.
6. Sprinkle the cooked pastry evenly with semolina to prevent the fish juices making the pastry soggy.
7. Reassemble the fillets on the cooked pastry, dotting them with plenty of butter and sprinkling with lemon juice, tarragon, salt and pepper as you go.
8. Roll out the rest of the pastry into a large sheet, slightly thinner this time, and lay it over the fish. Cut round the fish, leaving a good 2.5cm/1 inch border beyond the edge of the bottom layer of pastry. Carefully tuck the top 'sheet' under the cooked pastry, shaping the head and tail of the fish carefully.
9. Brush with beaten egg. Using the back of a knife, mark the pastry in a criss-cross pattern to represent fish scales, or mark the scales with the rounded end of a teaspoon. Cut some pastry trimmings into fine strips and use them to emphasize the tail fins and gills, and use a circle of pastry for the eye. Brush again with egg.
10. Bake for 15 minutes to brown and puff up the pastry, then turn down the oven to 150°C/300°F/gas mark 3 for a further 30 minutes to cook the fish. Cover the crust with wet greaseproof paper if the pastry looks in danger of over-browning. To test if the fish is cooked, push a fine skewer through the pastry and fish from the side: it should glide in easily.
11. For the sauce, melt half the butter in a saucepan, add the flour and cook, stirring, for 1 minute or until the butter and flour are pale biscuit-coloured and foaming. Draw off the heat, then add the stock and wine. Return to the heat and stir until boiling and smooth. Boil rapidly until you have a sauce of coating consistency.
12. Add the tarragon and the cream. Season with salt and pepper as necessary. Beat in the remaining butter, bit by bit. Pour into a warmed sauceboat.
13. Slide the salmon en croûte on to a board or salmon dish.
14. Hand the sauce separately.

WHITE BURGUNDY

Salmon Fish Cakes

SERVES 4
225g/8oz cooked salmon, flaked
170g/6oz cooked potato, mashed
salt and freshly ground black pepper
30g/1oz melted butter
15ml/1 tablespoon chopped parsley
1 egg, beaten
dry white breadcrumbs
90ml/6 tablespoons oil for frying
150ml/1/4 pint parsley sauce (see page 221)

1. Mix the fish and potato together. Season well with salt and pepper.
2. Add the melted butter, parsley and enough beaten egg to bind the mixture until soft but not sloppy. Allow to cool.
3. Flour your hands and shape the mixture into 8 flat cakes 2.5cm/1 inch thick. Brush with beaten egg and dip into breadcrumbs.
4. Heat the oil in a frying pan and fry until the fish cakes are brown on both sides.
5. Serve with parsley sauce.

DRY WHITE

Salmon Koulibiac

SERVES 4
rough puff pastry made with 170g/6oz flour
110g/4oz long-grain rice
285g/10oz cooked salmon, flaked
55g/2oz butter
1 onion, finely diced
30g/1oz mushrooms, chopped
15ml/1 tablespoon chopped parsley
juice of 1/2 lemon
2 hardboiled eggs, coarsely chopped
salt and freshly ground black pepper
1 egg, beaten with a pinch of salt

1. Set the oven to 200°C/400°F/gas mark 6.
2. Place the rice in a large saucepan of boiling water and cook for 10-12 minutes. Drain in a colander or sieve and swish plenty of hot water through it. Stand the colander on the draining board. With the handle of a wooden spoon, make a few draining holes through the pile of rice to help the water and steam escape. Leave

for 30 minutes.
3. Roll a third of the pastry into a rectangle as thick as a coin. Leave to relax for 10 minutes in the refrigerator.
4. Place the pastry on a wetted baking sheet. Prick lightly with a fork and bake until golden brown, about 15 minutes. Leave on a wire rack to cool. Do not turn the oven off. Rinse the baking tray under cold water until cool.
5. Melt the butter over moderate heat and add the onion. When nearly cooked add the mushrooms and cook gently for 1 minute.
6. Put the rice in a bowl and fork in the onion, mushrooms, parsley, lemon juice, salmon, eggs and plenty of seasoning.
7. Place the cool pastry base on the wet baking sheet and pile on the rice mixture. Shape it with your hands into a neat mound, making sure that it completely covers the base.
8. Roll the remaining pastry into a blanket large enough to cover the mixture with an overlap of 2.5cm/1 inch. With a sharp knife cut the corners off the blanket at right angles to the cooked base. Working carefully with a palette knife, lift the base and tuck the pastry blanket underneath it. Seal with beaten egg. Repeat with the other 3 sides. Refrigerate for 10 minutes.
9. Meanwhile, shape the discarded corners into leaves, drawing in the veins and stem with the back of a knife.
10. Brush with egg, decorate with the pastry leaves and brush with egg again. Bake in the oven for 30 minutes, until the pastry is golden brown. Serve hot or cold.

NOTE I: If a sauce is required, serve plain soured cream, seasoned with salt and pepper.
NOTE II: This is also delicious made with cooked chicken flesh instead of salmon.

WHITE BURGUNDY

Salmon Mayonnaise

This recipe is for boned salmon mayonnaise. It is an excellent idea to bone the salmon for a large party as it makes it easy to serve.

1 whole salmon, cleaned

For the court bouillon:
150ml/$^1/_4$ pint vinegar
3 bay leaves
1 onion, sliced
large bunch of parsley
1 carrot, peeled and sliced
12 peppercorns
5ml/1 teaspoon salt

For the garnish:
290ml/$^1/_2$ pint mayonnaise (see page 224)
cucumber slices, blanched
lemon wedges
bunch of watercress, trimmed

1. Half fill a fish kettle with water and add the remaining court bouillon ingredients. Simmer together for 20 minutes. Strain and cool.
2. Put the fish in the cold court bouillon and bring slowly to the boil. Poach gently for 5 minutes.
3. Remove from the heat and leave the fish to cook and cool in the cooking liquid. Check it every 10 minutes or so and when the salmon is cooked, remove it carefully and leave to get cold. The salmon is cooked when the eyes are cloudy, the skin lifts easily and the flesh is opaque.
4. Tidy up the salmon, mitre the tail and remove the fins. Skin the top half of the salmon, leaving the head and eyes intact. Lift off the two top fish fillets and turn them over on to a serving plate so that they are skinned side down. Remove any remaining little bones. Spread with the mayonnaise.
5. Cut the back bone out from the two bottom fillets and remove any remaining little bones. Lift the bottom fillets and turn them over on to the top fillets to reassemble the fish with the mayonnaise sandwiched between. Skin the 2 top fillets.
6. Now decorate the salmon how you like, using cucumber slices, lemon wedges and watercress. Any extra mayonnaise can be thinned down with hot water and handed separately.

NOTE: Starting with a cooled court bouillon is considered to produce moister flesh, but it is not always practicable. If the fish has to be put into a hot court bouillon allow about 6 minutes for every 450g/1lb and remove as soon as it is cooked.

SANCERRE/POUILLY-FUME

Boned Salmon Trout with Tomatoes

This is a low-fat alternative to salmon mayonnaise.

SERVES 8
1.8kg/4lb salmon trout, cleaned

For the court bouillon:
1 onion, sliced
1 bay leaf
1 parsley stalk, bruised
6 peppercorns
150ml/1/4 pint white wine vinegar

For the tomato stuffing:
2 onions, finely chopped
arachide oil
20 tomatoes, peeled, deseeded and chopped
salt and white pepper
5ml/1 teaspoon fresh thyme leaves

To garnish:
1 cucumber
lemon wedges
bunch of watercress, trimmed

1. Put all the court bouillon ingredients into a large fish kettle and add enough water to come 7.5cm/3 inches up the sides.
2. Add the trout, bring to the boil, reduce the heat and poach gently for 4 minutes. Remove from the heat and leave the trout in the liquid for 8-10 minutes. Check that it is cooked, remove and lift out to get completely cold.
3. Meanwhile prepare the stuffing. Cook the onions in a very little oil for 3 minutes. Add the tomatoes, season and cook, stirring, for a further 25 minutes to reduce to a thick sauce. Liquidize and leave to cool.
4. Skin the fish, leaving the head and tail intact. Carefully remove the top 2 fillets and remove the backbone. Sandwich them back in place with the tomato sauce.
5. Decorate with fine strips of cucumber skin and garnish with lemon wedges and a bunch of watercress.

NOTE: If there is any tomato stuffing left over it can be thinned to the consistency of a sauce with stock and served as an accompaniment.

WHITE LOIRE

Flat Salmon Pie

SERVES 4
pâte à pâte made with 450g/16oz flour (see page 531)
55g/2oz Gruyère or Cheddar cheese, grated
30g/1oz grated Parmesan
85g/3oz unsalted butter, melted
55g/2oz fresh white breadcrumbs
225g/8oz smoked salmon, chopped
30ml/2 tablespoons chopped dill
1 large garlic clove, crushed
140ml/5 fl oz soured cream
freshly ground black pepper
lemon juice
beaten egg

1. Make up the pâte à pâte and roll out into two rectangles, one to fit a Swiss roll tin, the other slightly larger.
2. Set the oven to 200°F/400°F/gas mark 6.
3. Lightly grease and flour the back of a Swiss roll tin or baking sheet. Put the smaller rectangle of pastry on it and prick all over with a fork. Bake for 15 minutes until half-cooked. Loosen it on the baking sheet so that it does not stick and leave to cool.
4. Mix together the Gruyère or Cheddar cheese, the Parmesan, the melted butter and the breadcrumbs. Scatter half of this mixture all over the half-cooked pastry, leaving 1cm/1/2 inch clear round the edge.
5. Scatter the smoked salmon on top of the cheese mixture. Then scatter over the dill.
6. Mix the garlic with the soured cream and spread all over the salmon. Season well with pepper but not salt.

7. Sprinkle evenly with lemon juice and top with the rest of the cheese mixture. Wet the edge of the bottom piece of pastry lightly with beaten egg and put the top sheet of pastry in place, pressing the edges to seal it well.
8. Use any pastry trimmings to decorate the pie and brush all over with beaten egg.
9. Bake until the pastry is crisp and pale brown. Serve hot or cold.

NOTE: Off-cuts and trimmings of smoked salmon can be bought more cheaply than slices, and do well for this dish.

ALSACE RIESLING

Boned Stuffed Trout

SERVES 2
2 x 225g/8oz trout, cleaned and boned (see page 240)
55g/2oz butter
15ml/1 tablespoon very finely shredded white of leek
15ml/1 tablespoon very finely shredded carrot
55g/2oz button mushrooms, very thinly sliced
5ml/1 teaspoon chopped thyme
lemon juice
30ml/2 tablespoons white wine
salt and freshly ground black pepper
55g/2oz feta cheese, diced

To garnish:
lemon wedges
small bunch of watercress

1. Set the oven to 200°C/400°F/gas mark 6.
2. Melt the butter in a saucepan and gently cook the leek and carrot for 2 minutes. Add the mushrooms and cook for a further minute. Add the thyme, lemon juice and wine and cook until the liquid has evaporated. Season with salt and freshly ground black pepper. Allow to cool. Add the feta cheese.
3. Stuff the fish with this mixture and lay in a lightly greased roasting tin. Cover and bake in the oven for 15 minutes.
4. Remove to a warm serving dish and garnish with lemon wedges and watercress.

DRY WHITE

Grilled Sardines

SERVES 4
16 small or 8 large fresh sardines
oil
pepper
lemon juice
parsley to garnish

1. To clean the sardines: slit along the belly and remove the innards. Rinse the fish under cold running water and with a little salt gently rub away any black matter in the cavity. Cut off the gills.
2. Heat the grill. Score the fish with 3 or 4 shallow diagonal cuts on each side, brush with oil, season with pepper and sprinkle with lemon juice.
3. Grill for about 2 minutes on each side, brushing with the hot oil and the juices that run from the fish.
4. Lay the sardines on a warmed platter. Pour over the juices from the grill pan and serve at once.

CRISP DRY WHITE

Fried Scallops with Garlic

SERVES 4
16 scallops
55g/2oz butter
1 small garlic clove, crushed
salt and freshly ground black pepper
juice of 1/2 lemon
a little chopped parsley

1. Remove the muscle from the scallops (found on the opposite side from the coral or roe).
2. Melt the butter in a frying pan. Add the scallops, garlic and pepper. Cook over a moderate heat, turning occasionally for 3 minutes.
3. Add the lemon juice and parsley and sprinkle with salt. Serve immediately.

LIGHT DRY WHITE

Scallops au Gratin

SERVES 4
150ml/1/4 pint white wine
1 bay leaf
1/4 onion
8 large or 12 small scallops
450g/1lb mashed potato (see page 187)
30g/1oz butter
30g/1oz flour
15ml/1 tablespoon cream
lemon juice
salt and freshly ground black pepper
dried breadcrumbs
a little extra butter to finish

To serve:
4 scallop shells

1. Put the wine with 150ml/1/4 pint water, the bay leaf and onion into a saucepan. Bring to the boil. Turn down the heat, add the scallops and poach very gently for 5 minutes.
2. Lift the scallops from the liquid. Pull away the hard muscle (opposite the coral or roe) and cut each scallop into 2 or 3.
3. Divide them between 4 scallop shells. Pipe or spoon the mashed potato around the edge of the shells.
4. Melt the butter in a pan, add the flour and cook for 30 seconds. Strain over the liquid in which the scallops were cooked and stir until the sauce is thick and smooth. Add the cream and season with lemon juice, salt and pepper.
5. Spoon over the scallops. Sprinkle with the crumbs, dot with butter and brown under the grill.

MUSCADET

Scallops with Green Pasta

This low-fat dish is delicious as long as you are not expecting a rich creamy sauce for the pasta!

SERVES 4
570ml/1 pint water
60ml/4 tablespoons dry white wine
4 slices lemon
2 bay leaves
2.5cm/1 inch piece root ginger, peeled
3 Jerusalem artichokes
2 carrots
10 fresh scallops
110g/4oz mangetout, topped and tailed
3 spring onions, chopped
15ml/1 tablespoon chopped fresh coriander

To serve:
450g/1lb fine green pasta

1. Put the water, wine, lemon, bay leaves and ginger into a saucepan and boil rapidly until reduced to about 425ml/3/4 pint. Strain into a large clean wide saucepan (a sauté pan is ideal). Pick the ginger out of the sieve, chop about 5mm/1/4 inch of it very finely and add it to the poaching liquor.
2. Peel the artichoke and carrots and cut into very fine strips. Leave in acidulated water until ready to cook.
3. Clean the scallops very well. Remove and discard the muscle (found opposite the orange roe) and cut the scallops in half horizontally.
4. Heat up the poaching liquor and when simmering add the mangetout and spring onions. Cook for 2 minutes. Add the drained carrots and artichokes and cook for a further minute. Add the scallops and cook for about 2 minutes until tender.
5. Meanwhile, cook the green pasta in plenty of rapidly boiling water, drain it and pile it in a large shallow dish.
6. Lift the scallops and vegetables from the poaching liquor and arrange over the pasta. Garnish with the coriander.
7. Reduce the cooking liquor, by boiling rapidly, to a few tablespoons and hand it separately.

LIGHT DRY WHITE

Fried Scallops with Bacon

SERVES 4
12 scallops
4 rashers of back bacon
15ml/1 tablespoon chopped parsley
15ml/1 tablespoon lemon juice
salt and freshly ground black pepper

1. Clean the scallops, pull away the hard muscle (found opposite the coral) and discard. Cut in half horizontally.
2. Cut the bacon into slivers and fry until beginning to brown. Reduce the heat and add the scallops. Fry slowly for 1 minute on each side. Add the parsley and lemon juice, season and serve immediately.

CHABLIS

Didier Oudill's Braised Scallops in their Shells

This recipe has been taken from Michel Guérard's *Cuisine Gourmande.*

SERVES 4
12 scallops in their shells
75g/2¾oz butter
125g/4½oz flaky pastry (see page 527)
salt and pepper
½ beaten egg

For the garnish:
55g/2oz butter
110g/4oz leeks, cut into julienne
110g/4oz carrots, cut into julienne
110g/4oz button mushrooms, cut into julienne
salt and pepper
5ml/1 teaspoon chopped tarragon
15ml/1 tablespoon chopped shallot

1. Open the scallops with a strong knife and detach the scallop from the lower shell. Scoop out the scallops with a spoon, catching all their juice in a strainer lined with a fine cloth and placed over a bowl. Pull away and discard the membrane or frill and the black stomach parts, wash the scallops thoroughly in running water, and dry them on a cloth. Separate the corals and cut the white parts in 2 across the middle to obtain 24 rounds.
2. Scrub 8 of the shells (top and bottoms) under running water and keep them on one side.
3. Heat the butter in a saucepan and cook the leeks and carrots for 5 minutes. Then add the mushrooms and cook for a further 3 minutes. Add salt, pepper and tarragon. Cover and simmer for 2 minutes.
4. Roll out the pastry and cut it into 8 strips 25 x 2.5cm/10 x 1 inch. Heat the oven to 250°C/480°F/gas mark 9.
5. Divide half the vegetable garnish among the 8 shells and sprinkle with the shallot.
6. Put the coral and 3 rounds of the white part of the scallop on each shell and season with salt and pepper.
7. Cover the scallops with the rest of the vegetables, sprinkle them with the strained scallop juice and divide the butter between them.
8. Put 8 empty shells on top of the filled shells and edge each with a strip of the pastry, brushed with beaten egg, to seal completely. Bake for 10-12 minutes, according to the size of the scallops, and serve in the shells.

NOTE: A low-fat version of this recipe can be prepared without the butter. Steam the vegetables for the garnish instead of frying them.

CHABLIS

Fried Scampi

SERVES 4
450g/1lb scampi
salt and freshly ground black pepper
lemon juice
oil for deep-frying
290ml/½ pint fritter batter (see page 534)
deep-fried parsley (see page 631)

1. If using frozen scampi sprinkle with pepper and lemon juice and defrost slowly.
2. Heat the oil until a crumb dropped into it will sizzle and brown.
3. Dip the scampi in the batter and fry until golden brown. Drain on absorbent paper. Sprinkle with salt.
4. Garnish with fried parsley and serve at once.

VERY DRY WHITE

Sea Bass with Black Bean Sauce

A 1.85kg/4lb sea bass sounds like a huge amount for 6 people, but its very deliciousness necessitates such generosity! Black beans can be bought from Chinese supermarkets in tins or vacuum packs. If you like, the sauce can be thickened at the end with 10ml/2 teaspoons cornflour.

SERVES 6
1.85kg/4lb sea bass, cleaned and scaled
15ml/1 tablespoon sunflower oil
salt and freshly ground black pepper
4 slices of lemon

To serve:
black bean sauce (see page 232)
spring onion bows (see page 631)

1. Set the oven to 190°C/375°F/gas mark 5.
2. Brush a large piece of tin foil with the oil. Place the fish on it, season with salt and pepper, cover with the lemon slices, wrap up loosely, but secure the edges firmly, and place on a baking sheet.
3. Bake for 40 minutes.
4. Remove from the foil wrapping to a warmed serving dish, garnish with the spring onion bows, dribble over a little of the sauce and hand the rest separately.

WHITE BURGUNDY

Sea Bass with Wild Rice

SERVES 4
1.25kg/3lb sea bass, cleaned and scaled
lemon juice
freshly ground black pepper
55g/2oz brown rice, soaked overnight
55g/2oz wild rice
30g/1oz pinenuts, browned
30g/1oz sultanas
15ml/1 tablespoon chopped fresh dill
oil for greasing
1 onion, sliced
1 bay leaf
30ml/2 tablespoons white wine

To garnish:
bunch of watercress, trimmed

1. Set the oven to 180°C/350°F/gas mark 4.
2. Season the inside of the sea bass with a little lemon juice and black pepper. Wash both the rices very well and cook them for 30 minutes in plenty of boiling water. Drain and rinse them under cold water until they are completely cold. Drain them well. Add the pinenuts, sultanas and dill. Season to taste.
3. Put the sea bass on a sheet of well-oiled tin foil; stuff the cavity with the rice mixture. Scatter the onion over the fish, add the bay leaf and sprinkle on the wine. Draw the tin foil up to make a parcel.
4. Place the parcel on a large baking sheet and cook it in the oven for 40-50 minutes. Serve this fish hot or cold, garnished with watercress.

WHITE BURGUNDY

Skate with Brown Butter and Capers

SERVES 4
900g/2lb skate wing
570ml/1 pint court bouillon (see page 219)
75g/3oz unsalted butter
15ml/1 tablespoon lemon juice
15ml/1 tablespoon capers, slightly crushed

1. Wash the skate and divide into 4 portions.
2. Place the skate in the cold or warm court bouillon in a shallow pan. Cover with a lid and bring slowly to the boil. Poach very gently for 15-20 minutes.
3. Remove the fish and drain on kitchen paper. Gently scrape away any skin. Place the skate on a hot serving dish and keep warm in the oven while you make the sauce.
4. Pour off the court bouillon, reheat the pan and melt the butter. When the butter is foaming and a rich golden brown, remove the pan from the heat, add the lemon juice and capers and pour over the skate.

VERY DRY WHITE

Skate with Spinach and Bacon

SERVES 2
1 skate wing, filleted into 2
55g/2oz button mushrooms
15g/$^1/_2$oz flat-leafed parsley, chopped
15g/$^1/_2$oz butter
juice of $^1/_2$ lemon
salt and pepper
4 rashers of streaky bacon
1 small piece pig's caul (about 30cm/12 inches square)
oil
2 garlic cloves
30ml/2 tablespoons balsamic vinegar
150ml/$^1/_4$ pint chicken stock (see page 219)

For the spinach:
450g/1lb fresh spinach, cooked and chopped
30g/1oz butter
1 garlic clove, crushed

1. Set the oven to 200°C/400°F/gas mark 6.
2. Sauté the mushrooms and half the parsley in the butter. Add the lemon juice and season to taste.
3. Divide the mushroom mixture between the two fillets and roll them up into a ball. Wrap in the bacon and then in the caul. Secure, if necessary, with a cocktail stick.
4. Heat a little oil in a casserole, add the skate balls and the garlic. Sauté until the bacon is golden.
5. Cover and cook in the preheated oven for 15-20 minutes.
6. Discard the caul and garlic and keep the skate warm.
7. Put the casserole back on the heat. Add the vinegar and reduce by half. Then add the chicken stock and reduce by half again. Add the remaining parsley.
8. Sauté the spinach in the butter and garlic.
9. Put the spinach on 2 plates, arrange the skate on top and pour over the reduced vinegar and stock.

CRISP DRY WHITE

Sole au Gratin

SERVES 4
This recipe was given to me by Mrs Levis of the Sign of the Angel in Lacock. The dish should be prepared 24 hours in advance.

3 sole, filleted and skinned
75ml/5 tablespoons sunflower oil
1 lemon, quartered
1 large sprig fresh tarragon
15g/$^1/_2$oz butter, melted
grated cheese
dry white breadcrumbs

To serve:
lemon wedges
parsley

1. Arrange the sole, black skin downwards, in a shallow dish. Pour over the oil. Lightly squeeze the lemon quarters over the sole, and leave them in the dish. Arrange the tarragon over the fish and leave to marinate for 24 hours.

2. Preheat the grill to a high setting.
3. Brush a large baking sheet with a good lip with the melted butter. Arrange the sole fillets on top. Dust evenly with the cheese and crumbs and grill until golden brown.
4. Arrange on individual plates and garnish with the lemon wedges and sprigs of parsley.

DRY WHITE

Sole Bonne Femme

SERVES 4

3 medium sole, skinned and filleted
70g/2½oz butter
1 shallot, finely chopped
170g/6oz mushrooms, finely sliced
2.5ml/½ teaspoon lemon juice
290 ml/½ pint hot fish stock, made from the trimmings
1 glass white wine
salt and white pepper
15g/½oz flour
150-200ml/5-7 fl oz double cream

1. Set the oven to 180°C/350°F/gas mark 4.
2. Melt 15g/½oz butter, add the shallots and mushrooms and cook slowly for 10 minutes or until the shallots are soft. Add the lemon juice.
3. Put the shallots and mushrooms in the bottom of an ovenproof dish. Arrange the fillets, folding the ends underneath, on top. Pour over the stock and wine and season with salt and pepper. Cover with a lid and bake in the oven for 10-15 minutes.
4. Lift the fillets on to a plate and keep warm. Strain the fish liquid into a saucepan and reserve the mushrooms as a garnish.
5. Reduce the fish liquid to 125ml/4 fl oz by boiling rapidly.
6. Melt 30g/1oz butter, add the flour and cook for 30 seconds. Remove from the heat and add the fish fumet (reduced fish stock). Stir well, return to the heat and bring slowly to the boil, stirring continuously until very thick.
7. Cut the remaining butter into small cubes. Gradually beat the double cream into the fish sauce – if it looks as though it might curdle, beat it vigorously. Take the sauce off the heat and gradually beat in the cubes of butter to make it shiny. The sauce should now be of coating consistency, but if it is too thick a little milk can be added. Season to taste with salt, white pepper and lemon juice.
8. Reheat the mushrooms. Arrange the fish fillets on a warm serving dish. Coat the cream sauce over the fish, spoon the mushrooms down the centre and serve.

CHABLIS

Sole with Mustard and Bacon

SERVES 4

12 fillets lemon or Dover sole
mustard
6 thin rashers, smoked back bacon
290ml/½ pint fish stock (see page 219)
1 large onion, chopped
8 tomatoes, peeled and chopped
10 sage leaves, roughly chopped
salt and freshly ground black pepper
45ml/3 tablespoons Greek yoghurt
fish glaze to season (see page 220)

1. Spread a little mustard on the skinned side of each fillet of sole. Fold into neat parcels, skinned side inside.
2. Wrap a little piece of bacon over each sole parcel and set aside.
3. Meanwhile, make the sauce. Put the stock, onion, tomatoes, sage, salt and pepper into a saucepan and simmer together for 30 minutes. Remove from the heat and allow to cool down.
4. Process the sauce ingredients together very well until smooth, return to the rinsed-out saucepan and boil rapidly, stirring frequently, to a fine purée. Add the yoghurt and taste. It may be necessary to add a little extra fish glaze.
5. Grill the fillets of sole, bacon side up, for 4 minutes. Arrange on a warmed serving dish and hand the sauce separately.

FULL DRY WHITE

Filets of Sole Meunière

SERVES 4
3 lemon sole, skinned and filleted
seasoned flour
55g/2oz butter, clarified (see page 138)
15ml/1 tablespoon chopped mixed herbs, including parsley
5ml/1 teaspoon lemon juice
lemon wedges

1. Wash the fillets of sole, dry thoroughly, and roll in the seasoned flour.
2. Melt half the butter in a thick frying pan and when foaming add the fillets with the skinned side uppermost. Cook over a moderate heat, turn over and brown on the other side.
3. Slide the fish on to a plate, with the butter from the pan, and keep warm.
4. Wipe the pan very well, removing any bits of fish. Melt the remaining butter in the frying pan, heat until a delicate brown, cool slightly and add the herbs and lemon juice. Pour over the fish and serve immediately, garnished with the lemon wedges.

DRY WHITE

Sole Colbert

In this recipe, the backbone of the fish is loosened while it is raw and removed after cooking.

SERVES 4
4 x 340g/12oz Dover soles
seasoned flour
beaten egg
dry white breadcrumbs
fat for deep-frying
110g/4oz maître d'hôtel butter (see page 235)
lemon wedges

1. Skin and trim the soles, leaving on the heads. With a small sharp knife make a cut on the side of the fish that had the black skin, down the centre through the flesh to the backbone. Working from the centre of the fish, raise the fillets, loosening them with a knife, and snip the bone just below the head and above the tail.
2. Dip the fish in seasoned flour, shaking away any excess. Brush with beaten egg and press on the dry white breadcrumbs. Be sure to egg-and-crumb the underside of the raised fillets.
3. Heat up the oil so that a crumb will sizzle in it. Fry the whole fish until a good golden brown, holding it down with a fish slice to prevent it curling up. Drain well on absorbent paper.
4. Allow to settle for 1-2 minutes. Then carefully pull out the backbone, cutting round the breadcrumb coating to prevent too much of it being pulled off.
5. Fill the cavity with slices of maître d'hôtel butter. Serve immediately with wedges of lemon.

NOTE: For a light lunch dish or first course 'slip' soles are suitable. They weigh 170-225g/6-8oz.

WHITE BURGUNDY

Grilled Dover Sole

1 Dover sole per person
melted butter
salt and pepper
lemon juice

1. Make a cut in the belly (near the head) of each fish and remove the entrails. Wash the fish thoroughly in cold water.
2. Now skin the fish: place the fish on a piece of greaseproof paper and pour a little pile of salt beside it. Snip off the fins with scissors. Make a cut across the black skin just above the tail with a sharp knife, being careful to cut only the skin and not the flesh. Dip your thumb and index finger in the salt and then gently work them under the black skin from the tail upwards until you have raised enough of the skin to be able to take a firm grasp of it. The salt prevents the skin slipping out of your grasp. Using a tea towel to help get a firm grip, pull the skin off the fish in one sharp tug. Repeat on the other (pale) side. This will prove rather more difficult, and is not strictly necessary.
3. Heat the grill. Brush both the grill and one

side of the fish with melted butter. Season with salt, pepper and lemon juice and place under the hot grill for about 4 minutes. Turn over and brush the second side with butter. Grill again.

NOTE I: This method of skinning a flat fish does not work very well for lemon soles.
NOTE II: Alternatively, the fish can be grilled by dipping them in melted butter and then seasoned flour, which makes the fish crisper.

DRY WHITE

Woven Sole with Sweet and Sour Sauce

This recipe has been adapted from a recipe in *La Potinière and Friends* by David and Hilary Brown.

SERVES 4
16 fillets of lemon sole taken from 4 fish
salt and freshly ground pepper
900g/2lb fresh spinach, cooked and chopped
30g/1oz butter
2 medium tomatoes, peeled, deseeded and chopped

For the sauce:
30g/1oz caster sugar
45ml/3 tablespoons sherry vinegar
75ml/5 tablespoons Noilly Prat or dry white vermouth
150ml/1/4 pint chicken stock
60ml/4 tablespoons double cream
15g/1/2oz unsalted butter

1. Cut the sole lengthways into 1cm/1/2 inch strips. Lay side by side and cut all of them to the same length - approximately 10cm/4 inches. Each person needs 7 strips.
2. Lay 4 strips side by side on the work surface. Weave the other 3 strips in and out at a 90 degree angle to the original 4 strips. Eventually you will have a square of woven strips of fish.
3. Lift each plait on to a piece of buttered greaseproof paper on a baking sheet. Cover and refrigerate until needed.
4. Preheat the oven to 450°F/240°C/gas mark 9.
5. To make the sauce, melt the sugar in a small heavy pan. Cook over a medium heat until the sugar turns golden brown. Add the vinegar and reduce by boiling for 1 minute. Add the Noilly Prat and the stock, bring to the boil and reduce by half. Add the cream and simmer until the sauce will coat the back of a spoon. Then whisk in the butter.
6. To serve, remove the cover from the fish, sprinkle with salt and a little cold water. Place in the oven and cook for 4-5 minutes.
7. While it is cooking, reheat the spinach by tossing in half the melted butter. Season with salt and pepper. Warm the tomato by tossing in the remaining butter.
8. Reheat the sauce and taste. It may need seasoning.
9. Divide the spinach between 4 warmed plates. Spoon the sauce around the spinach and with a fish slice carefully lay the woven sole on top of the spinach. Top each fish with the warm tomato.

WHITE ALSACE

Lemon Sole with Cucumber

SERVES 4
3 x 675g/1 1/2lb lemon soles, skinned and filleted
1 large cucumber, peeled, halved lengthways and thickly sliced
seasoned flour
55g/2oz butter
salt and pepper
lemon juice

1. Blanch the cucumber in a pan of boiling salted water for 1-2 minutes. Drain and dry well.
2. Dip the fillets in seasoned flour. Lay them on a plate but do not allow them to touch each other - they will become soggy.
3. Heat half the butter in a frying pan. When foaming, put in a batch of fillets. Turn them over when a golden brown; allow about 1 minute on each side. Dish on to a shallow platter and keep warm. Cook the remaining fillets.

4. Melt the remaining butter in the pan. Add the cucumber and fry quite briskly for 1 minute. Remove from the heat, add salt, pepper and lemon juice. Return to the heat, boil up and tip over the fish. Serve at once.

DRY WHITE

Lemon Sole with Burnt Hollandaise

SERVES 4
12 fillets lemon sole, skinned

For the fish stock:
skin, bones and trimmings from the fish
1 onion, sliced
1 carrot, sliced
425ml/$^3/_4$ pint water
2 slices lemon
6 peppercorns
1 bay leaf
pinch of salt
1 parsley stalk

150ml/$^1/_4$ pint hollandaise sauce (see page 225)
45ml/3 tablespoons double cream

1. Place all the ingredients for the stock in a pan. Bring to the boil and simmer for 25-30 minutes. Strain and allow to cool.
2. Set the oven to 180°C/350°F/gas mark 4.
3. Roll the fillets up, skinned side inside. Lay them in an ovenproof dish or roasting pan and pour over the stock. Cover and poach in the oven for 15-20 minutes. Alternatively, poach carefully on the hob.
4. While the fish cooks, heat up the grill and make the hollandaise sauce, which must be very thick.
5. Drain the fish well and arrange on a heat-resistant serving dish. Mix the sauce with the cream and coat each fillet with a spoonful. Brown quickly under the grill and serve immediately.

WHITE BURGUNDY

Stuffed Squid Provençal

SERVES 4
12 small squid
30ml/2 tablespoons olive oil
1 onion, finely chopped
4 spring onions, finely chopped
2 garlic cloves, crushed
6 tomatoes, peeled and roughly chopped
30ml/2 tablespoons chopped mixed herbs
45ml/3 tablespoons finely chopped parsley
30ml/2 tablespoons fresh white breadcrumbs
2 egg yolks
salt and freshly ground black pepper
30ml/2 tablespoons brandy
150ml/$^1/_4$ pint white wine
425ml/$^3/_4$ pint tomato sauce (see page 231)
3 anchovies, soaked in milk, drained and chopped
15ml/1 tablespoon capers, chopped
12 black olives, pitted

1. Set the oven to 150°C/300°F/gas mark 2.
2. Prepare the squid (see page 165), keeping the tentacles for the stuffing.
3. Start the stuffing. Heat half the olive oil in a saucepan, and sweat the onions, spring onions and garlic in it, adding the roughly chopped tentacles to the pan for the last minute, to lightly cook them.
4. Mix the tomatoes, mixed herbs, 30ml/2 tablespoons of the parsley, the breadcrumbs and the cooled onion mixture together. Bind the stuffing with the egg yolks, beat well and season with salt and freshly ground black pepper.
5. Fit a piping bag with a medium plain nozzle and fill with the stuffing. Pipe into the whole squid, being careful not to overfill, or the squid will burst during cooking. Seal the ends of each squid with a cocktail stick.
6. Heat the rest of the olive oil in a frying pan and brown the squid evenly all over. Then flame with the brandy. Remove the squid from the frying pan, and place in a casserole dish.
7. Add the wine to the frying pan and reduce by boiling to half its original quantity. Add the tomato sauce, the anchovies and capers, and bring to the boil. Pour over the squid.
8. Cover the casserole dish and place in the oven

for 1 hour, or until the squid are cooked.
9. Remove the squid from the casserole dish, with a perforated spoon, on to a serving dish and keep warm while finishing the sauce.
10. If the sauce is too thin, reduce by boiling rapidly in a saucepan. Check for seasoning, and spoon over the squid. Garnish with the black olives and the remaining parsley.

RHONE/PROVENCE ROSE

Stir-fried Squid

SERVES 4
900g/2lb fresh or frozen squid
15ml/1 tablespoon sunflower oil
1 garlic clove, peeled and slivered
1cm/½ inch fresh ginger root, peeled and chopped
2 pieces lemon grass, chopped
4 spring onions, sliced
5-10ml/1-2 teaspoons sugar
15ml/1 tablespoon Shaoxing wine, vermouth or sherry

1. Clean the squid (see page 165). Drain well.
2. Heat the oil in a wok, add the garlic, ginger and lemon grass and cook slowly for 1 minute. Add the squid and stir-fry over a very high heat for 1 minute. Reduce the heat, add the spring onions and cook slowly for a further minute. Add the sugar and wine and cook for 1 more minute.

WHITE ALSACE

Trout with Hazelnuts

SERVES 4
55g/2oz hazelnuts
4 medium-sized rainbow trout
seasoned flour
85g/3oz clarified butter (see page 138)
lemon juice
salt and pepper
lemon wedges
chopped parsley

1. Set the oven to 170°C/325°F/gas mark 3. Brown the hazelnuts in the oven. Rub them in a clean cloth to remove the skins. Chop them roughly.
2. Clean the trout very well (if not properly cleaned they will taste very bitter). Dip them in the flour and shake off any excess.
3. Fry briefly on both sides in all but 15ml/1 tablespoon of the butter. Transfer to an ovenproof dish, pouring over the butter from the pan. Bake for 15 minutes (or until firm to the touch).
4. Fry the hazelnuts in the remaining butter.
5. Arrange the trout on a warm serving dish, pour over the hazelnuts and butter, then sprinkle with lemon juice, and salt and pepper. Garnish with lemon wedges and sprinkle with parsley.

NOTE I: This is similar to the classic trout with almonds, in which split or flaked almonds are simply fried in butter and sprinkled over the fish.
NOTE II: The fish may be cooked entirely in the frying pan, but they must be fried slowly, for about 7 minutes a side.

DRY WHITE

Sea Trout en Papillote

SERVES 2
340g/12oz fillet of sea trout, skinned
55g/2oz butter
15ml/1 tablespoon very finely shredded white of leek
15ml/1 tablespoon very finely shredded carrot
55g/2oz button mushrooms, thinly sliced
5ml/1 teaspoon freshly chopped tarragon or fennel leaves
salt and freshly ground black pepper
lemon juice
30ml/2 tablespoons white wine
oil for brushing

1. Heat the oven to 220°C/425°F/gas mark 7.
2. Fold a large sheet of greaseproof paper in half and cut out 2 semicircles, with a radius of 20cm/8 inches.
3. Melt half the butter and add the leek and carrot. Cook slowly without browning for 5 minutes, then add the mushrooms. Cook for 2 more minutes, then add the tarragon or fennel,

and season with salt and pepper. Allow to cool.
4. Cut the fish into 4 or 6 diagonal slices about 1cm/½inch thick.
5. Brush the inside of the paper rounds with a little oil, leaving the edges clear. Divide the vegetable mixture between the two papillotes, spooning it on to one side only of the paper round. Divide the fish slices between the papillotes on top of the vegetables. Squeeze a few drops of lemon on each and sprinkle on the wine. Dot with the remaining butter and add salt and pepper.
6. Fold the free half of the papillote paper over to make a parcel rather like an apple turnover. Fold the edges of the two layers of paper over twice together, twisting and pressing hard to seal.

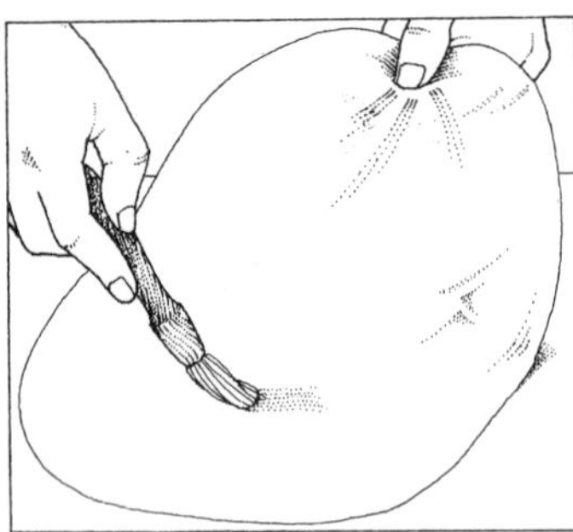

Brush the paper with a little oil

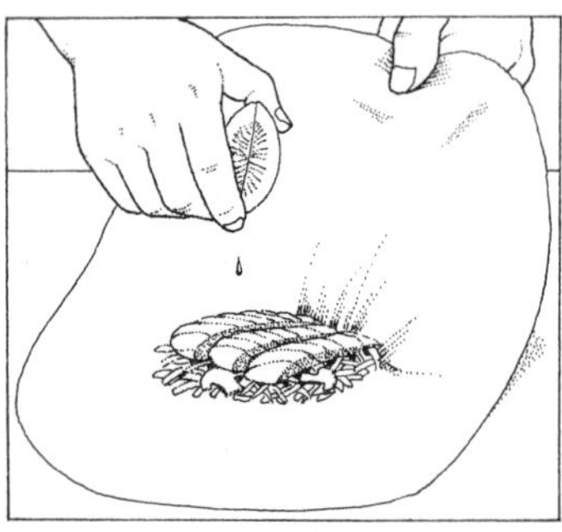

Squeeze a few drops of lemon on to the fish

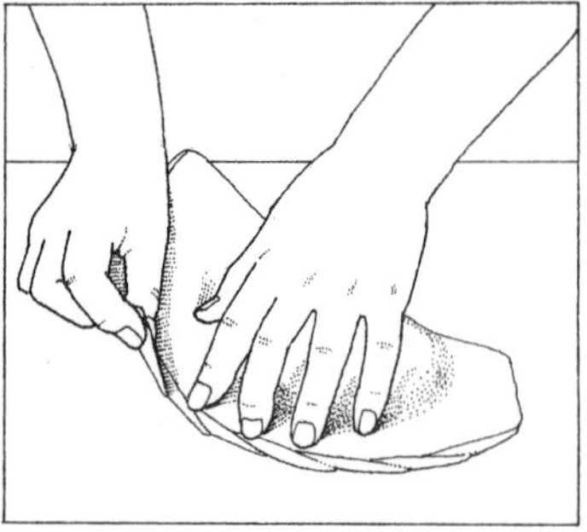

Fold the edges of the paper together; twist and press to make a really good seal

7. Lightly brush a baking sheet with oil and put it into the oven for 5 minutes to heat. Then put the papillotes on the baking sheet, taking care that they do not touch each other. Bake for 12 minutes.
8. Serve immediately on hot plates. Each diner unwraps his own puffed-up parcel.

NOTE I: Halibut, haddock, salmon, indeed almost any fish, can be cooked in this way. Whole trout weighing 340g/12oz will take 15 minutes to cook. Breast of chicken, boned and skinned, is good too, and takes 20 minutes in a piece, 15 if in slices.
NOTE II: For a richer dish serve with beurre blanc (see page 227).
NOTE III: Papillotes are generally made from circular papers, as in the above recipe, but are better made from heart-shaped pieces if whole small fish or long fillets of fish are to be enwrapped.

WHITE BURGUNDY

Steamed Trout Fillets in Lettuce

This recipe is taken from *Easy to Entertain* by Pat Lucada.

SERVES 4
2 shallots, very finely chopped
15ml/1 tablespoon oil
170g/6oz mushrooms, finely chopped
squeeze of lemon juice
salt and pepper
8 large lettuce leaves, or cabbage leaves
4 large trout (pink fleshed if possible), filleted and skinned

1. Sweat the shallots in the oil, stirring constantly. Add the mushrooms, lemon juice, salt and pepper. Sauté until the mushrooms give off their juices, then boil hard until all the juice has evaporated.
2. Blanch the lettuce in a large quantity of boiling salted water for 1-2 minutes, until just limp. Refresh in a bowl of cold water, then spread out on tea towels or absorbent paper to dry.
3. Trim the fillets and remove any bones with tweezers. By running your finger against the grain of the flesh, you can feel where they are.

Pat the fillets dry and season with salt and pepper. Place a spoonful of the mushroom mixture on each fillet and roll up. Wrap in a lettuce leaf and place seam down in a steamer. Continue with the other fillets. Steam until tender, about 10 minutes.

DRY WHITE

Steamed Trout Fillets with Tomato and Ginger Sauce

SERVES 4

8 trout fillets
15ml/1 tablespoon oil
8 basil leaves, chopped
lemon juice
salt and freshly ground white pepper

For the tomato and ginger sauce:
340g/12oz fresh ripe tomatoes, peeled and deseeded
55g/2oz fresh ginger, sliced
45g/½oz butter

For the watercress and coriander garnish:
60ml/4 tablespoons water
15g/½oz butter
1 bunch watercress, leaves and young shoots only
small bunch coriander, leaves only
15ml/1 tablespoon cream
salt and freshly ground black pepper

1. Put the trout fillets on a sheet of lightly oiled tin foil. Brush the fish with oil and sprinkle with the chopped basil, lemon juice, salt and pepper. Cover with foil and refrigerate until ready to cook.
2. Put the tomatoes and ginger into a liquidizer and then pass through a sieve. Warm over a low heat but do not boil. Just before serving, whisk in the butter to give the sauce a shine.
3. To cook the watercress and coriander: bring the water to the boil and mix in the butter. Add the watercress and coriander and cook for 2 minutes. Drain well in a colander. Return the leaves to the saucepan, add the cream, salt and pepper and set aside until ready to serve.
4. To cook and serve the fish: lay the parcel of fish on a wire rack and cook over a pan of boiling water on top of the stove for 3-4 minutes.
5. Place a spoonful of the watercress mixture on each plate. Arrange 2 fillets of fish on top and surround with the sauce. Serve immediately.

WHITE ALSACE

Trout in Filo Pastry with Orange Beurre Blanc

SERVES 4

4 x 225g/8oz trout, filleted and skinned
85g/3oz butter
1 large carrot, cut into julienne strips
1 leek, cut into julienne strips
4 sheets of filo pastry
60ml/4 tablespoons dry white wine
salt and pepper
orange beurre blanc (see page 227)

1. Heat the oven to 200°C/400°F/gas mark 6.
2. Cut the trout into 2.5cm/1 inch wide strips and divide them into 4.
3. Melt a little of the butter in a frying pan, add the carrot and leek and cook until soft but not coloured.
4. Melt the remaining butter. Cut each filo sheet in half and brush with butter. Sandwich the halves together.
5. Divide the vegetables between the 4 filos and then place the fish on top of the vegetables. Sprinkle 15ml/1 tablespoon of wine over each, brush with melted butter and season with salt and pepper.
6. Draw the edges of the pastry together so that the parcels look like 'Dick Whittington' sacks.
7. Place each sack on a floured baking sheet, dab with melted butter and cook in the oven for 8-10 minutes, or until the pastry is crisp and golden brown.
8. Serve immediately with orange beurre blanc.

VERY DRY WHITE

Turbot Sausages with Watercress Sauce

This recipe assumes that you have a food processor.

SERVES 4
340g/12oz fillet of turbot, skinned
110g/4oz fillet of whiting or haddock, skinned
2 eggs, separated
290ml/½ pint cream
salt and pepper
cayenne
beaten egg
fine dried crumbs
butter for frying

For the sauce:
30g/1oz butter
30g/1oz flour
290ml/½ pint fish stock (see page 219)
570ml/1 pint cream
1 bunch of watercress, trimmed
salt and freshly ground black pepper

For the garnish:
watercress leaves

1. Keeping everything as cool as possible, process the fish, then add the egg yolks, cream and seasonings. Whisk the whites and fold them in.
2. Roll the mixture up in cling film in the shape of sausages.
3. Poach for 10-15 minutes in simmering water. Allow to cool, then brush with egg and roll in crumbs.
4. For the sauce, melt the butter and add the flour. Cook for 30 seconds. Remove from the heat. Add the stock and cream. Return to the heat, bring up to the boil and simmer for 4 minutes. Add the watercress and whizz briefly. Season with salt and pepper.
5. Fry the sausages in butter. Serve with the sauce and decorate with watercress leaves.

WHITE BURGUNDY

Deep-fried Whitebait

SERVES 4
450g/1lb whitebait
oil or fat for deep-frying
seasoned flour
lemon wedges
cayenne

1. Sort through the whitebait, discarding any broken fish.
2. Heat the deep fat until a crumb will sizzle vigorously in it.
3. Put the whitebait in a sieve and spoon over the flour. Shake and toss carefully until every fish is coated. Do this in batches if necessary.
4. Place a small handful of whitebait (too many will stick together) into the fat and cook for no more than 2 minutes. Remove and repeat until all the fish are fried. They should be crisp and pale brown.
5. Drain on absorbent paper. Serve at once with lemon wedges and offer cayenne pepper.

NOTE: If for any reason the whitebait cannot be served at once, they should be spread out in a thin layer on a baking sheet and kept, uncovered, in a just-warm oven until wanted. They will become soggy if piled up or covered.

WHITE LOIRE

Fish in Batter

SERVES 4
4 cutlets or steaks of any white fish
oil for deep-frying
10ml/2 teaspoons oil
55g/2oz plain flour
pinch of salt
1 egg yolk
45ml/3 tablespoons warm water
lemon wedges

1. Heat the oil until a crumb will sizzle gently in it.
2. Mix the 10ml/2 teaspoons oil with the flour and add the salt, egg yolk and water.
3. Dip the fish into this batter, hold it with tongs and lower it into the hot fat. Increase the

temperature of the oil.
4. Cook for 4-10 minutes depending on the thickness of the fish pieces.
5. Drain well on absorbent paper and sprinkle lightly with salt. Serve with wedges of lemon.

WHITE LOIRE

Seafood Pancakes

SERVES 4
8 pancakes (see page 533)
110g/4oz cooked prawns, peeled
110g/4oz frozen scampi (raw)
110g/4oz frozen scallops (raw)
slice of onion
6 peppercorns
bay leaf
parsley stalk
15g/½oz butter
15g/½oz flour
75ml/5 tablespoons milk
salt and pepper

To finish:
30g/1oz butter, melted
grated cheese

1. Make the pancakes and set aside. Then make the filling.
2. If the prawns are frozen, defrost them slowly.
3. Place the frozen scampi and scallops in a small pan. Cover with cold water, add the onion, peppercorns, bay leaf and parsley stalk. Bring slowly to boiling point. Immediately draw the pan off the heat and leave for 4 minutes, then strain, keeping the liquid.
4. Boil the liquid rapidly until reduced by half. Discard the onion and flavourings.
5. Remove the tough piece of muscle from the scallops (found on the opposite side of the roe) and cut each scallop into 2 or 3 pieces.
6. Melt the butter, add the flour and cook for 30 seconds. Take off the heat. Add 75ml/5 tablespoons of the reserved fish stock and mix well. Pour in the milk and return the pan to the heat. Bring slowly to the boil, stirring continuously. Season with salt and pepper. Simmer for 2 minutes to give a smooth thick mixture.
7. Mix the fish with the sauce. Divide the mixture between the pancakes and roll up.
8. Heat the grill.
9. Lay the pancakes side by side in a well-buttered ovenproof dish. Brush melted butter over the top of the pancakes and sprinkle them with grated cheese. Grill until lightly browned.

CRISP DRY WHITE

Poached Fish, Hot or Cold

Use salmon, haddock, etc., either whole or in a large piece. If the fish weighs over 1.5 kg/3lb, double the court bouillon quantities.

For the fish:
see above

For the court bouillon:
about 1 litre/2 pints water
5ml/1 teaspoon salt
150ml/¼ pint wine vinegar
1 medium onion, sliced
bunch of fresh parsley
sprig of thyme
1 bay leaf
6 peppercorns

For cold fish:
watercress, trimmed
cucumber slices, blanched
mayonnaise

For hot fish:
lemon wedges
boiled potatoes
melted butter

1. Simmer together all the court bouillon ingredients for 1 hour. Strain and cool.
2. Put the fish in the cold court bouillon and heat gently, bringing up to poaching temperature. Do not allow the water to simmer or boil – it should barely move. Poach for 4 minutes.
3. If the fish is to be served cold, turn the heat off now and leave the fish to cool. It will finish

cooking as it does so. Check the fish every 10 minutes or so, and when cooked, remove it carefully from the court bouillon and leave to get cold. When cold, skin the fish, garnish it with watercress and cucumber and hand the mayonnaise separately.
4. If the fish is to be served hot, poach it for 4 minutes per 450g/1lb, then carefully lift it out. Skin it if necessary, garnish with lemon wedges, surround with hot potatoes and pass the melted butter separately.

NOTE: Starting with a cooled court bouillon is considered to produce moister flesh, but it is not always practicable. If the fish has to be put into a hot court bouillon allow 6 minutes per 450g/1lb and remove at once.

DRY WHITE

Fish Pie

SERVES 6
900g/2lb fillet of haddock, whiting, cod or a mixture of any of them
425ml/3/4 pint milk
1/2 onion, sliced
6 peppercorns
1 bay leaf
salt and pepper
5 hardboiled eggs, quartered
15ml/1 tablespoon chopped parsley
30g/1oz butter
30g/1oz flour
30ml/2 tablespoons cream
675g/1 1/2lb mashed potatoes (see page 187)
butter

1. Set the oven to 180°C/350°F/gas mark 4.
2. Lay the fish fillets in a roasting pan.
3. Heat the milk with the onion, peppercorns, bay leaf and a pinch of salt.
4. Pour over the fish and cook in the oven for about 15 minutes until the fish is firm and creamy looking.
5. Strain off the milk, reserving it for the sauce. Flake the fish into a pie dish and add the eggs. Sprinkle over the parsley.
6. Heat the butter in a saucepan, stir in the flour and cook for 1 minute. Draw off the heat and gradually add the reserved milk
7. Return to the heat and stir, bringing slowly to the boil. Taste and add salt and pepper as needed. Stir in the cream and pour over the fish, mixing it with a palette knife or spoon.
8. Spread a layer of mashed potatoes on the top and mark with a fork in a criss-cross pattern. Dot with butter. Place on a baking sheet and brown in the oven for about 10 minutes, or longer if the pie has been made in advance.

DRY WHITE

Fritto Misto

SERVES 4
450g/1lb mixed raw prawns, crayfish tails, crab meat, sole, whiting and whitebait (prepared weight)
lemon juice
salt and pepper
oil or fat for deep-frying

For the batter:
5g/1/4oz fresh yeast
150ml/1/4 pint tepid water
110g/4oz plain flour
pinch of salt
15ml/1 tablespoon olive oil
1 egg white

For the garnish:
deep-fried parsley (see page 631)

1. First make the batter. Mix the yeast with the water. Sift the flour and salt into a bowl. Make a well in the centre and pour in the frothing yeast liquid and oil.
2. With a wooden spoon, beat the mixture, gradually drawing in the flour. Leave in a warm place to rise for 30 minutes.
3. Sprinkle the fish with lemon juice and pepper and leave for 30 minutes or so.
4. Beat the egg white until stiff and fold it into the batter.
5. Drain the fish and dry on absorbent paper. Dip into the batter, coating each piece completely.
6. Heat the oil until a drop of batter will fizzle slowly. Deep-fry the pieces, a few at a time, until

the batter is golden brown. Drain on absorbent paper, sprinkle with salt and pile on to a serving dish. Garnish with deep-fried parsley.

SOAVE

Salmon and Plaice Ravioli with Basil Sauce

The egg whites and cream can be added in the processor but they must be very cold and not over-beaten. If too warm the mixture will split (curdle) and there is no way to rescue it. The described method is foolproof.

SERVES 4
pasta made with 1 egg (see page 532)

For the filling:
55g/2oz skinned salmon fillet
55g/2oz skinned plaice fillet
1cm/½ inch root ginger, peeled and sliced
squeeze of lemon juice
salt and ground white pepper
1 egg white
120ml/4 fl oz double cream, chilled
2.5ml/½ teaspoon ground mace

For the sauce:
170ml/6 fl oz extra virgin olive oil
1 large garlic clove, peeled and sliced
10 basil leaves, torn
2 tomatoes, peeled, deseeded and finely diced
squeeze of lemon juice

1. Make the pasta and leave to relax, covered in cling film.
2. Put the salmon and plaice, ginger and lemon juice into a food processor and pound well or chop finely and push through a sieve. (This is quite a task.)
3. Put the fish in a bowl. Season with salt and pepper and set in a roasting tin of ice to keep the mixture chilled. Beat well, gradually adding the egg white, then the cream, making sure that the mixture does not become too runny. It should hold its shape. Taste and season with mace, and more salt and pepper if necessary. Refrigerate until ready to use.
4. Roll out the pasta very thinly into a square. Brush lightly with water. Place teaspoonfuls of filling at intervals of 3cm/1½ inches in even rows, over half the pasta. Fold the other half of the pasta over the mounds of fish mousseline. Press together, firming all round each mound of filling. Cut between the rows, making sure that the edges are sealed. Set aside.
5. Put a large saucepan of salted water on to boil.
6. Make the sauce. Heat the oil, add the garlic and leave to cook very slowly for about 3-4 minutes.
7. Add the basil, tomatoes, lemon juice, salt and pepper. Cook for 2-3 minutes.
8. Cook the ravioli in the boiling water for 3-4 minutes. Drain well.
9. Serve the ravioli with the basil and olive oil sauce drizzled over the top.

DRY WHITE

Tartare of Salmon and Tuna

This recipe is taken from *New American Classic Cookery* by Jeremiah Towers.

SERVES 4
1 cucumber
salt and freshly ground pepper
120ml/4 fl oz fresh lemon juice
30ml/2 tablespoons sesame oil
225g/8oz salmon fillet, boned and skinned
225g/8oz tuna fillet, skinned, all dark meat removed
30ml/2 tablespoons olive oil
4 tomatoes, peeled, deseeded and finely chopped
rocket and chopped chives to garnish

1. Peel the cucumber, score lengthwise with a fork, and cut into very thin slices. Whisk salt and pepper into half the lemon juice; then whisk in the sesame oil. Toss the cucumber slices in the sauce and let stand for 1 hour.
2. Finely chop the salmon and tuna separately. Into each of the chopped fish, stir half the remaining lemon juice, a tablespoon of olive oil and salt and pepper to taste.

3. To serve: arrange the cucumber on 4 plates with the slices overlapping. Spoon the 2 tartares in separate mounds in the centre of each plate.
4. Toss the chopped tomato in the bowl in which the cucumber marinated and divide between the plates. Garnish with rocket and chives.

CALIFORNIAN SAUVIGNON

Grilled Seafood Kebabs

SERVES 4
225g/8oz turbot fillet
12 small scallops, cleaned
1 red pepper, deseeded and cut into large pieces
2 rashers of rindless streaky bacon

1. Heat the grill to its highest temperature.
2. Cut the turbot into pieces similar in size to the whole scallops.
3. Thread the turbot, scallops and pepper on to 4 large skewers. Place on the grill.
4. Cut the bacon in half lengthways and lay a piece on each kebab. Grill for 2 minutes. Turn over, keeping the bacon on top, and grill for a further 4 minutes. Remove and discard the bacon after 2 minutes.
5. Serve on a bed of saffron rice or freshly cooked pasta.

NOTE: The bacon is discarded in order to make this a low-fat dish, but it can be eaten if preferred.

WHITE LOIRE

Pot au Feu de la Mer

SERVES 6
170g/6oz monkfish, cubed
170g/6oz sole fillets, cubed
675ml/1½ pints fish stock
4 large scallops, muscle removed, halved
110g/4oz whole scampi
90ml/6 tablespoons dry white wine
8 spring onions, trimmed and cut into julienne strips
1 medium carrot, peeled and cut into julienne strips
1 large stick celery, cut into julienne strips
4 large cup mushrooms, turned
150ml/¼ pint double cream
salt and pepper

1. Poach the monkfish and sole in hot fish stock for 2 minutes. Remove and keep warm in a very low oven. Add the scallops and scampi and poach for 1 minute. Remove and keep warm.
2. Add the wine to the fish stock and reduce, by boiling rapidly, to 290ml/½ pint.
3. While the stock is reducing, blanch the spring onions, carrots and celery in boiling salted water for 1 minute, then drain well. Blanch the mushrooms until just cooked.
4. Add the cream to the reduced fish stock and boil to reduce to a creamy consistency. Taste and season as necessary. Add the fish.
5. Arrange the fish in its sauce on 4 plates and garnish with a scattering of warm julienne vegetables and the mushrooms.

WHITE BURGUNDY

Paella

This is a fairly basic recipe to which other seafood can be added as required.

SERVES 4
45ml/3 tablespoons oil
1 onion, sliced
85g/3oz bacon, diced
225g/8oz long-grain rice
8 filaments of saffron, soaked in 30ml/2 tablespoons hot water
170g/6oz squid, cleaned *(see page 165)*
1 pimento, sliced
salt and freshly ground black pepper
4 chicken joints, skinned
570ml/1pint chicken stock *(see page 219)*
55g/2oz peas, cooked
425ml/¾ pint unshelled cooked prawns

To garnish:
chopped parsley

1. Heat the oil in a deep-sided frying pan or paella dish, add the onion and bacon and cook for 2 minutes. Reduce the heat, add the rice and stir over a moderate heat until the rice begins to whiten.
2. Set the oven to 180°C/350°F/gas mark 5 if required (see below).
3. Add the saffron, squid and pimento, mix well and season with salt and pepper. Arrange the skinned chicken joints on top of the rice. Pour over the stock, bring to the boil, cover with greaseproof paper and bake for 35 minutes or simmer on top of the hob, checking that nothing catches, for about 30 minutes.
4. When the rice is tender, add the peas and most of the prawns, warm through and garnish with the remaining prawns and the parsley.

NOTE: If preferred, the prawns not used for garnish can be shelled before they are added to the paella.

DRY WHITE/ROSE

Plaited Fish with Tarragon Butter

For each person you will need 3 strips of fish, 2 of salmon and 1 of turbot or other firm-fleshed white fish. The strips should be about 15cm/6in x 1cm/½ inch, and free of skin and bones.

For the fish:
see above

For the stock:
1 glass white wine
1 carrot, peeled and shredded
1 leek, peeled and shredded
1 onion, sliced
bay leaf
good bunch of parsley
fish heads, bones, skins
1 litre/2 pints water
12 peppercorns
pinch of salt

For the sauce:
140g/5oz butter, chilled
5ml/1 teaspoon flour
30ml/2 tablespoons double cream
15ml/1 tablespoon chopped tarragon

1. Boil the stock ingredients together for 30 minutes. Strain.
2. Set the oven to 170°C/325°F/gas mark 3.
3. Plait the 3 strips of fish for each person and lay neatly in a roasting tin. Pour over the stock and poach in the oven for about 8 minutes until just firm. Lift out and dish up on a plate. Keep covered.
4. Reduce the stock by boiling rapidly to 290ml/½ pint.
5. Melt 30g/1oz of the butter in a small, heavy saucepan with sloping sides and stir in the flour. Cook for 1 minute. Remove from the heat, and gradually add the reduced stock. Return to the heat and stir until boiling. You should have a barely thickened sauce.
6. Cut the remaining butter into small dice and whisk it, a piece at a time, into the boiling sauce. It will form an emulsion. Keep whisking until all the butter is incorporated. Add the cream and tarragon, taste, season and pour round the fish.

CRISP DRY WHITE

Poultry and Game

Poultry and Game

TO PREPARE AND DRAW A GAME BIRD FOR THE OVEN

Some birds are easier to pluck than others, ducks being notoriously tedious. All birds are easier to pluck if still warm when tackled. Work away from draughts, as the feathers fly about, and pluck straight into a dustbin. Tug the feathers, working from the tail to the head, pulling against the way the feathers grow. If the bird is very young or if there is a lot of fat, pull downwards towards the tail to avoid tearing the flesh.

Once plucked, the bird should be singed. This can be done with a burning taper, or directly over a gas flame, but care should be taken to singe only the down and small feathers, and not to blacken the flesh. The bird should then be rubbed with a clean teatowel to remove any remaining stubble. It is now ready for drawing.

Surprisingly, birds keep better, when hanging, with their insides intact. Once eviscerated they must be cooked within a day or two. So when you are ready to cook the bird, take it down, and proceed as follows.

1. Pluck it.

2. Cut round the feet, at the drumstick joint, but do not cut right through the tendons. Pull the legs off the bird, drawing the tendons out with them. If the bird is small this is easy enough - just bend the foot back until it snaps, and pull, perhaps over the edge of a table. Turkeys are more difficult: snap the feet at the drumstick joint by bending them over the end of the table, then hang the bird up by the feet from a stout hook, and pull on the bird. The feet plus tendons will be left on the hook, the turkey in your arms. All too often birds are sold with the tendons in the legs, making the drumsticks tough when cooked.

3. Now for the head and neck. Lay the bird breast side down on a board. Make a slit through the neck skin from the body to the head. Cut off the head and throw it away. Pull back the split neck skin, leaving it attached to the body of the bird (it will come in useful to close the gap if you are stuffing the bird). Cut the neck off as close to the body as you can.

4. Put a finger into the neck hole, to the side of the stump of neck left on the bird, and move the finger right round, loosening the innards from the neck. If you do not do this you will find them difficult to pull out from the other end.

5. With a sharp knife slit the bird open from the vent to the parson's (or pope's) nose, making a hole large enough to just get your hand in. Put your hand in, working it so the back of your hand is up against the arch of the breastbone, and carefully loosen the entrails from the sides of the body cavity, all the way round. Pull them out, taking care not to break the gall bladder, the contents of which would embitter any flesh they touched. Covering the gutting hand with a cloth helps extract the intestines intact. The first time you do this it is unlikely that you will get everything out in one motion, so check that the lungs and kidneys come too. Have another go if necessary. Once the bird is empty, wipe any traces of blood off with a clean damp cloth.

The neck and feet go into the stockpot with the heart and the cleaned gizzard. To clean the gizzard, carefully cut the outside wall along the natural seam so that you can peel it away from the inner bag of grit. Throw the grit bag away, with the intestines and the gall bladder. Do not put the liver in the stockpot: it may make the stock bitter. It may be fried and served with the dish, or fried, chopped and added to the sauce, or kept frozen until enough poultry liver has been collected to make pâté. But if the liver is to be used, carefully cut away the discoloured portion of it where it lay against the gall bladder (it will be bitter) and trim off any membranes.

The bird is trussed to keep it in a compact neat shape, usually after stuffing. Trussing large birds is unnecessary as the bird is to be carved up anyway, and trussing serves to prevent the inside thigh being cooked by the time the breast is ready. Small birds, especially game birds where underdone thighs are desirable, are trussed, but their feet are left on. Their feet may simply be tied together for neatness' sake, and the pinions skewered under the bird. Or they may be trussed in any number of ways, one of which is described below.

1. Arrange the bird so that the neck flap is folded over the neck hole, and the pinions turned under and tucked in tight. They will, if folded correctly, hold the neck flap in place, but if the bird is well stuffed the neck flap may have to be skewered or sewn in place.

2. Press the legs down and into the bird to force the breast into a plumped-up position. Thread a long trussing needle with thin string and push it through the wing joint, right through the body and out of the other wing joint.

3. Then push it through the body again, this time through the thighs. You should now be back on the side you started.

4. Tie the two ends together in a bow to make later removal quick.

5. Then thread a shorter piece of string through the thin end of the two drumsticks and tie them together, winding the string round the parson's nose at the same time to close the vent. Sometimes a small slit is cut in the skin just below the end of the breastbone, and the parson's nose is pushed through it.

Small birds such as quail are invariably cooked whole, perhaps stuffed, and perhaps boned (see page 280). But medium-sized ones, like chickens and guinea fowl, are often cut into two, four, six or eight pieces. Use a knife to cut through the flesh and poultry shears or scissors to cut the bones.

TO SPLIT A BIRD IN HALF:
Simply use a sharp knife to cut right through flesh and bone, just on one side of the breastbone, open out the bird and cut through the other side, immediately next to the backbone. Then cut the backbone away from the half to which it remains attached. The knobbly end of the drumsticks and the fleshless tips to the pinions can be cut off before or after cooking. In birds brought whole to the table they are left on.

TO JOINT A BIRD INTO FOUR:
First pull out any trussing strings, then pull the leg away from the body. With a sharp knife cut through the skin joining the leg to the body, pull the leg away further and cut through more skin to free the leg. Bend the leg outwards and back, forcing the bone to come out of its socket close to the body. Turn the bird over, feel along the backbone to find the oyster (a soft pocket of flesh at the side of the backbone, near the middle). With the tip of the knife, cut this away from the carcase at the side nearest the backbone and farthest from the leg. Then turn the bird over again, and cut through the flesh, the knife going between the end of the thigh bone and the carcase, to take off the leg, bringing the oyster with it. Using poultry shears or a heavy knife, split the carcase along the breastbone. Cut through the ribs on each side to take off the fleshy portion of the breast, and with it the wing. Trim the joints neatly to remove scraps of untidy skin.

For six joints, proceed as above but split the legs into thigh portions and drumsticks. The exact join of the bones can easily be seen if the leg is laid on the board, skin side down. Cut through the fat line. With a cleaver, or the heel end of a knife, chop the feet off the drumsticks.

TO JOINT INTO EIGHT:
1. Turn the chicken over so the backbone is uppermost. Cut through to the bone along the line of the spine.

2. Where the thigh joins the backbone there is a fleshy 'oyster' on each side. Cut round them to loosen them from the carcase so that they come away when the legs are severed.

3. Turn the bird over and pull a leg away from the body. Cut through the skin only, as far round the leg as possible, close to the body.

4. Pull the leg away from the body and twist it down so that the thigh bone pops out of its socket on the carcase and is exposed.

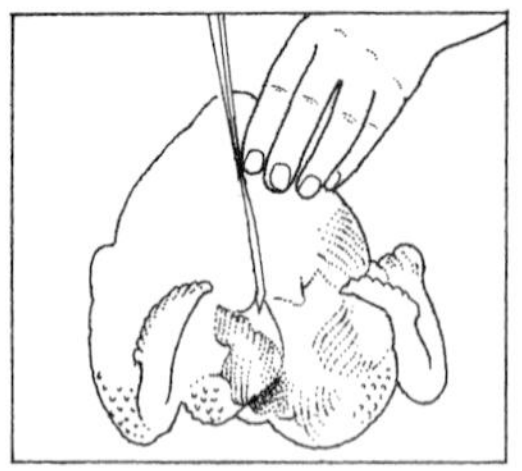
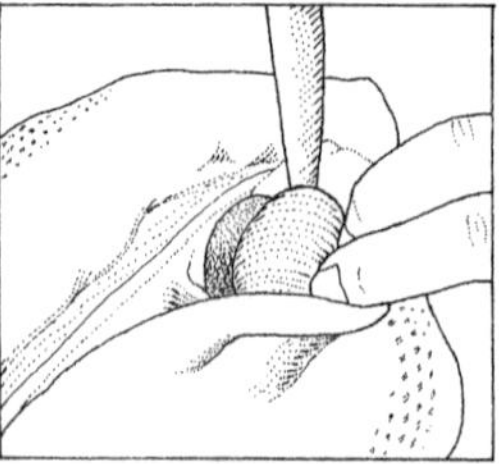

Jointing a chicken: Stages 1 and 2 (numbers refer to text)

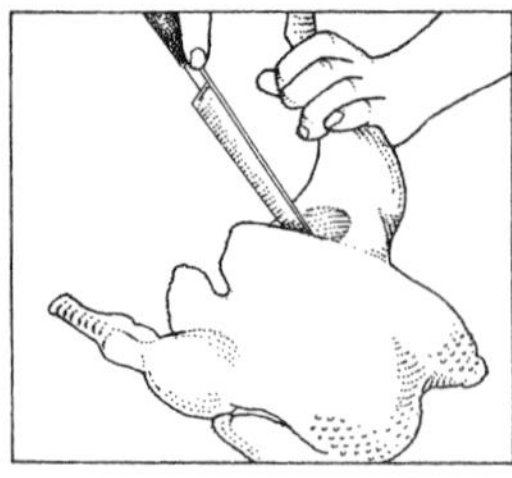
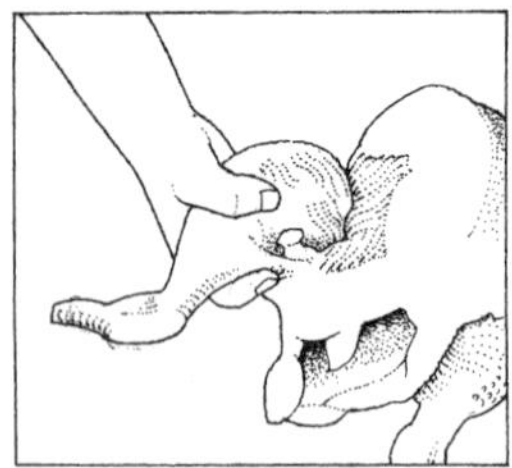

Stages 3 and 4

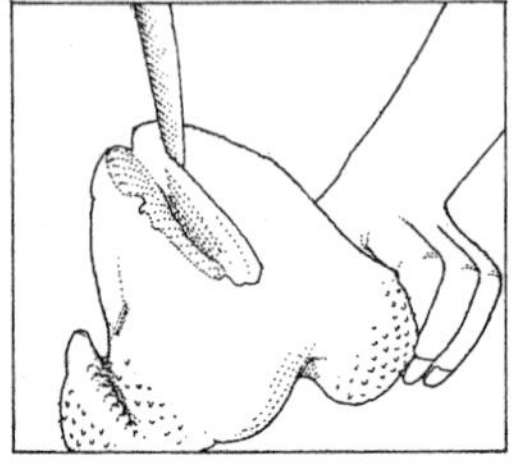
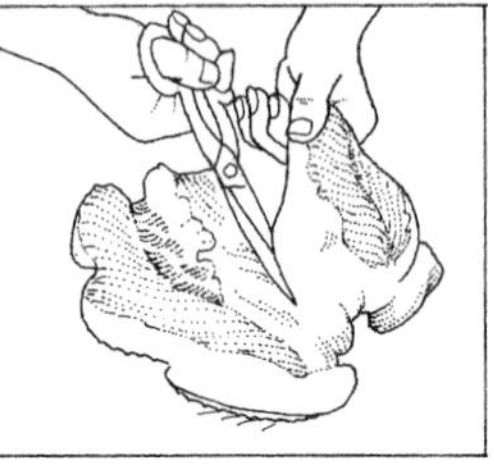

Stages 6, 7 and 8

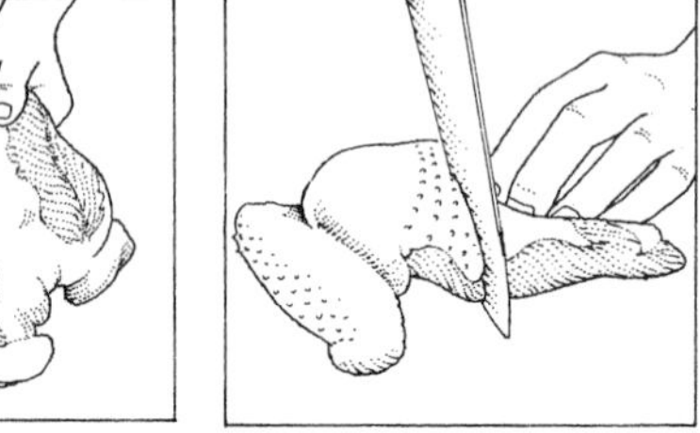
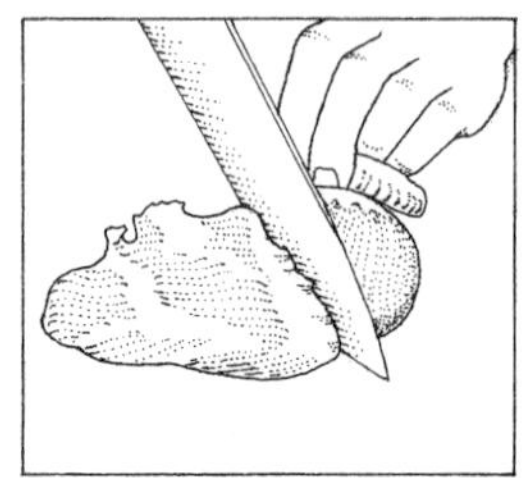

Stages 9 and 11

5. Cut the leg off, taking care to go between thigh bone and carcase and to bring the 'oyster' away with the leg. (Turn over briefly to check.) Repeat the process for the other leg.
6. Carefully cut down each side of the breast bone to free the flesh a little.
7. Use scissors to cut through the small bone close to the breast. Cut away the breastbone.
8. Open up the bird. Cut each wing and breast off the carcase with scissors. Start at the tail end and cut to and through the wing bone near the neck.
9. Cut the wing joint in two, leaving about one third of the breast attached to the wing.
10. Cut off the pinions from each wing. They can go into the stockpot with the carcase.
11. Separate the drumsticks and thighs, lay the legs skin side down on the board, and cut through where the thigh and lower leg bones meet, on the obvious fat line.
12. With a cleaver, or the heel end of a heavy knife, chop the feet off the drumsticks.

BARDING

Poultry liable to dry out during cooking is often barded: lay fatty bacon or rindless pork back fat strips over the body of the bird, and secure or tie in place. The barding is removed during cooking to allow the breast to brown.

BONING

1. Put the chicken breast side down on a board. Cut through to the backbone.
2. Feel for the fleshy 'oyster' at the top of each thigh and cut round it. Cut and scrape the flesh from the carcase with a sharp knife held as close as possible to the bone.
3. Continue along both sides of the backbone until the ribcage is exposed. At the joint of the thigh and pelvis, cut between the bones at the

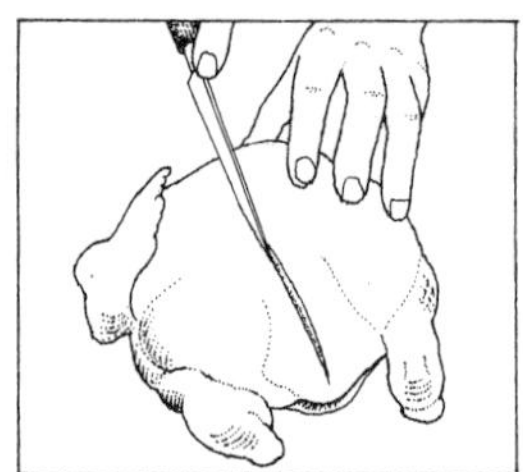
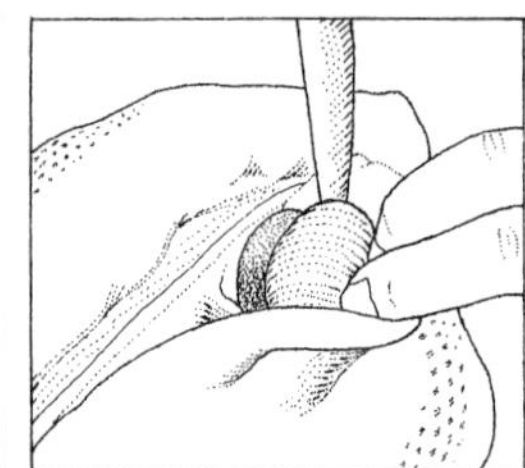

Boning a chicken: Stages 1 and 2 (numbers refer to text)

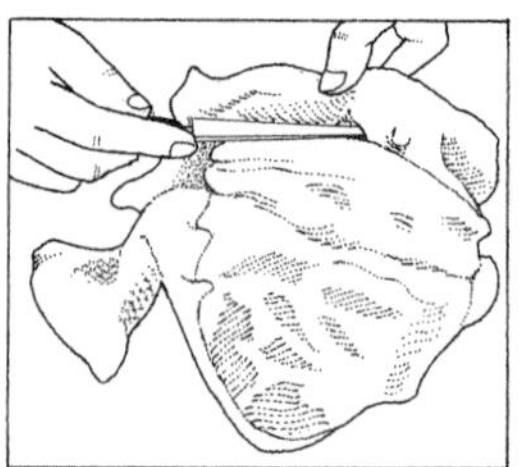
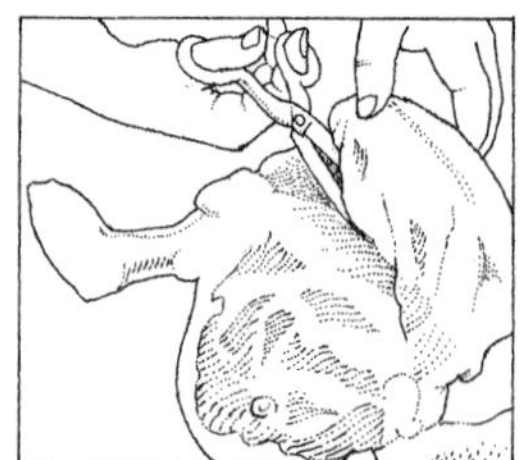

Stages 3 and 4

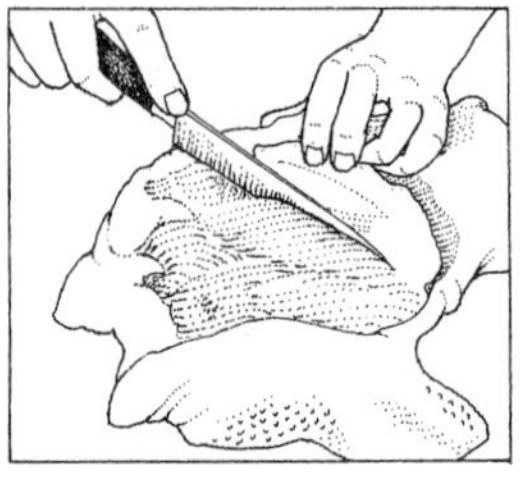
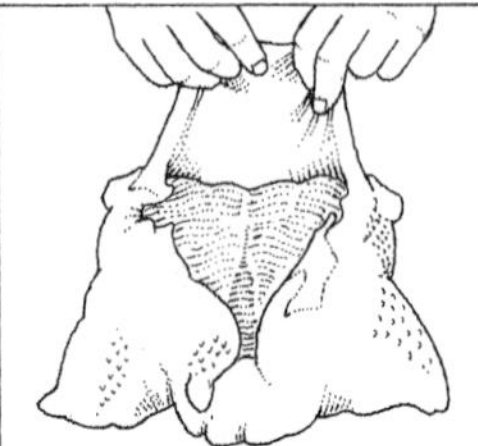

Stages 10 and 12

socket so that the legs stay attached to the flesh and skin, and not to the body carcase.
4. Keep working right round the bird then use scissors to cut away most of the ribcage, leaving only the cartilaginous breastbone in the centre.
5. Using a heavy knife, cut through the foot joints to remove the knuckle end of the drumsticks.
6. Working from the inside thigh end scrape one leg bone clean, pushing the flesh down towards the drumstick until you can free the thigh bone. Repeat on the other leg.
7. Working from the drumstick ends, scrape the lower leg bones clean in the same way and remove them. Remove as many tendons as possible from the legs as you work.
8. Now for the wings. Cut off the pinions with a heavy knife.
9. Scrape the wing bones clean as you did the leg bones.
10. Carefully free the breastbone with the knife, working from the middle of the bird towards the tail.
11. Take great care not to puncture the skin, which has no flesh under it at this point so is easily torn.
12. You should now have a beautifully boned bird. Keep the neck flap of skin intact to fold over once the chicken is stuffed.

Roasting Tables

If using a fan (convection) oven, reduce the cooking times by 15 per cent or lower the oven temperature by 20°C/40°F.

Meat		**Temperature**			**Cooking time**	
		°C	°F	Gas	per kg	per lb
Beef	Brown	220	425	7	20 mins +	
	Rare roast	160	325	3	35 mins	15 mins
	Medium roast				45 mins	20 mins
Pork	Roast	200	400	6	65 mins	25 mins
Veal	Brown	220	425	7	20 mins+	
	Roast	180	350	4	55 mins	25 mins
Lamb	Brown	220	425	7	20 mins	
	Roast	190	375	5	55 mins	20 mins
Chicken		200	400	6	35-45 mins	15-20 mins
	NOTE: Few chickens, however small, will be cooked in much under an hour.					
Turkey	Small (under 6kg/13lb)	200	400	6	25 mins	12 mins
	Large	180	350	4	35 mins	15 mins
	NOTE: For more detailed timings see chart over. (Few turkeys, however small, will be cooked in under 2 hours.)					
Duck, goose	Small (under 2.5kg/5lb)	190	375	5	45 mins	20 mins
	Large	180	350	4	55 mins	25 mins
Pigeon		200	400	6	25-35 minutes	
Grouse		190	375	5	25-35 minutes	
Guinea fowl		190	375	5	70 minutes	
Partridge		190	375	5	20-25 minutes	
Pheasant		190	375	5	45-60 minutes	
Wild duck		200	400	6	40 minutes	
Woodcock		190	375	5	20-30 minutes	
Quail		180	350	4	20 minutes	
Snipe		190	375	5	15-20 minutes	
Teal		210	425	7	25 minutes	

Thawing and cooking times for turkeys

Although the thawing time in this table can be relied, on the cooking times are dependent on an accurate oven. For safety's sake, plan the timing so that, if all goes right, the bird will be ready 1 hour before dinner. This will give you leeway if necessary. When the bird is cooked, open the oven door to cool the oven, then put the turkey on a serving dish and put it back in the oven to keep warm.

Thawing in a warm room (over 18°C/65°F) or under warm water is not recommended, as warmth will encourage the growth of micro-organisms, which might result in food poisoning.

Weight of bird when ready for the oven, regardless of whether it is boned, stuffed or empty	Thawing time at room temperature 18°C/65°F hours	Thawing time in refrigerator 5°C/40°F hours	Cooking time at 180°C/ 350°F Gas mark 4 hours	Cooking time at 200°C/ 400°F Gas mark 6 hours
4 -5 kilos/8-10lb	20	65	-	2
5 -6 kilos/11-13lb	24	70	-	2-2 1/2
6 -7 kilos/14-16lb	30	75	3-4	-
8 -9 kilos/17-20lb	40	80	4-5	-
9 -11 kilos/21-24lb	48	96	5-6	-

Chicken Elizabeth

The Cordon Bleu School devised this dish for the Coronation celebrations in 1953.

SERVES 4

1.35 kg/3lb roasting chicken, washed and dried
chicken stock or water with 1 bay leaf, 6 peppercorns, salt, 2 parsley stalks, 1 slice lemon and 2 teaspoons fresh thyme
225ml/8 fl oz Elizabeth sauce (see page 224)

To serve:
rice salad (see page 210)
bunch of watercress

1. Place the chicken, untrussed, in a saucepan of simmering chicken stock or in a pan of water with the flavourings.
2. Cover the pan and cook gently for 1 1/4-1 1/2 hours or until the chicken is tender and the drumsticks feel loose and wobbly. Remove from the stock and set aside to cool.
3. Remove the flesh from the chicken bones, and when it is quite cold mix with the sauce, keeping a little back.
4. Pile the chicken into the middle of a serving dish and coat with the reserved sauce. Surround with the rice salad and garnish with watercress.

NOTE: It is easier to strip chicken flesh from the bones while the bird is still lukewarm. But on no account should the sauce be added to the flesh until the chicken is stone cold.

WHITE LOIRE

Poached Chicken with Parsley Sauce

SERVES 4

1.35 kg/3lb chicken, cleaned but not trussed

For the court bouillon:
1 onion, sliced
2 carrots
2 parsley stalks
salt
6 peppercorns
2 sticks celery
2 bay leaves

For the parsley sauce:
30g/1oz butter
30g/1oz flour
150ml/1/4pint milk
about 150ml/1/4 pint chicken stock taken from the cooking liquid
30ml/2 tablespoons single cream (optional)
30ml/2 tablespoons chopped parsley
salt and freshly ground black pepper

1. Put the chicken into a large saucepan with the onion, carrots, parsley stalks, salt, peppercorns, celery and bay leaves. Half submerge the bird with water and put on a well-fitting lid.
2. Bring to the boil, reduce the heat and simmer gently for 1 1/2 hours or until the chicken is cooked, when the legs feel loose and wobbly.
3. Remove the chicken from the pan and strain the stock.
4. Carefully skim the stock of all the fat. When you have spooned off as much grease as possible, lay successive sheets of absorbent paper on the surface of the liquid to remove the rest of the fat.
5. Now start the parsley sauce: melt the butter, add the flour and cook for 1 minute. Remove from the heat.
6. Gradually add the milk and chicken stock. Return to the heat and bring to the boil, stirring continuously.
7. Simmer for 2 minutes, then add the cream (if using) and set aside.
8. Skin the chicken and remove the bones, leaving the flesh in large pieces.
9. Reheat the sauce and add the parsley. Season if necessary with salt and pepper. Add more stock if the sauce is too thick. Add the chicken to the sauce, turn gently, and tip into a serving dish.

NOTE: Do not add the parsley to the sauce in advance as it will lose its colour.

WHITE ALSACE

Curried Chicken and Ham Pie

SERVES 4
55g/2oz butter
1 onion, chopped
5ml/1 teaspoon curry powder
2.5ml/1/2 teaspoon turmeric
45g/1 1/2oz flour
290ml/1/2 pint stock reserved after cooking the chicken
150ml/1/4 pint creamy milk
5ml/1 teaspoon chopped fresh parsley
5ml/1 teaspoon chopped fresh mint
pinch of crushed cardamom seeds
pinch of dry English mustard
salt and freshly ground black pepper
squeeze of lemon juice
2 hardboiled eggs, chopped
110g/4oz ham, cut into 1cm/1/2 inch dice
1.35 kg/3lb chicken, poached, boned and cut into large chunks
wholemeal pastry made with 225g/8oz flour (see page 527)
1 beaten egg mixed with 1 pinch of salt and 5ml/1 teaspoon water (egg wash)

1. Set the oven to 200°C/400°F/gas mark 6.
2. Melt the butter and add the onion. Cook gently until soft but not coloured.
3. Stir in the curry powder and turmeric and cook for 1 minute.
4. Add the flour and cook over a gentle heat for 1 minute. Draw the pan off the heat. Add the chicken stock and stir well. Return to the heat. Bring slowly up to the boil, stirring continuously until the sauce is thick and shiny.
5. Add the milk and stir again until the sauce returns to the boil.
6. Add the parsley, mint, cardamom seeds, mustard and seasoning. Simmer for 2-3 minutes.
7. Taste, adding more salt if necessary, and add the lemon juice. Allow to cool.
8. Stir in the hardboiled eggs, the ham and the chicken. Pour the mixture into a pie dish.
9. Roll the pastry on a floured board into a rectangle about 5mm/1/4inch thick.
10. Cut a band of pastry slightly wider than the edge of the pie dish. Brush the rim of the dish

with water and press on the band of paste. Brush with a little beaten egg or water and lay the pastry lid over the pie. Cut away any surplus pastry from the sides with a knife.
11. Press the pie edges together and mark a pattern with the point of a small knife, or pinch with the fingers into a raised border. Shape the pastry trimmings into leaves for decoration. Make a small hole in the pastry to allow the steam to escape.
12. Brush the pastry with beaten egg and decorate with the pastry leaves. Brush again with egg.
13. Bake for 30-35 minutes until golden brown.

Note: If the pie is not to be baked as soon as it has been assembled it is essential that the curry sauce and the chicken are both completely cold before they are combined. Keep the pie refrigerated or frozen until baking. If frozen, thaw in the refrigerator before cooking.

DRY WHITE/ROSE

Chicken and Sweetbread Filling for Vol-au-Vents or Feuilletés

SERVES 4
pair of calves sweetbreads or 225g/8oz lambs sweetbreads
45g/1½oz butter
1 small onion, very finely chopped
55g/2oz button mushrooms, sliced
30g/1oz flour
150ml/¼ pint creamy milk
15ml/1 tablespoon sherry
150ml/¼ pint chicken stock
15ml/1 tablespoon chopped parsley
squeeze of lemon juice
225g/8oz cooked chicken, cut in chunks
salt and freshly ground black pepper
1 large vol-au-vent case (see page 529) or 4 feuilletté cases

1. Soak the sweetbreads in cold water for 4 hours. Change the water every time it becomes pink (probably 4 times). There should be no blood at all when the sweetbreads are ready for cooking.
2. Place them in a pan of cold water and bring up to the boil. Poach for 2 minutes.
3. Drain the sweetbreads and rinse under running cold water. Dry well. Pick them over, removing all the skin and membrane and chop coarsely.
4. Melt the butter and add the onion and cook slowly until soft but not coloured - this may take 10 minutes.
5. Add the sweetbreads. Stir in the mushrooms and leave over a gentle heat for 1 minute. Remove the sweetbreads and mushrooms with a perforated spoon.
6. Stir the flour into the pan and cook for 1 minute. Draw off the heat and stir in the milk, sherry and stock. Bring slowly to the boil, stirring continuously. Simmer for 1 minute.
7. Add the parsley, lemon juice, chicken pieces, sweetbreads, mushrooms and seasoning.
8. Tip the mixture carefully into the pastry case and reheat in the oven for 5 minutes.

SPICY DRY WHITE

Chicken and Yoghurt Cream Curry

SERVES 4
1.8 kg/4lb chicken
seasoned flour mixed with a pinch each of turmeric, cayenne, dried English mustard and crushed coriander
30ml/2 tablespoons oil
2 medium onions, chopped
1 garlic clove, crushed
5ml/1 teaspoon cumin powder
10ml/2 teaspoons turmeric
290ml/ ½ pint chicken stock
1 bay leaf
10ml/2 teaspoons tomato purée
juice of 1 lemon
30ml/2 tablespoons chopped fresh mint
15ml/1 tablespoon cream
10ml/2 teaspoons plain yoghurt
8g/¼oz blanched almonds, browned
To serve:
boiled rice

1. Joint the chicken into 8 pieces and dip in the well-seasoned flour. Heat the oil in a sauté pan and brown the chicken all over. With a perforated spoon remove the pieces and place them in a roasting dish or casserole.
2. Heat the oven to 180°C/350°F/gas mark 4.
3. Now fry the onions and garlic until they turn brown. Add the cumin and turmeric and cook for 2 minutes. Add the stock, bay leaf, tomato purée, lemon juice and mint. Taste and add salt and pepper as necessary. Bring slowly to the boil, stirring continuously.
4. Pour this over the chicken joints. Cover and cook in the oven for 45-50 minutes or until the chicken is tender. Turn off the oven.
5. Lift the chicken joints out of the sauce on to a serving dish. Cover and keep warm. Meanwhile heat the curry sauce, adding the cream, yoghurt and almonds. Pour over the chicken and serve with boiled rice.

SPICY DRY WHITE

Chicken with Whole Spices

SERVES 4

1 x 1.8kg/4lb chicken, skinned and jointed into 8 pieces
70g/2½oz clarified butter (see page 138)
10ml/2 teaspoons turmeric
1.25ml/¼ teaspoon ground ginger
4 cardamom pods
1cm/½ inch splintered cinnamon
3 cloves, ground
good pinch ground mace
good pinch cayenne
1.25ml/¼ teaspoon black pepper
½ bay leaf, crumbled
5ml/1 teaspoon ground mustard seeds
2 garlic cloves, crushed
5 onions, sliced

1. Lightly fry the chicken in half of the butter with the turmeric and ginger.
2. Shell the cardamoms and crush the seeds with the cinnamon, cloves, mace, cayenne, pepper, bay leaf and mustard seeds in a pestle and mortar.
3. Add the garlic, onions, crushed spices and remaining butter to the sauté pan. Place over a fierce heat and when it sizzles reduce the temperature, cover and cook slowly for 45 minutes.

LIGHT RED

Tandoori Chicken

SERVES 4

1 x 1.8kg/4lb chicken, cut into 8 joints and skinned
4 garlic cloves, crushed
290ml/½ pint low-fat yoghurt
1 heaped teaspoon of each of the following:
ground coriander
ground cumin
ground fenugreek
sweet paprika
ground ginger
1.25ml/¼ teaspoon chilli powder
1.25ml/¼ teaspoon dry English mustard

To serve:
yoghurt
lemon wedges

1. Mix the garlic, yoghurt and spices together in a large bowl.
2. Cut a few slashes into the flesh of each chicken joint, add to the yoghurt and spice mixture, mix well, cover and refrigerate overnight or for as long as possible.
3. Set the oven to 200°C/400°F/gas mark 6. Put the chicken joints on to a wire rack on a roasting tin and bake for 1 hour. The chicken should get very brown but not burnt – it may be necessary to cover it with tin foil halfway through the cooking in order to stop it burning.
4. Serve with yoghurt and lemon wedges.

NOTE: This can also be made using strips of chicken breasts. They should be marinated in the yoghurt and spices for 1 hour and then grilled for 10 minutes.

LAGER OR RED RHONE

Gougère

A gougère is a cheese choux pastry case which may be filled with a variety of mixtures such as haddock (see page 243), chicken or game (see below).

SERVES 4

105g/3¾oz plain flour
pinch of salt
pepper and cayenne
85g/3oz butter
225ml/7 fl oz water
3 eggs, lightly beaten
55g/2oz strong Cheddar cheese, cut into 5mm/¼ inch cubes
425ml/¾ pint filling (see below)
15ml/1 tablespoon browned crumbs
15ml/1 tablespoon grated cheese.

1. Set the oven to 200°C/400°F/gas mark 6.
2. Sift the flour with the seasonings.
3. In a large saucepan slowly heat the butter in the water and when completely melted bring up to a rolling boil. When the mixture is bubbling all over, tip in all the flour, take off the heat and beat well with a wooden spoon until the mixture will leave the sides of the pan. Allow to cool for about 10 minutes.
4. Beat in the eggs gradually until the mixture is smooth and shiny and of a 'dropping consistency' – you may not need the last few spoonfuls of egg. Stir in the diced cheese.
5. Spoon the mixture round the edge of a flattish greased ovenproof dish. Bake for 25 minutes. Pile the filling into the centre and sprinkle with the crumbs and grated cheese. Bake until the choux is well risen and golden and the filling is hot (about 15 minutes).

Chicken or Game Filling for Gougère

SERVES 4

1 medium onion, finely sliced
30g/1oz butter
110g/4oz large mushrooms, sliced
20g/¾oz flour
290ml/½ pint chicken stock
salt and freshly ground black pepper
10ml/2 teaspoons chopped fresh parsley
340g/12oz cooked game or chicken, shredded

1. Soften the onion in the butter over gentle heat. Add the mushrooms. Cook for 1 minute.
2. Stir in the flour. Cook for 1 minute.
3. Draw the pan off the heat and stir in the stock. Return to the heat. Bring up to the boil, stirring continuously. Season. Simmer for 1 minute.
4. Add the parsley and game or chicken and use as required.

RED BURGUNDY

Vinegar Chicken

SERVES 4

30g/1oz clarified butter (see page 138)
1.8 kg/4lb chicken, cut into 8 joints
5 large garlic cloves, unpeeled
75ml/5 tablespoons wine vinegar
290ml/½ pint dry white wine
30ml/2 tablespoons brandy
10ml/2 teaspoons pale French mustard
1 heaped teaspoon tomato purée
290ml/½ pint very fresh double cream
2 tomatoes, skinned and deseeded

1. Heat the butter and in it brown the chicken pieces, skin side first. Add the unpeeled garlic and cover the pan. Cook gently for 20 minutes or until the chicken is tender. Remove the chicken (keep warm) and pour off all the fat.
2. Add the vinegar to the pan, stirring well and scraping any sediment from the bottom. Boil rapidly until the liquid is reduced to about 30ml/2 tablespoons.
3. Add the wine, brandy, mustard and tomato purée to the remaining vinegar in the pan, mix well and boil to a thick sauce (about 5 minutes at a fast boil).
4. In a small heavy-bottomed saucepan boil the cream until reduced by half, stirring frequently to prevent burning. Take off the heat and fit a small wire sieve over the saucepan. Push the vinegar sauce through this, pressing the garlic cloves well to extract their pulp.
5. Stir the sauce and add salt and pepper as

necessary. Cut the tomato into thin strips and stir into the sauce. Arrange the chicken on a hot serving dish, and spoon over the sauce.

NOTE I: The deliciousness of this dish – and it is delicious – depends on the vigorous reduction of the vinegar and wine. If the acids are not properly boiled down the sauce is too sharp.
NOTE II: Five cloves of garlic seems a lot, but the resulting smooth sauce does not taste particularly strongly of garlic.

LIGHT RED

Chicken with Tomato and Coriander

SERVES 4
1.35kg/3lb chicken
seasoned flour
30ml/2 tablespoons oil
2 onions, finely chopped
1 garlic clove, crushed
400g/14oz tin plum tomatoes
1 bayleaf
10ml/2 teaspoons tomato purée
salt and freshly ground black pepper
30ml/2 tablespoons roughly chopped coriander

1. Joint the chicken into 8 pieces and dip in the seasoned flour.
2. Heat the oil in a sauté pan and brown the chicken all over. With a perforated spoon, take up the pieces and place them in a roasting dish or casserole.
3. Heat the oven to 180°C/350°F/gas mark 4.
4. Add the onions to the sauté pan and cook slowly for 10 minutes or until beginning to soften. Add the garlic and cook for a further minute. Add the tomatoes, bay leaf and tomato purée. Season with salt and pepper. Bring slowly to the boil, stirring continuously.
5. Pour this over the chicken joints. Cover and cook in the oven for 45-50 minutes or until the chicken is tender. Turn off the oven.
6. Lift the chicken joints out of the sauce. Trim them and arrange on a serving plate. Keep warm in the turned-off oven.
7. Skim any fat off the sauce, boil rapidly to a syrupy consistency. Stir the sauce well to amalgamate the tomatoes and to prevent the sauce from 'catching'. Add three-quarters of the coriander. Adjust the seasoning and pour the sauce over the chicken. Garnish with the remaining coriander.

LIGHT RED

Coq au Vin

SERVES 4
110g/4oz lean bacon, diced
55g/2oz clarified butter (see page 138)
8 button onions, peeled
12 button mushrooms
1.35 kg/3lb roasting chicken, jointed into 8 pieces
290ml/½ pint red wine
chicken stock
1 small garlic clove, crushed
bouquet garni (1 bay leaf, 1 sprig each of thyme and parsley and 1 celery stick, tied with string)
salt and pepper
20g/¾oz flour

To serve:
buttered rice
12 small triangular croûtons
15ml/1 tablespoon chopped parsley

1. Drop the bacon into a pan of boiling water for 30 seconds. Drain and dry well.
2. Put half the butter in a large heavy saucepan and slowly brown the bacon in it. Remove and reserve the bacon.
3. Add the onions, shaking the pan to brown them evenly all over.
4. Add the mushrooms (do not bother to peel them unless the skins are very tough). Fry fast for a further 2 minutes, then lift out all the fried food. Do not wash the pan.
5. Add the remaining butter to the juices in the pan and brown the chicken (skin side first) slowly and well on all sides. Tip off all the fat.
6. Return the vegetables and bacon pieces to the pan, and add the wine and enough stock to nearly cover the chicken pieces.
7. Add the crushed garlic, bouquet of herbs and salt and pepper.
8. With a wooden spoon move the pieces about

and stir the sauce until it comes to the boil. Stir well to loosen any sediment. Cover with a well-fitting lid and simmer slowly until the onions and chicken are tender (about 45 minutes).

9. Remove the bouquet garni. Lift out all the solid ingredients and put them on to a serving dish. Keep warm while you make the sauce.

10. Skim all the fat from the cooking liquid, putting 15ml/1 tablespoonful fat into a cup. Measure the liquid and make it up to 290ml/1/2 pint with more chicken stock or water. (If there is more than 290ml/1/2 pint boil the liquid rapidly to reduce it.)

11. Mix the flour with the fat in the cup, stir well and add a little of the hot cooking liquid to this paste. Return this mixture to the pan and bring gradually to the boil, stirring continuously. Simmer for 2 minutes until the sauce is smooth and shiny.

12. Neaten the chicken joints, arrange in a deep platter and spoon the sauce over the chicken. Garnish with the croûtons and chopped parsley.

NOTE: If there is time, marinate the chicken joints in the wine and bouquet garni for a few hours or overnight – this will improve the taste and colour. Dry the joints well before frying, or browning them will be difficult.

RED BURGUNDY

Chicken Sauté Normande

SERVES 4

1.8 kg/4lb roasting chicken, jointed into 8 pieces
45g/1 1/2oz clarified butter (see page 138)
1 shallot, chopped
15ml/1 tablespoon Calvados
10ml/2 teaspoons flour
225ml/8 fl oz dry cider
150ml/1/4 pint chicken stock
salt and freshly ground black pepper
bouquet garni (bay leaf, parsley stalks and 4 sprigs of thyme, tied together with string)
30ml/2 tablespoons cream

For the garnish:
2 dessert apples, peeled, cored and sliced
15g/1/2oz butter
chopped parsley

1. Heat the butter and in it brown the chicken pieces, skin side first.

2. Add the shallot and sauté for 2-3 minutes.

3. Add the Calvados, light it with a match and shake the pan until the flames die down. Remove the chicken joints.

4. Stir in the flour, cook for 1 minute. Remove from the heat. Add the cider. Blend well and add the stock. Return it to the heat and bring slowly to the boil, stirring continuously. Season and add the bouquet of herbs. Simmer for 2 minutes.

5. Replace the chicken, cover and simmer gently for 35-40 minutes until tender.

6. Meanwhile prepare the garnish by frying slices of peeled apple in the butter until golden brown on each side. Keep warm.

7. When the chicken is tender, lift it out and trim the joints neatly. Arrange on an ovenproof platter and keep warm.

8. Strain the sauce into a clean saucepan and reduce by boiling rapidly to the required consistency. Add the cream and season to taste.

9. Garnish with apple slices and sprinkle with chopped parsley.

LIGHT FRUITY RED

Chicken with Thyme

This chicken dish is delicious but great care must be taken not to allow the sauce to curdle – make sure that there is virtually no fat in the 75ml/ 5 tablespoons of liquor before you add the butter.

SERVES 4

1.8 kg/4lb chicken, jointed into 8 pieces
200g/7oz unsalted butter
2 sprigs thyme
1/2 lemon
pinch of sugar
salt and freshly ground black pepper
60ml/4 tablespoons white wine
150ml/1/4 pint water
30ml/2 tablespoons chopped thyme
bunch of watercress

Salad of Roast Tomatoes and Spring Onions.

Above: Dry-fried Prawns with Coriander. Right: Sea Bass with Black Bean Sauce.

Left: Skate with Spinach and Bacon. Above: Steamed Trout Fillets with Tomato and Ginger Sauce.

Above: Chicken with Prunes. Right: Mustard Grilled Chicken.

Left: Warm Chicken Salad. Above: Stuffed Boned Duck.

Above: Venison with Lemon and Redcurrant Sauce and Rösti Potatoes. Right: Partridge with Lentils.

Left: Cold Game Pie with Orange and Endive Salad. Above: Steak and Kidney Pudding.

Above: Gaeng Ped Nua (Spicy Red Beef). Right: Bacon Noisettes with Sweet Onion Purée.

Above: Lamb Steak à la Catalane with Lentils.

1. Heat 30g/1oz of the butter in a large sauté pan. Cut the remaining butter into small pieces and chill in the refrigerator.
2. Brown the chicken joints, skin side down. Add the thyme, lemon, sugar, salt, pepper, white wine and water. Cover and simmer for 25-30 minutes or until tender.
3. Remove the chicken from the pan and keep warm while you make the sauce. Discard the lemon and thyme. Skim off all the fat.
4. Add 75ml/5 tablespoons of water to the pan and mix well, scraping up any sediment. Reduce, by boiling rapidly, to about 75ml/5 tablespoons of liquor, and, when simmering, using a wire whisk, gradually add the well-chilled butter piece by piece. The process should take about 2 minutes and the sauce should become thick and creamy. Add the chopped fresh thyme. Season to taste and garnish with watercress.

DRY WHITE/ROSE

Chicken Paprika

SERVES 4
1.8 kg/4lb chicken
15ml/1 tablespoon oil
15ml/1 tablespoon butter
1 onion, finely sliced
30ml/2 level tablespoons paprika
200g/7oz can tomatoes
100ml/3½ fl oz white wine
570ml/1 pint chicken stock
1 bay leaf
2 slices lemon
1 parsley stalk
salt and freshly ground black pepper
150ml/¼ pint white sauce (see page 221)

For the garnish:
15ml/1 tablespoon soured cream
chopped parsley

1. Wash the chicken and wipe dry. Set the oven to 200°C/400°F/gas mark 6.
2. Heat the oil in a frying pan and when hot add the butter. When the butter is foaming, add the chicken and brown it well all over. Take it out and put into a casserole.
3. Fry the onion in the oil and butter and when just beginning to brown, reduce the heat and add the paprika. Cook for 2-3 minutes. Stir in the tomatoes, wine and stock. Add the bay leaf, lemon slices and parsley stalk. Season well. When boiling, pour over the chicken.
4. Cover and bake in the oven for about 1 hour or until the chicken is cooked.
5. When the chicken is tender, take it out of the casserole, remove the bay leaf, parsley stalk and lemon slices. Carefully skim off the fat with a spoon, or soak up and lift off the fat by laying absorbent paper on the surface of the sauce. Liquidize the sauce and push it through a sieve.
6. Beat the paprika sauce into the prepared white sauce until completely incorporated and smooth.
7. Joint the chicken neatly into 8 pieces and arrange on a serving dish. Heat up the sauce and spoon it over the chicken. Trickle over the soured cream and sprinkle with chopped parsley.

LIGHT RED

Jambonneaux de Poulet

SERVES 2
55g/2oz cooked ham, minced
55g/2oz cooked chicken livers, mashed
55g/2oz butter, softened
salt and freshly ground black pepper
2 legs taken from 1 large chicken
45g/1½oz clarified butter for frying (see page 138)
110g/4oz mixed finely chopped onion, celery and carrot (mirepoix)
75ml/5 tablespoons Madeira
225ml/8 fl oz chicken stock
1 bay leaf
sprig of watercress

1. Beat together the ham, chicken livers and softened butter. Taste and add pepper or salt if needed.
2. Remove the bone from the chicken legs without splitting the skin, working carefully from the thick end. Stuff the ham mixture into the boned-out chicken legs. With a trussing needle and fine string sew up the chicken joints

so that they resemble miniature hams.
3. Melt half the butter in a flameproof casserole. When it is foaming and hot, add the chicken legs and brown lightly all over, then remove from the pan. Add the remaining butter to the casserole with the mirepoix of vegetables. Fry until the vegetables are lightly brown.
4. Place the jambonneaux (chicken legs) on top of the vegetables. Heat the Madeira in a small pan or ladle held over the flame. When hot set it alight with a match and pour it, flaming, into the pan. Add the chicken stock, bay leaf, salt and pepper. Bring to the boil, cover and simmer slowly for 1 hour. Check to ensure that not all the liquid is evaporating - if so, simply add extra water.
5. When the chicken is cooked (when pierced with a skewer the juices that run out should be clear, not pink), remove to a plate and keep warm. Remove the string.
6. Strain the cooking liquor and press the vegetables to extract most of the juice. Boil to reduce to a syrupy consistency, checking the seasoning. Serve the sauce separately in a warmed gravy boat. Garnish the jambonneaux with a sprig of watercress.

DRY WHITE

Chicken Legs with Orange Vinaigrette

SERVES 4
6 chicken legs (thigh and drumstick intact)
110g/4oz sausagemeat
4 cooked French beans, chopped
1 cooked carrot, diced
30ml/2 tablespoons cream
1 small garlic clove, crushed
pepper and salt
55g/2oz butter, melted

For the orange vinaigrette:
45ml/3 tablespoons salad oil
5ml/1 teaspoon frozen concentrated orange juice
2.5ml/½ teaspoon onion juice
salt and freshly ground black pepper

1. Set the oven to 200°C/400°F/gas mark 6.
2. Bone 4 chicken legs, working up from both ends with a small sharp knife and scraping the flesh back from the bones until you can pull them out. Bone the other 2 legs, but less carefully, and skin them. Mince the flesh of these 2 and mix with the sausagemeat.
3. Mix the diced beans and carrot with the minced meat and the cream, garlic and a little salt and pepper. Spoon this mixture into the 4 boned legs. Dip 4 small pieces of muslin into the melted butter, wrap the chicken legs in this muslin and tie them up firmly. The parcels should look rather like crackers.
4. Bake the parcels for 35 minutes. Unwrap and leave to get cold and then chill in the refrigerator.
5. Slice the legs into thin rings and arrange on a platter. Whisk together the orange vinaigrette ingredients and spoon over the chicken.

FULL DRY WHITE

Tarragon Chicken

SERVES 4
1.8 kg/4lb roasting chicken
55g/2oz clarified butter (see page 138)
slice of lemon
4 sprigs tarragon
salt and pepper
150ml/¼ pint chicken stock
20g/¾oz flour, sifted
150ml/¼ pint double cream
salt and pepper

1. Heat the oven to 200°C/400°F/gas mark 6. Wipe the inside and outside of the chicken. Place a small nut of the butter, the lemon slice and half the tarragon inside the cavity. Season inside and out with salt and pepper.
2. Melt the remaining butter in a casserole the size of the chicken and brown all sides of the bird in it. Place the giblets (except the liver) in the casserole, pour over the stock, cover with a lid and place in the oven. Leave to cook for 1¼ hours or until the juice runs out clear, rather than pink, when the thigh is pierced with a skewer.
3. Remove the chicken, draining the juices back into the casserole. Joint the chicken neatly and put the pieces in a covered dish. Keep warm.

4. Skim all the fat from the stock. Mix 15ml/1 tablespoon of this fat with the flour in a teacup. When thoroughly blended pour more of the stock into the cup and mix well. Return this to the casserole and stir over direct heat until boiling. Simmer for 5 minutes.
5. Strain into a clean saucepan and add the remaining sprigs of tarragon. Simmer for 1-2 minutes, then stir in the cream. Taste and season if necessary.
6. Spoon over the chicken joints and serve.

WHITE BURGUNDY

Boned Stuffed Chicken

The filling for Leith's Good Food's Boned Duck (see page 307) is also delicious in a boned chicken.

SERVES 6
1.8 kg/4lb chicken
55g/2oz butter, melted

For the stuffing:
15g/½oz butter
1 small onion, finely chopped
225g/8oz good quality sausagemeat
30ml/2 tablespoons fresh white breadcrumbs
1 small apple, chopped
pinch of sage
1 egg
salt and freshly ground black pepper

For the garnish:
bunch of watercress

1. Bone the chicken completely, including the legs and wings (see page 280).
2. Make the stuffing: melt the butter, add the onion and cook until soft but not coloured. Mix together the sausagemeat, onion, breadcrumbs, apple, sage and egg and season well with salt and pepper. Beat very well.
3. Use this stuffing to fill the boned chicken. Draw up the sides and wrap the chicken in a piece of muslin saturated with the melted butter. Tie the chicken at either end so that it resembles a Christmas cracker.
4. Set the oven to 200°C/400°F/gas mark 6.
5. Place the chicken on a wire rack over a roasting tin and bake for 1½ hours.
6. Unwrap the chicken and serve hot or cold garnished with the watercress.

DRY WHITE/ROSE

Boned Chicken with Spinach and Ricotta

SERVES 6
1.8kg/4lb chicken, boned (see page 280)
110g/4oz ricotta cheese
1 egg, beaten
1.35kg/3lb spinach, cooked and chopped
2 sticks celery, finely chopped
pinch of mace
lemon juice
salt and freshly ground pepper
chicken stock

1. Open the chicken out on a board, skin side down. Remove any excess fat. Season the flesh with a little pepper.
2. Beat together the ricotta cheese and egg until quite smooth. Add the spinach, celery and mace and season with lemon juice, salt and pepper.
3. Stuff the chicken with this mixture, wrap in a piece of muslin and tie the ends up tightly.
4. Place the chicken in a large saucepan and add enough chicken stock to nearly cover the chicken. Bring the stock to the boil, reduce the heat and simmer the chicken for 1¼ hours.
5. When cooked, remove the chicken from the stock and allow to cool. When completely cold, remove the muslin and slice the chicken.

LIGHT RED

Boned Chicken with Leeks

SERVES 6
1.35kg/3lb chicken, boned (see page 280)
6 leeks
1 large carrot, peeled
mint leaves, washed
110g/4oz ricotta cheese
salt and freshly ground black pepper

To serve:
red pepper sauce (see page 231)

1. Preheat the oven to 200°C/400°F/gas mark 6.
2. Lay the chicken skin side down. Remove any large pieces of fat and season it lightly. Rearrange the flesh, by gently pushing it (particularly the thighs and breast) so that it is fairly evenly distributed over the skin.
3. Cut the leeks in half lengthways and blanch for 2 minutes in boiling water. Refresh them under running cold water. Drain well on absorbent paper. Pare the peeled carrot into long thin ribbons. Blanch for 1 minute. Refresh under running cold water and drain on absorbent paper.
4. Layer the leeks, carrot ribbons, mint and ricotta in the centre of the chicken. Try to imagine how it will look when carved and make it look attractive. Season it lightly.
5. Fold the sides of the chicken up to make a roll. Wrap the chicken in a damp piece of muslin. Tie the ends of the cloth together.
6. Bake the chicken for $1^1/4$ hours on a wire rack in a roasting tin. Unwrap and leave it to get completely cold.
7. Carve the chicken into slices and serve the red pepper sauce separately.

DRY WHITE

Boned Stuffed Poussins

SERVES 2
2 poussins
85g/3oz butter
1 large onion, finely chopped
110g/4oz button mushrooms, sliced
55g/2oz fresh white breadcrumbs
30ml/2 tablespoons finely chopped fresh parsley
grated rind of $^1/4$ lemon
30g/1oz prunes, soaked overnight
30g/1oz dried apricots, soaked overnight
salt and freshly ground black pepper
$^1/2$ egg, beaten
170g/6oz mixed chopped onion, carrot, turnip and celery (mirepoix)
290ml/$^1/2$ pint chicken stock (made from the bones of the poussin)
1 bay leaf
bunch of watercress

1. Bone the poussins without removing the legs or wings (see page 280).
2. Make the stuffing: melt 30g/1oz of the butter, add the onion and cook slowly until soft but not coloured. Add the mushrooms and cook for 1 minute further.
3. Mix the onions and mushrooms with the breadcrumbs, parsley and lemon rind. Stone and chop the prunes and chop the apricots. Add them both to the stuffing. Season with salt and pepper and add the egg. Beat very well.
4. Lay the poussins, skin side down, flat on the table top. Divide the stuffing between them and sew them up using cotton or very fine string. Try to shape them to their original form.
5. Melt half the remaining butter in a flameproof casserole. When it is foaming, add the poussins and brown lightly all over, then remove them from the pan.
6. Add the remaining butter to the casserole with the mirepoix of diced vegetables. Fry until the vegetables are lightly browned.
7. Set the poussins on top of the vegetables. Add the chicken stock, bay leaf, salt and pepper. Bring to the boil, cover and simmer slowly for 40-50 minutes.
8. When the poussins are cooked (when pierced with a skewer the juices that run out should be

clear, not pink), place them on a plate and remove the cotton or string. Keep warm.

9. Press the vegetables through a sieve to extract most of their juices, and discard the vegetables. Boil to reduce to a syrupy consistency. Season to taste.

10. Garnish the poussins with watercress and serve the sauce separately.

WHITE ALSACE

Boned Stuffed Poussins with Shiitake Mushrooms and Wild Rice

SERVES 4

4 poussins, boned
85g/3oz shiitake mushrooms, sliced
4 spring onions, chopped
30g/1oz butter
85g/3oz rice, cooked
30g/1oz wild rice, cooked
30g/1oz pistachio nuts, roughly chopped
1 egg, beaten
salt and freshly ground black pepper
a little oil
15g/½oz butter
1 small onion, finely chopped
1 small carrot, finely chopped
1 stick celery, finely chopped
290ml/½ pint chicken stock
1 bay leaf

To garnish:
bunch of watercress

1. Bone the poussins without removing the legs or wings (see page 280).

2. Make the stuffing: cook the mushrooms slowly in the butter, with the spring onions, for 3 minutes. Add to the rices with the pistachio nuts. Bind with the beaten egg and season to taste with salt and pepper.

3. Lay the poussins, skin side down, flat on the table top. Divide the stuffing between them and sew them up using cotton or very fine string. Try to shape them to their original form.

4. Heat the oil in a flameproof casserole, add the butter and when foaming add the poussins, 2 at a time, and brown lightly all over. Remove to a plate.

5. Add the onion, carrot and celery to the pan and fry until lightly browned. Set the poussins on top of the vegetables. Add the chicken stock, bay leaf, salt and pepper. Bring up to the boil, cover and simmer for 40-50 minutes.

6. When the poussins are cooked, remove to a warmed serving plate. Remove the string or cotton.

7. Meanwhile, make the sauce: skim the fat from the top of the cooking juices. Strain the sauce, with a little mirepoix, into a clean saucepan. Boil rapidly to a syrupy consistency. (Check that the sauce is not too strong – if necessary it can be thickened with a little beurre manié and need not be reduced.) Taste and season.

8. Arrange the poussins on a warm serving plate. Garnish with watercress.

9. Heat the sauce and pour into a warm sauce-boat. Serve the sauce separately.

LIGHT RED

Chicken Croquettes

SERVES 4

55g/2oz butter
1 small onion, chopped
30g/1oz mushrooms, chopped
55g/2oz flour
290ml/½ pint milk, or milk and chicken stock mixed
salt and pepper
5ml/1 teaspoon chopped parsley
oil for deep-frying
1 egg yolk
lemon juice
285g/10oz cooked chicken, diced finely or minced
seasoned flour
1 egg, beaten
dry white breadcrumbs

1. Melt the butter and add the onion. When the onion is soft but not coloured, add the mushrooms and cook for 1 minute.

2. Add the flour and cook, stirring, for 1 minute. Draw the pan off the heat and stir in the milk.

Return to the heat and bring slowly up to the boil, stirring continuously. Simmer for 2-3 minutes, season and add the parsley. Remove from the heat and allow to get completely cold. It should be very thick.
3. Meanwhile, heat the oil until a crumb will sizzle in it.
4. When the sauce is cold, beat in the egg yolk, add a squeeze of lemon juice and stir in the chicken flesh.
5. With floured hands, shape the mixture into cylinders about 3.5cm/1½ inches long.
6. Coat with beaten egg and dip into breadcrumbs.
7. Deep-fry the croquettes until golden brown. Drain well and serve at once.

LIGHT RED

Chicken Kiev

SERVES 4
110g/4oz butter, softened
15ml/1 tablespoon chopped fresh parsley
squeeze of lemon juice
salt and freshly ground black pepper
4 chicken supremes
seasoned flour
beaten egg
dried white breadcrumbs
oil for deep-frying

1. Mix the butter with the parsley, lemon juice, salt and pepper. Divide the butter into 4 pieces, shape into rectangles and chill well.
2. Remove the skin and bone from the chicken breasts. You should have 4 equal-sized pieces of chicken. With a sharp knife split the breasts almost in half horizontally and open them out so that you have a chicken escalope. Put them between sheets of wet greaseproof paper and, using a rolling pin, carefully beat the chicken pieces to flatten the meat out thinly.
3. Place a piece of the prepared butter in the centre of each chicken piece. Roll up so that the butter is completely wrapped. Dust lightly with seasoned flour. Dip into beaten egg, then roll carefully in the crumbs. Chill for 30 minutes.
4. Brush with more beaten egg and roll again in dried crumbs. Leave to chill for another 30 minutes.
5. Heat the oil until a crumb will sizzle vigorously in it. Fry the chicken pieces in the oil for 8 minutes. Drain well on absorbent paper and serve.

NOTE I: Crushed garlic is frequently added to the butter inside the chicken. Though frowned on by classic chefs, this is quite delicious. Other flavourings, such as chopped tarragon, smooth liver pâté, mashed anchovies, or a duxelles of mushrooms, can be good too. But the butter is the essential ingredient, providing flavour, moisture and drama all at once.
NOTE II: If desired, the small wing bone at the shoulder end of the breast can be left in place. When the chicken escalope is rolled up, the bone protrudes from the 'parcel', giving the breast the appearance of a drumstick.

BEAUJOLAIS

French Roast Chicken

SERVES 4
1.8 kg/4lb roasting chicken with giblets
butter
pepper and salt
slice of onion
bay leaf
few parsley stalks

For the gravy:
About 10ml/2 teaspoons flour
190ml/⅓ pint chicken stock or vegetable water

1. Set the oven to 200°C/400°F/gas mark 6.
2. Smear a little butter all over the chicken. Season inside and out with pepper only (no salt). Put the bird breast side down in the roasting tin.
3. Put all the giblets (except the liver) and the neck into the pan with the chicken. Add the onion, bay leaf and parsley stalks. Pour in a cup of water. Roast the bird for 30 minutes.
4. Take out, season all over with salt, turn the bird right side up and baste it with the fat and juices from the pan. Return to the oven.
5. Check how the chicken is doing periodically. It will take 60-80 minutes. It is cooked when the

leg bones wobble loosely and independently from the body. Baste occasionally as it cooks, and cover with foil or greaseproof paper if it is browning too much. Remove the cooked chicken to a serving dish and keep warm while making the gravy.
6. Place the pan with its juices on a low heat on top of the cooker. Skim off most of the fat.
7. Whisk in enough flour to absorb the remaining fat.
8. Add the chicken stock or vegetable water and stir until the sauce boils. Strain into a gravy boat.

LIGHT RED

English Roast Chicken

SERVES 4
1.8 kg/4lb roasting chicken
slice of lemon
15g/1/2oz butter
freshly ground black pepper

For the stuffing:
30g/1oz butter
1 onion, finely chopped
55g/2oz fresh breadcrumbs
1 small cooking apple, peeled and grated
10ml/2 teaspoons chopped mixed fresh herbs
grated rind 1/2 lemon
beaten egg
salt and pepper

For the garnish:
4 chipolata sausages
4 rashers rindless streaky bacon

For the gravy:
5ml/1 teaspoon flour
290ml/ 1/2 pint chicken stock (made from the neck and giblets, see page 219)

To accompany:
bread sauce (see page 232)

1. Set the oven to 200°C/400°F/gas mark 6.
2. Rub the chicken all over with the lemon slice.
3. Start the stuffing by melting the butter and frying the onion until soft but not coloured.
4. Put the breadcrumbs, cooking apple, herbs and lemon rind together in a mixing bowl.
5. Add the softened onion and enough beaten egg to bind the mixture together. Do not make it too wet. Season to taste.
6. Stuff the chicken from the neck end, making sure the breast is well plumped. Draw the neck skin flap down to cover the stuffing. Secure with a skewer if necessary.
7. Smear a little butter all over the chicken and season with salt and pepper. Roast for about 1 1/2 hours or until the juices run clear when the thigh is pierced with a skewer.
8. Meanwhile, make each chipolata sausage into two cocktail-sized ones by twisting gently in the middle. Cut each bacon rasher into short lengths and roll them up.
9. After the chicken has been cooking for 1 hour in the oven put the sausages and bacon rolls in the same pan, wedging the bacon rolls so that they cannot come undone.
10. Baste occasionally and check that the sausages and bacon are not sticking to the side of the tin and getting burnt.
11. When the chicken is cooked, lift it out on to a warm serving dish. Trim off the wing tips and tops of the drumsticks, surround with the bacon rolls and sausages and keep warm while you make the gravy.
12. Slowly pour off all but 15ml/1 tablespoon fat from the roasting pan, taking care to keep any juices. Add the flour and stir over heat for 1 minute. Add the chicken stock and stir until the sauce boils. Simmer for 3 minutes. Taste and add more pepper and salt if necessary. Strain into a gravy boat.
13. Serve the chicken with bread sauce and gravy.

NOTE I: English chicken is usually stuffed from the neck end or breast but the stuffing may be put into the body cavity if preferred.
NOTE II: The chicken looks neater if it is trussed after stuffing, but it is more difficult to get the thighs cooked without the breast drying out if this is done.

LIGHT RED

Chicken with Prunes

SERVES 4
1.8 kg/4lb chicken with giblets
30g/1oz butter
few slices onion
slice of lemon
salt and freshly ground black pepper
1 bay leaf
few slices carrot

For the sauce:
15g/½oz butter
12 shallots, peeled
12 stoned cooked prunes
15ml/1 tablespoon sugar
15ml/1 tablespoon vinegar

For the garnish:
bunch of watercress

1. Set the oven to 200°C/400°F/gas mark 6.
2. Wipe the chicken. Place half the butter, half the onion and the lemon in the breast cavity. Put, breast side down, in a roasting dish with 5mm/¼inch water. Spread the remaining butter over the chicken and season with salt and pepper. Add the giblets (except the liver), the bay leaf, remaining onion and carrot to the water.
3. Roast for 1-¼hours, basting 3 or 4 times and turning the bird over at half-time. When the chicken is cooked, clear juices will run from the thigh when pierced with a skewer.
4. Meanwhile, prepare the sauce: melt the butter and when foaming add the shallots. Cover and cook slowly, shaking the pan occasionally to prevent them burning but allowing them to brown all over. Add the prunes to the pan and reduce the heat to a minimum.
5. Slowly melt the sugar in a heavy saucepan, tilting and turning it as necessary to get an even pale caramel colour. Add the vinegar – be sure to stand back as it will hiss and splutter. Add 30ml/2 tablespoons chicken stock from the bottom of the roasting pan. Simmer until the caramel is dissolved. Season if necessary.
6. Joint the chicken and arrange on a serving dish. Spoon over the prunes and shallots and glaze with the caramel sauce. Garnish with watercress.

CLARET

Lemon Chicken

SERVES 4
55g/2oz unsalted butter
juice of 2 small lemons
2 double poussins
10ml/2 teaspoons sugar
paprika
salt and freshly ground black pepper
watercress

1. Melt the butter in a large saucepan and add the lemon juice.
2. Add the whole poussinss and cover the pan with the lid.
3. Cook on a gentle heat for 30 minutes, turning the chickens to brown slightly on all sides. They should now be partially cooked, and the butter and lemon juice in the pan should be brown but not burnt.
4. Take out the birds and split them in two.
5. Heat the grill. Lay the portions of chicken cut side up on the grill tray. Brush them with some of the lemon juice and butter from the saucepan. Sprinkle with half of the sugar and plenty of paprika and pepper. Grill slowly for about 15 minutes or until a really good brown.
6. Turn the joints over and again brush with lemon juice and butter and sprinkle with sugar, paprika and pepper. Grill for a further 15 minutes until cooked through and very dark – almost, but not quite, charred. Sprinkle with salt.
7. Arrange on a heated dish, pour over the juices from the grill pan and garnish with sprigs of watercress.

WHITE ALSACE

Mustard Grilled Chicken

Although this is called grilled chicken it is partially baked to ensure that the chicken is cooked without becoming burnt.

SERVES 4
30g/1oz butter
30ml/2 tablespoons French mustard
2kg/4½lb chicken

juice of 1 lemon
15ml/1 teaspoon sugar
15ml/1 teaspoon paprika
freshly ground black pepper
few sprigs of watercress

1. Mix together the butter and mustard.
2. Preheat the oven to 200°C/400°F/gas mark 6.
3. Joint the chicken into 8. Cut off the wing tips and the knuckles. Remove any small feathers.
4. Spread each chicken joint on the underside with half the mustard mixture. Sprinkle with half the lemon juice, sugar and paprika. Season with pepper. Bake for 10 minutes.
5. Turn the chicken over and spread again with the mustard mixture. Sprinkle with the rest of the paprika, lemon juice and sugar. Season with pepper. Bake for a further 10 minutes.
6. Heat up the grill.
7. Arrange the joints under the grill in such a way that the larger joints are closest to the strongest heat and that the breast joints are near the edge of the grill.
8. Grill until dark and crisp but be very careful not to let the joints burn.
9. Arrange the joints neatly on a flat serving dish. Pour over the juices from the pan and garnish with watercress.

LIGHT RED

Spatchcock Grilled Chicken

SERVES 4
4 x 450g/1lb poussins
salt and freshly ground black pepper
pinch of cayenne
lemon juice
55g/2oz butter
15g/½oz Parmesan cheese, grated

For the garnish:
watercress
French dressing (see page 228)
sauce Robert (see page 223)

1. Split the chickens down one side of the backbone with a pair of poultry shears or kitchen scissors. Cut down the other side of the backbone to remove it. Open out the chickens and flatten well on a board by pressing with the heel of your hand. Skewer the birds in position, i.e. flat and open.
2. Season well with salt, pepper and cayenne and sprinkle with lemon juice. If possible, leave for 1 hour.
3. Heat the grill. Brush the cut side of the chickens with melted butter. Place under the grill for about 12 minutes or until a good golden brown, brushing with the pan juices frequently. Turn over, brush again and grill for a further 7 minutes or until the chicken is cooked.
4. Brush once more with the hot butter and sprinkle with the Parmesan cheese. Grill until golden brown and crisp. Arrange on a serving dish and garnish with watercress dipped in French dressing. Serve with sauce Robert.

LIGHT RED

Chicken and Beanshoot Salad

SERVES 6
1.8 kg/4lb cooked chicken, preferably poached
450g/1lb beanshoots
1 small onion, finely chopped
15ml/1 tablespoon chopped mint
French dressing (see page 228)
soy sauce

1. Cut the chicken flesh into 2.5cm/1 inch strips, discarding the skin and bones. Mix with the washed but raw beanshoots.
2. Add the onion and mint to the French dressing and mix with the chicken and beanshoots.
3. Pile into a serving dish and sprinkle liberally with soy sauce.

DRY WHITE

Chicken Chaudfroid

This is a cold chicken coated with a white sauce, glazed with aspic jelly, and garnished with slices of truffle or mushroom. The chicken should be cooked the day before serving because the stock in which it is cooked becomes the aspic jelly. The recipe calls for a whole chicken but poached chicken supremes can be used in its place.

SERVES 4
1.8 kg/4lb chicken, not trussed
1 onion, sliced
½ carrot
2 bay leaves
sprig of parsley
6 peppercorns
2.5ml/½ teaspoon salt

For the aspic jelly:
860ml/1½ pints chicken stock (see page 219)
55g/2oz gelatine
75ml/5 tablespoons white wine
75ml/5 tablespoons sherry
15ml/1 tablespoon tarragon vinegar
3 egg whites
3 egg shells, crushed

For the chaudfroid sauce:
1 bay leaf
4 peppercorns
slice of onion
blade of mace
sprig of parsley
425ml/¾ pint milk
30g/1oz butter
30g/1oz flour
salt
150ml/¼ pint chicken aspic
15g/½oz gelatine
75ml/5 tablespoons cream

For the garnish:
fine slices cooked button mushroom or truffle or tarragon leaves
1 punnet mustard and cress

1. On the first day, place the chicken in a saucepan, just cover with cold water, add the vegetables, herbs, peppercorns and salt. Bring to the boil, cover and simmer gently until the chicken is tender (about 1¼ hours). When it is cooked, a skewer will glide easily into the thigh, and the drumstick should feel loose.
2. Remove the bird from the pan, allow it to cool, loosely cover with cling film, and place it in the refrigerator overnight. Strain the stock, taste and season and leave it to cool. If possible, refrigerate it (this will set the fat and make it easier to remove the next day).
3. The next day, remove all the fat from the chicken stock. Put the stock (which should be about 860ml/1½ pints) and gelatine into a clean pan. Add the wine, sherry and vinegar. Place over a gentle heat to dissolve the gelatine. Allow to cool.
4. Put the egg white and the crushed shells into the stock. Place over the heat and whisk steadily with a balloon whisk until the mixture begins to boil. Stop whisking immediately, and draw the pan off the heat. Allow the mixture to subside. Take care not to break the crust formed by the egg white.
5. Bring the aspic just to the boil again, and again allow to subside. Repeat this once more (the egg white will trap the sediment in the stock and clear the aspic). Allow to cool for 2 minutes.
6. Fix a double layer of fine muslin or white kitchen paper over a clean basin and carefully strain the aspic through it, taking care to hold the egg-white crust back. When all the liquid is through (or almost all of it) allow the egg white to slip into the muslin or kitchen paper. Then strain the aspic again – this time through both egg white crust and cloth. Do not try to hurry the process by squeezing the cloth, or murky aspic will result.
7. Make the chaudfroid sauce: place the bay leaf, peppercorns, onion slice, mace and parsley sprig in a saucepan with the milk. Set over a gentle heat and bring slowly to the boil. Leave to cool for 20 minutes.
8. Melt the butter, add the flour and cook for 1 minute. Draw off the heat and slowly, stirring all the time, strain the milk into the pan. Return the pan to the heat and bring slowly up to the boil, stirring continually until you have a slightly thickened shiny sauce. Season well with salt and simmer gently for 5 minutes.
9. In a small pan put 100ml/3 fl oz of the aspic,

and sprinkle on the gelatine. Allow to soak for 10 minutes, then heat gently until clear and warm. Strain this into the white sauce with the cream. Taste and add more salt if necessary. The sauce must be very smooth and shiny: it can be strained through a tammy cloth or strainer or whizzed in a liquidizer to give it a good sheen. Stir the sauce as it cools and begins to set. When it is the consistency of thick cream it is ready to use for coating.

10. To prepare the chicken, skin and joint it very neatly into 4 or 8 pieces, removing the wing tips and drumstick knuckles. Place the pieces on a wire rack with a tray underneath.

11. Coat each chicken joint very carefully with the nearly set chaudfroid sauce. Allow to set and if necessary give it a second coating, scraping extra sauce (which will need reheating slightly to return it to coating consistency) from the tray underneath the wire rack.

12. When nearly set, arrange the slices of mushroom or truffle or tarragon leaves in a formal simple pattern on each chicken piece. Allow to set.

13. Coat with some of the cool but still liquid aspic. Allow to set. Give a second and perhaps third coating, allowing each coating to set before attempting the next.

14. Pour the remaining aspic on to a shallow tray. Allow to set, then cut it into neat dice. Use it to cover a large flat serving dish and make a slight dome in the centre. Arrange the chicken chaudfroid around this and surround with small clumps of mustard and cress.

NOTE I: Chaudfroid is classically decorated with sliced truffles. These are delicious if fresh but disappointing as well as expensive if bought in tins. Mushrooms make an inexpensive and satisfactory substitute. Fresh tarragon leaves are pretty and give the dish a delicious flavour.
NOTE II: If the aspic is less than crystal clear it is wise not to chop it, which seems to emphasize its murkiness.

WHITE BURGUNDY

Chicken Baked in a Brick

If you have no chicken brick an earthenware casserole with a well-fitting lid will do, but the brick, which is chicken-shaped, is particularly good as it closely fits the chicken, with little space for the evaporation of juices. It is a modern version of the ancient method of covering a gutted bird, feathers and all, in wet clay, then baking it. When the hardened clay was broken off, the feathers came away with it, leaving the chicken cooked, succulent and tender. Modern bricks, not made of wet clay, are designed for plucked birds!

SERVES 4
1.8 kg/4lb chicken
handful of fresh herbs
lemon
melted butter or olive oil
salt and freshly ground black pepper

1. Clean the chicken. Place the herbs and lemon inside the body cavity.

2. Brush the chicken with the butter or oil and season with salt and pepper.

3. Cover with the lid. Place in a cold oven. Set the oven to 230°C/450°F/gas mark 8 and bake for 2 hours. Serve the juices with the chicken.

NOTE I: If the chicken is to be served cold, when cooked, remove the lid and leave to cool.
NOTE II: The chicken can also be put into a hot oven. It will then take about $1^1/_2$ hours.
NOTE III: The manufacturers of chicken bricks generally advise the user not to wash the brick in detergent. Simply rinse in very hot water and put back in the warm oven to dry out.

DRY WHITE/ROSE

Chicken à la King

SERVES 6

1.8 kg/4lb chicken, not trussed
1 small onion, sliced
1 small carrot, sliced
2 bay leaves
few parsley stalks
salt
6 peppercorns
45g/1½oz butter
1 onion, finely sliced
1 small green pepper, deseeded and sliced
1 tinned pimento, sliced
110g/4oz mushrooms, sliced
45g/1½oz flour
15ml/1 tablespoon sherry
150ml/¼ pint milk
45ml/3 tablespoons single cream
freshly ground black pepper

To serve:
boiled rice

1. Put a large pan of water on to simmer with the onion, carrot, bay leaves, parsley stalks, salt and peppercorns. Add the whole chicken, breast side up. Cover and simmer until tender (about 1 hour). To test if the chicken is cooked, push a skewer into the thickest part of the thigh. It should glide in easily. Also the drumstick should be loose and wobbly.
2. Remove the chicken from the stock and allow both to become completely cold.
3. Skim the fat off the stock. Reduce the stock by rapid boiling until it measures 425ml/¾pint.
4. Skin the chicken and remove the bones.
5. Melt the butter, add the sliced onion and cook gently for 2 minutes. Add the green pepper and cook for a further minute. Add the pimento, mushrooms and flour and cook, stirring for 1 minute.
6. Remove the pan from the heat and add the reduced stock. Mix well and return the pan to the heat. Bring slowly to the boil, stirring continuously. Add the sherry. Simmer for 1-2 minutes.
7. Add the milk and cream and reheat without boiling. Season with salt and pepper.
8. Add the chicken in large pieces and allow to warm through without boiling. Check the seasoning.
9. Serve with boiled rice.

AUSTRALIAN/CALIFORNIAN CHARDONNAY

Poussins with Pernod

SERVES 4

4 x 450g/1lb one-portion poussins
seasoned flour
30g/1oz butter
2 shallots, finely chopped
75ml/5 tablespoons Pernod

For the garnish:
lemon wedges
chopped parsley

1. Bone the poussins completely (see page 280).
2. Open the poussins out; put them between 2 pieces of wet greaseproof paper and flatten them with a wooden mallet or rolling pin.
3. Dip them in seasoned flour and shake off any excess flour.
4. Melt the butter in a large sauté pan. When foaming, brown the poussins for about 2 minutes on each side. Reduce the temperature and add the shallots. Continue to sauté the poussins for about 2 further minutes on each side.
5. Increase the temperature and pour in the Pernod. When hot, set the alcohol alight with a match and turn off the heat. When the flames die away, scrape the pan with a spoon to loosen any sediment stuck to the bottom.
6. Take out the poussins; arrange on a warm serving dish. Boil up the pan juices and pour, sizzling, over the poussins. Garnish with lemon wedges and parsley and serve immediately.

NOTE : Two-portion poussins are called 'double' poussins, whereas one-portion birds are 'single' birds.

SPICY DRY WHITE

Chicken Curry with Almonds

SERVES 8

8 chicken breasts
60ml/4 tablespoons sunflower oil
85g/3oz blanched almonds
10ml/2 teaspoons ground cardamom
5ml/1 teaspoon ground cloves
5ml/1 teaspoon ground chilli
20ml/4 teaspoons ground cumin
20ml/4 teaspoons ground coriander
10ml/2 teaspoons ground turmeric
2 onions, finely chopped
2 garlic cloves, crushed
2.5cm/1inch piece root ginger, finely chopped
400g//14oz tinned tomatoes, chopped
150ml/1/4 pint water
salt and freshly ground black pepper
30ml/2 tablespoons Greek yoghurt
few leaves coriander to garnish

1. Set the oven to 190°C/375°F/gas mark 5.
2. Pick over the chicken breasts, removing any fat or gristle. Set aside.
3. Put 15ml/1 tablespoon oil into a saucepan and fry the almonds until golden brown but not burnt. Set aside. Add the remaining oil and in it slowly cook the spices for 1 minute.
4. Liquidize together the almonds and cooked spices with enough water to make a smooth paste.
5. Rinse out the saucepan, add 30ml/2 more tablespoons of oil and in it fry the onions, garlic and ginger until the onions are golden brown.
6. Reduce the heat and add the tomatoes, spice and almond paste, seasoning and 150ml/1/4 pint water. Stir well and simmer for 2 or 3 minutes.
7. Tip the sauce into an ovenproof dish. Add the chicken breasts and spoon over some of the sauce. Cover with tin foil and bake for 40 minutes or until the chicken is cooked.
8. Transfer the chicken to a warm serving dish. Swirl the yoghurt into the sauce. Pour over the chicken breasts and garnish with fresh coriander.

RED RHONE

Chicken with Coriander and Saffron Sauce

This recipe has been adapted from a recipe by Shirley Gill in *Taste* magazine.

SERVES 4

1 sachet powdered saffron
30g/1oz butter
2 onions, chopped
2 garlic cloves, crushed
150ml/1/4 pint Greek yoghurt
400g/14oz tin chopped tomatoes
75-90ml/5-6 tablespoons chopped coriander
salt and freshly ground black pepper
4 chicken breasts, skinned

To garnish:
coriander leaves

1. Heat the saffron in a small dry saucepan for 3 seconds. Pour on 45ml/3 tablespoons of hot water and stir to dissolve.
2. Melt the butter in a sauté pan and fry the onions and garlic for 5-8 minutes until lightly golden. Stir in the saffron liquid. Add the yoghurt, 15ml/1 tablespoon at a time, stir and fry until it is well incorporated into the sauce. Add the tomatoes, coriander and seasoning.
3. Put the chicken breasts into the saucepan and bring slowly to the boil. Cover and simmer over a low heat for 30 minutes or until the chicken is tender.
4. Remove the lid, lift out the chicken breasts and keep warm.
5. Reduce the sauce by boiling rapidly, stirring occasionally to prevent it catching, until thickened. Pour over the chicken breasts and serve immediately. Garnish with a little fresh coriander.

SPICY DRY WHITE

Lemon Chicken with Mint and Yoghurt Sauce

SERVES 4

4 chicken breasts, skinned and boned

For the marinade:
grated rind and juice of 1 lemon
15ml/1 tablespoon chopped parsley
1.25ml/¼ teaspoon dried thyme or 15ml/ 1 tablespoon fresh thyme leaves
1.25ml/¼ teaspoon ground coriander
15ml/1 tablespoon sunflower oil

For the sauce:
150ml/¼ pint natural yoghurt
15ml/1 tablespoon chopped mint
salt and pepper
1 garlic clove, crushed

To garnish:
small bunch of watercress

1. Mix the marinade ingredients together and leave the chicken breasts in it overnight or as long as possible.
2. Heat the oven to 200°C/400°F/gas mark 6.
3. Place the chicken and the marinade in a roasting pan and cook for 30 minutes.
4. Meanwhile, mix all the sauce ingredients together.
5. When the chicken is cooked, arrange on a warm serving dish, garnish with watercress and serve the sauce separately.

FULL DRY WHITE

Chicken Breasts with Parma Ham and Spinach

SERVES 4

4 chicken breasts, boned, skinned and any fat removed
4 thin slices best quality Parma ham
4 large spinach leaves, blanched and refreshed
570ml/1 pint chicken stock (see page 219)

For the dressing:
60ml/4 tablespoons good quality olive oil
60ml/4 tablespoons salad oil
30ml/2 tablespoons tarragon vinegar
15ml/1 tablespoon parsley, chopped
15ml/1 tablespoon dill, chopped
5ml/1 teaspoon grainy mustard
salt and freshly ground black pepper

To garnish:
cherry tomatoes

1. Wrap each chicken breast in 1 piece of Parma ham and then in 1 large spinach leaf.
2. Place the chicken breasts in a saucepan side by side, not on top of each other, and pour over hot chicken stock.
3. Cover the saucepan with a lid and bring back to the boil and then turn down the heat and poach gently for 18-20 minutes or until the breasts feel just firm to the touch.
4. Meanwhile, make the herby dressing. Combine all the ingredients together in a liquidizer or food processor until a green purée is formed.
5. Flood 4 plates with some of the herby dressing and then lift the chicken breasts out of the saucepan and drain. Cut each chicken breast on the angle and arrange overlapping in a semi-circle on the herby dressing. Garnish with whole cherry tomatoes.

NOTE: This can be served hot or cold.

WHITE BURGUNDY

Chicken with Black Bean Sauce

SERVES 4

4 large chicken breasts, skinned and boned
10ml/2 teaspoons cornflour
45ml/3 tablespoons fermented black beans
30ml/2 tablespoons sunflower oil
2 spring onions, chopped
1 garlic clove, sliced

2.5cm/1inch piece root ginger
30ml/2 tablespoons soy sauce
30ml/2 tablespoons sherry
5ml/1 teaspoon sugar
290ml/½ pint water
10ml/2 teaspoons sesame oil

To garnish:
2 spring onions, chopped

1. Trim any fat off the chicken breasts and cut into bite-sized pieces. Mix with the cornflour and set aside.
2. Wash the beans again and again as they are very salty.
3. Heat 15ml/1 tablespoon of the oil in a small saucepan, add the spring onions, garlic and ginger and cook slowly for 1 minute.
4. Add the soy sauce, sherry, sugar, black beans and water. Bring to the boil and simmer slowly for 10 minutes.
5. Heat the remaining sunflower oil in a wok and quickly stir-fry the chicken. Add the black bean sauce and cook very slowly for a further 5 minutes.
6. Add the sesame oil and pile on to a warmed serving dish. Garnish with the chopped spring onions.

WHITE ALSACE

Chicken with Mushrooms and Coriander

SERVES 4
4 chicken breasts, skinned and boned
15g/½oz cornflour
1 large onion, finely sliced
15-30ml/1-2 tablespoons sunflower oil
10ml/2 teaspoons coriander seeds, very well crushed
225g/8oz field mushrooms, sliced
150ml/¼ pint chicken stock (see page 219)
salt and freshly ground black pepper
30ml/2 tablespoons medium sherry

To garnish:
fresh coriander leaves

1. Trim any fat from the chicken breasts and cut the flesh into large cubes. Toss in the cornflour and set aside.
2. Fry the onion in 15ml/1 tablespoon oil and when beginning to soften add the coriander seeds, increase the heat and allow the onion to brown and the seeds to toast. This will take 1-2 minutes.
3. Add the chicken and fry for 3 minutes. Remove the chicken from the pan and set aside. Add the second tablespoon of oil and the mushrooms and cook until beginning to soften. Return the chicken to the pan. Add the stock and season with salt and pepper. Stir well and simmer for 4 or 5 minutes.
4. Add the sherry and boil for 30 seconds. Pile on to a warm serving dish and garnish with the fresh coriander leaves.

LIGHT RED

Chicken Breasts with Leek and Watercress Sauce

SERVES 4
4 chicken breasts, boned and skinned
30g/1oz truffle, finely sliced (optional)
15g/½oz butter
85g/3oz white of leeks, finely chopped
1 small shallot, finely chopped
small bunch of watercress, carefully picked over
30ml/2 tablespoons port
290ml/½ pint chicken stock
2 egg yolks
75ml/2½fl oz double cream

1. With a sharp knife, make a horizontal incision in the thickest part of each chicken breast and insert slices of truffle.
2. Melt the butter, add the leeks and shallot and cook slowly until soft but not brown. Add all but 2 sprigs of the watercress, the port and stock and simmer for 10 minutes.
3. Add the chicken breasts and poach, covered, for 12 minutes. Turn the chicken over halfway through cooking. Remove from the pan, returning any watercress or leeks stuck to the

breasts to the saucepan. Keep warm while you make the sauce.
4. Chop the remaining watercress very finely.
5. Reduce the poaching liquid, by boiling rapidly, to concentrate its flavour, and liquidize until very smooth. Pour into a clean saucepan. Bring to just below boiling point.
6. Mix the egg yolks with the cream, add a little of the hot sauce to the yolks, stir and return to the saucepan. Stir over a moderate heat until thickened. It is essential that the sauce does not get near boiling point or it will curdle. Stir in the remaining watercress to improve the colour.
7. Arrange the chicken breasts, split in 2 if liked, on individual warmed plates. Spoon over the sauce.

DRY WHITE

Chicken Breasts with Ginger

SERVES 4
4 chicken breasts, boned and skinned
1 large onion, chopped
2 garlic cloves, crushed
5cm/2 inch piece of root ginger, chopped
5 cardamom pods, cracked
5ml/1 teaspoon ground turmeric
30ml/2 tablespoons soy sauce
30ml/2 tablespoons dry sherry (optional)

1. Place the chicken breasts in a bowl with the onion, garlic, ginger, cardamom pods, turmeric, soy sauce and sherry. Cover the bowl and leave for about 2 hours so that the chicken can absorb the flavour. Turn the chicken once or twice.
2. Line a flat baking dish with foil and arrange the breasts on it. Pour over the marinade and seal the chicken tightly in the foil so that none of the juice can escape.
3. Bake at 200°C/400°F/gas mark 6 for 30 minutes.

AUSTRALIAN/CALIFORNIAN CHARDONNAY

Chicken Breasts with Red Pepper Sauce

SERVES 4
4 chicken breasts
45ml/3 tablespoons finely shredded white of leek
30ml/2 tablespoons finely shredded carrot
salt and pepper

To serve:
red pepper sauce (see page 231)
watercress leaves to garnish

1. Skin and bone the chicken breasts and remove any fat.
2. Mix the leeks and carrots together, season and use as a stuffing.
3. Put the stuffing between the main part of the breasts and the loose fillet. Wrap each breast in a piece of cling film.
4. Poach the chicken breasts in water for 15 minutes. Remove from the saucepan, unwrap and leave to get completely cold.
5. Flood the base of 4 large plates with the pepper sauce.
6. Put a chicken breast on each plate and garnish with watercress leaves.

DRY WHITE/ROSE

Chicken Breasts with Juniper Berries

SERVES 4
4 chicken breasts
4 large Savoy cabbage leaves
12 juniper berries
150ml/¼ pint hot chicken stock
small bunch of watercress to garnish

1. Skin and bone the chicken breasts. Heat the oven to 190°C/375°F/gas mark 5.
2. Cut out the tough stalks and blanch the cabbage leaves in boiling water for 1 minute. Refresh under running cold water and drain well. Wrap each chicken breast and 3 juniper berries in a leaf.
3. Place in an ovenproof casserole. Pour over the

hot stock, cover and bake for 20 minutes.
4. Remove from the oven, lift out of the stock and serve individually garnished with a little watercress. They can look very pretty if sliced on the diagonal.

AUSTRALIAN/CALIFORNIAN CHARDONNAY

Chicken Fried Rice I

SERVES 4
4 chicken breasts, skinned and boned
oil
1 onion, chopped
1 garlic clove, crushed
2.5cm/1 inch piece root ginger, skinned and finely chopped
1 green chilli, finely chopped
170g/6oz basmati rice, soaked for 30 minutes
2.5ml/½ teaspoon ground turmeric
10ml/2 teaspoons dried lemon grass, or 5ml/1 teaspoon fresh lemon grass
290ml/½ pint chicken stock
salt and freshly ground black pepper

1. Cut away any fat from the chicken and cut into bite-sized pieces.
2. Fry the chicken lightly in a little oil in a large sauté pan. Remove from the pan. Add the onion and cook for 10 minutes. Add the garlic, ginger, chilli and rice and fry until the rice becomes a little opaque. Add the turmeric and cook for 1 minute.
3. Return the chicken to the sauté pan. Add the lemon grass and enough stock to just cover the rice. Season with salt and pepper.
4. Bring up to the boil and simmer slowly, adding more stock if necessary, until the rice is cooked. This will take about 30 minutes.

DRY WHITE

Chicken Fried Rice II

SERVES 4
450g/1lb fresh chicken, cubed
170g/6oz basmati rice, soaked in cold water for 30 minutes
30ml/2 tablespoons oil
1 small onion, finely chopped
1 garlic clove, crushed
1cm/½inch piece root ginger, peeled and chopped
1 green chilli, deseeded (under running cold water) and chopped
290ml/½ pint chicken stock (see page 219)
30ml/2 tablespoons soy sauce
salt and freshly ground black pepper
15ml/1 tablespoon pinenuts, browned
15ml/1 tablespoon sesame seeds, toasted
few leaves coriander

1. Pick over the chicken and remove any fat or gristle.
2. Drain and rinse the rice.
3. Heat the oil in a large ovenproof dish and lightly fry the chicken until golden brown. Remove from the pan. Add the onion and cook slowly for 10 minutes or until nearly soft. Add the garlic, ginger and chilli and cook for 1 minute.
4. Add the rice and stir until slightly opaque. Add the stock and bring up to the boil. Add the soy sauce and salt and pepper. Simmer for 5 minutes.
5. Return the chicken to the dish and continue to cook for another 25 minutes or until the stock is absorbed, the rice cooked and the chicken is tender.
6. Stir in the pinenuts and sesame seeds. Pile into a warm serving dish and garnish with the fresh coriander.

DRY WHITE

Oriental Chicken with Sesame Seeds

SERVES 4-6
1.8kg/4lb chicken
oil

For the marinade:
1 small garlic clove, crushed
1cm/½ inch piece fresh ginger, peeled and grated
45ml/3 tablespoons soy sauce
15ml/1 tablespoon sesame oil
7.5ml/½ tablespoon honey
7.5ml/½ tablespoon wine vinegar or sherry

large pinch ground turmeric
5ml/1 teaspoon tomato purée

For the vegetables:
55g/2oz mangetout, blanched
55g/2oz baby sweetcorn, blanched
55g/2oz button mushrooms, blanched
1 red pepper, deseeded and cut into strips on the diagonal
55g/2oz French beans, blanched
15ml/1 tablespoon sesame seeds, toasted

1. Skin the chicken and cut the flesh into strips the size of your little finger.
2. Mix together the ingredients for the marinade and add the chicken. Leave for 1 hour.
3. Heat the oil in a wok, add the chicken and stir-fry, with its marinade, until tender. This will take 4-5 minutes.
4. Add all the vegetables and when thoroughly heated pile into a warm serving dish and scatter over the warm toasted sesame seeds.

FULL DRY WHITE

Stir-fried Chicken with Cashews

450g/1lb boned and skinned chicken flesh
2.5cm/1 inch piece root ginger, peeled and sliced
2 small garlic cloves, peeled and sliced
10ml/2 teaspoons cornflour
15ml/1 tablespoon soy sauce
15ml/1 tablespoon dry sherry
150ml/¼ pint chicken stock
15ml/1 tablespoon sunflower or grapeseed oil
55g/2oz unsalted, peeled cashew nuts
2 spring onions, chopped

1. Trim the chicken of all fat and cut into even-sized pieces.
2. Put into a bowl with the ginger and garlic, cover and leave to stand.
3. Mix the cornflour with the soy sauce, sherry and chicken stock. Set aside.
4. Heat the oil in a wok. Add the nuts and stir-fry until lightly browned. Remove with a slotted spoon.
5. Add the chicken with the ginger and garlic and stir-fry until the chicken is cooked and tender. This will take 4-5 minutes.
6. Add the liquid ingredients and stir until well blended and thickened. Add a little water if it seems too thick. Taste and season if necessary. Pile into a warmed serving dish and sprinkle with the spring onions and nuts.

FULL DRY WHITE

Warm Chicken Salad

This salad can be adapted according to what salad ingredients there are in your refrigerator. It can easily be made into a complete meal with the addition of hot new potatoes. The essential ingredients (other than the chicken!) are the rocket, chives, walnut oil and balsamic vinegar. It is also very good made with breast of pheasant instead of the chicken.

SERVES 4
4 chicken breasts, skinned
seasoned flour
salad leaves such as, frisée, lamb's lettuce, gem lettuce, rocket
110g/4oz baby sweetcorn
110g/4oz broccoli
salt and freshly ground black pepper
sunflower oil
110g/4oz shiitake or chestnut mushrooms
1 bunch chives, chopped
60ml/4 tablespoons olive oil
15ml/1 tablespoon balsamic vinegar

1. Remove any fat from the chicken breasts, cut into bite-sized pieces and coat them lightly with the seasoned flour. Put them on to a plate, making sure that the pieces of chicken are not touching.
2. Put the salad leaves into a large salad bowl.
3. Cook the sweetcorn and broccoli in a small amount of salted boiling water and at the same time fry the chicken breasts in hot sunflower oil. They will take about 5 minutes. Once the chicken has browned on both sides, reduce the heat so that it cooks slowly. When the chicken is nearly cooked, fry the mushrooms in a second pan.
4. Drain the broccoli and sweetcorn. Lift the

chicken pieces on to absorbent paper.
5. Transfer all the ingredients to the salad bowl, mix together, season well and serve immediately.

SAUVIGNON

Stuffed Boned Duck

SERVES 6
1 large duck, boned
45g/1½oz butter
1 medium onion, finely chopped
85g/3oz mushrooms, sliced
1 small garlic clove, crushed
85g/3oz fresh white breadcrumbs
4 x 5cm/2 inch slices ham, cubed
85g/3oz pork belly, minced
1 egg
1 egg yolk
salt and freshly ground black pepper
bunch of watercress

1. Carefully remove any excess fat from the duck, especially from the vent end. Push the meat around gently so that it is evenly distributed on top of the skin.
2. To make the stuffing: melt the butter, add the onion and fry gently until it is soft and transparent. Add the mushrooms and garlic and cook for 2 more minutes.
3. Take the pan off the heat and add the breadcrumbs, diced ham, pork belly, egg and yolk and plenty of salt and pepper. Mix well.
4. Stuff the duck and wrap it in a piece of muslin or clean 'J' cloth and tie it at either end so it looks like a Christmas cracker.
5. Put on a wire rack in a roasting pan. Prick lightly and rub with salt. Roast for 1½ hours at 200°C/400°F/gas mark 6, or until the bird is brown and crisp all over.
6. Drain off the fat and place the duck on a platter. Serve hot or cold, garnished with watercress.

NOTE: If the butcher will not bone the duck, instructions can be found on page 280.

RED BURGUNDY

Leith's Good Food's Boned Duck

SERVES 4
1 duck, boned
1 large chicken breast, boned and skinned
½ small onion, chopped
110g/4oz dried apricots, sliced
chopped tarragon and parsley
30g/1oz pistachio nuts

1. Set the oven to 200°C/400°F/gas mark 6.
2. Carefully remove any excess fat from the duck, especially from the vent end.
3. Put the chicken breast and onion together in a food processor and whizz briefly. Add the apricots, tarragon, parsley and nuts. Mix well and season.
4. Stuff the duck and wrap it in a piece of muslin or a clean 'J' cloth and tie it at either end so it looks like a Christmas cracker.
5. Put on a wire rack in a roasting tin. Prick lightly and rub with salt. Roast for 1¼ hours. Serve cold with a tarragon cream dressing or hot with orange, port and redcurrant sauce.

SOFT LIGHT RED

Leith's Roast Duckling

SERVES 3
1 large duckling
salt and pepper
30g/1oz granulated sugar
15ml/1 tablespoon vinegar
150ml/¼ pint duck or chicken stock
juice and grated rind of 1 orange
10ml/2 teaspoons brandy
45g/1½oz flaked almonds
15g/½oz butter
1 celery stick, finely chopped
1 small onion, finely chopped

To garnish:
1 whole orange
bunch of watercress

1. Set the oven to 200°C/400°F/gas mark 6.
2. Prick the duck all over, dust it lightly with salt, and put it in the oven to roast for 1 hour. It needs no fat, but it is a good idea to lay it legs up for the first 30 minutes and turn it right side up for the next 30 minutes.
3. Take it out, drain well, and joint it. Put the pieces into a clean roasting pan, skin side up. Keep the roasting juices.
4. Put the sugar and vinegar in a thick-bottomed saucepan. Dissolve the sugar over gentle heat, then boil until the sugar caramelizes: it will go dark brown and bubbly, with large slow bubbles. Pour on the stock; it will hiss and splutter so take care. Stir until the caramel lumps disappear. Add the orange rind and juice, any roasting juices from the duck (but no fat) and the brandy. Pour over the duck.
5. Return to the oven and continue cooking until the joints are cooked through (another 20 minutes or so). Do not baste. Remove the duck joints to an ovenproof plate and keep warm. (If the skin is not truly crisp the duck can be returned to the oven for 10 minutes like this without the sauce.)
6. Fry the flaked almonds in the butter until golden brown. Scatter over the duck.
7. Skim the sauce to remove any fat, and strain it into a saucepan. Add the celery and onion, and boil until the celery is just beginning to soften but still a little crunchy (about 5 minutes). Taste the sauce and add salt and pepper. You should have a thin, fairly clear liquid with plenty of chopped celery and onion in it. Serve the sauce separately, or poured round, not over, the duck.
8. Cut the orange (with the skin on) in half and slice it. Surround the duck with the orange slices and put a bunch of watercress at each end of the dish.

NOTE: This recipe is a speciality of Leith's Restaurant in London.

CLARET

Roast Duck with Apple Sauce

SERVES 3
1 x 1.8kg/4lb duck
salt and freshly ground black pepper
1/2 onion
1/2 orange
5ml/1 teaspoon flour
290ml/1/2 pint duck or strong chicken stock
apple sauce (see page 232)

1. Set the oven to 200°C/400°F/gas mark 6. Wipe the duck clean inside and out. Season the cavity well with salt and pepper. Place the onion and orange inside the duck. Prick the skin all over and sprinkle with salt.
2. Put the duck upside down on a rack in a roasting pan and roast for 30 minutes. Then pour off the fat. Turn the duck over and continue roasting until cooked (about 1 hour). Test by sticking a skewer into the thigh – if the juices run out pink the duck needs further cooking.
3. Tip the juices from the cavity into a bowl and reserve them. Joint the duck into 6 pieces and arrange the joints on a serving dish; or leave whole for carving at the table. In any event keep it warm, without covering, as this would spoil the crisp skin.
4. To make the gravy, pour off all the fat in the roasting pan except for 15ml/1 tablespoon. Stir over a low heat, scraping the bottom of the pan to loosen all the sediment. Whisk in the flour and add the juices from inside the duck, and the stock, and whisk until smooth. Simmer, stirring, for 2 minutes. Season to taste.
5. Strain the gravy into a warm gravy boat. Fill a second gravy boat with hot or cold apple sauce.

RED LOIRE

Duck Breasts with Green Peppercorn Sauce

SERVES 4
4 large duck breasts, skinned
45g/1½oz unsalted butter

For the sauce:
150ml/¼ pint dry white wine
45ml/3 tablespoons brandy
120ml/8 tablespoons white stock
290ml/½ pint double cream
30ml/2 tablespoons wine vinegar
5ml/1 teaspoon sugar
15ml/1 tablespoon port
20g/¾oz green peppercorns, well rinsed
20g/¾oz tinned red pimento, cut into dice
salt and pepper

For the garnish:
2 firm dessert apples, peeled, cored and cut into 8
30g/1oz unsalted butter

1. To make the sauce: put the wine and brandy in a heavy pan and boil gently for about 5 minutes or until reduced to a third of the original volume.
2. Add the stock and boil for 5 minutes. Add the cream and boil for about 15 minutes, stirring occasionally so that it does not catch on the bottom, or until the sauce has reduced by about a third and is of pouring consistency (i.e. about as thick as single cream).
3. Put the vinegar and sugar into a small saucepan. Boil for 30 seconds or until it smells caramelized and is reduced to about 15ml/1 tablespoon. Cool for 1 minute and pour in the cream sauce. Stir well. It may be necessary to replace it over the heat to re-melt the caramel. Add the port, peppercorns and pimento. Season. Set aside until ready for use.
4. To cook the duck breasts and the apple garnish: melt the 45g/1½oz unsalted butter in a large heavy frying pan. When it stops foaming, add the duck breasts and fry fairly fast on both sides. Reduce the heat and fry slowly for 8-10 minutes.
5. Melt the butter for the garnish in a second frying pan and fry the apples very slowly until golden brown.
6. To serve: reheat the sauce in a double saucepan. Slice the duck breasts, lengthways, into fairly thin slices. They should be rose pink. Flood the base of 4 large plates with the sauce. Arrange a fan of sliced duck breast on each plate and garnish with 3 or 4 pieces of apple.

NOTE: An alternative way to serve this is to sprinkle the unskinned duck breasts with a little salt, roast in a hot oven for 15-20 minutes and then place them under a grill for a good crisp skin. Slice and serve as described above.

RED LOIRE

Peking Duck

The pancakes can be bought from oriental grocers, or follow the instructions below for making them.

SERVES 6
2.3kg/5lb oven-ready duck
45ml/3 tablespoons brandy
75ml/5 tablespoons clear honey
45ml/3 tablespoons soy sauce
1 bunch spring onions
10cm/4 inch piece cucumber

For the Chinese pancakes:
250g/9oz flour, plus extra for dusting
200ml/7fl oz boiling water
45ml/3 tablespoons sesame oil

For the sauce:
15ml/1 tablespoon sesame oil
2.5cm/1 inch piece ginger, peeled and sliced
30ml/2 tablespoons soya paste
200g/7oz plum jam
5ml/1 teaspoon chilli powder
30g/1oz caster sugar

1. Place the duck in a colander in a pan. Pour over a kettle full of boiling water to loosen the skin. Pat dry, inside and out, with kitchen paper.
2. Brush the brandy over the duck – the alcohol has a drying effect on the skin and will help to make it really crispy. Tie a piece of string

around the wings and hang the duck up in a cool airy place. Put a bowl or tray underneath to catch any drips.

3. Leave the duck for 4 hours – until the skin is very dry. Mix together the honey and soy sauce and brush over the duck. Leave to dry for 1 hour, then brush again and leave to dry for 3 hours.

4. Meanwhile, make the pancakes: sift the flour into a mixing bowl and gradually add the water to make a soft dough. Place on a lightly floured surface and knead well until smooth. Place in a bowl, cover with a clean damp tea towel and leave to rest for 30 minutes.

5. Knead the dough again for 5 minutes, and dust with a little flour if it is sticky. Roll out to a roll about 2.5cm/1 inch in diameter. Cut the roll into 16 x 2.5cm/1 inch segments, then roll each segment into a smooth ball.

6. Work with 2 dough balls at a time. Dip one side of one ball in the sesame oil. Place the oiled side on top of the other ball, then flatten the balls together slightly with the palm of your hand. Lightly flour your work surface, then roll out to a circle of about 15cm/6 inches diameter. Repeat with the remaining balls of dough. .

7. Heat a heavy-based frying pan over a low flame. Place a double pancake in the pan and cook for about 1 minute, or until dry on one side. Turn over and cook for 1 minute on the other side. Pull the pancakes apart and stack on a plate. Cooking the pancakes together will keep them moist, making them easier to roll around the filling.

8. Make the sauce: heat the oil in a small pan and fry the ginger for 2 minutes to lightly flavour the oil. Remove the ginger with a slotted spoon. Add the soya paste, plum jam, chilli powder and sugar and heat gently until smooth. Pour into a serving bowl and then set aside.

9. Preheat the oven to 190°C/375°F/gas mark 5. Place the duck on a rack in a roasting tin and roast for 1½ hours. It is essential that the duck be placed on a rack, otherwise the fat in the pan will stop the skin browning underneath. Do not open the door during the cooking time.

10. Meanwhile, cut the spring onions into 5cm/2 inch pieces, and shred lengthways into thin strips. Cut the cucumber in half and then into batons. Arrange on a serving dish.

11. Transfer the duck to a board. Remove the skin and cut into squares. Carve the meat into slices and place both on a serving dish. To serve, dip the meat and crispy skin, in the plum sauce and brush over a pancake. Put the meat, skin, spring onion, and cucumber in the middle and roll up to eat.

NOTE: Instead of making the plum sauce, you can use hoisin sauce. Flavour the oil with the ginger, then add 125ml/4 fl oz hoisin sauce and heat gently.

SPICY DRY WHITE

Cold Duck Breast Salad

SERVES 6

6 duck breasts
salt and freshly ground black pepper
225g/8oz mangetout, cooked and refreshed
110g/4oz broccoli florets, cooked and refreshed
110g/4oz pinenuts, toasted
4 spring onions, sliced

For the French dressing:
15ml/1 tablespoon lemon juice
60ml/4 tablespoons grapeseed oil
salt and freshly ground pepper
15ml/1 tablespoon double cream

1. Set the oven to 230°C/450°F/gas mark 8.

2. Place the duck breasts, skin side up, in a roasting pan. Season with salt and pepper and roast for 15 minutes. Remove from the oven and allow to cool.

3. Once cool, refrigerate. There should be meat juices in the pan. Remove any fat and then reduce the juices to 30ml/2 tablespoons and allow to cool.

4. Make the French dressing by mixing all the ingredients together, and add the cool, reduced duck juice. Check the seasoning.

5. Slice the duck breasts diagonally and then toss in the French dressing with the mangetout and broccoli. Arrange on a plate and scatter the pinenuts and spring onions over the top.

FULL DRY WHITE

Roast Goose Mary-Claire

A 4. 5kg/10lb goose may sound huge for 6 people but most of a goose seems to be carcase! Therefore this goose has a lot of delicious, Middle Eastern-style stuffing. It is a similar stuffing to that made by Leith's Good Food for its famous roast stuffed duck. Be careful not to overcook the goose or it will become dry and tough.

SERVES 6
4.5kg/10lb goose
salt and freshly ground black pepper
1/2 lemon

For the stuffing:
30g/1oz butter
1 onion, finely chopped
285g/10oz chicken breast, minced (or cut in 4 if using a food processor)
15ml/1 tablespoon sage, lightly chopped
340g/12oz dessert apples, peeled and chopped
10 dried apricots, soaked for 2 hours, drained and chopped
55g/2oz unsalted pistachio nuts, lightly chopped
55g/2oz shredded beef suet
85g/3oz fresh breadcrumbs
1 egg

To finish:
15ml/1 tablespoon honey

For the gravy:
570ml/1 pint potato water or goose stock
30ml/2 tablespoons Calvados

To garnish:
bunch of watercress

1. Wipe the goose all over. Season the inside with salt and pepper and rub with a cut lemon.
2. Set the oven to 190°C/375°F/gas mark 5.
3. Make the stuffing: melt the butter, add the onion and cook for about 10 minutes until soft but not coloured. Beat together the chicken, onion, sage, apple, apricots, pistachio nuts and suet. Add enough of the breadcrumbs to make a firm but not solid stuffing. Season to taste. Add the egg and beat really well. You can make it in a food processor, but leave out the pistachios and stir them in at the end.
4. Fill the goose cavity with the stuffing. Weigh the goose, with stuffing, to establish the cooking time. Allow 15 minutes to 450g/1lb and 15 minutes over.
5. Prick the goose all over and sprinkle with salt. Place on a wire rack over a roasting pan. Roast, basting occasionally, but do not worry if you forget as a goose is very fatty. Every so often you will have to remove fat from the roasting tin with a plastic baster. Do not throw it away as it is wonderful for cooking. If the goose gets too dark, cover it with tin foil.
6. Ten minutes before the bird is cooked, spread the honey evenly over the skin. This will help to make it crisp. When the goose is cooked, place on a serving plate and return to the oven, which you have turned off.
7. Make the gravy: carefully spoon off all the fat in the roasting pan, leaving the cooking juices behind. Scrape off and discard any burnt pieces stuck to the bottom of the pan. Add the stock and, if you can, a little of the stuffing. Bring up to the boil,whisk well and simmer for about 15 minutes. Increase the heat and boil until syrupy, add the Calvados, season to taste and boil for 30 seconds. Taste and strain into a warm gravy boat.
8. Garnish the goose with watercress.

RED BURGUNDY

Confit D'Oie (Preserved Goose)

This recipe, still common in France, is for goose flesh preserved in fat. The pieces of goose are lifted from the jar and wiped clean of fat before being served either cold or reheated, or used in composite dishes. The confit takes 3 days to complete. Use a very fat goose, but if you cannot get one, use 2 average or 3 small ducks instead.

4.5 kg/10lb goose
900g/2lb salt
7g/1/4oz saltpetre
4 cloves, crushed
2 bay leaves, pounded

pinch of thyme
1.8 kg/4lb goose fat
450g/1lb lard

1. Cut the goose into quarters.
2. Mix together the salt, saltpetre, cloves, bay leaves and thyme and rub some of this over the whole surface of the goose.
3. Put the goose into a large (about 1.8kg/4lb) glazed earthenware pot and add the remaining spiced salt. Cover and leave for 24 hours.
4. Slowly melt the goose fat in a large saucepan. Remove the goose pieces from the salt, wipe clean and put into the fat. Place over slow heat and cook very gently for 3 hours. To test if the goose is cooked, prick it with a skewer. The juices that run out should be clear, and the flesh should feel tender.
5. Drain the pieces of goose and remove the bones. Strain a thick layer of fat in which the goose was cooked into a large glazed earthenware jar.
6. When this fat has completely solidified arrange the pieces of goose on top, taking care to prevent them touching the wall of the jar.
7. Cover the pieces of goose with just-liquid cool goose fat. Put into a cool place.
8. Leave for 2 days. Strain some more liquid goose fat into the jar to seal any holes which may have occurred.
9. When this is set, melt the lard and pour a layer about 1cm/½inch thick over the surface. When this is set, put a circle of greaseproof paper on top, pressing it down to exclude any air. Cover the top of the jar with a double thickness of paper and tie with string. You can keep the confit d'oie in this way for at least a month.

FULL RED

Cold Boned Goose with Aspic

SERVES 10
1 medium-sized goose
1 carrot, chopped
1 onion, chopped
2 leeks, chopped
1 celery stick, chopped
6 peppercorns
bouquet garni (bay leaf, parsley stalk, mace and thyme)

For the aspic:
150ml/¼ pint dry cider
55g/2oz gelatine
2 egg shells, crushed
2 egg whites

For the stuffing:
30g/1oz butter
1 onion, finely chopped
225g/8oz dessert apples, peeled, cored and chopped
225g/8oz cooking apples, peeled, cored and chopped
85g/3oz breadcrumbs
4 dates, finely chopped
170g/6oz sausagemeat
30ml/2 tablespoons chopped mint
salt and freshly ground black pepper
1 egg, beaten

For the garnish:
1 small orange
bunch of watercress

1. Bone the goose completely, including the legs and wings (see page 280).
2. To make the stock for the aspic: place the goose bones and giblets (except the liver) in a large pan with the carrot, onion, leeks, celery, peppercorns and bouquet garni. Bring to the boil, cover and simmer for 1 hour.
3. To make the stuffing: melt the butter, add the onion and cook slowly until soft but not coloured. Add the apples and cook for 1 further minute. Allow to cool.
4. Stir the apple and onion mixture into the breadcrumbs, dates and sausagemeat. Add the mint and season well. Add enough beaten egg just to bind the mixture together.
5. Lay the goose, skin side down, on a wooden board. Remove any excess fat. Pile on the stuffing and roll up the goose into a neat roll, making sure that all the untidy ends are tucked in. Sew up neatly using a needle and fine string. Wrap the goose in a piece of muslin or a clean tea towel and tie it securely.
6. Strain the stock and taste for seasoning. Put the goose into a heavy saucepan or fish kettle and pour on the stock. Bring to the boil, cover tightly and simmer slowly for 2 hours. Turn the

goose over once during cooking. Drain, reserving the stock for the aspic.

7. As soon as the goose is cool enough to handle, tighten the wrappings, and put on a plate. When cold, refrigerate.

8. Pour the stock into a bowl and leave to cool overnight. If the stock can be transferred to the refrigerator once it is cold so much the better – it will set the fat and make removing it easier. Next day lift or skim off any fat from the goose stock. It must be absolutely fat-free.

9. Put 860ml/1½ pints of the goose stock (make up with water if not enough) into a very large saucepan with the cider and gelatine. Place over a gentle heat.

10. Place the crushed shells in a bowl, add the egg white and whisk until frothy. Pour into the warming stock and keep whisking steadily with a balloon whisk until the mixture boils and rises. Stop whisking immediately, and draw the pan off the heat. Allow the mixture to subside. Take care not to break the crust formed by the egg white.

11. Bring the stock up to the boil again, and again allow to subside. Repeat this once more (the egg white will trap the sediment in the stock and clear the aspic). Allow to cool for 10 minutes.

12. Fix a double layer of fine muslin over a clean basin and carefully strain the aspic through it, taking care to hold the egg-white crust back. When all the liquid is through (or almost all of it) allow the egg white to slip into the muslin. Then strain the aspic again – this time through both egg-white crust and cloth. Do not try to hurry the process by squeezing the cloth or you will get murky jelly. Allow to cool until on the point of setting.

13. Unwrap the goose and wipe away all the grease. Place it on a wire rack with a tray underneath.

14. Coat it with the nearly set aspic. Place in the refrigerator until set.

15. Cut the orange, skin and all, across into very thin even slices. You should end up with 7 or 8. Dip the orange slices in a little cool aspic and arrange them in a neat overlapping row down the centre of the goose. Leave to set. Coat the goose with more aspic. Once this layer has set, add further layers until really shiny. Place on a serving dish.

16. Set the remaining aspic in a shallow tray. Cut into neat squares and use to surround the goose. Garnish with watercress.

NOTE: If the aspic is less than crystal clear, it is wise not to chop it as this seems to emphasize its murkiness.

RED BURGUNDY

Roast Turkey

A large square of fine muslin (butter-muslin) is needed for this recipe.

SERVES 12
5.35 kg/12lb turkey

For the oatmeal stuffing:
1 large onion, finely chopped
20g/¾oz butter
340g/12oz medium oatmeal
5ml/1 teaspoon rubbed dried sage or 4 leaves fresh sage, chopped
170g/6oz shredded beef suet
salt and freshly ground black pepper

For the sausagemeat and chestnut stuffing:
450g/1lb sausagemeat
450g/1lb unsweetened chestnut purée
110g/4oz fresh breadcrumbs
1 large egg, beaten
salt and freshly ground black pepper

To prepare the turkey for the oven:
170g/6oz butter
giblets
½ onion
2 bay leaves
few parsley stalks
290ml/½ pint water

For the garnish:
1 chipolata sausage per person
1 streaky bacon rasher per person

For the gravy:
10ml/2 teaspoons flour
stock or vegetable water

1. Weigh the turkey. Calculate the cooking time with the help of the chart on page 282.

2. Make the oatmeal stuffing: cook the onion in

the butter until beginning to soften. Mix with the oatmeal, sage, and shredded suet. Add enough water just to bind the mixture together, and taste and season as required. Stuff into the cavity of the turkey.
3. Make the sausagemeat and chestnut stuffing: mix together the sausagemeat, chestnut purée, breadcrumbs and beaten egg. Taste and season as required. Stuff this into the neck end of the turkey, making sure that the breast is well plumped. Draw the skin flap down to cover the stuffing. Secure with a skewer.
4. Set the oven to 180°C/350°F/gas mark 4.
5. Melt the butter and in it soak a very large piece of butter-muslin (about 4 times the size of the turkey) until all the butter has been completely absorbed.
6. Season the turkey well with salt and pepper. Place it in a large roasting pan with the giblets (except the liver) and neck. Add the onion, bay leaves and parsley stalks and pour in the water. Completely cover the bird with the doubled butter-muslin and roast in the prepared oven for the time calculated (a 5. 3 kg/12lb turkey should take 3-3½ hours).
7. Meanwhile, prepare the garnishes: make each chipolata sausage into 2 cocktail-sized ones by twisting gently in the middle. Take the rind off the bacon and stretch each rasher slightly with the back of a knife, cut into 2 and roll up. Put the sausages and bacon rolls into a second roasting pan, with the bacon rolls wedged in so that they cannot unravel. Half an hour before the turkey is ready, put the sausages and bacon in the oven.
8. When the turkey is cooked, the juices that run out of the thigh when pierced with a skewer should be clear. Remove the muslin and lift the bird on to a serving dish. Surround with the bacon and sausages and keep warm while making the gravy.
9. Lift the pan with its juices on to the top of the cooker and skim off the fat. Whisk in the flour and add enough chicken stock or vegetable water to make up to about 425ml/¾ pint. Stir until boiling, then simmer for a few minutes. Taste and add salt and pepper if necessary. Strain into a warm gravy boat.

RED BURGUNDY

Christmas Turkey Stuffed with Ham

SERVES 20
2.3 kg/5lb piece of boiled bacon or ham, skinned
6.7 kg/15lb turkey, boned (see page 280)

For the stuffing:
30g/1oz butter
1 large onion, finely chopped
900g/2lb pork belly, minced
450g/1lb unsweetened tinned chestnut purée or mashed cooked fresh chestnuts
225g/8oz fresh white breadcrumbs
2 eggs, lightly beaten
5ml/1 teaspoon dried sage
30ml/2 tablespoons chopped parsley
salt and freshly ground black pepper

For the roasting:
55g/2oz butter
1 onion, sliced
3 bay leaves
2 parsley stalks
425ml/¾ pint water

For the gravy:
30ml/2 tablespoons flour
about 290ml/½ pint turkey stock
bunch of watercress

1. Set the oven to 200°C/400°F/gas mark 6.
2. To make the stuffing: melt the butter, add the onion and cook until soft but not coloured.
3. When cold, mix with all the other stuffing ingredients.
4. Open the turkey out flat on a board, skin side down. Spread the stuffing on the turkey and put the ham or bacon on top.
5. Draw up the sides and sew together with a needle and fine string. Turn the bird right side up and try to push it into an even, rounded shape.
6. Smear the butter all over the turkey and put it into a roasting tin. Add the giblets (except the liver) and the neck. Add the onion, bay leaves and parsley stalks. Pour in the water. If the turkey looks too flat, wedge the sides with bread tins to hold it in shape.
7. Roast the bird for 1 hour, lower the temperature to 180°C/350°F/gas mark 4 and

roast for a further 3 hours. Baste occasionally as it cooks and cover with foil or greaseproof paper if it is browning too much.
8. When the turkey is cooked, a skewer will glide through the thigh easily. Lift it out on to a serving dish and keep warm while you make the gravy.
9. Lift the pan with its juices on to the top of the cooker. Pour off as much fat as possible.
10. Using a wooden spoon or wire whisk, stir in enough flour to absorb the remaining fat. Add 290ml/$^1/_2$ pint stock and stir until the sauce boils. Strain into a warm gravy boat.
11. Garnish the turkey with the watercress and serve the gravy separately.

NOTE I: This turkey is delicious served cold with a herby mayonnaise.
NOTE II: The turkey may be stuffed the day before cooking. If this is done, care should be taken that both the turkey and stuffing are well chilled before the bird is stuffed. Refrigerate until ready to cook.
NOTE III: If the turkey is roasted covered in 2 layers of muslin completely saturated in melted butter there is no need for basting during cooking, and when the cloths are removed the bird will be brown and crisp.

RED BURGUNDY

Jugged Hare

SERVES 6
1 hare, skinned and jointed, with its blood
dripping
225g/8oz mirepoix of carrot, onion and celery
bouquet garni (1 bay leaf, 2 parsley stalks, sprig of thyme)
570ml/1 pint good brown stock (see page 218)
salt and freshly ground black pepper
15ml/1 tablespoon redcurrant jelly
45ml/3 tablespoons port

1. Wash and wipe dry the pieces of hare, removing any membranes. Heat the dripping in a large saucepan and fry the joints until well browned, adding more dripping if the pan becomes dry. Lift out the joints and brown the mirepoix.
2. Return the hare to the pan. Add the bouquet garni, stock, salt and pepper. Cover and simmer for 2 hours or until the hare is really tender.
3. Arrange the joints in a casserole.
4. Strain the stock into a saucepan. Add the redcurrant jelly and port and simmer for 5 minutes. Draw the pan off the heat.
5. Mix the blood with a cupful of the hot stock. Pour back into the pan without allowing the sauce to boil. The blood will thicken the sauce slightly.
6. Taste the sauce, adding salt and pepper if necessary. Pour over the hare joints in the casserole and serve.

NOTE: The sauce depends on the blood to thicken it. If very little blood (less than 150ml/$^1/_4$ pint) comes with the hare, the basic stock must be thickened with a little beurre manié - flour and butter kneaded together in equal quantities - and whisked in small blobs into the boiling stock. This must be done before the addition of the blood, which would curdle if boiled.

CLARET

Venison Casserole

SERVES 4
675g/1$^1/_2$lb venison

For the marinade:
1 onion, sliced
1 carrot, sliced
1 celery stick, sliced
1 garlic clove, crushed
6 juniper berries
slice of lemon
1 bay leaf
290ml/$^1/_2$ pint red wine
30ml/2 tablespoons wine vinegar
6 peppercorns

For the casserole:
15ml/1 tablespoon oil
30g/1oz butter
110g/4oz onions, peeled
1 garlic clove, crushed
110g/4oz button mushrooms

10ml/2 teaspoons flour
150ml/$^1/_4$ pint beef stock
15ml/1 tablespoon cranberry jam
salt and freshly ground black pepper
55g/2oz fresh cranberries
15g/$^1/_2$oz sugar
110g/4oz cooked whole chestnuts
chopped parsley

1. Cut the venison into 5cm/2inch cubes, trimming away any tough membrane or sinew.
2. Mix the ingredients for the marinade together and add the meat. Mix well, cover and leave in a cool place or in the refrigerator overnight.
3. Set the oven to 170°C/325°F/gas mark 3.
4. Lift out the venison cubes and pat dry with absorbent paper. Strain the marinade, reserving the liquid for cooking.
5. Heat half the oil in a heavy saucepan and brown the cubes of meat, frying a few at a time. Lay them in a casserole. If the bottom of the pan becomes brown or too dry, pour in a little of the strained marinade, swish it about, scraping off the sediment stuck to the bottom, and pour over the cubes of meat. Then heat a little more oil and continue browning the meat.
6. When all the meat has been browned, repeat the déglaçage (boiling up with a little marinade and scraping the bottom of the pan).
7. Now melt the butter and fry the onions and garlic until the onions are pale brown all over. Add the mushrooms and continue cooking for 2 minutes.
8. Stir in the flour and cook for 1 minute. Remove from the heat, add the rest of the marinade and the beef stock, return to the heat and stir until boiling, again scraping the bottom of the pan. When boiling, pour over the venison.
9. Add the cranberry jam. Season with salt and pepper.
10. Cover the casserole and place in the heated oven for about 2 hours or until the meat is really tender.
11. Meanwhile cook the cranberries briefly with the sugar in 30-45ml/2-3 tablespoons water until just soft but not crushed. Strain off the liquor. Lift the venison pieces, mushrooms and onions with a perforated spoon into a serving dish.
12. Boil the sauce fast until reduced to a shiny, almost syrupy, consistency. Add the chestnuts and cranberries and simmer gently for 5 minutes.
13. Pour the sauce over the venison and serve garnished with chopped parsley.

FULL RED

Braised Venison

SERVES 6-8
2.7 kg/6lb haunch of venison
30g/1oz butter
15ml/1 tablespoon oil
2 onions, sliced
225g/8oz carrots, sliced
4 celery sticks, sliced
salt and freshly ground black pepper
1 bay leaf
thyme
sage
150ml/$^1/_4$pint red wine
about 290ml/ $^1/_2$ pint beef stock
30g/1oz butter
30g/1oz flour
15ml/1 tablespoon cranberry jelly

1. Heat the oven to 150°C/300°F/gas mark 2.
2. Prepare the venison by trimming away any tough membranes and sinews.
3. Heat the butter and oil in a large flameproof casserole and brown the venison well on all sides. Remove from the casserole.
4. Add the onions, carrots and celery, and fry for 5 minutes until lightly browned.
5. Season with salt and pepper, add the bay leaf and a sprinkling of thyme and sage. Lay the venison on top of the half-cooked vegetables. Add the wine and enough stock to come about a quarter of the way up the meat.
6. Bring to simmering point, cover tightly and put in the oven for $1^1/_2$ hours.
7. When it is cooked lift out the meat, carve neatly and place on a serving dish. Keep warm, covered with a lid or foil.
8. Strain the liquid from the vegetables into a saucepan.
9. Mix the butter and flour together to make a beurre manié. Add this to the liquid bit by bit, stirring, and bring to the boil. Stir in the cranberry jelly and correct the seasoning.
10. Just before serving spoon a thin layer of

sauce over the venison to make it look shiny and appetizing; serve the remaining sauce in a sauce boat.

FULL RED

Peppered Venison Steak

SERVES 4
4 x 140g/5oz venison collops (steaks) cut from the fillet
30ml/2 tablespoons whole peppercorns
30g/1oz unsalted butter
15ml/1 tablespoon oil (preferably olive)
30ml/2 tablespoons brandy
150ml/¼ pint double cream
salt

1. Wipe the steaks and trim off any gristle.
2. Crush the peppercorns coarsely in a mortar or under a rolling pin and press them into the surface of the meat on both sides.
3. Cover the steaks and leave them for 2 hours at room temperature for the flavour to penetrate the meat.
4. Heat the oil in a heavy-based pan, add the butter and when it is foaming fry the steaks as fast as you dare. Get them to the degree you like them (generally they need about 2 minutes per side for blue, 3 minutes for rare, 3½ minutes for medium and 4 minutes for well done).
5. Pour in the brandy and set it alight. Add the cream and a pinch of salt. Mix the contents of the pan thoroughly, scraping up any sediment stuck to the bottom.
6. Place the steaks on a heated platter.
7. Boil up the sauce again, then simmer to a syrupy consistency and pour over the meat. Serve at once.

NOTE: If the venison is very fresh and you want a gamier taste, marinate it for 2 days in equal quantities of red wine and oil, flavoured with a sliced onion, 6 juniper berries and a bay leaf. Dry well before frying.

VERY FULL RED

Venison Steaks with Lemon and Redcurrant Sauce

SERVES 4
For the sauce:
1 lemon
110g/4oz redcurrant jelly
1 cinnamon stick
30ml/2 tablespoons port
45g/1½oz butter, chilled and cut into small pieces

For the steaks:
4 x 1cm/½ inch venison steaks taken from the leg or loin
salt and freshly ground black pepper
15ml/1 tablespoon crushed juniper berries
55g/2oz butter
30ml/2 tablespoons olive oil
60ml/4 tablespoons port

To garnish:
small bunch of watercress

1. First prepare the sauce: pare the rind from the lemon and cut into fine needleshreds. Cut the lemon in half and extract the juice. Reserve.
2. Heat the redcurrant jelly gently with the cinnamon stick, port and needleshreds. Simmer for 10 minutes, add the strained lemon juice and beat in the butter.
3. Trim the venison steaks of any tough membranes and season them with salt, pepper and juniper berries.
4. Heat the butter and oil in a heavy frying pan and cook the steaks over a high heat to brown on both sides. Reduce the heat and cook for a total of about 8 minutes, depending on size.
5. Remove the steaks to a serving dish. Pour the fat out of the frying pan and deglaze with the port. Pour over the steaks.

FULL RED

Roast Pheasant

SERVES 4
2 medium pheasants
salt and pepper
butter
2 strips of pork fat

For the gravy:
5ml/1 teaspoon flour
15ml/1 tablespoon ruby port
5ml/1 teaspoon redcurrant jelly

1. Wipe the birds and remove any remaining feathers.
2. Set the oven to 200°C/400°F/gas mark 6.
3. Season the birds inside and put a knob of butter in each body cavity.
4. Tie slices of pork fat over the breasts (this is called barding and is to prevent drying out during cooking).
5. Spread a little butter over the rest of the birds and season with salt and pepper.
6. Place in a roasting pan, pour 5mm/1/4 inch water into the pan and cook for about 40-50 minutes, basting frequently.
7. When cooked lift the pheasants out of the pan and keep warm while you make the gravy.
8. Sprinkle the flour into the roasting juices and add the port and redcurrant jelly.
9. Place the roasting pan over heat and stir and scrape the bottom until the liquid boils.
10. Add a little more water or stock if it is too thick. Boil for 2 minutes, then season well and strain into a warmed gravy boat.
11. Serve the pheasants whole on a warm plate. Serve the gravy separately.

CLARET

Galantine of Pheasant

SERVES 6
1 large pheasant, cleaned
225g/8oz raw chicken meat, minced
170g/6oz sausagemeat
2 shallots, chopped
30ml/2 tablespoons Madeira
15ml/1 tablespoon chopped fresh parsley
salt and freshly ground black pepper
2 slices cooked tongue, cut into strips
1 flat dark mushroom, sliced

For the stock:
1 carrot, sliced
1 onion, sliced
1 celery stick, chopped
6 peppercorns
1 bay leaf
1 parsley stalk
salt
pinch of thyme

To garnish:
bunch of watercress

1. Bone the pheasant completely, including the legs and wings (see page 280). Cut off any excess fat from the vent end.
2. Place the bones in a pan of water with the stock ingredients, bring to the boil, cover and simmer gently for about 1 hour.
3. Meanwhile, prepare the farce (stuffing): mix together the raw chicken meat, sausagemeat, shallot, Madeira and parsley. Season with salt and pepper.
4. Open the bird on a board, skin side down. Push the meat around gently so that it is evenly distributed on top of the skin. Spread with half the farce and lay on the tongue and the mushroom slices. Season and cover with the remaining farce. Fold over the sides of the bird and stitch them together with a needle and fine string. Wrap the bird in a piece of muslin and tie the ends together.
5. Strain the stock. Place the pheasant in a heavy pan and pour over the stock. Bring to the boil, cover tightly with a lid and simmer slowly for 1 1/2 hours, turning the pheasant over once during the cooking.
6. Lift out the bird and, when cool, tighten the muslin cloth round it and leave overnight, refrigerated.
7. Unwrap the cold pheasant, wipe off any grease and slice. Arrange the slices on a flat serving plate and garnish with watercress.

RED BURGUNDY

Whiskied Pheasant

This recipe is one that Nicola Cox has demonstrated at Leith's School; it was, rightly, very popular.

SERVES 2
1 plump pheasant
55g/2oz butter
1 onion
55ml/2 fl oz whisky
200-300ml/$^1/_3$-$^1/_2$ pint double cream
15ml/1 tablespoon Dijon mustard
salt and freshly ground black pepper
1 lemon

To garnish:
bunch of watercress

1. Set the oven to 190°C/375°F/gas mark 5.
2. Melt the butter in a casserole and gently fry the finely chopped onion until golden; add the pheasant and brown on all sides.
3. Pour over the whisky and flame, shaking the pan until the flames die down. Season, then cover the casserole closely and put in the oven for 40-50 minutes until the pheasant is tender.
4. Remove and joint the pheasant; keep warm.
5. Place the pan over high heat and boil up the juices until only 30-45ml/2-3 tablespoons remain, stirring all the time; then add the double cream gradually, boiling down until you have a coating sauce.
6. Remove the pan from the heat, add the mustard and season to taste. Add the lemon juice, pour over the pheasant and serve garnished with the watercress.

FULL RED

Mustard Rabbit

Preparation for this dish begins a day in advance.

SERVES 4
1 rabbit, skinned and cleaned
French mustard
5ml/1 teaspoon chopped tarragon
45g/1$^1/_2$oz butter or bacon dripping
85g/3oz bacon or salt pork, diced
1 onion, finely chopped
1 garlic clove, crushed
5ml/1 teaspoon flour
570ml/1 pint chicken stock (see page 219)

For the garnish:
chopped parsley

1. If the rabbit's head has not been removed, cut if off with a sharp heavy knife. Then cut the rabbit into 6 neat joints.
2. Soak the rabbit in cold salted water for 3 hours. Drain and dry well. (This is to whiten the rabbit.)
3. Spread 30ml/2 tablespoons of mustard mixed with the tarragon over the pieces of rabbit and leave in a cool place overnight.
4. The next day set the oven to 170°C/325°F/gas mark 3.
5. Heat the butter or dripping and brown the joints all over. Remove them with a perforated spoon and place in an ovenproof casserole.
6. Add the bacon, onion and garlic to the frying pan. When the onions are soft and just browned, stir in the flour and cook for 1 minute.
7. Take the pan off the heat and stir in the stock. Return to the heat and bring the sauce slowly to the boil, stirring continuously.
8. Pour this sauce over the rabbit. Put into the oven for about 1$^1/_2$ hours or until the rabbit is tender.
9. Lift the rabbit on to a warm serving dish. Add 5ml/1 teaspoon of mustard to the sauce, taste and add salt and pepper if necessary. Boil for 1 minute. If the sauce is now rather thin, reduce it by boiling rapidly until shiny and rich in appearance. Pour the sauce carefully over the rabbit pieces.
10. Sprinkle with the parsley.

FULL RED

Pigeon Kebabs

SERVES 4
breasts from 4 pigeons
freshly ground black pepper
16 short rashers rindless steaky bacon
16 flat brown mushrooms
oil
chopped savory or thyme

1. Heat the grill.
2. Skin each pigeon breast and cut into 4 pieces. Season with pepper. Stretch the bacon on a board with the back of a knife. Wrap each breast piece loosely in a strip of bacon.
3. Skewer the wrapped breasts alternately with the mushrooms on 4 short skewers.
4. Brush well with oil, sprinkle with savory or thyme and season with pepper.
5. Grill the kebabs for about 6 minutes, turning the skewer every 2 minutes. The breasts should be slightly pink inside and the bacon evenly brown. Serve immediately as the meat toughens if kept for any length of time.

MEDIUM RED

Pigeon with Garlic

This recipe has been adapted from *Nouvelle Cuisine* by the Troisgros brothers. The quantity of garlic called for is not a mistake!

SERVES 4

4 pigeons
100g/3½oz butter
24 garlic cloves, unpeeled
7g/¼oz foie gras (optional) or 30g/1oz chicken liver pâté (see page 139)
22.5ml/1½ tablespoons of brandy
7.5ml/5 tablespoons chicken stock
salt and freshly ground black pepper

1. Clean the pigeons and reserve the livers.
2. Put 7g/¼oz butter into each pigeon and truss them, just cutting the nerve at the joint of the legs so that they do not curl up. Season with salt and pepper.
3. Separate the cloves of garlic but do not peel them. Push the foie gras or chicken liver pâté through a sieve.
4. Preheat the oven to 220°C/425°F/gas mark 7. Heat the remaining butter in a heavy pan, put in the pigeons and brown them lightly on all sides. Surround with the cloves of garlic and cook for 20 minutes in the oven, basting frequently.
5. Put the pigeons on a plate in a warm place with 8 cloves of garlic and their cooking butter. In the same pan, sauté the pigeon livers with the remaining cloves of garlic, deglaze with the cognac and press the livers and garlic through a sieve on to the foie gras.
6. Put the stock, or failing that, water, into the pan, bring to the boil and thicken with the garlic and liver purée. Untruss the pigeons, lift off the breasts, skin them and simmer for 2-3 minutes in the sauce and taste for seasoning.
7. Serve the breasts on a heated serving dish, lightly coated with the sauce and surrounded by the whole cloves of garlic.

RED BURGUNDY

Jack Horner's Pie

SERVES 8

8-10 (depending on size) pigeon breasts, boned and skinned
oil or dripping
1 onion, finely chopped
1 large carrot, sliced
10ml/2 teaspoons flour
290ml/½ pint brown stock (use water in preference to a packet stock cube)
150ml/¼ pint red wine
salt and freshly ground black pepper
15ml/1 tablespoon orange juice
10ml/2 teaspoons redcurrant jelly
170g/6oz prunes, soaked overnight
puff pastry made with 225g/8oz flour (see page 528)
beaten egg

1. Remove any membranes from the pigeon breasts and cut each into 3 or 4 pieces.
2. Heat a little oil or dripping in a frying pan and brown the pieces of pigeon breasts, a few at a time, until brown all over. Remove them to a plate as they are done.
3. Fry the onion and carrot in the pan until slightly softened and pale brown.
4. Stir in the flour and cook for 1 minute. Remove from the heat and add the stock and wine. Return to the heat, bring to the boil and simmer, stirring to scrape any sediment from the bottom of the pan, for 2 minutes. Season with salt and pepper.
5. Return the pigeon breasts to the frying pan (or if it is too small, tip the lot into a saucepan). Add the orange juice and jelly and simmer slowly for 1 hour. Be very careful not to let the

liquid evaporate and the pan burn. If it boils, add extra water.
6. Add the prunes and simmer for a further 1/2 hour. Taste and add extra seasoning if required. Tip into a pie dish and leave to get cold.
7. Set the oven to 200°C/400°F/gas mark 6.
8. Roll out the pastry to the thickness of a coin. Cut a long strip just wider than the rim of the pie dish, brush the lip of the dish with water and press down the strip.
9. Brush the strip with water and lay over the sheet of pastry. Press it down firmly. Cut away any excess pastry.
10. Cut a 1cm/1/2 inch hole in the centre of the pie top and cover with a leaf-shaped piece of pastry (the hole is to allow the escape of steam).
11. Decorate the top with more pastry leaves. Brush all over with egg. Leave in the refrigerator to relax for 10 minutes.
12. Bake in the oven for 30 minutes, or until the pastry is well risen and golden brown.

VERY FULL RED

Roast Woodcock

SERVES 4
4 woodcock
4 rashers bacon
salt and freshly ground black pepper
4 rounds white bread 13cm/5 inches in diameter, toasted on one side (see croûtes, page 325)
5ml/1 teaspoon flour
150ml/1/4 pint stock
squeeze of lemon juice
watercress to garnish

1. Pluck the woodcock. Remove the heads and draw the gizzards through the neck openings, but do not draw the entrails. Truss neatly.
2. Set the oven to 180°C/350°F/gas mark 4.
3. Cover each bird with a rasher of bacon and season well. Place in a roasting pan and roast for about 25 minutes, removing the bacon after 15 minutes to allow the breasts to brown thoroughly.
4. Spread the entrails on the untoasted side of the bread and place a bird on top of each. Keep warm while you prepare the gravy.
5. Tip off all except a scant tablespoon of the fat from the roasting pan.
6. Add the flour and cook for 1 minute until a russet brown.
7. Pour in the stock and bring up to the boil, stirring continuously with a spoon, scraping the bottom of the pan to loosen the sediment as it comes to the boil.
8. Season with salt, pepper and lemon juice. Strain the gravy into a warmed boat.
9. Place the woodcock on a serving dish and garnish with watercress.

RED RHONE

Roast Partridge with Port and Grapes

This is a low-fat recipe; if required, a little cream can be added to the sauce to enrich it!

SERVES 4
4 small partridges
1 dessert apple
1 onion, chopped
15ml/1 tablespoon port
55g/2oz seedless grapes

1. Set the oven to 375°F/190°C/gas mark 5.
2. Clean the partridges. Cut the apple into 4 and put a quarter inside each partridge.
3. Put the chopped onion in a roasting pan. Pour on 425ml/3/4 pint water.
4. Put the partridges on a wire rack on top of the roasting pan. Roast, basting with water occasionally, for 40 minutes.
5. Remove from the oven. Tip the apple and any meat juices from the partridges into the roasting pan. Bring up to the boil and stir vigorously to pulverize the apple. Simmer for 2-3 minutes.
6. Push through a sieve, pressing well to extract all the flavour, into a clean saucepan. It should be the required consistency; however, if it is too thin, boil rapidly to reduce to a syrupy consistency.
7. Add the port and boil for 30 seconds; add the grapes and allow them to warm through.
8. Serve the partridges on a warm plate and serve the sauce separately.

RED BURGUNDY

Guinea Fowl Braised with Caramel and Oranges

SERVES 4
2 guinea fowl
10ml/2 teaspoons sunflower oil
55g/2oz shallots, chopped finely
30g/1oz granulated sugar
15ml/1 tablespoon wine vinegar
175ml/6 fl oz chicken stock (see page 219)
juice of 2 oranges, strained
salt and freshly ground black pepper

To garnish:
1 orange, segmented
small bunch of watercress

1. Preheat the oven to 190°C/375°F/gas mark 5.
2. Remove any feathers from the guinea fowl and wipe their insides clean with a damp cloth.
3. Heat the oil in a flameproof casserole. Add the guinea fowl and brown them all over. Remove them from the casserole.
4. Reduce the heat and add the shallots; cook them for 2 minutes. Add the sugar and vinegar, dissolving the sugar over a gentle heat, and then boil the liquid until the sugar caramelizes. Pour on the stock – it will hiss and splutter so take care – and stir over a gentle heat, until the caramel lumps disappear. Add the orange juice. Season well with salt and pepper. Return the guinea fowl to the casserole and bring the cooking liquor up to the boil.
5. Cover the casserole and pot-roast it for 1 hour.
6. Remove the guinea fowl and joint them as you would a chicken (see page 280). Arrange the pieces on a warm serving plate. Skim as much fat as possible from the cooking liquor. Strain it into a clean saucepan, skim it again and boil rapidly for 3 minutes.
7. Garnish the guinea fowl with segments of orange and a small bunch of watercress, and serve the hot sauce separately.

RED BURGUNDY

Quail with Chestnuts and Calvados

8 small quail
2 dessert apples, peeled, cored and diced
freshly ground black pepper
1 onion, sliced
1 bay leaf
45ml/3 tablespoons Calvados
1 x 140g/5oz tin unsweetened chestnuts
chicken stock

1. Set the oven to 200°C/400°F/gas mark 6.
2. Season the quail with pepper and stuff with the apple.
3. Place the quail in a roasting pan with the onion, bay leaf, Calvados and 4 of the chestnuts. Add enough chicken stock to come a quarter of the way up the quail. Cover with tin foil and roast in the oven for 25 minutes. Remove the foil and roast for a further 10 minutes.
4. Remove the quail to a warm serving dish and keep warm in the turned-off oven.
5. Strain the cooking liquid into a saucepan, pressing the vegetables to extract their flavour. Skim off any fat from the liquid, then reduce by boiling until syrupy. You should have about 290 ml/$^1/_2$ pint.
6. Add the remaining chestnuts and warm through in the sauce.
7. Spoon the liquid over the quail, garnish with chestnuts and hand any extra sauce separately.

LIGHT RED

Cold Game Pie (I)

This pie takes 2 days to complete.

SERVES 6-8
pâte à pâté made with 450g/1lb flour (see page 531)
1 grouse
1 partridge
1 pigeon
2 hare joints
110g/4oz venison
2 large carrots
2 large onions
2 sticks celery

60ml/4 tablespoons oil
110g/4oz butter
290ml/ 1/2 pint red wine
1 litre/1 3/4 pints good stock
4 bay leaves
a little fresh thyme
parsley stalks
salt and freshly ground black pepper
30g/1oz gelatine
beaten egg

1. Split the birds in half. Cut the venison into small cubes. Chop the carrot, onion and celery roughly.
2. Heat about 15ml/1 tablespoon each of butter and oil in a heavy pan, and when the butter is foaming, add a good handful of the chopped vegetables. Keep the heat at a medium temperature - enough to fry and brown the vegetables without burning the butter. Keep turning the vegetables to get an even colour all over. When they are all done, lift them out with a perforated spoon and transfer to a large deep saucepan.
3. Add more oil and butter and brown the venison, the hare and finally the birds. If the bottom of the pan becomes sticky and brown, deglaze it with half a glass of the wine or stock: pour in the liquid and boil up, stirring with a metal spoon or fish slice and scraping the bottom of the pan to loosen the sediment. Tip this liquid in with the browned ingredients and continue frying the meats.
4. When all the ingredients are browned and transferred to the deep saucepan, deglaze the pan again, pouring the juices in with the meats. Add the rest of the wine, the stock, and, if necessary, a little water (the ingredients must be just covered). Add the herbs and salt and pepper. Cover with a lid and simmer for 1 1/2 hours or until everything is tender.
5. Strain off the liquid and leave until completely cold. Skim thoroughly, then transfer to a saucepan and boil to reduce to about 570ml/1 pint. Add the gelatine to the liquid and leave to soak.
6. When the meat is cool enough to handle, remove all the bones from the birds and hare and cut the flesh into small pieces (about the size of the cubes of venison). Discard the cooked vegetables, the bay leaves and parsley stalks. Let the meat cool completely.
7. Set the oven to 190°C/375°F/gas mark 5. Lightly grease a 1.8kg/4lb pie mould or a loose-bottomed cake tin.
8. Roll two-thirds of the pastry into a round big enough to cover the base and sides of the mould or tin. Dust the pastry with a little flour. Now fold it in half, away from you. Place one hand on the fold of the semi-circle and with the other gently push and pull the sides so that you form a 'bag' roughly the shape and size of the pie mould or cake tin. Open out the bag and fit it into the greased mould or tin.
9. Fill the pie with the meat. Roll out the remaining pastry into a round big enough to cover the top of the pie. Dampen the bottom edge, then press this 'lid' on to the pastry case, pinching the edges together.
10. Decorate with pastry trimmings, shaped into leaves, and make a neat pea-sized hole in the middle of the top. Brush with beaten egg.
11. Bake for 50 minutes. While the pie is in the oven, heat up the stock to melt the soaked gelatine. Allow to cool.
12. Remove the pie carefully from the mould or tin and stand on a flat baking sheet. Brush with beaten egg all over and return to the oven for a further 20 minutes. Take out and allow to cool.
13. Using a small funnel, pour the cooled, but not quite set, stock into the pie through the hole in the pastry lid. Allow the liquid to seep down into the pie, then pour in some more: this can be a slow process, but the pie should take about 570ml/1 pint of liquid, and it is important that you add it to prevent the filling becoming crumbly and dry.

NOTE: If buying such small quantities of hare and venison proves difficult, use 225g/8oz lean chuck steak instead.

CLARET

Cold Game Pie (II)

Preparation for this dish must start 2 or 3 days in advance.

SERVES 6

For the forcemeat:
110g/4oz poultry livers
1 pheasant, boned (see page 280) and skinned
450g/1lb pork belly, derinded
3 shallots, finely chopped
2 sage leaves, finely chopped
5ml/1 teaspoon chopped thyme
1 garlic clove, crushed
10ml/2 teaspoons salt
5ml/1 teaspoon coarsely ground black pepper
15ml/1 tablespoon brandy
45ml/3 tablespoons dry white wine

For the jelly:
1 stick celery
1 carrot, sliced
1 slice of onion
1 bay leaf
sprig of parsley
sprig of marjoram
bones, giblets (except the liver) and skin of the pheasant
15g/½oz gelatine

For the pastry crust:
pâte à pâté made with 450g/1lb flour (see page 531)
piece of pig's caul about 30cm/12 inches square
beaten egg

1. Trim any discoloured parts and sinew from the livers.
2. Reserve 1 pheasant breast, the pheasant liver and 1 other poultry liver. Mince the rest of the pheasant meat with the remaining livers and the pork belly. Add the shallot, sage, thyme, garlic, salt, pepper, brandy and wine. Mix well and put into a deep bowl.
3. Lay the breast meat and livers on top, and cover. Refrigerate for 24 hours.
4. Make up the pâte à pâté.
5. Use two-thirds of it to line a 20cm/8 inch raised pie mould or a loose-bottomed cake tin.
6. Line the empty pie shell with the pig's caul, allowing the sides to hang down over the edge.
7. Put half the minced mixture into the mould. Cut the pheasant breast into strips and lay them on top of the forcemeat.
8. Lay the livers on top of the pheasant strips. Cover with the rest of the forcemeat, pressing down well to eliminate any air pockets.
9. Draw the caul up over the forcemeat to envelop it.
10. Set the oven to 190°C/375°F/gas mark 5.
11. Use the remaining pastry to cover and elaborately decorate the top of the pie. Press the edges of the top firmly to the base pastry. Make a hole in the middle of the pastry top to allow steam to escape.
12. Brush with beaten egg.
13. Bake the pie for 15 minutes, then turn the oven down to 150°C/300°F/gas mark 2, for a further 1¾ hours. Allow to cool overnight.
14. Make the stock by simmering the jelly ingredients (except the gelatine) in 1 litre/2 pints water for 2 hours. Strain through muslin or a double 'J'-cloth and chill overnight.
15. Remove all traces of fat from the stock. Pour it into a saucepan and sprinkle on the gelatine. Leave to soak for 10 minutes, then bring slowly to the boil. Boil until there is approximately 290ml/½ pint of liquid left.
16. Leave until cold but not set – it should be syrupy. Carefully pour, little by little, into the pie, through the hole in the pastry. A small funnel will make this operation easier. Continue until the liquid level is visible, and will no longer gradually sink. If by some mischance the pastry case has a hole in it allowing the liquid to leak out, plug the hole with softened butter.
17. Chill the pie until the liquid is set: about 2 hours.

NOTE: If pouring the liquid into the pie proves difficult, carefully make, with the tip of a knife, another hole in the cooked pastry towards the edge, and pour the liquid through this.

CLARET

Partridge with Lentils

2 partridges, drawn, trussed and larded
salt
30g/1oz lard
30g/1oz unsmoked bacon, chopped
30g/1oz onion, chopped
110g/4oz Puy lentils, soaked in cold water for 1 hour and drained
grated rind of 1/2 lemon
1 bay leaf
110g/4oz Gyula sausage or similar dried, smoked pork sausage
290ml/1/2 pint chicken stock
75ml/1/8 pint soured cream

1. Preheat the oven to 170°C/325°F/gas mark 3.
2. Sprinkle the partridges with salt. Melt the lard in a large frying pan and fry the partridges until they are golden brown all over. Remove from the pan.
3. Fry the bacon and onion in the same pan until golden brown.
4. Put the lentils into a large pan with the lemon rind and bay leaf. Add the partridges, sausage, bacon and onion. Pour over enough stock to just cover the ingredients. Cover the pan with a lid and put it into the oven. Cook until the partridges are tender, about 45 minutes. If the partridges are ready before the lentils, remove them and the sausages from the pan.
5. When the lentils are tender, pour over the soured cream and bring the liquid to the boil.
6. Carve the partridges and cut the sausages into thin slices. Place the lentils in a deep serving dish, put the partridge pieces on top and garnish with the sliced sausage.

Croûtes for Roast Game Birds

When roasting small game birds, such as snipe or woodcock, the 'trail', or entrails, is left inside and only the gizzard removed. After roasting, the liver and juices are spread on the uncooked side of a slice of bread which has been fried or toasted on one side only. The roasted bird is served on this croûte.

Larger birds like pheasant and grouse are drawn before roasting, but the liver may be returned to the body cavity to cook with the bird. This, plus any other scrapings from the inside of the bird, is spread on the uncooked side of the croûte, which is then cut diagonally in half and served as a garnish to the whole roast bird.

Fried Crumbs for Roast Game Birds

55g/2oz butter
60ml/4 tablespoons dry white breadcrumbs

Melt the butter and fry the crumbs very slowly until they have absorbed most of it, and are golden in colour and crisp. Serve in a warm bowl, handed to the diners with the sauce or sauces.

NOTE: Fresh white crumbs can be used, but rather more butter will be needed as they are very absorbent, and great care should be taken to fry slowly so that the crumbs become crisp before they turn brown.

Meat

Meat

THE YOUNGER the animal, and the less exercise it has taken, the more tender its meat will be, but its flavour will be less pronounced. For example a week-old calf will be tender as margarine, and about as flavourless. An ox that has pulled a cart all its long life will be quite the reverse – good on flavour, but tough as old boots. A relatively young, and therefore tender, animal will have white or pale fat, rather than yellow; the meat will be less dark, and the bones more pliable than in an older, tougher animal. So rump steak with a bright red hue and white fat may well be more tender than the dark flesh and yellow fat of older meat, but it will probably lose in flavour what it gains in texture.

Because tenderness is rated highly today, the most expensive cuts of meat are those from the parts of the animal's body that have had little or no exercise. For example, the leg, neck and shoulder cuts of beef are tougher (and therefore cheaper) than those taken from the rump or loin.

But apart from the age of the animal, there are other factors that affect tenderness. Meat must not be cooked while the muscle fibres are taut due to rigor mortis, which can last, depending on the temperature at which the carcase is stored, for a day or two. The state of the animal prior to slaughter can also affect the tenderness of the meat; for example, if it is relaxed and peaceful the meat is likely to be more tender. Injections of certain enzymes (proteins that produce changes in the meat without themselves being changed) given to the animal before slaughter will produce the same result artificially.

But the most crucial factor affecting tenderness is the length of time that meat is stored before cooking. If hung in temperatures of 2°C/35°F it will, due to enzyme activity, become increasingly tender. Temperatures should not be higher than this, because although the enzyme activity would be greater, the risk of spoilage due to bacterial action would become high. For beef, 7 days is the minimum hanging time, while 3 weeks or a month are more desirable. However, with the commercial demands for quick turnover, the weight-loss during storage and the expense of storing, good hanging is rare these days. Some enzyme activity continues if the meat is frozen, and the formation, and subsequent melting, of ice-crystals (which, in expanding, bruise the fibres of the meat) means that freezing meat can be said to tenderize it. However, the inevitable loss of juices from the meat (and subsequent risk of dryness after cooking) is a disadvantage that outweighs the minimal tenderizing effect.

Hanging is most important in beef, as the animals are comparatively old, perhaps 2 or 3 years, when killed. It is less important for carcases of young animals, such as calves and lambs, as their meat is relatively tender anyway.

Because, inevitably, some bacterial action (as well as enzyme action) must take place during hanging, the flavour of well-hung meat is stronger, or gamier, than that of under-hung meat. The colour will also deepen and become duller with hanging. But the prime reason for hanging meat is to tenderize it, rather than to increase or change its flavour. This is not so with game, including venison, which is hung as much to produce a gamey flavour as to tenderize the meat.

The last, and probably most important, factor that affects the ultimate tenderness of meat is the method of cooking. Half-cooked or rare meat will be tender simply because its fibres have not been changed by heat, and will still retain the softness of raw meat. But as the heat penetrates the whole piece of meat the fibres set rigidly and the juices cease to run. Once the whole piece of meat is heated thoroughly, all the softness of raw meat is lost and it is at its toughest. This explains the natural reluctance of chefs to serve well-done steaks – it is almost impossible to produce a tender well-done grilled steak.

But, paradoxically, further cooking (though not fast grilling or frying) will tenderize that tough steak. This is seen in stewing, when long, slow cooking gradually softens the flesh. A joint from an older animal, which has done much muscular work during its lifetime and is coarse-grained and fibrous, can be made particularly tender by prolonged gentle cooking. This is because much of the connective tissue present in such a joint, if subjected to a steady temperature of, say, 100°C/200°F, will convert to gelatine, producing a soft, almost sticky tenderness.

Joints with finer graining and little connective tissue, such as rump or sirloin, will never become gelatinous, and are consequently seldom cooked other than by roasting or grilling, when their inherent tenderness (from a life of inaction) is relied on. But they will never be as tender as the slow-cooked shin or oxtail, which can be cut with a spoon.

It does not matter that few people have any idea which part of the animal their meat comes from. But it is useful to know, if not how to do the butcher's job, at least which cuts are likely to be tender, expensive, good for stewing, or not worth having, and what to look for in a piece of meat.

Roasting Meat

1. Weigh the joint and establish the length of cooking time (see below).
2. Preheat the oven (electric ovens take much longer to heat up than gas ovens).
3. Prepare the joint for roasting; see the relevant recipe.
4. Heat some dripping in a roasting pan and if the meat is lean, brown the joint over direct heat so that it is well coloured. Pork and lamb rarely need this but many cuts of beef do.
5. Place the joint in the pan, on a grid if you have one available, as this aids the circulation of hot air; roast for the time calculated.

ROASTING TIMES

Obviously a long thin piece of meat weighing 2.3 kg/5lb will take less time to cook than a fat round piece of the same weight, so that the times below are meant only as a guide. The essential point is that meat must reach an internal temperature of 60°C/140°F to be rare, 70°C/150°F to be medium pink, and 80°C/170°F to be well done. A meat thermometer stuck into the thickest part of the meat, and left there during cooking, eliminates guesswork.

BEEF: Beef is generally roasted in the hottest of ovens for 20 minutes to brown the meat (or it may be fried all over in fat before being transferred to the oven). Whatever the method, count the cooking time after the browning has been done, and allow 10-15 minutes per 450g/1lb for rare meat, 20 minutes for medium and 25 for well done, roasting the meat in a preheated oven set at 190°C/375°F/gas mark 5.

LAMB: Put the lamb into the hottest of ovens for 15 minutes, then allow 15 minutes to 450g/1lb at 190°C/375°F/gas mark 5. This will produce very slightly pink lamb. If lamb without a trace of pinkness is wanted, allow an extra 20 minutes after the calculated time is up.

PORK: Pork must be well cooked. Allow 40 minutes to 450g/1lb at 170°C/325°F/gas mark 3. If crackling is required, roast at 200°C/400°F/gas mark 6 for 25 minutes to 450g/1lb, plus 25 minutes over.

VEAL: Brown in hot fat over direct heat. Or roast for 20 minutes at maximum temperature. Then allow 25 minutes per 450g/1lb at 180°C/350°F/gas mark 4.

Cuts of meat

BEEF

For roasting: sirloin, fore rib, fillet
For pot-roasting: topside, silverside, brisket, thick flank
For stewing, braising and boiling, and for salting and boiling: chuck, shin, brisket, flank, neck, topside, silverside
For grilling and frying: fillet, rump and sirloin. But the names for steaks can be confusing:

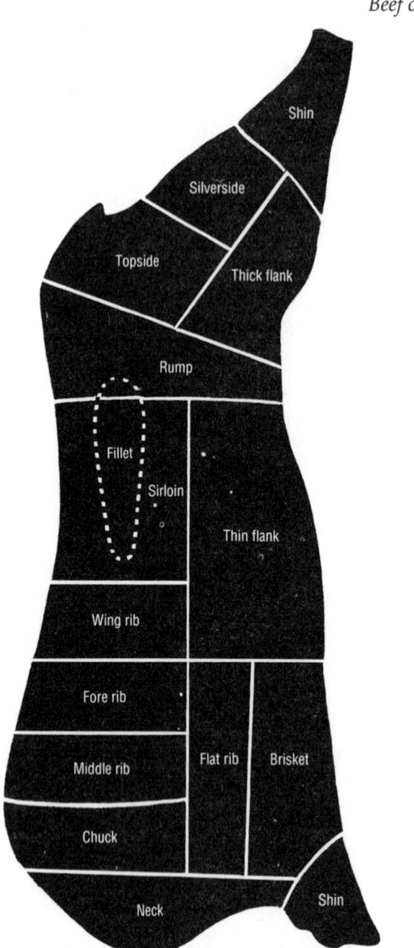

Beef cuts

Rump steaks (rumsteak or bifsteak in French): These are thick (about 2cm/3/4inch) slices cut across the grain of the rump, and then, if for individual servings, cut into smaller neat pieces.

Fillet steak: This comes in various guises. Cut across into neat thick (2cm/1 inch) slices, it becomes tournedos. A neat piece for 2 or 3 people, weighing perhaps 225g/8oz cut from the thick end (but with all the coarser meat trimmed from it), can be grilled, spitted or roasted as a châteaubriand. Medallions are thin neat slices cut across the fillet.

Sirloin steak: The name sirloin covers steak from the upper side of the true sirloin, wing rib and fore rib. The French entrecôte means only the true tender sirloin, which is cut in individual steaks or as T-bone steaks (on the rib, with the sirloin on one side of the T and the fillet or undercut on the other). French côte de boeuf or our rib of beef are thick steaks on the rib bone, from the slightly less tender wing rib or fore rib. Porterhouse is a double-sized T-bone, or double-sized wing rib.

For pies: chuck, brisket, thick flank, shin (foreleg), shin or leg (hind leg).

VEAL

The cuts of veal, and their names, more closely resemble those of a lamb or sheep than those of grown-up beef.

As veal is more tender than beef, more of the animal is suitable for quick cooking (roasting, frying). But as there is little fat on a calf, care must be taken to moisten the meat frequently during cooking to prevent dryness. Because of the absence of fat, veal is seldom grilled.

Dutch veal is milk-fed and expensive. It has a pale pink colour and the best cuts are exceptionally tender. But the taste is mild to the point of insipidity, and it needs good seasoning, usually plenty of lemon, pepper or a good sauce. English veal is cheaper, has more flavour,

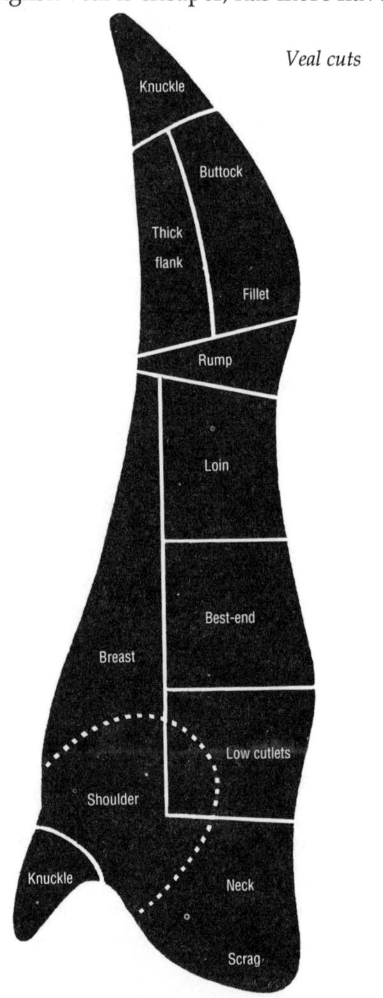

Veal cuts

and generally has a slightly more reddish hue. This is because the animals are killed older than their Dutch fellows, and are generally, though not always, grass-fed. But veal should never look bloody or really red.

For roasting: leg, loin, best end, breast
For braising and stewing: leg, shoulder, middle neck, scrag, breast
For frying (and possibly grilling if frequently basted): cushion (fillet), loin chops, best end cutlets, rump, round (buttock)
For stock: knuckle, foot or scrag end of neck.
NOTE: The more tender cuts from the forequarter, from a top-quality milk-fed calf, may also be boned out and sliced for escalopes.

PORK

Pork used to be eaten mainly in winter, or as bacon, because of the difficulty of keeping it fresh. But with modern methods of refrigeration, pork is eaten all the year round.

The flesh should be pale pink, not red or bloody. Pork killed for the fresh meat market is generally very young and tender, carrying little fat. Suckling pigs, killed while still being milk-fed, may be roasted or barbecued whole, and are traditionally served with the head on, and with an apple or an orange between the jaws.

Crackling is the roasted skin of pork. The skin must be scored deeply with a sharp knife before roasting. Salt is rubbed on the skin, making it crisp and bubbly when cooked.

For roasting: any part of the pig (bar the head, trotters and knuckle) are suitable
For grilling and frying: spare rib chops, loin chops, chump chops from the saddle, best end cutlets, belly bones or American spare ribs (usually with a marinade), fillet, tenderloin, trotters
For boiling: leg, belly, hand and spring, trotters
For pies: any meat is suitable
For sausages: any fatty piece, especially belly.

BACON

Bacon pigs are killed when heavier than pigs destined for the fresh pork market, so the comparable cuts of bacon should contain more fat than those of fresh pork.

Almost the whole of the pig is salted in brine for up to a week, then matured. Green bacon is sold at this stage. Smoked bacon is hung in cool smoke for up to a month. Gammon is bacon from a hind leg, and ham is bacon from a hind leg that has been brined or cured in dry salt separately from the rest of the pig. Gammon is cured while still attached to the body. Hams are salted and possibly smoked according to varying local traditions. Parma ham and Bayonne ham, for example, are salted and smoked but not cooked further before eating. English hams are generally cooked before eating hot or cold. The most famous are the well-hung Braddenham ham and the sweet mild York ham. American Virginia hams are said to owe their sweet flavour to the fact that the hogs are fed on peanuts and peaches, and the hams are cured in salt and sugar and smoked over apple and hickory wood for a month. Westphalian ham from Germany is eaten raw in thin slices like Parma ham. Paris ham is similar to English York ham.

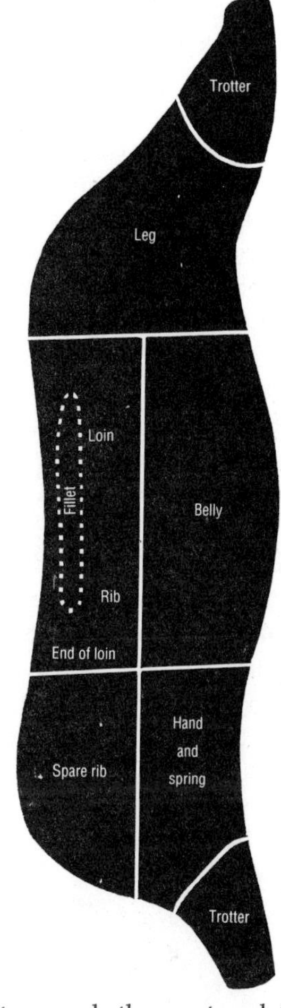

Pork cuts

Since good refrigeration is now widely available, pork need no longer be salted as a preservative measure. Today pork is turned into bacon mainly for the flavour. Smoked bacon keeps slightly longer than green (unsmoked) but, again, modern smoking is done more for the flavour than for preservation.

Commercially produced bacon is generally mild. Bacon cured at home, without chemical preservatives, vacuum packs, etc. , is likely to have more flavour and saltiness, but needs soaking before cooking.

Smoked and green bacon flesh look similarly reddish-pink. It should not be dry, hard, dark or patchy in colour. Smoked rind is yellowish-brown; green bacon rind is white.

English bacons vary according to manufacturer and price, some being saltier than others, so care should be taken if boiling without prior soaking. It is wise to soak large pieces to be cooked whole, such as gammons or forehocks. Smaller cuts, steaks and rashers, rarely need soaking.

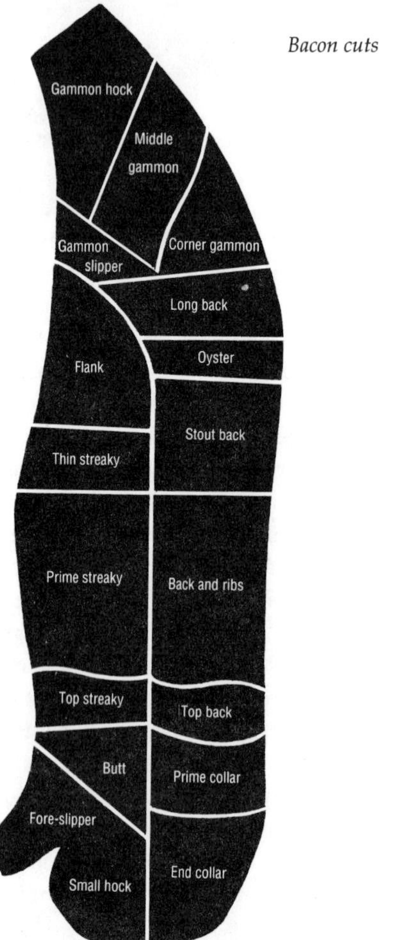

Bacon cuts

Danish pigs are all cured in the same manner, giving a good quality, mild-tasting, not very salty bacon.

For boiling and stewing: all cuts are suitable, but the lean pieces (forehock, gammon, collar) are sometimes casseroled or stewed whole, tied with string
Streaky and flank are used diced for soups, or to add flavour to stews
For frying or grilling: all cuts are suitable but rashers are usually cut from the back, streaky or collar. Steaks are cut from the gammon or prime back
For baking (usually boiled first): large lean pieces are generally used (whole gammon or ham, whole gammon hock, large piece of back, whole boned and rolled forehock or either of the collars).

LAMB AND MUTTON

Animals weighing more than 36 kg/80lb are graded as mutton. Real mutton is seldom available in butchers' shops since all the animals are killed young enough to be called lamb. But there is a difference between the small sweet joints of the new season's spring lamb, and the larger lambs killed later in the year.

Really baby lambs, killed while still milk-fed, are extremely expensive, with very pale, tender flesh. A leg from such a lamb would feed only 2 or perhaps 3 people at most.

British lamb is very fine in flavour, but good imported New Zealand lamb is usually cheaper. As a general rule, New Zealand lamb joints come from smaller animals than the full-grown English lambs, but it should be remembered that 3 grades of New Zealand lamb are imported into Britain, ranging from excellent to very tough. All New Zealand lamb comes into the country frozen, so it stands to reason that some lambs have been more recently killed than others. The best time to buy New Zealand lamb is from Christmas through to the summer months.

Lamb should be brownish-pink rather than grey in colour, but not bloody. Because the animal is killed young, almost all the cuts are tender enough for grilling, frying or roasting, but the fattier, cheaper cuts are used for casseroles and stews too.

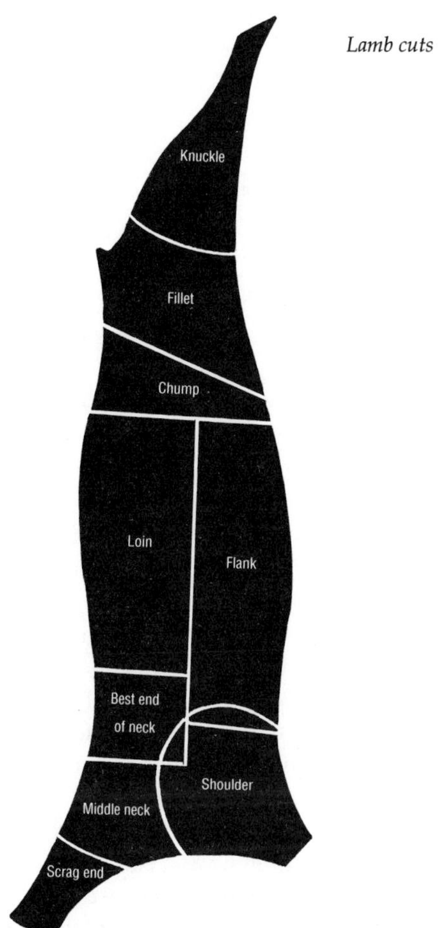

Lamb cuts

For roasting: saddle or loin, best end of neck (rack of lamb), shoulder, leg, breast
For braising: chump chops, loin, leg
For grilling and frying: best end cutlets, loin chops, chump chops, steaks from fillet end of leg
For boiling and stewing: knuckle, scrag and middle neck, breast, leg.

Butchery and meat preparation

Most cuts of meat are available ready prepared from the shop or market. But it is useful to know how to bone and tie certain French and English cuts that a busy butcher may be unwilling to tackle.

BONING

Boning is easier than most people imagine. A short sharp knife is essential. Tunnel-boning – where the bone, say from a leg, is extracted from the hole from which it protrudes, without opening out the meat – is more difficult than open-boning, where the flesh is split along the bone, the bone worked out and the meat rolled up and tied or sewn. But, whether tunnel-boning or open-boning, it is essential to work slowly and carefully, keeping the knife as close to the bones as possible, and scraping the meat off the bone rather than cutting it. Any meat extracted inadvertently with the bone can be scraped off and put back into the joint.

With most bones it is possible, when tunnel-boning, to work from both ends – for example, a leg of lamb can be worked on where the knuckle bone sticks out of the thin end, and the leg bone out of the fillet end. But in most cases it is simpler to cut neatly through the flesh, along the length of the bone, from the side nearest to the bone, and work the bone out all along its length. After all, some sewing or tying is necessary at the ends of the joints even if tunnel-boned, and it is simpler to sew up the length of the joint.

Trainee butchers are taught to use the knife in such a way that should it slip it will not hurt them. This means never pulling the knife directly towards the body. In addition, the knife is held firmly like a dagger when working, with the point of the knife down. But the safest precaution that cooks can take is to see that their knifes are sharp. Blunt knives need more pressure to wield, and are therefore more inclined to slip.

BUTTERFLY JOINTS

To make a butterfly joint, open-bone a leg of lamb. Hold a sharp, sturdy butcher's knife like a dagger and cut, from the knuckle end, down the non-fleshy side of the leg and gradually work out the three bones.

LAMB 'EN BALLON'

This is a stuffed boned shoulder of lamb that is tied up to look like a balloon (see page 368 for a recipe). To reassemble the shoulder, spread the stuffing on one half of the boned lamb and fold the other half close up over to cover it. If the shoulder has been tunnel-boned, push the stuffing into it. Turn the shoulder over, skinned side up. Tie the end of a 3m/9ft piece of string firmly round the shoulder, making a knot in the middle at the top. Take the string around again, but this time at right angles to the first line,

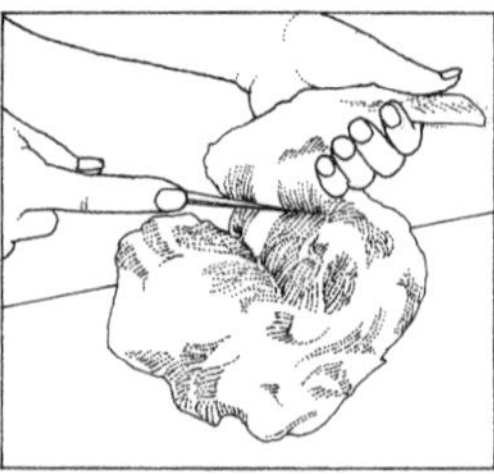

To make a butterfly joint, work from the knuckle end

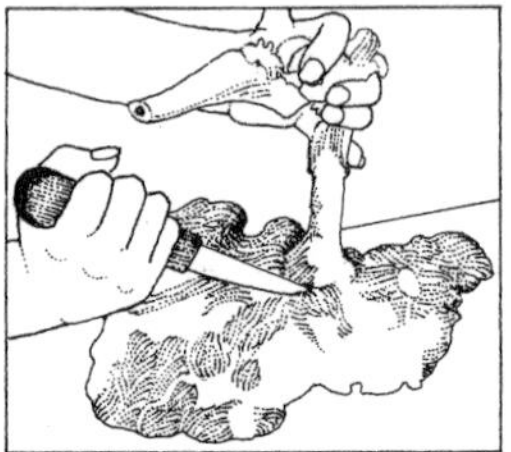

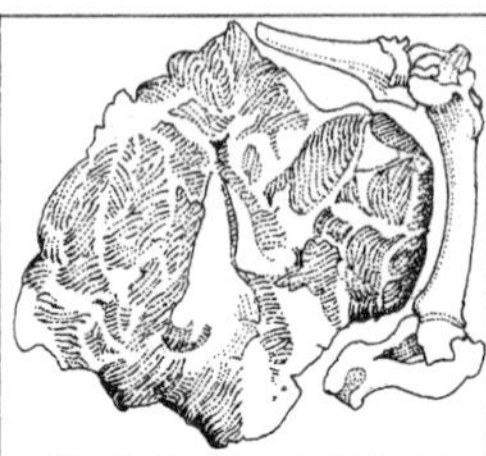

Gradually ease out the three bones

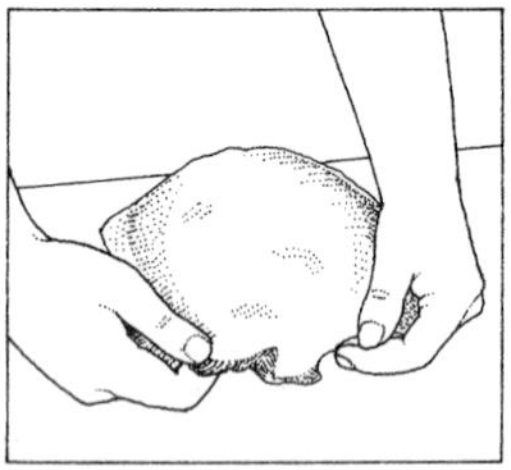

After stuffing, fold the butterfly flaps under the joint

again tying at the first knot. Continue this process until the 'balloon' is trussed about 8 times. Tuck in any loose flaps of meat or skin.

ROLLING AND TYING

Once a joint, such as a loin, is boned, remove most of the fat and lay it, meat side up, on the board. Season it or spread sparingly with stuffing. Roll it up from the thick end and use short pieces of thin cotton (not nylon) string to

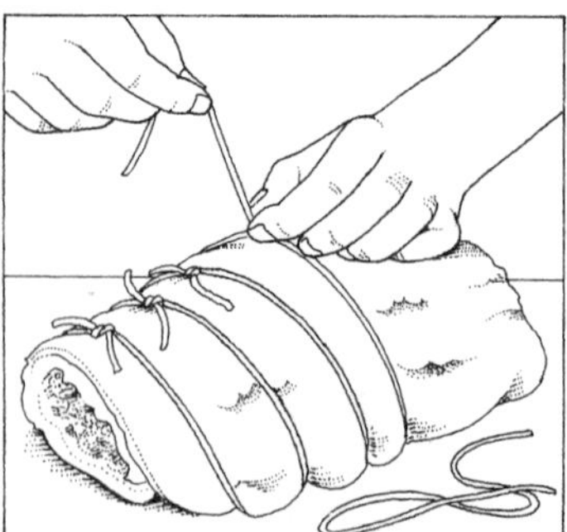

Tie with short pieces of string or cotton

tie round the meat at 2.5cm/1 inch intervals. These can easily be cut off when serving, or the carver can slice between them when cutting the meat into thick slices.

SEWING UP WHOLE JOINTS AFTER STUFFING

Use a larding needle or large darning or upholstery needle. Some of these are curved slightly which makes the job easier.

Use thin old-fashioned white string, not nylon which will melt under heat. If the string is not very thin it can be 'untwined' quite easily and used as required. Leave a good length of string at the beginning and end, but do not tie elaborate knots, which are difficult to undo when dishing the meat. Simple, large, fairly loose stitches are best – the whole length of string can be pulled out in one movement when dishing.

LARDING

Some very lean or potentially tough meat is larded before roasting. This promotes tenderness and adds flavour. The technique is most commonly used for slow-roasted dishes like boeuf à la mode or roast veal. A special larding needle is used.

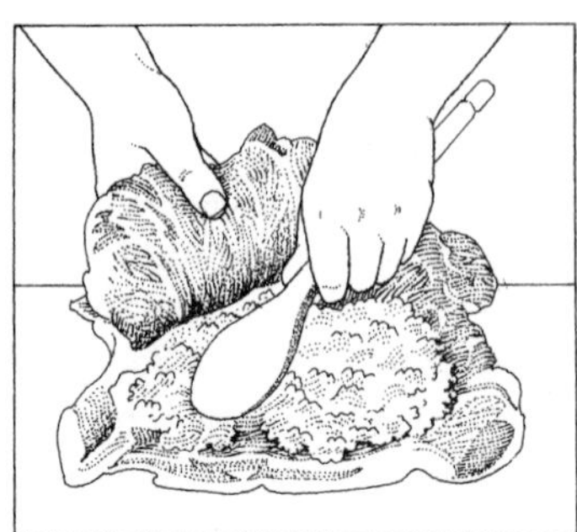

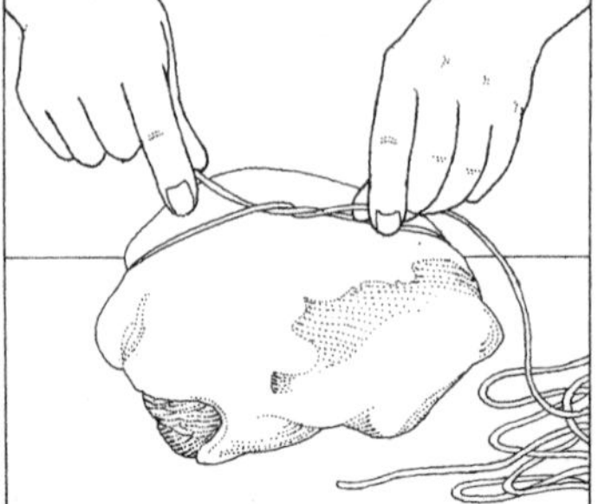

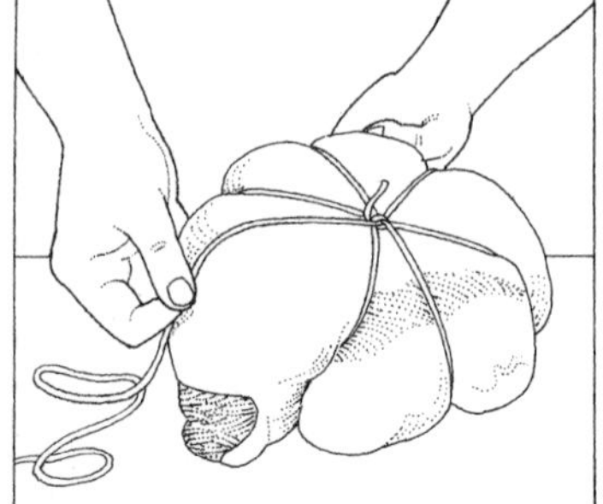

To assemble lamb en ballon, stuff a boned shoulder and tie

To lard a joint, cut the larding fat (usually rindless back pork fat) into thin strips and put one of them into the tunnel of the needle, clamping down the hinge to hold it in place. The fat should extend a little way out of the needle. Thread through the meat, twisting the needle gently to prevent the fat pulling off. Then release the clamp, and trim the 2 ends of fat close to the meat. Repeat this all over the lean meat at 2.5cm/1 inch intervals.

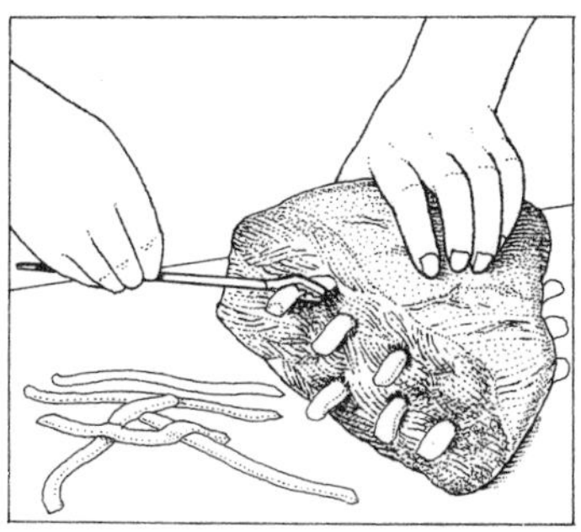

To lard: thread with strips of pork fat

Preparing beef

STEAKS FOR GRILLING OR FRYING
Cut across the grain of the meat, if possible into thickish slices. Trim neatly, and cut rump slices into 2 or 3 individual steaks.

MINUTE STEAKS
Cut large thin steaks. Put them between 2 sheets of paper or polythene and bat gently with a cook's mallet or rolling pin to flatten the meat.

TOURNEDOS STEAKS
Cut 2.5cm/1 inch slices across the trimmed fillet.

FOR STEWING
Remove the gristle, but not all the fat (it will add moisture and flavour). Cut into 2.5cm/1 inch cubes, or larger. Too-small pieces shred up, becoming dry and tough during cooking.

FOR STROGANOFF
Cut into small strips about the thickness of a pencil across the grain of the meat.

FOR ROASTING
If the meat has no fat on it, tie a piece of pork fat, or fatty bacon, round it. Tie up as described on page 334.

Preparing lamb

SADDLE
This consists of both loins of lamb, left attached at the backbone, in the same way as a baron of beef.

First remove the skin: with a small knife lift a corner of the skin, hold this firmly with a tea towel to get a good grip and tug sharply to peel off. Trim off any very large pieces of fat from the edges of the saddle, but leave the back fat. Tuck the flaps under the saddle. Cut out the kidneys but keep them (they can be brushed with butter and attached to the end of the saddle with wooden skewers 30 minutes before the end of the roasting time). Using a sharp knife, score the back fat all over in a fine criss-cross pattern.

The pelvic or aitch bone, protruding slightly from one end of the saddle, can be removed, or left in place and covered with a ham frill when the saddle is served.

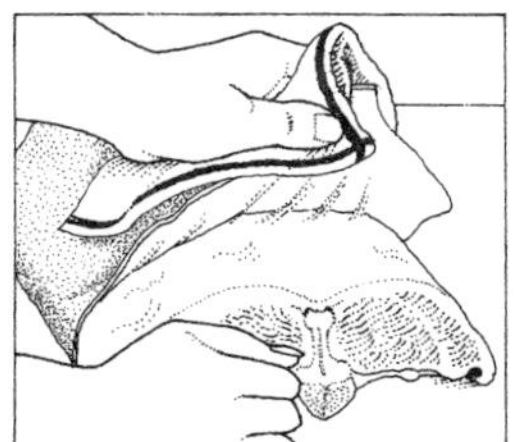

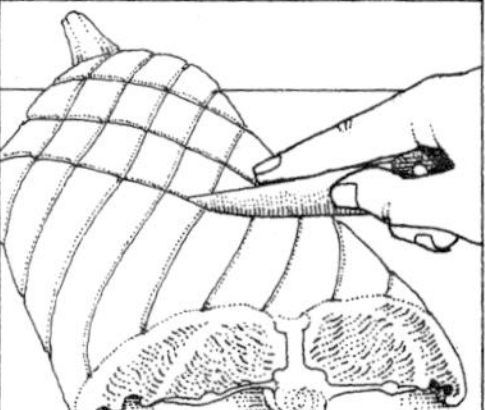

Preparing a saddle of lamb

FRENCH-TRIMMED BEST END CUTLETS
Skin the best end: lift a corner of the skin from the neck end with a small knife, hold it firmly, using a cloth to get a good grip, and peel it off. Chine if the butcher has not already done so. This means sawing carefully through the chine bone (or spine) just where it meets the rib bones. Take care not to saw right through into the eye of the meat. Now remove the chine bone completely. Chop off the cutlet bones so that the length of the remaining bones is not more than twice the length of the eye of the meat. Remove the half-moon shaped piece of flexible cartilage found buried between the layers of fat and meat at the thinner end of the best end. This is the tip of the shoulder blade. It is simple to work out with a knife and your fingers. Remove the line of gristle to be found under the meat at the thick end.

If thin small cutlets are required, cut between each bone as evenly as possible, splitting the

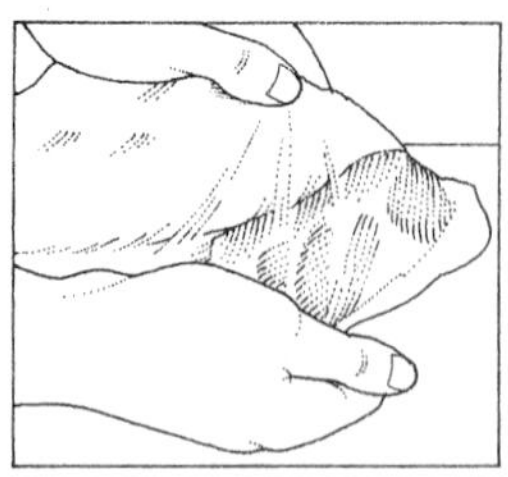
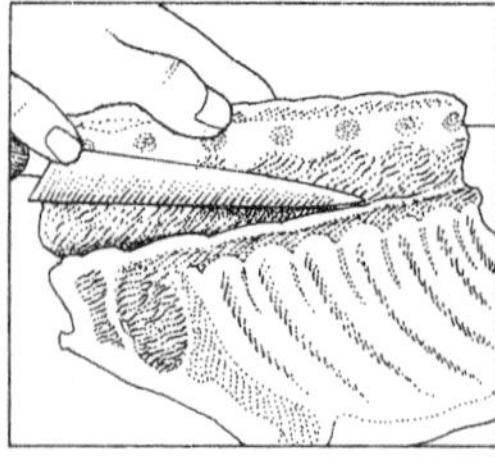

For cutlets: skin and chine

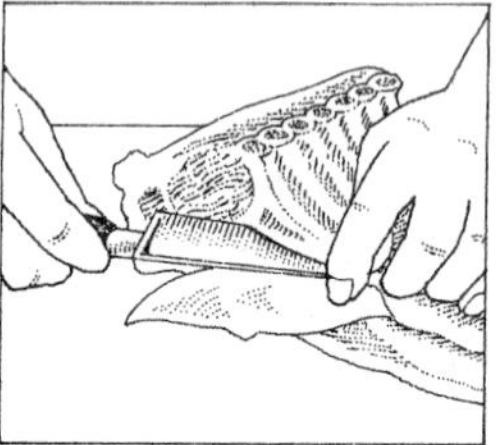
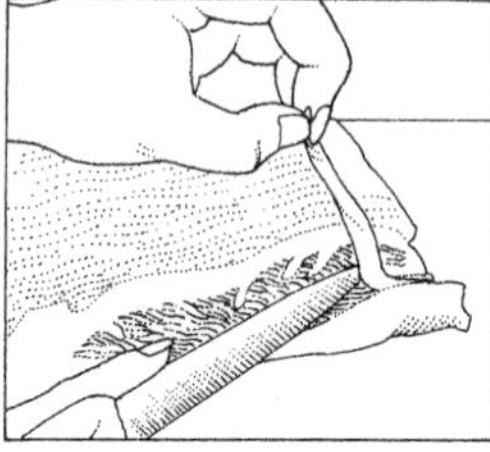

Remove the shoulder blade and gristle

rack into 6 or 7 small cutlets. If fatter cutlets are required, carefully ease out every other rib bone. Then cut between the remaining bones into thick cutlets. Now trim the fat from the thick end of each cutlet, and scrape the rib bones free of any flesh or skin.

NOISETTES

These are boneless cutlets, tied into a neat round shape with string. They are made from the loin or best end. Skin the meat: lift a corner of the skin with a small knife, holding it firmly with a cloth to get a good grip, and pull it off.

Chine the meat (see page 335). Now remove first the chine bone and then all the rib bones, easing them out with a short sharp knife. Remove the half-moon-shaped piece of flexible cartilage found buried between the layers of fat and meat at the thinner end of the best end. This is the top of the shoulder blade. Remove the line of gristle to be found under the meat at the thick end.

Trim off any excess fat from the meat and roll it up tightly, starting at the meaty thick side and

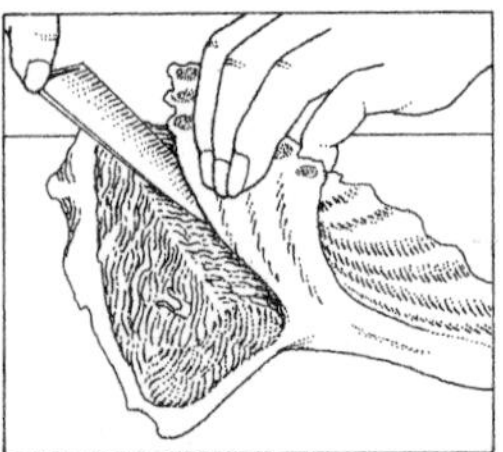
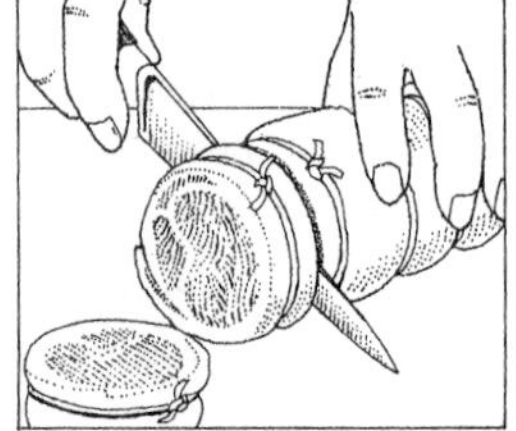

For noisettes: ease out the bones, then roll, tie and cut

working towards the thin flap. Tie the roll neatly with separate pieces of string placed at 3cm/1½inch intervals. Trim the ragged ends of the roll to neaten them. Now slice the roll into pieces, cutting accurately between each string. The average English best end will give 4 good noisettes. The string from each noisette is removed after cooking.

COLLOPS

These are small slices of meat taken from the best end neck of lamb. They are a very extravagant lamb steak (see page 363 for a recipe). Lay the best end neck down and prepare the meat partly as for noisettes (see above), i.e. remove the chine bone, gristle and shoulder blade. With a sharp knife (and making small cuts close to the rib bones), ease the bones, in one piece, away from the meat. Gradually separate the whole 'eye' of the meat (the fat-free cylinder) from the bones. Using a sharp flexible knife, remove all fat and membranes from the meat. Finally, slice into meat rounds or 'collops'.

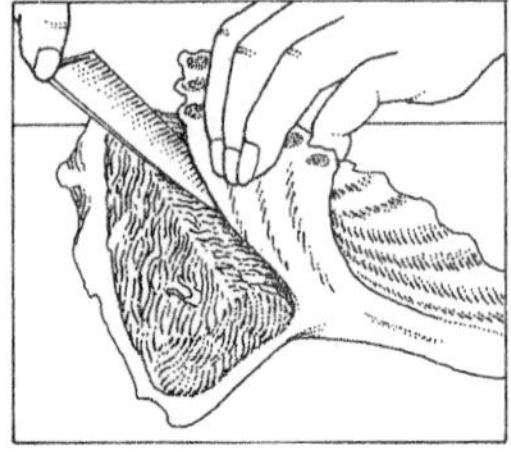
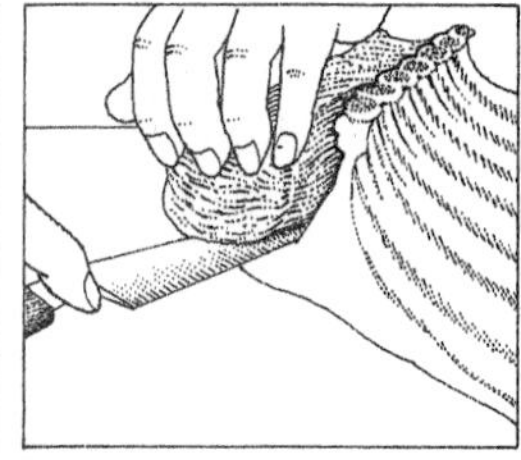

For collops: ease out the bones and separate the eye

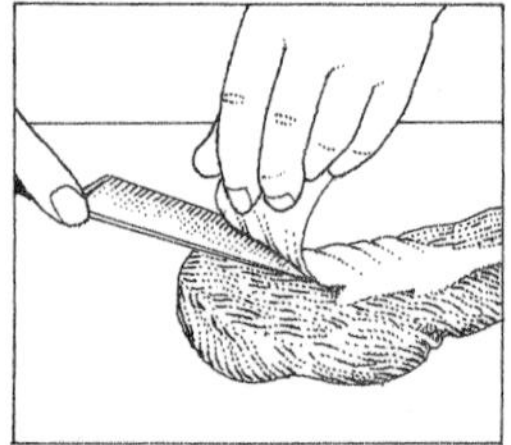
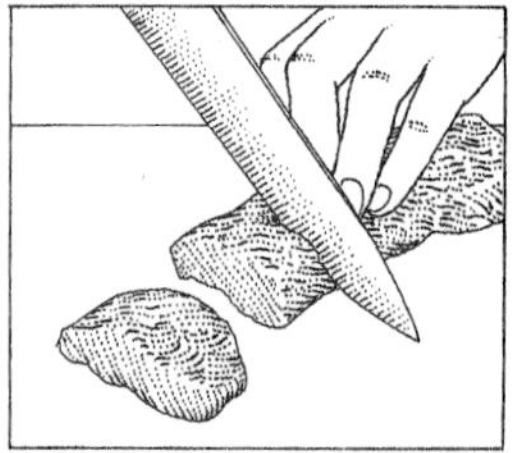

Remove fat and membrane, and slice

CROWN ROAST

Two racks (best ends) are needed. The rack is prepared similarly to one destined for cutlets (see page 335) but the rib bones are left slightly longer, and the rack is not split into cutlets.
However it is skinned and chined, the shoulder cartilage and the line of gristle are removed. The excess fat is cut off (stages 1 and 2 on facing page)

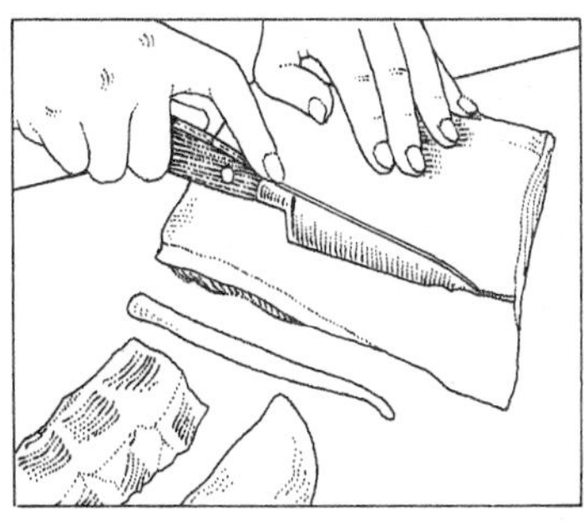

Stage 1

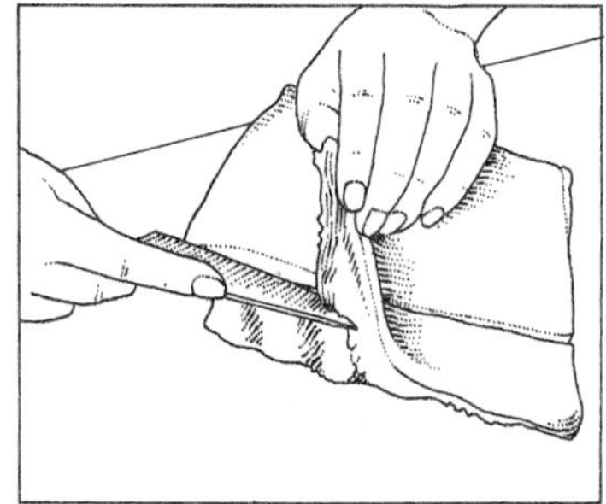

Stage 2

Stage 3

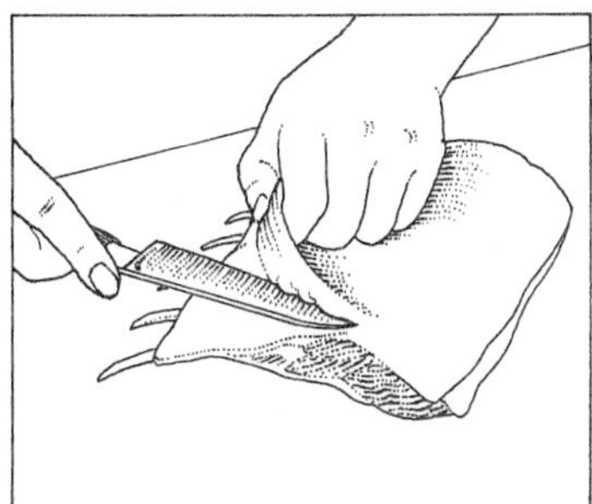

Stage 4

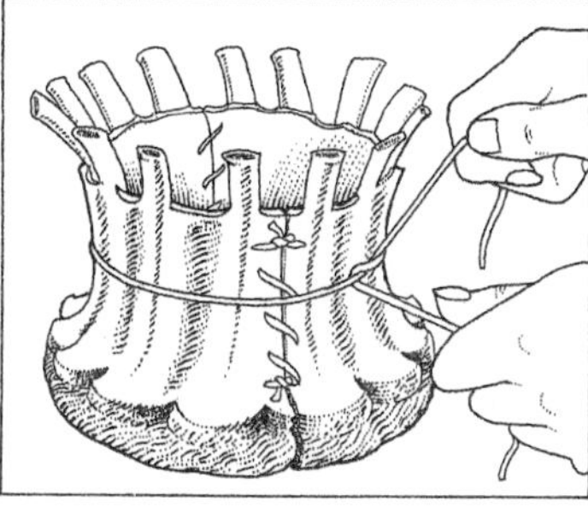

Stage 5

To make a crown roast: see the numbered stages in the text below

and the the top inch of the bones are scraped clean (stage 3 above). Remove an even layer of fat from the prepared rack (stage 4 above). Bend each best end into a semi-circle, with the fatty side of the ribs inside. To facilitate this it may be necessary to cut through the sinew between each cutlet, from the thick end for about 2.5cm/1 inch. But take care not to cut into the fleshy eye of the meat. Sew the ends of the racks together to make a circle, with the meaty part forming the base of the crown. Tie a piece of string round the 'waist' of the crown (stage 5 above). A crown roast is traditionally stuffed, but this can result in undercooked inside fat.

GUARD OF HONOUR (RACK OF LAMB)
Prepare 2 best end racks exactly as for the crown roast, above. Score the fat in a criss-cross pattern. Hold the 2 best ends, one in each hand, facing each other with the meaty part of the racks on the board, and the fatty sides on the outside. Jiggle them so that the rib bones interlock and cross at the top. Sew or tie the bases together at intervals. Stuff the arch if required.

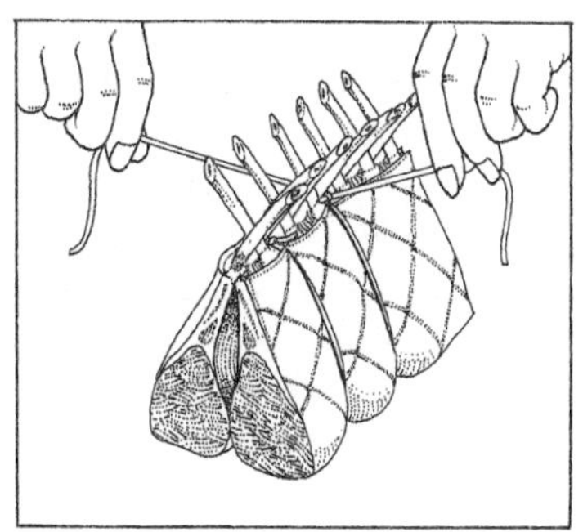

To assemble a guard of honour: tie the prepared racks together

FOR ROASTING TABLE, see page 281

Preparing pork and bacon

CHOPS

Chops are trimmed of rind, and the fat snipped or cut across (from the outside towards the meat). This is because as the fat shrinks during cooking, it tends to curl the chops out of shape.

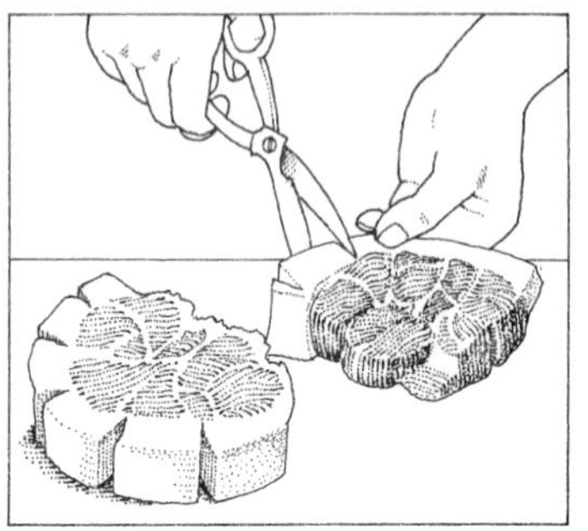

To prepare chops: snip the fat at even intervals

GAMMON STEAKS OR BACON CHOPS

Snip the surrounding fat as described above. Bacon chops (really thick rashers from the prime back) are sometimes cooked with the rind left on, but snipping is essential to prevent curling.

AMERICAN OR CHINESE SPARE RIBS

These are made from pork belly (not English spare rib). They can be cut before or after cooking. Simply cut between each belly bone, splitting the meat into long bones.

TO SCORE CRACKLING

It is vital that crackling should be scored evenly and thoroughly, each cut, which should penetrate the skin and a little of the fat below it, being even and complete. Unscored crackling is tough and difficult to carve. Make the cuts not more than 1cm/1/2 inch apart all over the skin. Score the crackling after boning but before rolling and tying the joint.

Carving meat

The most important factor in good carving is a really sharp knife, a fork with a safety guard, and a board or flat plate unencumbered by vegetables and garnishes. Common sense usually dictates how joints are to be tackled. Meat off the bone is simple: just cut in slices of whatever thickness you prefer, across the grain of the meat. Pork, beef and veal are traditionally carved in thinner slices than lamb.

LEGS

The legs of pork, lamb, bacon (gammon or ham), veal and venison are carved similarly. Put the leg meaty side up on the board or plate and grasp the knuckle bone with one hand, or pierce the joint firmly with a carving fork. Cut a small shallow 'V' or scoop out of the middle of the top of the meat. Carve slices of meat from both sides of the 'V'. Then turn the leg over and take horizontal slices from the other side.

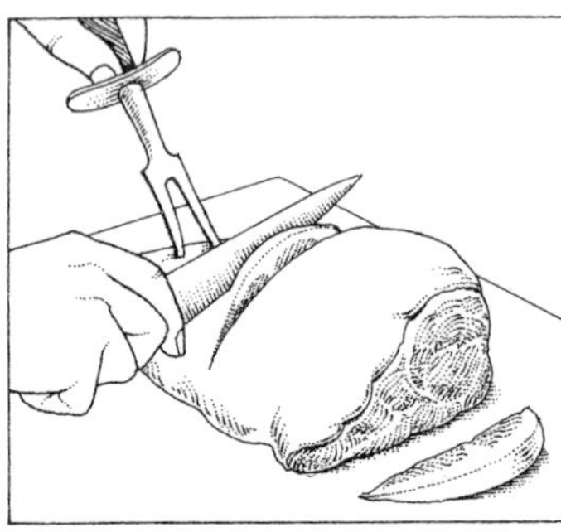

To carve a leg of lamb: carve slices of meat from both sides of the 'V'

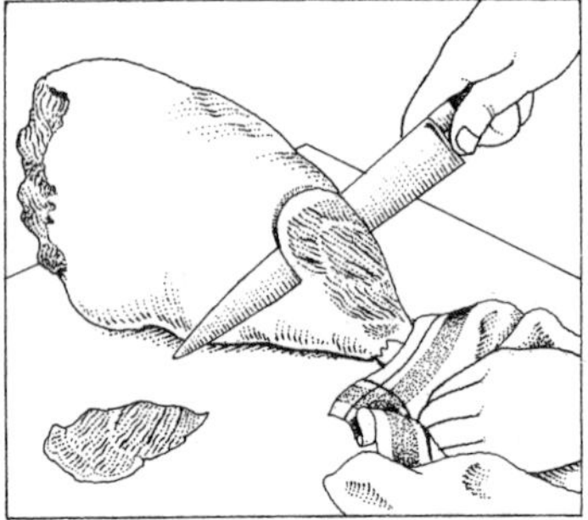

Alternatively, carve diagonally from the knuckle end

Legs can also be cut in diagonal slices from the knuckle end. This is more common with hams, but both methods are used for all legs.

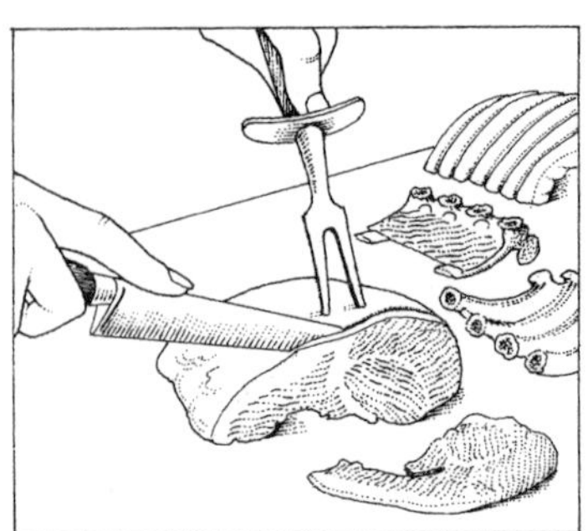

To carve a loin of pork: remove bones and crackling before slicing

LOINS

Loins and best end of pork, veal and lamb are often roasted on the bone to prevent shrinkage, but to carve them it is easier to remove the meat off the rib cage and slice to the desired thickness. To carve a loin of pork, the crackling can be removed in one piece. The meat is then sliced and the crackling can be cut, with scissors, in the same number of pieces as there are slices of meat. If boned, the meat is cut similarly, but in thinner slices, about 5mm/1/4 inch thick. Beef strip loin (boned sirloin) is cut in the same way, thinly in Britain, thickly in America.

Sirloin of beef on the bone is tackled from the top and bottom, the slices cut as thinly as possible on the top, the undercut or fillet slices being carved more thickly. Each diner should be given a slice or two from both top and bottom.

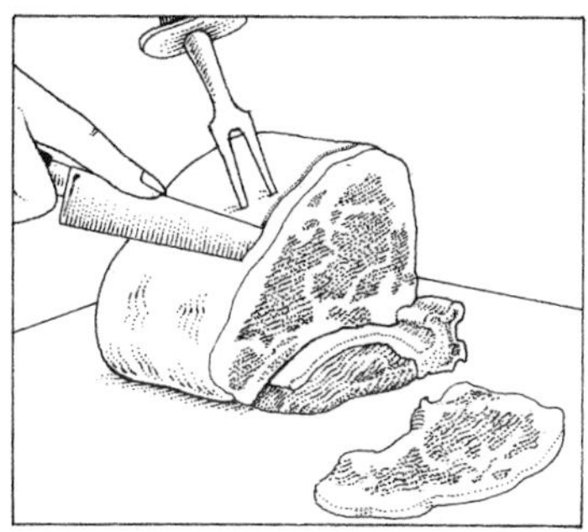

To carve a sirloin on the bone: slice from the top and undercut

SADDLE OF LAMB

The chump end of the saddle is cut in thin slices across the grain of the meat, at right angles to the backbone. But the main part of the saddle, lying each side of the backbone, is cut in thin strips or narrow slices down the length of the saddle. This can be done on the bone, but it is easier if you lift the whole side of the saddle off in one piece and cut into long slices.

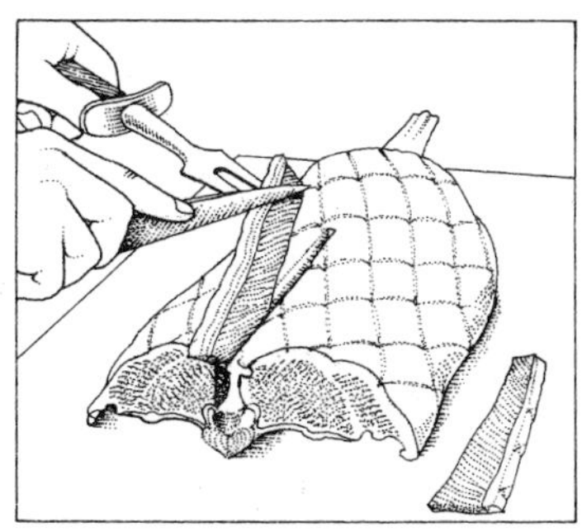

To carve a saddle: cut in thin strips, down the length of the saddle

CROWN ROAST AND GUARD OF HONOUR

Remove the string and split into cutlets.

SHOULDER OF LAMB

A shoulder is simple to carve as long as you know where the bones are. Place it fatty side up and cut like a cake on the side opposite to the bone.

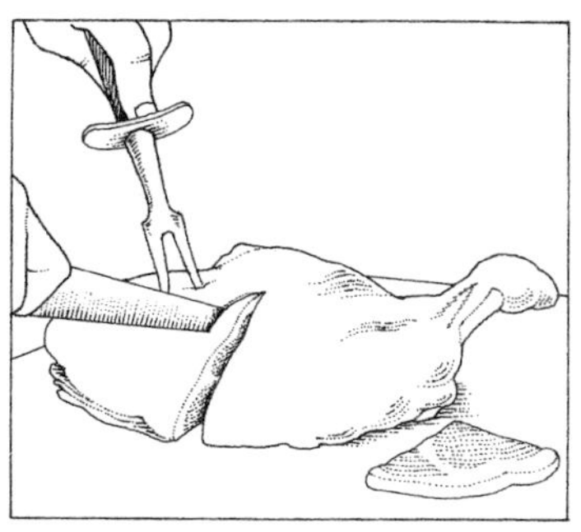

To carve a shoulder of lamb: cut like a cake

SMALL FORERIB OF BEEF

A single forerib of beef is cooked on the bone and then cut off the bone in one piece. Instead of slicing into thin horizontal slices it can be cut into shorter fatter vertical slices.

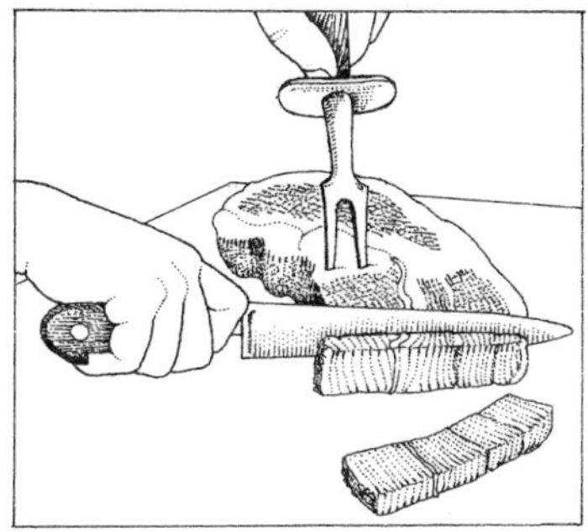

To carve a small forerib of beef: remove from the bone and slice horizontally

LARGE FORERIB OF BEEF

Place the roast on its side and make a 5cm/2 inch cut along the length of the rib. Stand the meat up, rib side down. Carve several slices and lift off and place on a warm serving dish. Turn the rib back on its side and make a second 5cm/2 inch cut along the length of rib. Carve.

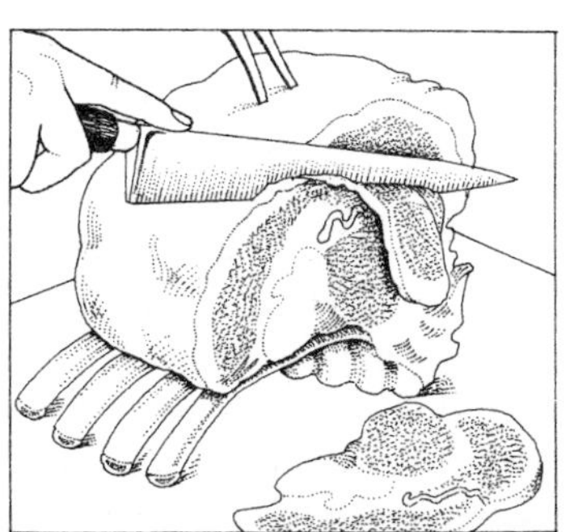

To carve a large forerib of beef

Steak and Kidney Pudding

SERVES 4
675g/1½lb chuck steak
225g/8oz ox kidney
flour
suet pastry made with 340g/12oz flour (see page 526)
salt and pepper
10ml/2 teaspoons chopped onions
10ml/2 teaspoons chopped fresh parsley

1. Cut the steak into cubes about 2.5cm/1 inch square.
2. Chop the kidney, discarding any sinews.
3. Place both steak and kidney in a large sieve. Pour over the flour and shake until the meat is lightly coated.
4. On a floured surface, roll out two-thirds of the suet pastry into a round about 1cm/½ inch thick. Flour the surface lightly to stop it sticking together when folded. Fold the pastry over to form a half-moon shape. Place the pastry with the straight side away from you and roll it lightly so that the straight side becomes curved and the whole rounded again. Now separate the layers, and you should have a bag, roughly the shape of a 1kg/2lb pudding basin. Use it to line the basin, easing the pastry where necessary to fit, and trimming off the top so that 1cm/½ inch sticks up over the edge.
5. Fill the lined basin with the meat, sprinkling plenty of seasoning, chopped onion and parsley in between the layers.
6. Add water to come three-quarters of the way up the meat.
7. Roll the remaining third of suet pastry 5mm/¼ inch thick, and large enough to just cover the pudding filling. Put in place, wet the edges and press them together securely.
8. Cover the pudding with a double piece of greaseproof paper, pleated down the centre to allow room for the pastry to expand, and a similarly pleated piece of foil. Tie down with string.
9. Place in a saucepan of boiling water with a tightly closed lid, or in a steamer, for 5-6 hours, taking care to top up with boiling water occasionally so as not to boil dry.
10. Remove the paper and tin foil and serve the pudding from the bowl.

NOTE I: Traditionally, steak and kidney puddings served from the bowl are presented wrapped in a white linen napkin.
NOTE II: As the filling of the pudding may, with long cooking, dry out somewhat, it is worth having a gravy boat of hot beef stock handy to moisten the meat when serving.
NOTE III: A delicious addition to steak and kidney pudding is to add a small can of smoked oysters to the meat filling.

CLARET

Steak and Kidney Pie

SERVES 4
675g/1½lb chuck steak
225g/8oz ox kidney
oil or dripping
1 onion, finely chopped
30g/1oz flour
425ml/¾ pint beef stock
salt and pepper
15ml/1 tablespoon chopped parsley
rough puff pastry made with 225g/8oz flour (see page 527)
beaten egg

1. Trim away the excess fat from the steak and cut the meat into cubes about 2.5cm/1 inch square. Slice the kidneys finely, discarding any sinew.
2. Heat the oil or dripping in a frying pan and brown a few pieces of meat at a time until browned all over, putting them on to a plate as they are done. Fry the onion in the same fat until soft and brown.
3. Stir in the flour and cook for 1 minute. Gradually add the stock, stirring continuously and scraping any sediment from the bottom of the pan. Bring to the boil and simmer for 1 minute. Return the meat to the pan, season with salt and pepper and simmer slowly until the meat is tender (about 2 hours). Add the parsley.
4. If the sauce is greasy, skim off the fat; if it is too thin, remove the meat to a pie dish and boil the sauce rapidly until syrupy. Pour the sauce over the meat and leave until completely cold.

5. Set the oven to 200°C/400°F/gas mark 6.
6. Roll out the pastry to the thickness of a coin. Cut a long strip just wider than the rim of the pie dish, brush the lip of the dish with water and press down the strip.
7. Brush the strip with water and lay over the sheet of pastry. Press it down firmly. Cut away any excess pastry.
8. Cut a 1cm/1/2 inch hole in the centre of the pie-top and cover with a leaf-shaped piece of pastry (the hole is to allow the escape of steam).
9. Decorate the top with more pastry leaves. Brush all over with egg. Leave in the refrigerator to relax for 10 minutes.
10. Bake in the oven for 30 minutes, or until the pastry is well risen and golden brown.

CLARET

Pancake Pie

SERVES 4
8 French pancakes *(see page 533)*
450g/1lb minced beef
1 large onion, chopped
1 celery stick, chopped
3 rashers rindless streaky bacon, diced
1 garlic clove, crushed
10ml/2 teaspoons flour
570ml/1 pint stock
15ml/1 tablespoon Madeira
10ml/2 teaspoons tomato purée
pinch of thyme
15ml/1 tablespoon chopped parsley
salt and freshly ground black pepper
150ml/1/4 pint soured cream and 150ml/1/4 pint yoghurt mixed together

1. Make the pancake batter first and allow it to stand while preparing the meat sauce. While the sauce simmers fry the pancakes. Keep them warm in the folds of a tea towel in a low oven while finishing off the sauce.
2. Fry half the mince in a hot frying pan.
3. Lift out with a perforated spoon and place in a saucepan.
4. Fry the remaining mince, and transfer this to the saucepan too.
5. When all the mince has been fried, fry the onion, celery, bacon and garlic until just turning brown. Tip off a little of the fat.
6. Add the flour and cook gently, stirring for 1 minute.
7. Stir in the stock and Madeira and bring to the boil, stirring continuously. Pour this into the saucepan.
8. Add the tomato purée, thyme, half the parsley and season with salt and pepper. Simmer gently for about 45 minutes (or until thick and syrupy).
9. When the meat sauce is cooked, reduce by rapid boiling if it is too runny. Season well.
10. Place one pancake on the serving dish, spoon over some meat sauce and cover with a second pancake.
11. Continue to layer the meat sauce and pancakes, finishing with a layer of meat sauce.
12. Sprinkle with the remaining parsley and serve immediately, with the soured cream and yoghurt sauce offered separately.

MEDIUM RED

Shepherd's Pie (I)

SERVES 4-5
1 onion, finely chopped
1 carrot, finely chopped
1 celery stick, finely chopped
675g/1 1/2lb minced beef
oil for frying
10ml/2 teaspoons flour
570ml/1 pint beef stock *(see page 218)*
1 bay leaf
5ml/1 teaspoon Worcestershire sauce (optional)
5ml/1 teaspoon tomato purée
salt and pepper

For the top:
675g/1 1/2lb mashed potato *(see page 187)*
butter

1. Fry half the vegetables with half of the mince in a large frying pan. Brown well all over. Brown the remaining mince with the remaining vegetables.
2. Remove with a draining spoon and place in a saucepan as the mince is browned.
3. Add the flour and cook for 30 seconds.
4. Add the beef stock and slowly bring to the boil, stirring continuously.
5. Now add the bay leaf, Worcestershire sauce,

tomato purée and seasoning.
6. Set the saucepan on a medium heat to simmer. Cover and leave to cook for 45 minutes. Check it every so often and add extra water if it becomes too dry.
7. Set the oven to 200°C/400°F/gas mark 6.
8. Remove the bay leaf from the mince and tip the meat into a pie dish, reserving some of the liquid if the mixture is very runny.
9. When slightly cooled, spread the potato over the top.
10. Fork it up to leave the surface rough, or draw the fork over the surface to mark with a pattern.
11. Dot the top with butter. Place in the oven for 20-30 minutes or until the potato is brown and crusty.

MEDIUM RED

Shepherd's Pie (II)

This is a low-fat dish – the mince is a component part, rather than a principal ingredient.

SERVES 4
10ml/2 teaspoons grapeseed oil
110g/4oz lean minced beef
1 onion, finely chopped
2 large carrots, finely chopped
2 celery sticks, finely chopped
10ml/2 teaspoons tomato purée
2.5ml/½ teaspoon allspice
10ml/2 teaspoons flour
290ml/½ pint brown stock
1 bay leaf
110g/4oz cooked chickpeas
salt and freshly ground black pepper

For the topping:
675g/1½lb potatoes, peeled and cut into chunks
150ml/¼ pint skimmed milk
30g/1oz low-fat spread, e.g. Outline
grated nutmeg
salt and freshly ground black pepper

1. Heat the oil in a large nonstick sauté pan. Add the beef and brown well all over. Reduce the heat and add the onion, carrot and celery. When the vegetables have softened, add the tomato purée, allspice and flour. Cook for 1 minute.
2. Remove from the heat, add the stock, stir well. Return to the heat and bring gradually up to the boil, stirring continuously. Add the bay leaf, season and simmer for 30 minutes.
3. Meanwhile, prepare the mashed potatoes. Cook the potatoes until soft in boiling water. Drain them and return to the empty saucepan. Mash over a medium heat allowing them to dry out as you do so but taking care that the potato does not stick to the bottom of the pan and burn. Push the mound of potato to one side of the saucepan and pour the milk into the exposed side of the pan. Put this side over direct heat and get the milk boiling. Add the low-fat spread and allow it to melt. Now beat the milk and low-fat spread into the potato. Season with nutmeg, salt and pepper.
4. Preheat the oven to 200°C/400°F/gas mark 6.
5. Add the chickpeas to the saucepan of vegetables and simmer for 2-3 minutes. Remove the bay leaf. With a large slotted spoon, transfer the meat and vegetables into a pie dish. Boil the gravy until reduced to a syrupy consistency. Pour it over the meat and vegetables and mix well. Leave to cool for 5 minutes.
6. Pile the potato on top of the pie filling and fork it up roughly. Reheat in the oven for 20 minutes.

MEDIUM RED

Boiled Silverside

SERVES 6
1.35kg/3lb piece of salt silverside
6 pieces of marrow bone
bouquet garni of 1 bay leaf, 2 parsley stalks, 6 peppercorns, 1 small onion, tied in muslin
6 medium onions
4 large carrots, quartered
2 turnips, quartered
12 dumplings (see page 343)
chopped parsley

1. Soak the beef in cold unsalted water for about 3 hours.
2. Put the bones and beef in a large pan of fresh unsalted water and bring slowly to the boil, skimming as the scum rises to the surface.
3. When simmering, add the bouquet garni and half-cover the pan. Simmer for about 3 hours.

Remove the bouquet garni and skim off any fat.
4. Now add the vegetables and simmer for 1 hour or until the meat and vegetables are tender.
5. Meanwhile, cook the dumplings: if there is room in the pot, float them in the liquid 20 minutes before the end of the cooking time. If not, take some of the stock (topping up with boiling water if necessary) and simmer them in a separate saucepan. Do not cover.
6. Place the beef on a large serving dish. Surround it with the vegetables, dumplings, and marrow bones. Cover and keep warm.
7. Taste the stock. If weak-flavoured, reduce by rapid boiling. Skim if necessary.
8. Ladle a cupful or so of hot liquid over the meat and vegetables, sprinkle with chopped parsley and serve at once. Serve more liquid separately in a sauceboat.

NOTE: Dumplings are always a little soggy cooked on the stove. For a drier, fluffier version, they should be baked in the oven.

CLARET OR RIOJA

Pot au Feu Ordinaire

This recipe has been adapted from Time Life's *The Good Cook: Beef and Veal.*

SERVES 4-6
1kg/2lb silverside or topside of beef, tied in a compact shape
1kg/2lb beef bones, sawn into 5-7.5cm /2-3 inch pieces
2.5 litres/4 pints water
15g/½oz salt
200g/7oz carrots
110g/4oz turnips
200g/7oz leeks
3 onions, 1 stuck with cloves
30g/1oz parsnip
30g/1oz celery

1. Put the bones in the bottom of a large saucepan with the meat on top. Add the water and the salt. Place over a very gentle heat, so that you can skim the liquid when it boils. It should take about 30 minutes to come to the boil – it must be skimmed constantly to make a very clear broth.
2. When the liquid boils, splash on 45ml/3 tablespoons of cold water. Skim again and, once the liquid starts to boil again, add another 45ml/3 tablespoons of cold water. This produces a third lot of scum, this time almost white. Skim. When the liquid starts to boil once more, add another 45ml/3 tablespoons of cold water. The little scum that rises this time should be perfectly white and clean. Skim it. Then add the vegetables and skim off any scum that rises. With a damp cloth, carefully wipe the inside edges of the pot so that no traces of scum remain.
3. Simmer, very slowly, for 3 hours. Keep checking it and should any scum rise to the surface, remove it with a perforated spoon. It can be cooked in a low oven or ideally in the slow oven of an Aga.
4. Traditionally the broth is served as a first course – either with noodles or with the vegetables cooked with the beef.
5. The beef is served sliced and garnished with freshly cooked vegetables. It can be accompanied by a selection of the following: pickled gherkins, coarse salt, horseradish sauce, capers, mustard and French dressing.

RED RHONE

Dumplings

SERVES 4
225g/8oz self-raising flour
pinch of salt
110g/4oz suet
about 75ml/5 tablespoons cold water
570ml/1 pint beef stock (see page 218)

1. Set the oven to 180°C/350°F/gas mark 4.
2. Sift the flour and salt into a bowl. Mix in the suet.
3. Make a dip or 'well' in the flour. Add a little water to the well and, using a palette knife, mix in the surrounding flour. Draw the mixture together with your hands and knead gently to a soft dough.
4. With floured hands, shape the mixture into dumplings about the size of a ping-pong ball.
5. Float the dumplings in a pan of simmering beef stock, and cook uncovered for 20-25 minutes.
6. Remove with a perforated spoon. They should be light and not too doughy.

Family Beef Stew

SERVES 4
900g/2lb stewing beef
dripping
2 large mild onions, sliced
6 medium carrots, cubed
2 medium turnips, cubed
570ml/1 pint beef stock (see page 218)
salt and pepper
1 bay leaf
2 parsley stalks
pinch of fresh thyme
30g/1oz pearl barley

1. Set the oven to 200°C/400°F/gas mark 6.
2. Remove any gristle and excess fat from the meat and cut it into 3cm/1½ inch cubes.
3. Melt a little of the dripping in a sauté pan. Brown the beef cubes on all sides, a few at a time, and transfer to an ovenproof casserole. If the bottom of the pan becomes too brown and sticky, pour in a little stock and swish it about, scraping the sediment from the bottom of the pan. Pour this into the casserole, and then melt a little more fat and continue browning the meat until all is transferred to the casserole.
4. Fry the onion, carrot and turnip until golden brown and place them in the casserole.
5. Pour the stock into the pan and bring to the boil, scraping any remaining sediment from the bottom. Stir in the seasoning, bay leaf, parsley, thyme and barley and pour on to the meat.
6. Cover the casserole and place in the oven. After 20 minutes reduce the heat to 150°C/300°F/gas mark 2 and cook for another 2 hours. Skim off any excess fat.

NOTE: This stew is even better if kept for a day before eating – the barley swells up even more and the flavour improves.

FULL RED

Beef Olives

SERVES 4
4 thin slices lean beef
seasoned flour
15ml/1 tablespoon beef dripping
425ml/¾ pint beef stock (see page 218)
225g/8oz mirepoix of carrot, onion and celery

For the stuffing:
120ml/8 tablespoons fresh breadcrumbs
30ml/2 tablespoons chopped suet
30ml/2 tablespoons chopped parsley
grated rind of 1 lemon
beaten egg to bind

1. Set the oven to 150°C/300°F/gas mark 2.
2. Put the slices of beef between wet greaseproof paper and flatten lightly with a rolling pin or mallet.
3. Mix all the ingredients for the stuffing together and season to taste with salt and pepper.
4. Divide the mixture between the pieces of beef and roll up, folding in the ends to make neat parcels. Tie the beef olives with fine string and roll them in seasoned flour.
5. Heat half the dripping in a frying pan and brown the beef olives on all sides. Remove them and then lightly brown the mirepoix in the remaining dripping.
6. Place the beef olives on top of the mirepoix in a shallow casserole or small roasting tin. Pour over the stock, bring to the boil and cover. Cook in the oven for 1½ hours.
7. Dish the beef olives on a warm plate. Remove the string. Skim any fat off the liquid and then strain, pressing as much of the softened vegetables through the sieve as possible. Pour this over the beef.

NOTE: If the sauce is too thin, either thicken it by reduction or by adding beurre manié (see page 217). If the sauce is too thick, thin it down with a little extra stock.

MEDIUM RED

Spaghetti Bolognese

SERVES 4 OR 6
450g/1lb spaghetti

For the sauce:
55g/2oz chicken livers
85g/3oz unsmoked bacon
oil
170g/6oz minced beef
15g/½oz butter
110g/4oz mixed onion and celery, finely diced
1 garlic clove, crushed
110g/4oz mushrooms, sliced
1 glass white wine or Madeira
290ml/½ pint beef stock (see page 218)
225g/8oz tin tomatoes
30ml/2 tablespoons tomato purée
salt and freshly ground black pepper
5ml/1 teaspoon chopped fresh marjoram
fresh Parmesan cheese, grated

1. Trim off and discard the discoloured parts from the chicken livers.
2. Dice the bacon and fry slowly in its own fat, in a large frying pan, until lightly browned. Increase the temperature and fry the chicken livers, adding a little oil if necessary, and then the mince. Fry until well browned all over.
3. With a draining spoon, lift the bacon, mince and livers into a saucepan. Melt the butter in the frying pan and add the onion, celery and garlic. Cook slowly, stirring occasionally, until soft and lightly coloured. Add the mushrooms and cook for 30 seconds. Tip into the pan of meat.
4. Pour the wine into the frying pan and bring to the boil, scraping the bottom of the pan with a wooden spoon to loosen all the sediment. Stir in the stock, tomatoes and tomato purée. Season well with salt, pepper and marjoram. Pour on to the meat in the saucepan. Cover and simmer for 45 minutes or until the meat is tender. If greasy, skim off as much of the fat as possible.
5. While the sauce is cooking push the spaghetti into a large pan of boiling salted water and stir until the water reboils. Boil uncovered for 10-12 minutes or until just tender. Tip into a colander, then rinse under running hot water. Drain well. Return to the rinsed-out pan and heat gently with 15ml/1 tablespoon of oil, turning carefully with a wooden spoon.
6. Place the spaghetti in a warm serving dish and pour over the Bolognese sauce. Serve with grated fresh Parmesan cheese sprinkled on top of the sauce or served separately.

VALPOLICELLA

Boeuf Bourguignonne

SERVES 4
900g/2lb chuck steak
15ml/1 tablespoon beef dripping
12 small button onions or shallots
30g/1oz butter
1 garlic clove, crushed
10ml/2 teaspoons flour
290ml/½ pint red wine
290ml/½ pint beef stock (see page 218)
bouquet garni (bay leaf, sprig of thyme, a few parsley stalks and 1 celery stick tied up with string)
salt and freshly ground black pepper
55g/2oz piece fatty bacon, diced
110g/4oz button mushrooms
chopped parsley for garnish

1. Set the oven to 150°C/300°F/gas mark 2.
2. Cut the beef into 3cm/1 inch cubes, discarding any fat and gristle.
3. Melt half of the dripping in a thick-bottomed casserole pan and brown the beef pieces very well, a few at a time. They must be brown on all sides. Put them into a bowl as they are done. If the bottom of the pan becomes very dark or too dry, pour in a little of the wine, swish it about, scraping off the sediment stuck to the bottom, and pour over the meat. Heat up a little more fat and continue to brown the meat. When it is all brown repeat the déglaçage (adding the wine and scraping the pan).
4. Peel the shallots by dunking them in boiling water for 30 seconds and then removing the skins. Dry them and fry in half the butter until well browned.
5. Add the garlic and stir in the flour. Cook, stirring, for 1 minute.
6. Add the wine and stock. Stir until boiling, again scraping the bottom of the pan.
7. Put the meat and sauce together in a casserole and add the bouquet garni. Season. Cover and place in the oven to cook for 2-3 hours or until

the meat is very tender.

8. Meanwhile, prepare the bacon and mushrooms: cut the bacon into 1cm/½ inch cubes and blanch in boiling water for 1 minute. Refresh and drain well. Wipe the mushrooms but do not peel or remove the stalk. Cut into quarters if large. Melt the remaining butter in a frying pan and, when foaming, add the bacon and mushrooms and cook fairly fast until delicately browned. Lift them out and add to the stew when it has been in the oven for 2 hours. Continue cooking for a further 30-60 minutes.

9. When the beef is cooked, use a perforated spoon to lift the meat, bacon and vegetables into a clean casserole. Remove the bouquet garni, taste and boil the sauce fast to reduce to a syrupy consistency. If the sauce is too salty do not reduce it but thicken with a little beurre manié.

10. Pour the sauce over the beef and serve sprinkled with the chopped parsley.

NOTE: This stew can be cooked on top of the cooker, over a low heat, for 1-2 hours, but slow oven-cooking produces a better result, with the meat as soft as butter but not shredded or falling apart and with no danger of 'catching' on the bottom.

RED BURGUNDY

Carbonnade de Boeuf

SERVES 4

900g/2lb chuck steak
15ml/1 tablespoon beef dripping
3 onions, finely sliced
1 garlic clove, crushed
10ml/2 teaspoons brown sugar
10ml/2 teaspoons flour
290ml/½ pint brown ale
290ml/½ pint brown stock (see page 218)
5ml/1 teaspoon wine vinegar
1 bay leaf
pinch of thyme
pinch of nutmeg
salt and freshly ground black pepper
4 slices French bread spread thickly with French mustard

1. Set the oven to 150°C/300°F/gas mark 2.

2. Cut the beef into small steaks, cutting across the grain of the meat. Melt half of the dripping in a large frying pan and fry the steaks, a few at a time, until browned all over, putting them into a flameproof casserole as they are done. If the bottom of the pan becomes very dark or too dry, pour in a little of the stock, swish it about, scraping off the sediment stuck to the bottom, and pour over the meat. Heat up a little more fat and continue to brown the meat. When it is all brown, repeat the déglaçage (adding the stock and scraping the pan).

3. Fry the onions slowly and, when beginning to brown, add the garlic and sugar. Cook for a further minute or until nicely brown.

4. Stir in the flour and cook, stirring, over the heat for 1 minute. Take off the heat and pour in the brown ale and the remaining stock.

5. Return to the heat and bring slowly to the boil, stirring continuously. Pour into the casserole and add the vinegar, bay leaf, thyme, nutmeg, salt and pepper.

6. Cover and bring to simmering point over direct heat, simmer for 5 minutes, then bake for 2-3 hours. Increase the oven temperature to 190°C/375°F/gas mark 5.

7. Put the slices of bread, mustard-side up, on top of the stew (they are there to absorb the fat) and return the casserole, without the lid, to the oven until the bread is brown and crisp (about 15 minutes).

BEER OR FULL RED

Beef Curry

SERVES 4

15ml/1 tablespoon oil
900g/2lb chuck steak, cut into 5cm/2 inch cubes
2 onions, sliced
2.5cm/1 inch piece fresh ginger, peeled and finely chopped
2 garlic cloves, crushed
5ml/1 teaspoon ground cardamom
2.5ml½ teaspoon ground cloves
2.5ml½ teaspoon ground chilli
5ml/1 teaspoon ground black pepper
10ml/2 teaspoons ground cumin
15ml/3 teaspoons ground coriander

2.5ml/½ teaspoon ground turmeric
5ml/1 teaspoon flour
400g/14oz tin tomatoes
salt and pepper

1. Heat the oil and fry the steak pieces, a few at a time, until well browned all over, removing them to a plate as they are done.
2. Fry the onion in the same oil (adding a little more if necessary), add the ginger and garlic and cook for 2 minutes.
3. Add all the ground spices and cook slowly for a further minute, taking care not to let them burn. Add the flour and cook for 30 seconds.
4. Add the tomatoes and bring slowly to the boil, stirring all the time.
5. Put back the meat, cover with a lid and simmer very slowly until the meat is tender – about 2 hours. Add a little water if it begins to dry out. It can also be cooked in a very slow oven for about 3 hours.

VERY FULL RED

Gaeng Ped Nua (Spicy Red Beef)

Ingredients for this recipe are available in specialist Thai shops.

SERVES 6-8
2 tablespoons Thai red curry paste
3 tablespoons oil
1.5kg/3lb braising steak, cut into strips
1 stalk of lemon grass, cut into strips
a few makrut (citrus) leaves
340g/12oz creamed coconut
2 tablespoons nam pla (Thai fish bouillon)
2.5ml/½ teaspoon sugar
2 red peppers, deseeded and cut into strips
1 bunch fresh basil

1. In a large wok or pan fry the curry paste in the oil for 1 minute. Add the strips of beef and stir-fry, then ensuring that the curry paste coats the meat, cover with water and add the lemon grass and broken-up makrut leaves.
2. Simmer until the meat is tender (about 1½ hours).
3. Mix the creamed coconut with 570ml/1 pint water and add it to the meat. Reduce until the sauce is thick.
4. Add the fish bouillon, sugar and red peppers and simmer until the peppers are just cooked.
5. Finally add the basil leaves.
6. Serve with steamed or boiled rice.

NOTE: If the sauce curdles (which it often does) it can be brought back with vigorous whisking.

FULL SPICY RED

Beef Curry with Almonds

This is an adaptation of a recipe by Josceline Dimbleby. As with many recipes using a large variety of dried spices, if you have not got them all do not worry, just use a little extra of the ones you do have. The cumin and coriander, however, are essential.

SERVES 4
900g/2lb chuck steak
30-60ml/2-4 tablespoons sunflower oil
5ml/1 teaspoon ground cardamom
2.5ml/½ teaspoon ground cloves
10ml/2 teaspoons ground black pepper
10ml/2 teaspoons ground cumin
15ml/1 tablespoon ground coriander
2.5ml/½ teaspoon ground turmeric
85g/3oz blanched almonds
2.5cm/1inch piece fresh ginger, peeled and very finely chopped
2 garlic cloves, crushed
2 onions, sliced
400g/14oz tin tomatoes
salt
30ml/2 tablespoons plain yoghurt

To garnish:
fresh coriander leaves

1. Trim the beef of as much fat and gristle as possible and cut into 3.5cm/1½ inch cubes.
2. Set the oven to 170°C/325°F/gas mark 3.
3. Put 15ml/1 tablespoon of the oil into a frying

pan, heat gently. Add the almonds and fry until golden brown. Set aside. Add a little more oil to the pan, add the dry spices and cook slowly for 1 minute.

4. Put the spices and nuts into a liquidizer and whizz to a smooth purée with 150ml/¼ pint water.

5. Wipe the frying pan clean. It is important to prevent the final curry having bits of burnt dried spices in it. Add 15ml/1 tablespoon oil, heat well and brown the beef cubes well on all sides, a few at a time. Transfer to an ovenproof casserole. If the bottom of the pan becomes too brown and sticky pour in a little water and swish it about, scraping the sediment from the bottom of the pan. Pour this into the casserole and then add a little more oil to the frying pan and continue to brown the meat until all is transferred to the casserole.

6. Add the ginger, garlic and onions and fry slowly until the onions are a deep golden brown. Add the spice and almond mixture and the tinned tomatoes. Stir well, bring to the boil and simmer for 1 minute. Season to taste with salt and pour over the meat. Place over a direct heat and bring back up to the boil. Cover and place in the oven. Bake for 2-3 hours or until the meat is very tender.

7. Check the curry 2 or 3 times during the cooking process and if it is becoming too dry add a little water.

8. Just before serving, stir the yoghurt into the curry and reheat without boiling. Pour into a warm serving dish and decorate with the fresh coriander leaves.

FULL SPICY RED

Fried Steak

SERVES 4

4 sirloin steaks cut 2cm/¾ inch thick or 4 fillet steaks cut 2.5cm/1 inch thick
freshly ground black pepper and salt
oil or dripping
maître d'hôtel butter (see page 235)

1. Season the steaks with pepper. Leave to warm to room temperature if they have been chilled. Sprinkle lightly with salt just before cooking.

2. Brush a frying pan with a little oil or dripping and place over good heat until it is beginning to smoke.

3. Brown the steaks quickly on both sides. For a blue or rare steak, keep the heat fierce for the whole cooking time. For better done steaks, lower the temperature to moderate after the initial good browning. Length of cooking time varies according to the thickness of the meat, the type of steak, the degree of heat, the weight of the frying pan, etc. With experience it is possible to tell from the feel of the steak how well cooked it is - it feels very soft when blue; very firm when medium. But if you want to be certain, there is nothing for it but to cut a tiny slit in the fattest part of the meat, and take a look. Don't do this until you are fairly sure that the steak is ready - too many cuts will mean loss of juices. Cooking times, assuming a good hot pan, would be approximately as below:

SIRLOIN	
Blue steak:	1 minute per side
Rare steak:	1½ minutes per side
Medium rare:	2 minutes per side
Medium steak:	2¼ minutes per side
FILLET	
Blue steak:	1½ minutes per side
Rare steak:	2¼ minutes per side
Medium rare:	3¼ minutes per side
Medium steak:	4½ minutes per side

4. Serve the steaks topped with a slice of maître d'hôtel butter.

MEDIUM RED

Hamburger

SERVES 4

675g/1½lb minced lean beef steak
1 small onion, grated
30ml/2 tablespoons parsley or mixed herbs
5ml/1 teaspoon Worcestershire sauce (optional)
seasoning

1. Heat the grill.

2. Mix all the ingredients together with a fork. Taste for seasoning.

3. With wet hands, shape the meat into flattish rounds, making sure that they are equal in size. Make a slight dip in the centre. They will shrink and thicken when they cook.
4. Grill steadily, turning once. Allow 3 minutes each side for rare burgers, 5 for well done.
5. Serve on a hot dish, or between heated soft buns sliced in half.

NOTE: See pages 595-608 for relishes.

MEDIUM RED

Green Dragon Walnut Meatballs

This recipe has been taken from *Marvellous Meals with Mince* by Josceline Dimbleby.

SERVES 4
For the meatballs:
1 large green pepper
450g/1lb minced beef or pork
2 garlic cloves, finely chopped
85g/3oz walnuts, chopped
15ml/1 tablespoon tomato purée
30ml/2 tablespoons soy sauce
5ml/1 teaspoon ground ginger
3-4 pinches of cayenne pepper
15ml/1 tablespoon caster sugar
salt
15ml/1 tablespoon sunflower oil for frying

For the sauce:
22.5ml/1½ tablespoons soy sauce
67. 5ml/4½ tablespoons water
15ml/1 tablespoon wine vinegar
7.5ml/½ tablespoon caster sugar
4-5 spring onions, finely chopped

1. Cut the pepper in half and take out the seeds and stem. Bring a small pan of salted water to the boil, put in the pepper, cover the pan and boil for 6-8 minutes, until soft. Drain and chop finely.
2. Put the mince in a bowl and add the chopped pepper, garlic, walnuts, tomato purée and soy sauce. Then add the ground ginger, cayenne pepper, sugar and a good sprinkling of salt.
3. Mix everything together very well with a wooden spoon. If you have a food processor the mixture can be whizzed together briefly: this prevents the meatballs from breaking up when they are cooked. Then, with wet hands, form the mixture into balls the size of a ping-pong ball.
4. Heat the sunflower oil in a large frying pan and fry the meatballs over a low to medium heat, turning to brown all over, for about 15 minutes. Transfer with a slotted spoon to a serving dish and keep warm in a low oven.
5. Pour most of the fat out of the pan but leave the residue of meat juices. Add the soy sauce, the water and the vinegar. Stir in the caster sugar and dissolve over a low heat. Then bubble fiercely for a minute or two until you have a thick, dark and syrupy sauce. Remove from the heat and stir in the chopped spring onions. Spoon the sauce over the meatballs and serve immediately.

RED RHONE

Meatballs

This version is lower in fat than are most meatballs.

SERVES 4
85g/3oz burghul (cracked wheat)
225g/8oz minced beef
15ml/1 tablespoon coriander, roughly chopped
4 spring onions, roughly chopped
1 garlic clove
10ml/2 teaspoons soy sauce
salt and freshly ground black pepper
15ml/1 tablespoon sunflower oil for frying
tomato sauce to serve (see page 231)

To garnish:
a few coriander leaves

1. Soak the burghul in cold water for 20 minutes. Drain and squeeze dry.
2. Put all the ingredients together in a food processor and process to a soft dough.
3. Wet your hands and shape the meat mixture into balls the size of a walnut and fry them slowly in the oil for about 5 minutes.
4. Heat the tomato sauce, pour it over the meatballs and decorate with the coriander leaves.

Kibbeh

This recipe for stuffed cracked wheat shells has been adapted from one by Claudia Roden in her book *Mediterranean Cookery.*

For the shells:
225g/8oz burghul (cracked wheat)
450g/1lb minced beef
1 onion, roughly chopped
salt and freshly ground black pepper

For the filling:
1 onion, finely chopped
30ml/2 tablespoons sunflower oil
55g/2oz pinenuts
285g/10oz minced beef
5ml/1 teaspoon ground cinnamon
2.5ml/½ teaspoon allspice
15ml/1 tablespoon chopped parsley
15ml/1 tablespoon chopped mint
salt and freshly ground black pepper
sunflower oil for deep-frying

To serve:
plain yoghurt
sesame oil

To garnish:
sprigs of watercress

1. First make the shells. Soak the cracked wheat in cold water for 20 minutes.
2. Process together the beef, onion, salt and pepper. Drain the cracked wheat and process the beef again, in batches, with the cracked wheat. Process until the mixture is very soft. Knead well by hand.
3. Meanwhile, make the filling. Fry the onion in the oil until soft but not brown, add the pinenuts and fry until golden brown. Add the beef and fry until lightly browned all over. Add the cinnamon, allspice, parsley, mint, salt and freshly ground black pepper.
4. With wet hands, take a small egg-sized portion of the shell mixture and roll into a ball. Make a hole in the centre and shape into a thin walled pot with a pointed bottom by turning and pressing it in your palm.
5. Place some stuffing inside the hole and pinch the top of the pot together to seal it. Shape the top to a point. Repeat with the rest of the mixtures, wetting your hands frequently.
6. Heat the oil and deep-fry 4 or 5 kibbeh at a time until golden brown. Drain well on absorbent paper.
7. Flavour the yoghurt with sesame oil.
8. Arrange the kibbeh on a large warm plate, decorate with watercress and serve the yoghurt sauce separately.

FULL RED

Tournedos Chasseur

SERVES 4
4 slices white bread
oil for frying
55g/2oz butter
4 x 170g/6oz fillet steaks
1 shallot, finely chopped
110g/4oz mushrooms
15ml/1 tablespoon dry white wine
290ml/ ½ pint demi-glace sauce (see page 223), or good beef gravy, slightly thickened
5ml/1 teaspoon chopped chervil

1. Cut the crusts off the bread, and trim each slice into a round or octagonal croûte. Heat some oil in a frying pan and fry the bread on both sides until crisp and brown. Keep warm on a serving platter.
2. Heat 5ml/1 teaspoon of the oil in a heavy frying pan and cook the steaks on both sides until done to your liking (4-5 minutes a side for well done, 1-2 minutes a side for rare). Lift them out when ready and place on top of the croûte. Keep warm.
3. In the same pan in which you fried the steaks, melt half the butter. Add the chopped shallot and cook over a moderate heat until just turning colour. Add the rest of the butter and fry the mushrooms in this, scraping the bottom of the pan to loosen any of the meat sediment left from the fried steaks (this will help the flavour of the sauce).
4. After about 2 minutes, pour in first the white wine, then the demi-glace sauce. Allow to bubble rapidly to reduce and thicken to a coating consistency. Add the chopped chervil and spoon carefully over the steaks.

CLARET

Filet de Boeuf à la Stroganoff

SERVES 4
340g/12oz fillet of beef
55g/2oz butter
1 medium onion, finely sliced
225g/8oz mushrooms, finely sliced
100ml/1 small glass white wine
150ml/¼ pint good beef stock
15ml/1 tablespoon oil
30ml/2 tablespoons brandy
salt and freshly ground black pepper
30ml/2 tablespoons cream
30ml/2 tablespoons soured cream

1. Cut the beef into 5cm/2 inch strips, the thickness of a finger.
2. Melt half the butter in a frying pan and gently cook the onion until soft and transparent. Add the mushrooms and toss over the heat for 1 minute. Add the wine and the stock. Boil rapidly to reduce the liquid to about 30ml/2 tablespoons. Stir well and then pour into a bowl, scraping the pan.
3. Now heat the oil and the remaining butter in the pan. Get it as hot as you dare. Drop in the beef strips. Fry over fast heat to brown and seal the edges without over-cooking the middle. Remove the strips to a plate as they are browned. Then turn the heat down.
4. Pour the brandy into the hot pan. Set it alight. As soon as the flames have died down, pour in the mushroom and stock mixture. Return the meat to the pan and stir in the cream. Taste the sauce. Add salt and pepper as necessary. If the sauce is too thin, remove the meat and boil the sauce rapidly to reduce it to a syrupy consistency.
5. Reheat, then tip into a warm serving dish and fork the soured cream in roughly. If the soured cream is very thick it can be watered down a little.

NOTE: The essence of a perfect beef Stroganoff is the speed at which the beef strips are cooked. If using tougher meat, there is nothing for it but gently to stew the beef (after adding the mushrooms and stock) until tender. This alternative can be very good.

RED BURGUNDY

Mixed Grill

Grilling times depend on the thickness of the foods, and the temperature of the grill. The suggestions below should be regarded as guidelines only.

SERVES 1
110g/4oz rump or sirloin steak
oil
freshly ground black pepper
55g/2oz calves liver
1 chipolata sausage
1 lambs kidney
1 rasher back bacon
1 whole tomato
2 large flat mushrooms
salt and freshly ground black pepper
watercress to garnish

When preparing a mixed grill, begin by grilling the meat that will take the longest time to cook and then gradually add the other ingredients so that everything is ready at the same time.

STEAK: flatten the steak slightly, brush it with oil and season with pepper. Do not use salt as this drains out the juices and makes the meat tough and dry. It can be salted just before cooking.
LIVER: remove the membrane that surrounds the liver, cut into thin pieces, brush with oil and season with pepper.
CHIPOLATA SAUSAGES: prick with a fork to allow the fat to escape during cooking. Do not add any extra fat.
KIDNEY: skin and halve the kidney, snipping out the 'core'. Brush with oil and season with pepper.
BACON: cut off the rind. Put the bacon on a board and, using the back of a knife, stretch it. This helps to prevent shrinking and curling during grilling.
TOMATO: cut in half, brush with a little oil and season with salt and pepper.
MUSHROOMS: wipe and peel the mushrooms, cut the stalk to 1cm/½ inch, brush with oil and season with salt and pepper.

1. Heat the grill.
2. When very hot, place the chipolata sausage under it.

3. After 1 minute, add the liver and the kidney.
4. After a further minute, add the steak and bacon. Cook for 1 minute.
5. Turn the sausage and steak over and cook for a further minute.
6. Add the tomatoes and mushrooms and grill for a further 2 minutes or so, turning the tomatoes over and turning the sausage if necessary.
7. As the items are ready, put them on a heated platter, draining the fat from the sausage and bacon carefully. Just before serving, garnish with a sprig of watercress.

NOTE: Mixed grill is traditionally served with potato chips or straw potatoes.

CLARET

Grilled Steak

SERVES 4
4 fillet steaks, cut 2cm/3/4 inch thick, or 4 sirloin steaks, cut 2.5cm/1inch thick
salt and freshly ground black pepper
butter, melted
maître d'hôtel butter (see page 235)

1. Season the steaks with pepper. Leave to warm to room temperature if they have been chilled. Sprinkle lightly with salt just before cooking.
2. Heat the grill. Do not start cooking until it is at maximum temperature.
3. Brush the grill rack and steak with a little melted butter.
4. Grill the steak quickly on both sides. For a blue or rare steak, keep the heat fierce for the whole cooking time. For better done steaks, lower the temperature to moderate after the initial good browning. Length of cooking time varies according to the thickness of the meat, the type of steak, the efficiency of the grill, etc. With experience it is possible to tell from the feel of the steak how well cooked it is – it feels very soft when blue, very firm when medium. But if you want to be certain, there is nothing for it but to cut a tiny slit in the fattest part of the meat and take a look. Do not do this until you are fairly sure that the steak is ready – too many cuts will mean loss of juices. Cooking times, assuming a good hot grill, would be approximately as below:

SIRLOIN	
Blue:	1 1/4 minutes per side
Rare:	1 3/4 minutes per side
Medium rare:	2 1/4 minutes per side
Medium:	2 3/4 minutes per side
FILLET	
Blue:	2 1/4 minutes per side
Rare:	3 1/4 minutes per side
Medium rare:	4 1/4 minutes per side
Medium:	5 minutes per side

5. Serve each steak topped with a slice of maître d'hôtel butter.

FULL RED

Steak Wellington

SERVES 4
4 x 170g/6oz fillet steaks or tournedos
salt and freshly ground black pepper
Worcestershire sauce
30g/1oz beef dripping
55g/2oz flat mushrooms, chopped
85g/3oz chicken liver pâté (see page 139)
rough puff pastry made with 225g/8oz flour (see page 527)
beaten egg
290ml/1/2 pint wild mushroom sauce (see page 229)
watercress

1. Set the oven to 230°C/450°F/gas mark 8. Trim any fat or membranes from the steaks. Season with pepper and a few drops of Worcestershire sauce.
2. Heat the dripping in a pan and brown the steaks quickly on both sides. The outside should be brown, the middle absolutely raw. Reserve the frying pan unwashed. Leave the meat to cool on a wire rack (this is to allow the fat to drip off the steaks rather than cooling and congealing on them).
3. Cook the mushrooms in the frying pan. Tip into a bowl.
4. Beat the mushrooms into the pâté. Taste and add seasoning if necessary. Spread one side of each steak with this mixture. Roll out the pastry until it is about the thickness of a large coin. Cut

into four 18cm/7 inch squares.
5. Place each steak, pâté side down, on a piece of pastry. Brush the edges with water and draw them together over the steak, making a neat and well-sealed parcel. Place them on a wet baking sheet, pâté side up, and brush with beaten egg. Make a small slit in the top of each parcel so that the steam can escape. Decorate with leaves made from the pastry trimmings. Brush these with egg too. Place in the refrigerator for 10 minutes so that the pastry can relax.
6. Now brush the steak parcels with a little more beaten egg and cook in the oven for 15 minutes, by which time the pastry should be golden brown and the meat pink.
7. While the steaks are cooking reheat the sauce.
8. Dish on a warm plate. Garnish with watercress and serve the sauce separately.

RED BURGUNDY

Fillet of Beef en Croûte

SERVES 8-10
1.8 kg/4lb piece of fillet from the thick end
freshly ground black pepper
Worcestershire sauce (optional)
30g/1oz beef dripping
puff pastry made with 340g/12oz flour (see page 528)
110g/4oz flat mushrooms
30g/1oz butter
110g/4oz chicken liver pâté (see page 139)
beaten egg

1. Set the oven to 230°C/450°F/gas mark 8.
2. Skin and trim the fillet and season well with pepper and Worcestershire sauce (if used). Melt the dripping in a roasting pan and when hot add the meat and brown on all sides. Roast in the oven for 20 minutes.
3. Take one-third of the pastry and roll it on a floured board until it is a little more than the length and breadth of the fillet. Place it on a wet baking sheet, prick with a fork and bake in the oven until golden brown, about 20 minutes. Do not turn the oven off. Leave the pastry on a wire rack to cool.
4. Remove the fillet from the roasting pan and allow to cool.
5. Chop the mushrooms very finely and quickly fry in the butter. Mix this with the pâté and spread the pâté over the cooked pastry base. Place the cold fillet on top of this and, with a sharp knife, cut away any pastry that is not covered by the fillet.
6. Roll the remaining pastry on a floured board into a 'blanket' large enough to cover the fillet easily. Lift up the new pastry and lay it gently over the fillet. With a sharp knife cut off the corners of the 'blanket'. Do not throw away these trimmings.
7. Lift one length of the raw pastry and brush the underside with beaten egg. With a palette knife, lift the base and tuck the 'blanket' neatly underneath it. Repeat with the other 3 sides. Shape the pastry trimmings into leaves. Brush the pastry-covered fillet with beaten egg. Decorate with the pastry leaves and brush again.
8. Place the fillet in the oven for 20 minutes or until the pastry is very dark brown and shiny. This recipe assumes that rare beef is desired, but longer cooking in the first instance, without the pastry, will ensure a more well-done fillet. For medium beef, give it a further 10 minutes and for well-done beef, a further 15 minutes.
9. Serve hot or cold. If served hot, it should be carved at the table or the juices will be lost and the meat may have a grey unappetizing look.

NOTE: The dish may be prepared in advance up to the final baking. It should be left ready for the oven on the baking sheet, loosely covered with plastic film or foil to stop the egg glaze drying. If prepared in advance it is important that the mushrooms and pâté should be stone cold before mixing together, and that the meat should be cold before covering with the pastry.

RED BURGUNDY

Fillet of Beef with Three Purées

SERVES 4
4 x 170g/6oz beef fillet steaks
pepper
15ml/1 tablespoon oil

For the mushroom filling:
30g/1oz butter
225g/8oz mushrooms, finely sliced
salt and freshly ground black pepper
pinch of thyme
lemon juice

For the onion purée:
30g/1oz butter
1 large Spanish onion, finely chopped
15ml/1 tablespoon double cream
salt and white pepper

For the spinach purée:
30g/1oz butter
450g/1lb fresh spinach, destalked and shredded
1 small garlic clove, crushed
pinch of nutmeg
55g/2oz Gruyère cheese, grated
55g/2oz anchovy fillets, soaked in milk

8 sheets of filo pastry
45g/1½oz butter, melted
1 beaten egg to glaze

1. Season the beef with pepper. Heat the oil in a frying pan and brown the fillets quickly on both sides and quickly round the edge. Remove and leave to cool on a wire rack.
2. For the mushroom filling: melt the butter in a saucepan. Add the mushrooms, season with salt and pepper and thyme. Cook until soft and add a little lemon juice. Allow to cool.
3. For the onion purée: in another saucepan melt the butter, add the onion and sweat until softened but not brown. This will take at least 20 minutes. Add the cream and season with salt and white pepper. Leave to cool.
4. For the spinach purée: melt the butter, add the spinach and garlic and toss until limp. Season with salt, pepper and nutmeg. Leave to cool. Preheat the oven to 220°C/425°F/gas mark 7.
5. Cut 2 sheets of filo pastry in half. Brush each layer with melted butter and pile the pastry layers on top of each other.
6. Take a quarter of the mushroom filling and place it in the centre of the pastry. Place a steak on top and wrap the pastry round it to form a parcel. Turn it over and place it seam side down on a baking tray. Repeat with the other 3 steaks.
7. Ten minutes before you want to serve the steaks, brush them with egg wash and place them in the oven.
8. Meanwhile, heat the onion purée in a saucepan. Toss the spinach in a pan. When the spinach is hot add the Gruyère and anchovy fillets.
9. To serve, place the pastry parcel on a plate with a spoonful of each purée beside it.

RED BURGUNDY

English Roast Beef

SERVES 10
2.5 kg/5lb sirloin or rib roast of beef
15ml/1 tablespoon flour
a little dry mustard
salt and freshly ground black pepper
horseradish cream (see page 220)

1. Weigh the beef to establish the cooking time (see below).
2. Set the oven to 220°C/425°F/gas mark 7.
3. Place the beef on a rack and sprinkle with flour, salt, a little mustard and plenty of pepper.
3. Place the rack and beef over a roasting pan and roast for 20 minutes.
4. Turn the oven down to 160°C/325°F/gas mark 3 and cook slowly for 20 minutes per 450g/1lb for medium rare meat or 15 minutes for very rare. Serve with horseradish cream in a separate dish.

NOTE I: If allowed to cool for 20 minutes before serving, the meat will be easier to carve, but, naturally, not so hot.
NOTE II: If thickened gravy is required in addition to 'God's gravy' – the juices that will run from the meat before and during carving – roast the joint directly in the pan, not on a rack over it. Then pour off most of the dripping, taking care not to lose any brown juices. Add

enough flour (usually about 10ml/2 teaspoons) to the remaining fat and juices and stir over the heat until the flour has browned, and any sediment from the bottom of the pan is loosened. Add up to 290ml/1/2 pint of stock and stir or whisk until boiling. Add salt and pepper to taste.

CLARET

Yorkshire Pudding

SERVES 4
125g/4oz plain flour
good pinch of salt
2 eggs
290ml/1/2 pint milk or milk and water mixed
60ml/4 tablespoons good beef dripping

1. Sift the flour and salt into a bowl. Make a well in the centre and break the eggs into it.
2. With a wooden spoon, beat the eggs, gradually drawing in more flour to the centre.
3. Beat in the milk little by little until the batter is smooth. Leave for 30 minutes before use.
4. Heat the oven to 200°C/400°F/gas mark 6.
5. Heat the dripping until hot in a roasting pan, ovenproof dish or Yorkshire pudding tin.
6. Pour in the batter. Bake for 30 minutes or until the pudding is risen and golden. Yorkshire puddings baked in individual patty moulds take about 15 minutes.

NOTE I: If the pudding is to be served with roast beef, you can place it between the open rack holding the beef, and the dripping pan below. In this way any dripping juices from the beef will fall on to the pudding and improve its flavour. However, this makes for a slightly flat pudding.

Alternatively, roast the beef directly in the tin (i.e. not on a wire rack) and half an hour before the beef is ready, increase the oven temperature to 200°C/400°F/gas mark 6 and pour the batter around the beef.

If the pudding is not quite cooked when the beef is ready, keep the beef warm and increase the oven temperature to 220°C/425°F/gas mark 7. Cook until well risen and golden brown.

NOTE II: If making the pudding as a sweet course, use flavourless oil instead of dripping and serve with honey, treacle or maple syrup.

Spiced Beef

This recipe takes 8 days to complete.

SERVES 8
1 garlic clove
1.35kg/3lb boneless sirloin of beef
55g/2oz brown sugar
30g/1oz ground allspice
2-3 bay leaves, chopped
85g/3oz salt
about 450g/1lb plain flour

1. Peel the garlic and cut it into thin slivers. Stick these into the beef flesh. Rub the surface of the joint with the sugar.
2. Leave in a cool place for 12 hours. Mix together the allspice, chopped bay leaves and salt.
3. Take a little of the salt mixture and rub it well into the meat.
4. Keep for a week, turning and rubbing with more salt and spice each day.
5. Set the oven to 190°C/375°F/gas mark 5.
6. Make enough of a fairly thick doughy paste (by mixing flour and water together) to completely envelop the beef.
7. Wrap the meat in the paste.
8. Put it, paste and all, into a roasting pan and pour in a small cup of water. Bake for 1 1/4 hours.
9. Remove and allow to cool. Snip off the crust and discard it before serving the beef.

NOTE : This is especially good eaten cold with Cumberland sauce (see page 232) or a sweet pickle.

CALIFORNIAN/AUSTRALIAN CABERNET SAUVIGNON

Steak Tartare

The beef in this recipe is served raw so it is essential that it is top quality and very fresh.

SERVES 4
450g/1lb fillet or rump steak
salt and freshly ground black pepper
about 60ml/4 tablespoons salad oil
3 egg yolks
Worcestershire sauce (optional)

about 45ml/3 tablespoons chopped onion
about 15ml/1 tablespoon chopped green pepper
about 15ml/1 tablespoon chopped fresh parsley
crisp lettuce to garnish

1. Chop or mince the steak finely and mix with the other ingredients to taste.
2. Shape into 4 rounds and arrange on a serving dish garnished with the lettuce leaves.

NOTE I: Because of the varying tastes of steak tartare eaters, in restaurants this dish is mixed to the customer's requirements at the table. The meat is presented in a hamburger shape on the plate, with the egg yolk in a half shell sitting on the top of it, and surrounded by the prepared chopped vegetables. The waiter then proceeds to beat the flavourings, oil and yolk into the meat with a fork.
NOTE II: Steak tartare is sometimes garnished with anchovy fillets or even caviar.
NOTE III: Steak tartare is surprisingly good with hot potatoes of some kind, rather than a salad. Chips or matchstick potatoes are best.

CLARET

Boeuf Philippe

SERVES 6
560g/1¼lb fillet of beef (ends will do)
Worcestershire sauce
freshly ground black pepper
15ml/1 tablespoon beef dripping
½ cauliflower
170g/6oz French beans
3 tomatoes
2.5ml/½ teaspoon horseradish sauce
1 garlic clove, crushed
45ml/3 tablespoons French dressing (see page 228)
8 black olives, stoned
bunch of watercress

1. Set the oven to 200°C/400°F/gas mark 6.
2. Season the meat with Worcestershire sauce and black pepper. Heat the beef dripping in a roasting pan over the cooker ring and add the beef. Brown evenly on all sides. If the beef is in one thick piece put it into the oven for 15 minutes, less if it is thin or in smaller pieces. It should be pink inside. Allow to cool.
3. Wash the cauliflower and cut into florets. Plunge these into a pan of boiling water for 4-5 minutes. Drain. Rinse under cold water to prevent further cooking. Drain again.
4. Wash and top and tail the beans. Cook in boiling salted water for 5 minutes, then rinse under cold water and drain.
5. Plunge the tomatoes into boiling water for 5 seconds and skin. Cut into quarters.
6. Add the horseradish sauce and crushed garlic to the French dressing. The salad is now ready for assembly but this should not be done until just before serving. The beef will lose its colour if dressed too soon, and the salad will look tired if left to stand for any length of time.
7. Cut the beef into thin slices and then into thin strips, cutting across the grain of the meat. Place in a basin with the other ingredients, reserving 1 tomato and 4 olives for decoration.
8. Using your hands, mix in three-quarters of the French dressing and pile into a serving dish. Place the reserved tomatoes and olives on top of the dish and brush with a little French dressing. Garnish with a bunch of watercress dipped into the remaining dressing.

CLARET

Sesame Beef Salad

SERVES 6
450g/1lb sirloin steak, about 5cm/2 inch thick
oil for frying
225g/8oz button mushrooms, sliced
225g/8oz mangetout, topped, tailed and blanched

For the marinade:
2 onions, sliced
75ml/5 tablespoons dry sherry
75ml/5 tablespoons light soy sauce
45ml/3 tablespoons sesame oil
plenty of ground black pepper

For the dressing:
90ml/6 tablespoons grapeseed oil
45ml/3 tablespoons white wine vinegar
15ml/1 tablespoon Dijon mustard
5ml/1 teaspoon runny honey

1. Remove any fat or gristle from the steak.
2. Mix together the marinade ingredients, add the steak and leave to marinate overnight. Turn the steak occasionally if not completely submerged in the marinade.
3. Place the dressing ingredients in a bowl and whisk until well emulsified.
4. Remove the beef from the marinade and pat dry. Strain the marinade (reserving the onions and marinade). Heat a little oil in a frying pan and brown the steak well on both sides. Turn the heat down to medium and cook for a further 4 minutes on each side (this timing assumes that you like rare steak; it can obviously be cooked for longer). Remove the steak, place on a wire rack and leave to get completely cold.
5. Add the onions from the marinade to the frying pan and cook over a high heat for about 4 minutes. Lift out and place in the dressing.
6. Add the mushrooms and the marinade to the frying pan and cook until the marinade has reduced to about 15ml/1 tablespoon.
Add to the dressing and allow to get completely cold.
7. When all the ingredients are cold, cut the steak into very thin strips and add to the dressing with the mangetout. Toss together and pile on to a serving dish.

FULL RED

Fondue Bourguignonne

The fondue pot is placed in the middle of the table. Guests spear cubes of meat with a long fondue fork (or steel knitting needle) and cook them in the sizzling oil. Then they dip them into one of the sauces (guests should be provided with their own small dishes of these as well as salt, pepper and mustard) before eating them. Each guest should also be provided with an ordinary eating fork (the long one gets too hot to put in the mouth) and plenty of paper napkins for mopping up drips.

oil for frying
curried mayonnaise
garlic cream
tomato dip
170g/6oz rump or fillet steak per person

1. Make the sauces or dips and put into small saucers or bowls for each person.
2. Cut the meat into small cubes, removing any fat, with a sharp knife shortly before the meal. If the meat is left ready cut in pieces for too long the juices may run out. This makes the meat dry when cooked; but if it is wet when lowered into the hot fat it will splutter dangerously.
3. Get the fondue oil ready: do not overfill the pot - it should be just over half full. Test that the oil is hot enough by dropping in a cube of bread. It should sizzle gently.

RED BURGUNDY

Green Peppercorn Steaks

SERVES 4

10ml/2 teaspoons green peppercorns (frozen or tinned)
oil
4 x 2.5cm/1inch thick fillet steaks
30ml/2 tablespoons brandy
30ml/2 tablespoons double cream
salt

1. Rinse the peppercorns if they are canned.
2. Brush a frying pan with oil. Heat until hot. Fry the steaks as fast as you dare on both sides. Get them to the degree you like them (see page 348). Leave to cool for 1 minute.
3. Pour in the brandy and set it alight.
4. When the flames die down, remove the steaks to a warm serving dish.
5. Add the peppercorns, cream and a pinch or two of salt to the frying pan. Mix well, scraping up any sediment. Boil up and pour over the steaks.

FULL RED

Dried Fried Shredded Beef

This recipe has been adapted from a recipe by one of our most admired outside lecturers, Yan Kit So.

SERVES 4-6
450g/1lb lean cut beef (rump steak, top round)
3-4oz/85-110g carrots, cut into julienne
3-4 celery sticks, cut into julienne
2.5ml/1/2 teaspoon salt
21/2 cups oil for deep-frying
5ml/1 teaspoon cornflour
2-3 dried red peppers, halved and deseeded
2.5ml/1/2 teaspoon ground roasted Szechuan peppercorns
5ml/1 teaspoon sesame oil

For the marinade:
30ml/2 tablespoons thin soya sauce
10ml/2 teaspoons sugar
15ml/1 tablespoon Shaoxing wine or sherry
5ml/1 teaspoon sesame oil
2.5ml/1/2 teaspoon ground roasted Szechuan peppercorns

For the thickening:
2.5ml/1/2 teaspoon cornflour
scant 5ml/1 teaspoon sugar
60ml/4 tablespoons water

1. Shred the beef across the grain into thread-like strips 7. 5cm/3 inches long. Put into a bowl.
2. Add all the ingredients for the marinade and combine well. Allow to stand at room temperature for 45-60 minutes so that the marinade permeates every sliver of beef.
3. Put the carrots and celery into a bowl and add a good pinch of salt to draw out the water. Drain after 20-30 minutes. Pat dry, if necessary.
4. Mix the ingredients for the thickening in a small bowl and set aside.
5. Heat the oil in a wok until very hot. Remove the beef from the marinade and coat evenly with the cornflour. Tip the beef gently into the oil and deep-fry for 2-3 minutes or until crisp. Turn off the heat, remove with a large hand strainer and drain on kitchen paper. Pour the oil into a container for future use. Wash and dry the wok.
6. Reheat the wok over moderate heat until hot. Add 30ml/2 tablespoons oil and swirl it around. Tip in the red peppers and fry until they are dark in colour. Remove and discard. Add the carrots and celery. Stir for a few minutes until dry before adding the beef. Continue to stir over gentle heat for another 3-4 minutes or until everything is quite dry and crisp. Add the thickening grandually, stir until the beef is coated.
7. Sprinkle with the ground Szechuan peppercorns and sesame oil before serving.

MEDIUM RED

Fillet of Beef Carpaccio

SERVES 6
675g/11/2lb fillet steak, cut across grain into very fine slices

For the sauce:
45ml/3 tablespoons yoghurt
45ml/3 tablespoons double cream
45ml/3 tablespoons mayonnaise (see page 224)
15ml/1 tablespoon made English mustard
salt and pepper
2.5ml/1/2 teaspoon creamed horseradish
lemon juice

1. Flatten the slices of beef between 2 sheets of cling film or wet greaseproof paper using a mallet or rolling pin. Carefully remove all sinews.
2. When the slices are as thin as possible, spread them over plates without letting them overlap.
3. Mix together the first 4 sauce ingredients.
4. Flavour to taste with the remaining ingredients.
5. Serve the sauce separately.

MEDIUM RED

Moussaka

SERVES 4
olive oil
675g/1½lb lean mutton, minced
1 large onion, finely chopped
½ garlic clove, crushed
3 tomatoes
150ml/¼ pint white wine
150ml/¼ pint water
salt and freshly ground black pepper
handful of fresh parsley, finely chopped
pinch of ground nutmeg
1 medium aubergine
1 large potato, peeled
15g/½oz dried breadcrumbs
15g/½oz butter
15g/½oz flour
1 bay leaf
290ml/½ pint milk
1 egg yolk
15ml/1 tablespoon cream
55g/2oz dry Cheddar cheese, grated

1. Heat a little olive oil in a large saucepan and brown the meat in it. Tip off any excess fat. Put the meat into a bowl.
2. Add the onions and garlic to the pan. Cook, stirring, for 5 minutes. Return the meat to the pan.
3. Dip the tomatoes in boiling water for 10 seconds, skin, chop and add to the meat.
4. Add the wine, water, salt, pepper, parsley and nutmeg and cook over a gentle heat, stirring often, until most of the liquid has evaporated. This will take 30 minutes.
5. Heat the oven to 170°C/325°F/gas mark 3. Cut the aubergine in thin slices, salt lightly and leave for about 30 minutes for some of the juice to drain out. Rinse and dry well on a cloth. Cook the potato in boiling salted water until just tender. Cool and slice.
6. Heat a little more oil in a frying pan and fry each slice of aubergine on both sides until well browned but not burnt.
7. Put them in the bottom of a large casserole. Sprinkle on the breadcrumbs.
8. Now tip in half the meat mixture. Put half the sliced potato in next, seasoning with salt and pepper, then the rest of the meat, and then the rest of the potato.
9. Melt the butter in a saucepan. Stir in the flour, add the bay leaf, then the milk and stir constantly while bringing slowly to the boil. Season with salt and pepper and leave simmering while you mix the egg yolks and cream in a bowl.
10. Pour the sauce on to the yolks and cream, stirring all the time. Add half the cheese.
11. Pour the sauce over the dish. Sprinkle the rest of the cheese on top.
12. Put the dish into the oven and test after 1 hour with a skewer; the whole mass should be soft. The top should be browned too, but if not, finish the browning under the grill.

NOTE: Many chefs insist that the custard top and the inclusion of potato make this dish not a true moussaka. But moussaka in its native Greece usually contains both, and the Greeks have as many variations on moussaka as we have on apple pie.

FULL SPICY RED

Babotie

SERVES 4
1 slice white bread
290ml/½ pint milk
1 onion, chopped
1 small apple, chopped
30g/1oz butter
15ml/1 tablespoon curry powder
450g/1lb cooked lamb, minced
15ml/1 tablespoon chutney
15g/½oz almonds, chopped
a few raisins
15ml/1 tablespoon vinegar or lemon juice
salt and freshly ground black pepper

For the top:
2 eggs
salt and pepper
2 lemon leaves

1. Soak the bread in the milk.
2. Grease an ovenproof dish and set the oven to 180°C/350°F/gas mark 4.
3. Cook the onion and apple slowly in the butter until soft but not coloured. Add the curry

powder and cook for a further minute.
4. Mix the apple and onion with the meat, chutney, almonds, raisins and vinegar or lemon juice. Squeeze the milk from the bread, reserving the milk, and fork the bread into the meat. Season with salt and pepper and pile into the dish.
5. Place in the oven until a slight crust has formed, about 10 minutes.
6. Meanwhile, mix the eggs with the milk in which the bread has been soaked. Season with salt and pepper.
7. Pour this over the meat mixture, place the lemon leaves on top and bake until the custard has set and browned about 30-35 minutes.

NOTE: Bay leaves can be substituted for lemon leaves.

LIGHT RED

Cottage Pie

SERVES 4
1 onion, chopped
15ml/1 tablespoon oil
340g/12oz cooked beef or lamb, minced
2 tomatoes, peeled and chopped
10ml/2 teaspoons Worcester sauce
15ml/1 tablespoon tomato chutney
5ml/1 teaspoon tarragon vinegar
15ml/1 tablespoon chopped thyme
15ml/1 tablespoon plain flour
425ml/3/4 pint beef stock (see page 218)
gravy browning (optional)
450g/1lb mashed potatoes (see page 187)
butter

1. Set the oven to 200°C/400°F/gas mark 6.
2. Heat the oil in a frying pan and gently cook the onion; allow to brown slightly.
3. Add the cooked meat, tomatoes, Worcestershire sauce, tomato chutney, tarragon vinegar and thyme. Sprinkle with the flour and stir into the meat. Cook over a gentle heat for 2 minutes.
4. Add the stock and bring to the boil stirring continuously. Simmer for 20 minutes adding more stock if necessary. Season with salt and pepper and add some gravy browning if required.
5. Tip into a pie dish and allow to cool slightly.
6. Spread the mashed potato on the top. Fork it up to leave the surface rough or draw the fork over the surface to mark with a pattern. Dot the top with butter.
7. Place the pie on a baking sheet in the oven for 20-30 minutes or until the potato is golden brown and crisp.

MEDIUM RED

Mung Beans with Lamb and Rosemary

This is a bean dish with meat – in other words, the lamb is not the principal ingredient, merely one of the flavours and textures integral to the finished recipe.

225g/8oz lean lamb, preferably leg (trimmed weight)
5ml/1 teaspoon sunflower oil
1 large onion, sliced
2 garlic cloves, crushed
1 litre/2 pints beef stock or water if not available
15ml/1 tablespoon tomato purée
15ml/1 tablespoon chopped rosemary
salt and freshly ground black pepper
225g/8oz mung beans, soaked for 4 hours
5 cloves, tied together in a small piece of muslin

1. Set the oven to 150°C/300°F/gas mark 2.
2. Cut the meat into 2.5cm/1 inch cubes. Fry in the oil, in a nonstick frying pan until well browned all over. Transfer to an ovenproof casserole. Fry the onion and garlic for 2 minutes. Add the stock, tomato purée, rosemary and pepper. Bring to the boil and pour over the meat.
3. Drain the beans, rinse and add to the casserole. Bring up to the boil, add the little bag of cloves, cover and transfer to the oven. Bake for 1 1/2 hours.
4. Season to taste with salt. Pile into a clean serving dish and sprinkle with the parsley.

NOTE: Do not add salt to the beans until after they are cooked.

FULL RED

Lancashire Hotpot

SERVES 4

900g/2lb middle neck of mutton or lamb
3 lambs kidneys (optional)
900g/2lb potatoes
salt and freshly ground black pepper
2 large onions, finely sliced
2 carrots, sliced
pinch of dried thyme or 5ml/1teaspoon chopped fresh thyme
1 bay leaf
570ml/1 pint brown stock (see page 218)
55g/2oz butter

1. Set the oven to 180°C/350°F/gas mark 4.
2. Cut the meat into chops, trimming away most of the fat.
3. Skin, split, core and quarter the kidneys.
4. Wash and peel the potatoes, discard any eyes and cut into slices about 5mm/¼inch thick.
5. Butter a casserole dish and line it with a layer of potatoes. Season well with salt, pepper and thyme.
6. Layer the cutlets, sliced onions, carrots and kidneys on top of the potatoes, seasoning well with salt, pepper and thyme and adding the bay leaf when the pot is half full. Finish with a neat layer of potatoes overlapping each other.
7. Pour in enough stock to come to the bottom of the top layer of potatoes.
8. Brush the top with plenty of melted butter and season well with salt and pepper.
9. Cover the casserole and bake in the oven for about 2 hours.
10. Remove the lid and continue to cook for a further 30-40 minutes until the potatoes are brown and crisp and the meat is completely tender.

CLARET

Navarin of Lamb

SERVES 4-6

900g/2lb middle neck of lamb
salt and freshly ground black pepper
30ml/2 tablespoons dripping
15ml/1 tablespoon flour
1 litre/2 pints brown stock (see page 218)
1 garlic clove, crushed
30ml/2 tablespoons tomato purée
bouquet garni (parsley, bay leaf and celery tied together with string)
12 button onions, peeled
pinch of sugar
1 turnip, cut into sticks
3 carrots, cut into sticks
3 potatoes, peeled and cut in chunks

1. Cut the lamb into pieces and season with salt and pepper.
2. Heat 15ml/1 tablespoon of dripping in a heavy pan and brown the meat on all sides. Pour off the fat into a frying pan. Sprinkle the meat with the flour. Cook for 1 minute, then stir in the stock, garlic and tomato purée. Add the bouquet garni. Stir until boiling, then simmer for 1 hour. Skim off any surface fat.
3. Heat a little more fat and soften and brown first the onions with the sugar, then the turnips, carrots and potatoes, adding more dripping as needed.
4. Add the browned vegetables to the meat stew, cover tightly and continue cooking over gentle heat, or in a moderate oven, for a further 30-40 minutes or until the meat is tender. Taste for seasoning.
5. Remove the bouquet garni. Allow the navarin to stand for 5 minutes, then skim off the surface fat and spoon the stew into a warm serving dish.

NOTE: Fresh peas or beans are sometimes added to the navarin after the final skimming. The stew must then be cooked until they are just tender.

CLARET

Bacon Noisettes with Sweet Onion Purée

SERVES 4
2 best end necks of lamb, chined
10 rashers of streaky rindless bacon
unsalted butter
bunch of watercress

For the purée:
30g/1oz butter
2 large onions, very finely chopped

1. First prepare the noisettes. Skin the best end necks. Remove the chine bone and then rib bones. Trim off any excess fat from the inside and outside of the meat so that you just have a thin piece of fat. Roll it up tightly from the thick end. Surround the rolls with the bacon and tie each best end into 4 or 5 noisettes. Slice. Press under a heavy weight until required. An hour is ideal.
2. Make the purée: melt the butter, add the onions and cook slowly until absolutely soft – this may well take 45 minutes. Increase the heat and cook until the onions are browned but not burnt. Liquidize and push through a sieve.
3. Fry the noisettes in the butter for 5 minutes per side, remove the string and arrange on a warm serving plate. Garnish with a small bunch of watercress and serve the warm onion purée separately.

MEDIUM RED

Noisettes of Lamb with Sherry and Mushrooms

SERVES 4
2 small best end of necks of lamb, each with 6-7 bones
dripping or lamb fat
1 large onion, finely chopped
225g/8oz large black mushrooms, sliced
10ml/2 teaspoons flour
290ml/½ pint brown stock
60ml/4 tablespoons sherry
salt and freshly ground black pepper
1 bay leaf
chopped parsley to garnish

1. First prepare the noisettes of lamb (see page 336).
2. Set the oven to 180°C/350°F/gas mark 4.
3. Heat the dripping or lamb fat in a frying pan and brown the noisettes well on both sides. Make sure that the edges also get browned. Lift with a perforated spoon and shake off any excess fat. Place them in a roasting pan.
4. Heat another spoon of dripping in the frying pan, add the onion, and fry until soft and turning colour. Add the mushrooms and cook for a further minute. Stir in the flour. Cook for 1 minute. Pour in the stock and sherry. Bring slowly to the boil, stirring all the time and scraping the bottom of the pan. Simmer for 2 minutes, season to taste and pour over the noisettes.
5. Add the bay leaf and cover with foil or a lid.
6. Bake in the oven until the meat is tender, for about 20 minutes (see note). Remove the bay leaf and lift out the noisettes on to a warm serving dish.
7. If the sauce is too thin, the mushrooms should be removed to the serving dish and the sauce boiled vigorously to reduce it to a syrupy consistency. Remove the string from the noisettes, spoon the sauce over, and scatter with parsley.

NOTE: If the noisettes are cooked in a roasting pan they will take about 20 minutes; in a china casserole dish, however, they may take up to 35 minutes.

CLARET

Noisettes of Lamb with Onion and Mint Sauce

SERVES 4
2 best end necks of lamb, each with 5-7 cutlet bones
salt and freshly ground black pepper
15ml/1 tablespoon chopped mint
dripping

60ml/4 tablespoons thick onion and mint sauce, warmed (see page 230)
small bunch of watercress

1. First prepare the noisettes of lamb, seasoning the meat with salt, pepper and mint before rolling up (see page 336).
2. Set the oven to 200°C/400°F/gas mark 6.
3. Heat 15ml/1 tablespoon of dripping in a heavy roasting pan and, over brisk heat, brown the noisettes quickly on both sides. Transfer to the oven. Baste once or twice until the meat is cooked but still slightly pink inside, about 15 minutes. Alternatively, the noisettes can be fried in the dripping, fast at first to brown them, then more gently for about 3 minutes on each side; or they may be plainly grilled, for about 4 minutes per side. Remove the string.
4. Arrange on a warm serving dish.
5. Spoon a little of the hot onion and mint sauce on top of each noisette and garnish with watercress.

NOTE: Cutlets (trimmed and shortened, but not boned into noisettes) can be used instead of the more elaborate noisettes.

CLARET

Collops of Lamb with Onion and Mint Sauce

SERVES 4
2 racks of lamb
onion and mint sauce (see page 230)

For the sauce:
bones from the racks
1 carrot, chopped
1 onion, chopped
10ml/2 teaspoons flour
5ml/1 teaspoon tomato purée
570ml/1¼ pints water
1 bay leaf
1 sprig mint
1 garlic clove, crushed

1. Prepare the meat: trim the fat from the rack of lamb and place in a roasting pan in a hot oven to render down. Reserve this dripping to brown the collops and the bones.
2. Remove the 'eye' or fillet from the best ends in one piece and trim off all the fat and gristle.
3. Prepare the sauce: cut up the remains of the rack of lamb and brown over a medium heat in a little of the dripping. Remove from the pan.
4. Add the carrots and onions and cook until well browned. Add the flour and cook, stirring until lightly coloured, then add the tomato purée and cook for a further minute.
5. Return the bones to the pan and add the water, herbs and garlic. Bring to the boil and leave to simmer for at least 1 hour.
6. Strain the sauce, pressing the vegetables lightly; skim off any fat. Reduce, by boiling rapidly, if necessary, and season to taste.
7. Set the oven to 240°C/475°F/gas mark 8. Brown the meat quickly in a little dripping and then place in the hot oven for 10 minutes. Turn the oven off and leave for 5 minutes to allow the juices to set.
8. Warm 4 large plates. Heat the sauce and onion and mint purée. Place a spoonful of the purée on each plate. Slice the fillet and arrange, in overlapping slices, on top of the purée. Spoon over some of the brown sauce and serve the rest separately.

CLARET

Lamb Daube

SERVES 4
900g/2lb lean lamb (preferably from the leg)
15ml/1 tablespoon oil
110g/4oz streaky bacon, diced
1 onion, chopped
150ml/¼ pint stock
55g/2oz flour

For the bouquet garni:
1 bay leaf
sprig of thyme
sprig of rosemary
sprig of parsley
1 small strip of orange rind

For the marinade:
290ml/½ pint red wine
1 medium onion, cut in rough slices

1 stick of celery, roughly chopped
1 garlic clove
sprig of parsley
1 bay leaf
sprig of rosemary
4 whole allspice berries

1. Trim the lamb and cut into large pieces.
2. Prepare the marinade by mixing all the ingredients together. Lay the pieces of meat in it and leave overnight.
3. Set the oven to 170°C/325°F/gas mark 3.
4. Drain the meat from the marinade and pat dry with a cloth. Keep the marinade.
5. Heat the oil in a heavy pan and brown the bacon and the onion. Lift out with a perforated spoon and place in a casserole.
6. Brown the meat in the same pan, a few pieces at a time. Lay them on top of the bacon and onion.
7. Strain the marinade into the empty pan. Add the stock. Bring to the boil, scraping the bottom of the pan to loosen any sediment. Pour over the meat.
8. Tie the bouquet garni herbs and orange rind together with a piece of string and sink them in the liquid in the casserole.
9. Make a stiff dough by adding water to the flour. Put the lid on the casserole and press a band of dough around the join of lid and dish to seal them completely.
10. Cook in the oven for 2 hours. Remove the lid. Remove the bouquet garni.
11. Lift the meat out and put it on a serving dish. Keep it warm.
12. Boil the sauce to reduce it to a syrupy consistency and pour over the meat.

RED BURGUNDY

Lamb Curry

SERVES 4
30g/1oz clarified butter (see page 138) or ghee
1 small onion, grated or chopped
675g/1½lb boneless lamb, preferably shoulder, cut into 4cm/1½ inch cubes
10ml/2 teaspoons turmeric
2.5ml/½ teaspoon ground ginger
1 garlic clove, crushed
7.5ml/1½ teaspoons ground coriander
1.25ml/¼ teaspoon salt
1.25ml/¼ teaspoon cayenne
425ml/¾ pint stock (preferably, but not necessarily, meat stock)
15ml/1 tablespoon chopped parsley
7.5ml/½ tablespoon chopped mint

1. Melt the butter in a large saucepan and brown the onion in it. Remove to a plate.
2. Put the meat in the pan and brown all over. Add the turmeric, ginger, crushed garlic and coriander. Return the onions and stir and cook for 1 minute over a low heat.
3. Season with salt and cayenne and add enough stock to come 1cm/½inch below the top of the meat. This level should be kept constant. Bring to the boil, cover and simmer gently until the meat is tender, about 1½hours, adding stock as necessary.
4. When the lamb is tender, remove the meat from the pan and keep warm. Reduce the liquid by boiling rapidly. Add the parsley and mint and pour over the meat.

NOTE I: More (or fewer) spices may be added according to taste.
NOTE II: Ghee is clarified fat sold in tins in Indian stores.

LAGER OR FULL SPICY RED

Accompaniments for Curries

BANANA AND COCONUT: Chop 2 bananas and squeeze the juice of 1 lemon over them. Mix in 30ml/2 tablespoons desiccated coconut.

TOMATO AND ONION: Chop 1 large onion and 3 skinned tomatoes finely. Mix together with salt and pepper, 15ml/1 tablespoon olive oil and a squeeze of lemon juice.

CHUTNEY AND CUCUMBER: Mix 1 cupful chopped cucumber into the same amount of sweet chutney (such as mango or apple).

GREEN PEPPER, APPLE AND RAISIN: Chop equal quantities of apple and green pepper finely, or mince them. Add 15ml/1 tablespoon raisins or sultanas and salt, pepper, lemon juice, cayenne and sugar to taste.

POPPADOMS: These are large flat wafers, available in most supermarkets. They are heated in the oven or under the grill, or fried in hot fat until crisp. They can be bought spiced or plain.

Lamb with Dill Sauce

SERVES 4

900g/2lb lean leg of lamb, cut into large chunks
1 onion, sliced
1 carrot, cut into sticks
15ml/1 tablespoon crushed dill seeds, or 3-4 sprigs fresh dill
1 bay leaf
12 peppercorns
1.25ml/$^1/_2$ teaspoon salt
720ml/1$^1/_4$ pints chicken stock (see page 219)
30g/1oz butter
15ml/1 tablespoon flour
1 egg yolk
45ml/3 tablespoons cream
10ml/2 teaspoons lemon juice
freshly ground black pepper

1. Put the meat, onion, carrot, dill stalks or seeds, but not the fresh leaves, bay leaf, peppercorns and salt into a saucepan.
2. Cover with the stock and bring slowly to the boil. Turn down the heat and cook as slowly as possible for 1$^1/_2$ hours, or until the meat is tender.
3. Lift out the cubes of meat, discarding the bay leaf and dill stalks, and place in a casserole or serving dish. Cover to prevent drying out, and keep warm.
4. Strain the stock, and skim off all the fat. Measure the remaining liquid and make up to 425ml/$^3/_4$ pint with water if necessary. Return to the saucepan.
5. Mix the butter and flour together to a smooth paste. Whisk this gradually into the hot stock, and whisk steadily until the sauce is smooth. Bring to the boil and simmer for 2 minutes.
6. Mix the egg yolk and cream in a bowl. Mix a little of the hot sauce into the cream mixture, and then stir this back into the sauce. Be careful not to boil the sauce now or the yolk will scramble. Flavour the sauce with the lemon juice and add salt and freshly ground black pepper to taste. Chop the dill leaves if you have them, and stir in. Pour over the meat and serve at once.

MEDIUM RED

Lamb Cutlets Grilled with Herbs

SERVES 4

12 French-trimmed lamb cutlets (see page 335)
30g/1oz butter, melted
15ml/1 tablespoon oil
a selection of chopped fresh herbs, e. g. thyme, basil, mint, parsley, marjoram and rosemary
salt and freshly ground black pepper

1. Heat the grill.
2. Brush the cutlets with melted butter and oil, sprinkle over half the herbs and season with salt and pepper.
3. Place the cutlets under the grill, about 8cm/3 inches away from the heat, and cook for 2-3 minutes.
4. Turn them over, baste with the fat from the bottom of the pan and sprinkle over the remaining herbs.
5. Grill for 2-3 minutes (2 minutes each side should give a succulent pink cutlet, 3 minutes a well-done cutlet).
6. Dish the cutlets on a warm serving dish and pour over the pan juices. Serve at once.

CLARET

Indonesian Mixed Meat Kebabs

SERVES 4

225g/8oz lean lamb, cut into 1cm/½ inch cubes
225g/8oz lean pork, cut into 1cm/½ inch cubes
2 medium onions, blanched and quartered
1 green pepper, blanched, deseeded and cut into 8
1 red pepper, blanched, deseeded and cut into 8
110g/4oz button mushrooms

For the marinade:
140g/5oz low-fat plain yoghurt
5ml/1 teaspoon ground ginger
1 garlic clove, crushed
pinch of ground cumin
pinch of ground coriander
juice and grated rind of ½ lemon
salt and freshly ground pepper

For the garnish:
small bunch of watercress

1. Mix the marinade ingredients in a bowl. Add the lamb and pork, then coat well. Cover and leave for several hours in a cool place, turning occasionally.
2. Heat the grill.
3. Thread the ingredients on to 4 skewers and baste with any extra marinade.
4. Place under the grill and cook for 5 minutes a side. Garnish with sprigs of watercress.

FULL SPICY RED

Lamb Cutlets Soubise

SERVES 4

8 French-trimmed cutlets (see page 335)
seasoned flour
beaten egg
dried breadcrumbs
55ml/2 fl oz oil
15g/½oz butter
watercress
290ml/ ½ pint soubise sauce (see page 222)

1. Dip each cutlet into flour, shake, and brush with beaten egg. Press on the breadcrumbs.
2. Heat the oil in a frying pan. When hot, add the butter. Fry the cutlets for 3-4 minutes on each side, until golden brown on the outside but not hard to the touch. Drain briefly on absorbent paper to remove any grease. Serve garnished with washed watercress. Serve the soubise sauce separately.

LIGHT/MEDIUM RED

Lamb Steak à la Catalane with Lentils

SERVES 4

4 lamb steaks 1cm/½ inch thick, cut across the upper leg, bones removed

For the marinade:
290ml/½ pint olive oil
6 garlic cloves, crushed
30ml/2 tablespoons thyme
1 large onion, finely sliced
24 peppercorns, slightly crushed
salt

For the lentils:
225g/8oz (raw weight) green/brown lentils, cooked
4 onions, finely chopped
4 garlic cloves, crushed
olive oil
30ml/2 tablespoons tomato purée
60ml/4 tablespoons chopped mixed herbs
salt and freshly ground black pepper
sesame oil

For the garnish:
watercress

1. Lay the lamb steaks in a roasting pan or shallow dish. Pour over the oil and add all the other marinade ingredients. Leave the steaks to marinate for at least 8 hours, preferably 24 hours, turning them over 2 or 3 times.
2. Sweat the onion and garlic in a little olive oil until completely soft and transparent.
3. Add the cooked lentils, the tomato purée and herbs, season well and sprinkle over sesame oil to taste. Keep warm.
4. Meanwhile get a thick frying pan or griddle

really hot, or preheat the grill for at least 10 minutes.
5. Remove most of the oil from the steaks and put them in the hot pan or under the grill. Fry or grill, turning once, until both sides are a good brown. Like beef steaks they can be eaten in any state from blue to well done, but if overcooked they become very tough. They are best pink in the middle. Serve immediately with a bouquet of watercress.

NOTE: The steak can be served whole with the lentils or cut into strips or cubes and put on top of the lentils.

MEDIUM RED

Lamb Cutlets in Pastry

SERVES 4
4 double best end lamb cutlets (see note)
dripping or oil for frying
30ml/2 tablespoons chopped ham
5ml/1 teaspoon tomato purée
55g/2oz mushrooms, chopped
15ml/1 tablespoon chopped parsley
salt and freshly ground black pepper
puff pastry made with 225g/8oz flour (see page 528)
1 egg beaten with salt (egg wash)
tomato sauce (see page 231)
watercress to garnish

1. Set the oven to 230°C/450°F/gas mark 8.
2. Trim off the excess fat from the cutlets and fry briskly in a little dripping or oil to brown the meat. The cutlets must be brown on both sides but raw in the middle. Leave to cool on a wire rack (this prevents the fat from solidifying on the cutlet). Scrape any congealed fat off the cutlets.
3. Mix the ham, tomato purée, mushrooms and parsley together. Season with salt and pepper.
4. Roll out the pastry into a 23cm/9 inch square. Cut it diagonally into 4 triangles.
5. Put a quarter of the filling on to the centre of each triangle and put a cutlet on top of this, so that the meaty part is exactly in the middle of the piece of pastry.
6. Fold over the flaps of pastry on to the top of the cutlet, leaving the bone sticking out. Make sure the pastry 'seams' slightly overlap. Trim away any excess pastry, but keep the trimmings.
7. Turn the cutlets over and place them on a wet baking sheet. Brush the tops with egg wash. Cut 4 large leaves out of the pastry trimmings and put one on each cutlet. Brush again with egg.
8. Bake in the oven for 15-20 minutes or until the pastry is a good brown. The meat inside will be faintly pink. For well-done cutlets, cover the pastry with foil to prevent burning, and continue baking for a further 5 minutes.
9. Serve tomato sauce separately.

NOTE: Double cutlets are thick ones achieved by cutting through the best end so that each piece of meat has 2 bones to it. One bone is then carefully removed. It is vital that all fat is removed.

CLARET

Roast Stuffed Shoulder of Lamb

SERVES 6
1 shoulder of lamb, 1.8kg/4lb boned
15g/½oz butter
1 large onion, finely chopped
55g/2oz chicken livers, trimmed and diced
55g/2oz mushrooms, sliced
1 garlic clove, crushed
15ml/1 tablespoon mixed chopped fresh herbs (mint, thyme, parsley and rosemary)
squeeze of orange juice
salt and freshly ground black pepper
½ cup cooked rice
30ml/2 tablespoons sultanas
small bunch of watercress

For the gravy:
10ml/2 teaspoons flour
5ml/1 teaspoon tomato purée
290ml/½ pint stock
1 glass red wine (100ml/3½ fl oz)

1. Weigh the lamb and establish its cooking time: 20 minutes to the 450g/1lb and 10 minutes over.
2. Set the oven to 190°C/375°F/gas mark 5.
3. Melt the butter in a frying pan and add the

onion. Fry gently until soft.
4. Add the livers and turn the heat up. Fry fairly fast to brown the livers on all sides.
5. Add the mushrooms, garlic, herbs and orange juice. Cook gently until the mushrooms are soft. Season with salt and pepper.
6. Remove from the heat and mix into the cooked rice. Add the sultanas.
7. Push this stuffing into the shoulder of lamb, sewing up the edges with thin string.
8. Roast for the established cooking time. It should be cooked all the way through.
9. Lift the meat from the roasting pan and keep warm on a serving platter in the switched-off oven.
10. To make the gravy: pour off most of the fat from the roasting pan, and then stir in first the flour and then the tomato purée. Cook for 30 seconds.
11. Add the stock and wine, and stir over the heat until the sauce boils, scraping the brown bits from the bottom of the pan as you go. Simmer for 2-3 minutes. Season to taste. Strain into a warm gravy boat.
12. Garnish the lamb with the watercress.

MEDIUM RED

Shoulder of Lamb Stuffed with Feta

This dish is served with a tomato and mint salsa.

SERVES 6
1 shoulder of lamb, 1.8kg/4lb boned
85ml/3 fl oz red wine
20g/3/4oz flour

For the stuffing:
225g/8oz feta cheese, cut into 1cm/1/2 inch cubes
10ml/2 teaspoons green peppercorns
1 shallot, chopped
85g/3oz fresh breadcrumbs
30ml/2 tablespoons thinly sliced sun-dried tomatoes, or 2 tomatoes, skinned, deseeded and finely chopped
15ml/1 tablespoon fresh thyme leaves
1 egg, beaten
salt and freshly ground black pepper

To garnish:
sprigs of watercress

To serve:
tomato and mint salsa (see page 230)

1. Set the oven to 200°C/400°F/gas mark 6.
2. Trim the lamb of any excess fat leaving a thin layer on the outside.
3. Mix together the stuffing ingredients, beat lightly and season with salt and freshly ground black pepper.
4. Season the inside of the lamb and stuff it carefully. Using thin string sew the lamb up, but not too tightly.
5. Weigh the lamb and for pink lamb allow 20 minutes per 450g/1lb. For better done lamb cook the shoulder for a further 30 minutes.
6. Put the lamb into a roasting tin and bake for the required cooking time.
7. Half an hour before the lamb is ready pour the red wine over the joint.
8. When the lamb is cooked remove it from the oven and place in a warm place to rest for 10 minutes.
9. Pour off all but 15ml/1 tablespoon of fat from the roasting tin, place the tin on the heat and stir in the flour. Cook, stirring, for 1 minute. Add some water and also any extract that may have been produced during cooking. Bring to the boil and simmer for 5 minutes.
10. Just before serving remove the string from the lamb. Serve with the gravy and hand the tomato and mint salsa separately. Garnish the lamb with a small sprig of watercress.

FULL RED

Shoulder of Lamb 'En Ballon'

This dish is served with a sweet port gravy.

SERVES 6-8
1 boned shoulder of lamb
butter
salt and pepper
sprigs of rosemary
290ml/1/2 pint stock or water

2 glasses port (140ml/5 fl oz)
watercress to garnish (optional)

For the stuffing:
30ml/2 tablespoons parsley
85g/3oz smoked ham, chopped
salt and pepper

For the glaze:
30ml/2 tablespoons redcurrant jelly

1. Set the oven at 190°C/375°F/gas mark 5.
2. Mix the stuffing ingredients together and push into the lamb, or, if the lamb has been opened out, spread it on one half and fold the other half over to cover it.
3. Using a long piece of string, tie the shoulder so that the indentations made by the string resemble the grooves in a melon or the lines between the segments of a beachball (see page 333).
4. Weigh the lamb.
5. Smear all over with butter and sprinkle with salt and pepper. Scatter a few rosemary leaves on top. Pour the stock into the pan.
6. Roast for 25 minutes per 450g/1lb. Half an hour before the cooking time is up, smear the lamb with 30ml/2 level tablespoons redcurrant jelly and return to the oven.
7. Remove the strings carefully and lift the lamb on to a warm serving dish. Leave to rest for 15 minutes before serving. It will retain heat even if not placed in a warming cupboard.
8. Meanwhile, make the gravy. Skim the fat from the juices in the pan. Add the port and bring to the boil. Boil vigorously until the sauce is syrupy and reduced to about one-third of a pint. Taste and add salt and pepper if necessary. Strain into a gravy boat. Garnish the lamb with watercress if wished.

CLARET

Crown Roast of Lamb

SERVES 4-6
1 crown roast or 2 matching racks (best ends of lamb) with 7 cutlets each, chined
55g/2oz butter
good sprig of rosemary
bunch of watercress

To serve hot:
5ml/1 teaspoon flour
290ml/½ pint good stock
salt and freshly ground black pepper

To serve cold:
redcurrant jelly

1. If the butcher has not trimmed and tied the meat into a crown, follow the instructions on page 336.
2. Set the oven to 200°C/400°F/gas mark 6. Melt the butter in a roasting pan. Add the crumbled rosemary and put in the crown of lamb. Wrap up the ends of the bones with wet brown paper, then with foil to prevent them from burning. It is easier to cover a few bones at a time than to cover the whole crown. Brush over the melted butter.
3. Roast for 1½ hours if pink lamb is wanted, or 2 hours for well-done lamb. Lift out the crown.
4. To serve hot: skim or pour off virtually all of the fat from the roasting pan, taking care not to pour away any of the meat juices. Stir in the flour, scraping any sediment off the bottom of the pan. Add the stock and stir until boiling. Simmer for 2 minutes. Season to taste.
5. Decorate each bone with a cutlet frill. Garnish with watercress in the centre. Hand the gravy separately.
6. To serve cold: slice the meat between the bones to separate the cutlets. Trim off the excess fat from each cutlet, but take care to keep the cutlets in the right order, so you can reassemble the crown. Tie a ham frill round the reassembled crown and decorate each bone with a cutlet frill. Garnish with watercress in the centre. Serve with redcurrant jelly.

CLARET

Rack of Lamb with Mustard and Breadcrumbs

SERVES 2

10ml/2 teaspoons pale French mustard
15ml/1 tablespoon fresh white breadcrumbs
15ml/1 tablespoon chopped fresh herbs (mint, chives, parsley and thyme)
1.25ml/¼ teaspoon salt
2.5ml/½ teaspoon freshly ground black pepper
best end of neck, chined, trimmed and skinned
10ml/2 teaspoons unsalted butter

1. Set the oven to 220°C/425°F/gas mark 7.
2. Trim off as much fat as possible from the meat.
3. Mix together the French mustard, breadcrumbs, herbs, salt, pepper and butter. Press a thin layer of this mixture over the rounded, skinned side of the best end.
4. Place it, crumbed side up, in a roasting tin and roast for 25-30 minutes for a 7-cutlet best end, less for a smaller one. This will give pink, slightly underdone lamb. Serve with the butter and juices from the pan poured over the top.

FULL RED

Roast Saddle of Lamb

A saddle of lamb is a cut consisting of both loins, left in a single piece. It can weigh anything from 2-4.5kg/4½-10lb New Zealand lamb cuts are generally smaller than British.

1 saddle of lamb
dripping
1 garlic clove (optional)
salt and freshly ground black pepper
rosemary

For the gravy:
425ml/¾ pint brown stock (see page 218)
10ml/2 teaspoons flour

To serve:
redcurrant jelly or soubise sauce

1. Heat the oven to 200°C/400°F/gas mark 6.
2. Trim off any excess fat from underneath the saddle and remove the kidneys. Trim away all but 2.5cm/1 inch of the 2 flaps.
3. Skin the saddle: the best way to do this is to lift the skin at one corner with a sharp knife and hold it tightly in a tea towel to prevent it slipping out of your grip. Give a sharp tug and pull off all the skin in one piece. This sounds more difficult than it is. Score the fat in a criss-cross pattern with a sharp knife (see page 335).
4. Heat 30ml/2 tablespoons dripping in a roasting pan. When it is hot, add the saddle of lamb, tucking the flaps underneath and basting well.
5. Stick a few small pieces of skinned garlic into the saddle near the bone. Season with salt, pepper and a scattering of rosemary.
6. Roast for 15 minutes to the 450g/1lb and 15 minutes over for pink lamb. If the saddle is extremely large, it should be covered with damp greaseproof paper halfway through roasting to prevent it from becoming too brown.
7. Lift the meat on to a warm serving platter. Pour away all but 15ml/1 tablespoon fat from the pan, taking care not to lose any of the meat juices or sediment. Stir the flour into the pan to absorb the remaining fat. Cook, stirring, over the heat for 1 minute. Add the stock and stir until boiling, taking care to scrape up any stuck sediment on the bottom of the pan. Simmer for 2 minutes and season with salt and pepper as necessary.
8. To carve the saddle, cut thin strips parallel to the backbone, down the length of the meat. The thicker, chump end may be cut across in slices if preferred but the main part is usually carved lengthways (see page 339).

CLARET

Roast Leg of Lamb

SERVES 4

1 small leg of lamb
salt and freshly ground black pepper
3 large sprigs of rosemary
2 glasses of red wine (200ml/7 fl oz)

For the gravy:
10ml/2 teaspoons flour
290ml/½ pint stock
salt and freshly ground black pepper

1. Set the oven to 200°C/400°F/gas mark 6.
2. Weigh the joint to establish the cooking time. Allow 15 minutes to 450g/1lb and 20 minutes extra.
3. Wipe the lamb. Season with salt and pepper and place in a roasting pan, with the sprigs of rosemary on top. Place in the preheated oven.
4. Half an hour before the end of the cooking time, pour the wine over the lamb.
5. When the lamb is cooked, the juices that run out of the meat when pierced with a skewer will be faintly pink. Remove the joint from the oven and place it on a warm serving dish, discarding the sprigs of rosemary. Keep warm while making the gravy.
6. Carefully pour off all but 15ml/1 tablespoon fat from the roasting pan, leaving any meat juices in the pan.
7. Add the flour to the remaining liquid in the pan and, using a wire whisk or wooden spoon, stir it over a gentle heat until a delicate brown. Remove from the heat and stir in the stock. Return to the heat, stirring all the time, and simmer for 2 minutes.
8. Season with salt and pepper as necessary and strain into a warm gravy boat.

NOTE: For well-done lamb allow 25 minutes per 450g/1lb and 20 minutes extra. When cooked the juices that run out of the meat, when pierced with a skewer, should be clear.

COTES DU RHONE

Gigot of Lamb with Stuffed Artichoke Hearts

SERVES 4-5
1 small leg of lamb
salt and freshly ground black pepper
1 garlic clove, peeled and cut into slivers (optional)
large pinch of rosemary leaves
10ml/2 teaspoons dripping
8 globe artichokes or 8 canned artichoke bottoms
225g/8oz celeriac
110g/4oz mashed potato
30g/1oz butter
10ml/2 teaspoons flour
150ml/¼ pint stock
small bunch of watercress

1. Set the oven to 200°C/400°F/gas mark 6.
2. Wipe the lamb. Season with salt and pepper. If liked, spike thin slivers of garlic into the meat near the bone. Sprinkle with rosemary. Weigh the lamb to establish the cooking time.
3. Heat the dripping in a roasting pan, add the lamb, baste well and put in the hot oven. Roast, for 15 minutes per 450g/1lb and 15 minutes over. When pierced with a skewer, the juices that run out of the meat should be faintly pink.
4. To prepare the artichokes, wash them and cook in a pan of boiling salted water for about 45 minutes or until the leaves will pull away easily from the whole. Peel away all the leaves, keeping them to serve with a vinaigrette dressing as a first course. Using a teaspoon, scrape out the prickly choke of each artichoke, and trim the base with a sharp knife so that it will stand steady.
5. While the artichokes are cooking, peel the celeriac and boil in salted water until quite tender. Drain well. Push the flesh through a sieve. Beat in the mashed potato, half the butter, and salt and pepper to taste.
6. Pile this mixture into the artichoke bottoms. Brush with the remaining butter and place on a greased baking sheet.
7. When the lamb is tender, remove from the oven. Turn the heat down to 150°C/300°F/gas mark 2, and put the artichokes into the oven so that they will heat up as the oven cools.
8. Place the lamb on a warm serving dish, removing the pieces of garlic if used.
9. Carefully pour off all but 15ml/1 tablespoon fat from the roasting pan, leaving any meat juices in the pan.
10. Add the flour to the remaining liquid in the pan and, using a wire whisk or wooden spoon, stir it over a gentle heat until a delicate brown. Remove from the heat and stir in the stock. Return to the heat, stirring all the time, and simmer for 2 minutes.

11. Season with salt and pepper as necessary and strain into a warm gravy boat. Surround the lamb with the artichokes and garnish with watercress.

RED RHONE

Butterfly Leg of Lamb

SERVES 6-8
1 large leg of lamb, butterfly boned (see page 333)
15ml/1 tablespoon soy sauce
½ onion, sliced
4 sprigs thyme
2 bay leaves
3 garlic cloves, peeled and sliced
30ml/2 tablespoons good quality olive oil
salt and freshly ground black pepper

For the gravy:
290ml/½ pint water or vegetable water
50ml/2 fl oz red wine (½ glass)

For the garnish:
small bunch of watercress

1. Weigh the boned leg of lamb.
2. Open out the leg of lamb and place it skin side down on a large plate. Scatter over the soy sauce, sliced onion, thyme, bay leaves, garlic, oil and pepper. Fold the 2 'butterfly' ends inwards to encase the flavourings, cover and leave to marinate overnight.
3. Set the oven to 230°C/450°F/gas mark 8.
4. Open out the boned leg and lay it, flesh side down, in a roasting pan. Sprinkle the fatty side fairly liberally with salt and roast for 20 minutes, and then reduce the oven to 200°C/400°F/gas mark 6 and roast for a further 8 minutes per 450g/1lb. In other words, a 1.8kg/4lb leg (boned weight) will cook for about 50 minutes.
5. Turn off the oven. Transfer the meat to a serving plate and leave it in the turned-off oven while making the gravy.
6. With a large metal spoon, skim off as much of the fat from the cooking juices as possible. Add the water and wine and place over a direct heat. Bring up to the boil and stir well to loosen any sediment stuck to the bottom of the pan. Simmer for 4-5 minutes. Taste and add extra salt, pepper or soy sauce as necessary and strain into a warm gravy boat.
7. Garnish the lamb with the watercress and serve the gravy separately.

MEDIUM RED

Lamb Cutlets Reform

SERVES 4
beaten egg
salt and pepper
10ml/2 teaspoons very finely chopped ham
dry white breadcrumbs
12 lamb cutlets, French trimmed (all fat removed and bones shortened to about 5cm/2 inches)
15ml/1 tablespoon oil
15g/½oz butter

For the sauce:
150ml/¼ pint demi-glace (see page 223)
white of 1 hardboiled egg
1 gherkin
30g/1oz mushrooms
½ slice cooked tongue
150ml/¼ pint sauce poivrade (see page 223)

For the garnish:
paper cutlet frills
watercress sprigs

1. Set the oven to 230°C/450°F/gas mark 8.
2. Season the beaten egg with salt and pepper. Brush the cutlets with this.
3. Mix the ham with the breadcrumbs and press the cutlets in this mixture, coating both sides well.
4. Heat the oil in a heavy roasting pan and add the butter. Fry the cutlets briskly in the fat to brown them on both sides and then transfer to the oven for 5 minutes until they are tender but still pink. Drain well on absorbent paper.
5. While the cutlets are baking, prepare the sauce: put the demi-glace into a saucepan. Cut the egg white, gherkin, mushrooms and tongue into very thin strips. Add them to the sauce and heat for 3-4 minutes. Add poivrade sauce to taste. Pour into a warm gravy boat.
6. Place a cutlet frill on each cutlet bone. Lay the

cutlets in an overlapping circle on a warm serving dish. Garnish with watercress. Serve the sauce separately.

NOTE: The cutlets can be simply fried or grilled if preferred. They are finished in the oven to clear the cooker top so that there is room to make the sauce and prepare any vegetables.

CLARET

Forcemeat Balls

Forcemeat balls are traditionally made to accompany jugged hare.

MAKES 20-24
450g/1lb good quality pork sausagemeat
1 medium onion, finely chopped
15ml/1 tablespoon finely chopped parsley
15ml/1 tablespoon finely chopped fresh sage, or 5ml/1 teaspoon dried sage
grated rind of 1/4 lemon
30g/1oz fresh breadcrumbs
salt and pepper
plain flour for rolling
55g/2oz clarified butter

1. Mix together the sausagemeat, onion, parsley, sage, lemon rind and breadcrumbs. Season with salt and pepper.
2. Using wet hands, shape into balls the size of a ping-pong ball. Roll in flour.
3. Melt the butter in a frying pan and toss the balls over the heat until cooked and well browned - approximately 8-10 minutes.

Simple Sausages

This sausagemeat mixture can be used to fill sausage skins or simply be made into skinless sausages as described below.

SERVES 4
450g/1lb minced fatty pork (e. g. from the belly)
1 medium onion (optional)
4 slices white bread, crusts removed, crumbed
1 egg
3 leaves of fresh, chopped sage, or 5ml/1 teaspoon rubbed dried sage
salt and pepper
fat for frying

1. Mix the pork belly and onion (if used) together.
2. Stir the breadcrumbs into the meat with the egg and the sage.
3. Add plenty of salt and pepper and mix thoroughly. Taste and season further if necessary.
4. Wet your hands, and form the mixture into sausage shapes.
5. Fry the sausages in hot fat, turning them frequently. They should cook slowly, and will take about 12 minutes if 2.5cm/1 inch diameter.

Pork Chops with Rosemary

SERVES 4
1 small onion, finely chopped
5ml/1 teaspoon finely chopped parsley
5ml/1 teaspoon finely chopped rosemary
1 egg
salt and freshly ground black pepper
4 x 170g/6oz pork chops, neatly trimmed
dried white breadcrumbs
oil

1. Mix the onion, parsley, rosemary and egg together in a bowl. Season well with salt and pepper. Coat each pork chop with the egg mixture and then dip in breadcrumbs, covering them well.
2. Heat the oil in a frying pan. Add the chops and fry until golden brown on both sides, and tender all the way through, 12-15 minutes.

MEDIUM RED

Spare Ribs

SERVES 4
1.25kg/2½lb skinned pork belly pieces (American spare ribs)

For the marinade:
30ml/2 tablespoons runny honey
30ml/2 tablespoons soy sauce
½ garlic clove, crushed
juice of 1 lemon
salt and pepper

1. Mix together the ingredients for the marinade and soak the spare ribs in it for at least 1 hour. The longer they marinate the better.
2. Set the oven to 180°C/350°F/gas mark 4.
3. Put the ribs, with the marinade, into a roasting pan and bake, basting occasionally, for 1½ hours.

MEDIUM RED

Glazed Bacon Joint

SERVES 4-6
1.35 kg/3lb forehock of bacon
1 onion
1 carrot
1 bay leaf
fresh parsley stalks
peppercorns
30ml/2 tablespoons demerara sugar
5ml/1 teaspoon dry English mustard
handful of cloves

1. Soak the bacon overnight in cold water. This removes excess salt.
2. Place it in a large pan of cold water and add the onion, carrot, bay leaf, parsley stalks and peppercorns. Bring slowly to the boil, cover and simmer for 1¼ hours.
3. Leave the joint to cool slightly in the stock. Then lift out and carefully pull off the skin without removing any of the fat.
4. Mix the sugar and mustard together and press it all over the joint to form an even coating.
5. Using a sharp knife, cut a lattice pattern across the bacon through the sugar and fat. Press on again any sugar that falls off. Stick a clove into each diamond segment, or into the cuts where the lines cross.
6. Set the oven to 220°C/425°F/gas mark 7 and bake the joint for about 20 minutes, or until brown and slightly caramelized.

NOTE I: If you haven't time to soak salty bacon overnight, cook it for 30 minutes in plain water and then transfer to a pan of simmering water with the bay leaf etc.
NOTE II: The cooking stock is useful for making soups, especially pea or lentil soup.
NOTE III: The bacon joint can be decorated with a ham frill: to make one, cut a piece of greaseproof paper to about 12 x 30cm/5 x 12 inches. Fold it loosely in half lengthways, without pressing down the fold. Make 5cm/2 inch cuts, 1cm/½inch apart, parallel to the end of the paper, cutting through both thicknesses from the folded side towards the open sides. Make the cuts all along the strip. Now open out the paper and re-fold it lengthways in the opposite direction. Wrap the frill round the ham bone and secure with a paper clip.

RED BURGUNDY

Roast Pork

SERVES 4
1.35 kg/3lb loin of pork, with skin intact
oil
salt

For the gravy:
10ml/2 teaspoons flour
290ml/½ pint well-flavoured stock

To serve:
small bunch of watercress
apple sauce (see page 232)

1. Set the oven to 220°C/425°F/gas mark 7.
2. Score the rind (crackling skin) with a sharp knife in cuts about 5mm/¼inch apart, cutting through the skin but not right through the fat.
3. Brush the skin with oil and sprinkle with salt to help give a crisp crackling.
4. Place in a roasting pan and roast for 1 hour 40 minutes (25 minutes to 450g/1lb, plus 25

minutes extra). After half an hour reduce the oven temperature to 190°C/375°F/gas mark 5.
5. Once the pork is cooked, turn off the oven, put the pork on a serving dish and replace it in the oven leaving the door ajar if it is still very hot.
6. Tip all but 10ml/1 dessertspoonful fat from the roasting pan, reserving as much of the meat juices as possible.
7. Add the flour and mix over the heat until well browned.
8. Draw off the heat, add the stock and mix well with a wire whisk or wooden spoon. Return to the heat and bring slowly up to the boil, whisking all the time. Simmer for a few minutes until the gravy is shiny. Season with salt and freshly ground black pepper to taste. Strain into a warm gravy boat.
9. Garnish the pork with watercress and serve with gravy and apple sauce.

NOTE: Remove the crackling before carving, then cut it with scissors into thin strips.

RED BURGUNDY

Loin of Pork with Prunes

SERVES 4

1.35kg/3lb loin of pork without skin or much fat
oil for frying
15g/½oz butter
1 onion, finely chopped
290ml/½ pint brown stock (see page 218)
1 glass red wine (100ml/3½ fl oz)
110g/4oz stoned prunes (the kind that don't need soaking)
1 bay leaf
15ml/1 tablespoon redcurrant jelly
2 sprigs fresh thyme
150ml/¼ pint single cream
small bunch of watercress

1. Set the oven to 150°C/300°F/gas mark 2.
2. Heat the oil in a flameproof casserole dish. Add the butter and, when foaming, add the pork. Fry until lightly browned all over. Add the onion and fry until golden.
3. Add the stock, wine, one-third of the prunes, the redcurrant jelly, bay leaf and thyme. Bring up to the boil, cover and place in the oven. Bake for 1½ hours.
4. Remove the pork from the casserole and slice neatly. Arrange in overlapping slices on a serving dish and keep warm while you make the sauce.
5. Strain the cooking liquor, removing any excess fat. Boil until reduced to a syrupy consistency. Add the cream and remaining prunes.
6. Spoon the sauce over the pork and garnish with watercress.

MEDIUM RED

Pork Chops Vallée D'Auge

SERVES 4

4 x 170g/6oz pork chops
salt and freshly ground black pepper
1 large onion, very finely chopped
1 celery stick, chopped
10ml/2 teaspoons Calvados or brandy
30g/1oz ham, sliced
150ml/¼ pint dry cider
2 dessert apples
lemon juice
caster sugar
15ml/1 tablespoon butter
1 egg yolk
150ml/¼ pint double cream
watercress to garnish

1. Set the oven to 180°C/350°F/gas mark 4.
2. Prepare the pork chops by cutting away any excess fat. Dry with absorbent paper and sprinkle with salt and pepper.
3. Put the fat trimmed from the pork chops in a large frying pan and place over moderate heat. When the fat has melted and the pieces are shrivelled and crisp, remove the bits with a perforated spoon.
4. Put the chops in the pan and fry over a fairly high heat on each side until well browned. Put them into a casserole without any fat, cover and place in the warm oven.
5. Lower the heat under the frying pan, add the

onion and celery and fry gently until soft but not coloured. Add the Calvados and set alight with a match. Add the ham and cider. Allow to simmer for 2 minutes.
6. Pour over the pork chops and leave covered in the oven for about 15 minutes or until the chops are completely tender.
7. Meanwhile, peel and core the apples and cut them into rings. Brush each ring with lemon juice and sprinkle with sugar. Melt the butter in the frying pan and fry the apple rings until barely soft, and slightly brown on both sides.
8. Remove the chops from the oven and keep them warm with the apple rings while you prepare the sauce.
9. Strain the liquor from the casserole (reserve the ham and vegetables) and bring it up to simmering point in a clean pan. Mix the egg yolk with the cream in a bowl and add a little of the hot stock to the mixture. Return this to the saucepan and set over a gentle heat until the sauce becomes creamy and slightly thick, but take great care not to curdle it by boiling.
10. Put the reserved ham and vegetables on to a warm serving plate. Arrange the chops on top and coat with the creamy sauce. Arrange the apple rings around the dish and garnish with watercress.

CIDER OR LIGHT RED

Pork Fillets in Cider

SERVES 4
15ml/1 tablespoon oil
15g/½oz butter
1 medium onion, finely chopped
675g/1½lb pork tenderloin (fillet), trimmed
290ml/½ pint cider
seasoning
1 bay leaf
1 small cooking apple
1 eating apple
15ml/1 tablespoon single cream

To garnish:
chopped parsley

1. Set the oven to 180°C/350°F/gas mark 4.
2. Heat the oil in a frying pan. Add the butter and when hot add the pork fillets and brown quickly, all over. Remove to a plate. Reduce the heat, add the onion and cook slowly until soft. Return the pork fillets to the pan. Add the cider and bay leaf. Bring up to the boil and tip into a casserole dish. Season, cover and bake for 10-15 minutes.
3. Peel and core the apples and dice into cubes. Add to the fillets and continue cooking for a further 10-15 minutes, until the pork and apples are tender. Remove from the oven.
4. Take out the fillets and keep warm. Strain the cooking liquor, remove the bay leaf from the sieve, and place the apples and onions in a serving dish. Keep warm.
5. Boil the cooking liquor rapidly until reduced to a syrupy consistency. Add the cream. Taste and adjust the seasoning if necessary.
6. Slice the pork fillets thickly, arrange on top of the apples and onions, pour over the sauce and sprinkle with parsley.

CIDER OR LIGHT RED

Pork Fillets with Red and Green Peppers

SERVES 4
675g/1½lb pork fillets (tenderloin)
30ml/2 tablespoons sunflower oil
1 garlic clove, crushed
1 large onion, sliced
1 red pepper, deseeded and sliced
1 green pepper, deseeded and sliced
5ml/1 teaspoon ground cumin
5ml/1 teaspoon ground coriander
5ml/1 teaspoon ground cinnamon
5ml/1 teaspoon ground turmeric
2.5ml/½ teaspoon ground mild chilli powder
30ml/2 tablespoons Greek yoghurt
15ml/1 tablespoon roughly chopped fresh mint

1. Trim off any fat and membrane from the pork fillet with a sharp, flexible knife. Cut the meat into 5mm/¼inch slices.
2. Heat the oil in a large sauté pan and brown the meat, a few pieces at a time, until evenly coloured all over. Remove the meat to a plate.
3. Add the garlic, onion and peppers to the pan and allow to soften without browning for a few

minutes. Add the dry spices and cook for a further 2 minutes. Stir regularly and add a little extra oil if they are in danger of getting too dry or burnt.
4. Take the pan off the heat. Return the pork and add just enough water to cover the meat and vegetables. Return to the heat and bring gradually up to the boil stirring continually.
5. Simmer for about 10 minutes or until the meat is tender. Remove the meat from the pan and reduce the sauce, by boiling rapidly, to half. Return the meat to the pan, add the yoghurt, let it heat through without boiling. Take off the heat, add the mint and serve immediately.

RED RHONE

Medallions of Pork with Prunes

This recipe has been adapted from *Cuisine à la Carte* by Anton Mosimann.

SERVES 4
8 pork medallions (2.5cm/1 inch thick), well trimmed, including the kidney
8 small prunes, with stones removed
seasoned flour
15ml/1 tablespoon olive oil
20g/¾oz butter
100ml/4 fl oz white wine
150ml/¼ pint brown veal stock
40g/1¼oz butter, diced

For the garnish:
50g/2oz turned carrots, blanched
50g/2oz turned turnips, blanched
8 small prunes, blanched with stones removed
20g/¾ oz butter
a little chopped parsley

1. Flatten the pork medallions lightly between 2 sheets of wet greaseproof paper.
2. Place the prunes in cold water in a pan, cover and bring to the boil.
3. Remove from the heat and set aside for 30 minutes in the water.
4. Pour off the water, cut the prunes in half and dry on a cloth.
5. Push the prunes through the pork medallions. Dust with seasoned flour.
6. Heat the oil and butter in a large frying pan.
7. Put in the pork medallions and slowly sauté on both sides until juicy, constantly using a spoon to baste during the process.
8. Remove the medallions from the pan and keep warm. Pour off all the fat from the pan.
9. Add the white wine and veal stock and reduce, by boiling rapidly, to about 150ml/¼ pint. Strain through a sieve, reheat and gradually add the butter, bit by bit, whisking all the time until smooth and glossy. Season to taste and pour over the medallions.
10. Sauté the carrots, turnips and prunes for the garnish in the butter and scatter around the pork.
11. Garnish with parsley and serve immediately.

MEDIUM RED

Jambalaya

SERVES 4-6
450g/1lb pork tenderloin fillet
30-45ml/2-3 tablespoons oil
1 onion, finely chopped
2 sticks celery, finely chopped
2 frankfurters, sliced
55g/2oz garlic sausage, diced
110g/4oz rice
10ml/2 teaspoons ground ginger
2.5ml/½ teaspoon turmeric
2.5ml/½ teaspoon paprika
290ml/½ pint chicken stock
lemon juice
salt and freshly ground black pepper
110g/4oz shelled cooked prawns

1. Trim the fillet and cut it into 1cm/½ inch cubes. Heat half the oil in a heavy saucepan and quickly fry the pork until well browned. Lift the pieces out and put them aside. Add the onion and celery to the saucepan, reduce the heat and fry gently until soft and evenly coloured. Lift them out.
2. Now fry the frankfurters and garlic sausage, adding more oil if necessary and turning them until evenly browned. Lift them out. Heat the remaining oil, stir in the rice and fry, stirring constantly, until opaque. Add the ginger,

turmeric and paprika and fry for 30 seconds.
3. Add the chicken stock and put all the fried food back. Bring to the boil, season with a dash of lemon juice, salt and pepper. Reduce the heat, cover and simmer until all the stock has been absorbed and the rice is cooked, about 20 minutes. Add the prawns and warm them in the rice for a minute or two before serving.

RED RHONE

Sweet and Sour Pork

SERVES 4

675g/1½lb lean pork
2.5ml/½ teaspoon salt
15ml/1 tablespoon cornflour
oil for deep-frying
1 green pepper

For the sweet and sour sauce:
5ml/1 teaspoon cornflour
60ml/4 tablespoons water
30ml/2 tablespoons sugar
30ml/2 tablespoons vinegar
30ml/2 tablespoons tomato purée
30ml/2 tablespoons orange juice
30ml/2 tablespoons soy sauce
30ml/2 tablespoons finely chopped pineapple
2.5ml/½ teaspoon oil

1. Start with the sauce: blend the cornflour with the water and mix it with the sugar, vinegar, tomato purée, orange juice and soy sauce.
2. Fry the chopped pineapple in the oil for 1 minute. Add this to the sauce.
3. Cut the pork into 2cm/¾inch cubes. Sprinkle with salt and toss in the cornflour.
4. Heat the oil in the fryer until a crumb will sizzle vigorously in it. Deep-fry the pork for 4 minutes. Drain on absorbent paper.
5. Heat 15ml/1 tablespoon oil in a wide pan. Deseed and slice the green pepper and fry it quickly for 30 seconds. Lower the temperature, add the sauce and cook for 1 minute. Add the pork and cook together for 1 minute. If the sauce seems too thick add a little water before serving.

BEER OR RED BURGUNDY

Jambon Persillé

SERVES 6

1 x 900g/2lb piece mild gammon or unsmoked lean bacon
1 slice of onion
1 bay leaf
½ carrot
2 parsley stalks
6 peppercorns
1 litre/2 pints veal stock plus 15g/½oz gelatine if the stock is not jellied
150ml/¼ pint dry white wine
15ml/1 tablespoon tarragon vinegar
2 egg shells
2 egg whites
45ml/3 tablespoons finely chopped parsley

1. Soak the bacon in cold water overnight.
2. Simmer it in fresh water to cover with the onion, bay leaf, carrot, parsley stalks and peppercorns until tender, about 1½ hours. Leave to cool in the liquid.
3. Put the veal stock into a large clean saucepan. If it is not set to a solid jelly, sprinkle in the gelatine. Add the wine and vinegar. Put over gentle heat to dissolve the gelatine or to melt the jelly, then allow to cool.
4. Put the crushed shells and egg whites into the stock. Place over the heat and whisk steadily with a balloon whisk until the mixture begins to boil. Stop whisking immediately and draw the pan off the heat. Allow the mixture to subside. Take care not to break the crust formed by the egg white.
5. Bring the aspic just up to the boil again, and again allow to subside. Repeat this once more; the egg-white will trap the sediment in the stock and clear the aspic. Allow to cool for 2 minutes.
6. Fix a double layer of fine muslin or white kitchen paper over a clean basin and carefully strain the aspic through it, taking care to hold the egg-white crust back. When all the liquid is through, or almost all of it, allow the egg white to slip into the muslin or kitchen paper. Then strain the aspic again – this time through both egg-white crust and cloth. Do not try to hurry the process by squeezing the cloth, or murky aspic will result. Allow to cool.
7. Cut the ham into thick slices and then into neat strips. Arrange a neat layer in the bottom

of a mould or soufflé dish which has been rinsed out with cold water or very lightly oiled.
8. Pour in enough almost-cold jelly to hold the ham in place when the jelly sets. Leave in the refrigerator to set.
9. Mix the parsley into half the just-liquid jelly and pour 1cm/½inch into the soufflé mould. Allow to set. Arrange a second layer of ham on top and set it in place with clear jelly.
10. Continue the layers in this way, finishing with clear jelly. Chill well.
11. To turn out: dip the mould into hot water to loosen the jelly. Invert a plate over the mould and turn the plate and mould over together. Give a slight shake to dislodge the jelly and remove the mould.

NOTE: A good but less elegant jambon persillé is made with uncleared veal jelly, chopped parsley and cubes of cooked ham simply combined in a dish and allowed to set.

RED BURGUNDY

Juniper Pork Chops

SERVES 4
4 pork chops at least 2cm/¾inch thick
4 juniper berries
salt and freshly ground black pepper
7g/¼oz butter
75ml/5 tablespoons dry white wine
60ml/4 tablespoons double cream
watercress

1. Lightly crush the juniper berries with a rolling pin or in a mortar.
2. Cut off the excess fat from the chops leaving only 0.5cm/¼inch all the way round. Sprinkle with pepper.
3. Heat the fat cut from the chops in a frying pan and cook until the liquid fat has run out and the pieces are crisp. Remove the pieces with a perforated spoon and throw away.
4. Put the chops in the hot pan. Fry for 5-7 minutes on each side until browned. Take out the chops and keep warm in a low oven.
5. Pour off the pork fat from the pan and melt the butter in it. Toss the juniper berries in this for 1 minute. Add the wine, bring up to the boil and reduce, by boiling rapidly, to half the original quantity. Add the cream, and reduce, by boiling rapidly, to a thin but syrupy sauce, taste and season. Pour over the chops.
6. Garnish with watercress.

LIGHT RED

Grilled Pork Chops with Apple Rings

SERVES 4
4 x 170g/6oz pork chops
a little oil
freshly ground black pepper
3-4 fresh sage leaves or a pinch of dried sage

To garnish:
2 dessert apples
butter for frying
5ml/1 teaspoon sugar
few sprigs watercress

1. Heat the grill.
2. Trim the rind from the chops and snip short cuts through the fat towards the meat, about 1cm/½inch apart to prevent curling up during grilling. Brush lightly with oil.
3. Season with pepper and crumbled or chopped sage.
4. Grill the chops for 8-10 minutes on each side, or until tender right through. Keep warm on a heated platter.
5. Peel the apples, core them and slice across into thick rings.
6. Melt a small knob of butter in a frying pan and when it is frothing lay in the apple rings. Sprinkle with a little sugar and fry lightly on both sides until golden brown but not mushy. The sugar will caramelize, giving a brown toffee-like coating to the apples.
7. Garnish the chops with the fried apple rings and watercress.

MEDIUM RED

Stir-fried Pork

Although this recipe uses pork fillet it is still reasonably low in saturated fat.

SERVES 4

450g/1lb pork (tenderloin fillet), trimmed
15ml/1 tablespoon dry sherry
15ml/1 tablespoon soy sauce
1cm/½ inch piece of fresh ginger, peeled and grated
1 bunch spring onions, cut into rings
110g/4oz baby sweetcorn, blanched
110g/4oz mangetout, topped and tailed
freshly ground black pepper

For the sauce:
15ml/1 tablespoon dry sherry
15ml/1 tablespoon soy sauce

1. Cut the pork into 'little finger'-sized strips, and marinate for at least one hour in the sherry, soy sauce and ginger.
2. In a nonstick frying pan or wok, cook the pork with a little of the marinade for 4 minutes.
3. Add the rest of the marinade and the spring onions, baby corn and mangetout. Cook for a further 4 minutes. Add the sauce and reheat.
4. Season with pepper and serve.

NOTE: If not using a nonstick frying pan or wok, the pork will have to be fried in a little oil.

LIGHT RED

Pork Medallions with Ginger Sauce

SERVES 6-8

For the marinade:
225ml/8 fl oz teriyaki sauce
110g/4oz runny honey
110ml/4 fl oz medium dry sherry
10ml/2 teaspoons finely chopped fresh ginger
30ml/2 tablespoons sesame oil
3 pork fillets, cut into 2.5cm/1 inch medallions
oil for frying

1. Whisk together the marinade ingredients and pour over the pork medallions. Cover and allow to marinate for 2 hours, turning the meat occasionally.
2. Drain off the marinade. Strain into a saucepan, bring to the boil and allow to reduce a little until the sauce has thickened slightly.
3. Heat a little oil in a frying pan. Fry the medallions a few at a time until they are cooked through. Serve with the sauce.

NOTE: This goes very well with stir-fried batons of parsnip and carrot.

LIGHT RED

Pork Pie

SERVES 8-10

675g/1½lb pork (tenderloin fillet)
pâte à pâté made with 450g/1lb flour (see page 531)
45g/1½oz butter
45g/1½oz flour
225ml/8 fl oz chicken stock (see page 219)
55ml/2 fl oz dry white wine
2 eggs
55ml/2 fl oz double cream
salt and freshly ground black pepper
15ml/1 tablespoon chopped parsley
30ml/2 tablespoons chopped thyme leaves
beaten egg to glaze

1. Set the oven to 200°C/400°F/gas mark 6.
2. Trim the pork fillet, discarding any fat, sinew or gristle. Place in a roasting pan and roast uncovered for 30 minutes. Remove from the oven and allow to cool.
3. Place a third of the pastry in the refrigerator. Divide the remaining pastry in half. Roll out one piece into a long strip to fit the sides of a 20cm/8 inch spring-clip tin. Press it round the sides neatly. Roll out the second piece to fit the base of the tin. Press the base and sides together carefully. Prick the base well and place it in the refrigerator to chill.
4. Meanwhile, make the filling: mince the pork fillet finely.
5. Melt the butter in a heavy saucepan, stir in the flour and stir over the heat for 1 minute.

Remove the pan from the heat, add the stock and wine and mix well. Return to the heat and stir or whisk until it comes up to the boil. Simmer for 5 minutes, stirring occasionally. (If the sauce is too thick add some water, but it should be a thick panade.)

6. Remove the pan from the heat, separate the eggs and beat the yolks into the sauce with the cream. Season carefully with salt, freshly ground black pepper, parsley and thyme. Add the minced pork.

7. Whisk the egg whites until stiff and fold into the mixture. Taste and add more seasoning if necessary.

8. Place the filling in the pastry case making it slightly domed in the centre.

9. Roll out the remaining pastry for the lid. Dampen the bottom edge with water and press the lid on to the pastry case. Trim and crimp the edges. Make a neat hole in the middle of the lid. Decorate with pastry trimmings made into leaves.

10. Brush with egg glaze and cook on a baking sheet in the oven for 40 minutes. Serve cold.

LIGHT RED/ROSE

Flat Ham Pie

SERVES 6

pâte à pâté made with 450g/1lb flour (see page 531)
55g/2oz Gruyère or Cheddar cheese, grated
30g/1oz grated Parmesan
45g/1½oz butter, melted
55g/2oz fresh white breadcrumbs
225g/8oz ham
30ml/2 tablespoons chopped dill or chives
1 large garlic clove, crushed
150ml/¼ pint soured cream
freshly ground black pepper
juice of ½ lemon
beaten egg

1. Make up the pâte à pâté and roll out into rectangles, one to fit a Swiss roll tin, the other slightly larger.

2. Set the oven to 200°C/400°F/gas mark 6.

3. Lightly grease and flour the back of a Swiss roll tin or a rectangular baking sheet. Put the smaller rectangle of pastry on it and prick all over with a fork. Bake for 15 minutes and leave to cool.

4. Mix together the Gruyère or Cheddar, the Parmesan, the melted butter and the breadcrumbs. Scatter half of this all over the baked pastry, leaving a good 1cm/½inch clear all round the edge.

5. Chop the ham into small pieces and scatter it on top of the cheese mixture. Then scatter over the dill or chives.

6. Mix the garlic with the soured cream and spread all over the ham. Season well with pepper but no salt.

7. Sprinkle evenly with the lemon juice and top with the rest of the cheese mixture. Wet the edge of the bottom piece of pastry with lightly beaten egg and put the top sheet of pastry in place, pressing the edges to seal it well.

8. Use any pastry trimmings to decorate the pie and brush all over with beaten egg.

9. Bake until the pastry is crisp and pale brown. Serve hot or cold.

LIGHT RED/ROSE

Veal Escalopes with Rosemary

SERVES 4

4 x 140g/5oz veal escalopes
salt and freshly ground black pepper
30g/1oz butter
5ml/1 teaspoon fresh rosemary or 2. 5ml/½ teaspoon dried rosemary
30ml/2 tablespoons dry white wine
15ml/1 tablespoon single cream

1. If the escalopes are not very thin, place them between 2 sheets of wet greaseproof paper or polythene and gently beat with a mallet or rolling pin. Season with salt and pepper.

2. In a frying pan over a moderate heat melt the butter with the rosemary. When the butter is foaming, fry the escalopes (one or two at a time if they won't fit in the pan together) for 3-4 minutes on each side until a very delicate brown. Take out the veal with a perforated spoon or fish slice and keep warm in a very low oven.

3. Pour the wine into the pan and heat, scraping the surface of the pan with a wooden spoon to incorporate any sediment. Boil up well and add the cream. Taste and correct the seasoning if necessary. Pour over the veal and serve immediately.

LIGHT RED

Veal Escalopes with Ragoût Fin

SERVES 4

110g/4oz calves sweetbreads
20g/3/4oz butter
1 small onion, finely chopped
30g/1oz bacon, diced
55g/2oz button mushrooms, sliced
15ml/1 level tablespoon chopped parsley
7g/1/4oz flour
150ml/1/4 pint well-flavoured chicken stock
salt and freshly ground black pepper
4 x 170g/6oz veal escalopes
extra butter for frying
squeeze of lemon juice

For the garnish:
sprigs of watercress
lemon wedges

1. Soak the sweetbreads in cold water for 4 hours, changing the water every time it becomes pink; probably 4 times. There should be no blood at all when the sweetbreads are ready for cooking.
2. Place them in a pan of cold water and bring up to boiling point, but do not allow to boil. Simmer for 2 minutes. Rinse under cold running water and dry well.
3. Pick over the sweetbreads, removing all the skin and membrane. Chop them coarsely.
4. Melt the butter and add the onion. Cook slowly until soft but not coloured. Add the bacon and sweetbreads and cook for 3 minutes. Stir in the mushrooms and parsley and leave over a gentle heat for 1 minute.
5. Mix in the flour and cook for 1 minute. Remove from the heat and stir in the stock. Return to the heat and bring slowly to the boil, stirring continuously. Season with salt and pepper. Simmer for 1 minute and set aside to cool and solidify.
6. Place the veal escalopes between 2 pieces of wet greaseproof paper or polythene and, with a rolling pin or mallet, beat them lightly until quite thin.
7. Divide the sweetbread mixture between the escalopes and fold them in half.
8. Melt some butter in a large frying pan and when foaming, add the escalopes. Brown lightly on both sides. Reduce the temperature and cook slowly for 4-5 minutes. Lift out the escalopes on to a warm serving plate.
9. Increase the heat under the frying pan and brown the butter, remove from the heat and add a squeeze of lemon juice. Pour over the escalopes and serve garnished with watercress and lemon wedges.

MEDIUM RED

Veal Marsala

SERVES 4

4 x 170g/6oz veal escalopes
30g/1oz butter
salt and freshly ground white pepper
30ml/2 tablespoons Marsala
60ml/4 tablespoons double cream
lemon juice

1. Put the veal escalopes between 2 sheets of wet greaseproof paper and beat lightly with a mallet or rolling pin until thin.
2. Melt the butter in a frying pan and, when it is foaming, fry the escalopes briskly to brown them lightly on both sides (2-3 minutes per side). Dish them on a warm plate and keep warm.
3. Tip off any fat in the pan. Add 30ml/2 tablespoons water and the Marsala, swill it about and bring to the boil. Add the cream, season well with salt, pepper and a few drops of lemon juice.
4. Return the veal to the pan to heat through gently.

LIGHT RED/VALPOLICELLA

Veal Steaks with Wild Mushrooms

SERVES 4

4 veal steaks
110g/4oz mixed wild mushrooms, sliced
425ml/3/4 pint brown stock (see page 218)
1 glass white wine (100ml/3 1/2 fl oz)
170g/6oz unsalted butter, chilled and diced

1. Melt 15g/1/2oz of the butter in a frying pan and, when it is foaming, fry the veal steaks to brown them lightly on both sides (2-3 minutes per side). Dish them on a warm plate.
2. Add the mushrooms and fry for 1 minute.
3. Add the stock and wine and boil, scraping the bottom of the pan to incorporate the sediment, for 3 minutes. Remove the mushrooms with a perforated spoon and arrange on the veal steaks. Continue to boil the stock until reduced to 75ml/5 tablespoons.
4. Allow the stock to cool slightly. Using a wire whisk and plenty of vigorous continuous whisking, add the butter. The process should take about 2 minutes and the sauce should thicken. Taste, season and pour over the veal steaks.

LIGHT RED

Hungarian Veal Steaks with Aubergine

SERVES 4

1 large aubergine
salt and pepper
30g/1oz seasoned flour
675g/1 1/2lb boneless veal (sirloin or fillet)
225g/8oz larding pork or 110g/4oz thin rindless streaky bacon
oil for frying
30g/1oz clarified butter
1 shallot, finely chopped
5ml/1 teaspoon paprika
45ml/3 tablespoons white wine
150ml/1/4 pint single cream
290ml/1/2 pint mornay sauce (see page 221)
15ml/1 tablespoon grated cheese
15ml/1 tablespoon dry white breadcrumbs

1. Set the oven to 130°C/250°F/gas mark 2.
2. Slice the aubergine in 1cm/1/2inch thick slices. Sprinkle with salt and leave to release its juices (to degorge). Rinse well, pat dry and dip in seasoned flour.
3. Roll up and bard the meat (wrap it carefully in the pork fat, cut into thin strips, or in the streaky bacon). Tie the roll at 3cm/1 1/2inch intervals with string. Slice through the meat between the strings to give 4 even-sized steaks, surrounded by fat or bacon and each encircled with string.
4. Heat the oil and fry the aubergine until golden brown and tender. Remove from the pan, drain on absorbent paper and keep warm in the oven.
5. Dust the veal steaks with seasoned flour. Heat the butter in the pan and fry the veal steaks for 6-8 minutes on each side. Remove and keep warm in the oven.
6. Add the shallot to the pan and cook slowly for 2 minutes, then add the paprika and continue cooking for a further 2 minutes. Pour on the wine and boil to reduce it by half. Cool slightly, pour in the cream and season with salt and pepper. Reheat, boil to reduce if a little thin and then keep on one side.
7. Heat the grill. Reheat the mornay sauce.
8. Lay the aubergine slices in an ovenproof dish. Remove the strings from the veal steaks and lay them on top of the aubergines. Coat with the mornay sauce. Sprinkle with cheese and crumbs and brown under the grill. Reheat the paprika sauce and trickle it around the dish.

MEDIUM RED

Grilled Medallions of Veal with Goats Cheese and Aubergine Purée

SERVES 4

For the purée:
2 medium aubergines
1 garlic clove, unpeeled
about 150ml/¼ pint olive oil
225g/8oz olives, stoned and finely chopped
black pepper

For the meat:
4 medallions of veal
4 slices of goats cheese
60ml/4 tablespoons fresh white breadcrumbs

To garnish:
frisée lettuce, tossed in a hazelnut oil French dressing

1. Set the oven to 200°C/400°F/gas mark 6.
2. Brush the aubergines lightly with oil and put into a roasting pan. After half an hour add the unpeeled garlic and bake until they are soft. This will take about half an hour.
3. Allow the aubergines and garlic to cool.
4. Peel the aubergines, put the flesh into a clean cloth and squeeze lightly to extract the bitter juices. Peel the garlic and chop the aubergines and garlic together. Add half the oil and the olives. Season with pepper and leave for at least 30 minutes for the flavour to develop.
5. Heat the grill to its highest temperature. Baste the medallions of veal with some of the remaining oil and grill for 2 minutes per side.
6. Put the goats cheese slices on the veal medallions, brush lightly with oil and sprinkle with the breadcrumbs. Grill until lightly coloured.
7. Place the medallions of veal on 4 warm plates. Place a generous spoonful of the warm aubergine and olive purée on each plate.
8. Garnish with the frisée tossed in hazelnut dressing.

MEDIUM RED/CHIANTI

Veal Cutlets and Grilled Vegetables with Aïoli

SERVES 8

For the aïoli:
6 garlic cloves, peeled and crushed
3 egg yolks
45ml/3 tablespoons fresh white breadcrumbs
2.5ml/½ teaspoon salt
60ml/4 tablespoons white wine vinegar
290ml/½ pint olive oil
15ml/1 tablespoon boiling water

For the vegetables:
2 aubergines, cut in slices lengthways
olive oil
3 large red peppers, halved and deseeded
6 medium courgettes, cut into thin diagonal slices
4 onions, sliced
6 tomatoes, skinned, quartered and deseeded
balsamic vinegar
mint, finely chopped
basil, finely chopped

For the veal:
8 veal cutlets
olive oil
salt and freshly ground black pepper

1. To make the aïoli: put the garlic, egg yolks, breadcrumbs, salt and vinegar in a food processor. Process to a paste and slowly add the oil to make a thick sauce. Add the boiling water.
2. Salt the aubergines and leave in a colander for 20 minutes. Rinse and pat dry with kitchen paper. Paint each side lightly with olive oil and grill until dark brown but not burnt.
3. Grill the peppers skin side up until they are charred and blistered. Remove the skin and cut the flesh into strips.
4. Grill the courgettes.
5. Sauté the onions in a little oil until light brown.
6. Layer the vegetables, including the tomatoes in a bowl, sprinkling each layer with balsamic vinegar, mint and basil. Set aside to marinate at room temperature for 1 hour.
7. Brush both sides of the cutlets with olive oil

and sprinkle with salt and pepper. Grill under a preheated grill for 5-7 minutes each side, depending on the thickness of the meat.
8. To serve: place the cooked cutlets and some of the marinated vegetables on warm individual plates. Serve a spoonful of aïoli beside the vegetables.

LIGHT FRUITY RED

Osso Bucco

SERVES 4
4 large meaty pieces knuckle of veal, cut across with the bone and marrow in the centre
45ml/3 tablespoons good quality olive oil
1 large or 2 small onions, finely chopped
1 large carrot, finely chopped
2 garlic cloves, crushed
10ml/2 teaspoons flour
10ml/2 teaspoons tomato purée
340g/12oz ripe tomatoes, skinned and choppped
150ml/1/4 pint dry white wine
290ml/1/2 pint good veal stock
salt and freshly ground black pepper
bouquet garni (sprig each of parsley and thyme, stick of celery and 1 bay leaf, tied together with string)
1 tablespoon chopped parsley

1. Put 15ml/1 tablespoon of the oil into a saucepan, add the onion, carrot and garlic and cover with a well-fitting lid. Leave on a gentle heat to cook without browning.
2. Brown the meat on both sides in the rest of the oil in a large pan, one or two pieces at a time. Remove to a plate as they are browned.
3. When all are done sprinkle the flour into the pan and stir well. Add the tomato purée, cooked vegetables, tomatoes, wine, stock, salt and pepper and bring to the boil.
4. Replace the veal, sink the bouquet garni in the liquid and put on the lid. Simmer for 1 1/2 hours or until the veal is very tender but not quite falling off the bone.
5. Take the veal out and place on a warmed serving platter with a fairly deep lip. Cover with foil and keep warm while you boil the sauce rapidly until thick. Stir frequently and watch that it does not catch and burn at the bottom.
6. Remove the bouquet garni. The sauce should be pushed through a sieve, then poured over the meat, but it is often served without sieving. Osso bucco looks, and is, a substantial peasant dish, made brighter by a last-minute scattering of chopped parsley.

ITALIAN MEDIUM RED/CHIANTI

Blanquette de Veau

SERVES 4
900g/2lb pie veal
slice of lemon
bouquet garni (4 parsley stalks, 2 bay leaves, blade of mace or pinch of nutmeg)
salt and pepper
2 carrots, peeled and cut into sticks
2 onions, peeled and sliced
5ml/1 teaspoon cornflour
1 egg yolk, or 2 for a very rich sauce
150ml/1/4 pint double cream

For the garnish:
8 fried bread triangles made from 2 slices crustless white bread
chopped parsley

1. Trim the fat from the meat but do not worry about the gristle. Put the veal in a pan of cold water with a slice of lemon. Bring slowly to the boil, skimming carefully. Add the bouquet garni with a little salt. Remove the lemon slice. Simmer gently for 30 minutes.
2. Add the carrots and onions and continue to simmer until the meat is really tender and the vegetables cooked, probably a further 30-40 minutes.
3. Strain the liquid into a jug. Skim off any fat. There should be 290ml/1/2 pint. If there is less, add a little water. If there is more return the liquid to the pan and reduce, by rapidly boiling. Pick over the meat, removing any fat or gristle, and put the meat and vegetables into an ovenproof serving dish. Remove the bouquet garni.
4. Mix the cornflour in a cup with a few spoons of cold water and add some of the hot liquid from the veal to this. Stir while bringing to the boil. You should now have a sauce that is very slightly thickened: about the consistency

of thin cream. If it is still too thin, do not add more cornflour, but boil rapidly until reduced to the correct consistency. Add salt and pepper.
5. Mix the egg yolks and cream together in a bowl. Add some of the sauce, mix well, and return to the pan. Do not boil or the eggs will scramble. Reheat gently, stirring until the egg yolks have thickened the sauce to the consistency of double cream, then pour over the meat and vegetables.
6. Served garnished with triangles of fried bread with their corners dipped in chopped parsley.

FULL DRY WHITE

Veal Florentine

SERVES 4
1 garlic clove, crushed
6 tomatoes, skinned and sliced
55g/2oz butter
900g/2lb spinach, cooked and chopped
salt and freshly ground black pepper
pinch of nutmeg
Four 140g/5oz veal escalopes
290ml/½ pint cheese sauce (see page 221)
15ml/1 tablespoon grated cheese
15ml/1 tablespoon dried breadcrumbs

1. Set the oven to 180°C/350°F/gas mark 4.
2. Fry the garlic and the tomatoes lightly in a quarter of the butter without allowing the tomatoes to get too soft. Place them in a dish big enough to hold the veal in one layer.
3. Toss the spinach in a little butter in the pan. Season with salt, pepper and nutmeg. Spread the spinach on top of the tomatoes.
4. Put the veal between 2 pieces of wet greaseproof paper and flatten by batting evenly with a rolling pin. Cut across the grain into strips.
5. Heat the remaining butter in a large frying pan. Fry the veal strips in this until lightly browned all over. Put them on top of the spinach and season well with salt and pepper.
6. Heat the cheese sauce and pour evenly over the veal and spinach. Sprinkle with the grated cheese and breadcrumbs.
7. Bake for 15 minutes or until bubbly and hot, then grill to brown the top, if necessary.

NOTE: Chicken Florentine can be made in the same way using strips of poached chicken in place of fried veal. They both make excellent party dishes.

DRY WHITE/SOAVE

Hungarian Veal Goulash

SERVES 4
900g/2lb pie veal
450g/1lb onions, sliced
20g/¾oz butter
15ml/1 tablespoon paprika
290ml/½ pint veal stock
squeeze of lemon juice
1 glass white wine (100ml/3½ fl oz)
10ml/2 teaspoons tomato purée
salt and freshly ground black pepper
5ml/1 teaspoon flour
150ml/¼ pint soured cream
chopped parsley to garnish

1. Cut the veal into 5cm/2 inch cubes. Trim off as much fat as possible but do not worry about any skin and gristle.
2. In a large saucepan, cook the onions in the butter until soft. Add the paprika and cook for a further minute.
3. Add the veal, stock, lemon juice, wine, tomato purée, salt and pepper, bring to the boil and simmer until the meat is tender, 45-60 minutes.
4. Strain the stock into a jug. Skim off any fat. There should be about 290ml/½ pint. If there is less, add some water. If there is more, reduce by boiling rapidly. Pick off any skin or gristle from the veal and place the meat in an ovenproof dish. Return the stock to the pan, mix the flour with a little of the soured cream and add some of the hot veal stock to it. Mix thoroughly and return the paste to the veal stock. Bring slowly to the boil, stirring continuously; cook for 2 minutes.
5. Check the seasoning and pour the sauce over the veal. Streak in the remaining soured cream and scatter chopped parsley on top.

MEDIUM RED

Veal and Ham Raised Pie

SERVES 4
657g/1½lb boned shoulder of veal
110g/4oz ham
salt and freshly ground black pepper
1 onion, chopped
30ml/2 tablespoons chopped fresh parsley
hot watercrust pastry made with 450g/1lb flour (see page 531)
1 egg, beaten
290ml/½ pint aspic (see page 219)

1. Set the oven to 190°C/375°F/gas mark 5.
2. Cut the veal and ham into small cubes. Trim away most of the fat and all the skin and gristle. Season with salt and pepper, chopped onion and parsley. Leave on one side while you make the pastry and mould the pastry case (see page 531).
3. Fill the pie with the seasoned meat, making sure that you press it firmly into the corners and cover with the remaining pastry. Press the edges together. Make a neat hole in the middle of the lid. Secure a lightly buttered double-layered piece of greaseproof paper around the pie with a paper clip.
4. Bake for 15 minutes. Reduce the oven to 170°C/325°F/gas mark 3. Cook for a further hour. Half an hour before the pie is due to come out of the oven remove the paper 'collar' and brush the pastry evenly all over with the beaten egg. Take the pie out of the oven, and allow to get quite cold.
5. Warm the aspic enough to make it just liquid but not hot. Using a funnel, fill up the pie with jelly. Allow the liquid to set slightly and then add more liquid until you are sure that the pie is completely full. This will take some time. Leave in the refrigerator for the jelly to reset.

NOTE: A richer and, frankly, better result is achieved with a pâte à pâté crust, though the classic English pie is made as above. The recipe for pâte à pâté is found on page 531, and the pork pie recipe on page 380 gives instructions for shaping and baking.

LIGHT RED/ROSE

Nicola Cox's Veal Roast

Nicola Cox regularly demonstrates at Leith's School of Food and Wine and is always very popular. She has written numerous cookery books and runs Farthinghoe Fine Food and Wine.

SERVES 8
2 kg/4¼lb boneless roasting veal (a long solid piece of loin is best)
salt and pepper
10ml/2 teaspoons chopped mixed fresh herbs
30ml/2 tablespoons cognac
30ml/2 tablespoons Madeira or sherry
30ml/2 tablespoons olive oil
3 large thin slices of ham
6 large thin slices Gruyère
85g/3oz onions, finely sliced
85g/3oz carrots, finely sliced
55g/2oz butter
15ml/1 tablespoon oil
2-3 rashers fat bacon

1. Make 3 long parallel cuts 2.5cm/1 inch apart the whole length of the meat, but do not cut quite through. The meat should now look rather like the leaves of a book.
2. Sprinkle inside the slits with salt, pepper, herbs, cognac, Madeira and olive oil.
3. Wrap in foil and leave in the bottom of the refrigerator for 6 hours, or overnight.
4. Make 3 'sandwiches' of ham pressed between slices of cheese. Pack one between each leaf of meat.
5. Press the meat together again to re-form the roast and tie up with string. If it is a bit untidy don't worry; it will pull together in the cooking.
6. Set the oven to 170°C/325°F/gas mark 3.
7. In a large casserole, gently brown the onion and the carrot in the butter and oil for 5 minutes.
8. Remove the vegetables and then in the same casserole brown the veal over fairly high heat until sealed on all sides; this will take 15-20 minutes. Return the vegetables to the casserole.
9. Cover the meat with the bacon, foil and then the lid. Cook in the oven for 2¼-2½ hours, basting occasionally with the juices in the casserole.

10. When tender, put the meat in a warm place for 15-20 minutes to settle before carving.
11. Skim the fat off the liquid in the pan. If necessary boil the juices to reduce to 190ml/1/3 pint. Strain into a sauce boat.
12. Carve the meat in slices across the grain so that each slice has a larding of ham and cheese.

CHIANTI

Larded Loin of Veal

SERVES 6
1kg/2lb piece loin of veal (weight without bones)
strips of bacon fat
30g/1oz butter
10ml/2 teaspoons Dijon mustard
mixed herbs, chopped
salt and freshly ground black pepper
15ml/1 tablespoon dripping
5ml/1 teaspoon flour

1. Set the oven to 180°C/350°F/gas mark 4. Weigh the veal to establish the cooking time.
2. With a very sharp knife, cut away the rind and most of the fat from the loin, leaving about 1cm/1/2 inch of fat on the joint.
3. Take long strips of bacon fat one by one and press into the tunnel of a larding needle. Push the needle through the lean part of the meat, gently turning it so that the lard does not come loose. When the fat is through the length of the meat, pull the needle away leaving the fat embedded in the meat. Repeat this 8 or 9 times making sure that there is an equal distance between each lard.
4. With a sharp knife, make criss-cross incisions into the outer layer of fat.
5. Spread the butter and half of the mustard over the lean side of the joint. Spread mustard only on the fat side, making sure that this goes well into the incisions. Sprinkle with mixed herbs, salt and pepper, and tie up neatly with string.
6. Put the dripping in a roasting pan and melt over a gentle heat. When it begins to spit, put the joint into it, baste, and place in the oven. Roast for 25 minutes per 450g/1lb.
7. Remove the joint to a warm serving dish. Skim the excess fat from the pan. With a whisk or wooden spoon, scrape the bottom of the pan and beat in the flour. Stir until boiling, then simmer for 2 minutes.
8. Check the seasoning and pour into a warm sauce boat. Serve with the joint.

MEDIUM RED

Cold Veal with Green Peppercorns

SERVES 10
2kg/4 1/2lb piece of boned shoulder veal
30g/1oz unsalted butter
1 glass white wine (100ml/3 1/2 fl oz)
bunch of watercress to garnish

For the stuffing:
1 onion, finely chopped
30g/1oz butter
140g/5oz button mushrooms, sliced
1 small green pepper, deseeded and chopped
1 garlic clove, crushed
70g/2 1/2oz fresh white breadcrumbs
salt and freshly ground black pepper
450g/1lb minced pork belly
5ml/1 teaspoon well-rinsed green peppercorns
15ml/1 tablespoon chopped mixed herbs
1 egg, lightly beaten

1. First prepare the stuffing: cook the onion in the butter until soft. Add the mushrooms, green pepper and garlic and cook for a further 2 minutes. Mix with the breadcrumbs, salt, pepper, pork, peppercorns, herbs and beaten egg. Beat well.
2. Lay the veal out flat, season with salt and pepper and spread with the stuffing. Roll and tie up. It should be a cylindrical shape.
3. Lightly brown the meat in the unsalted butter in a large flameproof casserole. When browned all over, add the wine. Cover with tin foil as a lid and bake in a preheated oven, at 180°C/350°F/gas mark 4, for 2 1/2 hours.
4. Remove from the casserole and if it is to be served cold, allow to cool before removing the string. If it is to be served hot, remove the string, and serve in thin overlapping slices. Garnish with watercress.

SPICY DRY WHITE

Brains with Brown Butter

SERVES 4
4 calves brains
860ml/1½ pints court bouillon (see page 219)
salt and pepper
55g/2oz butter
about 3 gherkins
about 10 capers
chopped parsley
45ml/3 tablespoons lemon juice

1. Wash the brains well and soak in cold water for 2-3 hours. Drain them.
2. Bring the court bouillon to the boil, add the brains and poach for 15 minutes. Remove and drain thoroughly.
3. Cut the brains into slices, removing any membranes. Lay on a heated serving dish and season with salt and pepper.
4. Chop the gherkins, capers and parsley.
5. Heat the butter in a pan until just turning brown. Immediately add the gherkins, capers and parsley. Boil up, remove from the heat, add the lemon juice, pour over the brains and serve immediately.

CLARET

Kidneys Turbigo

SERVES 4
9 lambs kidneys
butter for frying
225g/8oz small pork sausages
12 baby onions or shallots, peeled
225g/8oz button mushrooms
30ml/2 tablespoons sherry
425ml/¾ pint stock
bouquet garni (1 celery stick, 1 bay leaf, sprigs of parsley and thyme, tied together with string)
salt and pepper
30g/1oz butter
30g/1oz flour
140ml/5 fl oz carton soured cream

1. Skin the kidneys, halve them and remove the core with a pair of scissors.
2. Heat the butter in a frying pan. Brown the kidneys quickly, a few at a time, on both sides. They should cook fast enough to go brown rather than grey. Remove them into a sieve set over a bowl as you go.
3. Now fry the sausages, then the onions, and finally the mushrooms in the same way. Put them on to a plate - not with the kidneys.
4. Put everything back into the pan, except for the kidney juice in the bowl - the blood can be very bitter. Pour over the sherry and stock and sink the bouquet garni in the liquid. Add salt and pepper and cover with the saucepan lid.
5. Cook very gently for about 1 hour or until the kidneys and onions are tender. Make sure that the kidneys are submerged during cooking.
6. Lift the meat and vegetables on to a serving dish and discard the bouquet garni.
7. Work the butter and flour together to a paste (beurre manié). Drop about half of it into the sauce and whisk or stir briskly while bringing slowly to the boil. If the sauce is still on the thin side, add the rest of the butter and flour mixture in the same way, whisking out the lumps. Boil for 1 minute.
8. Add half of the soured cream, stir, but do not boil, and pour over the dish. Serve the remaining cream separately.

NOTE: Classic turbigo does not have the soured cream but the addition is delicious.

FULL RED

Lambs Kidneys with Mushrooms in Mustard Sauce

SERVES 2

6 lambs kidneys
30g/1oz butter
110g/4oz large flat mushrooms, chopped
30ml/2 tablespoons double cream
10ml/2 teaspoons Dijon mustard
salt and freshly ground black pepper
chopped parsley

1. Skin, split and core the kidneys with a pair of scissors. Cut into fine slices.
2. Melt the butter and brown the kidneys quickly all over. Add the mushrooms and cook for 1 minute.
3. Reduce the heat and stir in the cream, mustard, salt and pepper. Serve the lambs kidneys immediately, garnished with chopped parsley.

RHONE

Veal Kidneys Robert

SERVES 2-3

150ml/¼ pint dry white wine
450g/1lb veal kidneys
45g/1½oz butter
5ml/1 teaspoon Dijon mustard
10ml/1 dessertspoon chopped parsley
squeeze of lemon juice
salt and freshly ground black pepper
30ml/2 tablespoons double cream

1. Put the wine in a saucepan and boil until reduced by half.
2. Remove the membranes and cores from the kidneys, and slice them quite finely.
3. Fry a handful of kidney slices at a time in hot butter, shaking the pan until the kidneys are brown but still pink inside.
4. Return all the kidneys to the pan and add the mustard, wine, parsley, lemon juice and seasoning. Bring to the boil, stirring continuously. Stir in the cream. Taste, adding salt and pepper if necessary.
5. Turn into a warm dish and sprinkle with parsley.

FULL RED

Veal Kidneys in Pastry Puffs

If ceps, chanterelles or morels are not available, use oyster or small button mushrooms instead.

SERVES 4

puff pastry made with 340g/12oz flour (see page 528)
1 beaten egg to glaze

For the filling:
290ml/½ pint white wine
340g/12oz veal kidneys
70g/2½oz unsalted butter
55g/2oz ceps, sliced
55g/2oz small chanterelles
55g/2oz small morels
10ml/2 teaspoons Dijon mustard
15ml/1 tablespoon chopped parsley
squeeze of lemon juice
salt and freshly ground black pepper
90ml/6 tablespoons double cream

1. Set the oven to 220°C/425°F/gas mark 7.
2. Roll the pastry into a large rectangle. Cut it into 4 x 10cm/4 inch diamonds, i. e. each side should measure 10cm/4 inches. Place them on a damp baking tray and brush with glaze. With a sharp knife, trace a line about 1cm/½inch from the edge of each diamond, without cutting all the way through the pastry. A small diamond is thus traced, which will form the hat for the pastry case. Make a design inside this diamond with the knife. Flour the blade of the knife and use this to 'knock up' the sides of pastry. Chill for 15 minutes.
3. Bake in the preheated oven for 20 minutes or until all puffed up and brown. With a knife, outline and remove the 'hats' and scoop out any uncooked dough inside. Transfer the cases and hats to a rack to cool. Reduce the oven to 180°C/350°F/gas mark 4.
4. Meanwhile, prepare the filling: put the wine

into a saucepan and boil until reduced by half.
5. Remove the membranes and cores from the kidneys and slice them quite finely.
6. Fry the wild mushrooms very slowly, in a little of the butter, for about 3 minutes. Set aside.
7. Fry the kidneys, a small handful at a time, in the remaining butter. Fry them very slowly. Remove to a sieve set over a bowl. Bitter juices will run out of the kidneys and these should be discarded.
8. Return the pastry cases to the oven for 4 minutes to reheat.
9. Put the wine, mustard, parsley, lemon juice, salt, pepper and cream into the frying pan. Bring to the boil and reduce, by boiling rapidly, for 1 minute. Add the kidneys and mushrooms to the sauce.
10. Divide the filling between the 4 pastry cases. Put on the hats and serve immediately.

RED BURGUNDY

Calves Liver Lyonnaise

SERVES 4
450g/1lb calves liver
55g/2oz butter
1 large onion, finely sliced
seasoned flour
salt and freshly ground black pepper
290ml/½ pint brown stock (see page 218)
15ml/1 tablespoon orange juice
15ml/1 tablespoon mixed finely chopped fresh herbs (rosemary, sage, thyme)
chopped parsley

1. Set the oven to 190°C/375°F/gas mark 5.
2. Skin the liver by removing the fine outer membrane. Cut it into slices. Remove any large 'tubes'.
3. Heat half the butter in a frying pan and slowly cook the onion until first soft and transparent and finally evenly pale brown. Set aside.
4. Dip the slices of liver into the seasoned flour, shaking off any excess.
5. Heat the rest of the butter until foaming. Fry the liver pieces in it, a few at a time, for about 2 minutes each side. The liver should be nicely browned on the outside but pale pink in the middle. Drain well. Arrange in overlapping slices with the onions in an ovenproof dish. Keep warm.
6. Sprinkle enough of the seasoned flour (about 5ml/1 teaspoon) into the frying pan to absorb the remaining fat. Cook for 1 minute, stirring and scraping any sediment from the bottom of the pan. Gradually stir in the stock and the orange juice. Allow to boil. Season with pepper and salt and add the herbs. Simmer for 1 minute. Pour this gravy over the liver, garnish with chopped parsley and serve immediately.

RED BURGUNDY

Liver and Bacon

SERVES 4
450g/1lb calves or lambs liver
seasoned flour
55g/2oz butter
1 onion, thinly sliced
6 rashers rindless bacon
290ml/½ pint beef stock (see page 218)
small glass sherry (optional)
watercress to garnish

1. Remove the film of membrane from the liver and cut the meat into thin slices. Dip the slices in seasoned flour and keep well separated on a plate.
2. Heat half of the butter in a frying pan and fry the onion slowly in it until soft and brown. Tip the onion into a saucer.
3. Heat the grill. Cook the bacon under it until crisp and brown but not brittle. Turn off the grill and leave the bacon under it to keep warm.
4. Heat the rest of the butter in the frying pan and fry the liver slices, a few pieces at a time, adding more butter if necessary. Note that liver is easily spoiled by overcooking. Dish on a shallow platter and keep warm.
5. Put the onion, and any of its fat, back into the pan and add a sprinkling of the seasoned flour – just enough to absorb the fat. Cook for 1 minute. Pour in the stock and stir well as it comes to the boil. Add the sherry, if using.
6. Boil the sauce rapidly to reduce in quantity and thicken it. This will also give a richer

appearance and concentrate the flavour. Taste and season as necessary.
7. Pour the sauce over the liver, top with the bacon and garnish with watercress. Serve at once as liver toughens on standing.

FULL RED

Oxtail Stew

SERVES 4
2 oxtails, cut into 1cm/½ inch lengths
seasoned flour
340g/12oz carrots
225g/8oz onions
30g/1oz beef dripping
150ml/¼ pint red wine
570ml/1 pint water or stock
5ml/1 teaspoon chopped thyme
salt and freshly ground black pepper
2.5ml/½ teaspoon sugar
5ml/1 teaspoon tomato purée
juice of ½ lemon
2 slices white bread
45ml/3 tablespoons oil
30ml/2 tablespoons chopped parsley

1. Wash and dry the tails. Trim off any excess fat and toss in seasoned flour.
2. Peel the carrots and slice them thickly. Slice the onions.
3. Melt the dripping in a heavy saucepan and add the oxtail, a few pieces at a time, browning the sides evenly and well. Remove to a plate as they are done.
4. Brown the carrots and onions in the same pan.
5. Replace the oxtail. Pour over the wine and water or stock and add the thyme, salt, pepper and sugar. Bring to the boil and simmer for 2 hours.
6. Set the oven to 150°C/300°F/gas mark 2.
7. Take out the pieces of meat and vegetables and place in a casserole.
8. With a small ladle or spoon, skim off the fat which will rise to the top of the remaining liquid. Add the tomato purée and lemon juice and bring quickly to the boil.
9. Pour this over the oxtail, cover with a lid, and place in the preheated oven for approximately 3 hours, or until the meat is almost falling off the bone.
10. Remove the crusts from the bread and cut the slices into 4 triangles. Heat the oil in a heavy frying pan and gently fry the triangles in the fat, one side after the other, until crisp right through and evenly brown. Drain on absorbent paper.
11. When the oxtail is tender, take it out of the oven, place the croûtes around the edge of the dish and sprinkle with the chopped parsley.

NOTE I: If the sauce is too thin, remove the meat and vegetables to a serving dish and boil the sauce rapidly until reduced to the desired consistency.
NOTE II: When buying oxtail choose short fat tails with a good proportion of meat on them. Long stringy thin tails are poor value - pale in flavour and short on meat.

FULL RED

Pressed Tongue

SERVES 4
1 ox tongue, fresh or salted
salt
6 peppercorns
bouquet garni (celery stick, bay leaf, sprigs of parsley and thyme, tied together with string)
2 onions
2 carrots
1 celery stick
425ml/¾ pint aspic made from beef stock and gelatine (see page 219)

1. If the tongue is salted, soak it in fresh water for 4 hours. If the tongue is fresh, soak it in brine (salty water) for 1-2 hours.
2. Place it in a saucepan and pour in enough water to cover completely.
3. Add salt if the tongue is fresh. Add the peppercorns, bouquet garni, onions, carrots and celery.
4. Bring gently to the boil, skimming off any scum. Cover tightly and simmer for 3-4 hours, or until tender when pierced with a skewer. Leave to cool for 1 hour in the liquid.
5. Take out and remove the bones from the root of the tongue and peel off the skin.
6. Curl the tongue tightly and fit it into a deep

round cake tin or tongue press.
7. Pour a little cool jellied stock or aspic into the tin.
8. Place a plate which just fits inside the tin on top of the tongue. Stand a heavy weight (about 4kg/8lb) on the plate and leave overnight in the refrigerator.
9. To carve: slice thinly across the top of the round.

NOTE: The stock in which the tongue is cooked is suitable for use in making the jellied stock if it is not too salty.

RED BURGUNDY

Haggis

Even in Scotland haggis is seldom made at home today, mainly because a sheep's pluck, consisting of the liver, heart and lights (lungs), makes too much haggis for a modern-sized family, and cleaning the stomach of the sheep (which forms the skin of the haggis) is a tedious and messy business, requiring much washing and careful scraping. This is a simplified haggis, cooked in a pudding basin instead of a sheep's stomach.

SERVES 4
2 onions
2 sheeps hearts
450g/1lb lambs liver
55g/2oz oatmeal
85g/3oz chopped suet
5ml/1 teaspoon chopped sage
pinch of allspice
salt and freshly ground black pepper
butter for greasing the bowl

1. Peel the onions and put them, with the cleaned hearts and liver, into a pan of water. Boil for 40 minutes, then lift them out of the liquid.
2. Mince the hearts, liver and onions and mix with the oatmeal, suet, sage, allspice and plenty of salt and pepper. Add enough of the cooking liquid to give a soft dropping consistency.
3. Grease a pudding basin, fill with the mixture, cover with greaseproof paper and foil and tie down with string.
4. Steam for 2 hours. Serve hot.

NOTE: Very good haggis can be bought in reliable shops. Do not prick haggis before boiling or baking - it may burst. A haggis should be boiled for 30 minutes per 450g/1lb, but for a minimum of 1 hour. It can also be baked, wrapped in tin foil, at 180°C/350°F/gas mark 4 for 30 minutes per 450g/1lb, but for a minimum of 1 hour. Place the wrapped haggis in a casserole, add a little water and cover tightly.

WHISKY OR CLARET

Supper Dishes

Frogs Legs with Rosemary and Ginger

SERVES 4

45g/1½oz butter, softened
large pinch ground ginger
small piece root ginger, finely chopped
1 sprig rosemary, roughly chopped
½ garlic clove, crushed
salt and pepper
8 frogs legs
150ml/¼ pint dry white wine

1. Mix together the softened butter, ginger, rosemary, garlic, salt and pepper and beat well. Spread this mixture over the frogs legs.
2. Fry the frogs legs briefly on both sides to just colour.
3. Pour over the wine and simmer for 7 minutes. If the wine evaporates too much, add a little water.
4. Remove the legs and keep them warm. Bring the sauce up to a rolling boil and reduce, whisking all the time until slightly thickened.
5. Pour the sauce over the frogs legs and serve immediately.

SPICY DRY WHITE

Chestnut Crumble

Chestnuts are very low in fat. This is a very 'cranky' recipe but, in spite of that, delicious.

SERVES 4

900g/2lb fresh chestnuts (if not available, use whole tinned chestnuts)
2 celery sticks, chopped
1 carrot, peeled and chopped
white part of 2 leeks, chopped
425ml/¾ pint white or vegetable stock
freshly ground black pepper

For the topping:
3 slices wholemeal bread made into crumbs
1 large carrot, peeled and grated
15ml/1 tablespoon finely chopped fresh mint

1. Make a slit in the skin of each chestnut and place in a large pan of cold water. Bring to the boil and cook slowly for 20 minutes. Remove from the water and peel. Chestnuts are far easier to peel when they are still hot, so keep the water hot and return them to the pan for a minute or two as and when necessary.
2. While the chestnuts are cooking, lightly boil the vegetables in the stock until they are just tender.
3. Heat the oven to 200°C/400°F/gas mark 6.
4. Mix together the chestnuts, vegetables and stock. Season well with pepper and pile into a pie dish.
5. Mix together the breadcrumbs, carrot and chopped mint and sprinkle it over the chestnut pie. Bake for 20 minutes.

Walnut and Buckwheat Croquettes

SERVES 4

225g/8oz cooked buckwheat
110g/4oz walnuts, broken
4 garlic cloves, crushed
10ml/2 teaspoons oregano
1 egg, beaten
salt and freshly ground black pepper
wholewheat breadcrumbs, toasted
oil for frying

1. Mix all the ingredients, except the breadcrumbs and oil, together, and mould into croquette shapes. Roll in breadcrumbs and refrigerate for 30 minutes. Fry gently in oil over a medium heat.

Wild Mushrooms in a Cage

This recipe has been adapted from one of Paul Gayler's recipes in *Take Six Cooks.*

SERVES 4

For the vegetable stock:
100g/3½oz unsalted butter
¼ onion, peeled and diced
½ leek, cleaned and diced
½ celery stick, diced

30g/1oz carrots, peeled and diced
30g/1oz cabbage, shredded
1.25ml/¼ teaspoon crushed garlic
1.25ml/¼ teaspoon crushed black peppercorns
5ml/1 teaspoon sea salt
150ml/¼ pint white wine
290ml/½ pint water
30ml/2 tablespoons double cream

4 slices wholemeal bread
45g/1½oz unsalted butter
2 shallots, finely chopped
100g/3½oz selection of wild mushrooms, e. g. morels, trompettes, oyster, chanterelles, etc., washed and roughly chopped if large
70ml/2½ fl oz Madeira
70ml/2½ fl oz white wine
150ml/¼ pint double cream
salt and freshly ground black pepper
100g/3½oz puff pastry
beaten egg for egg wash

To garnish:
chervil leaves

1. Set the oven to 200°C/400°F/gas mark 6.
2. First prepare the vegetable stock: melt 30g/1oz of the butter in a medium-sized saucepan and add the diced vegetables and garlic. Sweat gently, covered with a lid, for about 5 minutes or until soft. Add the peppercorns, salt and wine. Bring to the boil and simmer, without a lid, until reduced by half.
3. Add the water and bring to the boil, skimming frequently. Simmer gently for 20-25 minutes. Pass through a fine sieve. Skim off any fat that rises to the top and keep until required.
4. Cut out 4 x 9cm/3½ inch diameter circles of wholemeal bread. Brush with 30g/1oz melted butter and place in a patty tin. Press another patty tin, of the same size, on top and place in the oven for 10 minutes. Remove the top tin and continue to dry out the croustades in the oven.
5. Melt 15g/½oz of the butter in a sauté pan, add the shallots and cook gently for 2 minutes. Then add the wild mushrooms and continue cooking for 1 minute. Add the Madeira and white wine and cook until reduced by half, then add the cream and continue reducing until the mushrooms are coated with the cream. Adjust the seasoning and allow to cool.
6. Fill the croustades with the mushroom mixture.
7. Roll out the pastry very thinly and cut out 4 circles 6.5cm/2½ inches in diameter. Make 1cm/½ inch parallel gashes into the pastry at regular intervals across the diameter.
8. Brush the pastry with egg wash and put on top of the mushrooms, pulling downwards to stick on the croustade. Rest the pastry in the refrigerator for 30 minutes.
9. Brush the 'cages' with egg wash and place in the preheated oven for 5-8 minutes.
10. Make a sauce from the vegetable stock: cook the stock until reduced by half, add the double cream and reduce again until thickened. Whisk in the remaining butter, adding a little at a time to form an emulsion. Adjust the seasoning.
11. To serve: pour a little sauce on to a serving plate, remove the 'cages' from the oven and place on the centre of the plate. Garnish with the chervil. Serve immediately.

CRISP DRY WHITE

Exotic Vegetable Couscous

225g/8oz couscous
425ml/¾ pint tomato juice
425ml/¾ pint water
1 garlic clove, crushed
5ml/1 teaspoon ground cumin
few sprigs of coriander
salt and freshly ground black pepper

For the vegetables:
10 baby carrots, scraped, with a little green left on
10 baby turnips, scraped, with a little green left on
10 fresh okra pods, trimmed
10 ears fresh baby corn
6 tiny purple finger aubergines (if available)
10 pearl onions, skinned
225g/8oz thin asparagus, trimmed

For the sauce:
5ml/1 teaspoon ground cumin
5ml/1 teaspoon ground coriander
2.5ml/½ teaspoon chilli powder
30ml/2 tablespoons tomato purée

1. Cover the couscous with cold water and leave to absorb the liquid for 20 minutes.
2. Put the tomato juice, water, garlic, cumin, coriander, salt and pepper into a large saucepan. Bring up to the boil and simmer for 15 minutes. Strain and return to the saucepan.
3. Set the couscous to steam above the tomato sauce. Ideally it should be put into a muslin-lined steamer or special couscoussière, but a wire sieve lined with a 'J' cloth will do. Put the sieve in place and cover with a pan lid or cloth to prevent the steam escaping too much. Simmer for 20 minutes.
4. Fork the couscous to remove any lumps. Add all the vegetables, except the asparagus, to the tomato sauce and simmer for 5 minutes. Add the asparagus and simmer for a further 5 minutes.
5. Pile the couscous on to a dish and keep warm. Do not worry if it feels a little tacky; it always does.
6. Drain the vegetables, reserving the liquor, and arrange them on top of the couscous. Drizzle over 30ml/2 tablespoons of the tomato sauce. Garnish with the fresh coriander leaves.
7. Mix the remaining tomato sauce with the sauce ingredients and serve it separately. It is very hot.

DRY WHITE

Hot Sweet Potato Stew

SERVES 4
120ml/4 fl oz oil
15ml/1 tablespoon yellow mustard seeds
5ml/1 teaspoon ground mace
2 green chillies, chopped
5 garlic cloves, crushed
30g/1oz root ginger, peeled and sliced
2 onions, peeled and sliced
225g/8oz sweet potatoes, sliced
225g/8oz parsnip, sliced
450g/1lb tomatoes, or 400g/14oz tinned, chopped
15ml/1 tablespoon garam masala
lemon juice to taste
salt and freshly ground black pepper

1. Heat the oil in a large pan, add the mustard seeds and mace and cook until the seeds pop.
2. Reduce the heat, add the chilli, garlic, ginger and onion, and fry gently.
3. Add the sweet potato, parsnip and tomatoes. Cover and simmer very gently until the vegetables soften. Add the garam masala. Season to taste with lemon juice, salt and pepper.

MEDIUM DRY WHITE

Lentil 'Cassoulet'

SERVES 4
olive oil
340g/12oz lamb fillet taken from the shoulder, sliced
1 large onion, finely sliced
1 garlic clove, crushed
450g/1lb brown lentils
400g/14oz tin tomatoes
water to moisten
1 glass red wine (100ml/3½ fl oz)
5 cloves, tied in a muslin bag or a clean 'J'-cloth
salt and freshly ground black pepper
15ml/1 tablespoon herbes de Provence
1 large spicy sausage, sliced

1. Heat the oil in a large, flameproof casserole and lightly brown the lamb on both sides. Remove to a plate. Reduce the heat and add the onion and garlic; cook until beginning to soften.
2. Add the lentils, lamb, tomatoes and enough water to cover. Bring gradually to the boil and add the wine, cloves, salt and pepper and herbs.
3. Cover and simmer very slowly until the lentils are soft but not mushy. This will probably take about 1 hour. Check it every so often to make sure that it is not getting too dry. If so, add extra water.
4. Add the sausage about 10 minutes before the lentils are cooked. Serve with a green salad.

FULL RED

Chorizos

This recipe is from Jane Grigson's *Charcuterie and French Pork Cookery*.

MAKES 20
For the filling:
450g/1lb lean pork (neck or shoulder)
225g/8oz back fat

1 small red pepper
1 small chilli
75ml/2½ fl oz red wine
15ml/1 tablespoon salt
1.25ml/¼ teaspoon granulated sugar
a good pinch saltpetre
1.25ml/¼ teaspoon ground mixed spice
1.25ml/¼ teaspoon cayenne pepper
1 large garlic clove, crushed
sausage skins (2.5cm/1 inch diameter), washed (available in some good butchers)

1. Mince the pork and fat, using the coarse plate of the mincer.
2. Cut the pepper and chilli in half, remove the seeds and stalks, put through the mincer and add to the pork.
3. Add the other ingredients and mix well.
4. Fill the sausage skins with this mixture, but do not pack too tightly or the sausages will burst. Twist every 12.5-15cm/5-6 inches.
5. Smoke lightly or dry above the stove at a temperature of between 15°-19°C/60°-70°F overnight.
6. Cook as required.

MEDIUM RED

Venison Sausages

MAKES ABOUT 80 SAUSAGES
1.8kg/4lb boned venison meat (haunch or shoulder)
900g/2lb rump steak
675g/1½lb pork fat
225g/8oz anchovy fillets (tinned)
20ml/2 dessertspoons juniper berries, crushed
1 garlic clove, crushed
15ml/3 teaspoons ground ginger
22.5ml/1½ tablespoons salt
15ml/1 tablespoon rubbed sage
5ml/1 teaspoon ground mace
5ml/1 teaspoon mignonette or cracked black pepper
425ml/¾ pint red wine
150ml/¼ pint Jamaica rum
340g/12oz Cox's apples, grated with skins left on
oil for frying
sausage skins, washed (available in some good butchers)

1. Mince together the meats, fat and anchovy fillets. Mince again. Mix in all the other ingredients and beat well.
2. Fry a small amount in a little oil to test for seasoning before filling the skins.
3. Fill the sausage skins with the mixture; do not pack too tightly or they will burst. Twist every 10-12.5cm/4-5 inches.
4. Cook as required.

FULL RED

Boudin Blanc

This recipe has been adapted from *The Observer French Cookery School.*

MAKES ABOUT 10 SAUSAGES
150ml/¼ pint double cream
100g/3½oz breadcrumbs
2 metres/6 yards pork intestine
225g/8oz lean veal
225g/8oz fat pork
225g/8oz boned chicken breast, or a further 225g/8oz lean veal
1 onion, chopped
3 eggs
5ml/1 teaspoon ground allspice
salt and white pepper
oil for frying

For cooking:
1.5 litres/2½ pints water
750ml/1¼ pints milk

1. Scald the cream by bringing it just to the boil, pour it over the breadcrumbs and leave to cool.
2. Soak the pork intestine in cold water.
3. Work the veal, fat pork and chicken, if used, twice through the fine blade of a mincer, adding the onion before the second mincing. Alternatively, work the meat and onion a little at a time in an electric food processor. Put the mixture in a bowl and stir in the soaked breadcrumbs, eggs, allspice and plenty of salt and pepper. Sauté a small ball of the mixture in a little oil and taste for seasoning – the mixture should be quite spicy. Beat with a wooden spoon or your hand until very smooth.
4. To fill the sausages: drain the pork intestine –

it should be pliable. Tie one end, insert the sausage-stuffer or funnel in the other and spoon in the filling, shaking it down the skins. Do not fill them too tightly or they will burst during cooking. Tie into 15cm/6 inch sausages. Prick before cooking.

5. Bring the water and milk to the boil in a large pan. Lower the sausages into the pan. Cover and poach very gently for 18-20 minutes. Allow the sausages to cool to tepid in the liquid, then drain them and leave to cool completely. They can be cooked up to 24 hours ahead and kept covered in the refrigerator. They are very good fried and served with slices of fried apple.

LIGHT RED

Cassoulet

SERVES 12

900g/2lb dried haricot beans
225g/8oz salt pork or unsmoked bacon
1 onion, studded with 8 cloves
bouquet garni
2 garlic cloves, crushed
450g/1lb pork bladebone
225g/8oz Toulouse sausage (or Cumberland sausage)
675g/1½lb boned breast of lamb
8 large tomatoes, skinned and quartered
30ml/2 tablespoons chopped thyme leaves
30ml/2 tablespoons chopped parsley
salt and freshly ground black pepper
60ml/4 tablespoons fresh white breadcrumbs

1. Wash the beans well with cold water and leave to soak overnight.

2. Rinse well and place in a pan of fresh cold water, making sure they are covered. Add the rind of the salt pork or bacon, the onion and cloves, bouquet garni and garlic.

3. Bring to the boil, skim and allow to simmer for 1¾ hours or until the beans are tender.

4. Meanwhile, roast the lamb, pork and sausages in a preheated oven at 190°C/375°F/gas mark 5, for 30 minutes or until the meat is cooked and the sausages brown.

5. Remove the meat from the oven, tip off and reserve the fat, slice the sausages into 1cm/½ inch pieces and cut the meat into 2.5cm/1 inch chunks.

6. When the beans are cooked strain them, reserving 570ml/1 pint of the cooking liquor. Discard the rind, onion and bouquet garni.

7. Set the oven to 170°C/325°F/gas mark 3.

8. Place a layer of beans in a deep ovenproof dish. Cover with a layer of the meat, sausage, tomatoes and herbs. Season generously with salt and pepper. Continue to layer up finishing with a layer of beans. Pour over the cooking liquor and reserved fat, and sprinkle the breadcrumbs on the top.

9. Place uncovered in the oven for 1½ hours. If the breadcrumbs become dry and crusty, stir them into the cassoulet and add more liquid if necessary. Sprinkle more breadcrumbs on top. At the end of the cooking time the meat and beans should be very tender and creamy and the top crisp and brown.

NOTE: This is delicious if it is made a couple of days in advance. It is also very good and traditional if *confit d'oie* (preserved goose) is added with the meat in place of the pork.

FULL RICH RED

Black Pudding with Apple Sauce

SERVES 4

2 black puddings
oil
apple sauce (see page 232)

1. Slice the black puddings into 1.5cm/½ inch slices and fry slowly in a little oil for a couple of minutes per side.

2. Arrange on a warm plate and serve the apple sauce separately.

LIGHT RED

Roman-style Grilled Mozzarella Cheese

1 thin stick of Italian bread
4 x 110g/4oz packets mozzarella cheese
45ml/3 tablespoons olive oil
salt and freshly ground black pepper
10 anchovy fillets in oil, drained and soaked in milk
140g/5oz unsalted butter

1. Cut the bread and the mozzarella cheese into 2cm/3/4inch thick slices.
2. Preheat the grill to its highest temperature.
3. Skewer the bread alternately with the cheese on 4 short skewers.
4. Pack the bread and cheese really closely together.
5. Place the skewers on an oiled baking sheet.
6. Brush the slices of bread liberally with the olive oil and season with salt and pepper.
7. Lower the grill temperature slightly and grill for 6-8 minutes, turning occasionally, making sure that the bread doesn't burn.
8. Meanwhile, drain the anchovies from the milk. Heat the butter and, when melted, remove the pan from the heat. Add the anchovies and mash with a fork until they are well emulsified. Season to taste.
9. Remove the skewers from the grill, place on a large flat serving dish, and pour some of the sauce over each skewer.

DRY WHITE

Pizza

This recipe has been taken from *A Taste of Venice* by Jeanette Nance Nordio.

MAKES 2 X 25CM/10 INCH PIZZAS
10g/1/3oz fresh yeast
pinch of sugar
150ml/1/4 pint lukewarm water
200g/7oz plain flour
2.5ml/1/2 teaspoon salt
60-75ml/4-5 tablespoons olive oil
190ml/1/3pint pizzaiola sauce (see page 229)
225g/8oz mozzarella, diced or grated
45ml/3 tablespoons grated Parmesan cheese

1. Cream the fresh yeast with a pinch of sugar and 30ml/2 tablespoons of the lukewarm water.
2. Sift the flour with the salt and make a well in the centre. Pour in the yeast mixture, the remaining water and the oil. Mix together until it turns into a soft but not wet dough. Add more water or flour if necessary.
3. Turn out on to a floured surface and knead well for about 5 minutes until the dough is smooth. Place in a clean bowl and cover with greased polythene. Leave in a warm place until the dough has doubled in bulk.
4. Preheat the oven to 230°C/450°F/gas mark 8. Divide the dough in 2. Roll each piece into a circle about 25cm/10 inches across. Place on greased and floured baking trays.
5. Crimp or flute the edges slightly to help keep in the filling. Spread with the tomato sauce. Sprinkle with the cheese and pour over a little oil. The pizzas can 'sit' for up to an hour before they are baked.
6. Bake near the bottom of the oven for 5 minutes and then reduce the temperature to 200°C/400°F/gas mark 6 for a further 15 minutes.

LIGHT/MEDIUM RED

Chicago Pizza Pie

It is essential that the tinned tomatoes are very well drained.

MAKES 2 X 20CM/8 INCH PIZZAS
5ml/1 teaspoon fresh yeast
290ml/1/2 pint lukewarm water
450g/1lb plain flour
2.5ml/1/2 teaspoon salt
30ml/2 tablespoons olive oil
225g/8oz mozzarella cheese, thinly sliced
60ml/4 tablespoons tomato purée
good pinch of oregano or marjoram
15ml/1 tablespoon chopped basil
900g/2lb tin Italian tomatoes, very well drained
110g/4oz Italian sausage or salami, chopped
salt and freshly ground black pepper

1. Dissolve the yeast in the lukewarm water. Sift the flour and the salt together and mix to a soft dough with the yeasty water. Mix in the olive

oil with a knife and then knead for 10 minutes until elastic and smooth.
2. Grease 2 deep sandwich tins or flan tins with a little more olive oil and divide the dough between the tins. Put in a warm place, such as the airing cupboard, for about 1 hour to rise, then push the dough flat on the bottom of the tins and press to come up the sides. Heat the oven to 250°C/500°F/gas mark 9.
3. Cover the dough with half the mozzarella cheese and put the tins back in the warm place to rise again. When puffy, after about half an hour, push the dough again with the back of a large spoon and once again press the edges up the sides of the tins.
4. Mix the tomato purée, marjoram and basil together and spread this all over the dough. Cut each tinned tomato in half and discard the juice. Put them into the pizzas. Add the rest of the mozzarella cheese and the salami. Sprinkle with a little more marjoram, season well and bake for 20 minutes.

MEDIUM RED

Pizza Calzone

SERVES 2
pizza dough made with 250g/8oz flour
2 slices ham, cut into strips
170g/6oz mozzarella, cut into slices
6 tomatoes, skinned and sliced
salt and freshly ground black pepper
15ml/1 tablespoon chopped basil
extra virgin olive oil

1. Set the oven to 240°C/475°F/gas mark 8.
2. Divide the dough in 4 and place on 4 floured baking sheets. Using the heel of your hand, push and punch the dough into 4 ovals about 15cm/6 inches in diameter.
3. Arrange the ham, mozzarella and tomato over half of each pizza base leaving the edge clear. Season with salt and pepper and sprinkle over the basil and a little olive oil.
4. Fold over the uncovered half of the pizza and press the edges firmly together.
5. Bake for 15 minutes.

LIGHT/MEDIUM RED

Savoury Choux Buns

MAKES 30
3-egg choux pastry (see page 529)
30g/1oz fresh Parmesan, grated
good pinch of dry English mustard
good pinch of cayenne pepper

For the filling:
290ml/½ pint white sauce (see page 221)
450g/1lb spinach, cooked and roughly chopped
30g/1oz pinenuts, toasted
30g/1oz cashew nuts, toasted
salt and pepper

1. Set the oven to 200°C/400°F/gas mark 6.
2. Combine the Parmesan cheese, mustard and cayenne pepper with the choux pastry.
3. Put teaspoons of the choux mixture on to a wet baking sheet.
4. Bake for 35-40 minutes. The buns should swell and become brown and feel firm to the touch. If they are taken out when only slightly brown, they will collapse on cooling.
5. Once cooked, make a small hole in the base of each bun and return to the oven with the base uppermost for 5-10 minutes.
6. While the buns are cooking, mix together the white sauce, spinach and nuts. Season to taste and reheat.
7. Split the buns in half and spoon in the filling. Serve warm.

Cornish Pasties

SERVES 4
shortcrust pastry made with 225g/8oz flour (see page 525)
110g/4oz chuck steak, finely diced
1 large onion, finely chopped
1 large potato, finely chopped
30ml/2 tablespoons water
salt and freshly ground black pepper
egg wash to glaze

1. Make and chill the pastry.
2. Prepare the filling by mixing together the meat, onion and potato. Add the water and seasoning and mix thoroughly.
3. Set oven to 200°C/400°F/gas mark 6.

4. Divide the chilled pastry into 4 and roll each out to the thickness of a coin. Cut out a 20cm/8 inch diameter circle using a plate as a template.
5. Spoon the meat and vegetable mixture into the centre of each circle. Brush around the edge with water. Carefully bring the sides up and over the filling so that the pasties look like closed purses. Using floured fingers, crimp the edges. Place on a baking sheet. Brush with egg glaze and chill for 5-10 minutes.
6. Brush again with glaze before baking near the top of the oven for 10-15 minutes. Reduce the oven to 180°C/350°F/gas mark 4 and bake for a further 45-50 minutes. Check occasionally, moving to a lower shelf if necessary.

MEDIUM RED

Toad in the Hole

SERVES 4
450g/1lb pork sausages
60ml/4 tablespoons beef dripping

For the batter:
110g/4oz plain flour
good pinch of salt
2 eggs
150ml/¼ pint water mixed with 150ml/¼ pint milk

1. Sift the flour and salt into a large wide bowl. Make a well or hollow in the centre of the flour and break the eggs into it.
2. With a whisk or wooden spoon, mix the eggs to a paste and very gradually draw in the surrounding flour, adding just enough milk and water to the eggs to keep the central mixture a fairly thin paste. When all the flour is incorporated, stir in the rest of the liquid. The batter can be made more speedily by putting all the ingredients together in a liquidizer or food processor for a few seconds, but take care not to over-whisk or the mixture will be bubbly. Leave to 'rest' at room temperature for 30 minutes before use. This allows the starch cells to swell, giving a lighter, less doughy final product.
3. Turn the oven to 220°C/425°F/gas mark 7.
4. Heat 15ml/1 tablespoon dripping in a frying pan and fry the sausages until evenly browned all over, but do not cook them through.
5. Heat the rest of the dripping in an ovenproof shallow metal dish or roasting pan until smoking hot, either in the oven or over direct heat. Add the sausages to it and pour in the batter.
6. Bake for 40 minutes or until the toad in the hole is risen and brown. Serve with hot gravy.

FULL RED

Crespelle alla Fiorentina

SERVES 4-6
30g/1oz butter
1 medium onion, finely chopped
55g/2oz prosciutto (Parma ham), chopped
290ml/½ pint béchamel sauce (see page 221)
225g/8oz ricotta cheese
675g/1½lb spinach, cooked and chopped
55g/2oz fresh Parmesan cheese, grated
55g/2oz pinenuts, toasted
salt and freshly ground black pepper
grated nutmeg
425ml/¾ pint tomato sauce (see page 231, double the recipe)
16 French pancakes (see page 533)

1. Melt the butter in a sauté pan, add the onion and cook slowly until soft but not coloured. Add the prosciutto and cook over a medium heat for 1 minute. Tip into a bowl and leave to cool.
2. Add 75ml/5 tablespoons of the béchamel, the spinach, ricotta cheese, Parmesan cheese and toasted pinenuts to the onion and prosciutto. Mix well and season to taste with salt, pepper and grated nutmeg.
3. Preheat the oven to 200°C/400°F/gas mark 6.
4. Tip a little of the tomato sauce into a large ovenproof gratin dish.
5. Divide the spinach filling between the pancakes and roll them up. Arrange them in a single layer on top of the tomato sauce.
6. Cover with the remaining tomato sauce and

bake for 30 minutes or until the pancakes are thoroughly hot.
7. Reheat the béchamel sauce and, just before serving, dribble it over the crespelle.

MEDIUM RED

Bocconcini di Parma

SERVES 4-6
16 pancakes (see page 533), made with a pinch of nutmeg added to the batter
900g/2lb ricotta cheese
4 egg yolks
1 whole egg
170g/6oz freshly grated Parmesan cheese
55g/2oz butter, softened
freshly grated nutmeg
salt and freshly ground black pepper

1. Drain the ricotta and put it in a bowl. Using a wooden spoon, start to break it up, adding the egg yolks, egg, Parmesan cheese and butter. Mix well and season to taste with nutmeg, salt and pepper. Refrigerate for half an hour.
2. Place a pancake on a board and spread 3 heaped tablespoons of the stuffing along one side. Roll it up. Place the rolled pancake, seam side down on a baking sheet. Repeat until all the pancakes are stuffed. Refrigerate for half an hour.
3. Preheat the oven to 190°C/375°F/gas mark 5.
4. Grease a 33 x 22cm/13½ x 8 inch baking dish with butter. Using a very sharp knife cut each pancake into thirds. Arrange them standing up in the baking dish, side by side. Bake for 20 minutes and serve hot.

DRY WHITE

Baked Stuffed Aubergines

SERVES 4
2 medium-sized aubergines
285g/10oz minced beef
1 onion, finely chopped
½ green pepper, chopped
55g/2oz mushrooms, chopped
1 garlic clove, crushed
5ml/1 teaspoon flour
290ml/½ pint beef stock (see page 218)
1 bay leaf
10ml/2 teaspoons tomato purée
5ml/1 teaspoon chopped parsley
salt and pepper
lemon juice
290ml/½ pint tomato sauce (see page 231)
15g/½oz butter, melted
grated Gruyère or strong Cheddar cheese
dried breadcrumbs

1. Cut the aubergines in half lengthways and scoop out the centre, leaving the shell with about 5mm/¼ inch of flesh attached. Sprinkle lightly with salt and leave upside down to drain.
2. Chop up the aubergine flesh and sprinkle with salt. Leave to drain on a tilted board or in a sieve for 20 minutes.
3. Fry the mince until evenly brown.
4. Rinse and dry the aubergine flesh. Add to the mince with the onion, green pepper, mushroom and garlic and cook for a further 3-4 minutes.
5. Stir in the flour. Cook for 1 minute, then add the beef stock, bay leaf, tomato purée, parsley, pepper and lemon juice. Bring to the boil, stirring continuously, then cover and simmer for 20-25 minutes. Remove the bay leaf.
6. Set the oven to 200°C/400°F/gas mark 6.
7. Wash and dry the aubergine shells, brush with the melted butter and fill with the mince mixture. Sprinkle over the grated cheese and crumbs.
8. Bake in the preheated oven for 30 minutes, or until the shells are tender and the cheese well browned and crusty. Serve with the tomato sauce.

MEDIUM RED

Bubble and Squeak

SERVES 4

450g/1lb mashed potatoes (see page 187)
450g/1lb cooked vegetables, such as cabbage or onion or leek
salt and freshly ground pepper
55g/2oz good dripping or butter

1. Mix the potato with the other vegetables. Season to taste.
2. Melt the dripping or butter in a heavy-based pan.
3. Put in the vegetable mixture, pressing it down flat on the hot dripping. Cook slowly to heat through and allow a crust to form on the bottom of the mixture.
4. Now flip the cake over on to a plate and return it to the pan to brown the second side.
5. Slide on to a warm serving dish and serve immediately.

NOTE: Bubble and squeak is really a leftover fry-up and it does not matter if the cake is neat and even or crumbly and broken. But if you prefer it to be round and neat so that you can cut it into slices, a beaten egg added to the mixture will ensure that the ingredients hold together.

LIGHT RED

Stuffed Peppers

SERVES 4

4 green or red peppers
30g/1oz butter
1 medium onion, finely diced
1 garlic clove, crushed
110g/4oz mushrooms, finely sliced
30g/1oz split blanched almonds
140g/5oz long-grain rice
290ml/½ pint chicken stock (see page 219)
5ml/1 teaspoon chopped rosemary
30g/1oz raisins
15ml/1 tablespoon chopped parsley
salt and pepper
290ml/½ pint tomato sauce (see page 231)

1. Cut off the tops of the peppers and remove the core and seeds.
2. Drop the peppers into boiling water for 5 minutes. Plunge immediately into cold water to cool.
3. Set the oven to 190°C/375°F/gas mark 5.
4. Melt the butter in an ovenproof casserole and cook the onion until transparent. Add the garlic, mushrooms and almonds. Sauté (fry briskly, while tossing the contents of the pan in the butter) for a further 2 minutes. Stir in the rice and fry for a further minute.
5. Pour on the stock and bring to the boil. Add the rosemary, raisins, parsley and seasoning. Cover and bake in the oven for 20 minutes.
6. When the rice is cooked, fill the peppers with it and place them in a deep ovenproof dish. Pour on the tomato sauce. Cover with wet greaseproof paper and a lid and put back into the oven for 30 minutes.

LIGHT RED

Risotto

This is not a classic risotto, merely a simplified version that can often be used for leftovers such as cold roast lamb. For a classic recipe using arborio rice, see page 406.

SERVES 4-6

55g/2oz butter
110g/4oz streaky bacon, diced
1 large onion, diced
2 large garlic cloves, crushed
1 green pepper, deseeded and sliced
3 sticks celery, diced
110g/4oz mushrooms, sliced
30ml/2 tablespoons tomato purée
2.5ml/½ teaspoon dried or 5ml/1 teaspoon fresh basil (optional)
2.5ml/½ teaspoon dried or 5ml/1 teaspoon fresh thyme
salt and freshly ground black pepper
170g/6oz piece of ham, diced
225g/8oz cooked rice
4 medium tomatoes, skinned and chopped
30g/1oz Parmesan cheese
chopped parsley

1. Melt the butter in a large sauté pan. Gently fry the bacon in it.
2. Add the onion and garlic and cook until the onion is transparent. Add the green pepper, celery and mushrooms. Sweat with the lid on for 10 minutes.
3. Stir in the tomato purée. If the mixture looks dry, add a tablespoon or two of water. Add the herbs, salt and pepper. Stir in the ham and rice and gently heat for 5 minutes.
4. Add the tomatoes to the rice mixture with the Parmesan. Heat through and correct the seasoning.
5. Pile into a warm serving dish and garnish with plenty of parsley.

LIGHT RED

Risotto with Three Cheeses

SERVES 4-6
110g/4oz Gorgonzola, crust removed
110g/4oz mozzarella cheese
150ml/1/4 pint lukewarm milk
85g/3oz butter
15ml/1 tablespoon olive oil
450g/1lb arborio rice
860ml/1 1/2 pints chicken stock (see page 219)
salt and freshly ground black pepper
30 shelled pistachio nuts, blanched and skinned (or use toasted pinenuts)
110g/4oz freshly grated Parmesan cheese

1. Cut the Gorgonzola and mozzarella into small cubes. Place in a bowl, pour over the milk and leave to stand for 20 minutes.
2. Heat the butter and oil in a flameproof casserole over a medium heat. When the butter is melted, add the rice and cook very slowly for 4 minutes.
3. Meanwhile, heat the chicken stock and gradually add it to the rice, stirring continuously and gently until all the stock has been absorbed; this will take about 15 minutes.
4. Add the milk with the cheeses to the pan and stir continuously until well amalgamated. This will take about 5 minutes.
5. Taste for seasoning and add the pistachio nuts and Parmesan cheese. Serve.

NOTE: This risotto has to be made at the last minute as it does not keep warm well.

LIGHT RED

Risotto alla Milanese

SERVES 4
85g/3oz unsalted butter
1 large onion, finely chopped
400g/14oz risotto rice (arborio)
150ml/1/4 pint white wine
1.75 litres/3 pints chicken stock (see page 219)
about 15 saffron filaments
salt and freshly ground pepper
30g/1oz unsalted butter
55g/2oz freshly grated Parmesan cheese

1. Melt the butter in a large saucepan and gently cook the onion until soft and lightly coloured. Add the rice and the wine, bring to the boil and cook until the wine is absorbed, about 3 minutes. Stir gently all the time.
2. Meanwhile, in a second pan reheat the chicken stock and add the saffron filaments to it. Let the stock simmer gently.
3. Start adding the hot chicken stock to the rice a little at a time, stirring gently. Allow the stock to become absorbed between each addition. Keep stirring constantly. Season with salt and pepper, and keep adding the stock until the rice is cooked but still *al dente*, about 20 minutes.
4. Remove the pan from the heat, add the butter and the Parmesan cheese and mix well with a wooden spoon until the butter is melted and the cheese absorbed. Serve straight away, with additional Parmesan if desired.

LIGHT RED

Macaroni Cheese

SERVES 4
110g/4oz macaroni
oil
20g/3/4oz butter
20g/3/4oz flour
salt, pepper, cayenne pepper and a pinch of dry English mustard
425ml/3/4 pint milk
170g/6oz grated cheese
7.5ml/1/2 tablespoon breadcrumbs

1. Boil the macaroni in plenty of salted water with 15ml/1 tablespoon of oil. The water must boil steadily to keep the macaroni moving freely and prevent it sticking to the pan; the lid is left off to prevent boiling over. Cook the macaroni until it is just tender. Drain well and rinse under boiling water.
2. Melt the butter, add the flour, cayenne pepper and mustard. Cook, stirring, for 1 minute. Draw the pan off the heat. Pour in the milk and mix well. Return to the heat and stir until boiling. Simmer, stirring all the time, for 2 minutes.
3. Stir the macaroni into the sauce and reheat if necessary. Season the sauce to taste. Stir in all but 15ml/1 tablespoon of cheese and turn the mixture into an ovenproof dish.
4. Heat the grill.
5. Mix the reserved cheese with the crumbs and sprinkle evenly over the sauce; make sure that all the sauce is covered or it will form brown blisters under the grill.
6. Grill fairly quickly until the top is browned and crisp.

LIGHT FRUITY RED

Spaghetti Carbonara

SERVES 4
340g/12oz spaghetti
15ml/1 tablespoon oil
100g/3 1/2 oz streaky bacon, cut into small strips
4 egg yolks
30ml/2 tablespoons single cream
55g/2oz fresh Parmesan cheese, grated
freshly ground black pepper

1. Cook the spaghetti in plenty of boiling salted water.
2. Put the oil into a fairly large frying pan, add the strips of bacon and fry them lightly over a moderate heat until the bacon fat has melted. Remove the pan from the heat and set aside, keeping the pan warm.
3. Meanwhile, beat the egg yolks in a bowl with a whisk; then whisk in the cream and half of the Parmesan, and add a generous amount of black pepper. When the spaghetti is still firm to the bite (*al dente*), drain it; transfer it to the pan with the bacon, place over a medium heat and pour the egg mixture over it. Stir quickly and serve straight away.
4. Serve the remaining Parmesan separately.

LIGHT RED

Spaghetti con Vongole

This recipe has been taken from *A Taste of Venice* by Jeanette Nance Nordio.

SERVES 4
450g/1lb spaghetti
900g/2lb baby clams in their shells
90ml/6 tablespoons olive oil
2 garlic cloves, peeled and bruised
4 large tomatoes, skinned and chopped
salt and freshly ground black pepper
15ml/1 tablespoon chopped parsley

1. Wash and scrub the clams thoroughly.
2. Heat 15ml/1 tablespoon oil, add the clams, cover and shake until the clams have opened. Discard any that have remained closed. Remove the clams and strain the juices. Reserve both.
3. Heat the remaining oil in a saucepan, add the

garlic and cook until golden brown; remove and discard. Add the tomatoes, clam juice and seasoning and cook for about 30 minutes. Add the clams and cook gently for 1-2 minutes. Add the parsley.
4. Meanwhile, cook the spaghetti in plenty of boiling salted water to which 15ml/1 tablespoon of oil has been added. When *al dente,* drain and mix with the tomato sauce. Serve immediately and give the guests finger bowls.

DRY WHITE

Spaghetti en Papillote

This is an unusual way to serve spaghetti but it keeps it moist and succulent.

SERVES 4
150ml/1/4 pint good quality olive oil
1 large garlic clove, peeled
400g/14oz tin Italian tomatoes, drained
salt and freshly ground black pepper
1.25ml/1/4 teaspoon chilli powder
225g/8oz spaghetti
450g/1lb fresh tomatoes, skinned, deseeded and slivered
30ml/2 tablespoons finely chopped parsley
28 large black Greek olives, pitted

1. Heat all but 30ml/2 tablespoons of the oil in a heavy saucepan. When warm, add the garlic and leave to infuse over a gentle heat for 2 minutes. Remove and add the drained tomatoes, taking care as the oil will spit. Simmer for 20 minutes, stirring occasionally. Season with salt, pepper and the chilli powder.
2. Process or liquidize until smooth and return to the rinsed-out saucepan. Simmer for a further 10 minutes until it reduces to a thick shiny sauce.
3. Set the oven to 190°C/375°F/gas mark 5.
4. Cook the spaghetti in plenty of fast-boiling salted water with 15ml/1 tablespoon oil until just tender.
5. While the spaghetti is cooking, arrange 4 x 30cm/12 inch circles of double greaseproof paper on a board.
6. Drain the spaghetti, mix it with the fresh tomatoes, the remaining oil, half the parsley, the olives and the tomato sauce. Mix well and season to taste if necessary.
7. Divide the spaghetti mixture between the 4 circles of greaseproof paper. Close each parcel up, trap a little air in the parcel and secure the edges firmly by twisting and turning them together.
8. Place in a shallow, wet roasting pan and bake for 15 minutes.
9. Remove from the oven and place on warm individual plates. Open the parcels with scissors and sprinkle the remaining parsley over each serving.

MEDIUM RED

Pasta with Tomato and Egg Sauce

SERVES 4
2 large Spanish onions, sliced
15ml/1 tablespoon olive oil
2 x 400g/14oz tins of tomatoes, chopped
salt and pepper
285g/10oz pasta butterflies or spirals
15ml/1 tablespoon chopped fresh basil
3 eggs, beaten lightly
freshly grated Parmesan cheese

1. Cook the onions very slowly in the olive oil until soft but not coloured - this should take 15-20 minutes.
2. Add the tomatoes, salt and pepper, stir well and bring the mixture up to the boil. Let it simmer for 10 minutes.
3. Meanwhile, cook the pasta in rapidly boiling water to which 5ml/1 teaspoon of oil and a little salt has been added. When the pasta is cooked, drain it well and refresh with hot water.
4. Take the tomato sauce off the heat, season it, add the basil and then gradually pour in the lightly beaten eggs. The sauce should become rich and creamy.
5. Mix a little of the sauce with the pasta, pile it into a serving dish and pour the remaining sauce over it.
6. Serve sprinkled with a little freshly grated Parmesan cheese.

MEDIUM RED

Greek Parsley Pasta

SERVES 4
1 batch 3-egg pasta (see page 532)
1 bunch Greek parsley
pesto sauce (see page 228)

1. Roll the pasta out, very thinly, on a lightly floured board. Roll to a rectangle. Cut in half. Keep well covered to prevent it drying out.
2. Take one sheet of pasta and arrange individual parsley leaves at 3cm/$1^1/_2$inch intervals, in even rows, all over it. Cover loosely with the other sheet of pasta and press down firmly. Roll again until the Greek parsley can be seen between the layers of pasta.
3. Using a pastry cutter, cut between the rows, making sure that all the edges are sealed.
4. Simmer in boiling salted water for 2-3 minutes or until just tender. Drain well and toss in warm pesto sauce.

MEDIUM RED

Pasta Roulade with Tomato Sauce

SERVES 4
1kg/2lb spinach, cooked and chopped
30g/1oz butter
225g/8oz ricotta cheese
85g/3oz toasted pinenuts
nutmeg
salt and freshly ground black pepper
15ml/1 tablespoon roughly chopped fresh basil
1 batch 3-egg pasta (see page 532)

To serve:
fresh tomato sauce (see page 231)
freshly grated Parmesan cheese

1. Melt the butter in a saucepan, add the spinach and cook for 1 minute, stirring continuously to prevent sticking. Add the ricotta, pinenuts, seasonings and basil. Leave to cool.
2. Roll out the pasta into a large thin circle. Spread the spinach filling evenly over the surface, then roll up like a Swiss roll. Wrap the roll in a clean 'J' cloth or muslin and tie the ends with string, like a cracker.
3. Cook in a large saucepan or fish kettle of salted simmering water for approximately 20 minutes.
4. Set the oven to 200°C/400°F/gas mark 6. Slice thickly and arrange in an ovenproof dish. Pour over the tomato sauce, scatter over the Parmesan cheese and reheat in the oven for 20 minutes.

MEDIUM RED

Tagliatelle with Oyster Mushrooms and Sage

SERVES 3-4
225g/8oz tagliatelle
oil
salt and freshly ground pepper
55g/2oz butter
450g/1lb oyster mushrooms, sliced
15ml/1 tablespoon chopped sage

1. Cook the tagliatelle in plenty of boiling salted water, to which 15ml/1 tablespoon of oil has been added, until tender. Drain well and keep warm.
2. Melt the butter in a large saucepan and cook the oyster mushrooms for 1-2 minutes until soft. Add the tagliatelle and sage, season to taste with salt and pepper and serve immediately.

DRY WHITE

Tricolour Pasta Salad

SERVES 4 or 6
225g/8oz pasta twists
1 red pepper, deseeded and quartered
450g/1lb broccoli
90ml/6 tablespoons French dressing (see page 228)
30ml/2 tablespoons chopped parsley

1. Cook the pasta in plenty of boiling salted water until just tender. Rinse under running water until completely cold and drain well.

2. Grill the pepper until the skin is well charred, scrape off the skin and cut the flesh into 5mm/1/4 inch wide strips.
3. Cut the broccoli into small florets and cook in boiling water for 1 minute. Rinse under cold water and drain well.
4. Toss the pasta, peppers and broccoli in the French dressing and parsley. Serve chilled.

LIGHT DRY WHITE

Ravioli with Spinach and Ricotta Filling

SERVES 4
egg pasta made with 340g/12oz flour (see page 532)

For the filling:
450g/1lb spinach, cooked and choppped
110g/4oz ricotta cheese
1 egg
salt and freshly ground black pepper
grated nutmeg
freshly grated Parmesan cheese

To serve:
pesto sauce (see page 228)

1. Mix the spinach with the ricotta cheese and beat well with the egg. Season to taste with salt, pepper, nutmeg and Parmesan cheese.
2. Roll the pasta into a very thin rectangle. Cut accurately in half. Keep well covered to prevent drying out.
3. Take one sheet of pasta and place half-teaspoons of filling, in even rows, all over it. Brush round the piles of filling with a little water. Cover loosely with the other sheet of pasta and press firmly round each mound of filling. Check carefully that you have no bubbles of air.
4. Cut between the rows, making sure that all the edges are sealed. Allow to dry on a wire rack for 30 minutes.
5. Simmer for 6-10 minutes until tender. Drain well and serve with the pesto sauce.

BARDOLINO OR VALPOLICELLA

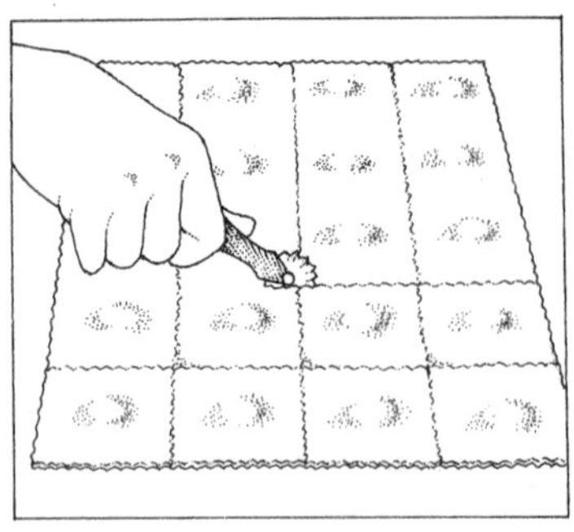

Cut between the rows of pasta, checking carefully that you have no bubbles of air.

Pasta-Filled Bread

SERVES 6
Italian bread made with 900g/2lb flour (see page 565)
450g/1lb tagliatelle
oil
pesto sauce (see page 228)
2 avocado pears, peeled and sliced

1. Cut the top quarter off the Italian bread and keep it to use as a lid. Hollow out the centre of the loaf. This will be used as a container for the pasta.
2. Cook the pasta in boiling salted water to which 15ml/1 tablespoon oil has been added, until just tender. Drain well. Toss in the pesto sauce, add the avocado pears. (Do not worry if they break up.) Tip the filling into the hollowed-out loaf.
3. Place the lid on the top and serve immediately.

NOTE The pasta stays warm in the loaf for a while. Once the pasta is eaten, the loaf, which will be soaked in pesto sauce, is delicious to eat.

LIGHT DRY WHITE

Lasagne Verdi Bolognese

SERVES 4
green pasta (see page 532, using half quantities)
freshly grated Parmesan cheese

For the meat sauce:
15ml/1 tablespoon dripping or oil
340g/12oz minced beef
1 onion, finely diced

stick of celery, finely diced
4 garlic cloves, chopped
30g/1oz flour
290ml/ 1/2 pint stock
1 glass white wine (100ml/3 1/2 fl oz)
salt and freshly ground black pepper
15ml/1 tablespoon chopped parsley
5ml/1 teaspoon chopped marjoram
pinch of cinnamon
15ml/1 tablespoon tomato purée

For the cream sauce:
45g/1 1/2oz butter
1 bay leaf
45g/1 1/2oz flour
570ml/1 pint creamy milk
salt and freshly ground black pepper
nutmeg

1. Cut the pasta into strips 15cm/6 inches long and 3cm/1 inch wide. Allow to dry for 1 hour.
2. Heat the fat and brown the mince well. Add the vegetables and the garlic and fry, stirring continuously, for 2 minutes.
3. Stir in the flour. Cook for 30 seconds. Pour in the stock and the wine, and add the salt, pepper, parsley, marjoram, cinnamon and tomato purée. Bring to the boil, stirring. Simmer slowly for 45 minutes, then boil rapidly, stirring, until the sauce is very thick and syrupy.
4. To make the cream sauce: melt the butter, add the bay leaf and flour and cook, stirring, for 1 minute. Draw off the heat.
5. Add the milk and return to the heat. Bring slowly to the boil, stirring continuously until you have a thick, creamy sauce. Simmer for 2 minutes. Season to taste and remove the bay leaf.
6. To cook the lasagne: drop the pasta a few pieces at a time into a large pan of fast-boiling salted water. They will take about 3 minutes if home-made, 12 minutes if out of a packet, to become tender. Rinse under boiling water and leave to dry – do not stack the pasta pieces on top of each other as they will stick.
7. Set the oven to 190°C/375°F/gas mark 5. Butter an ovenproof dish and cover the bottom with a layer of pasta, then spoon on a thin layer of meat sauce. Cover with a layer of cream sauce. Arrange a layer of pasta on top of this. Continue the layers in this manner finishing with cream sauce. Sprinkle with cheese.
8. Bake for 20-25 minutes, until bubbling and just brown on top.

MEDIUM RED

Ravioli

SERVES 4
egg pasta made with 370g/12oz flour (see page 532)

For the meat filling:
85g/3oz cooked beef, minced
85g/3oz cooked veal, minced
15g/1/2oz butter
10ml/2 teaspoons white breadcrumbs
10ml/2 teaspoons chopped parsley
10ml/2 teaspoons beef stock
5ml/1 teaspoon tomato purée
salt and freshly ground black pepper
pinch of ground nutmeg
pinch of ground cinnamon
1 small egg, beaten

To serve:
freshly grated Parmesan cheese
melted butter or oil or tomato sauce (see page 231)

1. Fry the meats in the butter for 5 minutes. Stir in the breadcrumbs, parsley, stock, tomato purée, salt, pepper, nutmeg and cinnamon. Taste and add more seasoning if required.
2. Add enough egg to bind the mixture together. Allow to cool.
3. Roll the pasta into a very thin rectangle. Cut accurately in half. Keep well covered to prevent drying out.
4. Take one sheet of pasta and place half-teaspoons of filling at 3cm/1 1/2 inch intervals, in even rows, all over it. Cover loosely with the other sheet of pasta and press together firmly all round each mound of filling. Cut between the rows, making sure that all the edges are sealed. Allow to dry on a wire rack for 30 minutes.
5. Simmer the ravioli in near-boiling salted water for 15-20 minutes or until just tender. Drain well. Serve with tomato sauce, oil or melted butter, and serve grated Parmesan cheese separately.

LIGHT RED

Cannelloni

SERVES 4

egg pasta (see page 532 using half quantities)
290ml/ 1/2 pint tomato sauce (see page 231)
45g/1 1/2oz strong Cheddar or Gruyère cheese, grated, or 30g/1oz Parmesan, grated

For the filling:
10ml/2 teaspoons oil or dripping
340g/12oz minced beef
1 onion, chopped
1 stick of celery, chopped
1 garlic clove, crushed
10ml/2 teaspoons tomato purée
10ml/2 teaspoons flour
180ml/6 fl oz beef stock (see page 218)
1 bay leaf
15ml/1 tablespoon chopped parsley
15ml/1 tablespoon port or Madeira
salt and freshly ground black pepper

1. Cut the pasta into 10cm/4 inch strips about 6cm/2 1/2 inches wide. Allow to dry for 1 hour.
2. Heat the oil and add the meat. Brown well all over. Add the onion, celery, garlic and tomato purée and cook for 2 minutes.
3. Add the flour and cook for 30 seconds. Draw the pan off the heat, add the stock, bay leaf and parsley, stir well and return to the heat. Bring slowly to the boil, stirring continuously.
4. Season, cover and simmer for 10 minutes. Then add the port or Madeira and continue to simmer for 10 minutes. Check the sauce every so often and if it is getting too dry add a little extra stock. Remove the bay leaf.
5. Set the oven to 200°C/400°F/gas mark 6. Heat the grill.
6. Cook the pasta in boiling salted water until just tender (about 5 minutes if home-made, 12 if bought). Drain well, and pat dry with a tea towel or cloth.
7. Divide the meat mixture between the strips of pasta and roll them up to form the cannelloni. Place them in a greased ovenproof dish.
8. Pour over the tomato sauce and sprinkle with grated cheese. Bake for 15 minutes, then place under the grill until nicely browned.

NOTE I: For a blander version, trickle over a little white sauce or double cream before grilling the finished dish.
NOTE II: Commercially made cannelloni is usually tube-shaped, and the filling is inserted with a teaspoon.

LIGHT RED/VALPOLICELLA

Cannelloni with Spinach and Mushroom Filling

SERVES 4

900g/2lb spinach, cooked and chopped
55g/2oz butter
225g/8oz flat black mushrooms, sliced
425ml/3/4 pint creamy white sauce (see page 221)
salt and freshly ground black pepper
12 cooked cannelloni
55g/2oz Cheddar cheese, grated
15ml/1 tablespoon dried white breadcrumbs

1. Set the oven to 180°C/350°F/gas mark 4.
2. Melt the butter, add the mushrooms and fry for 3 minutes. Allow the juices to evaporate. Stir in the spinach and 150ml/1/4 pint of the white sauce and season with salt and pepper.
3. Stuff the mixture into the cannelloni, or roll up in the pancakes. Lay them in an ovenproof dish. Add three-quarters of the cheese to the remaining sauce and use to coat the cannelloni. Sprinkle the remaining cheese and crumbs on top.
4. Bake in the oven for 20 minutes or until the top is lightly browned.

NOTE: This filling can also be used to stuff French pancakes (see page 533)

ITALIAN MEDIUM RED

Lemon and Garlic Gnocchi with Warm Borlotti Beans

SERVES 4

1 batch well-seasoned gnocchi (see page 181)
3 cloves garlic, unpeeled
oil
110g/4oz fine white breadcrumbs
1 lemon, finely grated
45ml/3 tablespoons chopped parsley
freshly ground black pepper
1 beaten egg

To serve:
oil for frying
2 x 400g/14oz tinned borlotti beans, drained
150ml/1/4 pint extra virgin olive oil
2 garlic cloves, peeled
1 small red chilli, deseeded
30ml/2tablespoons chopped basil
juice of 1 lemon
salt and freshly ground black pepper

1. Preheat oven to 400°F/200°C/gas mark 6.
2. Make the gnocchi and leave to chill in a shallow square tin which has been rinsed with water.
3. Paint the 3 cloves of garlic with a little oil and cook, about 10 minutes, peel and crush.
4. Mix together the garlic, breadcrumbs, lemon rind and parsley, season with black pepper.
5. Divide the chilled gnocchi into 8 even pieces. Dip into beaten egg and then coat evenly in the breadcrumbs.
6. Heat enough oil in a frying pan to come half-way up the gnocchi, fry until golden brown on both sides. Drain well and keep warm in the oven.
7. Meanwhile heat the virgin olive oil, remove from the heat, add the garlic and chilli and leave to infuse for 1/2 hour. Strain.
8. Heat the infused oil and when hot, quickly fry the basil. When it turns bright green reduce the heat, add the borlotti beans and heat through, add the lemon juice, salt and pepper to taste.
9. Divide the warmed beans between four warm plates, and put 2 gnocchi on each plate.

SPICY DRY WHITE

Potato Tart

This doesn't sound very exciting but is in fact a truly delicious tart.

SERVES 6-8

225g/8oz plain flour
pinch of salt
85g/3oz butter
30g/1oz lard
1 egg yolk
very cold water

For the tomato filling:
45ml/3 tablespoons olive oil
1 onion, finely chopped
8 medium tomatoes, peeled, deseeded and chopped
15ml/1 tablespoon tomato purée
1 sprig thyme
pinch of sugar
salt and freshly ground black pepper

For the potato filling:
6 waxy potatoes, peeled and cut into even chunks
30ml/2 tablespoons olive oil

For the onion filling:
85g/3oz unsalted butter
5 medium onions, thinly sliced

To serve:
150ml/1/4 pint crème fraîche
freshly grated nutmeg

1. Set the oven to 200°C/400°F/gas mark 6.
2. Sift the flour with the salt. Rub in the fats until the mixture looks like breadcrumbs.
3. Mix the yolk with 45ml/3 tablespoons water and add to the mixture. Mix to a firm dough, first with a knife and then with one hand, adding more water if necessary.
4. Roll the pastry out and line a 23cm/9 inch flan ring. Chill in the refrigerator for 20 minutes and then bake blind (see page 152) for 15 minutes in the preheated oven.
5. To make the tomato filling, heat the oil over a low heat and cook the onion gently for about 10 minutes. Add the tomatoes, tomato purée, thyme, sugar, salt and pepper. Increase the heat and cook until all the liquid evaporates. This will take about 35 minutes.

6. Brush the potatoes with oil and sprinkle with salt. Roast in the preheated oven until tender, about 1 hour. Cut into 5mm / 1/4inch slices. Turn the oven up to 230°C / 450°F / gas mark 6.
7. To make the onion filling: melt the butter, add the onions and cook slowly until soft and creamy – about 30 minutes.
8. Spread the onions on the pastry base and cover with the tomato filling, then arrange the sliced potatoes around the top. Cover with crème fraîche and sprinkle with nutmeg. Bake in the preheated oven for 15 minutes or until brown. Serve at room temperature.

LIGHT RED

Cheese and Nut Balls

SERVES 6

110g/4oz fresh brown breadcrumbs
85g/3oz chopped mixed nuts, e.g. hazelnuts, almonds, walnuts, toasted
15ml/1 tablespoon chopped mixed herbs, e.g. parsley, mint, thyme
1 large onion, finely chopped
5ml/1 teaspoon tomato purée
110g/4oz Cheddar cheese, grated
1 egg, lightly beaten
salt and freshly ground pepper
seasoned flour
oil for frying

1. Mix together all the ingredients except the flour. Season well with salt and plenty of freshly ground black pepper.
2. Using wet hands shape the mixture into balls the size of a ping pong ball, roll in seasoned flour and deep-fry in oil until brown.

LIGHT RED

Caroline's Ricotta Pie

Caroline Yates is on the staff at Leith's and sometimes cooks us the most perfect vegetarian lunches. This was one of her most popular recipes.

For the 'pie':
840g/1 3/4lb ricotta cheese
4 egg yolks
1 egg
170g/6oz fresh Parmesan cheese, grated
55g/2oz unsalted butter, softened
salt and freshly ground black pepper
grated nutmeg

To serve:
pesto sauce (see page 228)

1. Set the oven to 190°C / 375°F / gas mark 5.
2. Mix together the ricotta, egg yolks, egg, Parmesan cheese and butter. Beat well and season to taste with salt, pepper and nutmeg.
3. Turn into a buttered 1 litre / 2 pint ovenproof dish.
4. Bake for 30 minutes. Cool slightly. Turn out on to a plate. Drizzle with the pesto sauce and serve while still warm.

MEDIUM RED

Grilled Polenta with Prosciutto Salad

SERVES 6-8

2 litres/3 1/2 pints chicken stock (see page 219)
400g/14oz coarse cornmeal
285g/10oz fresh Parmesan cheese, grated
salt and freshly ground black pepper
85ml/3 fl oz olive oil infused with a sliced garlic clove
1 medium aubergine
225g/8oz wild mushrooms, sliced
110g/4oz sun-dried tomatoes, sliced
170g/6oz prosciutto, thinly sliced
1 red pepper, grilled, peeled and sliced
1 yellow pepper, grilled, peeled and sliced
1 large red chilli, finely sliced
85g/3oz black olives, pitted

400g/14oz tin of artichoke hearts, drained and cut in half
10ml/2 teaspoons balsamic vinegar
few basil leaves for garnish

1. Heat the stock in a large saucepan until simmering. Slowly pour in the cornmeal, stirring all the time until thick. Reduce the heat as much as possible, cover the pan and cook, stirring frequently for 30-40 minutes. Add 250g/9oz of the Parmesan cheese and season with pepper. Cover and set aside to cool slightly.
2. Pour the polenta on to a damp baking sheet and smooth the surface with a wet spatula. The polenta should be about 1cm/1/2 inch thick.
3. When the polenta is cool cut into diamond shapes, place on a lightly greased baking sheet, brush with the flavoured olive oil and grill under a hot grill. When brown and crisp turn the shapes over, brush with more oil and grill on the other side. Dust with the remaining Parmesan cheese.
4. Cut the aubergines into long 1cm/1/2 inch wide strips and lightly salt them. Leave for 30 minutes then rinse and dry the aubergine, brush with olive oil and grill until soft.
5. Toss the mushrooms with the sun-dried tomatoes and their oil over a high heat for 3 minutes. Remove with a slotted spoon, add the prosciutto and increase the heat. Fry, stirring, until crisp and brown.
6. Mix together the peppers, chilli, aubergines, mushrooms, tomatoes, prosciutto, olives and artichoke hearts. Mix 30ml/2 tablespoons olive oil with the vinegar, season and sprinkle over the salad.
7. Arrange the polenta around the edge of a large serving plate, put the salad in the centre and garnish with basil leaves.

ITALIAN MEDIUM RED

Aubergine Charlotte

This is a useful supper dish – a layered up aubergine and tomato 'pie' which is good served with a crisp green salad and Basmati rice.

SERVES 4
4 large aubergines
salt and freshly ground black pepper
1 onion, finely chopped
olive oil
1 garlic clove, crushed
15 tomatoes, peeled, deseeded and chopped
290ml/1/2 pint yoghurt
stock

1. Slice and salt the aubergines and leave to 'degorge' in a colander for 30 minutes. Meanwhile, cook the onion in a little oil for 3 minutes. Add the garlic, tomatoes, salt and pepper and cook for a further 25 minutes.
2. Rinse and dry the aubergines. Steam for 20 minutes.
3. Set the oven to 180°C/350°F/gas mark 4.
4. Arrange a layer of aubergine slices along the bottom and up the sides of a loaf or Charlotte tin.
5. Layer up two-thirds of the tomatoes, the yoghurt and remaining aubergines finishing with a layer of aubergines.
6. Cover and bake for 40 minutes.
7. Cool for 5 minutes. Tip off any excess liquid. Turn out and serve hot with the tomatoes which have been thinned to the consistency of a sauce with a little stock.

Above: Butterfly Leg of Lamb

Above: Veal Cutlets and Grilled Vegetables with Aïoli. Right: Oxtail Stew.

Left: Cassoulet. Above: Pizza.

Above: Greek Parsley Pasta. Right: Salmon and Plaice Ravioli with Basil Sauce.

Left: Caroline's Ricotta Pie. Above: Grilled Polenta and Prosciutto Salad.

Above: Cassis Cream Pie. Right: Three-Chocolate Bavarois.

Left: Striped Chocolate and Grand Marnier Bavarois. Above: Black Coffee Jelly with Greek Yoghurt.

Above: Ballymaloe's Jelly of Fresh Raspberries. Right: Charlotte's Higgledy Piggledy Tart.

Above: Poached Pear and Polenta Tart.

Sweet Sauces

Crème Chantilly

150ml/¼ pint double cream
30ml/2 tablespoons iced water
5ml/1 teaspoon icing sugar
2 drops vanilla essence

1. Put all the ingredients into a chilled bowl and whisk with a balloon whisk, steadily but not too fast, for about 2 minutes or until the cream has thickened and doubled in volume.
2. Whisk faster for 30-40 seconds until the mixture is very fluffy and will form soft peaks.

NOTE: Chilling the ingredients and the bowl gives a lighter, whiter result.

Crème Pâtissière

290ml/ ½ pint milk
2 egg yolks
55g/2oz caster sugar
20g/¾oz flour
20g/¾oz cornflour
vanilla essence

1. Scald the milk.
2. Cream the egg yolks with the sugar and when pale, mix in the flours. Pour on the milk and mix well.
3. Return the mixture to the pan and bring slowly up to the boil, stirring continuously. (It will go alarmingly lumpy, but don't worry, keep stirring and it will get smooth.) Allow to cool slightly and add the vanilla essence.

Crème Anglaise (English Egg Custard)

290ml/ ½ pint milk
15ml/1 tablespoon sugar
1 vanilla pod or few drops of vanilla essence
2 egg yolks

1. Heat the milk with the sugar and vanilla pod and bring slowly to the boil.
2. Beat the yolks in a bowl. Remove the vanilla pod and pour the milk on to the egg yolks, stirring steadily. Mix well and return to the pan.
3. Stir over gentle heat until the mixture thickens so that it will coat the back of a spoon; this will take about 5 minutes. Do not boil. Pour into a cold bowl.
4. Add the vanilla essence if using.

Easy Crème Anglaise

1 egg yolk
30g/1oz caster sugar
30g/1oz flour
225ml/8 fl oz milk
2 drops vanilla essence

1. Beat the egg yolk and sugar together. Add the flour, beat well.
2. Heat the milk and bring slowly to the boil. Pour the milk on to the egg yolk, sugar and flour. Mix well and return to the pan.
3. Bring to the boil, stirring continuously. Allow it to thicken. Pour into a bowl and add the vanilla essence.

Orange Crème Anglaise

570ml/1 pint milk
zest of 1 orange
1 vanilla pod
85g/3oz sugar
6 egg yolks
30ml/2 tablespoons Grand Marnier
1 drop of orange essence

1. Heat the milk with the orange zest and vanilla pod and bring slowly to the boil.
2. Whisk the sugar and egg yolks together until pale. Pour the milk on to the egg yolks, stirring steadily. Remove the vanilla pod.
3. Return the milk to the pan and cook over a gentle heat, stirring well until it will coat the back of a spoon. This will take about 5 minutes.
4. Strain into a bowl and add the Grand Marnier and orange essence. Allow to cool before using.

Mocha Custard

290ml/½ pint milk
8 coffee beans
55g/2oz chocolate
2 egg yolks
15g/½oz caster sugar

1. Put the milk into a small saucepan with the coffee beans. Place over a low heat and bring up to the boil. Turn off the heat and leave to infuse for 10 minutes.
2. Break the chocolate into small even-sized pieces and put them into a bowl over (not in) a saucepan of simmering water. Allow to melt completely.
3. Beat the egg yolks with the sugar until pale and creamy.
4. Strain the milk into the bowl of melted chocolate and add to the egg-yolk mixture.
5. Pour this mixture into a rinsed-out saucepan and place over a medium heat, stirring until the mixture thickens so that it will coat the back of a spoon, but do not boil. This should take 3-4 minutes.

Sugar Syrup

285g/10oz granulated sugar
570ml/1 pint water
pared rind of 1 lemon

1. Put the sugar, water and lemon rind in a pan and heat slowly until the sugar has completely dissolved.
2. Bring to the boil and cook to the required consistency. Allow to cool.
3. Strain. Keep covered in a cool place until needed.

NOTE: Sugar syrup will keep unrefrigerated for about 5 days, and for several weeks if kept cold.

Caramel Sauce

225g/8oz granulated sugar
290ml/½ pint water

1. Place the sugar in a heavy-bottomed saucepan with half the quantity of water.
2. Dissolve the sugar slowly without stirring it or allowing the water to boil.
3. Once all the sugar has dissolved turn up the heat and boil until it is a good caramel colour.
4. Immediately, tip in the remaining water (it will fizz dangerously, so stand back).
5. Stir until any lumps have dissolved, then remove from the heat and allow to cool.

Toffee Sauce

30ml/2 tablespoons brandy
110g/4oz butter
55g/2oz demerara sugar
30ml/2 tablespoons double cream

1. Place all the ingredients in a saucepan and heat until melted. Bring to the boil and allow to thicken slightly.

Apricot Sauce

110g/4oz dried apricots, soaked overnight
110g/4oz tinned apricots
570ml/1 pint water

1. Drain the dried apricots and put them into a saucepan with the tinned apricots and water. Bring up to the boil and simmer until tender.
2. Liquidize and then push through a sieve. If the sauce is too thin, reduce it by rapid boiling to the required consistency. If it is too thick, add a little water.

NOTE: This sauce can be served hot or cold.

Apricot Sauce with Kernels

85g/3oz granulated sugar
290ml/½ pint water
225g/8oz apricots, halved
juice of ½ lemon

1. Dissolve the sugar in the water over a gentle heat. Do not allow to boil until the sugar has completely dissolved (this will prevent the syrup from crystallizing).
2. Add the apricots to the pan with the stones and lemon juice.
3. Bring to the boil and cook until the apricots are soft (about 15 minutes).
4. Remove the stones, but keep them.
5. Boil the apricots rapidly for a further 5-10 minutes, or until the pulp is reduced to a syrupy consistency. Push the apricot sauce through a nylon or stainless steel sieve. Taste and add extra sugar if necessary.
6. Crack the stones and remove the kernels. Chop the kernels roughly and add to the sauce. Serve hot or cold.

Raspberry Jam Sauce

45ml/3 tablespoons raspberry jam
85g/3oz sugar
125ml/¼ pint water

1. Put the sugar and water in a saucepan and heat slowly until the sugar has dissolved. Then boil rapidly until the syrup feels tacky between finger and thumb.
2. Add the jam, stir until smooth, then sieve to remove the pips.

Hot Chocolate Sauce

170g/6oz unsweetened chocolate, chopped
60ml/4 tablespoons water
15ml/1 tablespoon golden syrup
5ml/1 teaspoon instant coffee powder, dissolved in 15ml/1 tablespoon boiling water
15g/½oz butter

1. Put the chocolate into a bowl set over, not in, a pan of boiling water. When melted, add the water, golden syrup, coffee and butter and stir until thin and shiny.

Apple Purée

450g/1lb cooking apples
110g/4oz sugar
60ml/4 tablespoons water

1. Peel and core the apples. Cut them into chunks. Put them with the sugar and water in a heavy saucepan and simmer gently until they are a soft pulp. Beat out any lumps with a wooden spoon.
2. If the purée is too sloppy, boil it rapidly to reduce and thicken it, but leave the lid half on as it splashes dangerously.

Apple Marmalade

3 cooking apples
a little butter
strip of lemon rind
about 85g/3oz brown sugar

1. Wash the unpeeled apples, quarter and core them. Rub the bottom and sides of a heavy saucepan with butter.
2. Slice the apples thickly into the pan and add the lemon rind. Cover and cook gently, stirring occasionally, until completely soft.
3. Push through a sieve. Rinse out the pan and return the purée to it. Add at least 55g/2oz brown sugar to 570ml/1 pint purée. Cook rapidly until the mixture is of dropping consistency (about 4 minutes). Allow to cool. Add more sugar if necessary.

Brandy Butter

Cream equal quantities of unsalted butter and caster sugar together until very light. Add finely grated orange rind and brandy to flavour fairly strongly.

Melba Sauce

225g/8oz fresh or frozen (not tinned) raspberries
icing sugar

1. Defrost the raspberries if frozen. Push them through a nylon or stainless sieve to remove all seeds.
2. Sift in icing sugar to taste. If too thick, add a few spoonfuls of water.

Raspberry Coulis

340g/12oz fresh raspberries
juice of 1/2 lemon
70ml/2 1/2 fl oz sugar syrup (see page 419)

1. Whizz all the ingredients together in a food processor, and push through a conical strainer.

NOTE: If it is too thin, it can be thickened by boiling rapidly in a heavy saucepan. Stir well to prevent it 'catching'.

Sweet Gooseberry Sauce

225g/8oz ripe gooseberries
150ml/1/4 pint water
110g/4oz sugar
pinch of ground ginger

1. Put all the ingredients in a thick-bottomed saucepan. Bring gradually to the boil and then simmer until the gooseberries pop open and change to a yellowish colour.
2. Push through a sieve and reheat.

Puddings

Orange Fool

SERVES 4

2 small oranges
290ml/½ pint double cream
30ml/2 tablespoons icing sugar

1. With a potato peeler, pare about half the rind off 1 orange. The strips should have no white pith on the underside. Using a very sharp fruit knife, cut into tiny thin strips about 2.5cm/1 inch long.
2. Place these needleshreds in a pan of boiling water for 5 minutes. Rinse in cold water until completely cool. Drain.
3. Grate the remaining orange rind and squeeze the juice.
4. Whip the cream. When stiff, stir in the orange juice, grated rind and sugar.
5. Spoon into small glasses or little china pots or coffee cups. Scatter over the needleshreds of orange rind to decorate.

SWEET WHITE

Lemon Syllabub

SERVES 4

290ml/½ pint double cream
finely grated rind of ½ lemon
juice of 2 lemons
30ml/2 tablespoons white wine
icing sugar to taste, sifted
thinly pared peel of ½ lemon

1. Place the cream in a bowl with the lemon rind. Whip, adding the lemon juice, wine and icing sugar at intervals. Spoon into individual glasses.
2. Cut the lemon peel into very thin needleshreds. Drop them into boiling water and cook for 2 minutes. Drain and dry them. Scatter on top of the syllabub.

SWEET WHITE

Ginger Syllabub

SERVES 4

60-90ml/4-5 tablespoons Advocaat liqueur
30ml/2 tablespoons ginger marmalade
290ml/½ pint double cream
1-2 pieces preserved ginger

1. Mix the Advocaat and ginger marmalade together.
2. Whip the cream lightly and stir in the marmalade mixture.
3. Spoon into small glasses, little china pots or coffee cups.
4. Put 2-3 thin slivers of preserved ginger on top of each syllabub. Chill before serving.

NOTE I: For a smoother texture the ginger marmalade and the Advocaat can be liquidized or sieved together.
NOTE II: In the absence of ginger marmalade use orange marmalade well flavoured with finely chopped bottled ginger and its syrup.

RICH SWEET WHITE

Treacle Lick

This recipe was given to me by Mrs Levis of the Sign of the Angel in Lacock, Wiltshire. It is very rich and stirs up strong reactions – it is loved or loathed.

SERVES 4

6 eggs, separated
225g/8oz fine brown sugar
450g/1lb black treacle, warmed
570ml/1 pint double cream, whipped
150ml/¼ pint rum

1. Beat together the egg yolks and sugar until pale and creamy.
2. Add the warmed treacle.
3. Fold in the very lightly whipped double cream. Add the rum.
4. Whisk the egg whites until stiff but not dry. Fold into the egg and treacle mixture. Pile in individual glasses and leave to chill and set.

FORTIFIED SWEET WHITE

Apricot Mousse

SERVES 4
225g/8oz good quality dried apricots, soaked overnight
15ml/1 tablespoon sugar
290ml/½ pint water
7g/¼oz gelatine
150ml/¼ pint double cream, lightly whipped
2 egg whites

For the decoration:
whipped cream
apricot pieces

1. Drain the apricots and put them into a heavy saucepan with the sugar and water. Simmer them slowly until they are tender.
2. Liquidize the cooked apricots with enough of the liquor to make a smooth, soft purée. Taste and add more sugar if necessary.
3. Put 45ml/3 tablespoons water into a small saucepan, sprinkle on the gelatine and set aside to 'sponge' for 5 minutes.
4. Dissolve the gelatine over a gentle heat and when clear and warm, stir it into the purée. Leave it to set slightly, then fold in the lightly whipped cream.
5. Whisk the egg whites until stiff but not dry and, using a large metal spoon, fold into the apricot mixture.
6. Pour into a soufflé dish and leave to set in the refrigerator for 2-3 hours.
7. When set, decorate with rosettes of cream and apricot pieces.

SWEET WHITE

Orange Mousse

This is a very low-fat, sugar-free mousse.

SERVES 4-6
150ml/¼ pint water
15g/½oz or 1 envelope of gelatine
200ml/7 fl oz carton frozen concentrated orange juice, defrosted
15ml/1 tablespoon brandy
290ml/½ pint low-fat natural yoghurt
2 egg whites

1. Put 3 tablespoons of the water into a small saucepan. Sprinkle on the gelatine and leave it to become spongy. Dissolve the gelatine over a gentle heat; do not allow it to boil. When it is clear and warm, add it to the orange juice with the remaining water and the brandy. Stir this into the yoghurt.
2. Refrigerate the mixture until it is just beginning to set.
3. Whisk the egg whites until they are stiff but not dry. Fold them into the setting orange base and pour the mixture into a glass bowl. Leave it to set in the refrigerator for a few hours.

NOTE: To make orange ice cream, make the mousse as above and freeze until solid. Remove from the freezer 20 minutes before serving.

SWEET WHITE

Chocolate Mousse

SERVES 4
4 eggs
110g/4oz chocolate

1. Chop the chocolate into even-sized pieces. Put into a bowl over (not in) a saucepan of simmering water. Allow it to melt.
2. Separate the eggs. Stir the melted chocolate into the egg yolks. Mix well.
3. Whisk the egg whites until quite stiff and fold them into the chocolate mixture.
4. Turn immediately into a soufflé dish or into individual pots or glasses.
5. Chill until set, preferably overnight, but for at least 4 hours.

FORTIFIED SWEET WHITE

Rich Chocolate Mousse

SERVES 4
70g/2½oz granulated sugar
110ml/4 fl oz water
3 egg yolks
170g/6oz plain chocolate, chopped
340ml/12 fl oz double cream, lightly whipped

1. Put the sugar and water in a small saucepan, heat gently until the sugar has completely dissolved and then bring to the boil.
2. Boil 'to the thread' (when a little syrup is placed between a wet finger and thumb and the fingers are opened it should form a thread about 2.5cm/1 inch long).
3. Allow to cool slightly.
4. Pour the sugar syrup over the egg yolks, whisking all the time. Carry on whisking until the mixture is thick and mousse-like.
5. Carefully melt the chocolate in a bowl over hot water. Fold the chocolate into the egg mixture.
6. Immediately and carefully fold in the lightly whipped cream. Use as required.

NOTE: Use couverture chocolate if available.

LIQUEUR MUSCAT

White Chocolate Mousse

SERVES 4
30ml/1 fl oz milk
110g/4oz white chocolate, chopped
2 drops vanilla essence
2 egg yolks
15g/½oz caster sugar
7g/¼oz gelatine
100ml/3½ fl oz double cream, lightly whipped
3 egg whites

1. In a small pan heat the milk. Add the chocolate and stir over a gentle heat until melted. Add the vanilla essence.
2. Beat the egg yolks with the sugar until pale and creamy.
3. Put 45ml/3 tablespoons water in a small saucepan, sprinkle on the gelatine and set aside to 'sponge' for 5 minutes.
4. While the chocolate is still warm add it to the yolk and sugar mixture.
5. Dissolve the gelatine over a gentle heat and when clear and warm stir it into the chocolate mixture.
6. Leave the chocolate mixture in the refrigerator to thicken and begin to set, then fold in the cream.
7. Whisk the egg whites until stiff but not dry and fold into the chocolate mousse mixture.
8. Turn into individual serving dishes and chill until set.

SWEET SPARKLING

Chocolate and Chestnut Mousse Cake

SERVES 4-6
140g/5oz semi-sweet dark chocolate
45g/1½oz unsalted butter
225g/8oz tinned unsweetened chestnut purée
4 eggs
55g/2oz caster sugar
1 egg white
icing sugar
lightly whipped double cream

1. Line the base and sides of a 20cm/8 inch diameter, 5cm/2 inch deep, cake tin with greaseproof paper. Lightly oil the paper and dust it out with flour.
2. Melt the chocolate and butter in a small saucepan. Tip into a bowl and beat well until smooth.
3. Set the oven to 180°C/350°F/gas mark 4.
4. Sieve the chestnut purée into the chocolate and butter mixture.
5. Separate the eggs. Whisk the egg yolks with the sugar until thick, pale and mousse-like. Add this to the chocolate and chestnut mixture and mix well.
6. Whisk the egg white until stiff but not dry. Fold into the chocolate mixture. Pour into the prepared cake tin.
7. Bake for 50 minutes. Leave in the tin to set and cool for 5 minutes. Turn out and dust lightly with the icing sugar. Serve the whipped double cream separately.

LIQUEUR MUSCAT

Chocolate Mousse and Ginger Syllabub in Chocolate Cases

SERVES 6
chocolate mousse (see page 425)
ginger syllabub (see page 424)

For the chocolate cases:
225g/8oz best quality plain chocolate

To decorate:
chocolate shapes (see page 633)

1. First make the chocolate cases: break up the chocolate and place it in a pudding basin. Set it over (not in) a saucepan of simmering water. Stir until the chocolate is smooth and melted. Do not overheat or the chocolate will lose its gloss.
2. Brush melted chocolate thinly over the insides of 8 small paper cases. (It is easier if you make double paper cases by slipping one case inside another.) Repeat the process until you have a reasonably thick, but not clumsy, layer. Leave to harden. Carefully peel away the paper.
3. Make up the chocolate mousse and ginger syllabub according to the recipes but do not dish them up.
4. Divide the chocolate mixture between the 8 chocolate cases. Spread flat and leave to set slightly. Spoon over the ginger syllabub. Decorate each case with a chocolate shape.

FORTIFIED SWEET WHITE

Caramel Mousse

SERVES 4
10g/1/3oz gelatine
squeeze of lemon
170g/6oz granulated sugar
3 eggs
45g/1½oz caster sugar
150ml/¼ pint double cream

For the decoration:
55g/2oz granulated sugar
whipped double cream

1. In a small pan, soak the gelatine in the lemon juice with 30ml/2 tablespoons water.
2. Melt the granulated sugar in another pan with 45ml/3 tablespoons water and boil until it turns to a brown caramel. Pour in 75ml/5 tablespoons of water very carefully – it will hiss alarmingly. Cook over a gentle heat until the caramel is dissolved. Leave to cool slightly.
3. Whisk the eggs and caster sugar in a bowl over a pan of simmering water until mousse-like and thick. Remove from the heat and whisk occasionally until beginning to cool.
4. Heat the soaked gelatine very gently until it is quite runny and clear. Do not boil. Stir into the mousse with the caramel sauce. Stir gently over a bowl of ice until beginning to thicken and set.
5. Lightly whip the cream and add it to the mixture.
6. Pour into a dish and refrigerate until set.
7. Meanwhile, make the caramel chips for the decoration: lightly oil a flat dish or baking sheet. Put the sugar in a heavy-bottomed small saucepan and heat gently, without any water, until it first melts, then turns to caramel. When it is evenly brown, pour immediately on to the oiled dish or baking sheet. Allow to cool until hard as glass, then immediately break into small chips with the end of a rolling pin. Keep dry and cool until needed.
8. Decorate the mousse with rosettes of whipped cream and caramel chips.

FORTIFIED SWEET WHITE

Charlotte Russe

SERVES 4-6
15 sponge fingers (see page 576)
150ml/¼ pint clear lemon jelly

For the custard:
vanilla pod or 2. 5ml/½ teaspoon vanilla essence
425ml/¾ pint milk
45g/1½oz caster sugar
5 egg yolks
45ml/3 tablespoons sherry
15g/½oz gelatine
60ml/4 tablespoons water
235ml/8 fl oz double cream, lightly whipped

For the decoration:
4 glacé cherries cut in half
a few pieces of angelica

1. Make the lemon jelly. When it is cool but not set, wet a charlotte mould and pour in a thin layer (about 5mm/1/4 inch) of jelly. Decorate the base with cherries and angelica and leave to set. Pour in the rest of the jelly and refrigerate again until nearly set. When it is almost set, arrange the sponge fingers, sugared side outside, standing up around the sides of the mould with their ends in the jelly.
2. Make the custard: put the vanilla in the milk and heat gently.
3. In a bowl, mix the sugar and egg yolks well together. When the milk is almost boiling, remove the pod and pour on to the yolks, stirring vigorously. Set the bowl over a pan of simmering water and stir until thick enough to coat the back of the spoon. Strain and allow to cool. Add the sherry.
4. In a small pan, soak the gelatine in the water, then dissolve over gentle heat. When runny and clear, stir into the cooling custard. When the custard is almost set, fold in the partially whipped cream and turn the mixture into the mould, spreading it flat. Put in the refrigerator to set.
5. Trim off any biscuits sticking up above the level of the filling. Run a knife between the biscuits and the mould to make sure they are not stuck. Dip the bottom of the mould briefly into hot water to dislodge the jelly. Invert a plate over the mould, turn the 2 over together and lift off the mould.

SWEET WHITE

Chocolate Terrine with Orange and Cointreau Sauce

This is a very pretty terrine of 3 coloured chocolate mousses. It can be served individually plated or as a whole.

SERVES 4
white chocolate mousse (see page 426)

For the milk chocolate mousse:
170g/6oz milk chocolate, broken up
30g/1oz unsalted butter
15g/1/2oz gelatine
3 eggs, separated
30g/1oz sugar
150ml/1/4 pint double cream, lightly whipped

For the dark chocolate mousse:
170g/6oz dark chocolate, broken up
45ml/3 tablespoons water
30g/1oz unsalted butter
15g/1/2oz gelatine
3 eggs, separated
30g/1oz sugar
45ml/3 tablespoons double cream, lightly whipped

For the orange sauce:
290ml/1/2 pint fresh orange juice
5ml/1 teaspoon arrowroot
juice of 1/4 lemon
30ml/2 tablespoons Cointreau

To garnish:
chocolate leaves

1. Make the white chocolate mousse and tip into a lightly oiled 1. 75 litre/3 pint terrine or loaf tin. Leave to set for 20 minutes.
2. Next prepare the milk chocolate mousse: melt the chocolate and butter together.
3. Put 45ml/3 tablespoons water into a small saucepan and sprinkle on the gelatine.
4. Whisk the egg yolks with the sugar until very thick.
5. Dissolve the gelatine over a low heat until clear and warm.
6. Add the melted chocolate and gelatine to the egg yolk and sugar mixture. Stir gently until the mixture is on the point of setting. Fold in the lightly whipped cream.
7. Whisk the egg whites until stiff but not dry and fold into the mousse mixture. Pile on top of the white chocolate mousse. Leave to set for 20 minutes.
8. Next prepare the dark chocolate mousse: melt the chocolate with the water and butter.
9. Pour 45ml/3 tablespoons water into a small saucepan and sprinkle on the gelatine.
10. Whisk the egg yolks with the sugar until very thick.

11. Dissolve the gelatine over a low heat until clear and warm.
12. Add the melted chocolate and gelatine to the egg yolk and sugar mixture. Stir gently until the mixture is on the point of setting. Fold in the lightly whipped cream.
13. Whisk the egg whites until stiff but not dry and fold into the chocolate mousse. Pile on top of the milk chocolate mousse and leave to set for 20-30 minutes.
14. Finally prepare the orange sauce: put the orange juice into a saucepan and bring up to the boil. Mix the arrowroot with a little cold water. Add some of the hot orange juice and pour into the remaining orange juice. Return to the boil, stirring continuously, and simmer for 1 minute. Leave to cool and add the Cointreau.
15. To serve: flood the base of a pudding plate with the orange sauce and cover with one slice of the chocolate terrine. Decorate with chocolate leaves.

FORTIFIED MUSCAT

Prune Mousse

SERVES 4
110g/4oz prunes, stoned
30ml/1 fl oz Armagnac (or brandy)
7g/¼oz gelatine
110g/4oz granulated sugar
150ml/¼ pint water
2 egg whites
150ml/¼ pint double cream, lightly whipped

1. Soak the prunes for a day in the Armagnac and purée them in a liquidizer or food processor.
2. Soak the gelatine in 45ml/3 tablespoons water.
3. Put the sugar and water together in a small saucepan and heat gently until the sugar has completely dissolved. Once it has completely dissolved, bring to the boil. Allow it to boil 'to the thread' (when a little syrup is placed between a wet finger and thumb and the fingers are opened it should form a thread about 2.5cm/1 inch long). Leave to cool for half a minute.
4. Whisk the egg whites and pour on the cooked sugar syrup, whisking all the time until they have formed a thick shiny meringue.
5. Dissolve the gelatine over a gentle heat and when clear, runny and warm, add it to the prune purée.
6. Gradually whisk the purée into the meringue mixture. Fold in the lightly whipped cream. Pour into a serving dish and allow to set.

SWEET WHITE

Cassis Cream Pie

SERVES 6
For the base:
2 eggs, separated
55g/2oz caster sugar
30g/1oz plain flour, sifted
15ml/1 tablespoon blackcurrant jelly or sieved jam

For the mousse and glaze:
340g/12oz blackcurrants
75ml/5 tablespoons crème de cassis liqueur
3 eggs, separated
110g/4oz caster sugar
15g/½oz gelatine
150ml/¼ pint double cream
30ml/2 tablespoons blackcurrant jelly or sieved jam

1. Set the oven to 220°C/425°F/gas mark 7.
2. Grease and flour a 20cm/8 inch diameter loose-bottomed cake tin.
3. Make the base: set a bowl over a pan of simmering water and put into it the egg yolks and half the caster sugar. Keeping the water simmering under the bowl but not touching the bottom of it, whisk the mixture with an electric or balloon whisk until it is pale, mousse-like and very thick. Remove from the heat.
4. Whisk the egg whites until stiff and fold in the rest of the sugar.
5. Fold the yolk and white mixtures together, then fold in the flour.
6. Turn into the cake tin and bake for 15 minutes until evenly brown and slightly shrunk from the tin sides.
7. Remove the cake from the tin and cool, upside down, on a wire rack.
8. When cold, spread evenly with the blackcurrant jelly or jam.
9. Wash the cake tin and oil its sides. The mousse will set in this.

10. Make the blackcurrant purée by simmering the fruit with 30ml/2 tablespoons water. Keep stirring and boiling as much as possible until the juice has evaporated without the fruit catching and burning on the bottom of the pan.
11. Push the fruit through a sieve to extract the seeds, scraping the paste-like purée from the back of the sieve with a clean (not covered in blackcurrant seeds) spoon. Take one-third of the purée and reserve it for the top. Mix the rest with 30ml/2 tablespoons cassis.
12. Make the mousse: once again set a bowl over simmering water and whisk the yolks, 30ml/2 tablespoons cassis and two-thirds of the sugar. It will be more liquid than the first mixture and will take longer; it should thicken sufficiently to leave a ribbon-like trail when the whisk is lifted. Remove from the heat and whisk occasionally as it cools.
13. Put 45ml/3 tablespoons water into a small saucepan and sprinkle over the gelatine. Leave to soak for 10 minutes.
14. Stir the blackcurrant purée into the egg-yolk mixture.
15. Put the gelatine over very gentle heat to dissolve it. When runny and clear, stir into the blackcurrant mixture.
16. Whip the cream until it will just hold its shape, and fold into the mousse.
17. Whisk the egg whites until stiff and fold in the remaining sugar.
18. Fold the blackcurrant mousse and the meringue mixtures together lightly and without overmixing – a few air pockets are preferable to a mixture with all the air stirred out of it.
19. Fit the cooled and jam-spread cake back into the cake tin, and pour the mousse into it. Level the top and freeze until very solid.
20. To remove the mousse from the tin: loosen the sides by wrapping the cake tin in a cloth dipped in very hot water. Push the nearly or completely frozen mousse out of the tin on the loose bottom. With a fish slice, ease the pie on to a serving plate. Allow to thaw in the refrigerator. (The only reason the pie is frozen is to make getting it out of the tin easier. But if a deep flan ring on a baking sheet is used instead of the tin, or a spring-form cake pan – with sides that unclip – then freezing is not necessary.)
21. To make the glazed top: gently heat together the reserved blackcurrant purée, the sieved jam or jelly and the crème de cassis. Stir until melted, then boil hard for a few seconds to get a shiny clear syrup.
22. Cool the glaze until just liquid, pour over the set mousse, and ease to the edges with a palette knife. Prick any air bubbles with the knife.

SWEET WHITE

Cold Lemon Soufflé

SERVES 4
7g/¼oz gelatine
3 eggs
juice and rind of 2 large lemons
140g/5oz caster sugar
150ml/¼ pint double cream, lightly whipped

For the decoration:
whipped double cream
wafer-thin lemon slices
browned nibbed almonds

1. In a small saucepan, soak the gelatine in the lemon juice.
2. Separate the eggs. Place the yolks, lemon rind and sugar in a mixing bowl and whisk together with an electric mixer (or with a balloon whisk or rotary beater with the bowl set over a saucepan of simmering water). Whisk until very thick. If whisking by hand over hot water, remove from the heat and whisk for a few minutes longer, until the mixture is lukewarm.
3. Dissolve the gelatine over a gentle heat and, when warm, add it to the mousse mixture. Stir gently until the mixture is on the point of setting, then fold in the cream. Taste and if too tart, sift in a little icing sugar; if too bland, add a little more lemon juice.
4. Whisk the egg whites until stiff but not dry and fold them into the soufflé with a large metal spoon.
5. Pour the mixture into a soufflé dish and leave to set in the refrigerator for 2-3 hours. Decorate with rosettes of cream, lemon slices and nuts.

NOTE: This dish can be given a more soufflé-like appearance by tying a double band of oiled paper round the top of the dish so that it projects about 2.5cm/1 inch above the rim, before pouring in the mixture. (The dish must be of a size that would not quite contain the mixture without the added depth given by the paper band.) Pour it in to come about 2.5cm/1 inch up the paper, above the top of the dish. When the soufflé is set, carefully remove the paper and press the almonds round the exposed sides.

SWEET WHITE

Cold Raspberry Soufflé

SERVES 4
3 eggs
110g/4oz sugar
45ml/3 tablespoons water
15g/½oz gelatine
340g/12oz raspberries
150ml/¼ pint double cream

For the decoration:
browned chopped or nibbed almonds
150ml/¼ pint double cream, whipped
whole raspberries

1. To prepare the soufflé dish (which should be 15cm/6 inches in diameter), tie a double piece of greaseproof paper around the outside and secure the ends with a paper clip or pin. The paper should stick up about 2.5cm/1 inch above the rim. Brush the inside of the projecting paper with oil.
2. Separate the eggs. Whisk the yolks with the sugar either over a gentle heat (with the bowl set over a pan of simmering water), or in an electric mixer, until light and fluffy, and thick enough for the whisk to leave a 'ribbon trail' when lifted.
3. Remove from the heat and whisk again until the mixture is almost cold.
4. Put the water into a small saucepan and sprinkle over the gelatine. Leave to soak.
5. Liquidize the raspberries and sieve the purée into the egg-yolk mixture.
6. Dissolve the gelatine over a gentle heat - do not allow it to boil - and when warm and clear stir it into the raspberry mixture. Stir gently until on the point of setting. Fold in the whipped cream. Taste and sift in a little icing sugar if too tart.
7. Whisk the whites until stiff but not dry and fold them into the soufflé mixture. Pile into the dish and flatten the top neatly. The soufflé mixture should come at least 2cm/¾inch above the edge of the dish. Refrigerate for at least 4 hours.
8. Remove the oiled paper carefully. Spread the exposed sides thinly with cream. Press almonds gently on to the cream. Pipe rosettes of whipped cream round the top and garnish each with a whole raspberry.

SWEET WHITE

Cold Passionfruit Soufflé

SERVES 4
8 passionfruit
7g/¼oz gelatine
juice and rind of 1 lemon
15ml/1 tablespoon water
3 eggs
110g/4oz caster sugar
150ml/¼ pint double cream

For decoration:
1 passionfruit

1. Cut the passionfruit in half. Scoop out and sieve all the flesh.
2. In a small saucepan, soak the gelatine in the lemon juice and water.
3. Separate the eggs. Place the yolks, lemon rind and sugar in a mixing bowl and whisk together with an electric mixer (or with a balloon whisk or rotary beater with the bowl set over a saucepan of simmering water). Whisk until very thick. If whisking by hand over hot water, remove from the heat and whisk for a few minutes longer (until the mixture is lukewarm). Gradually add the passionfruit pulp.
4. Dissolve the gelatine over a gentle heat and when warm add it to the mousse mixture. Stir gently until the mixture is on the point of setting, then fold in the cream. Taste and if too tart sift in a little icing sugar; if too bland add a little more lemon juice.
5. Whisk the egg whites until stiff but not dry

and fold them into the soufflé with a large metal spoon.
6. Pour the mixture into a soufflé dish and leave to set in the refrigerator for 2-3 hours. When set decorate with the seeds of 1 passionfruit.

NOTE: This dish can be given a more soufflé-like appearance by tying a double band of oiled paper round the top of the dish so that it projects about 3cm/1¼ inches above the rim, before pouring in the mixture. (The dish must be of a size that would not quite contain the mixture without the added depth given by the paper band.) Pour it in to come about 2.5cm/1 inch up the paper, above the top of the dish. When the soufflé is set, carefully remove the paper and press the almonds round the sides.

SWEET WHITE

Hot Orange Soufflé

SERVES 4
45g/1½oz butter
45g/1½oz flour
grated rind of 1 large orange
290ml/½ pint fresh orange juice
55g/2oz caster sugar
4 egg whites
icing sugar

1. Butter a soufflé dish and dust with caster sugar. Set the oven to 200°C/400°F/gas mark 6. Preheat a baking sheet.
2. Melt the butter and add the flour. Cook for 1 minute and draw off the heat. Add the orange rind and juice. Return the pan to the heat and bring very gently up to the boil, stirring continuously. Simmer for 2 minutes and add the sugar. Taste and add more if necessary, remembering that the egg whites will dilute the taste. Cool.
3. When the orange sauce is cool, whisk the whites until stiff and fold them into it. Pour into the prepared soufflé dish - do not fill more than two-thirds of the dish. Run your finger around the top of the soufflé mixture. This gives a 'top hat' appearance to the cooked soufflé.
4. Bake in the hot oven, on the hot baking sheet, for 20-25 minutes. Dust lightly with icing sugar just before serving.

NOTE: When making a soufflé always remove the oven shelf above the soufflé dish - just in case the souffle rises unexpectedly well!

RICH SWEET WHITE

Hot Chocolate Soufflé

To make a successful hot chocolate soufflé you must have everything organized before you start to cook and work as quickly as possible. It is quite difficult to do.

SERVES 4
butter, melted
55g/2oz plus 5ml/1 teaspoon caster sugar
110g/4oz dark bitter chocolate
4 egg yolks
30ml/2 tablespoons brandy (optional)
5 egg whites
icing sugar

1. Set the oven to 200°C/400°F/gas mark 6. Preheat a baking sheet. Prepare the soufflé dish by brushing the inside with melted butter and dusting it with 5ml/1 teaspoon caster sugar.
2. Chop the chocolate with a large knife and put it into a bowl over a saucepan of gently simmering water, stirring until the chocolate has completely melted.
3. Beat the remaining sugar and the egg yolks together for 1 minute with a wooden spoon until thick and fluffy. Add the brandy if used. Add the egg-yolk mixture to the chocolate, mixing well - it will thicken slightly.
4. Whisk the whites until they will stand in soft peaks when the whisk is withdrawn from the bowl. Whisk in 5ml/1 teaspoon caster sugar, until stiff and shiny. Gently but thoroughly fold them into the mixture.
5. Turn into the soufflé dish but do not fill more than two-thirds of the dish. Run the handle of a wooden spoon around the top edge of the soufflé mixture. This gives a 'top hat' appearance to the cooked soufflé. Bake on the hot baking sheet for 20-25 minutes.
6. Test by giving the dish a slight shake or push. It if wobbles alarmingly, it needs further cooking; if it wobbles slightly it is ready. Dust with icing sugar and serve at once.

NOTE: When making a soufflé always remove the oven shelf above the soufflé dish, just in case the soufflé rises unexpectedly well!

FORTIFIED SWEET WHITE

Hot Apricot Soufflé

SERVES 4

110g/4oz good quality dried apricots, soaked overnight in 190ml/⅓ pint water
20g/¾oz butter, plus extra for greasing the dish
30g/1oz caster sugar, plus extra for dusting
20g/¾oz flour
190ml/⅓ pint orange juice
grated rind of 1 orange
5 egg whites

1. Butter a 1 5cm/6 inch (1 litre/2 pint) soufflé dish and dust it with caster sugar. Set the oven to 200°C/400°F/gas mark 6.
2. Poach the apricots in the water until very tender and then liquidize with the cooking liquor.
3. Melt the butter in a small saucepan, add the flour and cook for 1 minute. Remove from the heat and add the orange juice and orange rind. Return the pan to the heat and bring to the boil, stirring continually. Simmer for 2 minutes. Add the apricots.
4. Whisk the egg whites until just stiff, add the sugar and whisk again until stiff.
5. Add 15ml/1 tablespoon of egg white to loosen the soufflé base and then gently fold in the rest of the egg whites. Pour into the prepared soufflé dish.
6. Using the end of a wooden spoon, run it around the top of the soufflé mixture. This is so that when the soufflé is cooked it will look like a top hat.
7. Bake in the hot oven for 12-15 minutes.

SWEET SPARKLING

Junket

SERVES 4

570ml/1 pint fresh milk
10ml/2 teaspoons sugar
5ml/1 teaspoon rennet

1. Heat the milk with the sugar to blood temperature (lukewarm).
2. Stir well and pour into a serving bowl.
3. Stir in the rennet and leave to set at room temperature. Once set, the dish may be refrigerated.

NOTE: To vary the flavour of plain junket, spoon over a little whipped cream and sprinkle with crumbled ratafia biscuits; sprinkle the surface with grated nutmeg; or flavour with coffee essence, orange rind or grated chocolate.

Baked Custard

SERVES 4

3 whole eggs plus 1 egg yolk
3 drops vanilla essence
425ml/¾ pint very creamy milk or milk plus single cream
55g/2oz caster sugar
1 bay leaf
grated nutmeg

1. Set the oven to 170°C/325°F/gas mark 3.
2. Lightly beat the eggs, extra yolk and vanilla essence together with a wooden spoon; don't make them frothy.
3. Heat the milk to boiling point with the sugar, stirring as you do so.
4. Remove from the heat, cool for a second or two, and then pour on to the eggs, stirring all the time with a wooden spoon, not a whisk, to avoid creating bubbles.
5. Strain the mixture into an ovenproof dish. Straining removes any egg 'threads' which would spoil the smooth texture of the finished custard. Add the bay leaf and sprinkle with grated nutmeg.
6. Stand the custard dish in a roasting pan of hot water and bake in the oven for 40 minutes. It is set when there is a definite skin on the top and when the middle of the custard is no longer liquid (although it will still wobble).
7. Serve hot, warm or chilled.

Rice Pudding

SERVES 4
a nut of butter
15ml/1 tablespoon sugar
55g/2oz round (pudding) rice
570ml/1 pint milk
vanilla essence
ground nutmeg

1. Set the oven to 150°C/300°F/gas mark 2.
2. Rub the butter round a pie dish. Put the sugar, rice, milk and vanilla essence into the dish. Sprinkle with nutmeg.
3. Stir, and bake in the oven for 3-4 hours, by which time it should be soft and creamy with an evenly coloured brown skin.

Bread and Butter Pudding

SERVES 4
2 slices of plain bread
30g/1oz butter
30ml/2 tablespoons currants and sultanas, mixed
10ml/2 teaspoons candied peel
2 eggs and 1 yolk
15ml/1 rounded tablespoon sugar
290ml/½ pint creamy milk
vanilla essence
ground cinnamon
demerara sugar

1. Spread the bread with butter. Cut into quarters. Arrange in a shallow ovenproof dish, buttered side up, and sprinkle with currants, sultanas and candied peel.
2. Make the custard: mix the eggs and yolk with the sugar and stir in the milk and vanilla essence.
3. Pour the custard carefully over the bread and leave to soak for 30 minutes. Sprinkle with ground cinnamon and demerara sugar.
4. Heat the oven to 180°C/350°F/gas mark 4.
5. Place the pudding in a roasting pan of hot water and cook in the middle of the oven for about 45 minutes or until the custard is set and the top is brown and crusty.

NOTE: The pudding may be baked without the bain-marie (hot-water bath) quite successfully, but if used it will ensure a smooth, not bubbly custard.

SWEET WHITE

Crème Caramel

SERVES 4-5
110g/4oz granulated sugar
4 eggs
30ml/2 tablespoons caster sugar
570ml/1 pint milk
vanilla essence

1. Set the oven to 150°C/300°F/gas mark 2. Warm a soufflé or other ovenproof dish in it.
2. Place the granulated sugar in a heavy pan with 60ml/4 tablespoons water and allow it to melt slowly. When melted, boil rapidly until it has turned to a good brown toffee. Pour into the hot soufflé dish and coat all over by carefully tipping the dish. Leave until cold.
3. Beat the eggs and caster sugar together with a wooden spoon.
4. Scald the milk and stir this into the egg mixture. Add the vanilla essence. Strain into the prepared dish.
5. Stand in a bain-marie and cook in the oven for 1 hour or until the custard has set.
6. Allow to cool until tepid or stone-cold, then turn out on to a dish with a good lip.

FORTIFIED SWEET WHITE

Queen's Pudding

SERVES 4
290ml/ ½ pint milk
15g/½oz butter
30g/1oz caster sugar for the custard
60ml/4 tablespoons fresh white breadcrumbs
grated rind of 1 lemon
2 eggs
30ml/2 tablespoons raspberry jam, warmed
110g/4oz caster sugar for the meringue

1. Set the oven to 180°C/350°F/gas mark 4.
2. Heat the milk and add the butter and sugar. Stir until the sugar dissolves, then add the breadcrumbs and lemon rind.
3. Separate the eggs. When the breadcrumb mixture has cooled slightly, mix in the egg yolks. Pour into a pie dish and leave to stand for 30 minutes.
4. Bake for 25 minutes or until the custard mixture is set. Remove and allow to cool slightly.
5. Turn down the oven to 150°C/300°F/gas mark 2.
6. Carefully spread the jam over the top of the custard. (This is easier if you melt the jam first.)
7. Whip the egg whites until stiff. Whisk in 10ml/2 teaspoons of the meringue sugar. Whisk again until very stiff and shiny and fold in all but half a teaspoon of the remaining sugar.
8. Pile the meringue on top of the custard and dust the top lightly with the reserved sugar.
9. Bake until the meringue is set and straw coloured (about 10 minutes).

NOTE I: This is particularly good served hot with cold whipped cream.
NOTE II: When making a meringue mixture with a powerful electric mixer, gradually add half the sugar when the whites are stiff. Whisk again until very shiny and then add the remaining sugar and whisk lightly until just incorporated.

SWEET WHITE

Semolina

SERVES 4
few drops oil
570ml/1 pint milk
85g/3oz semolina
2 eggs
85g/3oz caster sugar
juice of 1 lemon
few drops vanilla essence
60-75ml/4-5 tablespoons double cream

1. Heat the milk in a heavy saucepan and when boiling, gradually stir in the semolina.
2. Reduce the heat and simmer for 10 minutes or until the semolina is cooked. Remove from the heat and allow to cool slightly.
3. Separate the eggs. Whisk the yolks and sugar until light and fluffy and stir into the semolina mixture.
4. Beat in the lemon juice, vanilla essence and cream.
5. Whisk the egg whites until stiff and fold into the semolina mixture with a metal spoon.

Petits Pots de Crème

SERVES 4-6
290ml/½ pint milk
just over 290ml/½ pint single cream
30g/1oz caster sugar
1 vanilla pod or 2 drops essence
4 egg yolks
1 large egg

For the flavourings:
5ml/1 teaspoon coffee essence
45g/1½oz chocolate, melted

1. Set the oven to 150°C/300°F/gas mark 2.
2. Place the milk and cream with the sugar and vanilla pod in a pan and scald (bring to the point when the liquid is about to boil but is not yet bubbling). Remove the pod. (If using vanilla essence, add it once the milk is scalded.)
3. Beat the yolks with the whole egg and pour on the scalded milk. Strain and divide into 3 equal parts.
4. Flavour one-third of the custard with coffee essence, one-third with melted chocolate and leave one-third plain. Pour into ramekin dishes. Stand the dishes in a roasting pan full of near-boiling water. Bake, covered with a sheet of paper or foil, for 35-40 minutes. Remove the covering, being careful not to let any condensed water drop on to the crèmes. Lift out of the water and allow to cool.

NOTE: Chocolate-flavoured custards may take longer to cook (about 45 minutes).

Crème Brûlée

Crème brûlée is best started a day in advance.

SERVES 4-5
290ml/½ pint double cream
1 vanilla pod or 5ml/1 teaspoon vanilla essence
4 egg yolks
15ml/1 tablespoon caster sugar

For the topping:
caster sugar

1. Put the cream with the vanilla pod into a pan and heat up to scalding point, making sure it does not boil. Remove the vanilla pod.
2. Set the oven to 170°C/325°F/gas mark 3.
3. Beat the egg yolks with the caster sugar and when light and fluffy, stir in the warm cream. Place the mixture in the top of a double saucepan, or in a bowl over a pan of simmering water, on a gentle heat. Stir all the time until the custard coats the back of the spoon. If using vanilla essence, add it now.
4. Pour the custard into an ovenproof serving dish, place in a roasting pan half-filled with hot water and bake for 12 minutes to create a good skin on top. Refrigerate overnight. On no account break the top skin.
5. Next day heat the grill.
6. Sprinkle the top of the custard with a 5mm/¼inch even layer of caster sugar. To do this, stand the dish on a tray or large sheet of greaseproof paper and sift the sugar over the dish and tray or paper. In this way you will get an even layer. Collect the sugar falling wide for re-use.
7. When the grill is blazing hot, put the custard under it, as close as you can get it to the heat. The sugar will melt and caramelize before the custard underneath it boils. Watch carefully, turning the custard if the sugar is browning unevenly.
8. Allow to cool completely before serving. The top should be hard and crackly.
9. To serve: crack the top with the serving spoon and give each diner some custard (which should be creamy and barely set) and a piece of caramel. Crème brûlée is also good made in individual ramekin dishes. In this event, bake the custard for only 5 minutes.

NOTE: If making crème brûlée for more than 4 or 5 people, either make in individual ramekin dishes or in more than one large dish.

FORTIFIED SWEET WHITE

Almond Bavarois with Apricot Sauce

110g/4oz ground almonds
1 vanilla pod
290ml/½ pint milk
2 eggs, separated
55g/2oz caster sugar
45ml/3 tablespoons water
15g/½oz gelatine
grated rind of 1 orange
3 drops almond essence
150ml/¼ pint double cream, lightly whipped

To serve:
apricot sauce (see page 419)

1. Set the oven to 180°C/350°F/gas mark 4.
2. Place the almonds on a baking sheet and place in the oven for 20 minutes or until lightly roasted. Allow to cool.
3. Put the vanilla pod into a saucepan with the milk and scald but do not boil.
4. Whisk the egg yolks and sugar together in a bowl over (not in) simmering water and keep whisking until very thick.
5. Remove the vanilla pod from the milk and stir the milk into the egg yolk and sugar mixture. Return to the saucepan and reheat, stirring continuously with a wooden spoon until you have a custard that will coat the back of a spoon. It will curdle if allowed to boil. Strain.
6. Put 45ml/3 tablespoons water into a small saucepan and sprinkle on the gelatine. Leave to sponge.
7. Dissolve the gelatine over a gentle heat, and when clear and warm pour into the custard mixture. Stir occasionally until on the point of setting.
8. Stir in the ground almonds, the orange rind and the almond essence.
9. Fold in the cream.
10. Whisk the egg whites until stiff but not dry

and fold into the bavarois mixture. Tip into 8 very lightly oiled ramekin dishes. Cover and leave to set.

11. To serve: flood the base of a pudding plate with the apricot sauce and turn an almond bavarois out on top of the sauce.

SWEET WHITE

Orange Bavarois with Meringues

SERVES 4

For the meringues:
1 egg white
55g/2oz caster sugar

For the bavarois:
45ml/3 tablespoons water
10ml/2 level teaspoons gelatine
5 lumps sugar
1 orange
425ml/3/4 pint milk
3 egg yolks
22.5ml/1 1/2 tablespoons caster sugar
150ml/1/4 pint double cream

To serve:
grated chocolate

1. First prepare the meringues: whisk the egg white until stiff, add 10ml/2 teaspoons of the sugar and continue whisking until stiff again; then fold in the rest. Put this mixture into a forcing bag and pipe into tiny button meringues on baking parchment using a 5mm/1/4inch plain pipe. Dry in a slow oven (130°C/260°F/gas mark 1/2) for about 40 minutes. Immediately peel off the paper and leave to cool.

2. Put the water into a small saucepan and sprinkle on the gelatine. Leave to soak.

3. Rub the sugar lumps over the orange until the sugar is well coloured by the oils in the rind. Put the lumps into the milk and dissolve over a gentle heat.

4. Cream the egg yolks and caster sugar together until thick and light, then pour the milk on to the mixture. Return to the pan and put over a gentle heat to thicken the custard. Stir constantly and do not allow to boil. When the custard will coat the back of the wooden spoon, strain into a bowl and allow to cool.

5. Put the gelatine over gentle heat and when clear and runny, add to the custard.

6. Stand the custard in a roasting pan or bowl full of ice and stir gently until the mixture thickens.

7. Whip the cream lightly, then fold 30ml/2 tablespoons of it into the custard. Pour at once into a lightly oiled plain mould. Refrigerate until set (about 3 hours).

8. Whip the rest of the cream a little stiffer. When the custard is set turn it out on to a plate and mask with the rest of the whipped cream. Cover with the meringues and sprinkle with grated chocolate.

NOTE I: Rubbing the sugar lumps over the orange rind extracts the orange flavour, but is a little tedious. An alternative method is to pare the rind finely from the orange and infuse it in the hot milk, then strain it.

NOTE II: If making a meringue mixture with a powerful electric mixer, gradually add half the sugar when the whites are stiff. Whisk again until very shiny and then add the remaining sugar and whisk lightly until just incorporated.

SWEET WHITE

Coffee Cream Bavarois

SERVES 4

7g/1/4oz gelatine
225ml/8 fl oz milk
20g/3/4oz unsweetened chocolate
3 egg yolks
85g/3oz caster sugar
15ml/1 tablespoon instant coffee
150ml/1/4 pint double cream

For the decoration:
grated chocolate
double cream, whipped

1. In a very small saucepan, soak the gelatine in 30ml/2 tablespoons water.

2. Place the milk and broken-up chocolate in a

saucepan and heat gently until the chocolate has completely melted.
3. Mix the egg yolks and sugar together. Stir in the warm milk and chocolate mixture. Beat well. Return to the saucepan.
4. Dissolve the coffee in 30ml/2 tablespoons boiling water and add it to the mixture. Stir continuously with a wooden spoon for 3-5 minutes. It is ready when the custard will coat the back of the spoon. Be careful not to overheat or the mixture will curdle.
5. Cool by standing the pan in a bowl of cold water.
6. Dissolve the gelatine over a gentle heat; when melted and clear, stir it into the cooling custard. Stir occasionally until on the point of setting. Lightly whip the cream and fold it into the coffee mixture.
7. Turn into a large dish or into individual pots and leave in the refrigerator to set. Decorate with grated chocolate and whipped cream.

NOTE: An attractive way to present this bavarois is to serve individual moulds on a plate flooded with crème anglaise (see page 418) and decorated with tiny chocolate shapes (see page 633).

FORTIFIED SWEET WHITE

Three Chocolate Bavarois

375ml/13 fl oz milk
8 egg yolks, beaten
45g/1½oz caster sugar
140g/5oz white chocolate, grated
140g/5oz milk chocolate, grated
140g/5oz dark chocolate, grated
20g/¾oz powdered gelatine, soaked in 90ml/6 tablespoons cold water
720ml/1¼ pints double cream, lightly whipped

To serve:
290ml/½ pint crème anglaise, flavoured with grated orange rind and/or 15ml/1 tablespoon Grand Marnier (see page 418)

1. Line a 900g/2lb loaf tin with a piece of greaseproof paper cut to fit the bottom of the tin. Lightly oil the tin.
2. Bring the milk to the boil in a saucepan. Beat the eggs and sugar together with a wooden spoon and pour over the milk. Return the mixture to the saucepan and heat gently, stirring constantly with a wooden spoon until the mixture thickens slightly and coats the back of the spoon.
3. Place each variety of chocolate in a separate bowl and divide the custard equally between them, pouring through a sieve to remove any egg threads. Stir well to melt the chocolate.
4. Melt the gelatine gently over a low heat. When clear and warm, add half the gelatine to the white chocolate custard. Stir gently and when the mixture is on the point of setting, fold in one-third of the lightly whipped cream. Pour into the base of the loaf tin. Refrigerate until set.
5. Once the white chocolate bavarois has set, reheat the remaining gelatine and add half of it to the milk chocolate custard. When it is on the point of setting, fold in another third of the lightly whipped cream. Pour over the set white chocolate bavarois, very carefully. Refrigerate until set.
6. Once the milk chocolate bavarios has set, reheat the last of the gelatine and add it to the plain chocolate custard. When it is on the point of setting fold in the remaining cream. Pour very carefully over the set milk chocolate bavarois and refrigerate until set.
7. To serve: turn the bavarois out carefully, using a knife to loosen it, or dip the tin very quickly in boiling water. Remove the greaseproof paper from the top. Slice the bavarois with a hot knife and serve with the flavoured crème anglaise.

FORTIFIED SWEET WHITE

Striped Chocolate and Grand Marnier Bavarois

This recipe has been adapted from *The Roux Brothers on Pâtisserie.*

SERVES 8
1 x 3 egg quantity sponge fingers mixture (see page 577)

1 x 3 egg quantity sponge fingers mixture made with 30g/1oz sifted cocoa powder instead of arrowroot
55ml/2 fl oz sugar syrup (see page 419)
30ml/1 fl oz Grand Marnier
30g/1oz plain chocolate, grated

For the Grand Marnier bavarois:
150ml/1/4 pint milk
45g/1 1/2oz sugar
2 egg yolks
4g/1/8oz gelatine (5ml/1 teaspoon)
30ml/1fl oz Grand Marnier
150ml/5fl oz double cream, lightly whipped

For the chocolate bavarois:
55g/2oz plain chocolate
150ml/1/4 pint milk
55g/2oz sugar
2 egg yolks
15g/1/2oz flour
4g/1/8oz gelatine (5ml/1 teaspoon)
150ml/1/4 pint double cream, lightly whipped

1. Preheat the oven to 200°C/400°F/gas mark 6.
2. Using 2 separate piping bags fitted with 5mm/1/4 inch plain nozzles, pipe out the plain and chocolate sponge mixtures alternately in diagonal lines on a baking sheet lined with silicone paper.
3. Bake in the oven for 10-15 minutes.
4. Invert the sponge on to a clean tea towel. Carefully peel off the paper and turn the sponge on to a cooling rack.
5. When the sponge is cool trim the edges with a serrated knife. Cut 2 bands the depth of a 20cm/8 inch spring clip tin (i. e. 7.5cm/3 inches). From the remaining sponge, cut out a circle slightly smaller than the diameter of the tin.
6. Line the sides of the tin with the bands of sponge, and place the circle of sponge in the bottom of the tin.
7. Mix the sugar syrup with the Grand Marnier and brush the sponge with the mixture.

THE GRAND MARNIER BAVAROIS:
8. Heat the milk with the sugar and when dissolved bring slowly to the boil.
9. Beat the yolks in a bowl. Pour the milk on to the egg yolks, stirring steadily. Return to the pan.
10. Stir over a gentle heat until the mixture thickens. Do not boil. Strain and allow to cool.
11. Soak the gelatine in 30ml/2 tablespoons water.
12. Dissolve the gelatine over a gentle heat and, when clear and warm, add to the custard with the Grand Marnier.
13. Fold in the lightly whipped cream.

THE CHOCOLATE BAVAROIS:
14. Soak the gelatine in 30ml/2 tablespoons water.
15. Cut the chocolate in small, even-sized pieces. Heat the milk with half the sugar and the chocolate.
16. Cream the egg yolks and remaining sugar and stir in the flour.
17. Pour the milk on to the egg-yolk mixture, stirring well. Return the custard to the pan and bring up to the boil, stirring all the time. Simmer for 2 minutes. Allow to cool.
18. Dissolve the gelatine over a gentle heat and, when clear and warm, add to the chocolate mixture.
19. Fold in the lightly whipped cream.

TO ASSEMBLE:
20. Pour the chocolate bavarois into the prepared sponge case. Ladle over the Grand Marnier bavarois to make an irregular marbled effect. (If necessary stir both mixtures together quickly.)
21. Allow to set for 4 hours in the refrigerator.
22. To serve, unclip the tin and remove the sides. Trim off any excess sponge with a pair of scissors. Scatter grated chocolate around the edges of the pudding.

NOTE: If possible use couverture for the plain chocolate.

FORTIFIED SWEET WHITE

Coeurs à la Crème

These are best started 4 days in advance.

SERVES 4
225g/8oz cottage cheese, drained
55g/2oz icing sugar
290ml/1/2 pint double cream
2 egg whites
290ml/ 1/2pint single cream

1. On the first day: push the cheese through a sieve. Stir the sugar and double cream into it and mix thoroughly.
2. Whisk the egg whites until stiff. Fold into the cheese mixture.
3. Line a small sieve with a clean piece of muslin and place over a bowl. Turn the cheese mixture into the muslin and leave to drain in a cool place for 3-4 days.
4. To serve, turn out the cheese on to an attractive serving dish. Pour over the single cream and serve with fresh summer fruits.

NOTE I: Classically, coeurs à la crème are made in small heart-shaped moulds (hence the name). If you do not have heart-shaped moulds, individual sweet cheeses can be made by securing muslin with rubber bands over small ramekin dishes filled with the cheese mixture, and then inverting the ramekins on to a wire rack to drain.
NOTE II: For a less rich cream, substitute soured cream or yoghurt for the single cream.

Iced Sabayon

SERVES 4
4 egg yolks
60ml/4 tablespoons caster sugar
150ml/1/4 pint white wine
30ml/2 tablespoons Marsala
150ml/1/4 pint double cream, whipped

1. Put the egg yolks, sugar and wine into a bowl. Set over a saucepan of simmering water. Whisk for 15-20 minutes until thick and creamy. Remove from the heat and continue to whisk until cool. Add the Marsala and fold in the cream.
2. Serve well chilled.

NOTE: Sabayon can only 'sit' for about an hour before splitting.

FORTIFIED SWEET WHITE

Zabaglione

SERVES 4
4 egg yolks
85g/3oz caster sugar
120ml/8 tablespoons Marsala

1. Put the egg yolks and sugar into a bowl over a pan of simmering water and whisk until frothy and pale.
2. Gradually whisk in the Marsala until the mixture is very thick. Take care that the bowl does not touch the simmering water. If it does, the eggs will scramble.
3. Pour into individual glasses and serve at once.

FORTIFIED SWEET WHITE

Jellies

These are fruit juices or syrups set with gelatine. Some are clarified in a similar manner to aspic and clear soups.

You will need:
1. Jelly bag, usually made of flannel, or a large double muslin cloth.
2. Balloon whisk.
3. Large saucepan.

POINTS TO REMEMBER:
1. All equipment must be spotlessly clean and grease-free. Scalding in boiling water will ensure this.
2. Weigh all ingredients carefully.
3. Follow the whisking and clearing methods very carefully. Short cuts will only lead to murky jelly.
4. When turning out jellies, it is a good idea to wet the serving plate. If the unmoulded jelly is not dead centre, you can then slide it gently to the correct position. If the plate is dry, the jelly will cling to it and be difficult to budge.
5. Recipes often say to wet a jelly mould – if using a china mould, it may be necessary to grease it with a flavourless oil to ensure that it turns out.

Orange Jelly and Caramel Chips

SERVES 4

For the orange jelly:
45ml/3 tablespoons water
20g/¾oz gelatine
570ml/1 pint orange juice
290ml/ ½ pint double cream, whipped lightly

For the caramel:
55g/2oz granulated sugar

1. Start with the jelly: put the water in a small saucepan. Sprinkle on the gelatine and allow to stand for 10 minutes. Dissolve over a very gentle heat without allowing the gelatine to boil. Do not stir.
2. When the gelatine is clear and liquid, mix with the orange juice and pour into a wet plain jelly mould or pudding basin.
3. Chill in the refrigerator for 2-4 hours, or until set.
4. Meanwhile, start the caramel: put the sugar in a heavy pan and set over a gentle heat.
5. Lightly oil a baking sheet.
6. When the sugar has dissolved, boil rapidly to a golden caramel. Immediately pour on to the baking sheet. Leave to harden and cool completely.
7. Break up the caramel into chips.
8. Loosen the jelly round the edges with a finger. Invert a serving plate over the jelly mould, turn the mould and plate over together, give a sharp shake and remove the mould. If the jelly won't budge, dip the outside of the mould briefly into hot water to loosen it.
9. Spread over the cream to completely mask the jelly.
10. Just before serving, scatter the caramel over the jelly (do not do this in advance as the caramel softens quickly).

Clear Lemon Jelly

SERVES 6
860ml/1½ pints water
225g/8oz sugar
rind of 4 lemons, thinly pared
290ml/½ pint lemon juice
4 small sticks cinnamon
120ml/8 tablespoons sherry
55g/2oz gelatine
green colouring (optional)
whites and crushed shells of 3 eggs

1. Make the lemon jelly: put all the ingredients except the gelatine, egg whites, egg shells and green colouring into a very clean pan. Sprinkle on the gelatine and place over a medium heat. Stir until the gelatine and sugar have dissolved. Taste, adding more sugar if necessary, and cool. Remove the cinnamon stick.
2. Put the crushed shells and the egg whites into the jelly. Place over a moderate heat and whisk steadily with a balloon whisk until the mixture begins to boil. Stop whisking immediately and draw the pan off the heat. Allow the mixture to subside. Take care not to break the crust formed by the egg whites.
3. Bring just up to the boil again, and allow to subside. Repeat this once more (the egg white will trap the sediment in the liquid and clear the jelly). Allow to cool for 2 minutes.
4. Fix a double layer of fine muslin over a clean basin and carefully strain the jelly through it, taking care to hold the egg-white crust back. Keep back as much of the lemon rind as you can as it tends to clog up the sieve. Do not try to hurry the process by squeezing the cloth, or murky jelly will result. If the jelly begins to set before it is completely strained, warm it up again to melt it just enough to filter through the muslin.
5. Colour it delicately with the green colouring, if required.
6. Pour into a wet jelly mould. Leave refrigerated until set (at least 4 hours, but preferably overnight).
7. Turn out the jelly: loosen the top edge all around with a finger. Dip the mould briefly into hot water. Place a dish over the mould and invert the 2 together. Give a good sharp shake and remove the mould.

Black Jelly with Port

SERVES 4
450g/1lb blackcurrants
225g/8oz sugar
190ml/ 1/3 pint ruby port
20g/3/4oz gelatine
whipped cream or English egg custard (see page 418)

1. Put the currants and sugar into a saucepan and heat slowly. Push through a sieve.
2. Add the port to the purée and enough water to bring the liquid up to 570ml/1 pint.
3. Put 45ml/3 tablespoons water in a small saucepan and sprinkle the gelatine over it. Allow to soak for 10 minutes. Heat very gently until the gelatine is clear and liquid, but do not boil. Pour into the blackcurrant mixture and mix well. Pour into a wet jelly mould or dish. Refrigerate until set.
4. To turn out, briefly dip the mould into hot water – just enough to loosen it without melting the jelly. Put the serving dish over the mould and invert it so that the jelly falls on to the plate. Serve with whipped cream or English custard.

NOTE: If the serving plate is wetted, it is easier to shift the jelly to the middle should it end up slightly off-centre.

Black Coffee Jelly with Greek Yoghurt

This is a sugar-free jelly and will be a shock to people with a sweet tooth!

SERVES 4
570ml/1 pint black coffee
concentrated apple juice
30g/1oz gelatine
Greek yoghurt

1. Make up the black coffee using freshly ground coffee beans and, while still warm, sweeten to taste with the concentrated apple juice. Leave to cool.
2. Put 45ml/3 tablespoons of the cool coffee into a small saucepan, sprinkle on the gelatine and set aside to 'sponge' for 5 minutes.
3. Dissolve the gelatine over a gentle heat. When warm, pour into the coffee and spoon into suitable small moulds. Refrigerate until set. This will take about 1 hour.
4. Turn the moulds out on to individual plates and place a good dollop of Greek yoghurt on to each plate.

Claret Jelly (I)

SERVES 4
570ml/1 pint claret or other red wine
570ml/1 pint water
rind of 2 lemons
170g/6oz granulated sugar
2 small cinnamon sticks
2 bay leaves
30ml/2 tablespoons redcurrant jelly
45g/1 1/2oz gelatine
2 egg whites and the egg shells
drop of cochineal or carmine colouring (optional)

1. First make the jelly: put all the ingredients except the gelatine, egg whites, shells and red colouring into a very clean pan, sprinkle on the gelatine and place over a medium heat. Stir until the gelatine and sugar have dissolved. Taste, adding more sugar if necessary, and cool. Remove the bay leaves, cinnamon sticks and lemon rind.
2. Put the crushed shells and the egg whites into the jelly. Place over a moderate heat and whisk steadily with a balloon whisk until the mixture begins to boil. Stop whisking immediately and draw the pan off the heat. Allow the mixture to subside. Take care not to break the crust formed by the egg whites.
3. Bring just up to the boil again, and again allow to subside. Repeat this once more (the egg whites will trap the sediment in the liquid and clear the jelly). Allow to cool for 2 minutes.
4. Fix a double layer of fine muslin over a clean basin and carefully strain the jelly through it, taking care to hold the egg-white crust back. Do not try to hurry the process by squeezing the cloth, or murky jelly will result.
5. Add a drop of red colouring if necessary. Pour into a wet jelly mould, and leave refrigerated until set.
6. Invert a wet plate over the mould and turn the 2 over together. Give a sharp shake and remove the mould.

Claret Jelly (II)

This is a sugar-free jelly. It will taste quite sour, so if you have a sweet tooth, a little concentrated apple juice can be added.

SERVES 4
290ml/½ pint claret
1 small cinnamon stick
pared rind of 1 orange
3 cloves
1 bay leaf
120ml/8 tablespoons orange juice
15g/½oz or 1 envelope gelatine

1. Put the wine, cinnamon, orange rind, cloves and bay leaf into a saucepan. Place it over a low heat and leave the contents to infuse for 30 minutes. Once the pan is reasonably warm, turn off the heat and just let the wine stand.
2. Meanwhile, pour the orange juice into a small, heavy pan and sprinkle on the gelatine. Leave it to become spongy.
3. Strain the infused wine into a bowl. Melt the gelatine over a gentle heat; when it is warm and runny, add it to the wine. Stir it well and pour the mixture into a wet 570ml/1 pint jelly mould.
4. Refrigerate the jelly until it sets, 2-3 hours.
5. To serve, dip the mould briefly in hot water for just long enough to loosen the jelly without melting it. Put a damp serving dish over the mould and invert it so that the jelly falls out on to the plate. Edge it into the centre if necessary; wetting the serving dish makes it possible to move the jelly more easily.

NOTE: An alternative way to serve the pudding is to pour the jelly into the base of a plate and, when it is set, cover with a beautiful arrangement of prepared fresh fruit.

Banana and Grape Chartreuse

SERVES 6
clear lemon jelly (see page 441)
110g/4oz white grapes
1 banana

1. Prepare the lemon jelly.
2. Rinse a ring mould out with water. Pour a layer of lemon jelly in the bottom of the mould, about 1cm/½inch deep. Put into a cold place to set.
3. If using seedless grapes just wash them. If not, cut in half and take out the seeds. (If the skins are tough or spotted, the grapes should be peeled: dip them into boiling water for a few seconds to make this easier.)
4. Arrange the grapes and slices of banana in the ring mould. Pour in enough cool but not quite set jelly to come halfway up the grapes and leave in the refrigerator to set. Pour in the rest of the cool jelly so that the fruit is just covered and leave to set. Continue to layer the grapes and banana in this way until the mould is full.
5. To turn out the jelly, dip the outside of the mould briefly in hot water. Invert a wet plate over the jelly mould and turn the 2 over together. Give a sharp shake and remove the mould.

LIGHT SWEET WHITE

Ballymaloe's Jelly of Fresh Raspberries with a Mint Cream

Sally Procter of Leith's spent a happy few days at Ballymaloe cookery school run by Dorina Allen in Ireland and came back with several excellent recipes. This is a particularly delicious pudding for the summer.

560g/1¼lb fresh raspberries
225g/8oz sugar
290ml/½ pint water
4 sprigs fresh mint
10ml/1 dessertspoon Framboise liqueur
15ml/1 tablespoon lemon juice
15ml/1 tablespoon gelatine

For the mint cream:
15 fresh mint leaves
15ml/1 tablespoon lemon juice
190ml/⅓ pint cream

To garnish:
mint leaves

1. Pick over the raspberries and reserve about 110g/4oz of the best ones for decoration.
2. Put the sugar, water and mint leaves into a small heavy pan. Bring slowly to the boil. Simmer for a few minutes. Cool. Add the Frambroise and lemon juice.
3. Put 45ml/3 tablespoons water into a small saucepan. Sprinkle on the gelatine and leave to sponge.
4. Oil 6 ramekin dishes very lightly.
5. Strain the flavoured syrup into a bowl. Dissolve the gelatine over a gentle heat and when clear and warm add it to the strained syrup. Add the raspberries.
6. Pour three-quarters of the jelly into the ramekin dishes, making sure that all the raspberries are used up. Refrigerate until beginning to solidify and then spoon over the remaining jelly. This is to ensure that the jellies have flat bottoms when turned out.
7. Meanwhile, make the mint cream: crush the mint leaves in a pestle and mortar with the lemon juice. Add the cream and stir. The lemon juice will thicken the cream. If the cream becomes too thick, add a little water.
8. Divide the mint cream between 6 plates and spread it over the surface of each. Turn out a raspberry jelly on top of the cream in the centre of the plate. Decorate with the reserved raspberries and extra mint leaves.

LIGHT SWEET WHITE

Meringues

Flaming Baked Alaska

1 large sponge cake
150ml/¼ pint sugar syrup
choice of 340g/12oz fresh fruits (peaches, strawberries, etc.)
570ml/1 pint vanilla, chocolate or strawberry ice cream
4 egg whites
pinch of salt
225g/8oz caster sugar
45ml/3 tablespoons brandy

1. Put the sponge cake on a plate and sprinkle with a little of the sugar syrup.
2. Arrange the fruit on top of the cake and cover with ice cream. Place in the freezer.
3. Set the oven to 230°C/450°F/gas mark 8.
4. Meanwhile, make the meringue: whisk the egg whites, with a pinch of salt, to a stiff snow. Whisk in 45ml/3 tablespoons sugar and continue to whisk until the mixture is stiff and shiny. Fold in the remaining sugar with a metal spoon.
5. Place the meringue in a piping bag with a star nozzle and pipe it over the cake and ice cream.
6. Place the pudding in the oven until it has turned golden brown.
7. Meanwhile, heat the brandy and when the meringue is browned, light the brandy and pour it flaming over the meringue. Serve immediately.

RICH SWEET WHITE

Italian Meringue

This meringue is much more laborious to make than Swiss meringue, but it has the advantage that once mixed it is extremely stable. Provided it is covered with polythene or a damp cloth to prevent drying out, the cook can leave it for hours before using it without risk of disintegration and, as it hardly swells at all in the oven, it is ideal for piped meringue baskets, vacherins, etc. It cooks rather faster than Swiss meringue (see page 449), is chalkier and more powdery, and stays a brilliant white. Although it is not as nice to eat as Swiss meringue, it is useful if catering for large numbers, and delicious if filled with strawberries and cream.

225g/8oz lump sugar
90ml/6 tablespoons water
4 egg whites

1. Put the sugar and water in a heavy saucepan.
2. Without stirring, bring it slowly to the boil. If any sugar crystals get stuck to the side of the pan, brush them down into the syrup with a clean wet brush. Use a sugar thermometer if available.
3. The syrup is ready when it reaches 116°C/240°F. Alternatively, test for the 'soft ball' stage (see note).
4. While the syrup is gently boiling to the correct stage, whisk the egg whites to stiff peaks.
5. If the whites are in an electric mixer, pour the bubbling hot syrup on to them in a steady stream while whisking, taking care not to pour the syrup on to the wires of the whisk – it cools fast against the cold metal and can harden and stick to the whisk. If whisking the whites by hand, and in the absence of anyone to pour as you whisk, pour the syrup on to the whites in stages, about one-third at a time, whisking hard between each addition and working as fast as possible. The syrup must be bubbling hot as it hits the egg white to partially cook it.
6. Once the syrup is all in, whisk hard until the mixture is stiff and shiny and absolutely stable. If the whisk is lifted, the meringue should not flow at all.
7. Keep covered with polythene or a damp cloth if not using at once.

NOTE: To test the syrup, drop a teaspoonful into a cup of cold water. If the syrup has reached the right temperature, it will set into a soft ball which can be squashed between the fingers. If the syrup forms a hard ball, like a hard-boiled sweet, it has reached too high a temperature to make Italian meringue.

Galette au Chocolat Cordon Bleu

This very rich chocolate meringue pudding has come to Leith's via the imagination of the Cordon Bleu Cookery School.

SERVES 6
5 egg whites
285g/10oz caster sugar
45g/1½oz cocoa

For the filling:
400g/14oz tin black cherries
Kirsch
110g/4oz plain chocolate
75ml/2½ fl oz water
570ml/1 pint double cream

For the decoration:
icing sugar (to dust)
150ml/¼ pint double cream
chocolate caraque

For the cherry sauce:
the cherries not used in the cake
5ml/1 teaspoon arrowroot
the drained cherry juice

1. Set the oven to 140°C/275°F/gas mark 1. Line 3 x 18cm/7 inch baking sheets with bakewell paper.
2. Whisk the egg whites until stiff, add 15ml/1 tablespoon of the measured sugar and continue whisking for about 30 seconds. Sift the cocoa with the remaining sugar and quickly cut and fold into the whites. Spread or pipe the mixture into 3 x 18cm/7 inch rounds on the bakewell paper. Bake for 1-1¼ hours or until dry and crisp.
3. Drain the cherries and leave to macerate in a little Kirsch, reserving the juice.
4. Break the chocolate into small pieces, put into a pan with the water and stir continuously over a gentle heat until melted. Allow to cool slightly.
5. Start whisking the cream and, as it thickens, add the chocolate, and then continue whisking until the cream holds its shape.
6. Sandwich each meringue round with a layer of chocolate cream, topped with a quarter of the cherries. Dust the top of the galette with icing sugar, decorate with rosettes of plain cream and chocolate caraque. Serve the cherry sauce separately.
7. To make the cherry sauce, mix the arrowroot with 15ml/1 tablespoon cold water. Heat up the cherry juice in a small saucepan. Add a little of the hot cherry juice to the arrowroot. Return to the saucepan and boil, stirring continuously, for 45 seconds until slightly thickened and shiny. Add the remaining cherries. Serve hot or cold.

FORTIFIED SWEET WHITE

Almond Dacquoise with Apricot Puree

SERVES 6
5 egg whites
pinch of salt
large pinch cream of tartar
285g/10oz caster sugar
110g/4oz ground almonds
290ml/½ pint double cream

For the purée:
225g/8oz fresh apricots, halved and stoned
sugar to taste

1. Preheat the oven to 140°C/275°F/gas mark 1.
2. Line 2 baking sheets with bakewell paper and mark a 22.5cm/9 inch diameter circle on each.
3. Whisk the egg whites, with a pinch of salt and the cream of tartar, until stiff, then add 40ml/2½ tablespoons of the sugar. Whisk again until very stiff and shiny.
4. Fold in the rest of the sugar. Fold in the ground almonds.
5. Divide the mixture between the 2 baking sheets and spread the meringue to the correct size.
6. Bake for 1 hour. Cool slightly, remove from the bakewell paper and leave to become completely cold.
7. While the meringues are baking, make the apricot purée. Put the apricots into a saucepan with 30ml/2 tablespoons sugar and enough water to come halfway up the apricots. Cook slowly, stirring occasionally, until the apricots are tender.

8. Process the poached apricots with enough of the liquid to make a thick purée. Taste and add extra sugar if required. Cool.
9. Whip the cream. Sandwich the cake together with half the cream mixed with the apricot purée. Decorate the top of the dacquoise with rosettes of cream.

NOTE: When making a meringue mixture with a powerful electric mixer, add half the sugar when the whites are stiff. Whisk again until very shiny and then add the remaining sugar and whisk lightly until just incorporated.

SWEET WHITE

Meringue Cuite

'Cooked' meringue is a professional chef's meringue used largely for frosting petits fours, for fruit pie tops and as unbaked frosting for cakes. It is only worth making if an electric whisk is handy, when it is easy. It produces an even chalkier and finer-textured meringue than Italian meringue and, if used on baked confections, comes out of the oven shiny, smooth and pale-biscuit coloured.

Like Italian meringue, meringue cuite is very stable in the oven, hardly swelling at all and unlikely to cook out of shape. For this reason it is often used for intricate work such as the meringue basket on page 450. When baked at very low temperatures, it emerges smooth and shiny white.

The proportions of egg white to sugar are the same as for most meringues, but the sugar used is confectioner's (icing) sugar, rather than caster. Sometimes a 50-50 mixture of caster and icing sugar is used and occasionally, when the meringue is for a fine cake frosting that will not be baked, the sugar content can be increased above the normal 55g/2oz per small egg white to 85g/3oz.

4 egg whites
225g/8oz icing sugar
3 drops vanilla essence

1. Use a whisking bowl that will fit snugly on a saucepan of simmering water, without the bottom of the bowl being in direct contact with the water. Whisk the whites until stiff and set them over the water.
2. Add the sifted icing sugar. It flies about in sugar-dust clouds so take care. Whisk until thick and absolutely stable – there should be no movement at all when the whisk is lifted. Add the vanilla essence.
3. Keep covered with polythene or a damp cloth if not using at once.

NOTE: If the mixture is whisked in a strong machine, a good result can be achieved without beating over heat. But it takes a good 15 minutes to get a perfect 'cuite' consistency.

Noix au Café

SERVES 4-6
225g/8oz sugar
90-105ml/6-7 tablespoons water
4 egg whites
5ml/1 teaspoon coffee essence

1. Put the sugar and water into a heavy saucepan. Dissolve over a gentle heat and then cook quickly, without stirring, to 116°C/240°F. Use a sugar thermometer for this, or wait until it gets to the soft ball stage (see page 446).
2. Whisk the egg whites until stiff. Pour on the sugar syrup. Pour it steadily on to the egg whites, whisking all the time, but taking care that the syrup does not strike the whisk wires (where it would cool and set solidly). Continue whisking until all the sugar has been absorbed, and the meringue is completely cool. Beat in the coffee essence.
3. Set the oven to 140°C/275°F/gas mark 1. Line 2 baking sheets with bakewell paper (vegetable parchment). It can be held in place with a few dots of the uncooked meringue.
4. Reserve a quarter of the mixture for the filling. Place the remaining mixture in a forcing bag fitted with a medium-sized plain nozzle. Pipe walnut-sized mounds on the prepared baking sheets. Bake for 1-1½ hours or until dry and crisp, when they will lift easily off the paper.
5. When completely cool, sandwich them together with the reserved coffee meringue mixture.

Strawberry Meringue Basket

This is a classic meringue cuite recipe. In order to make this 18cm/7 inch diameter basket, you will need to make the meringue in 2 batches – it is too great a quantity to be managed at once.

SERVES 8

For the meringue cuite:
8 egg whites
450g/1lb icing sugar
6 drops vanilla flavouring

For the filling:
450g/1lb fresh strawberries, hulled
425ml/3/4 pint double cream, whipped

1. Set the oven to 140°C/275°F/gas mark 1. Line 2 large baking sheets with silicone 'bakewell' paper. Draw 2 18cm/7 inch diameter circles on each piece of paper and turn over.
2. Make up the first batch of meringue cuite. Put half the egg whites with half the sifted sugar into a mixing bowl and set over, not in, a pan of simmering water. Whisk, with a large hand balloon whisk or electric hand whisk, until the meringue is thick and will hold its shape. This may well take up to 10 minutes of vigorous beating. (A very good imitation meringue cuite can be made by whisking the egg whites and sugar together in a powerful mixer without bothering to heat the meringue. However, hand whisks tend to overheat in the time it takes to achieve the correct solidity of meringue if not beaten over heat.)
3. Add half of the vanilla flavouring. Remove the bowl and whisk for a further 2 minutes.
4. Remove the meringue from the heat and put into a forcing bag fitted with a 1cm/1/2 inch plain nozzle. Squeeze gently to get rid of any pockets of air. Hold the bag upright in your right hand and, using your left hand to guide the nozzle, pipe a circular base on the first baking sheet, on one of your pencilled circles. Pipe 3 18cm/7 inch empty rings on the 3 remaining pencilled circles.
5. Bake for 45-60 minutes until dry and crisp. Cool on a wire rack.
6. Make up the second batch of meringue cuite using the remaining ingredients. Return the round of cooked meringue to the baking sheet. Use a little uncooked mixture to fix the hoops on the round, one on top of the other.
7. Put the remaining mixture into a forcing bag fitted with a rose nozzle. Cover the hoops with the meringue.
8. Bake at the same temperature for 45-60 minutes until set and crisp. Cool.
9. Fill with the lightly whipped cream and strawberries just before serving.

LIGHT SWEET WHITE

Meringues (Swiss Meringues)

This quantity makes 50 miniature or 12 large meringues.

4 egg whites
pinch of salt
225g/8oz caster sugar

For the filling:
whipped cream

1. Set the oven to 110°C/225°F/gas mark 1/2.
2. Place silicone paper on 2 baking sheets.
3. Whisk the egg whites with a pinch of salt until stiff but not dry.
4. Add 30ml/2 tablespoons of the sugar and whisk again until very stiff and shiny.
5. Fold in the rest of the sugar.
6. Drop the meringue mixture on to the paper-covered baking sheets in spoonfuls set fairly far apart. Use a teaspoon for tiny meringues; a dessertspoon for larger ones.
7. Bake in the oven for about 2 hours until the meringues are dry right through and will lift easily off the paper.
8. When cold, sandwich the meringues together in pairs with whipped cream.

NOTE : If making a meringue mixture with a powerful electric mixer, when the whites are stiff gradually add half the sugar. Whisk again until very shiny, then add the remaining sugar and whisk lightly until just incorporated.

Walnut and Lemon Meringue Cake

SERVES 6
4 egg whites
pinch of salt
225g/8oz caster sugar
140g/5oz walnuts
290ml/½ pint double cream
60ml/4 tablespoons lemon curd (see page 604)

1. Set the oven to 190°C/375°F/gas mark 5.
2. Line 2 20cm/8 inch cake tins with lightly oiled tin foil or simply line the base with silicone paper and oil the sides of the tin.
3. Whisk the egg whites with a pinch of salt until stiff, then add 30ml/2 tablespoons of the sugar. Whisk again until very stiff and shiny.
4. Fold in the rest of the sugar.
5. Chop the nuts roughly, reserving a handful, and stir into the mixture.
6. Divide the mixture between the 2 tins, smoothing the tops slightly.
7. Bake the cakes for 40 minutes. Turn them out on a wire rack and peel off the paper.
8. Whip the cream and mix half of it with the lemon curd. Sandwich the cakes with this.
9. Use the rest of the whipped cream and nuts for the top.

NOTE: When making a meringue mixture with a powerful electric mixer, when the whites are stiff add half the sugar gradually. Whisk again until very shiny and then add the remaining sugar and whisk lightly until just incorporated.

SWEET WHITE

Pavlova

SERVES 4-6
4 egg whites
pinch of salt
225g/8oz caster sugar
5ml/1 teaspoon cornflour
5ml/1 teaspoon vanilla essence
5ml/1 teaspoon white wine vinegar or lemon juice
290ml/½ pint double cream, lightly whipped
30g/1oz roughly chopped walnuts
450g/1lb fresh pineapple, cored and cut into cubes

1. Set the oven to 140°C/275°F/gas mark 1.
2. Put a sheet of silicone paper on a baking sheet.
3. Whisk the egg whites with a pinch of salt until stiff. Gradually add the sugar, beating until you can stand a spoon in the mixture.
4. Add the cornflour, vanilla and vinegar or lemon juice.
5. Pile the mixture on to the prepared baking sheet, shaping to a flat oval or a circle 3cm/1½ inches thick. Bake for about 1 hour. The meringue is cooked when the outer shell is pale biscuit coloured and hard to the touch. Remove carefully and gently peel off the paper.
6. When quite cold, spoon on the whipped cream and sprinkle on the fruit and nuts.

NOTE: Any fruits in season can be substituted for nuts and pineapple.

SWEET WHITE

Meringue Baskets

MAKES 6
2 egg whites
pinch of salt
110g/4oz caster sugar

For the filling:
double cream, lightly whipped
strawberries or raspberries

1. Place the silicone paper on 2 baking sheets. Set the oven to 100°C/200°F/gas mark ½.
2. Whisk the egg whites with a pinch of salt to a stiff snow. Whisk in 30ml/2 tablespoons of the

sugar and continue to whisk until the mixture is stiff and shiny. Fold in the remaining sugar with a metal spoon.

3. Put the mixture into a forcing bag fitted with a rose pipe, and pipe on to the silicone paper to form little baskets.

4. Leave to dry in the oven for 2 hours. Take out and allow to cool.

5. Place a little cream in each basket and fill with strawberries or raspberries.

NOTE I: Meringue baskets are often made with meringue cuite (see page 448), which is very solid and does not rise out of shape in the oven.

NOTE II: An electric mixer gives a similar result to meringue cuite, but the hand-made uncooked kind tastes better, even if it looks less professional. If making a meringue mixture in an electric machine, gradually add half the sugar when the whites are stiff, whisk again until very stiff, then whisk in the remaining sugar until just incorporated.

Banana and Grape Vacherin

SERVES 6

4 egg whites
pinch of salt
225g/8oz caster sugar
1 banana
lemon juice
85g/3oz black grapes
85g/3oz green grapes
290ml/ ½ pint double cream, lightly whipped

1. Set the oven to 100°C/200°F/gas mark ½. Cover 2 baking sheets with silicone paper.

2. Whisk the egg whites with the salt until stiff but not dry, then add 30ml/2 tablespoons of the sugar. Whisk again until very stiff and shiny. Fold in the remaining sugar.

3. Fill a forcing bag fitted with a medium-sized plain nozzle with the meringue. Pipe into 2 rounds the size of a dessert plate.

4. Place in the oven to dry out slowly for 2-3 hours. The meringue is ready when light and dry, and the paper will peel off the underside easily.

5. Cut the banana into chunks and toss in the lemon juice. Halve and deseed the grapes.

6. Spread three-quarters of the cream on one of the meringue cases and scatter over the banana and all but 4 each of the black and green grapes. Place the second meringue on top of this. Using the rest of the cream, pipe rosettes around the top. Decorate each alternate rosette with a grape half.

NOTE: If making a meringue mixture with a powerful electric mixer, gradually add half the sugar when the whites are stiff. Whisk again until very shiny and then add the remaining sugar and whisk lightly until just incorporated.

SWEET WHITE

Hazelnut Meringue Cake with Raspberry Sauce

SERVES 6

110g/4oz hazelnuts
4 egg whites
pinch of salt
225g/8oz caster sugar
drop of vanilla essence
2.5ml/½ teaspoon white vinegar
225g/8oz raspberries
icing sugar
squeeze of lemon juice
290ml/½ pint double cream

1. Set the oven to 190°C/375°F/gas mark 5. Line 2 20cm/8 inch cake tins with lightly oiled tin foil.

2. Place the hazelnuts on a baking sheet and bake until dark brown. Remove the skin by rubbing the nuts in a tea towel. Leave to get completely cold. Set aside 5 nuts and grind the rest. Do not over-grind or they will become greasy and make the meringue heavy. Weigh the nuts. You will need 100g/3½oz for the meringue.

3. Whisk the egg whites with a pinch of salt until stiff and then gradually beat in the caster sugar a tablespoon at a time, the vanilla and

vinegar, beating until very stiff. Fold in the nuts very gently with a large metal spoon. Pile the mixture into the prepared tins, spreading evenly with a spatula.
4. Bake for 40 minutes. Allow to cool in the tin. Lift out the meringues in the tin foil and then peel away all the foil.
5. While the meringue is cooling, liquidize the raspberries with icing sugar and lemon juice. Push through a sieve and taste for sweetness. If very thick, add a little water.
6. To decorate, whip the cream and sandwich the meringue together with two-thirds of it. Dust the top with icing sugar. Pipe 5 large rosettes of cream round the edge of the top of the meringue and decorate each with a reserved hazelnut. Serve the raspberry sauce separately.

RICH SWEET WHITE

Meringue Mont Blanc

SERVES 6
For the meringue:
3 egg whites
pinch of salt
170g/6oz caster sugar
icing sugar

For the filling:
440g/15oz tin sweetened chestnut purée
150ml/¼ pint double cream, lightly whipped

For decoration:
chocolate caraque or coarsely grated chocolate

1. Set the oven to 100°C/200°F/gas mark ½. Cover a baking sheet with a piece of silicone paper.
2. Whisk the egg whites with a pinch of salt until stiff but not dry, add 22.5ml/1½ tablespoons of the sugar and whisk again until very stiff and shiny. Fold in the remaining sugar.
3. Pile the meringue into a forcing bag with a 1cm/½ inch plain nozzle. Pipe the mixture into an 18cm/7 inch circle on the prepared baking sheet, starting from the centre and spiralling outwards. Pipe a rim 3cm/1½ inches deep. Dust lightly with icing sugar.
4. Bake in the oven for at least 2 hours until the meringue is dry and crisp. When cooked, remove carefully and allow the meringue to cool.
5. Beat the tinned chestnut purée until soft. Pile into the meringue case, cover with the lightly whipped cream and arrange the chocolate caraque on top.

NOTE: If making a meringue mixture with a powerful electric mixer, gradually add half the sugar when the whites are stiff. Whisk again until very shiny and then add the remaining sugar and whisk lightly until just incorporated.

SWEET SPARKLING WHITE

Floating Islands

MAKES 12 ISLANDS
For the custard:
240ml/8 fl oz milk
290ml/½ pint cream
10ml/2 teaspoons caster sugar
vanilla pod or 3 drops vanilla essence
10ml/2 level teaspoons cornflour
4 egg yolks

For the meringue:
3 egg whites
salt
170g/6oz caster sugar

To serve:
grated chocolate

1. Place the milk, the cream and the sugar in a saucepan with the vanilla. Bring gently to the boil, remove from the heat and leave to infuse for 30 minutes. Remove the vanilla pod.
2. Mix the cornflour with a little water. Stir a little of the hot milk mixture into it and then pour it back into the milk. Place over a gentle heat and bring slowly to the boil, stirring continuously. Simmer for 4 minutes to cook the cornflour.
3. Beat the egg yolks and then pour the cream mixture on to the yolks in a thin stream, beating well all the time. The custard will probably thicken at once to a consistency that will coat

the back of a wooden spoon. If it does not, return to the saucepan and stir steadily over very gentle heat until it does so. Take care not to boil or it will curdle. Pour into a shallow wide serving dish, and cover with plastic film to prevent a skin forming.
4. Meanwhile, make the islands: half fill a deep frying pan with water and set over the heat.
5. Whisk the whites with a pinch of salt until stiff by not dry. Whisk in the caster sugar very gradually until you have a smooth shiny meringue mixture.
6. The water mixture should now be simmering. Put 3 or 4 tablespoons of meringue mixture into the frying pan and cook gently for only 30 seconds on each side, by which time they will have almost doubled in size. (Do not add more than 3 or 4 islands at a time and do not overcook.) Lift out with a perforated spoon and leave on a wire rack or tea towel to drain completely. Lay the islands carefully on the 'lake' of custard.
7. Sprinkle the islands with the chocolate.

SWEET WHITE

Floating Islands with Caramel

floating islands (see page 452)
85g/3oz sugar

1. Place the sugar in a heavy pan and set over a gentle heat until it has dissolved and cooked to a golden brown.
2. Remove from the heat, and immediately trickle over the islands already in the custard.

RICH SWEET WHITE

Floating Islands with Coffee Custard

floating islands (see page 452)
5ml/1 teaspoon instant coffee
10ml/2 teaspoons boiling water

1. Proceed as for floating islands but dissolve the coffee in boiling water and add it to the custard sauce just before removing it from the heat.

RICH SWEET WHITE

Floating Islands with Orange

floating islands (page 452, omitting the vanilla)
rind of 1 orange
1 tablespoon Grand Marnier

1. Proceed as for floating islands, but infuse the rind in the cream and milk mixture in place of the vanilla pod.
2. Add the Grand Marnier to the custard before pouring into the serving dish.

SWEET WHITE

Baked and Steamed Puddings

Apple Charlotte

SERVES 4
1kg/2lb apples
85g/3oz sugar
30ml/2 tablespoons apricot jam
15g/½oz butter
8 slices stale, medium-sliced crustless bread
110g/4oz melted butter

For the apricot glaze:
45ml/3 tablespoons apricot jam
60ml/4 tablespoons water

1. Core and slice the apples and put them into a heavy pan. Add the sugar and cook, without water, until very soft. Boil away any extra liquid and push through a sieve. Whisk in the apricot jam.
2. Butter a charlotte mould or deep cake tin.
3. With a pastry cutter stamp one piece of bread into a circle to fit the bottom of your mould or tin and cut it into six equal sized triangles. Cut the remaining bread into strips.
4. Set the oven to 200°C/400°F/gas mark 6.
5. Dip the pieces of bread into the melted butter. Arrange the triangles to fit the bottom of the mould and arrange strips in overlapping slices around the sides.
6. Spoon in the apple purée and fold the buttery bread back over it.
7. Bake for 40 minutes. Allow to cool for 10 minutes.
8. Meanwhile, make the apricot glaze. Put the jam and water into a small heavy pan and heat, stirring occasionally, until warm and completely melted.
9. Turn out the pudding: invert a plate over the mould and turn the mould and plate over together. Give a sharp shake and remove the mould.
10. Brush the charlotte with the apricot glaze and serve with cream or custard.

NOTE: This looks a little clumsy but tastes delicious.

SWEET WHITE

Chocolate Roulade

SERVES 6
5 eggs
140g/5oz caster sugar
225g/8oz dark sweetened chocolate, roughly chopped
75ml/3 fl oz water
5ml/1 teaspoon strong instant coffee
290ml/½ pint double cream
icing sugar

To prepare the tin:
oil, flour, caster sugar

1. Take a large roasting pan and cut a double layer of greaseproof paper slightly bigger than it. Lay this in the tin; don't worry if the edges stick up untidily round the sides. Brush the paper lightly with oil and sprinkle with flour and then caster sugar. Set the oven to 200°C/400°F/gas mark 6.
2. Separate the eggs and beat the yolks and the sugar until pale and mousse-like.
3. Put the chocolate, water and coffee into a thick-bottomed saucepan and melt over a gentle heat. Stir into the yolk mixture.
4. Whisk the whites until stiff but not dry. With a metal spoon, stir a small amount thoroughly into the chocolate mixture, to 'loosen' it. Fold the rest of the whites in gently. Spread the mixture evenly on the paper.
5. Bake for about 12 minutes until the top is slightly browned and firm to touch.
6. Slide the cake and paper out of the roasting pan on to a wire rack. Cover immediately with a damp tea towel (to prevent the cake from cracking) and leave to cool, preferably overnight.
7. Whip the cream and spread it evenly over the cake. Roll up like a Swiss roll, removing the paper as you go. Put the roll on to a serving dish and, just before serving, sift a little icing sugar over the top.

NOTE I: The cake is very moist and inclined to break apart. But it doesn't matter. Just stick it together with the cream when rolling up. The last-minute sifted icing sugar will do wonders for the appearance.
NOTE II: If this cake is used as a Yule log the tendency to crack is a positive advantage: do not cover with a tea towel when leaving

overnight. Before filling, flip the whole flat cake over on to a tea towel. Carefully peel off the backing paper, then fill with cream and roll up. The firm skin will crack very like the bark of a tree. Sprigs of holly or marzipan toadstools help to give a festive look. A dusting of icing sugar will look like snow.

FORTIFIED SWEET WHITE

Hazelnut Roulade

SERVES 4-6
3 eggs
55g/2oz caster sugar
15ml/1 tablespoon plain flour
1.25ml/1/4 teaspoon baking powder
55g/2oz browned ground hazelnuts
icing sugar
150ml/1/4 pint double cream, whipped

1. Set the oven to 180°C/350°F/gas mark 4.
2. Prepare a paper case as for a Swiss roll. It should be the size of a piece of A4 paper. Grease it lightly.
3. Separate the eggs and beat the yolks and the sugar together until pale and mousse-like.
4. Sift the flour with the baking powder and fold it into the egg-yolk mixture along with the nuts.
5. Whisk the egg whites until stiff but not dry and fold into the mixture.
6. Spread the mixture into the prepared paper case.
7. Bake for about 20 minutes until the top is slightly browned and firm to touch.
8. Remove the roulade from the oven and allow to cool, covered with a sheet of kitchen paper.
9. Sprinkle icing sugar on to a piece of greaseproof paper and turn the roulade on to it. Remove the original piece of paper.
10. Spread the whipped cream evenly over the roulade and roll it up like a Swiss roll.

NOTE: Serve the hazelnut roulade with a raspberry coulis, or add fresh fruit to the cream before rolling up the roulade.

RICH SWEET WHITE

Spiced Ginger Roll

SERVES 4
For the roll:
110g/4oz plain flour
5ml/1 teaspoon mixed spice
5ml/1 teaspoon ground ginger
70g/2 1/2oz butter
30ml/2 tablespoons black treacle
30ml/2 tablespoons golden syrup
1 egg
150ml/1/4 pint water
5ml/1 teaspoon bicarbonate of soda
caster sugar

For the filling:
450g/1lb cooking apples
30g/1oz butter
5ml/1 teaspoon ground cinnamon
55g/2oz sugar

To serve:
whipped cream

1. First make the filling: peel and core the apples. Slice them roughly.
2. Melt the butter in a saucepan and add the cinnamon, sugar and apples. Cover with a lid and cook very gently, stirring occasionally, until the apples become pulpy. Beat until smooth, adding more sugar if the apples are still tart.
3. Set the oven to 180°C/350°F/gas mark 4. Prepare a Swiss roll tin by greasing the inside, then covering the base with greaseproof paper, and greasing again. Dust with caster sugar.
4. Sift the flour, mixed spice and ginger together. Melt the butter in a pan with the treacle and syrup. Whisk the egg with the water and soda. Draw the syrup mixture off the heat and pour in the egg and water. Mix well.
5. Now pour this into the flour and whisk together for 30 seconds. Pour into the prepared tin and bake for 12-15 minutes or until firm to the touch.
6. Turn out on to a sheet of greaseproof paper dusted with caster sugar. Remove the paper now stuck to the back of the cake. Spread the cake with the apple purée, roll up like a Swiss roll and serve, preferably with whipped cream.

NOTE: The pudding is not pretty, being squashy and dark brown, but the taste is wonderful. A last-minute dusting with icing sugar will help the appearance.

RICH SWEET WHITE

Baked Cheesecake

SERVES 6
For the crust:
12 digestive biscuits, crushed
85g/3oz butter, melted

For the filling:
225g/8oz best-quality soft cream cheese
75ml/5 tablespoons double cream
1 whole egg and 1 yolk
5ml/1 teaspoon vanilla essence
sugar to taste (about 15ml/1 tablespoon)

For the topping:
70ml/2½ fl oz soured cream
5ml/1 teaspoon caster sugar

1. Set the oven to 170°C/325°F/gas mark 3.
2. Mix the crust ingredients together and line the base of a shallow pie dish or flan ring with the mixture.
3. Bake for 10 minutes or until hard to the touch.
4. Beat the cream cheese and then add the remaining filling ingredients. Beat well until smooth and pour into the crust.
5. Return to the middle of the oven and bake until the filling has set (about 20 minutes).
6. Take out and allow to cool.
7. Spread with the soured cream mixed with the sugar.

NOTE: The top can be decorated with nuts, sultanas or fresh fruit such as redcurrants or halved deseeded grapes, but is very good as it is.

LIGHT SWEET WHITE

Treacle Sponge

SERVES 4-6
30ml/2 tablespoons golden syrup
10ml/2 teaspoons fine white breadcrumbs
110g/4oz butter
110g/4oz caster sugar
grated rind of 1 lemon
2 eggs, beaten
110g/4oz self-raising flour
pinch of salt
5ml/1 teaspoon ground ginger
75ml/3 fl oz milk

To serve:
custard or cream

1. Grease a pudding basin with a knob of butter.
2. Mix together the syrup and breadcrumbs in the basin.
3. In a mixing bowl, cream the butter and, when very soft, add the sugar. Beat until light and fluffy. Add the lemon rind.
4. Gradually add the eggs, beating very well between each addition.
5. Sift and fold in the flour with the salt and ginger.
6. Add enough milk to make the mixture just loose enough to drop from a spoon.
7. Turn into the pudding basin, cover and steam for 1½ hours.
8. Turn out and serve with custard or cream.

RICH SWEET WHITE

Simpson's Treacle Roll

SERVES 4
225g/8oz self-raising flour
110g/4oz suet, shredded
225g/8oz golden syrup

1. Sift the flour with a good pinch of salt into a bowl. Stir in the shredded suet and add enough water to mix first with a knife, and then with one hand, to a soft dough.
2. Roll it on a floured surface to a large rectangle.
3. Spread the surface with the golden syrup.
4. Roll it up and fold the sides underneath.

5. Wrap it first in greased greaseproof paper and then in a cloth.
6. Place in the top half of a steamer and steam for 1 1/2 hours. Serve with whipped cream or custard.

RICH SWEET WHITE

Sussex Pond Pudding

This recipe has been taken from Jane Grigson's *English Food.*

SERVES 6
225g/8oz self-raising flour
110g/4oz chopped fresh beef suet
150ml/1/4 pint milk and water
110g/4oz slightly salted butter
110g/4oz demerara sugar
1 large lemon or 2 limes, very well washed

1. Mix the flour and suet together in a bowl. Make into a dough with milk and water. The dough should be soft, but not too soft to roll out into a large circle. Cut a quarter out of this circle, to be used later as the lid of the pudding.
2. Butter a 1.4 litre/2 1/2 pint pudding basin lavishly. Drop the three-quarter circle of pastry into it and press the cut sides together to make a perfect join. Put half the remaining butter, cut up, into the pastry, with half the sugar.
3. Prick the lemon (or limes) all over with a larding needle, so that the juices will be able to escape, then put the fruit on to the butter and sugar. Add the remaining butter, again cut in pieces, and sugar.
4. Roll out the pastry that was set aside to make the lid. Lay it on top of the filling, and press the edges together so that the pudding is sealed completely. Put a piece of foil right over the basin, with a pleat in the middle. Tie it in place with string, and make a string handle over the top so that the pudding can be lifted easily.
5. Put a large pan of water on to boil, and lower the pudding into it; the water must be boiling, and it should come halfway or a little further up the basin. Cover and leave to boil for 3-4 hours. If the water gets low, replenish it with boiling water.
6. To serve: put a deep dish over the basin after removing the foil lid, and quickly turn the whole thing upside down: it is a good idea to ease the pudding from the sides of the basin with a knife first. Serve immediately. The buttery juices will flow out of the pudding to form a 'pond'.

RICH SWEET WHITE

Christmas Pudding

MAKES 2.3kg/5lb
170g/6oz raisins
110g/4oz currants
200g/7oz sultanas
85g/3oz mixed peel, chopped
225g/8oz mixed dried apricots and figs, chopped
290ml/1/2 pint brown ale
30ml/2 tablespoons rum
grated rind and juice of 1 orange
grated rind and juice of 1 lemon
110g/4oz prunes, stoned and soaked overnight in cold tea, then drained and chopped
1 dessert apple
225g/8oz butter
340g/12oz dark brown sugar
30ml/2 tablespoons treacle
3 eggs
110g/4oz self-raising flour
15ml/1 teaspoon mixed spice
2.5ml/1/2 teaspoon cinnamon
pinch of ground nutmeg
pinch of ground ginger
pinch of salt
225g/8oz fresh white breadcrumbs
55g/2oz chopped hazelnuts, toasted

1. Soak the dried fruit overnight in a mixture of beer, rum, orange juice and lemon juice. Mix with the prunes.
2. Grate the apple, skin and all.
3. Cream the butter with the sugar. Beat until light and fluffy. Add the orange rind, lemon rind and treacle.
4. Whisk the eggs together and gradually add them to the mixture, beating well between each addition.
5. Fold in the sifted flour, spices, salt and breadcrumbs and stir in the dried fruit and soaking liquor.
6. Divide the mixture between greased pudding

basins, cover with 2 layers of greaseproof paper and one piece of foil. Tie with string and steam for 10-12 hours.

LIQUEUR MUSCAT

Sweet Soufflé Omelette

SERVES 2
2 eggs
15ml/1 tablespoon apricot jam
15ml/1 tablespoon lemon juice
30g/1oz caster sugar
15g/½oz butter
icing sugar to decorate

1. Separate the eggs.
2. Set the oven to 180°C/350°F/gas mark 4.
3. Warm the jam with the lemon juice.
4. Beat the yolks with the caster sugar until light and fluffy.
5. Whisk the egg whites until stiff but not too dry. (The mixture should form a 'medium' peak when the whisk is lifted from it, not too floppy, not too rigid.)
6. Heat a 15cm/6 inch frying pan and melt the butter in it.
7. Fold the egg whites into the yolks and when the butter is foaming, but not coloured, pour in the omelette mixture.
8. Lower the heat and cook for 1 minute until the underside has just set.
9. Place in the oven for 5 minutes or until the omelette top is just set - do not overcook.
10. Get 2 long skewers red-hot in a gas flame. Leave them there while baking the omelette.
11. Spread the warmed jam over half the omelette and fold in 2 with a spatula - you may need to cut the omelette a little in the middle.
12. Slip on to a heated flat serving dish. Sprinkle the surface with icing sugar.
13. Brand a criss-cross pattern in the sugar with the red-hot skewers. Serve immediately.

NOTE I: It is not strictly necessary to finish the cooking in the oven, but it avoids the risk of burning the bottom before the top is set.
NOTE II: The branding with the hot skewer is not essential either, but the omelette should be sprinkled with icing sugar before serving.

SWEET WHITE

Banana Fritters

SERVES 8
8 bananas
150ml/¼ pint fritter batter (see below)
oil for shallow-frying
icing sugar

1. Peel the bananas and cut in half lengthways.
2. Dip immediately into the prepared batter.
3. Heat 5mm/¼ inch of oil in a frying pan and when hot, fry the fritters for about 2 minutes on each side until golden brown. Drain well and dust with icing sugar.

RICH SWEET WHITE

Sweet Fritter Batter

125g/4oz plain flour
pinch of salt
2 eggs
15ml/1 tablespoon oil
50g/1¾oz sugar
150ml/¼ pint milk

1. Sift the flour with the salt into a bowl.
2. Make a well in the centre, exposing the bottom of the bowl.
3. Put one whole egg and one yolk into the well and mix with a wooden spoon or whisk until smooth, gradually incorporating the surrounding flour and the milk. A thick cream consistency should be reached.
4. Add the oil and sugar. Allow to rest for 30 minutes.
5. Whisk the remaining egg white and fold into the batter with a metal spoon just before using.

NOTE: This batter can be made speedily in a blender. Simply put all the ingredients, except the egg white, into the machine and whizz briefly.

Eve's Pudding

SERVES 4
butter for greasing
675g/1½lb cooking apples
150ml/¼ pint water
160g/5½oz sugar
grated rind of 1 lemon
30g/1oz butter
1 small egg, beaten
55g/2oz self-raising flour
pinch of salt
15ml/1 tablespoon milk

For the crust:
45g/1½oz butter

1. Set the oven to 200°C/400°F/gas mark 6. Butter a pie dish.
2. Peel, core and slice the apples and place them in a heavy saucepan with the water, 110g/4oz sugar and half the lemon rind. Stew gently until just soft, then tip into the pie dish.
3. Cream the butter until soft and beat in the remaining sugar. When light and fluffy, add the beaten egg by degrees and mix until completely incorporated.
4. Sift the flour with the salt and fold it into the butter and egg mixture.
5. Add the remaining lemon rind and enough milk to bring the mixture to a dropping consistency. Spread this over the apple.
6. Bake in the oven for about 25 minutes or until the sponge mixture is firm to the touch and has slightly shrunk at the edges.

SWEET WHITE

Black Cherry Clafoutis

SERVES 6
a little butter
55g/2oz plain flour
pinch of salt
55g/2oz caster sugar
3 eggs
290ml/½ pint milk
15ml/1 tablespoon oil
15ml/1 tablespoon dark rum
900g/2lb black cherries, stoned
icing sugar

1. Set the oven to 180°C/350°F/gas mark 4. Butter a shallow ovenproof dish.
2. Sift the flour and salt into a large bowl and add the sugar. Beat in the eggs, one by one, with a wire whisk.
3. Add the milk slowly, continuing to beat the mixture in order to obtain a smooth batter. Add the oil and rum.
4. Put the black cherries into the ovenproof dish and pour in the batter covering the fruit.
5. Bake for 40-45 minutes and then lower the heat to 150°C/300°F/gas mark 2 for a further 30-40 minutes, until it looks golden brown.
6. To test whether the clafoutis is cooked, insert a sharp knife or skewer into the middle and it should come out clean.
7. Serve warm sprinkled with icing sugar.

NOTE: This pudding can be made with blackberries or any soft berry fruits instead of cherries.

SWEET WHITE

Steamed Valencia Pudding

SERVES 4
15g/½oz butter for greasing the basin
handful of large stoned raisins
110g/4oz butter
grated rind of 1 lemon
110g/4oz caster sugar
2 eggs
110g/4oz self-raising flour
about 75ml/3 fl oz milk

To serve:
English egg custard (see page 418)

1. Grease a pudding basin. Line the sides of the basin with split raisins (split side against the basin), arranging them in a pattern if you like.
2. Cream the butter and when very soft add the lemon rind and the sugar. Beat until light, pale

and fluffy.
3. Gradually add the eggs, beating well between each addition.
4. Fold in the flour, sifted with salt, and add enough milk to make the mixture just loose enough to drop from a spoon. Turn into the pudding basin.
5. Cover with a pleated piece of double greaseproof paper or foil and tie down. (The paper is pleated to allow for expansion.)
6. Steam for 2 hours. Turn out and serve the custard separately.

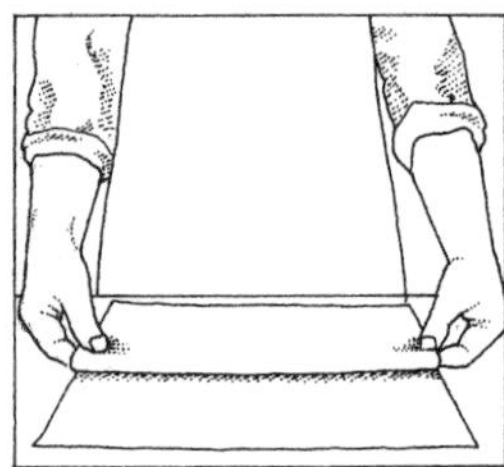
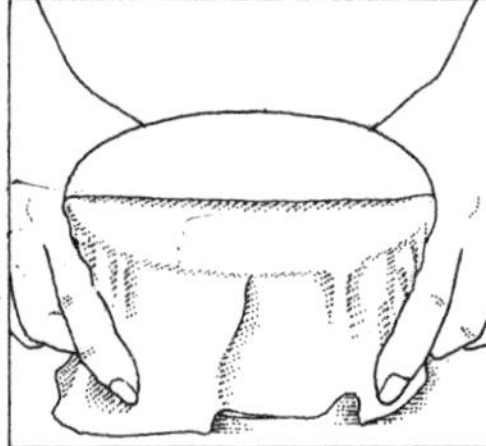

Cover with pleated double greaseproof paper.

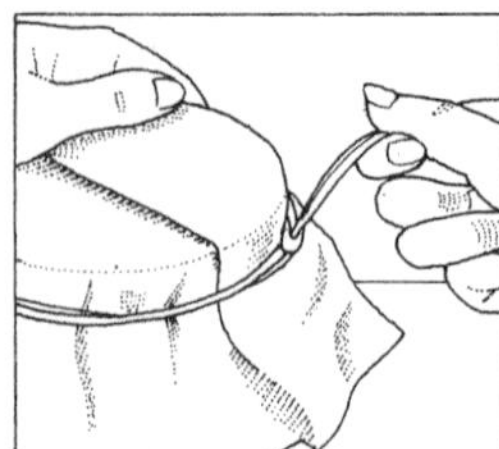
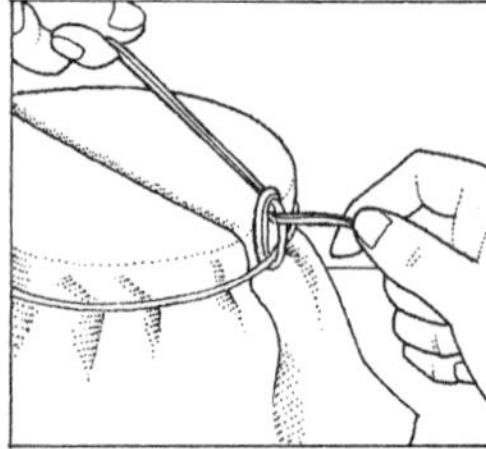

Tie down and make a string handle for easy removal.

RICH SWEET WINE

Sticky Toffee Pudding

SERVES 4-6
225g/8oz dates, chopped
290ml/½ pint tea
110g/4oz butter
170g/6oz caster sugar
3 eggs
225g/8oz self-raising flour
5ml/1 teaspoon bicarbonate of soda
5ml/1 teaspoon vanilla essence
5ml/1 teaspoon Camp coffee

To serve:
toffee sauce (see page 419)

1. Set the oven to 180°C/350°F/gas mark 4.
2. Soak the dates in the hot tea for 15 minutes.
3. Prepare an oiled moule à manqué cake tin with a circle of oiled greaseproof paper on the base.
4. Cream together the butter and sugar until pale.
5. Beat in the eggs, one at a time, and then fold in the sifted flour.
6. Add the bicarbonate, vanilla essence and Camp coffee to the date/tea water and then fold into the cake mixture.
7. Turn into the prepared moule à manqué tin and bake on the middle shelf of the oven for 1-1½ hours or until a skewer will come out clean.
8. Pour the warm toffee sauce over the hot pudding and serve immediately.

RICH SWEET WHITE

Le Gascon

This is a very complicated recipe but the end result justifies all the effort.

SERVES 8-10
3 egg quantity sponge fingers (see page 577)
3 egg chocolate génoise (see page 547)
30ml/2 tablespoons Armagnac or brandy
150ml/¼ pint sugar syrup (see page 419)
3 egg quantity rich chocolate mousse (see page 425)
2 egg white quantity prune mousse (see page 429)
110g/4oz chocolate quantity glaçage koba (see page 463)

1. Trim one end of the sponge fingers and line the sides of a 20cm/8 inch spring clip tin, making sure all the fingers are the same height.
2. Cut the chocolate génoise in half horizontally and place one half cut side up in bottom of tin.
3. Add the Armagnac to the sugar syrup.
4. Brush both cakes with the sugar syrup.
5. Pour the chocolate mousse into the centre until it comes halfway up the sponge fingers. Allow it to set.
6. Place the other half of the génoise cut-side up on top of the set chocolate mousse and brush with the sugar syrup.
7. Pour the prune mousse on top leaving a space of 5mm/¼inch at the top. Allow it to set.

8. Pour the glaçage koba over the top and level with a palette knife if necessary. Leave to set.

FORTIFIED SWEET RED

Pineapple and Apricot Gâteau

SERVES 6

225g/8oz fresh apricots
5 thin slices fresh pineapple
150ml/¼ pint sugar syrup (see page 419)
3 eggs
105g/3¾oz caster sugar
85g/3oz plain flour
pinch of salt
2.5ml/½ teaspoon ground cinnamon
finely grated rind of ½ lemon
290ml/½ pint double cream
30g/1oz chopped nuts
3 drops vanilla essence
15ml/1 tablespoon icing sugar
apricot glaze

1. Cut the apricots in half and poach them with the pineapple in the syrup until tender (about 20 minutes). Take care that the apricots do not overcook. Leave to cool.
2. Grease 2 20cm/8 inch sandwich tins and dust them with flour. Set the oven to 180°C/350°F/gas mark 4.
3. Whisk the eggs with the sugar in an electric beater (or with a hand whisk with the bowl set over a saucepan of simmering water) until thick and mousse-like. If the beating has been over heat, continue to beat while the mixture cools.
4. Fold in the flour with the salt, cinnamon and lemon rind. Pile the mixture into the sandwich tins and spread with a spatula. Bake for 20 minutes. Allow to cool in the tins for 2-3 minutes and then turn out on to a wire rack to cool completely.
5. Whisk the double cream until stiff. Stir in the chopped nuts, vanilla and icing sugar. Sandwich the cakes together with the cream. Decorate the top with the poached fruits and brush with warm apricot glaze.

SWEET WHITE

Glaçage Koba (Chocolate Icing)

75ml/2½ fl oz milk
225g/8oz plain chocolate, chopped
30ml/1 fl oz double cream
55g/2oz butter
15g/½oz powdered glucose
4 tablespoons sugar syrup (see page 419)

1. Bring the milk to the boil and add the chocolate, cream, butter and glucose. Stir over a gentle heat until well mixed and all the chocolate has melted.
2. Add the sugar syrup.
3. Allow the icing to cool to a coating consistency. If it gets too thick, place over a pan of simmering water and stir until the correct consistency is obtained.

NOTE: Use chocolate couverture, if available.

Pastry and Yeast Puddings

Apple and Orange Crumble

SERVES 4
3 oranges
900g/2lb cooking apples
45ml/3 tablespoons demerara sugar
pinch of cinnamon

For the crumble:
170g/6oz plain flour
pinch of salt
110g/4oz butter
55g/2oz sugar

1. Peel the oranges as you would an apple, with a sharp knife, removing all the pith. Cut out the orange segments leaving behind the membranes.
2. Peel and core the apples. Cut into thick slices. Mix with the orange segments and their juice. Add the sugar and cinnamon. Tip into an ovenproof dish.
3. Set the oven to 200°C/400°F/gas mark 6.
4. Sift the flour and salt into a bowl. Rub in the fat and when the mixture resembles coarse breadcrumbs mix in the sugar. Sprinkle it over the apples and oranges.
5. Bake on a hot baking sheet for 45 minutes or until hot and slightly browned on top.

NOTE: If using wholemeal flour for the crumble topping, use 140g/5oz of melted butter. Instead of rubbing it into the flour, mix briskly with a knife.

SWEET WHITE

Plum Pie

This recipe leaves the stones in the plums – if preferred, the plums can be cut in half and stoned. If the plums are large or not very ripe they should be pre-cooked in a little sugar syrup before they are baked.

SERVES 6
225g/8oz plain flour
pinch of salt
55g/2oz lard
85g/3oz butter
30-45ml/2-3 tablespoons cold water
caster sugar to dredge

For the filling:
675g/1½lb small plums
45ml/3 tablespoons demerara sugar
2.5ml/½ teaspoon ground cinnamon

1. Preheat the oven to 220°C/425°F/gas mark 7.
2. Sift the flour with the salt into a bowl. Rub in the fats until the mixture resembles coarse breadcrumbs.
3. Stir in enough water to bind the paste together. Push together into a ball, wrap up and chill in the refrigerator while you prepare the filling.
4. Wash the plums and place them in a pie dish with the cinnamon and sugar.
5. Roll out the pastry on a floured board. Cut a band of pastry wider than the rim of the pie dish. Wet the rim and press the band on all the way round. Brush with water and lay over the rolled-out pastry. Trim the edges, press them down firmly and mark with a fork or press into a frilly edge with fingers and thumb.
6. Shape the pastry trimmings into leaves. Brush the top of the pie with water and decorate with the leaves. Brush the leaves with water and dredge the whole pie with caster sugar.
7. Cut 1 or 2 small slits in the pastry top to allow the steam to escape. Bake on the top shelf for 25-35 minutes.

RICH SWEET WHITE

Treacle Tart

SERVES 4
110g/4oz plain flour
pinch of salt
55g/2oz butter
10ml/2 teaspoons caster sugar
1 egg yolk
very cold water

For the filling:
120ml/8 tablespoons golden syrup
grated rind of ½ lemon and 10ml/2 teaspoons of the juice
pinch of ground ginger (optional)
60ml/4 tablespoons fresh white breadcrumbs

1. Set the oven to 190°C/375°F/gas mark 5.
2. Sift the flour with the salt. Rub in the butter until the mixture looks like breadcrumbs. Add the sugar.
3. Mix the yolk with 30ml/2 tablespoons water, and add to the mixture.
4. Mix to a firm dough, first with a knife, and finally with one hand. It may be necessary to add water but the pastry should not be too wet. (Though crumbly pastry is more difficult to handle, it produces a shorter, lighter result.)
5. Roll the pastry out to 5mm/1/4 inch thick, and line a pie plate or flan ring with it. Prick the bottom with a fork - do not prick all the way through the pastry.
6. Heat the syrup with the lemon juice and rind to make it a little runny. Add the ginger if using.
7. Pour half the syrup into the pastry case.
8. Sprinkle with crumbs until they are soaked. Pour in the remaining syrup and sprinkle in the remaining crumbs.
9. Bake for about 30 minutes or until the filling is almost set and the edge of the pastry is brown. The filling should be a little on the soft side if the tart is to be eaten cold because it hardens as it cools. Ideally, serve lukewarm.

SWEET SPARKLING

Lemon Meringue Pie

SERVES 4
170g/6oz plain flour
pinch of salt
85g/3oz butter
5ml/1 teaspoon caster sugar
1 egg yolk
very cold water

For the filling:
30g/1oz cornflour
290ml/1/2 pint milk
30g/1oz sugar
2 egg yolks
grated rind and juice of 1 lemon

For the meringue:
2 egg whites
110g/4oz caster sugar
little extra caster sugar

1. First make the pastry: sift the flour with the salt. Rub in the butter until the mixture looks like breadcrumbs. Add the sugar.
2. Mix the yolk with 30ml/2 tablespoons water. Add this to the mixture.
3. Mix to a firm dough, first with a knife, and finally with one hand. It may be necessary to add more water, but the pastry should not be too wet. (Though crumbly pastry is more difficult to handle, it produces a shorter, lighter result.)
4. Roll out the pastry and use it to line a 20cm/8 inch flan ring. Leave it in the refrigerator for about 30 minutes to relax (this prevents shrinkage during cooking).
5. Heat the oven to 190°C/375°F/gas mark 5. Bake the pastry blind (see page 152).
6. Reduce the oven temperature to 170°C/325°F/ gas mark 3.
7. Meanwhile, make the filling: mix the cornflour (which should be very accurately weighed) with a tablespoon of the milk.
8. Heat the remaining milk. Pour this on to the cornflour paste, stir well and return the mixture to the pan. Boil for 3-4 minutes, stirring continuously. Add the sugar.
9. Allow to cool slightly, then beat in the egg yolks, lemon rind and juice.
10. Pour this mixture immediately into the pastry case. Remove the flan ring and return to the oven for 5 minutes to set the filling. Make the meringue: whisk the egg whites until stiff. Add 15ml/1 tablespoon of the caster sugar and whisk again until very stiff and solid.
11. Fold in the remaining sugar. Pile the meringue on to the pie. It is essential to cover the filling completely or the pie will weep. On the other hand, if you have used a small flan ring do not use all the meringue - the pie will be too sweet and may well weep. Dust with a little extra caster sugar.
12. Place in the oven for 5 minutes or until the meringue is a pale biscuit colour.

NOTE I: Lemon curd (see page 604) makes a good alternative to the lemon custard filling.
NOTE II: When making a meringue mixture with a powerful electric mixer, add half the sugar when the whites are stiff. Whisk again until very shiny and then add the remaining sugar and whisk lightly until just incorporated.

Custard Tart

SERVES 6
rich shortcrust pastry made with 140g/6oz flour (see page 525)

For the filling:
4 eggs
55g/2oz sugar
290ml/$^{1}/_{2}$ pint milk
290ml/$^{1}/_{2}$ pint single cream
few drops vanilla essence
grated nutmeg

1. Set the oven to 190°C/375°F/gas mark 5. Line a 20cm/8 inch flan ring or dish with the shortcrust pastry. Bake blind for 15-20 minutes (see page 152).
2. Lower the oven to 170°C/325°F/gas mark 3.
3. Lightly beat the eggs with the sugar. Pour on the milk and cream and add the vanilla essence. Strain into the prepared flan case and sprinkle a little grated nutmeg over the top.
4. Bake for 1 hour or until the custard has set.

Butterscotch Pie

SERVES 4
rich shortcrust pastry made with 110g/4oz flour (see page 525)
30g/1oz butter
55g/2oz demerara sugar
290ml/$^{1}/_{2}$ pint milk
15ml/1 tablespoon cornflour
pinch of ground ginger
30ml/2 tablespoons double cream, lightly whipped
chopped walnuts to decorate

1. Set the oven to 190°C/375°F/gas mark 5.
2. Line a 15cm/6 inch flan ring with the pastry and bake blind (see page 152). Cool on a wire rack.
3. Slowly melt the butter. Add the sugar and cook until dark brown and oily; this may well take 10 minutes.
4. Carefully pour on three-quarters of the milk (the milk will splutter alarmingly and the butter and sugar will become toffee-like). Simmer slowly until the sugar has dissolved.
5. In a cup, blend the cornflour with the remaining milk. Pour a little hot milk into the cup and mix well. Pour this back into the butterscotch milk and stir while it boils and thickens. Draw off the heat and stir in the ginger. Allow to cool.
6. Add the cream. Pour the mixture into the pastry case and sprinkle over the chopped nuts.

FORTIFIED SWEET WHITE

Mincemeat Flan

SERVES 8
rich shortcrust pastry made with 225g/8oz flour (see page 525) or pâte sucrée (see page 530)
caster sugar

For the filling:
1 small cooking apple
55g/2oz butter
85g/3oz sultanas
85g/3oz raisins
85g/3oz currants
45g/1$^{1}/_{2}$oz mixed peel, chopped
45g/1$^{1}/_{2}$oz chopped almonds
grated rind of large lemon
2.5ml/$^{1}/_{2}$ teaspoon mixed spice
15ml/1 tablespoon brandy
85g/3oz brown sugar
1 banana, chopped

1. Heat the oven to 190°C/375°F/gas mark 5.
2. Roll the pastry out to 5mm/$^{1}/_{4}$ inch thick, and line a 25cm/10 inch flan ring, keeping the pastry trimmings for the lattice decoration.
3. Bake blind for 20 minutes (see page 152).
4. For the mincemeat: grate the apple, skin and all. Melt the butter and add it, with all the other filling ingredients, to the apple. Mix well.
5. Fill the flan with the mincemeat. Cut the pastry trimmings into thin strips and lattice the top of the flan with them, sticking the ends down with a little water. Brush the lattice with water and sprinkle with caster sugar. Return to the oven for 10-12 minutes, removing the flan ring after 5 minutes to allow the sides of the pastry to cook to a pale brown.

FORTIFIED SWEET WHITE

Rhubarb Lattice Flan

SERVES 4-5

rich sweet shortcrust pastry made with 170g/6oz flour (see page 525)
675g/1½lb rhubarb
30g/1oz caster sugar
caster sugar for sprinkling

For the glaze:
5ml/1 teaspoon arrowroot
15ml/1 tablespoon redcurrant jelly

1. Make the pastry and line a 20cm/8 inch flan ring, reserving the trimmings. Chill for 20 minutes.
2. Set the oven to 190°C/375°F/gas mark 5.
3. Prepare the rhubarb: cut it into 3cm/1½ inch lengths and stew very gently in 15ml/1 tablespoon water with the sugar until tender. Drain the fruit very well and reserve the juice.
4. Bake the pastry case blind for 20-25 minutes (see page 152).
5. Arrange the rhubarb neatly in the flan case.
6. Mix the arrowroot with enough of the fruit juice to make it smooth. Put the arrowroot mixture and the juice into a saucepan and bring it to the boil, stirring all the time. Add the jelly and boil for 30 seconds. Cool until warm, then pour into the flan, all over the fruit.
7. Roll out the pastry trimmings into long strips 5mm/¼ inch wide. Twist the strips like barley sugar and arrange them in a lattice pattern over the flan, sticking the ends down with a little water. Brush each strip with water and sprinkle with caster sugar.
8. Return the flan to the oven until the pastry becomes a pale golden brown. Leave to cool on a wire rack.

SWEET WHITE

Pecan Pie

SERVES 8-10

For the pastry:
225g/8oz plain flour
pinch of salt
55g/2oz lard
85g/3oz butter
10ml/2 teaspoons sugar
30-45ml/2-3 tablespoons cold water

For the filling:
450g/1lb shelled pecan nuts
4 eggs
225g/8oz soft brown sugar
170g/6oz golden syrup
2.5ml/½ teaspoon salt
55g/2oz unsalted butter, melted
vanilla essence
30ml/2 tablespoons flour

1. Preheat the oven to 200°C/400°F/gas mark 6.
2. Sift the flour and salt into a bowl. Rub in the fats until the mixture resembles breadcrumbs.
3. Add the sugar and stir in enough water to bind the pastry together.
4. Roll out the pastry and use it to line a 28cm/11 inch flan case. Leave it in the refrigerator for about 30 minutes to relax. (This prevents shrinkage during cooking.)
5. Bake the pastry blind (see page 152).
6. Meanwhile, make the filling: chop half the pecan nuts. Whisk the eggs in a large bowl until frothy. Add the sugar, syrup, salt, melted butter and vanilla essence and beat well until thoroughly mixed. Stir in the sifted flour, making sure there are no lumps of flour in the mixture.
7. Scatter the chopped nuts over the cooked pastry case and pour over the filling. Arrange the remaining halved pecan nuts on top.
8. Bake on a baking sheet for 10 minutes and reduce to 170°C/325°F/gas mark 3 for 30-40 minutes or until the centre is just set. Serve warm or cold.

NOTE: The filling will separate slightly when it is cooked but this is normal and quite delicious.

FORTIFIED SWEET WHITE

Individual Apple Tarts

MAKES 8
rich shortcrust pastry made with 170g/6oz flour (see page 525)
4 dessert apples
caster sugar
Calvados
apricot glaze

1. Set the oven to 220°C/425°F/Gas Mark 7.
2. Make the rich shortcrust pastry. Divide into 8 pieces.
3. On a floured work surface, roll out each piece of pastry as thinly as possible. Cut into 12.5cm/5 inch circles, place on a baking sheet and chill for 20 minutes.
4. Peel the apples. Cut in half and carefully remove the cores, using the point of a knife.
5. Slice the apples finely and arrange half an apple on each piece of chilled pastry. Take care to pack the apples tightly to allow for shrinkage during cooking.
6. Sprinkle each tart evenly with 10ml/2 teaspoons caster sugar.
7. Place in the hot oven on the top shelf for 15 minutes or until golden brown. If it is not quite brown, place it under the grill for 1-2 minutes.
8. Sprinkle with a little Calvados and brush with warm apricot glaze.

SWEET WHITE

Redcurrant and Blackcurrant Flan

SERVES 6
sweet pastry made with 170g/6oz flour (see page 525)

For the sponge lining:
2 eggs
55g/2oz caster sugar
55g/2oz flour, sifted

For the filling:
170g/6oz redcurrants, fresh or frozen
170g/6oz blackcurrants, fresh or frozen
85g/3oz caster sugar

For the glaze:
45ml/3 tablespoons redcurrant jelly

To serve:
whipped cream

1. Strip the redcurrants and blackcurrants off the stalks by holding each sprig of berries by the stalk in one hand and using a fork in the other to dislodge the berries. (If they are frozen, thaw and drain them.)
2. Put the black and redcurrants in separate bowls and add half the sugar to each bowl, shaking to distribute the sugar without crushing the fruit. Leave for 4 hours. (Alternatively, simmer the fruits very gently with the sugar and a few spoons of water for 3 or 4 minutes to soften and cook them.)
3. Make up the pastry and use it to line a deep 18cm/7 inch diameter flan ring. Refrigerate for 20 minutes.
4. Set the oven to 200°C/400°F/gas mark 6.
5. Bake the flan case blind for 15 minutes (see page 152).
6. Make the sponge lining while the flan case is in the oven. Put the eggs and sugar into a bowl and set it over (not in) a pan of simmering water. Whisk steadily until the mixture is thick and mousse-like and the whisk will leave a ribbon-like trail when lifted. Remove from the heat and fold in the sifted flour. Remove the 'blind beans' from the half-cooked flan case. Pour the mixture in and return to the oven.
7. Bake for a further 10 minutes, then remove the flan ring and turn down the oven to 190°C/375°F/gas mark 5. Continue cooking until the pastry case is crisp and pale biscuit coloured, then remove and allow to cool.
8. Strain the fruit well (tipping both juices into a small saucepan) and arrange the black- and redcurrants in alternate quarters of the flan.
9. Add the redcurrant jelly to the juice and boil rapidly until syrupy and smooth. Cool until near setting, then spoon over the tart to give it a good clear glaze.
10. Serve with whipped cream.

SWEET WHITE

Rhubarb Tart

SERVES 4-6

For the filling:
675g/1½lb trimmed rhubarb
15ml/1 tablespoon caster sugar

For the pastry:
225g/8oz flour
pinch of salt
55g/2oz butter
55g/2oz lard
5ml/1 teaspoon caster sugar

For the flan mixture:
2 eggs
125g/4½oz caster sugar
150ml/¼ pint crème fraîche or single cream

1. Cut the rhubarb into 2.5cm/1 inch lengths and sprinkle with the sugar.
2. Set the oven to 190°C/375°F/gas mark 5.
3. Sift the flour into a medium-sized bowl with a pinch of salt. Rub the butter and lard into the flour until the mixture looks like breadcrumbs. Stir in the sugar. Add enough cold water to bind the pastry together.
4. Roll out the pastry and use it to line a 24cm/9 inch flan ring. Refrigerate it for 30 minutes.
5. Place the rhubarb and sugar in a shallow pan and cook over a gentle heat until the rhubarb softens slightly but still holds its shape. Allow to cool.
6. Bake the pastry blind (see page 152) in a preheated oven for 10-15 minutes. Allow to cool. Turn the oven down to 150°C/300°F/gas mark 2.
7. Mix the flan mixture ingredients together with a wooden spoon.
8. Arrange the rhubarb, without its juice, carefully in the baked flan case. Pour over the flan mixture and cook in the oven for 20-30 minutes. This tart is best served cold but not refrigerated.

SWEET WHITE

Charlotte's Higgledy Piggledy Tart

SERVES 8-10

walnut pastry made with 225g/8oz flour (see page 526)
150ml/¼ pint double cream, lightly whipped
290ml/½ pint crème pâtissière (see page 418)
soft seasonal fruit such as apricots, oranges, plums, kiwis, bananas and strawberries
apricot glaze

1. Line a 25cm/10 inch flan ring with the pastry. Relax for 30 minutes.
2. Preheat the oven to 375°F/190°C/gas mark 5.
3. Bake the flan case blind for 20 minutes (see page 152). Leave to cool.
4. Fold the cream into the almost cold crème pâtissière and pile into the flan case. Spread flat.
5. Prepare the fruit as for a fruit salad and arrange in a higgledy piggledy fashion.
6. Brush or spoon some warm apricot glaze over the top.

SWEET WHITE

Apple Flan Ménagère

SERVES 4

rich sweet shortcrust pastry made with 110g/4oz flour (see page 525)

For the filling and topping:
675g/1½lb medium-sized dessert apples
caster sugar
45ml/3 tablespoons warm apricot glaze

1. Set the oven to 190°C/375°F/gas mark 5.
2. Roll out the pastry and line a 15cm/6 inch flan ring. Chill again for 10 minutes.
3. Bake blind for 20 minutes (see page 152).
4. Peel, quarter and core the apples. Using a stainless steel knife, thinly slice them into the flan ring (the apples will shrink considerably during cooking, so make sure that the flan is well filled). When the flan is nearly full, arrange the apple slices very neatly in overlapping circles.

5. Dust well with caster sugar and bake in the oven for about 20 minutes.
6. Remove the metal flan ring and return to the oven for a further 7-8 minutes.
7. When the flan is cooked, brush with apricot glaze and slide on to a wire rack to cool.

SWEET WHITE

Danish Shortcake

SERVES 4
85g/3oz plain flour
pinch of salt
55g/2oz butter
30g/1oz caster sugar
30g/1oz ground hazelnuts, browned
225g/8oz strawberries

For the redcurrant glaze:
60ml/4 tablespoons redcurrant jelly
15ml/1 tablespoon lemon juice

1. Set the oven to 190°C/375°F/gas mark 5.
2. Sift the flour, with a pinch of salt, into a bowl. Rub in the butter until the mixture resembles breadcrumbs. Stir in the sugar and nuts. Knead together to form a stiff dough.
3. On a lightly greased baking sheet, roll or press the pastry into a cake-sized flat round. Put in the refrigerator to relax for 10-15 minutes.
4. Bake in the oven for 15-20 minutes until pale brown all over. Loosen and leave to cool and harden on the tray.
5. To make the glaze: melt the redcurrant jelly with the lemon juice, but do not allow it to boil. Keep warm.
6. Place the cooked shortcake on a serving dish, arrange the strawberries neatly over the top and brush thickly with the melted redcurrant glaze.

SWEET WHITE

Tarte Tatin

SERVES 6
For the pastry:
170g/6oz plain flour
55g/2oz ground rice
140g/5oz butter
55g/2oz caster sugar
1 egg, beaten

For the topping:
110g/4oz butter
110g/4oz granulated sugar
900g/2lb cooking apples
grated rind of 1 lemon

1. Set the oven to 190°C/375°F/gas mark 5.
2. To make the pastry: sift the flour and ground rice into a large bowl. Rub in the butter until the mixture looks like breadcrumbs. Stir in the sugar. Add the egg and bind the dough together. Chill while you prepare the top.
3. To make the topping: melt the butter in a 25cm/10 inch frying pan with a metal handle. Add the granulated sugar and take off the heat. Peel, core and thickly slice the apples. Arrange the apple slices over the melted butter and sugar in the base of the frying pan. Sprinkle on the grated lemon rind.
4. Place the frying pan over a high flame until the butter and sugar start to caramelize. It may take 6-7 minutes and you will be able to smell the change – it is essential that the apples get dark. Remove from the heat.
5. Roll the pastry into a circle 5mm/1/4 inch thick, to fit the top of the pan. Lay it on top of the apples and press down lightly. Bake in the oven for 25-30 minutes.
6. Allow to cool slightly, turn out on to a plate and serve warm.

NOTE: If you do not have a frying pan with a metal handle, cook the apples in an ordinary frying pan. Let the butter and sugar mixture become well caramelized and tip into an ovenproof dish. Cover with the pastry and then bake in the oven on a hot baking sheet.

SWEET WHITE

Upside-Down Apricot Tart

This recipe has been adapted from one in *The Josceline Dimbleby Collection* published by Sainsbury's.

SERVES 6

For the pastry:
170g/6oz plain flour, plus extra for rolling
85g/3oz caster sugar
a pinch of salt
85g/3oz butter
1 egg, whisked

For the filling:
340g/12oz dried apricots
55g/2oz butter
85g/3oz caster sugar

1. Soak the dried apricots in a bowl of water for 2 hours.
2. Make the pastry: sift the flour, caster sugar and salt into a bowl. Gently melt the butter in a saucepan and stir into the flour mixture with a wooden spoon. Then thoroughly mix in the whisked egg until the dough is smooth. Press the mixture together into a ball, cover with cling film and leave in the refrigerator for at least 1 hour.
3. To make the filling: drain the apricots and pat dry with absorbent paper. Smear the base and sides of a 25cm/10 inch flan dish or tin (not one with a loose base) with the butter. Sprinkle the caster sugar all over and arrange the apricots neatly in circles on top of the sugar, rounded side down.
4. Now take the pastry from the refrigerator and roll out on a floured surface to a little more than the size of the flan dish. (If the pastry breaks, just press it together again and don't worry if it looks messy as it won't show.) Press the edges of the pastry firmly down within the flan dish. Pierce 2 or 3 holes in the pastry.
5. Heat the oven to 200°C/400°F/gas mark 6. Cook the tart in the centre of the oven for 25 minutes. Then turn down the oven to 170°C/325°F/gas mark 3 and cook the tart for a further 30-35 minutes. Remove from the oven and cool slightly. Then turn out the tart upside down on to a serving plate and eat while warm.

SWEET WHITE

Martha Stewart's Fudge Tart

This tart is served with crème anglaise and orange sauce.

140g/5oz semi-sweet chocolate, finely chopped
170g/6oz unsalted butter, cut into small pieces
340g/12oz granulated sugar
95g/3½oz flour
6 eggs, lightly beaten
deep 20cm/8 inch pâte brisée (see page 525) tart case, baked and cooled

For the crème anglaise:
570ml/1 pint milk
1 vanilla pod
170g/6oz granulated sugar
6 egg yolks
10ml/2 teaspoons cornflour
30ml/2 tablespoons brandy

For the orange sauce:
170ml/6 fl oz freshly squeezed orange juice
30ml/2 tablespoons Grand Marnier
225g/8oz granulated sugar
15ml/1 tablespoon grated orange rind

1. Preheat the oven to 180°C/350°F/gas mark 4.
2. To make the filling: melt the chocolate and butter together in a basin over simmering water. When melted, remove from the heat and stir well to mix. Set aside to cool.
3. Mix together the sugar, flour and eggs in a mixing bowl and whisk until well blended. Stir in the chocolate-butter mixture. Pour the filling into the tart case and bake for approximately 50 minutes, until the filling is just set. Remove to a wire rack and let it cool completely.
4. To make the crème anglaise: put the milk and vanilla pod in a saucepan. Bring up to the boil. Turn off the heat and leave to infuse for 6 minutes. Remove the vanilla pod. Using an electric mixer, beat the sugar and egg yolks

together until thick and fluffy. Add the cornflour. Mixing on low speed, gradually add the infused milk. When thoroughly incorporated, transfer the mixture to a heavy saucepan. Cook over low heat, stirring constantly, until the sauce thickens to a light, creamy mixture. (Do not let the mixture boil, or the egg yolks will curdle.) Remove the mixture from the heat and whisk in the brandy. Strain the mixture through a fine sieve and cool. Refrigerate until ready to use.
5. To make the orange sauce: mix together the orange juice, Grand Marnier and sugar in a heavy saucepan and cook over low heat, stirring constantly, until thick and syrupy and reduced by half. Remove from the heat, stir in the grated orange rind and leave to cool.
6. To serve: place a slice of the tart on a plate and spoon some crème anglaise around it. Drizzle a small amount of orange sauce into the crème anglaise in swirls.

FORTIFIED SWEET WHITE

Tarte al' Coloche

This recipe has been taken from *Pâtissière* by the Roux Brothers. The tart takes its name from the bubbling caramel, which puffs up and *coloches* (bubbles). It makes a divine winter pudding, creamy and delicate, with the apples all coated in caramel. Christian Germain, the chef patron of the Château de Montreuil in France, makes the best tarte al' coloche in the world!

SERVES 8
pâte brisée made with 340g/12oz flour (see page 525)
pinch of flour
15ml/1 tablespoon butter, for greasing
12 medium dessert apples, preferably Cox's
1/2 cinnamon stick or a pinch of ground cinnamon
4 turns of the pepper mill
100g/3 1/2oz butter
140g/5oz sugar
500ml/18 fl oz double cream
2 eggs

1. Preheat the oven to 220°C/425°F/gas mark 7.
2. Make the pastry base: on a lightly floured surface, roll out the pastry to a thickness of about 3mm/1/8 inch.
3. Grease a flan ring and place it on a baking sheet. Line the ring with pastry, cutting off any excess with a sharp knife. Lightly crimp up the edges of the pastry to form a sort of frill above the edge of the ring. Leave to rest in the refrigerator for 20 minutes before baking.
4. Peel, quarter and core the apples. Place 4 quartered apples in a saucepan with 30ml/2 tablespoons water and the cinnamon. Cover the pan and cook gently until soft. Remove the cinnamon stick and add the pepper. Beat vigorously until the apples have the consistency of a compôte. Set aside at room temperature.
5. Bake the pastry blind: line the base and sides of the pastry with greaseproof paper. Fill with baking beans and bake in the preheated oven for 20 minutes. As soon as the pastry is half-cooked, remove the beans and paper and leave the base in a warm place. Reduce the oven temperature to 200°C/400°F/gas mark 6. In a large, thick-bottomed pan, melt the butter, then immediately add the sugar. Cook gently until it becomes a very pale caramel. Add the remaining apple quarters and roll them in the caramel for 4 minutes. They should be cooked but still firm. Set aside in a cool place.
6. To assemble the tart: spread the apple compôte over the base of the tart, then arrange the quarters on top. Pour the remaining caramel into a bowl and stir in the cream and eggs. Beat together lightly, then pour the mixture over the apples. Bake the tart in the preheated oven for 25 minutes.
7. Serve the tart warm and cut it at the table. Sprinkle lightly with icing sugar if wished.

RICH SWEET WHITE

Walnut, Pear and Apple Tart

SERVES 10
For the pastry:
225g/8oz flour
pinch of salt
5ml/1 teaspoon ground cinnamon
140g/5oz butter
110g/4oz caster sugar
55g/2oz walnuts, finely chopped
1 egg, beaten

For the filling:
3 cooking apples
3 William or Comice pears
30g/1oz butter
200g/7oz caster sugar
10ml/2 teaspoons ground cinnamon
juice of 1 lemon
110g/4oz sultanas
3 eggs
150ml/¼ pint double cream
170g/6oz walnuts, chopped

1. First make the pastry: sift the flour with the salt and cinnamon. Rub in the butter until the mixture resembles breadcrumbs. Mix in the sugar, then the walnuts.
2. Add the beaten egg to the mixture and mix to a firm dough. Leave the pastry to relax in the refrigerator for 30 minutes.
3. Roll out the pastry and use it to line a deep loose-bottomed 30cm/12 inch flan ring. Leave it in the refrigerator for about 30 minutes to relax.
4. Heat the oven to 190°C/375°F/gas mark 5.
5. Bake the pastry blind (see page 152).
6. Meanwhile, make the filling: peel and core the apples and pears and cut into chunks.
7. Melt the butter in a large heavy saucepan and, when foaming, add the apples and pears. Scatter on 85g/3oz of the caster sugar, the cinnamon, lemon juice and sultanas.
8. Toss the fruit over a medium heat for about 5 minutes, then strain, reserving the juice.
9. Spoon the lightly cooked pears and apples into the cooked pastry case.
10. Mix together the eggs, the remaining caster sugar, double cream and strained juice. Pour this mixture over the fruit and scatter the chopped walnuts over the top.
11. Place the flan in the oven and bake for 50 minutes, or until the centre is firm. (Cover with wet greaseproof paper if the tart begins to look too dark.)
12. Serve warm or cold.

SWEET WHITE

Poached Pear and Polenta Tart with Soft Cream

SERVES 8
425ml/¾ pint red wine
55g/2oz sugar
6 whole cloves
3 strips of lemon zest
2.5ml/½ teaspoon ground cinnamon
5 pears

For the pastry:
140g/5oz butter at room temperature
140g/5oz sugar
3 egg yolks
200g/7oz flour
85g/3oz polenta
2.5ml/½ teaspoon salt
extra 15ml/1 tablespoon polenta

For the soft cream:
150ml/¼ pint double cream
pear poaching liquid (see recipe)
brandy to taste
few drops of vanilla essence

1. Bring the wine, sugar, cloves, lemon zest and cinnamon to the boil in a medium-sized saucepan and simmer until reduced by about a fifth.
2. Peel the pears and cut them in half. Remove the cores carefully with an apple corer. Slice them into 1cm/½ inch pieces. Put the pear slices into the red-wine mixture and cook carefully over a low heat for approximately 40 minutes or until the pears are tender. Lift them out with a draining spoon and allow them to cool to room temperature.
3. Strain the red wine to remove the lemon zest and cloves. Put the syrup back on the heat, bring to the boil and reduce by half. Some of this will be used to flavour the cream. Set the oven to 200°C/400°F/gas mark 6.
4. To make the pastry: cream the butter and sugar together until well blended. Add the egg yolks one at a time, beating well between each addition. Sift the flour, polenta and salt together and mix into the creamed mixture. Beat until the dough comes together, then knead lightly on a

floured surface, adding more flour if necessary, until the pastry is no longer sticky. Rest the pastry in the refrigerator for 20 minutes.

5. Cut the dough in half. Press one half of the dough on to the base and sides of a 22cm/9 inch flan ring. Sprinkle the base with the extra polenta. Spoon the drained pears into the pastry shell.

6. Roll out the remaining dough to 1cm/½ inch thickness. Using a fluted biscuit cutter, cut out as many circles as possible from the dough. Place them on top of the pears, starting on the outside. Overlap the shapes and continue to cover the top.

7. Bake the tart in the preheated oven for about 30 minutes, covering with greaseproof paper if necessary after 20 minutes.

8. To make the soft cream: whip the double cream until soft peaks are formed. Flavour with some of the poaching liquid, the cognac and the vanilla essence to taste. Serve with the warm tart.

SWEET WHITE

Normandy Apple Flan

SERVES 6

This recipe has been taken from *The Observer French Cookery School* by Anne Willen of La Varenne.

pâte brisée made with 200g/7oz flour (see page 525)
100g/3½oz butter
1 egg yolk
3.5ml/¾ level teaspoon salt
30-45ml/2-3 tablespoons cold water
3-4 ripe dessert apples

For the frangipane:
100g/3½oz butter
100g/3½oz caster sugar
1 egg, beaten
1 egg yolk
10ml/2 teaspoons Calvados or Kirsch
100g/3½oz blanched almonds, ground
30ml/2 tablespoons flour

To finish:
150ml/¼ pint apricot jam glaze

1. Make the pâte brisée and wrap and chill for at least 30 minutes.

2. Set the oven at 200°C/400°F/gas mark 6, and place a baking sheet in the oven to heat. Roll out the dough, line a 25cm/10 inch tart tin with it, prick lightly with a fork, flute the edges and chill again until firm.

3. To make the frangipane: cream the butter, gradually beat in the sugar and continue beating until the mixture is light and soft. Gradually add the egg and yolk, beating well after each addition. Add the Calvados and Kirsch, then stir in the ground almonds and the flour. Pour the frangipane into the chilled pastry, spreading it evenly.

4. Peel the apples, halve them and scoop out the cores. Cut them crosswise in very thin slices and arrange them on the frangipane to make the spokes of a wheel, keeping the slices of each half apple together. Press them down gently until they touch the pastry dough base.

5. Bake the pie on the hot baking sheet near the top of the heated oven for 10-15 minutes until the pastry dough is beginning to brown. Turn down the oven to 180°C/350°F/gas mark 4, and continue cooking for 30-35 minutes or until the apples are tender and the frangipane is set.

6. Transfer to a rack to cool. A short time before serving, brush the tart with melted apricot jam glaze and serve at room temperature.

NOTE: Normandy apple tart is best eaten the day it is baked, but it can also be frozen. Just before serving, reheat to lukewarm in a low oven.

SWEET WHITE

Raisin and Yoghurt Tartlets

MAKES 18

sweet wholemeal pastry made with 170g/6oz flour (see page 527)
1 large egg
55g/2oz caster sugar
15ml/1 tablespoon plain flour
pinch of ground nutmeg
pinch of ground cinnamon
10ml/2 teaspoons lemon juice

grated rind of 1/2 lemon
150ml/1/4 pint yoghurt
55g/2oz raisins

1. Set the oven to 200°C/400°F/gas mark 6.
2. Roll out the pastry thinly and use it to line 18 tartlet tins. Leave to relax in the refrigerator for 15 minutes.
3. Bake blind for 10 minutes (see page 152). Remove the paper and beans. If the pastry is not quite cooked, return to the oven for 5 minutes. Leave to cool on a wire rack.
4. Reduce the oven to 180°C/350°F/gas mark 4.
5. Put the egg and the sugar into a pudding bowl. Stand this over (not in) a pan of simmering water. Whisk until the mixture thickens sufficiently to leave a 'ribbon' trail.
6. Fold in the flour, spices, lemon juice, rind, yoghurt and raisins.
7. Fill the tartlet cases with the mixture and bake for 20-25 minutes, or until the filling is just firm. Leave to cool on a wire rack.

LIGHT SWEET WHITE

Apple Florentine

SERVES 4
900g/2lb cooking apples
55g/2oz butter
50g/2oz demerara or barbados sugar
5ml/1 teaspoon ground cinnamon
grated rind of 1 lemon
rough puff pastry made with 225g/8oz flour (see page 527)

For the spiced cider:
150ml/1/4 pint cider
pinch each of ground nutmeg and ginger
1 stick cinnamon
pared rind of 1/2 lemon
55g/2oz sugar

To serve:
icing sugar
ice cream or whipped cream

1. Set the oven to 200°C/400°F/gas mark 6.
2. Peel, core and quarter the apples.
3. Melt the butter in a frying pan and, when foaming, add the apples. Fry until delicately browned.
4. Tip into a pie dish and mix in the sugar, cinnamon and lemon rind. Allow to cool.
5. Roll out the pastry on a floured board to 5mm/1/4 inch thickness.
6. Cut a strip of pastry very slightly wider than the edge of the dish. Brush the rim with water and press the strip down all round it.
7. Lift the pastry with the aid of the rolling pin and lay it on the pie. Press down the edge and trim the sides.
8. Mark round the edge with the prongs of a fork or the tip of a knife or crimp the edges with finger and thumb. Brush with cold water and dust with caster sugar.
9. Bake the pie for 25-30 minutes until golden brown.
10. Prepare the spiced cider: heat all the ingredients together in a pan over gentle heat for 10 minutes without boiling. Strain.
11. Remove the pie from the oven and, with a sharp knife, lift off the crust in one piece. Pour in the spiced cider.
12. Return the crust on to the pie and dust with icing sugar. Serve hot with ice cream or whipped cream.

NOTE: 'Florentine' is an obsolete word for pie.

SWEET WHITE

Millefeuilles

SERVES 4-6
rough puff pastry made with 225g/8oz flour (see page 527) or puff pastry (see page 528)
30ml/2 tablespoons strawberry jam
290ml/1/2 pint double cream, whipped
225g/8oz icing sugar, sifted

1. Set the oven to 220°C/425°F/gas mark 7.
2. On a floured board, roll the pastry into a large thin rectangle about 30 x 20cm/12 x 8 inches. Place on a wet baking sheet. Prick all over with a fork.
3. Leave to relax, covered, for 20 minutes. Bake until brown. Allow to cool.
4. Cut the pastry into 3 neat strips, each 10 x 20cm/4 x 8 inches. (Keep the trimmings for

decoration.) Choose the piece of pastry with the smoothest base, and reserve. Spread a layer of jam on the 2 remaining strips and cover with cream. Place them on top of each other and cover with the third, reserved, piece of pastry, smooth-side uppermost. Press down gently but firmly.
5. Mix the icing sugar with boiling water until it is thick, smooth and creamy. Be careful not to add too much water. Coat the icing over the top of the pastry and, while still warm, sprinkle crushed cooked pastry trimmings along the edges of the icing. Allow to cool before serving.

NOTE I: To 'feather' the icing, put 15ml/1 tablespoon of warmed, smooth liquid jam in a piping bag with a 'writing' nozzle. Pipe parallel lines of jam down the length of the newly iced millefeuilles, about 2cm/3/4 inch apart. Before the icing or jam is set, drag the back of a knife across the lines of jam. This will pull the lines into points where the knife crosses them. Repeat this every 5cm/2 inches in the same direction, and then drag the back of the knife in the opposite direction between the drag-lines already made.
NOTE II: Millefeuilles are also delicious covered with fresh strawberries and glazed with redcurrant glaze (see page 152) instead of icing the top.

SWEET SPARKLING WHITE

Jalousie

SERVES 4
rough puff pastry made with 110g/4oz flour (see page 527)
225g/8oz fresh apple marmalade (see page 420)
30ml/2 tablespoons smooth apricot jam
milk
caster sugar

1. Set the oven to 230°C/450°F/gas mark 8.
2. Roll the pastry into 2 thin rectangles, one about 2.5cm/1 inch bigger all round than the other. The smaller one should measure around 13 x 20cm/5 x 8 inches, and the larger 18 x 25cm/7 x 10 inches. Leave to relax for 20 minutes.
3. Prick the smaller one all over and bake until crisp and brown. Take it out and turn it over on the baking sheet. Allow to cool.
4. Melt the jam in a small pan, and brush over the top of the cooked pastry. Spread the apple marmalade all over the cooked piece of pastry, on top of the jam.
5. Lay the larger piece of pastry on the board, dust it lightly with flour and fold it, gently so that nothing sticks, in half lengthways. Using a sharp knife, cut through the folded side of the pastry, at right angles to the edge, in parallel lines, as though you were cutting between the teeth of a comb. Leave an uncut margin about 2.5cm/1 inch wide, all round the other edges, so that when you open up the pastry you will have a solid border.
6. Now lay the cut pastry on top of the pastry covered with jam and apple marmalade and tuck the edges underneath. Brush the top layer carefully all over with milk (this is a bit messy as the apple keeps coming up between the pastry crust). Sprinkle well with sugar.
7. Bake in the oven until well browned, about 20 minutes. Serve cold or warm.

NOTE: Jalousie literally means shutters, and these are what the pie looks like.

RICH SWEET WHITE

Individual Apple Tarts with Calvados Crème Anglaise

SERVES 4
puff pastry made with 225g/8oz flour (see page 528)
4 dessert apples
caster sugar
egg glaze
apricot glaze

To serve:
15ml/1 tablespoon Calvados
290ml/1/2 pint crème anglaise (see page 418), chilled

1. Set the oven to 200°C/400°F/gas mark 6.
2. Roll out the pastry and cut into 4 circles 2mm/1/8 inch thick and 12.5cm/5 inches in diameter. Place on a damp baking sheet. With a sharp knife, trace an inner circle about 1cm/1/2 inch from the edge of the pastry. Do not cut

all the way through the pastry.
3. Peel, core and slice the apples finely and arrange in concentric circles within the border of each pastry tart. Using a sharp knife, mark a pattern on the pastry border.
4. Sprinkle lightly with caster sugar. Brush the pastry rim with egg glaze, taking care not to let it drop down the sides of the pastry.
5. Flour the blade of a knife and use this to 'knock up' the sides of the pastry. Chill for 15 minutes.
6. Bake for 20 minutes. Leave to cool slightly and then brush liberally with warm apricot glaze.
7. Add the Calvados to the well-chilled crème anglaise. Serve the tarts warm with the cold custard.

SWEET WHITE

Feuilletée de Poires Tiède

SERVES 4
2 William pears
290ml/½ pint sugar syrup (see page 419)
puff pastry made with 340g/12oz flour (see page 528)
290ml/½ pint double cream, lightly whipped
290ml/½ pint crème anglaise (see page 418)
55ml/2 fl oz Poire William liqueur
icing sugar

1. Peel the pears, cut in quarters and remove the cores. Poach carefully in the sugar syrup until they are soft.
2. Set the oven to 220°C/425°F/gas mark 7.
3. On a lightly floured board, roll the pastry into 4 neat rectangles 10 x 6cm/4 x 2½ inches. Relax in the refrigerator for 20 minutes.
4. Bake until brown for 15 minutes. Cut in half horizontally, remove any uncooked dough and return to the turned-off oven to dry out. Remove from the oven.
5. Fold the lightly whipped cream into the crème anglaise. Flavour with the liqueur.
6. Sandwich the pastry slices together with the cream mixture and slices of warm poached pear. Dust the pastry lightly with icing sugar.

SWEET WHITE

Gâteau Pithivier

SERVES 6
puff pastry made with 450g/1lb flour (see page 528)
1 egg beaten with 2. 5ml/½ teaspoon salt
110g/4oz apricot jam glaze

For the almond filling:
125g/4½oz butter, softened
125g/4½oz sugar
1 egg
1 egg yolk
125g/4½oz whole blanched almonds, skinned and ground
15g/½oz flour
30ml/2 tablespoons rum

1. Make the puff pastry and chill.
2. For the filling: cream the butter in a bowl, add the sugar and beat thoroughly. Beat in the egg and the yolk; then stir in the almonds, flour and rum.
3. Roll out half the puff pastry to a circle, about 27cm/11 inches in diameter. Using a pan lid as a guide, cut out a 25cm/10 inch circle from this with a sharp knife, angling the knife slightly. Roll out the remaining dough slightly thicker than for the first round and cut out another 25cm/10 inch circle. Set the thinner circle on a baking sheet, mound the filling in the centre, leaving a 2.5cm/1 inch border, and brush the border with egg glaze. Set the second circle on top and press the edges together firmly.
4. Scallop the edge of the gâteau by pulling it in at intervals with the back of a knife. Brush the gâteau with egg glaze and, working from the centre, score the top in curves like the petals of a flower. Do not cut through to the filling. Chill the gâteau for 15-20 minutes. Set the oven to 220°C/425°F/gas mark 7.
5. Bake the gâteau in the heated oven for 30-35 minutes or until it is firm, puffed and brown. Brush the gâteau while still hot with melted apricot glaze. Transfer to a rack to cool.

SWEET SPARKLING WHITE

Tarte Française

SERVES 4
puff pastry made with 110g/4oz flour (see page 528)
egg glaze
45ml/3 tablespoons warm apricot glaze
squeeze of lemon
fruit as for a fruit salad, e.g. 2 oranges, small bunch of black grapes, small bunch of white grapes, small punnet of strawberries, 1 banana

1. Roll out the pastry into a rectangle the size of an A4 sheet of paper.
2. Cut out a 'picture frame' 2.5cm/1 inch wide. Dust liberally with flour and fold into 4. Carefully set aside.
3. Roll out the remaining pastry until it is a little larger than A4 size.
4. Set the oven to 220°C/425°F/gas mark 7.
5. Transfer the pastry to a baking sheet and prick it well all over. Using a pastry brush dampen the edges. Place the 'picture frame', still folded, on to the pastry and unfold. Trim the edges neatly. Brush off any excess flour. Knock up the pastry and brush the frame with egg glaze (take care not to dribble the glaze down the sides as the pastry will stick together). Chill in the refrigerator for 20 minutes.
6. Bake for 15 minutes or until crisp and brown.
7. Remove from the oven and leave to cool on a wire rack.
8. Use a little of the apricot glaze to brush the surface of the pastry.
9. Cut up the fruit as you would for a fruit salad and lay the pieces in rows on the pastry as neatly and closely together as possible. Be careful about colour (do not put 2 rows of white fruit next to each other, or tangerine segments next to orange segments, etc.). When complete, paint carefully with the warm glaze.

SWEET WHITE

Chocolate Profiteroles

MAKES 30
For the profiteroles:
3 egg quantity choux pastry (see page 529)

For the filling and topping:
570ml/1 pint whipped cream, sweetened with 15ml/1 tablespoon icing sugar
110g/4oz chocolate, chopped
15g/½oz butter
30ml/2 tablespoons water

1. Set the oven to 200°C/400°F/gas mark 6.
2. Put teaspoons of the choux mixture on a wet baking sheet, about 8cm/3 inches apart.
3. Bake for 20-30 minutes. The profiteroles should swell, and become fairly brown. If they are taken out when only slightly brown, they will be soggy when cool.
4. Make a hole the size of a pea in the base of each profiterole and return to the oven for 5 minutes to allow the insides to dry out. Cool on a wire rack.
5. When cold fill each profiterole with the sweetened cream, using a forcing bag fitted with a small plain nozzle.
6. Put the chocolate, butter and water into a bowl and melt over a pan of simmering water.
7. Dip the tops of the profiteroles in the chocolate and allow to cool.

NOTE: If no piping bag is available for filling the profiteroles, they can be split, allowed to dry out, and filled with cream or crème pâtissière when cold, and the icing can be spooned over the top. However, made this way they are messier to eat in the fingers.

FORTIFIED SWEET WHITE

Coffee Éclairs

MAKES 20-25
3 egg quantity choux pastry (see page 529)

For the filling and topping:
425ml/¾ pint double cream, lightly whipped and sweetened with 15ml/1 tablespoon icing sugar, or crème pâtissière (see page 418)
225g/8oz icing sugar
30ml/2 tablespoons very strong hot black coffee

1. Heat the oven to 200°C/400°F/gas mark 6. Wet 2 baking sheets.
2. Make up the choux pastry.

3. Using a forcing bag with a 1cm/½inch plain nozzle, pipe 5cm/2 inch lengths of choux pastry on to the baking sheets (keep them well separated as choux pastry swells during cooking). Bake for 25-30 minutes until crisp and pale brown.
4. Make a pea-sized hole in each one with a skewer to allow the steam to escape and return to the oven for 5 minutes to dry the insides out. Place on a wire rack to cool.
5. Put the sweetened cream (or the crème pâtissière) into a forcing bag fitted with a medium nozzle. Pipe the cream into the éclairs through the hole made by the skewer, until well filled.
6. Mix the icing sugar and very hot coffee together and beat with a wooden spoon until smooth. The mixture should be just runny.
7. Dip each éclair upside down into the icing so that the top becomes neatly coated.
8. Set aside to dry. Alternatively, the icing can be carefully spooned along the top ridge of each éclair.

NOTE: The éclairs may be split lengthways when cooked, allowed to dry out, and filled with cream or crème pâtissière when cold. The tops are then replaced and the icing spooned over but they are then messier to eat in the fingers.

FORTIFIED SWEET WHITE

Deep-fried Profiteroles

MAKES ABOUT 30
3 egg quantity choux pastry (see page 529)
oil for deep-frying
290ml/½ pint crème pâtissière (optional), (see page 418)
icing sugar, sifted

1. Heat the oil in a deep-fryer until a crumb will sizzle gently in it. Drop teaspoonfuls of the choux mixture into the fat, one at a time, so that they do not stick together. Cook for about 5 minutes or until the balls are brown and crisp. Drain well.
2. They can be split open and filled with warm crème pâtissière if wished. Dust with icing sugar and serve immediately.

NOTE: A thin apricot glaze is delicious served as a hot sauce.

SWEET SPARKLING WHITE

Gâteau St Honoré

SERVES 6
pâte sucrée made with 110g/4oz flour (see page 530)
3 egg quantity choux pastry (see page 529)
570ml/1 pint crème pâtissière (see page 418, double quantity)
110g/4oz granulated sugar

1. Line an 18cm/7 inch flan ring with the pâte sucrée and bake it blind at 190°C/375°F/gas mark 5 (see page 152) for 20 minutes until biscuit coloured.
2. Make the profiteroles: increase the oven temperature to 200°C/400°F/gas mark 6. Wet 2 baking sheets.
3. Put teaspoonfuls of the choux mixture on to the baking sheets and bake for 25 minutes until hard and pale brown.
4. Make a pea-sized hole in the base of each choux bun with a skewer and return to the oven for 5 minutes to dry the insides out. Place on a wire rack to cool.
5. Using a forcing bag fitted with a plain nozzle, pipe the crème pâtissière into 17 even-sized profiteroles, piping the mixture through the previously made holes. Spread the remaining crème pâtissière into the bottom of the empty flan case. Pile the profiteroles into a pyramid on top of the filling.
6. Slowly heat the sugar in a heavy saucepan until it caramelizes to a pale liquid toffee.
7. Pour the caramel over the profiteroles.

NOTE: Vast pyramids of profiteroles filled as here, or with whipped cream, form the traditional French wedding cake or croque en bouche. Sometimes icing sugar is sifted over the whole creation.

SWEET SPARKLING WHITE

Apricot Ring

SERVES 6

110g/4oz apricots
150ml/1/4 pint sugar syrup (see page 419)
3 egg quantity choux pastry (see page 529)
30ml/2 tablespoons apricot jam
140g/5oz icing sugar
290ml/1/2 pint double cream, whipped
30g/1oz almonds, browned

1. Set the oven to 200°C/400°F/gas mark 6.
2. Wash and halve the apricots and remove the stones. Poach in the sugar syrup until just tender (about 15 minutes). Drain well and leave to cool.
3. Pipe the choux paste mixture into a circle about 15cm/6 inches in diameter on a wet baking tray. Cook for about 30 minutes until brown and crisp.
4. Split horizontally with a bread knife. Scoop out any uncooked paste and discard; leave on a wire rack to cool.
5. Heat the jam and spread it on the base of the choux ring.
6. Mix 30g/1oz of the icing sugar with the whipped cream and fold in the apricots.
7. Spoon the mixture on to the base and press the lid on firmly.
8. Mix the rest of the icing sugar with a little boiling water until just runny. Coat the top of the choux ring with the icing and, while still wet, sprinkle with browned almonds.

SWEET WHITE

Apple Strudel

SERVES 6

strudel pastry made with 285g/10oz flour (see page 530) rolled to at least 40 x 60cm/15 x 24 inches

For the filling:
900g/2lb cooking apples
handful of currants, sultanas and raisins
30g/1oz brown sugar
2.5ml/1/2 teaspoon cinnamon
pinch of ground cloves
45ml/3 tablespoons crumbs, browned
grated rind and juice of 1/2 lemon
85g/3oz melted butter
icing sugar

1. Heat the oven to 200°C/400°F/gas mark 6. Grease a baking sheet.
2. Prepare the filling: peel, core and slice the apples in such a way that they don't have very sharp corners which will pierce the delicate pastry, and mix together with the dried fruit, sugar, spices, crumbs, lemon rind and juice.
3. Flour a large tea towel. Lay the pastry on this. If you have not got a big enough piece of pastry, several smaller ones will do, but they must be overlapped well.
4. Brush with butter. Spread the filling over the pastry evenly. Using the tea towel to help, roll up as for a Swiss roll, trying to maintain a fairly close roll. Lift the cloth and gently tip the strudel on to the baking sheet. Brush with melted butter.
5. Bake in the oven until a golden brown (about 40 minutes). Dust with icing sugar while still warm.

NOTE: In delicatessens, strudels are generally sold in one-portion sizes. To make these you will need leaves of pastry about 22cm/9 inches square. As they are easier to handle, they can be lifted without the aid of the cloth – just flour the table top to prevent sticking. Bake for 20 minutes.

SWEET WHITE

Strawberry Tartlets

These are low-fat strawberry tartlets – hardly the traditional ones made from rich, sweet pastry and filled with a mass of cream cheese and sugar!

SERVES 4

5 large sheets of filo pastry
grapeseed oil
1 batch pear sorbet (see page 512)
250g/8oz strawberries, hulled and cut in half

1. Preheat the oven to 200°C/400°F/gas mark 6.
2. Layer up the pastry and using a large round pastry cutter, cut out 8 rounds of filo pastry, making 40 circles.
3. Brush the bases of 8 upturned ovenproof cups with oil and cover each with a round of filo pastry. Brush the pastry with a very little extra oil and add another 4 rounds of pastry in the

same way to each cup.
4. Bake the tartlets for 10-15 minutes until they are a pale golden brown. Remove them from the oven, loosen them carefully from the cups and leave them to cool on a wire rack.
5. Five minutes before serving, place a spoonful of pear sorbet in each filo tartlet and arrange the strawberries on top.

SWEET WHITE

Baklava

Claudia Roden's book *A New Book of Middle Eastern Food* is fascinating to read and an excellent book from which to cook. At Leith's she is one of our very special guest lecturers. The students love to see her make both this baklava and the konafa.

170g/6oz unsalted butter, melted
450g/1lb filo pastry (24 sheets)
340g/12oz pistachios, walnuts or almonds, ground or finely chopped

For the syrup:
450g/1lb sugar
290ml/1/2 pint water
30ml/2 tablespoons lemon juice
30ml/2 tablespoons orange blossom water

1. First make the syrup: put the sugar, water and lemon juice into a saucepan, dissolve over a gentle heat and then simmer until thick enough to coat the back of a wooden spoon. Add the orange blossom water and simmer for a further 2 minutes. Leave to cool and then refrigerate.
2. Preheat the oven to 160°C/325°F/gas mark 3.
3. Brush melted butter on the base and sides of a deep baking sheet. Put half the filo sheets into the roasting pan, brushing each sheet with melted butter and overlapping or folding the sides over where necessary.
4. Spread the nuts evenly over the pastry, spoon over 60ml/4 tablespoons of the sugar syrup and then cover with the remaining sheets of filo, brushing each one as you layer it up. Brush the top layer with butter. Cut diagonally into lozenge shapes with a sharp, serrated knife.
5. Bake for 45 minutes, increase the oven temperature to 220°C/425°F/gas mark 7 and bake for a further 15 minutes or until well risen and golden brown.
6. Remove from the oven and pour the chilled syrup over the hot baklava. Leave to cool.
7. When cold, cut into lozenge shapes as before and place on a serving dish.

RICH SWEET WHITE/SPARKLING

Konafa

450g/1lb konafa pastry, available in delicatessens
225g/8oz unsalted butter, melted

For the syrup:
450g/1lb sugar
290ml/1/2 pint water
30ml/2 tablespoons lemon juice
30ml/2 tablespoons orange flower water

For the filling:
90ml/6 tablespoons ground rice
60ml/4 tablespoons sugar
1 litre/1 3/4 pints milk
150ml/1/4 pint double cream

1. First make the syrup: put the sugar, water and lemon juice into a saucepan, dissolve over a gentle heat and then simmer until thick enough to coat the back of a wooden spoon. Add the orange blossom water and simmer for a further 2 minutes. Leave to cool and then refrigerate.
2. Mix the ground rice and sugar to a smooth paste with 150ml/1/4 pint of the milk. Bring the rest of the milk up to the boil and gradually add the ground rice paste slowly, stirring vigorously. Simmer, stirring to prevent it catching on the bottom, until very thick. Allow to cool, add the cream and mix well.
3. Preheat the oven to 160°C/325°F/gas mark 3.
4. Put the konafa pastry into a large bowl. Pull out and separate the strands as much as possible with your fingers so that they do not stick together too much. Pour in the melted butter and work it in very well. Put half the pastry in a large, deep ovenproof dish. Spread the filling evenly over and cover with the remaining pastry. Flatten it with the palm of your hand.
5. Bake for 1 hour, increase the oven temperature

to 220°C/425°F/gas mark 7 and bake for a further 10-15 minutes or until golden brown.
6. Remove from the oven and pour the cold syrup over the hot konafa.

NOTE: Konafa can be made with a variety of fillings, such as cheese, nuts and cinnamon or sliced bananas. They can also be made as individually rolled pastries instead of one large pastry.

RICH SWEET WHITE/SPARKLING

Almond Pastry Fruit Flan

SERVES 6
almond pastry made with 110g/4oz flour (see page 530)

For the glaze:
45ml/3 tablespoons apricot jam
squeeze of lemon juice
15ml/1 tablespoon water

a selection of: oranges, pears, grapes, cherries, strawberries, bananas, apples, plums etc., depending on the season

1. Set the oven to 200°C/400°F/gas mark 6.
2. On a baking sheet roll or press the pastry into a 20cm/8 inch circle. Decorate the edges with a fork or the point of a sharp knife (pressed broad side into the pastry) or by pinching between fingers and thumb. Prick lightly all over.
3. Bake for about 15 minutes until a pale biscuit colour. Loosen with a palette knife and allow to cool slightly and harden on the baking sheet. Slip on to a wire rack to cool completely.
4. Meanwhile, prepare the apricot glaze: melt the jam with the lemon juice and water. Boil up, sieve and keep warm until ready for use. Do not stir too much or the glaze will be bubbly.
5. Prepare the fruits as you would for a fruit salad, but leaving any that discolour (such as apples or pears) until you assemble the flan.
6. Brush the pastry with some of the apricot glaze (this helps to stick the fruit in place and prevents the pastry from becoming too soggy).
7. Arrange the fruit in neat overlapping circles, taking care to get contrasting colours next to each other. Brush with apricot glaze as you go, especially on apples, pears or bananas. When all the fruit is in place, brush with the rest of the glaze.

NOTE: This flan should not be put together too far in advance as the pastry will become soggy in about 2 hours.

SWEET WHITE

Apricot Tart Bourdaloue

SERVES 4-6
pâte sucrée made with 170g/6oz flour (see page 530)

For the bourdaloue cream:
290ml/½ pint milk
2 egg yolks
55g/2oz caster sugar
15g/½oz flour
20g/¾oz cornflour
30ml/2 tablespoons ground almonds
15ml/2 tablespoons double cream
15ml/1 tablespoon Kirsch (optional)
2 egg whites

For the decoration:
140g/5oz sugar
290ml/½pint water
450g/1lb apricots

1. First prepare the pâte sucrée: wrap up and leave to relax for at least 30 minutes in the refrigerator.
2. Now prepare the apricots: place the sugar and water together in a heavy pan and set over a gentle heat. Halve the apricots and place them in the pan once the sugar has dissolved. Poach in the gently simmering sugar syrup until soft – be careful not to overcook them. Drain very well and set the apricots and syrup aside.
3. Set the oven to 190°C/375°F/gas mark 5. Line an 18cm/7 inch flan ring with the pâte sucrée and bake blind (see page 152) until a pale biscuit colour (about 15 minutes). Remove the paper,

blind beans and flan ring and bake for a further 5 minutes until the sides are evenly coloured. Slide on to a rack to cool.
4. To prepare the bourdaloue cream: scald the milk. Cream the egg yolks with half the sugar and when pale mix in the flours. Pour on the milk and mix well. Return the mixture to the pan and bring slowly to the boil, stirring continuously. (It will go alarmingly lumpy, but don't worry, keep stirring and it will get smooth.) Pour into a bowl. Allow to cool slightly. Mix in the ground almonds, cream and, if liked, add the Kirsch.
5. Whisk the egg whites and when stiff add the rest of the sugar and whisk again until stiff and shiny. Stir in to the cool bourdaloue mixture.
6. To put the flan together: fill the flan case with the bourdaloue cream and spread it flat with a spatula or palette knife. Arrange the well-drained apricots over the cream so that the tart is completely covered. Boil up the sugar syrup in which the apricots were cooked until thick enough to form a thread when tested between finger and thumb. Cool. Brush over the apricots.

RICH SWEET WHITE

Candied Lemon Tart

SERVES 6
pâte sucrée made with 170g/6oz flour (see page 530)
4 eggs
1 egg yolk
200g/7oz caster sugar
150ml/1/4 pint double cream
juice and grated rind of 2 lemons
icing sugar

To glaze:
1 lemon
150ml/1/4 pint sugar syrup

1. Set the oven to 170°C/325°F/gas mark 3.
2. Line a 18cm/7 inch flan ring with pâte sucrée. Relax for 30 minutes and then bake blind for 15 minutes (see page 152). Leave to cool on a wire rack. Reduce the oven to 150°C/300°F/gas mark 2.
3. For the filling: mix the eggs and extra yolk with the sugar and beat lightly with a whisk until smooth. Add the cream and whisk again. Add the lemon juice and rind. It will thicken alarmingly but do not worry.
4. Put the pastry case back on to a baking sheet and spoon in the lemon filling. Bake for 50 minutes; if it becomes too brown, cover the top with a piece of tin foil.
5. While the pie is cooking, prepare the glazed lemon rind. With a potato peeler, pare the rind from the lemon very finely, making sure that there is no pith on the back of the strips. Cut into very fine shreds.
6. Simmer these shreds in the sugar syrup until tender, glassy and candied. Leave to cool on greaseproof paper.
7. When the tart is cooked, remove the flan ring and leave to cool.
8. When cool, dust thickly and evenly with sifted icing sugar and arrange the candied shreds on top.

SWEET WHITE

Strawberry Tartlets

MAKES 20
pâte sucrée made with 170g/6oz flour (see page 530)

For the filling:
225g/8oz petit Suisse cheese
55g/2oz caster sugar
450g/1lb strawberries, hulled
60ml/4 tablespoons redcurrant jelly, melted

1. Set the oven to 190°C/375°F/gas mark 5.
2. Roll out the pastry thinly and use it to line tartlet tins. Bake blind for about 15 minutes or until a pale biscuit colour (see page 152). Remove the papers and the 'blind' beans. If the pastry is not quite cooked, return to the oven for 5 minutes. Carefully take out the pastry cases and leave to cool on a wire rack.
3. Cream the cheese with the caster sugar and place a teaspoonful of this mixture at the bottom of each case. Arrange the strawberries, cut in half if necessary, on top of the cheese and brush lightly with warm melted redcurrant jelly.

SWEET WHITE

Sablé aux Fraises

This recipe has been adapted from *The Roux Brothers on Pâtissèrie.*

SERVES 6

pâte sablé made with 280g/10oz flour (see page 526)
675g/1½lb strawberries, hulled and sliced
425ml/¾ pint raspberry coulis (see page 421)
55g/2oz icing sugar

1. Set the oven to 200°C/400°F/gas mark 6.
2. Divide the dough into 2 pieces to make for easier rolling.
3. Roll out the doughs very thinly and cut into a total of 18 x 10cm/4 inch circles. Bake in the preheated oven for 8 minutes or until a pale golden. Lift on to a wire rack and leave to cool.
4. Cut the strawberries in half and mix them with two-thirds of the raspberry coulis. Leave to macerate.
5. Place a pastry base on 6 pudding plates. Arrange a few macerated strawberries on top. Cover with a second pastry base and more strawberries. Cover with a third piece of pastry and sprinkle generously with icing sugar.
6. Serve the coulis separately or poured around the sablés.

NOTE: Do not assemble this pudding in advance as the pastry will become soggy.

Peach Pastry Cake

SERVES 6

70g/2½oz hazelnuts
85g/3oz butter
55g/2oz caster sugar
110g/4oz plain flour
pinch of salt
3 fresh peaches
190ml/⅓ pint whipped cream
icing sugar

1. Toast the nuts in a hot oven. When brown, rub in a dry cloth to remove the skins. Cool. Grind the nuts taking care not to overgrind them or they will be oily.
2. Beat the butter and when soft add the sugar and beat until light and fluffy.
3. Sift the flour with the salt and stir into the mixture with the nuts.
4. Set the oven to 190°C/375°F/gas mark 5.
5. Divide the paste into 3 and press out into thin flat rounds of 15cm/6 inch diameter. Chill for 30 minutes.
6. Place on baking sheets and bake for 10-12 minutes. Cut 1 into 6 portions before it cools. Allow to cool on a wire rack. They will become crisp as they cool.
7. Skin and slice the peaches. Mix the peach slices with the whipped cream. Using half this mixture as a filling, sandwich the 2 whole rounds of biscuit together. Spread the other half of the filling on the top.
8. Set the cut portions of biscuit into the cream mixture, placing each at a slight angle. Dust with icing sugar before serving.

Doughnuts

MAKES 8

225g/8oz plain flour
pinch of salt
7g/¼oz fresh yeast
45g/1½oz sugar
30g/1oz butter
2 egg yolks
150ml/¼ pint warm milk
fat for deep-frying
caster sugar flavoured with cinnamon

1. Sift the flour with the salt into a warm bowl.
2. Cream the yeast with 5ml/1 teaspoon of the sugar.
3. Rub the butter into the flour. Make a well in the centre.
4. Mix together the egg yolks, yeast mixture, remaining sugar and warm milk. Pour this into the well in the flour.
5. Using the fingertips of one hand, mix the central ingredients together, gradually drawing in the surrounding flour. Mix to a smooth soft dough.
6. Cover the bowl with a piece of greased polythene and leave to rise in a warm place for 45 minutes.
7. Knead the dough well for at least 10 minutes. Roll out on a floured board to 1cm/½inch thick. With a plain cutter, press into small rounds. Place on a greased tray and leave to

prove (rise again) until doubled in size.
8. Heat the fat until a crumb will sizzle vigorously in it. Put the doughnuts into the fryer basket and lower into the fat. Fry until golden brown, then drain on absorbent paper.
9. Toss in caster sugar and cinnamon.

Rum Baba

SERVES 4
For the sugar syrup:
170g/6oz loaf sugar
225ml/8 fl oz water
30ml/2 tablespoons rum

For the yeast mixture:
110g/4oz plain flour
15g/½oz fresh yeast
15g/½oz caster sugar
90ml/6 tablespoons warm milk
2 egg yolks
grated rind of ½ lemon
55g/2oz butter

For the decoration (optional):
fresh fruit such as grapes and raspberries
150ml/¼ pint double or whipping cream, lightly whipped

1. First make the sugar syrup: dissolve the sugar in the water and boil rapidly for 3 minutes. The syrup should be boiled to the 'thread' (when a little syrup is put between finger and thumb and the fingers are opened, the syrup should form a short thread). Add the rum.
2. Now make the yeast mixture: sift the flour into a warmed bowl.
3. Mix the yeast with 2.5ml/½ teaspoon of the sugar, 5ml/1 teaspoon of the flour and enough milk to make a batter-like consistency.
4. Whisk the egg yolks, remaining sugar and lemon rind until fluffy.
5. Clarify the butter: melt it slowly in a saucepan, see that it separates and strain through a clean 'J' cloth or muslin, leaving the sediment behind.
6. Make a well in the centre of the flour and add the yeast and beaten eggs. With your fingers, mix together and gradually draw in the flour from the sides, adding more milk as you take in more flour. When all the flour has been incorporated, beat with your hand until soft and smooth.
7. Gradually add the clarified butter, kneading and slapping the dough until it looks like a very thick batter and no longer sticks to the palm.
8. Cover and leave to rise in a warm place (e.g. the airing cupboard) for about 45 minutes. It should double in size.
9. Set the oven to 190°C/375°F/gas mark 5. Grease a 1 litre/1½ pint savarin (ring) mould with plenty of butter.
10. When the dough has risen, beat it down again and use to fill the mould. It should half-fill the tin.
11. Cover and leave to prove (rise again) for 10-15 minutes in a warm place.
12. Bake in the oven for 30-35 minutes.
13. Turn out on to a wire rack and, while still warm, prick with a toothpick and brush with plenty of rum syrup until the baba is really soaked and shiny. Put on a serving dish.
14. Serve plain or surround with fresh fruit and pile the whipped cream in the centre.

NOTE: If using dried or easy-blend yeast see note on page 488.

Savarin aux Fruits

In the absence of a savarin mould, use an ordinary cake tin. The fruit should then be piled on top of the cake.

SERVES 4
For the savarin:
110g/4oz plain flour
7g/¼oz fresh yeast
15g/½oz caster sugar
2 egg yolks
grated rind of ½ lemon
90ml/6 tablespoons lukewarm milk
55g/2oz butter, softened

For the syrup:
170g/6oz loaf sugar
225ml/8 fl oz water
2 drops vanilla essence

For the fruit mixture:
675-900g/1½-2lb in total of bananas, cherries, plums, grapes, oranges, apricots, apples and pineapple

To serve:
290ml/½ pint crème Chantilly (see page 418)

1. Sift the flour into a warmed bowl. Mix the yeast with 2. 5ml/½ teaspoon of the sugar, add 15ml/1 teaspoon flour and enough milk (about 60ml/4 tablespoons) to give a batter-like consistency.
2. Whisk the egg yolks, remaining sugar and lemon rind until fluffy.
3. Make a well in the centre of the flour and add the yeast and egg mixtures. Mix them together with the fingers of one hand, and then gradually draw in the flour from the sides, adding milk as you take in more flour. When all the flour has been incorporated, beat with your hand until very soft and smooth.
4. Gradually add the butter, kneading and slapping the dough until it looks like a thick batter, and no longer sticks to the palm of your hand.
5. Cover and leave to rise in a warm place for about 45 minutes. It should double in size.
6. Dissolve the sugar in the water and boil rapidly for 2 minutes, or until syrupy. When cool, add the vanilla essence.
7. Prepare the fruit as for a fruit salad and moisten with 1-2 spoons of the syrup.
8. Heat the oven to 190°C/375°F/gas mark 5. Butter a savarin or large ring mould thickly. When the dough has risen, beat it down again and fill the savarin mould. It should half-fill the tin. Cover and leave to prove (rise again) for 10-15 minutes in a warm place.
9. Bake in the oven for 30-35 minutes until golden brown. Turn out on to a wire rack and, while still hot, prick all over with a toothpick and brush with plenty of warm sugar syrup.
10. Allow to cool. Put on a serving dish and again brush with syrup until the cake is completely soaked. Fill the centre with the fruit. Serve with crème Chantilly.

NOTE: If using dried yeast, use half the amount called for, mix it with 45ml/3 tablespoons of the liquid (warmed to blood temperature) and 5ml/1 teaspoon sugar. Leave until frothy, about 15 minutes, then proceed. If the yeast does not go frothy, it is dead and unusable. If using easy-blend yeast, use half the quantity called for and add it to the dry ingredients.

Orange and Grand Marnier Pancakes

SERVES 4
grated rind of 1 large orange
290ml/½ pint crème pâtissière (see page 418)
30ml/2 tablespoons Grand Marnier
8 cooked French pancakes (see page 533)
icing sugar

1. Heat the grill.
2. Mix the orange rind with the crème pâtissière and the Grand Marnier.
3. Divide the mixture between the pancakes.
4. Fold each pancake in half and dust heavily with icing sugar.
5. Place under a hot grill until the icing sugar begins to caramelize.

Crêpes Suzette

SERVES 4-6
12 French pancakes (see page 533)

For the orange butter:
85g/3oz unsalted butter
30g/1oz caster sugar
grated rind of 1 orange
30ml/2 tablespoons orange juice
30ml/2 tablespoons orange Curaçao

To flame:
caster sugar
30ml/2 tablespoons orange Curaçao
15ml/1 tablespoon brandy

1. Put the butter, sugar, orange rind, juice and Curaçao into a large frying pan and simmer gently for 2 minutes.
2. Put a pancake into the frying pan and, using a spoon and fork, fold it in half and then in half again. Add a second pancake and repeat the process until the pan has been filled.
3. Sprinkle the pancakes with caster sugar and pour over the orange Curaçao and brandy. Light a match, stand back, and light the alcohol. Spoon it over the pancakes until the flames have died down. Serve immediately.

Fruit Puddings

Poached Apples

SERVES 4
170g/6oz sugar
570ml/1 pint water
450g/1lb dessert apples
stick of cinnamon
squeeze of lemon juice

To serve:
cream (optional)

1. Dissolve the sugar in the water. When completely dissolved, boil rapidly until you have a thin syrup (3-4 minutes).
2. Peel, core and quarter the apples. Place them in the sugar syrup with the cinnamon.
3. Bring slowly to the boil, then reduce the heat and poach gently for 20 minutes or until the apples are tender.
4. Remove the apples with a draining spoon and arrange in a shallow dish.
5. Reduce the syrup a little by further boiling, then add the lemon juice. Pour over the fruit just before serving.
6. Serve hot with cream, or chilled with or without cream.

LIGHT SWEET WHITE

Alain Senderens' Soupe aux Fruits Exotiques

This recipe was taken from Robert Carrier in *The Sunday Express.*

SERVES 4
1 small papaya
16 lychees
20 strawberries
2 kiwi fruits
8 passionfruits
15ml/1 tablespoon finely chopped mint

For the syrup:
90ml/6 tablespoons sugar
mint sprig
1 clove
1.25ml/1/4 teaspoon mixed Chinese spices (from good food stores and Chinese specialist shops)
thinly sliced zest of 1 lime
thinly sliced zest of 1/4 lemon
1 vanilla pod, split lengthways
2.5ml/1/2 teaspoon finely chopped root ginger
2 coriander seeds

1. To make the syrup: put the sugar, mint sprig, clove, Chinese spices, thinly sliced zest of lime and lemon, split vanilla pod, finely chopped root ginger, coriander seeds and 425ml/3/4 pint water into a heavy bottomed saucepan and bring slowly to the boil, stirring to dissolve the sugar. Reduce, by boiling rapidly, for 1 minute. Remove the pan from the heat and leave to infuse until cool.
2. Meanwhile, peel the papaya and cut the flesh into even-sized pieces. Skin the lychees and remove the stones. Wash and hull the strawberries. Peel the kiwi fruits and slice thinly.
3. When the syrup is cool, strain through a fine sieve into a bowl. Add the prepared fruits. Cut the passionfruits in half and spoon out the seeds and juice into the bowl of syrup. Chill for 2-3 hours.
4. To serve: divide the prepared fruits into 4 shallow bowls; spoon over the syrup and decorate with finely chopped mint.

LIGHT SWEET WHITE

Baked Apples

smallish cooking apples
brown sugar
sultanas

1. Wash the apples and remove the cores with an apple corer. With a sharp knife cut a ring just through the apple skin about two-thirds of the way up each apple.
2. Put the apples in an ovenproof dish and stuff the centres with a mixture of brown sugar and sultanas.
3. Sprinkle 10ml/2 teaspoons brown sugar over each apple. Then pour 5mm/1/4 inch of water

into the dish.
4. Bake in a moderate oven preheated to 180°C/350°F/gas mark 4 for about 45 minutes or until the apples are soft right through when tested with a skewer.

SWEET WHITE

Gratin de Fruits

SERVES 6
4 ripe peaches
4 ripe plums
4 ripe apricots
2 eggs
2 egg yolks
85g/3oz caster sugar
dash of Kirsch (optional)
55g/2oz flaked almonds

1. Skin and slice the peaches. Halve and stone the plums and apricots. Arrange on 6 small gratin dishes.
2. Heat up the grill.
3. Put the eggs, egg yolks and sugar into a bowl. Set over (not in) a pan of simmering water. Whisk for 10-15 minutes until thick and creamy. It is important that the eggs should thicken, not scramble. Add the Kirsch.
4. Spoon the sauce over the fruits. Sprinkle with the almonds and grill until evenly browned. Serve immediately.

SWEET WHITE

Fresh Fruit in Biscuit Cups

SERVES 8
1 quantity iced sabayon
8 biscuit cups (see page 507)
6 kiwi fruits, peeled and sliced
170g/6oz seedless grapes

1. Divide the iced sabayon between the 8 biscuit cups.
2. Decorate with the kiwi fruit and seedless grapes. Serve immediately.

Green Fruit Salad

3 kiwi fruits
225g/8oz greengages
225g/8oz white grapes
1 small ripe melon with green flesh
1 green dessert apple
apple juice

1. Peel and slice the kiwis. Stone and quarter the greengages and halve and seed the grapes.
2. Using a melon baller, scoop the melon flesh into balls, or simply cut into even-sized cubes. Slice and core the apples but do not peel.
3. Mix the fruits together, moisten with the apple juice and chill well before serving.

LIGHT SWEET WHITE

Blackcurrant Kissel

SERVES 4
450g/1lb blackcurrants
caster sugar to taste (about 170g/6oz)
10ml/2 teaspoons arrowroot

1. Wash the blackcurrants and remove the stalks.
2. Barely cover with water and add the sugar. Stew gently for about 20 minutes. Push through a sieve. Return to the saucepan and bring back to the boil.
3. Mix a little cold water with the arrowroot and mix to a smooth paste.
4. To the arrowroot add a cupful of the boiling purée and mix thoroughly. Add the arrowroot mixture to the fruit, stirring, and allow to thicken. Simmer for 1 minute. Pour into a serving bowl. Sprinkle evenly with caster sugar to prevent a skin forming.

LIGHT SWEET WHITE

Red Fruit Salad

SERVES 4

675g/1½lb assorted raspberries, strawberries, redcurrants, watermelon, plums or any fresh red fruit
orange juice

1. Wash the fruit.
2. Check the raspberries, discarding any bad ones.
3. Hull and halve the strawberries.
4. Wash, top and tail the redcurrants with the prongs of a fork.
5. Cut the melon flesh into cubes, discarding most of the seeds, but reserving the juice.
6. Halve and stone the plums.
7. Put the fruit into a glass dish and moisten with the fruit juice, if required. Chill well.

NOTE: Red fruit salad is also very good if sprinkled with a little triple-distilled rose water in place of the orange juice. A teaspoonful will be plenty.

LIGHT SWEET WHITE

Pineapple in the Shell

1 large pineapple

1. Cut the top and bottom off the pineapple so that you are left with a cylinder of fruit. Do not throw away the leafy top. With a sharp knife cut round inside the skin, working first from one end and then from the other, so that you can push the fruit out in one piece. Try not to pierce or tear the skin.
2. Slice the pineapple finely. Stand the pineapple skin in a shallow bowl, put the fruit back in it and replace the top. Kirsch can be sprinkled in too if liked.

Fresh Papaya with Limes

Simply serve halved papayas, with the seeds removed, with a wedge of fresh lime. Allow one half of a papaya per head.

Turned Mangoes with Limes

I had never seen mangoes served like this until I saw Arabella Boxer's *Sunday Times Cookery Course.* I was immensely impressed as, delicious as they are, mangoes always present the difficulty of how to eat them.

½ mango and 2 lime wedges a head

1. Cut a thick slice as close to the flat stone as possible.
2. Repeat on the other side. (Use the remaining mango flesh for another dish.)
3. With a small, sharp knife, make diagonal cuts through the flesh right down to the skin – be careful not to pierce the skin.

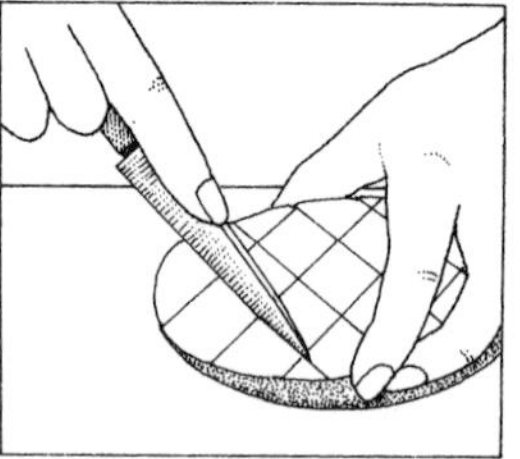

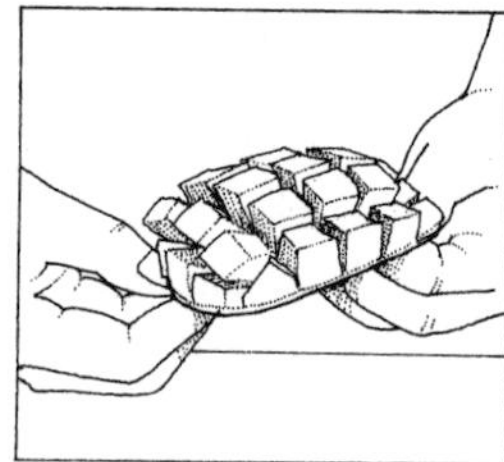

Cut the flesh to give a lattice finish. Turn mango inside out.

4. Push the skin up in such a way that the mango is domed and can be eaten with a spoon. Serve with lime wedges.

Summer Fruit Compote

SERVES 4-6

110g/4oz black cherries, pitted
225g/8oz strawberries
juice of 1 orange
juice of 1 lemon
30ml/2 tablespoons sugar
30ml/2 tablespoons Kirsch
225g/8oz raspberries
110g/4oz red cherries, pitted
110g/4oz blueberries
225g/8oz blackberries
225g/8oz loganberries

1. Process together half the black cherries, half the strawberries, the orange and lemon juice, the sugar and Kirsch. Taste and add more sugar if necesary.
2. Mix the remaining fruit together and pour the puree over it. Mix gently and pile into a serving bowl.
3. Keep the compote covered and refrigerated if not using immediately but serve at room temperature.

LIGHT SWEET WHITE

Watermelon Salad

SERVES 6
1 large watermelon
110g/4oz strawberries
15ml/1 tablespoon triple-distilled rose water

To decorate:
white gypsophilla (if available)

1. Cut off the top of the watermelon. Remove as much of the flesh as possible. Discard the seeds and cut the flesh into neat pieces.
2. Hull and halve the strawberries.
3. Mix together the strawberries, watermelon flesh and rose water. Pile back into the watermelon shell and replace the top.
Put on a large plate and decorate with the white gypsophilla.

Arranged Fruit Salad

SERVES 4
2 ripe passionfruits
1 large ripe mango
45ml/3 tablespoons orange juice
seasonal fruit, chilled e.g. 4 kiwi fruits, peeled and sliced, 110g/4oz strawberries, hulled, 110g/4oz black grapes, peeled and halved
4 sprigs mint

1. Process (but do not liquidize) the passionfruit pulp, mango flesh and orange juice together for 2 minutes.
2. Sieve the purée on to the base of 4 pudding plates so that each one is well flooded.
3. Arrange the prepared fruit in a pretty pattern on each plate. Decorate each with a sprig of mint.

NOTE: If you do not have a food processor, this sauce can be made in a liquidizer if the passionfruit are sieved before 'whizzing'.

Strawberries with Quark and Black Pepper

Quark is the German equivalent of the French fromage blanc. It is a very low-fat cheese made from skimmed milk.

Serve unhulled strawberries with a dip of Quark let down with water and seasoned with freshly ground black pepper.

Hot Winter Fruit Salad

SERVES 4
450g/1lb good quality mixed dried fruits, such as prunes, apricots, figs and apples
cold tea
15ml/1 tablespoon Calvados
60ml/4 tablespoons orange juice
3-4 cloves
1 x 5cm/2 inch piece cinnamon stick
1.25ml/¼ teaspoon mixed spice
pared rind of 1 lemon
1 star anise

1. Soak the mixed dried fruits in the Calvados and enough tea to just cover. Leave overnight.
2. Pour into a saucepan, add the orange juice, cloves, cinnamon, mixed spice, lemon rind and star anise. Bring up to the boil and simmer slowly until the fruits are soft. This will take about 20 minutes.
3. Remove the cloves, cinnamon, lemon rind and star anise. Serve hot or cold.

Oranges in Caramel

1 large orange per person
caramel sauce (see page 419)

1. With a potato peeler, pare the rind of 1 or 2 oranges very finely, making sure that there is no pith on the back of the strips. Cut into fine shreds.

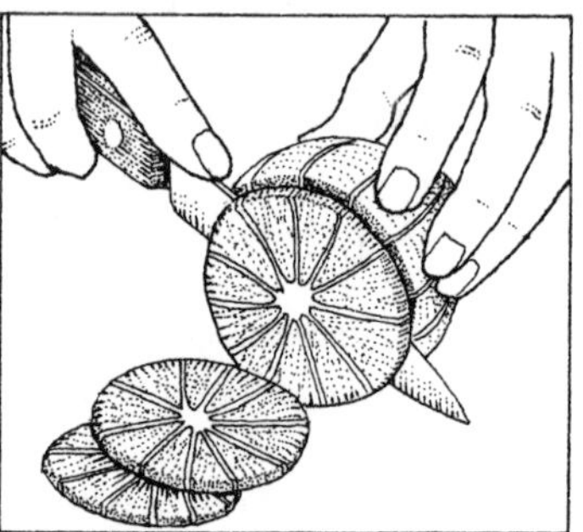

How to prepare an orange.

2. Simmer these needleshreds in caramel sauce or sugar syrup until soft and almost candied. They should be very sticky and quite dark.
3. Peel the remaining oranges with a knife as you would an apple, making sure that all the pith is removed.
4. Slice each orange horizontally. Remove pips.
5. Place the oranges in a glass bowl and pour over the cold caramel sauce. Chill well.
6. Scatter with needleshreds of orange before serving.

FORTIFIED SWEET WHITE

Butterscotch Figs

SERVES 4
8 ripe figs
140g/5oz caster sugar
55g/2oz unsalted butter
pinch of ground cinnamon
60ml/4 tablespoons Grand Marnier

To serve:
150ml/¼ pint double cream, lightly whipped

1. Preheat the oven to 150°C/300°F/gas mark 2.
2. Prick the figs with a fork. Place them in a casserole dish and sprinkle over 30g/1oz of the sugar. Add a little water and bake for 30 minutes. Baste the figs occasionally.
3. Meanwhile, melt the butter in a large sauté pan, add 60ml/4 tablespoons water and the sugar and boil until lightly browned. Add the figs, sprinkle with a little ground cinnamon and toss gently with 2 wooden spoons so that they become lightly caramelized all over.
4. Heat the Grand Marnier in a small saucepan and then pour it over the figs to flame.
5. Serve the figs in a little sauce and serve the cream separately.

FORTIFIED SWEET WHITE

Apricot Cheesecake

SERVES 4
For the crust:
170g/6oz digestive biscuits, crushed
85g/3oz melted butter
pinch of cinnamon

For the filling:
45ml/3 tablespoons water
15g/½oz gelatine
200g/7oz tin good quality apricots
225g/8oz soft cheese
150ml/¼ pint whipped cream
grated rind and juice of ½ lemon
70ml/2½ fl oz soured cream
sugar to taste (about 45g/1½oz)

For the decoration:
150ml/¼ pint whipped cream
browned nibbed almonds

1. Place an oiled flan ring on a flat, lipless baking sheet. Mix together the crust ingredients and put the mixture into the flan ring, pressing down firmly. Leave in the refrigerator for 20 minutes to harden.
2. Put the water into a small pan. Sprinkle on the gelatine and set aside to 'sponge'.
3. Liquidize the apricots, reserving 3 halves for decoration. Beat the cheese until soft, then mix in all the other filling ingredients.
4. Melt the gelatine over a gentle heat until clear and warm. Pour this into the cheese mixture, stirring well. Pile the filling into the flan ring and spread it flat with a palette knife. Leave in the refrigerator to set.

5. To serve: with a sharp knife, loosen the flan ring from the cheesecake and remove gently, being careful not to knock the edges. With 2 palette knives, or fish slices, carefully lift or slide the cake on to a serving dish. If this proves difficult, the biscuit base can be loosened by placing the baking sheet above a gentle heat for 30 seconds. Decorate the edges with rosettes of whipped cream and apricot quarters. Sprinkle nibbed almonds over the cream and serve.

NOTE: In the absence of a lipless baking sheet, use the back of a tray or roasting pan. The cake is easier to slide off a flat surface.

RICH SWEET WHITE

Pineapple and Date Salad

SERVES 4
2 small pineapples
12 fresh dates

1. Cut the pineapples in half lengthways, making sure that each half has an equal amount of green leaves. With a grapefruit knife, carefully remove the flesh, leaving the shells intact. Cut the flesh into cubes. Halve and stone the dates.
2. Mix the dates with the pineapple, keeping back 4 or 5 for the top. Pile the mixture into the shells and put the reserved date halves, shiny side up, on top.

NOTE I: Preserved dates are good too, though not as good as fresh ones.
NOTE II: If the pineapple is very sharp, it may be sweetened with sifted icing sugar.

Bristol Apples

SERVES 4
110g/4oz sugar for the syrup
290ml/$^1/_2$ pint water
4 dessert apples
2 oranges
55g/2oz sugar for the caramel
oil

1. Place the sugar for the syrup and the water in a pan and set over a gentle heat until the sugar dissolves. Boil rapidly for 3 minutes.
2. Peel, quarter and core the apples and place in the sugar syrup. Simmer very gently until just tender; this should take about 20 minutes. Remove the apples and allow them to cool.
3. With a sharp knife or potato peeler, thinly pare the rind from 1 orange, taking care to pare the rind only, leaving behind the bitter pith. Cut the rind into very fine even-sized needleshreds. Put into the syrup and boil until thick and tacky.
4. Peel the oranges with a sharp knife as you would an apple, making sure that all the pith is removed. Cut into neat segments, discarding any pips and membrane.
5. Put the sugar for the caramel into a thick-bottomed pan and let it dissolve over heat, without stirring.
6. Meanwhile, oil a baking sheet.
7. As the sugar bubbles, it will become a dark-golden colour. Pour this on to the oiled baking sheet and leave it to set into a thin layer like brown glass. When cold, break into chips, and put somewhere cool and dry.
8. Arrange the apples and oranges in a glass bowl, pour over the sugar syrup and chill in the refrigerator. When ready to serve, scatter over the broken caramel chips and the needleshreds.

RICH SWEET WHITE

Yoghurt, Honey and Dates

unsweetened natural Greek yoghurt
very cold runny honey
best dates, fresh or dried
thick cream
Jordan almonds, shelled but with the inner, brown skin left on, i.e. unblanched (optional)

1. For each person half-fill a pudding bowl or glass with yoghurt.
2. Stone the dates and chop them roughly. Put a few on the top of each helping of yoghurt.
3. Spoon a good dollop of thick cream over the top, then trickle over 5ml/1 teaspoon runny honey.

4. If using the almonds, scatter a few on now. (They may be used as well as, or instead of, the dates.)

Redcurrant, Mint and Yoghurt Pudding

This is a quick and simple light, low-fat, sugar-free summer pudding. It is better made with Greek yoghurt, but this has a higher fat content than most low-fat yoghurts. It can also be made with blackcurrants.

SERVES 4
290ml/1/2 pint plain, low-fat yoghurt
450g/1lb redcurrants, topped and de-stalked
concentrated apple juice to taste (optional)
15ml/1 tablespoon chopped fresh mint
1 egg white

Mix together the yoghurt and the redcurrants. Sweeten to taste with a little apple juice. Add the mint. Whisk the egg white until stiff but not dry and fold into the yoghurt and redcurrant mixture.

NOTE: It should not be made more than 2 hours in advance or it will begin to weep.

Raspberry and Almond Malakoff

SERVES 6
170g/6oz caster sugar
170g/6oz unsalted butter
290ml/1/2 pint double cream
170g/6oz ground almonds
45ml/3 tablespoons Kirsch
225g/8oz raspberries
1 large packet boudoir biscuits (sponge fingers)

1. Beat the sugar and butter until really fluffy, soft and white.
2. Whip the cream and fold with the ground almonds, Kirsch and finally the raspberries into the butter and sugar mixture.
3. Put an oiled circle of greaseproof paper (oiled side up) into the bottom of a 15cm/6 inch straight-sided cake tin or soufflé dish.
4. Line the sides with the biscuits, standing up round the edge. Spoon the mixture into the middle, pressing down gently and smoothing the top level.
5. Put into the refrigerator for 4 hours.
6. With a bread knife, cut the tops of the biscuits to the level of the mixture. Turn the Malakoff out on to a serving plate. Remove the circle of paper.

NOTE: The top can be decorated with rosettes of whipped cream and a few fresh raspberries, but it looks very pretty without further adornment.

SWEET WHITE

Peaches with Raspberry Coulis

SERVES 4
4 large ripe peaches
290ml1/2 pint raspberry coulis (see page 421)
about 30g/1oz blanched flaked almonds, browned

1. Place the peaches in a pan of boiling water for 10 seconds and then remove the skins. Stone and cut into segments.
2. Flood the base of 4 plates with the raspberry coulis. Arrange a peach prettily on each plate and scatter over the browned flaked almonds.

LIGHT SWEET WHITE

Summer Fruit Parcels

SERVES 6
For the fruit purée:
1/4 melon
4 peaches
2 apricots
dash of bitter almond essence
2 split vanilla pods

For the parcels:
2 bananas
1 orange
8 greengages
8 Victoria plums

24 raspberries
1 pear
3 split vanilla pods
fresh mint leaves
55ml/2 fl oz Grand Marnier

6 sheets of foil, 35cm/14 inches square

1. Heat the oven to its highest setting.
2. First make the fruit purée: cube the melon flesh, halve and stone the peaches and apricots and cut the flesh into cubes. Put the fruit into a small saucepan with 150ml/1/4 pint water, the almond essence and vanilla pods. Cover and simmer the fruit for about 10 minutes or until a light purée is formed. Remove the vanilla pods. Liquidize the purée and then sieve it. You should have about 290 ml/1/2 pint purée.
3. To prepare the remaining fruit: cut the bananas in half lengthways and then cut each piece in half. Peel the orange with a knife as you would an apple, making sure that all the pith is removed, and then cut the orange into segments. Halve and stone the greengages and plums. Pick over the raspberries. Peel, core and quarter the pear and cut the flesh into 12.
4. Lay out the foil and place 45ml/3 tablespoons purée on each piece. Arrange the fruit on top. Add half a vanilla pod to each parcel, 2 or 3 mint leaves and a dash of Grand Marnier. Fold up the edges of the foil to form sealed parcels and place them on a baking sheet in the hot oven for 7 minutes. Serve immediately on individual plates.

LIGHT SWEET WHITE

Greek Iced Fruit Salad

a selection of fruit: cantaloupe melon, red apples, bananas, black grapes, oranges, strawberries, cherries, etc.
lemon juice
crushed ice

1. Put all the fruit, unprepared, into the refrigerator for a few hours to chill well.
2. Prepare the fruit for eating with the fingers, i.e. peel the oranges and break into segments, picking off any pith. Wash, quarter and core the apples and slice, using a stainless steel knife. Break the grapes into bunches of 3 or 4 grapes each. Peel the bananas and cut into largish pieces. Cut the melon into quarters, remove the peel and cut the flesh into fingers. Leave the strawberries whole and unhulled, washing them only if they are sandy. Wash the cherries, leaving the stalks intact.
3. Arrange the fruit attractively on a very well chilled dish and sprinkle with lemon juice. Sprinkle with ice just before serving.

NOTE I: Apples can be peeled of course, but shiny red ones look good unpeeled.
NOTE II: Fruit that is liable to discolour, such as bananas, pears and apples, should be cut up shortly before serving.
NOTE III: To crush ice cubes, put them in a strong plastic bag or cloth and beat with a rolling pin.

Chinese Apple Fritters

SERVES 6
450g/1lb sugar
150ml/1/4 pint water
3 dessert apples
lemon juice
85g/3oz cornflour
oil for frying
30ml/2 tablespoons sesame seeds
5ml/1 teaspoon wine vinegar

1. Have ready a bowl of iced water.
2. Place the sugar and water together in a heavy pan and set over a gentle heat to dissolve without boiling.
3. Peel, core and quarter the apples. Cut into chunks. Sprinkle with lemon juice and roll in cornflour.
4. Put the oil on to heat.
5. Meanwhile, toast the sesame seeds in a small heavy dry pan.
6. Deep-fry the apples in hot oil for about 4 minutes until golden brown. Drain well on absorbent paper.
7. When the sugar has dissolved, boil rapidly until the mixture caramelizes (goes toffee-

brown), then add the vinegar, taking care as the mixture will splutter and sizzle. Add the sesame seeds and stand the saucepan in a roasting pan of warm water. (This will prevent the caramel becoming too hard.)

8. Turn a few apples at a time in the caramel and sesame seeds.

9. Dip each fritter into cold water to rapidly cool the caramel and harden it, and then drain and serve immediately.

FORTIFIED SWEET WHITE

Melon with Ginger Wine

small melons, e.g. Ogen
ginger wine

1. Buy Ogen melons, either tiny individual ones or slightly bigger ones that can be split between 2 people.

2. Scoop out the seeds of the melons and pour 15ml/1 tablespoon ginger wine into each. Chill well before serving.

Pears in Red Wine

SERVES 4
150ml/1/4 pint water
150ml/1/4 pint red wine
110g/4oz sugar
15ml/1 tablespoon redcurrant jelly
pared rind of 1 lemon
pinch of cinnamon or 1 cinnamon stick
4 firm pears
30g/1oz browned almond flakes
140ml/5 fl oz double cream, whipped

1. Place the water, wine, sugar and jelly in a thick-bottomed saucepan and heat gently until the sugar has dissolved. Add the lemon rind and cinnamon.

2. Peel the pears very neatly without removing the stalks. Place upright in the pan and cover with a lid. The pears should be completely covered by the wine and water mixture so choose a tall narrow pan. If this is not possible, wet the pears in the mixture thoroughly and turn them during cooking.

3. Bring the mixture to the boil and then set to simmer slowly for at least 20 minutes. The pears should be a deep crimson colour and very tender. The longer and slower the pears cook the better. (They can even be cooked overnight in an extremely low oven.)

4. Reduce the pears from the pan and place in a glass bowl. Reduce the wine liquid by rapid boiling to a syrupy consistency and strain it over the pears. Allow to cool. Chill.

5. Sprinkle over the browned nuts just before serving and serve the whipped cream separately.

RICH SWEET WHITE

Pear Sabayon with Pear Sorbet

SERVES 4
4 Conference pears
570ml/1 pint sugar syrup, (see page 419)
4 egg yolks
45ml/3 tablespoons caster sugar
55ml/2 fl oz Poire William, or eau de vie
150ml/¼ pint double cream, lightly whipped
pear sorbet (see page 512)
few sprigs of mint to garnish

1. Peel the pears very neatly, without removing the stalks. Place upright in a pan with the sugar syrup and cover with a lid. The pears should be completely covered by the sugar syrup. Choose a tall narrow pan. If this is not possible, wet the pears in the syrup thoroughly and turn them during cooking.
2. Bring to the boil and then set to simmer slowly for about 1 hour. The pears should be glassy and very tender. Remove from the syrup, allow to cool and then refrigerate until cold.
3. While the pears are poaching, prepare the sabayon sauce. Put the egg yolks and sugar into a bowl. Set over a saucepan of simmering water. Whisk, for at least 10 minutes, until thick and creamy. Remove from the heat and whisk until cool. Add the liqueur and lightly whipped cream. Chill.
4. To serve: flood the base of 4 pudding plates with the sabayon sauce. Slice the pears in such a way that they can be rearranged on the sabayon as a whole, but slightly flattened, pear. Garnish each plate with a large scoop of pear sorbet and a sprig of mint.

SWEET WHITE

Raspberries and Fromage Blanc with Fresh Figs

This is a low-fat, sugar-free pudding.

SERVES 4
225g/8oz fresh raspberries
concentrated apple juice
60ml/4 tablespoons low-fat fromage blanc
4 ripe figs, cut into quarters

To garnish:
sprigs of mint

1. Liquidize the raspberries with enough water to make a smooth purée. Taste and add a little apple juice to sweeten, if required. Strain and pour on to one side of 4 pudding plates.
2. Mix the fromage blanc with a little water and pour on to the other half of the pudding plates.
3. Marble the fromage blanc and raspberry purée together with a large fork and arrange the figs on top of the sauces. Garnish with the sprigs of mint.

LIGHT SWEET WHITE

Raspberry Plate

SERVES 4
450g/1lb raspberries and cooked blackcurrants
140g/5oz icing sugar
60ml/4 tablespoons crème de cassis liqueur
150ml/¼ pint double cream
fresh fruit to serve
mint to garnish

1. Liquidize together the cooked blackcurrants, icing sugar and cassis. Strain.
2. Pour this sauce on to one side of 4 plates and pour double cream on the other side. Squiggle with a fork where they join to marble slightly.
3. Pile fresh raspberries or a fruit salad of sliced figs, blackberries, damsons and blueberries in the middle of each plate and top each with a sprig of mint.

Creamed Cheese with Fresh Fruit

This dessert is simple to prepare and is particularly suitable for a buffet party.

SERVES 4-6
225g/8oz cottage cheese
290ml/½ pint double cream, lightly whipped
55g/2oz icing sugar
2 drops vanilla essence
3 figs, quartered
3 kiwis, peeled and sliced
4 oranges, peeled and segmented

1. Put the cottage cheese into a sieve and drain very well.
2. Push the cheese through the sieve (or process briefly in a processor) and fold in the lightly whipped double cream. Sweeten with the sifted icing sugar and add the drops of vanilla essence.
3. Pile on to a large oval dish and shape into a shallow mound. Arrange the fruit attractively on top of the cheese.

LIGHT SWEET WHITE

Summer Pudding

SERVES 4-6
900g/2lb redcurrants, blackcurrants, blackberries, raspberries and strawberries (or just some of these fruits, mixed)
30ml/2 tablespoons water
170g/6oz sugar
6-9 slices stale white bread

To serve:
double cream, lightly whipped

1. Cook the redcurrants, blackcurrants and blackberries with the water and sugar until just soft but still bright in colour. Add the raspberries and strawberries. Drain off most of the juice and reserve.
2. Dip slices of the bread into the reserved fruit juice and use it to line a pudding basin.
3. While the fruit is still just warm, pour it into the bread-lined basin. Cover with a round piece of bread dipped in the fruit juice. Tip the remaining juice into a saucepan and reduce, by boiling rapidly, to a syrupy consistency. Leave to cool.
4. Stand the pudding basin on a dish. Press a saucer or plate on top of the pudding and put a 450g/1lb weight on top. Leave in a cool place overnight. Remove the saucer and weight.
5. Invert a serving dish over the bowl and turn both over together. Give a sharp shake and remove the bowl. Spoon over the reserved, reduced fruit juice. Serve the cream separately.

SWEET WHITE

Ice Creams and Sorbets

Ice Creams and Sorbets

ICE CREAM is a foam stabilised by freezing much of the liquid (even when frozen some of the liquid is left unfrozen). There are tiny ice crystals composed of pure water and solid globules of milk fat and there are tiny air cells.

The liquid prevents the formation of a solid block. The ice crystals stabilise the foam by trapping air and fat in its structure and if ice creams contain a good proportion of fat they freeze to a smooth creaminess without too much trouble. If they consist of mostly sugar and water or milk they need frequent beating during the freezing process to prevent too large ice crystals forming. In any event the more a mixture is beaten and churned during freezing the more air will be incorporated and the creamier in texture it will be.

The tiny air cells are very important as they break up the solid liquid to make a lighter, softer texture. Ice cream without air would be difficult to serve, scoop or eat.

MAKING AND STORING

AN ICE-CREAM MAKER The best modern method of churning ice cream is with an ice-cream maker with a built-in chiller and electric motor. These machines are expensive, scaled-down versions of the commercial machines used by caterers. Their chief advantages are that they operate independently of the freezer, and are powerful and large enough to churn even a thick mixture to smoothness. The main disadvantages are the expense and the fact that they take up valuable work space when not in use (they are too heavy for cupboard storage).

AN ELECTRIC SORBETIERE is useful if making small quantities of ice cream from a fairly thin mixture - a custard or a syrup. But few are powerful enough to churn a mixture containing solid pieces (such as pieces of meringue or raisins, for example) or thick mixtures made from, say, mashed bananas. Also, sorbetières must be put into a freezer as they have no built-in chilling equipment and care must be taken when setting up the machine that the lead that connects the churn placed in the freezer to the plug on the wall will not be damaged by closing the freezer door, nor prevent the door closing tight.

A FOOD PROCESSOR will not chill the mixture, of course, but it is powerful enough to churn it to smoothness in a few minutes. Freeze the mixture in a shallow tray until solid, then break it up and process the frozen pieces, using the chopping blade, to pale creaminess. Return to the tray and refreeze.

BUCKET CHURNS can be bought with electric motors or with a handle for manual operation. Most have a good large capacity and are reliable and powerful, but they require a supply of ice and of salt. Coarsely crushed ice is packed in layers, sprinkled with coarse salt, between the metal ice-cream container and the outer bucket. The ice-cream in the container is churned steadily by a strong paddle for 25 minutes or so, until the ice cream is thick. It can be left, without fear of melting, in the churn for an hour or so after making.

MIXING ICE CREAMS BY HAND Finally, ice cream can be made without any special equipment. All that is needed is a shallow ice-cube tray or roasting pan, a bowl, and a strong whisk. The ice cream is half frozen in the tray, then tipped into the bowl (which is chilled) and whisked until smooth. This is repeated until icy shards are eliminated.

SUGAR AND FLAVOURINGS Extreme cold inhibits our sense of taste, the tastebuds being too cold to operate effectively. For this reason ice creams must be sweetened or flavoured more than seems right when tasting the mixture at room temperature.

STORAGE

Theoretically, ice cream can be stored for very long periods, but, certainly in a domestic freezer, there is some deterioration. Ice crystals may form on the surface of the ice cream after a week or so, meringue-based ices or ices containing gelatine may become rubbery, and if raw fruit (such as puréed peach) has been used, the colour will change for the worse. For total perfection, ice cream should be eaten the day it is made. But a few days' freezing is acceptable. If ices are frozen for longer periods, and obviously they often will be, poor texture can be rectified by allowing the ice cream to soften slightly, re-whisking it and re-freezing it. Or the frozen mixture can be re-beaten in a processor. If fruit ices are to be stored for longer than a few days, the fruit should be cooked to preserve the colour.

THAWING

Unless the mixture is very soft, it is wise to put it into the refrigerator for half an hour before serving to allow the ice to soften slightly. Or it may be softened sufficiently to scoop into balls, then put into a chilled serving dish and returned to the freezer until needed.

Ther are three basic methods of making ice cream.

CUSTARD-BASED METHOD (see page 504)

MOUSSE-BASED PARFAITS In a mousse-based parfait the air that will give the creaminess to the frozen mixture is beaten into the egg base over heat before cooling and freezing. This means that there is no need to churn or beat once the mixture is in the freezer, and it can be poured into a china soufflé dish with a paper collar tied round (see page 508) it so that it looks deceptively like a risen soufflé or an iced soufflé.

MERINGUE-BASED ICE CREAMS These are similar to the mousse-based parfaits, but the air is incorporated into the egg whites, as for meringue, before the flavouring fruit purée is added. The method is suitable for fruit ice creams, where the acidity of the fruit nicely cuts the sweet meringue.

THEN THERE ARE FROZEN YOGHURTS Yoghurt, because it is so low in fat, is not easy to freeze smoothly without the aid of a machine that beats or stirs constantly during freezing. It thaws and melts too fast for the processor method. The addition of large quantities of cream or sugar would make a smoother and more stable mixture but as frozen yoghurt is often served as a healthy alternative to a fattening dessert, such additions would defeat the cook's object.

SORBETS AND GRANITA Sorbets (sherberts or water ices) are made by freezing flavoured syrups or purées. The essential thing is to get the proportions right. Too much sugar and the sorbet will be oversweet, syrupy and too soft to hold its shape. Too little and it will be icy, crystalline and hard. Chefs use a saccharimeter to measure the amount of sugar in a syrup (a 'pese-syrop' to get the desired 37 per cent sugar), but good results can be had if the mixture contains about one-third sugar and two-thirds other ingredients. Once this figure is in the cook's head, he or she can make almost any sorbet with two-parts liquid (unsweetened) and one-part sugar, bringing the syrup slowly to the boil, cooling it, and freezing it, whisking as necessary.

There is no question that a machine gives the best results. If no machine is available the addition of a little gelatine (1 tablespoon for every 300ml/$^1/_2$ pint of liquid) or the addition of whisked egg whites does help prevent the formation of large ice crystals, and slows up melting.

If slightly less sugar is used, and the mixture is forked rather than beaten while freezing, a granita results - a granular, fast-melting sorbet.

The recipes for ice creams assume that you do not have an ice-cream maker – if you do, simply follow the manufacturer's instructions. Light, sweet wines go with most ice creams, particularly Italian Muscato with fruit ices. Also, try sweet sparkling wine or champagne.

Plum or Apricot Ice Cream

SERVES 6
900g/2lb plums or apricots
110/4oz granulated sugar
3 egg yolks
150ml/1/4 pint double cream

1. Stew the fruit with 150ml/1/4 pint water and 55g/2oz of the sugar. When tender, push both fruit and juice through a nylon or stainless steel sieve. You should have 290ml/1/2 pint purée. Taste and check for sweetness.
2. Dissolve the rest of the sugar in 150ml/1/4 pint water without boiling it. Then boil rapidly 'to the thread'. (To test, take a little syrup out of the pan with a wooden spoon, dip your fingers in cold water and then dip your finger and thumb into the syrup. The syrup should feel very tacky and form short threads when finger and thumb are drawn apart.)
3. Allow to cool for 1/2 minute. Beat the egg yolks with a whisk. Pour on the sugar syrup, whisking all the time, until the mixture is thick, pale and mousse-like, and quite cold.
4. Whip the cream until thick but not totally stiff. Add to the fruit purée with the yolk mixture. Turn into an ice tray.
5. Freeze for about 45 minutes or until beginning to freeze around the edges. Remove the ice cream, stir thoroughly and return to the freezer to freeze completely.
6. If the ice cream is not perfectly smooth, tip it into a chilled bowl, beat until smooth and creamy and refreeze.

Ginger Ice Cream

SERVES 6
85g/3oz granulated sugar
150ml/1/4 pint water
4 egg yolks
10ml/2 teaspoons ground ginger
570ml/1 pint double cream, lightly whipped
4 pieces stem ginger, cut into fine strips

1. Put the sugar and water into a small heavy pan. Dissolve over a gentle heat. Boil for 3 minutes. Remove from the heat and cool for 1 minute.
2. Put the egg yolks into a large bowl with the ground ginger, whisk lightly and pour on the warm sugar syrup (do not allow the syrup to touch the whisk if doing this in a machine). Fold in the cream. Freeze.
3. When the ice cream is half-frozen, whisk again and add the stem ginger. Freeze again.
4. Remove from the freezer half an hour before it is to be eaten and scoop into a glass bowl.

Vanilla Ice Cream

This ice cream is made with a custard base.

SERVES 6-8
570ml/1 pint milk
290ml/1/2 pint single cream
225g/8oz caster sugar
8 egg yolks
few drops vanilla essence

1. Set the freezer or ice compartment to the coldest setting. Put the milk, cream and sugar into a heavy saucepan and bring slowly to the boil. Beat the yolks with the vanilla in a large bowl.
2. Pour the scalding milk mixture on to the yolks, whisking as you do so. Strain into a roasting pan or into 2 ice trays. Cool.
3. Freeze until solid but still soft enough to give when pressed with a finger.
4. Tip the ice cream into a cold bowl, break it up, then whisk with a rotary beater until smooth, pale and creamy. If you have a food processor, all the better. Refreeze.

NOTE: If the ice cream is made more than 6 hours in advance, it will be too hard to scoop.

Put it in the refrigerator for 40-60 minutes before serving to allow it to soften.

Damson Ice Cream

SERVES 6-8
450g/1lb damsons
340g/12oz caster sugar
150ml/1/4 pint water
2 large egg whites
juice and finely grated rind of 1 small orange
290ml/1/2 pint double cream

1. Wash the damsons and put them, still wet, with 110g/4oz of the sugar in a thick-bottomed saucepan. Stew gently, covered, over very gentle heat or bake in the oven until soft and pulpy.
2. Push through a sieve, removing the stones.
3. Dissolve the remaining 225g/8oz sugar in the water and bring to the boil.
4. Boil steadily for 5 minutes.
5. While the syrup is boiling, beat the egg whites in an electric mixer or by hand until stiff. Pour the boiling syrup on to the egg whites, whisking as you do so. The mixture will go rather liquid at this stage, but keep whisking until you have a thick meringue.
6. Stir in the orange rind and juice and the purée.
7. Whip the cream until thick but not solid, and fold it into the mixture.
8. Freeze. It is not necessary to re-whisk the ice cream during freezing.

NOTE: The damson purée can be replaced by a purée of cooked plums, greengages, rhubarb, dried apricots or prunes, or a raw purée of soft fruit, such as fresh apricots or peaches.

Coffee Ice Cream

This ice cream is made with a custard base.

SERVES 4-6
4 egg yolks
85g/3oz caster sugar
pinch of salt
425ml/3/4 pint single cream
25ml/5 teaspoons instant coffee

1. Whisk the egg yolks, sugar and salt until light and frothy.
2. Place the cream and coffee together in a pan and heat slowly until the coffee dissolves.
3. Add the cream to the egg-yolk mixture, whisking all the time.
4. Pour the mixture into the top of a double saucepan or into a bowl set over a pan of simmering water.
5. Stir continuously until thick and creamy.
6. Strain into a bowl and allow to cool, whisking occasionally.
7. Chill, then freeze.
8. When the ice cream is half-frozen, whisk again and return to the freezer.

Raspberry Ice Cream

This ice cream is made with a mousse base.

SERVES 4-6
450g/1lb raspberries
85g/3oz icing sugar
70g/2 1/2 oz sugar
110ml/4 fl oz water
a little vanilla essence
3 egg yolks
290ml/1/2 pint single or double cream
squeeze of lemon

1. Liquidize or crush the raspberries and push through a nylon or stainless steel sieve.
2. Sweeten with the icing sugar.
3. Place the sugar and water in a saucepan and dissolve over a gentle heat.
4. When completely dissolved, boil 'to the thread'. (When a little syrup is put between finger and thumb and the fingers opened, it should form a sticky thread about 2.5cm/1 inch long.)
5. Cool for 1 minute. Add the vanilla essence.
6. Pour the sugar syrup on to the egg yolks and whisk until the mixture is thick and mousse-like.
7. Cool and add the cream, fruit purée and lemon juice.
8. Taste for sweetness and add more icing sugar if necessary.
9. Chill, then freeze.
10. If the ice cream is not quite smooth when half-frozen, whisk it once more and return to the freezer.

Chocolate Ice Cream

This ice cream is made with a custard base.

SERVES 4
340g/12oz plain chocolate, cut up into small pieces
570ml/1 pint milk
1 egg
1 egg yolk
55g/2oz caster sugar
570ml/1 pint double cream
5ml/1 teaspoon vanilla essence

1. Dissolve the chocolate in the milk over a gentle heat.
2. Whisk the egg and yolk with the sugar in a basin set over a pan of simmering water. Whisk until light and fluffy.
3. When the chocolate has melted and the milk nearly boiled, pour on to the egg mixture and whisk well. Strain and allow to cool.
4. Whip the cream lightly and fold it into the chocolate mixture with the vanilla essence. Put into a bowl and freeze.
5. When half-frozen, re-whisk and re-freeze.

NOTE: Chocolate mint crisps or mint cracknel, crumbled up and added to the mixture at the time of the final whisking, give a delicious flavour and crunchy texture.

Lemon Curd Ice Cream

SERVES 6
4 egg yolks
grated rind and juice of 2 lemons
125g/4½ oz caster sugar
110g/4oz unsalted butter, at room temperature, cut into small pieces
570ml/1 pint natural yoghurt

1. Put the egg yolks, lemon rind and juice, sugar and butter into a small saucepan. Put over a gentle heat and stir until the butter has melted and the curd coats the back of the spoon.
2. Allow the curd to cool and then stir the yoghurt into it. Cover closely and freeze.
3. Take the ice cream out of the freezer and put it into the refrigerator about an hour before serving.

Pistachio Parfait

SERVES 6
225g/8oz caster sugar
60ml/2½ fl oz water
3 egg whites
570ml/1 pint double cream
few drops of green colouring
15ml/1 tablespoon vanilla essence
5ml/1 teaspoon almond essence
75g/2½ oz pistachio nuts, chopped

1. Put the sugar and water in a heavy saucepan.
2. Without stirring, bring it slowly to the boil.
3. Boil until the syrup will form a thread when dropped from a spoon.
4. While the syrup is gently boiling at the correct stage, whisk the egg whites to stiff peaks.
5. If the whites are in a machine, pour the bubbling hot syrup on to them in a steady stream while whisking, taking care not to pour the syrup on to the wires of the whisk – it cools fast against the cold metal and can harden and stick to the whisk. If whisking the whites by hand, and in the absence of anyone to pour while you whisk, pour the syrup on to the whites in stages, about one-third at a time, whisking hard between each addition, and working as fast as possible. The syrup must be bubbling hot as it hits the egg white to partially cook it.
6. When all the syrup has been added, whisk hard until the mixture is stiff and shiny and absolutely stable. If the whisk is lifted, the meringue should not flow at all.
7. Lightly whip the cream and colour it a delicate green.
8. Fold the cream into the meringue mixture. Add the essences and chopped nuts.
9. Freeze and remove from the freezer half an hour before serving.

Pistachio Ice Cream in Biscuit Cups

SERVES 8
For the biscuit mixture:
85g/3oz butter
85g/3oz caster sugar
3 egg whites
85g/3oz plain flour

For the ice cream:
570ml/1 pint milk
225g/8oz caster sugar
1 vanilla pod
290ml/1/2 pint single cream
8 egg yolks, beaten
110g/4oz pistachio nuts, chopped

For the sauce:
3 whole eggs
3 egg yolks
140g/5oz sugar
45ml/3 tablespoons Framboise liqueur
340g/12oz fresh raspberries, sieved

1. Set the oven to 220°C/425°F/gas mark 7.
2. To make the biscuit cups, melt the butter, add the sugar, stir, over a very gentle heat, until dissolved and allow to cool.
3. Gradually beat in the unwhisked egg whites, using a wire whisk. Fold in the sifted flour. Baking 2 biscuits at a time, spread the mixture out in 8 very large paper-thin rounds on a greased and floured baking sheet. (Warm the sheet for easier spreading.)
4. Bake for 4 minutes. The biscuits should be just brown at the edges and pale in the middle.
5. While still hot and pliable, shape the discs of biscuit over greased upturned jam jars. Remove the jam jars when the paste has set. (If the cups are not quite crisp when cold, return them to the oven on the jam jars.)
6. Make the ice cream: bring the milk, sugar, vanilla pod and cream very slowly to the boil. Pour on to the beaten yolks, stirring well. Remove the vanilla pod.
7. If the mixture is still very thin and runny return it to a gentle heat and stir continuously until it will coat the back of the spoon. Immediately pour into a cold bowl and allow to cool. Add the nuts.
8. Freeze, either in an ice-cream maker or in ice trays in the freezer, taking it out and beating 2 or 3 times during the freezing process to prevent large ice crystals forming.
9. When nearly ready to serve, fill each biscuit cup with ice cream, stand on a platter and put back into the coldest part of the refrigerator or into the freezer while making the sauce.
10. Whisk the whole eggs, yolks, sugar and liqueur together in a bowl. Then stand over a saucepan of simmering water and keep whisking. It will thicken like zabaglione. Stir in the sieved berries and serve, lukewarm, with the biscuit cups.

Individual Mango Parfaits with Passionfruit Sauce

SERVES 8
2 ripe mangos
3 egg yolks
110g/4oz icing sugar
200ml/8 fl oz double cream
lemon juice

For the sauce:
4 passionfruits
orange juice
sugar syrup (see page 419)

To decorate:
8 sprigs of mint

1. Lightly oil 8 ramekins.
2. Process the mango flesh until smooth.
3. Whisk the egg yolks and icing sugar until very thick and light.
4. Lightly whip the double cream.
5. Fold the mango purée and cream into the egg-yolk mixture.
6. Add the lemon juice to taste; it may also be necessary to add extra icing sugar.
7. Pour the mixture into the prepared ramekins, cover with cling film and place in the freezer for at least 4 hours.
8. Prepare the sauce: mix the passionfruit pulp with a little orange juice and sugar syrup to taste.

9. To serve: turn the parfaits out on to individual plates, spoon over a little passionfruit sauce and decorate with a sprig of mint.

Hazelnut Ice

SERVES 8
150g/5oz granulated sugar
45ml/3 tablespoons water
150g/5oz roasted, skinned hazelnuts

For the Italian meringue:
150g/5oz sugar
8 egg whites
6 egg yolks
290ml/½ pint double cream, lightly whipped

To serve:
raspberry coulis (see page 421)

1. Prepare a 15cm/6 inch soufflé dish: tie a double piece of greaseproof paper around the outside of the dish. The paper should stand about 5cm/2 inches above the rim. Lightly brush the inside of the 'paper collar' with oil.
2. Lightly oil a baking sheet.
3. Melt the granulated sugar in a pan with water. When the sugar has dissolved, boil until it turns to a pale caramel. Add 130g/4½oz of the still-warm hazelnuts and cook for a further 2 minutes until a rich brown. Pour on to the oiled baking sheet.
4. Cool, then pound or liquidize.
5. To make the Italian meringue: make the sugar syrup by dissolving the sugar in the water over a gentle heat, then boil until the syrup reaches the soft ball stage (116°C/240°F using a sugar thermometer). In a large bowl, whisk the egg whites until stiff, then gradually add the sugar syrup; whisking all the time. Continue to whisk until really thick and shiny.
6. Put the egg yolks into a bowl and add the powdered nut mixture. Place the bowl over a saucepan of simmering water and whisk until the mixture is thick and fluffy. Whisk off the heat until the mixture has cooled. (If using an electric mixer, you need not beat the mixture over heat.)
7. Fold the cream into the egg mixture and then fold in the meringue.
8. Pour into the prepared soufflé dish and place in the freezer for at least 8 hours.
9. To serve: remove the greaseproof paper. Roughly chop the remaining hazelnuts and scatter on top of the soufflé. Serve the raspberry coulis separately.

Vanilla and Prune Ice Cream

SERVES 4
290ml/½ pint milk
290ml/½ pint double cream
2 vanilla pods, split lengthways
6 egg yolks
100g/3½ oz sugar
8 prunes, stoned, cut in half and marinated in brandy for 24 hours

To serve:
2 ripe peaches, halved

1. Scald the milk and cream with the vanilla pods.
2. Beat the egg yolks and sugar until creamy, add the milk mixture gradually and whisk together.
3. Return it to the saucepan and cook over a low heat, stirring constantly, until the custard coats the back of the spoon. Strain through a sieve into a bowl and allow to cool.
4. Freeze the mixture in a shallow tray.
5. Once frozen, take the ice cream out of the freezer and allow to soften at room temperature. Either place in a food processor and whizz to remove the ice crystals or use an electric beater. Fold in the prunes and brandy.
6. Place the ice cream back in the container and refreeze.
7. Serve with the peaches.

Peach and Banana Ice Cream with Grape Sauce

Ice creams made from yoghurt inevitably have a crystal-like texture. The more they are whisked, the smoother they become. If you have an ice-cream machine, however, they will be almost as smooth as other ice creams.

SERVES 4-6
4 ripe peaches
2 bananas
450g/1lb low-fat yoghurt
concentrated apple juice (optional)

For the sauce:
750ml/1¼ pints black grape juice

1. Peel and stone the peaches. Peel and chop the bananas.
2. Process or liquidize together the peaches, bananas and yoghurt until very smooth.
3. Taste and sweeten with the apple juice if required (it will taste less sweet once frozen).
4. Place in the freezer until half-frozen. Tip into a chilled bowl and whisk well. Replace in the freezer until half-frozen and whisk again. Freeze again until firm.
5. Meanwhile, put the grape juice into a saucepan and reduce, by boiling, to a quarter of its original quantity.
6. Remove the ice cream 30 minutes before serving with the grape sauce.

Dried Apricot Ice Cream

SERVES 4
225g/8 oz dried apricots, soaked overnight
1 strip of lemon rind
290ml/½ pint double cream, lightly whipped
lemon juice to taste

1. Put the apricots, the soaking water and the lemon rind into a saucepan and bring up to the boil.
2. Simmer the apricots until they are soft. This will take approximately 20 minutes.
3. Remove the lemon rind and liquidize the apricots with the water until smooth. Allow to cool.
4. Fold the cream into the apricot purée. Add the lemon juice to taste.
5. Chill. Freeze. When half-frozen, whisk well and return to the freezer.

NOTE: If you have a food processor, once the ice cream has frozen allow it to soften, cut it into pieces and process it well. If you have a *gelato chef* (electric ice-cream maker), add the unfrozen mixture to the machine and follow the manufacturer's instructions.

Brown Bread Ice Cream

SERVES 4
110g/4oz brown breadcrumbs
110g/4oz dark brown sugar
2 eggs, separated
290ml/½ pint double cream
150ml/¼ pint single cream
2 drops vanilla essence

1. Set the oven to 200°C/400°F/gas mark 6.
2. Place the breadcrumbs in the oven for 15 minutes or until dry.
3. Mix the sugar and breadcrumbs and return to the oven for a further 15 minutes or until the sugar caramelizes. Remove, allow to cool and crush lightly.
4. Beat the egg yolks, add the creams and fold in the caramelized crumbs. Add the vanilla essence.
5. Whisk the egg whites to soft peaks and fold into the mixture. Freeze until required.

Coffee and Ricotta Ice Cream

Claudia Roden inspired this very simple and, I think, completely delicious ice cream.

SERVES 4
255g/9oz ricotta cheese
15ml/1 tablespoon fine ground coffee
30ml/2 tablespoons caster sugar

1. Beat the ricotta cheese, add the coffee and sugar and mix until smooth. Freeze for 2-3 hours.
2. Remove from the freezer 20 minutes before serving.

Black Cherry Frozen Dessert

This is a cheat's bombe – simple to make and delicious to eat.

SERVES 8
400g/14oz tin morello cherries
110g/4oz raspberries
110g/4oz meringues (see page 449)
570ml/1 pint double cream, or 675g/1½lb vanilla ice cream (see page 504)
1 tablespoon brandy or Kirsch (optional)
icing sugar to taste

For the sauce:
10ml/2 teaspoons arrowroot
15ml/1 tablespoon brandy or Kirsch

1. Drain the cherries well, reserving the juice. Break up the meringues roughly.
2. Whip the cream until stiff, add the brandy or Kirsch and sweeten to taste. (If using ice cream, allow it to soften but not to melt.) Mix in the cherries, raspberries and meringue. Add sugar to taste.
3. Spoon the mixture into a bombe mould or bowl and put immediately into the freezer. It will take at least 2 hours, and probably 4, to harden. It can then be turned out on to a plate and put back in the freezer until needed.
4. Mix the arrowroot with a little water. Heat the reserved cherry juice in a saucepan, pour some of the hot juice on to the arrowroot, stirring, and then pour the arrowroot and juice into the saucepan. Bring to the boil, stirring. Allow to simmer for 1 minute after boiling. Add the brandy or Kirsch and serve hot with the bombe.

NOTE: This dessert can be made with fresh or frozen strawberries, pineapple or peaches, but the fruit should be chopped rather than left whole or in large pieces.

Mincemeat 'Bombe'

SERVES 8
290ml/½ pint double cream
45ml/3 tablespoons rum
225ml/8 fl oz natural yoghurt
8 meringue shells (see page 449), crushed
5ml/1 teaspoon freshly grated nutmeg

For the mincemeat sauce:
1 large dessert apple
55g/2oz raisins
55g/2oz sultanas
55g/2oz chopped hazelnuts, lightly toasted
55g/2oz soft dark brown sugar
2.5ml/½ teaspoon mixed spice
grated rind and juice of ½ lemon
grated rind and juice of 1 orange
60ml/4 tablespoons rum

1. Lightly oil and line 8 ramekin dishes with discs of greaseproof paper.
2. Whip the cream until it holds its shape. Whisk in the rum and fold in the yoghurt, the meringue and nutmeg. Turn into the ramekin dishes and freeze until firm.
3. Peel, core and chop the apple, add the remaining ingredients for the sauce, adding more orange juice or rum to taste.
4. To serve: run a knife around the ramekins and turn the ice cream out on to plates. Place in the refrigerator for 10 minutes before serving.
5. Heat the sauce until very hot but not boiling and hand it separately.

Peach Melba

SERVES 4
170g/6oz raspberries
icing sugar
2 large fresh peaches
425ml/3/4 pint vanilla ice cream (see page 504)

1. First prepare the Melba sauce: push the raspberries through a sieve and beat in icing sugar to taste.
2. If the peaches are not completely ripe, split and stone them and poach gently in a little sugar syrup (see page 419) until tender. Drain well and peel. If they are ripe, simply dip in boiling water for 4-5 seconds and then peel and halve them.
3. Serve in individual glasses. Place a spoonful of vanilla ice cream in each glass, cover with half a peach, round side up, and coat with Melba sauce. Serve immediately.

NOTE: The original peach Melba, created by Escoffier for the great opera singer, consisted of plain vanilla ice cream and fresh peaches resting in the hollowed-out back of a swan fashioned in ice. Escoffier later added the refinement of a pure raspberry purée.

Melon and Champagne Sorbet

SERVES 4-6
1 large Ogen melon
340g/12oz granulated sugar
75ml/5 tablespoons water
juice of 1 lemon
425 ml/3/4 pint champagne

1. Cut the melon into quarters. Remove the skin and seeds and liquidize or process until smooth.
2. Put the sugar and water into a heavy saucepan. Dissolve slowly on a gentle heat.
3. When the sugar has completely dissolved, boil rapidly until the syrup is tacky and a short thread can be formed if the syrup is pulled between finger and thumb.
4. Mix together the melon purée, lemon juice, champagne and warm syrup. Allow to cool.
5. Freeze overnight or until icy, then whisk until smooth and return to the freezer. Serve in well-chilled goblets.

NOTE: If you have an ice-cream machine, it makes short work of this sorbet. It is a soft sorbet because of the high alcoholic content.

Tomato Sorbet

SERVES 4-6
110g/4oz granulated sugar
290ml/1/2 pint water
500ml/17 fl oz tomato juice
juice of 1/2 lemon
fresh mint or basil leaves, roughly chopped
15ml/1 tablespoon Worcestershire sauce
Tabasco
salt and freshly ground black pepper
1 egg white

1. Dissolve the sugar in the water over a gentle heat. When clear, increase the heat and boil to the thread, i.e. when the syrup is tacky and a short thread can be formed if the syrup is pulled between finger and thumb. Cool for 1 minute.
2. Meanwhile, mix together the tomato juice, lemon and herbs. Season to taste with Worcestershire sauce, Tabasco, salt and pepper. Add the cooling sugar syrup. Transfer to a metal container and cool completely before freezing.
3. Once the sorbet has formed large crystals and is almost set, remove from the container and break up with a fork.
4. Whisk the egg white until stiff but not dry and fold into the tomato mixture. Return to the container and freeze again. Remove 10-15 minutes before serving.

NOTE: If using a food processor, when the sorbet is partially frozen, remove from the container, roughly chop and then quickly process. Add the unwhipped egg white through the lid funnel as the blade is moving. Process for approximately 1 minute. Return the mixture to the container and re-freeze.

Apple Sorbet

SERVES 4
4 Cox's apples
160g/5½ oz caster sugar
juice of 1 lemon
30ml/2 tablespoons Calvados
1 egg white

1. Peel, core and quarter the apples.
2. Put the apples into a saucepan with the sugar and enough water to just cover them. Poach gently for 20 minutes.
3. Remove the apples and reduce the cooking liquor, by boiling rapidly, until thick and syrupy. (Do not let it begin to caramelize.) Purée the apples, sugar syrup and lemon juice together in a liquidizer or food processor.
4. Allow to cool and then freeze.
5. When nearly frozen, return the sorbet to the processor and whizz briefly. Gradually add the unwhisked egg white to the food processor. It will fluff up tremendously. Return to the container and freeze until firm.

Pear Sorbet

SERVES 4
4 ripe William pears
160g/5½ oz caster or icing sugar
juice of 2 lemons
1 egg white, lightly whisked

1. Peel, core and quarter the pears.
2. Put the pears into a saucepan with the sugar and enough water to just cover the pears. Poach gently for 20 minutes.
3. Remove the pears and reduce the cooking liquor by boiling rapidly until thick and syrupy. (Do not let it begin to caramelize.) Purée the pears, sugar syrup and lemon juice together in a liquidizer or food processor.
4. Allow to cool and then freeze.
5. When nearly frozen, fold in the egg white and freeze until firm.

NOTE: If you have a food processor, allow the sorbet to freeze and then defrost until half-frozen. Whizz in the food processor and gradually add the egg white, unwhisked. It will fluff up.

Trois Sorbets

SERVES 4
pear sorbet (see above)
passionfruit sorbet (see page 513)
strawberry sorbet (see page 513)
fresh raspberries
fresh strawberries
fresh orange segments

For the coulis rouge:
225g/8oz raspberries
15ml/1 tablespoon water
15ml/1 tablespoon caster sugar

1. Prepare the coulis rouge: heat together the raspberries, water and caster sugar. Bring to the boil for 30 seconds to allow the sugar to dissolve. Push through a sieve and spoon on to 4 pudding plates so that the base of each dish is completely covered. Leave to get completely cold.
2. Arrange the sorbets and fresh fruit on the plates as illustrated.

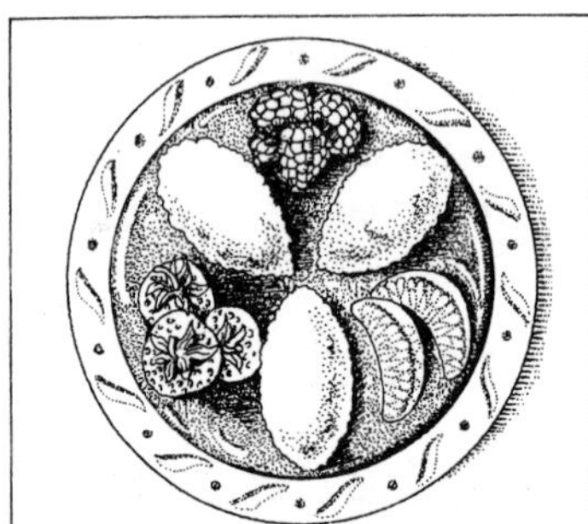

Pear, passionfruit and strawberry sorbet with fresh fruits.

Redcurrant Water Ice

SERVES 4
450g/1lb sugar
425ml/¾ pint water
7g/¼ oz gelatine
425ml/¾ pint redcurrant juice

1. Dissolve the sugar in the water over a low heat and, when completely dissolved, boil to the thread (i.e. when a little syrup is put between finger and thumb and the fingers opened, it should form a sticky thread 2.5cm/1 inch long).
2. In a small saucepan, soak the gelatine in 30ml/ 2 tablespoons redcurrant juice.
3. Add the rest of the juice to the sugar syrup.

4. Dissolve the gelatine over a low heat and when clear, stir into the redcurrant mixture.
5. Allow to get quite cold. Whisk very thoroughly, preferably in a food processor or ice-cream maker.
6. Chill, then freeze.

Lemon Sorbet

SERVES 4
pared rind and juice of 3 lemons
170g/6oz granulated sugar
570ml/1 pint water
1/2 egg white

1. Place the lemon rind, sugar and water together in a thick-bottomed saucepan. Dissolve the sugar over a gentle heat and, when completely clear, boil rapidly until you have a thick syrup (i.e. sufficiently thick for a thread to form between finger and thumb when the fingers are dipped in the syrup and then moved apart).
2. Allow to cool. When the syrup is cold, add the lemon juice and strain.
3. Freeze for 30 minutes or until the syrup is beginning to solidify.
4. Whisk the egg white until stiff and fold into the lemon-syrup mixture.
5. Freeze until solid.

NOTE: If you have a food processor, allow the lemon syrup to freeze and then whisk until soft. Pour in the egg white, through the funnel, whisking all the time. Freeze until solid.

Strawberry Sorbet

SERVES 4
170g/6oz caster sugar
570ml/1 pint water
juice of 1/2 lemon or small orange
340g/12oz fresh or frozen strawberries
2 egg whites

1. Place the sugar and water together in a thick-bottomed saucepan. Dissolve over a gentle heat and, when clear, boil gently for 5 minutes. Add the lemon or orange juice and cool.
2. Liquidize or mash the strawberries to a pulp and add the syrup. Put in a bowl in the freezer for 30 minutes or until the syrup is beginning to solidify.
3. Whisk the egg whites until stiff and fold into the half-frozen mixture. Return to the freezer until solid.

NOTE: If you have a food processor, allow the strawberry syrup to freeze, then whisk until soft. Pour in the egg white, through the funnel, whisking all the time. Freeze until solid.

Passionfruit Sorbet

SERVES 6
170g/6oz granulated sugar
425ml/3/4 pint water
pared rind and juice of 1 lemon
450g/1lb passionfruit pulp (from about 32 passionfruits)
1/2 egg white

1. Dissolve the sugar in the water. Add the lemon rind. Boil rapidly for 5 minutes, or until the syrup is tacky.
2. Sieve the passionfruit pulp and add to the syrup with the lemon juice. Cool.
3. Place in the deep freeze and leave until icy and half-frozen.
4. Tip into a chilled bowl and whisk well. Refreeze until almost solid.
5. Whisk the egg white until very stiff.
6. Tip the sorbet into another chilled bowl and break up. Whisk until smooth and fold in the egg white.
7. Freeze again until firm.
8. If the ice is not absolutely creamy and smooth, give it one more freezing and whisking.

NOTE: If you have a food processor, allow the passionfruit, syrup and lemon juice to freeze. Defrost slightly and then whisk until soft. Pour the egg white in, through the funnel, whizzing all the time. Freeze until solid.

Brandy Snap Tortes

SERVES 10
brandy snap mixture made with 110g/4oz flour (see page 575)
450g/1lb damson ice cream, slightly softened (see page 505)
raspberry coulis (see page 421)
110g/4oz raspberries and blueberries
sprig of fresh mint
icing sugar for dusting

1. Set the oven to 190°C/375°F/gas mark 5. Grease a baking sheet and palette knife.
2. Make the brandy snap mixture, adding an extra 5ml/1 teaspoon ground ginger. Bake the 20 brandy snaps on the baking sheet as in the recipe but lift them, flat, on to a wire rack and leave them to cool and harden.
3. Put a brandy snap 'flat' on to 10 pudding plates. Cover with some of the damson ice cream and flatten slightly. Cover with a second brandy snap flat. Arrange some more ice cream on top of the brandy snaps and cover with a third brandy snap.
4. Pour the raspberry coulis around the tortes.
5. Mix the raspberries and blueberries together. Arrange them on the coulis and decorate with a small sprig of mint.
6. Dust lightly with icing sugar.

Rich Vanilla Ice Cream

This ice cream is made with a mousse base.

SERVES 6-8
70g/2½ oz granulated sugar
120ml/8 tablespoons water
1 vanilla pod
3 egg yolks
425ml/¾ pint double cream

1. Put the sugar, water and vanilla pod into a saucepan and dissolve the sugar over a gentle heat, stirring.
2. Beat the egg yolks well. Half whip the cream.
3. When the sugar has dissolved, bring the syrup up to boiling point and boil 'to the thread'. Allow to cool for 1 minute. Remove the vanilla pod.
4. Whisk the egg yolks and gradually pour in the sugar syrup. Whisk until the mixture is very thick and will leave a trail.
5. Cool, whisking occasionally. Fold in the cream and freeze.
6. When the ice cream is half frozen, whisk again and return to the freezer.

NOTE: To boil to the thread: to test, dip your finger into cold water, then into a teaspoon of the hot syrup, which should form threads between your thumb and forefinger when they are drawn apart.

Composite Puddings

Coffee Rum Tipsy Cake

SERVES 4

2 plain sponge cakes or 2 boxes small bought sponge cakes
150ml/1/4 pint boiling water
45ml/3 tablespoons instant coffee
60ml/4 tablespoons sugar
15ml/1 tablespoon rum
140g/5oz icing sugar
85g/3oz butter
290ml/1/2 pint double cream
55g/2oz whole blanched almonds

1. Break up the cakes roughly and put them in a large bowl.
2. Pour the boiling water on to the coffee and sugar, and stir until the sugar has dissolved.
3. Add the rum and pour over the cake. Do not mix it in too much (the cake should retain a 'marbled' look, half white, half brown), but turn with a metal spoon.
4. Press the cake into a mixing bowl, and leave it with a weight on top (a 1kg/2lb can of fruit standing on a side plate will do) while you make the icing.
5. Beat the icing sugar and butter together until very light and creamy.
6. Whip the cream until just firm enough to hold its shape.
7. Brown the nuts under the grill.
8. Unmould the cake on to a plate. Using a palette knife dipped in hot water, spread the butter icing over the cake.
9. Then spread a layer of whipped cream over the icing and stud with the almonds.

LIQUEUR MUSCAT

Paskha

A rich, creamy cheese mixture, this is traditionally moulded in a tall wooden container, like a cut-off metronome. You can use a tall flowerpot or plastic pot instead.

This recipe has been taken from the *Observer Guide to European Cookery* by Jane Grigson.

SERVES 8

125ml/4 fl oz double cream
10cm/4 inch piece of vanilla pod, split
2 large egg yolks
85g/3oz sugar
110g/4oz unsalted butter, creamed
675g/1 1/2lb curd cheese or ricotta cheese
55-85g/2-3oz candied fruit and peel, chopped
55-85g/2-3oz blanched almonds, chopped

For decoration:
blanched almonds
candied fruit and peel
glacé fruits or raisins

1. In a small pan, bring the cream, with the vanilla pod, to the boil.
2. Beat the egg yolks with the sugar until creamy, then whisk in the cream.
3. Return the pan to the heat and cook, without boiling, until thick. Remove the vanilla pod and cool the custard. Then mix it with the remaining ingredients.
4. Pour the mixture into your chosen mould, lined with muslin – this helps you to turn it out, and gives a good surface pattern to the cream cheese.
5. Chill for at least 10 hours or up to 3 days. Stand the pot in a dish so that the whey can drain (some may ooze out, depending on the type of cheese that is used). Turn out and decorate. Serve with kulich (see page 553), or any brioche (see page 569) mixture you prefer, but flavoured with candied peel and cardamom.

NOTE: Chopped chocolate is a delicious addition to paskha.

FORTIFIED SWEET WHITE

Trifle

SERVES 6

1 sponge cake, preferably stale
raspberry jam
60ml/4 tablespoons sherry
30ml/2 tablespoons brandy
425ml/¾ pint milk
30ml/2 tablespoons sugar
5 egg yolks
2 drops vanilla essence
290ml/½ pint double cream
30g/1oz split blanched almonds
6 glacé cherries
angelica (optional)
a few ratafia biscuits (optional)

1. Cut the sponge cake into thick pieces. Sandwich the pieces together sparingly with jam. Pile them into a large glass dish.
2. Pour over the sherry and brandy and leave to soak while you prepare the custard.
3. Put the milk and sugar into a saucepan and bring to the point of boiling.
4. In a large bowl, lightly beat the yolks with a wooden spoon. Pour the scalding milk on to them, stirring with a wooden spoon.
5. Return the mixture to the saucepan and reheat carefully, stirring all the time, until it thickens enough to coat the back of the spoon. Care must be taken not to boil the custard, lest it curdles. Add the vanilla essence.
6. Strain on to the cake and leave to get quite cold.
7. Whip the cream until fairly stiff and spread or pipe over the trifle.
8. Decorate with the almonds, glacé cherries, angelica cut into diamond shapes and ratafia biscuits.

SWEET SPARKLING

Zuccotto

SERVES 8

2 x 225g/8oz Madeira cakes (see page 540)
45ml/3 tablespoons brandy
30ml/2 tablespoons Maraschino
30ml/2 tablespoons Cointreau
170g/6oz chocolate
55g/2oz roasted split almonds
55g/2oz hazelnuts, roasted and skinned
290ml/½ pint double cream, whipped
110g/4oz icing sugar
290ml/½ pint mocha custard (see page 419)

1. Line a 1.5 litre/2½ pint round-bottomed pudding basin with damp muslin or a clean damp 'J' cloth.
2. Cut the Madeira cakes into 9mm/¾ inch thick slices. Mix the brandy, Maraschino and Cointreau together and use to moisten each slice of cake. Line the pudding bowl with these slices as neatly as possible (as for a summer pudding). Reserve 2 slices for the top.
3. Chop the chocolate into tiny even-sized pieces. Mix half the chocolate with the nuts and fold into half the cream. Pile into the pudding basin and spread evenly over the sliced Madeira cake.
4. Melt the remaining chocolate in a small pan and mix with the remaining cream. Pile into the pudding basin and spread flat.
5. Cover the chocolate filling with the remaining slices of Madeira cake. Cover and refrigerate overnight.
6. The next day turn the zuccotto out on to a serving dish and coat with the cold mocha custard. Serve the rest of the custard in a sauceboat.

FORTIFIED SWEET WHITE

Nice Biscuit Refrigerator Cake

SERVES 4

190ml/1/3 pint double cream
45ml/3 tablespoons milk
30ml/2 tablespoons sherry
15 Nice or 'morning coffee' biscuits
225g/8oz sweetened chestnut purée (tinned)
110g/4oz chocolate
30g/1oz butter
a few walnut halves

1. Whip the cream until thick.
2. Mix the milk and sherry together.
3. Soak 3 biscuits in the milk and sherry and place them side by side on a serving dish.
4. Spread half the cream over this.
5. Soak the next 3 biscuits and place them on top of the cream.
6. Spread this with half the chestnut purée.
7. Repeat these 2 layers.
8. Top with 3 biscuits.
9. Place the chocolate in a pan with a very little water and heat gently until smooth and thick. Beat in the butter.
10. Pour over the biscuits and, when nearly set, decorate with the walnuts. Refrigerate.

LIQUEUR MUSCAT

Carrot Halva

This is a typical Indian pudding, this recipe has been adapted from one by Madhur Jaffrey.

SERVES 6

450g/1lb carrots, finely grated
6 cardamom pods
680ml/1 1/4 pints milk
85g/3oz clarified butter or ghee
140g/5oz sugar
55g/2oz pistachio nuts, chopped

1. Put the carrots, cardamom pods and milk in a pan. Bring up to the boil and simmer for 1-1 1/2 hours or until most of the liquid has evaporated. Remove the cardamom pods.
2. In another pan, melt the butter. Stir the carrot mixture into the melted butter and cook for 5-7 minutes. Add the sugar and nuts. Cook for 5 minutes.
3. Pile the mixture into a serving dish and serve at room temperature.

FORTIFIED SWEET WHITE

Tiramisù

SERVES 8

6 egg yolks
100ml/3 1/2 fl oz Marsala
100ml/3 1/2 fl oz dry white wine
85g/3oz icing sugar (or more to taste)
500g/1lb 2oz marscarpone or cream cheese
24 Savoy biscuits ('ladies' fingers)
100ml/3 1/2 fl oz Marsala
1/2 cup strong black coffee
unsweetened cocoa powder, for sprinkling

1. Mix the first 5 ingredients together to make a cream, but if making this for children or teetotallers leave out the Marsala and white wine.
2. Dip the biscuits in the Marsala and coffee mixed (once again leave out the Marsala if so desired), but take care not to make biscuits so soggy that they break. Line a dish about 25cm/10 inches square with a layer of biscuits and a layer of the cream.
3. Repeat, until all the ingredients have been used, ending with a cream layer. Sprinkle a thin

layer of unsweetened cocoa powder on top and place dish in refrigerator for a few hours before serving.

RICH SWEET WHITE

Chocolate Crumble Cake

SERVES 4
85g/3oz dark chocolate
85g/3oz butter
45g/1½ oz caster sugar
60ml/4 tablespoons golden syrup
340g/12oz broken biscuits
85g/3oz glacé cherries
85g/3oz flaked almonds

1. Chop the chocolate and melt it slowly with the butter, sugar and syrup, stirring all the time.
2. Add the crushed biscuits, cherries and almonds.
3. Grease a sheet of greaseproof paper and the inside of a 20cm/8 inch flan ring.
4. Press the mixture on to the paper and flatten it, using the flan ring to get a round shape.
5. Allow to cool until set hard.
6. Cut into small wedges.

LIQUEUR MUSCAT

French Toast with Apples

For the soaking liquid:
30ml/1 fl oz single cream
2 eggs
30ml/2 tablespoons cognac
45g/1½ oz sugar

For the French toast:
4 slices baguette, 2.5cm/1 inch thick
55g/2oz unsalted butter
3 cooking apples, peeled, quartered, cored and cut each quarter into 3

For the vanilla crème anglaise:
500ml/18 fl oz milk
1 vanilla pod
5 egg yolks
85g/3oz caster sugar

For the butterscotch sauce:
225g/8oz caster sugar
150ml/¼ pint water
210ml/8 fl oz double cream
45g/1½oz unsalted butter

1. Whisk together the cream, eggs, cognac and sugar. Strain into a shallow dish. Add the baguette slices and set aside.
2. To make the crème anglaise: scald the milk with the vanilla pod.
3. Beat the yolks and sugar together, pour in the milk and mix well. Return to the pan and stir over a gentle heat until the mixture thickens and will coat the back of a spoon. Do not allow to boil. Strain into a bowl and cover closely with a disc of paper to prevent a skin from forming.
4. To make the butterscotch sauce: put the sugar and water in a saucepan over a medium heat. Allow the sugar to dissolve before bringing to the boil. Cook to a golden brown and remove from the heat. Immediately add the cream and return to the heat. Stir to dissolve any lumps of sugar. Add the butter.
5. Put the apple pieces in the butterscotch sauce: and cook very gently until they are soft. Take great care as cooking apples fall apart very easily. Set them aside.
6. Drain the baguette slices. Heat the butter in a frying pan. Cook the slices on both sides until golden brown.
7. To assemble: ladle the vanilla crème anglaise on to 4 plates. Set a slice of toast on each plate and arrange the apples on top. Strain over the caramel sauce and serve.

Pastry, Pasta, and Batters

Pastry, Pasta and Batters

PASTRY comes in many forms. All of them are made from a mixture of flour and liquid, and usually contain fat. Variations in quantities and the ingredients themselves give each type its distinctive texture and taste.

The three commonest types of pastry are short (or crumbly), flaky, and choux pastry, all of which have variations. The degree of shortness (or crisp crumbliness) depends on the amount and type of fat (the shortening factor) incorporated into the flour, and the way in which the uncooked pastry, or 'paste', is handled.

THE INGREDIENTS

FATS Butter gives a crisp, rich shortcrust pastry with excellent flavour. Solid margarine gives a similar result that is slightly less rich and flavourful. Lard gives very short but rather tasteless pastry. It gives excellent results when used with butter. Solid cooking fat and vegetable shortening give a crust similar to lard. Suet is used only in suet crust, which is a soft and rather heavy pastry. A raising agent is usually added to the flour to combat the pastry's doughiness, and to make it more cake-like in texture.

FLOUR in shortcrust pastry is usually plain, all-purpose flour. Weak or cake flour is also suitable for pastry making. Wholemeal flour produces a delicious nutty flavoured crust, but is more absorbent than white flour and will need more liquid, which makes it harder and heavier. For this reason, a mixture of wholewheat and white flour, usually half and half, is generally used to make 'wholemeal' pastry. Self-raising flour is occasionally used in pastry making. It produces a soft, thicker, more cakey crust. It is also sometimes used to lighten cheese dough and other heavy pastes like suet crust. Whatever the flour, it should be sifted, even if it has no lumps in it, to incorporate air and give the pastry lightness.

The less liquid used in pastry making the better. Some very rich doughs, such as almond pastry, which contains a high proportion of butter and eggs, can be kneaded without any water or milk at all. Others need a little liquid to bind them. Water gives the pastry crispness and firmness. Too much makes pastry easy to handle but gives a concrete hard crust that shrinks in the oven. The addition of egg or egg white instead of water will give a firm but not hard crust. Egg yolk on its own produces a rich, soft and crumbly crust.

MAKING PASTRY

RUBBING IN Shortcrust pastry is made by rubbing fat into sifted flour and other dry ingredients with the fingertips, then adding other ingredients such as egg yolks and any liquid. Everything should be kept as cool as possible. If the fat melts, the finished pastry may be tough. Cut the fat, which should be firm and cold but not hard, into tiny pieces using a small knife and floured fingers. The flour prevents the fat from sticking to the fingers and beginning to melt, and the smaller the pieces of fat, the better the chances of even distribution. Mix the pieces of fat into the flour, then rub in, handling the fat as quickly and lightly as possible so it does not stick to the fingertips. Pick up a few pieces of floury fat and plenty of flour with the fingertips and thumbs of both hands. Hold your hands about 25cm/10 inches above the bowl, thumbs up and little fingers down, and gently and quickly rub the little pieces of fat into the flour, squashing the fat lightly as you go. Do not try to mash each piece of fat; a breadcrumb texture, not doughy lumps, is what is wanted. Drop the floury flakes of fat from a height; this cools the fat and aerates it, making the finished pastry lighter. Shake the bowl regularly so that the big unrubbed pieces of fat come to the surface. When the mixture looks like very coarse – not fine – breadcrumbs, stop.

ADDING LIQUID Rich shortcrust pastry, with a higher proportion of fat, needs little, if any, water added. Although over-moist pastry is easy to handle and roll out, the baked crust will be tough and may well shrink in the oven as the water evaporates in the heat. The drier and more difficult to handle the pastry is, the crisper the shortcrust will be. Add only as much water as is needed to get the pastry to hold together, and sprinkle it, 5ml/1 teaspoonful at a time, over as large a surface as possible.

Mixing should be kept to a minimum. Mix the pastry with a fork or knife so you handle it as little as possible. As soon as it holds together in lumps, stop mixing. Lightly flour your hands and quickly and gently gather into a ball, rolling it around the bowl to pick up crumbs.

RELAXING It is important to chill pastry for at least 30 minutes before rolling it out, or at least before baking. This allows cells to swell and absorb the liquid evenly. 'Relaxed' pastry will not shrink drastically or unevenly as just-made pastry will. Most pastries benefit from chilling, especially in hot weather, or if they are used to line tart tins, when shrinkage can spell disaster. Relaxing is less important, though still a good idea, for pastes used to cover pies. To prevent the surface of the pastry from drying out and cracking in the dry atmosphere of the refrigerator, cover it lightly with cling film or a damp cloth. Ideally pastry is relaxed before and after rolling.

ROLLING OUT Lightly dust the work surface with flour. Do not use much as this can alter the proportion of flour to the other ingredients. Once rolled, allow the pastry to relax in a cool place before baking, especially if it was not relaxed before rolling out.

TYPES OF PASTRY

SHORTCRUST: See recipe on page 525.
RICH SHORTCRUST: See recipe on page 525.

SUET CRUST PASTRY. This is made like shortcrust pastry except that the fat (suet) is generally chopped or shredded before use. Because self-raising flour (or plain flour and baking powder) is used in order to produce a less heavy dough pastry, it is important to cook the pastry soon after making it, while the raising agent is at its most active. During cooking the raising agent causes the dough to puff up and rise slightly and as it hardens, air will be trapped. This makes the suet crust lighter and more bread-like (see page 526).

PATE SUCRÉE, ALMOND PASTRY AND PATE A PATÉ
These and other very rich pastries are extreme forms of rich shortcrust, with all the liquid replaced by fat or eggs. Traditionally they are made by working together the egg yolks and fat, and sometimes sugar, with the fingertips until soft and creamy (see page 530). The flour is then gradually incorporated until a soft, very rich paste is achieved. To mix the paste, use only the fingertips of one hand. Using both hands, or the whole hand, leads to sticky pastry. The warmth of the fingertips is important for softening the fat, but once that is done, mixing and kneading should be as light and quick as possible. The pastry can be brought together very quickly by using a palette knife. Because of the high proportion of fat, no water is added.

Modern processors enable the most unskilled cook to make these pastries in seconds.

Simply put all the ingredients (the fat in smallish pieces) into the machine and process until the paste forms a ball. This may take a minute or so. The mixture first becomes crumbly, then as it warms up the butter softens and largish lumps appear. When these are gathered into one or two cohesive lumps the paste is made. Do not over-process as the paste will become sticky and taste greasy. The speed of the processor makes for very good pastry. These pastries become crisp as they cool. When biscuit coloured and cooked they will feel soft in the centre. When completely cool, slide off the baking sheet using a palette knife.

HOT WATERCRUST This is made by heating water and fat together and mixing them into the flour. Because of the high proportion of water, this pastry is inclined to be hard. Its strength and firmness allows it to encase heavy mixtures, such as an English pork pie, without collapsing. Also, as the fat used is generally lard, the pastry can lack flavour, so add a good spoon of salt. Many old recipes recommend throwing the pastry away uneaten once it has done its duty as container. Our recipe for veal and ham pie (see page 387) is a better-tasting modification of hot water crust, containing butter and egg.

Do not allow the water to boil before the fat has melted. If the water reduces by boiling, the proportion of water to flour will not be correct. Quickly mix the water and melted fat into the flour in a warm bowl, then keep it covered with a hot damp cloth. This prevents the fat from becoming set and the pastry from flaking and drying out.

CHOUX PASTRY Like Yorkshire pudding batter, this pastry contains water and eggs and depends on the rising of the steam within it to produce a puffy hollow pastry case. It is easy to make if the recipe is followed closely. The following points are particularly important:

1. Measure ingredients exactly. Proportions are important with choux.

2. Do not allow the water to boil until the butter has melted, but when it has, bring it immediately to a full rolling boil. Boiling the water too soon will cause too much evaporation.

3. Have the sifted flour ready in a bowl so that the minute the rolling boil is achieved, you can tip in the flour, all in one go.

4. Beat fast and vigorously to get rid of lumps before they cook hard.

5. Do not over-beat. Stop once the mixture is leaving the sides of the pan.

6. Cool slightly before adding egg, otherwise the egg will scramble.

7. Do not beat in more egg than is necessary to achieve a dropping consistency. If the mixture is too stiff, the pastry will be stodgy. If it is too thin, it will rise unevenly into shapeless lumps.

8. Bake until it is a good, even brown, otherwise the inside of the pastry will be uncooked.

9. If the pastry is to be served cold, split the buns/rings, or poke a hole in each of them with a skewer, to allow the steam inside to escape. If steam remains trapped inside, the pastry will be soggy and a little heavy. Opened-up pastry or small buns with holes in them can be returned to the oven, hole uppermost, to dry out further.

10. Serve the pastry on the day it is made (or store frozen), as it stales rapidly and does not keep well in a tin. See page 480 for chocolate profiteroles recipe.

FLAKY PASTRY AND PUFF PASTRY These are begun rather like the first stage for preparing shortcrust pastry, though the consistency is initially softer and less 'short', as they contain a high proportion of water. Then more fat, either in a solid block or in small pieces, is incoporated into the paste, which is rolled, folded and re-rolled several times. This process creates layers of pastry which, in the heat of the oven, will rise into light thin leaves. For instance, puff pastry, which is folded in three and rolled out six times, will have 729 layers.

As the whole aim is to create the layers without allowing the incorporated fat to melt, start with everything cool, including the bowl, the ingredients and even the worktop if possible. Short, quick strokes (rather than long steady ones) allow the bubbles of air so carefully incorporated in the pastry to move about while the fat is gradually and evenly distributed in the paste. Work lightly and do not stretch the paste, for the layers you have built up will tear and allow the air and fat to escape. Chill the pastry between rollings or at any point if there is a danger of the fat breaking through the pastry, or if the pastry becomes sticky and warm. It sounds like a complicated business, but it is a lot easier done than said: follow the instructions on page 528 (puff pastry), page 527 (rough puff pastry) and page 527 (flaky pastry).

Pastry rises evenly to a crisp crust in a steamy atmosphere. For this reason flaky and puff pastries (which are expected to rise in the oven) are sometimes baked with a roasting tin full of water at the bottom of the oven, or on a wet baking sheet. The oven temperature is set high to cause rapid expansion of the trapped layers of air and quick cooking of the dough before the fat has time to melt and run out.

STRUDEL PASTRY This differs from most other pastries in that it actually benefits from heavy handling. It is beaten and stretched, thumped and kneaded. This treatment allows the gluten to expand and promotes elasticity in the dough. The paste is rolled and stretched on a cloth (the bigger the better) until it is so thin that you should be able to read fine print through it. Keep the paste covered and moist when not in use. When the pastry is pulled out, brush it with butter or oil to prevent it cracking and drying, or keep it covered with a damp cloth. Strudel pastry can be bought in ready-rolled leaves from specialist food shops, especially Greek-owned ones. Called 'phyllo' or 'filo' pastry, it is used to make the Middle Eastern baklava. Detailed instructions for strudel pastry appear on page 530.

Shortcrust Pastry (Pâte Brisée)

170g/6oz plain flour
pinch of salt
30g/1oz lard
55g/2oz butter
very cold water

1. Sift the flour with the salt.
2. Rub in the fats until the mixture looks like coarse breadcrumbs.
3. Add 30ml/2 tablespoons water to the mixture. Mix to a firm dough, first with a knife, and finally with one hand. It may be necessary to add more water, but the pastry should not be too damp. (Though crumbly pastry is more difficult to handle, it produces a shorter, lighter result.)
4. Chill, wrapped, for 30 minutes before using. Or allow to relax after rolling out but before baking.

Rich Shortcrust Pastry

170g/6oz plain flour
pinch of salt
100g/3½oz butter
1 egg yolk
very cold water

1. Sift the flour with the salt.
2. Rub in the butter until the mixture looks like breadcrumbs.
3. Mix the yolk with 30ml/2 tablespoons water and add to the mixture.
4. Mix to a firm dough, first with a knife, and finally with one hand. It may be necessary to add more water, but the pastry should not be too damp. (Though crumbly pastry is more difficult to handle, it produces a shorter, lighter result.)
5. Chill, wrapped, for 30 minutes before using, or allow to relax after rolling out but before baking.

NOTE: To make sweet rich shortcrust pastry, mix in 15ml/1 tablespoon caster sugar once the fat has been rubbed into the flour.

Sweet Pastry

170g/6oz plain flour
large pinch of salt
2.5ml/½ teaspoon baking powder
100g/3½ oz unsalted butter
55g/2oz caster sugar
1 egg yolk
55ml/2 fl oz double cream

1. Sift the flour, salt and baking powder into a large bowl.
2. Rub in the butter until the mixture looks like coarse breadcrumbs. Stir in the sugar.
3. Mix the egg yolk with the cream and add to the mixture.
4. Mix to a firm dough, first with a knife and finally with one hand. Chill, wrapped, for 30 minutes before using, or allow to relax after rolling out but before baking.

Pâte Sablée

285g/10oz flour
pinch of salt
225g/8oz butter, softened
110g/4oz icing sugar, sifted
2 egg yolks
2 drops vanilla essence

1. Sift the flour on to a board with the salt. Make a large well in the centre and put the butter in it. Place the egg yolks and sugar on the butter with the vanilla essence.
2. Using the fingertips of one hand, 'peck' the butter, yolks and sugar together. When mixed to a soft paste, draw in the flour and knead lightly until the pastry is just smooth.
3. If the pastry is very soft, chill before rolling or pressing out to the required shape. In any event the pastry must be allowed to relax for 30 minutes before baking, either before or after rolling out.

Martha Stewart's Walnut Pastry

225g/8oz plain flour
pinch of salt
110g/4oz butter
140g/5oz ground walnuts
45g/1½ oz sugar
beaten egg

1. Sift the flour and salt into a bowl. Rub in the butter until the mixture resembles coarse breadcrumbs. Add the walnuts.
2. Stir in the sugar and add enough beaten egg (probably half an egg) to just bind the mixture together. Knead lightly. Chill before use.

NOTE: If you have a food processor, simply beat all the ingredients together until lightly combined. Chill before use.

Suet Pastry

As suet pastry is most often used for steamed puddings, instructions for lining a pudding basin are included here.

butter for greasing
340g/12oz self-raising flour
salt
170g/6oz shredded beef suet
water to mix

1. Grease a 1.1 litre/2 pint pudding basin.
2. Sift the flour with a good pinch of salt into a bowl. Stir in the shredded suet and add enough water to mix, first with a knife, and then with one hand, to a soft dough.
3. On a floured surface, roll out two-thirds of the pastry into a round about 1cm/½inch thick. Sprinkle the pastry evenly with flour.
4. Fold the round in half and place the open curved sides towards you.
5. Shape the pastry by rolling the straight edge away from you and gently pushing the middle and pulling the sides to form a bag that, when spread out, will fit the pudding basin.
6. With a dry pastry brush, remove all excess flour and place the bag in the well-greased basin.
7. Fill the pastry bag with the desired mixture.
8. Roll out the remaining piece of pastry and use it as a lid, damping the edges and pressing them firmly together.
9. Cover the basin with buttered greaseproof paper, pleated in the centre, and a layer of pleated tin foil. (Pleating the paper and foil allows the pastry to expand slightly without bursting the wrappings.) Tie down firmly to prevent water or steam getting in during cooking.

NOTE: Occasionally suet pastry is used for other purposes than steamed puddings, in which case it should be mixed as above and then handled like any other pastry, except that it does not need to relax before cooking.

Wholemeal Pastry

140g/5oz butter
110g/4oz wholemeal flour
110g/4oz plain flour
pinch of salt
water

1. Rub the butter into the flours and salt until the mixture looks like coarse breadcrumbs.
2. Add 30ml/2 tablespoons water to the mixture.
3. Mix to a firm dough, first with a knife and then with one hand. It may be necessary to add more water, but the pastry should not be too damp. (Although crumbly pastry is more difficult to handle, it produces a shorter, lighter result.)
4. Chill in the refrigerator for at least 30 minutes before using, or allow the rolled-out pastry to relax before baking.

NOTE I: To make sweet wholemeal pastry, mix in 30ml/2 tablespoons sugar once the fat has been rubbed into the flour.
NOTE II: All wholemeal flour may be used if preferred.

Herby Wholemeal Pastry

110g/4oz plain flour
110g/4oz wholemeal flour
a pinch of salt
110g/4oz butter, chopped
15g/1 tablespoon chopped thyme
water

1. Sift the flours with the salt and put any bran caught in the sieve back into the flour.
2. Rub the butter into the flour until the mixture looks like coarse breadcrumbs. Add the thyme.
3. Add enough water to the mixture and mix first with a knife and then with one hand to a firm dough. Chill in the refrigerator for 10 minutes and use as required.

Rough Puff Pastry

225g/8oz plain flour
pinch of salt
140g/5oz butter
very cold water

1. Sift the flour and salt into a cold bowl. Cut the butter into knobs about the size of a sugar lump and add to the flour. Do not rub in but add enough water to just bind the paste together. Mix first with a knife, then with one hand. Knead very lightly.
2. Wrap the pastry up and leave to relax for 10 minutes in the refrigerator.
3. On a floured board, roll the pastry into a strip about 30 x 10cm/12 x 4 inches long. This must be done carefully: with a heavy rolling pin, press firmly on the pastry and give short sharp rolls until the pastry has reached the required size. The surface of the pastry should not be over-stretched and broken.
4. Fold the strip into 3 and turn so that the folded edge is to your left, like a closed book.
5. Again roll out into a strip 1cm/½inch thick. Fold in 3 again and leave, wrapped, in the refrigerator for 15 minutes.
6. Roll and fold the pastry as before, then chill again for 15 minutes.
7. Roll and fold again, by which time the pastry should be ready for use, with no signs of streakiness.
8. Roll into the required shape.
9. Chill again before baking.

Flaky Pastry

225g/8oz plain flour
pinch of salt
85g/3oz butter
85g/3oz lard
150ml/¼ pint cold water

1. Sift the flour with a pinch of salt. Rub in half the butter. Add enough cold water to mix with a knife to a doughy consistency. Turn out on to a floured board and knead until just smooth.
2. Roll into an oblong about 10 x 30cm/4 x 12 inches long. Cut half the lard into tiny pieces and dot them evenly all over the top two-thirds

of the pastry, leaving a good margin.
3. Fold the pastry in 3, folding first the unlarded third up, then the larded top third down and pressing the edges to seal them. Give a 90-degree anti-clockwise turn so that the folded closed edge is to your left.
4. Repeat the rolling and folding process (without adding any fat) once more so that the folded, closed edge is on your left.
5. Roll out again, dot with the remaining butter as before, and fold and seal as before.
6. Roll out again, dot with the rest of the lard, fold, seal and roll once more.
7. Fold, wrap the pastry and 'relax' (or chill) for 10-15 minutes.
8. Roll and fold once again (without adding any fat) and then use as required.

NOTE I: As a general rule, flaky pastry is rolled out thinly, and baked at about 220°C/425°F/gas mark 7.
NOTE II: If the pastry becomes too warm or sticky and difficult to handle, wrap it up and chill it for 15 minutes before proceeding.

Puff Pastry

225g/8oz plain flour
pinch of salt
30g/1oz lard
150ml/1/4 pint icy water
140-200g/5-7oz butter

1. If you have never made puff pastry before, use the smaller amount of butter: this will give a normal pastry. If you have some experience, more butter will produce a lighter, very rich pastry.
2. Sift the flour with a pinch of salt. Rub in the lard. Add the icy water and mix with a knife to a doughy consistency. Turn on to the table and knead quickly until just smooth. Wrap in polythene or a cloth and leave in the refrigerator for 30 minutes to relax.
3. Lightly flour the table top or board and roll the dough into a rectangle about 10 x 30cm/4 x 12 inches long.
4. Tap the butter lightly with a floured rolling pin to get it into a flattened block about 9 x 8cm/3 1/2 x 3 inches. Put the butter on the rectangle of pastry and fold both ends over to enclose it. Fold the third closest to you over first and then bring the top third down. Press the sides together to prevent the butter escaping. Give it a 90-degree anti-clockwise turn so that the folded, closed edge is on your left.
5. Now tap the pastry parcel with the rolling pin to flatten the butter a little; then roll out, quickly and lightly, until the pastry is 3 times as long as it is wide. Fold it very evenly in 3, first folding the third closest to you over, then bringing the top third down. Give it a 90-degree anti-clockwise turn so that the folded, closed edge is on your left. Again press the edges firmly with the rolling pin. Then roll out again to form a rectangle as before.
6. Now the pastry has had 2 rolls and folds, or 'turns' as they are called. It should be put to rest in a cool place for 30 minutes or so. The rolling and folding must be repeated twice more, the pastry again rested, and then again given 2 more 'turns'. This makes a total of 6 turns. If the butter is still very streaky, roll and fold it once more.

Bouchée Cases

MAKES ABOUT 20
puff pastry made with 225g/8oz flour (see above)
beaten egg

1. Set the oven to 220°C/425°F/gas mark 7.
2. Roll out the pastry to 5mm/1/4 inch. With a 4cm/1 1/2 inch round pastry cutter, stamp it out in rounds. With a slightly smaller cutter, cut a circle in the centre of each round, but be careful not to stamp the pastry more than halfway through.
3. Brush the tops with beaten egg, taking care not to get egg on the sides, which would prevent the pastry layers separating and rising.
4. Bake on a wet baking sheet until brown and crisp; about 12 minutes.
5. Take off the pastry 'lids' and scrape out any raw pastry left inside. Return the bouchée cases to the oven for 4 minutes to dry out. Cool on a wire rack.

NOTE: Bouchée cases, if they are to be eaten hot, should either be filled while they are still very hot with a cooked hot filling, or (if they are cooked and cold) with a cooked cold filling. Hot fillings will tend to make the pastry soggy during the reheating process. If both filling and pastry go into the oven cold, the pastry will have time to become crisp again before the filling is hot.

Vol-au-Vents

MAKES 1 OR 2
puff pastry made with 225g/8oz flour (see page 528)
beaten egg
salt

1. Set the oven to 220°C/425°F/gas mark 7.
2. Roll the pastry to 1cm/½inch thickness and cut into a round about the size of a dessert plate. Place on a wet baking sheet. Using a cutter half the size of the pastry round, cut into the centre of the pastry, but take care not to cut right through to the baking sheet.
3. Flour the blade of a knife and use this to 'knock up' the sides of the pastry: try to slightly separate the leaves of the pastry horizontally; this means that the edge will flake readily when cooking. (It counteracts the squashing effect of the cutter used to cut out the round, which may have pressed the edges together, making it more difficult for the pastry to rise in even layers.)
4. Mix a pinch of salt into the beaten egg. Brush the pastry carefully with this egg wash, avoiding the knocked-up sides; if they are covered with egg, the pastry will not rise.
5. With the back of the knife blade, make a star pattern on the borders of the vol-au-vent case and mark a lattice pattern on the inner circle. (The back rather than the sharp edge of the blade is used as this will not cut into the pastry; the idea is to make a pattern without cutting through the surface of the pastry.)
6. Bake in a hot oven for 30 minutes, and carefully lift off the top of the inner circle. Keep this for the lid of the case when filled. Pull out and discard any partially cooked pastry from the centre of the case.
7. Return the case to the oven for 2 minutes to dry out. The vol-au-vent is now ready for filling. Ideally the heated pastry case is filled with hot filling, and then served.

NOTE: Flaky or rough puff pastry is also suitable. But the method of cutting is different: cut the pastry into 2 rounds the size of a side plate. Stamp a circle right out of the centre of one of them. Brush the uncut round with egg and place the ring of pastry on top. Bake the middle small round of pastry too, and use it for the vol-au-vent lid.

Choux Pastry

85g/3oz butter
220ml/7 fl oz water
105g/3¾ oz plain flour, well sifted
pinch of salt
3 eggs

1. Put the butter and water together in a heavy saucepan. Bring slowly to the boil so that by the time the water boils the butter is completely melted.
2. Immediately the mixture is boiling really fast, tip in all the flour and draw the pan off the heat.
3. Working as fast as you can, beat the mixture hard with a wooden spoon: it will soon become thick and smooth and leave the sides of the pan. Beat in the salt.
4. Stand the bottom of the saucepan in a basin or sink of cold water to speed up the cooling process.
5. When the mixture is cool, beat in the eggs, a little at at time, until it is soft, shiny and smooth. If the eggs are large, it may not be necessary to add all of them. The mixture should be of adropping consistency – not too runny. ('Dropping consistency' means that the mixture will fall off a spoon rather reluctantly and all in a blob; if it runs off, it is too wet, and if it will not fall off even when the spoon is jerked slightly, it is too thick).
6. Use as required.

Filo or Strudel Pastry

285g/10oz plain flour
pinch of salt
1 egg
150ml/$^{1}/_{4}$ pint water
5ml/1 teaspoon oil

1. Sift the flour and salt into a bowl.
2. Beat the egg and add the water and oil. First with a knife and then with one hand, mix the water and egg into the flour, adding more water if necessary to make a soft dough.
3. The paste now has to be beaten: lift the whole mixture up in one hand and then, with a flick of the wrist, slap it on to a lightly floured board. Continue doing this until the paste no longer sticks to your fingers, and the whole mixture is smooth and very elastic. Put it into a clean floured bowl. Cover and leave in a warm place for 15 minutes.
4. The pastry is now ready for rolling and pulling. To do this, flour a tea towel or large cloth on a table top and roll out the pastry as thinly as you can. Now put your hand (well floured) under the pastry and, keeping your hand fairly flat, gently stretch and pull the pastry, gradually and carefully working your way round until the paste is paper thin. (You should be able to see through it easily.) Trim off the thick edges.
5. Use immediately, as strudel pastry dries out and cracks very quickly. Brushing with melted butter or oil helps to prevent this. Or the pastry sheets may be kept covered with a damp cloth.

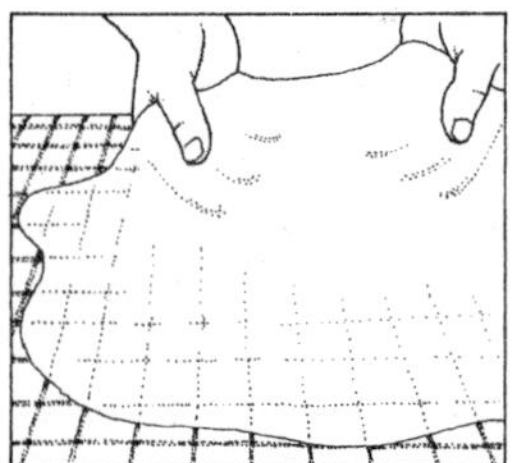
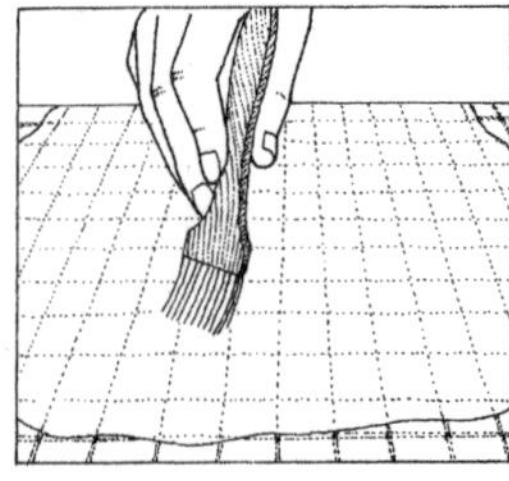

Stretch and pull until almost transparent; brush with butter.

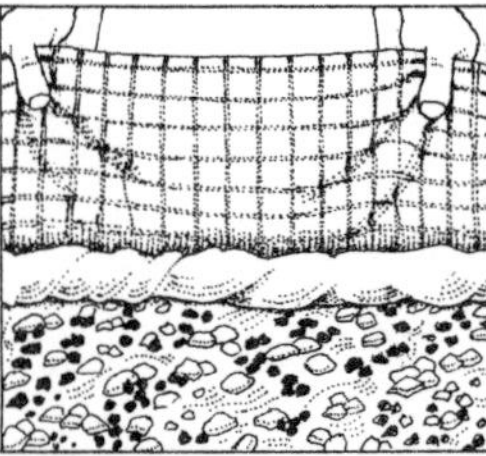
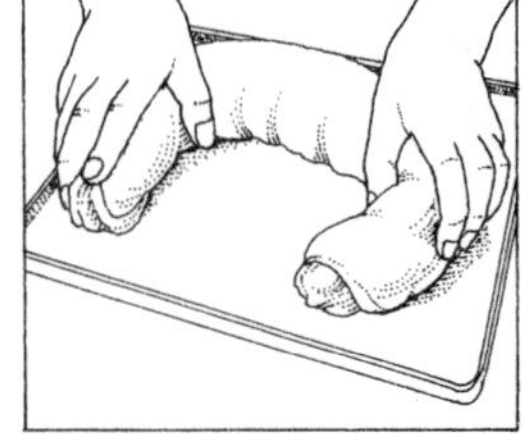

Fill as required (see page 482), roll up (using the tea towel).

NOTE: If the paste is not for immediate use wrap it well and keep refrigerated (for up to three days) or frozen. Flour the pastry surfaces before folding up. This will prevent sticking.

Pâte Sucrée

170g/6oz plain flour
pinch of salt
85g/3oz butter, softened
3 egg yolks
85g/3oz sugar
2 drops vanilla essence

1. Sift the flour on to a board with a pinch of salt. Make a large well in the centre and put the butter in it. Place the egg yolks and sugar on the butter with the vanilla essence.
2. Using the fingertips of one hand, mix the butter, yolks and sugar together. When mixed to a soft paste, draw in the flour and knead until the pastry is just smooth.
3. If the pastry is very soft, chill before rolling or pressing out to the required shape. In any event the pastry must be allowed to relax for 30 minutes either before or after rolling out, but before baking.

Almond Pastry (Pâte Frollée)

Care must be taken when making this because if it is over-kneaded the oil will run from the almonds, resulting in an oily paste.

110g/4oz plain flour
pinch of salt
45g/1$^{1}/_{2}$ oz ground almonds
45g/1$^{1}/_{2}$ oz caster sugar
1 egg yolk or beaten egg
2 drops vanilla essence
85g/3oz butter, softened

1. Sift the flour with the salt on to a board or table top. Scatter over the ground almonds.

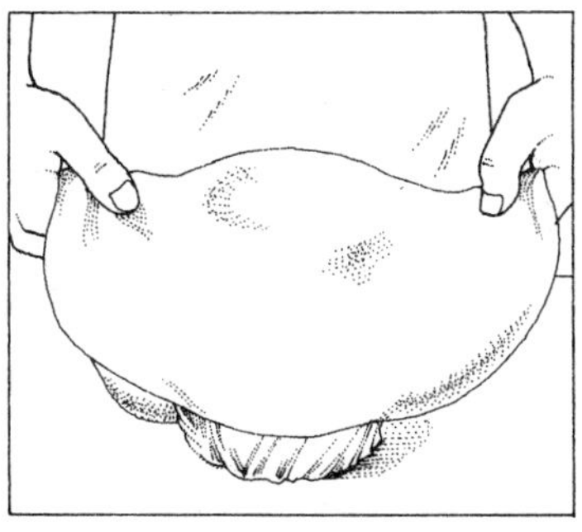
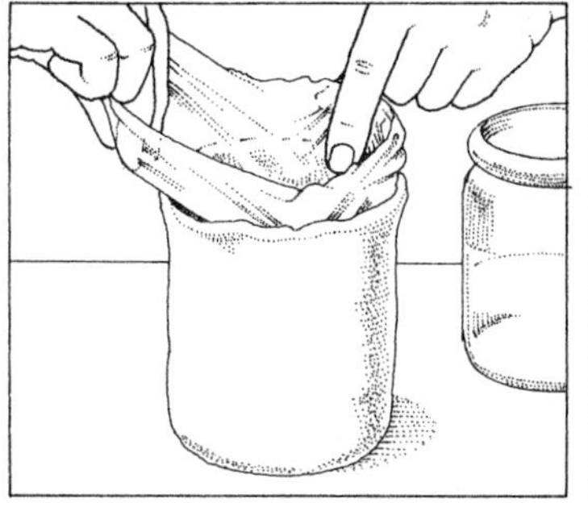
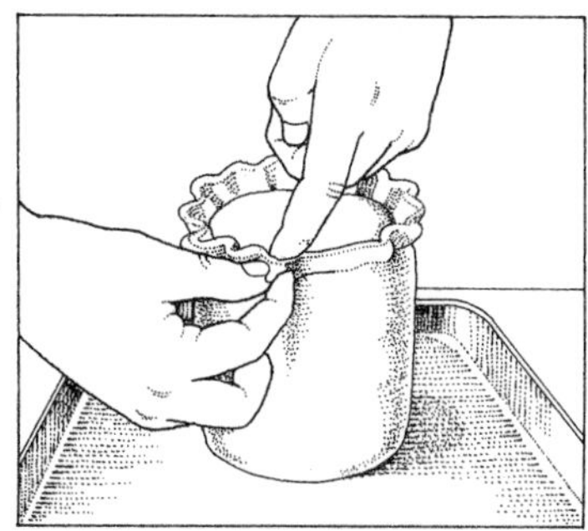

Drape pastry over prepared jar; when cool, remove jar and carefully draw out the paper. Crimp the edges together and bake.

Make a large well in the centre and put in the sugar, beaten egg or yolk and vanilla essence.
2. Using one hand only, mix the egg and sugar with your fingertips. When creamy, add the softened butter and continue to mix, gradually drawing in the flour and almonds.
3. Knead gently to a paste and chill. Allow to relax for 30 minutes before baking.

Pâte à Pâté

225g/8oz plain flour
2.5ml/1/2 teaspoon salt
165g/5 1/2 oz butter, softened
2 small egg yolks
up to 30ml/2 tablespoons water

1. Sift the flour and salt on to the table top. Make a large well in the centre and put the butter and yolks in it. Work the yolks and butter together with the fingers of one hand and draw in the surrounding flour, adding the water to give a soft, malleable, but not sticky paste.
2. Wrap and leave to rest in the refrigerator for 30 minutes. Use as required.

Hot Watercrust Pastry

This pastry is used for raised pies, such as pork pie and game pie.

225g/8oz plain flour
2.5ml/1/2 teaspoon salt
1 beaten egg
100ml/3 1/2 fl oz water
40g/1 1/4 oz butter
40g/1 1/4 oz lard

1. Wrap a piece of paper around the outside of a wide jar or small straight-sided saucepan. The paper can be held in position by tucking it in the opening of the jar or saucepan. Leave it upside down while you make the pastry.
2. Sift the flour and salt into a bowl. Make a dip in the middle, break the egg into it and toss a liberal covering of flour over the egg.
3. Put the water, butter and lard into a saucepan and bring slowly to the boil.
4. Once the liquid is boiling, pour it on to the flour, mixing with a knife as you do so. Knead until all the egg streaks have gone and the pastry is smooth.
5. Wrap in a piece of cling film and leave in the refrigerator for 10 minutes.
6. Reserve about a third of the paste for the lid, keeping it covered or wrapped and in a warm place. Roll out the remaining paste to a circle and drape it over the jar or saucepan. Working fast, shape the pastry to cover the jar or saucepan to a depth of about 7cm / 2.5 inches. Leave to chill in the refrigerator.
7. As the pastry cools it will harden. When hard, turn the jar or saucepan over and remove it carefully, leaving the paper inside the pastry case. Carefully draw the paper away from the pastry and when it is all loosened take it out. Stand the pastry case on a baking sheet and fill as required. Use the reserved third of the pastry to make the lid, wetting the rim of the pie case to make it stick down well. Bake as required.

Provençal Pastry

340g/12oz plain flour
190ml/⅓ pint virgin olive oil
salt
190ml/⅓ pint lukewarm water

1. Sift the flour into a bowl, add the oil, salt and water and mix as quickly and lightly as possible to a smooth dough.
2. Form into a ball, cover with cling film and relax in the refrigerator for half an hour. Use as required.

NOTE: A delicious alternative to the virgin oil is to use a herb and chilli flavoured olive oil (available in specialist shops).

Egg Pasta

450g/1lb strong flour
pinch of salt
4 eggs
15ml/1 tablespoon oil

1. Sift the flour and salt on to a wooden board. Make a well in the centre and drop in the eggs and oil.
2. Using the fingers of one hand, mix together the eggs and oil and gradually draw in the flour. The mixture should be a very stiff dough.
3. Knead until smooth and elastic (about 15 minutes). Wrap in polythene and leave to relax in a cool place for 1 hour.
4. Roll one small piece of dough out at a time until paper thin. Cut into the required sized noodles.
5. Allow to dry (unless making ravioli), hanging over a chair back if long noodles, lying on a wire rack or dry tea towel if small ones, for at least 30 minutes before boiling. Ravioli is dried after stuffing.

NOTE: If more or less pasta is required the recipe can be altered on a pro-rata basis, for example a 340g/12oz quantity of flour calls for a pinch of salt, 3 eggs and 12ml/1 scant tablespoon of oil.

Commonest noodle shapes

Cannelloni: rectangles about the size of a side plate. They are rolled and generally stuffed (like a pancake) after boiling, then reheated.
Tagliatelle (fettucine): thin ribbons of pasta, usually served with a sauce.
Lasagne: wide strips usually used in alternate layers with a savoury mixture.
Ravioli: flat sheets used to form small stuffed envelopes, which are then boiled and served with or without sauce.
Spaghetti: originally made by pulling the dough into thin strands, now usually made by machine.
Macaroni: made commercially into short tube-like pieces.

Green Pasta

225g/8oz spinach, cooked
340g/12oz strong flour
pinch of salt
2 eggs
15ml/1 tablespoon cream

1. Chop or liquidize the spinach and push through a sieve to get a fairly dry paste.
2. Sift the flour and salt on to a wooden board. Make a well in the centre and in it put the eggs, spinach and cream. Using the fingers of one hand, mix together the eggs, spinach and cream, gradually drawing in the flour. The mixture should be a stiff dough.
3. Knead until smooth and elastic (about 15 minutes). Wrap in polythene and leave to relax in a cool place for 1 hour.
4. Roll one small piece of the dough out at a time until paper thin. Cut into the required size. Allow to dry (hanging over a chair back if long noodles, or lying on a wire rack or clean tea towel if small) for at least 30 minutes before cooking.

Flavoured pasta

Follow the recipe for egg pasta (see page 532) and add the flavourings with the eggs.

Tomato Pasta Add approximately 10ml/ 2 teaspoons tomato purée.
Herb Pasta Add plenty of chopped very fresh herbs to taste, e.g. parsley, thyme and tarragon.
Beetroot Pasta Add 1 small cooked, puréed beetroot.
Saffron Pasta Add 1 packet of infused saffron powder.
Chocolate Pasta Add 55g/2oz melted cooked chocolate.

Saffron Noodles

225g/8oz strong plain flour
2 whole eggs
3 egg yolks
15ml/1 tablespoon of olive oil
2.5ml/½ teaspoon saffron filaments soaked in 30ml/2 tablespoons boiling water
salt and ground white pepper

1. Put all the ingredients into a food processor and process until the mixture forms a dough. (If a food processor is not available, sift the flour into a bowl, add the salt and pepper, make a well in the centre add the eggs, oil and saffron liquid. Gradually mix the flour into the liquid using your hand. Eventually draw it together into a ball of dough and knead until elastic.
2. Roll out the pasta as thinly as possible. Dust with flour and roll up like a Swiss roll. Cut as thinly as possible. Unravel the pasta, dust with flour and place on a tray to dry slightly. (This is much easier if you have a pasta machine).

French Pancakes (Crêpes)

MAKES ABOUT 12
110g/4oz plain flour
pinch of salt
1 egg
1 egg yolk
290ml/½ pint milk, or milk and water mixed
15ml/1 tablespoon oil
oil for cooking

1. Sift the flour and salt into a bowl and make a well in the centre, exposing the bottom of the bowl.
2. Into this well, place the egg and egg yolk with a little of the milk.
3. Using a wooden spoon or whisk, mix the egg and milk and then gradually draw in the flour from the sides as you mix.
4. When the mixture reaches the consistency of thick cream, beat well and stir in the oil.
5. Add the rest of the milk; the consistency should now be that of thin cream. (Batter can also be made by placing all the ingredients together in a liquidizer for a few seconds, but take care not to over-whizz or the mixture will be bubbly.)
6. Cover the bowl and refrigerate for about 30 minutes. This is done so that the starch cells will swell, giving a lighter result.
7. Prepare a pancake pan or frying pan by heating well and wiping with oil. Pancakes are not fried in fat like most foods – the purpose of the oil is simply to prevent sticking.
8. When the pan is ready, pour in about 15ml/ 1 tablespoon batter and swirl about the pan until evenly spread across the bottom.
9. Place over heat and, after 1 minute, using a palette knife and your fingers, turn the pancake over and cook again until brown. (Pancakes should be extremely thin, so if the first one is too thick, add a little extra milk to the batter. The first pancake is unlikely to be perfect, and is often discarded.)
10. Make up all the pancakes, turning them out on to a tea towel or plate.

NOTE I: Pancakes can be kept warm in a folded tea towel on a plate over a saucepan of simmering water, in the oven, or in a warmer. If allowed to

cool, they may be reheated by being returned to the frying pan or by warming in the oven.
NOTE II: Pancakes freeze well, but should be separated by pieces of greaseproof paper. They may also be refrigerated for a day or two.

Fritter Batter

125g/4½ oz plain flour
pinch of salt
2 eggs
15ml/1 tablespoon oil
285ml/10 fl oz milk

1. Sift the flour with the salt into a bowl.
2. Make a well in the centre, exposing the bottom of the bowl.
3. Put 1 whole egg and 1 yolk into the well and mix with a wooden spoon or whisk until smooth, gradually incorporating the surrounding flour and the milk. A thick creamy consistency should be reached.
4. Add the oil. Allow to rest for 30 minutes.
5. When ready to use the batter, whisk the egg white until stiff but not dry. Fold it into the batter with a metal spoon. Use the batter to coat the food and fry immediately.

Waffles

MAKES 8-10
2 eggs
170g/6oz plain flour
pinch of salt
15ml/1 tablespoon baking powder
30g/1oz caster sugar
290ml/½ pint milk
55g/2oz butter, melted
vanilla essence
extra melted butter

To serve:
butter
honey, maple syrup or jam

1. Separate the eggs.
2. Sift the flour, salt, baking powder and sugar together. Make a well in the centre and drop in the egg yolks.
3. Stir the yolks, gradually drawing in the flour from the edges and adding the milk and melted butter until you have a thin batter. Add the vanilla essence.
4. Grease a waffle iron and heat it up.
5. Whisk the egg whites until stiff but not dry and fold into the batter.
6. Add a little melted butter to the hot waffle iron, pour in about 60ml/4 tablespoons of the mixture, close and cook for 1 minute per side.
7. Serve hot with butter and honey, maple syrup or jam.

NOTE: The first waffle always sticks to the iron and should be discarded.

Scotch Pancakes or Drop Scones

MAKES 40
225g/8oz plain flour
2.5ml/½ teaspoon salt
2.5ml/½ teaspoon bicarbonate of soda
2.5ml/½ teaspoon cream of tartar
½ beaten egg
290ml/½ pint milk

To serve:
butter
jam

1. Sift together the flour, salt, bicarbonate of soda and cream of tartar.
2. Make a well in the centre of the mixture and into it pour half the milk.
3. Stir the milk and gradually draw in the flour from the sides of the bowl.
4. Add the egg and beat well.
5. Stir in more milk until the batter is the consistency of thick cream and will just run from a spoon. Cover and leave to stand for 10 minutes.
6. Meanwhile lightly grease a heavy frying pan or griddle iron and heat it. When really hot, drop 2 or 3 spoonfuls of batter on to the surface, keeping them well separated.
7. Cook for 2-3 minutes. When the undersides of the pancakes are brown, bubbles rise to the surface. Lift the pancakes with a fish slice, turn over and brown the other side.

Cakes

Cake-making

SUCCESSFUL cake-making is a most satisfying activity for the cook. It is also most demanding on account of the accuracy needed in measuring the ingredients and the skill necessary in preparing certain cakes. Confidence is best built by beginning with the easier cakes, such as gingerbread or fruit cake. The first attempts at making more difficult cakes such as a génoise sponge are often disappointing. Happily, practice, with good ingredients, proper utensils, careful weighing and measuring, precise oven temperatures and exact timing – in short, careful attention to detail – makes perfect.

Most cakes are made by mixing fat, sugar, flour, eggs and liquid. Air or another gas is incorporated to make the mixture rise during baking. As it bakes, strands of gluten in the flour are stretched by the gas given off until the heat finally hardens the cake. It is even rising that gives a cake a light sponge-like texture.

INGREDIENTS

Fats Butter makes the best flavoured cakes. Margarine, particularly the soft or 'tub' variety, is useful for speed but has less flavour than butter. Vegetable shortenings are flavourless but give light cakes. Lard cakes are often delicious but heavy, and for this reason lard is little used in cake making. Oils are not much used as they do not easily hold air when they are creamed or beaten, and the resulting cakes can therefore be heavy.

SUGARS The finer creaming possible with caster (fine granulated) sugar makes it most suitable for cake making. Very coarse granulated sugar can give a speckled appearance to a finished cake unless the sugar is ground down first in a blender or food processor. Soft brown sugars give colour and flavour to dark cakes like gingerbread, but they give sponge cakes a drab look and too much caramel flavour.

Golden syrup, honey, treacle and molasses are used in cakes made by the melting method. Such cakes are cooked relatively slowly, as these thick liquid sugars tend to caramelize and burn at higher temperatures.

EGGS Unless specified, most recipes assume a medium-sized egg weighing 55/2oz (UK size 3). The eggs should be used at room temperature – cold eggs tend to curdle the mixture and this results in the cake having a tough, coarse, too open texture. When using whisked egg whites in a cake, be sure not to allow even a speck of yolk into the whites. Any yolk or fat on the whisk will prevent proper whisking of the whites, reducing their air-holding ability and the lightness of the finished cake.

FLOURS Plain white flour is used in cake making unless otherwise specified. The high proportion of 'soft' or low-gluten wheat used in European plain flour makes it particularly suitable for cake making. In North America, plain or 'all-purpose' flour is made with more 'hard' than soft wheat, so cornflour, which is also weak (low in gluten), is sometimes substituted for some of the all-purpose flour, or special soft 'cake flour' is used. Although a little gluten is needed to allow the mixture to stretch and expand as it rises, too much would give a tough, chewy cake.

Self-raising flour has a raising agent (baking powder) added to it and should be used only if specified in the recipe. All flours, even if labelled 'ready-sifted', should be sifted before use to eliminate any lumps and to incorporate air.

RAISING AGENTS

Air is incorporated into cake mixtures by agitating the ingredients. Methods include sifting the flour, beating the butter and beating or creaming it again with the sugar to a fluffy, mousse-like consistency, and whisking the eggs. The heat of the oven causes the air trapped in the mixture to rise and leaven or lighten the cake, either by itself or in conjunction with other raising agents.

Steam raises some mixtures even when air has not been beaten into them. Flour mixtures with a high proportion of liquid in them, like Yorkshire pudding, will rise in a hot oven since, as the water vaporizes and the steam rises, the uncooked flour mixture rises with it. While in this puffed-up state, the mixture hardens in the oven heat with the steam trapped inside. The pockets of air created by steam are uneven and very open, as in choux pastry (see page 529), so steam is not used on its own for making cakes. But steam is a contributing factor in raising wet cake mixtures such as gingerbread.

Bicarbonate of soda, or baking soda, is a powder which, when mixed into cake mixtures, quickly gives off half its substance as carbon dioxide. In a cake the trapped gas causes the mixture to puff up. Heat sets the mixture once it has risen. By the time the cake cools, the gas will have escaped and will have been replaced by air. Unfortunately, the bicarbonate of soda remaining in the cake can give it a slightly unpleasant smell and taste, and a yellowish colour. For this reason, bicarbonate of soda is most often used in strong-tasting cakes such as gingerbread and those flavoured with chocolate, treacle or molasses. The carbon dioxide reaction is speeded up by acidic substances, so bicarbonate of soda is usually used in cake mixtures with ingredients such as sour milk, vinegar, buttermilk, soured cream, cream of tartar and yoghurt. This makes it especially suitable for quickly mixed items like fruit cakes, scones, soda bread and gingerbread. It also gives them a soft texture and spongy crust with a deep colour. Unfortunately the process destroys some of the vitamins present in the flour.

Baking powder in commercial forms consists of bicarbonate of soda and an acid powder that varies according to the brand, plus a starch filler, usually cornflour, arrowroot or ground rice. The starch keeps the mixture dry by absorbing any dampness in the air, which might cause the soda and the acid in the powder to react. The presence of the filler explains why more commercial baking powder than mixed 'bi-carb' and cream of tartar would be needed to raise the same cake. A 'delayed action' or 'double action' baking powder is sold in the USA that needs heat as well as moisture to produce carbon dioxide. It is not widely known in Europe. The advantage of it is that it can be added to mixtures in advance of baking - it starts to work only once in the oven.

Yeast cakes caused to rise by the growth of yeast cells are really sweetened enriched breads. They are traditional in East European cookery. The kulich on page 553 is a classic example.

PREPARING A CAKE TIN

All tins should be greased before use to prevent the cake mixture from sticking or burning at the edges or bottom. Melted lard or oil are the most suitable fats. Always turn the tin upside down after greasing to allow any excess fat to drain away. Use a paint brush to get a thin layer. Bread tins and nonstick sandwich tins need no preparation other than greasing. Tins for cakes made by the melting or creaming methods should be greased, then the base lined with greaseproof paper, cut exactly to size and the paper brushed out with more melted lard or oil. (To cut the paper accurately draw round the tin, then cut just inside the line). For cakes made by the whisking method, a dusting of caster sugar and flour should be given after lining and greasing.

For fruit cakes, grease the tin, then line the sides and base with greaseproof paper as follows:

1. Cut 2 pieces of greaseproof paper to fit the base of the cake tin.

2. Cut another piece long enough to go right round the sides of the tin and to overlap slightly. It should be 2.5cm/1 inch deeper than the height of the cake tin.

3. Fold one long edge of this strip over 2.5cm/1 inch all along its length.

4. Cut snips at right angles to the edge and

about 1cm/½inch apart, all along the folded side. The snips should just reach the fold.
5. Grease the tin, place one paper base in the bottom and grease again.
6. Fit the long strip inside the tin with the folded cut edge on the bottom (the flanges will overlap slightly) and the main uncut part lining the sides of the tin. Press them well into the corners.
7. Grease the paper and lay the second base on top of the first.
8. Brush the base again with more melted lard or oil and dust the lined pan with flour.

METHODS USED IN CAKE-MAKING

RUBBING IN The rubbing-in method gives a fairly substantial cake (such as rock cakes) with a crumbly moist texture. The raising agent is always bicarbonate of soda. In rock cakes the agent is in the self-raising flour. The cake is delicious served sliced and spread with butter, or eaten as a warm pudding with custard.

MELTING The melting method is used for very moist cakes like gingerbread. The fat, sugar, syrup and any other liquid ingredients are heated together to melt, then cooled slightly. The flour and other dry ingredients are sifted together and the warm sugar mixture is stirred, not beaten, into the dry mixture along with the eggs. The raising agent is always bicarbonate of soda. These cakes are the perfect cake for the beginner – easy, reliable and delicious.

CLASSIC CREAMING Creaming fat and sugar to a mousse-like consistency, and thereby incorporating air, is the secret of lightness in cakes like Victoria sponge, although a little chemical raising agent is usually added to ensure rising. First the butter or margarine is creamed or beaten until it is smooth and very light in colour, but the fat is never allowed to melt. If it did the carefully incorporated air beaten into it would escape. The sugar is then beaten in by degrees, until the mixture is pale and fluffy.

The eggs are lightly beaten and added, also by degrees, to the creamed mixture. The mix is beaten after each addition to thoroughly incorporate it. At this point the batter can curdle, especially if the eggs are too cold, but beating in 15ml/1 tablespoon of sifted flour taken from the recipe after each addition of eggs should prevent this. Cakes made from curdled mixtures are acceptable, but they have a less delicate, more open and coarse texture than those made from uncurdled mixture.

Plain flour, if used, should be sifted with the baking powder and salt. Self-raising flour should be sifted with salt. The flour mixture is then folded carefully into the creamed mixture with a metal spoon and with as little mixing as possible to ensure minimum air loss in the batter.

ALL-IN-ONE CREAMING The all-in-one method is an easy version of the creaming method, because all the ingredients are beaten together at the same time, but a strong electric mixer is necessary to make these cakes really successful. Soft 'tub' margarine gives a lighter result than butter.

CREAMING FOR FRUIT CAKES Another version of the creaming method is suited to fruit cakes. Softened butter and sugar are creamed in a mixing bowl to incorporate air. The eggs and any other liquid are gradually beaten into the creamed mixture, with the flour added with the last few additions of egg to reduce the risk of curdling. After the mixture is well combined, the dry fruit is folded in well to distribute it throughout the cake. The mixture should have a soft, dropping consistency (it should fall reluctantly off a spoon given a slight shake, neither sticking obstinately nor running off) and be spread out evenly in the prepared tin, with a slight dip in the centre of the mixture to counteract the cake 'peaking'.

Because fruit cakes are generally large and dense and contain a high proportion of fruit, which burns easily, they are cooked extremely slowly. To prevent burning they can be placed on a folded newspaper in the oven and can be covered in several layers of greaseproof or brown paper, but not foil, which traps the steam and produces too doughy a result.

WHISKING In the whisking method, the only raising agent is air that has been trapped in the cake batter during mixing. As the air expands in the heat of the oven, the cake rises. Cakes like Swiss roll and génoise commune are made by this method.

The simplest whisked sponge contains no fat. Sugar and eggs are whisked together until they are thick and light, then flour is folded in gently to keep in as much air as possible. In a lighter but more complicated whisked sponge, the eggs are separated and the yolks are whisked with the sugar and flour. The whites are whisked in another bowl, then folded into the batter. Sometimes half the sugar is whisked with the yolks, and half with the whites to give a meringue.

The sugar and eggs (or egg yolks only) are whisked in a bowl set over a pan of barely simmering water. Make sure that the bowl does not touch the water or the heat will scramble the eggs. The gentle heat from the steam speeds up the dissolving of the sugar and slightly cooks and thickens the eggs, so encouraging the mixture to hold the maximum number of air bubbles. The mixture should change colour from yellow to almost white and increase to four times its original volume. The mixture is ready when a lifted whisk will leave a ribbon-like trail. Traditionally, a balloon whisk is used, but a hand-held electric one works excellently. If a powerful food mixer is used, the heat can be dispensed with, though the process is speeded up if the mixture is put into a warmed bowl.

When the flour is folded in, great care should be take to fold rather than stir or beat, as the aim is to incorporate the flour without losing any of the beaten-in air, which alone will raise the cake. The correct movement is more of lifting the mixture and cutting into it, rather than stirring it.

Although they are light and springy, a drawback to these cakes is that they go stale quickly. Always plan to make fatless sponge on the day of serving, or freeze the cake once it is cool.

The génoise is a whisked sponge that has just-runny butter folded into it with the flour. Butter gives it flavour and richness and makes it keep a day or two longer than fatless sponges. The butter should be poured in a stream around the edge of the bowl and then folded in. If the butter is poured heavily on top of the whisked mixture, it forces out some of the air, and needs excessive mixing, with the danger of more air loss.

Whisked cakes are cooked when the surface will spring back when pressed with a finger. The cakes should be cooled for a few minutes in the tin and then turned out on to a cake rack. The baking paper should be carefully peeled off to allow the escape of steam.

Victoria Sandwich

oil for preparing 2 x 15cm/6 inch cake tins
110g/4oz butter
110g/4oz caster sugar
2 eggs
110g/4oz self-raising flour
water
30ml/2 tablespoons raspberry jam
caster sugar

1. Set oven to 190°C/375°F/gas mark 5.
2. Prepare the cake tins by lining the bottom of each with a disc of greaseproof paper and lightly brushing out each tin with oil.
3. Cream the butter and sugar together until light and fluffy.
4. Mix the eggs together in a separate bowl, and gradually beat into the creamed mixture a little at a time, adding 15ml/1 tablespoon of flour if the mixture begins to curdle at any stage.
5. Fold in the sifted flour, adding enough water to bring the mixture to a dropping consistency.
6. Divide the mixture between the tins and bake in the middle of the oven for about 20 minutes, or until the cakes are well risen, golden and feel spongy to the fingertips.
7. Allow the cakes to cool for a few minutes in the tins, then turn out on to a wire rack to cool completely.
8. Sandwich the cakes together with raspberry jam.
9. Dust the top of the cake with caster sugar.

Lemon Victoria Sponge

oil or melted lard for preparing the cake tins
170g/6oz butter
170g/6oz sugar
grated rind of 1 lemon
3 large eggs
170g/6oz self-raising flour

For the filling and topping:
lemon curd (see page 604)
feather icing (see page 585)

1. Set the oven to 190°C/375°F/gas mark 5.
2. Prepare 2 x 20cm/8 inch cake tins (see page 539).
3. Cream the butter and when soft add the sugar and beat until light and fluffy. Add the lemon rind.
4. Beat in 1 egg at a time, each time with 5ml/1 teaspoon flour.
5. Beat very well. Fold in the remaining flour. Add a little water – the consistency should be such that the mixture should fall reluctantly off a spoon.
6. Divide the mixture between the tins and bake for 20-25 minutes or until the cakes are well risen, golden and feel spongy to the fingertips.
7. Allow the cakes to cool for a few minutes in the tins, then turn out on to a wire rack to cool completely.
8. Sandwich the cakes with lemon curd.
9. Ice the top and 'feather' it as described in the icing recipe.

Madeira Cake

melted lard for greasing
170g/6oz unsalted butter
170g/6oz caster sugar
grated rind and juice of 1 lemon
pinch of ground cinnamon
3 eggs
110g/4oz self-raising flour
55g/2oz ground almonds
milk, if necessary
1 slice candied lemon (citrus peel)

1. Prepare an 18cm/7 inch cake tin (see page 539).
2. Set the oven to 170°C/325°F/gas mark 3.
3. Cream the butter and beat in the sugar until light and fluffy. Add the lemon rind and cinnamon.
4. Beat in the eggs one at a time, adding a little flour as you beat, to prevent the mixture from curdling. Add the lemon juice.
5. Fold in the remaining flour and the ground almonds with a metal spoon.
6. Add enough milk to bring the mixture to a dropping consistency (it should drop rather than run off a spoon).
7. Spoon the mixture into the cake tin and spread with a palette knife or spatula. Arrange the citrus peel on top of the cake.
8. Bake for $1^1/_4$ hours.
9. Cool the cake for 10 minutes in the tin before gently easing out on to a wire rack.

Marbled Chocolate Cake

1 x 4 egg Victoria sponge cake mixture (see page 539)
15ml/1 tablespoon cocoa powder
15ml/1 tablespoon warm milk
110g/4oz chocolate
15g/$^1/_2$ oz butter

1. Lightly grease a 20cm/8 inch ring mould with butter. Set the oven to 190°C/375°F/gas mark 5.
2. Make up the Victoria sandwich mixture and divide into 2 bowls.
3. Mix the cocoa powder with the warm milk and add it to one bowl.
4. Place spoonfuls of the mixture, alternating the colours into the ring mould. Use a skewer in a figure-of-eight motion to swirl the colours together.
5. Bake for 20-25 minutes or until the cake is well risen and feels spongy. Allow to cool for a few minutes in the tin, then turn out on to a wire rack to cool completely.
6. Break up the chocolate into small even pieces. Put into a bowl, add the butter and place over, not in, a pan of simmering water. Stir until completely melted.

7. Pour the chocolate over the cake, making sure that it is completely covered. Leave to cool and harden.

Christmas Cake

110g/4oz glacé cherries
55g/2oz mixed peel
450g/1lb raisins
285g/10oz sultanas
110g/4oz currants
225g/8oz butter
225g/8oz soft brown sugar
5 eggs, beaten
285g/10oz flour
10ml/2 teaspoons mixed spice
30ml/2 tablespoons black treacle
grated lemon rind
2 wine glasses of beer or sherry (200ml/7 fl oz)
110g/4oz ground almonds

1. Set the oven to 170°C/325°F/gas mark 3 and prepare a 22cm/9 inch round cake tin (see page 539).
2. Cut up the cherries and mix with the rest of the fruit.
3. Cream the butter until soft. Add the sugar and beat together until light and fluffy.
4. Add the beaten eggs slowly, beating well between each addition. If the mixture curdles, beat in 5ml/1 teaspoon of flour.
5. Fold in the flour, mixed spice, lemon rind, black treacle and beer or sherry.
6. Stir in the ground almonds and fruit.
7. Place the mixture in the prepared tin and make a deep hollow in the middle.
8. Bake for 2½ hours or until a skewer emerges clean from being stuck in the middle of the cake.
9. Allow to cool on a wire rack.

Coffee Almond Layer Cake

110g/4oz butter
110g/4oz caster sugar
85g/3oz plain flour
pinch of salt
5ml/1 teaspoon baking powder
2 eggs
10ml/2 teaspoons instant coffee, dissolved in 30ml/2 tablespoons hot water
55g/2oz ground almonds

For the filling:
170g/6oz unsalted butter
340g/12oz icing sugar
10ml/2 teaspoons instant coffee powder
55g/2oz flaked toasted almonds to decorate

1. Butter 2 x 18cm/7 inch sandwich tins (see page 539). Set the oven to 190°C/375°F/gas mark 5.
2. Cream the butter and beat in the sugar until light and fluffy.
3. Sift the flour, salt and baking powder. Beat the eggs lightly.
4. Add the eggs and flour alternately by degrees to the butter and sugar mixture. Stir in the coffee and the ground almonds. Divide the mixture between the tins and smooth the tops with a spatula.
5. Bake for 20-25 minutes or until the cake is firm and golden brown. Allow to cool in the tins for 5 minutes, then turn out on to wire racks and leave until stone cold.
6. Meanwhile, make the filling: beat the butter and sugar until light and fluffy and stir in the coffee.
7. Sandwich the cake layers with half the butter icing and spread the remainder around the sides and top of the cake. Decorate with flaked almonds.

Simnel Cake

A festive Easter cake: the 11 balls of marzipan are said to represent the apostles (without Judas). Sometimes they are made into egg shapes, the symbol of spring and rebirth.

large pinch each of salt and baking powder
225g/8oz plain flour
55g/2oz rice flour
110g/4oz glacé cherries
225g/8oz butter
225g/8oz caster sugar
grated rind of 1 lemon
4 eggs, separated
225g/8oz sultanas
110g/4oz currants
30g/1oz candied peel, chopped
340g/12oz marzipan (see page 589)
beaten egg
110g/4oz glacé icing (see page 585)

1. Set the oven to 180°C/350°F/gas mark 4. Prepare a 20cm/8 inch cake tin with a double lining of greased and floured greaseproof paper. Wrap the outside of the cake tin with a double thickness of brown paper to insulate the cake from direct heat.
2. Sift the salt, baking powder and flours. Cut the cherries in half.
3. Cream the butter until soft. Add the sugar and beat until light and fluffy. Add the lemon rind.
4. Beat in the egg yolks. Whisk the whites until stiff.
5. Fold one-third of the sifted flour into the mixture. Fold in the egg whites by degrees, alternating with the remaining flour and the fruit and peel.
6. Put half the mixture into the prepared tin, spreading a little up the sides of the tin.
7. Take just over one-third of the marzipan paste. Roll it into a smooth round. Place in the cake tin. Cover with the remaining mixture.
8. With a palette knife make a dip in the centre of the cake to counteract any tendency to rise in the middle.
9. Bake for 2 hours, then reduce the oven heat to 150°C/300°F/gas mark 2. Bake for a further 30 minutes.
10. Roll the remaining marzipan into a circle the same size as the top of the cake. Cut a piece from the centre about 12.5cm/5 inches in diameter and shape into 11 small even-sized balls.
11. Heat the grill. Lay the ring of marzipan on top of the cake and brush with egg wash. Arrange the marzipan balls on top of the ring and brush again with beaten egg. Grill until golden brown.
12. When cold pour a little glacé icing into the centre of the cake. Tie a ribbon around the side.

Chocolate and Orange Cake

For the cake:
85g/3oz dark sweetened chocolate
5ml/1 teaspoon vanilla essence
340g/12oz soft brown sugar
290ml/½ pint milk
grated rind of ½ orange
110g/4oz butter
2 eggs
225g/8oz plain flour
5ml/1 level teaspoon bicarbonate of soda

For the filling:
grated rind of ½ orange
290ml/½ pint thick cream, whipped
caster sugar to taste

For the icing:
110g/4oz dark sweetened chocolate
60ml/4 tablespoons milk

1. To make the cake set the oven to 190°C/375°F/gas mark 5. Line the bottom of 3 sandwich tins with greaseproof paper and brush them with melted lard or butter.
2. Put the chocolate, vanilla, half the sugar and half the milk into a saucepan. Cook, stirring until quite smooth. Add the grated orange rind.
3. Beat the butter with the rest of the sugar until very light and creamy. Beat in the eggs, then add the chocolate mixture and beat again. Sift in the flour and soda and beat well to get rid of all lumps. Add the rest of the milk and stir. The mixture should now have the consistency of pancake batter.
4. Divide the mixture between the 3 cake tins and bake in the middle of the oven for about 30

minutes or until the rounds have a very slightly shrivelled look around the edges. Do not worry if they do not feel very firm – they should be very moist and rather sticky. Allow to cool for 3 minutes before turning out on to a wire rack to cool. Peel off the paper.
5. To make the filling: mix the orange rind into the whipped cream and sweeten to taste. Make a triple-deck cake with the cream filling between the 3 layers of cake.
6. To make the icing: put the chocolate and milk into a saucepan. Heat, stirring, until smooth and thick. Cool slightly and pour or spread over the top of the cake.

Chocolate Fudge Cake

110g/4oz butter
110g/4oz caster sugar
2 eggs
30ml/2 tablespoons golden syrup
30g/1oz ground almonds
110g/4oz self-raising flour
pinch of salt
30g/1oz cocoa powder

For the icing:
110g/4oz granulated sugar
110ml/4 fl oz milk
140g/5oz plain chocolate, chopped
55g/2oz butter
30ml/2 tablespoons double cream
vanilla essence

1. Preheat the oven to 180°C/350°F/gas mark 4.
2. Grease and line the base of an 18cm/7 inch diameter deep cake tin with a circle of greaseproof paper.
3. Cream the butter until soft, add the sugar. Beat until light and fluffy.
4. Whisk the eggs together and add a little at a time to the butter and sugar mixture, beating well between each addition. If the mixture curdles, beat 5ml/1 teaspoon flour into it.
5. Stir in the golden syrup and ground almonds.
6. Sift together the self-raising flour and cocoa powder and fold into the mixture.
7. The cake mixture should have a reluctant dropping consistency; if it is too thick add a little water or milk.
8. Pile the mixture into the cake tin, spread flat with a palette knife and bake for 40 minutes or until the cake is well risen and feels spongy.
9. Turn out and cool on a wire rack.
10. Meanwhile, make the icing: put the sugar and milk into a pan over a low heat. Allow the sugar to dissolve and then bring it up to the boil. Simmer, without stirring, for 8 minutes.
11. Take the pan off the heat and stir in the chocolate; add the butter, cream and vanilla essence. Stir until completely melted.
12. Put into a bowl, cover and allow to chill for 2 hours until the icing is spreadable.
13. When the cake is cool, split it in half horizontally and sandwich back together again using a quarter of the icing. Spread the remaining icing on the top and sides of the cake, swirling it to give a frosted appearance.

Rice Cake

110g/4oz butter
225g/8oz caster sugar
finely grated rind of 1/2 lemon
4 eggs
225g/8oz ground rice

1. Set the oven to 180°C/350°F/gas mark 4. Line an 18cm/7 inch cake tin with a double layer of greased and floured greaseproof paper.
2. Cream the butter in a mixing bowl. Beat in the sugar until light and fluffy. Add the lemon rind and mix well.
3. Separate the eggs. Add the yolks to the mixture one at a time, beating hard all the time.
4. Whisk the egg whites until fairly stiff but not dry. Take a spoonful of egg white and mix it in. Stir in half the ground rice. Add half the remaining egg white. Add the rest of the ground rice, then the rest of the egg white.
5. Pour into the tin. Make a slight hollow in the centre of the mixture to counteract any tendency to rise in the middle.
6. Bake for 45 minutes or until firm to the touch and slightly shrunken at the edges.
7. Cool in the tin for 5 minutes, then turn out on to a wire rack to cool completely.

Squashy Rhubarb Cake

For the cake:
85g/3oz butter
85g/3oz sugar
2 small eggs
85g/3oz self-raising flour, sifted with a pinch of salt
milk

For the filling:
675g/1½lb rhubarb, cut into 2.5cm/1 inch pieces
15ml/1 tablespoon sugar

For the crumble top:
55g/2oz butter
85g/3oz plain flour
30g/1oz sugar

To finish:
icing sugar

1. Prepare a deep 20cm/8 inch cake tin (see page 537). Set the oven to 190°C/375°F/gas mark 5.
2. First make the crumble mixture: rub the butter into the flour and add the sugar. Set aside.
3. Now make the cake: cream the butter until soft and well beaten. Add the sugar and beat until very pale, light and fluffy.
4. Lightly beat the eggs and add them to the sugar mixture, beating in a little at a time, and folding in a spoonful of flour if the mixture curdles.
5. Fold in the rest of the flour and add a few dribbles of milk if the mixture is now too stiff. It should be of a dropping consistency – it will fall off a spoon rather reluctantly.
6. Turn the cake mixture into the prepared cake tin and spread it flat.
7. Cover carefully with the raw rhubarb pieces and sugar. Sprinkle with the crumble mixture.
8. Bake for about 45 minutes or until the cake feels firm on top. Leave to cool in the tin.
9. Just before serving, remove from the tin and sift over a thin layer of icing sugar.

NOTE: If using tinned rhubarb, you will need a 450g/1lb tin.

Pain de Gênes (Rich Almond Cake)

110g/4oz blanched almonds
3 eggs
140g/5oz caster sugar
55g/2oz potato starch or plain flour
2.5ml/½ teaspoon baking powder
good pinch of salt
85g/3oz butter
15ml/1 tablespoon Amaretto or Kirsch
icing sugar

1. Set the oven at 180°C/350°F/gas mark 4. Brush a moule-à-manqué or 20cm/8 inch cake tin with butter, line the bottom with a circle of greaseproof paper and brush it again.
2. Grind the almonds finely.
3. Whisk the eggs and sugar together until light and fluffy.
4. Sift the flour, baking powder and salt into a bowl. Stir into the nuts. Half fold this into the eggs and sugar mixture.
5. Melt the butter and carefully fold it into the cake mixture with the minimum of stirring. Add the Kirsch or Amaretto. Pour into the cake tin.
6. Bake for 30-35 minutes or until the cake is brown on top and springs back when lightly pressed with a finger.
7. Allow the cake to cool for 5 minutes in the tin, then loosen the sides with a knife and turn out on to a wire rack to cool. When cold, sift a thin layer of icing sugar over the top.

Whisked Sponge

3 eggs
85g/3oz caster sugar
22.5ml/1½ tablespoons lukewarm water
85g/3oz plain flour, sifted
pinch of salt

1. Set the oven to 180°C/350°F/gas mark 4. Prepare a cake tin (see page 537).
2. Place the eggs and sugar in a bowl and fit it over (not in) a saucepan of simmering water. Whisk the mixture until light, thick and fluffy. (If using an electric mixer no heat is required.)
3. Remove the bowl from the heat and continue

Above: Individual Apple Tarts.

Above: Gâteau Pithivier. Right: Sablé aux Fraises.

Left: Summer Fruit Compote. Above: Arranged Fruit Salad.

Above: Raspberries and Fromage Blanc with Fresh Figs. Right: Summer Pudding.

Left: Lemon Curd Ice Cream. Above: Individual Mango Parfaits with Passionfruit Sauce.

Above: Pistachio Parfait. Right: Brandy Snap Tortes.

nougatine

Left: Gâteau Nougatine. Above: Scones.

Above: Petits Fours. Right: Pickles.

Above: Canapés.

whisking until slightly cooled. Add the water.
4. Sift the flour and salt and, with a large metal spoon, fold into the mixture, being careful not to beat out any of the air.
5. Turn the mixture into the prepared tin and bake in the middle of the oven for about 30 minutes.
6. Test to see if it is cooked. (When the cake is ready, it will shrink slightly and the edges will look crinkled. When pressed gently it will feel firm but spongy and will sound 'creaky'.)
7. Turn out on to a wire rack to cool.

Swiss Roll

melted lard or oil for greasing
85g/3oz plain flour, sifted
pinch of salt
3 eggs
85g/3oz caster sugar
22.5ml/1 1/2 tablespoons warm water
2-3 drops vanilla essence
caster sugar
45ml/3 tablespoons warmed jam

1. Heat the oven to 190°C/375°F/gas mark 5. Prepare a Swiss roll tin by brushing a little melted lard or oil on the bottom and sides. Place in it a piece of greaseproof paper cut to fit the bottom of the tin exactly and brush again with melted fat. Dust with flour and sugar. (If no Swiss roll tin is available, a baking sheet fitted with a tray of doubled greaseproof paper can be used instead.)
2. Sift the flour with the salt.
3. Put the eggs and sugar in a bowl and fit it over (not in) a saucepan of simmering water. Whisk the mixture until light, thick and fluffy. (If using an electric mixer, no heat is required.) Continue beating until the mixture is cool again.
4. Using a large metal spoon, fold the water, essence and flour into the egg mixture.
5. Pour the mixture into the tin.
6. Bake for 12-15 minutes. It is cooked when, if touched with a finger gently, no impression remains. The edges will also look very slightly shrunk.
7. Lay a piece of greaseproof paper on the work-top and sprinkle it evenly with caster sugar. Using a knife, loosen the edges of the cooked cake, then turn it over on to the sugared greaseproof paper. Remove the rectangle of greaseproof paper from the bottom of the cake.
8. While the cake is still warm, spread it with the jam.
9. Using the paper under the cake to help you, roll the cake up firmly from one end. Making a little cut across the width of the cake just where you begin to roll helps to get a good tight Swiss roll.
10. Dredge the cake with caster sugar.

NOTE: If the cake is to be filled with cream, this cannot be done while it is hot. Roll the cake up, unfilled, and keep it wrapped in greaseproof paper until cool. Unroll carefully, spread with whipped cream, and roll up again.

Normandy Apple and Nut Cake

For the apple filling:
3 cooking apples (about 450g/1lb)
a little butter
Strip of lemon rind
about 85g/3oz brown sugar

For the cake:
125g/4 1/2 oz caster sugar
40g/1 1/2 oz ground hazelnuts, toasted until brown
4 egg yolks
50g/1 3/4 oz plain flour
50g/1 3/4 oz arrowroot
3 egg whites

To serve:
icing sugar
150ml/1/4 pint double cream

1. Wash the unpeeled apples, quarter and core them. Rub the bottom and sides of a heavy saucepan with butter. Slice the apples thickly into the pan and add the lemon rind and 60ml/4 tablespoons of water. Cover and cook gently, stirring occasionally until completely soft.
2. Push through a sieve. Rinse out the pan and return the purée to it. Add at least 55g/2oz brown sugar to 570ml/1 pint purée. Cook rapidly until the mixture is of a dropping consistency (about 4 minutes). Leave to cool.

3. Set the oven to 180°C/350°F/gas mark 4. Butter a sandwich tin or moule-à-manqué and dust it out with flour.
4. Beat together the sugar, nuts and egg yolks. When creamy and white, fold in the sifted flours.
5. Whisk the egg whites until stiff but not dry and fold them into the cake mixture. Spread in the prepared tin.
6. Bake for 40 minutes. Leave on a wire rack to cool.
7. Split the cake and sandwich it with the apple. Dredge the top with icing sugar.
8. Serve with whipped cream.

Génoise Commune

4 eggs
125g/4½ oz caster sugar
55g/2oz butter, melted but cool
125g/4½ oz plain flour

1. Set the oven to 190°C/375°F/gas mark 5. Prepare a moule-à-manqué or deep sandwich tin (see page 537).
2. Break the eggs into a bowl. Add the sugar. Place the bowl over a saucepan of simmering water and whisk until the mixture has doubled in bulk, and will leave a ribbon trail on the surface when the whisk is lifted. Lift the bowl off the heat and continue to whisk until the mixture has cooled. (If using an electric beater, whisking need not be done over heat.) Whisk in the butter quickly – if you work too slowly the cake will collapse.
3. Sift the flour over the cake mixture and fold it in thoroughly but gently with a large metal spoon.
4. Pour the mixture into the prepared tin. Bake for 30-35 minutes. Allow to cool slightly before turning out on to a wire rack.

Génoise Fine

4 eggs
125g/4½ oz caster sugar
100g/3½ oz butter, melted, but cool
100g/3½ oz plain flour

1. Prepare a moule-à-manqué or deep sandwich tin with oil, greaseproof paper, sugar and flour. Set the oven to 190°C/375°F/gas mark 5.
2. Break the eggs into a large bowl and add the sugar. Set the bowl over (not in) a pan of simmering water and whisk until light, fluffy and doubled in bulk. Take off the heat and whisk until cool. Whisk in the butter quickly – if you work slowly the cake will collapse.
3. Sift the flour over the cake mixture and fold it in thoroughly but gently with a large metal spoon.
4. Turn into the prepared tin and bake for 30-35 minutes. Leave to cool in the tin for a few minutes then turn on to a wire rack to cool.

NOTE: This is sometimes called a 'butter sponge'. However, this description is not culinarily correct, as a true sponge contains no fat.

Coffee Génoise with Chocolate Caraque

For the cake:
4 large eggs
125g/4½ oz caster sugar
55g/2oz butter, melted but cool
100g/3½ oz plain flour
10ml/2 teaspoons coffee powder

For the coffee butter cream filling and icing:
110g/4oz sugar
150ml/¼ pint milk
2 egg yolks
225g/8oz unsalted butter
coffee essence

For the chocolate caraque:
30g/1oz dark chocolate
browned chopped almonds for decoration
icing sugar

1. Prepare a moule-à-manqué or deep sandwhich tin (see page 537). Set the oven to 190°C/375°F/gas mark 5.
2. Break the eggs into a bowl, add the sugar and set the bowl over a saucepan of simmering water. Whisk until the mixture has doubled in bulk. Whisk intermittently off the heat until the mixture has cooled. (If using an electric mixer, beating need not be done over heat.) Quickly whisk in the butter – if you work too slowly the cake will collapse.
3. Sift the flour and coffee powder over the cake mixture and fold it in thoroughly but gently with a large metal spoon. Turn into the prepared cake tin.
4. Bake for about 35 minutes or until cooked – the edges should look slightly shrivelled. Allow to cool slightly in the tin and then turn out on to a wire rack. Peel off the paper and allow to cool completely.
5. To make the butter cream: add the sugar to the milk and bring to the boil. Beat the egg yolks, pour on the milk, mix well and return all the mixture to the saucepan. Stir over a gentle heat without boiling until slightly thickened. Strain and leave to cool completely.
6. Beat the butter until creamy and gradually whisk in the custard mixture. Flavour with coffee essence.
7. To make the chocolate caraque: melt the chocolate on a plate over a pan of boiling water. Spread thinly on a marble slab or other hard cold surface. When just set, use a long knife to shave off curls of chocolate: hold the knife with one hand on the handle and one hand on the tip of the blade. Hold it horizontally and scrape the chocolate surface by pulling the knife towards you. Chill the curls to harden them.
8. To decorate: split the cake in half and sandwich with one-third of the butter cream. Spread the tops and sides with the remainder. Press browned chopped almonds on to the sides of the cake. Cover the top with a pile of caraque chocolate and sift over a very fine dusting of icing sugar.

NOTE: If you do not want to make caraque, the cake can be very simply and attractively decorated in the following manner. Melt the chocolate meant for the caraque and stir it into the coffee butter cream. Spread the icing as smoothly as possible on top of the cake. Lightly place a lacy paper doily over it. Sift icing sugar over cake and doily. Carefully remove the doily, taking pains to prevent the icing sugar on it from falling on to the cake.

Chocolate Génoise

4 eggs
110g/4oz caster sugar
55g/2oz unsalted butter, melted but cool
85g/3oz plain flour, sifted
30g/1oz cocoa powder, sifted

1. First prepare a 20cm/8 inch moule-à-manqué cake tin. Brush it lightly with oil or melted lard. Line the base with a piece of greaseproof paper cut to size and brush again with oil or lard. Dust first with caster sugar and then with flour. Tip out any excess.
2. Whisk the eggs and sugar together until very light and fluffy. If you have a machine, this should take 5 minutes. If not, the whisking has to be done with a balloon whisk in a bowl set over a saucepan of simmering water and it can take up to 10 minutes. Be careful not to allow the base of the bowl to become too hot.
3. The mixture should then be whisked until cool. It is ready when it leaves a ribbon trail when the whisk is lifted. Do not over-whisk and stop if it begins to lose bulk. Whisk in the butter quickly. If you work too slowly the cake will collapse.
4. Fold the flour and cocoa powder into the mixture with a large metal spoon.
5. Tip into the prepared cake tin, give a light tap on the work surface to get rid of any large air pockets and bake in a preheated oven at 190°C/375°F/gas mark 5 for 25-35 minutes. Leave to cool in the tin for 2 minutes and then turn out on to a wire rack to cool completely.

Very Rich Chocolate Cake

This recipe is an adaptation of a Martha Stewart cake.

For the cake:
55g/2oz sultanas, chopped
55ml/2 fl oz brandy
3 eggs, separated
140g/5oz caster sugar
200g/7oz dark chocolate, chopped evenly
30ml/2 tablespoons water
110g/4oz unsalted butter
55g/2oz plain flour
85g/3oz ground almonds

For the icing:
140g/5oz dark chocolate, cut into small pieces
150ml/¼ pint double cream

1. Soak the sultanas in the brandy overnight.
2. Set the oven to 180°C/350°F/gas mark 4.
3. Prepare a moule-à-manqué or 20cm/8 inch cake tin: lightly brush with oil, line the bottom with a circle of greaseproof paper and grease again.
4. Separate the eggs and beat the yolks and sugar until pale and mousse-like.
5. Put the chocolate and water in a bowl set over a saucepan of simmering water. Stir until melted, then stir in the butter piece by piece until the mixture is smooth. Stir into the egg yolk mixture.
6. Sift the flour and very carefully fold it into the egg yolk and chocolate mixture with the ground almonds, sultanas and brandy.
7. Whisk the egg whites until stiff but not dry and fold into the chocolate mixture.
8. Turn the mixture into the prepared tin and bake for 35-40 minutes (the centre should still be moist). Leave to get completely cold in the tin.
9. Remove the cake from the tin and put it on a wire rack to ice it.
10. Prepare the icing: heat together the chocolate and cream. Stir until all the chocolate has melted and the mixture is smooth. Allow to cool and thicken to a coating consistency before pouring it over the cake.
11. Allow the icing to harden for at least 2 hours.

Chocolate and Orange Gâteau

For the candied orange peel
1 orange
110g/4oz granulated sugar
150ml/¼ pint water
30ml/2 tablespoons golden syrup
55g/2oz caster sugar

For the chocolate sponge cake:
55g/2oz plain flour
55g/2oz cornflour
45ml/3 tablespoons cocoa powder
pinch of baking powder
4 eggs
salt
110g/4oz caster sugar

For the orange syrup:
55g/2oz granulated sugar
85ml/3 fl oz water
45ml/3 tablespoons orange juice or Grand Marnier

For the orange filling:
55g/2oz orange marmalade
30ml/2 tablespoons orange juice or Grand Marnier

For the whipped ganache filling:
340g/12oz plain chocolate
220ml/8 fl oz double cream

For the ganache glaze:
225/8oz plain chocolate
220ml/8 fl oz double cream

CANDIED ORANGE PEEL

1. Peel the zest off the orange and cut into strips 2mm/⅛ inch wide. Put the zest into a small saucepan and cover with water. Bring to the boil and simmer for 5 minutes. This softens the zest and removes the bitter flavour. Drain and rinse under cold water.
2. Bring the granulated sugar, the water and golden syrup slowly up to the boil, ensuring that the sugar has dissolved before the liquid boils. Remove from the heat.
3. Stir in the zest and allow it to stand for 30 minutes. Bring it back up to the boil and set

aside for a further 30 minutes.
4. Remove the strips from the syrup, one at a time, with a fork, and put them on a wire rack to dry.
5. Spread the caster sugar on a plate and roll the cooled orange zest in it. Put in a warm dry place to dry out, keeping the pieces sparate. These can be made one week ahead.

CHOCOLATE ORANGE CAKE
1. Set the oven to 180°C/350°F/gas mark 4. Grease a 22cm/9 inch cake tin and line the bottom with a disc of greased greaseproof paper.
2. Sift the flours, cocoa and baking powder together.
3. Place the eggs, a pinch of salt and the sugar in a bowl and fit over, not in, a saucepan of simmering water. Whisk until the mixture is light, thick and fluffy and holds a good trail. (This can be done using a free-standing electric mixer without the simmering water.)
4. Carefully fold the sifted dry ingredients into the egg mixture in 2 batches.
5. Turn the mixture into the prepared tin and bake in the centre of the preheated oven for about 35 minutes or until the cake is firm to the touch and is just shrinking away from the edges of the tin. Loosen the cake and turn on to a wire rack to cool completely.

ORANGE SYRUP
1. In a saucepan dissolve the sugar in the water and bring to the boil. Allow to boil for a minute and then allow to cool. Once the syrup is cool stir in the orange juice or liqueur.

ORANGE FILLING
1. In a small bowl stir together the marmalade and orange juice or liqueur.

WHIPPED GANACHE FILLING
1. Chop the chocolate into small pieces. In a saucepan bring the cream up to boiling point. Remove from the heat and stir in the chocolate. Let the mixture stand for 2 minutes and then beat until smooth.
Cool at room temperature. Do not refrigerate.

GANACHE GLAZE
1. Make in exactly the same way as the whipped ganache filling. This may be made 2 hours in advance. Do not refrigerate.

TO ASSEMBLE THE CAKE
1. Beat the ganache filling with an electric hand mixer for 2 minutes until it has lightened in colour and texture.
2. Split the sponge cake horizontally into 3 layers. Using a pastry brush, moisten the bottom layer of the cake with some of the syrup. Spread with half the orange filling and then with a quarter of the whipped ganache.
3. Put the second layer of sponge on top, moisten that with syrup, spread with the remaining orange filling and then a further quarter of the whipped ganache. Cover with the top layer of cake and moisten with the remaining syrup.
4. Spread the top and sides with whipped ganache, reserving some for decoration. Refrigerate for at least 30 minutes or until the ganache becomes firm.
5. Place the gâteau on a wire rack over a tray. Pour the cool ganache glaze over the top and sides. Smooth with a palette knife. Refrigerate until set.
6. Put the remaining whipped ganache into a piping bag with a star nozzle and pipe out 12 rosettes around the edge of the gâteau. Decorate with the candied orange peel, just before serving.

NOTE: This cake can be assembled and refrigerated overnight. It tastes better if given a day to mature. It also freezes well – without the candied orange zest.

Gâteau Nougatine

For the cake:
110g/4oz hazelnuts
4 eggs
1 egg white
117g/4½oz sugar
55g/2oz softened butter
100g/3½ oz plain flour

For the royal icing:
1 small egg white
170g/6oz icing sugar
squeeze of lemon juice

For the nougat:
45g/1½ oz finely chopped almonds
85g/3oz caster sugar
2.5ml/½ teaspoon powdered glucose or pinch of cream of tartar

For the crème au beurre mousseline:
85g/3oz lump or granulated sugar
45ml/3 tablespoons water
2 egg yolks
110-140g/4-5oz unsalted butter

For the chocolate fondant icing:
225g/8oz loaf sugar
2.5ml/½ teaspoon liquid glucose or pinch of cream of tartar
115ml/4 fl oz water
30g/1oz unsweetened chocolate
1 drop vanilla essence

1. Set the oven to 180°C/350°F/gas mark 4.
2. Prepare a moule-à-manqué tin with greaseproof paper, oil, sugar and flour.
3. Start with the cake: brown the nuts. Remove the skins. Cool and grind.
4. Separate the eggs. Beat the yolks and 1 egg white with all but 15ml/1 tablespoon sugar, until white and creamy.
5. Whisk the remaining egg whites until stiff. Whisk in the reserved sugar.
6. Quickly beat the soft butter into the egg-yolk mixture. Mix the sifted flour with the nuts, lightly mix into the cake mixture and finally fold in the meringue mixture.
7. Pile into the cake tin. Bake for 40-50 minutes. Cool on a wire rack.
8. For the royal icing: whisk the egg white until frothy. Beat the icing sugar into it with the lemon juice until very smooth, white and stiff. Cover with a damp cloth until ready for use.
9. Oil a baking sheet.
10. Make the nougat: bake the chopped almonds until pale brown. Keep warm. Put the sugar and glucose into a heavy pan and place over a moderate heat. When golden, add the warmed almonds and continue to cook for 1 minute.
11. Turn on to the oiled baking sheet. Turn it over with an oiled palette knife, using a half-mixing, half-kneading motion. While still warm and pliable, roll as thinly as possible with an oiled lemon.
12. For the crème au beurre mousseline: dissolve the sugar in the water. Boil until the syrup will form short threads when stretched between finger and thumb. Whisk the yolks as you pour on the sugar syrup in a steady stream. Whisk until thick and mousse-like. Cream the butter and, when soft, add the mousse to the butter.
13. For the chocolate fondant icing: dissolve the sugar and 2.5ml/½ teaspoon liquid glucose in the water over a low heat without boiling. Cover and bring to the boil. Boil to soft ball (110-115°C/230-240°F). Meanwhile, scrub a stainless steel worktop and sprinkle with water. Stop the sugar syrup from cooking further by dipping the bottom of the pan into a bowl of very cold water. Cool slightly.
14. Chop the chocolate and melt it over a pan of simmering water. Pour the sugar syrup slowly on to the moistened stainless steel top. With a wet palette knife, fold the outsides of the mixture into the centre. When opaque but still fairly soft, add the melted chocolate and vanilla essence and continue to turn with a spatula and work until the fondant becomes fairly stiff. Put in a bowl and stand over a saucepan of simmering water to soften.
15. To assemble, split the cake into 3 layers. Crush the nougat with a rolling pin and mix half of it with half the butter cream (crème au beurre mousseline). Sandwich the cake together with this. Pour the melted chocolate fondant icing over the top. Spread butter cream around the sides and press on the remaining crushed nougat.
16. When the chocolate has set, fill a piping bag fitted with a writing nozzle with the royal icing and pipe the word 'nougatine' across the top.

Black Cherry Cake

400g/14oz tin black cherries
Kirsch
290ml/½ pint double cream
chocolate génoise (see page 547)
85g/3oz dark chocolate, grated
45ml/3 tablespoons water
110g/4oz icing sugar
about 55g/2oz browned split almonds
icing sugar for dusting

1. Remove the stones from the cherries and sprinkle the fruit with a little Kirsch.
2. Whip the cream until it will just hold its shape.
3. Split the cake into 3 thin rounds. On the bottom layer spread about one-third of the cream and sprinkle with half the cherries. Place the next layer of cake on top. Spread on another third of cream and the rest of the cherries. Place the top round on and flatten gently with your hands.
4. Place the chocolate in a pan with the water and stir over gentle heat until smooth, taking care not to boil.
5. Sift the icing sugar into a bowl and blend in the chocolate, adding a little extra water if necessary. Do this drop by drop to make a thick, pouring consistency. Pour over the top of the cake and allow to set.
6. Spread the remaining cream around the sides of the cake and press the browned split almonds against it.
7. Cut 3 strips of paper about 25cm/10 inches long and about 2.5cm/1 inch wide. Place them over the cake about 2.5cm/1 inch apart and sift over a heavy dusting of icing sugar.
8. Remove the paper strips carefully to reveal a striped brown and white top.

Dobez Torte

This is a cake with 5 layers. The mixture will not deteriorate if all the layers cannot be baked at the same time because of a lack of baking sheets or space in the oven.

SERVES 6
For the cake:
4 eggs
170g/6oz caster sugar
140g/5oz plain flour
pinch of salt

For the butter cream:
85g/3oz granulated sugar
60-75ml/4-5 tablespoons water
3 egg yolks
225g/8oz unsalted butter
coffee essence
55g/2oz skinned, toasted and ground hazelnuts

For the decoration:
140g/5oz sugar
30ml/2 tablespoons browned chopped almonds or ground browned hazelnuts
6 whole browned, skinned hazelnuts

1. Set the oven to 190°C/375°F/gas mark 5. Grease and flour 5 baking sheets and mark a 20cm/8 inch circle on each sheet (use a flan ring or saucepan lid in the floured surface).
2. Start with the cake: whisk the eggs, adding the sugar gradually. Set the bowl over (not in) a pan of simmering water and whisk until the mixture is thick and mousse-like. Remove from the heat and whisk intermittently until cool. Sift the flour and salt and fold into the egg mixture with a metal spoon. Divide the mixture between the 5 baking sheets and spread into circles as marked.
3. Bake for 8 minutes. Trim the edges and leave to cool on a wire rack.
4. Prepare the butter cream: dissolve the sugar in the water and, when clear, boil rapidly to the thread. (To test, put a little sugar syrup on to a wooden spoon, dip your index finger and thumb into cold water and then into the syrup in the spoon. When you pull your finger and thumb apart there should be a thread of syrup between them.) Allow to cool slightly for about 1 minute.
5. Whisk the yolks in a bowl and then pour the

syrup slowly on to them, whisking all the time. Keep whisking until you have a thick mousse-like mixture. Cream the butter well and beat in the egg and sugar mixture. Cool. Flavour 30ml/2 tablespoons of the buttercream with coffee essence and keep for decoration. Mix the ground hazelnuts and the remaining coffee essence into the remaining mixture.
6. Lay one piece of cake on a wire rack over an oiled tray. Melt the sugar for the caramel in a little water and, when dissolved, boil fiercely until a good caramel colour and pour immediately over the piece of cake, covering it completely.
7. Allow to harden slightly and mark into 6 portions with an oiled knife. (The idea is to cut through the setting caramel but not through the cake.) Trim the edges of excess caramel.
8. Sandwich the cake layers together with the coffee and hazelnut butter cream, placing the one with caramel on top. Spread the coffee and hazelnut butter cream thinly around the sides and press on the nuts.
9. Using a forcing bag with a large fluted nozzle, pipe a rosette with the remaining plain butter cream on top of each portion of cake. Decorate each rosette with a whole browned hazelnut.

Black Sticky Gingerbread

225g/8oz butter
225g/8oz soft brown sugar
225g/8oz black treacle
340g/12oz plain flour
10ml/2 teaspoons ground ginger
15ml/1 tablespoon ground cinnamon
10ml/2 teaspoons bicarbonate of soda
2 beaten eggs
290ml/½ pint milk

1. Grease a 20 x 30cm/8 x 12 inches roasting pan and line the base with greaseproof paper.
2. Preheat the oven to 150°C/300°F/gas mark 2.
3. Melt the butter, soft brown sugar and treacle in a pan.
4. Sift the flour, ground ginger and cinnamon, then stir in the melted mixture with the beaten eggs. Warm the milk to blood heat, pour it on to the bicarbonate of soda, stir it in and add it to the mixture. Stir well and pour the mixture into the prepared tin.
5. Bake the gingerbread for about 1½ hours . Cover the top with greaseproof paper after 1 hour.
6. When the gingerbread is cold, cut it into fingers and serve it spread with butter. This gingerbread keeps very well: in fact, it improves.

Apple and Ginger Cake

This is a very low-fat, low-sugar, almost cranky cake. It is moist in the centre and heavier than a normal sponge.

110g/4oz pear and apple spread
170g/6oz plain wholemeal flour
2 eggs, beaten
3 small dessert apples, peeled and grated
55g/2oz cashew nuts
2.5ml/½ teaspoon ground ginger
1.25ml/¼ teaspoon bicarbonate of soda

For the filling:
55g/2oz skimmed-milk soft cheese
15ml/1 tablespoon low-fat natural yoghurt or 1% fat fromage frais
concentrated apple juice to taste

To finish:
a very small quantity of icing sugar

1. Preheat the oven to 190°C/375°F/gas mark 5.
2. Put the pear and apple spread in a large basin. Add the flour and beat it in well. Add the eggs, grated apples, cashew nuts, ginger and bicarbonate of soda and beat really well.
3. Pile the mixture into 2 x 18cm/7 inch nonstick sponge tins and bake the cakes for 35 minutes.
4. Allow the cakes to cool in the tins for 5 minutes and then turn them out on to a wire rack to cool completely.
5. Mix the soft cheese with the yoghurt or fromage frais and beat well. Add a little concentrated apple juice to sweeten the filling. Use to sandwich the cakes together.
6. Place a paper doily on top of the cake and dust the top very lightly with icing sugar. Remove the doily carefully.

All-in-One Chocolate Cake

85g/3oz self-raising flour
pinch of salt
30g/1oz cocoa powder
2 eggs
110g/4oz caster sugar
110g/4oz butter
2-3 drops of vanilla essence
30-45ml/2-3 tablespoons warm water
soured cream and chocolate icing (see page 584)

1. Set the oven to 180°C/350°F/gas mark 4.
2. Sift the flour and salt into a bowl. Add the cocoa powder.
3. Add the eggs, sugar, butter and vanilla essence.
4. Beat with an electric whisk for 2 minutes.
5. Add the warm water and beat for a further minute.
6. Turn into a 10cm/7 inch cake tin and bake for 25-30 minutes. Turn out and leave to cool.
7. Split the cake in half and sandwich it together with half of the icing. Use the remaining icing to cover the top of the cake.

Kulich

This Russian Easter cake recipe has been adapted from a recipe in the *Observer Guide to European Cookery* by Jane Grigson.

570g/1¼ lb flour, sifted
1 packet dried yeast
180ml/6 fl oz warm milk
1.25ml/¼ teaspoon salt
3 egg yolks
140g/5oz sugar
3 cardamom pods, seeded and crushed
140g/5oz butter, softened
3 egg whites, stiffly whisked
75g/2½ oz raisins
30g/1oz each candied fruit and blanched almonds, chopped

For decoration (optional):
blanched almonds, chopped, candied fruit and peel or white glacé icing

1. Mix 225g/8oz of the flour with the yeast in a mixing bowl, then stir in the milk. Put the mixture into a polythene bag, put in a warm place and leave till spongy and doubled in size - about 1 hour.
2. Mix in the salt, 2½ egg yolks (set aside about half a yolk for glazing the kulich afterwards), sugar, cardamom and butter. Then fold in the egg whites and 225g/8oz more flour. The dough will be on the wet and sticky side. Add the rest of the flour gradually until the dough leaves the sides of the bowl. If it is a little sticky, do not worry too much. Put in a warm place and leave to rise again - about 2-3 hours this time.
3. Knock down the dough and add the fruits and almonds. Divide between 2 buttered and floured tall round moulds. If you have no suitable moulds (such as large brioche tins) use coffee tins. The dough should come half or two-thirds of the way up the tins. Leave to prove for about 1 hour.
4. Preheat the oven to 180°C/350°F/gas mark 4. Bake the kulichs in the oven for about 45 minutes. Check after 35 minutes by inserting a cocktail stick or thin skewer, which should come out clean. When the dough is cooked, the cake should have the appearance of a chef's hat.
5. When ready, turn out and brush with the remaining egg yolk and decorate, if you like, with chopped fruit and nuts, or icing, pouring it on so that it dribbles down the sides. Stick a candle in the top of each cake (if it is Easter).

Bread-making

Bread-making

With the advent of factory-made bread, bread-making became, for a while, almost a lost art amongst home cooks. Recently it has become a rediscovered craft and many people make the time to produce their own bread. Bread-making can be improved by understanding what is happening to the dough as it rises and cooks and what factors affect it. Once the process is understood, the cook can branch out from plain white bread to breads that contain nuts, herbs, fruits, vegetables, cheeses and different seeds and grains.

YEAST

Baker's yeast, the most usual leavening agent for bread, is a single-celled organism that belongs to the fungus family. For yeast to reproduce it needs warmth, moisture and food. Given the right conditions it can reproduce very quickly, giving off carbon dioxide as it does so. This is trapped in the dough or batter and so aerates it. The optimum temperature for yeast to reproduce is 25°C/80°F. Too much heat can kill it so care must be taken to ensure that the liquid used in making bread is lukewarm. A high concentration of sugar, fat or salt can slow down its rate of reproduction. If a dough is high in these ingredients then more yeast must be used. There are three types of yeast available: fresh, dried and easy-blend dried yeast.

Fresh yeast should be beige, crumbly-soft and sweet-smelling. It is usually thought of as the most satisfactory form of baker's yeast as it is less likely to produce 'beery' bread. Fresh yeast keeps for five days or so wrapped loosely in the refrigerator, and can be frozen for short periods, though results after freezing are unpredictable. If it is difficult to obtain, use dried yeast, or buy fresh yeast in a suitable quantity, divide it into 30g/1oz pieces, wrap them individually, then overwrap and freeze. Use as soon as the yeast thaws, and do not keep frozen for more than a month.

Dried yeast is bought in granular form in airtight sachets. It will remain active for about six months in a cool dry place. If substituting dried for fresh yeast when following a recipe, halve the weight of yeast called for. Dried yeast takes slightly longer to work than fresh yeast, and must first be 'sponged' in liquid, partly to reconstitute it, partly to check that is is still active. To avoid any beery taste, use rather less than the amount of dried yeast called for and allow a long rising and proving time. Using too much yeast generally means too fast a rise, resulting in bread with a coarse texture that goes stale quickly.

Easy-blend dried yeast is mixed directly with the flour, not reconstituted in liquid first. Sold in small airtight packages, it is usually included in bought bread mixtures. One 7g/¼oz package usually equals 15g/½oz conventional dried yeast or 30g/1oz fresh yeast.

FLOUR

Flour is the main ingredient in bread and gives it its individual character. Wheat flour is the most common because it contains a large amount of gluten, a form of protein that absorbs liquid to produce elastic strands in the dough. As the yeast works, it gives off carbon dioxide, which is trapped in the expanding dough, making it rise and puff up. When the loaf is cooked and set rigidly, the gas leaks out and is replaced by air.

RYE, MAIZE, MILLET and other flours contain less gluten than wheat flour. Because these flours lack the essential elasticity of wheat gluten, some wheat flour is usually added to the dough to produce a light-textured, well-risen loaf.

WHITE FLOUR is ground from wheat with the outer bran and inner germ removed, leaving 70-75 per cent of the original wheat. Removing the wheatgerm means the flour keeps longer, while removing the bran makes the flour lighter and finer. On the other hand, it will have fewer vitamins. For this reason white flours, whether bleached or unbleached, have B vitamins and other nutrients added to them in most countries. With or without such additions, bread made from white flour will have less flavour and less fibre than that made from wholegrain flour.

STRONG FLOUR is white flour made from varieties of wheat known as 'hard' wheat, which contain a particularly high proportion of gluten. Also called bread flour, the best comes from North America and is usually known as durum wheat. It is highly suitable for bread-making, giving the dough a remarkable capacity to expand and rise and produce a light, well-risen, springy loaf.

WEAK, SOFT OR HOUSEHOLD FLOUR is made from wheat grown mainly in Europe. It has less expansive gluten, produces a less elastic dough and bakes to a heavier, more crumbly bread. It makes excellent cakes and biscuits, where crumbliness and non-elasticity are advantages.

PLAIN FLOUR is general, all-purpose flour claimed to be suitable for sauces, cakes and breads, even though it does not have the high gluten content of strong flour. In Europe, where plain flour contains more soft wheat, it is less suitable for making breads than the plain or all-purpose flour used in North America, which contains more hard wheat.

SELF-RAISING FLOUR is usually made from soft wheat. A raising agent – usually a mixture of bicarbonate of soda and cream of tartar – is mixed with the flour. It is not used in yeast cookery, though some 'breads', such as wholemeal soda bread, are made with it.

WHOLEMEAL OR WHOLEWHEAT FLOUR is milled from the whole grain so that it contains the germ and the bran. Most of the B vitamins are in the wheatgerm, while bran provides roughage necessary for the digestive system. Bread made from wholemeal flour is undoubtedly healthier, but regardless of its natural gluten, it produces a heavier loaf. Also, the oil in the wheatgerm means that wholemeal bread will not keep as well as a white loaf. A mixture of wholemeal and white flour is a good compromise.

STONEGROUND FLOUR is usually wholemeal flour that has been milled between stone rollers rather than by modern milling methods. It is a coarser and heavier flour, even in its white version, than factory-milled flour, so more yeast or a longer rising time is needed to make it rise. It is claimed that more of the wheat's nutrients are retained as the grain is kept cooler during stone-grinding.

WHEATMEAL FLOUR, judging by its name, should refer to any wheat flour. However, the term is used by commercial bakers to describe brown bread flour that is not wholemeal. The colour may simply come from dye. Containing little or no bran or wheatgerm, it makes a lighter loaf. It is usually no more nutritious or 'healthy' than refined white flour.

OTHER BREAD INGREDIENTS

LIQUIDS For plain everyday bread the only liquid needed is water. It gives a crisp crust and a fairly hard or chewy bread. Milk produces a softer bread and a golden crust and is said by some to increase the keeping quality of bread. Beer gives the bread an individual, malty taste.

SALT is very important in bread. Not only does it affect the flavour but also the rising action of the yeast, the texture of the loaf and the crust. Without salt the flavour of the loaf can be bland. If a quick rising time is required, more yeast and less salt are needed, as in a pizza dough for example. If a dough does not seem to be rising very fast it is worth tasting it. If it tastes noticeably salty, the dough will produce a tough, badly risen loaf.

SUGAR is often included in savoury recipes for bread as a starter for the yeast. Too much sugar retards the yeast, so sweet doughs usually have a high proportion of yeast. White, demerara and brown sugars are used in doughs as well as molasses, black treacle and golden syrup. Honey can be substituted for golden syrup.

FATS added to a yeast dough include butter, lard, oil and vegetable fats. Butter gives a very good flavour and a good-looking crust. It can impede the action of the yeast and so a dough that is heavily enriched with butter, e.g. brioche dough, may not rise as much as an ordinary dough. Oil makes bread wonderfully easy to knead even when added in small quantities, for example 30ml/2 tablespoons to 675g/1½lb flour. Olive oil is the best oil to use, but alternatives are sunflower, peanut or sesame oils.

STAGES IN BREAD-MAKING

It is important to create the right conditions for the yeast to grow so that the dough will be elastic and accommodate the maximum carbon dioxide.

1. If the yeast is fresh, first cream it in a warm, not hot, cup with about 5ml/1 teaspoonful of sugar until smooth, then with a spoonful of lukewarm water. Dried yeast should be mixed with a little sweetened lukewarm water and left in a warm place for about 15 minutes. Once the yeast liquid is frothy, or 'sponges', add it to the flour, and mix in any remaining ingredients specified. If it does not froth, the yeast is dead and should not be used. Some recipes, usually those enriched with fat and sugar, require the yeast mixture and all the liquid to be beaten with a small proportion of the flour to a yeasty batter, called the starter, and left in a warm place until it 'sponges'. Then the rest of the flour is added and the mixing completed. This method used to be common to all breads. The process takes longer but is said by old-fashioned bakers to produce the lightest, most even-textured bread.
2. Kneading, or manipulating, the dough, is the next stage. It is necessary in order to distribute the yeast cells evenly and promote the dough's elasticity. The length of the time for kneading varies according to the type of flour and the skill of the kneader, but the dough must lose its stickiness and become smooth, elastic and shiny – this usually takes about 15 minutes.

Techniques vary, but the most common one is to push the lump of dough down and away with the heel of the hand, then to pull it back with the fingers, slap it on the worktop and repeat the process, turning the dough slightly with each movement. Table-top electric mixers with dough hooks or robust food processors can also be used for kneading. They take less time than kneading by hand, but follow the manufacturer's instructions closely.
Once kneaded, the dough is formed into a ball and put into a lightly oiled, warm – not hot – bowl, and turned to coat it evenly with grease to prevent hardening and cracking. The bowl is covered with a piece of cling film, oiled polythene or a damp cloth, put in a warm (32°C/90°F) draught-free place and left until about 1½ times its original size. The dough should spring back when pressed lightly with a floured finger. The longer the rising takes the better. Too rapidly risen or over-risen bread has a coarse texture and a beery smell.
3. Knocking back is the next process. The risen dough is knocked down, or punched with the knuckles to push out air that may have formed large, unevenly shaped holes. Punched to its original size, it is then kneaded briefly to make it pliable. Extra sugar or dried fruit are usually added at this point, before the dough is shaped and put into a loaf tin or on to a baking sheet.
4. Proving is the second rising of the dough. When this is completed, the loaf will have doubled in bulk and should look the size and shape you hope the finished bread will be. Proving can be done in a slightly warmer place, about 40°C/100°F, for a shorter time, about 20 minutes, because the previous rising and further kneading will have made the dough even more elastic and it will rise more easily. With a second rising, the bread will be lighter when baked.
5. The bread will continue to rise in the oven for a short time partly because of the rising steam in the loaf and partly because the yeast keeps working until the dough reaches 60°C/140°F. Then the heat of the oven will cook the dough into a rigid shape. Called 'oven spring', this final rising is likely to push the top crust away from the body of the loaf. To avoid too much oven spring, bread is baked at a fairly high temperature to kill the yeast quickly.
6. The baked bread should be golden brown and have shrunk slightly from the sides of the tin. To make sure that the bread is done, it should

be turned out on to a cloth and tapped on the underside. If it sounds hollow, it is done. If not, it should be returned to the oven, on its side, without the tin. Bread is cooled on a wire rack. After two hours, it will slice easily. Once stone cold it may be stored in a bread tin or a plastic bag. A lukewarm loaf stored in an airtight container will become soggy, if not mouldy.

SODA BREAD

Soda bread has bicarbonate of soda as a raising agent. However, in order to activate the soda an acid must be included in the ingredients. This is usually cream of tartar, which must be sifted with the bicarbonate of soda and the other dry ingredients to incorporate it thoroughly. When liquid is added to the dough, the alkali (bicarbonate of soda) and acid (cream of tartar) enter a chemical reaction and form carbonic acid gas. As soon as this is liberated the dough must go into the oven or the bread will not work and the flavour will be impaired. In some recipes the cream of tartar is replaced by sour milk or buttermilk. These doughs are the exact opposite of yeast doughs. High-speed mixing and quick light handling are required, rather than careful mixing and vigorous kneading.

SHAPES FOR ROLLS

These shapes are made using approximately 55g/2oz made-up bread dough each. Once the dough has had its first rising, knock it back and divide into equal-sized pieces of dough. A 450g/1lb flour quantity of bread dough will make 16 rolls. Rolls have to be made and shaped quickly or the first rolls will have overproved before the last rolls have been shaped.

PLAIN ROLLS Roll the dough on the work surface into a ball, pinching with the fingers to create a smooth surface on the underside. Turn the roll over, place on a baking sheet and press down slightly.

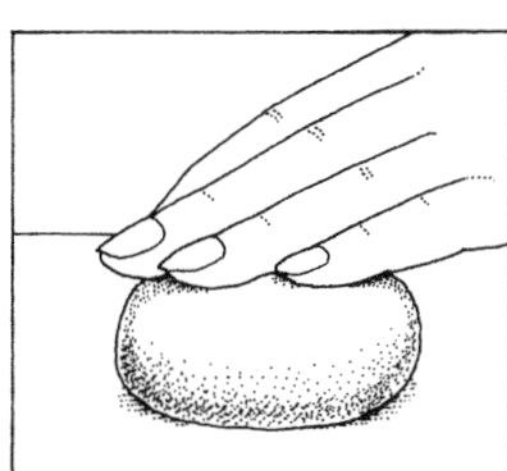
Plain roll

BAPS As above except that when they are placed on the baking sheet press down firmly to make them round and flattish.

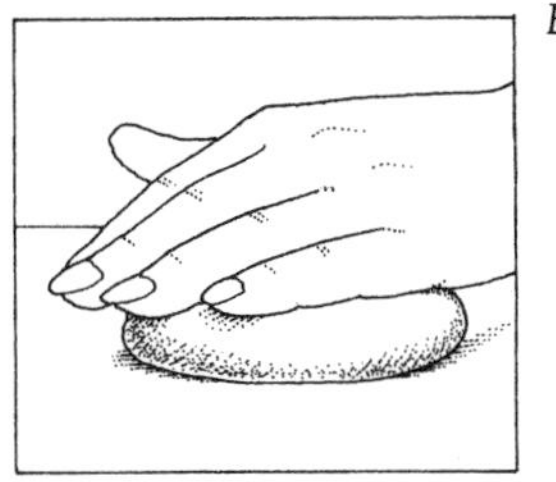
Bap

KNOTS Shape the dough, with your hands, into a sausage about 10cm/4 inches long. Carefully, without stretching, tie into a knot.

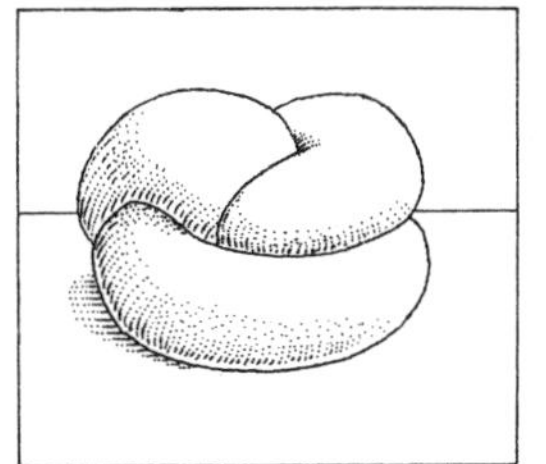
Knot

PLAITS Divide the dough into 3 equal pieces and shape each piece into a sausage about 10cm/4 inches long. Put 2 pieces parallel to each other 2.5cm/1 inch apart, and put the third one across them, threading it under the left-hand piece and over the right-hand piece. Starting from the middle take the left-hand piece and place it over the right-hand piece and proceed as for a plait (see diagrams). When one end is completed turn the plait over so that the unplaited pieces are towards you and proceed as before.

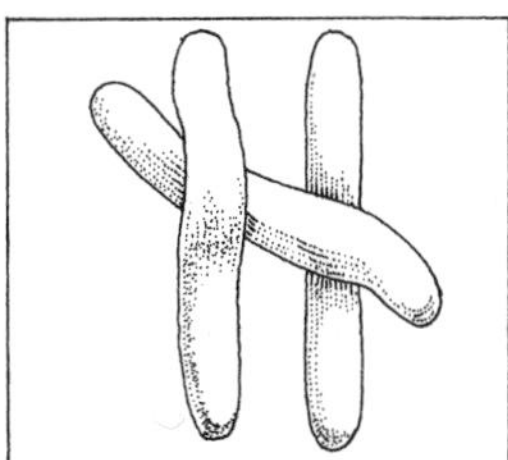

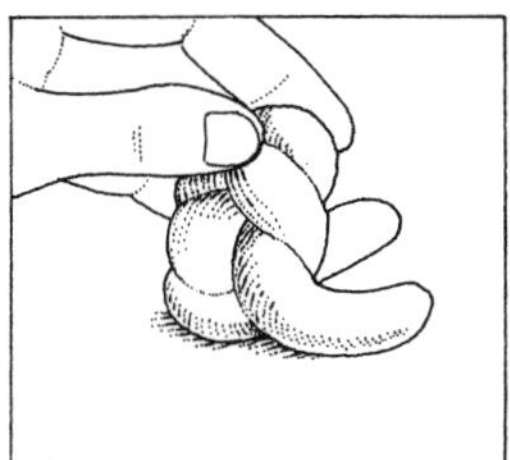

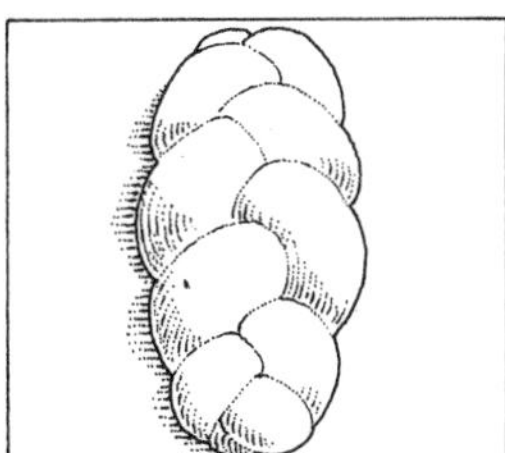

1. Preparing to plait
2. Turning the plait over
3. The completed plait

TWISTS OR WREATHS Divide the dough in two and shape each into a sausage approximately 12cm/5 inches long. Twist each piece around the other to look like a rope, then draw round into a circle pressing the ends together.

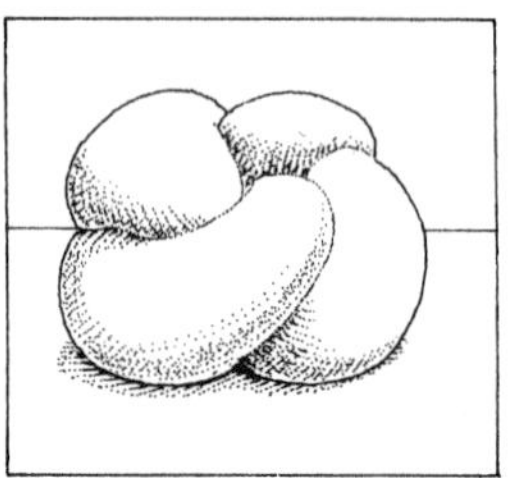
Twist

BLOOMERS Make as for plain rolls, except oval and not round. Make 3 diagonal slashes into the surface before proving.

Bloomer

CROWNS Shape as for plain rolls, and cut a cross into the surface before proving.

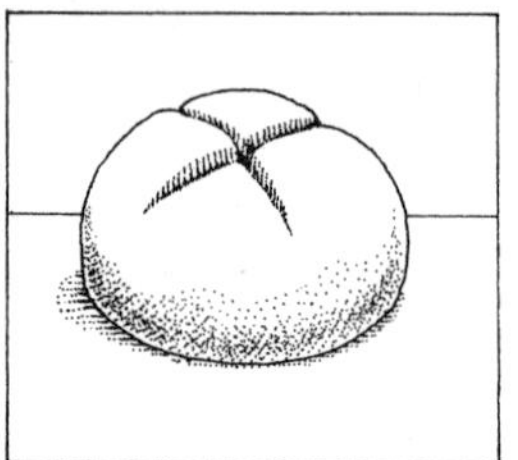
Crown

COTTAGE LOAVES Divide the dough into 2 pieces, one three-quarters larger than the other. Shape both into balls as for plain rolls. Make a small indentation in the centre of the top of the larger one and place the smaller roll on it. Using a floured finger or a wooden spoon handle, press a hole through both rolls to the baking sheet below, thus fixing the top to the bottom.

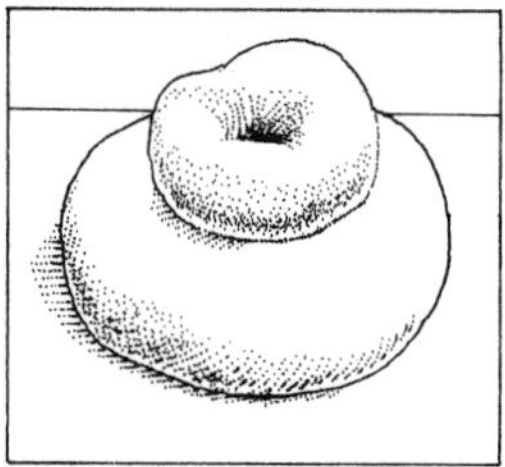
Cottage loaf

CATHERINE WHEEL Shape the dough into a sausage approximately 15cm/6 inches long. Coil the dough round from the centre, forming a Catherine wheel.

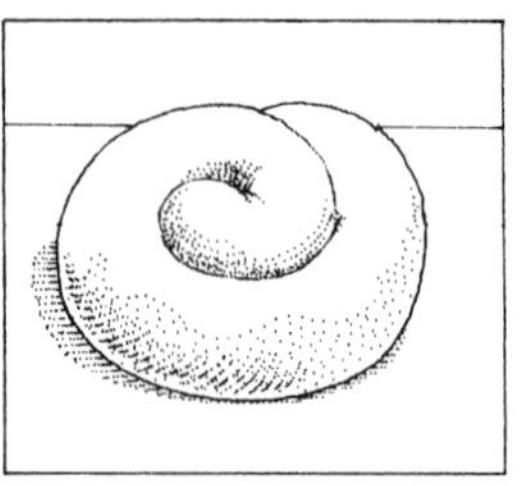
Catherine wheel

PAWNBROKER Divide the dough into 3 equal pieces. Form each into a neat ball and place next to each other on the baking sheet to make a triangle.

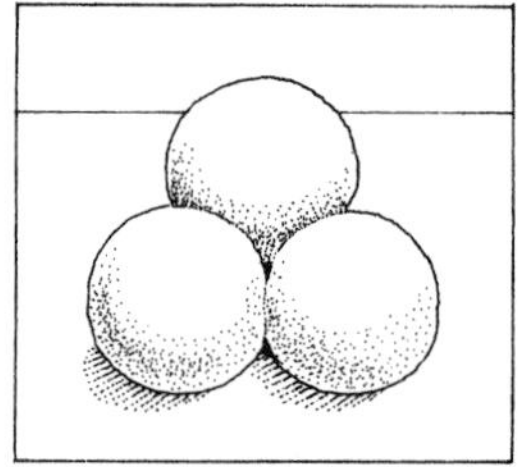
Pawnbroker

PROPELLER Shape the dough as for plain rolls and with a pair of scissors make 1cm/½inch snips at an angle of 45 degrees all round the edge. Prove.

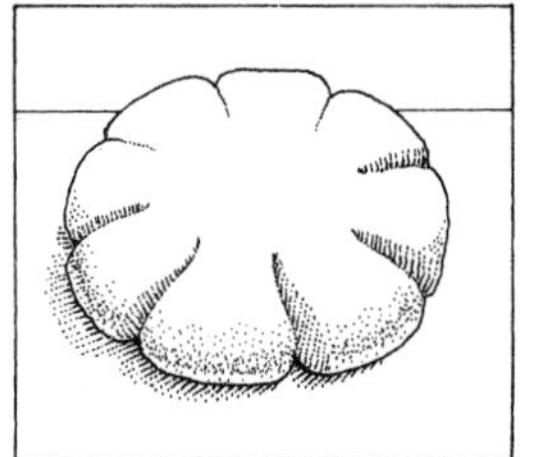
Propeller

MALTESE CROSS Shape the dough as for plain rolls and with a pair of scissors snip into the dough in 4 places as illustrated. Prove.

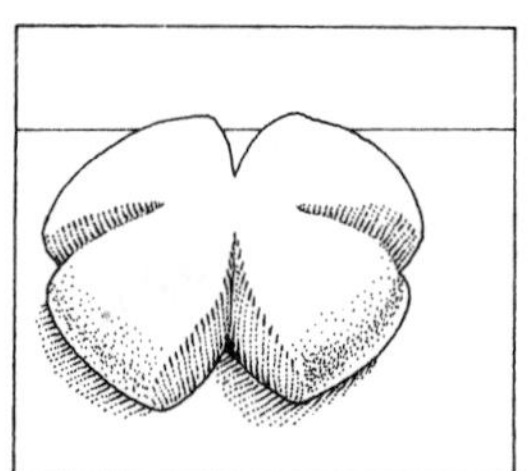
Maltese Cross

HEDGEHOGS Shape the dough into an elongated plain roll. Pinch with finger and thumb at one end to form the nose and eyes. With a pair of scissors make tiny snips into the dough to form the prickles. Use peppercorns or currants for the eyes.

White Bread

You will need a 1 kg/2lb bread tin. If it is old and used, you may not need to grease or flour it, but if it is new and not nonstick, brush it out very lightly with flavourless oil and dust with flour.

15g/½ oz fresh yeast
290ml/½ pint lukewarm milk
5ml/1 teaspoon caster sugar
30g/1oz butter
450g/1lb plain flour (preferably 'strong')
5ml/1 teaspoon salt
1 egg, lightly beaten
egg glaze

1. Dissolve the yeast with a little of the milk and the sugar in a teacup.
2. Rub the butter into the sifted flour and salt as you would for pastry.
3. Pour in the yeast mixture, the milk and the beaten egg and mix to a softish dough.
4. Add a small amount of flour if the dough is too sticky. When the dough will leave the sides of the bowl, press it into a ball and tip it out on to a floured board.
5. Knead until it is elastic, smooth and shiny (about 15 minutes).
6. Put the dough back in the bowl and cover it with a piece of lightly greased polythene.
7. Put it somewhere warm and draught-free and leave it to rise until it has doubled in size. This should take at least 1 hour. Bread that rises too quickly has a yeasty, unpleasant taste; the slower the rising the better - overnight in a cool larder is better than half an hour over the boiler!
8. Knead for a further 10 minutes or so.
9. Shape the dough into an oblong and put it into the loaf tin.
10. Cover with the polythene again and allow to rise again until it is the size and shape of a loaf. Brush with egg glaze.
11. Set the oven to 220°C/425°F/gas mark 7. Bake the loaf for 10 minutes, then turn the oven down to 190°C/375°F/gas mark 5 and bake for a further 25 minutes or until it is golden and firm.
12. Turn the loaf out on to a wire rack to cool. It should sound hollow when tapped on the underside. If it does not, or feels squashy and heavy, return it to the oven, without the tin, for a further 10 minutes.

NOTE: If using dried yeast or easy-blend see page 556.

Plaited White Loaf

450g/1lb warmed plain flour (preferably 'strong')
5ml/1 teaspoon salt
290ml/½ pint tepid milk
15g/½ oz butter
15g/½ oz fresh yeast
5ml/1 teaspoon caster sugar
1 egg, beaten
milk and poppy seeds for glazing

1. Sift the flour and salt into a warm mixing bowl. Make a well in the centre.
2. Heat the milk, melt the butter in it and allow to cool until tepid. Cream the yeast and sugar together. Mix the milk, egg and creamed yeast together and pour into the well.
3. Mix and knead until smooth and elastic (this should take 10-15 minutes). The dough should be soft.
4. Cover the bowl with a piece of oiled polythene and put to rise in a warm place for about an hour. It should double in bulk.
5. Heat the oven to 200°C/400°F/gas mark 6.
6. Divide the dough into 3 equal pieces and knead on a floured board. Form a long sausage with each piece and plait them together (see diagram, page 559). Place on a greased baking sheet.
7. Cover again with the oiled polythene and prove (allow to rise) in a warm place for 15 minutes.
8. Brush with milk, sprinkle with poppy seeds and bake for about 25 minutes or until the loaf is golden and sounds hollow when tapped on the underside.

NOTE: If using dried yeast or easy-blend see page 556.

Brown Soda Bread

Many soda bread recipes call for buttermilk, but we have found that it works well using milk.

900g/2lb wholemeal flour, **or** *675g/1½lb wholemeal flour and 225g/8oz plain white flour*
10ml/2 teaspoons salt
10ml/2 teaspoons bicarbonate of soda
20ml/4 teaspoons cream of tartar
10ml/2 teaspoons sugar
45g/1½ oz butter
570-860ml/1-1½ pints milk (if using all wholemeal flour, the recipe will need more liquid than if made with a mixture of 2 flours)

1. Set the oven to 190°C/375°F/gas mark 5.
2. Sift the dry ingredients into a warm dry bowl.
3. Rub in the butter and mix to a soft dough with the milk.
4. Shape with a minimum of kneading into a large circle about 5cm/2 inches thick. With the handle of a wooden spoon, make a cross on the top of the loaf. The dent should be 2cm/¾ inch deep.
5. Bake on a greased baking sheet for 25-30 minutes. Allow to cool on a wire rack.

Wholemeal Baps

MAKES 12 BAPS
20g/¾ oz fresh yeast
290ml/½ pint lukewarm milk
5ml/1 teaspoon caster sugar
225g/8oz wholemeal flour
225g/8oz plain white flour (preferably 'strong')
5ml/1 teaspoon salt
55g/2oz butter
1 egg, lightly beaten
sesame seeds

1. Dissolve the yeast with a little of the milk and the sugar in a teacup.
2. Warm a large mixing bowl and sift the flours and salt into it. Rub in the butter as you would for pastry.
3. Pour in the yeast mixture, the milk and nearly all the beaten egg and mix to a fairly slack dough.
4. When the dough will leave the sides of the bowl, press it into a ball and tip it out on to a floured board. Knead it until it is elastic, smooth and shiny (about 15 minutes).
5. Put the dough back in the bowl and cover it with a piece of lightly greased polythene. Put it somewhere warm (on a shelf above a radiator, on the grill rack over a pan of very gently simmering water on the cooker, in the airing cupboard or just in a draught-proof corner of the kitchen). Leave it there until the dough has doubled in size. This should take at least 1 hour.
6. Take the dough out of the bowl, punch it down and knead it again for 10 minutes.
7. Set the oven to 200°C/400°F/gas mark 6.
8. Divide the dough into 12 pieces and shape them into flattish ovals (using a rolling pin if you like). Put on a floured baking sheet and prove (allow to rise again) for 15 minutes. Brush with the remaining beaten egg. Sprinkle with the sesame seeds.
9. Bake for 20 minutes or until firm. Leave to cool on a wire rack. Covering the baps with a tea towel will ensure a very soft crust.

NOTE: If using dried yeast or easy-blend see page 556.

Wholemeal Bread

This wholemeal bread is simple to make as it has only one rising. As with all bread made from purely 100% wholemeal flour it will be heavier than bread made from a mixture of flours. The flour and water quantities are approximations as wholemeal flours vary enormously. The dough should be moist but not sticky. Use the smaller quantity called for and then add extra flour or water as necessary.

550g-600g/1lb 4oz-1lb 6oz stoneground 100% wholemeal flour
290-340ml/10-12 fl oz warm water
45ml/3 tablespoons buttermilk
15g/½ oz fresh yeast (for dried yeast halve this quantity)
5ml/ 1 teaspoon salt

1. Warm the flour with the salt in a mixing bowl in the bottom of a low oven for about 5 minutes. Warm 2 x 675g/1½lb nonstick loaf tins.
2. Mix the buttermilk with the warm water. Add a little of the liquid to the yeast with a pinch of flour.

If using dried yeast, set the mixture aside to sponge for 10 minutes. It is ready when it is frothy.
3. Make a well in the centre of the flour, pour in the yeast mixture and nearly all the water and buttermilk. Mix to a dough. Add extra flour or liquid as required. Knead well.
4. Fill the warmed tins three-quarters full of dough. Smooth the tops and cover with a piece of greased polythene. Leave in a warm place for 45 minutes or until the dough has risen to the top of the tins.
5. While the dough is rising, preheat the oven to 225°C/450°F/gas mark 8.
6. Bake the bread for 15 minutes. Reduce the heat to 195°C/375°F/gas mark 5 and bake for a further 25 minutes.
7. The bread should sound hollow when it is tapped on the underside. If it does not or feels squashy and heavy, then return to the oven, without the tin, for a further 5-10 minutes. Leave to cool on a wire rack.

Ballymaloe Brown Bread

30g/1oz yeast
5ml/1 teaspoon black treacle
350-425g/12-15 fl oz water at blood heat
450g/1lb wholemeal flour
5ml/1 teaspoon salt
15ml/1 tablespoon sesame seeds

1. Grease a 13 x 20cm/5 x 8 inch loaf tin.
2. Mix the yeast with the treacle and 150ml/1/4 pint of the water, and leave in a warm place for about 5 minutes, by which time it should look creamy and slightly frothy on top.
3. Sift the flour and salt into a large bowl. Make a well in the centre and add the yeast mixture and enough of the remaining liquid to make a wettish dough that would be just too wet to knead.
4. Put the dough in the loaf tin and smooth down the surface. Sprinkle with the sesame seeds and pat down. Place the tin in a warm place and cover with a dry tea towel. Leave to rise for 15-30 minutes.
5. Preheat the oven to 230°C/470°F/gas mark 9.
6. Place the bread in the hot oven for 45-50 minutes. After about 30 minutes, remove the bread from the tin and replace it in the oven to continue cooking. When cooked, it should sound hollow when tapped on the bottom.

NOTE: If using dried or easy-blend yeast see page 556.

Beer Bread

55g/2oz butter
20ml/1 dessertspoon soft brown sugar
290ml/1/2 pint brown ale
30g/1oz fresh yeast
5ml/1 teaspoon salt
1 egg
225g/8oz wholewheat flour
225g/8oz plain white flour (preferably 'strong')

1. Use a little of the butter to brush out a 1kg/2lb loaf tin.
2. Bring the sugar, beer and the rest of the butter to boiling point, then allow to cool until lukewarm.
3. Use 1-2 spoons of this liquid to cream the yeast. Add the creamed yeast, salt and lightly beaten egg to the beer mixture.
4. Warm a large mixing bowl and sift the flours into it. Make a well in the centre and pour in the liquid. Mix, first with a knife, and then with your fingers, to a soft but not sloppy dough. Knead for 10 minutes or until smooth and a little shiny. The dough should be very elastic.
5. Put the dough back in the bowl and cover it with a piece of greased polythene. Put in a warm place until it has doubled in bulk.
6. Take out, punch down and knead until smooth again. Shape the dough into a loaf shape and put into the tin. Cover with the greased polythene again and put back in the warm place to prove (rise again to double its bulk). It should now look the shape of the finished loaf.
7. While it is proving, heat the oven to 200°C/400°F/gas mark 6. Bake the loaf in the middle of the oven for 35 minutes or until it is brown on top and the bread sounds hollow when tapped on the underside. Cool on a wire rack.

NOTE: If using dried yeast or easy-blend, see page 556.

Raisin Bread

225g/8oz black grapes, deseeded
110g/4oz raisins
85ml/3 fl oz sweet white wine
30g/1oz fresh yeast
140ml/5 fl oz warm milk
310g/11oz flour
pinch of salt
130g/5oz sugar

1. Preheat the oven to 180°C/350°F/gas mark 4.
2. Soak the grapes and raisins in the white wine.
3. Dissolve the yeast in some of the warm milk.
4. Sift the flour with the salt. Add 110g/4oz of the sugar. Make a well in the centre and add the yeast mixture and enough warm milk to make a soft but not sticky dough.
5. Knead for 5 minutes or until the dough is smooth and springy. Put in a clean bowl, covered, in a warm place, to rise for one hour or until double its original size.
6. Knock down the dough and re-knead for 2 minutes. Cut the dough in half and shape into 2 x 20cm/8 inch circles. Place one on a floured baking sheet and cover with three-quarters of the soaked grapes and raisins. Cover with the second piece of dough and place the remaining grapes and raisins on top. Leave covered, in a warm place, until 1½ times its original size.
7. Sprinkle with the remaining sugar and bake in the preheated oven for about 45 minutes or until the loaf is risen and brown and sounds hollow when tapped underneath.

Blue Poppy Seed and Fresh Mint Bread

675g/1½lb wholemeal flour
5ml/1 teaspoon salt
110g/4oz blue poppy seeds
45ml/3 tablespoons roughly chopped mint
55g/2oz fresh yeast
5ml/1 teaspoon muscavado sugar
570ml/1 pint lukewarm water
15ml/1 tablespoon oil

1. Sift the flour and the salt into a large mixing bowl. Stir in the poppy seeds and chopped mint and make a well in the centre.
2. Cream the yeast and sugar together. Mix the oil with the lukewarm water.
3. Put the yeast mixture and the water and oil into the well and mix with a round-bladed knife until a soft, pliable dough is obtained, adding more water if necessary.
4. When the dough will leave the sides of the bowl, press it together into a ball and tip it out on to a lightly floured work surface.
5. Knead it until it is smooth and elastic (about 10 minutes).
6. Put the dough back into the bowl, which has been washed and lightly oiled, and cover it with a piece of lightly oiled cling film. Leave the dough to rise in a warm place until it has approximately doubled in size. This should take at least 1 hour.
7. Turn the dough out on to the floured work surface, punch it down and knead for a further 10 minutes or so until it is smooth.
8. Shape the dough into an oval, place on a floured baking sheet and leave to rise again for about 15 minutes covered with the oiled cling film. Set the oven to 220°C/425°F/gas mark 7.
9. Dust the top of the loaf with a little flour and bake for 20 minutes. Turn the oven down to 190°C/375°F/gas mark 5 and bake the loaf for a further 20 minutes or until it is brown and sounds hollow when tapped on the underside.
10. Leave the loaf to cool on a wire rack.

NOTE: If using dried or easy-blend yeast see page 556.

Italian Bread

This is a basic olive oil bread which can be adapted easily by adding a variety of herbs such as rosemary or sage or by adding grated cheese.

30g/1oz fresh yeast
225ml/8 fl oz warm water
450g/1lb strong plain flour
10ml/2 teaspoons salt
30ml/2 tablespoons olive oil

1. Dissolve the yeast in the warm water.
2. Sift the flour and salt on to a work surface, and make a well in the centre. Pour in the dissolved yeast and olive oil. Gradually draw in

the flour and when all the ingredients are well mixed, knead the dough for 8 minutes.
3. Put the dough in a lightly floured bowl. Cover with a damp tea towel and leave to rise in a warm place. This will take about 1 hour.
4. Knead again and shape as required, prove until 1 1/2 its original size and bake at 230°C/450°F/gas mark 8 for 10 minutes. Reduce the oven to 190°C/375°F/gas mark 5 and bake for about 45 minutes. Remove to a cooling rack and leave to get completely cold.

NOTE: If using dried yeast or easy-blend see page 556.

Potato Bread

450g/1lb potatoes, peeled, cooked and mashed with 150ml/1/4 pint milk and a knob of butter
30g/1oz yeast
425ml/3/4 pint lukewarm water
675g/1 1/2lb flour, preferably 'strong'
10ml/2 teaspoons salt

1. Allow the potatoes to cool until lukewarm.
2. Dissolve the yeast in the lukewarm water. Mix it with the mashed potatoes.
3. Sift the flour into a bowl with the salt. Add the potato and yeast mixture and mix well. When the mixture will leave the sides of the bowl, press it into a ball and tip it out on to a floured surface.
4. Knead until it is elastic, smooth and shiny; this will probably take 15 minutes.
5. Put the dough back in the bowl and cover it with a piece of lightly greased polythene.
6. Put it somewhere warm and draught-free and leave it to rise until it has doubled in size. This should take at least 1 hour.
7. Knead for a further 10 minutes or so.
8. Shape into 3 loaves, cover with polythene and leave to prove (rise again) for 15 minutes. Dust lightly with flour.
9. Set the oven to 220°C/425°F/gas mark 7. Bake the loaves for 10 minutes. Turn the oven down to 190°C/375°F/gas mark 5 and bake for a further 25 minutes or until golden brown and firm.
10. Turn out on to a wire rack to cool. The bread should sound hollow when tapped on the underside. If not, return to the oven for a further few minutes.

NOTE I: This recipe can be used for making attractive bread rolls. For details of making bread rolls see page 559.
NOTE II: If using dried yeast or easy-blend see page 556.

Sourdough Bread

This bread is made with a 'starter' of soured dough. The starter has to be made 3 days before the bread by which time it will have fermented and soured. Each time 150ml/1/4 pint of starter is used, 150ml/1/4 pint of flour and water paste (using 100ml water and 50g flour) must be replaced. The sourdough starter will last for about 7 days covered in the refrigerator. However, it will last indefinitely if you use and feed it and store it in the refrigerator.

For the sourdough starter:
7g/1/4oz yeast
290ml/1/2 pint warm water
110g/4oz wholemeal flour

For the sourdough bread:
225g/1/2lb wholemeal flour
25g/3/4oz fresh yeast
5ml/1 teaspoon sugar
10ml/2 teaspoons salt
150ml/1/4 pint sourdough starter (see above)
675g/1 1/2lb strong white flour

1. Make the sourdough starter. Dissolve the yeast in the warm water and leave for 10 minutes. Add to the wholemeal flour and make a runny paste. Cover and leave at room temperature for several days.
2. Make the sourdough bread. Preheat the oven to 200°C/400°F/gas mark 6.
3. Mix the wholemeal flour with 350ml/12 fl oz of boiling water. Cool until lukewarm.
4. Mix the yeast mixture into the soaked wholemeal flour using a whisk to remove any lumps.
5. Add enough strong plain flour to produce a soft but not sticky dough.
6. Knead for about 10 minutes or until smooth and elastic.
7. Put into a clean bowl and cover with a damp tea towel or greased polythene. Leave in a

warm place to rise for about 1 hour or until doubled in bulk.

8. Punch down and knead the dough lightly. Cut in half and shape into two round loaves. Place on greased baking sheets, cover and leave to rise until one and a half times its original size.

9. Bake in the preheated oven for 35-40 minutes or until the loaves sound hollow when tapped underneath.

Cheese and Caraway Bread

675g/1½lb wholemeal flour
5ml/1 teaspoon salt
30ml/2 tablespoons caraway seeds
170g/6oz Cheddar cheese, finely grated
55g/2oz fresh yeast
5ml/1 teaspoon muscavado sugar
15ml/1 tablespoon oil
570ml/1 pint lukewarm water
milk to glaze

For the topping:
30g/1oz grated cheese
15ml/1 tablespoon caraway seeds

1. Sift the flour and the salt into a large mixing bowl. Stir in the caraway seeds and grated cheese and make a well in the centre.

2. Cream the yeast and sugar together until liquid and mix the oil with the lukewarm water.

3. Put the liquid ingredients into the well, and mix with a round-bladed knife until a soft, pliable dough is obtained, adding more water if necessary.

4. When the dough will leave the sides of the bowl, press it together into a ball and tip it out on to a lightly floured surface.

5. Knead it until it is smooth and elastic (about 10 minutes).

6. Put the dough back into the bowl, which has been washed and lightly oiled, and cover it with lightly oiled cling film. Leave the dough to rise in a warm place until it has approximately doubled in size. This should take at least 1 hour.

7. Turn the dough out on to the floured surface , punch it down and knead for a further 10 minutes or so until smooth.

8. Shape the dough into a large circle, place it on a floured baking sheet, cover with the oiled cling film and leave to rise for about 15 minutes. Set the oven to 220°C/425°F/gas mark 7.

9. Brush the loaf with milk and sprinkle on the topping of grated cheese and caraway seeds. Bake it for 20 minutes and then turn the oven down to 190°C/375°F/gas mark 5. Continue baking for a further 30 minutes or until the loaf is brown and sounds hollow when it is tapped on the underside.

10. Leave the loaf to cool on a wire rack.

Cheese Gannet

15g/½ oz fresh yeast
1.5ml/⅓ teaspoon sugar
225g/8oz wholemeal flour
5ml/1 teaspoon salt
55g/2oz butter
105ml/3 fl oz milk
2 eggs, beaten
110g/4oz cheese, grated, preferably strong Cheddar or Gruyère
pinch of cayenne
pinch of English mustard
freshly ground black pepper
a little milk for glazing

1. Cream the yeast with the sugar and leave for 10 minutes.

2. Sift the flour with the salt into a warmed bowl.

3. Melt the butter in the milk and, when at blood heat, mix with the eggs and the creamed yeast. Pour this liquid into the flour and mix to a soft dough.

4. Cover and leave to rise in a warm place (do not worry if it does not rise very much – it will when cooking).

5. Set the oven to 220°C/425°F/gas mark 7.

6. Mix three-quarters of the cheese into the dough and season well with cayenne, mustard and pepper.

7. Pile into a well-greased 20cm/8 inch sandwich tin and flatten so that the mixture is about 2.5cm/1 inch deep. Put back in the warm place to prove (rise again) for 10-15 minutes.

8. Bake in a hot oven for 35-40 minutes.

9. Five minutes before the end of cooking, brush lightly with the milk and sprinkle with the remaining cheese.

NOTE I: The mixture can be divided into 6 round rolls: put 5 around the edge of a Victoria sandwich tin and one in the middle. Leave to prove and then bake. It will look like a crown loaf.
NOTE II: If using dried yeast or easy-blend see page 556.

Grissini

This recipe has been taken from Arabella Boxer's *Mediterranean Cookbook.*

7g/$^1/_4$ oz fresh yeast
10ml/2 teaspoons sugar
45ml/3 tablespoons warm water
5ml/1 teaspoon sea salt
150ml/$^1/_4$ pint boiling water
225g/8oz strong flour
15ml/1 tablespoon olive oil
1 egg, beaten
55g/2oz sesame seeds

1. Set the oven to 150°C/300°F/gas mark 2.
2. Dissolve the yeast and sugar in the lukewarm water.
3. Dissolve the sea salt in the boiling water, allow to cool to blood temperature and then mix with the yeast.
4. Sift the flour into a large bowl, make a well in the centre, pour in the yeast mixture and the oil. Mix to a soft dough.
5. Tip the dough on to a floured board and knead for 3-4 minutes, until smooth and elastic. Cover with a damp cloth and leave for 5 minutes. Knead for 3 minutes and then divide into 20 equal pieces.
6. Roll each piece of dough out until it is as thick as your little finger. Place on oiled baking sheets and prove (allow to rise again) for 10-15 minutes.
7. Brush with beaten egg, sprinkle with sesame seeds and bake for about 45 minutes until crisp and golden brown.

Chelsea Buns

MAKES 12
15g/$^1/_2$ oz fresh yeast
85g/3oz caster sugar
450g/1lb plain flour (preferably 'strong')
5ml/1 teaspoon salt
85g/3oz butter
1 egg
225ml/7$^1/_2$ fl oz tepid milk
2.5ml/$^1/_2$ teaspoon mixed spice
55g/2oz sultanas
55g/2oz currants
apricot glaze (see page 584)

1. Cream the yeast with 5ml/1 teaspoon of sugar.
2. Sift the flour into a warm dry bowl with the salt. Rub in half the butter and stir in half the sugar.
3. Beat the egg and add to the yeast mixture with the tepid milk.
4. Make a well in the centre of the flour and pour in the liquid. Using first a knife and then your hand, gradually draw the flour in from the sides of the bowl and knead until smooth.
5. Cover the bowl and leave to rise in a warm place until doubled in bulk (about 1 hour).
6. Punch the dough down again and knead again on a floured board. Roll into a square about 23cm/9 inches across.
7. Mix the remaining butter with half the remaining sugar and spread over bun mixture.
8. Sprinkle the remaining sugar, spice and fruit over the butter and sugar mixture. Set the oven to 220°C/425°F/gas mark 7.
9. Roll it up like a Swiss roll and cut into 3.5cm/$^1/_2$ inch slices.
10. Arrange the buns cut side up on the baking sheet and leave to prove for 15 minutes.
11. Sprinkle with sugar. Bake for 20-25 minutes. Brush with apricot glaze.
12. Leave the buns to cool on a wire rack before separating.

Hot Cross Buns

MAKES 12
20g/$^3/_4$ oz fresh yeast
55g/2oz caster sugar
220ml/7 fl oz milk
2 eggs, beaten
450g/1lb plain flour (preferably 'strong')
2.5ml/$^1/_2$ teaspoon salt
7.5ml/$^1/_2$ tablespoon mixed spice
85g/3oz butter
170g/6oz currants
30g/1oz finely chopped peel
a little sweetened milk for glazing

1. Cream the yeast with 5ml/1 teaspoon of the sugar.
2. Warm the milk to blood heat. Mix about two-thirds of the milk, the beaten eggs and the yeast.
3. Sift the flour, salt and spice into a mixing bowl. Rub in the butter. Add the remaining sugar. Make a well in the centre of the flour. Tip in the warm milk mixture and beat until smooth, adding more milk if necessary to produce a soft, sticky dough.
4. Turn the dough on to a floured board. Knead until the dough is very elastic.
5. Place in a lightly oiled bowl. Sprinkle with flour. Cover with a damp tea towel or an oiled sheet of polythene. Leave to rise in a warm place for about 1$^1/_2$ hours until doubled in bulk.
6. Set the oven to 200°C/400°F/gas mark 6.
7. Turn out on to a floured board again and knock down. Knead again for a few minutes, then work in the currants and peel, making sure that they are distributed evenly.
8. Shape into small round buns. Mark a cross on top of each bun with a knife. Place on baking trays and leave to prove for approximately 15 minutes or until doubled in bulk. Brush the tops with sweetened milk.
9. Bake for about 15 minutes. Brush again with sweetened milk, bake for 2 minutes more, then cool on a wire rack.

NOTE I: The crosses can be made by laying strips of shortcrust pastry or by piping a cross of flour and water paste on top of the buns just before baking.
NOTE II: If using dried yeast or easy-blend see page 556.

Stollen

450g/1lb strong white flour
5ml/1 teaspoon caster sugar
15g/$^1/_2$ oz fresh yeast, or 1$^1/_2$ teaspoons dried yeast
250ml/8 fl oz warm milk
5ml/1 teaspoon salt
85g/3oz butter
110g/4oz currants
110g/4oz sultanas
30g/1oz chopped mixed peel
30g/1oz walnuts or almonds, chopped
10ml/2 teaspoons grated orange or lemon rind
1 egg
55g/2oz glacé cherries
icing sugar for dusting

1. Prepare a yeast batter: mix together 110g/4oz flour, the sugar, yeast and warm milk. Set aside until bubbly. This will take about 20 minutes in a warm place.
2. Mix the remaining flour with the salt. Rub in 55g/2oz of the butter. Add the currants, sultanas, mixed peel, nuts and citrus rind.
3. Beat the egg, add it to the yeast batter with the flour, fruit and nuts. Mix well to a soft but not too sticky dough.
4. Knead until smooth and elastic. This will take about 10 minutes. Shape into a ball and leave in a warm place in a clean bowl covered with cling wrap or in a polythene bag, until doubled in bulk. This will take at least 1 hour. The dried fruits and nuts slow down the rising and proving of a bread dough.
5. Knead again (knock down) for 2 minutes and shape into an oval 30 x 20cm/12 x 8 inches.
6. Melt the remaining butter and brush half of it over the bread dough. Spread the glacé cherries over half the dough. Fold the other half over the dough and press down lightly. Cover with greased polythene and leave to prove until 1$^1/_2$ times its original size – this may take between 15 minutes and half an hour.
7. Set the oven to 190°C/375°F/gas mark 5.
8. Brush the remaining butter over the proved loaf and bake for 20-25 minutes. Leave to cool on a wire rack. Dust with icing sugar.

NOTE: An alternative version is to use 225g/8oz made-up marzipan to stuff the Stollen in place of the cherries and butter. Roll the marzipan into a sausage and place in the middle of the dough. Roll up and seal the ends by pinching them together. Bake as before.

Brioche

MAKES 12 SMALL BRIOCHES OR 1 LARGE ONE.
25ml/5 level teaspoons caster sugar
30ml/2 tablespoons warm water
225g/8oz flour
pinch of salt
2 eggs, beaten
55g/2oz melted butter, cool
7g/1/4oz fresh yeast

For the glaze:
1 egg mixed with 15ml/1 tablespoon water and 15ml/1 teaspoon sugar

1. Grease a large brioche mould or 12 small brioche tins.
2. Mix the yeast with 5ml/1 teaspoon of the sugar and the water. Leave to dissolve.
3. Sift the flour with a pinch of salt into a bowl. Sprinkle over the sugar. Make a well in the centre. Drop in the eggs, yeast mixture and melted butter and mix with the fingers of one hand to a soft but not sloppy paste. Knead on an unfloured board for 5 minutes or until smooth. Put into a clean bowl, cover with a damp cloth or greased polythene and leave to rise in a warm place until doubled in bulk (about 1 hour).
4. Turn out and knead again on an unfloured board for 2 minutes.
5. Place the dough in the brioche mould (it should not come more than halfway up the mould). If making individual brioches, divide the dough into 12 pieces. Using three-quarters of each piece, roll them into small balls and put them in the brioche tins. Make a dip on top of each brioche. Roll the remaining paste into 12 tiny balls and press them into the prepared holes. Push a pencil, or thin spoon handle, right through each small ball into the brioche base as this will anchor the balls in place when baking
6. Cover with greased polythene and leave in a warm place until risen to the top of the tin(s). The individual ones will take 15 minutes, the large one about 30 minutes.
7. Set the oven to 200°C/400°F/gas mark 6.
8. Brush the egg glaze over the brioches. Bake the large one for 20-25 minutes, or small ones for 10 minutes

NOTE: If using dried yeast or easy-blend see page 556.

Croissants

This recipe has been taken from the Roux brothers' book on pâtissèrie. We have tried literally dozens of croissant recipes and this is the first one we have found that works well. The dough for croissants should be made 10-12 hours in advance. You will need a template to make the croissants. It should be an isosceles triangle 15 x 18cm/6 x 7 inches.

MAKES 16-18
45g/1 1/2oz sugar
10g/1 1/2 teaspoon salt
300ml/11 fl oz cold water
15g/1/2oz fresh yeast
30g/1oz milk powder
500g/1lb 2oz strong flour
280g/10oz butter
1 egg yolk beaten with 15ml/1 tablespoon milk to glaze

1. Dissolve the sugar and salt in one-third of the cold water. In a separate bowl, beat the yeast into the remaining water, then beat in the milk powder.
2. Sift the flour into a bowl and, with one hand, mix in both the liquids. Mix to a smooth soft dough but do not knead.
3. Cover the dough and leave to rise in a warm place for about 30 minutes. The dough should double in size.
4. Knock back the dough by quickly flicking it over with your fingers to release the carbon gases – do not overwork. Cover with polythene and place in the refrigerator for 6-8 hours.
5. Shape the dough into a ball and cut a cross in the top. Roll out the dough at the 4 quarters so that it looks like 4 large 'ears' surrounding a small head.
6. Put the butter in the centre and fold the 'ears' over, ensuring that the butter is completely enclosed and will not ooze out.

7. Lightly flour the table and then carefully roll the dough away from you into a rectangle 40 x 70cm/16 x 27 inches. Brush off the excess flour and fold the dough into 3. Wrap in polythene and refrigerate for 20 minutes.
8. Repeat the rolling, folding and chilling (as in step 7) at least twice more until the dough is no longer streaky.
9. Preheat the oven to 200°C/400°F/gas mark 6.
10. Roll out the dough to a 40 x 76cm/16 x 30 inch rectangle, flouring the surface lightly and flapping up the dough occasionally to aerate it.
11. With a large knife, trim the edges and cut the dough lengthways into 2 equal strips.
12. Lay one short edge of the triangular template along one long edge of the dough and mark out the outline with the back of a knife. Invert the triangle and mark out as before. Once all the triangles are marked out (16-18 in all), cut them with a sharp knife.
13. Arrange the triangles on a baking sheet, cover tightly with polythene and refrigerate for a few moments. If the dough becomes too warm, it may soften and crack.

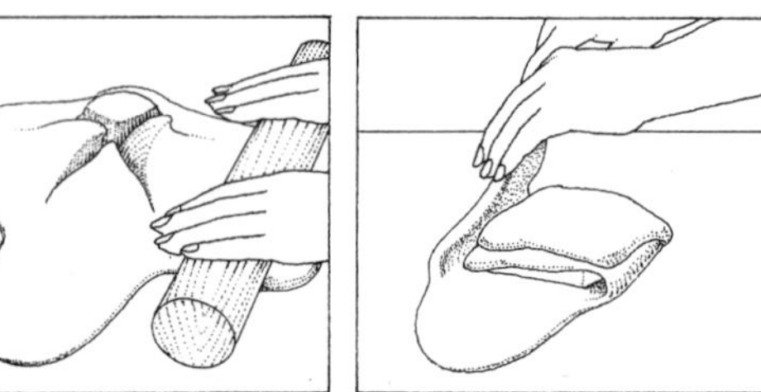

Steps 5 and 6 in the text above

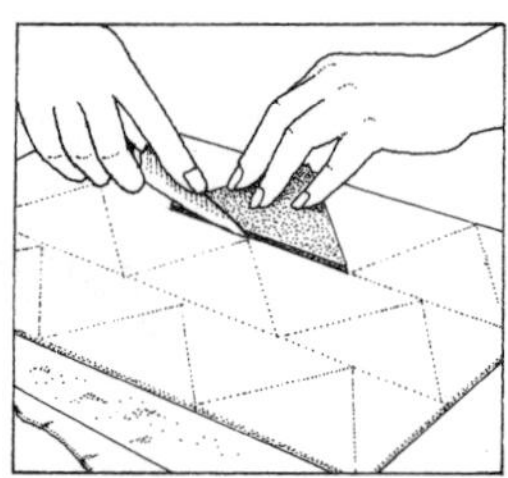

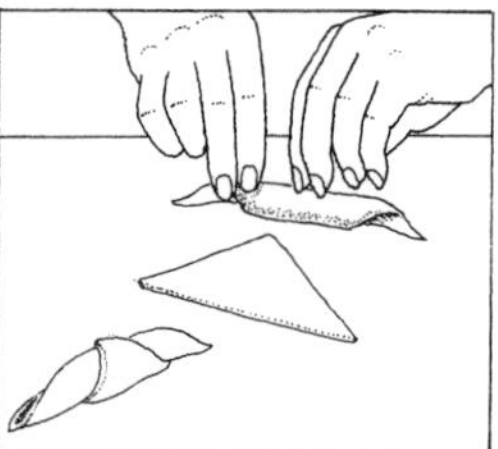

Steps 11 and 13 in the text above

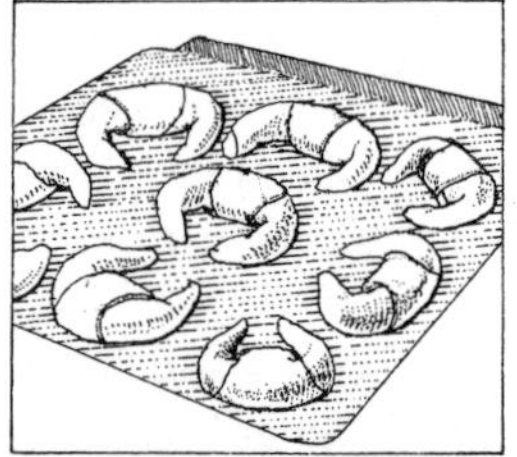

The finished croissants

14. Place the triangles, one at a time, on the work surface with the long point towards you. Stretch out the 2 shorter points and begin to roll the triangle towards you. Make sure that the central point is in the middle and underneath so that it does not rise up during cooking.
15. As soon as they are shaped, place the croissants on a baking sheet, turning in the corners to make a crescent shape. Since the sides of the oven are the hottest, the last row of croissants must face inwards or the points may dry out or burn.
16. Lightly brush the croissants with egg wash, working from the inside outwards so that the layers of dough do not stick together. Leave to rise in a warm draught-free place until they have doubled in size.
17. Lightly re-glaze the croissants with egg wash. Bake the croissants in the preheated oven for 15 minutes. Transfer to a wire rack to cool.

NOTE: If using dried or easy-blend yeast see page 556.

Buns, Scones and Biscuits

Coffee Buns

MAKES 12
110g/4oz butter
110g/4oz caster sugar
2 eggs
110g/4oz self-raising flour
10ml/2 teaspoons instant coffee powder
1.25ml/1/4 teaspoon vanilla essence
55g/2oz chopped walnuts
55g/2oz chocolate

1. Set the oven to 180°C/350°F/gas mark 4. Grease and flour 12 bun tins or paper moulds.
2. Cream the butter and sugar until light and fluffy.
3. Beat in the eggs, a little at a time.
4. Fold in the flour, coffee, vanilla essence and chopped nuts. Add a little water if necessary to make a soft dropping consistency.
5. Fill the tins or paper moulds two-thirds full and bake for 15-20 minutes. Leave to cool on a wire rack.
6. Grate the chocolate. Melt it on a plate over a pan of boiling water.
7. Spread each bun with a little melted chocolate and leave to cool and harden.

Scones

MAKES 6
225g/8oz plain flour
15ml/1 tablespoon baking powder
2.5ml/1/2 teaspoon salt
55g/2oz butter
30g/1oz sugar (optional)
150ml/1/4 pint milk

For glazing:
1 egg, beaten

1. Set the oven to 220°C/425°F/gas mark 7. Flour a baking sheet.
2. Sift the flour with the other powder ingredients.
3. Rub in the butter until the mixture resembles breadcrumbs. Stir in the sugar if required.
4. Make a deep well in the flour, pour in all the liquid and mix to a soft, spongy dough with a palette knife.
5. On a floured surface, knead the dough very lightly until it is just smooth. Roll or press out to about 2.5cm/1 inch thick and stamp into small rounds.
6. Brush the scones with beaten egg for a glossy crust or sprinkle with flour for a soft one.
7. Bake the scones at the top of the hot oven for 7 minutes or until well risen and brown. Leave to cool on a wire rack, or serve hot from the oven.

NOTE: 30g/1oz sultanas or other dried fruit may be added to the dried ingredients. For cheese scones, substitute 30g/1oz grated strong cheese for half the butter, and omit the sugar.

Shortbread

MAKES 6-8
110g/4oz butter
55g/2oz caster sugar
110g/4oz plain flour
55g/2oz rice flour

1. Set the oven to 170°C/325°F/gas mark 3.
2. Beat the butter until soft, add the sugar and beat until pale and creamy.
3. Sift in the flours and work to a smooth paste.
4. Place a 15cm/6 inch flan ring on a baking sheet and press the shortbread paste into a neat circle. Remove the flan ring and flatten the paste slightly with a rolling pin. Crimp the edges. Prick lightly.
5. Mark the shortbread into 6 or 8 wedges, sprinkle lightly with a little extra caster sugar and bake for 40 minutes until a pale biscuit colour. Leave to cool for 2 minutes and then lift on to a cooling rack to cool completely.

Iced Biscuits

MAKES 20
110g/4oz unsalted butter
110g/4oz caster sugar
1 egg, beaten
a few drops vanilla flavouring
285g/10oz plain flour
pinch of salt

For the glacé icing:
225g/8oz icing sugar
boiling water
colouring (optional)

1. Set the oven to 190°C/375°F/gas mark 5.
2. Beat the butter and, when soft, add the sugar and beat again until light and fluffy. Gradually beat in the egg. Add the vanilla flavouring.
3. Sift the flour with the salt and mix it into the butter, sugar and egg.
4. Roll the paste out thinly (about the thickness of a heavy coin) and stamp into rounds with a cutter. Place on an ungreased baking sheet.
5. Bake for 8-10 minutes until just beginning to brown at the edges. Leave to cool on a wire rack.
6. Make the glacé icing: sift the icing sugar into a bowl. Add enough boiling water to mix to a fairly stiff consistency.
7. Colour the icing as required.
8. Spoon the icing smoothly and evenly over the top of the biscuits. Leave to dry and harden.

Peanut Butter Cookies

MAKES ABOUT 40 BISCUITS
140g/5oz butter
110g/4oz caster sugar
110g/4oz soft brown sugar
1 large egg, beaten
110g/4oz crunchy peanut butter
2.5ml/½ teaspoon vanilla essence
200g/7oz plain flour
2.5ml/½ teaspoon salt
5ml/1 teaspoon baking powder

1. Heat the oven to 180°C/350°F/gas mark 4.
2. Cream the butter and both sugars together until smooth and soft. Beat in the egg, then the peanut butter, and add the vanilla.
3. Sift the flour with the salt and the baking powder into the mixture and stir until smooth. Do not over-beat or the dough will be oily.
4. Roll the mixture into small balls with the fingers and place well apart on 3 ungreased baking sheets. Flatten with the prongs of a fork.
5. Bake for 10-15 minutes, to an even, not too dark, brown.
6. While hot, ease off the baking sheets with a palette knife or fish slice and cool on a wire rack. Once stone cold and crisp, store in an airtight container.

Flapjacks

MAKES 16
170g/6oz butter
110g/4oz demerara sugar
55g/2oz golden syrup
225g/8oz rolled oats

1. Set the oven to 190°C/375°F/gas mark 5
2. Melt the butter in a saucepan.
3. Weigh out the sugar, then weigh the syrup by spooning it on top of the sugar (thus preventing it sticking to the scale pan) and add to the melted butter to heat through.
4. Remove the pan from the heat and stir in the oats.
5. Spread the mixture into a well-greased shallow tin.
6. Bake in the oven for about 30 minutes until golden brown.
7. Remove from the oven, mark immediately into bars and leave in the tin to cool.

Easter Biscuits

MAKES 8

55g/2oz butter
55g/2oz caster sugar
grated rind of 1/2 lemon
1/2 egg or 1 yolk
110g/4oz plain flour
2.5ml/1/2 teaspoon caraway seeds
55g/2oz currants
30g/1oz granulated sugar

1. Set the oven to 180°C/350°F/gas mark 4. Cover a baking sheet with a piece of greaseproof paper.
2. Cream together the butter, caster sugar and lemon rind. Beat in the egg.
3. Fold in the flour, caraway and currants.
4. Roll out the dough on a floured board to 5mm/1/4 inch thick. Cut into large rounds and carefully lift them on to the baking sheet. Prick with a fork and sprinkle with granulated sugar.
5. Bake for 10-15 minutes until set and pale golden.
6. Remove from the oven and leave on a wire rack to crisp and cool.

NOTE: If the dough becomes soft and difficult to handle, wrap it up and chill for 15 minutes before proceeding.

Gingerbread Men

MAKES 10

340g/12oz plain flour
10ml/2 teaspoons ground ginger
5ml/1 teaspoon bicarbonate of soda
110g/4oz butter
170g/6oz soft brown sugar
1 egg, beaten
60ml/4 tablespoons golden syrup
currants

1. Set the oven to 190°C/375°F/gas mark 5. Grease a baking sheet.
2. Sift the flour into a bowl. Add the ginger and the bicarbonate of soda.
3. Rub in the butter until the mixture looks like breadcrumbs. Mix in the sugar and beaten egg.
4. Warm the syrup slightly to make it runny, and stir enough into the flour mixture to make a soft dough.
5. With one hand knead until quite smooth, then roll out on the table or board as thinly as possible (about 5mm/1/4 inch).
6. With a gingerbread-man cutter, stamp out the men. If you do not have a cutter, do the best you can cutting round a gingerbread-man paper template.
7. Using the currants, give each man a row of buttons, 2 eyes and a mouth.
8. With a fish slice, lift the shapes on to the greased baking sheet and bake for about 12 minutes or until just coloured. Lift on to a wire rack. They will become crisp as they cool.

Almond and Apricot Cookies

MAKES 18

85g/3oz butter
85g/3oz granulated sugar
110g/4oz ground almonds

For the decoration:
apricot jam
flaked almonds, browned

1. Set the oven to 180°C/350°F/gas mark 4.
2. Cream the butter and, when soft, add the sugar and beat until light and fluffy. Stir in the ground almonds and roll the paste into balls the size of a marble. Chill for 10 minutes.
3. Place each ball in a paper case and put the cases into patty moulds. Bake in the oven for 15-20 minutes. Allow to cool in their cases.
4. Remove from the cases, spread with a little apricot jam and decorate with a browned flaked almond.

Gingernuts

MAKES 20-25
30g/1oz demerara sugar
55g/2oz butter
85g/3oz golden syrup
110g/4oz flour
2.5ml/½ teaspoon bicarbonate of soda
7ml/1 heaped teaspoon ground ginger

1. Set the oven to 180°C/350°F/gas mark 4. Grease a baking sheet.
2. Melt the brown sugar, butter and syrup together slowly, without boiling. Make sure the sugar has dissolved. Allow to cool.
3. Sift the flour, bicarbonate of soda and ground ginger into a mixing bowl. Make a well in the centre.
4. Pour the melted mixture into the well and knead until smooth. Roll into balls and flatten, on the prepared baking sheet, into biscuits about 3.5cm/1½ inches diameter.
5. Bake for 20-25 minutes or until golden brown. The gingernuts will not be crisp until they cool and set.

Brandy Snap Cups

MAKES 8
110g/4oz sugar
110g/4oz butter
110g/4oz or 60ml/4 tablespoons golden syrup
110g/4oz flour
juice of 1 lemon
large pinch of ground ginger

To serve:
whipped cream or ice cream

1. Set the oven to 190°C/375°F/gas mark 5. Grease a baking sheet, palette knife and one end of a wide rolling pin or a narrow jam jar or bottle.
2. Melt the sugar, butter and syrup together. Remove from the heat.
3. Sift in the flour, stirring well. Add the lemon juice and ginger.
4. Put the mixture on the baking sheet in teaspoonfuls about 15cm/6 inches apart. Bake for 5-7 minutes. They should go golden brown but still be soft. Watch carefully as they burn easily. Remove from the oven.
5. When cool enough to handle, lever each biscuit off the baking sheet with a greased palette knife.
6. Working quickly, shape them around the end of the rolling pin or greased jam jar to form a cup-shaped mould.
7. When the biscuits have taken shape, remove them and leave to cool on a wire rack.
8. Serve filled with whipped cream or ice cream.

NOTE I: If the brandy snaps are not to be served immediately they must, once cool, be put into an airtight container for storage. They become soggy if left out. Similarly, brandy snaps should not be filled with moist mixtures like whipped cream or ice cream until shortly before serving, or they will quickly lose their crispness.
NOTE II: Do not bake too many snaps at one time as once they are cold, they are too brittle to shape. They can be made pliable again if returned to the oven.

Brandy Snaps

The mixture for these is exactly the same as for brandy snap cups (above) but the biscuits are shaped round a thick wooden spoon handle and not over the end of a rolling pin or jam jar. They are filled with whipped cream from a piping bag fitted with a medium nozzle.

Miniature brandy snaps (served as petits fours after dinner) are shaped over a skewer. They are not generally filled.

Filigree Baskets

These make excellent 'cups' or baskets in which to serve ice cream and sorbets.

MAKES 6
2 egg whites
110g/4oz caster sugar
125g/4½ oz plain flour
2.5ml/½ teaspoon vanilla flavouring

1. Cut a template out of cardboard. For a basket big enough to hold a ball of sorbet, the stencil should be about 5cm/2 inches deep and 20cm/8 inches long at its widest.
2. Grease and flour a greaseproof-paper-lined baking sheet and mark the shape of the template in the flour coating.
3. Set the oven to 200°C/400°F/gas mark 6.
4. Whisk the egg whites and sugar together until the whisk will leave a ribbon-like trail when lifted.
5. Sift in the flour, add the vanilla and beat until smooth.
6. Put the mixture into a piping bag fitted with a nozzle with a 'mouth' about 2mm/⅛ inch across, or into a paper piping bag with the point snipped to provide the small nozzle mouth.
7. Pipe the shapes on to the floured paper.
8. Bake for 4-6 minutes or until just pale brown.
9. Remove from the oven and ease the biscuits off the tray. Have ready 6 smallish tea cups.
10. Return the biscuits to the hot oven for 30 seconds or just long enough for them to become very pliable again. While hot, curl them round and drop them into the tea cups. Allow to cool.
11. Once cold, store in an airtight container until needed.

Langues de Chat

MAKES 30-40
100g/3½ oz butter
100g/3½ oz caster sugar
3 egg whites
100g/3½ oz plain flour

1. Set the oven to 200°C/400°F/gas mark 6. Grease a baking sheet or line with silicone paper.
2. Soften the butter with a wooden spoon and add the sugar gradually. Beat until pale and fluffy.
3. Whisk the egg whites slightly and add gradually to the mixture, beating thoroughly between each addition.
4. Sift the flour and fold into the mixture with a metal spoon. Put into a forcing bag fitted with a medium-sized plain nozzle. Pipe into fingers the thickness of a pencil and about 5cm/2 inches long.
5. Tap the baking sheet on the table to release any over-large air bubbles from the fingers. Bake for 5-7 minutes or until biscuit-coloured in the middle and brown at the edges. Cool slightly, then lift off the baking sheet with a palette knife. Cool completely before putting into an airtight container.

Macaroons

MAKES 25
110g/4oz ground almonds
170g/6oz caster sugar
5ml/1 teaspoon plain flour
2 egg whites
2 drops vanilla essence
rice paper for baking
split almonds for decoration

1. Set the oven to 180°C/350°F/gas mark 4.
2. Mix the almonds, sugar and flour together.
3. Add the egg whites and vanilla. Beat very well.
4. Lay a sheet of rice paper or vegetable parchment on a baking sheet and with a teaspoon put on small heaps of the mixture, well apart.
5. Place a split almond on each macaroon and bake for 20 minutes. Allow to cool.

NOTE I: To use this recipe for petits fours the mixture must be put out in very tiny blobs on the rice paper. Two macaroons can then be sandwiched together with a little stiff apricot jam and served in petits fours paper cases.
NOTE II: Ratafia biscuits are tiny macaroons with added almond essence.

Sponge Fingers

MAKES 30
6 eggs
140g/5oz caster sugar
110g/4oz flour
30g/1oz arrowroot

1. Set the oven to 200°C/400°F/gas mark 6. Line 2 large baking sheets with silicone baking paper. Draw parallel lines 12.5cm/5 inches apart on the paper.
2. Separate 5 of the eggs. Beat the yolks with the whole egg and 110g/4oz of the caster sugar in a large bowl until they are nearly white.
3. Whisk the egg whites until stiff and gradually whisk in the remaining caster sugar. Fold the egg whites into the egg-yolk and sugar mixture. Carefully fold in the sifted flour and arrowroot.
4. Fit a 5mm/1/4 inch plain nozzle into a piping bag and fill the bag with the mixture. Pipe 12.5cm/5 inch fingers between the parallel lines on the baking paper. The fingers should be just touching.
5. Place in the top of the oven for about 10 minutes or until the sponge has risen and is biscuit-coloured.
6. Remove them from the oven, invert on to a clean tea towel and immediately and carefully peel off the paper. Turn the sponge fingers on to a wire rack to cool.

Tuiles à l'Orange

MAKES 25
2 egg whites
110g/4oz caster sugar
55g/2oz butter
55g/2oz plain flour
grated rind of 1 orange

1. Set the oven to 190°C/375°F/gas mark 5. Grease a baking sheet, or line with silicone paper.
2. Whisk the egg whites until stiff. Add the sugar and whisk thoroughly.
3. Melt the butter. Add it to the meringue mixture by degrees with the sifted flour. Fold in the orange rind.
4. Spread out teaspoonfuls very thinly on the prepared baking sheet, keeping them well apart to allow for spreading during cooking. Bake until golden brown (5-6 minutes).
5. Oil a rolling pin or the handle of a large wooden spoon. Loosen the tuiles from the baking sheet while still hot. While they are still warm and pliable curl them over the rolling pin or round the wooden spoon handle. When they are quite firm slip them off. When cold, store in an airtight container.

NOTE: Using silicone paper guarantees that the tuiles will not stick.

Tuiles Amandines

MAKES 25
30g/1oz blanched almonds
2 egg whites
110g/4oz caster sugar
55g/2oz plain flour
2.5ml/1/2 teaspoon vanilla essence
55g/2oz melted butter

1. Set the oven to 180°C/350°F, gas mark 4. Lightly grease at least 3 baking sheets and a rolling pin or line baking sheets with silicone paper.
2. Cut the almonds into fine slivers or shreds.
3. Place the egg whites in a bowl. Beat in the sugar with a fork. The egg white should be frothy but by no means snowy. Sift in the flour and add the vanilla and almonds. Mix with the fork.

4. Cool the butter (it should be melted but not hot) and add it to the mixture. Stir well.
5. Place the mixture in teaspoonfuls at least 13cm/5 inches apart on the baking sheets and flatten well.
6. Bake in the oven until a good brown at the edges and pale biscuit-coloured in the middle (about 6 minutes). Remove from the oven and cool for a few seconds.
7. Lift the biscuits off carefully with a palette knife. Lay them, while still warm and pliable, over the rolling pin to form them into a slightly curved shape. As soon as they are stone cold put them into an airtight tin or plastic bag to keep them crisp.

NOTE: Using silicone paper guarantees that the tuiles will not stick.

Venetian Biscuits

MAKES 24
110g/4oz blanched almonds
450g/1lb flour
pinch of salt
5ml/1 teaspoon baking powder
140g/5oz granulated sugar
85g/3oz plain chocolate, chopped into small pieces
4 large eggs, lightly beaten
1 egg white, to glaze

1. Preheat the oven to 190°C/375°F/gas mark 5. Grease a baking sheet.
2. Place the almonds on the baking sheet and bake in the oven until golden brown. Cool. Chop two-thirds and grind the remaining third finely.
3. Sift the flour, salt and baking powder into a bowl. Add the sugar, chocolate and almonds. Mix well.
4. Make a well in the centre and add the beaten eggs. Gradually incorporate the dry ingredients with the eggs. The dough should be firm.
5. Divide the dough into 4 and roll each piece into a long thin sausage shape approximately 2cm/ 3/4 inch in diameter and 20cm/8 inches long.
6. Place the rolls on the baking sheet at least 5cm/2 inches apart. Lightly whisk the egg white until just frothy and brush over the tops of the rolls.
7. Place in the preheated oven and bake for 20 minutes.
8. Remove the rolls from the oven, reduce the heat to 105°C/225°F/gas mark 1/4. Cut the rolls at a 45-degree angle at 1cm/1/2 inch intervals and return them individually to the baking sheet. Put back in the oven for a further 30 minutes. Allow to cool completely before serving.

NOTE: Raisins or glacé fruit can be used in place of the chocolate. The biscuits are meant to be eaten after being dipped in a liqueur, e. g. Amaretto or Grappa.

Florentine Biscuits

MAKES 20
55g/2oz butter
55g/2oz sugar
10ml/2 teaspoons honey
55g/2oz plain flour
45g/1 1/2oz chopped candied peel
45g/1 1/2oz chopped glacé cherries
45g/1 1/2oz chopped blanched almonds
85g/3oz chocolate, melted

1. Set the oven to 180°C/350°F/gas mark 4. Grease and flour 2 baking sheets.
2. Melt the butter, sugar and honey together in a heavy pan. Draw off the heat and add the flour, peel, cherries and almonds. Mix until smooth.
3. Drop teaspoonfuls of the mixture on to the baking sheets, leaving plenty of space for them to spread during cooking. Spread slightly with the spoon.
4. Bake for 8-10 minutes until golden. Leave on the tray for 2 minutes and then place on a wire rack to cool.
5. When cold spread the flat sides with melted chocolate. When the chocolate is on the point of setting, mark it with wavy lines with the prongs of a fork. Leave until the chocolate cools and hardens.

Danish Pastries

Most Danish pastries require almond filling and icing as well as the basic dough. Instructions for these are given first, followed by the individual instructions for Pinwheels, Almond Squares etc.

When rolling out Danish pastry, care should be taken to prevent the butter breaking through the paste and making the resulting pastry heavy. Use a heavy rolling pin, bring it fairly firmly down on to the pastry and roll with short, quick, firm rolls. Do not 'push' it. Avoid using too much flour. If the paste is becoming warm and unmanageable, wrap it up and chill it well before proceeding.

The icing should not be made until the pastries are baked. Danish pastries are frequently scattered with flaked browned almonds while the icing is still wet. Sometimes sultanas, small pieces of tinned pineapple or apple purée are included in the filling.

MAKES 6

For the pastry:
15g/½ oz fresh yeast
15ml/1 tablespoon caster sugar
100ml/3 fl oz milk, warmed
225g/8oz plain flour
pinch of salt
1 egg, lightly beaten
110g/4oz unsalted butter, softened

For the almond paste filling:
45g/1½ oz butter
45g/1½ oz icing sugar
30g/1oz ground almonds
2 drops vanilla essence

For the glaze:
1 egg, beaten

For the glacé icing:
110g/4oz icing sugar
boiling water to mix

1. Dissolve the yeast with 15ml/1 teaspoon of the sugar and the milk.
2. Sift the flour with a pinch of salt into a warmed bowl. Add the remaining sugar. Make a well in the centre and drop into it the egg and the yeast mixture.
3. Using a round-bladed knife, mix the liquids, gradually drawing in the surrounding flour to make a soft dough. If extra liquid is required, add a little more water.
4. When the dough leaves the sides of the bowl, turn it on to a floured surface and bring together gently until fairly smooth. Roll into a longish rectangle 5mm/¼inch thick.
5. Divide the butter into hazelnut-sized pieces and dot it over the top two-thirds of the dough, leaving a 1cm/½inch clear margin round the edge. Fold the pastry in 3, folding the unbuttered third up over the centre section first, and then the buttered top third down over it. You now have a thick 'parcel' of pastry. Give it a 90-degree turn so that the former top edge is on your right. Press the edges together.
6. Dust lightly with flour and roll into a long rectangle again. Fold in 3 as before. Chill for 15 minutes.
7. Roll and fold the pastry once or twice again, turning it in the same direction as before, until the butter is worked in well and the paste does not look streaky. Chill for at least 30 minutes or overnight, before proceeding with one of the recipes below.
8. To make the almond paste, cream the butter, add the sugar and beat well until light and soft. Mix in the ground almonds and flavour with vanilla essence. Mix well but do not overbeat or the oil will run from the almonds, making the paste greasy.
9. When ready to use the glacé icing: mix enough boiling water into the sugar to give an icing that will run fairly easily – about the consistency of cream.

NOTE: If using dried yeast or easy-blend see page 556.

Almond Squares

1. Follow the instructions on page 579.
2. Set the oven to 200°C/400°F/gas mark 6.
3. Roll the pastry on a floured baking sheet into a rectangle 25 x 20cm/10 x 7inches. Cut into 5cm/2 inch squares.
4. Put a spoonful of the filling into the centre of each piece of pastry. Fold each corner into the middle and press it down lightly into the almond paste to stick it in position.
5. Prove for 15 minutes (put into a warm, draught-free place to allow the dough to rise). Press down the middle of the squares.
6. Brush with beaten egg and bake for 15-20 minutes.
7. When cool, spoon over the freshly made glacé icing.

Crosses

1. Follow the instructions on page 579.
2. Set the oven to 200°C/400°F/gas mark 6.
3. Roll the pastry out thinly on a floured baking sheet and cut it into 13cm/5 inch squares.
4. Cut through each square and then overlap the 2 opposite corners.
5. Fill the central hole with almond paste filling or apple purée.
6. Prove for 15 minutes in a warm, draught-free place.
7. Brush with beaten egg and bake for 15-20 minutes.
8. When cool, dust with icing sugar or spoon over freshly made glacé icing.

Pinwheels

1. Follow the instructions on page 579.
2. Set the oven to 200°C/400°F/gas mark 6.
3. Roll the pastry out thinly on a floured baking sheet and cut it into 13cm/5 inch squares. From each corner, towards the centre of each square, make a cut about 3cm/1½inches long. Put a blob of almond filling in the uncut centre of each square.
4. Fold alternate points of pastry (one from each corner) into the middle and press on to the filling to secure. This leaves one unfolded point at each corner, and the pastry should now resemble a child's pinwheel.
5. Prove in a warm place for 15 minutes (allow to rise and puff up). Press down the corners.
6. Brush with beaten egg and bake for 15-20 minutes.
7. When cool, spoon on the freshly made glacé icing.

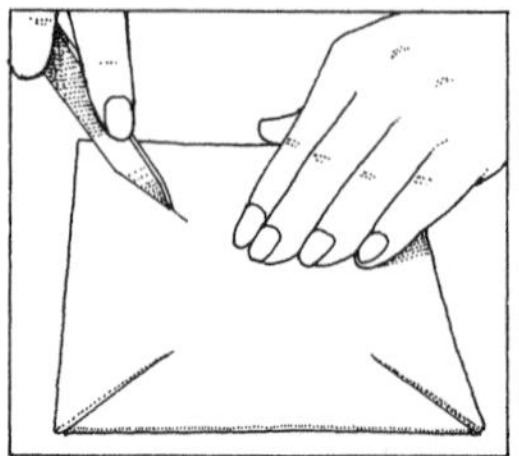
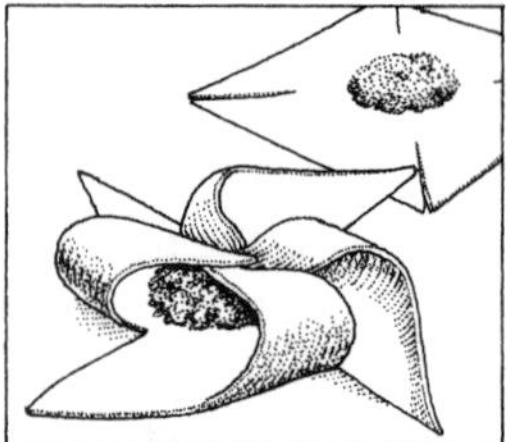

Cut and fill as in recipe

Cinnamon Wheels

In this recipe the almond paste is replaced with a cinnamon filling.

For the cinnamon filling:
55g/2oz butter
55g/2oz sugar
10ml/2 teaspoons cinnamon
small handful of dried fruit and chopped mixed peel

1. Follow the instructions on page 579, omitting the almond filling.
2. To make the filling, cream the butter with the sugar. Add the cinnamon and mix well.
3. Set the oven to 200°C/400°F/gas mark 6.
4. Roll the pastry to a rectangle 25 x 20cm/12 x 8 inches. Place on a floured baking sheet.
5. Spread the butter mixture over the dough, leaving a narrow margin all around. Scatter over the dried fruit and chopped peel.
6. Roll the pastry, from one end, into a thick roll. Cut into 2.5cm/1 inch slices. With a lightly floured hand, flatten each slice to the size of the palm of your hand. Put somewhere warm and draught-free to rise (prove) for 15 minutes.
7. Brush with egg glaze and bake for 15 minutes.
8. Allow to cool slightly and spoon over the freshly made glacé icing.

Crescents

1. Follow the instructions on page 579.
2. Set the oven to 200°C/400°F/gas mark 6. Roll out the pastry, on a floured baking sheet, into a rectangle 30 x 15cm/12 x 6 inches. Cut into 7.5cm/3 inch squares and cut each square diagonally in half.
3. Place a small piece of almond paste at the base (long side) of each triangle. Roll it up from the base to the tip and curve into a crescent shape.
4. Put into a warm, draught-free place to rise (prove) for 15 minutes.
5. Bake for 15-20 minutes or until a good brown. When cool, spoon over the freshly made glacé icing.

Palmiers

Palmiers are usually made from leftover pieces of puff pastry.

1. Set the oven to 200°C/400°F/gas mark 6.
2. Do not roll the trimmings up into a ball as you would with shortcrust pastry – this would spoil the carefully created layers in the paste. Lay the strips or pieces flat on top of each other, folding them if necessary.
3. Using caster sugar instead of flour, roll the pastry out into an oblong 5mm/¼ inch thick. Sprinkle well with caster sugar. Fold each end of the pastry to the centre, and then fold the pastry in half. Cut the roll across into slices 1cm/½ inch wide.
4. Lay the slices flat on a wet baking sheet, far apart, and flatten well with a sugared rolling pin or your hand. Bake for 10 minutes or until pale brown, with the underside caramelized. Turn over and bake for a further 10 minutes. Cool on a wire rack.

NOTE: These are delicious if sandwiched together with strawberry jam and whipped cream.

Eccles Cakes

MAKES 6
rough puff pastry made with 225g/8oz flour (see page 527)

For the filling:
15g/½ oz butter
55g/2oz brown sugar
110g/4oz currants
30g/1oz chopped mixed peel
2.5ml/½ teaspoon ground cinnamon
1.25ml/¼ teaspoon ground nutmeg
1.25ml/¼ teaspoon ground ginger
grated rind of ½ lemon
5ml/1 teaspoon lemon juice

For the glaze:
1 egg white
caster sugar

1. Set the oven to 220°C/425°F/gas mark 7.
2. Roll the pastry to the thickness of a coin. Cut out rounds 12.5cm/5 inches in diameter. Put aside to relax.
3. Melt the butter in a pan and stir in all the other filling ingredients. Cool.
4. Place a good teaspoon of filling in the centre of each pastry round.
5. Damp the edges of the pastry and press together in the centre, forming a small ball. Turn the balls over and lightly roll them until the fruit begins to show through the pastry.
6. With a sharp knife, make 3 small parallel cuts on the top.
7. Lightly beat the egg white with a fork. Brush the top of the Eccles cakes with this and sprinkle with caster sugar.
8. Place on a wet baking sheet and bake for 20 minutes or until lightly browned.

Icings, Fillings and Petits Fours

Apricot Glaze

45ml/3 tablespoons apricot jam
30ml/2 tablespoons water
juice of 1/2 lemon

1. Place all the ingredients together in a thick-bottomed pan.
2. Bring slowly up to the boil, stirring gently (avoid beating in bubbles) until syrupy in consistency. Strain.

NOTE: When using this to glaze food, use when still warm, as it becomes too stiff to manage when cold. It will keep warm standing over a saucepan of very hot water.

Chocolate Butter Icing

110g/4oz plain chocolate, chopped
55g/2oz unsalted butter
110g/4oz icing sugar, sifted
1 egg yolk

1. Melt the chocolate in a heavy saucepan with 15ml/1 tablespoon water, stirring continuously.
2. Beat together the butter and sugar until light and fluffy.
3. Beat in the egg yolk followed by the melted chocolate.

Crème au Beurre Meringue

This is a light soft frosting for cake.

For the meringue:
2 egg whites
110g/4oz icing sugar
170g/6oz unsalted butter

Suggested flavourings:
grated lemon or orange rind
melted chocolate
coffee essence

1. Put the egg whites with the sugar into a mixing bowl and set over a pan of simmering water. Whisk until the meringue is thick and will hold its shape. Remove from the heat and continue to whisk until slightly cooled.
2. Beat the butter until soft and gradually beat in the meringue mixture.
3. Flavour to taste as required.

Soured Cream and Chocolate Icing

140g/5oz plain chocolate
150ml/1/4 pint soured cream
10ml/2 teaspoons caster sugar

1. Break up the chocolate and place in a double saucepan.
2. Add the soured cream and sugar. Melt together over a gentle heat. Leave to cool and thicken.

Crème au Beurre Mousseline

This is a rich creamy cake filling.

55g/2oz granulated sugar
60ml/4 tablespoons water
2 egg yolks
grated rind of 1/2 lemon
110g/4oz unsalted butter

1. Dissolve the sugar in the water and when completely dissolved boil rapidly to about 105°C/215°F. At this point the syrup, if tested between finger and thumb, will form short threads. Take off the heat immediately.
2. Whisk the yolks and lemon rind and pour on the syrup. Keep whisking until thick.
3. Soften the butter and whisk gradually into the mixture. Allow to cool.

NOTE: This makes quite a small quantity of icing. However, it is very rich.

Glacé Icing

225g/8oz icing sugar
boiling water

1. Sift the icing sugar into a bowl.
2. Add enough boiling water to mix to a fairly stiff coating consistency. The icing should hold a trail when dropped from a spoon but gradually find its own level. It needs surprisingly little water.

NOTE: Hot water produces a shinier result than cold. Also, the icing, on drying, is less likely to craze, crack or become watery if made with boiling water.

Feather Icing

icing sugar
boiling water
colouring or chocolate

1. Sift the icing sugar into a bowl (225g/8oz will be sufficient for an 18cm/7 inch sponge).
2. Add enough boiling water to mix to a fairly stiff coating consistency. The icing should hold a trail when dropped from a spoon but gradually find its own level.
3. Take 30ml/2 tablespoons of the icing and colour it with food colouring or chocolate.
4. Place in a piping bag fitted with a fine writing nozzle.
5. Spread the remaining icing smoothly and evenly over the top of the cake, using a warm palette knife.
6. While it is still wet, quickly pipe lines, about 2.5cm/1 inch apart, across the top of the cake.
7. Now draw lines at right angles to the coloured lines with a pin or a sharp knife, dragging the tip through the coloured lines to pull them into points. If the pin is dragged in one direction through the coloured icing lines, Pattern A will result: if the pin is dragged alternately in opposite directions through the coloured icing lines, Pattern B will result.

Pattern A

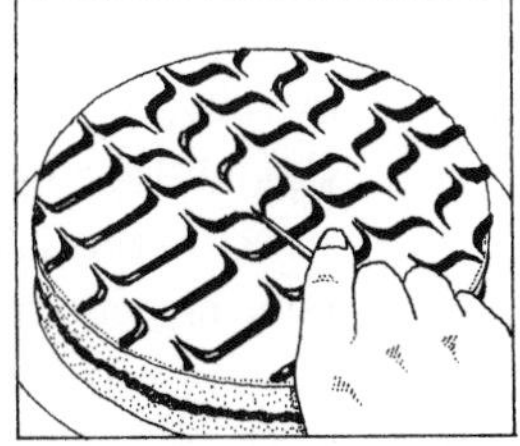

Pattern B

NOTE: Smooth melted jam can be used instead of coloured icing for the feathering.

Sugar Paste

Sugar paste is a simple mock fondant icing and is easy to mould and shape; it is very useful for decorating childrens' party cakes.

15ml/1 tablespoon liquid glucose
1 egg white
450g/1lb icing sugar, sifted

1. Warm the liquid glucose (in the bottle in a pan of hot water).
2. Beat together the glucose, egg white and icing sugar. Shape into a ball.
3. Knead on a surface dusted with icing sugar until pliable. This will take 5 minutes.

NOTE I: Store in a plastic bag in the refrigerator for up to 3 months.
NOTE II: Sugar paste can be coloured as required. Simply add food colouring and knead until thoroughly incorporated.

Fondant Icing

225g/8oz loaf sugar
115ml/4 fl oz water
2.5ml/½ teaspoon liquid glucose or pinch of cream of tartar plus 5ml/1 teaspoon water

1. Dissolve the sugar in the water over a low heat without boiling.
2. Mix in the glucose or cream of tartar. Cover and bring to the boil. Boil to 'soft ball' consistency (to a temperature of 110-115°C/230-240°F at which, if a spoonful is dropped into a bowl of cold water, it will form a soft ball when rubbed between the fingers). Stop the sugar syrup from cooking any further by dipping the bottom of the pan into a bowl of cold water. Let

it cool slightly.
3. Moisten a cold hard surface and pour the sugar syrup on to it in a steady stream. With a metal spatula fold the outsides of the mixture into the centre.
4. Continue to turn with a spatula and work until the fondant becomes fairly stiff. Knead into balls. Place in a bowl and cover with a damp cloth for 1-2 hours.
5. If the fondant is to be stored, place in a screw-top jar. When ready to use, put it in a bowl and stand over a pan of simmering water to melt.

NOTE I: A sugar thermometer is almost essential. It is vital to get the syrup exactly the right consistency: not too liquid, nor too hard.
NOTE II: To make coffee fondant icing, proceed as above but add 10ml/2 teaspoons coffee essence to the syrup before pouring on to the work surface.

Royal Icing

Icing a cake with royal icing is an advanced skill, and these notes are intended as a reminder for those who have already iced a cake or two. Royal icing is traditionally used (over a layer of marzipan) for the coating and decoration of special-occasion fruit cakes. It keeps very well.

1. More than with any other cooking, it is vital to clean up as you go along. It is almost impossible to produce delicate and neat work from a cluttered work surface. Get all the nozzles and piping bags lined up before you begin icing.
2. Never overfill the piping bag. This leads to the sticky icing squeezing out of the top.
3. Keep all full piping bags under a damp cloth or in a plastic bag to prevent the icing in the nozzle drying out.
4. Always keep the icing covered with a damp cloth when not in use to prevent it drying out.
5. Always clean the nozzles immediately after use, using a pin to ensure that no icing is left in the tip.
6. Practise the required pattern on the work surface before tackling the cake. Don't try complicated things like roses and scrolls before you have mastered thoroughly the easier decorations like trellis, shells, stars and dots.
7. Follow the instructions slavishly.
8. Never lick your fingers or equipment. Even a little wet icing can make you feel sick.
9. 450g/1lb sugar makes enough for a 20cm/8 inch cake; 900g/2lb sugar makes enough for a 25cm/10 inch cake.

For 1 coat of icing for a 20cm/8 inch cake:
1 egg white
450g/1lb icing sugar

Mix the egg white with 45ml/3 tablespoons of the sugar, and add lemon juice or glycerine if required (see below). Gradually add the remaining sugar and mix very well until the icing is soft, very white, fluffy and will hold its shape . More sugar can be added if the mixture is too sloppy. Blue colouring, if used (see below), is added last.

FLAVOURINGS AND COLOURINGS

1. 1 drop blue food colouring makes white icing very bright white.
2. 15ml/1 teaspoon lemon juice to each 225g/8oz sugar makes the icing a little sharper and less sickly.
3. 2.5ml/1/2 teaspoon glycerine to each 225g/8oz sugar produces a softer icing which will not splinter when cut. Without glycerine, royal icing eventually hardens to an unbreakable cement. More glycerine can be added, but this will give a softer icing unsuitable for a tiered cake. None need be used if the cake is to be eaten within 24 hours of icing.

CONSISTENCY

A cake is normally covered with 2-3 coats of icing and decorated with either piping or 'run-in' work. The consistency varies for each coat.
FIRST COATING: very thick – the icing should stand up in points if the beating spoon is lifted from the bowl.
SECOND COATING: a little thinner (the points should flop over at the tips, like rabbit ears).
THIRD COATING: the icing should be of thick pouring consistency.
FOR PIPING: consistency as for the first coating.
FOR RUN-IN WORK: as for the third coating.

BUBBLES

Royal icing should be beaten as little as possible: if making it by hand or in an electric machine, stop as soon as it is smooth and glossy. If there are any bubbles, leave the icing, covered with a damp cloth, in the refrigerator overnight.

APPLYING THE FIRST COAT

It is easier to apply the first layer of royal icing in two (for a round cake) or three (for a square cake) stages rather than all at once. The top is iced first and allowed to dry for 24 hours before icing the sides. On a square cake two of the opposite sides are iced and allowed to dry before the second two sides are iced.

Place a small spoonful of icing on a cake board about 5cm/2 inches larger in diameter than the cake, and put the cake on top. It will now stick to the board. Spoon half the icing on to the top of the cake with a palette knife and spread to the edge, using a paddling action to remove any air bubbles. Then, using a clean metal ruler, a 'straight edge' or large palette knife placed in the centre of the cake, draw the icing forwards and backwards across the cake until it is completely smooth and level and can be drawn off the cake.

Carefully remove any icing that has fallen down the sides of the cake. Leave to dry for 24 hours. Put the cake and board on an icing turntable or upturned bowl and spread the icing evenly around the sides, using a special icing scraper or a palette knife held at an angle of 45 degrees to the cake. Try to turn the cake around in one movement as you ice in order to ensure a smooth finish. For a square cake, ice two of the opposite sides.

Store the cake for at least 24 hours in a clean, cool, dry place to dry before you ice the other two sides. If the storage place is damp, it will prevent the icing from drying and it will slowly slip down the sides of the cake. If it is too warm, the cake will 'sweat' and oil from the marzipan will be drawn into the icing.

APPLYING THE SECOND COAT

This may not be necessary if the first layer is very smooth. If it is not perfect, smooth it down with fine sandpaper. Brush the surface well with a grease-free brush to remove any loose icing. Ice the cake as for the first coating, but use a slightly thinner icing.

APPLYING THE THIRD COAT OR FLOAT

A three-tier wedding cake or a less than perfectly iced cake may need a third layer of icing. If this is necessary, proceed when the second coating is dry. Prepare the surface as previously instructed.

Before converting the icing into the desired pouring consistency, pile a little thick icing into an icing bag fitted with a no. 1 or 2 writing nozzle and cover it with a damp cloth.

Add a little egg white to the remaining icing and beat until smooth and of a pouring consistency. Leave in a tightly covered container for 30 minutes. (Stretching a piece of polythene wrap over the bowl will do.) This is to make the air bubbles rise to the surface. If you do not do this, air bubbles will break all over the surface of the cake, making little holes in the icing.

With the writing tube, pipe an unbroken line of icing around the top edge of the cake.

Now pour the runny icing into a piping bag, remove the nozzle and guide it over the top of the cake, flooding the surface and carefully avoiding the piped line. With the handle of a teaspoon, work the flooding to the edge of the cake. The piped line will prevent the icing running off.

DECORATING WITH ICING

You must have a clear idea of the design before you begin. If it is a geometric pattern, draw it on a piece of tracing paper and place this on the cake. Using a large pin, prick where the lines meet. Remove the paper and you will be left with guidelines made by the pinpoints. Join these up with more pricked holes so that the design is visible. Half-fill the piping bags, fitted with the chosen nozzles, with the icing mixed to the correct consistency. Put them under a wet cloth until needed. Get everything you will need ready on or near your work surface (e.g. more bags and extra nozzles, a large spoon, a palette knife, a small basin of hot water for washing the nozzles).

DIRECT PIPING

STAR PIPING: fit the bag with a star nozzle. Hold the pipe upright, immediately above and almost touching the top of the cake, and squeeze gently from the top of the bag. Stop pressing and lift the bag away. Always stop pressing before lifting the bag away.

DOT OR PEARL PIPING: use a plain nozzle, and pipe as for stars. If the dots are too small, do not try to increase their size by squeezing out more icing; use a larger nozzle.

STRAIGHT LINES: with a plain nozzle, press the bag as for making a dot but leave the icing attached to the cake surface - do not draw away by lifting the bag. Hold the point of the nozzle about 4cm/1½ inches above the surface of the cake and, pressing gently as you go, guide rather than drag the icing into place. The icing can be directed more easily into place if it is allowed to hang from the tube.

TRELLIS WORK: with a plain nozzle, pipe parallel lines 5mm/¼ inch apart. Pipe a second layer over the top at right angles or at an angle of 45 degrees to the first. Then pipe another layer as closely as possible over the first set of lines, then another set over the second layer, and so on until you have the desired height of trellis. Six layers (three in each direction) is usual for an elaborate cake.

SHELLS: use a star nozzle. Hold the bag at an angle of about 45 degrees. Pipe a shell, release the pressure on the bag and begin a new shell one-eighth of the way up the first shell, so that each new shell overlaps its predecessor.

SCROLLS: use a star nozzle. Hold the bag at an angle of about 45 degrees. Pipe a scroll first from left to right and then from right to left.

RUN-IN WORK: using a writing nozzle, pipe the outline of a design (e.g. leaf, Father Christmas, etc.) on to oiled foil, oiled greaseproof, waxed or bakewell paper. 'Float' runny icing in the centre, and leave to set. Lift off and stick on to the cake with wet icing.

NOTE: Variations of pressure when piping both shells and scrolls make the icing emerge in the required thicknesses. Shells and scrolls can be made into very attractive borders when combined with trellis work and edged with pearls.

CAUSES OF FAILURE

BROKEN LINES

- Icing too stiff.
- Pulling rather than easing into place.
- Making the icing with a mixer set at too high a speed, causing air bubbles.

WOBBLY LINES

- Squeezing the icing out too quickly.
- Icing too liquid.

FLATTENED LINES

- Icing too liquid.
- Bag held too near the surface.

INDIRECT PIPING

Indirect piping is done on to oiled moulds or waxed paper and, when dry, the piped shapes are stuck to the cake with a little wet icing.

TRELLISED SHAPES: pipe as for direct piping on to waxed paper or oiled moulds (the backs of teaspoons, patty tins, cups or glasses). Leave for 24 hours, then warm over a very gentle heat to dislodge them. Slide off the mould and fix to the cake with a little wet icing.

FLOWERS: you need confectioner's 'flower nails' and petal nozzles. The icing should be thick. The petals are piped individually on to the oiled surface of the 'flower nail', the biggest petals first and then the smaller ones. If the flower nail is covered with oiled foil, the flower can be removed carefully after piping so that the nail can be used for the next flower. When dry, green icing leaves (piped and dried separately) can be attached to the back of the flowers with a little wet icing.

When making coloured flowers, it is helpful to tint the icing to a pale colour first. After they have dried, they can be touched up with a paint brush to give the flowers a more natural appearance. By varying the angle at which the piping bags are held, flatter petals (for daisies, violets and primroses) or thicker, more rounded petals (for roses) can be made. Sweet peas are made with 2-3 flat petals slightly overlapping each other with a smaller upright rounded petal piped on top of each flat one.

Marzipan or Almond Paste (Uncooked)

225g/8oz caster sugar
225g/8oz icing sugar
450g/1lb ground almonds
2 egg yolks
2 whole eggs
10ml/2 teaspoons lemon juice
6 drops vanilla essence

1. Sift the sugars together into a bowl and mix with the ground almonds.
2. Mix together the egg yolks, whole eggs, lemon juice and vanilla essence. Add this to the sugar mixture and beat briefly with a wooden spoon.
3. Lightly dust the working surface with icing sugar. Knead the paste until just smooth (overworking will draw the oil out of the almonds, giving a too greasy paste).
4. Wrap well and store in a cool place.

TO COVER A ROUND CAKE WITH UNCOOKED MARZIPAN

For a 22cm/9 inch diameter cake you will need:

uncooked marzipan made with 450g/1lb ground almonds
apricot glaze (see page 584)
icing sugar

1. If the cake is not level, carefully shave off some of the top and turn it upside down.
2. Measure around the side with a piece of string.
3. Lightly dust a very clean work surface with icing sugar and roll out two-thirds of the marzipan to a strip the length of the piece of string and the depth of the cake. Trim it neatly.
4. Roll out the remaining marzipan to a circle the size of the cake top.
5. Brush the sides of the cake with apricot glaze and, holding the cake firmly between both hands, turn it on to its side and roll it along the prepared strip of marzipan. Turn the cake right side up again. Use a round-bladed knife to smooth the join. Take a jam jar or straight-sided tin and roll it around the side of the cake.
6. Brush the top with apricot glaze and, using a rolling pin, lift the circle of marzipan on to the cake. Seal the edges with the knife and smooth the top with a rolling pin.
7. Leave to dry on a cake board 5cm/2 inches larger in diameter than the cake.

TO COVER A SQUARE CAKE WITH UNCOOKED MARZIPAN

For a 20cm/8 inch square cake you will need:

uncooked marzipan made with 450g/1lb ground almonds
apricot glaze (see page 584)
icing sugar

1. If the cake is not level, shave off a little of the top. Turn it upside down.
2. Measure one side of the cake with a piece of string.
3. Lightly dust a very clean work surface with icing sugar and roll out two-thirds of the marzipan into 4 strips the length of the piece of string and the depth of the cake. Trim neatly.
4. Roll the remaining marzipan, with any trimmings, to a square to fit the top of the cake.
5. Brush one side of the cake with apricot glaze. Turn the cake on to its side and, holding it firmly between both hands, place the glazed edge on one strip of marzipan. Trim the edges and repeat with the other three sides. Smooth the joins with a round-bladed knife. Take a jam jar or straight-sided tin and roll it around the sides of the cake, keeping the corners square.
6. Brush the top of the cake with apricot glaze and, using a rolling pin, lift the square of marzipan on to the cake. Seal the edges with the knife and smooth the top with a rolling pin. Leave to dry on a cake board about 5cm/2 inches wider, all round, than the cake.

NOTE: Square cakes are normally covered with uncooked marzipan. The cooked paste is too pliable and it is therefore difficult to get square corners.

Cooked Marzipan

This recipe gives a softer, easier-to-handle paste than the more usual uncooked marzipan.

2 eggs
170g/6oz caster sugar
170g/6oz icing sugar
340g/12oz ground almonds
4 drops vanilla essence
5ml/1 teaspoon lemon juice
icing sugar for kneading

1. Lightly beat the eggs.
2. Sift the sugars together and mix with the eggs.
3. Place the bowl over a pan of boiling water and whisk until light and creamy or until the mixture just leaves a trail. Remove from the heat and leave to get cold.
4. Add the almonds, vanilla and lemon juice.
5. Lightly dust the working surface with icing sugar. Carefully knead the paste until just smooth. (Overworking will draw out the oil from the almonds giving a too greasy paste.) Wrap well and store in a cool place.

TO COVER A ROUND CAKE WITH COOKED MARZIPAN
For a 20cm/8 inch diameter cake, you will need:

cooked marzipan made with 340g/12oz ground almonds
apricot glaze (see page 584)
icing sugar

1. If the cake is not very level shave off the top carefully. Turn it upside down, so that the level bottom becomes the top of the cake. Brush lightly with apricot glaze.
2. Lightly dust a very clean worktop with icing sugar and roll out the marzipan to a circle 20cm/8 inches larger in diameter than the cake.
3. Place the glazed cake upside down in the centre of the marzipan and, using your hands, carefully work the marzipan up the sides of the cake.
4. Take a jam jar or straight-sided tin and roll it around the sides of the cake to make sure that the sides are quite straight, and the edges square.
5. Turn it the right way up and place on a cake board 5cm/2 inches larger in diameter than the cake.

NOTE: Once a cake has been covered with marzipan, it should be left for a minimum of 2 days, but ideally a week, before icing, otherwise the marzipan colour can leak into the icing.

Marzipan Dates

MAKES ABOUT 20
about 20 dates (fresh or dried)
225g/8oz marzipan
green colouring (optional)

1. Split the dates lengthways almost in half. Take out the stones carefully, making sure that the dates stay whole.
2. Form the marzipan into a long sausage about 5mm/¼ inch in diameter. Cut it into lengths about the size of the dates.
3. Place a piece of marzipan in each date and half-close the opening. Place in tiny paper cases.

NOTE: The marzipan can be coloured pale green by the addition of a few drops of green colouring. Work the colour into the marzipan by kneading with one hand.

Tommies

MAKES ABOUT 20
70g/2½oz caster sugar
110g/4oz butter
85g/3oz ground hazelnuts
140g/5oz plain flour
honey
225g/8oz dark chocolate

1. Set the oven to 180°C/350°F/gas mark 4.
2. Cream the sugar and butter together until white.
3. Stir in the hazelnuts and flour.
4. As soon as the mixture becomes a paste, wrap and leave it in the refrigerator for 30 minutes.
5. Roll out thinly and cut into 2.5cm/1 inch rounds with a biscuit cutter or an upturned glass.
6. Place on a baking sheet and bake for 12 minutes. Put on a wire rack to cool.
7. Spread honey on half the biscuits, then sandwich them with the others. Return to the cooling rack.
8. Warm the chocolate on a plate over a pan of hot

water until it has melted and there are no lumps.
9. Spoon over the chocolate to cover the biscuits completely.
10. When set (and if there is enough chocolate left), fill a small piping bag fitted with a writing nozzle with melted chocolate and pipe a design over the set chocolate. Store in an airtight container.

Chocolate Cherries

These chocolates should be made a week in advance to allow the full flavour of the brandy to be infused into the cherries. You will need 24 small foil cups to make these sweets.

MAKES 24
24 black cherries, stoned
75ml/5 tablespoons brandy
225g/8oz couverture chocolate
170g/6oz fondant icing (see page 585)

1. Put the cherries into a bowl. Heat up the brandy and pour it over the cherries. Leave to stand for as long as possible.
2. Break up the chocolate into even-sized pieces and place in a bowl set over, not in, a pan of simmering water. When the chocolate has melted, use a teaspoon to line the little foil cups with it. Pour out any excess chocolate. Leave to dry.
3. Melt the fondant with 10ml/2 teaspoons of the brandy from the cherries in a bowl over, not in, a pan of simmering water.
4. Pour enough fondant to come a third of the way up each foil cup.
5. Drain the cherries very well. Add one to each cup. Fill almost to the top with more fondant. Leave to harden for 5-10 minutes.
6. Spoon over enough chocolate, swirling it to seal the edges, to cover the fondant icing completely. Leave to cool and harden. Serve in the foil cups.

Nougat

This recipe has been adapted from one by Mary B. Bockmeyer in *Candy and Candy Making*. You will need rice paper to make nougat.

MAKES 850g/1¾lb
225g/8oz granulated sugar
140g/5oz clear honey
22.5ml/1½ tablespoons liquid glucose
110ml/4 fl oz water
2 egg whites
5ml/1 teaspoon vanilla essence
285g/10oz blanched and toasted almonds, chopped and warmed
110g/4oz skinned pistachio nuts, chopped and warmed

1. Line a 20cm/8 inch square tin with rice paper.
2. Put the sugar, honey, liquid glucose and water in a saucepan and stir over a very gentle heat until the sugar dissolves. Boil rapidly until it reaches the soft crack stage (143°C/290°F).
3. Whisk the egg whites lightly, and gradually pour on the hot syrup, whisking continuously. Whisk until stiff, then add the vanilla essence and chopped nuts. The mixture must be stiff; if not, place in the top of a double boiler and stir until it dries it out a little.
4. Turn into the prepared tin. Cover with a second piece of rice paper. Place a board on top and weight lightly for 15 hours.
5. Cut into diamond shapes and serve.

Chocolate Truffles

MAKES 24
255g/9oz chocolate couverture, coarsely chopped
100ml/3½ fl oz double cream
vanilla pod
20g/¾oz unsalted butter
cocoa powder

1. Melt the chocolate in a bowl set over (not in) a pan of simmering water. Leave to cool.
2. Put the cream into a saucepan, add the vanilla pod and bring up to scalding point. Leave to cool. Remove the vanilla pod.
3. Beat the butter until very soft. Mix it into the chocolate, add the vanilla cream and leave to chill, until firm, in the refrigerator.
4. Shape into small balls and roll lightly in cocoa powder.

Whisky Truffles

MAKES 24
225g/8oz milk chocolate
60ml/4 tablespoons double cream
45ml/3 tablespoons whisky
30g/1oz unsalted butter
cocoa powder, to finish

1. Break the chocolate into even-sized pieces and melt in a bowl over (not in) a saucepan of simmering water.
2. In another saucepan, bring the cream up to the boil, take off the heat and mix with the melted chocolate.
3. When well mixed, add the whisky and beat in the butter.
4. Put in the refrigerator to harden.
5. Roll the mixture into a sausage shape, chop into lengths, roll into balls the size of a walnut and toss in the cocoa powder.

Mint and Tea Chocolates

MAKES 24
225g/8oz milk chocolate
110ml/4 fl oz double cream
7g/¼ oz Indian tea leaves
4 mint leaves, roughly chopped

1. Break the chocolate into even-sized pieces and melt in a bowl over (not in) a saucepan of simmering water.
2. In another saucepan, bring the cream up to the boil, turn off the heat, and add the tea and chopped mint. Allow to infuse for 1 minute and then strain.
3. Mix the flavoured cream with the melted chocolate and place in the refrigerator to harden slightly.
4. Roll out the chocolate mixture between 2 sheets of greaseproof paper until 1cm/½ inch thick. Allow to harden completely in the refrigerator.
5. Using a 2.5cm/1 inch plain round cutter, cut out the chocolates.
6. They can be served as they are or dipped in lukewarm melted chocolate. Alternatively, the mixture can be rolled into a sausage shape, cut into lengths, rolled with the palms of the hands into balls and dipped in cocoa powder.

Coffee and Orange Mini Meringues

MAKES 20
For the meringues:
3 egg whites
170g/6oz soft brown sugar
5ml/1 teaspoon instant coffee powder

For the filling:
425ml/¾ pint double cream
15ml/1 tablespoon Grand Marnier
grated rind of 1 orange

1. Set the oven to 110°C/225°F /gas mark ½.
2. Place silicone paper on 4 baking sheets.
3. Whisk the egg whites until stiff but not dry.
4. Gradually add 22.5ml/1½ tablespoons of sugar and whisk again until stiff and very shiny.
5. Whisk in the remaining sugar gradually, with the instant coffee powder.
6. Put the meringue into a forcing-bag fitted with 1 cm/½ inch plain nozzle. Pipe the meringue into small whirls.
7. Bake in the oven for about 2 hours until the meringues are dry and will lift easily off the paper. Leave to cool.
8. Whip the cream, fold in the Grand Marnier and orange rind. Sandwich the meringues together in pairs.

Orange Tartlets

MAKES 24
rich shortcrust pastry made with 170g/6oz flour (see page 525)

For the candied orange zest:
1 medium orange
340g/12oz granulated sugar
45ml/3 tablespoons liquid glucose
90ml/6 tablespoons water

For the orange curd:
1 large orange
1 medium lemon
55g/2oz unsalted butter
110g/4oz caster sugar
4 egg yolks

1. To make the candied orange zest: remove the zest from the orange with a potato peeler or small sharp knife and cut into 5mm/1/4 inch strips. Put into a small saucepan with enough water to cover and boil for 5 minutes to remove the bitter taste. Drain and refresh under running cold water.
2. Bring 225g/8oz of the sugar, the liquid glucose and water up to the boil in the saucepan. Remove from the heat and stir in the zest. Allow to stand for 30 minutes. Bring the liquid back to the boil and allow to stand for another 30 minutes. Remove the zest with a fork and transfer to a wire rack to cool.
3. Put the remaining sugar on a plate and roll the orange strips in sugar. Once they are dry they can be stored in an airtight container at room temperature for up to a week.
4. Preheat the oven to 180°C/350°F/gas mark 4.
5. Line small tartlet tins or petit four tins with the pastry. Prick with a fork and place in the refrigerator to relax.
6. Bake the tartlet cases blind for 10 minutes (see page 152). Remove the paper and beans and bake until the pastry is dry and light brown. Cool.
7. Next make the curd: grate the rind of the orange and half the lemon on the finest gauge of the grater, taking care to grate only the rind, not the pith.
8. Squeeze the juice from the orange and lemon.
9. Put the rind, juice, butter, sugar and lightly beaten egg yolks into a heavy saucepan or double boiler and heat gently, stirring all the time, until the mixture is thick.
10. Strain into a bowl and allow to cool.
11. To assemble: using a piping bag and very small plain nozzle, pipe a round of curd into each shell. Cut the orange peel into small diamonds and use them to garnish the tartlets.

Preserving

Preserving

THE TERM 'preserves' covers all food that has been treated to keep for longer than it would if fresh. Frozen food, dried food, salted food and smoked food are all preserves. But in household language, the word means jams, jellies, marmalades, pickles and sometimes bottled food; in short, the sort of preserves found on a good countrywoman's larder shelf.

Jellies are clear preserves, made from strained fruit juice. They should be neither runny nor too solid. Jams are made from crushed fruit. They should almost hold their shape, but be more liquid than jelly. Conserves are jams containing a mixture of fruits, generally including citrus fruit, and sometimes raisins or nuts. Marmalade is jam made exclusively from citrus fruit. Fruit butters are made from smooth fruit purées, cooked with sugar to the consistency of thick cream. Fruit cheeses are made in the same way but cooked until very thick. Butters and cheeses, because they are not set solidly and generally contain less sugar than jams, should be potted in sterilized jars. Curds generally contain butter and eggs, are best kept refrigerated, and will not keep for more than a couple of months.

Jams, jellies and marmalades

These preserves depend on four main factors to make them long-lasting:

1. The presence of pectin. This is a substance, converted from the gum-like pectose found to some degree in all fruit, which reacts with the acids of the fruit and with the sugar to form a jelly-like set. Slightly under-ripe fruit is higher in pectin than over-ripe fruit, and some types of fruit are higher in pectin than others, notably apples, quinces, damsons, sour plums, lemons and redcurrants. Jam made from these will set easily. Jam from low-pectin fruit such as strawberries, rhubarb, mulberries and pears may need added commercial pectin or lemon juice (or a little high-pectin fruit) to obtain a good set.

TO TEST FOR PECTIN: before you add the sugar, take a teaspoon of the simmered fruit juice and put it into a glass. When it is cold add 15ml/1tablespoon methylated spirit. After a minute a jelly will have formed. If it is in 1 or 2 firm clots there is adequate pectin in the fruit. If the jelly clots are numerous and soft the jam will not set without the addition of more pectin.

2. A high concentration of sugar. Sugar is itself a preservative, and without sufficient sugar the pectin will not act to form the set.

3. The presence of acid which, like sugar, acts with the pectin to form a gel or set. Acid also prevents the growth of bacteria, and it helps to prevent the crystallization of the sugar in the jam during storage. If the fruit is low in acid, then tartaric acid, ascorbic acid or lemon juice may be added.

4. The elimination and exclusion of micro-organisms. The jam itself is sterilized by rapid boiling. Jam jars need not normally be sterilized since the heat of the jam should be sufficient to sterilize them. However, harmless moulds do sometimes form round the rim and on the surface of jams potted in this way, and sterilizing the jars does help to prevent this. Jam jars may be soaked in solutions bought at chemists for sterilizing babies' bottles etc. Ordinary household bleach will also be effective, but the bottles should be rinsed in boiling water afterwards. The jam funnel should be sterilized with the jars. It is not necessary to sterilize ladles or spoons except by leaving them in the bubbling jam for a minute or two. Jelly cloths or bags need not be sterilized as the juice is dripped through them before being boiled.

Once put into the clean, dry jars, the jam is sealed to prevent the infiltration of mildew spores etc. Melted paraffin wax (melted white candles will do) poured over the surface of the jam makes a good old-fashioned and most effective seal, but most cooks rely on ordinary paper jam covers and a bit of luck.

Ideally, the jam should be sealed while boiling hot, i.e. before any fresh mildew spores can enter. However, if liquid wax is used on hot jam, it may disturb the flat surface, so the slightly cooled but still clear wax is poured on once the jam is set. Two applications of wax are necessary if the first covering shrinks away from the sides of the jar, leaving a gap.

Perhaps the best method of sealing is to use metal screw-tops. They should be sterilized and checked for a tight fit. The jam should be poured up to the shoulder of the jars, leaving a good 1cm/$^1/_2$ inch. The caps are screwed on tightly as soon as the jars are filled. The cooling jar will form a partial vacuum in the neck, tightly sealing the jar. Plastic lids do not give a reliable seal.

If, in spite of all precautions, mould appears on the top of the jams, it can be scraped off and the jam beneath is perfectly good to eat. But it should be eaten quite quickly as mould spores in the air could re-infect it. Scraping off visible mould will not prevent the invisible spores from multiplying. Jam that is fizzy or fermented should be thrown away.

YIELD

The amount of finished jam obtained from a given quantity of fruit varies according to type, jellies giving comparatively little, marmalades and whole fruit jams much more. As a general rule, the mixture will yield between 1$^1/_2$ times and double the weight of sugar used. It is wise to over-estimate the amount of jars needed, rather than to have to prepare more at the last minute.

EQUIPMENT

Making jam is easy enough, but it requires a little organization. First the equipment should be assembled. You will need:

Accurate scales
Preserving pan or a large heavy pan with a solid base
Sharp knives
Grater
Mincer
Long-handled wooden spoons
Perforated spoon
Metal jug with a large lip or a jam funnel
Jam jars
Jam covers, labels and rubber bands (available from chemists and stationers) or metal screw-top lids
Sugar thermometer (not essential but useful)
Perforated skimmer (not essential but useful)

POINTS TO REMEMBER

1. Make sure all equipment is absolutely clean.
2. Use dry, unblemished, just-ripe fruit.
3. Use preserving, lump, granulated or caster sugar. Modern white sugars are highly refined and therefore suitable. They need little skimming and give a clear preserve. Using preserving sugar has a slight advantage because the crystals are larger and the boiling liquid circulates freely round them, dissolving them rapidly. Caster sugar is inclined to set in a solid mass at the bottom of the pan and takes longer to dissolve. Brown sugar gives an unattractive colour to preserves.
4. Covering lukewarm jam could lead to mildew. If the jam is covered immediately, any bacteria or mildew spores present in the atmosphere are trapped between jam and seal and will be killed by the heat. If the atmosphere is lukewarm and steamy, perfect incubating conditions are created.

BASIC PROCEDURE

1. Wash and dry the jam jars and warm them in the oven.
2. Pick over the fruit, wash or wipe and cut up if necessary.
3. Put the fruit and water in the pan and set to simmer.
4. Warm the sugar in a cool oven. When it is added to the fruit it will then not lower the temperature too much, necessitating prolonged cooking which could impair the colour of the jam.
5. Bring the fruit to a good boil. Tip in the sugar and stir, without reboiling, until the sugar has dissolved.
6. Once the sugar has dissolved, boil rapidly, stirring gently but frequently.

7. When the mixture begins to look like jam – usually after about 10 minutes – test for setting. It is important not to overboil since this can make the colour too dark and the texture too solid. It will also ruin the flavour. Overboiling can sometimes even prevent a set by destroying the pectin. If you are using a thermometer, you can check the setting point: 105°C/220°F for jam and 106°C/222°F for marmalade. To test for setting, put a teaspoon of the jam on to an ice-cold saucer and return it to the ice compartment or freezer to cool rapidly. When cold, push it gently with a finger. The jam should have a slight skin, which will wrinkle if setting point is reached. If a finger is drawn through the jam, it should remain separated, not run together. Also, clear jam or jelly should fall from a spatula not in a single stream, but forming a wavy curtain and dripping reluctantly from more than one point.
8. As soon as a setting test proves positive, draw the jam off the heat. Skim carefully and then, if the jam contains whole fruit or large pieces of fruit, allow to cool for 15 minutes. This will prevent the fruit rising to the top of the jam jars.
9. Put the hot jars close together on a wooden board or tray. Fill them with hot jam with the aid of a jug or jam funnel.
10. Seal at once with screw-tops or put waxed paper discs, waxed side down, on the surface of the jam, and cover the tops of the jars with cellophane covers, securing them with a rubber band. Brush the cellophane tops with water to slightly stretch them. Carefully pull them tight. As they dry they will shrink tightly around the jars.
11. Wipe the sides of the jars with a hot, clean, damp cloth to remove any drips of jam.
12. Label each jar with the type of jam and the date.
13. Leave undisturbed overnight.
14. Store in a cool, airy, dark place.

MILDEW on the surface of the jam is probably caused by one of the following:
1. Using wet jars.
2. Covering the jam when lukewarm.
3. Imperfect sealing.
4. Damp or warm storage place.
5. Equipment that is less than spotless.
The mildew should be removed, and the jam consumed fairly quickly.

CRYSTALLIZATION of the sugar in jam is caused by:
1. Insufficient acid in the fruit.
2. Boiling the jam before the sugar has dissolved.
3. Adding too much sugar.
4. Leaving jam uncovered.
5. Storing in too cold an atmosphere, e.g. a fridge.

FERMENTATION of jam is caused by:
1. Insufficient boiling leading to non-setting.
2. Insufficient acid leading to non-setting.
3. Insufficient pectin leading to non-setting.
4. Insufficient sugar leading to non-setting.
5. A storage place that is too warm.
6. Jars that are less than spotless.

Pickles

Pickles are foods, usually vegetables or fruit, preserved in vinegar. Fruit for pickles is generally cooked in sugared vinegar, and stored in this sweetened vinegar syrup. Vegetables are usually, but not always, pickled raw, and are generally salted in dry salt, or steeped in brine, before being immersed in the vinegar. Salting draws moisture out of the food. If salting is omitted, the juices from the vegetables leak into the vinegar during storage, diluting it and impairing its keeping quality. Salt also has preservative powers, and its penetration into the food helps to prevent it 'going bad', but the main preservative in pickles is vinegar, which prevents the growth of bacteria.

The best salt is pure rock salt or crushed block salt. Pure sea salt is good too, but very expensive. Table salt has additives to make it conveniently free-flowing, but these may cause the pickle to go cloudy.

NOTE: Brass, old-fashioned iron or copper preserving pans or saucepans should not be used in the preparation of foods containing vinegar. The acid reacts with the metal, spoiling both colour and flavour.

BRINING

Brine is a solution of salt in water, and is suitable for the steeping of vegetables for pickling. Firm vegetables such as shallots should be pierced with a needle to allow the brine to penetrate.

225g/8oz pure salt (not table salt)
3 litres/4 pints water

1. Heat the salt and water slowly together until the salt has dissolved.
2. Allow to cool.
3. Prepare (peel, cut up, prick, etc.) the vegetables to be pickled, put them into a bowl and pour over the cold brine. Put a plate on top to keep the food submerged.
4. After 24 hours (usually, but check individual recipes) drain well, pat dry and pack into clean jars ready for pickling.

DRY-SALTING

This is particularly suitable for 'wet' vegetables such as marrow and cucumber.

110g/4oz dry pure salt (not table salt) per 1 kg/2lb prepared vegetables

1. Prepare (peel, cut up, etc.) the vegetables. If they are tough (like onions or shallots) pierce them deeply with a needle.
2. Put them in a bowl, sprinkling each layer liberally with salt. Cover and keep cool for 24 hours.
3. Drain off all the liquid, rinse the vegetables in cold water and pat dry in a clean cloth.
4. Pack into clean jars ready for pickling.

THE VINEGAR

Pickling vinegar should be strong, containing at least 5 per cent acetic acid. Most brand vinegars contain sufficient acid, but homemade vinegars or draught vinegars are not suitable. Brown malt vinegar is the best for flavour, especially if the pickle is to be highly spiced or is made with strong-tasting foods. White vinegar has less flavour, but obviously gives a clearer pickle. Wine vinegar is suitable for delicate mild-tasting foods. Commercial cider vinegar is good too. The vinegar may be spiced and flavoured according to taste by the addition of cayenne, ginger or chillies, or aromatic spices such as cardamom seeds, cloves or nutmeg. Whole spices are best as they can be removed easily, and will not leave the vinegar murky. Ready-spiced pickling vinegar may also be purchased.

Chutneys

Chutneys are the easiest preserves to make. They are mixtures, always sweet and sour, somewhere between a pickle and a jam. They are generally made of fruit, or sometimes soft vegetables such as tomato or marrow, with vinegar, onion and spices.

Both sugar and salt, themselves preservatives, are present in chutneys, but they are there for flavour more than for their keeping powers. As with jams, boiling the ingredients destroys micro-organisms, but with chutneys obtaining a set is not necessary – like pickles, they depend on vinegar for their keeping qualities.

Fruit and vegetables for chutneys should be sliced or cut small enough to be lifted with a teaspoon, but not so small as to be unidentifiable in the chutney. As the ingredients are seldom used whole, you can use damaged or bruised fruit, with the imperfect bits removed.

Chutneys improve with keeping. They can generally be eaten after two months (before this their taste is harsh) but are at their best between 6 months and 2 years. If the chutney is to be kept for more than 6 months a more secure seal than a jam cover is advisable. See the notes for jars and lids on page 597.

BASIC PROCEDURE FOR CHUTNEY

1. Prepare the ingredients: wash fruit and vegetables, peel where necessary, cut up, etc. Wash dried fruit if bought loose. Chop or mince onions. Use a stainless steel fruit knife for fruit or vegetables liable to discolour.
2. Put all the ingredients, except the sugar and vinegar, into a saucepan (not an unlined copper, brass or old-fashioned iron one: see note on page 598). The spices should be tied in a muslin bag if they are to be removed later.
3. Add enough of the vinegar to easily cover the other ingredients.
4. Cook slowly, covered or not, until the fruit or vegetables are soft, and most of the liquid has evaporated.
5. Add the sugar and the rest of the vinegar and stir until the sugar has dissolved.
6. Boil to the consistency of thick and syrupy jam.
7. Put into clean, hot jars. Cover as for jam if to be eaten within 6 months. Use non-metal lids or stoppers if it is to be kept longer.

NOTE: In recipes for chutneys that do not require prolonged cooking to soften the ingredients (e.g. apricot and orange chutney, page 607) the sugar and vinegar may be added with the other ingredients, the whole being boiled together.

Bottling fruit

The preservation of food by bottling works on the principle of destruction by heat of all micro-organisms present in the fruit or syrup. Because a partial vacuum is created in the jar, by expelling air during processing, a tight seal is formed between the lid and jar, keeping the sterilized contents uncontaminated.

The procedure described here applies to the bottling of fruit only. Because vegetables and meat contain little or no acid, and are therefore likely to harbour bacteria they need considerably longer processing at higher temperatures to become safe. This lengthy heating tends to spoil the texture and flavour of the food. In general, bottling meat and vegetables is not worth the effort, time and risks involved. But fruit and tomatoes, because they are fairly acid, do not contain bacteria; and the relatively harmless yeasts and moulds are more easily destroyed.

Fruit may be bottled in plain water or in salted water.

JARS

Kilner jars come with a glass lid and a rubber ring. The lid is kept in place by a metal screw-band. The rubber ring must not be re-used as it will not give a good seal twice, and is perishable. Kilner jars are closed loosely before processing, and only tightened fully when they come out of the sterilizer or saucepan, while still hot. As the hot air inside cools it will contract, pulling the lid on tightly as it does so.

Parfait jars are similar to Kilner jars but the lid is held in place by a metal gimp or clip. It is clipped shut before processing. There is sufficient spring in the gimp to allow the escape of steam during heating. The lid tightens automatically as the jar cools after processing.

PREPARING THE FRUIT

Fruit can be bottled raw or cooked. If the fruit is cooked the processing time need only be long enough for sterilization, not for tenderizing the fruit. If raw, the fruit is cooked and sterilized at the same time, and may need longer processing. Fruits that cook to a pulp easily, such as berries and cooking apples, are generally processed from raw as the minimum time at great heat is the objective. Other fruits, such as pears and peaches, which require an uncertain time to soften, are frequently pre-cooked as it is then possible to tell if they are tender. Pre-cooking has a further advantage. Once the fruit is cooked and softened, more of it can be packed into the jars. Also, it will not rise up in the jar when sterilized. Fruit bottled from raw frequently rises.

POINTS TO REMEMBER

1. Make sure the bottling jars are not cracked and that the tops are in good condition. Jars must have new rubber rings fitted each year. Screw bands or metal clips should work properly and jars should be clean.
2. Make the sugar syrup before peeling the fruit.
3. Choose perfect, not over-ripe fruit.
4. If fruit needs cutting or peeling, use a stainless steel knife.
5. If it is likely to discolour (apples or pears), drop the pieces into cold water containing a teaspoonful of ascorbic acid (vitimin C powder or a fizzy Redoxon tablet will do) until you are ready to process them.
6. Pack the fruit (cooked or raw) up to the necks of the jars.

PROCESSING THE FRUIT

The fruit can be processed (or sterilized) in the following ways:

1. In a sterilizer (sometimes called a pressure canner). This is a purpose-made machine like a large pressure cooker. It is reliable and easy to use, but by no means essential. Follow the manufacturer's instructions.
2. In a pressure cooker, which works like a sterilizer but holds fewer jars and will not hold tall ones. About 2.5cm/1inch of water in the bottom is sufficient, as no evaporation will take place. The process is very quick, and the jars and fruit sterilize in the steam. Wedge the jars with cloths to stop them rattling. Allow the pressure to fall before opening the cooker. Consult the maker's manual.
3. In a deep saucepan or bath of boiling water.

Stand the jars in the container and wedge them with cloths to stop them rattling or cracking. Fill with hot water right over the tops of the jars, or at least up to their necks. Cover as best you can with a lid or foil and teatowels to keep in the steam.

NOTE I: Processing in the oven is not recommended. The temperatures cannot be reliably checked and the jars sometimes crack or explode, or boil over.
NOTE II: If the fruit has been cooked in an open pan with its syrup, it is possible to get a good seal by closing the jar as soon as the hot fruit and boiling syrup are in it, without further sterilization, but the method is not reliable and processing according to the table on page 000 is recommended.

TESTING FOR SEALING
After processing, the jars should be lifted on to a board. Kilner jars should be screwed up tight. Jars should be left undisturbed for 24 hours. They must then be tested for sealing. Remove the bands on the Kilner jars, or loosen the clips on the Parfait jars. It should be possible to lift the jars by the lids, without breaking the seal. If the lid of a jar comes off, the jar must be reprocessed with a new rubber ring or the contents must be eaten within a day or two.

STORING
Wipe the jars with a damp clean cloth, label them with the date of bottling, and store in a dark place. They will keep for at least 18 months, probably for many years.

Gooseberry and Orange Jam

MAKES 675G/1½LB
450g/1lb gooseberries
grated rind and juice of 2 oranges
150ml/¼ pint water
450g/1lb warm preserving sugar

1. Top and tail the gooseberries.
2. Put them with the rind and juice of the oranges and the water into a preserving pan. Simmer until soft and yellowish.
3. Add the warmed sugar, allow it to dissolve, then boil rapidly until setting point is reached.
4. Pour into warm dry jars.
5. Cover and label the jars.
6. Leave undisturbed overnight. Store in a cool, dark, airy place

Blackcurrant and Rhubarb Jam

MAKES 1.3KG/3LB
450g/1lb blackcurrants
450g/1lb rhubarb
150ml/¼ pint water
900g/2lb preserving sugar

1. Wash the blackcurrants and, using the prongs of a fork, remove the stalks.
2. Cut the rhubarb into 0.5cm/¼ inch chunks.
3. Put the rhubarb, blackcurrants and water in a pan and boil for 30 minutes.
4. Warm the sugar and add it to the pan.
5. When the sugar has dissolved, boil rapidly until the jam reaches setting point (about 10-15 minutes).
6. Pour into warm dry jars.
7. Cover and label the jars.
8. Leave undisturbed overnight. Store in a cool, dark, airy place.

Plum or Damson Jam

MAKES 675g/1½lb
900g/2lb barely ripe plums or damsons
900g/2lb preserving sugar

1. Halve and stone the plums. Crack half the stones and remove the kernels.
2. Put the fruit and sugar together in a bowl and leave to stand overnight. (Do not use a metal container.)
3. Next day, transfer to a large saucepan or preserving pan and heat slowly until the sugar has dissolved. Then boil fast until the jam reaches setting point (about 7-10 minutes). Add the kernels while the jam is still bubbling.

4. Pour into warm dry jars.
5. Cover and label the jars.
6. Leave undisturbed overnight. Store in a cool, dark, airy place.

NOTE I: If the plums are difficult to stone, or damsons or greengages are used, simply slit the flesh of each fruit before mixing with the sugar. During boiling, the stones will float to the top and can be removed with a perforated spoon.
NOTE II: Macerating the fruit with the sugar in this way helps to soften the fruit before cooking and allows the cook to dispense with added water. Cooking is quicker as less liquid must be driven off.

Strawberry and Redcurrant Jam

MAKES 1.5kg/3½lb
900g/2lb strawberries
450g/1lb redcurrants
900g/2lb preserving sugar, warmed

1. Hull the strawberries and, using the prongs of a fork, remove the stalks of the redcurrants.
2. Put the redcurrants into a saucepan with 15ml/1 tablespoon water. Cook to a pulp – about 5 minutes.
3. Add the whole strawberries and bring to the boil.
4. Add the warmed sugar and, when dissolved, boil rapidly for 10-12 minutes until the jam reaches setting point. Cool for 15 minutes. This will prevent the berries rising in the jars.
5. Pour into warm dry jars.
6. Cover and label the jars. Leave undisturbed overnight.
7. Store in a cool, dark, airy place.

NOTE: The making of a little syrup with fruit, sugar and lemon juice before adding the bulk of the fruit is done to provide some liquid in which to cook the fruit. Stirring it in a dry pan would lead to crushing and mashing. If possible the fruit should remain whole, suspended in the jam.

Orange Marmalade

MAKES 1.5kg/3½lb
900g/2lb Seville oranges
2 lemons
2.85 litres/5 pints water
1.5 kg/3lb preserving sugar

1. Cut the oranges and lemons in half and roughly squeeze them into a large bowl. (Do not bother to extract all the juice: squeezing is done simply to make removing the pips easier.)
2. Remove the pips and tie them up in a piece of muslin or a clean 'J' cloth.
3. Slice the fruit skins, finely or in chunks as required, and add them to the juice with the bag of pips and the water. Leave to soak for 24 hours.
4. Transfer to a preserving pan or large saucepan and simmer gently until the orange rind is soft and transparent-looking – about 2 hours.
5. Warm the sugar in a slow oven for 20 minutes or so, then tip into the orange pulp. Stir well while bringing the mixture slowly to the boil.
6. Once the sugar has dissolved, boil rapidly until setting point is reached (106°C/222°F). This may take as long as 20 minutes, but it usually takes less. Test after 5 minutes and then again at 3-minute intervals.
7. Allow to cool for 10 minutes, then pour into warm dry jars. Cover with jam covers and leave for 24 hours.
8. Label and store in a cool, dark, airy place.

NOTE: Soaking overnight helps to soften the fruit. It may be dispensed with, but longer simmering will then be necessary.

Clear Grapefruit Marmalade

MAKES 675g/1½lb
2 grapefruit
4 lemons
2.28 litres/4 pints water
900g/2lb preserving sugar

1. Wash the grapefruit and lemons. Cut in half and squeeze out the juice.
2. Strain the juice into a bowl with the water.

3. Shred or chop the peel and pith of both lemons and grapefruit. Put them in a loose muslin bag with the pips of the lemons only.
4. Put the bag in the pan of juice and water. Allow to soak overnight.
5. Transfer the juice and muslin bag to a preserving pan or saucepan and simmer until the skins in the bag are tender (1-2 hours) and the liquid in the pan has reduced by half.
6. Warm the sugar.
7. Remove the muslin bag, squeezing it to extract all the juice before discarding.
8. Add the warmed sugar, stir and bring to the boil.
9. Boil rapidly for 8-10 minutes and test for setting.
10. Pour the marmalade into warm dry jars and cover. Leave undisturbed for 24 hours. Store in a dark, dry place.

NOTE: If shreds of rind are wanted in the jelly, pare the rind from the pith and shred it separately. Add to the boiling liquid.

Three-fruit Marmalade

MAKES 2.7kg/6lb
900g/2lb oranges
3 lemons
1 grapefruit
2.7kg/6lb sugar

1. Scrub the fruit well and put into a large pan with 3. 3 litres/6 pints of water. Bring up to the boil and simmer until the fruit is tender. Test by piercing the skin with the handle of a wooden spoon. This will take about $1^1/2$ hours and the water will have reduced in quantity.
2. Leave the water in the pan and remove the fruit, allow to cool and cut in half. Scoop out the pips and tie them in a piece of muslin, leaving a long piece of string that can be tied to the pan handle.
3. Cut the fruit halves into strips or alternatively put them, in batches, in a liquidizer. Put back into the pan of water and add the sugar. Warm gently and stir until the sugar dissolves.
4. Bring to the boil and boil vigorously until setting point is reached. Heat the jam jars.
5. Leave for 15 minutes until the peel has settled. Stir the marmalade and discard the pips.
6. Fill the hot sterilized pots and seal. Leave for 24 hours. Label and store in a cool, dry place.

Redcurrant Jelly

redcurrants
450g/1lb preserving sugar to each 570ml/1 pint of juice extracted

1. Place the washed fruit in a stone or earthenware pot, cover and place in a moderate oven at 180°C/350°F/gas mark 4. If the jar or pot used is glass rather than pottery, stand it in a bain-marie before placing in the oven. Cook until the fruit is tender and the juice has run from it (about 1 hour). Mash the fruit with a fork 3 or 4 times during the cooking process.
2. Alternatively, cook the fruit until soft in a microwave oven, or in a saucepan with a little water, stirring frequently.
3. Turn into a scalded muslin or jelly bag and allow to drain overnight.
4. Measure the juice and pour into a preserving pan, and add 450g/1lb sugar to each 570ml/1 pint of juice.
5. Dissolve over a gentle heat and then boil rapidly until setting point is reached (about 5 minutes).
6. Pour into warm dry jars.
7. Cover with jam covers and leave for 24 hours.
8. Label and store in a cool, dark, dry place.

Hedgerow Jelly

Pick rosehips, haws (hawthorn berries), blackberries, crab apples, sloes, wild bullaces or plums, rowanberries and elderberries in any proportions you like, making sure, however, that there is a good proportion of high-pectin fruit among them.

If the rosehips are very hard, simmer them in water until soft, then add everything else, roughly cut up if large (eg. crab apples) but not peeled or pitted. Add enough water to cover three-quarters of the fruit. Simmer slowly, stirring occasionally, until mushy.

Drip overnight through a jelly bag or several layers of cloth, without stirring. Measure the juice and return to a clean pan, with 450g/1lb of granulated or preserving sugar for every 570ml/1pint of juice. Boil to 105°C/220°F for a set. Cover while hot if using screw-top jars; while cold if using paper or wax covers.

Apple and Sage Jelly

MAKES 1.8kg/4lb
2kg/4½lb cooking apples
1.1 litre/2 pints water
150ml/¼ pint cider vinegar
450g/1lb sugar to each 570ml/1 pint juice
55g/2oz sage leaves, finely chopped

1. Wash the apples and cut them into thick pieces without peeling or coring.
2. Put the apples and water into a saucepan, bring up to the boil, cover and simmer for about 1 hour. Add the vinegar and boil for a further 5 minutes.
3. Meanwhile scald a jelly bag twice with boiling water.
4. Hang the jelly bag from the legs of an upturned stool and place a bowl underneath it.
5. Pour the apple pulp and juice into the jelly bag and allow to drip steadily for about 1 hour or until the bag has stopped dripping. Do not squeeze the bag.
6. Measure the juice and pour into the preserving pan. Add 450g/1lb sugar to every 570ml/1 pint of juice. Put the jam jars to warm.
7. Bring up to the boil gradually, ensuring that the sugar has dissolved before the juice has boiled, and stirring constantly.
8. Boil briskly, uncovered, for about 10 minutes, and skim frequently. Test for setting point. When this has been reached, allow the jelly to cool slightly and stir in the sage.
9. Pour into the warm jam jars and cover.

Lemon Curd

MAKES 450g/1lb
2 large lemons
85g/3oz butter
225g/8oz granulated sugar
3 eggs

1. Grate the rind of the lemons on the finest gauge on the grater, taking care to grate the rind only, not the pith.
2. Squeeze the juice from the lemons.
3. Put the rind, juice, butter, sugar and lightly beaten eggs into a heavy saucepan or double boiler and heat gently, stirring all the time until the mixture is thick.
4. Strain into jam jars and cover.

NOTE I: This curd will keep in the refrigerator for about 3 weeks.
NOTE II: If the curd is boiled, no great harm is done, as the acid and sugar prevent the eggs from scrambling.

Orange Curd

MAKES 450g/1lb
juice of 1 lemon
grated rind of 2 oranges
juice of 1 orange
85g/3oz butter
225g/8oz granulated sugar
3 eggs

1. Put the juice, rind, butter, sugar and lightly beaten eggs into a heavy saucepan or double boiler and heat gently, stirring all the time until the mixture is thick.
2. Strain into a bowl and allow to cool. Strain into jam jars and cover.

Damson Cheese

MAKES ABOUT 900g/2lb
1kg/2lb damsons
150ml/¼ pint water
450g/1lb granulated sugar to each 570ml/1 pint purée

1. Wash and remove the stalks of the damsons. Put them into a saucepan with the water. Cook slowly until the fruit is very soft.
2. Sieve the fruit and discard the stones.
3. Measure the pulp and use 450g/1lb granulated sugar for every 570ml/1 pint of purée.
4. Put the pulp and sugar together in a large pan. When the sugar has completely dissolved, bring the pan to the boil.
5. Boil steadily until you can make a clear track through the purée with a wooden spoon, showing the base of the pan. Keep stirring, otherwise the cheese will burn on the bottom of the pan.
6. Pour into warmed jars and cover with waxed discs and cellophane circles.

NOTE: Traditionally, this cheese is served as an accompaniment to lamb or game. It needs therefore to be put into a straight sided jar or bowl so that it can be turned out and sliced. However, it is delicious spread on bread.

Bottled Apples

340g/12oz preserving sugar
1.1 litre/2 pints water
12 apples

1. Prepare the sugar syrup: dissolve the sugar in the water over a gentle heat and, when completely dissolved, boil rapidly for 2-3 minutes.
2. Peel, core and slice the apples.
3. Pack tightly into 1kg/2lb jars.
4. Pour over the hot syrup.
5. Cover with the lids (not screwed tight if Kilner jars) and place in the hot-water bath. Cover with boiling water.
6. Boil steadily for 20 minutes.
7. Remove the jars and (if Kilner jars) seal firmly.
8. Leave for 24 hours, then test for sealing.

Spiced Pears

560g/1lb 4oz preserving sugar
425ml/3/4 pint white malt vinegar or white wine vinegar
6 small whole pears, peeled
15g/1/2oz cinnamon stick
5 cloves
2 dried chillies (optional)
2 pieces stem ginger, diced

1. Heat the sugar with the vinegar over gentle heat and, when completely dissolved, bring to the boil.
2. Add the prepared pears, the spices and the ginger.
3. Simmer gently until the pears are tender but not broken (about 35 minutes).
4. Remove the pears with a draining spoon and pack into a preserving jar.
5. If the syrup is rather thin, boil it rapidly until fairly thick and tacky.
6. Pour over the pears, and add the spices and ginger.
7. Put on the lid (if using a Kilner jar do not tighten). Process in a boiling water bath for 10 minutes.
8. Lift out and (if using a Kilner jar) tighten the lid.
9. Leave for 24 hours, then test for sealing.

Bottled Raspberries

900g/2lb raspberries
340g/12oz granulated sugar

1. Pick over the fruit but do not wash it.
2. Pack into 1kg/2lb jars, sprinkling with dry sugar between the layers. Shake the jars to settle the fruit. Leave overnight.
3. Top up to absolutely full with more fruit and sugar.
4. Cover with the lids (not screwed too tightly if Kilner jars). Process in a boiling water bath for 10 minutes.
5. Lift out of the water and tighten the lids if using Kilner jars.
6. Leave for 24 hours, then test for sealing.

Pickling Vinegar

1.1 litre/2 pints malt vinegar
8g/¼oz blades of mace
8g/¼oz cinnamon stick
8g/¼oz allspice berries
8g/¼oz black peppercorns
8g/¼oz mustard seeds
4 whole cloves
1 chilli
15g/½oz sliced root ginger

1. Put everything into a large saucepan (not an unlined copper or brass or iron one) and heat gently, covered tightly, until on the point of simmering. Remove from the heat.
2. Leave for 3 hours, then strain through muslin or a jelly bag. The vinegar is now ready for use.

Pickled Shallots or Small Onions

An example of a raw pickle, salted in brine.

small, even-sized onions, or shallots
brine (see page 598)
pickling vinegar (see above)

1. Scald the onions to make peeling them easier. Peel them. Prick deeply all over with a needle or skewer.
2. Put the onions or shallots in a bowl and cover with brine. Leave for 48 hours.
3. Drain thoroughly and pat dry with a clean cloth.
4. Pack tightly, but without bruising, into clean jars.
5. Cover well with the cold pickling vinegar.
6. Seal and store for 6 months before eating.

Pickled Beetroot

An example of a cooked pickle not given preliminary salting.

small, even-sized beetroots
pure salt
pickling vinegar (see above)

1. Cook the beetroots, unpeeled, in boiling, heavily salted water (1 tablespoon to 1.1 litres/2 pints) until tender (1-2 hours).
2. Drain and allow to cool. Skin them.
3. Pack, without bruising, into jars.
4. Cover well with cold pickling vinegar.
5. Add 5ml/1 level teaspoon pure salt to each 1kg/2lb jar.
6. Seal and store.

NOTE: If a milder pickle is wanted, the vinegar may be diluted by an equal amount of water. But if this is done the beetroot must be packed in a preserving (Kilner or Parfait) jar, and must be given a sterilization treatment in a boiling water bath for 30 minutes, or in a pressure cooker or canner for 2 minutes.

Dill Cucumber Pickle

An example of a pickle dry-salted and packed in sweet spiced vinegar.

MAKES 900g/2lb
900g/2lb cucumbers
pure salt
pickling vinegar (see above)
1 fresh dill head, or 15ml/1 tablespoon dill seeds
10ml/2 teaspoons mustard seeds
2 garlic cloves, sliced
170g/6oz granulated or preserving sugar

1. If the cucumbers are small enough to leave whole, prick them all over with a needle. If large, cut them into chunks, without peeling. Put into a bowl, sprinkling each layer liberally with salt. Leave for 24 hours.
2. Put the spiced vinegar (about 1 litre/1¾ pints) into a saucepan and add the dill, mustard seed, garlic and sugar. Bring slowly to the boil, then cool.

3. Rinse the cucumber well and pat dry with a clean cloth.
4. Pack the cucumber into jars. Cover with the cooled vinegar, adding the flavourings.
5. Seal and store.

Green Tomato and Apple Chutney

MAKES 2.25kg/5lb
1.35 kg/3lb green tomatoes
900g/2lb apples (any kind)
2 large onions, chopped
110g/4oz sultanas
5ml/1 teaspoon salt
5ml/1 teaspoon ground ginger
2.5ml/1/2 teaspoon ground nutmeg
2.5ml/1/2 teaspoon white pepper
pinch of allspice
860ml/1 1/2 pints vinegar
340g/12oz granulated or preserving sugar

1. Chop the tomatoes. Peel, core and chop the apples.
2. Put everything except the sugar and a cupful of vinegar into a saucepan and simmer gently, giving an occasional stir, for 1 1/2 hours or until the ingredients are soft and the liquid almost gone.
3. Add the rest of the vinegar and the sugar, and stir slowly until the sugar has dissolved.
4. Boil fast, stirring, until thick.
5. Pour into hot dry jars. If it is to be eaten within 6 months, cover as for jam. If it is to be kept longer, use non-metal lids or stoppers.

Apricot and Orange Chutney

MAKES 675g/1 1/2lb
4 oranges
450g/1lb dried apricots (soaked overnight)
1 onion, thinly sliced
225g/8oz sultanas
400g/14oz demerara sugar
10ml/2 teaspoons rock salt
570ml/1 pint cider vinegar
15ml/1 tablespoon mustard seeds
5ml/1 teaspoon turmeric

1. Boil the oranges whole for 5 minutes. Pare the skin with a sharp knife, removing all pith left on the back.
2. Shred the rind into thin needleshreds.
3. Peel the oranges and discard all the pith. Chop up the flesh.
4. Place the orange rind and flesh together with all the other ingredients, except for 150ml/1/4 pint vinegar, in a large pan and simmer until the fruit is soft and pulpy and the mixture very thick. Add the remaining vinegar. Boil briefly.
5. Pour immediately into warm, dry jars and cover with jam covers if to be eaten within a few months, or more securely with non-metal lids or stoppers if to be kept longer.

Spiced Fruit Pickle

MAKES 1.3kg/3lbs
900g/2lb mixed fresh fruit, e.g. plums, apricots, peaches, rhubarb
455g/1lb sugar
425ml/3/4 pint cider vinegar
grated rind and juice of 1 orange
5ml/1 teaspoon ground ginger
20ml//4 teaspoons mustard seeds
6 cloves
1 cinnamon stick

1. Prepare the fruit by removing the stones and cutting into 1cm/1/2 inch pieces – leave the skins on.
2. Dissolve the sugar in the vinegar, add the orange rind and juice, ginger, mustard seed, cloves and cinnamon stick.
3. Add the fruit and bring to the boil. Simmer carefully for 15 minutes.
4. Strain the fruit and reduce the liquid by boiling until it is syrupy. Mix it with the fruit.
5. Pour the pickle into clean, sterilized jam jars and seal with jam seals.

NOTE: This can be used straight away but is better if left to mature for at least a month. Store in a cool, dark place.

Hot Piccalilli

MAKES 2.7kg/6lbs
450g/1lb salt
4.6 litres/8 pints boiling water
675g/1½lb cauliflower, broken into small florets
450g/1lb cucumber, diced with the skin left on
675g/1½lb pickling onions, skinned
450g/1lb green beans, topped and tailed and cut in 2.5cm/1 inch lengths
450g/1lb marrow, diced
45g/1½oz dry English mustard
15g/½oz turmeric
45g/1½oz ground ginger
1½ level tablespoons flour
170g/6oz caster sugar
1.1 litres/2 pints distilled vinegar

1. Mix together the salt and boiling water. Leave to cool.
2. Prepare the vegetables and cover with the brine (salt and water). Leave for 24 hours.
3. Drain and rinse the vegetables.
4. Mix the mustard, turmeric, ginger, flour and sugar together and mix to a smooth liquid with 570ml/1 pint vinegar.
5. Pour the other 570ml/1 pint vinegar into a large saucepan. Add the prepared vegetables, and simmer until tender but still crisp. Stir in the spiced flour mixture. Cook, stirring continuously, until the pickles come to the boil and the sauce thickens. Simmer for 3 minutes.
6. Pack into jars and cover when cold.

Breakfasts

Poached Eggs on Toast

SERVES 4
4 very fresh cold eggs
4 slices fresh toast, buttered
salt and pepper

1. Fill a large saucepan with water and bring to simmering point.
2. Crack an egg into a cup and tip into the pan, holding the cup as near to the water as possible.
3. Raise the temperature so that the water bubbles gently.
4. With a perforated spoon, draw the egg white close to the yolk.
5. Poach each egg for 2 or 3 minutes.
6. Lift out with the perforated spoon, drain on absorbent paper and, if the egg whites are very ragged at the edges, trim them.
7. Place each egg on a piece of toast and sprinkle with salt and pepper. Serve immediately.

Jugged Kippers

SERVES 4
4 kippers
butter
freshly ground black pepper

1. Place the kippers, tail up, in a tall stoneware jug. Pour over enough boiling water to cover the kippers and leave to stand for 5-10 minutes.
2. Serve immediately on a warm dish with a knob of butter and plenty of pepper.

NOTE: This is a simple labour-saving method of cooking kippers.

Kedgeree

SERVES 4
55g/2oz butter
140g/5oz long-grain rice, boiled (weighed before cooking)
340g/12oz smoked haddock fillet, cooked, skinned and boned, or cooked fresh salmon if preferred
3 hardboiled eggs, coarsely chopped
salt, pepper and cayenne

1. Melt the butter in a large shallow pan and add all the other ingredients.
2. Stir gently until very hot.

NOTE: If making large quantities, heat in the oven instead of on the top of the stove. Kedgeree will not spoil in a low oven (130°C/250°F/gas mark 1). Stir occasionally to prevent the sides getting hot before the middle and to distribute the heat evenly.

Muesli

Named after Bircher Muesli, a Swiss doctor and health fanatic, this should contain nothing but natural ingredients, and no refined cereals. It usually consists of flaked oats, crushed or flaked wheat (including the bran and wheatgerm) and can include other cereals too.

To make a family supply of Muesli mix together:
450g/1lb instant porridge oats
55g/2oz dried apricots, chopped
55g/2oz sultanas
110g/4oz dried apple flakes
55g/2oz hazelnuts, chopped
55g/2oz bran
30g/1oz flaked almonds
110g/4oz 'honey crunch' or 'granola' or other toasted cereal (optional, but improves the texture)
30g/1oz unrefined brown sugar

Porridge

SERVES 4
1.1 litre/2 pints water
5ml/1 good teaspoon salt
110g/4oz medium oatmeal

1. Boil the water in a saucepan and add the salt.
2. Sprinkle in the oatmeal, keeping the water on the boil and stirring all the time.
3. Simmer for 30 minutes, stirring occasionally. If necessary add a little more water.

NOTE: Porridge keeps for an hour or so in a cool oven if covered with a lid, but should not be made too far in advance. Traditionally it is served with salt in Scotland, but in the south milk and sugar are added.

Canapés, Savouries and Snacks

Smoked Salmon Catherine Wheels

MAKES ABOUT 80
1 very large square-edged loaf of brown bread
butter, well softened
450g/1lb thinly sliced smoked salmon
freshly ground black pepper
lemon juice

1. Put the loaf of bread on a board and carefully cut off the top crust all along the length of the loaf.
2. Butter the top of the bread, being careful not to crumble it.
3. Now cut as thin a horizontal slice as you can.
4. Again butter the loaf and cut off the next slice and so on through the loaf. You should end up with about 10 or 12 long slices.
5. Cut off the crusts and lay smoked salmon on all the slices. Sprinkle with black pepper and lemon juice.
6. Now, starting at one end, roll them up carefully.
7. Cut each roll into about 8 thin rounds.

NOTE I: Unravelling can be prevented if the rolls are wrapped in cling film and refrigerated for a few hours before slicing.
NOTE II: For larger rolls or 'Catherine wheels', 2 slices of bread may be used: roll up one, then roll the next round the first roll.

Smoked Salmon Triangles

MAKES 40 SMALL TRIANGLES
5 slices brown bread
butter for spreading
freshly ground black pepper
110g/4oz smoked salmon
lemon juice

1. Butter the bread, sprinkle with black pepper and lay the smoked salmon slices carefully on top.
2. Sprinkle with lemon juice, then cut off the crusts and cut each slice into 8 triangles.

Smoked Salmon on Rye with Horseradish

MAKES 50
12-14 slices rye bread
225g/8oz cream cheese
creamed horseradish
salt and pepper
225g/8oz smoked salmon
sprigs of fresh dill

1. Remove the crusts from the bread. Cut out 4 even-sized rectangles approximately 3 x 4cm / $1^1/_4$ x $1^1/_2$ inches.
2. Season the cream cheese with the horseradish, salt and pepper. Spread it on to the bread rectangles, mounding it neatly.
3. Cut the smoked salmon into long thin strips and coil it neatly on top of the cream cheese mixture.
4. Decorate each rectangle with a sprig of dill.

Smoked Oyster Tartlets

MAKES 20
1 carrot
1 leek, white part only
20 smoked oysters
20 boat or oblong tartlet cases, warmed
55g/2oz beurre blanc (see page 227)

1. Cut the carrots and leeks into very fine julienne strips. Place in a steamer, season and cook until tender.
2. Reheat the smoked oysters in their own juice. Drain well.
3. Place a little of the cooked vegetables in the base of each tartlet case, cover with a smoked oyster and coat with the beurre blanc. Serve immediately.

Peking Duck Coronets

MAKES 20
1 duck leg
Hoisin sauce
10 wonton skins
1 egg white, lightly beaten
1/2 cucumber
4 spring onions

1. Heat the oven to 200°C/400°F/gas mark 6.
2. Brush the duck leg with Hoisin sauce and bake for 40 minutes.
3. Cut the wonton skins in half. Shape into cones and brush with egg white.
4. Heat a pan of deep oil until a crumb will sizzle vigorously in it and deep-fry the wonton cornets for 1 minute. Drain well on absorbent paper. When required, they can be reheated in the oven.
5. Cut the cucumber and spring onions into very fine julienne strips.
6. Shred the duck finely.
7. Pipe or spoon a little Hoisin sauce into the base of each warm cornet. Stuff with the duck and julienne of vegetables. Serve immediately.

Spinach Roulade with Smoked Salmon and Soured Cream

MAKES 36 SLICES
450g/1lb fresh spinach or 170g/6oz frozen leaf spinach
7g/1/4oz butter
2 eggs, separated
salt and pepper
pinch of nutmeg

For the filling:
150ml/1/4 pint soured cream
110g/4oz smoked salmon, chopped
5ml/1 teaspoon chopped fresh dill

1. Set the oven to 190°C/375°F/gas mark 5.
2. Prepare a Swiss roll tin, 19 x 26cm/7 1/2 x 10 1/2inches, using silicone paper.
3. Cook the spinach and drain it thoroughly. Push through a sieve and beat in the butter.
4. Gradually beat the egg yolks into the spinach and season with salt, pepper and nutmeg. Whisk the egg whites until stiff but not dry, and fold them into the spinach. Pour this mixture into the prepared paper case and spread it flat. Bake for 10-12 minutes or until it feels dry to the touch.
5. Mix the filling ingredients together.
6. Turn the roulade out on to a piece of greaseproof paper and remove the original silicone paper.
7. Cut the roulade into 2 pieces, so that you have 2 oblongs. Spread each oblong with the filling and, starting with the longer edge, roll up each one as you would a Swiss roll. Wrap in damp greaseproof paper and return to the oven for 5 minutes. Allow to cool.
8. Remove from the greaseproof paper and slice each roll into about 18 pieces.

Smoked Salmon and Dill Parcels

2 large smoked trout
150ml/1/4 pint double cream, lightly whipped
squeeze of lemon juice
1/2 teaspoon horseradish cream
freshly ground black pepper
8 slices smoked salmon
sprigs of fresh dill

1. Cut off the heads and tails of the trout. Skin them and remove the bones. Mince or pound the flesh and mix with the whipped cream, lemon juice, horseradish and pepper to taste. It should be a firm pâté.
2. Cut the smoked salmon into squares 6cm/2 1/2 inches. Trim off the corners. Place a teaspoon of the pâté on to the centre of the smoked salmon and fold the ends together. Turn them over and place a small sprig of dill on each one.

Nori Seaweed Canapés

140g/5oz short-grain rice
200ml/7 fl oz water
pinch of salt
2 sheets Nori seaweed

For the mushroom filling:
8 dry mushrooms
37.5ml/2½ tablespoons caster sugar
pinch of salt
30ml/2 tablespoons vodka
7.5ml/½ tablespoon soy sauce

For the carrot filling:
1 carrot, finely diced
15ml/1 tablespoon oil
2 spring onions, finely sliced
1 small piece root ginger, finely chopped
30ml/2 tablespoons dry sherry
15ml/1 tablespoon sugar
7.5ml/½ tablespoon soy sauce

For the vinegar dressing:
22.5ml/1½ tablespoons rice wine or white wine vinegar
15ml/1 tablespoon caster sugar
2.5ml/½ teaspoon salt

1. Make the mushroom filling: soak the mushrooms in enough water to cover them for 30 minutes and add the remaining ingredients and simmer for 10 minutes or until the liquid has evaporated. Set aside.
2. Make the carrot filling: cook the carrots very slowly in the oil and, when just softened, add the spring onions and cook for 1 minute, then add the sherry, sugar and soy sauce and cook for a further 3 minutes or until glazed. Set aside.
3. Mix the ingredients together for the vinegar dressing and set aside.
4. Rinse the rice under cold running water until the water runs clear. Put the rice into a saucepan and add 200ml/7 fl oz cold water. Leave to stand for 30 minutes. Bring to the boil and cook for 5 minutes or until the water is absorbed. Turn off the heat and, leaving the lid on, leave the rice to sit for 15 minutes to dry out slightly.
5. Tip the rice into a large bowl, pour over the vinegar dressing and stir until cold, by which time the rice should be shiny.
6. Place the seaweed on a tea towel. Arrange strips of the fillings lengthways on top of the seaweed as illustrated. Leave a gap of 2.5cm/1 inch at the end.
7. Using the tea towel to help, carefully roll up the seaweed as you would a roulade (from the carrot edge). Press firmly and cut into 1cm/½ inch slices.

Stuffed Dates

MAKES 60
110g/4oz nibbed almonds
60 fresh dates (about 2 boxes)
340g/12oz cream cheese

1. Brown the almonds under the grill or in a hot oven and allow to cool.
2. Cut the dates open lengthways. Replace each stone with 5ml/1 teaspoon cream cheese.
3. Slightly close the dates, leaving the cream cheese showing. Dip the cheese into the nuts.

Celery and Cream Cheese

MAKES ABOUT 50
10 celery sticks
340g/12oz cream cheese
chives, finely chopped
salt and pepper

1. Wash and scrub the celery, and cut into 5cm/2 inch lengths. If the sticks are very wide, they should be split in two.
2. Cream the cheese and add the chives and seasoning.
3. Using a forcing bag fitted with a fluted nozzle, pipe the cheese into the hollow of the celery sticks. It may be necessary to trim the underside of each celery stick to prevent it rolling over when put on a plate.

Cocktail Sausages with Mustard Dip

MAKES 120
60 chipolata or 120 cocktail sausages (450g/1lb)

For the dip:
mustard mayonnaise

1. Set the oven to 200°C/400°F, gas mark 6.
2. Make the chipolata sausages into cocktail size by twisting each sausage into two. After twisting, cut them apart.
3. Put them in a greased roasting pan and bake for 20 minutes or until beginning to brown. The roasting pan should be shaken at intervals to prevent the sausages sticking. They should be stirred around to prevent those on the edges getting browner than those in the middle.
4. Drain well and pierce each with a cocktail stick. Serve the dip separately.

Anchovy Puff Pastry Fingers

MAKES 40
rough puff pastry made with 225g/8oz flour (see page 527)
40 anchovy fillets (about 1 tin)
90ml/6 tablespoons milk
beaten egg

1. Divide the pastry into two and roll each piece thinly to a rectangle 30 x 10cm/12 x 4 inches. Slide on to 2 baking sheets and put in the refrigerator to relax.
2. Soak the anchovies in milk for 15 minutes to remove any oil and excess salt. Drain and trim the fillets neatly.
3. Heat the oven to 200°C/400°F/gas mark 6.
4. Brush one piece of pastry with beaten egg, prick with a fork and place the anchovy fillets neatly on it. You should be able to lay out 2 neat rows of 20 fillets in each row.
5. Cover with the second piece of pastry and brush again with egg wash. Press well together and prick all over with a fork.
6. Bake in the oven for 10-12 minutes until golden brown. Leave to cool on a wire rack.
7. When cold, cut the pastry into neat fingers of 5 x 1cm/2 x 1/2 inch in such a way that each finger has an anchovy fillet sandwiched inside it
8. Warm through before serving.

Twisted Cheese Straws

MAKES 50
170g/6oz plain flour
pinch of salt
100g/3 1/2 oz butter
45g/1 1/2oz grated Parmesan or mixed Parmesan and Gruyère or Cheddar cheese
pinch of pepper
pinch of cayenne pepper
pinch of dry English mustard
beaten egg

1. Set the oven to 190°C/375°F/gas mark 5.
2. Sift the flour into a basin with a pinch of salt. Rub the butter into the flour with your fingertips until the mixture resembles fine breadcrumbs. Add the grated cheese and seasonings.
3. Bind the mixture together with enough egg to make a stiff dough. Refrigerate for 10 minutes.
4. Line a baking sheet with greaseproof paper. Roll the paste into a rectangle and cut into strips 9 x 2cm/3 1/2 x 3/4 inch. Twist each strip 2-3 times like a barley sugar stick. Bake for 8-10 minutes. They should be a biscuit brown.

Poppy and Sesame Seed Straws

110g/4oz puff pastry
1 beaten egg
30ml/2 tablespoons poppy seeds
30ml/2 tablespoons sesame seeds

1. Set the oven to 200°C/400°F/gas mark 6.
2. Roll out the pastry quite thinly, brush with beaten egg and cut in half.
3. Sprinkle one half with poppy seeds and the other half with sesame seeds.
4. Roll each piece of pastry out very thinly. Cut

into long strips and twist like barley sugar strips.
5. Bake in the oven for 10-12 minutes until a golden brown.

Cheese Sablés

MAKES 24
225g/8oz plain flour
salt and freshly ground black pepper
225g/8oz butter
225g/8oz Gruyère or strong Cheddar cheese, grated
pinch of dry mustard
pinch of cayenne pepper
beaten egg

1. Set the oven to 190°C/375°F/gas mark 5. Line 2 baking sheets with greaseproof paper. This will prevent the sablés burning at the edges.
2. Sift the flour with a pinch of salt into a bowl. Rub in the butter until the mixture resembles breadcrumbs.
3. Add the cheese, salt, pepper, mustard and cayenne. Work into a paste but do not over-handle or the pastry will become greasy and be tough.
4. Roll out on a floured board until 0.5cm/ 1/4 inch thick. Cut into rounds or triangles and brush with beaten egg.
5. Bake until golden brown (about 10 minutes). Leave to cool on a wire rack.

Stilton Grapes

110g/4oz Stilton cheese
110g/4oz cream cheese
110g/4oz seedless grapes
110g/4oz walnuts, finely chopped

Beat the cheeses together. Wrap a little of the mixture around each grape and roll in the nuts.

Warmed Mediterranean Prawns with Dipping Sauce

20 large Mediterranean prawns
sesame oil

For the marinade:
45ml/3 tablespoons soy sauce
15ml/1 tablespoon sesame oil
30ml/2 tablespoons sherry
1cm/1/2 inch piece fresh ginger, peeled and finely chopped
1 garlic clove, cut into slivers

For the dipping sauce:
15ml/1 tablespoon sesame oil
30ml/2 tablespoons soy sauce
15ml/1 tablespoon runny honey
45-60ml/3-4 tablespoons ginger syrup (from a jar of preserved ginger)
15ml/1 tablespoon red wine vinegar
4 spring onions, chopped

1. Shell the prawns and remove the black vein down the back of each prawn.
2. Mix together the marinade ingredients and add the prawns. Leave for 3-4 hours.
3. Make the dipping sauce: mix all the ingredients together except for the spring onions.
4. Fry the prawns fairly briskly in the sesame oil. They are cooked when they turn pink and begin to butterfly out.
5. Tip the prawns on to a platter. Put the dipping sauce in a bowl, add the spring onions and serve immediately.

NOTE: Serve cocktail sticks with the prawns.

Dill Pancakes with Smoked Trout Mousse

MAKES 16
150ml/1/4 pint pancake batter (see page 533)
15ml/1 tablespoon chopped dill
fresh dill to decorate

For the smoked trout mousse:
1 smoked trout
75ml/2½fl oz double cream, lightly whipped
squeeze of lemon juice
2.5ml/½ teaspoon horseradish cream
freshly ground black pepper

1. Mix the chopped dill with the pancake batter.
2. Make the pancakes as usual (see page 533), then stamp out into rounds using a small fluted cutter.
3. Make up the mousse: remove the skin and bones from the trout. Mince or pound the flesh and mix with the whipped cream, lemon juice, horseradish and pepper to taste.
4. Place a teaspoon of the mousse on to each pancake and pinch the edges together to form a cone.
5. Decorate each pancake with a sprig of dill.

Gravad Lax on Rye

MAKES 24
1 packet rye bread
mustard and dill mayonnaise
lollo rosso lettuce
55g/2oz gravad lax

1. Stamp out rounds of rye bread, using a small round cutter.
2. Spread a little mustard mayonnaise on to each round.
3. Place a little lollo rosso on top, spread with a little more mustard mayonnaise and arrange a piece of gravad lax on top.

Tiny Stuffed New Potatoes

MAKES 20
20 even-sized tiny new potatoes
French dressing (see page 228)
75ml/2½fl oz soured cream
black lumpfish roe
¼ red pepper, cut into tiny dice
small bunch chives, snipped

1. Peel or scrub the potatoes and cook in gently simmering salted water until tender – about 20 minutes. Drain and, while still warm, soak in the French dressing until cool.
2. Lift the potatoes out of the dressing and pat dry with absorbent paper. Cut a thin slice from the bottom of each potato so that they can stand upright.
3. With a melon baller carefully scoop a hollow out of the top of each potato. Pipe or spoon a little soured cream into each hollow.
4. Top one-third of the potatoes with the lumpfish roe, one-third with red pepper and the remaining potatoes with the chives.

Toasties Cases

MAKES 20
5 thin slices bread
butter for spreading

1. Set the oven to 180°C/350°F/gas mark 4. Stamp out rounds of bread using a small fluted cutter.
2. Spread them with butter and mould into tiny patty tins. Press an empty patty tin on top and bake in the oven until golden brown and crisp.

Toasties with Salmon Roe

MAKES 20
20 toastie cases (see above)
75ml/2½fl oz soured cream
1 small jar salmon roe

1. Fill the toasties with soured cream and top with a little salmon roe.

NOTE: These must be filled at the last minute as they go soggy very quickly.

Toasties with Tuna Pâté

MAKES 20
20 toastie cases (see page 617)
110g/4oz cream cheese
110g/4oz tuna fish
lemon juice
freshly ground black pepper
chervil or dill to decorate

1. Purée the cream cheese and tuna fish together until very smooth. Season to taste with lemon juice and black pepper.
2. Pipe into the toastie cases and decorate each with a sprig of chervil or dill.

NOTE: These must be filled at the last minute as they go soggy very quickly.

Mascarpone Tartlets with Salmon Roe

225g/8oz Mascarpone cream cheese
30 tartlet cases
1 small jar salmon roe
fresh dill

1. Beat the Mascarpone cheese lightly and use to fill a piping bag fitted with a fluted nozzle.
2. Pipe the cheese into the tartlet cases and top with a little salmon roe.
3. Garnish each tartlet with a small piece of dill.

Cherry Tomatoes with Cream Cheese and Mint

MAKES 20
20 cherry tomatoes
110g/4oz cream cheese
7.5ml/½ tablespoon chopped fresh mint
squeeze of lemon juice
salt and freshly ground black pepper

1. Slice a quarter of each tomato off at the rounded end. Scoop out the flesh and reserve.
2. Mix a little of the flesh with the cream cheese, mint, lemon, salt and pepper. Cut a very thin slice from the bottom of each tomato so that they can stand upright. Fill the tomatoes with the cream cheese mixture and stick the tops back at a jaunty angle.

Drop Scones with Caviar

MAKES 20
150ml/¼ pint drop scone batter (see page 534)
75ml/2½ fl oz soured cream
1 small jar black lumpfish roe

1. Make up small drop scones 3cm/1¼ inches in diameter. Spread each drop scone with a little soured cream and top with lumpfish roe.

Stuffed Mange Tout

MAKES 20
20 mange tout
110g/4oz cream cheese
a little milk
15ml/1 tablespoon finely chopped chives and parsley
salt and freshly ground black pepper

1. Blanch and refresh the mange tout, then top and tail and split them open. Soften the cream cheese with a little milk, add the herbs and season to taste. Fill the mange tout with the cheese mixture using a small piping nozzle and forcing bag.

Salami Wedges

MAKES 24
170g/6oz cream cheese
4 spring onions, chopped
4 gherkins, chopped
15ml/1 tablespoon finely chopped parsley
salt and freshly ground black pepper
15 slices round pepper salami

1. Mix the cream cheese with the spring onions, gherkins and herbs and season to taste.
2. Spread a little of the mixture evenly over a slice of salami. Place another slice of salami on top, then spread with some more cream cheese mixture.
3. Continue to layer up the cream cheese and salami until you have used 5 slices of salami. The quantity will make 3 'cakes'.
4. Wrap in cling film and chill.
5. Cut each cake into 8 wedges.

Tabouleh in Cucumber with Greek Yoghurt

1 large cucumber
75ml/2½ fl oz Greek yoghurt
½ quantity tabouleh recipe (see page 119)

1. Cut the cucumber into 1cm/½ inch slices. Stamp with a fluted cutter and, using a teaspoon or melon baller, make a hollow in the centre of each round.
2. Spoon or pipe a little Greek yoghurt into each cucumber cup and top with a mound of tabouleh.

Tartlets with Quail Eggs and Smoked Salmon

MAKES 20
75ml/2½ fl oz mayonnaise
20 tartlet cases
10 quail eggs, hardboiled
55g/2oz smoked salmon, cut into julienne strips
chervil or dill to decorate

1. Spoon or pipe a little mayonnaise into each pastry case.
2. Halve the quail eggs and place a half, yolk side showing, on top of the mayonnaise.
3. Place a little smoked salmon on the quail egg and decorate with a sprig of chervil or dill.

Tartlets with Smoked Salmon and Caviar

MAKES 20
75ml/2½ fl oz Greek yoghurt
20 tartlet cases
85g/3oz smoked salmon, cut into julienne strips
½ small jar black lumpfish roe

1. Spoon or pipe a little Greek yoghurt into each pastry case.
2. Fill the pastry case with the smoked salmon and top with a little black lumpfish roe.

Cherry Tomato, Avocado and Mozzarella Kebabs

MAKES 20
20 cherry tomatoes
1 avocado, cut into cubes
1 packet mozzarella cheese, cut into cubes
8 basil leaves, shredded
45ml/3 tablespoons French dressing (see page 228)

1. Using 20 bamboo sticks, thread a cherry tomato, a cube of avocado and a cube of mozzarella on to each stick.
2. Mix the basil with the French dressing and spoon a little over the avocado and mozzarella.

Mini Hamburgers

MAKES 40

For the buns:
30g/1oz fresh yeast
15ml/1 tablespoon sugar
150ml/1/4 pint lukewarm milk
225g/8oz plain flour
5ml/1 teaspoon salt
55g/2oz butter, melted
beaten egg
sesame seeds

For the hamburgers:
450g/1lb mince
15ml/1 tablespoon finely chopped parsley
5ml/1 teaspoon Worcestershire sauce
seasoning
oil for frying

For the garnish:
lollo rosso lettuce
tomato chutney

1. Set the oven to 200°C/400°F/ gas mark 6.
2. Make the buns: cream the yeast with the sugar. Stir in the milk. Sift the flour and salt into a large bowl. Pour in the yeast mixture and melted butter. Knead well and leave to rise.
3. Shape the dough into 40 small buns. Leave to prove, brush with beaten egg and sprinkle with sesame seeds. Bake in the oven until firm and golden.
4. Make the hamburgers: mix all the ingredients together and beat lightly. With wet hands, shape the meat into flattish rounds. Fry the hamburgers until brown on both sides. Keep warm.
5. Assemble the hamburgers: split the buns in half. Arrange a little lollo rosso lettuce and tomato chutney on each base, place a hamburger on top and finish off with the top of the bun.

Mini Yorkshire Puddings with Rare Roast Beef

MAKES 30

dripping or oil
290ml/1/2 pint Yorkshire pudding batter
170g/6oz fillet or sirloin steak
horseradish cream
watercress

1. Set the oven to 220°C/425°F/gas mark 7.
2. Heat the dripping or oil in small patty tins.
3. Pour in the batter and bake until risen and golden.
4. Meanwhile, grill or fry the steak and cut into thin slices.
5. Spoon or pipe a little horseradish cream into each Yorkshire pudding. Arrange a slice of beef on top and garnish with a tiny sprig of watercress.

Mini Baked Potatoes with Cheese and Bacon

MAKES 20

20 small new potatoes
55g/2oz streaky bacon, grilled and diced
55g/2oz Cheddar cheese, grated
a little melted butter
salt and freshly ground black pepper

1. Set the oven to 200°C/400°F/gas mark 6.
2. Scrub the potatoes and bake for about 45 minutes or until cooked.
3. Cut a slice from the top of each potato. Scoop out the centre and mix with the remaining ingredients.
4. Pile the filling back into the potatoes.
5. Heat through in the oven for about 8 minutes.

Mushrooms Stuffed with Spinach, Bacon and Garlic

MAKES 20
20 even-sized mushrooms
55g/2oz butter
225g/8oz spinach, washed, de-stalked, cooked and finely chopped
55g/2oz streaky bacon, grilled and cut into tiny dice
2 garlic cloves, crushed
salt and pepper
flour
1 egg, beaten
dry white breadcrumbs
oil for deep-frying

1. Wipe the mushrooms and remove the stalks.
2. Melt the butter, add the spinach, bacon, garlic and seasoning.
3. Pile the stuffing into the mushrooms.
4. Dip the mushrooms first into the flour, then into the beaten egg and lastly into the breadcrumbs.
5. Heat the oil and fry the mushrooms until golden brown.
6. Drain on absorbent paper, sprinkle with salt and serve immediately.

Spinach and Ricotta Strudels

MAKES 20
225g/8oz frozen chopped spinach
110g/4oz butter
110g/4oz ricotta cheese
salt and freshly ground black pepper
good pinch of grated nutmeg
4 sheets filo pastry
1 egg, beaten

1. Set the oven to 200°C/400°F/gas mark 6.
2. Defrost the spinach. Melt 30g/1oz of the butter and add the spinach, ricotta and seasonings.
3. Melt the remaining butter and brush it over the sheets of filo pastry.
4. Cut each sheet of pastry into strips 5cm/2 inches wide.
5. Place a spoonful of filling at one end of each strip. Form a triangle by folding the right-hand corner to the opposite side, and fold over and then across from the left-hand corner to the right edge. Continue folding until the strip of pastry is used up.
6. Brush the strudels with beaten egg. Place on a greased baking sheet and bake for about 10 minutes or until golden brown.

Mini Cornish Pasties

MAKES 20
For the cheese pastry:
110g/4oz plain flour
55g/2oz butter
15g/½oz Parmesan cheese, grated
pinch of cayenne pepper
pinch of dry mustard
½ egg, beaten
cold water

For the filling:
225g/8oz minced beef
1 small onion, finely chopped
1 small potato, diced
1 small carrot, diced
5ml/1 teaspoon flour
stock to moisten
salt and freshly ground black pepper
few drops of Worcestershire sauce
1 egg, beaten

1. Make the pastry: sift the flour into a mixing bowl and rub in the butter. Add the Parmesan, cayenne and mustard. Bind to a firm dough with the beaten egg and a little water. Chill.
2. Make the filling: brown the mince and vegetables in a non-stick saucepan. Add the flour and cook gently for 1 minute. Add the stock and seasonings and cook until the vegetables are just soft. Cool.
3. Set the oven to 200°C/400°F/gas mark 6.
4. Roll out the pastry thinly, and stamp out 5cm/2 inch rounds with a pastry cutter.
5. Place a teaspoon of filling in the centre of each. Brush the edges of the pastry with beaten egg and fold over into tiny Cornish pasties. Brush the pastry with beaten egg and bake for 10-15 minutes until golden brown.

Tandoori Chicken with Cucumber and Yoghurt Dip

MAKES 12
225g/8oz boneless chicken meat
150ml/5 fl oz carton natural yoghurt
pinch each of chilli, cumin and coriander powder
5ml/1 teaspoon garam masala
5ml/1 teaspoon tomato purée
juice and grated rind of 1/2 lemon
1 garlic clove, crushed
5ml/1 teaspoon fresh ginger, peeled and chopped
salt and ground black pepper

For the cucumber and yoghurt dip:
1/4 cucumber
150ml/5 fl oz carton natural yoghurt
15ml/1 tablespoon double cream
15ml/1 tablespoon finely chopped mint
salt and ground black pepper

1. Cut the chicken into bite-sized chunks.
2. Place all the remaining ingredients together in a liquidizer or food processor and blend until smooth.
3. Lay the pieces of chicken in a shallow dish, pour over the marinade, cover and chill overnight.
4. The following day, just before serving, lift the chicken out of the marinade and place in a roasting pan. Preheat the grill or oven to the highest temperature. Cook the chicken for about 10 minutes or until reddish brown and tender. Spear with cocktail sticks and serve on a round dish surrounding the cucumber and yoghurt dip.
5. To make the cucumber and yoghurt dip: chop the cucumber finely and pat dry with absorbent paper to get rid of any excess moisture. Mix all the ingredients together and season with salt and ground black pepper.

Chicken Saté with Peanut Sambal

MAKES 60 COCKTAIL PIECES
5 chicken breasts, skinned

For the marinade:
1 medium onion, finely chopped
1 garlic clove, crushed
5ml/1 teaspoon ground coriander
5ml/1 teaspoon ground ginger
45ml/3 tablespoons dark soy sauce
juice of 1 small lemon
10ml/2 teaspoons dark brown sugar
ground black pepper

For the peanut sambal:
1 small onion, finely chopped
15ml/1 tablespoon oil
2.5ml/1/2 teaspoon chilli powder
110g/4oz crunchy peanut butter
30ml/2 tablespoons dark soy sauce
30ml/2 tablespoons lemon juice
200ml/7 fl oz cold water
dark brown sugar and salt to taste

1. For the sambal: cook the onion in the oil very slowly. Add the chilli powder and cook for 10 seconds.
2. Remove from the heat and add the peanut butter, soy sauce, lemon juice and water.
3. Return to the heat and stir until the sauce is thick and smooth. Season to taste with sugar and salt.
4. Cut each chicken breast into 12 cubes.
5. Mix together the ingredients for the marinade and add the chicken pieces. Leave to infuse for at least one hour. Heat the grill.
6. Skewer the chicken pieces on long wet bamboo sticks and grill for about 3 minutes each side.
7. Serve the peanut sambal as a dip.

NOTE: The bamboo sticks are wetted to prevent them from burning.

RIESLING

Chicken Livers Wrapped in Bacon

MAKES ABOUT 60
450g/1lb chicken livers
60 small slices streaky bacon

1. Set the oven to 220°C/425°F/gas mark 7.
2. Trim and discard the discoloured part from the livers.
3. Roll small pieces of liver in bacon and lay them side by side in a roasting pan, fairly tightly packed to prevent unravelling.
4. Bake for about 15 minutes or until they are just beginning to go brown on top. Drain well.
5. Stick a cocktail stick into each roll. They are now ready to serve, but if they are to be reheated, remove them from the roasting pan and keep in a cool place until needed. If the cocktail sticks are stuck in before reheating, make sure that they are wooden and not plastic.

Welsh Rarebit

SERVES 2
55g/2oz Gruyère cheese
55g/2oz Cheddar cheese
10ml/2 teaspoons French mustard
salt, pepper and cayenne
1 egg, beaten
15ml/1 tablespoon beer
2 slices bread
butter for spreading

1. Heat the grill.
2. Grate the cheese and mix all but one level tablespoon with the mustard, seasoning, beaten egg and beer.
3. Toast the bread and spread with butter.
4. Spoon the cheese mixture on to the toast and spread it neatly, making sure that all the edges are covered.
5. Sprinkle over the remaining cheese and grill until nicely browned.

LIGHT RED

Roquefort Toasts

MAKES 16
2 slices steaky rindless bacon
110g/4oz Roquefort cheese
15ml/1 level tablespoon tomato chutney
5ml/1 teaspoon Worcestershire sauce
5ml/1 teaspoon grated onion
4 slices bread, cut into 4 squares

1. Set the oven to 200°C/400°F/gas mark 6.
2. Dice the bacon finely. Fry in a heavy pan until crisp but not brittle. Drain well on absorbent paper and break up into small pieces.
3. Mix the Roquefort, tomato chutney, Worcestershire sauce and onion into a smooth paste.
4. Divide the mixture between the squares of bread and spread it evenly, being sure to cover all the edges.
5. Bake for 5 minutes until crisp and brown.
6. Sprinkle with the fried bacon and serve immediately.

Croque Monsieur

SERVES 4
85g/3oz butter
8 slices thin white bread
4 slices ham
4 slices Edam or Gruyère cheese
freshly ground black pepper

1. Butter the bread.
2. Make 4 sandwiches, each with a slice of ham and a slice of cheese inside, seasoned with pepper but not salt. Press well together.
3. Toast under the grill until golden brown on both sides. Cut in half and serve immediately.

NOTE: The sandwiches may also be made in a sandwich machine or fried in 0.5cm/1/4 inch hot fat or oil, turning over as necessary and draining well before serving.

Sausage Rolls

MAKES 12

400g/14oz sausagemeat
30g/1oz chopped parsley
30g/1oz chopped onion
salt and pepper
shortcrust pastry made with 225g/8oz flour (see page 525)
1 egg, beaten

1. Set the oven to 200°C/400°F/gas mark 6.
2. Mix together the sausagemeat, parsley, onion and seasonings.
3. Roll out the pastry to a large rectangle about 0.25cm/1/8 inch thick and cut in half lengthways.
4. With wet hands, roll the meat mixture into 2 long sausages the same length as the pastry and place one down the centre of each piece.
5. Damp one edge of each strip and bring the pastry over the sausagemeat, pressing the edges together and making sure that the join is underneath the roll.
6. Brush with beaten egg. Cut into 5cm/2 inch lengths. Using a pair of scissors, snip a small 'V' in the top of each sausage roll. (This is to allow steam to escape during cooking. A couple of small diagonal slashes made with a sharp knife will do as well.)
7. Place on a baking sheet and bake for 25-30 minutes.

Cheese Aigrettes

MAKES ABOUT 30

105g/3 3/4oz plain flour
salt and pepper
2.5ml/1/2 teaspoon mustard
cayenne pepper
85g/3oz butter
225ml/7 1/2 fl oz water
3 eggs, lightly beaten
55g/2oz strong Cheddar cheese, finely diced
oil or fat for deep-frying
grated Parmesan cheese

1. Sift the flour with the seasonings.
2. Slowly heat the butter and water together in a large pan. Immediately the butter is completely melted, bring to a full rolling boil and tip in the flour. Take off the heat at once and beat with a wooden spoon until the mixture leaves the side of the pan. Allow to cool for 10 minutes.
3. Gradually beat in the eggs until the mixture is smooth and shiny and of a 'dropping' consistency (you may not need all the egg). Add the Cheddar cheese.
4. Heat the deep fat until a crumb will sizzle vigorously in it.
5. Shape the mixture into even-sized balls (using 2 teaspoons) and drop them into the hot fat. Fry only a few at a time, leaving plenty of room for them to rise. Cook for about 7 minutes or until they are puffed and golden.
6. Lift them out and drain on absorbent paper. Dust with grated Parmesan cheese and serve without delay.

LIGHT RED

Angels on Horseback

SERVES 3

12 oysters
6 rashers rindless streaky bacon
6 small slices bread
butter
watercress

1. Set the oven to 200°C/400°F/gas mark 6. Heat the grill.
2. Prepare the oysters: wrap a tea towel round your left hand. Place an oyster on your left palm with the flat side upwards. Slip a short, wide-bladed kitchen or oyster knife under the hinge and push it into the oyster. Press the middle fingers of your left hand on to the shell and, with your right hand, jerk up the knife and prize the 2 shells apart. Free the oyster from its base.
3. On a board, stretch the bacon with the back of a knife (this helps to prevent shrinking during cooking). Wrap half a rasher around each oyster. Place the rolls on a baking sheet, tightly packed side by side to prevent them unravelling. Bake for about 8 minutes.
4. Meanwhile, cut the bread into rounds and toast them. Butter the toast and set 2 'angels' on each round. Arrange on a serving dish and garnish with watercress.

Devils on Horseback

SERVES 3

12 prunes
mango chutney
6 rashers rindless streaky bacon
6 small slices bread
butter
watercress

1. Pour boiling water over the prunes and leave to soak for 30 minutes. Set the oven to 200°C/ 400°F/ gas mark 6. Heat the grill.
2. Remove the stones from the prunes and stuff each cavity with half a teaspoon of mango chutney.
3. On a board, stretch the bacon with the back of a knife (this helps to prevent shrinking during cooking). Wrap half a rasher around each prune.
4. Place on a baking sheet, packed tightly side by side to prevent them unravelling. Bake for about 8 minutes.
5. Meanwhile, cut the bread into rounds and toast them. Butter the toast and set 2 'devils' on each round. Arrange on a serving dish and garnish with watercress.

SPICY DRY WHITE

Pain Bagna

Cut a French stick in half horizontally, remove a little of the soft bread, rub each side with a cut clove of garlic and sprinkle liberally with extra virgin olive oil. Scatter over the base any of the following ingredients:

sliced avocado pear
sliced peeled tomatoes
sliced mushrooms
stoned black olives
chopped anchovy fillets
sliced artichoke hearts

Season with salt and freshly ground black pepper. Sandwich together.

VALPOLICELLA

Scotch Woodcock

SERVES 4

8 anchovy fillets
30g/1oz butter
freshly ground black pepper
4 slices bread, crustless
4 egg yolks
290ml/½ pint single cream
15ml/1 tablespoon chopped fresh parsley
pinch of cayenne pepper

1. Heat the grill.
2. Pound the anchovy fillets into the butter and add pepper to taste
3. Toast the bread and spread thinly with the anchovy paste. Put on a heated plate and keep warm.
4. Put the egg yolks, cream, parsley and cayenne pepper together in a saucepan. Stir or whisk over moderate heat until thick and creamy.
5. Pour over the toasts and serve immediately.

SPICY DRY WHITE

Camembert Fritters

SERVES 3

1 Camembert cheese, chilled
1 egg, beaten
dried white breadcrumbs
oil for deep-frying
deep-fried parsley (see page 631)

1. Cut the chilled Camembert into small wedges and roll each first in beaten egg, then in breadcrumbs. Chill again for 30 minutes.
2. Heat the oil in a deep-fryer until smoking hot. Test for heat by dropping in a crumb: if it starts to sizzle immediately, the fat is ready.
3. Fry until very pale brown. Drain well.
4. Serve the fritters at once, garnished with the parsley.

NOTE: These are delicious served with gooseberry sauce.

LIGHT RED

Mushroom Strudel

SERVES 4

225g/8oz rindless streaky bacon rashers
30g/1oz butter
2 small onions, finely chopped
450g/1lb button mushrooms, sliced
150ml/$^1/_4$ pint stock
salt and freshly ground black pepper
15ml/1 tablespoon chopped fresh parsley
strudel paste made with 225g/8oz flour, rolled and pulled out (see page 530)
melted butter
beaten egg

1. Set the oven to 200°C/400°F/gas mark 6.
2. Dice the bacon and fry in its own fat until cooked and slightly browned. Add the butter.
3. Reduce the heat, add the onion and cook until soft but not coloured. Add the mushrooms and cook briskly for 30 seconds. Add the stock.
4. Season with salt and pepper and add the chopped parsley. Boil rapidly until the liquid has evaporated. Allow to cool.
5. Cut the strudel leaves into 13cm/5 inch squares. Brush each square with melted butter.
6. With a draining spoon, place some mushroom mixture in the centre of each square.
7. Using both hands, draw the edges of the pastry together so that the strudel looks like a Dick Whittington sack. Pinch the 'neck' of the sack with your fingers to secure it tightly. Alternatively, roll each strudel up into a sausage shape. Brush the pastry bags with beaten egg. Bake on a greased baking sheet for 25 minutes or until the pastry is golden brown.

NOTE: When working with strudel paste it is vital to prevent the thin leaves drying out and cracking. Keep the paste covered with polythene or a damp cloth, and when the leaves are exposed to the air, work fast. Brush the strudels with butter as quickly as you can.

SPICY DRY WHITE

Mozzarella in Carrozza

SERVES 4

8 slices thin sandwich bread
4 large slices Mozzarella cheese
2 eggs, beaten with a little salt
oil for frying

1. Cut the crusts off the bread and make 4 rounds of cheese sandwiches. Cut into 4.
2. Leave the sandwiches to soak in the beaten egg for 30 minutes. Turn them over once so that both sides are saturated with the egg.
3. Press the edges of the sandwiches firmly together and fry in hot oil until golden brown. Drain well on absorbent paper.

LIGHT RED

Chick Pea Bread

When we tested this recipe at Leith's School, it was greeted with very mixed reactions. People either loved or loathed it. Our most elegant teacher said that she thought it was delicious but added she rather loved stodge. Looking at her I thought that it was very unlikely but let the comment pass.

110g/4oz chick pea flour (besan flour)
2.5ml/$^1/_2$ teaspoon salt
425ml/$^3/_4$ pint water
30ml/1 floz good quality olive oil

1. Preheat the oven to 220°C/425°F/gas mark 7.
2. Sift the flour and salt together into a bowl.
3. Make a well in the centre and gradually add the water, mixing as you do so until it is a smooth batter.
4. Stir in the olive oil.
5. Pour into a 20 x 15cm/8 x 6 inch greased baking tin.
6. Place in the preheated oven and cook for 25-30 minutes or until the bread has set.
7. Serve warm or cold with plenty of freshly ground black pepper.

NOTE: Chick pea flour is also called besan flour and is available from many Indian or Asian shops.

Baked Bread with Garlic and Oil

1 large French stick
5 garlic cloves, peeled
coarse salt
extra virgin olive oil

1. Heat the oven to 200°C/400°F/gas mark 6.
2. Slice the bread into 2cm/3/4 inch thick diagonal slices, and place on a baking sheet in the hot oven until golden brown.
3. Cut the garlic in half and, when the bread is golden brown, rub each side with the cut surface of the garlic.
4. Arrange the bread on a serving dish and sprinkle with the salt. Then dribble over the olive oil. Serve immediately.

NOTE: The baked bread may be served with the oil poured over it and the salt and garlic handed separately.

Barquettes of Puff Pastry with a Julienne of Vegetables

MAKES 14-16
170g/6oz puff pastry
2 carrots, peeled and cut into fine julienne strips
2 leeks, the white part only, washed and cut into fine julienne strips
salt and freshly ground black pepper
5ml/1 teaspoon fresh thyme leaves
110g/4oz chicken beurre blanc

1. Set the oven to 220°C/ 425°F/ gas mark 7.
2. Roll the pastry out thinly and use it to line 14-16 small pastry boats. Prick well and bake blind for 5 minutes (see page 152).
3. Steam the carrots and leeks together with the salt, pepper and fresh thyme leaves.
4. Arrange the vegetables in the warm boats and spoon over the beurre blanc. Use as a garnish for fish, poultry and veal dishes.

Filo Pastry Baskets filled with Tomatoes and Dill

These pretty baskets can be used to garnish chicken, lamb and fish dishes.

MAKES 20
1 1/2 sheets filo pastry
45g/1 1/2oz unsalted butter, melted
2 ripe tomatoes
2 large sprigs fresh dill, roughly chopped
salt and freshly ground black pepper

1. Heat the oven to 200°C/400°F/gas mark 6.
2. Brush each layer of filo pastry with melted butter to prevent it drying out and cracking.
3. Using a small pastry cutter, press out rounds of filo pastry and line 20 tiny tartlet tins, 2.5cm/1 inch in diameter. Each tartlet case uses 3 layers of filo pastry.
4. Cook for 5-7 minutes or until golden brown.
5. Meanwhile, prepare the tomato filling: plunge the tomatoes into boiling water and leave for 10 seconds. Transfer to a bowl of cold water to stop any further cooking. When cool, skin them. Cut them into quarters and remove the seeds. Chop the tomato flesh neatly into tiny dice.
6. Heat 15ml/1 tablespoon unsalted butter in a frying pan and quickly fry the tomatoes for about 30 seconds, taking care that they do not cook to a purée. Add the chopped dill and season to taste.
7. Place a spoonful of the tomato mixture in each pastry basket and serve immediately to prevent them going soggy.

Spring Onion Bows

Choose large cylindrical spring onions that do not have especially bulbous roots. Cut off a large part of the green tops and the roots. With a small, sharp knife cut vertical lines halfway through the onions at both ends (see illustration). Leave in icy water for 2 hours – by which time they will have opened out.

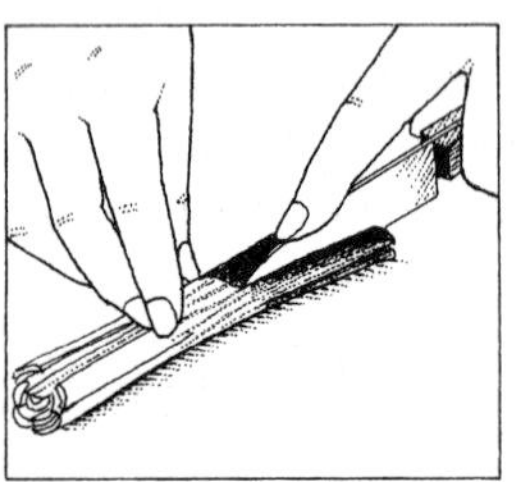

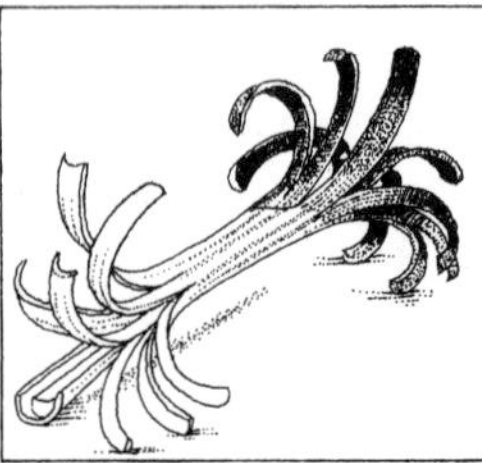

Slice from the ends towards the centre . Leave in iced water.

Deep-fried Parsley

Pick sprigs of fresh but dry parsley and place in a frying basket. Heat the oil until a crumb will sizzle in it, then lower the basket into the fat. It will hiss furiously. When the noise stops, the parsley is cooked. It should be bright green and brittle, with a very good concentrated flavour.

NOTE: To avoid splashing any hot fat, tie the parsley on to the end of a piece of string and lower into the fat from a height.

Marinated Goats Cheese

SERVES 6-12
6 crotin goats cheeses
2 garlic cloves, cut in half
4 sprigs fresh rosemary
4 sprigs fresh thyme
4 sprigs fresh oregano
2 fresh basil leaves
10 black peppercorns
10 coriander seeds
380ml/13 fl oz good quality olive oil

1. Cut the goats cheeses in half horizontally.
2. Arrange the cheese, garlic, herbs, peppercorns and coriander seeds in a preserving jar in alternate layers. Pour in enough olive oil to cover the cheeses.
3. Seal the jar and store in a cool place for at least a week but no longer than a month. If you leave it longer, the oil will turn rancid and the cheese will become too soft.
4. Serve the marinated cheese sprinkled with the oil from the jar, with piping hot slices of toasted French bread.

Clarified Butter

METHOD 1: Put the butter in a pan with a cupful of water and heat until melted and frothy. Allow to cool and set solid, then lift the butter, now clarified, off the top of the liquid.

METHOD 2: Heat the butter until foaming without allowing it to burn. Pour it through fine muslin or a double layer of 'J' cloth.

METHOD 3: Melt the butter in a heavy pan and skim off the froth with a perforated spoon.

NOTE: Clarified butter will act as a 'seal' on pâtés or potted meats, and is useful for frying as it will withstand great heat before burning.

Croûtons

2 slices bread from an unsliced slightly stale white loaf
oil for frying
salt

1. Cut the crusts off the bread and cut into small 0.5cm/1/4 inch cubes.
2. Heat the oil until a crumb will sizzle vigorously in it. Fry the bread for about 1 minute or until golden brown.
3. Drain on absorbent paper and then sprinkle with salt.

Walnut Bread

1½ slices brown bread per person
butter
chopped walnuts

1. Place a whole loaf in the freezer for half an hour. This will stiffen the loaf and make it easier to cut accurately.
2. Using a sharp knife, cut off one crust and spread the exposed bread with softened butter.
3. Cut a thin slice and repeat until you have enough slices.
4. Put each slice, butter side down, in a flat dish containing the walnuts, and press down slightly so that the walnuts stick to the butter.
5. Cut each slice in half diagonally.

Melba Toast

6 slices white bread

1. Light the grill and set the oven to 150°C/300°F/gas mark 2.
2. Grill the bread on both sides until well browned.
3. While still hot, quickly cut off the crusts and split the bread in half horizontally.
4. Put the toast in the oven and leave until dry and brittle.

NOTE: Melba toast can be kept for a day or 2 in an airtight tin but it will lose its flavour if kept longer, and is undoubtedly best served straight from the oven.

French Toast

MAKES 16 FINGERS
4 slices white bread
2 eggs
150ml/¼ pint milk
good pinch of nutmeg
55g/2oz butter
oil

1. Cut the crusts from the bread. Cut each slice into 4 fingers.
2. Beat the eggs, milk and nutmeg together in a pie dish or soup plate.
3. Dip the pieces of bread into this mixture, coating them well.
4. Melt half the butter with a tablespoon of oil in a heavy-bottomed frying pan. When the butter is foaming, fry the bread in it until golden brown on both sides. Drain on absorbent paper. Add the rest of the butter and more oil as needed, until all the bread fingers are cooked.

NOTE: French toast is sometimes served with crisp bacon, or with marmalade, maple syrup or a mixture of sugar and cinnamon, or with strawberries sprinkled with icing sugar.

Chocolate Shapes

170g/6oz best quality plain chocolate

1. First make a paper piping bag. Cut a 38cm/15 inch square of greaseproof paper and fold diagonally in half.
2. Hold the paper down with a finger on the middle of the long folded edge. Then bring one corner up to the apex opposite your steadying finger, and hold it with the apex corners together.
3. Wrap the other side corner right round the cone to join the other 2 corners. You should now be holding all 3 corners together.
4. Fold the corners over together.
5. Cut a tear in them so that you have a lug or flange. Fold down this flange to prevent the bag unravelling.
6. Meanwhile, break up the chocolate and place it in a pudding basin. Set it over (not in) a saucepan of simmering water. Stir until the chocolate is smooth and melted. Do not overheat or the chocoate will lose its gloss.
7. Fill the piping bag with some of the chocolate and snip the tip of the cone to make a small hole.
8. Use the chocolate-filled bag to pipe small elegant shapes on some greaseproof paper. Leave to cool and harden.
9. Tip the remaining chocolate on to a second piece of greaseproof paper. Leave to cool and, when almost hard, cut into shapes.
10. Use as required.

Praline

few drops oil
55g/2oz unblanched almonds (with the skins on)
55g/2oz caster sugar

1. Oil a baking sheet.
2. Put the almonds and sugar in a heavy pan, and set over a gentle heat. Stir with a metal spoon as the sugar begins to melt and brown. When thoroughly caramelized (browned), tip on to the oiled sheet.
3. Allow to cool completely, then pound to a coarse powder in a mortar or blender.
4. Store in an airtight jar.

NOTE: Whole praline almonds, as sold in the streets of Paris, are made in the same way, but are not crushed to a powder. They are sometimes used for cake decoration.

Membrillo

This is delicious eaten with cheese, or with cream cheese as a pudding or just as sweets.

1.8 kg/4lb quinces
290ml/$^1/_2$ pint water
granulated sugar

1. Chop the quinces and stew in the water until soft.
2. Sieve and weigh the pulp.
3. Mix the pulp with an equal quantity of sugar. Put into a saucepan, bring up to the boil and stir until the paste leaves the side of the pan. It will spit and splutter like mad so cover your hand with a cloth and stir the paste continuously.
4. Pile into flat trays lined with greaseproof paper and leave in an airing cupboard or another warm place for 3-4 days.
5. When it is completely firm, cut into small pieces and roll in icing sugar. Store between greaseproof paper in airtight tins.

Index